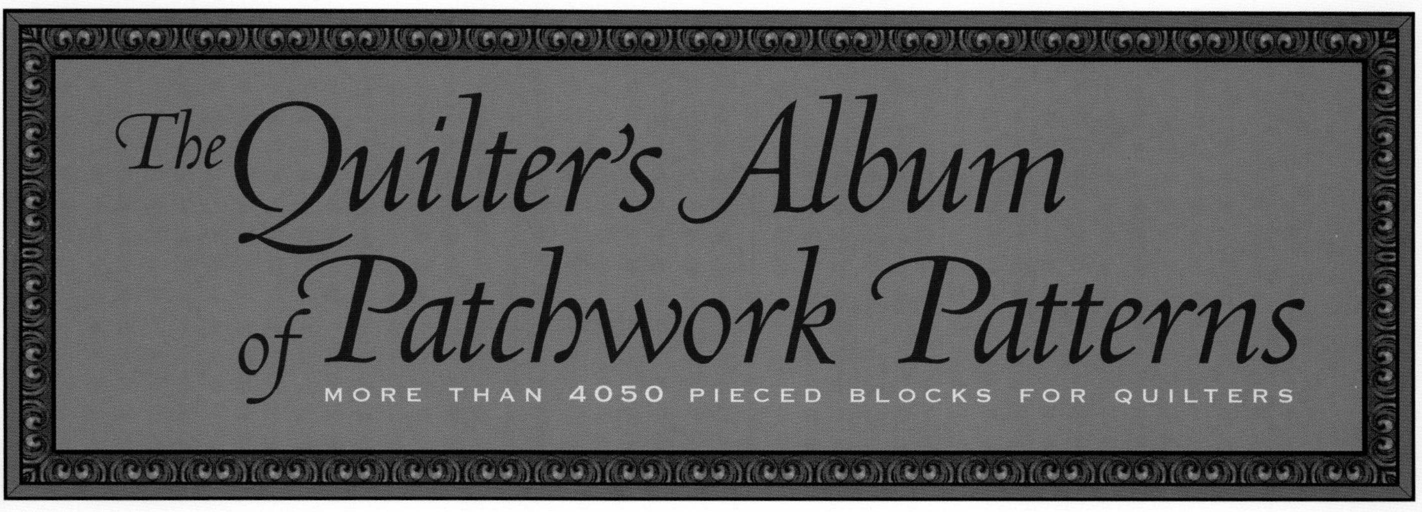

The Quilter's Album of Patchwork Patterns

MORE THAN 4050 PIECED BLOCKS FOR QUILTERS

Jinny Beyer

Breckling Press

Library of Congress Cataloging-in-Publication Data

Beyer, Jinny.
A quilter's album of patchwork patterns: more than 4050 pieced designs for quilters / Jinny Beyer.
p. cm.
Includes bibliographical references and index.
ISBN 978-1-933308-08-1
1. Patchwork--Patterns. 2. Quilting--Patterns. I. Title.

TT835.B432 2009
746.46'041--dc22

2009021009

This book was set in Centaur, Din Shriften and Edwardian Script
Editorial and production direction by Anne Knudsen
Interior design by Maria Mann
Quilt photography by Steve Tuttle

Published by Breckling Press
283 Michigan Ave., Elmhurst
IL 60126 USA

Printed and bound in China

International Standard Book Number: 978- 1-933308-08-1

Acknowledgments

This book would never have come to fruition without the generous help of so many people who were willing to share their knowledge, expertise, and documents with me. A very special tribute goes to the memory of Cuesta Benberry, who was an exceptional person in every way. She had the foresight to donate her lifelong quilt research and documents to the Museum of American Folk Art in New York, City. Her work was a tremendous source of information for me. Joyce Gross has been generous of her time and knowledge ever since I met her in the mid 1970s and has provided a wealth of information on quilt makers, particularly women from the early to mid twentieth century. Merikay Waldvogel sent me countless newspaper clippings that she accumulated through the years, most of them related to Laura Wheeler and Alice Brooks designs. She was also very willing to share information or answer questions by email and telephone. Wilene Smith openly shared her research through the years and was extremely helpful with early sources of quilt patterns, as well as dates and information on the Aunt Martha series of patterns. Hazel Carter, a long time friend, generously shared her collection of twentieth century quilt patterns, books, and clippings. Bunnie Jordan, Bettina Havig, Edith Leeper, Elaine Kelly, Connie Chunn, Sue Cummings, and Edward Price were all willing to share ideas and their research with me. Thank you also to Carole Nicholas, Karen Lumen and Ricki Selva for allowing me to show their quilts in the book.

I am particularly thankful and wish to acknowledge those who helped me with the physical aspect of collecting information and organizing it. My son, Sean Beyer, helped me tremendously with the research for the book. He spent countless hours at the Museum of American Folk Art in New York going through and copying the Cuesta Benberry materials that the museum had available. He also spent several months painstakingly working his way through microfilm files of newspapers at the Library of Congress and making copies of quilt columns and patterns from the 1920s to 1960. Robin Hollinger, Barb Hollinger, and Michelle Polchow helped with the sorting and organizing of the blocks.

Most of all I want to thank Anne Knudsen, president of Breckling Press for her willingness to tackle such a huge project. Neither of us knew when we began that it would end up being such a large book or that it would be as time consuming as it was. My thanks, too, to our book designer, Maria Mann of High-Tide Design, who was willing to make countless rounds of corrections, even up to the last moment before printing.

And, of course, thank you to my husband, John, who, for the last four years has had to live with the clutter of all the research spread over every available horizontal surface in the house.

Fans, Quilters' Quest Quilt, designed by Jinny Beyer, 2008, pieced by Carole Nicholas and quilted by Leslie Sevigney.

Introduction

My reasons for writing *The Quilter's' Album of Patchwork Patterns* are several fold. Back in 1980, I published *The Quilter's Album of Blocks & Borders*. It was a collection of 532 pieced blocks and 212 pieced borders. Over the years, I continued collecting designs, and have now amassed more than 4050 unique pieced quilt blocks. Of those, almost 500 are blocks I have designed over the last 35 years; the remainder are patterns found in quilt books, catalogs, periodicals, and newspapers dating from the late 1800s to about 1980. There are many more sources that I am sure to find, but at some point I knew I had to stop collecting and start working on a new book to make my research available to you.

In the early stages of writing the book, I knew I wanted to do more than provide an encyclopedia of quilt designs; I wanted to give quilters a way to recreate each and every block in quilts of their own. This meant that, along with pictures of each design, I needed to include tools for redrafting and resizing the block. I began by identifying the underlying grid each block was based on (in the book, you will see that the grid is identified immediately below the color picture of the block). To make it easier for you to "see" the grid, the book includes a set of transparent grid sheets. Just lay the correct grid over the top of each design and you can immediately see how it is broken into individual shapes for cutting, then piecing. Helpful too, a line drawing of each block is shown on the same page as the color picture, making it easy to see the basic structure without being distracted by the color fabric fills.

Because the base design grid is so important, I decided to categorize and sequence the blocks according to the grids used to draft them. Next, they are sub-categorized by the symmetry of the block, so that similar looking blocks are grouped together. Some designs are showcased again in "quick-reference" sections to major groups, such as baskets, trees, log cabins, butterflies, and so on. A list of these groups and where they can be found in the book is provided on page 19.

Another reason for publishing this book is to offer a source of inspiration for quilters. In color pictures, each design is "filled" with patterned fabrics, showing how patterns and color work together. A favorite technique of mine is to use border print fabrics inside block designs, and there are plenty of examples scattered throughout the book. I also like to play with mirror images to create optical illusions, so on page 43 I show you a technique of using mirrors to see multiple designs. Part 1 gives plenty of help in trying these techniques and more to create interesting effects in your own quilts.

Because quilt history has always been fascinating to me, I wanted this book to serve as a resource for historians, librarians, and everyone with an interest in patterned block designs. For this reason, the primary name I have given each block comes from the earliest source I could find for that block. (For most of the designs I used the earliest source as a guide to placement of light and dark colors in the block pictured.) Where I found the same basic design published under different names, I listed those sources as secondary names. You will see that some blocks have just one name, while others have a dozen or more secondary names. In some cases, the different names come from different regions of the country, but in others new names are simply the result of the whims of the designers. While there are about 4050 blocks in this book, there are more than 6200 names identifying those blocks. Appendixes list the pieced blocks that I have found by some of the more well-known pattern sources—Nancy Cabot, Nancy Page, Laura Wheeler, Alice Brooks, *Kansas City Star*, and *Ladies Art Company*—as well as blocks I have designed.

Whether you are a designer, a historian, a librarian or a quilter looking for ideas for your next quilt, it is my wish that *The Quilter's Album of Patchwork Patterns* will serve as a valuable reference to pieced quilt blocks for many years to come.

Jinny Beyer

Table of

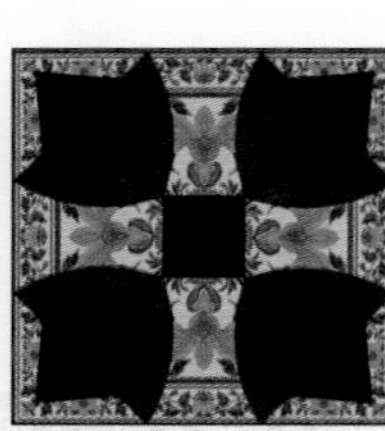

Contents

Antique Sunflower, circa 1840. Collection of Jinny Beyer.

PART 1

A Primer on Pieced Blocks

Patchwork Magic

There must be magic in old calico
For, as I lift this quilt so tenderly
And spread it out that its design may show,
I hear the years tip-toe away from me.
I see a low, white house through flakes of snow
That cover roof and path and naked tree;
And I am sitting in the cozy glow
Before its friendly hearth where I can see,
Beneath a fluted cap, a wrinkled face
As Granny sorts her patches – yellow, red
To sew with thrifty care, that she may place
A warmth and brightness on her best spare bed.
There must be magic in old calico
For I am living sixty years ago.

N.M. Bennett, *Farm Journal and Farmer's Wife* (Silver Anniversary issue), 1945

Mirage, Jinny Beyer, 2000.

Block Sources

It is common knowledge that many of today's quilt patterns first emerged during colonial times. Others became part of our culture as early Americans moved westward and the patterns followed. Passed down to family members and shared with friends, quilt patterns and quilt names have become part of our nation's folklore, reflecting as they do hard times, the beauties of nature, religious dedication, political tides, patriotism, and the pioneering spirit, among many other themes close to our hearts.

Early Sources

My journey to research quilt patterns and their names began in the mid 1970s and continues today. I found very few patterns in printed form prior to about 1850, though history has left behind quilts that show blocks were sewn before their designs were ever published. The earliest sources include *Petersen's,* a magazine for ladies published from 1842 to 1898, and *Godey's Lady's Book,* published from 1830 to 1880. The oldest printed design I found comes from the January 1835 issue of this celebrated women's magazine. It was an illustration of hexagons set side by side and was named *Honeycomb, Six-Sided,* or *Hexagon Patchwork.* When designs appeared in early periodicals, there was rarely a name given; most were named 'Mosaic,' if they were named at all. *Dictionary of Needlework,* published in 1882, does give simple names to a few patchwork designs, including *Canadian Patchwork, Twist Patchwork,* and *Right Angles Patchwork.*

Hexagon Patchwork, *Godey's Lady's Book,* Jan 1835. See 431-7.

Towards the end of the nineteenth century, more periodicals sprang up, including *Capper's Weekly, Dakota Farmer, Farm and Fireside, Farm and Home,* and a group of magazines published by the Vickery and Hill Company in Augusta, Maine. Among these were *American Woman, Comfort, Fireside Visitor, Good Stories, Happy Hours, and Hearth and Home.* (Smith) Typically, these magazines featured needlework columns, sometimes including quilt patterns. Unlike in earlier ladies magazines, most of the blocks were named.

The first significant printed contribution to the quilt world was the patterns offered by Ladies Art Company, established in 1889 in St. Louis, Missouri, by H.M. Brockstedt. Ladies Art Company sold quilt and other needlework patterns, listed by number. Patterns numbered 1 through 273 were offered in 1895, with patterns 273-400 following in 1896. The first known catalog, containing all 400 designs, was printed in 1897. Several of the blocks had appeared earlier in magazines, but the catalog presented them together for the first time. Subsequent issues contained even more designs, and by 1928 there were 530, most of them pieced blocks. (Chunn) Importantly, each block was assigned a specific name. Those names and the designs or variations of them have appeared over and over in periodicals and quilt books to this day. In the *Ladies Art Company* catalogs, each block was numbered, and the numbers make it easy to date the designs. The timeline shown here was compiled by Connie Chunn.

Ladies Art Company

- 1895: List only of blocks 1 to 273
- 1896: List only of blocks 1 to 400
- 1897: Catalog of designs 1 to 400
- 1901: Catalog with the addition of blocks 401-420
- 1906: Catalog with the addition of numbers 431-450
- 1922: Catalog with the addition of numbers 451-500
- 1928: Catalog with the addition of numbers 501-530
- ca. 1932: A few designs numbered 531 or higher sold as patterns or kits only

The frequency of publication of quilt patterns and designs in periodicals and magazines continued to grow into the twentieth century as new companies selling patterns came into being. Sometime around 1906, Clara Stone, who was a contributor to the Vickery and Hill magazines, published a quilt illustration booklet containing 188 pieced designs. Several of these had appeared earlier in magazines or the *Ladies' Art Company* catalog.

Milestone Books

Double X, Webster, 1915. See 74-5.

Spider Web, Finley, 1929. See 292-11.

Chimney Swallows, Hall, 1935. See 317-1.

One person very influential in the popular quilt movement in the early 1900s was Marie Webster. Webster began designing quilts when she was in her 50s and several appeared in color in *Ladies' Home Journal* in 1911 and 1912. Soon, quilters around the country were asking for her patterns. Along with her sister Emma Daughtery, Webster started a mail order business from her home. The Practical Patchwork Company sold original Marie Webster patterns and kits through the 1930s. (www.quiltershalloffame.org) In 1915, Webster made a major contribution to the quilt world with the publication of the first book devoted solely to quilting, *Quilts: Their Story and How to Make Them.* An extremely popular book, it helped fuel growing interest in quilts and is still used as a reference today. Marie Webster's home in Marion, Indiana, now houses the Quilters' Hall of Fame, founded in 1979 by Hazel Carter of Vienna, Virginia.

In 1929, another milestone was reached with the publication of *Old Patchwork Quilts and the Women Who Made Them* by Ruth Finley. From Ohio, and later New York, Finley was fascinated with women's folk art, and quilting soon became a passion. She loved to interview quilters and would travel the countryside looking for quilts and the women who made them. She wrote their stories down, and these became a core part of her book, which she researched for 14 years. (www.quiltershalloffame.org) Finley's book differs from Marie Webster's in that there are many more illustrations and photographs. It remains an important reference of quilt designs for quilters.

The Romance of the Patchwork Quilt in America, published in 1935 by Carrie Hall and Rose Kresinger, was another major contribution to the quilt world. A skilled needlewoman, Carrie Hall became caught up in the quilt revival in the early 1900s, as so many other quilters did. She decided to find all known quilt patterns and piece a block for each one. (Havig) These blocks, along with the stories and names that went with them, remain an important resource for quilters. Unfortunately, there were no line illustrations to accompany the blocks and they were photographed grouped together on the page, often quite small. This made it difficult to determine exactly how each block was drafted. Perhaps this partly explains why, in subsequent years, several traditional patterns were drafted in a variety of ways.

Carrie Hall offered her blocks for display, and traveled the country giving lectures about quilt history. As the demand for such programs began to wane in the late 1930s, she donated her entire collection of blocks in 1938 to the Thayer Museum at the University of Kansas (now known as the Spencer Museum of Art). More blocks went to the museum than appear in the book. Presumably Carrie Hall continued making blocks after the book was published. Even though the block collection was from known patterns, I have not found an earlier published source for all of them; for this reason, I have sourced many early patterns to the Hall blocks. Fortunately for today's quilt makers, in 1999 the entire collection was published in *Carrie Hall Blocks* by Bettina Havig. The blocks all appear in color and in sufficient size to determine how they are drafted.

Newspaper Sources

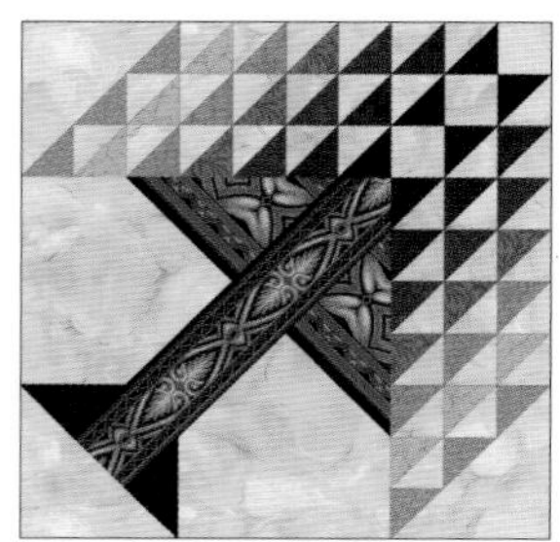
Pine Tree, *Kansas City Star,* Sep 19, 1928. See 208-9.

In the late 1920s newspapers around the country began printing syndicated columns devoted to quilting, and pattern companies advertised quilt patterns for sale. The bulk of the designs in this book came from various newspapers found in papers left by Cuesta Benberry to the Museum of American Folk Art in New York City, or on microfilm at the Library of Congress in Washington, D.C. While there may be others, the first newspaper that I have found to offer patterns on a regular basis is the *Kansas City Star* of Kansas City, Missouri. The column would first appear in the *Daily Star* newspaper on Saturday and run again in *The Weekly Star* the following Wednesday. The newspaper began its column on September 19, 1928 with the *Pine Tree* pattern, and offered patterns over a longer period of time than any other newspaper column devoted to quilting. The last pattern offered in the daily newspaper was *Little Boy's Breeches* on July 16, 1938, but the weekly newspaper continued offering patterns (although sporadically in the later years) until May 24, 1961, when the last pattern, *A Fan of Many Colors,* was printed. (*Kansas City Star*) In all, there were 1068 patterns given in the newspaper, more than three quarters of which were pieced designs. A few were repeated in later years with either the same or a different block name. The name of the *Weekly Kansas City Star* changed to *Weekly Star Farmer* in 1952 (Smith). To avoid any confusion, in this book I refer to all *Kansas City Star* patterns simply as *Kansas City Star,*.

Most of the patterns offered in the *Kansas City Star* through 1930 were McKim Studio designs. Ruby Short McKim had a needlework mail order business and had previously been published in other periodicals. The majority of patterns bearing her name when they appeared in the newspaper column were presented with identical art in McKim's book, *101 Patchwork Patterns,* published in 1931. Two other names associated with the early *Kansas City Star* patterns are Eveline Foland and Edna Marie Dunn, who were illustrators for the newspaper. The *Kansas City Star* patterns differed from most other columns that were to spring up in that the newspaper gave a complete pattern for the design; most others gave an image of the design and readers were expected to send for the pattern.

The first weekly syndicated quilt columnist that I found is Florence La Ganke, who is known best by her pen name, Nancy Page (see page 6). In its February 4, 1927 issue, the *Syracuse Herald* announced the launch of a new column by Page, covering many aspects of women's life. Notice that there is no mention of quilting or sewing.

> "Coming! Nancy Page, Friend and Counselor. Commencing Monday, *The Herald* will publish the daily adventures of Nancy Page, an attractive young married woman who meets and solves problems of Dress, Beauty, Food, Diet, Etiquette, Child Care, Economy, House Furnishings. Created by Florence La Ganke, the character of Nancy Page will grow upon all women readers. Into her presentation of the solutions to pressing problems of the home, Miss La Ganke weaves Romance, Individuality and Continuity ... You will be interested not only in the running story of the life of Nancy Page, but also in the methods she uses to meet life's baffling problems. *The Syracuse Herald*" (*Syracuse Herald,* February 24, 1927)

It was not until two years later that the column featured the first of Page's series of quilt patterns. Each week, Page would provide a different block pattern, until an entire quilt was completed. In 1932 she began offering individual quilt patterns. Several of these had already appeared in the *Ladies Art Company* catalog or other newspapers prior to being published in the Nancy Page column. Still, out of the 500-plus pieced blocks I found, Page was the earliest published source for more than half.

The most prolific of all the newspaper quilt columnists, Elizabeth Leitner Rising, wrote under the pen name Nancy Cabot. The first column was published in the *Chicago Tribune* on January 22, 1933. Cabot's column was subsequently syndicated to other newspapers around the country. While it did not run over as long a period of time as the *Kansas City Star* or Nancy Page columns, Cabot's column offered patterns on a daily, rather than weekly, basis until late July 1938 and then sporadically until early 1945. More than 2000 designs were offered, about half of which were appliqué blocks. It is interesting to note that the first pattern to appear in the *Kansas City Star* column and the Nancy Cabot column were both *Pine Tree* designs.

During the 1930s other quilting columns appeared in newspapers and magazines around the country, such as Jane Alan's Historic Quilt Blocks column, Patty Shannon's column in the *Kentucky Farmer's Home Journal,* and Anne Orr's column in *Good Housekeeping* and *Better Homes and Gardens.* I have not been able to find out if Jane Alan's name was a pen name. Her designs, appearing in several periodicals, were mostly the same as previously published blocks, but Alan provided patterns as well as pictures of the designs. An *Illinois State Register* clipping advertised her collection of patterns: "Jane Alan's Pioneer Days Collection of twenty authentic old designs with full-sized cutting patterns, is 25 cents. Send your order to Jane Alan, care of this paper."

Little Boy's Breeches, *Kansas City Star,* Jul 16, 1938. See 275-6.

A Fan of Many Colors, *Kansas City Star,* May 24, 1961. See 386-3.

Pine Tree, Nancy Cabot, *Chicago Tribune,* Jan 22, 1933. See 255-2.

Nancy Page

Quilt Club

"The Nancy Page Quilt Club met at Nancy's for the next to the last block. Her home was a riot of color, for there were pots of tulips everywhere, and that gave the members the clue for the day. 'Of course, our flower is the tulip.' On the table were bits of yellow, orange, deep red, lavender, purple and striped pink and white. 'You guessed right. It is the tulip, and since tulips are such gorgeous affairs, I am giving you a wide choice in colors. Take whatever you want...." (*Syracuse Herald*, July 7, 1929)

Florence La Ganke (later Florence La Ganke Harris) was a remarkable woman for her time. She was born in 1886 and from a very early age was on a fast track for success. The quilt world knows her best for her Nancy Page Quilt Club columns that appeared from the late 1920s well into the 1940s in newspapers in the United States and Canada. Few realize that quilting was just a small part of her accomplished career. La Ganke's particular studies were in foods, nutrition, and home economics. In 1919, at the age of 33, she traveled to California to direct the home economics division of the Oakland Public Schools.

"'Food is an adventure, cookery a romance,' declares Miss Florence M. La Ganke, who has come from the faculty of Teachers' College, Columbia University, to direct the department of home economics in the Oakland public schools and to demonstrate to students the difference between cookery, an art, and cooking, a drudgery." (*Oakland Tribune,* Aug 26, 1919)

After a few years, La Ganke returned to her mid-western roots and became the Home Economics editor of the *Cleveland Plains Dealer*. (*Lima News,* Jun 25, 1926) Shortly thereafter, in early 1937, she launched her syndicated Nancy Page column. The column was geared towards food, diet, child care, and other aspects of a woman's life of that time. (*Syracuse Herald,* Feb 24, 1927) La Ganke was the author of at least eight cookbooks and co-author of many others, including text books. At one time, she had her own radio program, "Home in the Sky". (*Evening Independent,* Massillon, Ohio, Oct 31, 1960)

Even after her column was retired, La Ganke remained respected in her field. She continued to write and lecture well into her 70s, and in 1949 she served as Economics Director for the national Potato Chip Institute, Inc. She was a judge for many cooking contests and even the Mrs. America contest.

Connected to the column was the Nancy Page Club, whose members met to discuss Early American Life. (*Syracuse Herald,* Feb 1, 1928) After about a year, the club changed its name to the Nancy Page Quilt Club. (*Manitoba Free Press*, Jan 25, 1929). The commentary was similar to that in the regular Nancy Page columns, with Nancy's friends meeting at her home and taking part in the discussions and give and take. The quilt club column appeared on Saturdays or Sundays in most newspapers and was the forum for a series of sampler-type quilts, mostly appliqué. At lease 20 quilts were a part of this series and only one was entirely pieced. Each quilt had a theme and each week a new block would be given until the quilt was complete. The introduction of the first quilt, *Grandmother's Garden* took up an entire half page of the newspaper and gave explicit instructions. The quilt design was a pieced basket with appliqué flowers. (*Syracuse Herald*, Mar 10, 1929) Each week a different set of flowers was offered.

With the popularity of quilts still increasing, the Nancy Page column further expanded its quilting portion to include patterns for the "club" members on Tuesdays (although some newspapers offered the column other days of the week). More than 600 patterns were offered. The earliest date I found for this new feature was June 6, 1932 in the *Nashville Banner*. Some were traditional designs that had been previously published by other columnists, but some were new or had new names. The Nancy Page columns were phased out of many newspapers in the mid to late 1930s but I found that the *Birmingham News* was one paper that carried them into the mid 1940s, most likely there were others as well."

Chain Link Quilt, Nancy Page, *Nashville Banner,* Sep 6, 1932. See 225-3.

Tea Leaves, Nancy Page, *Birmingham News,* Jul 4, 1939. See 123-12.

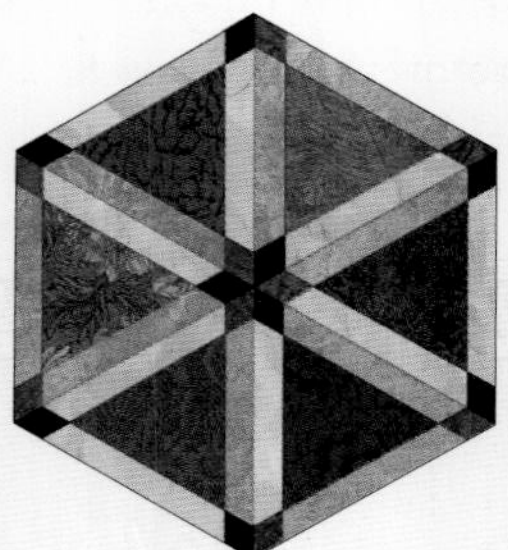

Diamond String, Nancy Page, *Nashville Banner,* Mar 6, 1934. See 397-5.

Polk Ohio, Nancy Page, *Birmingham News,* Oct 13, 1936. See 276-2.

The Patty Shannon column was written by Gladys Sanders for the *Kentucky Farmers Home Journal* and began in March 1936. Like the *Kansas City Star* and Jane Alan columns, Shannon's columns offered patterns for the blocks. (Waldvogel: "Also Known As Patty Shannon")

Catalogs

In addition to the columnists, several pattern companies printed catalogs of quilt patterns during the 1930s, and many advertised regularly in newspapers. The advertiser would typically offer an illustration of a design, perhaps a brief narrative, and information on where to send money to obtain the pattern. Most notable was Needlecraft Service, Inc., which produced designs by Alice Brooks and Laura Wheeler (see pages 8 to 9). Needlecraft Service, Inc. also identified patterns with such names as Mary Cullen and Anne Adams, but the art and catalog numbers were usually identical to previously offered designs.

Tropical Sun, *World Herald,* Mar 31, 1933. See 380-4.

Another noteworthy pattern company Home Arts Studios, founded by Hubert Ver Mehren of Des Moines, Iowa. Ver Mehren's primary business was the Iowa Button and Pleating Company, but in the late 1920s and into the early '30s he also sold quilt designs, producing at least two catalogs, *Colonial Quilts* and *Hope Winslow's Quilt Book.* Ver Mehren's designs were advertised in newspapers as well. Most of the designs I found for Home Art Studios appeared in various periodicals from late 1932 through early 1934. The last listing I found was for *Pinwheel Star* in the *World Herald* on March 13, 1934. Many of Ver Mehren's designs were quite complex. He produced patterns for several full-size quilts and many quilt blocks. One wonders if some of these elaborate patterns were ever actually pieced, but it is clear that he enjoyed creating geometric patterns. Two of the patterns Ver Mehren produced are shown here.

Golden Dahlia Quilt, *Des Moines Register,* Mar 5, 1933. See 290-5.

Catalog Offerings

The early quilt catalogs not only sold patterns, but many offered fabrics, pre-cut blocks, quilts, and even piecing and quilting services. Fabrics were often referred to as colorfast, or oil calico. (Oil-boiled calico was produced through a process of finishing the fabric that involved boiling the yardage in an oil mordant, rendering it much more colorfast.) It is fascinating to read some of these catalogs and to see the prices of the services offered. Here are a few examples.

The 1928 *Ladies Art Company* sold patterns for pieced blocks for 15c each; two for 25c; five for 50c; a dozen for $1.00. Each included paper pattern pieces and a colored cardboard diagram of the design. To order the colored cardboard diagram without the pattern pieces, the cost was 5c each; seven for 25c; fifteen for 50c; thirty-five for $1.00. The catalog also offered other sales and services, such as some of the following:

"Old-fashioned oil calico, figured. Width 24 inches. Price, per yard, 22c."

"Cotton Batting, very best White Rose. Twelve ounces to roll, 55c."

"Hand-quilting $12.00 to $18.00, according to the pattern. These prices include the finishing of the edge with plain binding, but no material is furnished."

Blazing Star, *Ladies Art Company,* 1897. See 277-8.

"Complete quilts made from any design in this book. Prices range from $25.00 to $45.00. Write for estimate."

Ladies Art Company also sold finished blocks. Prices varied according to the complexity of the blocks and ranged from $.35 to $1.75 each. They could also be ordered by the dozen, with a range of $4.00 to $20.00 per dozen.

"The blocks are made only in the size given below the illustration of this design. We make the design in any combination of colors desired, using the best muslin and colored materials."

Another pattern catalog, *Prize Winning Designs,* published by Colonial Pattern Company, offered many patterns and sold precut pieces for some designs.

Gold Brick, *Prize Winning Designs,* ca. 1931. See 185-8.

Asymmetrical Flowers

Sunflower, Laura Wheeler, *Cincinnati Enquirer,* Dec 7, 1935. **See 369-10.**

Tulip Garden, Alice Brooks, *Detroit Free Press,* Sep 7, 1936. **See 370-1.**

Morning Glory, Alice Brooks, *Detroit Free Press,* Aug 30, 1934. **See 370-2.**

Garden Treasure, Alice Brooks, *Detroit Free Press,* Oct 2, 1935. **See 370-4.**

Old Fashioned Garden, Alice Brooks, *Detroit Free Press,* Jul 3, 1934. **See 364-7.**

Mountain Pink, Laura Wheeler, *Indianapolis Star,* Jun 24, 1934. **See 264-1.**

Spring Fancy, Laura Wheeler, *Cincinnati Enquirer,* Apr 19, 1935. **See 365-1.**

Laura Wheeler and Alice Brooks

Many of the popular pattern designers and columnists of the 1930s and '40s selected and reworked designs that came from much earlier sources. Yet one set of designs stands out because of the originality of the blocks published: the Laura Wheeler and Alice Brooks patterns published by Needlecraft Service, Inc., 82 Eighth Avenue, New York City. According to notes left by Cuesta Benberry, this was a subsidiary of Graphics Enterprises, Inc., a mail-order pattern syndicate. I have found no evidence to indicate that Laura Wheeler or Alice Brooks were actual people. Most likely they were names attached to the patterns by the company.

Most of the Laura Wheeler and Alice Brooks patterns are unique. Many times, the exact same art appeared in different issues of different periodicals, yet Needlecraft Service, Inc. attributed it sometimes to Wheeler and other times to Brooks. There was only a pattern number or a pattern name to provide clues as to which name the design was associated with. (Numbers lower than 5000 were attributed to Wheeler; numbers over 5000 were attributed to Brooks.) Many of the designs have a character and style of their own, quite different from other, more traditional blocks. Of the more than 200 pieced patterns I found credited to Brooks and the more than 300 credited to Wheeler, only a handful of each were from an earlier source.

Designs with the Brooks and Wheeler names began to appear in newspapers across the country in 1933, usually with a one or two paragraph blurb and information on how to send for the pattern. Generally, each week's design was the same in all periodicals. Wheeler's designs were introduced first, with Brooks coming toward the end of 1933. The earliest Wheeler design I found was *Swing in the Center*, which was published in the *Illinois State Register* on April 24, 1933. The same pattern appeared in the *Cincinnati Enquirer* on July 3, 1933, when that newspaper launched a quilt block series. The first pattern I found attributed to Brooks was *Turkey Tracks, Detroit Free Press,* November 2, 1933. Through 1933 and 1934, Brooks and Wheeler quilt designs appeared frequently, sometimes as often as 10 or 11 designs per month. By Fall 1934, their frequency dropped to about six patterns a month. Their appearance became gradually more sporadic as other types of needlework patterns, including embroidery, crochet, and knitting, took over. By the late 1930s and '40s, it was rare to find a Brooks or Wheeler quilt pattern in newspapers or periodicals.

Rival newspapers in the same city sometimes featured different blocks. If a city newspaper ran an Alice Brooks pattern, its rival might, for instance, publish a Laura Wheeler design. It seems that the newspaper was able to set pricing, too, because, depending on the periodical, identical patterns were priced at either 10 cents or 15 cents. The majority of newspapers directed customers to Needlecraft Service, Inc. in New York City for fulfillment, but some, such as the *Detroit Free Press*, fulfilled orders themselves. Here is the blurb that accompanied the *Cincinnati Enquirer's* launch of the Laura Wheeler designs: "Send 10 cents for this pattern to the *Cincinnati Enquirer,* Needlework Department, 82 Eighth Avenue, New York City." On May 3, 1934 the blurb, asked for "10 cents in stamps or coin (coin preferred)." By the 1950s, the mailing address for Needlecraft Servies, Inc, changed to PO Box 161, Old Chelsea Station, NY 11, New York. Old Chelsea Station was the name of a New York branch post office, and some people began calling the company Old Chelsea Station Needlecraft Services. By the late 1970s, the name of Needlecraft Service, Inc. had disappeared from newspaper columns; either the pattern company changed its name or was acquired, because from that point the Alice Brooks and Laura Wheeler designs were credited to Grit Patterns.

An interesting characteristic of the Alice Brooks and Laura Wheeler patterns is that many of the blocks were designed to be placed "on point." Of the blocks I found, a fifth of the Brooks patterns and about a seventh of the Wheeler patterns are on point. This is just one of the ways in which the blocks were unusual. The innovative quality of the designs is particularly evident in those blocks that feature stylized flowers (about a fifth of the patterns). A glance through pages 360 to 370, where all the curved pieced flower patterns are grouped, will show how many of those are Brooks or Wheeler patterns. There are more pieced flower designs in the Laura Wheeler and Alice Brooks blocks than in patterns from any other company. Most have a similar free-form style and are often asymmetrical; some have bi-lateral symmetry with one half of the block mirroring the other. Almost half of the designs feature curved lines. (Less than a quarter of the *Kansas City Star* blocks, a fifth of the Nancy Cabot blocks, and a small scattering—only a twentieth—of the Nancy Page blocks have curved elements.) The grids Brooks and Wheeler used for their patterns are another distinctive feature; they quite often used such odd grids as 11 x 11, 13 x 13, or 25 x 25. Still more innovative, several of the blocks were designed to form interlocking patterns when placed side by side, making it a puzzle to find the basic block in Brooks and Wheeler designs. All of these attributes blended to give the Alice Brooks and Laura Wheeler designs an easily recognizable and distinctive style that stands out among other pattern creators of their period.

Interlocking Patterns

Tulip, Laura Wheeler, *Cincinnati Enquirer,* Aug 12, 1933. **See 307-9.**

Dogwood, Alice Brooks, *Detroit Free Press,* Jun 13, 1935. **See 370-7.**

Double Pinwheel, Laura Wheeler, *Cincinnati Enquirer,* Oct 10, 1935. **See 314-8.**

Kite, Laura Wheeler, *Tulsa Tribune,* Jun 3, 1981. **See 181-12.**

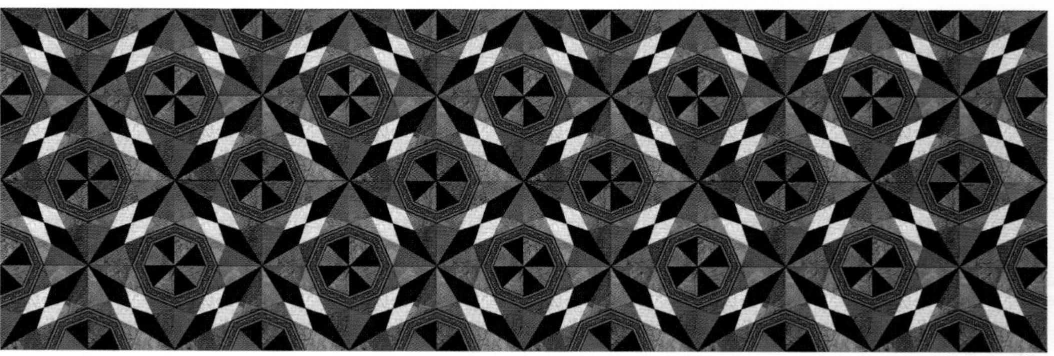

Tree of Temptation, *Grandmother Clark's Patchwork Designs, Book No. 22*, 1932. See 220-12.

"To be assured of a harmonious quilt top, you may order any of the above designs, all accurately cut out, ready for you to sew together. The material used is an unusually fine, soft fabric that is absolutely guaranteed against fading. You may have your choice of Pink, Rose, Blue, Green, Yellow, Orange or Orchid in small figured prints or plain colors. Quilts average 74 by 96 inches. Complete top, with border is included each, $3.98."

This catalog also sold white fabric for 25c per yard and printed fabric for 29c per yard. Also for sale were bundles of fabric, cut into strips 4½ inches wide and one yard long, 12 fabrics per bundle, for 59c.

The 1932 *Virginia Snow Studio Art Needlework Creations* catalog offered "Grandma Dexter Quilt Patches. A good assortment of fancy fast color prints sufficient to make ordinary size quilt. 35c."

Also for sale were, "Large Roll Quilt Patches. Contains a good assortment of fancy fast color prints. 2 lbs. to package, 65c."

In 1932, *Grandmother Clark's Patchwork Quilt Designs* advertised:

"Bundle Bargains—75c. We have made arrangements with a dress factory to supply our readers with left-over pieces suitable for quilt blocks. These pieces are all colors, all sizes, all shapes and all washable and have been done up into 2-pounds bundles."

Other Sources

Victory Quilt, *Kansas City Star*, Apr 22, 1942. See 439-13.

Not only were quilt designs abundant in newspapers and periodicals throughout the 1930s, either through columns or advertising, but they cropped up on the radio, too. There was at least one radio show devoted to women. A quilt block, with no name associated with it, appeared on Sundays in the *Topeka Daily Capital*. The text refers to the Women's Club of the Air on radio station WIBW. According to one column, WIBW was the Capper's station, run by *Capper's Weekly*, which is a possible source for the blocks presented. When *Star of Bethlehem* was presented on April 15, 1934, the accompanying text read, "The Women's Club of the Air offers this quilt pattern and you can learn how to obtain it at 2 p.m. Wednesday, during the club broadcast over WIBW." On April 22,1934, the text read, "More details will be given during the club program heard over the Capper station at 2 p.m." *Eastertide* was presented on April 1, 1934 with this byline, "Tune in Wednesday, at 2 p.m. The making of this block will be further described."

The craze of quilting died down during World War II, as everyone's attention turned to Victory Gardens, helping the troops, and the trials of war. It wasn't until the 1970s that another revival spurred new interest in quilting. Since that time the industry has certainly changed. Hundreds of books and patterns have been published, fabrics have been designed strictly for the quilt industry, and countless tools and rulers have been invented that the women of earlier decades would never have imagined possible.

My Own Blocks

Star Magnolia, Jinny Beyer, Quilter's Quest design, 2004. See 307-2.

This book would be at least four times its size if I had attempted to catalog all designs that have been created since the 1970s. I purposely limited myself to traditional quilt blocks, created for the most part before 1970. The exception is blocks that I created myself.

Since 1972, I have designed blocks for several purposes, including personal use. Some were designed specifically for my annual seminar at Hilton Head Island in South Carolina. In each of the 29 years the seminar was conducted, I created a series of blocks to give to participants. With the exception of appliqué designs, they are all included in this book.

Since 1984, I have designed fabric for quilters through RJR Fabrics. For most of the fabric collections I create a quilt and RJR has produced patterns for the design. I have also published patterns through my company and retail store, Jinny Beyer Studio. In recent years I have compiled or designed several quilt blocks for our local "Shop Hop" in the Maryland/Northern Virginia area. The blocks usually follow some type of theme, such as baskets, trees, flowers or fans, and each shop has a different pattern which is given out to participants. The idea is for the quilter who visits each shop to collect all of the blocks and then make a sampler quilt using all of the designs. Each shop creates its own quilt using the blocks. A few of the blocks are shown here.

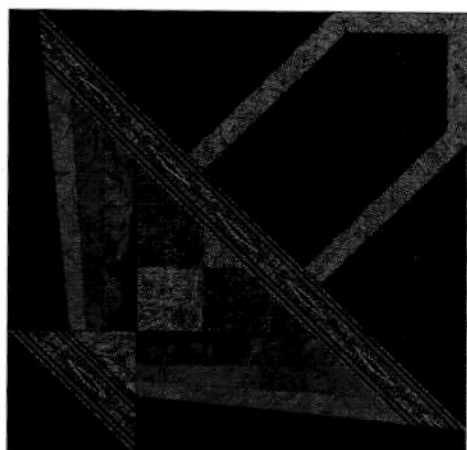

Birch Basket, Jinny Beyer, Quilter's Quest design, 2006. See 238-5.

Daffodil, Jinny Beyer, Quilter's Quest design, 2007. See 220-7.

Great Falls Fan, Jinny Beyer, Quilter's Quest design, 2008. See 433-10.

Unidentified Sources

As you look through the book, you will occasionally come across block designs that I have been unable to source accurately. While working on the book, I was fortunate enough to receive a large number of newspaper clippings, collected by various people. Some of these clippings were cut from newspapers as far back as the 1930s, when the person who clipped them had no thought of preserving the sources or dates. Thankfully, these were passed on to new generations of quilters, probably tucked into sewing baskets or books. Looking at the clippings, I could sometimes know that it was a Nancy Cabot or a Nancy Page design, usually because of a reference in the clipping itself. Sometimes I could track down the source, because the clipping invited readers to order patterns from a particular newspaper's needlework department. Often, however, the clippings proved impossible to trace. Rather than exclude those blocks and allow them to be lost to history, I added them to the book, sourcing them as: "unidentified newspaper clipping, date unknown."

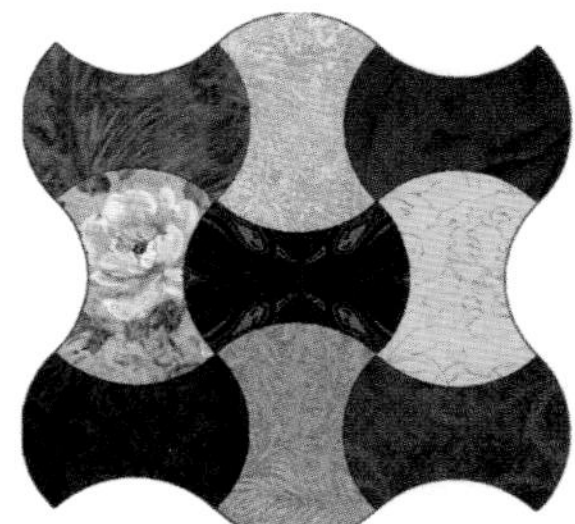

The Friendship Quilt, *Kansas City Star,* Nov 15, 1930. See 433-10.

Some quilt names are hard to find in published sources, yet we all know a particular design when we see it. Those blocks have become part of quilting folklore and we call them by the names our grandmothers passed down to us. For instance, the earliest published source I found for the block shown here was *Kansas City Star,* where it was named *The Friendship Quilt.* I have always known this pattern as *Apple Core,* yet I have not been able to find it in print by that name. In a very few cases like this, I have listed the source as: "source unknown, date unknown." I invite readers to help me track down early published sources for blocks like this.

When researching blocks from books and periodicals of the 1920s and '30s, I would often find a short block of text describing the pattern or giving its origin. I deciding to include these anecdotal references, but ask that you read them "with a grain of salt," since they are not always accurate. Writers of the time may have romanticized the names of patterns and how those names came about. Some of these comments, though, may be quite valuable. Remember that quilters during the 1930s were only a generation or two removed from early quilts made in the 1800s. Quilt folklore came to them through word of mouth and family stories that were close to their hearts. Some of the Nancy Cabot, Nancy Page, and *Kansas City Star* columns include patterns contributed by readers and attributed to their mothers or grandmothers. Commentary like this provides us with unique insight into the creation of blocks and their evolution from generation to generation.

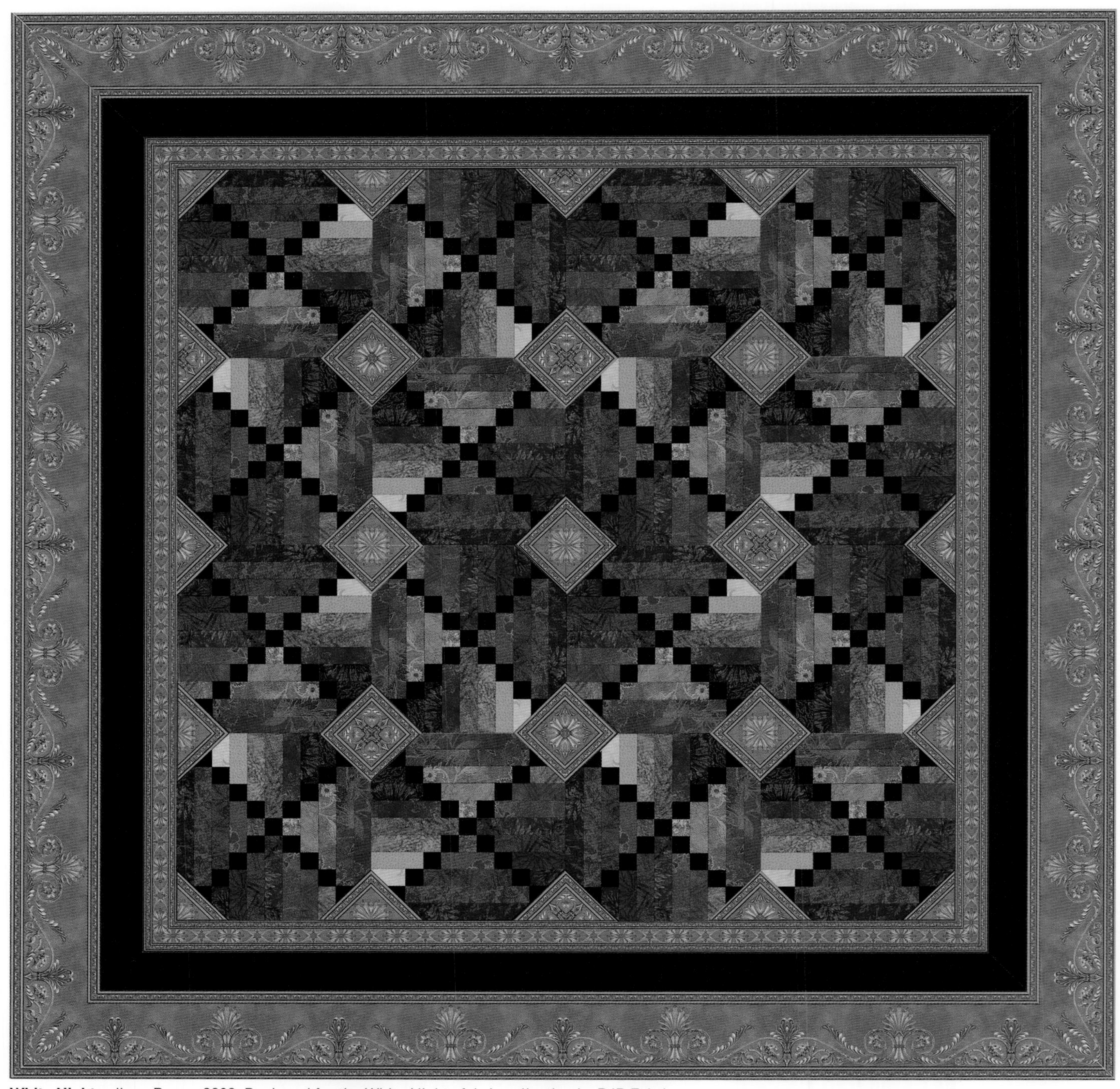

White Nights, Jinny Beyer, 2008. Designed for the White Nights fabric collection by RJR Fabrics.

How the Blocks Are Organized

Almost all of the geometric designs we use in patchwork have a basic underlying grid that acts as an invisible guide to drafting the patterns. Most designs are based on grids made up of a certain number of equal-size squares. Others are based on spokes radiating from the center of the block outwards, and some combine both grids and spokes. Using this simple base-grid system, the designs in this book are organized first into five major groups: square blocks; hexagonal blocks; continuous pattern blocks; one-patch blocks; and other blocks.

Within these major groups, the blocks are split into designs *without curved lines* and designs *with curved lines*. If even a small part of the design includes a curved line, such as a stem on a flower, that block is categorized as a curve-line block. Next, each block is assigned to a category, such as 2 x 2 base grid category, 3 x 3 base grid category, 5 x 5 base grid category, and so on. From there, the next level of organization differs for each of the five major groups. We will look first at square blocks.

How Square Blocks Are Organized

Once they have been divided into designs without curves and designs with curves, square blocks are then sequenced according to the number of squares that make up the grid used for drafting them, from smallest number to largest number. They are further organized according to the symmetry of the design. Some of the curved designs are broken down even further, depending on the similarity of the design to other blocks (see page 18).

To clarify how this organization system works, take a look at this:

Square blocks

No curves	Curves
Base grid category	Base grid category
Specific grid	Specific grid
Symmetry	Symmetry
Similarity	Similarity

Organization According to Base Grid

With the exception of those in the 8-pointed star category, blocks are based on a grid of squares, where each square is the same size.

2 x 2 base grid

2 x 2 Base Grid Category

The 2 x 2 base grid category contains more blocks than any other in this book. The base grid is a square broken into four same-size smaller squares—two squares across and two down.

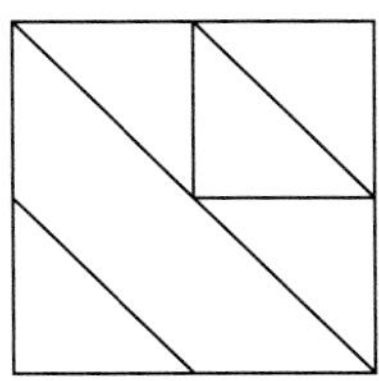

Duck's Foot

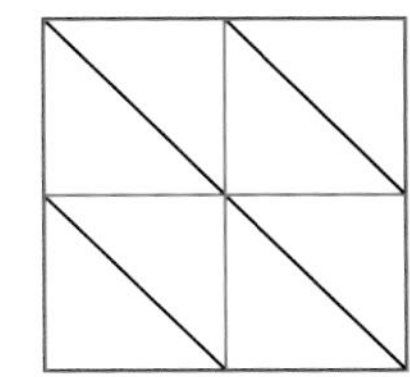

There are several additional grids that belong to the 2 x 2 category, each of them formed by dividing the squares of the base grid repeatedly in half. They are listed below. Note that some quilters may refer to 2 x 2 blocks as "4-patch" because they are based on a total of four squares (2 x 2 = 4). But for the purposes of easy classification in this book, they belong in the 2 x 2 base grid category. It includes: 2 x 2 base grid, 4 x 4 grid, 8 x 8 grid, 16 x 16 grid, 32 x 32 grid, and 64 x 64 grid (because of the tiny size of the squares, this grid is not shown here).

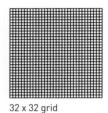

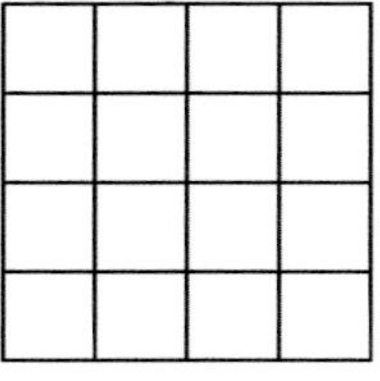
4 x 4 base grid

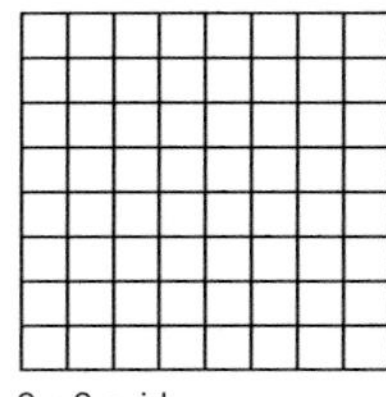
8 x 8 grid

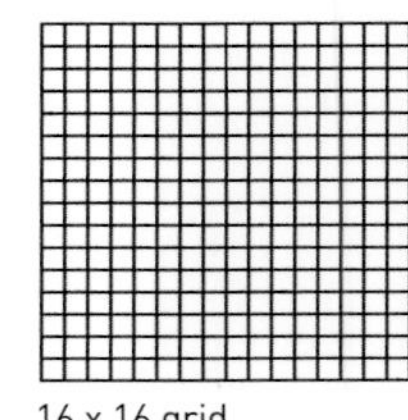
16 x 16 grid

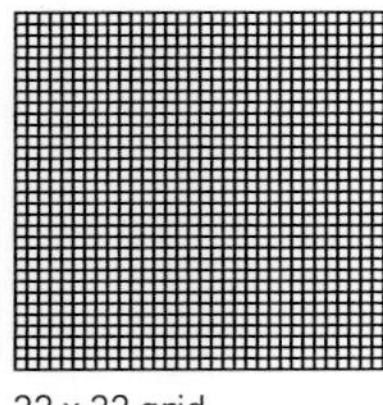
32 x 32 grid

3 x 3 Base Grid Category

In this category, all blocks are based on a grid of 3 squares across and 3 squares down. There are several additional grids that belong to this category, each of them formed by dividing the squares of the base grid repeatedly in half. Note that some quilters refer to designs in this category as "9-patch", but for the purposes of this book, the basic design grid is 3 x 3. This category includes 3 x 3 base grid, 6 x 6 grid, 12 x 12 grid, 24 x 24 grid, and 48 x 48 grid.

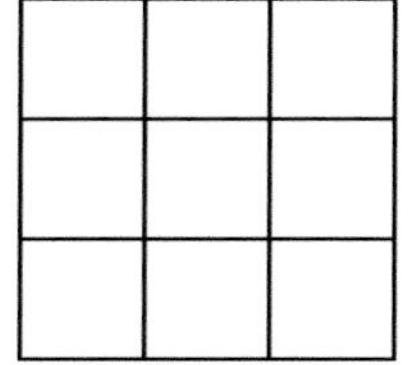
3 x 3 base grid

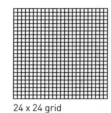

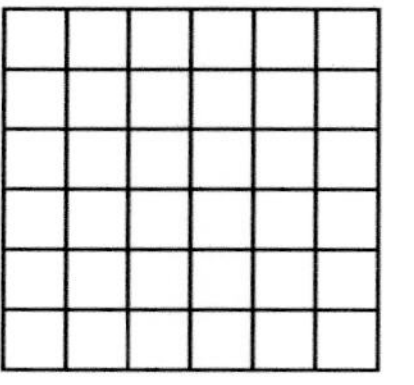
6 x 6 grid

12 x 12 grid

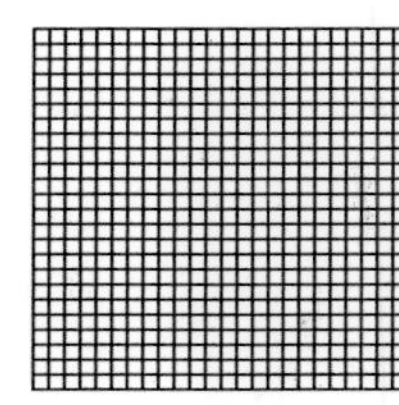
24 x 24 grid

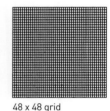

48 x 48 grid

5 x 5 Base Grid Category

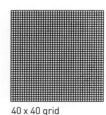

Here, the base grid is 5 x 5 (25 squares) and multiples of this category include designs based on grids of: 5 x 5 (base grid), 10 x 10 grid, 20 x 20 grid, and 40 x 40 grid.

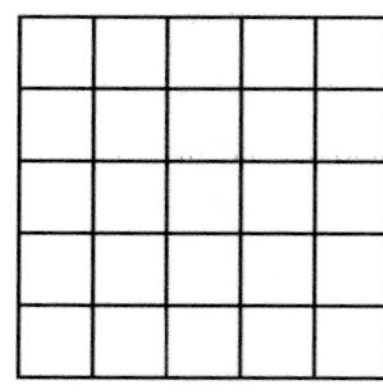
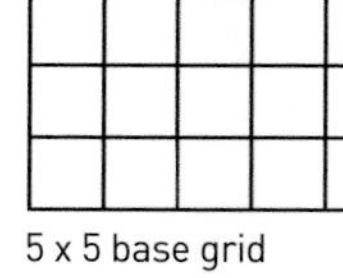
5 x 5 base grid

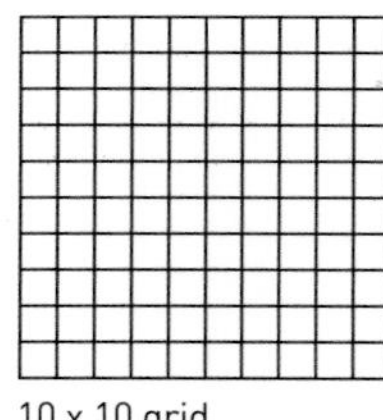
10 x 10 grid

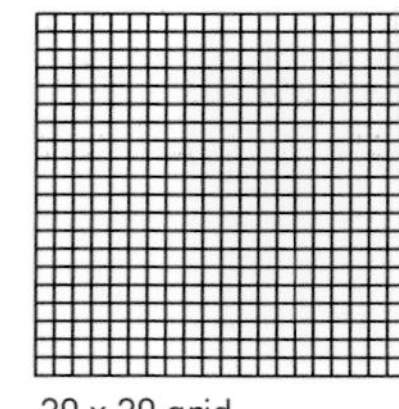
20 x 20 grid

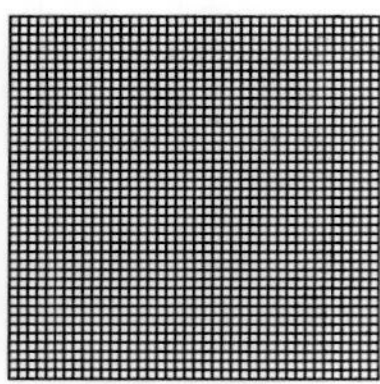
40 x 40 grid

7 x 7 Base Grid Category

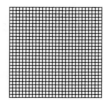

These designs are based on the following grids: 7 x 7 (base grid), 14 x 14 grid, 28 x 28 grid, and 56 x 56 grid (because of the tiny size of the squares, this grid is not shown).

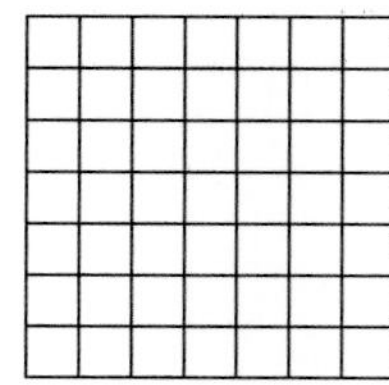
7 x 7 base grid

14 x 14 grid

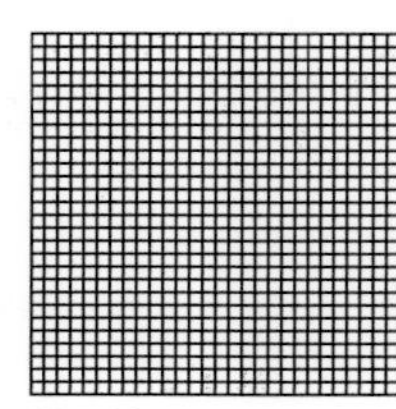
28 x 28 grid

Grid Sheets

The transparent grid sheets that accompany this book are to be used as a guide in understanding how to draft the blocks. Note the grid used for each design is given in the caption beneath the color block. For the block you wish to study, first locate the grid on the transparent sheets. Place the grid over the block. In most cases you will readily see how lines can be drawn from various parts of the grid to create the pattern.

9 x 9 base Grid Category

Because 9 is a multiple of 3, many of the designs in this category are related to ones in the 3 x 3 base grid category. (Since 9 is a base number that cannot be divided by two, 9 x 9—or 81 squares—gets its own category.) Two designs in this category are shown here. This category includes: 9 x 9 base grid, 18 x 18 grid, 36 x 36 grid, and 72 x 72 grid (because of the tiny size of the squares, this grid is not shown).

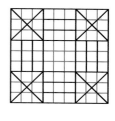

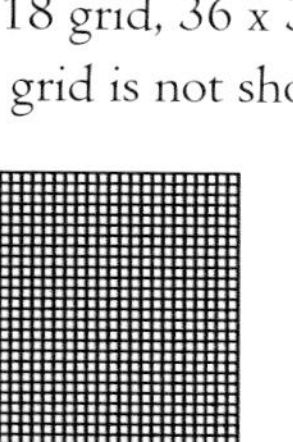

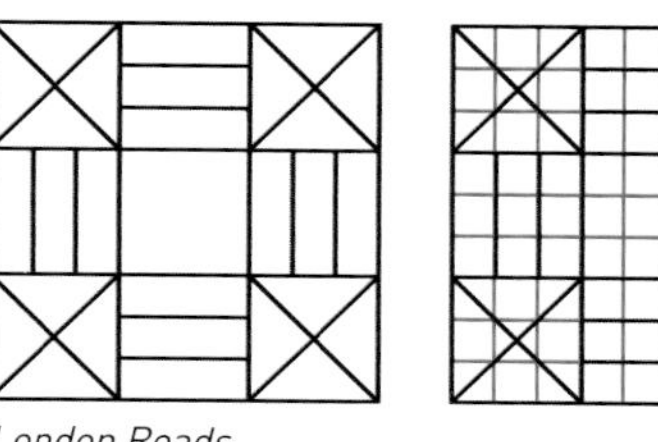

London Roads

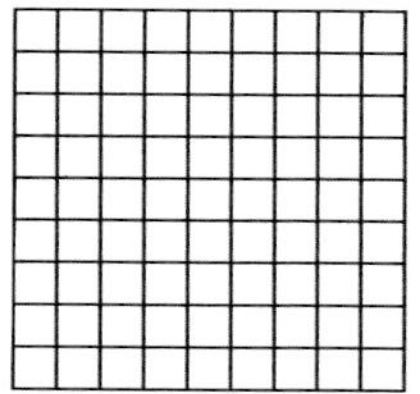

9 x 9 base grid

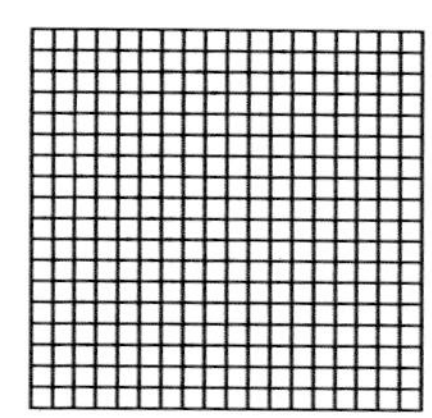

18 x 18 grid

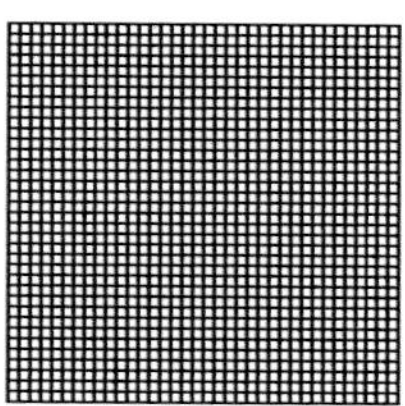

36 x 36 grid

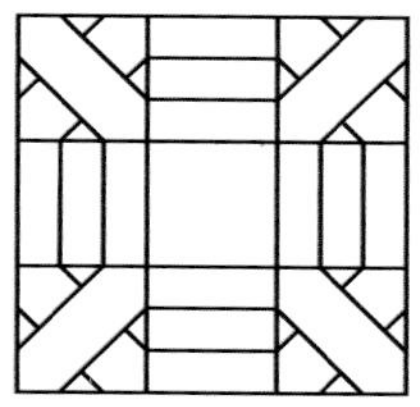

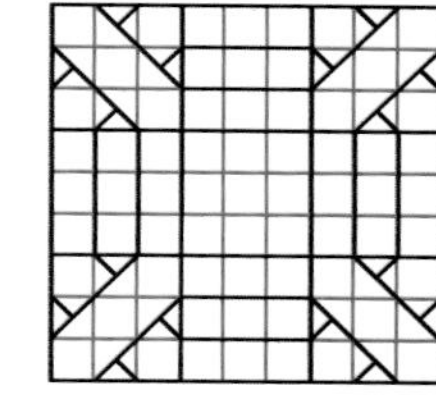

Tangled Garter

11 x 11 Base Grid Category

These designs are based on the following grids: 11 x 11 (base grid), 22 x 22 grid, and 44 x 44 grid (because of the tiny size of the squares, this grid is not shown).

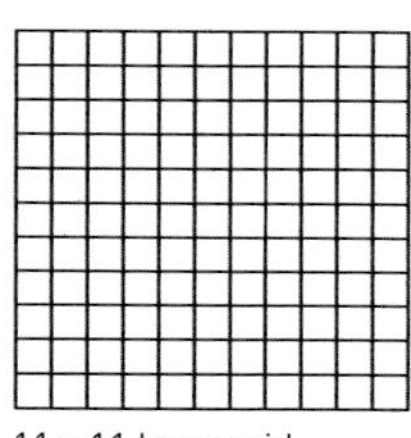

11 x 11 base grid

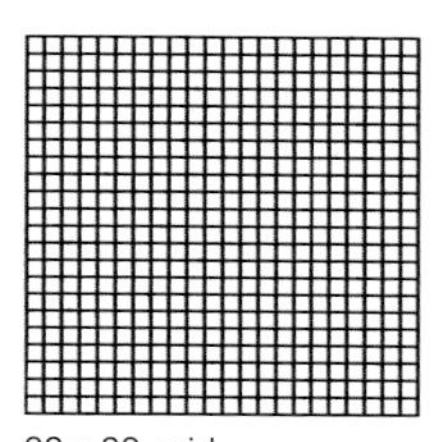

22 x 22 grid

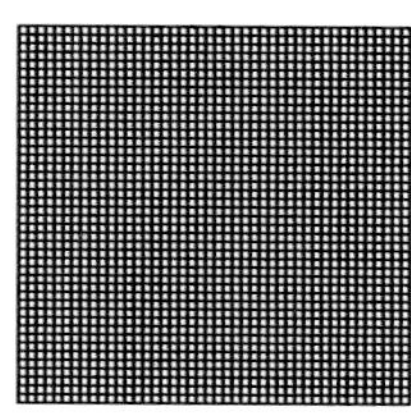

44 x 44 grid

13 x 13 Base Grid Category

These designs are based on the following grids: 13 x 13 (base grid), 26 x 26 grid, and 52 x 52 grid (because of the tiny size of the squares, this grid is not shown).

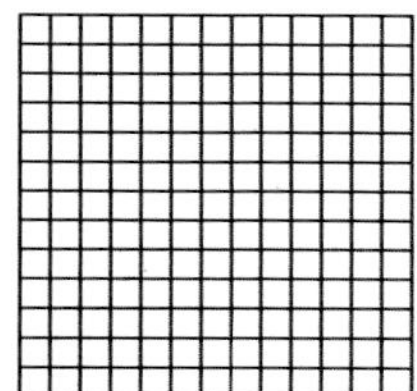

13 x 13 base grid

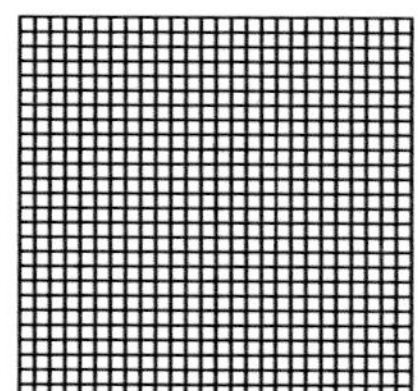

26 x 26 grid

15 x 15 Base Grid Category

Some of the designs in this category are related to ones in the 5 x 5 base grid category. (Similar to the relationship between the 3 x 3 and 9 x 9 categories, this happens because 15 is a multiple of 5 and it cannot be divided by two). The category comprises: 15 x 15 (base grid), 30 x 30 grid, and 60 x 60 grid (because of the tiny size of the squares, this grid is not shown).

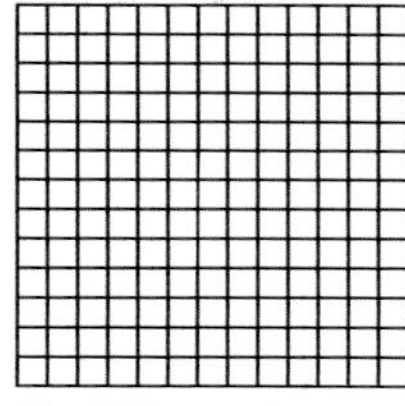

15 x 15 base grid

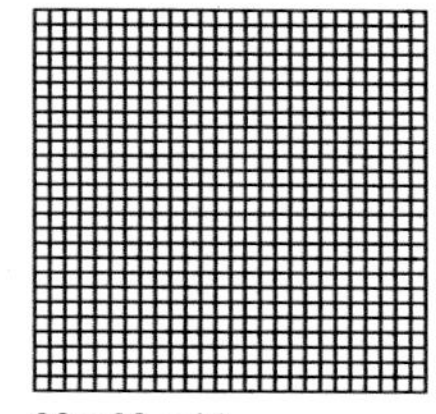

30 x 30 grid

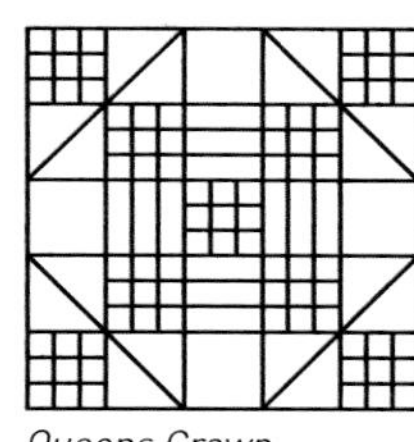

Queens Crown

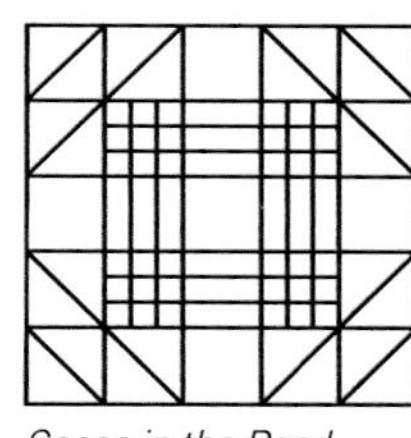

Goose in the Pond

Other Categories

Since there are fewer blocks in each, the following categories are presented together. Here is how they break down:

17 x 17 base grid (34 x 34 grid, 68 x 68 grid)
19 x 19 base grid (38 x 38 grid)
21 x 21 base grid (42 x 42 grid)
23 x 23 base grid (46 x 46 grid)
25 x 25 base grid (50 x 50 grid)
27 x 27 base grid (54 x 54 grid)
29 x 29 base grid
31 x 31 base grid (62 x 62 grid)
33 x 33 base grid
35 x 35 base grid (70 x 70)
41 x 41 base grid
51 x 51 base grid

The Exception: 8-Pointed Star Category

Blocks in the 8-pointed star category differ from grid-based blocks. Rather than being based on a grid of squares, these blocks are based on the pattern created when 16 lines radiate from the center of a square to its outside lines. Eight pointed star blocks are organized first according to symmetry groups, then according similarity of the designs.

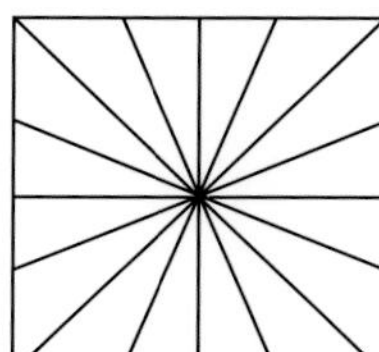

8-pointed star grid

Organization According to Symmetry of the Design

So far, we have grouped blocks according to base grid category, then (for all but 8-pointed star designs) according to the grid upon which they are based. As a third level of organization, the blocks are further categorized according to the symmetry of the block. Similar looking designs are grouped together within the symmetry groups and follow the sequence outlined below.

Traditional Block Symmetry

This is by far the most common type of patchwork block. If a grid of eight spokes is put over the design, dividing it into wedges, you will see that each wedge between the spokes is a mirror of the wedges on either side.

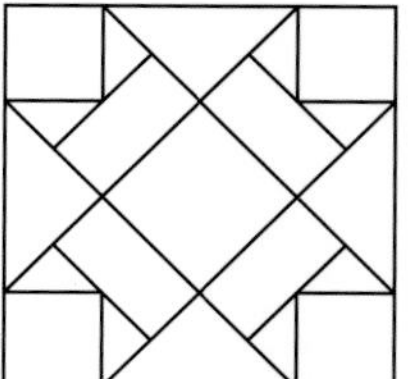

Centennial

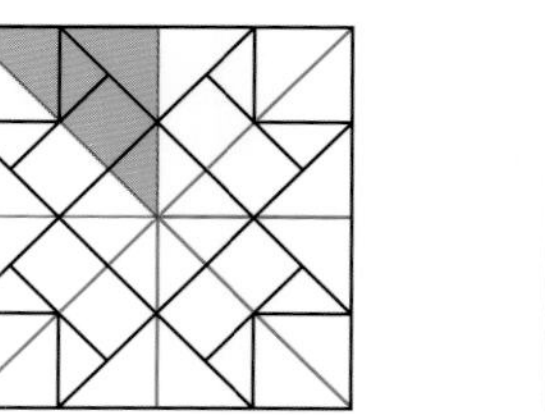

Farmer's Daughter

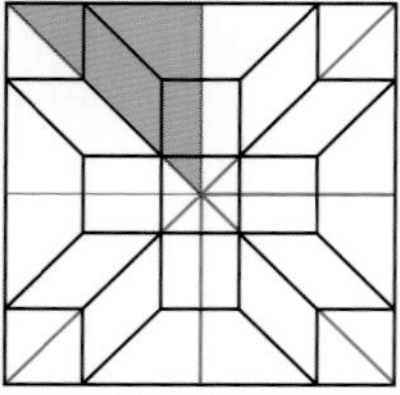

Pinwheel Symmetry

In this symmetry parts of the design are rotated, as shown here.

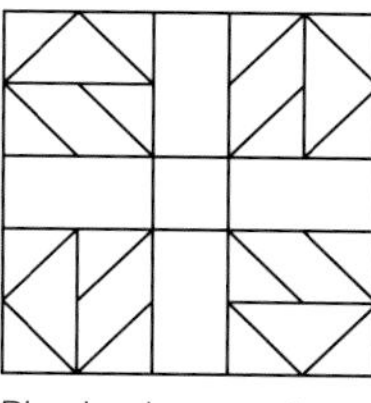

Pinwheel symmetry

Mirrored Symmetry

There are two types of mirrored symmetry illustrated by the designs in this book. The first is *bilateral symmetry*,, which occurs when one half of an image is the mirror of the other half. Designs such as some baskets, fans, or trees, for example, have bilateral symmetry where the mirror line goes diagonally across the block. Many of these designs are meant to be set "on point." In other bilateral symmetry designs, the mirror line goes either vertically or horizontally across the block.

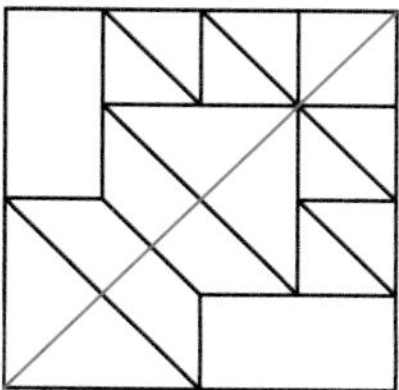

Sugar Bowl (diagonal)

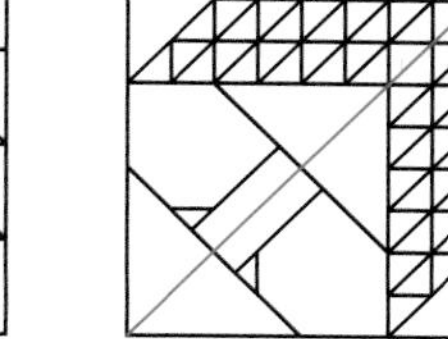

Tree of Life (diagonal)

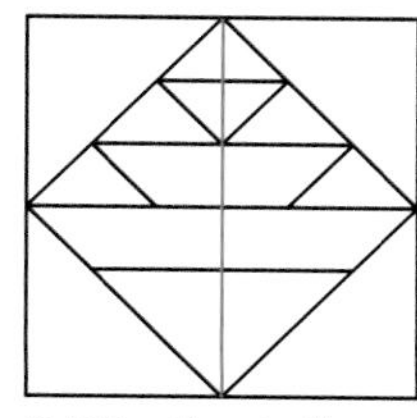

Sail Boat (vertical)

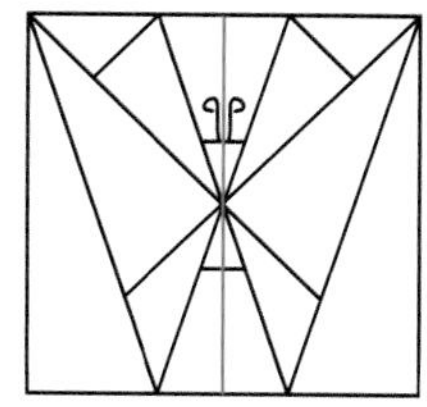

Pieced Butterfly (vertical)

The second type of mirrored symmetry is *double mirrored symmetry*, where the mirror line goes either diagonally across both corners (first pair of drawings), or where it goes both vertically and horizontally (second pair of drawings). Mirrored symmetry designs will be shown together, with the ones with diagonal symmetry appearing first and the ones with vertical and horizontal symmetry next.

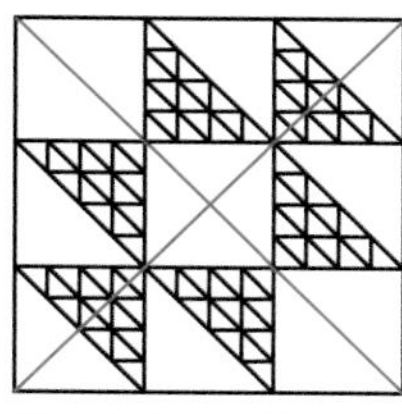

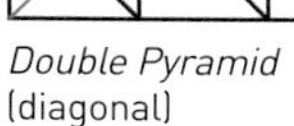

Double Pyramid (diagonal)

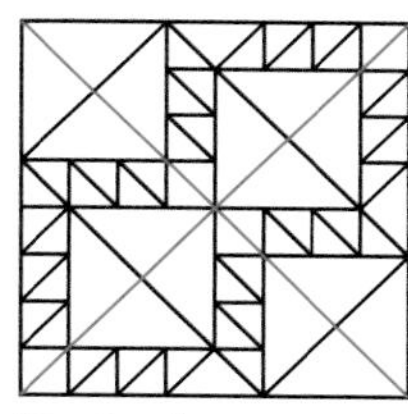

The Swallow (diagonal)

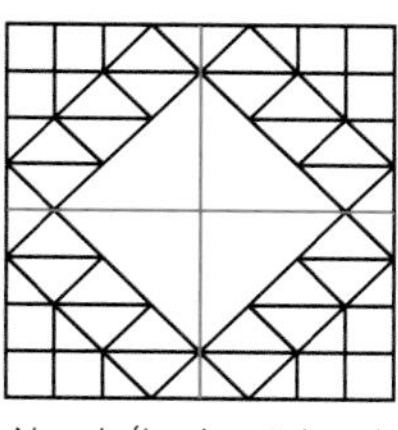

Navajo (horizontal and vertical)

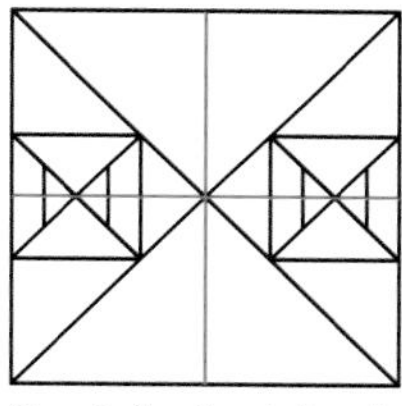

Spools (horizontal and vertical)

180-Degree Rotation

There are not many of these types of designs, but they are ones in which half of the design is rotated 180 degrees from the other half.

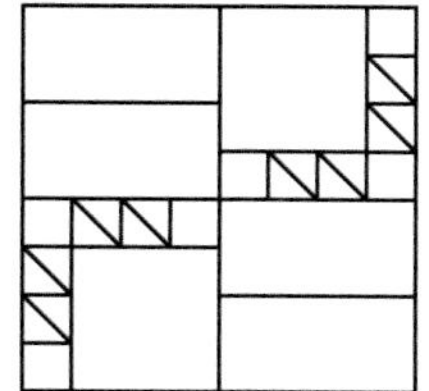

World's Fair Puzzle (180-degree rotation)

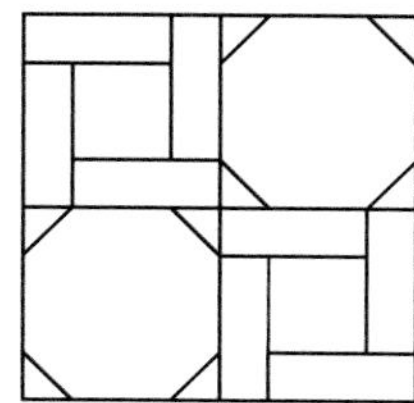

Round the Twist (180-degree rotation)

Asymmetrical Designs

Designs with no symmetry, like the ones shown here, are listed last within the category.

Sunflower

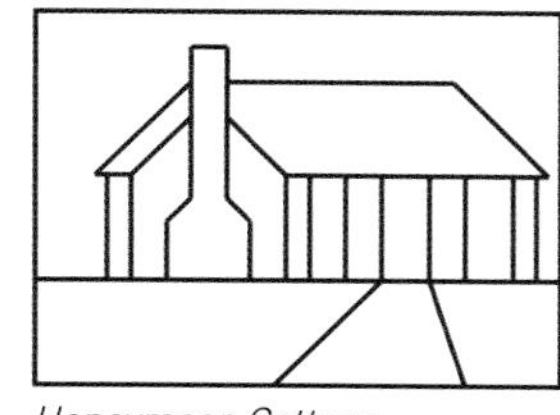

Honeymoon Cottage

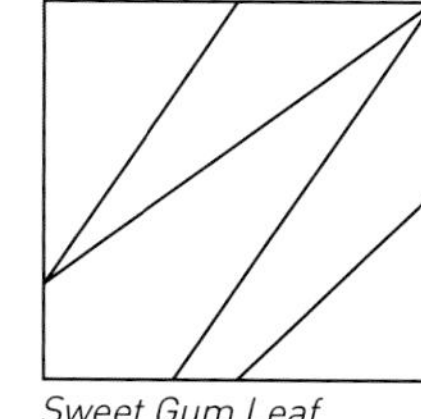

Sweet Gum Leaf

Organization According to Similarity of Design

There is one more level of organization that I have used for designs that have curved lines. That is the similarity of the designs, or the recognizability of the pattern. As with the square designs that don't have curves, a large percentage of the curved designs are first organized according to grid, then symmetry. But since most quilters are familiar with popular designs such as *Drunkard's Path, Fans, Mariner's Compass,* and so on, I have grouped those types of designs together in the following sub-categories, without regard to the grids used for drafting them. This makes it easier to find and identify the designs.

Drunkard's Path blocks (page 350)
Reel blocks (page 354)
Strawberry blocks (page 355)
Tulip blocks (page 357)
Flower blocks (page 360)
Wheel blocks (page 370)
Dresden Plate blocks (page 374)
Compass blocks (page 378)
Crossroads blocks (page 383)
Fan blocks (page 385)
Heart blocks (page 388)

How Hexagonal Blocks Are Organized

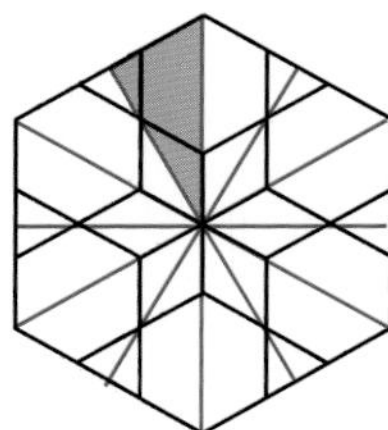

The Hexagon Star

Designs in this group are based on a hexagon and a grid of 12 spokes radiating from the center. Some are in the shape of a hexagon, while others are a hexagon within a square or rectangle. Just as in the square group, these designs are first split into those without curved lines and those with curved lines. The blocks are further sorted according to symmetry, as explained above, but with one exception. Those with traditional block symmetry do not have 8 spokes, but 12, with the portions between each spoke being the mirror of the adjacent ones.

Here is how the hexagon designs are organized:

Hexagonal blocks

No curves	Curves
Symmetry	Symmetry
Similarity	Similarity

How Continuous Pattern Blocks Are Organized

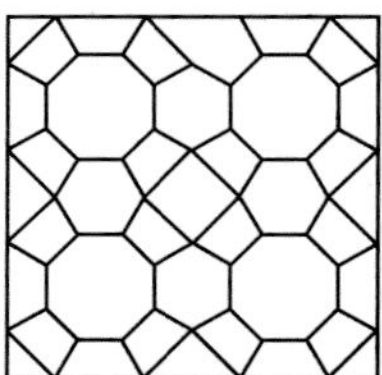

Summer Trellis

Joseph's Coat

Many quilt blocks have mosaic-type designs, where the pattern forms an overall design and does not break down into squares or hexagons. While some of the designs shown in this major group are in the form of squares, others, when put side by side, do not form squares. (If you wanted to sew them together, you would have to cut off part of multiple shapes, then make a seam.) The designs are divided into four categories—designs without curved elements, hexagons without curved elements, hexagons with curves elements, and other designs with curved elements. They are grouped within these categories according to the similarity of the patterns.

Continuous patterns

No curves	Curves
Hexagons without curves	Hexagons with curves
Other designs without curves	Other designs with curves
Similarity	Similarity

How One-Patch Blocks Are Organized

Some designs are made with only a single shape. I call these One-Patch designs. These patterns are sorted first by whether they are without curves or with curves, and within those sections they are organized according to shape, then according to similarity of design.

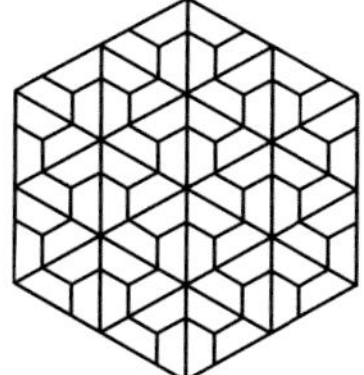

Ecclesiastic

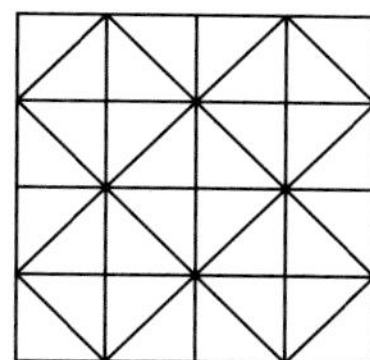

Old Tippecanoe

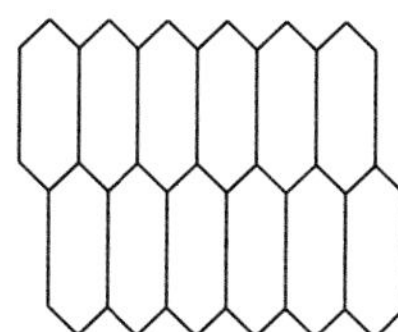

Honeycomb

One-patch blocks

No curves	Curves
Shape	Shape
Similarity	Similarity

How Pentagon Blocks Are Organized

There are very few designs in this category. They are grouped into designs based on whether they include or do not include curved elements.

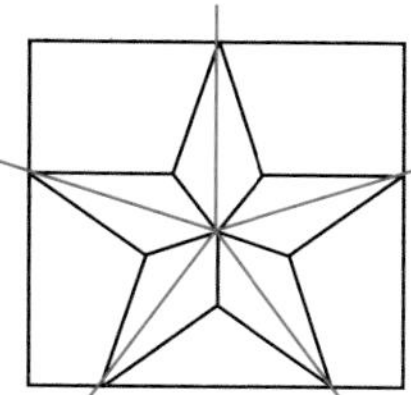

Five Pointed Star

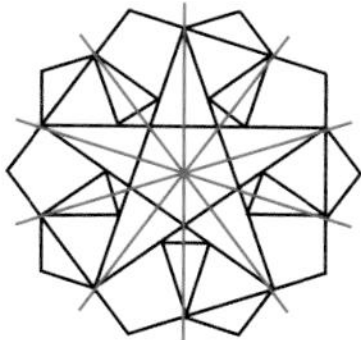

Layered Star

How 7-Pointed Star Blocks Are Organized

These blocks are designed to be used as a single block. They are based on 14 spokes radiating from the center outwards. There are very few designs, so they are organized into those without curves and those with curves.

Summer Rays

How Other Blocks Are Organized

The patterns in this category do not fit into any of the others. They are not square or hexagonal, and many are drafted with odd grids, such as 6 x 15 or 10 x 13. The designs without curves appear before the ones with curves, but there is no other level of categorization.

Quick Reference

As a further help to finding familiar blocks, several quick-reference sections are scattered throughout the book. If you are looking for a particular basket block, for instance, you will soon find different baskets are drafted on different grids, or that some have curves and others don't. The quick-reference section on page 319 collects all basket blocks together, so that you can easily distinguish between them and choose the one you want. Each one is referenced to the category in which it belongs, where you will find the full-size color image and line art. Here is a complete list of the quick-reference guides.

Presentation of the Blocks

Each block is shown in two ways. There is a large color illustration, showing how the block may look in fabric, and a small line drawing that shows how the block is drafted. For each block, the first name provided is the earliest published source I was able to find. As every quilter knows (and as explained in my chapter on Block Sources), over the years, some blocks have come to be known by multiple names. These additional names are listed in alphabetical order after the earliest source.

Be aware that I have not taken coloration or shading of the block into consideration when determining unique designs. In every case, I have identified a block as unique based on the line drawing from which that block is drafted. Oftentimes in quilt history, a block changes name based on the way it is colored or shaded. Ruth Finley had this to say,

> "Manipulation of patterns is further illustrated by the transformation of a *Jacob's Ladder* ... into *Stepping Stones* ... All *Jacob's Ladder* quilts are made in two tones only, the dark patches being very dark and the light patches correspondingly light. No intermediate shades are allowable, since the fundamental idea of the *Jacob's Ladder* is extreme contrast, resulting in a series of dark "ladders" running up and down the quilt or diagonally across. Now take this same block; reverse the light and dark patches and add a third intermediate tone, and you have ... *Stepping Stones* in Virginia and New England, in Pennsylvania *The Tail of Benjamin's Kite,* in Western Reserve *The Underground Railroad* and in the Mississippi and prairie countries *The Trail of the Covered Wagon* or just *Wagon Tracks.*" (Finley)

In terms of the way this block is drafted (and the line drawing used to draft it), all these named designs are identical. I have not shown multiple colorations of the same block, but have identified it only by the structure of the design, which is, after all, the most important element. In most cases, I have colored the block with the same light/dark placement as in the earliest source of that block. The exception is one-patch designs—designs made with a single shape. For squares, diamonds and hexagons, particularly, there are distinct names for the various designs depending on how they are colored.

At first examination, some designs seem to be identical to others, but when you look closely at the line drawings you will see slight differences, perhaps additional lines or other subtle variations. Most likely, these variations happened over time, as the block passed down from generation to generation. The result is that blocks that carry the same name often are structurally different and are drafted on different grids. Compare, for instance, these three versions of *Crowned Cross,* one from Ruth Finley, one from Carrie Hall and one from Nancy Page. Look, also, at the two variations of *Noon and Night,* one from Nancy Page and the other from Laura Wheeler. The two versions of *Mrs. Cleveland's Choice,* one from *Ladies Art Company* and the other from Nancy Cabot, are yet another example.

Crowned Cross

Ruth Finley. See 166-5.

Carrie Hall. See 199-5.

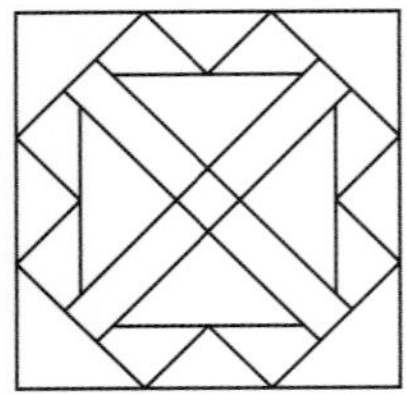

Nancy Page. See 166-7.

Noon and Night

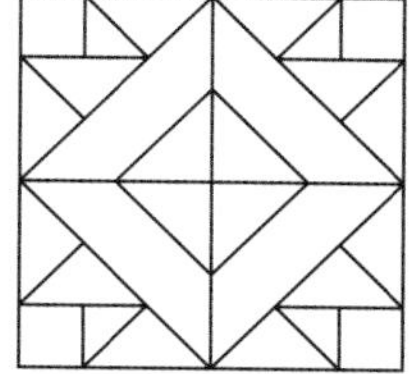

Nancy Page. See 154-10.

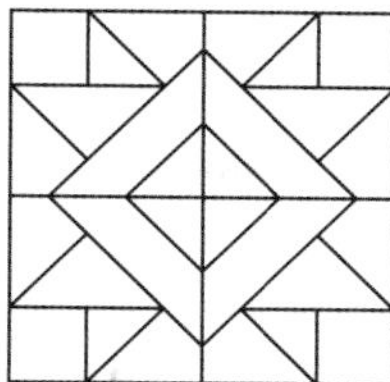

Laura Wheeler. See 210-2.

Mrs. Cleveland's Choice

Ladies Art Company. See 249-9.

Nancy Cabot. See 175-12.

Now look at these two *Illinois Star* patterns, one from *Prairie Farmer,* drafted in an 8 x 8 grid, and another from Nancy Cabot, drafted on a 28 x 28 grid. The Cabot pattern has a larger triangle at the sides and a narrower strip next to the triangle.

Illinois Star

Quilt Booklet No. 1. See 83-9.

Nancy Cabot. See 236-8.

In some cases, the only difference between two blocks may be that the art is "flipped". *Clay's Choice* is a good example. I have treated these as a single, unique design, not as two variations.

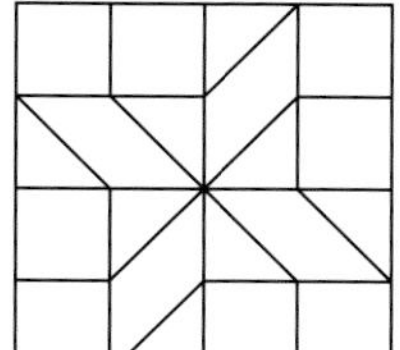

Clay's Choice. See 70-5.

If there is any variation at all in design structure, no matter how subtle, I have included that block as a unique design. For the most part, similar designs appear together, since they are usually based on the same grid; in instances where they are based on different grids, there is a cross reference to similar designs or to a quick-reference section.

I find the evolution of block designs to be fascinating and studying the sources of designs has helped me understand how blocks are constructed. The previous chapter describes the various historical sources of traditional pieced blocks. I hope reading both chapters will provide you with a deeper insight into the design of the blocks you choose for your quilts.

Fortune Teller, Ricki Selva, 2000. This quilt is a fragmented version of *Nova* (see page 47), a Hilton Head Seminar design by Jinny Beyer.

Using Base Grids to Draft Designs

Old quilts and quilt blocks can be found in so many places—antique stores, trunks in the attic, and old photographs. All of these are fascinating, particularly if you are interested in making similar quilts of your own. This book can help you figure out exactly how a long-ago quilter made her blocks. The key, which you have already read about in the previous chapter, is to understand the underlying grid that forms the basis of any quilt block. The first part of the chapter will help you spot the grid used to draft a design; the second part will provide steps to draft your own blocks.

Square Grids

It is very easy to find the grid underlying some patterns, because the designs themselves include the entire grid, with perhaps a few extra lines across some of the squares of the grid, such as the ones shown here.

Let's look at some examples. With *Star Flower,* it is easy to see that there are four equal divisions, therefore a 4 x 4 grid would be required to draft the block. Since 4 x 4 designs are categorized within the 2 x 2 base grid category, you will find the design in that section of the book. In *Wedding Ring,* there are clearly five equal divisions across the block. Since 5 cannot be divided evenly by any another number, the base grid must be 5 x 5. In *Greek Cross,* there are 7 equal divisions; 7 cannot be equally divided by any other number, so the base grid must be 7 x 7.

Star Flower. See 62-6.

Other patterns have the grid on part of the design. It is still quite easy to see what grid they are based on, as with *Flagstones, Village Green,* and *The Bridal Path.*

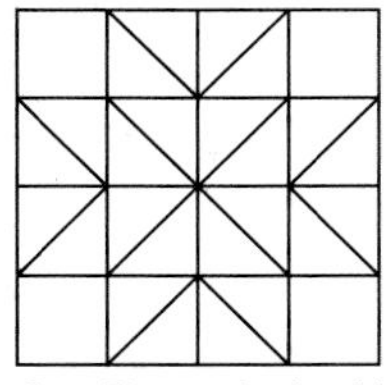

Star Flower, 4 x 4 grid

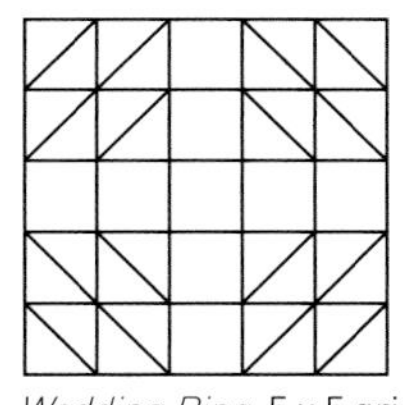

Wedding Ring, 5 x 5 grid

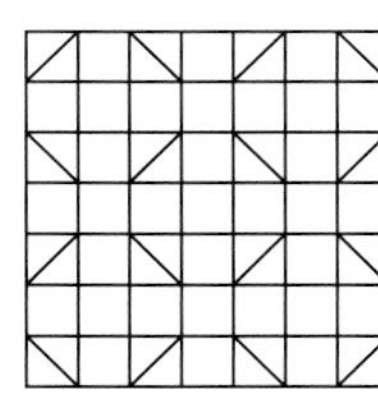

Greek Cross, 7 x 7 grid

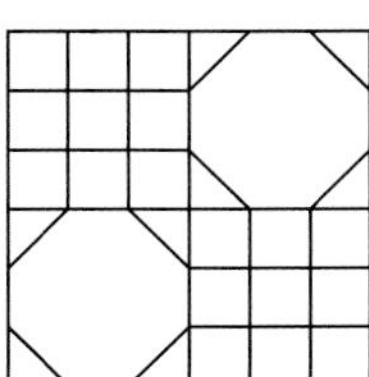

Flagstones, 6 x 6 grid

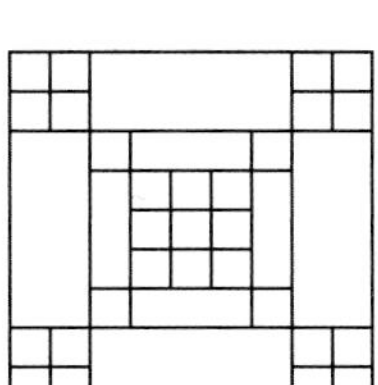

Village Green, 9 x 9 grid

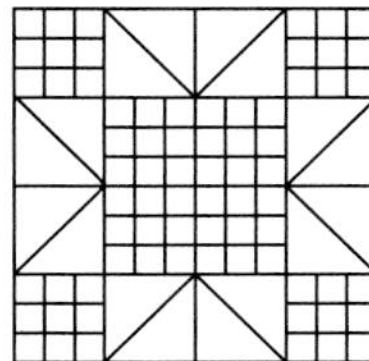

The Bridal Path, 12 x 12 grid

For a large majority of the blocks, the grid is not so easily apparent. In fact, many designs based on a grid of squares have no squares at all in the design. After figuring out the underlying grid for each of the 4,000-plus designs in this book, I came up with a few methods that work best for me. They require tracing paper, a straight edge ruler, and a pencil.

Method 1

Centennial, 8 x 8 grid. See 78-5.

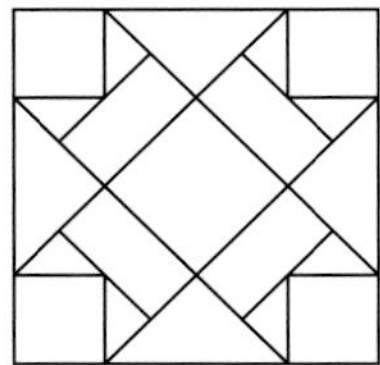

The first method is used for the less complex designs. Take, for example, the block *Centennial.*

1. Photocopy the block. If it is a portion of a quilt or antique block, try to get it as flat and square as possible. If you are copying a design from a book, you may need to find a photocopier with a "zoom" feature, so that you can enlarge the design to at least three inches square.

2. Align a piece of tracing paper so that its bottom edge falls along the bottom edge of the photocopied design and the perpendicular edge falls on the left side of the block.

3. Slowly move the paper to the right, keeping the bottom edge even with the bottom of the block, until you see the first place where lines from the design either touch the top or bottom edge of the block or intersect other lines within the design. Using the straight edge ruler, draw a line on the design showing that first intersection.

4. Move the paper to the right again until you come to the next intersection and draw a second line.

5. Keep moving the paper to the right and continue in this way until you have drawn perpendicular lines at all the intersections and places where the design touches the top and/or bottom edge of the block.

You will see that in the end there are eight equal divisions across the block. That means this design has a grid of 8 x 8 squares. But what is the category? Keep dividing eight in half until you get to the lowest number of squares; that will tell you that the base grid category is the 2 x 2. Therefore, the design will be found in the 2 x 2 base grid category, in the 8 x 8 grid section.

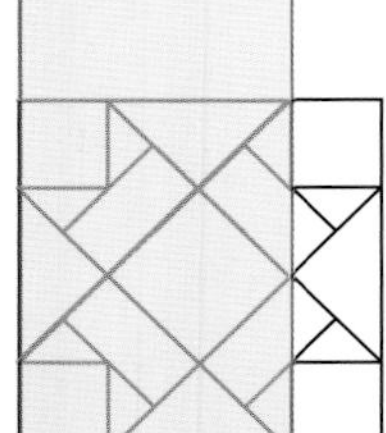

Step 2

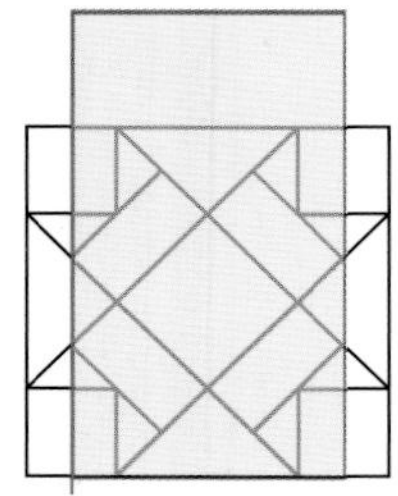

Step 3

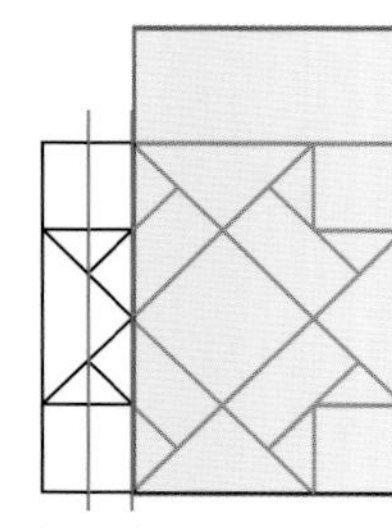

Step 4

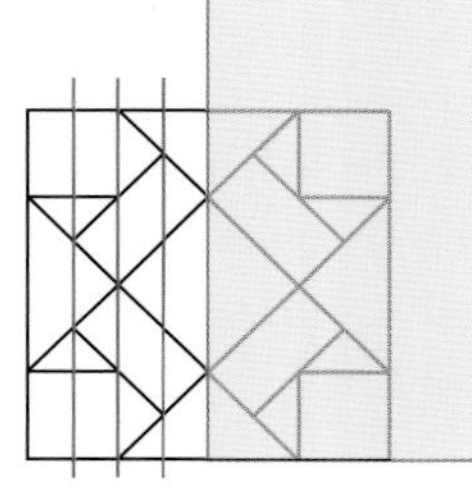

Step 5

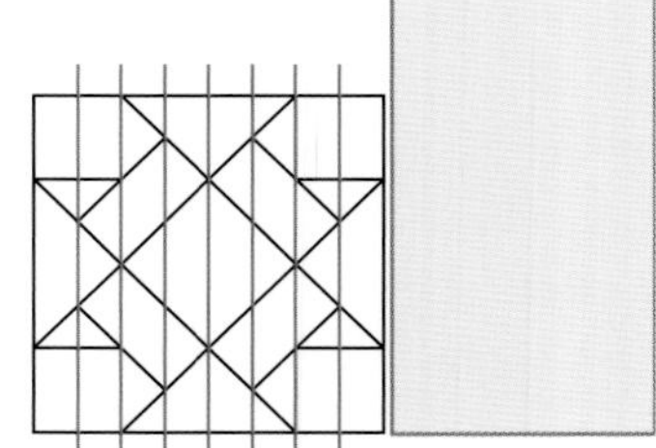

Centennial, 8 x 8 grid

Method 2

Box Quilt. See 258-9.

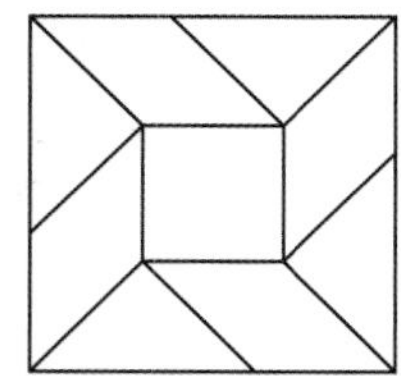

For more complex designs, try this similar method. Look at this variation of *Box Quilt*, published in *Ladies Art Company* catalog. On the surface, this looks like an easy block to identify. One can clearly see three divisions and it would appear that the divisions are equal, but are they? Complete steps 1-5 above and it is obvious that there is no clear-cut grid. There are two small sections that are same size, plus three larger sections, of which two are the same size and one is slightly smaller. When the first method does not help, follow these steps.

6. Find the smallest division. This is indicated along the length of the block in red. Place a piece of tracing paper over the block and mark that smallest division on the paper and the block.

7. Mark the block. Continue moving the tracing paper using the smallest division to mark along the top edge of the block, until the entire block has tic marks.

When the divisions are counted, you will see that there are 13 equal divisions. This means the base grid for this block is 13 x 13. The block can be found in the 13 x 13 base grid category with other designs that have a 13 x 13 grid.

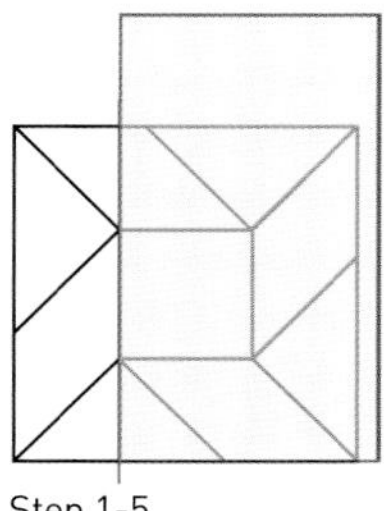

Step 1-5

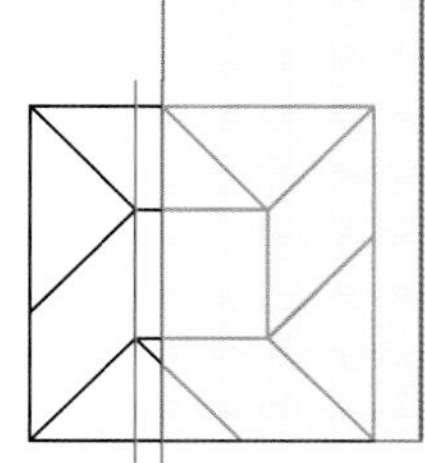

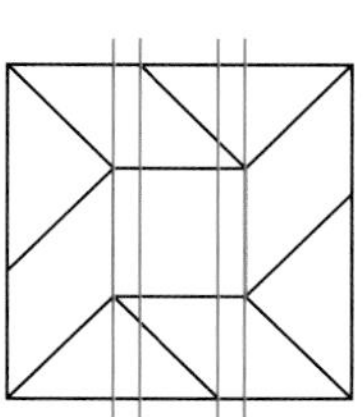

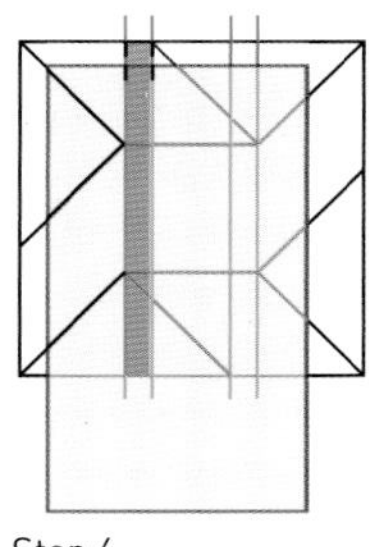

Step 6

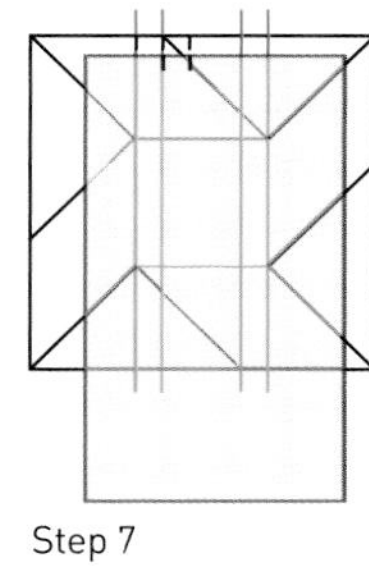

Step 7

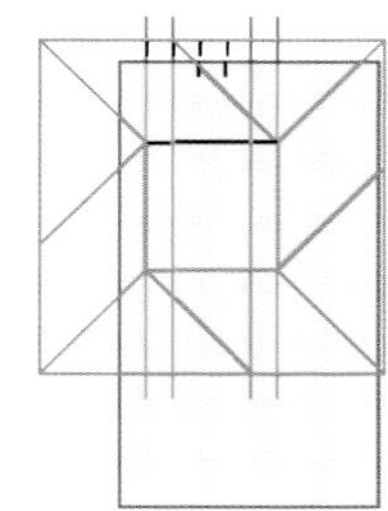

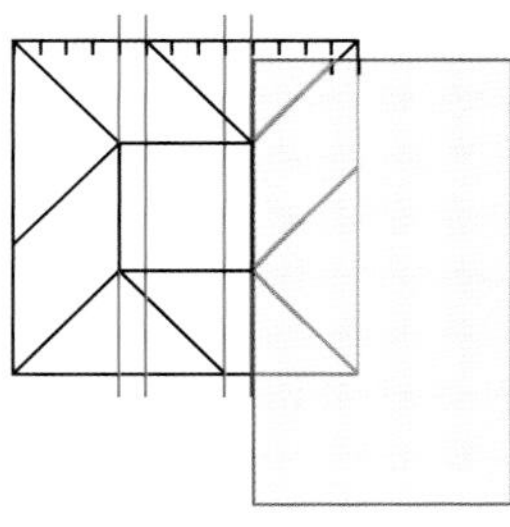

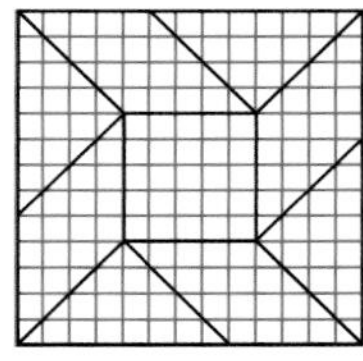

Box Quilt, 13 x 13 grid

Method 3

Look at this variation of *Bear's Paw*. Three clearly defined small divisions are apparent in the corners of the block, but it is obvious that the section in the middle is wider than one of the corner divisions, yet narrower than two of the corner divisions. Follow the steps to find the grid.

Bear's Paw. See 262-7.

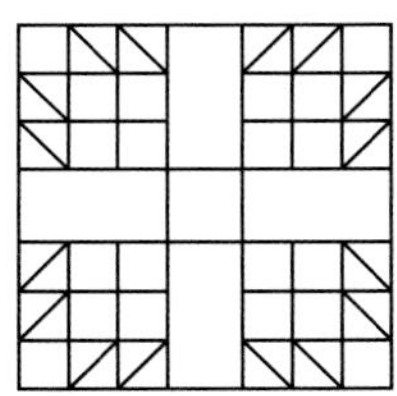

Bear's Paw

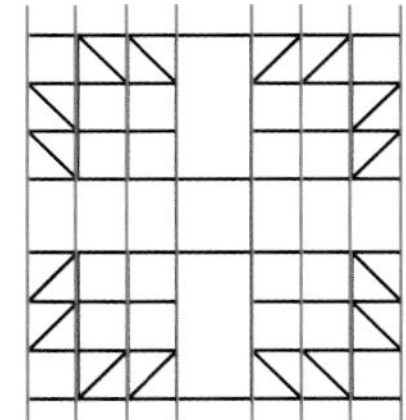

1. Place the tracing paper over the design and mark one of the smaller divisions onto the paper. (One of these is indicated by the red column.)
2. Bring that measurement to the middle section and make a mark.
3. You will clearly see a smaller division (marked in blue). Mark the width of that smaller division on the tracing paper.
4. Use the smaller division as a guide and put tic marks across the block.

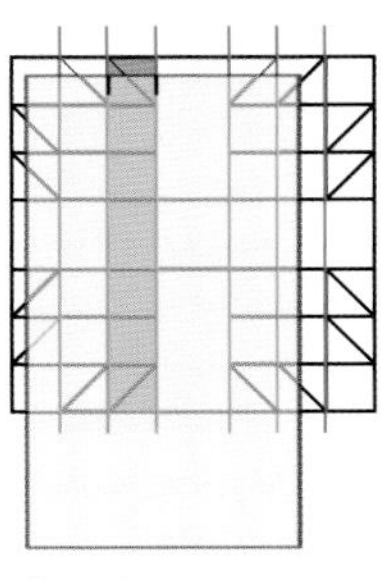

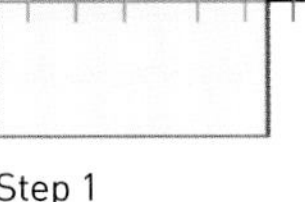

Step 1

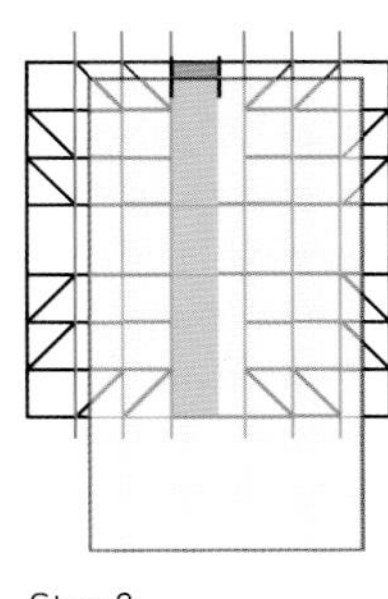

Step 2

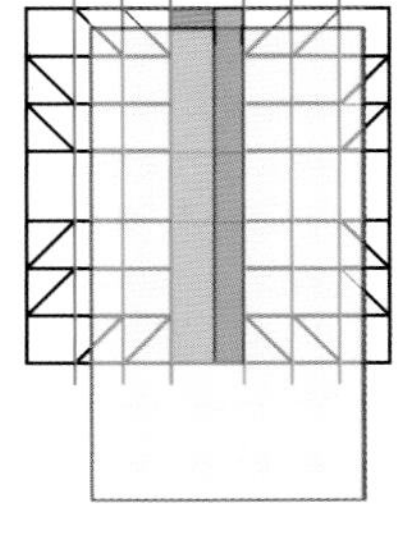

Step 3

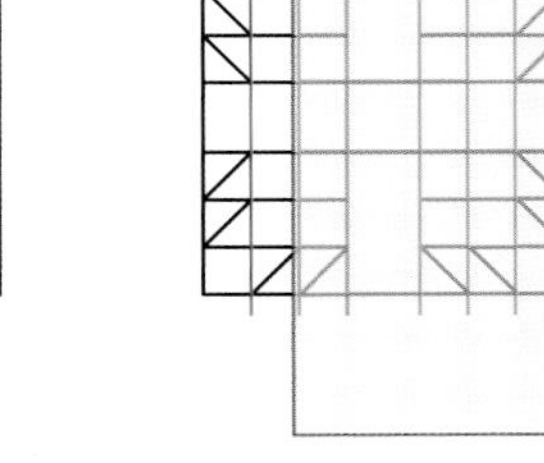

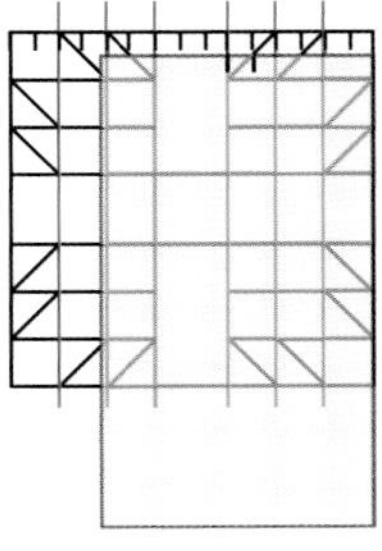

Step 4

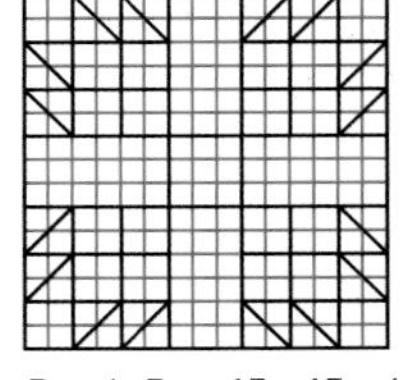

Bear's Paw, 15 x 15 grid

The center section contains three of the smaller divisions and the corner squares each contain two. There are 15 equal divisions. The base grid is 15 x 15 (because 15 cannot be equally divided by 2), and so this block can be found in the 15 x 15 base grid category, among the 15 x 15 grid designs.

8-Pointed Star Grids

Eight Pointed Star. See 276-1.

The 8-pointed star category is different from categories based on a grid of squares. Designs from this group are based on a series of 16 lines radiating at equal distance apart from the center of the block outwards. Take a look at the basic *Eight-Pointed Star* design.

At first glance, it is easy to assume that this design falls into a 4 x 4 or 3 x 3 base grid. But once you find the places where lines in the design intersect or come to the edges of the block, you discover that those divisions are not equal. Note too that it is impossible to find a smallest division to divide the rest of the block into, as was done above with the grids of squares. That is because this block is not based on a grid of squares. When a grid of 16 spokes radiating at equal angles from the center of the block is placed over the design, you can see where the points of the star hit the lines of the spokes. Furthermore, and this is one of the biggest clues to identifying designs in this category, the distance between the star points along the edge of the block is the same as the distance between the points diagonally across the corner. All of the star points are equal distance from each other.

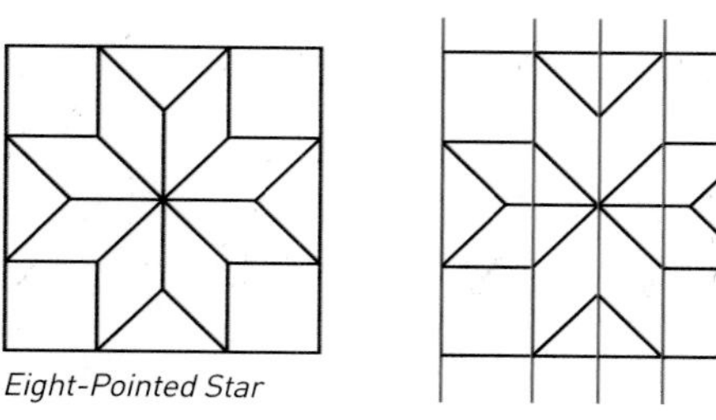

Eight-Pointed Star

Unequal divisions

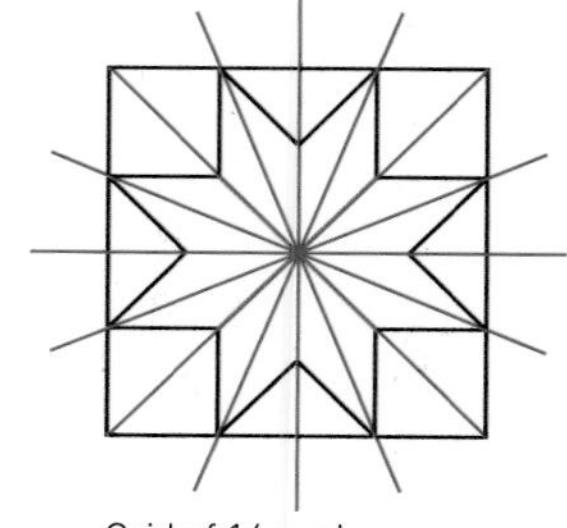

Grid of 16 spokes

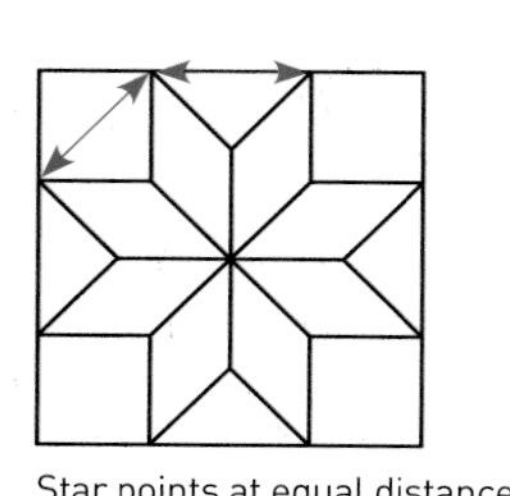

Star points at equal distance

Keep in mind that not all stars with eight points fall into the 8-pointed star category. Compare *Eight Pointed Star* with another star with eight points, *Godey Design*. A close look reveals that *Eight Pointed Star* is made up of 45-degree diamonds. That means that each side of the diamonds making up the star is the same length. The star in *Godey Design* is made up of parallelograms, where two sides of the shape are shorter than the other two. Furthermore, if the distance is measured between the points of the star, it becomes apparent that some points are farther apart than others. This design is based on a grid of 6 x 6 squares and can be found in the 3 x 3 base grid category, in the 6 x 6 section.

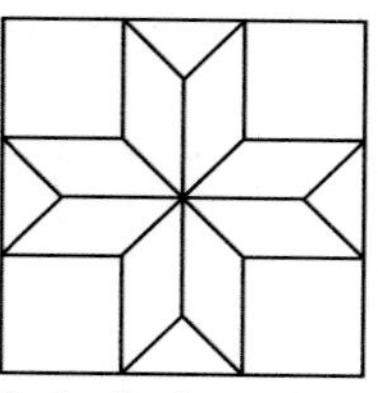

Godey Design

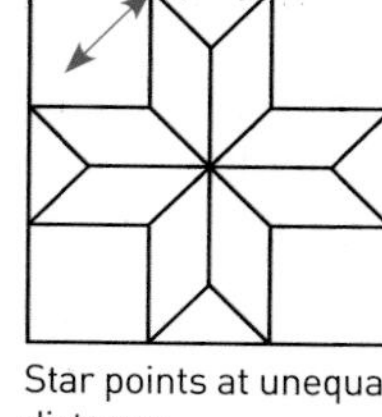

Star points at unequal distance

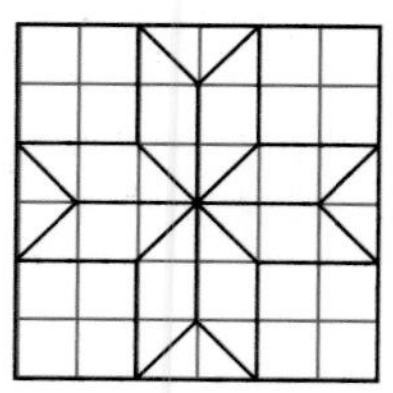

Godey Design, 6 x 6 grid

Here is the basic 8-pointed star grid. Many designs in the 8-pointed star category can be drafted using the lines of this grid. Others that are more complex require additional lines on the grid to draft the design.

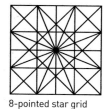

8-pointed star grid

The following clues will help you confirm that a design fits into the 8-pointed star category:

1. The design has an 8-pointed star made up of 45-degree diamonds, where all of the outer points are the same distance from each other. The star may fill the entire square, or it might be a smaller star within the design.

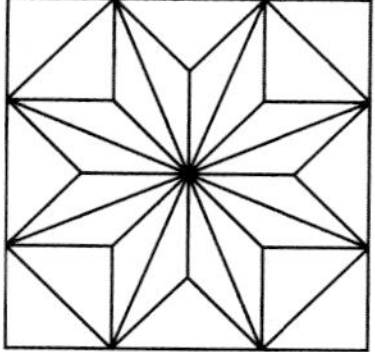
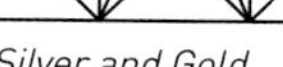
Silver and Gold

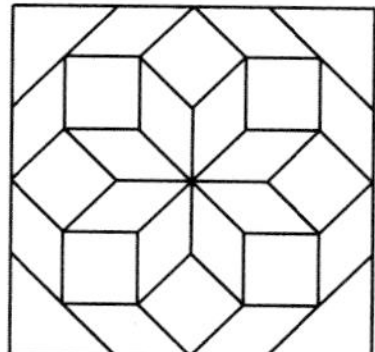
Rolling Star

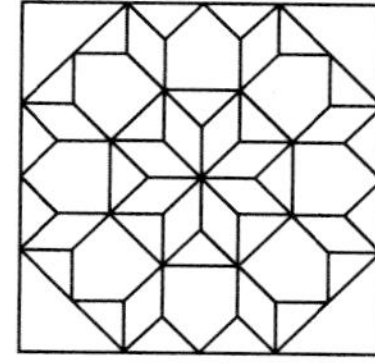
Star of Bethlehem

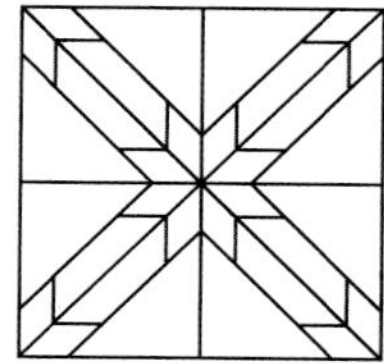
Indian Arrowhead

2. The design has partial stars that contain perfect 45-degree diamonds and the star points are equal distance from each other.

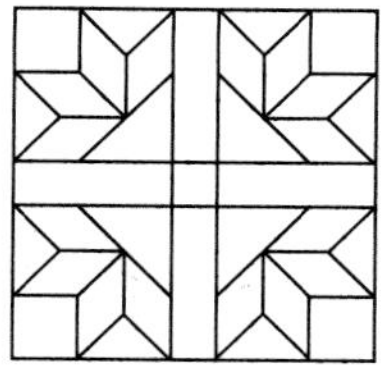
Crossroads

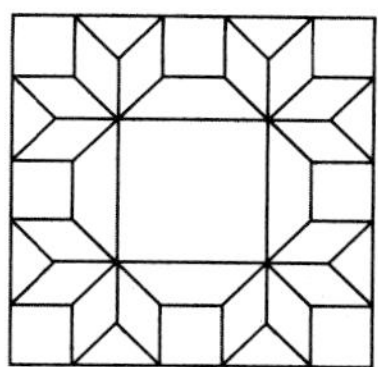
Lotus Star

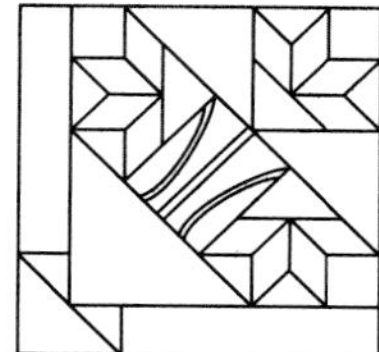
Basket of Lilies

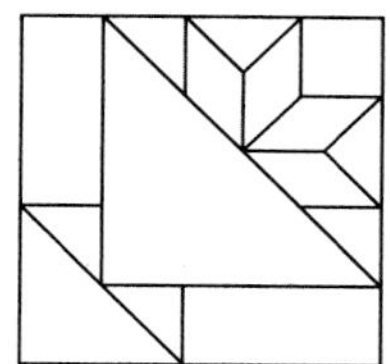
Cactus Basket

3. The design has stars with points at equal distance from each other, but only part of the complete diamonds shows.

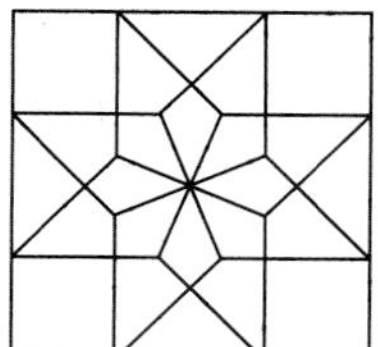
Enigma Star

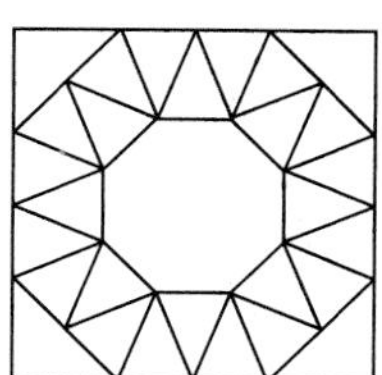
Jupiter Star

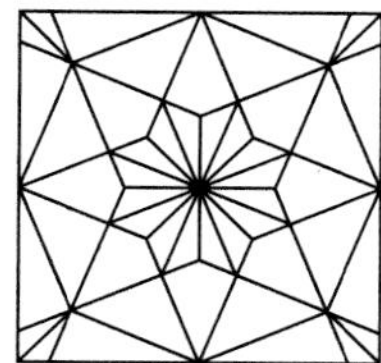
Pinwheel Star

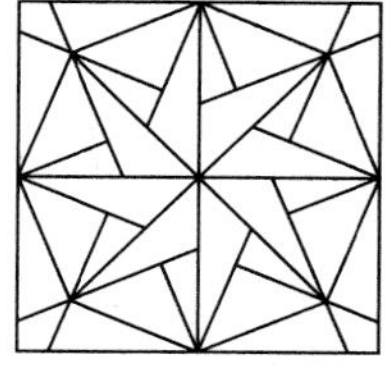
Lucky Star

4. The design has three divisions across the top and the middle division is the same width as the diagonal across the corner.

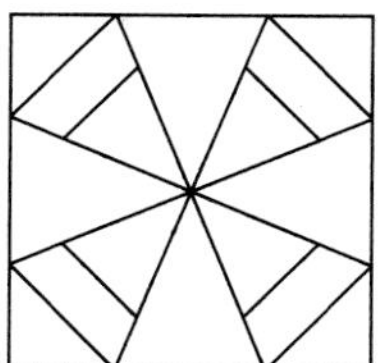
Propeller

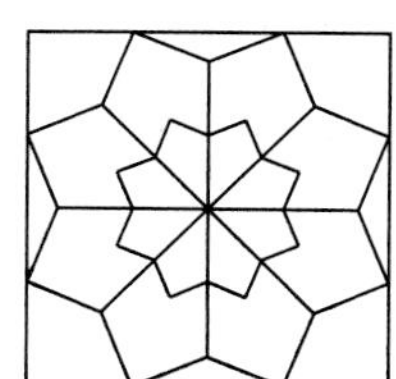
Double Star

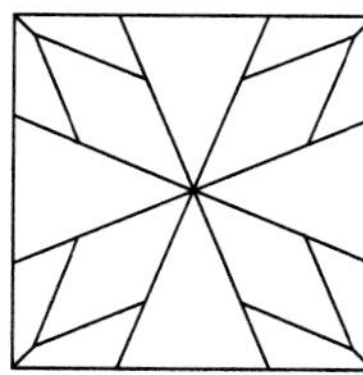
Illusions

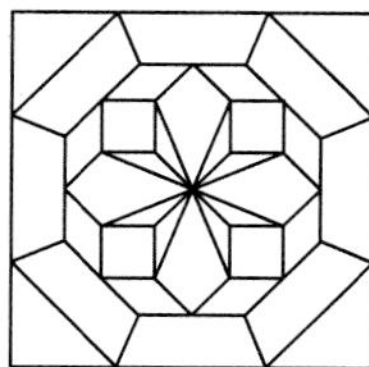
Court Jester

5. The design contains a perfect octagon.

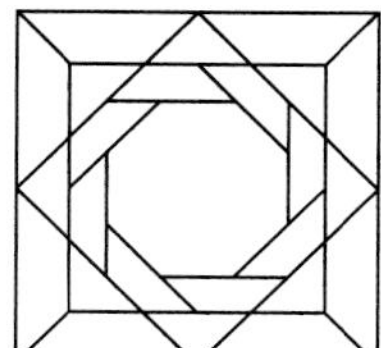
Interlocked Squares

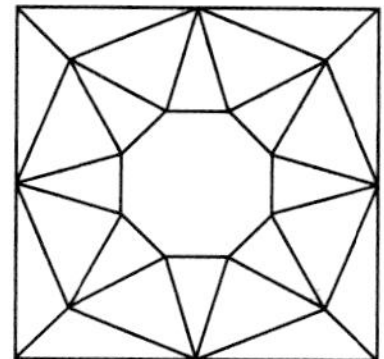
Rising Sun

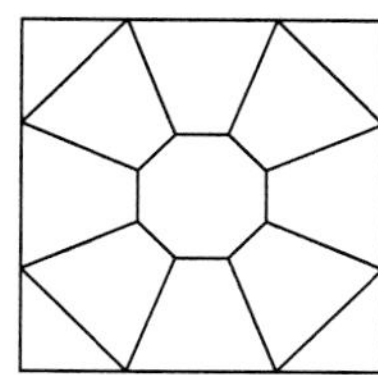
The Windmill

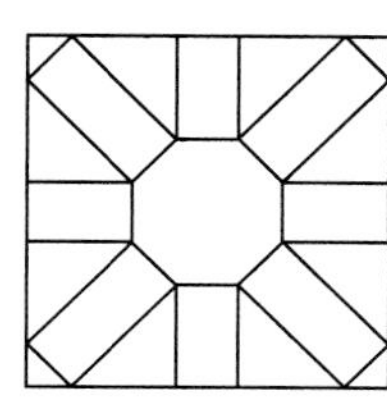
Midsummer Night

Hexagon Grids

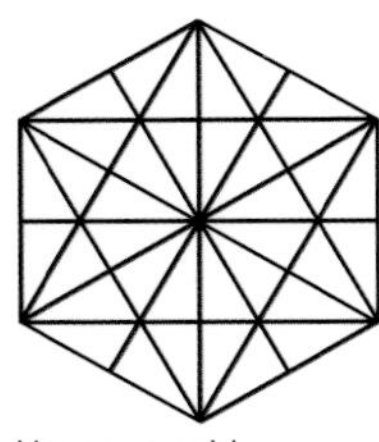

Hexagon grid

Designs based on a hexagon are quite easy to spot because almost all of them are in the shape of a hexagon, or contain a 6- or 12-pointed star. Just as the 8-pointed star grid contains a star with eight points, likewise the hexagon grid contains a star with six points. The basic hexagon grid is shown here, but for some of the more complex designs additional lines must be added to the grid (see page 18).

Other Designs

See pages 18 to 19 for a description of the continuous, one-patch and pentagon designs. As with hexagons, it is usually obvious which grid category these fall into.

Drafting Designs

The Original. See 121-8.

The words *geometry* and *drafting* scare a lot of people, bringing back memories of falling behind in math class at school or dreaded algebraic formulas and geometric theorems. Yet all we are doing when we create patchwork quilts is working with simple geometric designs. Men and women have been doing it for centuries in the making of the wonderful quilt patterns that have been passed to us today. The fact is that drafting patchwork designs is very easy and does not require math skills. All you need is a simple understanding of how the designs are structured. Then, with the help of paper, pencil, ruler, compass and a 45-degree right-angle triangle, you can draw any geometric pattern you please. The rest of this chapter will help you.

The computer is a valuable tool for drafting patterns. Any good graphics program will allow you to draft designs quickly and accurately, using the guidelines provided here. Even if you plan on using a computer, it is important to understand the basics, so that computer drafting becomes easier.

Drafting Designs Based on a Grid of Squares

First Step: Determine the Category and Grid

Beginner's Joy. See 57-11.

As we have seen, almost all geometric designs used in patchwork have a basic underlying grid that acts as an invisible guide to drafting the design. Most designs we work with are based on grids made up of a certain number of equal-size squares, as explained above. The key to successful pattern drafting is to be able to recognize what category a design falls into and what underlying grid forms the basis of the design. This part is easy, because it is all in this book, where blocks are organized by category and grid. (The grid used for drafting the design is noted under each colored design.) If you have trouble seeing how the design fits the grid, work with the transparent grid sheets and place them over the designs to see how the grid fits. If the design you want to draft is not in this book, then follow the guidelines on pages 23 to 27 for determining how to find the grid of a design.

Second Step: Draw a Perfect Square

To have an accurate pattern it is imperative that the square is accurate as well. Some people ask, why not use graph paper? The answer is that you will often need odd-size squares. If a square needs to be 8 ⅞," for instance, it would be very difficult to draft on graph paper, unless the graph-paper grid was in ⅛" increments.

There are various methods for drawing a perfect square. Here are three methods to choose from. First, determine the finished size of square, then follow these guidelines.

Method 1

I can't help but think that this method must have been the one used by ancient artisans and mathematicians. Like all geometric shapes, a perfect square can be drawn by creating a series of overlapping circles.

1. Determine the size you want the square to be and open a compass to half that exact size (the radius of the circle). Draw a circle and mark the center point A.
2. Without changing the setting on the compass, place it on the edge of the circle and draw a second circle that overlaps the first. Mark the center of that circle B.
3. Draw a line connecting A and B.
4. Place a right-angle triangle on line AB with the 90-degree angle at A, then draw a line up the side of the triangle until it hits the first circle at C.
5. Flip the triangle and place it on line AB with the 90-degree angle at B, then draw a line up the side of the triangle until it hits the second circle at D.
6. Connect C and D to finish the square.

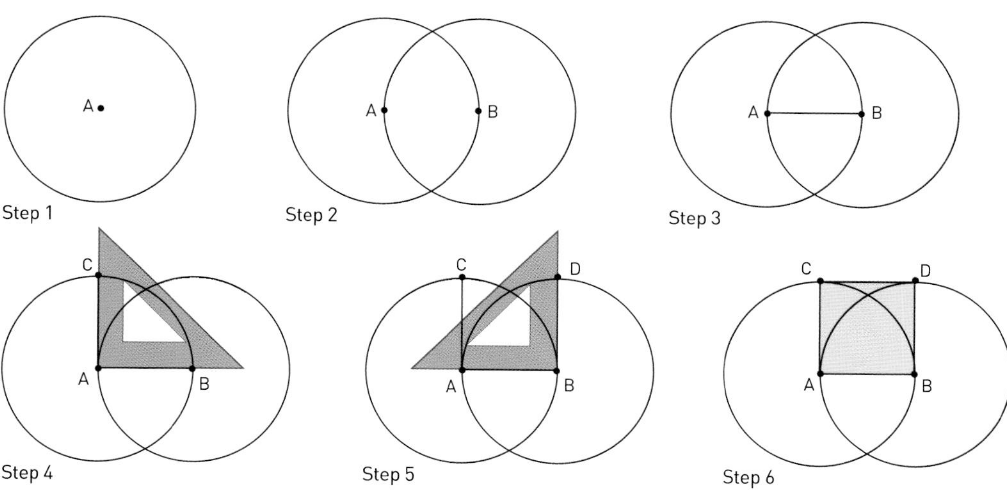

Method 2

1. Draw a horizontal line (AB) the length of the size of the finished square.
2. Place a large 45-degree right-angle triangle along the AB line with one side exactly on the line and the 90-degree at A. Draw a line the exact length of the first line up the side of the triangle.
3. Turn the triangle so it is along the newly drawn line, with the right angle stopping at the exact endpoint of the new line. Draw another line the exact length of the previous two.
4. Turn the triangle one last time with the right angle at the end of the new line and draw the final segment of the square.

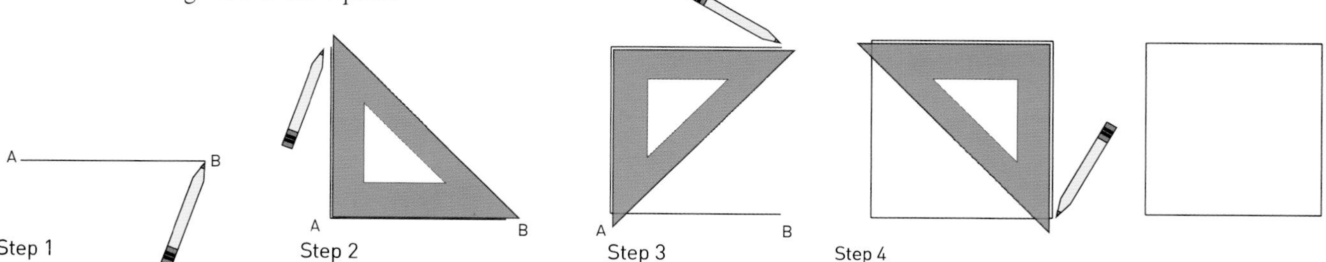

Method 3

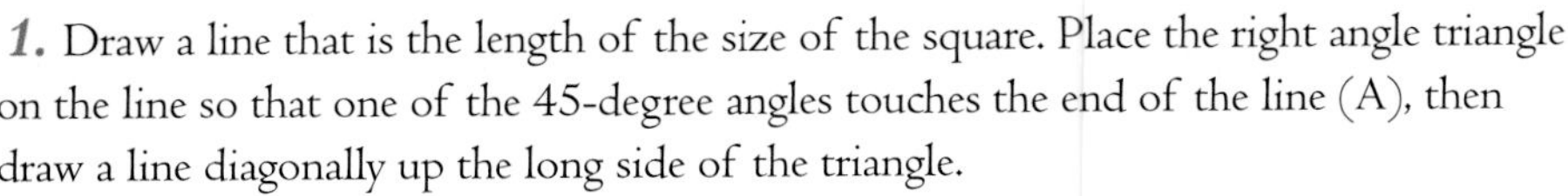

1. Draw a line that is the length of the size of the square. Place the right angle triangle on the line so that one of the 45-degree angles touches the end of the line (A), then draw a line diagonally up the long side of the triangle.

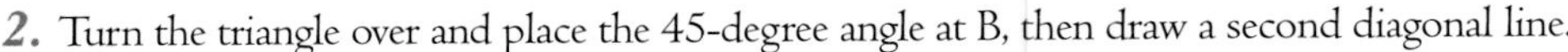

2. Turn the triangle over and place the 45-degree angle at B, then draw a second diagonal line.

3. Move the triangle to the right so that the right angle is at A. Draw a line up the side of the triangle until it hits the diagonal line at C.

4. Turn the triangle and put the right angle on B and draw another line until it touches the second diagonal line at D.

5. Connect C and D to complete the square.

A B

Step 1

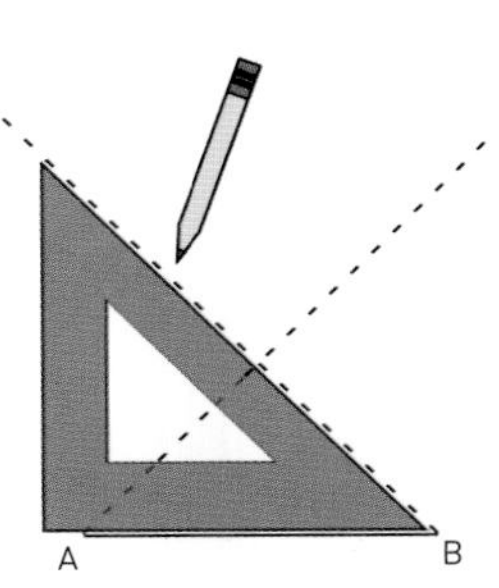

Step 2

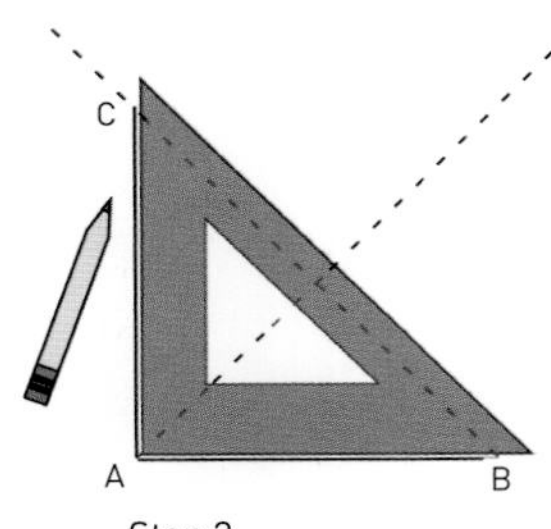

Step 3

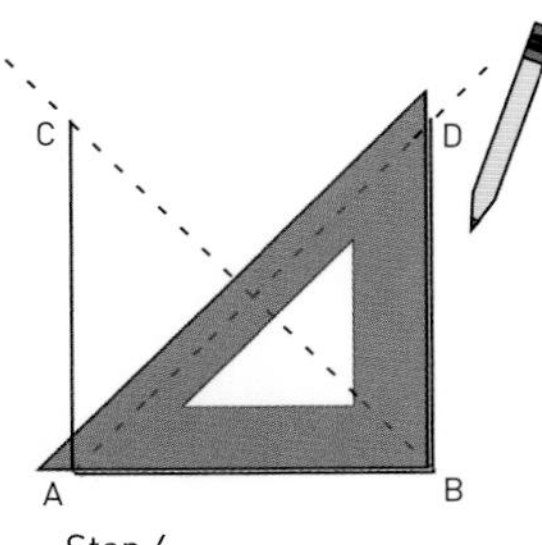

Step 4

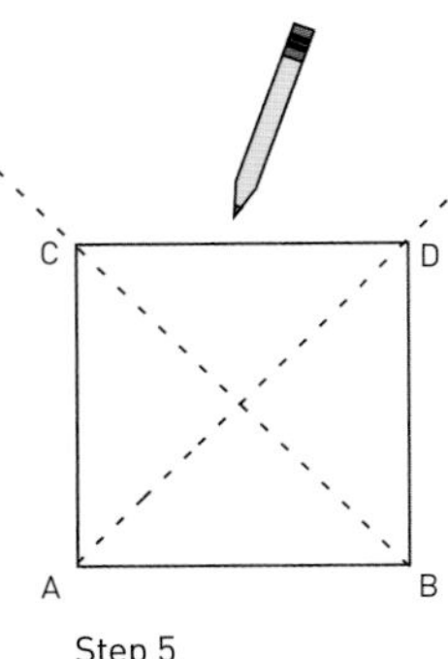

Step 5

Third Step: Draw the Grid on the Square

I used to create the grid on a piece of paper the old-fashioned way—by folding the paper into the number of segments needed. What I found is that that method is not always very accurate. Furthermore, while it is fairly easy to fold for the 2 x 2 and 3 x 3 base grid categories, some of the other categories are much more difficult. For the last several years I have used another method that is much more accurate and will allow you to put any grid on any size square. All you need is a ruler that is *longer* than the square you want to divide (a ruler with both inches and metrics is good) and a right-angle 45-degree triangle.

For illustration purposes, let's say that the design you want to draft is based on a 5 x 5 grid and you want to draft it in a 7¾" size. First, you will need to divide the square into five equal divisions in both directions in order to get the grid. If you do the math, you will realize that each division must measure 1.55". This would be difficult to do, since rulers don't have such specific increments. Besides, there is a much easier way. If the square were 10" instead of 7¾" it would be easy to divide into five equal parts. It would just be a matter of making a mark every 2". But wait, and here's the easy part. All you have to do is *pretend* that the square is 10". To do this:

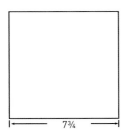

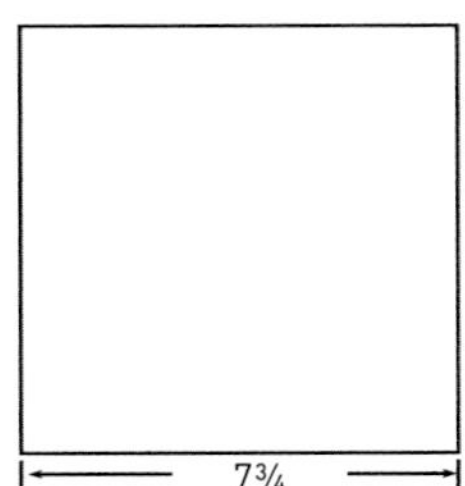

Step 1

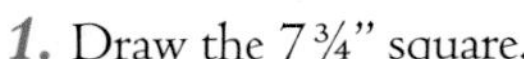

1. Draw the 7¾" square.

2. Place zero on your ruler somewhere along the left side of the square. Then angle the ruler so that the 10" mark falls somewhere on the right side (the opposite *parallel* side.)

3. Now make a mark every 2" along the edge of the ruler and you will see that that—from left to right—the square is divided into five equal divisions, each of them exactly 1.55" wide.

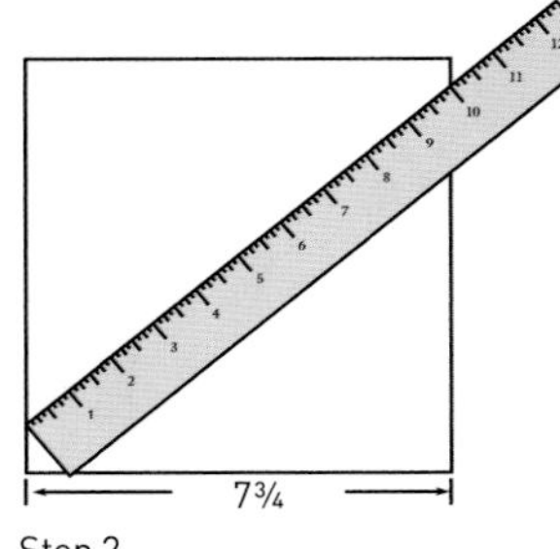

Step 2

4. Using a right-angle 45-degree triangle, align the bottom of the triangle along the bottom edge of the square. Move the triangle until the perpendicular side hits the first dot and then draw a straight line. Continue moving the triangle to each dot until all lines are drawn.

5. Now you need the lines going the other direction, so turn the paper one quarter turn and repeat the process again. You must make a *new* set of dots. So as not to get the dots confused, it is helpful to use a different colored pencil for this step.

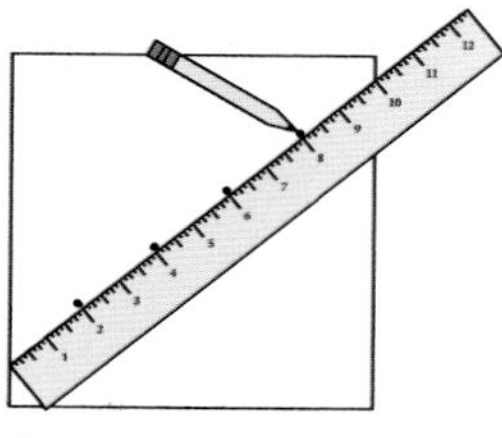
Step 3

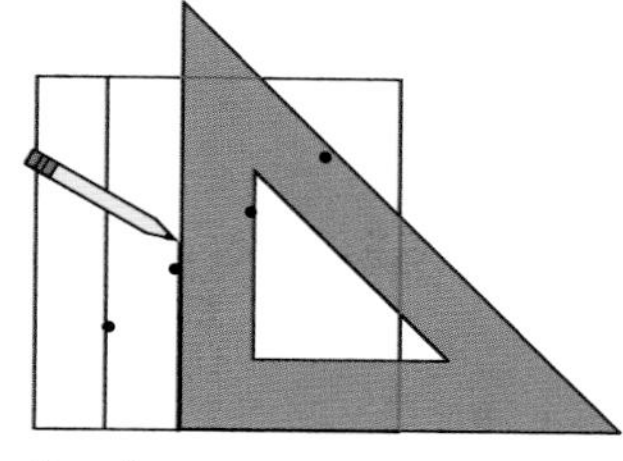
Step 4

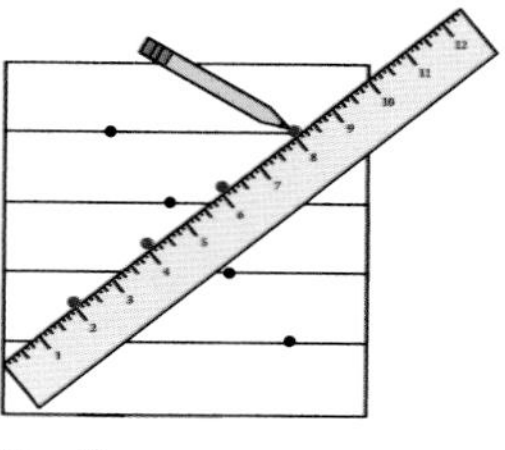
Step 5

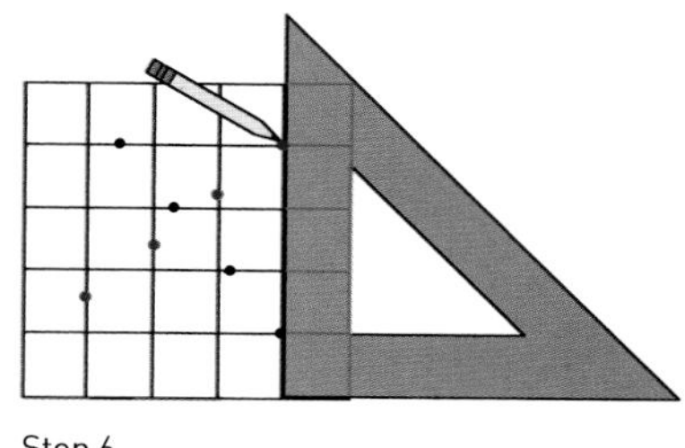
Step 6

If you want to divide this same square into 11 divisions for an 11 x 11 grid, then angle 11 across the square instead of 10 and mark every inch. This same process can be used for dividing any size square into any number of divisions. All that is needed is a ruler *longer* than the width of the square. Find a number on the ruler (whether it is the inch or metric side) greater than the width of the square, which can be easily divided by the number of divisions you are trying to achieve. Place zero on the left side of the square and angle the ruler until that number falls on the parallel side on the right side of the square, then simply mark off the increments. Because a metric ruler has smaller divisions, sometimes it is easier to use the metric side and sometimes the inch side.

Once in a while when dividing certain sized squares, a problem occurs. Let's say that you want to divide a 7" square into a 6 x 6 grid. The next number higher than 7 that can easily be divided by 6 is 12. When 12" is angled across the square, you see that the square is too small for the 12" to fit. When this occurs one of three things can be done. First, if the ruler has metric divisions, try that portion of the ruler. A 7" square is a little less than 18 centimeters. The next number higher than 18 that could easily be divided by seven is 21. Twenty-one easily fits the 7" space, so angle 21 across the paper and make a mark every 3 centimeters. If you don't have a metric ruler, another solution is to go to nine rather than 12. Nine divided by 6 is 1½". Nine will fit across the 7" square, so you just mark every 1½" instead of every 2".

A third way to handle the problem is to extend the right-hand edge of the square with a line. Use 12" and angle the ruler until zero is on the left side of the square and 12 hits the extended line. Even though some of the division's marks will be off the square, if your right triangle is large enough, you can still make perfect divisions of the square.

When teaching classes on pattern drafting, I find that some students have a hard time grasping the concept of dividing a space into a certain number of equal divisions, in the way described above. In ancient times, when so many incredibly intricate mosaic patterns were created, artisans didn't have a ruler with inches and centimeters marked on it. But they probably did have a stick or piece of wood upon which they marked off a certain number of equal spaces. Without rulers, they most likely used this device to divide a space into equal divisions. When I encounter students who have a problem with the concept of dividing the space, I pass out sheets of lined notebook paper and have them follow this next process of dividing a square into seven equal divisions. (It works with any divisions; seven is just an arbitrary choice). These are the steps:

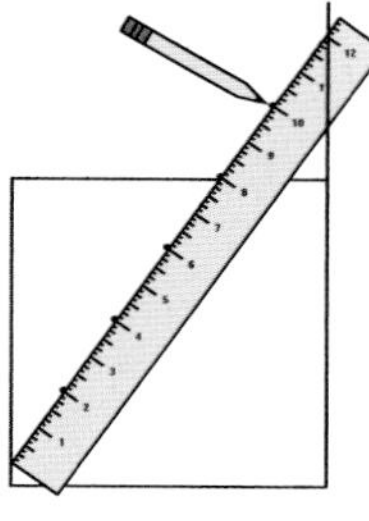
Angle the ruler

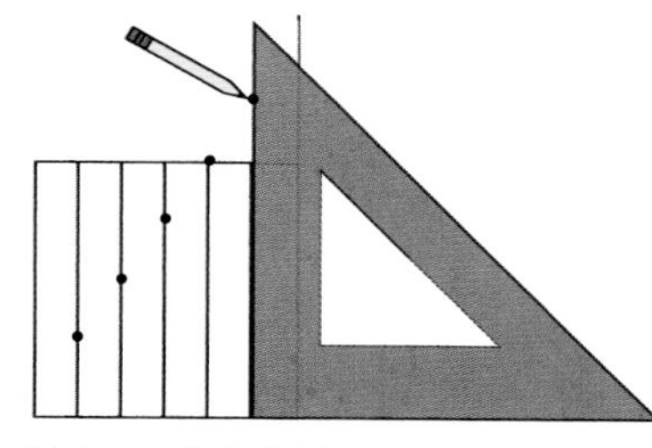
Make perfect divisions

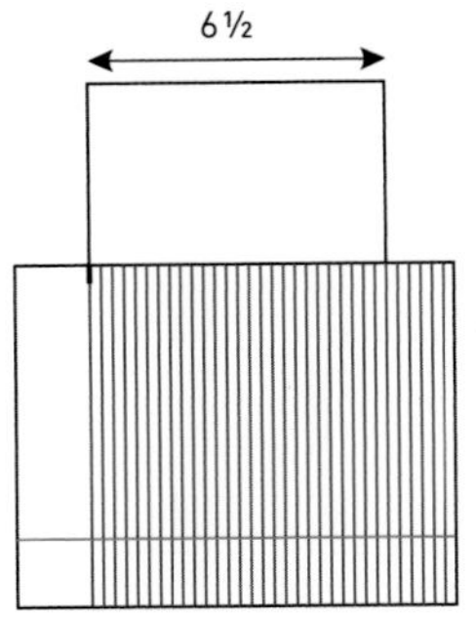

Step 2

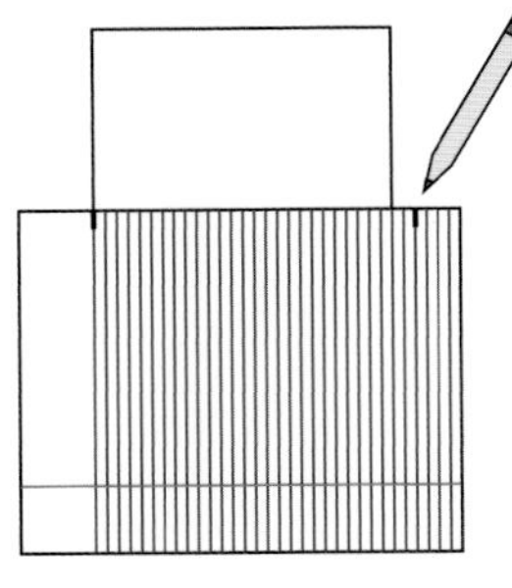
Step 3

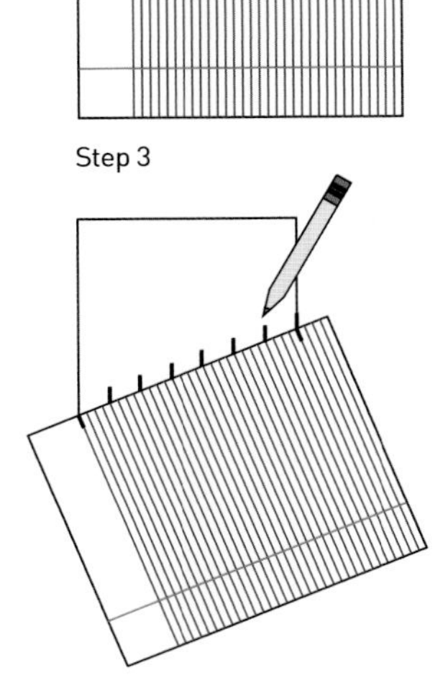
Step 4

1. Draw a square that is 6½". (Again this is an arbitrary choice.)

2. Turn the notebook paper sideways so the lines are running vertically to the square, then mark one of the lines towards the left hand side of the paper with a heavier line.

3. Put that heavier line on the left-hand side of the square and count how many divisions of the notebook paper there are until the right hand edge of the square is reached. That number is 26. Since you can't divide seven into 26 and get an equal division you go to the next number of divisions beyond the square that you could easily divide by 7, which would be 28. Make a heavy mark on that line as well.

4. Now angle the area between the two marks on the notebook paper across the square from the left side of the square to the opposite right hand parallel side. Since 28 divided by 7 is 4, make a mark every 4 spaces of the lined paper. When finished, you will see that the square will be divided into seven equal divisions.

5. Using a right triangle as before, line it up to each mark and draw straight lines dividing the square into seven vertical columns.

6. Turn the square one quarter turn clockwise and repeat the process (as explained in step 5 on page 31) to get the lines in the other direction.

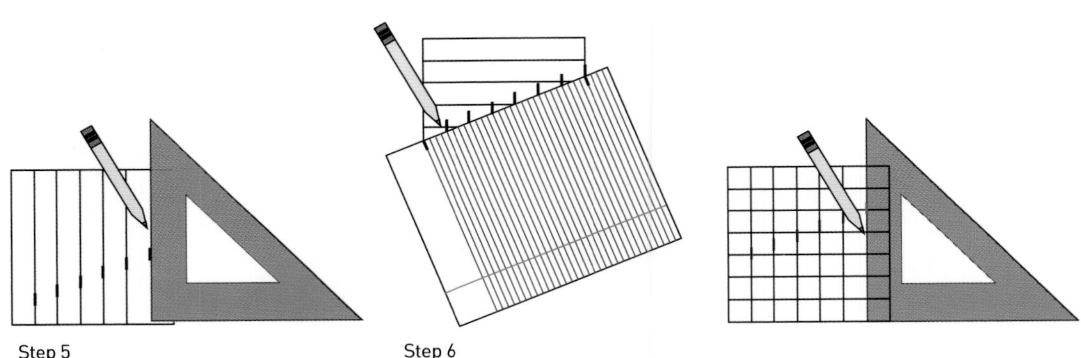
Step 5

Step 6

Fourth Step: Determine How the Design Is Created from the Grid

The next step is to determine how to use the grid to create the design. The transparent grid sheets that are included with the book contain the major grids in each category. Look at the caption below the color version of each design to see which grid is used. Here are some guidelines that should help.

1. Find the appropriate transparent grid to place over the design. For many of the designs you will be able to see which portions of the grid need to be connected to draw the pattern.

2. Even with the aid of a grid, it can sometimes be confusing. Find the portions of a design that are apparent and draw those in first. It might be a diagonal line across all the corners, or a square in the middle. Once that is done the other lines seem easier to see.

3. Some people visualize one corner of the block better than another. If that is the case, draw the lines you see, then turn the block a quarter turn and draw the same lines in the next corner.

4. Some designs have lines that do not go to the corner of the grid. If that occurs place a small ruler along the line and follow the ruler beyond the line to see where it stops. It will usually be at the corner of one of the squares of the grid.

Drafting Designs Based on an 8-Pointed Star Grid

Eight-pointed star designs are magical to me. I find the proportions in many of the designs much more pleasing than in designs based on a grid of squares. This grid is the basis for so many ancient designs; I find drafting the grid and going deeper into the intricacies of design is a giant puzzle.

As mentioned earlier, the base design in this category is the simple star with 8 points. Look at the star shown here. There are clearly three divisions across the top. But those divisions are not equal. This star cannot be drafted on a grid of squares, or the diamonds do not come out perfectly.

When the star points are marked alternately with A and B as shown, and when 16 spokes are superimposed over the design, you can see that every other spoke is an A or a B. Furthermore, if you start with a piece of paper that has the spokes already on it with the A/B points marked, and connect every A to every B, you will have the basic 8-pointed star grid. To draw a basic 8-pointed star, place a piece of tracing paper over the grid and draw only the portions needed for the star.

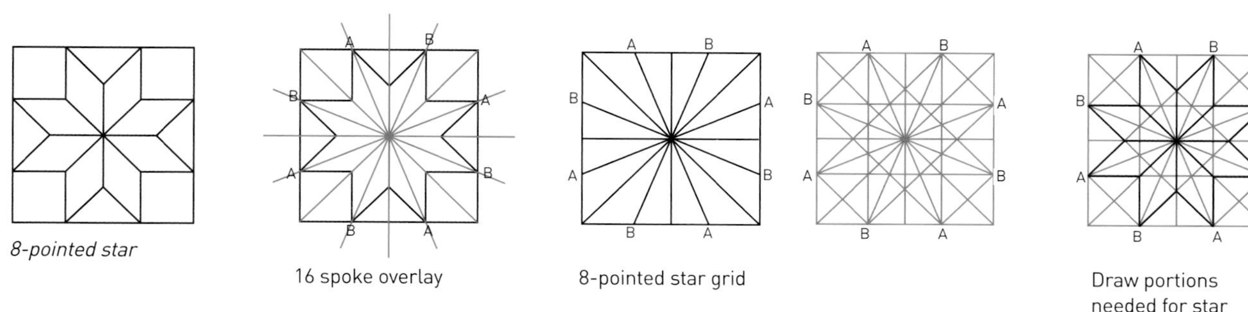

8-pointed star

16 spoke overlay

8-pointed star grid

Draw portions needed for star

So the question is how do you get the spokes on the paper, since they do not fall on the corners of any grid of squares? I used to fold a square of paper to get the grid but found that to be inaccurate. Now I use one of these methods.

Method 1

1. Draw a square and divide it diagonally from corner to corner.
2. Line up a right-angle 45-degree triangle with the center of the square and draw a line dividing the square in half from top to bottom.
3. Turn the square 90 degrees and repeat, dividing it in half the other direction.
4. Place a compass point at each of the four corners and open the compass until the pencil reaches the *center* of the block. Draw a quarter circle from each corner. The points where the quarter circles touch the *edges* of the square are the A/B points.
5. Mark the A/B points as shown.
6. Connect the A points to the As on the opposite side and the B points to the Bs on the opposite side to create the radiating lines. Draw the grid as shown above.

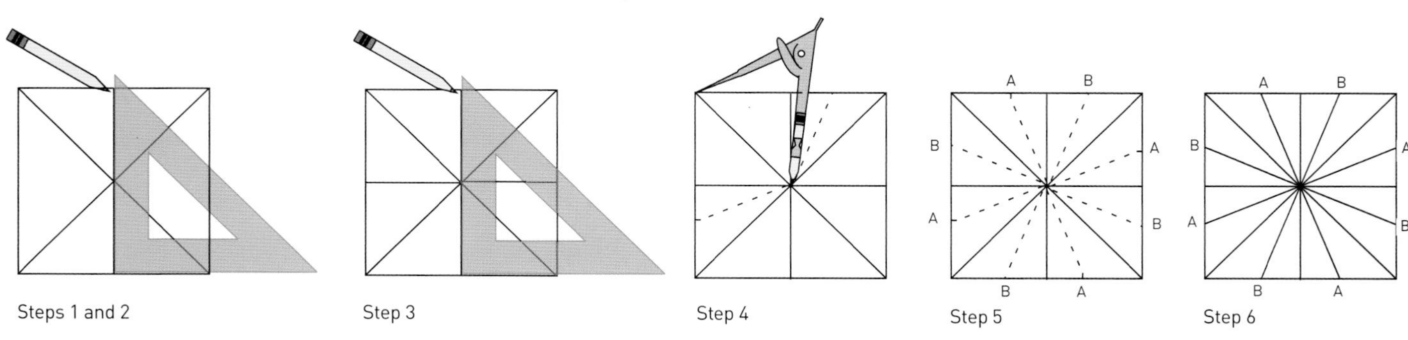

Steps 1 and 2

Step 3

Step 4

Step 5

Step 6

Method 2

1. Follow steps 1 to 3 above. Draw a circle inside the square.

2. Connect points X to get a square on point within the circle.

3. Draw another square so the corners are at the intersection of the circle and the diagonal lines that extend to the corners (Y).

4. Draw lines from the center through the places where the two inner squares intersect and extend them to the edges of the outer square. The A/B points are where those lines touch the edges of the square and the grid and star are drawn as in Method 1.

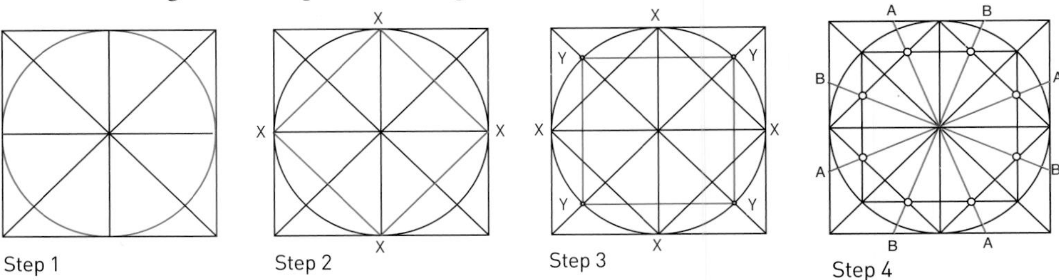

Step 1 Step 2 Step 3 Step 4

The star points on *Eight Pointed Star* touch the edges of the block, but many designs in the 8-pointed star category have smaller stars that are part of the pattern. Look at the *Rolling Star*. Now look at the smaller square that was drawn in Method 2, step 3. *Rolling Star* has a smaller star that is drafted inside that square. There is no need to draw a new set of spokes because you already have them on the grid. Just move the A/B points in along the spokes to the smaller square. When the grid is put over the design, it is easy to see which lines to follow to draw the pattern.

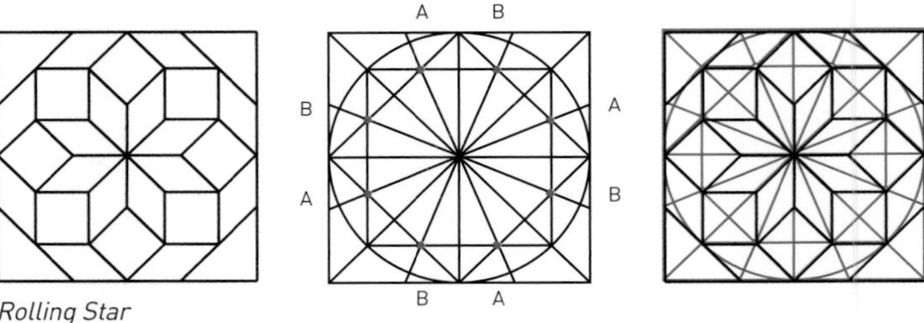

Rolling Star

Four Eight-Pointed Star Grids

Some patterns have still smaller stars that require smaller squares. Keeping this in mind and to make it easier to draft some of the 8-pointed star designs in this book, I have included four different 8-pointed star grids. They have all been drawn from the same basic 16 spokes. All four of these are on the transparent grid sheets that came with this book.

Grid 1

Grid 1 is based on Method 1 above, with a few extra lines. Added to that base grid are the same square that was drawn in step 3 of Method 2 above, and lines cutting through the middle of the star points that form an octagon. A large majority of the 8-pointed star patterns in this book can be drafted from this grid.

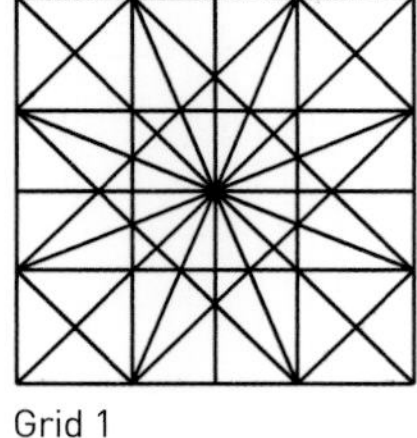

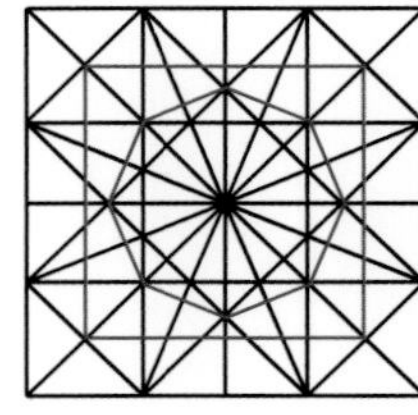

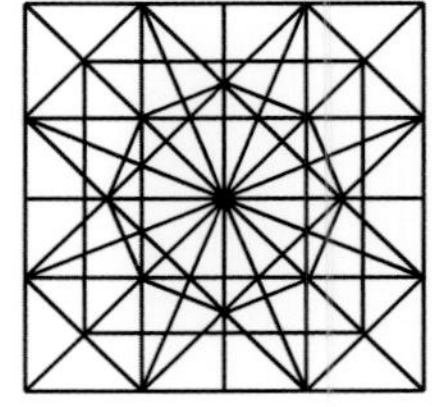

Grid 1

Grid 2

Grid 2 is also based upon Method 1, but this time the star is "on point." It is drawn exactly the same as the other star, except that the points of the diamonds come from the Xs and Ys, not the As and Bs. Connect the Xs to the Ys as shown, then add the final square and octagon.

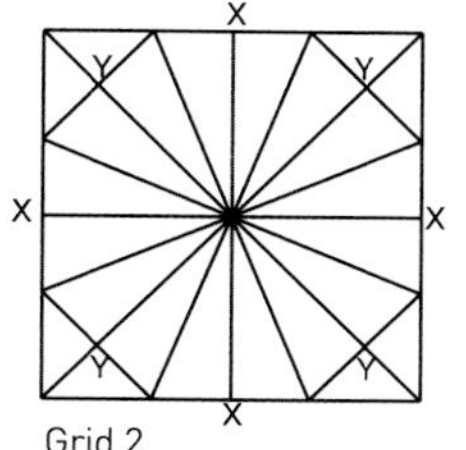

Grid 2

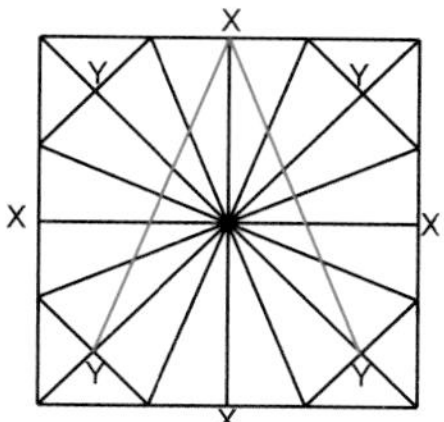

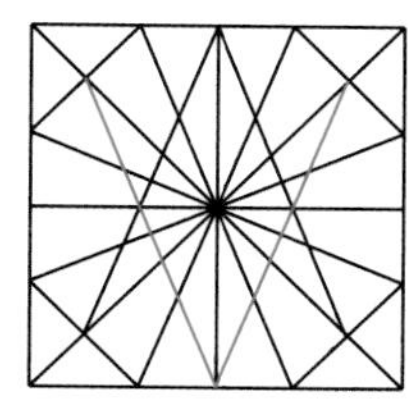

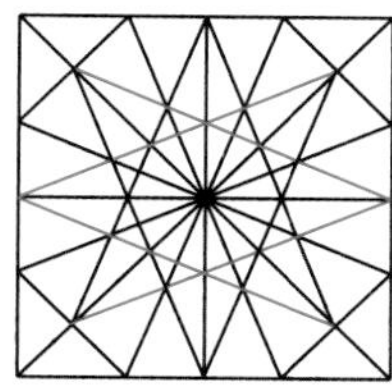

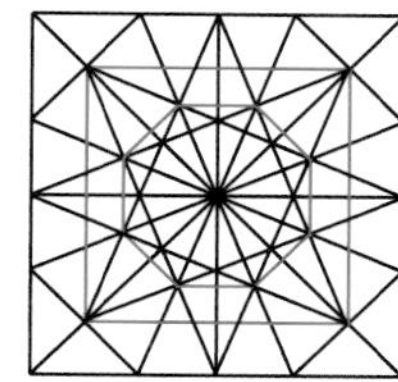

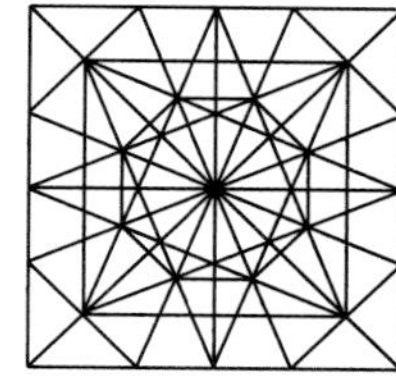

Grid 3

1. Use the grid created in Method 2 and add another still smaller square as shown.
2. Add another diagonally set square.
3. Add another smaller square and diagonally set square.
4. Continue adding squares.

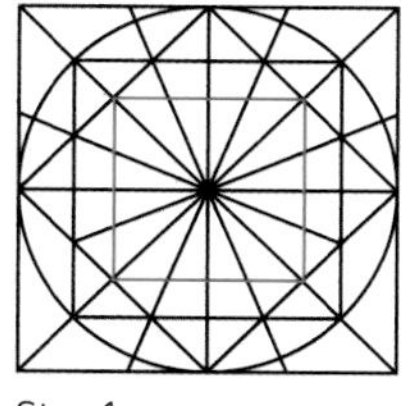
Step 1

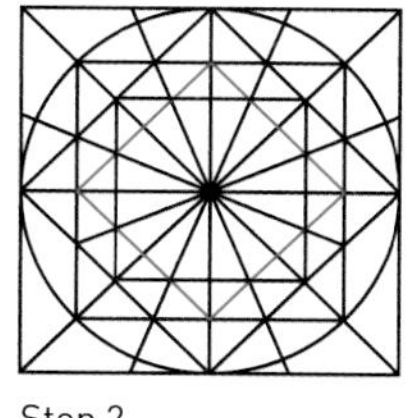
Step 2

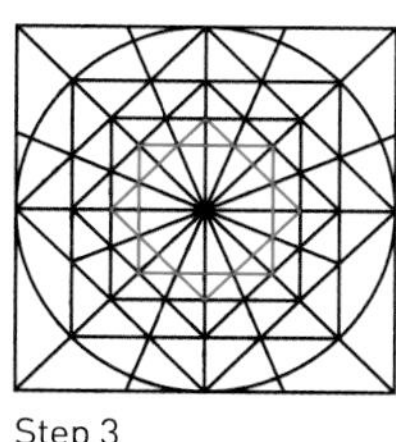
Step 3

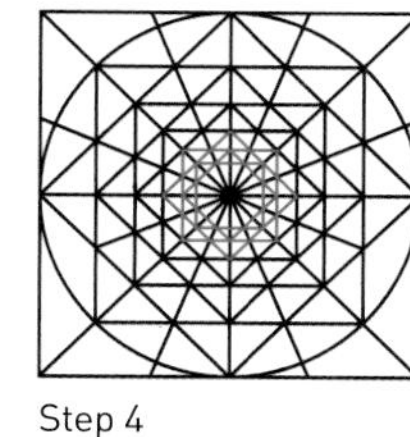
Step 4

Grid 3

This process produces increasingly smaller squares, many of which are used for designs in the 8-pointed star category, including those shown here.

Log Star

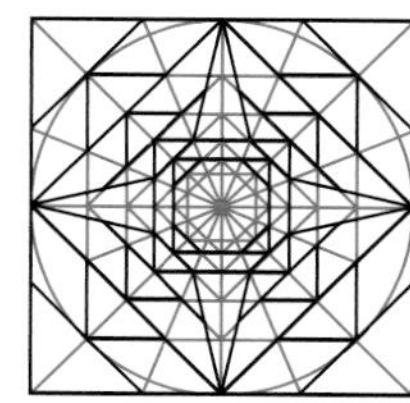

White Nights

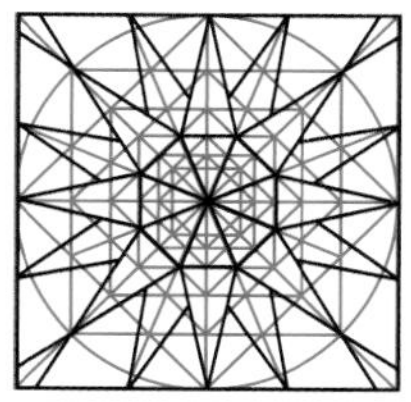

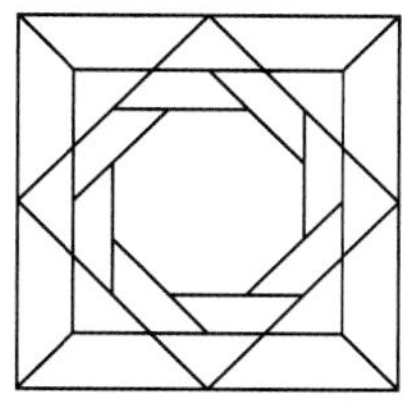
Interlocked Squares

Grid 4

Some designs are fairly complex and can use more reference points. This grid begins with grid one, but adds the star points from grid 2. There are also three additional squares that appear in various eight-pointed star patterns.

1. Square A is created by connecting the yellow dots shown.
2. A different set of dots is the reference for Square B.

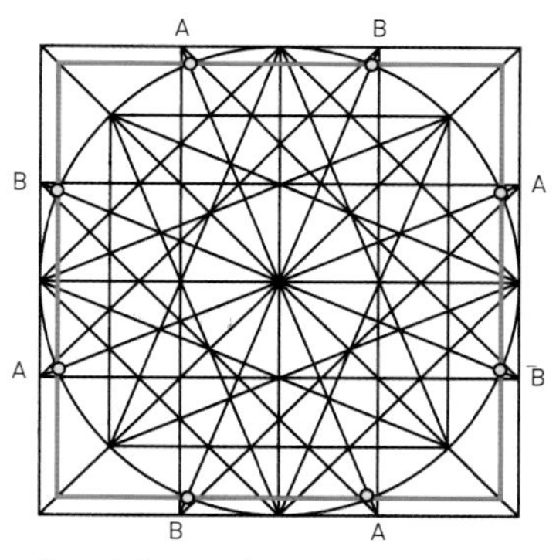

Step 1: Square A

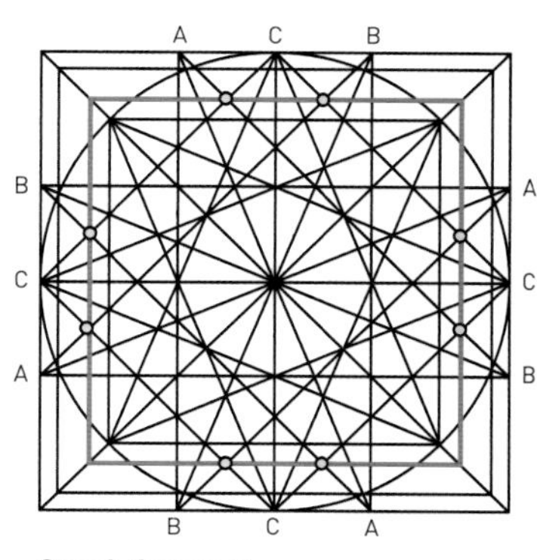

Step 2: Square B

3. To draw Square C, there need to be additional reference points. Draw lines from the corners of the block to the points on Square A, as shown. Note where those lines cross the lines that form part of the star (indicated by dots). Connect those dots to get the line for the top of the square. Repeat for the other three sides.

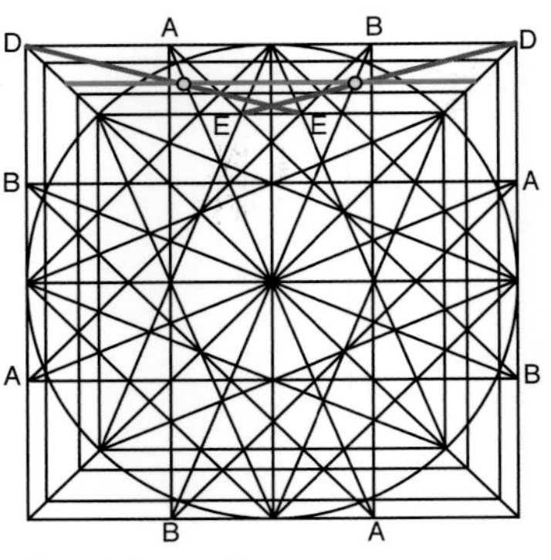

Step 3: Square C

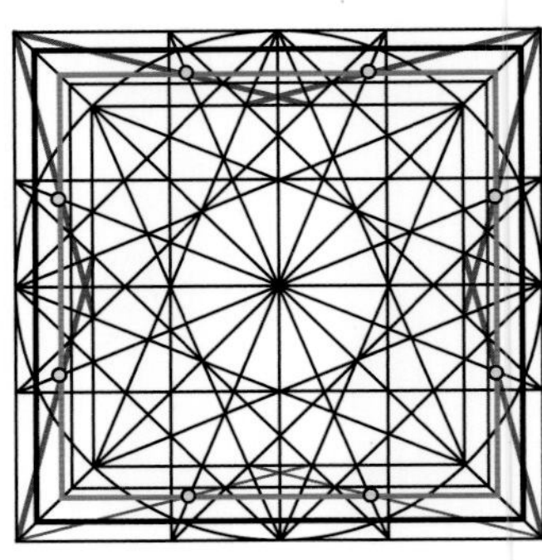

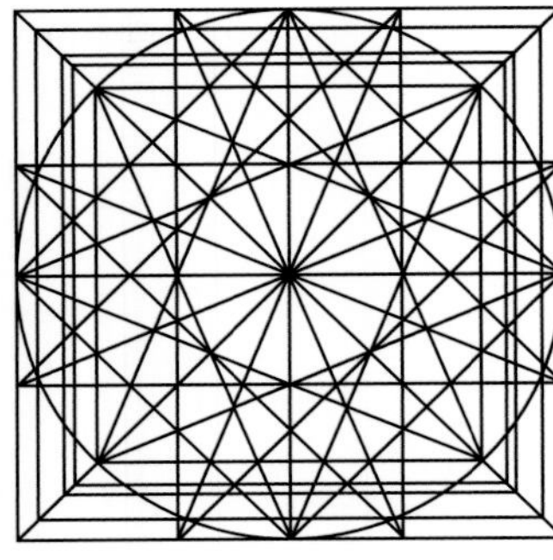

Step 4: 8-pointed star grid

In this book, the caption beneath the color art specifies which of the four grids applies to each block. Parts of any of the four grids can be used to draft the design since they are all based on the original 16 spokes. If you don't clearly see how to draft the design when one of the grids is placed over it, then try a different one. Bear in mind that some of the designs, such as baskets or lily patterns, use part of the grid. Sometimes parts of stars are drawn from the corner, so the grid might have to be placed in the corner. Portions of many designs do not go all the way to an intersection on the grid. If you are confused, put a ruler along the line, then see where the ruler ends. That could help. For example, look at *Shooting Star.* When grid 1 is placed over the design, there are no reference points for the center octagon. But the green line goes from the point of the star, along one side and extends to the reference point.

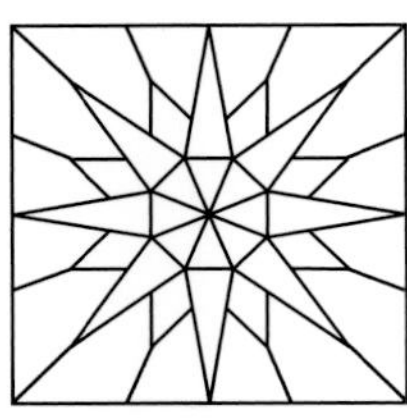

Shooting Star

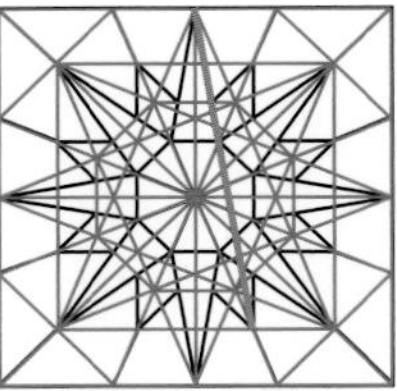

Shooting Star with grid 1

Combining Methods

There are numerous variations of the *Lone Star* where the diamond is broken into smaller diamonds. The easiest way to find those divisions is to break the squares and triangles around the edges of the star into however many divisions are needed, as illustrated with *Star upon Star* shown here. Follow the method of creating a grid as explained on pages 33 to 36.

Star upon Star

Several 8-pointed star designs are drafted using a combination of an 8-pointed star grid and a square grid. These are noted in the captions beneath the color blocks.

Drafting Hexagons

Elaborate hexagonal configurations of diamonds and triangles have been used for centuries in ancient art, and hundreds of mosaic designs based on the hexagon can be found in buildings and mosques throughout the Middle East. I find the hexagon one of the most exciting and versatile shapes to work with. Like most geometric shapes and designs, the circle is the beginning. I have several methods for drafting a hexagon, but the one given here seems the easiest.

1. Using a compass, decide what size you want the hexagon to be and draw a circle that size. Draw a line through the center of the circle, extending it to the edges at A and B.

2. Without changing the opening of the compass, place it at A and make another circle the same size as the first. Place the compass at B and make a third circle.

3. Notice where the two outer circles intersect with the middle one. Connect those points to get a hexagon.

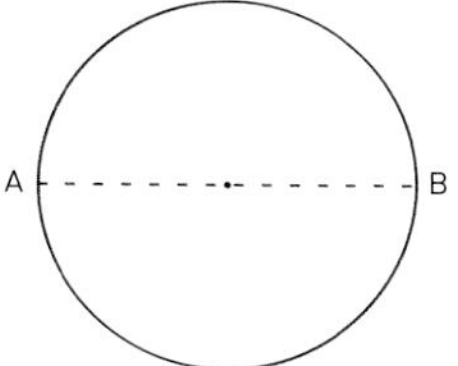

Step 1

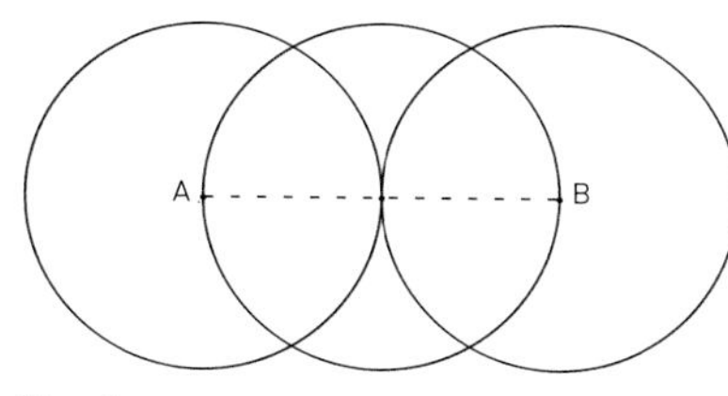

Step 2

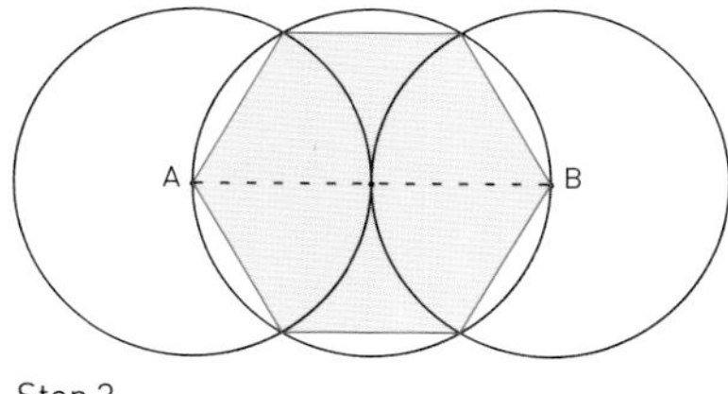

Step 3

Grid 1

Hexagon grid 1 is the basic grid for many hexagon designs.

1. Follow the method above to draw a hexagon.
2. Connect opposite angles to get the first set of spokes.
3. Draw an equilateral triangle inside the hexagon.
4. Draw a second equilateral triangle to complete the star.
5. Draw lines from the center through the intersection of the star point to get the remaining spokes.

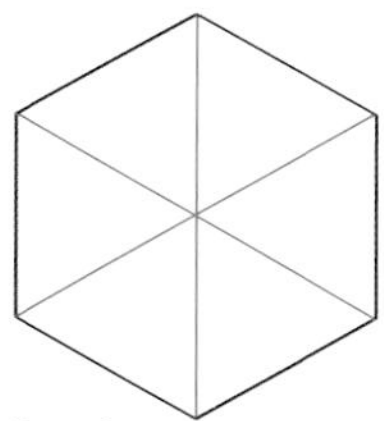
Step 2

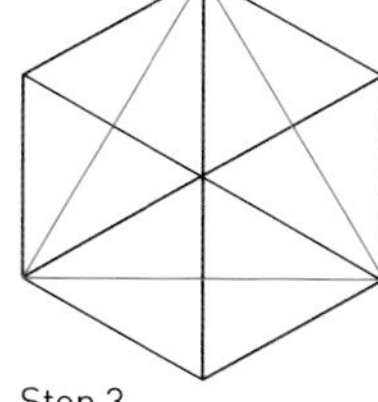
Step 3

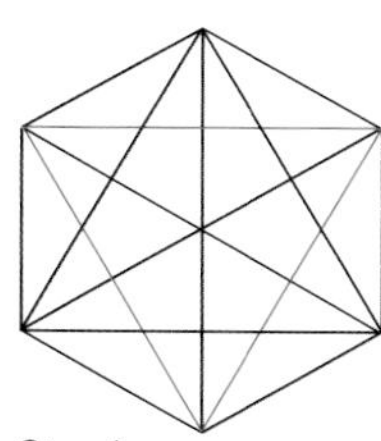
Step 4

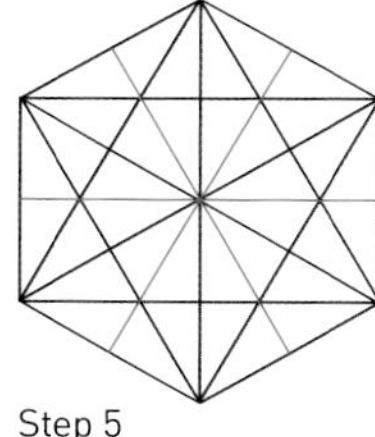
Step 5

Grid 2

Some more complex designs require more reference points to create the grid.

1. Follow steps 1-5 above, and then add these additional lines.
2. Draw a smaller star inside the small hexagon at the center of the grid.
3. Draw a larger star from the spokes that touch the middle of the hexagon.
4. Draw a small hexagon in the center of the grid.

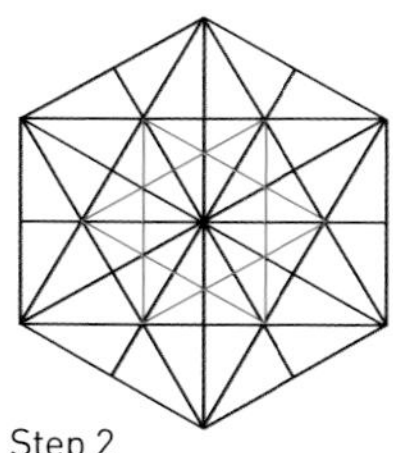
Step 2

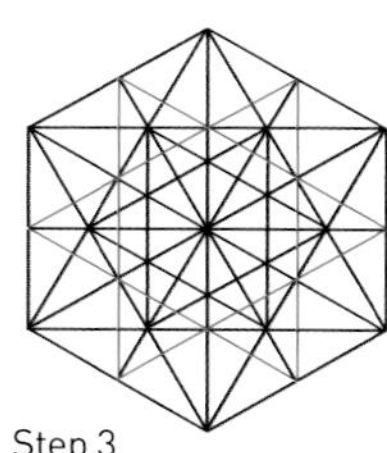
Step 3

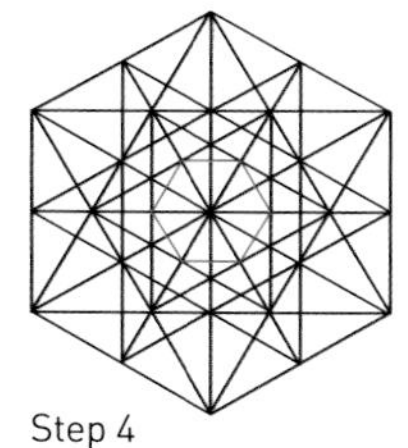
Step 4

Drafting Curved Designs

Mariner's Compass. See 379-2.

Many curved designs are drafted the same way as designs with no curves. You just need to know what grid to use and put the lines accordingly. Designs like *Sunflower, Mariner's Compass,* and *Dresden Plate* are similar to the hexagon and 8-pointed star in that they require spokes going from the center outwards at equal intervals. Space prohibits showing the drafting of all the various designs, but here a couple of examples to provide an overview.

Mariner's Compass

Probably my favorite of all curved blocks is *Mariner's Compass* and the many variations of this ancient design. Compass designs vary in the number of points, the size of the center circle and so much more. Let's start with the basic *Mariner's Compass.* This is based on the 8-pointed star grid.

1. Draft the 8-pointed star grid using Method 2 from page 34. Working clockwise, number the spokes 1, 2, 1, 2, around the circle.

2. Start at the top with number 1 and place a ruler from number 1 down towards the base of the square stopping at the circle at number 2. Do not draw the line all the way. Stop it when it hits the diagonal line going to the corner as shown.

3. Continue in this manner and add three additional points.

4. Add four new points between the first four. Start at one of the remaining number 1s on the circle and bring the line to the adjacent number 2 line where it intersects with the first set of points.

5. Now working with number 2s, place the ruler from a 2 to the next number 1 line. Draw from the point only until the line hits the point. Add the remaining 7 points. This makes a 16-pointed compass design.

6. Since the basic *Mariner's Compass* usually has another round of points, there needs to be another set of spokes. Draw a line from the intersection of two points through the center of the square and through the next intersection to the edge of the circle. Repeat for the remaining spokes.

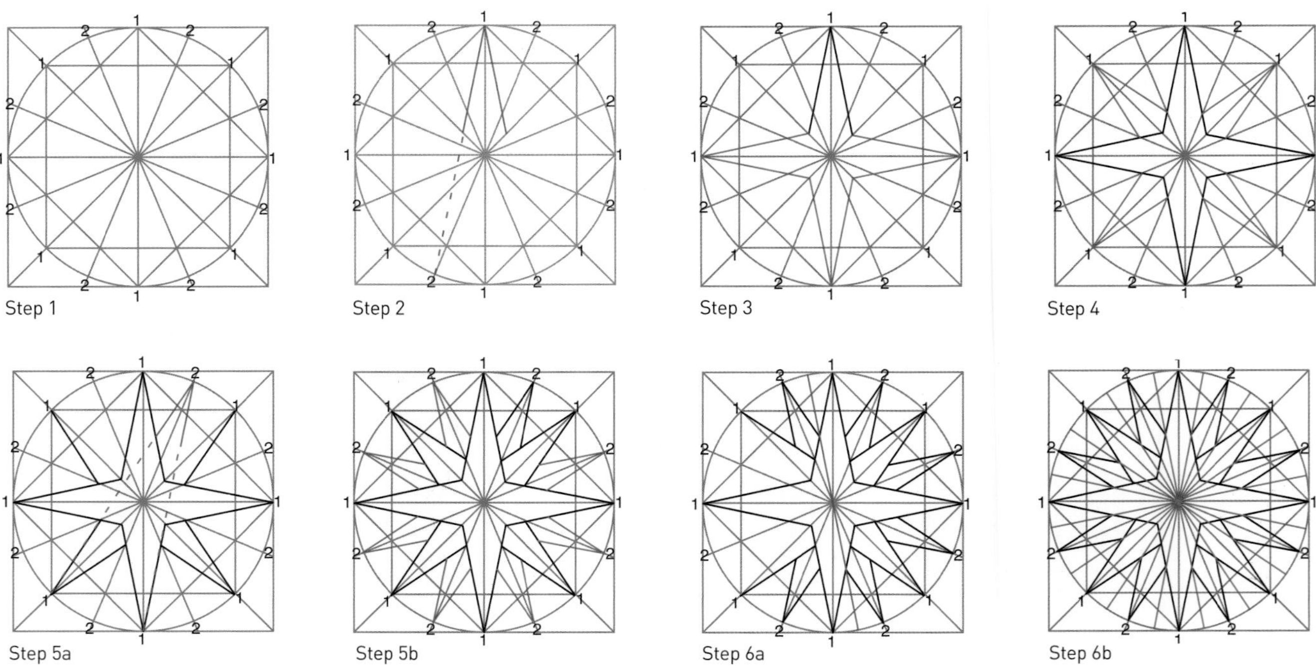

Step 1 Step 2 Step 3 Step 4

Step 5a Step 5b Step 6a Step 6b

7. Working the same as before place a ruler from one of the new spokes where it hits the circle and bring it down to the opposite side of the circle to the next new spoke over. Draw only until the line hits the points as shown. Add the remaining points in the same way.

8. Draw a circle in the middle of the design. Place a compass in the center and open it to where the first set of points meet and draw the circle.

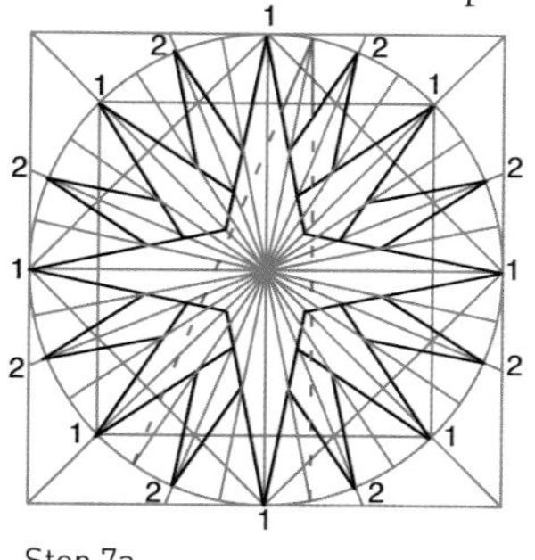
Step 7a

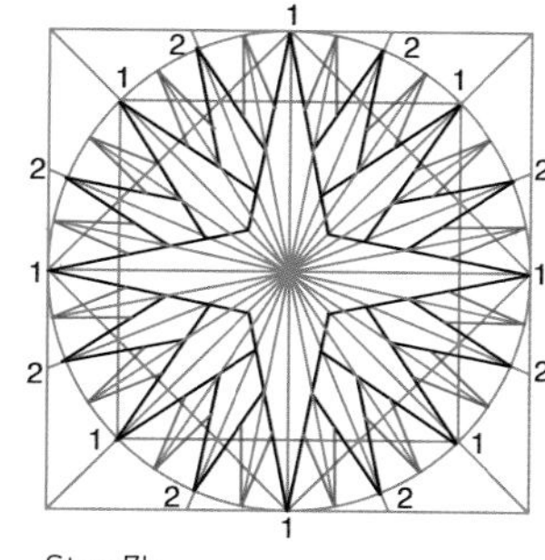
Step 7b

Step 8

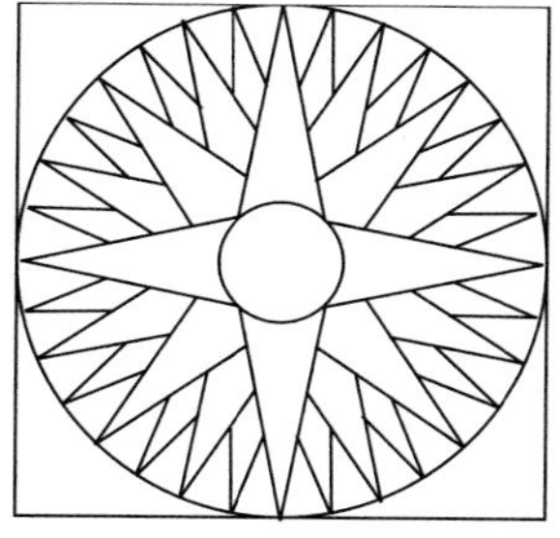
Mariner's Compass

Several designs in this book use this basic compass design, but either have fewer points or lines extended to add additional points. Some are shown here.

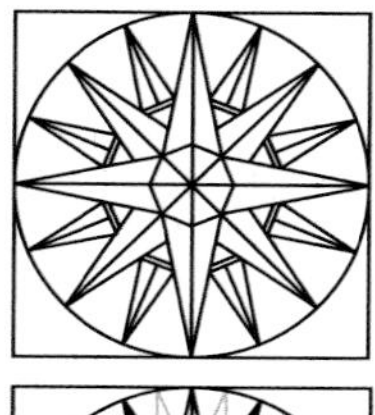

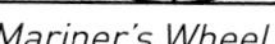
Mariner's Wheel

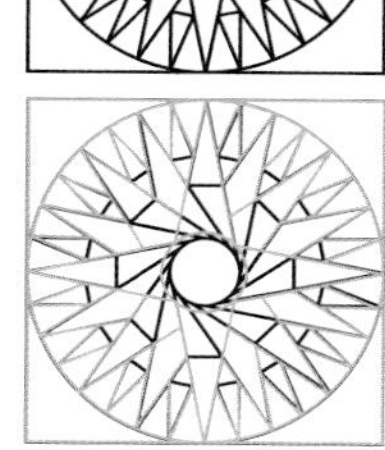
Nautilus

Mariner's Whirl

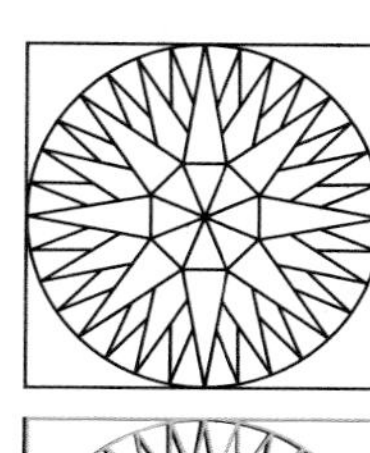
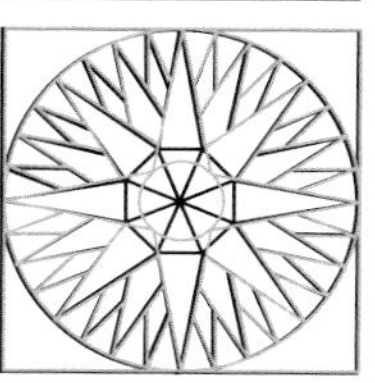
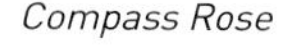
Compass Rose

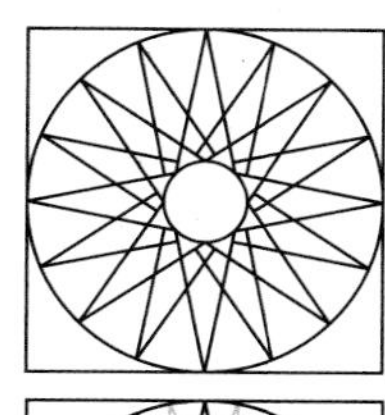
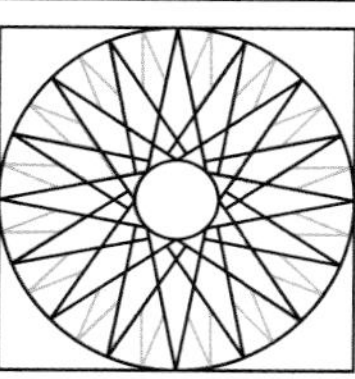
Golden Compass

Sunflower Designs

There are several *Sunflower* designs in this book and most use some combinations of grid, circles, and spokes. Let's take a closer look at one of them.

A 14 x 14 grid is necessary as a guide to drawing the three circles that are needed for drafting *Noonday* and 24 spokes are needed for drawing both layers of points. Follow this sequence of illustrations to see how the design is drawn. To divide the circle into 24 divisions:

Noonday. See 381-7.

1. Work from hexagon grid 1 on page 37. Draw a circle around the hexagon and extend the spokes (created in Step 5 of Hexagon Grid 1) to the edge of the circle.

2. Draw another star from those points.

3. Use the intersection of the outer points of the star as a guide, and bring a line from one of the intersections through the center of the circle and to the edges of the circle.

4. Add the remaining "spokes" to create the 24 divisions of the circle.

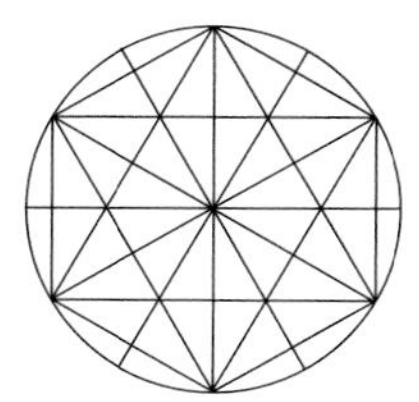
Step 1

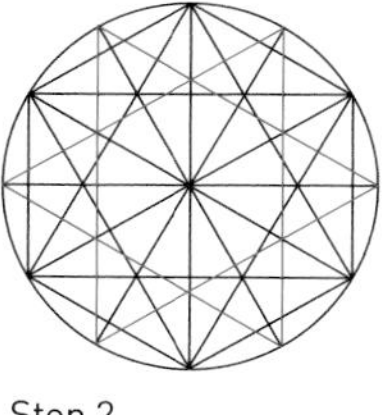
Step 2

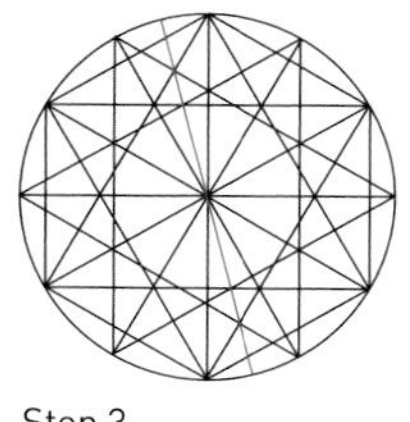
Step 3

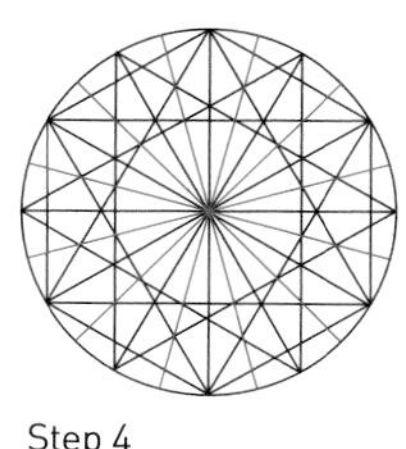
Step 4

To draft *Noonday:*

1. Draw the three circles on a 14 x 14 grid.

2. Add 24 spokes to the circles as shown.

3. Draw the inner set of points from where the spokes touch the medium sized circle down to the next spokes over where they touch the smallest circle.

4. Add the outer set of points from the large circle to where the spokes hit the first set of points.

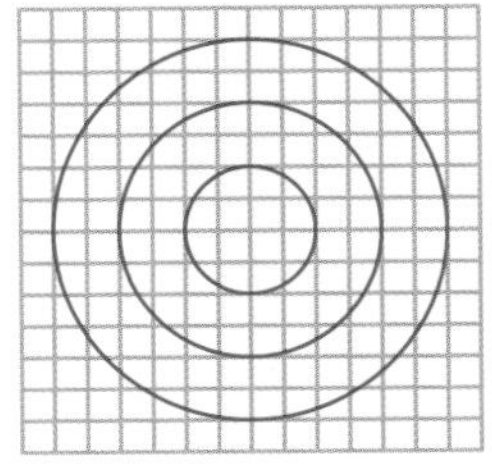

Step 1

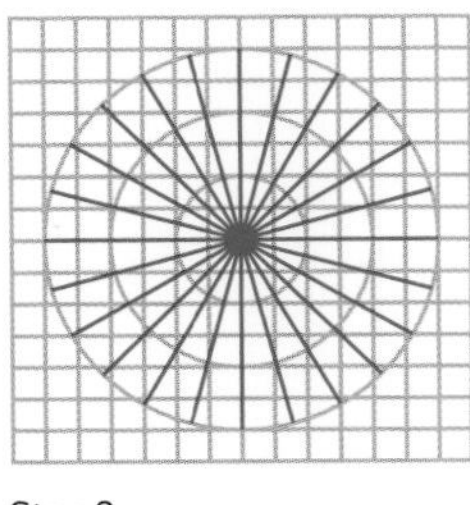

Step 2

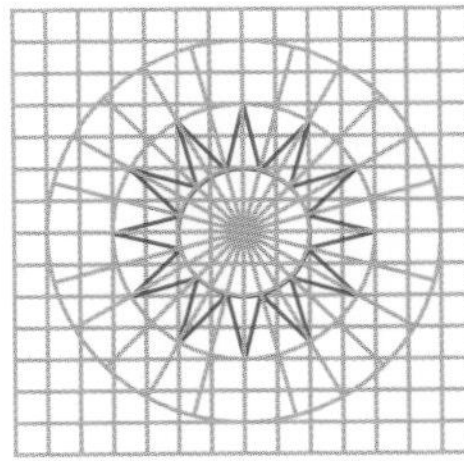

Step 3

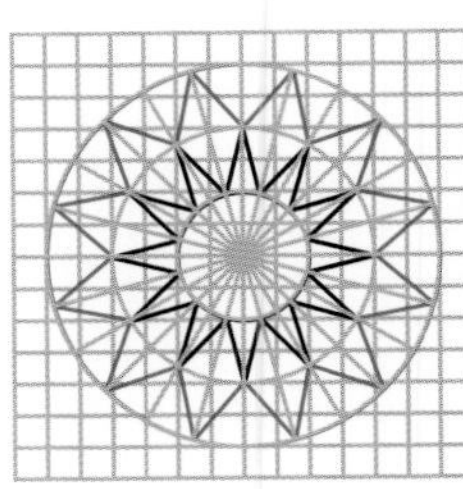

Step 4

Noonday

Drafting Pentagons

Evening Star. See 436-1.

There are not many designs that contain a pentagon, but there are a lot of *Sunflower* or *Dresden Plate* designs that require 10 or 20 divisions of the circle in order to draft them. As with other shapes, the pentagon can be drafted by working with a series of overlapping circles.

1. Determine how large you want the pentagon to be and draw two overlapping circles to that size. Construct the square (steps 1-6, page 29). Draw a line from the center of the left-hand circle through B and to the edge of the right-hand circle at C.

2. Draw a vertical line where the two circles overlap and mark "D" where that line crosses AB.

3. Place a compass point at D and open it out until it reaches the top right corner of the square at E. Make an arc and mark F where that arc crosses line BC.

4. Working with a right triangle, draw a perpendicular line straight up from F.

5. Draw a line extending the top of the square until it meets the perpendicular line at G.

6. Place the compass point at B and open it out to G. Do not change the opening of the compass.

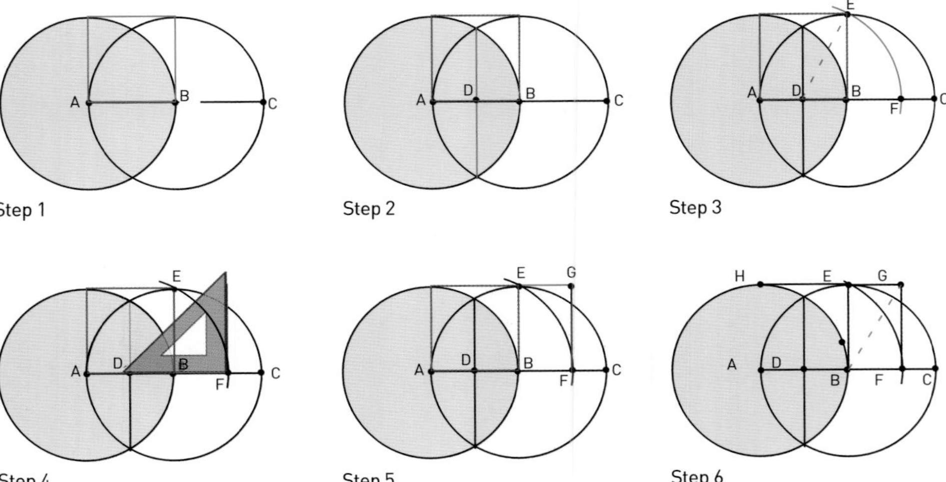

7. Place the compass point at H. Draw an arc. Mark I and J at intersects, as shown.
8. Place the compass point at I. Draw another arc. Mark K where the arc crosses the left circle.
9. Place the compass at K and draw another arc, marking L where that arc touches the circle.
10. Connect I, H, J, L, K, and I to draw the pentagon.

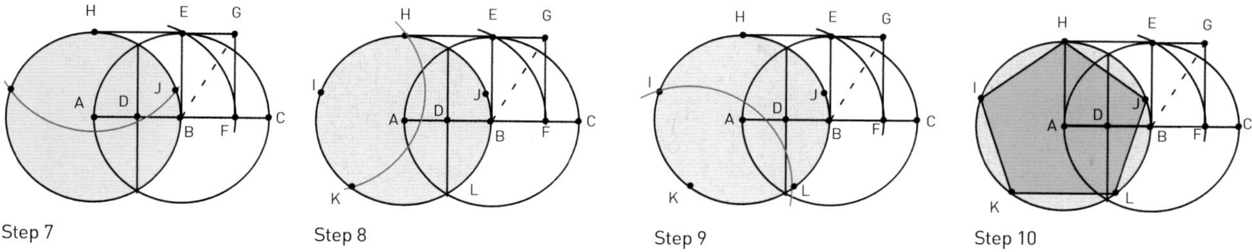

Step 7 Step 8 Step 9 Step 10

Drafting 5-Pointed Star Designs

To draw the 5-pointed star and also to get 10 or 20 divisions of the circle, follow these steps:

1. Starting at the angles of the pentagon, draw lines forming the five-pointed star.
2. To get 10 divisions of the circle, draw a line from one of the points through the center of the circle on through the intersection of the star points to the edge of the circle. Repeat for all five points and the circle is now divided into 10 divisions.
3. Draw a larger star from the points where the new spokes touch the circle.
4. Find one of the places where the 10 large points of the star touch and draw a line from there, through the center and to the edge of the circle. Add the remaining lines and the circle is divided into 20 equal divisions.

Forty divisions of the circle can be made by adding another set of points to the last spokes drawn. This is similar to the process used to create 32 points in the *Mariner's Compass.*

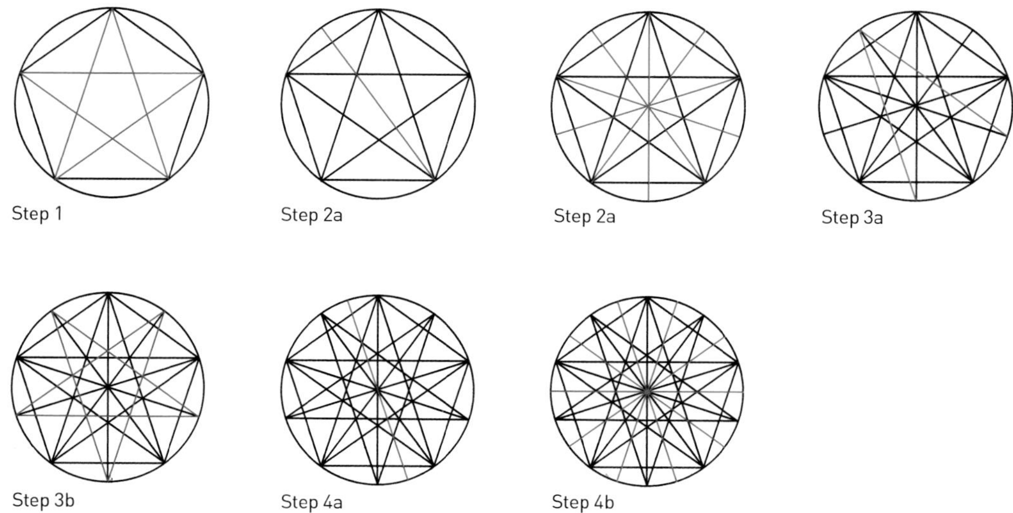
Step 1 Step 2a Step 2a Step 3a

Step 3b Step 4a Step 4b

Triple Play, Jinny Beyer, 2004.

Design Ideas

There are countless ways in which you can use the blocks in this book as idea-starters for creating quilts of your own. In this chapter, I will share many techniques I use to come up with ideas for new quilts. They are in no particular order, so feel free to dip in and out of this chapter as you browse through the book. Have fun experimenting—there are thousands of new quilts waiting to be made!

Begin in Black and White

The design process I use for every quilt begins in the same way. It's important to find the proper balance between lights and darks. Also, correct placement of contrast/value withing a design is key. For that reason, I design first in black and white. Only then do I go to fabric and group the colors lights through darks so that the balance I developed can carry over into color.

For block-style quilts and other designs made up of units, I used to rely on a photocopier to create my black and white designs. Now I use a computer, but the process is the same. Either tool simplifies the design process. I shade various parts of the working drawing in dark, medium, and light values, then I make multiple copies and put like-copies together to see how they look. Often I shade the design in several different versions, since it is only after putting multiple copies together that I can really predict what the effect will be. Often a colored-in version that is least attractive as a single block becomes more exciting when put together with other blocks.

Using Mirrors

Here is an easy way to see how square designs will look side by side without having to make multiple blocks. Position two small mirrors at right angles and adjacent to each other along one of the corners of the block. Many designs when set next to each other show interesting all-over or mosaic-type designs. With this simple mirror trick, you can see them. Try it with some of the blocks in the book. Note that, depending on the symmetry of the block, different things will occur.

Best of All.
See 157-6.

Traditional block symmetry

Coat of Arms.
See 201-4.

Traditional block symmetry

Tree of Life. See 218-1.

Bilateral symmetry.

Tetra. See 99-13.

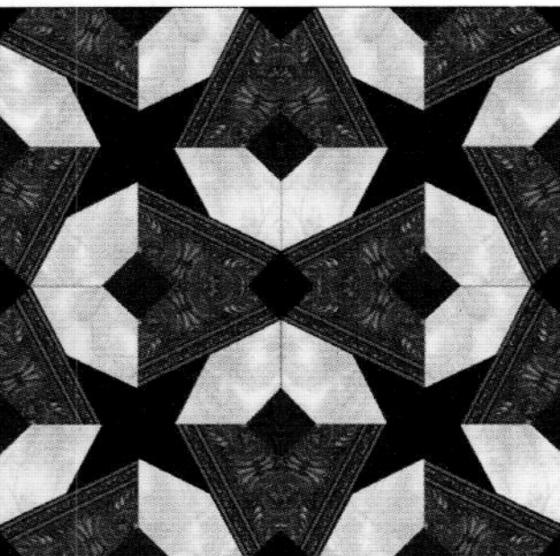
Pinwheel symmetry

For traditional style blocks, using mirrors is the same as placing the blocks side by side. For blocks with bilateral symmetry, different designs occur because of the mirroring effect. Blocks with pinwheel symmetry are interesting as well. Keep in mind if you like a design that results from mirroring a pinwheel-type design, half of the blocks will have to be made the mirror image of the other half.

Two-Block Design

While many traditional quilts repeat the same block throughout the quilt, there is no reason why you should limit your quilt to a single block. Here are a few guidelines on creating interesting two-block designs.

It is best to select blocks from the same category. The reason is that same-category designs are more apt to align nicely at the edges. Even though you will be alternating just two blocks, begin by choosing several from the category, since you never know which ones will look good together. It's important that you try not to visualize how designs will look next to each other. So many times those that seem least likely to go together end up looking the best.

Select some simple designs as well as more complicated ones. Sometimes a simple block compliments a more complex block. Try to find designs that are quite different from each other; if they are too similar, the resulting design is usually not very effective. I often look for at least one design that has a strong diagonal going towards the corners.

Use an odd number of blocks so that one of them can be centered in the middle of the quilt. Also, see how the blocks look on point rather than set square.

There are two ways to work with the designs in this book to experiment with pairing blocks. You can select a category, then photocopy in black and white a few of the pages. You will need at least five copies of each design. Cut out the blocks, select two designs to experiment with, then see how they look when alternated (lay out all five copies of each block). *Hint: Use a non-permanent glue stick so that you can put several different combinations together. If you have ready access to a photocopier, copy each layout before dismantling it so that you can compare layouts.* The second way to combine blocks is to work from the line drawings. It is probably best if you enlarge them on a photocopier. Shade them in light, medium, and dark, differently form the way the color versions are shaded in the book. Make at least five photocopies, then start alternating designs to create layouts. Another option is to work first with unshaded line drawings, arranging them into layouts. The line drawing alone might give you some ideas for shading.

Look at these examples of two-block layouts. The first combines two designs from the 8-pointed star category, *Cassiopeia* and *Silver Star.* The second combines two designs from the 5 x 5 base grid category, both 10 x 10 designs, *White Water* and *Millstone.*

Cassiopeia and *Silver Star:* See 289-9 and 285-6.

White Water and *Millstone:* See 196-6 and 200-5.

Fragmenting

"Fragmenting" block designs is a concept I developed several years ago. The idea is to take a design and break the various shapes down into smaller versions of the same shape. If you look at *Lone Star* blocks, where the diamond is an 8-pointed star made up of smaller diamonds, it's easy to understand how fragmenting works. It is a wonderful technique that lends itself well to color shading.

Lone Star. See 278-7.

When fragmenting, each shape should have the same number of divisions so that the lines intersect from one shape to another. Some designs work better than others. Obviously no curved designs can be used for this technique. Some patterns do not fragment well because the shapes in the design do not join evenly with adjacent shapes. The fragmentation lines, therefore, do not meet. Three designs are shown here, *Roads to Berlin, Andromeda,* and, on the next page, *Nova.*

Roads to Berlin is made up of very simple shapes. Each shape is broken down into five divisions and there are 25 smaller shapes within each of the original shapes of the design. There can be as many divisions of the block as you want, depending on how big you want each individual shape and how large the quilt is to be. One of the aspects of the first fragmented drawing of *Roads to Berlin* that I don't like is the way the triangles are broken up and how the lines from the parallelograms continue straight into the triangles. When this occurs, some of the lines can be eliminated. For instance, pretend that those triangles are half of a square, and break the design up into squares instead of triangles. If you do this, the only triangles are at the edges of the shape.

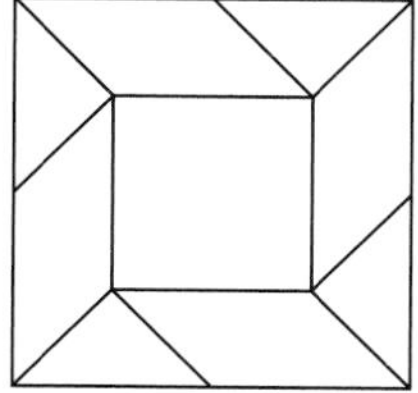

Roads to Berlin. See 66-7.

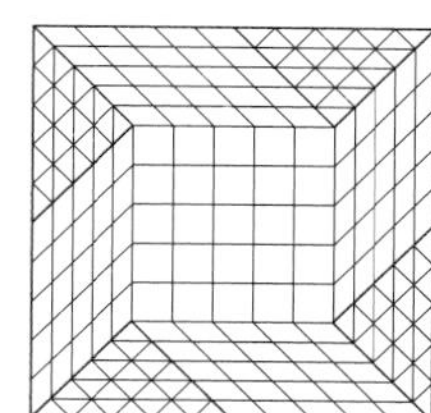
Fragmented

Alternate version

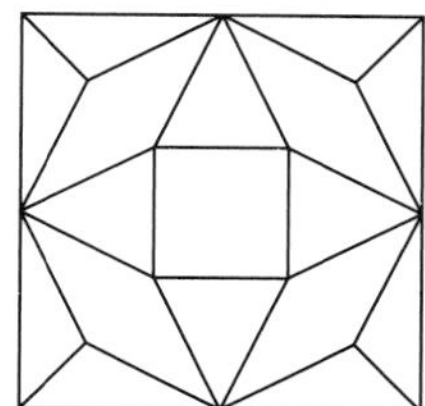
Andromeda. See 138-4.

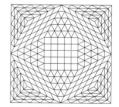

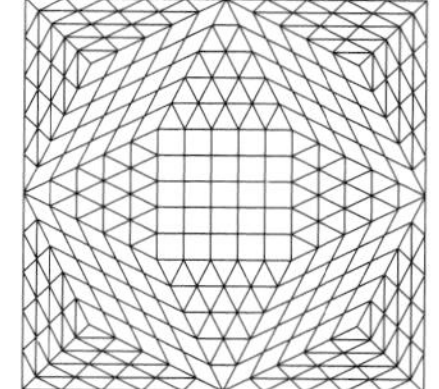
Fragmented

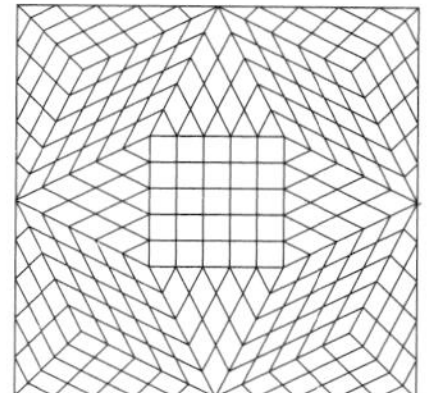
Alternate version

Andromeda is a little different. Even though this design also has triangles at the edge of the block, when they are broken down into smaller triangles, the lines do not continue straight across, so there is a stronger optical illusion to the resulting pattern. If you wish, try removing some of the lines and turning those triangles into parallelograms. Decide which of the two versions is more appealing. In the alternate version shown here, some of the lines in the triangles that surround the center square have also been removed, resulting in a shape made up of diamonds instead of triangles. The only triangles are at the edge of the shape. Compare this illustration with the first illustration to decide which version you prefer.

Designs to Fragment

Many designs are suitable for fragmenting. Here are a few.

8 Point Star. See 64-5
Mosaic No. 6. See 67-1
Beginner's Delight. See 68-1
Inspiration Point. See 80-10
Whirlwind. See 82-3
Ohio Star. See 83-6
Diamond Star. See 96-11
Michigan Beauty. See 97-1
Quartered Star. See 126-5
Vega. See 138-8
Godey Design. See 139-1
Moonstone. See 142-5
Building Blocks. See 142-10
Patience Corner. See 150-9
Hobby Nook. See 201-7
Bachelor's Puzzle. See 206-7
The Builder's Block Quilt. See 207-9
Orion. See 211-4
Dove at the Window. See 229-8
The Wandering Flower. See 237-8
The North Star. See 248-11
Aunt Sukey's Choice. See 259-4
Marion. See 260-3
Rolling Star. See 286-2
Square A. See 289-6
Silver Star. See 290-6
Glory Design. See 394-6
Elongated Box Pattern. See 406-1
Magic Squares. See 406-4
Variegated Diamonds. See 406-5
Box Quilt. See 406-6
Cube Lattice. See 406-7
Godey Design. See 430-7
Enchantment. See 431-3
Block Party. See 431-4

There are more individual pieces in *Nova*. Consequently when the various shapes are fragmented, some of the pieces will be quite small. Once again, try removing some of the lines in one or more of the smaller shapes. Compare the differences. See the quilt made with this design on page 22.

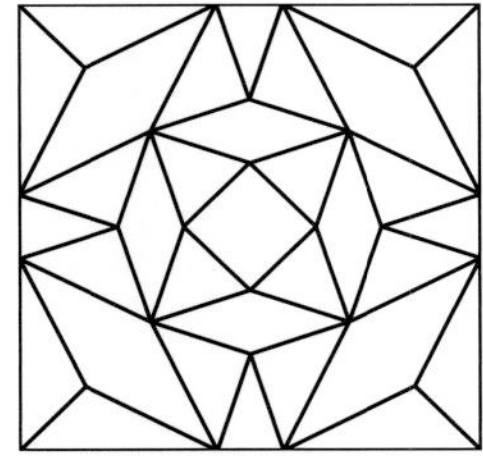

Nova. See 230-11.

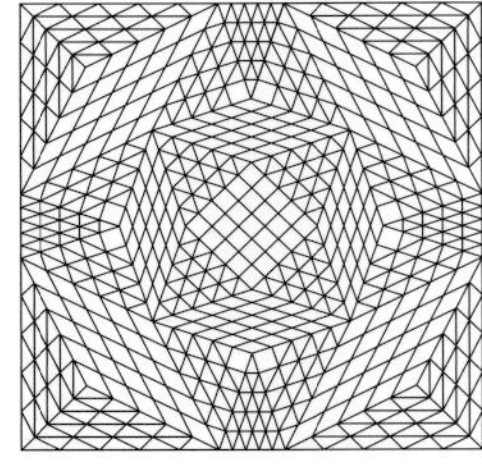

Fragmented

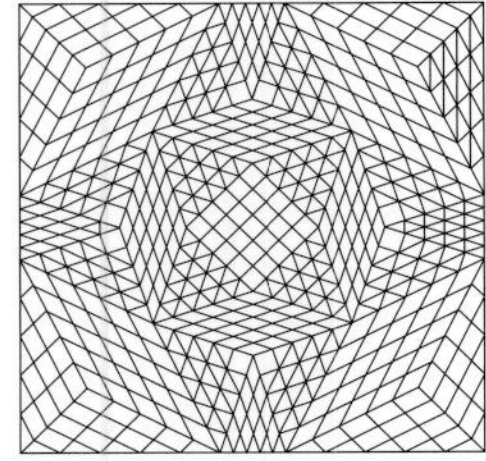

Alternate version

Another way to fragment is to add lines in one direction only, making strips rather than smaller versions of the original shape. The strips can run parallel along any side of the shape. This was done in a quilt I call *Faberge*. The original block is *Mediterranean Puzzle*. Here are the original block, the fragmented version, and the quilt design in color.

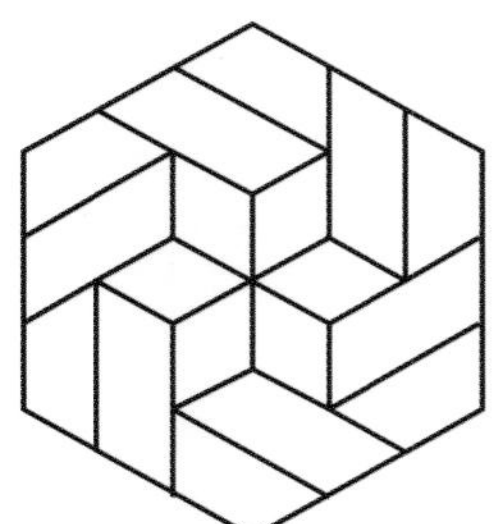

Mediterranean Puzzle. See 397-10.

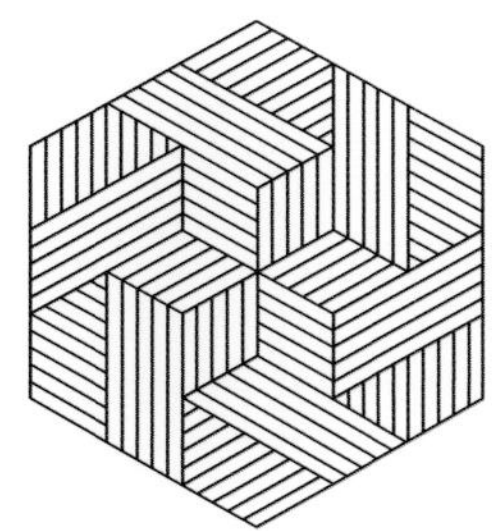

Fragmented

Faberge, Jinny Beyer, 2008. This quilt was designed for the Faberge Fabric collection by RJR Fabrics.

Experimenting with Fragmenting in Black and White

Once you have selected a design, draft it into a 6" or 7" square, divide the shapes down into a certain number of equal divisions, then connect the lines to create smaller versions of the larger shape. There should be no less than three divisions per shape, but I prefer at least four. For experimenting, you can just eyeball the divisions. As mentioned earlier, I design everything first in black and white. Next, I select one of the large shapes in the fragmented design and shade it from light to dark in as many ways as I can think of. The illlustration at top right shows shading in the triangles around the center square.

Repeat the process with each of the other shapes. The design at this point does not look like anything at all. The next step is to photocopy the shaded-in version several times, then cut out the individual shaded units and stack like-shapes together. Now rebuild the design using four diamonds that are shaded all the same, four triangles that are the same, and so on. Try several variations to see which you prefer. One of my favorite aspects of shading colors together is the opportunity to create "glowing" effects. This occurs when the lightest color falls next to the darkest one. The glowing effect is even evident in black and white, and even more spectacular when transferred to color.

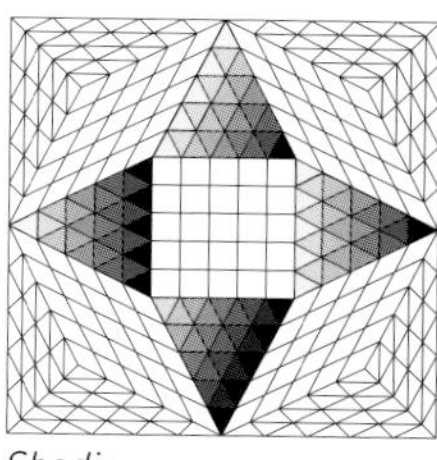

Shading

Fragmented

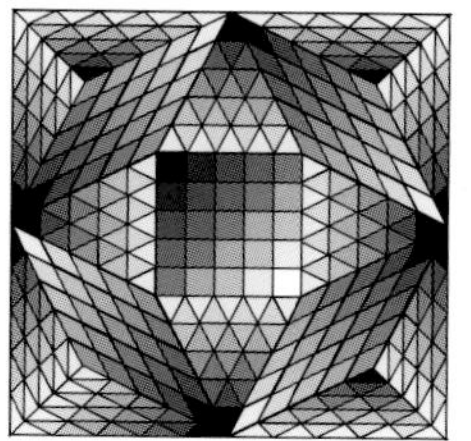

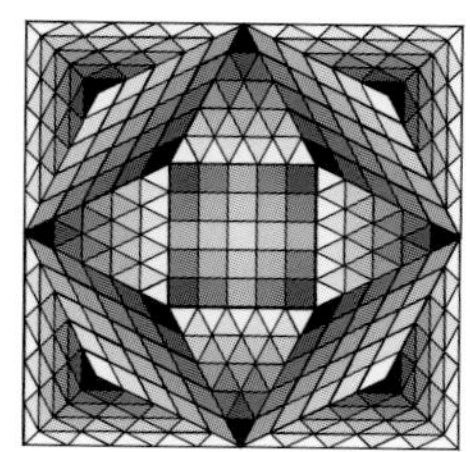

Multiple versions

Templates for Fragmented Designs

When I first developed the idea of fragmenting, I decided the size I wanted the finished quilt to be, drafted one fourth of it on a large piece of paper, then divided up the individual shapes using the technique for creating grids found in the previous chapter. This was a tedious job. Then one day I had one of those "light-bulb" moments. There is no need to work up new templates. You already have all the templates you need in the original design. All that is necessary is to draw the basic design in a size that produces individual shapes that are a good size to work with. Follow this step-by-step process:

1. Draft the block in a size that makes individual pieces in a size you want to work with. Determine the number of divisions you would like in each of the shapes in the finished quilt. As the number of divisions in the block increases, the size of the finished quilt will increase as well. Alternatively, determine the size of the finished quilt, then divide that size by how many divisions you want in each shape. The resulting number will tell you how large you need to draw the base design. As an example, look at *Andromeda* drafted into an 8" size. The four templates required have been highlighted.

2. If there are only two divisions per shape, use the same templates as the 8" block, then sew together four pieces per unit. The finished size will be 16" (2 repeats x 8" block = 16").

3. Using the same templates as the 8" pattern but making three divisions in each of the shapes, the result is a 24" block (3 repeats x the original 8" block = 24").

4. Using the same templates as the 8" pattern, but making four divisions in each of the shapes, the result is a 32" block (4 repeats x the original 8" block = 32").

For a larger quilt, either begin with an original block that is larger than 8" or continue adding divisions to each of the shapes—5 repeats x 8" = 40" quilt, 6 repeats x 8" = 48" quilt, and so on. The size of the original drafted shapes remains the same size. The number of repeats in each shape determines the size of the quilt.

If you want the quilt to be a specific size, such as 60", and you would like 5 divisions in each of the shapes, then divide 60" by 5, which equals 12". You will need to draft the design in a 12" block to get the correct size templates. If that makes the templates too large, then make 6 divisions. This way, the design can be drafted into a 10" square.

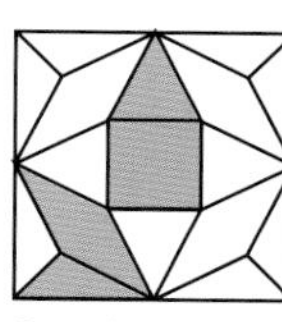
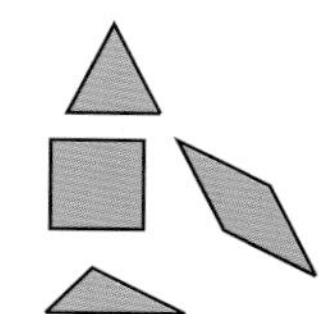

Step 1

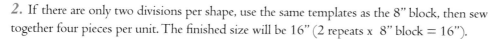

Step 2

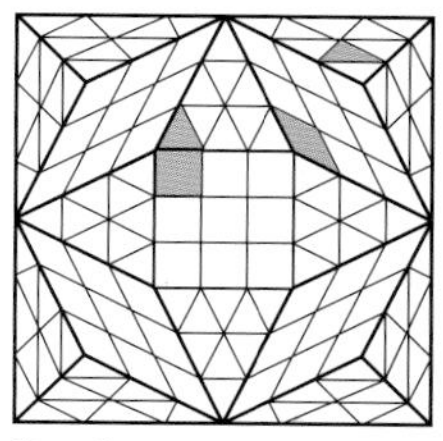

Step 3

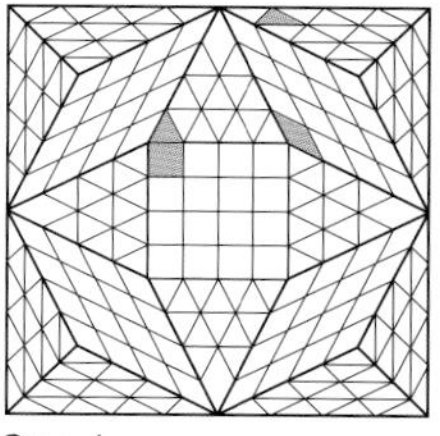

Step 4

Color and Fabric

If you are pleased with the black and white version of your block design, it is very important to adhere to the same light, medium, and dark placement when selecting fabrics. It is natural to select fabrics by groups of color, such as light green to dark green, light blue to dark blue, and so on. If you are working on a fragmented quilt, however, where the units are large, this would result in large areas of a single color. In these cases, my preference is to select a palette of colors that gradually shades from one color into another. This is illustrated in the colored version of *Andromeda* shown below. (I named this quilt *Mayflowers* because I was inspired by the colors of iris blooming in my yard in May. I eliminated lines in the corner pieces and in the triangles around the center square and instead used parallelograms and diamonds in those two shapes.)

Inspiration photo

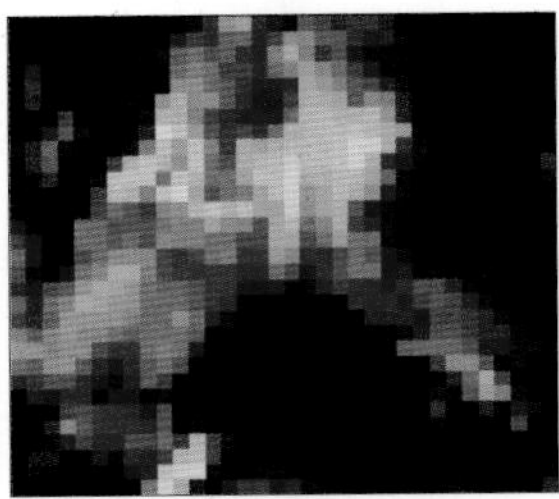

Pixilated version

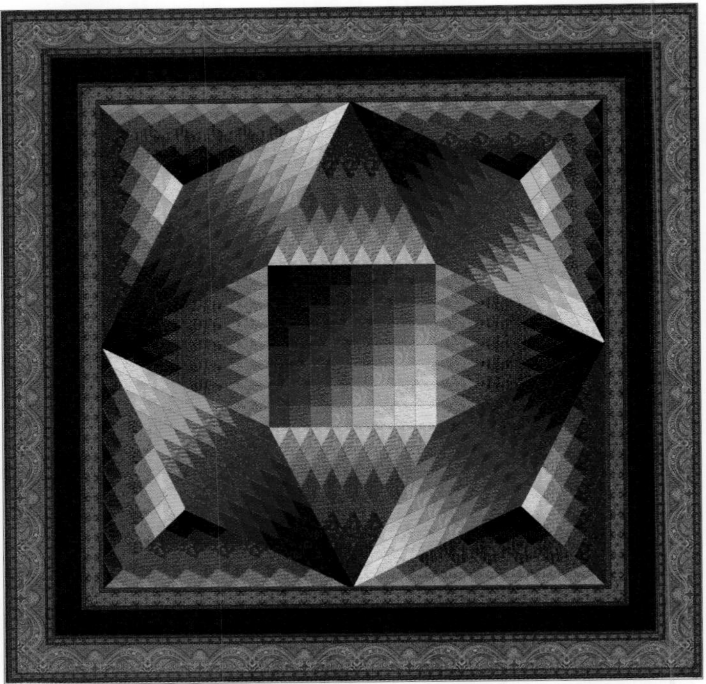

Mayflowers, Jinny Beyer, 2002. Designed for the Palette Fabric Collections by RJR Fabrics.

The central ideas behind my color philosophy is shading; it is very important to use as many hues as you need to get colors to shade smoothly into each other across a design. The photograph of the iris that inspired the color scheme of *Mayflowers* is shown here, along with a pixilated version showing the colors in the image. I love working with colors from nature, as there are always several shades of the colors and nature has enough variation in each of the colors to allow them to shade together.

Look closely at *Mayflowers* to see how the colors have been shaded together. First look at the diamonds. Because there are eight divisions of the shape, I needed 15 different fabrics in order to shade from light to dark. Two of the diamonds are the same and the other two have different fabric in them, but the light to dark shading remains the same. This allows the use of more colors, which, in turn, helps to better capture the color effects in the iris photograph. The colors in one diamond shade from beige through pale yellow to gold to orange/gold to orange then red, deep red, burgundy, eggplant and to black. The other one shades through peach to pink to reds and burgundy. I needed only eight fabrics for each of the other shapes, but, as before, those colors were not limited to a particular color family; instead, they shaded through other colors to give the design more variety.

Look at *Fortune Teller*, another fragmented quilt made by Ricki Selva (see page 22). She fragmented each section of the *Nova* block into five divisions. Notice how Ricki 's subtle use of color shading dramatically enhances the design. *County Clare* (see page 404) is another fragmented design. Each shape in the original block, *Cube Lattice* (see 406-7), has been broken down into three divisions or nine smaller shapes.

Creating Interlocking or Tessellating Designs

There are various ways to create interlocking or *tessellating* designs. One way is to shade the designs in a different manner. Look at *Snail Trail* shown here in both line and colored art. The line art is rather ordinary, but when it is colored in a non-traditional way a spectacular design emerges. When multiple blocks are put together they create an overall interlocking pattern. Look closely and see how the block is colored: two opposite quarter sections are colored dark and two are colored light. When four designs are rotated around either the dark or light corners, they create a motif that tessellates when multiple four-block units are put together.

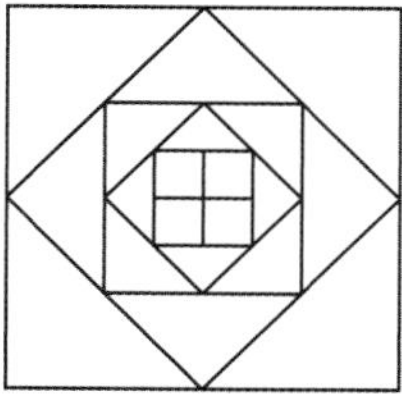

Snail Trail. See 93-11.

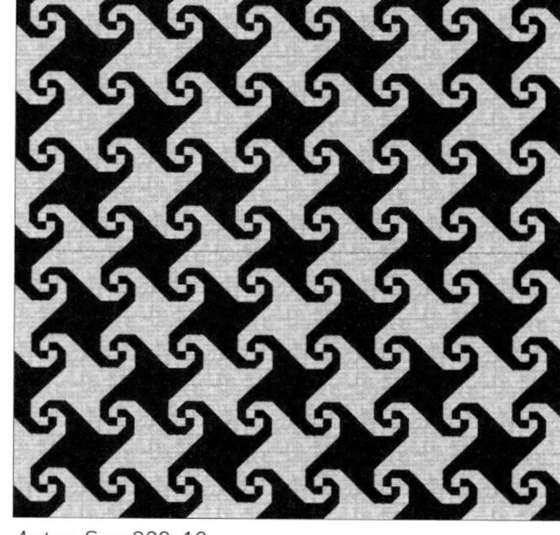

Aster. See 380-10.

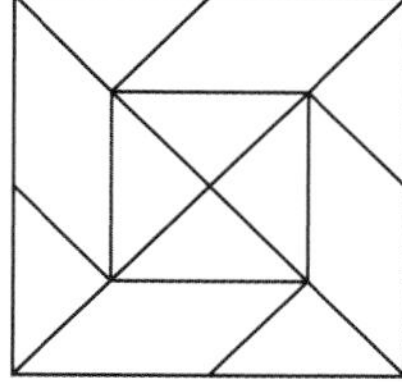

Two in One. See 66-9.

The same thing occurs when half the block is colored dark and the other half light, as illustrated with the block *Two in One*. If four blocks are rotated around either the dark or the light corner it creates a unit that when repeated over and over creates an interlocking design

The same effect can be achieved with many of the blocks in this book. Bear in mind that if there is a single square in the center of the block you will need to divide it diagonally from corner to corner both directions. Since you need to color either quarter or half sections light and dark, there must be an even number of pieces in the design. Have fun experimenting. For more information of how to create interlocking patterns from traditional designs see my book, *Designing Tessellations*.

Creative Fabric Use

Almost ever since I began quilt making, I have incorporated *border prints* and other mirror-imaged prints into my designs. I design my own fabrics and always include a border print in each new collection. I often include large-scale mirrored fabrics of designs such as paisleys, as well. Border prints are fabrics made up of repeat stripes with mirror-image designs. In my designs there are two different stripes—one narrow and one wider—and each is repeated at least four times across the width of the fabric. Each of these is separated by at least ½" so the stripes can be cut apart while still allowing a standard ¼" seam allowance on each one.

For most quilt blocks, we tend to cut fabrics quickly by layering them to cut up to four pieces at one time. Yet this type of speed cutting does not pay any regard to how the motifs that make each fabric so appealing fall within the piece. If we take a little extra time on certain portions of the block to "fussy cut" or center motifs from fabric within the individual shapes, the rewards are well worth the effort.

Border print fabrics and other prints with mirror-image motifs can greatly enhance the impact of a pieced block. I had great fun looking at some of the blocks in this book and figuring out where in that block a border print or other mirrored fabric might be used to enhance the design. While I wanted to adhere to the light, medium, dark placement of values that I found in the earliest known source for a design, for many of them I also used border prints and other mirrored fabrics in light, medium, and dark instead of an overall fabric pattern. As you look through this book, these blocks will be a lesson in themselves on ideas for working with mirrored fabrics in shapes within the patterns.

Border Prints Used in Shapes

One aspect of working with border prints that I particularly like is the fact that the various shapes can be outlined using a small stripe from the print. Therefore, when cutting out the pieces, I like to place the template on the fabric so the portion of the template that will form the *outside* of the shape will fall along one of the straight-line edges of the border print. I make sure that this line falls just within the sewing line so that it will still be visible when all the pieces of the shape are sewn together. This technique is described below.

Balkan Puzzle. See 428-3.

Caroline's Choice. See 73-8.

Four Knaves. See 196-2.

Border Print Squares

Many patchwork blocks in this book have squares as part of the design, where the square is further divided into four triangles. These blocks present a perfect opportunity to use a border print. Some designs where squares have been used in this way are shown here, you will be able to find many others throughout the book.

For my own quilts, if there is a square in the design and it is not broken down into triangles, I often alter the design by drawing lines diagonally from the corners. This gives me the opportunity to use a border print. When preparing the color art for this book, I did not do that, since I wanted to maintain the integrity of the original design, but if you like the look of a border-print square in the quilt blocks, try breaking the squares into triangles yourself. Follow these guidelines.

1. Divide the square diagonally from corner to corner to create four triangles, then using semi-transparent template material, make a template from one of the triangles that includes a ¼" seam allowance around all sides.

2. Draw a line down through the middle of the template. This line will be used as a guide for centering the motifs of the fabric. To do this, line one of the short sides of a right angle, 45-degree triangle along the *long* edge of the triangle template and bring the other short edge to the right angle on the template. Draw the line.

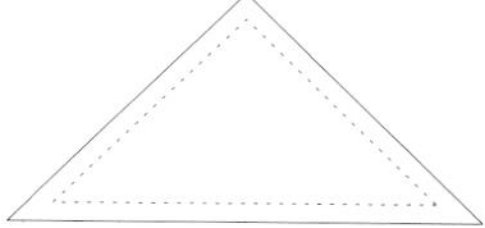

Step 1

3. Using the line marked in step 2 as a guide, center the template on one of the mirror-image motifs in the border-print fabric, making sure that a line from the border print falls just inside the sewing line on the long side of the triangle. This ensures that you will have a nice line or frame around the outside of the finished square. Trace some portion of the design directly onto the template. As you move the template to cut the other pieces, this mark can be used as a guide for lining up the template in the same exact place as the first triangle. Carefully draw around the template and cut the piece out. Then cut three more triangles identical to the first one.

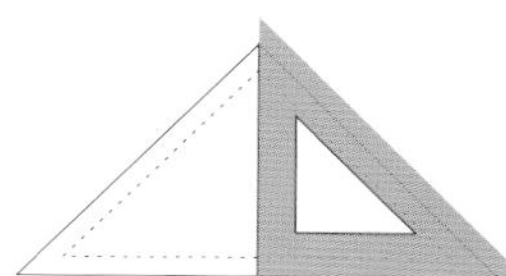

Step 2

4. Sew the four triangles together, carefully matching the design on the border print.

If you want to see what the finished shape will look like before actually cutting into the fabric, place the template onto the fabric in the place where you think you want to cut. Then carefully place two square mirrors onto the seam allowance of the template. Place these mirrors on the two sides that will be sewn to reform the shape. Gently remove the template and the image in the mirror will show you how the finished piece will look once it is sewn together.

Step 3

Step 4

It is amazing how many different squares you can cut from the same border strip by simply placing the template on a slightly different portion of the fabric. The squares shown here illustrate just a few possibilities from the border print shown above.

Border-Print Octagons and Hexagons

Octagons and hexagons can be made with a border print in exactly the same way as the square. If the design has an octagon or hexagon that is divided into triangles, follow the same process as the square, but this time cut eight or six identical triangles from the border print. Just as with the triangle template for creating a square, mark a line down the center of the template and then center that line on a mirror-imaged portion of the fabric. Draw a portion of the design on the template to use as a guide for cutting the remaining triangles. Make sure that all triangles are cut exactly the same. The octagon is illustrated here with *Atlantic Aster.* Notice also in this design how a narrow section of border print has been used to frame the points of the star. Those pieces are also cut identically except that half of them are mirror imaged.

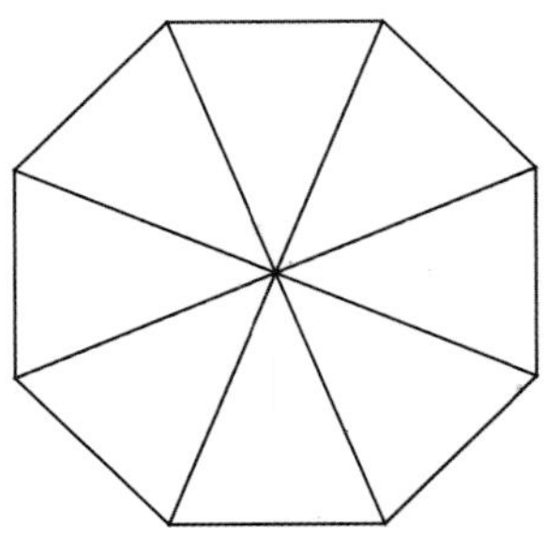

Atlantic Aster. See 380-10.

Border Print Diamonds

Triple Play. See 395-10.

Creating a diamond with a border-print fabric is a little different from the shapes covered so far, but it can give a spectacular effect. *Triple Play* is an example of a quilt where diamonds made from border prints have been used as part of the design (see page 42). Four separate pieces make up the completed diamonds and three diamonds—light, medium, and dark—join together to create a cube in the center of each block. This is a great design to use up left over pieces of border print fabrics.

To create a border-print diamond, four triangles must be cut. Two are exactly the same and the other two are the exact mirror image of the first two. This time, do not try to center a mirror-imaged portion of the border print in the middle of the template. The reason for this is that the triangle shape used to create the diamond is not symmetrical; therefore it would be impossible to center a motif in the middle of the template. What is important is that two of the pieces are the exact mirror image of the other two and that a line from the border print falls along the long side of the triangle to act as a frame around the completed shape.

To create a border print diamond, follow these steps:

1. If the diamond is not already divided into four triangles, divide it in half lengthwise and sideways. Make a template from one of the four triangles of the diamond, adding the ¼" seam allowance around all sides. Mark the grain line arrow onto the template along the *long* side of the triangle. This is very important as the arrow indicates the straight grain of fabric. The template must be placed onto the border print fabric so that a line from the fabric will fall just inside the sewing line. The arrow will help you to place the template correctly.

2. After positioning the template onto the border print, draw some portion of the design from the fabric onto the template. This will act as a guide for cutting the remaining pieces. Cut the first piece and then, using the marked design on the template as a guide, cut a second one exactly the same. Carefully flip the template horizontally and, once again using the marked design on the template as a guide, find the exact mirror image of the first piece. Cut two diamonds that are the exact mirror image of the first two.

3. Position the triangles according to the illustration, and then sew together.

Diamond Head is another example where a border print diamond has been used.

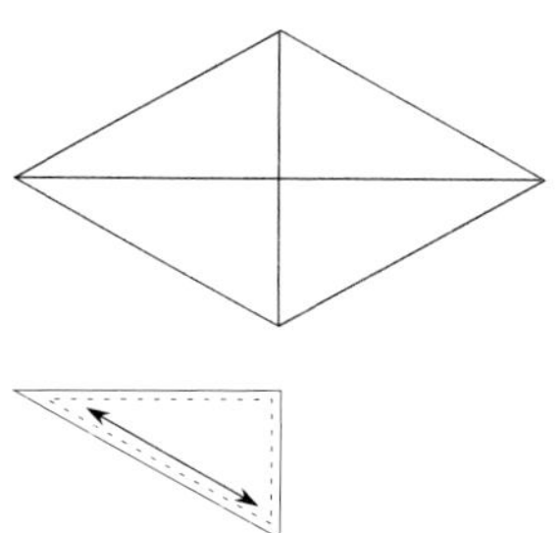
Step 1

Step 2

Step 3

Diamond Head. See 314-2.

Using Border Prints in Other Areas of a Design

Border prints are often effectively used in triangles, in basket patterns, as sashing, or in other rectangular areas of a block. Look at these examples.

Basket of Daffodils. See 306-9.

Lancelot. See 270-1.

Double Pinwheel. See 169-7.

Spider Web. See 169-9.

Mirrored Fabrics

Try using mirrored fabrics as well as border prints to create kaleidoscopic effects in quilts. Mirrored fabrics create particularly interesting effects in star, sunflower, and mariner's compass type patterns. The process is exactly the same as working with border-print fabrics. Center the template to be used over a mirror-imaged portion of the fabric. Mark part of the design onto the template so that the remaining pieces can be cut exactly the same. There are many examples throughout the book, but a few are repeated here.

As you can see in this section, border prints and mirror-imaged fabrics can add a unique look to a square, triangle, hexagon, octagon, diamond, or any other geometric shape within a patchwork block. Take some time to page through the book looking only for blocks that have these types of fabrics. That will be the biggest lesson you can have in learning creative ways to add uniqueness to a block.

The Zinnia Quilt. See 381-7.

Cone Flower. See 382-2.

Silver Star. See 285-6.

Star Bright. See 282-10.

Moonglow, Jinny Beyer, 1999.

PART 2

Square Blocks

"Piece work is dear to both young and o ld. The pride of the little girl making her first quilt and the grandame piecing for her great-granddaughter's wedding gift."

MRS. R. STOTENBUR (AGED 72) *FARM AND HOME,* 1898

2 x 2 Base Grid Category

Includes ● 2 x 2, ● 4 x 4, ● 8 x 8, ● 16 x 16, ● 32 x 32, and ● 64 x 64 grids

❶ **Arrowhead Puzzle,** Aunt Martha series: *Quilts,* ca. 1963.

❷ **Washington's Puzzle,** Nancy Cabot, *Chicago Tribune,* Oct 15, 1934. See 265-10. "In the history of today's quilt pattern, there is much room for speculation and equal opportunity for dispute. Both Virginians and Kentuckians claim the distinction of creating this block, but in neither state can be found a solution as to what puzzled the father of our country." Nancy Cabot, *Chicago Tribune,* Oct 15, 1934

❸ **Cotton Reels,** Goodman, 1973.

❹ **Homeward Bound,** Nancy Cabot, *Chicago Tribune,* Nov 12, 1937.

❺ **Hidden Square,** source unknown, date unknown.

❻ **Birds in the Air,** Gutcheon, *The Perfect Patchwork Primer,* 1973.

❼ **Duck's Foot,** source unknown, date unknown.

❽ **Sailboat,** source unknown, date unknown.

❾ **Wild Goose Chase,** *The Patchwork Book,* 1932. See 427-6. Also known as:
- **Birds in Flight,** *American Patchwork Quilts,* 1973.
- **Flying Geese,** source unknown, date unknown.

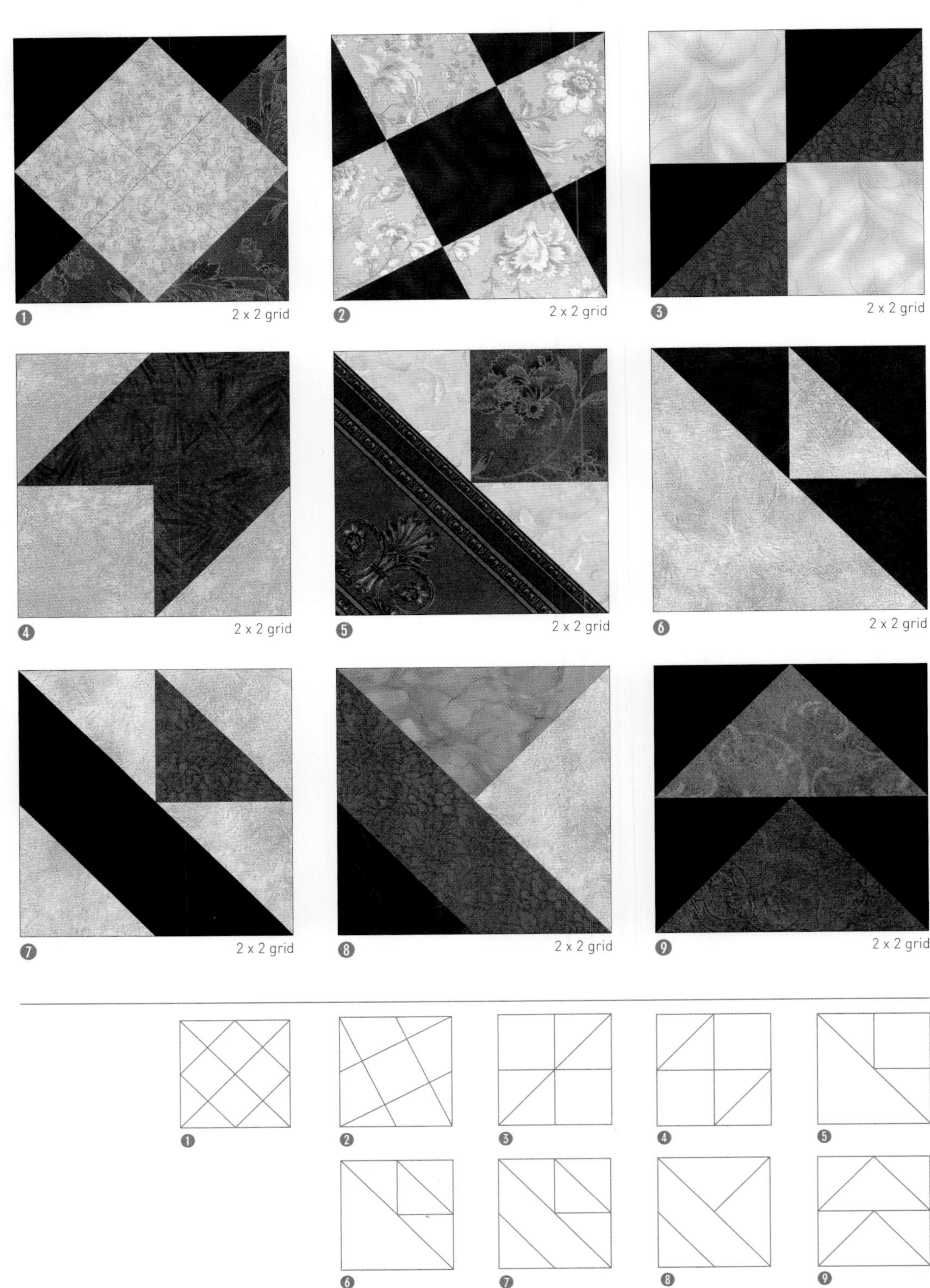

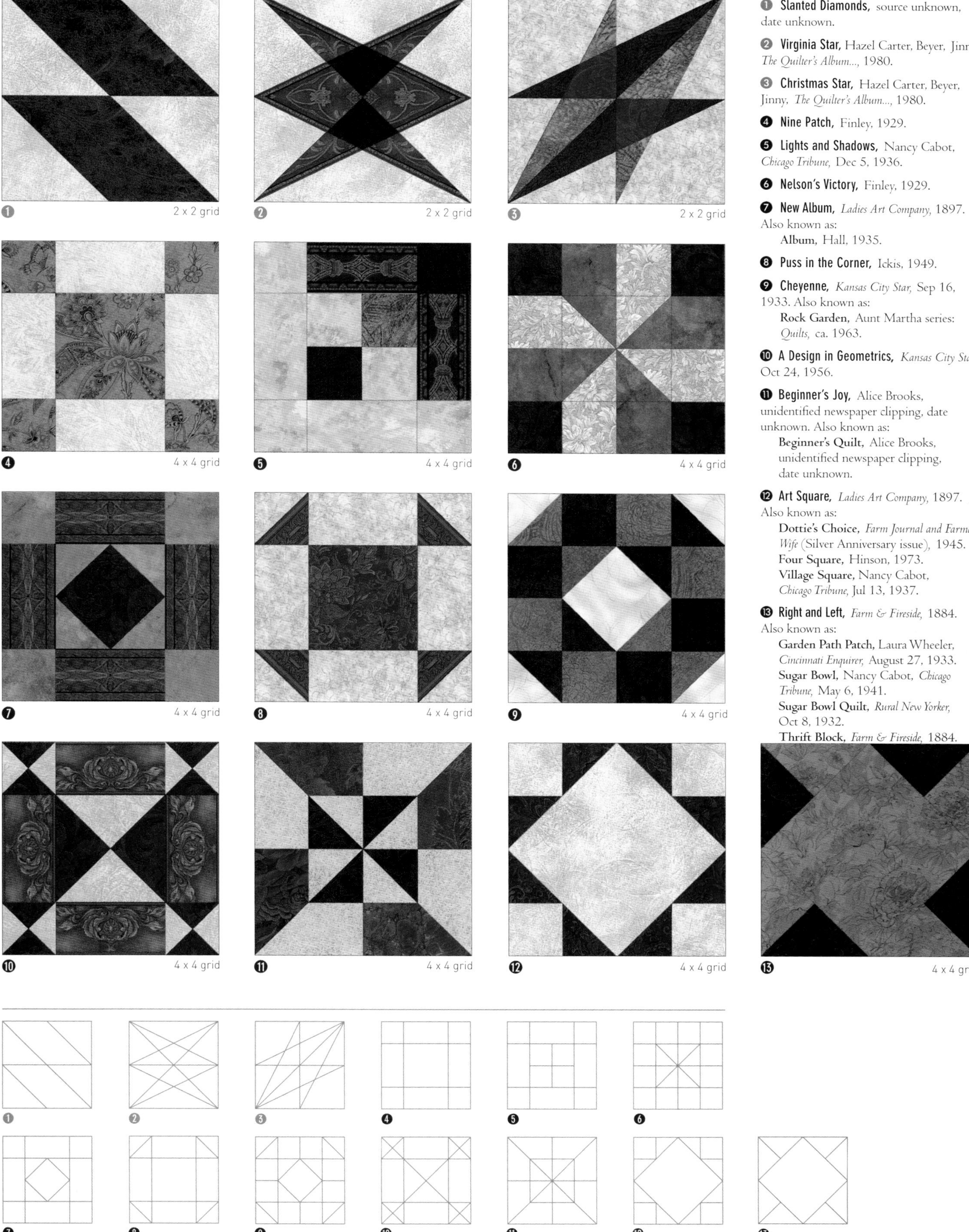

❶ **Slanted Diamonds,** source unknown, date unknown.

❷ **Virginia Star,** Hazel Carter, Beyer, Jinny, *The Quilter's Album...,* 1980.

❸ **Christmas Star,** Hazel Carter, Beyer, Jinny, *The Quilter's Album...,* 1980.

❹ **Nine Patch,** Finley, 1929.

❺ **Lights and Shadows,** Nancy Cabot, *Chicago Tribune,* Dec 5, 1936.

❻ **Nelson's Victory,** Finley, 1929.

❼ **New Album,** *Ladies Art Company,* 1897. Also known as:
  Album, Hall, 1935.

❽ **Puss in the Corner,** Ickis, 1949.

❾ **Cheyenne,** *Kansas City Star,* Sep 16, 1933. Also known as:
  Rock Garden, Aunt Martha series: *Quilts,* ca. 1963.

❿ **A Design in Geometrics,** *Kansas City Star,* Oct 24, 1956.

⓫ **Beginner's Joy,** Alice Brooks, unidentified newspaper clipping, date unknown. Also known as:
  Beginner's Quilt, Alice Brooks, unidentified newspaper clipping, date unknown.

⓬ **Art Square,** *Ladies Art Company,* 1897. Also known as:
  Dottie's Choice, *Farm Journal and Farmer's Wife* (Silver Anniversary issue), 1945.
  Four Square, Hinson, 1973.
  Village Square, Nancy Cabot, *Chicago Tribune,* Jul 13, 1937.

⓭ **Right and Left,** *Farm & Fireside,* 1884. Also known as:
  Garden Path Patch, Laura Wheeler, *Cincinnati Enquirer,* August 27, 1933.
  Sugar Bowl, Nancy Cabot, *Chicago Tribune,* May 6, 1941.
  Sugar Bowl Quilt, *Rural New Yorker,* Oct 8, 1932.
  Thrift Block, *Farm & Fireside,* 1884.

❶ **Southern Belle,** Clara Stone, *Practical Needlework,* ca. 1906.

❷ **Day or Night,** Alice Brooks, unidentified newspaper clipping, date unknown.

❸ **Twelve Triangles,** *Farm Journal and Farmer's Wife,* ca. 1941.

❹ **Economy,** *Ladies Art Company,* 1897. Also known as:
Economy Patch, Hall, 1935.

❺ **The King's Crown,** *Kansas City Star,* 1931.
Thrift Block, Nancy Cabot, *Chicago Tribune,* Sep 6, 1937.

❻ **Windmill,** Nancy Page, *Birmingham News,* Nov 7, 1933.

❼ **Windmill,** *Ladies Art Company,* 1897.

❽ **Our Editor,** Clara Stone, *Practical Needlework,* ca. 1906.

❾ **Peace and Plenty,** *Farm Journal and Farmer's Wife* (Silver Anniversary issue), 1945. Also known as:
Unknown Four Patch, Hinson, 1973.

❿ **The Blockade,** *Kansas City Star,* Jun 4, 1938. Also known as:
The Broken Dish, *Kansas City Star,* Apr 30, 1952.
A Four Corner Puzzle, *Kansas City Star,* Jul 21, 1943.

⓫ **Four Four Time,** *Farm Journal and Farmer's Wife,* ca. 1941.

⓬ **Mosaic No. 1,** *Ladies Art Company,* 1897. Also known as:
Mosaic No. 3, Nancy Cabot, *Chicago Tribune,* Jan 17, 1934.

Quick Reference: Boats

With our nation's long maritime history, it is no wonder that so many blocks depicting ships or boats have evolved. They are grouped here for easy identification.

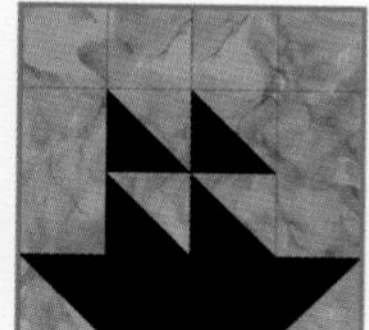

Fishing Boats, *Progressive Farmer.* **See 76-7.**

Ships in the Night, *Chicago Tribune.* **See 270-10.**

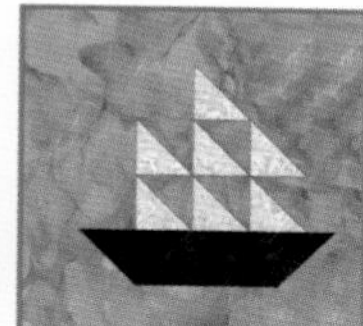

Dream Ship, *Chicago Tribune.* **See 173-5.**

The Sail Boat, *Kansas City Star.* **See 76-8.**

Sailboat Quilt, *Birmingham News.* **See 110-8.**

Ship of Dreams. Beyer, Alice. **See 76-6.**

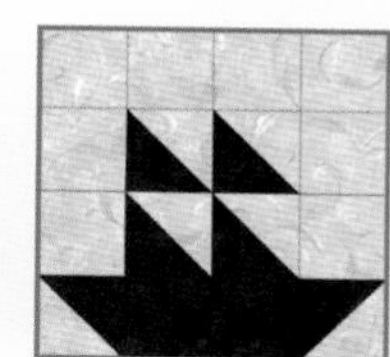

Fishing Boats, *Chicago Tribune.* **See 76-10.**

The Sailboat Oklahoma, *Kansas City Star.* **See 76-9.**

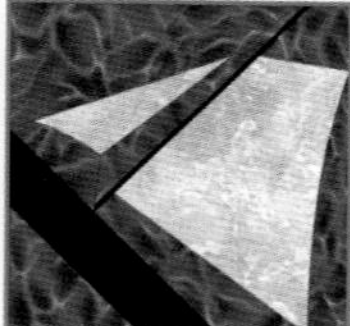

Sailboat, *Indianapolis Star.* **See 339-12.**

Sailboat, Hall. **See 127-6.**

West Wind, *Birmingham News.* **See 127-5.**

Ships at Sea, unidentified newspaper clipping. **See 72-8.**

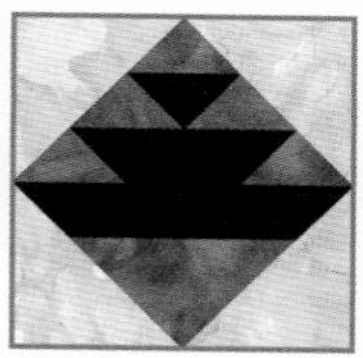

Sail Boat Block, *Kansas City Star.* **See 154-6.**

Sail Boat, Hall. **See 154-7.**

Ships at Sea, *Chicago Tribune.* **See 107-7.**

Ships at Sea, *Chicago Tribune.* **See 107-8.**

Ships at Sea, *The Farmer's Advocate.* **See 107-6.**

Ships a' Sea, *The Country Gentleman.* **See 107-9.**

Lost Ship, Hall. **See 107-11.**

Lost Ship, Hall. **See 208-11.**

Lost Ship Pattern, *Ladies Art Company.* **See 150-4.**

1 **Mosaic No. 2,** *Ladies Art Company,* 1897. Also known as:
- **Mosaic No. 8,** Nancy Cabot, *Chicago Tribune,* Sep 1, 1934.

2 **Mosaic No. 5,** *Ladies Art Company,* 1897.

3 **Triangle Squares,** *Virginia Snow Patchwork Designs,* ca. 1930.

4 **Windblown Square,** McKim, 1931. See 66-12 and 428-3. Also known as:
- **Balkan Puzzle,** Nancy Cabot, *Chicago Tribune,* Feb 15, 1933.
- **Flowing Ribbons,** Nancy Cabot, *Chicago Tribune,* Oct 31, 1935.
- **Whirlpools,** Nancy Page, *Birmingham News,* May 8, 1934
- **Windblown Star,** Nancy Cabot, *Chicago Tribune,* Feb 15, 1933.

5 **St. Valentine,** Clara Stone, *Practical Needlework,* ca. 1906.

6 **Marion's Choice,** Clara Stone, *Practical Needlework,* ca. 1906. Also known as:
- **Martha's Choice,** Nancy Page, *Birmingham News,* Jun 24, 1941.

7 **Mosaic No. 21,** *Ladies Art Company* 1897. Also known as:
- **Mosaic No. 6,** Nancy Cabot, *Chicago Tribune,* Jul 23, 1934.
- **Road to Paris,** *Old Fashioned Quilts,* ca. 1931.

8 **Mosaic No. 16,** *Ladies Art Company,* 1897. Also known as:
- **Canadian Gardens,** Nancy Page, *Birmingham News,* Sep 15, 1942.
- **Connecticut,** Nancy Page, *Birmingham News,* Sep 25, 1934.
- **Mosaic No. 12,** Nancy Cabot, *Chicago Tribune,* Oct 13, 1934.

9 **Hour Glass,** Nancy Page, *Nashville Banner,* Jan 30, 1934. Also known as:
- **Mrs. Lacey's Choice,** Nancy Page, *Birmingham News,* Apr 6, 1943.

10 **Square and Star,** *Ladies Art Company,* 1897. See 95-6. Also known as:
- **Godey's Lady's Book Block,** ca. 1938, per Havig.
- **Joseph's Coat,** Nancy Page, *Birmingham News,* Oct 15, 1935.
- **Squares and Triangles,** *Kansas City Star,* Jan 5, 1955.

11 **Godey Design,** *Godey's Lady's Book,* 1857. Also known as:
- **Mosaic No. 3,** *Ladies Art Company,* 1897.

12 **A Red & White Crisscross,** *Kansas City Star,* Sep 9, 1942.

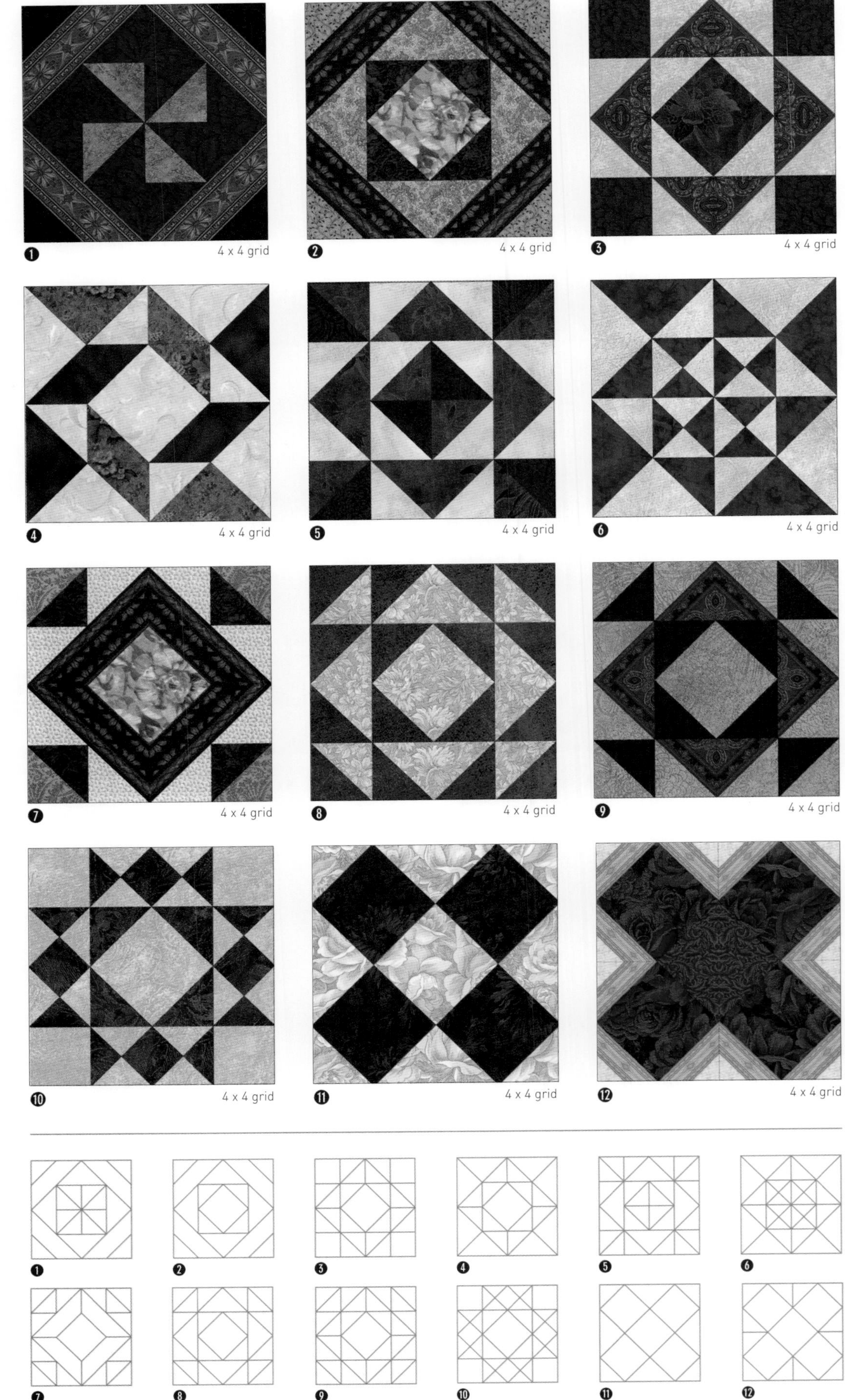

❶ **Triangles & Squares,** *Kansas City Star,* Sep 24, 1952.

❷ **Broken Sash,** Khin, 1980. See 119-7, 233-12 and 253-5.

❸ **Magic Cross,** *The Patchwork Book,* 1932.

❹ **Wheel of Time,** Clara Stone, *Practical Needlework,* ca. 1906.

❺ **Mosaic No. 19,** *Ladies Art Company,* 1897. Also known as:
  Castles in Spain, Nancy Page, *Birmingham News,* Feb 22, 1938.
  Mosaic No. 7, Nancy Cabot, *Chicago Tribune,* Aug 8, 1934.

❻ **A Snowflake,** *Ladies Art Company,* 1897. Also known as:
  Cross Stitch, Nancy Cabot, *Chicago Tribune,* Aug 19, 1937.
  Maud's Album Quilt, Nancy Page, *Birmingham News,* May 10, 1938.
  Old Italian Design, *The Farm Journal Quilt Patterns,* ca. 1935.
  Snow Block, Nancy Cabot, *Chicago Tribune,* Sep 29, 1934.

❼ **King's X,** *Farm Journal,* Martens, 1970.

❽ **The Arrowhead,** *Kansas City Star,* Mar 26, 1941.

❾ **The Cotton Boll Quilt,** *Kansas City Star,* Feb 12, 1941. Also known as:
  Mother's Choice, *Kansas City Star,* Dec 4, 1946.

❿ **Squire Smith's Choice,** Clara Stone, *Practical Needlework,* ca. 1906.

⓫ **Necktie,** *Ladies Art Company,* 1897. Also known as:
  Peek Hole, *The Patchwork Book,* 1932.

⓬ **Nelson's Victory,** Clara Stone, *Practical Needlework,* ca. 1906.

❶ **End of the Day,** *Farm Journal and Farmer's Wife* (Silver Anniversary issue), 1945. Also known as:
- **A Whirligig for Your Child,** *Kansas City Star,* Jun 20, 1956.

❷ **Mr. Roosevelt's Necktie,** *Practical Needlework,* ca. 1906. Also known as:
- **Oh Susannah,** ca 1938, per Havig.
- **Susannah,** Ruby McKim, *Kansas City Star,* Sep 7, 1929.
- **Susannah Patch,** *Ladies Art Company,* 1922.
- **Susannah's Patch,** Nancy Cabot, *Chicago Tribune,* Sep 18, 1936.

❸ **Sawtooth,** *Farm & Fireside,* 1884. Also known as:
- **Ann's Doll Quilt,** Nancy Page, *Nashville Banner,* Sep 19, 1933.
- **Eight Pointed Star,** Orlofsky, 1974.
- **Evening Star,** *Ladies Art Company,* 1897.
- **Nameless Star,** Nancy Cabot, *Chicago Tribune,* Oct 20, 1934.
- **Saw Tooth,** Ickis, 1949.
- **Square and Points,** *Kansas City Star,* Jun 3, 1933.
- **Variable Star,** Holstein, 1973

❹ **Indian Star,** *Kansas City Star,* Jul 17, 1937.

❺ **Sarah's Choice,** Clara Stone, *Practical Needlework,* ca. 1906.

❻ **Star Flower,** *Q Book 112, One Piece Quilts,* date unknown.

❼ **Ribbon Star,** *Ladies Art Company,* 1897. Also known as:
- **Cog Block,** *Kansas City Star,* Jul 27, 1955.
- **Eight Pointed Star,** *Farm Journal Quilt Patterns,* ca. 1935.
- **Evening Star,** Beyer, Jinny, *The Quilter's Album…,* 1980.
- **Joining Star,** Nancy Page, *Lowell Sun* May 21, 1934.

'The Joining Star' is part of the Nancy Page Quilt Series, 'Quilt of Many Stars'. It is used as the 'corner stones' of the sashing pieces: "When the Nancy Page quilt club members saw the tiny blocks which were used in the joining star they did not wonder that Nancy gave them this pattern at this time. Instead of waiting until all the body stars were made, the member could make one of these joining stars whenever she had leisure or was waiting for the men folks to come home for dinner." *Lowell Sun,* May 21, 1934

❽ **Robert's Choice,** Nancy Page, *Birmingham News,* Oct 20, 1942.

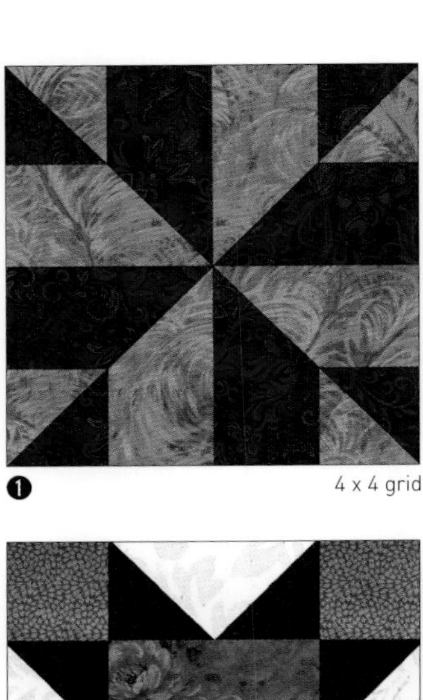

❶ 4 x 4 grid

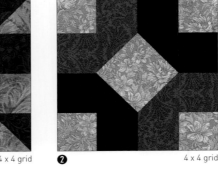

❷ 4 x 4 grid

❸ 4 x 4 grid

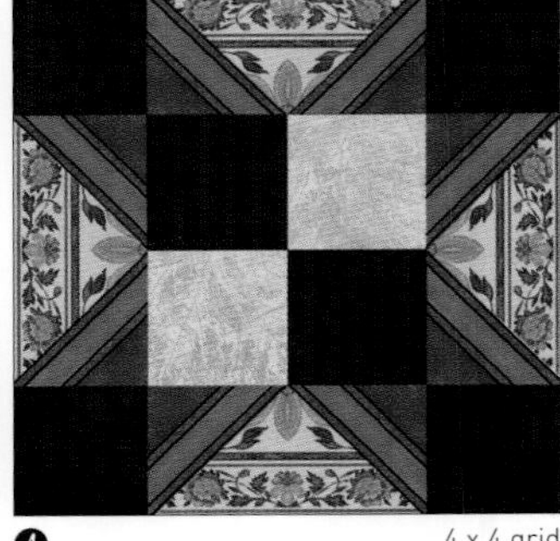

❹ 4 x 4 grid

❺ 4 x 4 grid

❻ 4 x 4 grid

❼ 4 x 4 grid

❽ 4 x 4 grid

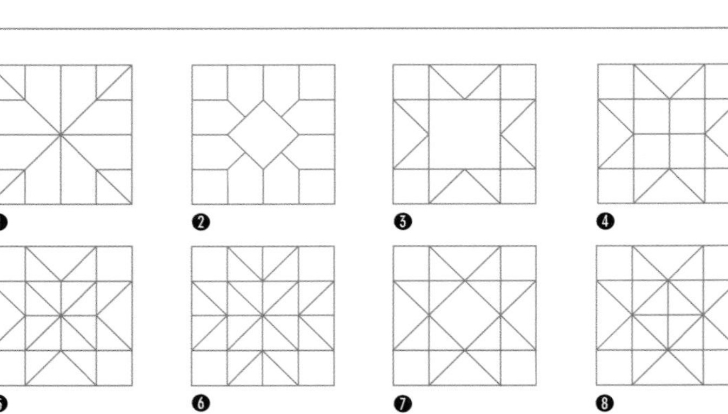

❶ ❷ ❸ ❹

❺ ❻ ❼ ❽

"With the opening of A Century of Progress exposition less than a month away, it is of timely interest to recall to notice the quilt with which the Columbian Exposition is commemorated. Specially designed and named after the World's Fair of '93, the pattern originally was made up in blue and white checked gingham, contrasted with plain white…." Nancy Cabot, *Chicago Tribune,* May 7, 1933

"The old-time patchwork quilt was an heirloom. It was not alone an economy; it was the needlewoman's interpretation of the things in her daily life and of the events of her time. Given such an occasion as the Fair at Chicago, she would have made a quilt to commemorate such an outstanding event. So, we today, following the spirit of the needlewoman of old, offer the 'World's Fair'—a quilt which in generations to come will call to mind the remarkable exposition we now are having at Chicago. Like the designs of old, it too has its meaning. Diversity of pattern—first you see one design, then it shifts to another—characterizes the variety of interests centered at the exposition. Its outstanding patchwork symbol is the palm—the symbol of the victory over obstacles necessary to assure us a Century of Progress." Laura Wheeler, *Cincinnati Enquirer,* Aug 10, 1933

The Chicago World Fairs

County and State Fairs have always been an inspiration for people to get out their fabrics and design new quilts, or to create new blocks to commemorate the event. The two world fairs held forty years apart in Chicago had a great impact on quilting, perhaps contributing to awareness of this unique craft as it gained popularity in the late 1800s and on through the 1930s.

The World's Columbian Exposition held from May 1 to October 30, 1893, celebrated the four hundredth anniversary of Christopher Columbus's landing in America. I found eight blocks containing the words "World" and "Fair", four of them are dated before 1933, so presumably they were named for this great Exposition. I found the first block shown here in the 1897 *Ladies Art Catalog*. It is also known as *Going to Chicago* and *Chicago World's Fair*. The next two are obviously based on the same design, but they have been drafted on different grids.

According to a Nancy Cabot column in the *Chicago Tribune* on June 11, 1935, the *Columbian Star* was also inspired by the 1893 Fair. We may speculate that other blocks, such as *Columbian Chain* and *Columbian Puzzle*, were also created for the Columbian Exposition.

Forty years after the Columbian Exposition, a second World Fair took place in Chicago, which also boosted the popularity of quilting. A Century of Progress International Exposition opened on May 27, 1933 to commemorate the one hundredth anniversary of the incorporation of the city. As part of the Exposition, Sears Roebuck sponsored the Sears National Quilt contest. This was the largest quilt contest ever held and more than 25,000 quilters from all over the country participated. The judging was first done at a local level and then at a regional level. The final competition was judged at the Fair itself. Participants were encouraged to be creative as they made quilts in the spirit of the Century of Progress theme. (Waldvogel & Brackman, 1993)

World's Fair Block, *Ladies Art Company.* **See 106-10.**

The World's Fair. *Ladies Art Company.* **See 326-4.**

World's Fair, Hall. **See 341-4.**

World's Fair Puzzle, *Ladies Art Company.* **See 108-5.**

World's Fair, *Grandma Dexter New Appliqué and Patchwork Designs.* **See 95-7.**

Columbian Star, *Ladies Art Company.* **See 156-6.**

World's Fair, *The Farmer's Wife Book of New Designs and Patterns.* **See 249-3.**

Century of Progress, *Chicago Tribune.* **See 399-4.**

Century of Progress, *Farm Journal and Farmer's Wife.* **See 120-6.**

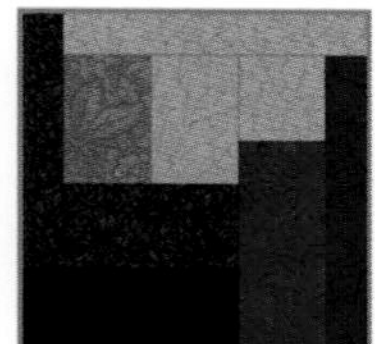
Century of Progress, *Chicago Tribune.* **See 111-3.**

Century of Progress, *Grandma Dexter Appliqué and Patchwork Designs, Book 36a.* **See 115-3.**

World's Fair, *Cincinnati Enquirer.* **See 121-10.**

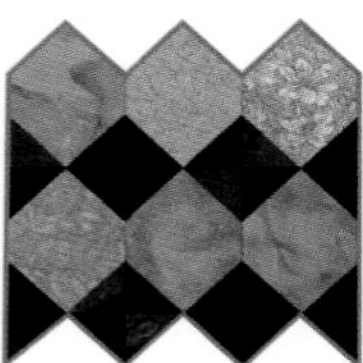
The World Fair Quilt, *Kansas City Star.* **See 407-5.**

❶ **Crystal Star,** *Kansas City Star,* Jun 16, 1934.

❷ **Star Puzzle,** *Ladies Art Company,* 1897. Also known as:
- **Barbara Frietchie,** Nancy Page, *Nashville Banner,* Oct 3, 1933.
- **Barbara Frietschie Star,** *Grandmother Clark's Authentic Early American Patchwork Quilts, Book No. 23,* 1932.
- **The Colorado Quilt,** *Kansas City Star,* Jan 8, 1941.
- **Pieced Star,** *Detroit Free Press,* Apr 5, 1933.
- **Wind Mill Quilt,** *Wallaces' Farmer,* 1928, per Brackman.

❸ **Swallow Tails,** Jinny Beyer, Hilton Head Seminar design, 1982; published in Beyer, Jinny, *Patchwork Portfolio.*

❹ **Odd Fellow's Cross,** Ickis, 1949.

❺ **8 Point Star,** *Grandma Dexter New Appliqué and Patchwork Designs, Book 36b,* ca. 1932. See 139-1 and 276-1. Also known as:
- **The Arrow Star,** *Kansas City Star,* Oct 20, 1934.
- **Columns,** Gutcheon, 1973.
- **Eight Pointed Star,** James, 1978.
- **Idaho Star,** Nancy Cabot, date unknown, per Alboum.
- **The Southern Star,** *Kansas City Star,* Mar 28, 1945.

❻ **Red and White Cross,** Nancy Cabot, *Chicago Tribune,* May 26, 1936.

❼ **Star of the Milky Way,** *Old Fashioned Quilts,* ca. 1931.

❽ **Starry Night,** *Q Book 110, Star Quilts,* date unknown.

❾ **Semi Octagon,** ca. 1938, per Havig. Also known as:
- **Will O' the Wisp,** *Farm Journal and Farmer's Wife* (Silver Anniversary issue), 1945.
- **The Windmill Blades,** *Kansas City Star,* Nov 10, 1954.

❿ **Star of the East,** *Farm Journal and Farmer's Wife* (Silver Anniversary issue), 1945. Also known as:
- **Midnight Stars,** date unknown, per Brackman.

⓫ **Four Petals,** *Farm Journal and Farmer's Wife* (Silver Anniversary issue), 1945.

⓬ **Priscilla,** Hall, 1935. Also known as:
World without End, Hall, 1935.

❶ 4 x 4 grid

❷ 4 x 4 grid

❸ 4 x 4 grid

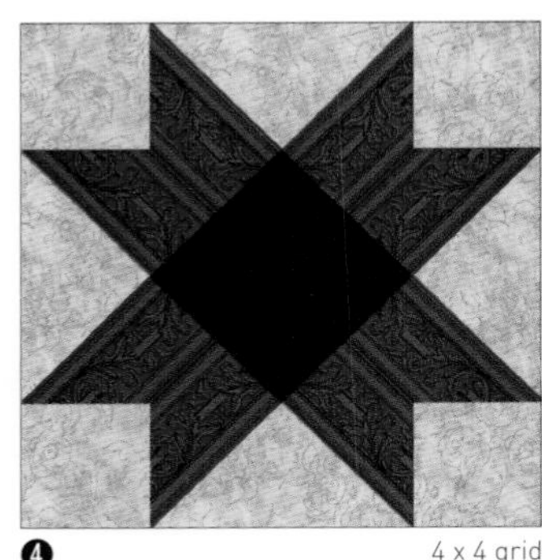
❹ 4 x 4 grid

❺ 4 x 4 grid

❻ 4 x 4 grid

❼ 4 x 4 grid

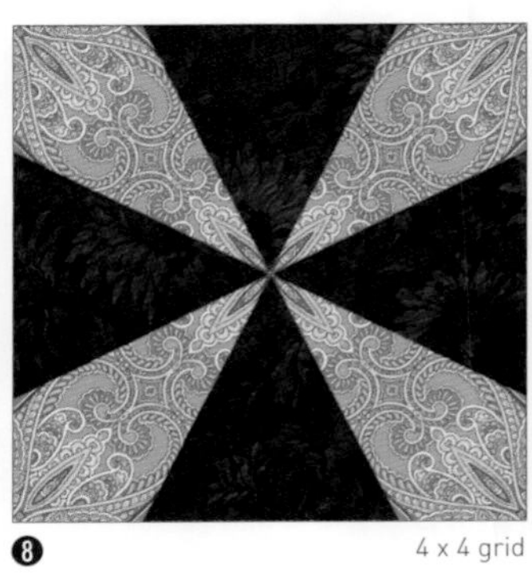
❽ 4 x 4 grid

❾ 4 x 4 grid

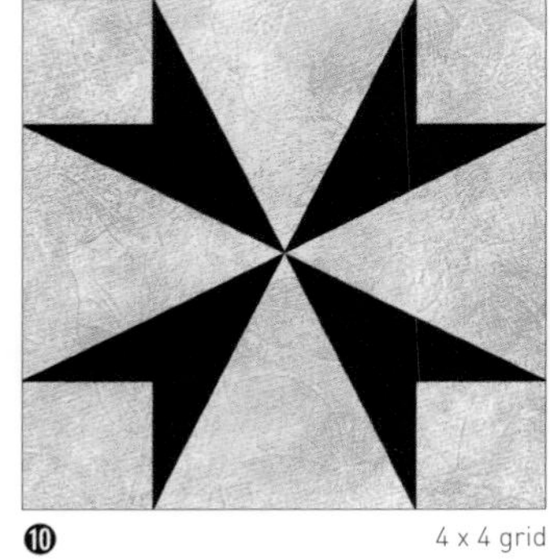
❿ 4 x 4 grid

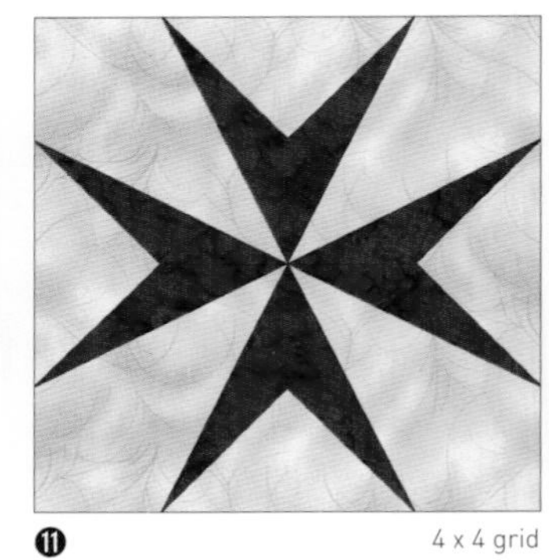
⓫ 4 x 4 grid

⓬ 4 x 4 grid

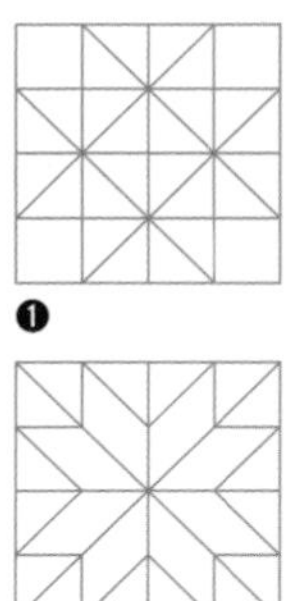
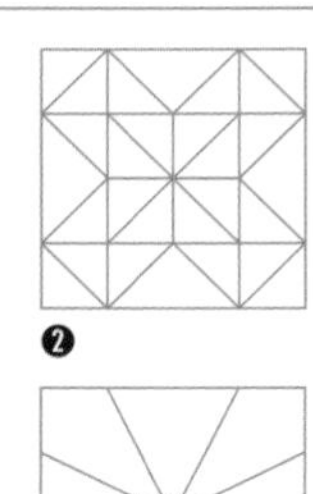
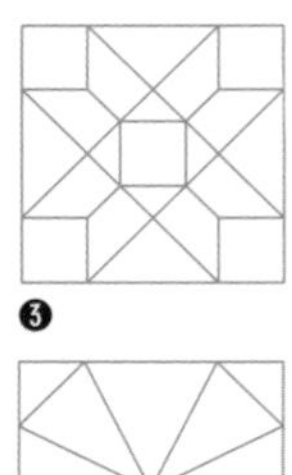
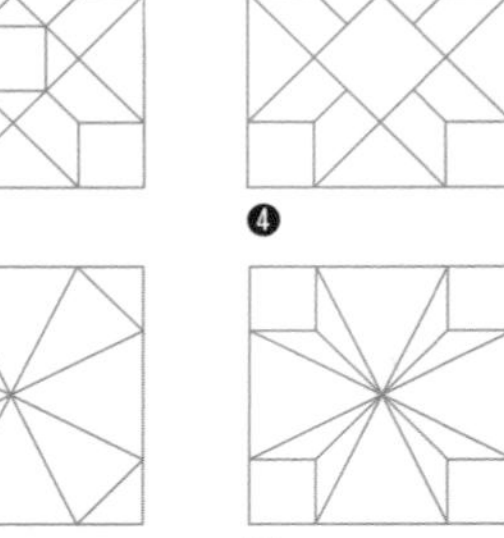
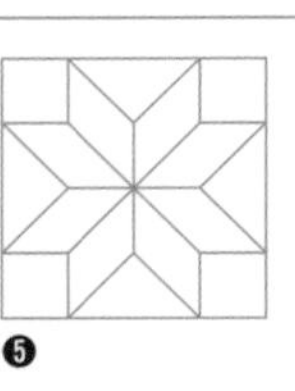
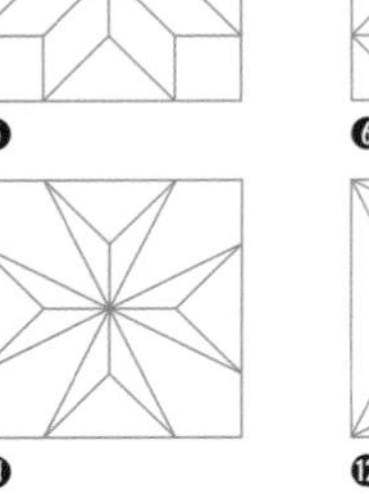
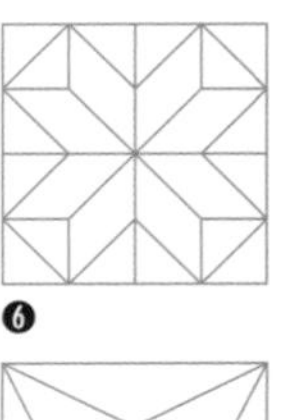

❶ ❷ ❸ ❹ ❺ ❻

❼ ❽ ❾ ❿ ⓫ ⓬

Quick Reference: Kaleidoscopes

Kaleidoscope-style blocks are quite popular because of the all-over design that is created when multiple blocks are put together. These designs have been drafted on many different grids over the years, but all have a similarity as can be seen in the ones presented here.

Priscilla, Hall. **See 64-12.**

Kaleidoscope, *Kansas City Star.* **See 264-4.**

World without End, *Chicago Tribune.* **See 227-1.**

Tippecanoe, Gutcheon, *The Perfect Patchwork Primer.* **See 65-1.**

The Priscilla, *Ladies World Magazine.* **See 226-12.**

Amethyst, *Kansas City Star.* **See 82-4.**

Rocky Road to Kansas, *Ladies Art Company.* **See 65-2.**

Hobby Nook, *Kansas City Star.* **See 201-7.**

The Dragon Fly, *Kansas City Star.* **See 201-8.**

The Wandering Flower, *Kansas City Star.* **See 237-8.**

World without End. Havig. **See 82-5.**

Kaleidoscopic Patch, *Chicago Tribune.* **See 413-9.**

Kaleidoscopic Patch, *Ladies Art Company.* **See 413-12.**

Diamond and Star, *Ladies Art Company.* **See 413-11.**

Starry Night, *Chicago Tribune,* **See 413.13.**

Priscilla, *Home Art Studios.* **See 413-10.**

❶ 4 x 4 grid

❷ 4 x 4 grid

❸ 4 x 4 grid

❶ **Tippecanoe,** Gutcheon, *The Perfect Patchwork Primer*, 1973. Also known as: Sugar Cone, James, 1978.

❷ **Rocky Road to Kansas,** *Ladies Art Company,* 1897.
"The four-pointed star is made of irregular shaped pieces sewed together 'Crazy' fashion, then cut into points using white as a background." Hall, 1935

❸ **Wheel of Destiny,** *Farm Journal and Farmer's Wife* (Silver Anniversary issue), 1945.

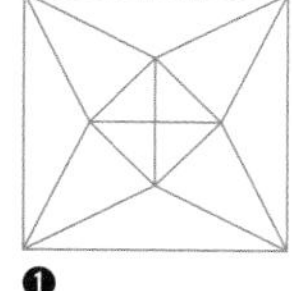

❶

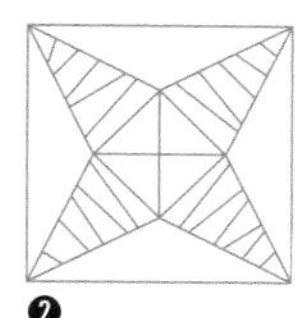

❷

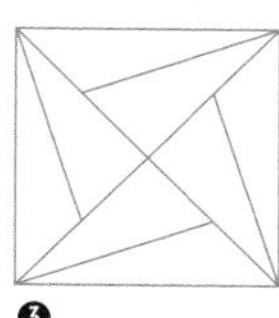

❸

❶ **Twin Sisters,** *Ladies Art Company,* 1897. Also known as:
- **Pinwheel,** Khin, 1980.
- **Twin Sisters Quilt,** Nancy Page, *Detroit Free Press,* Jan 20, 1942.
- **Water Wheel,** Ickis, 1949.
- **Whirlwind,** McKim, 1931.
- **Windmill,** *Grandma Dexter Appliqué and Patchwork Designs, Book 36a* ca. 1932.

❷ **Turnstile,** *Ladies Art Company,* 1928. Also known as:
- **Churn Dash,** Nancy Cabot, *Chicago Tribune,* Apr 20, 1937.
- **Modern Envelope,** *Kansas City Star,* Sep 26, 1945.
- **Old Windmill,** date unknown, per Brackman.
- **Pinwheel,** McKim, 1931.
- **The Whirligig,** *Kansas City Star,* Jul 26, 1950.
- **The Whirling Windmill,** *Kansas City Star,* Sep 19, 1951.
- **Whirlwind,** *The Patchwork Book,* 1932.
- **Wind Mill,** Hall, 1935.
- **Windmill,** Ruby McKim, *Kansas City Star,* Mar 29, 1930.
- **Windmill Quilt,** *Kansas City Star,* Mar 1, 1935.

❸ **The Spinner,** Nancy Page, *Birmingham News,* Feb 5, 1935. Also known as:
- **Brave World,** *Farm Journal and Farmer's Wife* (Silver Anniversary issue), 1945.
- **Forest Paths,** *Farm Journal and Farmer's Wife* (Silver Anniversary issue), 1945.

❹ **Windmill,** Aunt Martha series: *Quilts: Modern-Colonial,* ca. 1954.

❺ **Scrap Zig Zag,** *Kansas City Star,* Oct 26, 1955.

❻ **Susannah,** Gutcheon, *The Perfect Patchwork Primer,* 1973

❼ **Roads to Berlin,** *Kansas City Star,* Sep 13, 1944.

❽ **Double Windmill,** Nancy Cabot, *Chicago Tribune,* Mar 11, 1938. Also known as:
- **Sky Rockets,** Nancy Page, *Birmingham News,* May 28, 1940.

❾ **Two in One,** Alice Brooks, unidentified newspaper clipping, date unknown. Also known as:
- **Serendipity;** Jinny Beyer, Jinny Beyer Studio design 2000; published in Beyer, Jinny, *Quiltmaking by Hand.*

❿ **Bachelor's Puzzle,** Nancy Cabot, *Chicago Tribune,* Sep 28, 1933. See 142-10 and 206-7.

Little could Nancy Page know how many great men quilters there are today when she made this comment. "You all have heard of the 'Old Maid's Puzzle' quilt block. Well, here we have one which is quite as perplexing. Not that I think a man will ever piece this quilt—but odder things have been heard of—but I know you will have to keep your wits about you when you put the pieces together." Nancy Page, *Birmingham News,* Dec 17, 1940

⓫ **Flying Fish,** Nancy Cabot, *Chicago Tribune,* Mar 2, 1937.

⓬ **Balkan Puzzle,** *Grandmother Clark's Patchwork Quilt Designs, From Books 20-21-23,* 1932. See 60-4 and 428-3. Also known as:
- **Windblown Square,** Hinson, 1973.
- **Zig Zag Tile Quilt,** Hinson, 1973.

❶ **Mosaic No. 6,** *Ladies Art Company,* 1897. Also known as:

- **Mosaic No. 4,** Nancy Cabot, *Chicago Tribune,* Jun 22, 1934.
- **Zig Zag Tile,** Nancy Page, *Nashville Banner,* Jul 12, 1932.

❷ **Pinwheel,** Laura Wheeler, *Laura Wheeler Collection of Needlecraft Masterpieces,* ca. 1958.

❸ **Pin Wheel,** Finley, 1929. Also known as:

- **Paper Pinwheels,** Nancy Page, *Birmingham News,* Jul 12, 1938.
- **Pin Wheels,** Hall, 1935.
- **Pinwheel,** Laura Wheeler, *Cincinnati Enquirer,* Dec 10, 1933.
- **The Pinwheel,** Laura Wheeler, *Morning Herald,* Apr 27, 1933.

❹ **Churn Dash,** Finley, 1929. Also known as:

- **Churn Dash Quilt,** Nancy Page, *Nashville Banner,* Aug 23, 1932.
- **Churn Dasher,** Hall, 1935.

❺ **Churn Dash,** Nancy Cabot, *Chicago Tribune,* Feb 28, 1934.

❻ **Windmill,** ca. 1938, per Havig.

❼ **Next Door Neighbor,** Gutcheon, *The Perfect Patchwork Primer,* 1973.

❽ **State of Louisiana,** *Dakota Farmer* Feb 15, 1927. Also known as:

- **Louisiana,** *Hearth and Home,* date unknown.

❾ **Double Quartet,** *Grandmother Clark's Patchwork Quilt Designs, From Books 20-21-23,* 1932. Also known as:

- **The Flying X Quilt,** *Kansas City Star,* Oct 26, 1938.
- **The X Quartette,** *Kansas City Star,* Jul 12, 1939.

❿ **Seesaw,** Gutcheon, *The Perfect Patchwork Primer,* 1973.

⓫ **Millwheel,** Nancy Cabot, *Chicago Tribune,* May 3, 1937.

⓬ **Star of Destiny,** Clara Stone, *Practical Needlework,* ca. 1906.

❶ **Beginner's Delight,** Alice Brooks, unidentified newspaper clipping, date unknown.

❷ **July Fourth,** Nancy Page, *Birmingham News,* Jul 3, 1934. Also known as:
- **A Quilt Takes Patriotic Hues,** *Kansas City Star,* Jan 23, 1957.

❸ **Star of Beauty,** Clara Stone, *Practical Needlework,* ca. 1906. Also known as:
- **July Fourth,** Nancy Page, *Birmingham News,* Jul 3, 1934.
- **Next Door Neighbor,** *Ladies Art Company,* 1922.
- **Patriotic Quilt,** Jinny Beyer, Beyer, Jinny, *The Quilter's Album...,* 1980.

❹ **Autumn Flurries,** Nancy Page, *Birmingham News,* Dec 3, 1940. Also known as:
- **Winged Arrow,** Nancy Page, date unknown; published in *Quilter's Newsletter Magazine,* Sep 1986.
- **Winged Arrows,** Nancy Page, *Birmingham News,* Dec 3, 1940.

"The wind is blowing all four ways at once and sending these leaves or arrowheads or what ever you want to call them scurrying and flurrying. That's why I called this pattern by the name of 'Autumn Flurries.' It is known as 'Winged Arrows' too. Nancy Page, *Birmingham News,* Dec 3, 1940

❺ **Yankee Puzzle,** *Ladies Art Company,* 1897. Also known as:
- **Yankee Puzzles,** *Q Book 108, Centennial Quilts,* date unknown.

❻ **Year's Favorite,** *Farm Journal and Farmer's Wife* (Silver Anniversary issue), 1945.

❼ **Yankee Puzzle,** Nancy Page, *Birmingham News,* Aug 2, 1938.

❽ **Whirligig,** *The Patchwork Book,* 1932.

❾ **Patch Me If You Can,** *Dakota Farmer* Feb 15, 1927.

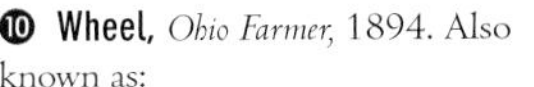

⑩ Wheel, *Ohio Farmer,* 1894. Also known as:

- **Catch Me If You Can,** *Pieced Quilt,* ca. 1900.
- **Devil's Dark House,** date unknown; published in Beyer, Jinny, *The Quilter's Album....*
- **Dutchman's Puzzle,** *Ladies Art Company,* 1897.
- **Fly Foot,** McKim, 1931.
- **Indian Emblem Quilt,** Eveline Foland, *Kansas City Star,* Nov 12, 1930.
- **Mosaic,** date unknown; published in Beyer, Jinny, *The Quilter's Album....*
- **Old Maid's Puzzle,** *Old Fashioned Quilts,* ca. 1931.
- **Swastika,** McKim, 1931.
- **Swastika Quilt,** *Kansas City Star,* May 3, 1939.
- **Virginia Reel,** *Workbasket,* date unknown, per Brackman.
- **Whirligig,** *Old Fashioned Quilts,* ca. 1931.
- **The Whirlwind,** *The Farmer's Advocate,* Apr 27, 1933.
- **Wild Goose Chase,** Gutcheon, *The Quilt Design Workbook,* 1976.
- **Winding Blades,** *Kansas City Star,* Aug 4, 1943.
- **Zig Zag,** Comfort, date unknown, per Brackman.

⑪ Return of the Swallows, *Kansas City Star,* Oct 2, 1946.

⑫ Mosaic No. 12, *Ladies Art Company,* 1897. Also known as:

- **Mosaic No. 5,** Nancy Cabot, *Chicago Tribune,* Jun 29, 1934.
- **Mosaic No. 9,** Nancy Cabot, *Chicago Tribune,* Sep 11, 1934.

Quick Reference: Red Cross Blocks

The goal of the American Red Cross, founded by Clara Barton on May 21, 1881, was to aid in domestic and overseas disaster relief efforts. True to the spirit of the American quilter, at least two blocks were named for this organization early on. One appeared in the 1897 *Ladies Art Company* catalog and another in the ca. 1906 Clara Stone booklet, *Practical Needlework.* During the build-up to and during World War II, several new patterns were named for the organization. They are shown here.

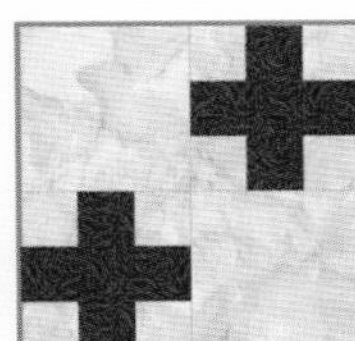

Red Cross *Kansas City Star.* **See 153-3.**

Red Cross, *Birmingham News.* **See 182-6.**

Red Cross, *Ladies Art Company.* **See 183-5.**

Red Cross, *Practical Needlework.* **See 184-7.**

The Red Cross Quilt, *Quilts.* **See 91-11.**

The Red Cross Quilt, *Kansas City Star.* **See 274-5.**

Red and White Cross, *Chicago Tribune.* **See 64-6.**

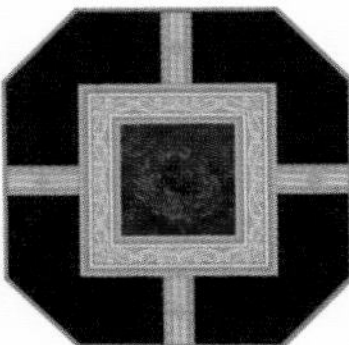

The Red Cross, *Kansas City Star.* **See 412-8.**

Red Cross Quilt, *Kansas City Star.* **See 412-9.**

Red Cross, *Birmingham News.* **See 91-1.**

The Red Cross Quilt, *Kansas City Star.* **See 85-8.**

❶ **Star of Friendship,** Alice Brooks, *Detroit Free Press,* Dec 21, 1933. Also known as:
: **Pinwheel Design,** Laura Wheeler, unidentified newspaper clipping, date unknown.

❷ **Wheels,** *Progressive Farmer,* 1976.

❸ **Pale Stars,** Nancy Page, *Birmingham News,* May 30, 1939.

❹ **Mosaic No. 18,** *Ladies Art Company,* 1897. Also known as:
: **Mosaic No. 11,** Nancy Cabot, *Chicago Tribune,* Oct 4, 1934.
: **Old Poinsettia Block,** Nancy Cabot, *Chicago Tribune,* Dec 31, 1937.
: **Spinning Stars,** Nancy Page, *Birmingham News,* Aug 27, 1935.

❺ **Shooting Star,** *Ladies Art Company,* 1897. Also known as:
: **Clay's Choice,** Finley, 1929.
: **Clay's Favorite,** Nancy Cabot, *Chicago Tribune,* Dec 13, 1937.
: **Harry's Star,** Finley, 1929.
: **Henry of the West,** Finley, 1929.
: **Henry's Star,** Nancy Cabot, *Chicago Tribune,* Apr 5, 1933.
: **Meteor Quilt,** unidentified newspaper clipping, date unknown.
: **The Star of Bethelem (sic),** *The Farmer's Advocate,* Apr 27, 1933.
: **Star of the West,** Finley, 1929.
: **Stardust Quilt,** Nancy Page, *Birmingham News,* Dec 7, 1937.

"Henry Clay's Efforts to Maintain Union Inspired Interesting Quilt. Keenly alive to the social distress of the 1800s, women of that day wove into their quilt patterns stories of unrest.

'This department today offers another design, 'Clay's Choice,' in the historical quilt series. About 1832 there was a considerable agitation in the south for disunion. Proposals to admit California, a free state, to the Union were met with violent protest, because it meant the upsetting of equality in the number of slave and free states. Other differences included the problems of slavery in the territory of New Mexico and Utah, the Texas boundary, slave trade between the states, and northern refusal of cooperation in returning fugitive slaves. Henry Clay, in an effort to maintain the Union, offered a compromise bill designed to soothe both sections. It provided for payment of $10,000 to Texas for relinquishing claims to New Mexico; admission of California as a free state; making states of New Mexico and Utah with no provisions as to slavery; abolition of slave trade in the District of Columbia, and efficient fugitive slave laws for the south. 'Clay's Choice' represents this move toward pacification. Other names for this quilt are 'Henry's Star' and 'Star of the West.'" Nancy Cabot, *Chicago Tribune,* Apr 5, 1933

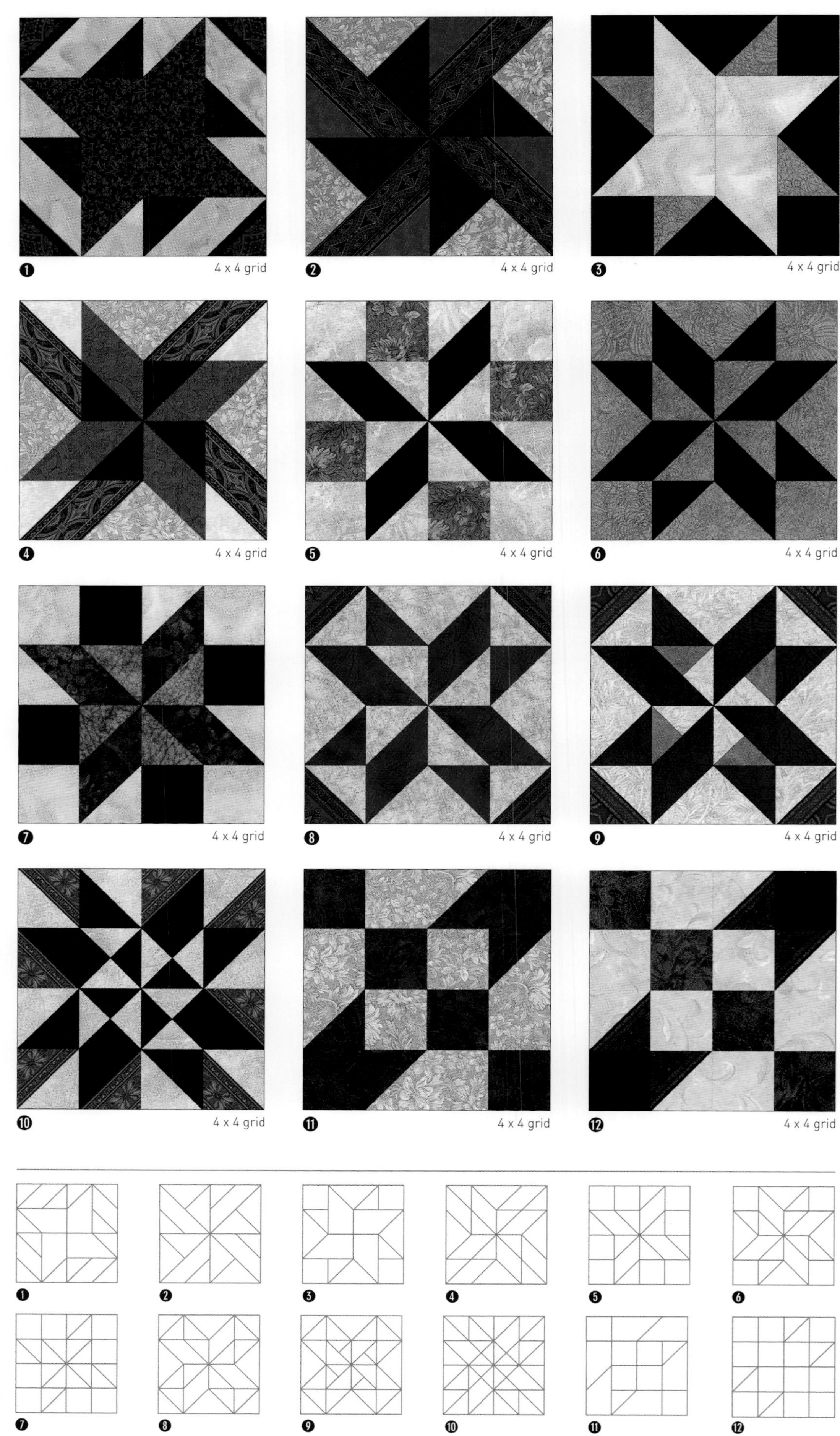

Quick Reference: Airplanes

Many quilt designs were created to commemorate events in history. Certainly the development of the airplane, man's first flight, the Wright brothers, Charles Lindburg, Amelia Earhart, and commercial airline flight caused great interest. As a result, several new quilt blocks were created with the airplane theme. Two blocks that I found from earlier sources were renamed. *Fish* first appeared in the ca. 1906 Clara Stone catalog *Practical Needlework*. It was named *Airplane Motif* in the April 2,1947 *Kansas City Star*. *Flying Bat* appeared in the 1897 *Ladies Art Company* catalog. It was later renamed *Airplanes* in the 1945 *Farm Journal and Farmer's Wife* catalog.

Several new blocks also appeared on the scene. The earliest airplane related quilt block I found was *The Aircraft Quilt* which appeared in the July 13, 1929 edition of *Kansas City Star*. The text that accompanied the block confirms the interest in naming quilt designs after important events.

Here are several quilt designs that relate to the airplane theme. Some depict the airplane itself, others the propeller, and one block represents the airport.

"Here is modern design in pieced quilts. Mrs. Otto Prell, Miami, Ok., sent The Star this design just as two transcontinental airplane lines are being inaugurated in their flight through Kansas City from coast to coast. May it have its place in the history of the world as emblematic of this age, just as our great-grandmothers designed the saw-tooth and the churn dash and the log cabin patterns which were symbolic of the time in which they lived." *Kansas City Star*, Jul 13, 1929

Aeroplane, Aunt Martha series: *The Quilt Fair Comes to You.* **See 335-3.**

Lone Eagle, per Havig. **See 342-2.**

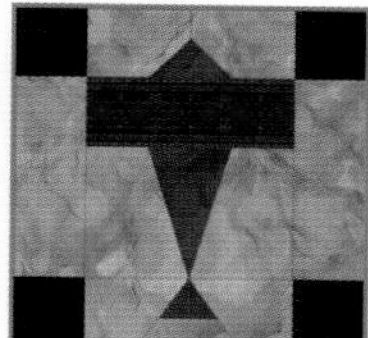

The Aircraft Quilt, *Kansas City Star.* **See 269-8.**

Airplane, per Havig. **See 256-11.**

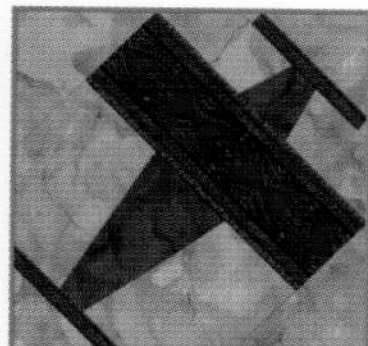

The Air Plane, *Kansas City Star.* **See 265-5.**

The Alta Plane, per Havig. **See 225-12.**

Airplane Motif, *Kansas City Star.* **See 288-11.**

Airplanes, *Farm Journal and Farmer's Wife Quilt* (Silver Anniversary issue). **See 278-2.**

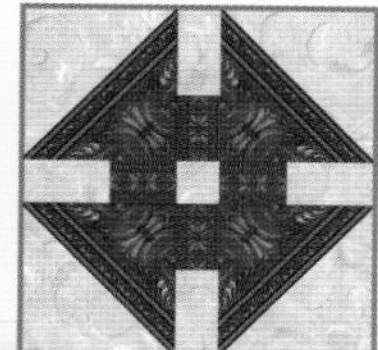

Aeroplane, *The Patchwork Book.* **See 112-2.**

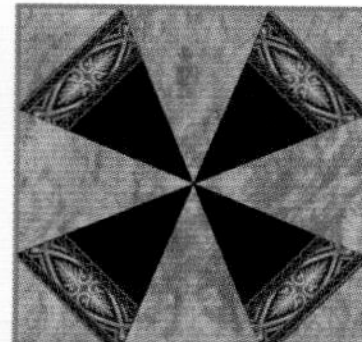

Propeller, Beyer, Jinny, *The Quilter's Album ....* **See 292-8.**

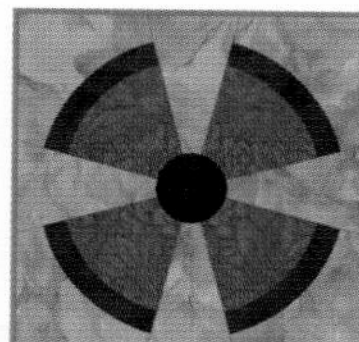

Air Ship Propeller, *Kansas City Star.* **See 372-8.**

Propeller, *Ladies Art Company.* **See 185-4.**

Lindy's Plane, Nancy Cabot, *Chicago Tribune.* **See 118-10.**

Airport, per Havig. **See 268-7.**

❻ **Diamond Star,** *Practical Needlework,* ca. 1906.

❼ **Shooting Star,** Nancy Cabot, *Chicago Tribune,* Aug 25, 1934.
"'Shooting Star" is an early American quilt pattern that claims Kentucky as its native state. Old fashioned quilters will cling to the original color scheme of blue, white, and a figured blue and white material. Young moderns will select pastel tints." *Chicago Tribune,* Aug 25, 1934

❽ **A Unique Design,** *Ladies Home Journal,* 1896. Also known as:
- **Lucky Pieces,** Nancy Page, *Birmingham News,* Sep 21, 1937.
- **Mosaic, No. 13,** *Ladies Art Company,* 1897.
- **Mosaic No. 3,** *Colonial Quilts,* 1932.
- **Pieced Star,** Nancy Page, *Birmingham News,* Jun 14, 1938.
- **Pierced Star,** Ickis, 1949.
- **Star Puzzle,** Jinny Beyer, Beyer, Jinny, *The Quilter's Album...,* 1980.

❾ **Star and Pinwheels,** Nancy Cabot, *Chicago Tribune,* Jul 3, 1937.

❿ **Solitaire,** Clara Stone, *Practical Needlework,* ca. 1906.

⓫ **Road to Oklahoma,** *Ladies Art Company,* 1897. Also known as:
- **New Four Patch,** Hall, 1935.
- **The Road to Oklahoma,** *Kansas City Star,* Jun 4, 1947.

⓬ **Road to Oklahoma,** Nancy Cabot, *Chicago Tribune,* Aug 16, 1937. Also known as:
- **The Arkansas Cross Roads,** *Kansas City Star,* Mar 19, 1941.
- **The Winged Four-Patch,** *Kansas City Star,* Jan 9, 1952.

❶ **Quilt in Light and Dark,** *Kansas City Star,* Sep 24, 1941. See 245-1.

❷ **Chisholm Trail Quilt,** *Kansas City Star,* May 31, 1939.

❸ **Wild Duck,** Nancy Page, *Birmingham News,* Feb 12, 1935. Also known as:

Lozenge Web, Nancy Cabot, *Chicago Tribune,* May 20, 1936.

❹ **Free Trade Block Quilt,** Home Art Studios, *Cincinnati Enquirer,* Apr 17, 1933.

❺ **The Scotch Quilt,** *15 Quilts for Today's Living,* 1968.

❻ **T Quilt,** *Farm and Home,* Nov 1898. "Piece work is dear to both young and old. The pride of the little girl making her first quilt and the grandame piecing for her great-granddaughter's wedding gift. The inclosed (sic) pattern for a T quilt may be set together with plain blocks, or the four corners at top of T's joined forming a large square of the darker color." Mrs. R Stotenbur (aged 72), *Farm and Home,* Nov 1898

❼ **The T Quilt Pattern,** *Kansas City Star,* Feb 1, 1939. Also known as:

T Quilt, Nancy Cabot, unidentified newspaper clipping, date unknown.

❽ **Ships at Sea,** Laura Wheeler, unidentified newspaper clipping, date unknown. See 107-6, 107-7 and 107-8.

❾ **Clay's Compromise,** Nancy Cabot, *Chicago Tribune,* Apr 9, 1933. "'Clay's Compromise,' another presentation in the series of historical quilt patterns being reproduced in this department, is designed to picture the result of Henry Clay's attempt to obtain judicious legislation for both the north and the south on the slavery problem of the 1800s. Faced with the problems of admission of California as a free state, slavery in the territory of New Mexico and Utah, the Texas boundary, slave trade between the states, and southern difficulty in retrieving fugitive slaves, Clay had drawn up his famous compromise bill. This compromise, however, encountered much opposition, and was debated several months in Congress by such men as Seward, Webster, and Calhoun before it could be passed. And at the end of that time, so many amendments had been made, and so many changes grafted, that the final settlement was a hodgepodge, having lost much of its original balance and simplicity. So if the quilt looks a little askew, remember that it represents Clay's bitter struggle." Nancy Cabot, Chicago Tribune, Apr 9, 1933

❿ **Aircraft,** Hall, 1935.

⓫ **Snowflake,** Clara Stone, *Practical Needlework,* ca. 1906.

⓬ **Ladies' Wreath,** *Ladies Art Company,* 1897.

❶ **Necktie,** Finley, 1929.

❷ **Three Patch Quilt,** Laura Wheeler, source unknown, date unknown.

❸ **Tam's Patch,** Gutcheon, *The Perfect Patchwork Primer,* 1973.

❹ **Carmen's Block,** Nancy Page, *Nashville Banner,* Jul 11, 1933. See 128-3. Also known as:

Autumn Leaves, Hinson, 1973.
Double Four Patch, *Q Book 126, All Time Quilt Favorites,* date unknown.
Four Patch, Hall, 1935.

❺ **The Sickle,** *Kansas City Star,* May 30, 1936.

❻ **Buckeye Beauty,** Clara Stone, *Practical Needlework,* ca. 1906. Also known as:

Double Four Patch, Nancy Page, *Birmingham News,* Mar 7, 1939.
Gay Scraps, Laura Wheeler, unidentified newspaper clipping, date unknown.
Give This One a Name, *Kansas City Star,* June 29, 1955.
Mrs. Keller's Choice, ca. 1938, per Havig.
Railroad, Martens, 1970.
World's Fair, *Old Fashioned Quilts,* ca. 1931.

❼ **Caroline's Choice,** *Progressive Farmer,* 1901. See 128-5 and 128-6. Also known as:

Double T, Ickis, 1949.
Flashing Windmills, Nancy Cabot, *Chicago Tribune,* Jul 2, 1938.
Flutter Wheel, Hall, 1935.
Pin Wheels, Hall, 1935.

❽ **Caroline's Choice,** Nancy Cabot, *Chicago Tribune,* Apr 13, 1936.

❾ **Crosses and Losses,** *Ladies Art Company,* 1897. Also known as:

Bouncing Betty, *Progressive Farmer,* ca. 1933.
Fox and Geese, Finley, 1929.
Hour Glass, *Grandma Dexter New Appliqué and Patchwork Designs, Book 36b,* ca. 1932.

❿ **Old Maid's Puzzle,** Nancy Cabot, *Chicago Tribune,* Jun 15, 1933.

⓫ **Flock of Geese,** Finley, 1929. Also known as:

Flock, Gutcheon, *The Perfect Patchwork Primer,* 1973.
Snowball, *Farm Journal Quilt Patterns,* ca. 1935.

⓬ **Double X No. 3,** *Ladies Art Company,* 1897.

❶ **Double X,** *Farm & Fireside,* Feb 15, 1893. Also known as:

- **Crosses and Losses,** Finley, 1929.
- **Double X, No. 2,** *Ladies Art Company,* 1897.
- **Fireflies,** James, 1978.
- **Fox and Geese,** Finley, 1929.
- **Goose and Goslings,** *Grandmother Clark's Patchwork Quilt Designs, From Books 20-21-23,* 1932.
- **Old Maid's Puzzle,** Hinson, 1973.
- **X,** Hinson, 1973.

❷ **Old Maid's Puzzle,** *Ladies Art Company,* 1897. Also known as:

- **Fox and Geese,** Finley, 1929.
- **Hour Glass,** Virginia Snow, *Grandma Dexter New Appliqué and Patchwork Designs, Book 36b,* ca. 1932.

❸ **Hovering Hawks,** Nancy Page, *Birmingham News,* Dec 28, 1937.

❹ **Hovering Hawks,** Finley, 1929. Also known as:

- **Ocean Wave,** *Grandmother Clark's Patchwork Quilt Designs, From Books 20-21-23,* 1932.
- **Ocean Waves,** Nancy Cabot, *Chicago Tribune,* Oct 14, 1936.
- **Road to Heaven,** James, 1978.
- **Triple X,** Finley, 1929.

❺ **Double X,** Webster, 1915. Also known as:

- **The Swallow,** date unknown; published in Beyer, Jinny, *The Quilter's Album....*
- **Winged Square,** source unknown, date unknown.

❻ **The Anvil,** Finley, 1929.

❼ **Indian Hatchet,** Nancy Page, *Birmingham News,* Oct 6, 1936.

❽ **The Disk,** *Ladies Art Company,* 1897. Also known as:

- **Cactus Basket,** Nancy Page, *Birmingham News,* Mar 17, 1936.
- **Flower Pot,** *Old Fashoined Quilts,* Apr 11, 1931.

❾ **Basket,** Nancy Page, *Nashville Banner,* Jan 2, 1934.

"Basket quilts are always popular . . . that was why I was glad to get this pattern from Mrs. Sullivan of Baltimore, Maryland. She says that her mother pieced one like this over eighty years ago." Nancy Page, *Nashville Banner,* Jan 2, 1934

❿ **Flower Basket,** *Ladies Art Company,* 1898. Also known as:

- **Betty's Basket,** Nancy Page, *Nashville Banner,* Jul 19, 1932.

⓫ **Sugar Bowl,** *Farm Journal Quilt Patterns,* ca. 1935.

⓬ **May Basket,** Alice Brooks, unidentified newspaper clipping, date unknown.

❶ 4 x 4 grid

❷ 4 x 4 grid

❸ 4 x 4 grid

❹ 4 x 4 grid

❺ 4 x 4 grid

❻ 4 x 4 grid

❼ 4 x 4 grid

❽ 4 x 4 grid

❾ 4 x 4 grid

❿ 4 x 4 grid

⓫ 4 x 4 grid

⓬ 4 x 4 grid

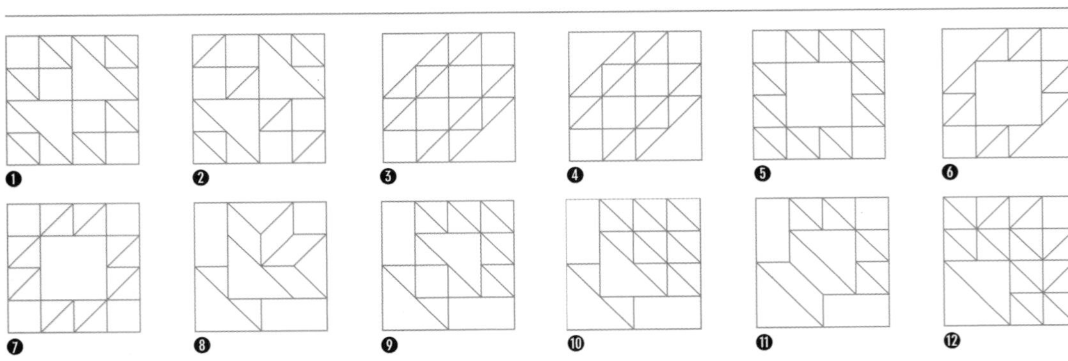

❶ **Flower Basket,** Nancy Cabot, *Chicago Tribune,* Feb 3, 1935. Also known as:
- **Simple Flower Basket,** Nancy Cabot, *Chicago Tribune,* Jan 26, 1938.

❷ **Mosaic No. 14,** *Ladies Art Company,* 1897.

❸ **Tea Leaf,** Gutcheon, *The Perfect Patchwork Primer,* 1973.

❹ **Belle's Favorite,** Clara Stone, *Practical Needlework,* ca. 1906.

❺ **Mosaic No. 22,** *Ladies Art Company,* 1897. Also known as:
- **Star of the West,** Nancy Page, *Birmingham News,* May 25, 1937.
- **Ten Inch Border,** Nancy Page, *Birmingham News,* Jan 24, 1939.

❻ **Mosaic No. 1,** Nancy Cabot, *Chicago Tribune,* May 11, 1934.

❼ **New England Star,** Holice Turnbow, Beyer, Jinny, *The Quilter's Album...,* 1980.

❽ **Starfish Quilt,** Alice Brooks, *Detroit Free Press,* Oct 12, 1934.

❾ **Mosaic No. 15,** *Ladies Art Company,* 1897. Also known as:
- **Mosaic No. 9,** ca. 1938, per Havig.

❿ **Mosaic No. 10,** *Ladies Art Company,* 1897.

⓫ **Ribbon Star,** ca. 1938, per Havig.

⓬ **Double Z,** *Ladies Art Company,* 1897. Also known as:
- **Brown Goose,** Finley, 1929.
- **Devil's Claws,** Finley, 1929.
- **Framed X,** *Farm Journal and Farmer's Wife* (Silver Anniversary issue), 1945.
- **Gray Geese,** Beyer, Alice 1934.
- **Gray Goose,** Finley, 1929.
- **Old Maid's Puzzle #2,** Clara Stone, *Practical Needlework,* ca. 1906.

❶ **Brown Goose Quilt,** Nancy Page, *Detroit Free Press,* Aug 9, 1932. Also known as:
- **Brown Goose,** Nancy Cabot, *Chicago Tribune,* Mar 9, 1934.
- **Devil's Claws,** Hinson, 1973
- **Double Z,** Hall, 1935.
- **Gray Goose,** Nancy Cabot, *Chicago Tribune,* Jul 9, 1933.
- **Old Gray Goose,** Nancy Cabot, *Chicago Tribune,* Jan 27, 1933.

❷ **Modern Quilt,** Alice Brooks, unidentified newspaper clipping, date unknown.

❸ **Left and Right,** Nancy Cabot, *Chicago Tribune,* Aug 27, 1935. See 99-4.

❹ **Mosaic No. 11,** *Ladies Art Company,* 1897. Also known as:
- **Triangles,** Nancy Page, *Birmingham News,* Nov 21, 1939.

❺ **Forward and Back,** Nancy Cabot, *Chicago Tribune,* Jan 16, 1937. Also known as:
- **Perpetual Motion,** Nancy Cabot, *Chicago Tribune,* Jan 16, 1937.
- **Tree Everlasting,** Nancy Cabot, *Chicago Tribune,* Jan 16, 1937.

❻ **Ship of Dreams,** Alice Brooks, Beyer, Alice, 1934. Also known as:
- **The Mayflower,** *Kansas City Star,* Aug 29, 1936.
- **A Sail Boat in Blue and White,** Nancy Cabot, *Chicago Tribune,* Jan 4, 1937.
- **Ship o' Dreams,** *Detroit Free Press,* Sep 13, 1934.
- **The Ship Quilt** *Mrs. Danner's Fourth Quilt Book,* 1958.
- **Tad Lincoln's Sailboat,** *Q Book 124, White House Quilts,* date unknown.

❼ **Fishing Boats,** *Progressive Farmer,* date unknown.

❽ **The Sail Boat,** *Kansas City Star,* May 15, 1957.

❾ **The Sailboat Oklahoma,** *Kansas City Star,* Jun 28, 1944.

❿ **Fishing Boats,** Nancy Cabot, *Chicago Tribune,* Jan 4, 1937.

⓫ **Squares upon Squares,** *Farm Journal and Farmer's Wife,* ca. 1941.

⓬ **Concorde Star,** Hazel Carter, Beyer, Jinny, *The Quilter's Album...,* 1980.

❶ 8 x 8 grid

❷ 8 x 8 grid

❸ 8 x 8 grid

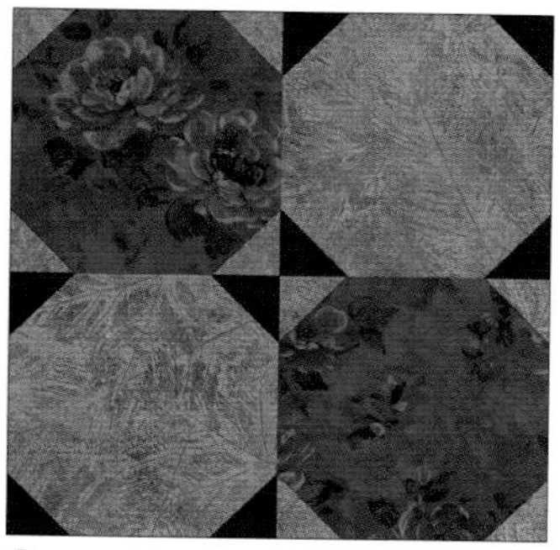

❹ 8 x 8 grid

❺ 8 x 8 grid

❻ 8 x 8 grid

❼ 8 x 8 grid

❽ 8 x 8 grid

❾ 8 x 8 grid

❿ 8 x 8 grid

⓫ 8 x 8 grid

⓬ 8 x 8 grid

❶ **Necktie,** Eveline Foland, *Kansas City Star,* Jan 30, 1932.

❷ **Magic Circle,** *Ladies Art Company,* 1897.

❸ **True Lover's Knot,** *Ladies Art Company,* 1897. Also known as:
- **Bow Tie in Pink and White,** *Kansas City Star,* Feb 22, 1956.
- **Dumbell Block,** Nancy Cabot, *Chicago Tribune,* Jan 30, 1932.
- **Magical Circle,** Nancy Cabot, *Chicago Tribune,* Oct 25, 1933.
- **Necktie,** Nancy Page, *Nashville Banner,* Sep 20, 1932.

❹ **The Marble Floor,** Eveline Foland, *Kansas City Star,* Oct 22, 1930. Also known as:
- **Hour Glasses,** Bacon, 1973.
- **Octagons,** Bacon, 1973.
- **Rob Peter to Pay Paul,** *Farm Journal Quilt Patterns,* ca. 1935.
- **Snowballs,** Nancy Cabot, *Chicago Tribune,* July 16, 1938.

❺ **Milford Center,** Nancy Page, *Birmingham News,* Jan 11, 1944.

❻ **Grandmother's Cross,** *Kansas City Star,* Jun 20, 1945.

❼ **Sarah's Favorite,** *Ladies Art Company,* 1897. Also known as:
- **Sally's Favorite,** Nancy Cabot, *Chicago Tribune,* Jun 1, 1934.
- **Sara's Favorite,** Hall, 1935.

❽ **Toad in a Puddle,** *Ladies Art Company,* 1897. Also known as:
- **Rambler,** Ruby McKim, *Kansas City Star,* Dec 29, 1928.
- **The Rambler,** Nancy Cabot, *Chicago Tribune,* Nov 16, 1938.

❾ **Spring Beauty,** Eveline Foland, *Kansas City Star,* Feb 20, 1932. Also known as:
- **Crimson Rambler,** Hall, 1935.
- **I Excel,** *Kansas City Star,* May 7, 1940.
- **IXL,** *Kansas City Star,* Mar 28, 1936.
- **Old Maid's Ramble,** Nancy Cabot, *Chicago Tribune,* Jul 31, 1934.
- **The Rambler,** Nancy Cabot, *Chicago Tribune,* Apr 11, 1933.

❿ **Railroad Crossing,** Nancy Page, *Birmingham News,* Oct 17, 1939.

⓫ **Old Maid's Ramble,** *Ladies Art Company,* 1897. Also known as:
- **Double Triangle,** *Rural New Yorker,* ca. 1931.
- **Vermont,** Nancy Page, *Birmingham News,* Feb 11, 1936.

⓬ **The Railroad,** *Q Book 121, Bicentennial Quilts,* date unknown.

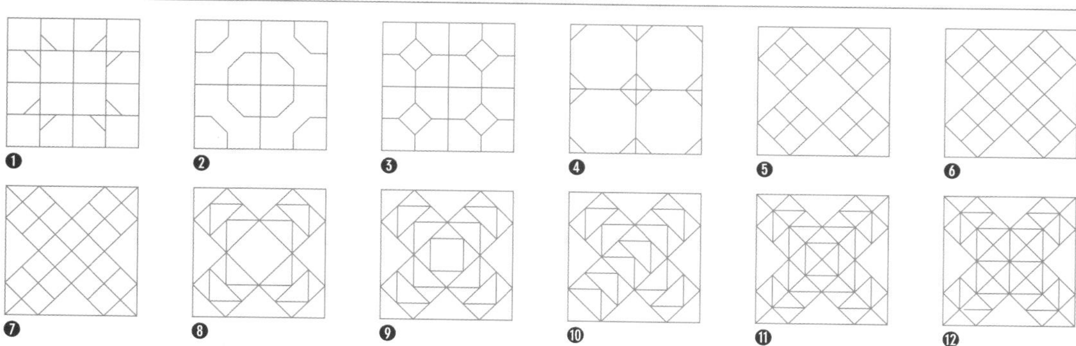

❶ **Alabama Rambler,** Nancy Cabot, *Chicago Tribune,* Oct 3, 1936.

❷ **Colorful Scraps,** Alice Brooks, unidentified newspaper clipping, date unknown.

❸ **Jamestown Square,** Nancy Cabot, *Chicago Tribune,* Mar 22, 1938.
"With so many of our beautiful coverlets coming from Virginia, it is only natural that we should be interested in the pieced block, 'Jamestown Square.' This is one of the old designs with an historic background, having been pieced for the first time in 1839 in yellow, blue, and white. The particular yellow material which composed the quilt was imported from England, and the residents of the town considered it to be one of the 'finest dimity.'" Nancy Cabot, *Chicago Tribune,* Mar 22, 1938

❹ **Susannah Patch,** Nancy Page, *Birmingham News,* Aug 19, 1941.

❺ **Centennial,** *Ladies Art Company,* 1897.

❻ **Missouri Star,** Nancy Cabot, *Chicago Tribune,* Jul 24, 1933.

❼ **Double T,** Ruby McKim, *Kansas City Star,* Nov 28, 1928. Also known as:
Eight Pointed Star, Nancy Cabot, *Chicago Tribune,* Sep 25, 1935.
Four T's, Ruby McKim, *Kansas City Star,* Nov 28, 1928.

❽ **Broken Star,** Nancy Cabot, *Chicago Tribune,* Jul 17, 1936.
"The outstanding charm of 'Broken Star' is that it may be pieced so rapidly that one square may be finished in twenty minutes. And neatly done as well." Nancy Cabot, *Chicago Tribune,* Jul 17, 1936

❾ **Flying Cloud,** Clara Stone, *Practical Needlework,* ca. 1906. Also known as:
Martha Washington, *Quilt Blocks from The Farmer's Wife,* 1932.
Martha Washington Star, Nancy Cabot, *Chicago Tribune,* Jun 28, 1933.
Martha Washington's Star, Peto, 1949.

❿ **Star of the East,** Laura Wheeler, unidentified newspaper clipping, date unknown.

⓫ **Beginner's Pride,** Laura Wheeler, unidentified newspaper clipping, date unknown.

⓬ **Four Patch Star,** Alice Brooks, unidentified newspaper clipping, date unknown.

❶ 8 x 8 grid

❷ 8 x 8 grid

❸ 8 x 8 grid

❹ 8 x 8 grid

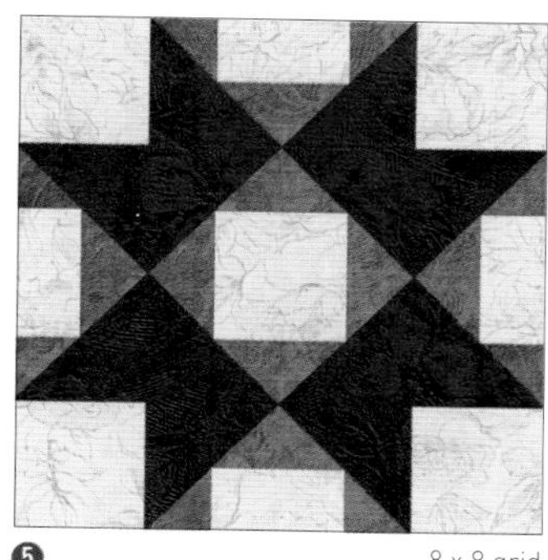

❺ 8 x 8 grid

❻ 8 x 8 grid

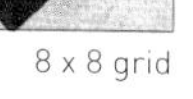

❼ 8 x 8 grid

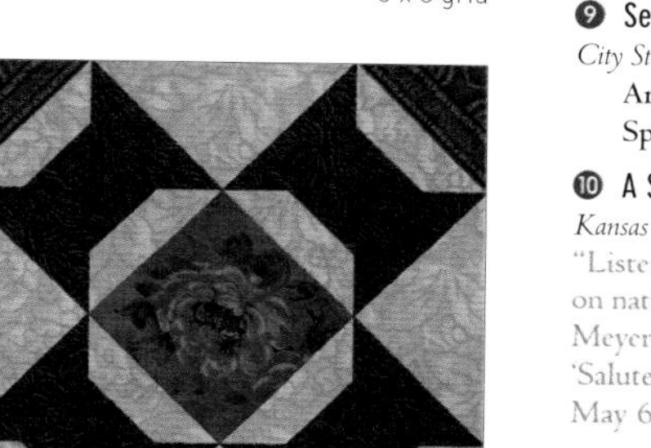

❽ 8 x 8 grid

❾ 8 x 8 grid

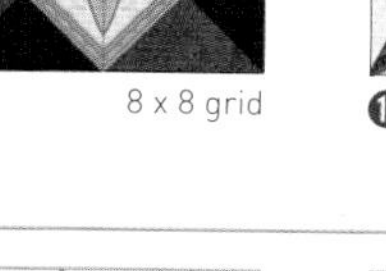

❿ 8 x 8 grid

⓫ 8 x 8 grid

⓬ 8 x 8 grid

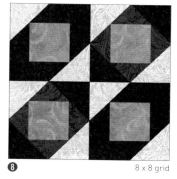

❶ Two in One Design, Alice Brooks, unidentified newspaper clipping, date unknown.

❷ Stars and Squares, *Ladies Art Company,* 1897. Also known as:

- **Double Star,** Jane Alan, *Illinois State Register,* May 21, 1933.
- **Rising Star,** Finley, 1929.
- **Rising Star and Square,** source unknown, date unknown.

❸ Eight Hands Around, *Ladies Art Company,* 1897. Also known as:

- **Eight Hands Round,** Ickis, 1949.

❹ Handy Andy, Gutcheon, *The Perfect Patchwork Primer,* 1973.

❺ Home Treasure, Hall, 1935. Also known as:

- **Cross and Square,** Nancy Cabot, *Chicago Tribune,* Nov 23, 1937.

❻ Home Treasure, Nancy Page, *Birmingham News,* May 7, 1940.

❼ Pride of Holland, *Farm Journal and Farmer's Wife* (Silver Anniversary issue), 1945.

❽ This and That, *Kansas City Star,* Nov 15, 1944.

❾ Secret Drawer, Eveline Foland, *Kansas City Star,* Oct 4, 1930. Also known as:

- **Arkansas Traveler,** Hall, 1935.
- **Spools,** Hall, 1935.

❿ A Salute to the Colors, Jinny Beyer, *Kansas City Star,* May 6, 1942. "Listening to daily talk by our soldiers on national loyalty inspired Miss Adelia Meyer, Chester, Neb, to design the 'Salute to the Colors." *Kansas City Star,* May 6, 1942

⓫ Memory Star, Jinny Beyer, Beyer, Jinny, *Soft-Edge Piecing,* 1995.

⓬ Federal Square, Nancy Cabot, *Chicago Tribune,* Jun 19, 1937.

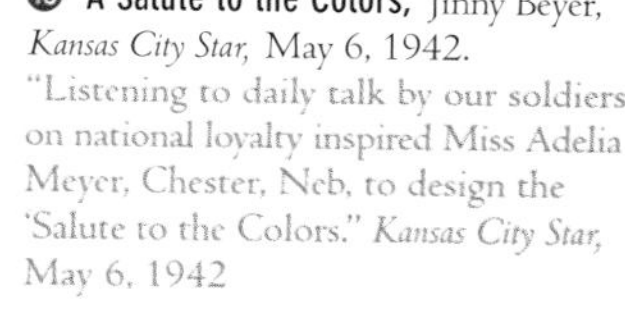
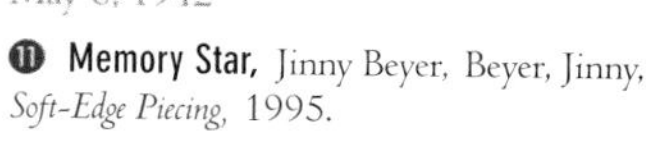
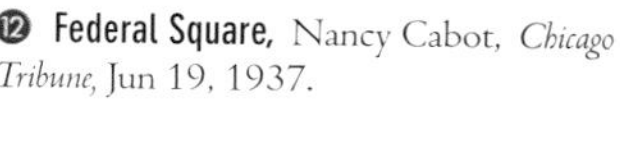

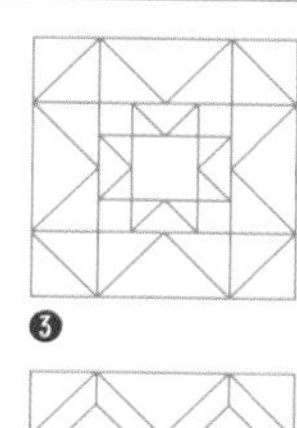
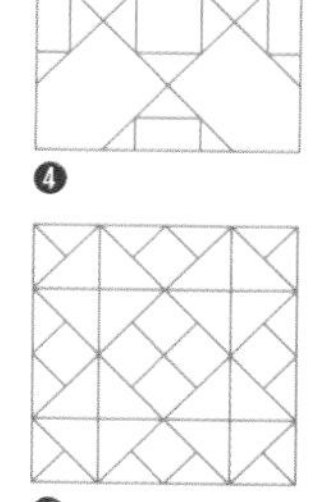
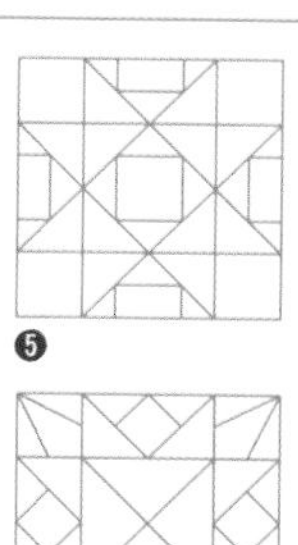
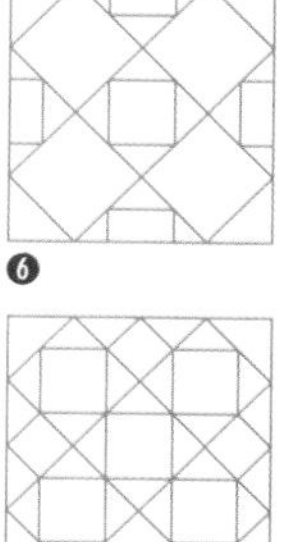
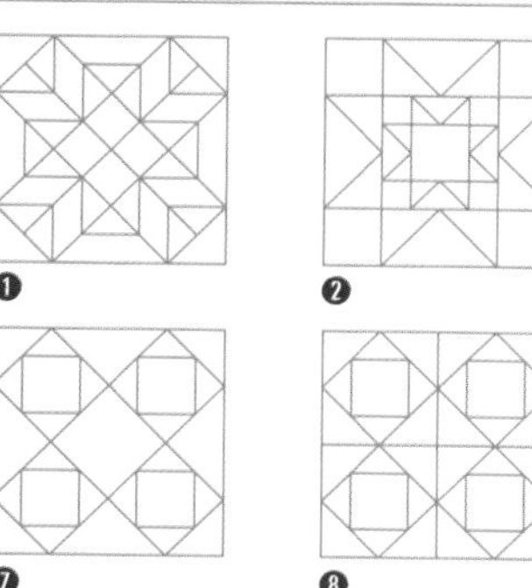
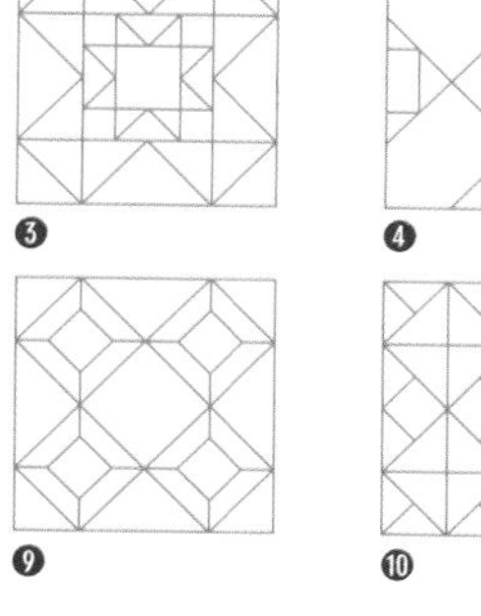
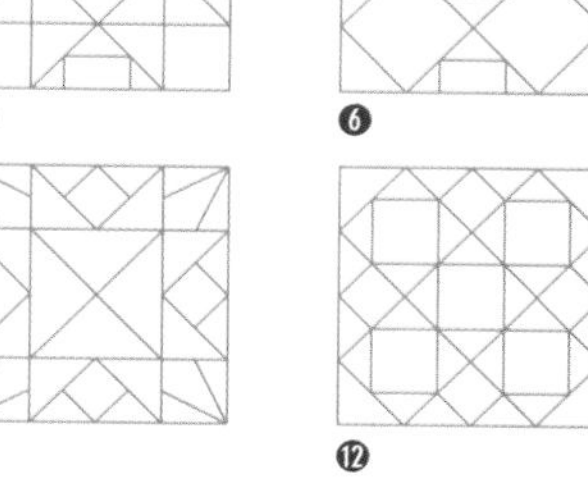

❶ ❷ ❸ ❹ ❺ ❻

❼ ❽ ❾ ❿ ⓫ ⓬

❶ **Heirloom,** Laura Wheeler, unidentified newspaper clipping, date unknown.

❷ **1904 Star,** Clara Stone, *Practical Needlework,* ca. 1906.

❸ **Four Patch,** Laura Wheeler, unidentified newspaper clipping, date unknown.

❹ **Texas Ranger,** *The American Woman,* Mar 1902. See 179-8. Also known as:
Iowa Star, *Old Fashioned Quilts,* 1931.

❺ **Signal Lights,** Nancy Page, *Nashville Banner,* Apr 3, 1934.

❻ **Lucky Star,** Laura Wheeler, *Cincinnati Enquirer,* Feb 8, 1934.

❼ **Cowboy's Star,** Nancy Page, *Birmingham News,* Mar 29, 1938.

❽ **Crossed Canoes,** *Ladies Art Company,* 1897. See 138-12 and 201-6.

❾ **The Milkmaid's Star,** *Kansas City Star,* Aug 4, 1948.

❿ **Inspiration Point,** Jinny Beyer, Hilton Head Seminar design, 1988; published in Beyer, Jinny, *Patchwork Portfolio.*

⓫ **Gemstone,** Jinny Beyer, Beyer, Jinny, *Patchwork Portfolio,* 1989.

⓬ **Sandpiper,** Jinny Beyer, Hilton Head Seminar design, 1984; published in Beyer, Jinny, *Patchwork Portfolio.*

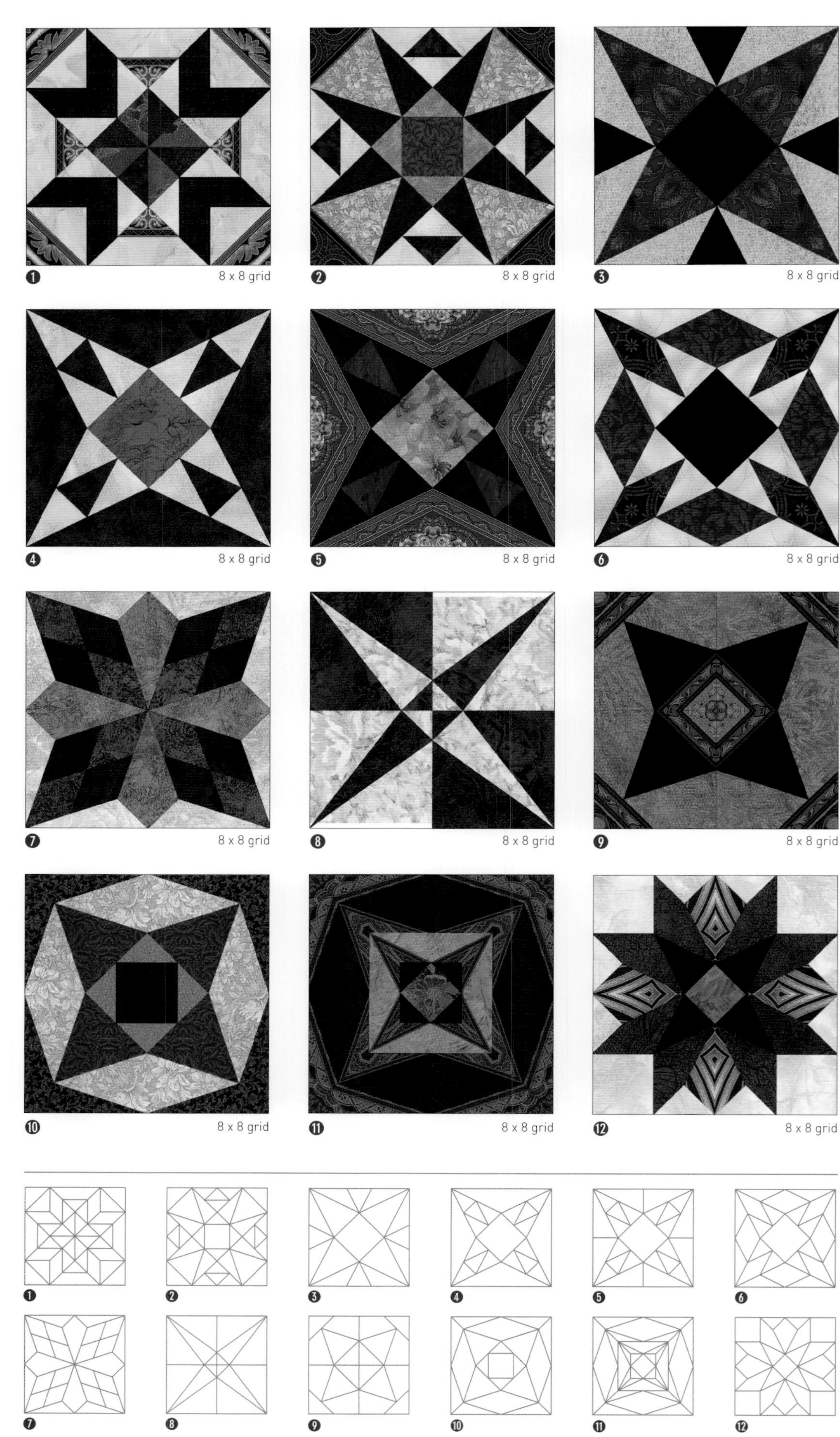

❶ **Lead Glass,** Jinny Beyer, Hilton Head Seminar design 1988; published in Beyer, Jinny, *Patchwork Portfolio.*

❷ **Square and Diamonds,** *Kansas City Star,* Apr 4, 1956.

❸ **Star and Cone,** *Eight Star Quilt Designs,* ca. 1936.

❹ **Twinkling Star,** Nancy Cabot, *Chicago Tribune,* Jun 28, 1938.

❺ **Starflower,** Nancy Page, *Birmingham News,* Feb 1, 1938.

❻ **Salzburg Connection,** Jinny Beyer, Beyer, Jinny, *Patchwork Portfolio,* 1989.

❼ **Polaris,** Jinny Beyer, Hilton Head Seminar design, 2000.

❽ **Royal Oak,** Jinny Beyer, Hilton Head Seminar design, 1982; published in Beyer, Jinny, *Patchwork Portfolio*

❾ **Grandmother's Two Patch,** Alice Brooks, *Detroit Free Press,* Oct 19, 1934.

❿ **Windmill Star,** *Kansas City Star,* May 12, 1934.

⓫ **Quasar,** Jinny Beyer, Hilton Head Seminar design, 1999.

⓬ **Spindles and Stripes,** *Kansas City Star,* Dec 5, 1950.

1 **Signs of Spring,** *Farm Journal and Farmer's Wife* (Silver Anniversary issue), 1945.

2 **Evening Star,** Alice Brooks, *Detroit Free Press,* May 4, 1940.

3 **Whirlwind,** Jinny Beyer, Hilton Head Seminar design, 1989; published in Beyer, Jinny, *Patchwork Portfolio.*

4 **Amethyst,** Eveline Foland, *Kansas City Star,* Feb 7, 1931. See page 65, 237-8, and 413-9. Also known as:
- **Crazy Quilt Star,** Beyer, Alice 1934.
- **Crazy Star Quilt,** Nancy Cabot, *Chicago Tribune,* Apr 15, 1935.
- **Windmill Star,** *Virginia Snow Studio Art Needlework Creations.* 1932.

5 **Diamond Star,** *Eight Star Quilt Designs,* ca. 1935. Also known as:
- **Golden Wedding Ring,** Hinson, 1973.
- **Priscilla,** Hall, 1935.
- **World Without End,** Hall, 1935.

6 **Key West Beauty,** Nancy Cabot, *Chicago Tribune,* Sep 8, 1936. Also known as:
- **Key West Star,** Gutcheon, *The Perfect Patchwork Primer,* 1973.

7 **Key West Beauty,** *Ladies Art Company,* 1922. Also known as:
- **Key West,** Nancy Cabot, *Chicago Tribune,* Feb 6, 1934.

8 **Dervish Star,** *Grandma Dexter New Appliqué and Patchwork Designs, Book 36b,* ca. 1932.

9 **Pinwheel,** Alice Brooks, unidentified newspaper clipping, date unknown.

10 **Dutch Mill,** *Ladies Art Company,* 1922.

11 **Priscilla's Dream,** *Detroit News,* per Brackman, 1938.

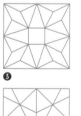

12 **Framed Bouquet,** Nancy Cabot, *Chicago Tribune,* Oct 10, 1935.

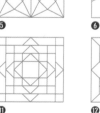

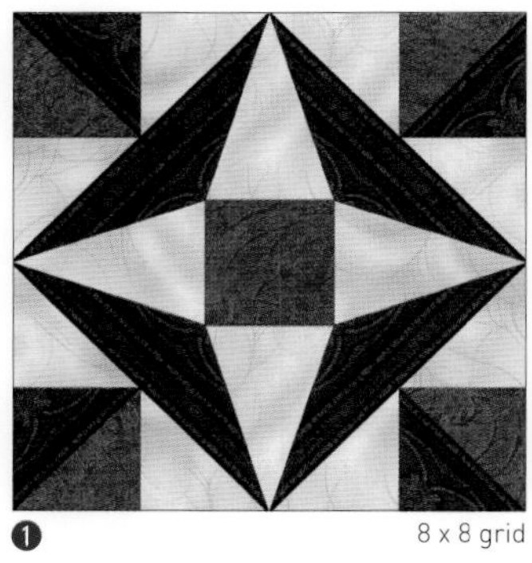

1 8 x 8 grid

2 8 x 8 grid

3 8 x 8 grid

4 8 x 8 grid

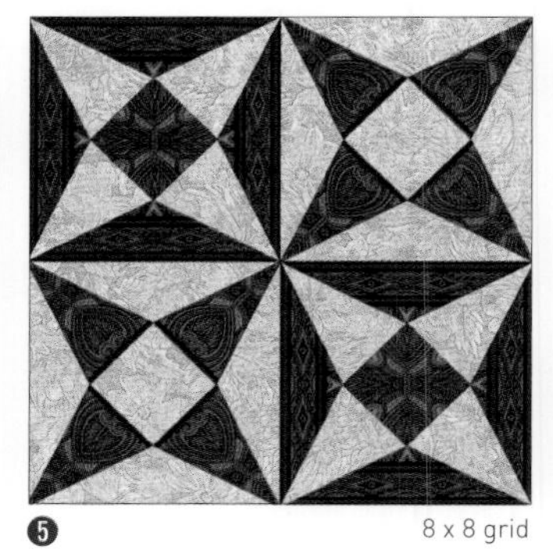

5 8 x 8 grid

6 8 x 8 grid

7 8 x 8 grid

8 8 x 8 grid

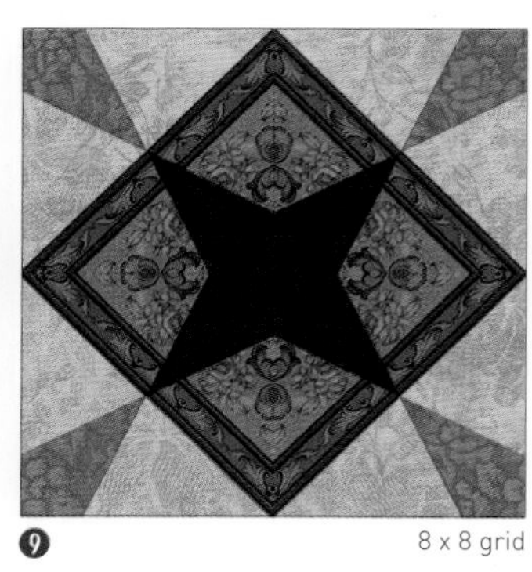

9 8 x 8 grid

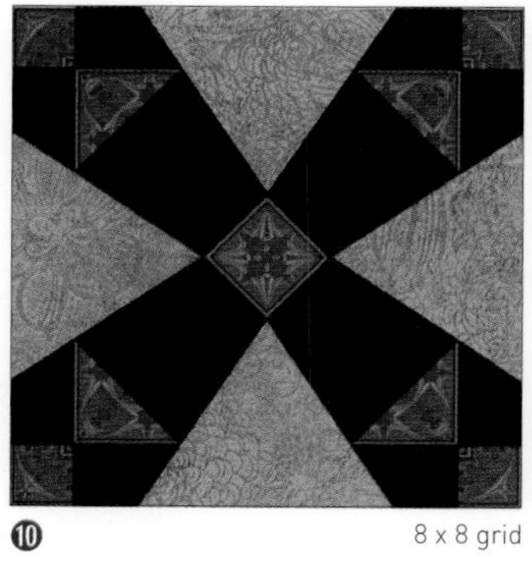

10 8 x 8 grid

11 8 x 8 grid

12 8 x 8 grid

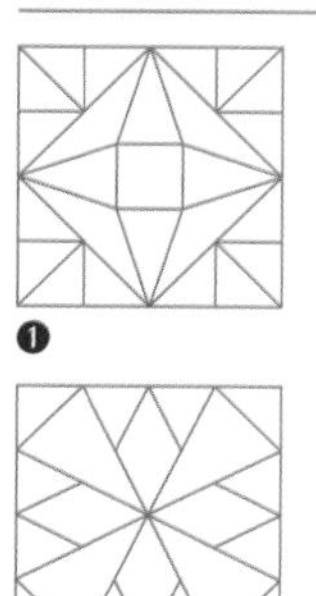

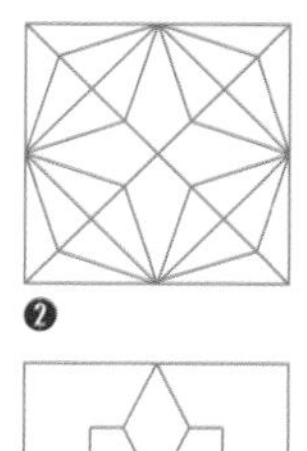

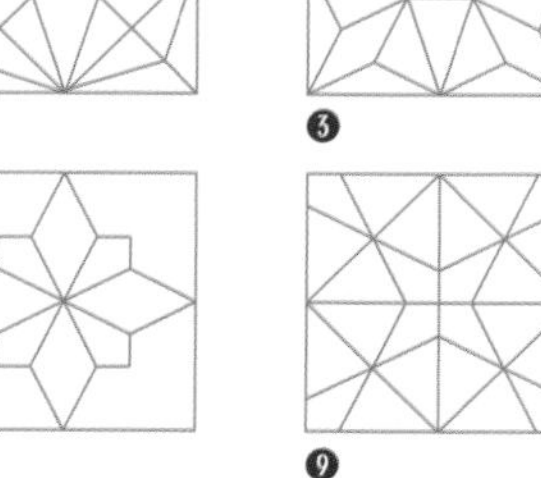

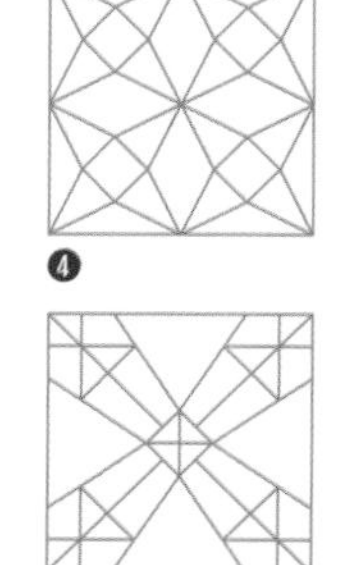

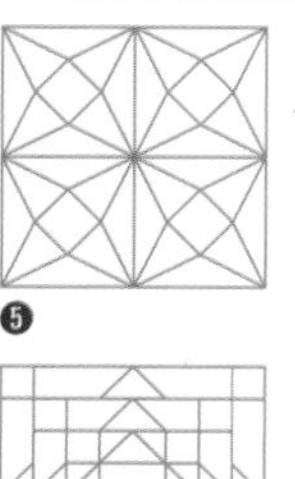

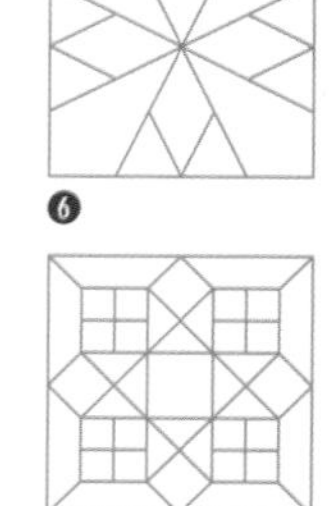

1 2 3 4 5 6

7 8 9 10 11 12

❶ **Stars of Twilight,** Home Art Studios, *Cincinnati Enquirer,* Apr 19, 1933.

❷ **Deco Tulip,** Jinny Beyer, Hilton Head Seminar design, 1991.

❸ **Diamond Star,** Home Art Studios, unidentified newspaper clipping, date unknown.

❹ **Flower Show,** Nancy Page, *Birmingham News,* Mar 14, 1944.

❺ **Star and Cubes,** *Grandma Dexter New Appliqué and Patchwork Designs, Book 36b,* ca. 1932.

❻ **Ohio Star,** Nancy Page, *Birmingham News,* Oct 22, 1935.

❼ **Quasar,** Jinny Beyer, Hilton Head Seminar design, 2000; published in Beyer, Jinny, *Quiltmaking by Hand.*

❽ **Chelsea,** Jinny Beyer, Hilton Head Seminar design, 1991.

❾ **Illinois Star,** *Quilt Booklet No. 1,* 1931. See 236-8.

❿ **Knight's Block,** Nancy Cabot, *Chicago Tribune,* Oct 14, 1935.

⓫ **Constellation,** Nancy Cabot, *Chicago Tribune,* Jan 7, 1936.

⓬ **Cog Wheels,** *Kansas City Star,* Nov 9, 1935.

❶ Diagonal Paths, Nancy Cabot, *Chicago Tribune,* Apr 18, 1936.

❷ Happy Birthday, Nancy Page, *Birmingham News,* Nov 24, 1942.

❸ The Rosebud, *Kansas City Star,* May 20, 1942.

❹ Philadelphia Block, Nancy Cabot, *Chicago Tribune,* Jan 19, 1938. See 183-1 and 253-3. Also known as:
: **Philadelphia Pavement,** Nancy Cabot, *Chicago Tribune,* Jan 19, 1938.

❺ Diamond Ring, Clara Stone, *Practical Needlework,* ca. 1906. Also known as:
: **Fanny's Favorite,** *Ladies Art Company,* 1922.
: **Linda's Favorite,** Nancy Page, *Birmingham News,* Jun 15, 1943.
: **My Favorite,** Nancy Cabot, *Chicago Tribune,* Aug 8, 1933.
: **Old Favorite,** Nancy Cabot, *Chicago Tribune,* Aug 5, 1937.

❻ Grandmother's Own, *Ladies Art Company,* 1897. Also known as:
: **Four Square,** *Farm Journal Quilt Patterns,* ca. 1935.

❼ Lattice Square, Nancy Cabot, *Chicago Tribune,* Nov 29, 1937. Also known as:
: **The Spool Quilt,** *Kansas City Star,* Dec 11, 1940.

❽ Easter Morning, Nancy Page, *Birmingham News,* Mar 19, 1940. Also known as:
: **Thrifty,** Laura Wheeler, unidentified newspaper clipping, date unknown.
: **Two Patch,** Alice Brooks, unidentified newspaper clipping, date unknown.

❾ Mosaic No. 4, *Ladies Art Company,* 1897.

❿ Star Sapphire, Jinny Beyer, Hilton Head Seminar design, 1994.

⓫ Johnnie Around the Corner, *Ladies Art Company,* 1897. Also known as:
: **The Broken Wheel,** *Kansas City Star,* Sep 29, 1943.

⓬ Churn Dash, *Ladies Art Company,* 1897. Also known as:
: **Picture Frame,** Clara Stone, *Practical Needlework,* ca. 1906.
: **The Picture Frame,** *Kansas City Star,* Sep 28, 1955.

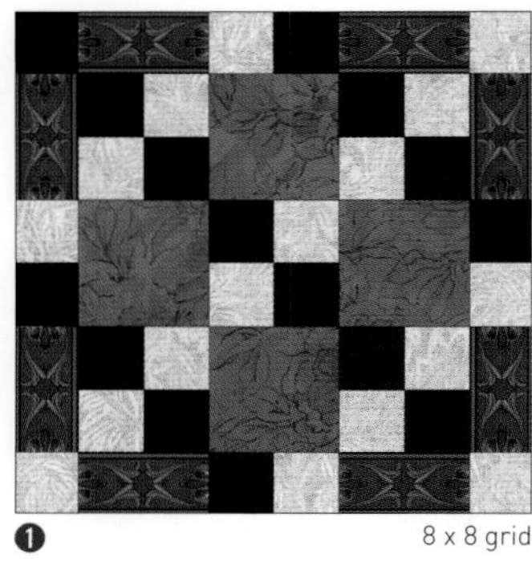

❶ 8 x 8 grid

❷ 8 x 8 grid

❸ 8 x 8 grid

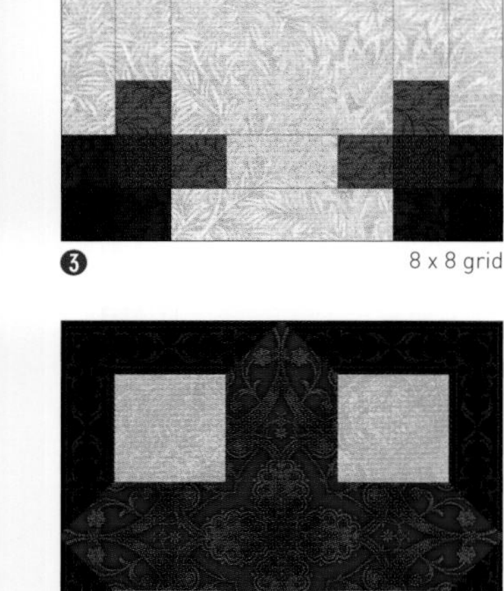

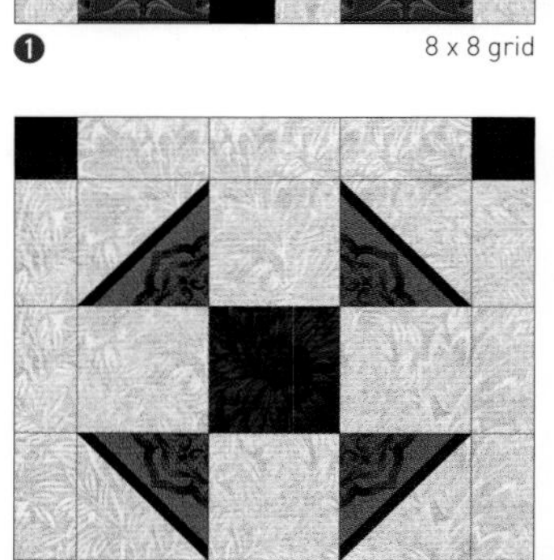

❹ 8 x 8 grid

❺ 8 x 8 grid

❻ 8 x 8 grid

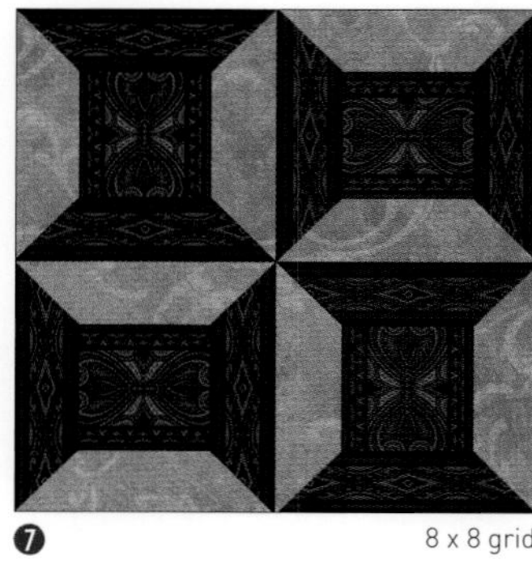

❼ 8 x 8 grid

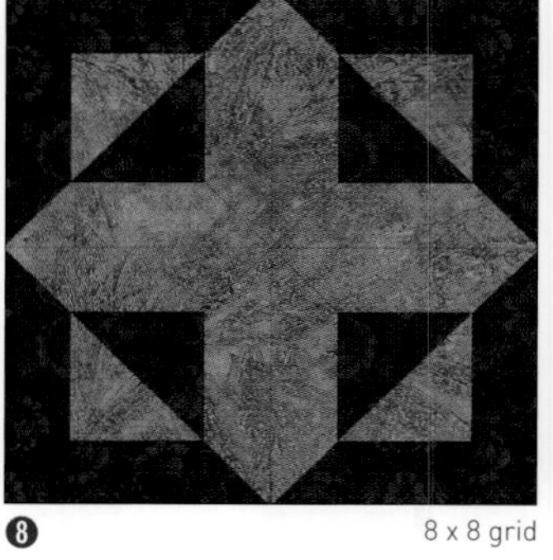

❽ 8 x 8 grid

❾ 8 x 8 grid

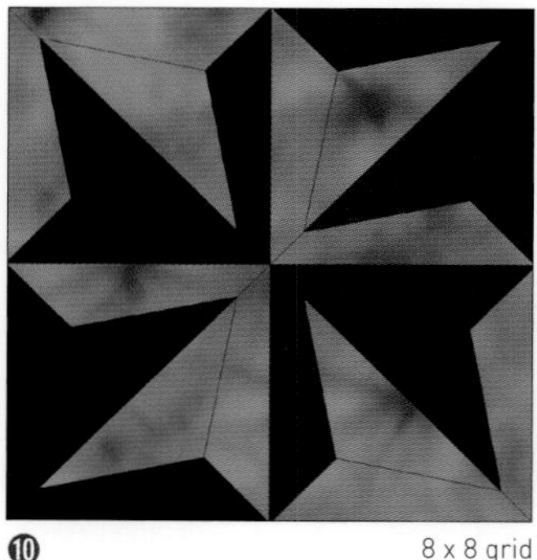

❿ 8 x 8 grid

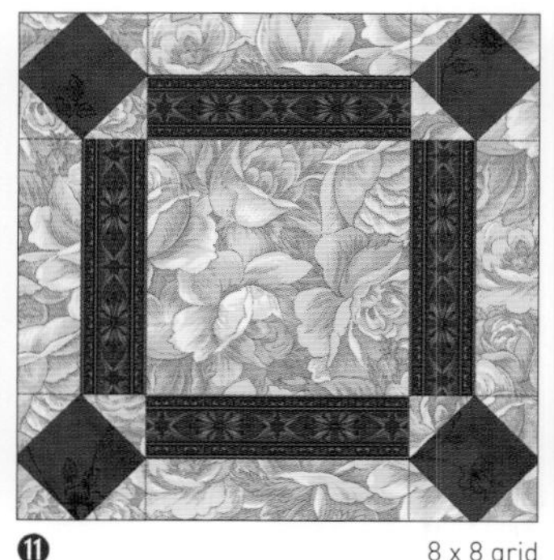

⓫ 8 x 8 grid

⓬ 8 x 8 grid

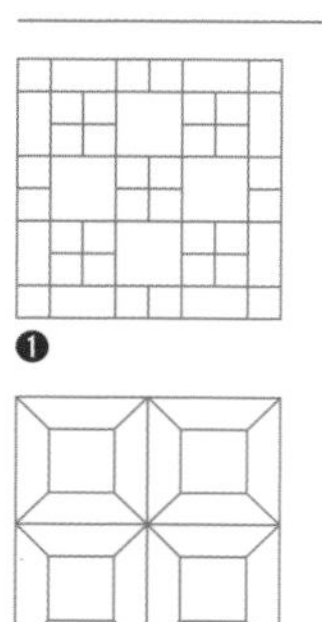

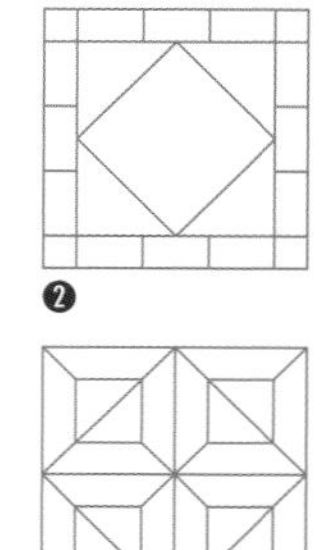

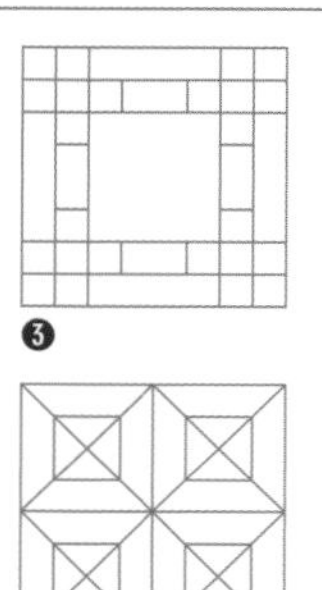

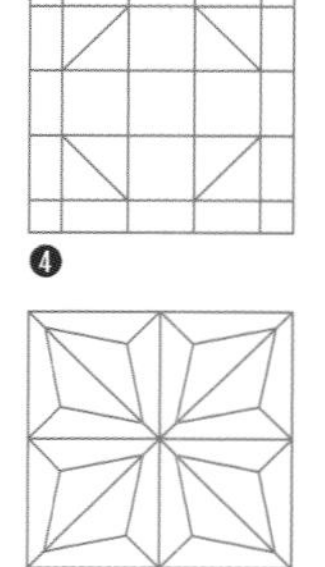

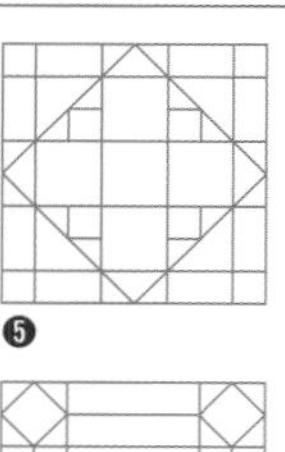

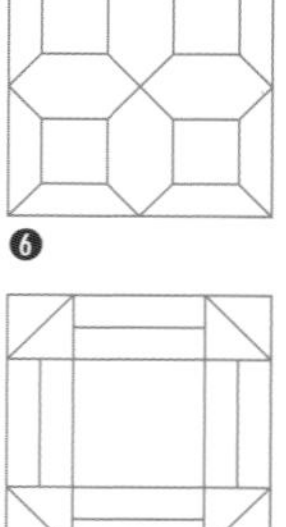

❶ ❷ ❸ ❹ ❺ ❻

❼ ❽ ❾ ❿ ⓫ ⓬

❶ **Frame a Print,** Aunt Martha series: *Patchwork Simplicity,* ca. 1977.

❷ **Coxey's Camp,** *Ladies Art Company,* 1897. Also known as:

> **Coxey's Army,** Nancy Cabot, *Chicago Tribune,* Jun 19, 1934.

❸ **Triangles and Stripes,** *Ladies Art Company,* 1897. Also known as:

> **Magic Box,** Nancy Page, *Birmingham News,* Dec 10, 1940.
>
> **Squares and Stripes,** Nancy Page, *Birmingham News,* Dec 10, 1940.

❹ **Old Fashioned Frame,** Nancy Page, *Birmingham News,* Jul 15, 1941. Also known as:

> **Victorian Frame,** Nancy Page, *Birmingham News,* Feb 16, 1943.

"This week and next I am showing a way in which a basic pattern may be changed slightly to give quite a different effect. Today I have a simple variation of the old-fashioned 'churn dash,' a pattern which has been popular for more than 100 years. I am calling the design an old-fashioned frame. You can imagine that the frame is in a brown figured print and the effect will be similar to that of the old-time brown wood frame that was made of four pieces crossed at the four corners." Nancy Page, *Birmingham News,* July 15, 1941

❺ **Jewel Box,** Jinny Beyer Studio design, 2000.

❻ **Ruins of Jericho,** Nancy Cabot, *Chicago Tribune,* Nov 27, 1937.

❼ **Maltese Cross,** Nancy Page, *Birmingham News,* Aug 28, 1934.

❽ **The Red Cross Quilt,** *Kansas City Star,* Oct 28, 1942.

❾ **Buffalo Ridge,** Nancy Cabot, date unknown; published in *Quilter's Newsletter Magazine,* Sep 1986.

❿ **Premium Star,** Nancy Cabot, *Chicago Tribune,* May 5, 1935. See 223-9, 223-10, 223-11, and 262-7. Also known as:

> **Bear Tracks,** Hinson, 1973.
>
> **Bear's Foot,** Hinson, 1973.
>
> **Bear's Paw,** Hinson, 1973.
>
> **Cross and Crown,** Hinson, 1973.
>
> **Duck's Foot in the Mud,** Hinson, 1973.
>
> **Goose Tracks,** Hinson, 1973.
>
> **Hand of Friendship,** Hinson, 1973.
>
> **Lily Design,** Hinson, 1973.
>
> **Path of Thorns,** Nancy Page, *Birmingham News,* Aug 6, 1935.

⓫ **Cross and Diamond,** Nancy Cabot, *Chicago Tribune,* Mar 27, 1937.

⓬ **Three Patch,** Alice Brooks, *Alice Brooks Designs,* date unknown.

Quick Reference: Bow Ties

The *Bow Tie* or *Necktie* has been a popular theme for quilts for years. It is amazing how many variations there are of such a simple design.

True Lover's Knot, *Ladies Art Company.* **See 77-3 .**

Magic Circle, *Ladies Art Company.* **See 77-2 .**

True Lover's Knot Aunt Martha series: *Quilts: Modern-Colonial.* **See 210-10.**

Bow Tie Quilt, Aunt Martha series: *Quilts: Modern-Colonial.* **See 253-1.**

Necktie, *Kansas City Star.* **See 77-1.**

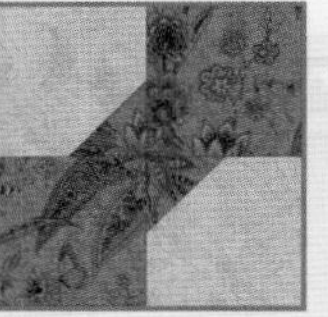
Necktie. Finley. **See 73-1.**

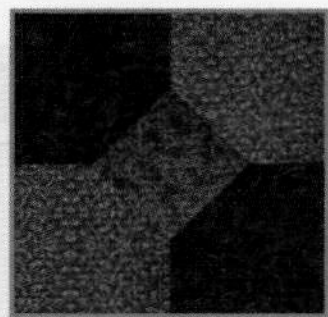
Necktie, *Ladies Art Company.* **See 61-11.**

Necktie, Aunt Martha series: *Quilts: Modern-Colonial.* **See 192-13.**

Bow Tie Quilt, *Blue Ribbon Patterns.* **See 111-8.**

Colonial Bow Tie, *Virginia Snow Studio ArtNeedle-work Creations.* **See 127-10.**

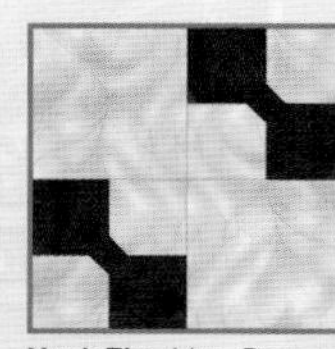
Neck Tie, *Mrs. Danner's Fifth Quilt Book.* **See 119-8.**

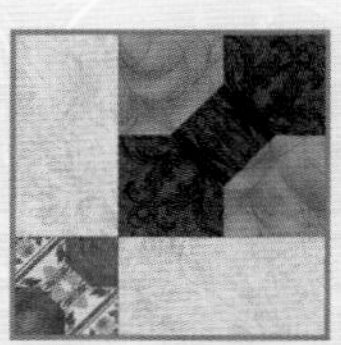
Midget Necktie, *Kansas City Star.* **See 151-8.**

Fred's Spool, *Practical Needlework.* **See 124-1.**

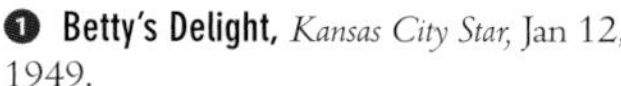
❶ **Betty's Delight,** *Kansas City Star,* Jan 12, 1949.

❷ **Four Square,** Nancy Cabot, *Chicago Tribune,* Mar 11, 1935.

❸ **Table for Four,** Nancy Page, *Birmingham News,* Jul 22, 1941.

❹ **Stepping Stones,** Virginia Snow, *Grandma Dexter New Appliqué and Patchwork Designs, Book 36b,* ca. 1932. Also known as:
- **Nose Gay,** Beyer, Alice, 1934.
- **Nosegay,** Nancy Cabot, *Chicago Tribune,* Apr 12, 1933.

❺ **Reflecting Star,** Jinny Beyer, Hilton Head Seminar design, 1983; published in Beyer, Jinny, *Patchwork Portfolio.*

❻ **Tuscan Sun,** Jinny Beyer, RJR Patterns, 2004.

❶ 8 x 8 grid

❷ 8 x 8 grid

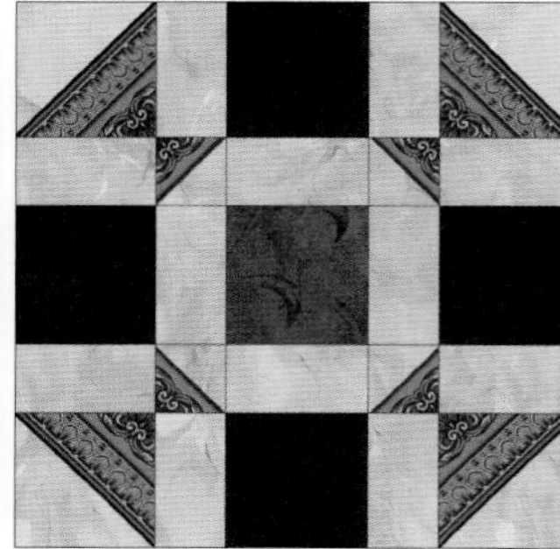
❸ 8 x 8 grid

❹ 8 x 8 grid

❺ 8 x 8 grid

❻ 8 x 8 grid

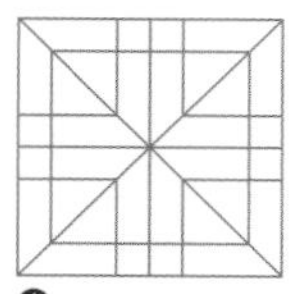
❶

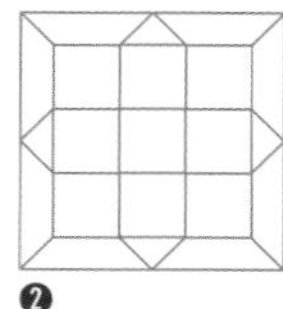
❷

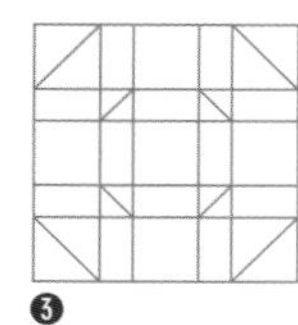
❸

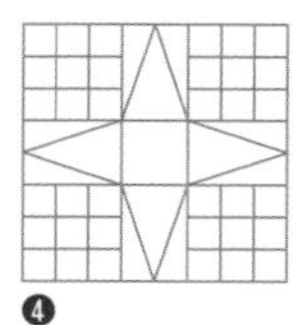
❹

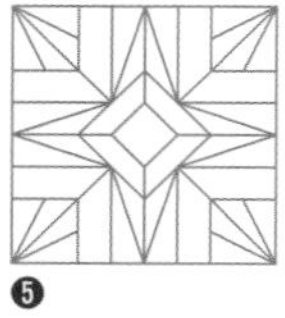
❺

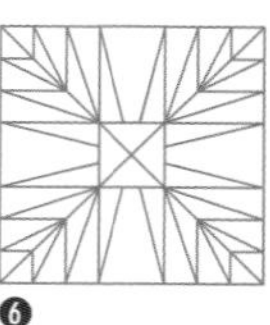
❻

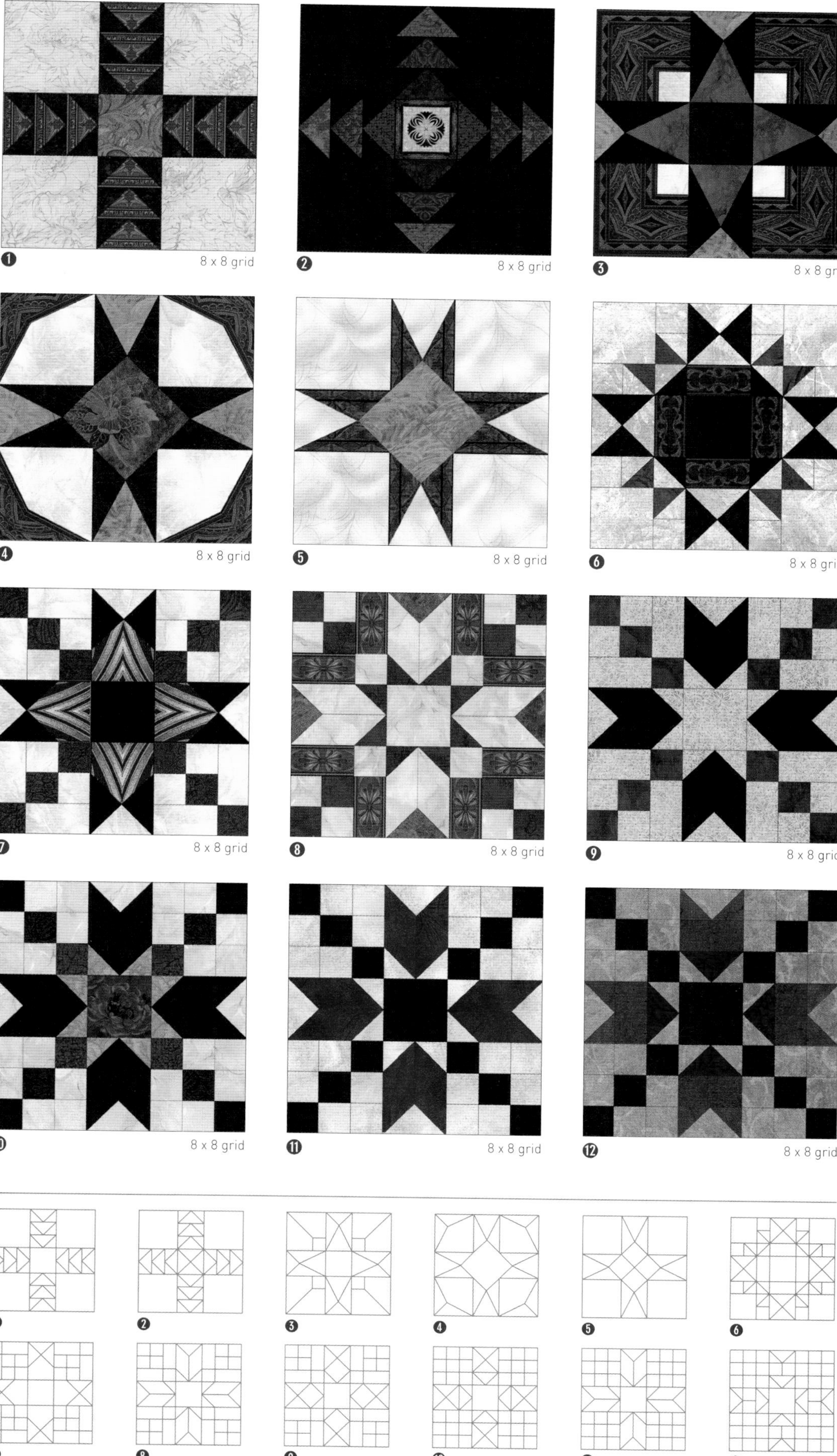

❶ **Road to California,** *Ladies Art Company,* 1897. Also known as:
- **Kite Tails,** Nancy Page, *Birmingham News,* June 9, 1942.
- **Stepping Stones,** Nancy Page, *Nashville Banner,* June 2, 1932.
- **Wild Goose Chase,** Nancy Page, *Birmingham News,* June 9, 1942.

❷ **Jacob's Ladder,** *Grandma Dexter Appliqué and Patchwork Designs, Book 36a,* ca. 1932.

❸ **La Mancha,** Jinny Beyer, *Hilton Head Seminar design,* 1993.

❹ **Ferris Wheel,** Jinny Beyer, Hilton Head Seminar design, 1995.

❺ **Pineapple Quilt,** Aunt Martha series: *Quilt Lover's Delight,* ca. 1960.

❻ **Rising Sun,** Nancy Page, *Birmingham News,* May 13, 1941.

❼ **Skipping Stones,** Jinny Beyer, Hilton Head Seminar design, 1988; published in Beyer, Jinny, *Patchwork Portfolio.*

❽ **Blackford's Beauty,** *Ladies Art Company,* ca. 1941. Also known as:
- **Arrow Point,** Aunt Martha series: *The Quilt Fair Comes to You,* ca. 1933.
- **Arrowhead,** *Farmer's Wife,* ca. 1920, per Brackman.
- **Black Beauty,** Nancy Cabot, *Chicago Tribune,* July 14, 1933.
- **Dover Square,** Nancy Page, *Birmingham News,* Sep 28, 1943.
- **Good Cheer,** Clara Stone, *Practical Needlework,* ca. 1906.
- **The Hunt,** *Farm Journal and Farmer's Wife,* ca. 1941.
- **Star and Stripe,** Nancy Cabot, *Chicago Tribune,* Feb 24, 1938.
- **Stepping Stones,** Ickis, 1949.

❾ **Arrowhead,** Home Art Studios, *Cincinnati Enquirer,* Mar 2, 1933.

❿ **Stepping Stones,** Eveline Foland, *Kansas City Star,* Sep 5, 1931. Also known as:
- **Arrowheads,** Hall, 1935.
- **The Winged Nine Patch,** *Kansas City Star,* Sep 11, 1940.

⓫ **Endless Chain,** Aunt Martha series: *The Quilt Fair Comes to You,* ca. 1933. Also known as:
- **Arrow Points,** Nancy Page, *Birmingham News,* Sep 18, 1934.

⓬ **Stepping Stones,** *Kansas City Star,* Feb 25, 1948.

❶ **Blackford's Beauty,** Nancy Cabot, *Chicago Tribune,* Apr 19, 1934.

❷ **Arrowhead,** *Quilt Blocks from The Farmer's Wife,* 1932.

❸ **Ruby Roads,** Nancy Cabot, *Chicago Tribune,* May 8, 1937.

❹ **Annapolis Block,** Nancy Cabot, *Chicago Tribune,* Jun 10, 1937.

❶ 8 x 8 grid

❷ 8 x 8 grid

❸ 8 x 8 grid

❹ 8 x 8 grid

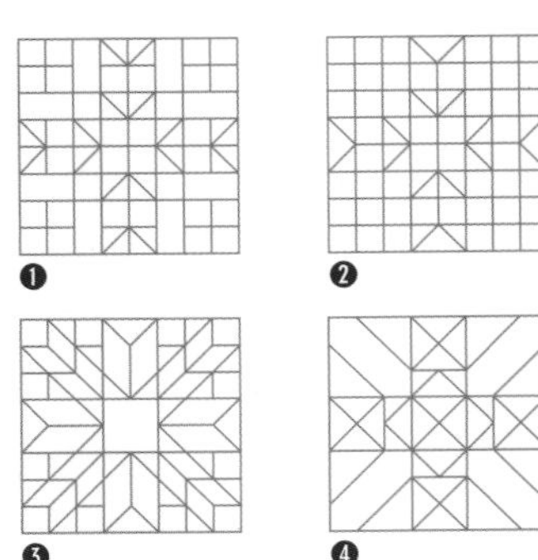

Quick Reference: Log Cabins

The Log Cabin quilt design has been a long time favorite of quilters. Log cabins were a part of the lives of early settlers who became part of the westward experience. It is no wonder that the Log Cabin would be depicted in a quilt. Even though the basic design had been made in Europe earlier and has been found on ancient artifacts, its popularity in the United States came in the second half of the 1800s.

The pattern has numerous names, depending for the most part on how the blocks are put together. When opposite sides are colored light and dark it is often called *Courthouse Steps.* When two adjacent sides are dark and the other two sides light, it is known as *Straight Furrow, Barn Raising,* and *Sunshine and Shadow.* Early quilts were often made with a red or yellow square in the center, representing the red of the fire or yellow of the candlelight.

The technique used for piecing many older Log Cabin quilts is similar to foundation piecing that is done today. It was called "press piecing" and Log Cabin quilts were sometimes called "pressed quilts." The process begins with a square of some sort of cloth, often muslin, that is cut to the size of the block. A small square is basted in the center, and then logs are added around the square. The first log is placed right side down on top of the central square, cut to size, then stitched in place through all layers. That strip is then "pressed" open and the next log is added in the same manner, this time cut to the width of the center square plus the width of the log. Pieces are continually added until all logs have been sewn.

Another style of design related to the Log Cabin is the Pineapple designs. They were made in a similar pattern, but the "logs" were added in an octagon.

"A block synonymous with beauty and antiquity is this old 'Interlaced Block.' The pattern is an early adaptation of the old pressed quilt known variously as 'Log Cabin Patch,' 'Straight Furrow,' and 'Barn Raising.'" Nancy Cabot, *Chicago Tribune,* Jun 11, 1934

"One of the oldest of the log cabin quilt designs, this fascinating block changes its title with the arrangement of its pieces. 'Straight Furrow' is a pioneer block that has traveled with courageous women from Connecticut to Virginia, to Kansas and Oregon, and back again. When it was first made, of silk and wool, it was known as a 'pressed' quilt, since it was sufficiently decorative without the quilting." Nancy Cabot, *Chicago Tribune,* March 30, 1934

Sunshine and Shadow, *Nashville Banner.* **See 155-2.**

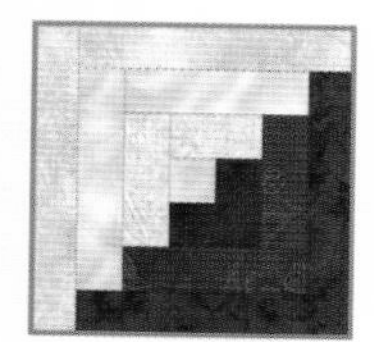
Log Cabin 'Light and Dark', *Q Book 102, Grandmother's Patchwork Quilts.* **See 226-5.**

Log Cabin. Holstein. **See 111-5.**

Straight Furrow, *Chicago Tribune.* **See 111-6.**

Log Cabin Straight Furrow. Holstein. **See 233-7.**

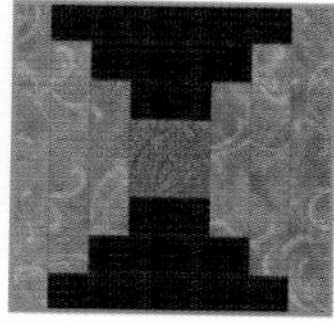
Log Cabin, *Chicago Tribune.* **See 111-7.**

Log Cabin. Hall. **See 246-1.**

White House Steps, *Ladies Art Company.* **See 246-3.**

Log Cabin, *Colonial Quilts.* **See 210-7.**

Log Cabin. Holstein. **See 210-8.**

Log Cabin. Hall. **See 254-7.**

Log Cabin, Jinny Beyer Studio design. **See 254-6.**

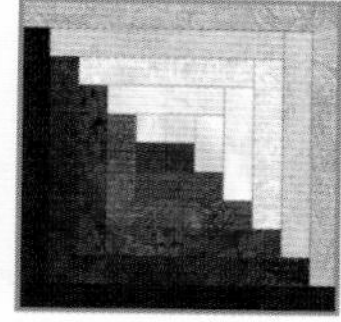
Log Cabin, *Illinois State Register.* **See 254-8.**

Log Cabin, *Ten Piecework Quilts for Southern Homes.* **See 259-1.**

Log Cabin, *Grandmother Clark's Old Fashioned Quilt Designs, Book 21.* **See 174-4.**

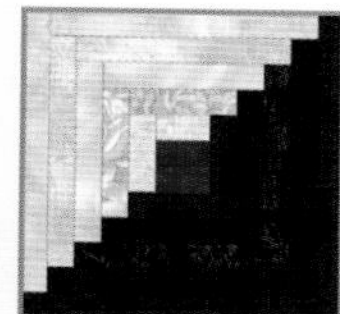
Old Fashioned Log Cabin, *Mrs. Danner's Fifth Quilt Book.* **See 174-5.**

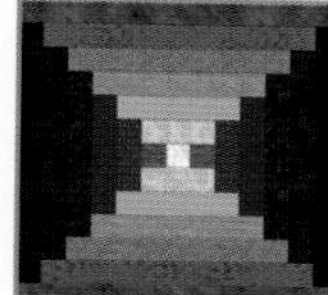
Log Cabin, *Kansas City Star.* **See 259-2.**

Log Cabin, Holstein. **See 233-7.**

New Log Cabin, *Chicago Tribune.* **See 233-9.**

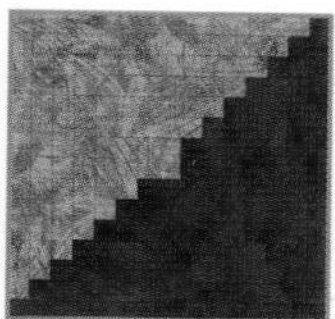
Log Cabin Straight Furrow, Holstein. **See 264-2.**

The Log Patch, *Ladies Art Company.* **See 120-9.**

Loghouse Quilting, *Saward.* **See 120-10.**

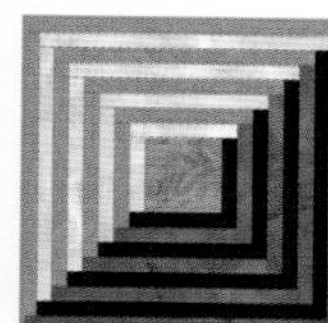
Log Cabin. Orlofsky. **See 272-1.**

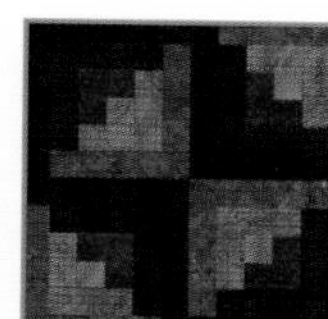
Cabin in the Woods, *Chicago Tribune.* **See 174-3.**

Log Cabin, *Kansas City Star.* **See 233-8.**

Interlaced Block, *Chicago Tribune.* **See 111-4 .**

Interlaced Blocks, *Ladies Art Company.* **See 254-9**

Carpenter's Square, *Ladies Art Company.* **See 254-10.**

Swastika Patch, *Ladies Art Company.* **See 246-4.**

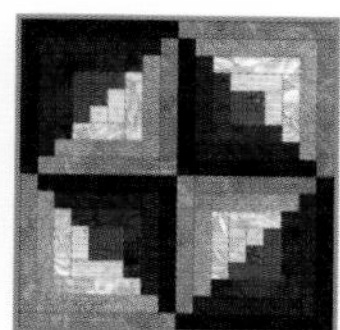
American Log Patchwork, *Ladies Art Company.* **See 250-10.**

Log Cabin, *Chicago Tribune.* **See 270-8.**

The Log Cabin Quilt, *Kansas City Star.* **See 179-6.**

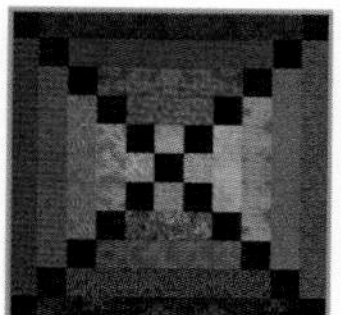
The Border Sea, *RJR Patterns.* **See 253-6.**

Aztec Steps, *Hilton Head Seminar design.* **See 121-1.**

Patagonia, *RJR Patterns.* **See 120-12.**

Monticello, *RJR Patterns.* **See 120-11.**

Somerset, *RJR Patterns.* **See 208-2.**

Stepping Stones, *Farmer's Wife Book of New Designs and Patterns.* **See 253-7.**

Mission Stairs, *RJR Patterns.* **See 170-3.**

Twister, *Hilton Head Seminar design.* **See 398-6.**

❶ **Virginia Crossroads,** Jinny Beyer, Beyer, Jinny, *Patchwork Portfolio,* 1989.

❷ **Flying Clouds,** Finley, 1929. Also known as:

- **Flying Checkers,** Nancy Page, *Birmingham News,* May 5, 1942.
- **Four Frogs,** Finley, 1929.
- **Summer Clouds,** Nancy Cabot, *Chicago Tribune,* Apr 5, 1938.

❸ **Heather Square,** Nancy Cabot, *Chicago Tribune,* Mar 20, 1937.

❹ **Double T,** *One Dozen Quilt Patterns,* ca. 1936. Also known as:

- **Rockets,** Judy Spahn, Beyer, Jinny, *The Quilter's Album...,* 1980.

❺ **T Square,** Clara Stone, *Practical Needlework,* ca. 1906.

❻ **Calibogue Sound,** Jinny Beyer, Hilton Head Seminar design, 1988; published in Beyer, Jinny, *Patchwork Portfolio.*

❼ **Lattice,** Nancy Page, *Nashville Banner,* Aug 29, 1933.

❽ **Devil's Puzzle,** Nancy Cabot, *Chicago Tribune,* Oct 19, 1934. See 229-11.
"'Devils Puzzle' is an intriguing pieced block both in name and design. It is composed entirely of pieced blocks which are set together without intervening strips and forms an endlesss pattern. It was designed, as you might not suspect, by a pious old soul who lived in Pennsylvania." Nancy Cabot, *Chicago Tribune,* Oct 19, 1934

❾ **Devil's Puzzle,** *Ladies Art Company,* 1897. See 229-11.

❿ **Carolina Crossroads,** Hilton Head Seminar design, 1985; published in Beyer, Jinny, *Patchwork Portfolio.*

⓫ **Crosswind,** Jinny Beyer, Hilton Head Seminar design, 1987; published in Beyer, Jinny, *Patchwork Portfolio.*

⓬ **Springtime,** *Detroit Free Press,* Book No. 6, Jul 29, 1933.

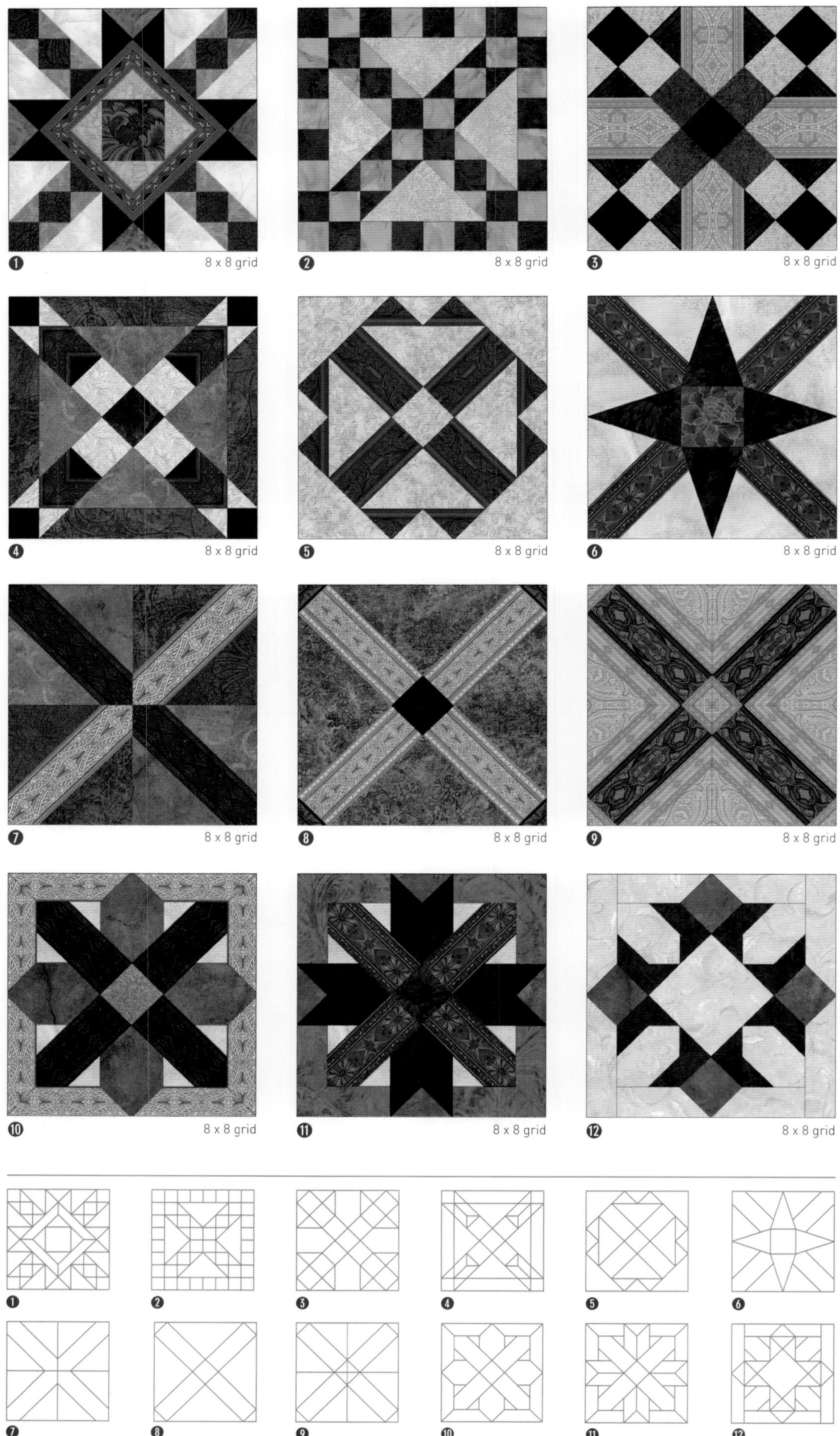

❶ **Brooklyn,** Nancy Page, *Birmingham News,* Sep 29, 1936. Also known as:

- **Red Cross,** Nancy Page, *Birmingham News,* Apr 6, 1937.

❷ **Yellow Brick Road,** Jinny Beyer, Beyer, Jinny, *Patchwork Portfolio.* 1989.

❸ **Linton Pathway,** *Old Fashioned Quilts,* 1931. See 159-1, 200-6.

❹ **Halley's Comet,** Jinny Beyer, Hilton Head Seminar design, 1986; published in Beyer, Jinny, *Patchwork Portfolio.*

❺ **Chicago Pavements,** Clara Stone, *Practical Needlework,* ca. 1906. Also known as:

- **Album,** Jinny Beyer, Beyer, Jinny, *The Quilter's Album...,* 1980.
- **Album Patch,** date unknown; published in Beyer, Jinny, The Quilter's Album. . . .
- **The Casement Window,** Eveline Foland, *Kansas City Star,* Mar 28, 1931.
- **Chimney Sweep,** Finley, 1929.
- **Courthouse Square,** Hall, 1935.
- **The Garden Patch,** *Kansas City Star,* Oct 23, 1940.
- **Tinted Chains,** Nancy Cabot, *Chicago Tribune,* Feb 19, 1938.

❻ **Court House Lawn,** Nancy Cabot, *Chicago Tribune,* Mar 8, 1937.

❼ **Whirling Squares,** Nancy Page, *Birmingham News,* Mar 14, 1939.

❽ **Roman Cross,** *Ladies Art Company,* 1897.

❾ **Washington Sidewalk,** *Ladies Art Company,* 1897. Also known as:

- **Crosspatch,** *The Patchwork Book,* 1932.
- **Friendship Chain,** Nancy Cabot, *Chicago Tribune,* Apr 13, 1934.
- **Roman Cross,** Nancy Cabot, *Chicago Tribune,* Nov 11, 1934.
- **Tennallytown Square,** Nancy Cabot, *Chicago Tribune,* Jul 8, 1938.
- **Washington,** Nancy Page, *Birmingham News,* Mar 24, 1936.
- **Washington's Sidewalks,** Nancy Cabot, *Chicago Tribune,* Apr 13, 1934.

❿ **Cross Patch,** *Old Fashioned Quilts,* ca. 1931. Also known as:

- **The Basket Weave Friendship Block,** *Kansas City Star,* Jul 1, 1953.
- **The Basket Weave Friendship Quilt,** *Kansas City Star,* Apr 9, 1958
- **A Friendship Quilt for Many Purposes,** *Kansas City Star,* Jul 20, 1960.
- **Casement Window,** Nancy Page, *Birmingham News,* Sep 13, 1932.
- **Courthouse Square,** Hall, 1935.
- **Friendship Quilt,** *Kansas City Star,* Aug 20, 1947.
- **Friendship's Chain,** *Farm Journal Quilt Patterns,* ca. 1935.
- **Military Cross Roads,** Nancy Page, *Birmingham News,* Oct 21, 1941.
- **Roman Cross,** Hall, 1935.
- **The Album,** *Kansas City Star,* Oct 30, 1935.

⓫ **Red Cross,** *Quilts,* 1945. Also known as:

- **The Red Cross Quilt,** *Kansas City Star,* Jan 15, 1947.

⓬ **Four Cross,** Clara Stone, *Practical Needlework,* ca. 1906.

1. **Kentucky Chain,** *Practical Needlework,* ca. 1906.
2. **Paths to Peace,** ca. 1938, per Havig.
3. **Chimney Sweep,** Nancy Cabot, *Chicago Tribune,* Jul 3, 1935.
4. **Aunt Mary's Double Irish Chain,** Clara Stone, *Practical Needlework,* ca. 1906.
5. **Wild Duck and Duckling,** Nancy Cabot, *Chicago Tribune,* Mar 22, 1935. Also known as:
   - **Duck and Ducklings,** *Farm Journal Quilt Patterns,* ca. 1935.
   - **Ducks and Ducklings,** Nancy Cabot, *Chicago Tribune,* July 31, 1937.
6. **Sunshine,** *Ladies Art Company,* 1897.
7. **Sunshine,** Nancy Cabot, *Chicago Tribune,* Jul 14, 1934.
8. **Sunshine,** Nancy Cabot, *Chicago Tribune,* Dec 25, 1936.
9. **Spring Has Come,** Nancy Page, *Birmingham News,* Mar 23, 1937.
10. **Delectable Mountains,** Hall, 1935.
11. **Jagged Edge,** Ickis, 1949.
12. **Mineral Wells,** Nancy Page, *Birmingham News,* Feb 13, 1940.

❶ **Mosaic,** *The Patchwork Book,* 1932.

❷ **Jubilee,** Nancy Page, *Birmingham News,* Sep 3, 1935. See 131-5, 159-3, 159-4, 409-11.

❸ **Ocean Wave,** Nancy Cabot, *Chicago Tribune,* Aug 22, 1936. See 131-5, 159-3, 159-4, and 409-11.

❹ **The Square Deal,** Eveline Foland, *Kansas City Star,* Aug 20, 1932.

❺ **Potholder Patch,** Alice Brooks, *Alice Brooks Designs,* date unknown.

❻ **Windmill,** *The Farmer's Wife Book of New Designs and Patterns,* 1934.

❼ **Monkey Wrench,** Hall, 1935. See 108-8 and page 342. Also known as:
Snail's Trail, Hall, 1935.

❽ **Cock's Comb,** Nancy Cabot, date unknown, per Brackman.

❾ **Cobblestone,** Jinny Beyer, Hilton Head Seminar design, 2001; published in Beyer, Jinny, *Quiltmaking by Hand.*

❿ **Scrap,** Clara Stone, *Practical Needlework,* ca. 1906. Also known as:
Mosaic Rose, Nancy Cabot, *Chicago Tribune,* May 19, 1938.
Square on Square, Nancy Page, *Nashville Banner,* May 30, 1933.

⓫ **Snail Trail,** *Ladies Art Company,* 1928. See 108-8. Also known as:
Indiana Puzzle, Beyer, *The Quilter's Album...,* 1980.
Journey to California, *Kansas City Star,* Apr 6, 1955.
Monkey Wrench, Ruby McKim, *Kansas City Star,* Jan 12, 1929.
Road to Oklahoma, *Kansas City Star,* Nov 6, 1957.
Snail's Trail, *Old Fashioned Quilts,* 1928.
Virginia Reel, *The Mountain Mist Blue Book of Quilts,* 1935.
Whirligig, date unknown; published in Beyer, Jinny, *The Quilter's Album....*

⓬ **Nautilus,** Clara Stone, *Practical Needlework,* ca. 1906.

❶ **Crimson Rambler,** Nancy Page, *Birmingham News,* Sep 6, 1938.

❷ **No Name Patch,** ca. 1938, per Havig.

❸ **Baton Rouge Block,** *Ladies Art Company,* 1922. Also known as:

- **Baton Rouge,** Nancy Cabot, *Chicago Tribune,* Jan 27, 1934.

❹ **Grandmother's Favorite,** Eveline Foland, *Kansas City Star,* Nov 5, 1930.

❺ **New Hampshire,** Nancy Page, *Birmingham News,* Oct 12, 1943.

❻ **Flying X,** Nancy Cabot, *Chicago Tribune,* Jun 7, 1938.

❼ **Ring Around the Posey,** Marcia Aasmundstad, Beyer, Jinny, *The Quilter's Album...,*1980.

❽ **Mosaic No. 7,** *Ladies Art Company,* 1897. See 96-5, 112-9, 167-10, 167-11, 167-12, and 217-10. Also known as:

- **Jack in the Pulpit,** Hall, 1935.
- **Mosaic No. 2,** Nancy Cabot, *Chicago Tribune,* May 19, 1934.
- **Toad in the Puddle,** Hall, 1935.

❾ **Broken Dishes,** *Michigan Farmer,* May 27, 1926. See 96-5, 112-9, 167-10, 167-11, 167-12, 167-12, and 217-10. Also known as:

- **Double Squares,** date unknown; published in Beyer, Jinny, *The Quilter's Album....*

❿ **Scotch Squares,** *Farmer's Wife,* Jan 1913. Also known as:

- **Scotch Plaid,** ca. 1938, per Havig.

⓫ **Around the Corner,** Nancy Cabot, *Chicago Tribune,* Apr 8, 1936.

⓬ **Pinwheel Square,** Marcia Aasmundstad, Beyer, Jinny, *The Quilter's Album...,* 1980.

❶ 8 x 8 grid

❷ 8 x 8 grid

❸ 8 x 8 grid

❹ 8 x 8 grid

❺ 8 x 8 grid

❻ 8 x 8 grid

❼ 8 x 8 grid

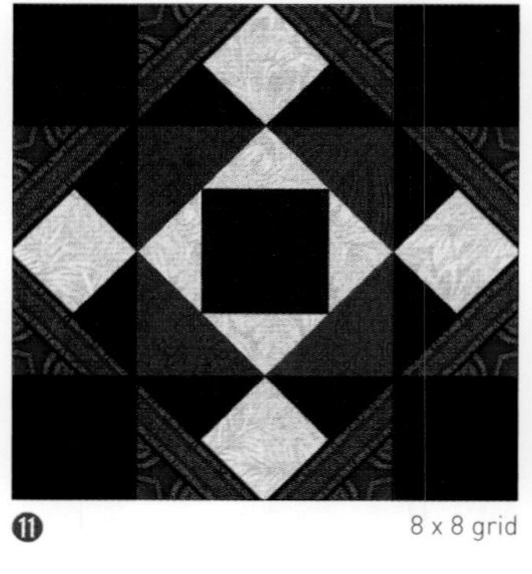

❽ 8 x 8 grid

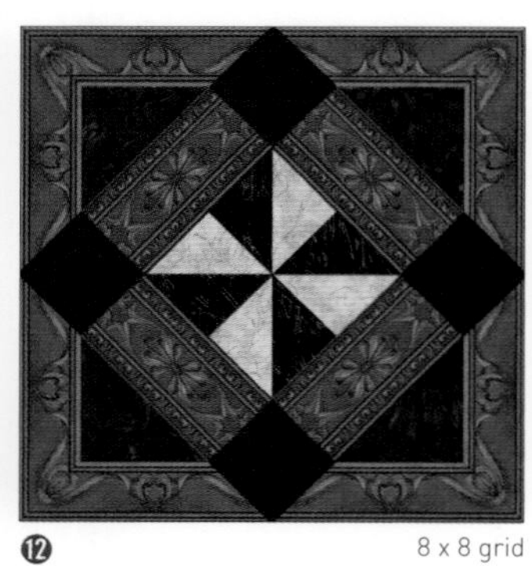

❾ 8 x 8 grid

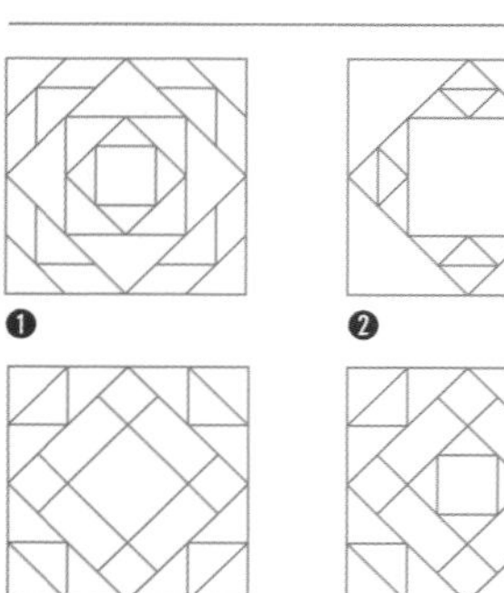

❿ 8 x 8 grid

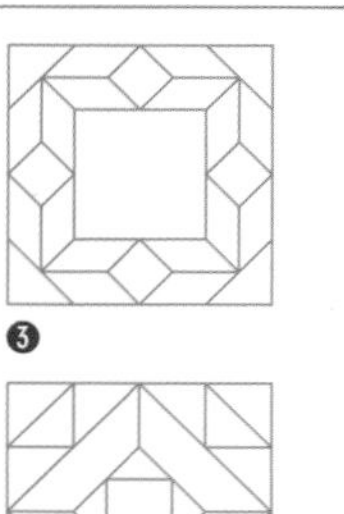

⓫ 8 x 8 grid

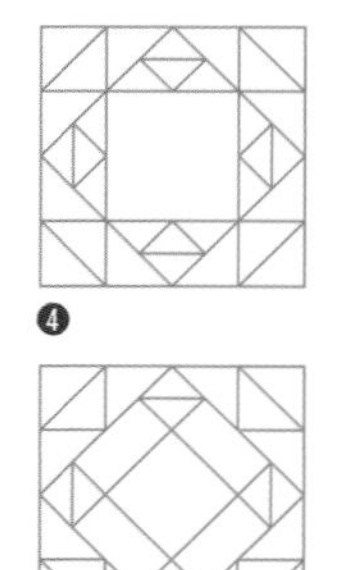

⓬ 8 x 8 grid

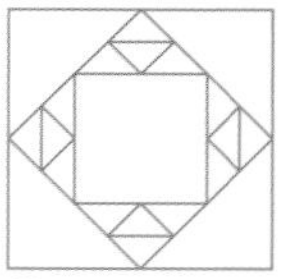

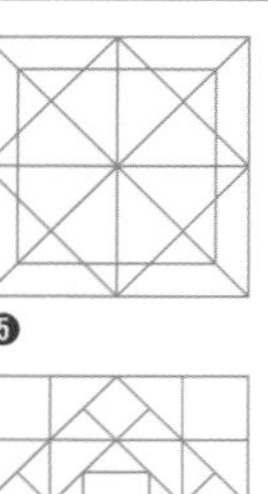

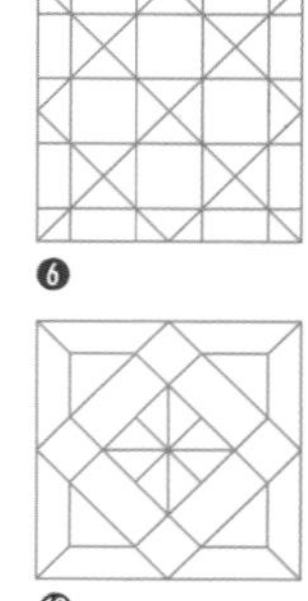

❶ ❷ ❸ ❹ ❺ ❻

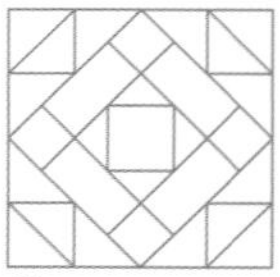

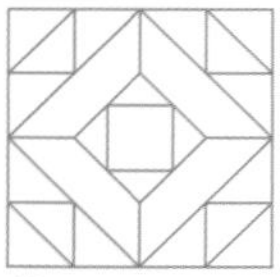

❼ ❽ ❾ ❿ ⓫ ⓬

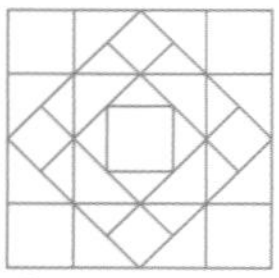

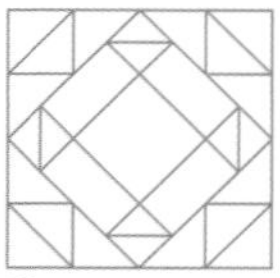

❶ **Forest Trail,** Laura Wheeler, *Illinois State Register,* Jun 27, 1933.
"This pattern is an unusual one in that the blocks when joined give a lovely interlacing pattern like paths that twist and turn and cross each other. It is an old pattern and has appeared in variations under other names. Of all the variations, this alone has the charm of the interlacing pattern." Laura Wheeler, *Illinois State Register,* June 27, 1933

❷ **Boston Star,** Nancy Page, *Birmingham News,* Jan 18, 1944.

❸ **Hull's Victory,** Clara Stone, *Practical Needlework,* ca. 1906.

❹ **Beacon Lights,** Nancy Page, *Birmingham News,* Aug 11, 1936.

❺ **Memory Block,** Nancy Cabot, *Chicago Tribune,* Jun 16, 1938.

❻ **Crown of Thorns,** Finley, 1929. See 60-10. Also known as:
   Georgetown Circle, Finley, 1929.
   Georgetown Circles, Gutcheon, *The Perfect Patchwork Primer,* 1973.

❼ **World's Fair,** Virginia Snow, *Grandma Dexter New Appliqué and Patchwork Designs, Book 36b,* ca. 1932.

❽ **Nameless,** Clara Stone, *Practical Needlework,* ca. 1906.

❾ **Flower Pot,** *Grandmother Clark's Patchwork,* 1932.

❿ **Quita's Favorite,** Nancy Page, *Birmingham News,* May 3, 1938.

⓫ **Flower Pot,** Nancy Cabot, *Chicago Tribune,* Jan 18, 1935.

⓬ **The Pyramids,** Nancy Cabot, *Chicago Tribune,* Jan 11, 1936.

❶ **Chained Star,** Nancy Page, *Birmingham News,* Dec 1, 1936.

❷ **Jeweled Scrap Quilt,** Laura Wheeler, *National Weeklies, Inc.,* date unknown.

❸ **Beginner's Star,** Alice Brooks, unidentified newspaper clipping, date unknown.

❹ **Four Patch,** Laura Wheeler, unidentified newspaper clipping, date unknown.

❺ **Gem Blocks,** *The Patchwork Book,* 1932. See 94-8, 94-9, 167-10, 167-12, 112-9, and 217-10.

❻ **Saddleback,** Jinny Beyer, Beyer, Jinny, *Patchwork Portfolio,* 1989.

❼ **Stacked Crystals,** Jinsny Beyer, Hilton Head Seminar design, 1995.

❽ **Spring House,** Jinny Beyer, Beyer, Jinny, *Patchwork Portfolio,* 1989.

❾ **Sand Castle,** Jinny Beyer, Hilton Head Seminar design, 1986; published in Beyer, Jinny, *Patchwork Portfolio.*

❿ **Morning Patch,** Nancy Page, *Birmingham News,* Apr 21, 1942.

⓫ **Diamond Star,** *Ladies Art Company,* 1897. See 141-12 and 211-12. Also known as:
Mother's Choice, Clara Stone, *Practical Needlework,* ca. 1906.
Open Box, Nancy Page, *Nashville Banner,* Apr 11, 1933.

⓬ **Sandhills Star,** *Kansas City Star,* Jan 18, 1939.

❶ **Michigan Beauty,** *Practical Needlework,* ca. 1906. Also known as:
- **Idaho,** Nancy Page, *Birmingham News,* Apr 14, 1936.
- **The Laurel Wreath,** "One Dozen Quilt Patterns," *Progressive Farmer,* ca. 1936.
- **Many Pointed Star,** "Eight Star Quilt Designs", *Progressive Farmer,* ca. 1935.
- **Paper Flowers,** Nancy Page, *Birmingham News,* Jul 18, 1939.

❷ **Mayflower,** Jinny Beyer, Beyer, Jinny, *Patchwork Portfolio,* 1989.

❸ **Lily Quilt Pattern,** *Ladies Art Company,* 1897. Also known as:
- **The Corner Star,** *Kansas City Star,* Aug 9, 1939.
- **The Crowfoot,** *Mrs. Danner's Fourth Quilt Book,* 1958.
- **The Springtime Blossom,** *Mrs. Danner's Third Quilt Book,* 1954.

❹ **Lily Quilt Pattern,** Nancy Cabot, *Chicago Tribune,* Sep 19, 1934.

❺ **Lily Quilt,** Nancy Page, *Birmingham News,* Oct 9, 1934. Also known as:
- **Sweet Gum Leaf,** Nancy Cabot, *Chicago Tribune,* Aug 17, 1936.

❻ **Devil's Claws,** *Ladies Art Company,* 1897. Also known as:
- **Bright Stars,** Nancy Cabot, *Chicago Tribune,* Apr 21, 1942.
- **Cross Plains,** Clara Stone, *Practical Needlework,* ca. 1906.
- **Crow Foot,** *Mrs. Danner's Quilts, Books 1 & 2,* 1971.
- **Devil's Claw,** Nancy Page, *Detroit Free Press,* Aug 25, 1933.
- **Four Stars,** Nancy Page, *Birmingham News,* Sep 3, 1940.
- **Glitter,** Nancy Page, *Birmingham News,* Dec 15, 1936.
- **Idaho Beauty,** Clara Stone, *Practical Needlework,* ca. 1906.

❼ **Devil's Claw,** Nancy Cabot, *Chicago Tribune,* Jun 18, 1934.

❽ **Stars and Cubes,** Nancy Page, *Birmingham News,* Apr 2, 1935. See 292-1.

❾ **Old Maid's Patience,** Nancy Cabot, *Chicago Tribune,* Jun 24, 1933.

❿ **Twinkle, Twinkle Little Star,** *Kansas City Star,* Jun 26, 1935. See 291-10.

⓫ **Eureka,** Nancy Cabot, *Chicago Tribune,* Nov 12, 1937.

⓬ **Mosaic Squares,** Nancy Cabot, *Chicago Tribune,* Jul 1, 1936.

❶ **Garden Path,** Laura Wheeler, *Cincinnati Enquirer,* Aug 27, 1933.
"The scrap bag indeed comes into its own with this quilt, for the charm of the pattern is enhanced by the diversity of the materials used. Just as our gardens bloom in all colors of the rainbow, so this quilt is gay in its varied patches. The 'path,' made by the squares formed by scraps of material, sets off the large flower motif that makes this striking pattern. Those who prefer can repeat the same materials throughout and a very handsome quilt will result." Laura Wheeler, *Cincinnati Enquirer,* Aug 27, 1933

❷ **Crown of Thorns,** Nancy Page, *Birmingham News,* Apr 11, 1939.

❸ **Crow's Foot,** *Ladies Art Company,* 1897. Also known as:
- **Arrow Heads,** Nancy Page, *Birmingham News,* Oct 8, 1935.
- **Crowfoot,** Nancy Cabot, *Chicago Tribune,* Dec 16, 1937.

❹ **Swing in the Center,** Nancy Cabot, *Chicago Tribune,* May 15, 1933. Also known as:
- **Turkey in the Straw,** Nancy Cabot, *Chicago Tribune,* May 15, 1933.

❺ **Eight Hands Around,** Nancy Cabot, *Chicago Tribune,* Dec 12, 1936. Also known as:
- **Castle Garden,** Nancy Cabot, *Chicago Tribune,* Jan 12, 1937.

❻ **Odd Fellow's Chain,** *Ladies Art Company,* 1897. Also known as:
- **San Diego,** Nancy Page, *Birmingham News,* Sep 24, 1935.

❼ **Odd Fellow's Chain,** Nancy Cabot, *Chicago Tribune,* Mar 8, 1935.

❽ **Merry Go Round,** *Capper's Weekly,* ca. 1930.

❾ **Thirteen Squared,** *Farm Journal and Farmer's Wife,* ca. 1941. Also known as:
- **Thirteen Squares,** Martens, 1970.

❿ **Hains Point,** Jinny Beyer, Beyer, Jinny, *Patchwork Portfolio,* 1989.

⓫ **Storm at Sea,** Eveline Foland, *Kansas City Star,* May 14, 1932. See 114-4 and 171-11. Also known as:
- **Ocean Waves,** Laura Wheeler, *Cincinnati Enquirer,* Sep 6, 1933.
- **Rolling Stone,** Laura Wheeler, *Cincinnati Enquirer,* Sep 6, 1933.

⓬ **Custer's Last Stand,** Nancy Cabot, *Chicago Tribune,* Apr 30, 1933.
"Commemorating the tragic battle of the Little Big Horn in 1876, this quilt pattern weaves a graphic story of 'Custer's Last Stand.' As you remember from your history, this battle was the climax of an expedition against the Sioux and their allies in what is now Montana. Custer, with 260 men, was sent to the junction of the Little Big Horn and the Big Horn rivers and was overwhelmed there by a horde of Sioux led by Sitting Bull. In a battle lasting twenty minutes, his entire force was defeated and massacred. The quilt design, with its squares and surrounding triangles, is symbolic of the small group of American cavalrymen standing off the encircling Indians." Nancy Cabot, *Chicago Tribune,* Apr 30, 1933

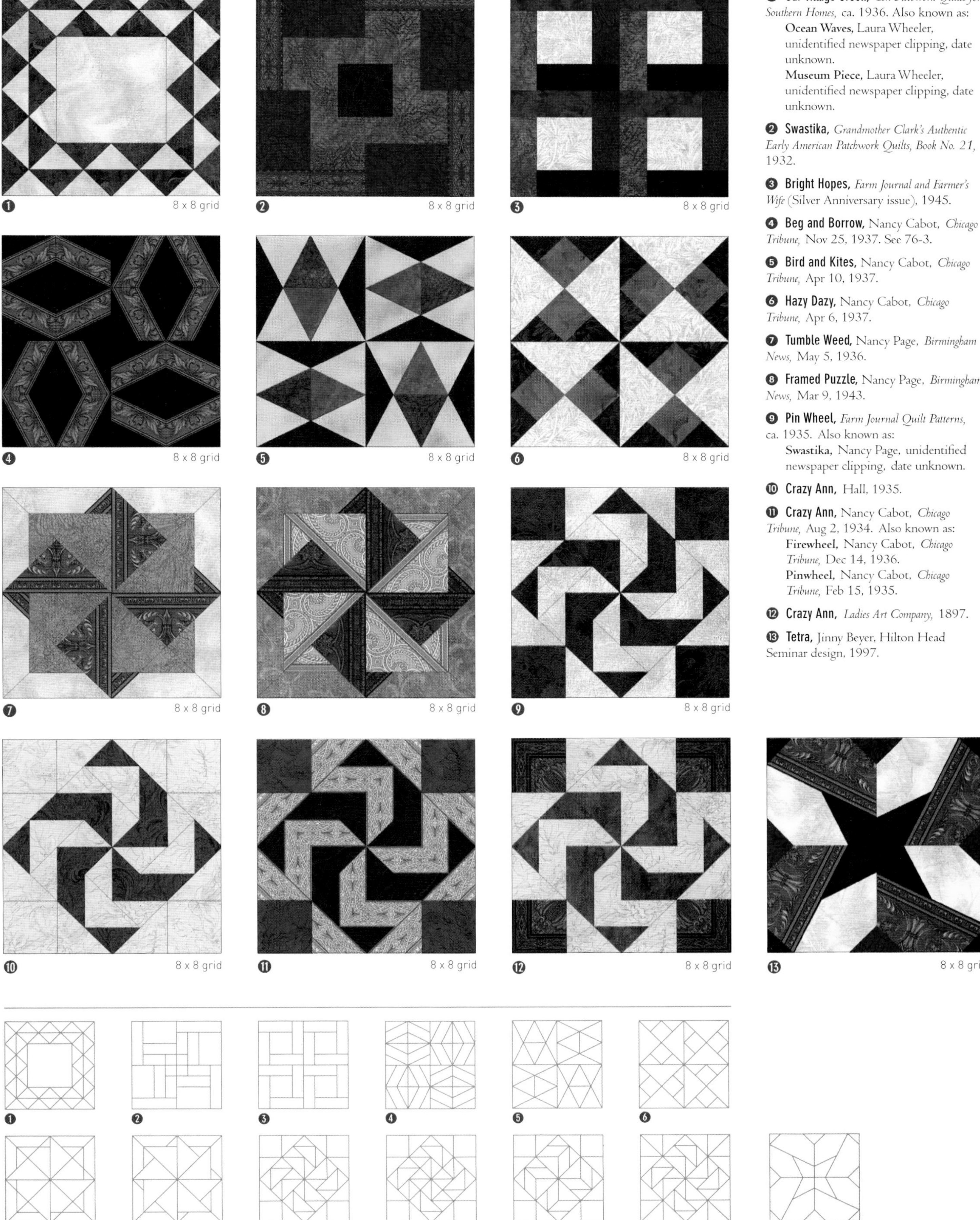

❶ **Our Village Green,** *Ten Piecework Quilts for Southern Homes,* ca. 1936. Also known as:
Ocean Waves, Laura Wheeler, unidentified newspaper clipping, date unknown.
Museum Piece, Laura Wheeler, unidentified newspaper clipping, date unknown.

❷ **Swastika,** *Grandmother Clark's Authentic Early American Patchwork Quilts, Book No. 21,* 1932.

❸ **Bright Hopes,** *Farm Journal and Farmer's Wife* (Silver Anniversary issue), 1945.

❹ **Beg and Borrow,** Nancy Cabot, *Chicago Tribune,* Nov 25, 1937. See 76-3.

❺ **Bird and Kites,** Nancy Cabot, *Chicago Tribune,* Apr 10, 1937.

❻ **Hazy Dazy,** Nancy Cabot, *Chicago Tribune,* Apr 6, 1937.

❼ **Tumble Weed,** Nancy Page, *Birmingham News,* May 5, 1936.

❽ **Framed Puzzle,** Nancy Page, *Birmingham News,* Mar 9, 1943.

❾ **Pin Wheel,** *Farm Journal Quilt Patterns,* ca. 1935. Also known as:
Swastika, Nancy Page, unidentified newspaper clipping, date unknown.

❿ **Crazy Ann,** Hall, 1935.

⓫ **Crazy Ann,** Nancy Cabot, *Chicago Tribune,* Aug 2, 1934. Also known as:
Firewheel, Nancy Cabot, *Chicago Tribune,* Dec 14, 1936.
Pinwheel, Nancy Cabot, *Chicago Tribune,* Feb 15, 1935.

⓬ **Crazy Ann,** *Ladies Art Company,* 1897.

⓭ **Tetra,** Jinny Beyer, Hilton Head Seminar design, 1997.

❶ **Flyfoot,** Laura Wheeler, *Illinois State Register,* May 10, 1933.
"Colonial architecture, based on the classic Greek, employed the fret motif among others in the decorations of doorways, mantles and other trim in the house. It is no wonder then that this fret was adapted by the quilt makers of those days, and comes to us as the Flyfoot. The name is really a corruption of the Greek name for the fret." *Portland Press Herald,* date unknown

❷ **Windmill,** Martens, 1970.

❸ **Windmill,** *Grandmother's Patchwork Quilt Designs, Book 20,* 1931.

❹ **The Jig Jog Puzzle,** *Kansas City Star,* May 7, 1938.

❺ **A Puzzle Meets a Quilt,** *Capper's Weekly,* ca. 1930. Also known as:
Interwoven Puzzle, *Q Book 116, Blue Ribbon Quilts,* date unknown.

❻ **Fox and Geese,** *Farm Journal and Farmer's Wife,* ca. 1941.

❼ **Wild Goose Chase,** date unknown, per Holstein.

❽ **Golden Tile,** Jinny Beyer, Hilton Head Seminar design, 2004.

❾ **Delft Mill,** Nancy Cabot, *Chicago Tribune,* Apr 7, 1937.

❿ **Dutch Windmill,** *Ladies Art Company,* 1928.

⓫ **Dutch Windmill,** Home Art Studios, unidentified newspaper clipping, date unknown.

⓬ **Kansas Troubles,** *Ladies Art Company,* 1897. See 207-7. Also known as:
Grand Right and Left, *Farm Journal and Farmer's Wife,* ca. 1941.
Kansas Trouble, *Kansas City Star,* Mar 3, 1934.
Lucasta's Block, Nancy Page, *Birmingham News,* Feb 27, 1940.

❶ 8 x 8 grid

❷ 8 x 8 grid

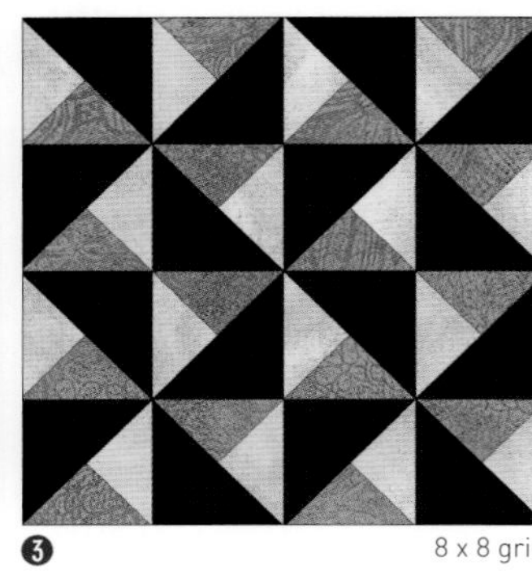
❸ 8 x 8 grid

❹ 8 x 8 grid

❺ 8 x 8 grid

❻ 8 x 8 grid

❼ 8 x 8 grid

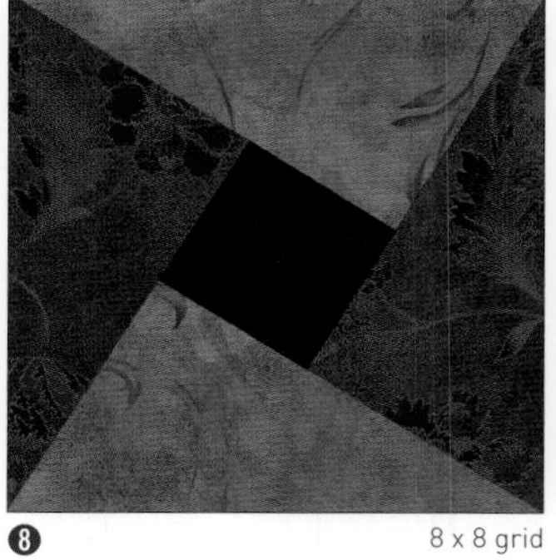
❽ 8 x 8 grid

❾ 8 x 8 grid

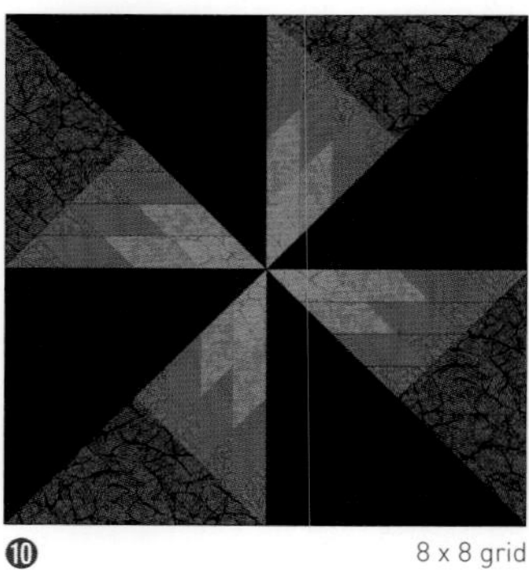
❿ 8 x 8 grid

⓫ 8 x 8 grid

⓬ 8 x 8 grid

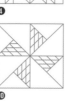

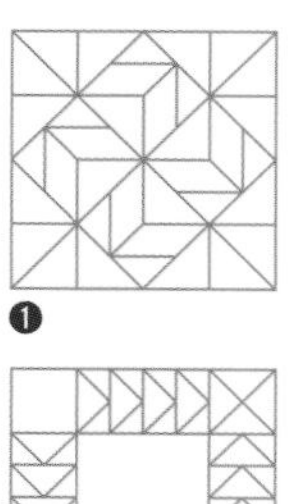
❶

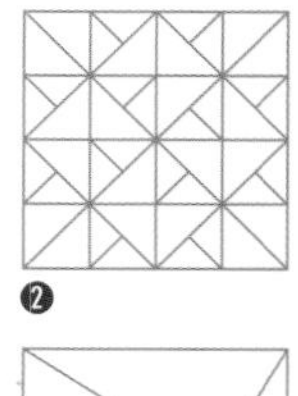
❷

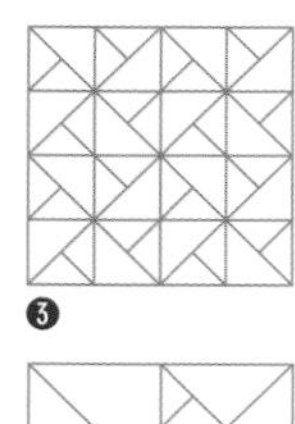
❸

❹

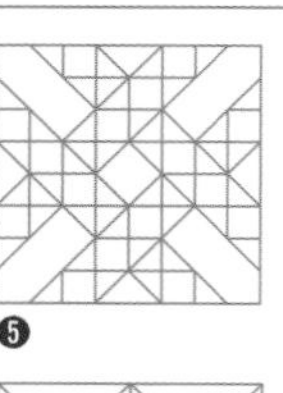
❺

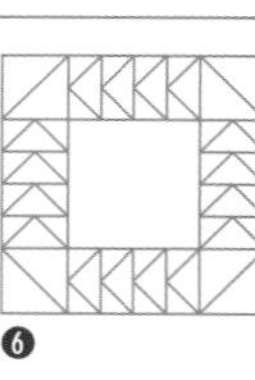
❻

❼

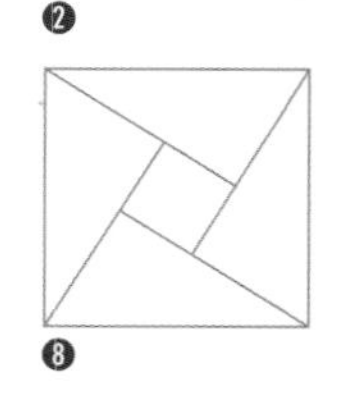
❽

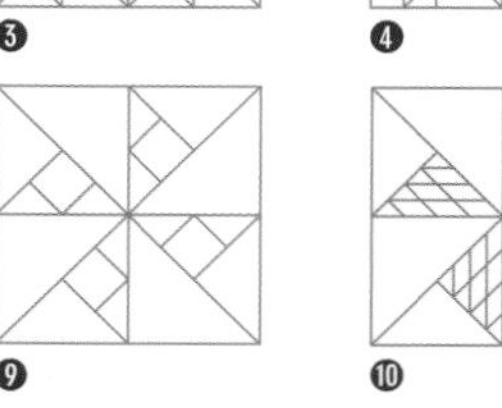
❾

❿

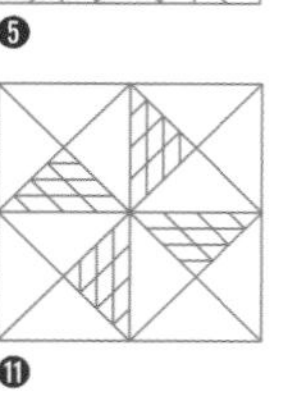
⓫

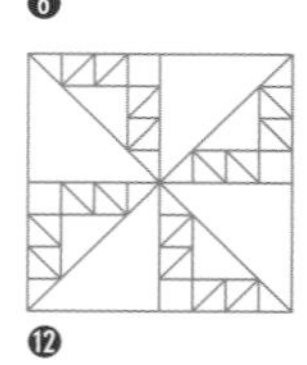
⓬

1. **Pink Shower,** *Farmer's Wife,* 1931.
2. **Irish Puzzle,** *Ladies Art Company,* 1897. See 207-7. Also known as:
   - **Blue and White,** Nancy Cabot, *Chicago Tribune,* Jan 19, 1934.
   - **Climbing Rose,** Finley, 1929.
   - **Flying Dutchman,** Finley, 1929.
   - **Forest Path,** Finley, 1929.
   - **Indian Trail,** Finley, 1929.
   - **Kansas Trouble,** *Quilts Heirlooms of Tomorrow,* date unknown.
   - **Kansas Troubles,** Hall, 1935.
   - **North Wind,** Finley, 1929.
   - **Old Maid's Ramble,** Finley, 1929.
   - **Prickly Pear,** Finley, 1929.
   - **Rambling Road,** Finley, 1929.
   - **Rambling Rose,** Finley, 1929.
   - **Storm at Sea,** Finley, 1929.
   - **Tangled Tares,** Finley, 1929.
   - **Weather Vane,** Finley, 1929.
   - **Winding Walk,** Finley, 1929.
3. **Bear's Paw,** *Ladies Art Company,* 1897. Also known as:
   - **Flying Dutchman,** Hinson, 1973.
   - **Forest Path,** Hall, 1935.
   - **Indian Trails,** Hall, 1935.
   - **Irish Puzzle,** Hall, 1935.
   - **North Wind,** Hall, 1935.
   - **Old Maid's Ramble,** Hall, 1935.
   - **Prickly Pear,** Hinson, 1973.
   - **Rambling Road,** Hall, 1935.
   - **Rambling Roads,** Hinson, 1973.
   - **Rambling Rose,** Hinson, 1973.
   - **Storm at Sea,** Hall, 1935.
   - **Tangled Tares,** Hinson, 1973.
   - **Weather Vane,** Hinson, 1973.
   - **Winding Walk,** Hall, 1935.
4. **Waves of the Sea,** *Kansas City Star,* Mar 6, 1937.
5. **Merry Go Round,** Ruby McKim, *Kansas City Star,* May 10, 1930. See 428-9. Also known as:
   - **Double S,** Nancy Page, *Birmingham News,* Feb 15, 1939.
   - **Eternal Triangle,** Hall, 1935.
6. **Eternal Triangle,** ca. 1938, per Havig. See 105-5 and 428-9. Also known as:
   - **Merry Go Round,** Hall, 1935.
7. **Little Penguins,** Nancy Cabot, *Chicago Tribune,* Feb 4, 1936.
8. **Yokahama Banner,** Nancy Cabot, *Chicago Tribune,* Apr 13, 1937.
9. **Slashed Album,** *Ladies Art Company,* 1897. Also known as:
   - **Around the Chimney,** *Kansas City Star,* Jul 7, 1932.
   - **Flying Bats,** Finley, 1929.
10. **Flying Bats,** Laura Wheeler, *Cincinnati Enquirer,* Jul 28, 1933. Also known as:
    - **Open Windows,** Nancy Cabot, *Chicago Tribune,* Jun 5, 1937.
11. **Over the Sahara,** Nancy Page, *Birmingham News,* Mar 30, 1943.
12. **Pinwheel,** Laura Wheeler, *Sioux City Journal,* Nov 26, 1938.

1 Adelaide Tile, Jinny Beyer, Jinny Beyer Studio design, 2006.

2 Whirligig, *Book of Quilts, The Farmer's Wife,* 1931. See 217-5. Also known as:
- **Whirligig Quilt,** Home Art Studios, *World Herald,* Sep 25, 1933.

3 Geode, Jinny Beyer, Hilton Head Seminar design, 1996.

4 Four Patch Beauty, Alice Brooks, unidentified newspaper clipping, date unknown.

5 Whirligig I, Marcia Aasmundstad, Beyer, Jinny, *The Quilter's Album...,*1980.

6 Whirligig II, Marcia Aasmundstad, Beyer, Jinny, *The Quilter's Album...,*1980

7 Dewey's Victory, Clara Stone, *Practical Needlework,* ca. 1906. Also known as:
- **Martha Washington,** *Kansas City Star,* Apr 29, 1936.
- **Martha Washington Star,** *Farmer's Wife,* 1926.
- **Octagonal Star,** *Old Fashioned Quilts,* ca. 1931.

8 Diamond Knot, Nancy Cabot, *Chicago Tribune,* Oct 21, 1935.

9 Summer Breezes, Nancy Page, *Birmingham News,* May 14, 1940.

10 Willy Nilly, Nancy Page, unidentified newspaper clipping, date unknown.

11 Chinese Coin, *Prize Winning Designs,* ca. 1931.

12 Friendly Hand, *Comfort,* ca. 1920, per Brackman. Also known as:
- **Chinese Coin,** date unknown, per Brackman.
- **Crosses and Losses,** date unknown, per Brackman.
- **Indiana Puzzle,** *Kansas City Star,* Feb 8, 1930.
- **Milky Way,** Nancy Cabot, *Chicago Tribune,* Jun 20, 1934.
- **Monkey Wrench,** *Mrs. Danner's Quilts, Books 1 & 2,* 1934.
- **Old Fashioned Indian Puzzle,** *Kansas City Star,* Apr 1, 1959.

1 8 x 8 grid

2 8 x 8 grid

3 8 x 8 grid

4 8 x 8 grid

5 8 x 8 grid

6 8 x 8 grid

7 8 x 8 grid

8 8 x 8 grid

9 8 x 8 grid

10 8 x 8 grid

11 8 x 8 grid

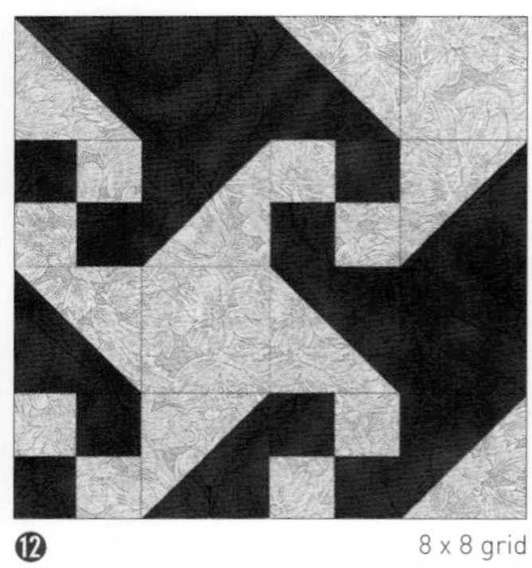
12 8 x 8 grid

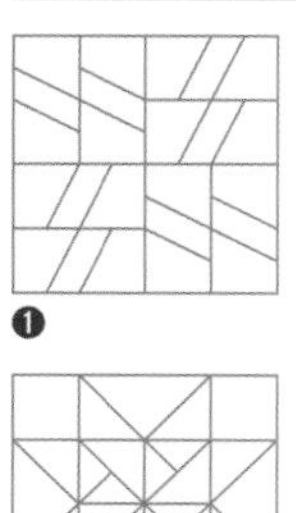
1 7

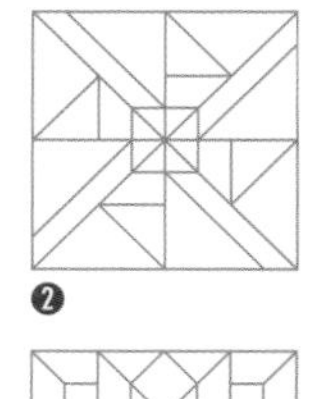
2

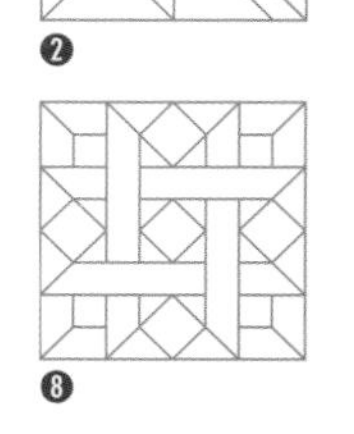
8

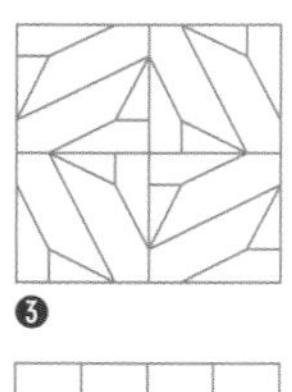
3

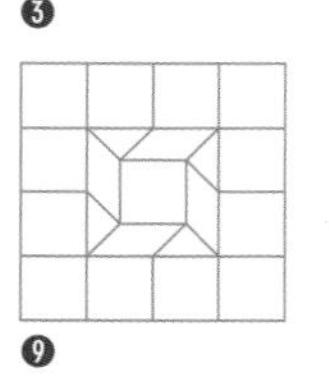
9

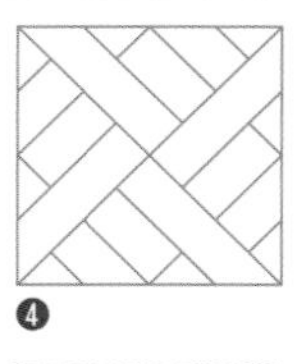
4

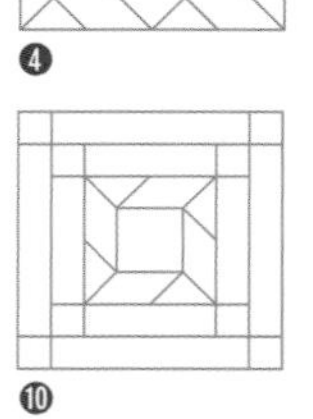
10

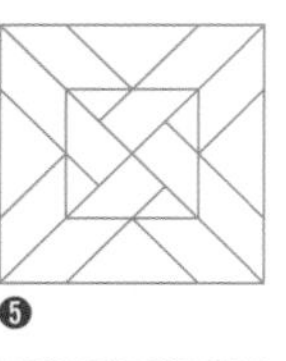
5

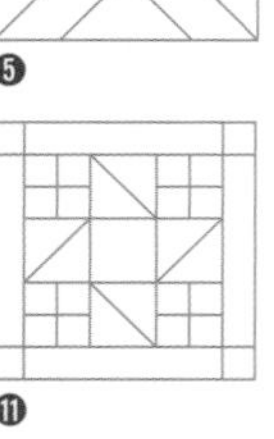
11

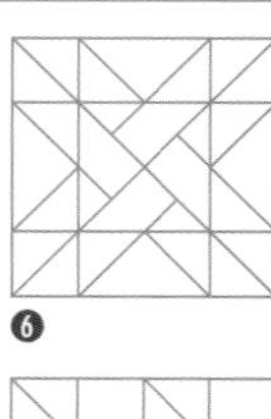
6

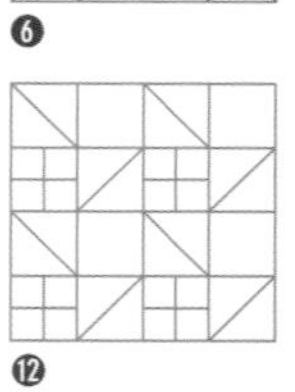
12

❶ Kaleidoscope, Nancy Page, *Birmingham News,* Nov 26, 1935.

❷ Spinning Jenny, Nancy Cabot, *Chicago Tribune,* Oct 12, 1936.

❸ Wind Blades, Jinny Beyer, Hilton Head Seminar design, 1996.

❹ Springfield Patch, *Ladies Art Company,* 1922. Also known as:

Monterey, Nancy Page, *Birmingham News,* Mar 1, 1938.

"Any one who has ever taken the drive along the Pacific Coast near Monterey remembers so happily and vividly the windblown cypress trees. I don't know but that the memory of the trees gave me the inspiration for this design. I can see the trees bent low by the wind as I look at this pattern." Nancy Page, *Birmingham News,* Mar 1, 1938

❺ Flower of the Morning, Alice Brooks, *Detroit Free Press,* Jan 19, 1934.

❻ Whirligig, Nancy Cabot, *Chicago Tribune,* Oct 29, 1936.

❼ Double Windmill, Nancy Cabot, *Chicago Tribune,* Oct 26, 1936.

"'Double Windmill' is one of those old Pennsylvania Dutch patterns which enjoyed popularity not only among the early settlers, but among present day quilt makers. It first was pieced in Philadelphia, as early as 1800, in two shades of blue, white, and red." Nancy Cabot, *Chicago Tribune,* Oct 26, 1936

❽ Spinning Hour Glass, Nancy Cabot, *Chicago Tribune,* Nov 5, 1936.

❾ Double Aster, Nancy Cabot, *Chicago Tribune,* Nov 12, 1936.

❿ Peony and Forget Me Nots, Nancy Cabot, *Chicago Tribune,* Nov 19, 1936.

⓫ Whirling Legs, ca. 1938, per Havig.

⓬ Autumn Stars, Nancy Cabot, *Chicago Tribune,* Nov 19, 1937.

❶ **Indian Maze,** Nancy Cabot, date unknown; published in *Quilter's Newsletter Magazine,* Sep 1986.

❷ **Lattice Work,** Jinny Beyer, Beyer, *Patchwork Portfolio,* 1989.

❸ **The Meteor,** *Prize Winning Designs,* ca. 1931.

❹ **Duck Tracks,** Nancy Page, *Birmingham News,* Dec 3, 1935.

❺ **Tiara,** Jinny Beyer, Jinny Beyer Studio design, 2008.

❻ **Copper Beech,** Jinny Beyer, Quilter's Quest design, 2004.

❼ **Pine Tree Quilt,** *Indianapolis Star,* Jan 20, 1937. Also known as:
Tulip Poplar, Jinny Beyer, Quilter's Quest Design, 2004.

❽ **Magnolia Bud,** Eveline Foland, *Kansas City Star,* Mar 26, 1932. See 116-7, 225-8, and 228-5. Also known as:
The Magnolia Bud, *Kansas City Star,* May 4, 1949.

❾ **Red, White and Blue,** *Farm Journal and Farmer's Wife* (Silver Anniversary issue), 1945.

❿ **Pansy,** McKim, 1931. Also known as:
Modernistic Pansy, Hall, 1935.

⓫ **Geese in Flight,** Nancy Cabot, *Chicago Tribune,* Apr 15, 1936.

⓬ **Star and Diamond,** Nancy Page, *Nashville Banner,* Aug 8, 1933.

❶ **Puss in the Corner,** Nancy Cabot, *Chicago Tribune,* Jul 28, 1938.

❷ **Rocky Mountain Puzzle,** Nancy Cabot, *Chicago Tribune,* Jun 22, 1936.

❸ **Blacks and Whites,** Nancy Cabot, *Chicago Tribune,* Nov 4, 1936.

❹ **Odds and Ends,** Nancy Cabot, *Chicago Tribune,* Mar 19, 1935.

❺ **Signature Quilt,** *Kansas City Star,* Feb 10, 1954.
"Everything to be desired for a friendship signature quilt is included in this pattern. There is a long white strip for the name, there are print blocks and 1-tone pieces, with the choice of color left to the needle crafter. The block was designed by Mrs. Clyde Offutt, Sleeper, Mo." *Kansas City Star,* Feb 10, 1954

❻ **The Signature Friendship Quilt,** *Kansas City Star,* Jun 17, 1953.
"Whether you like a name quilt for its sentimentality, or are in a money-making state of mind in behalf of a club, here is a design offering space for nine signatures in each square. Mrs. Ed Draper, Orlando, Ok., creator of the design, prefers the same color for all the 1-tone pieces." *Kansas City Star,* Jun 17, 1953

❼ **Primrose Path,** Finley, 1929. Also known as:
- **Bismark,** Nancy Cabot, *Chicago Tribune,* Mar 29, 1938.

❽ **The Xquisite,** *Ladies Art Company,* 1897. Also known as:
- **Xquisite,** Hall, 1935.

❾ **Railroad,** Nancy Cabot, *Chicago Tribune,* Apr 11, 1934.

"A young southern belle in 1860 selected for her first attempt at needlework the well known square and triangle patches and pieced them in an arrangement suggesting a railroad track. And thus this block, 'Railroad,' originated. Nancy Cabot, *Chicago Tribune,* Apr 11, 1934

❿ **The Exquisite,** Nancy Cabot, *Chicago Tribune,* Jun 21, 1934.

⓫ **Indian Plumes,** Hinson, 1973.

⓬ **Barrister's Block,** *Ladies Art Company,* 1897. Also known as:
- **Lawyer's Puzzle,** Finley, 1929.
- **The Saw,** date unknown, per Brackman.

❶ **New Barrister's Block,** Nancy Cabot, *Chicago Tribune,* Jan 24, 1938.

❷ **Wandering Lover,** *Hearth and Home,* 1895, per Smith.

❸ **Road to Oklahoma,** Alice Brooks, *Detroit Free Press,* Dec 16, 1933. "It's funny, but quilts have the habit of getting named one thing in New England, another thing in Dixie, and something entirely different out West! Here's the Road to Oklahoma—it's probably called the Road to Something Else, somewhere else. But no matter what its name, it's a lovely scrap quilt and gives you the chance to dip into the scrap bag—pull out the scraps higgledy-piggledy and sew them in. Of course you can make it in just four materials if you like, but however you do it, it's effective." Alice Brooks, *Detroit Free Press,* Dec 16, 1933

❹ **Upstairs and Down,** Nancy Cabot, *Chicago Tribune,* Oct 12, 1935.

❺ **Free Trade Block,** Finley, 1929. Also known as:
- **Coronation,** Nancy Page, *Birmingham News,* Mar 2, 1937.
- **Free Trade Patch,** Hall, 1935.

❻ **Dove in the Window,** Finley, 1929.

❼ **Starry Path,** *Farm Journal and Farmer's Wife,* ca. 1941.

❽ **Unknown,** *Dakota Farmer,* Feb 16, 1926.

❾ **Spool and Bobbin,** Nancy Cabot, *Chicago Tribune,* May 15, 1936.

❿ **New Four Patch,** *Farm & Fireside,* 1884. Also known as:
- **Chicago World's Fair,** source unknown, date unknown.
- **Going to Chicago,** Nancy Page, *Detroit Free Press,* July 4, 1933.
- **Jacob's Ladder,** Finley, 1929.
- **Railroad,** *Farm Journal Quilt Patterns,* ca. 1935.
- **Railroad Block,** Nancy Cabot, *Chicago Tribune,* July 10, 1936.
- **State House,** Nancy Cabot, *Chicago Tribune,* Jun 22, 1937.
- **World's Fair,** Nancy Cabot, *Chicago Tribune,* May 7, 1938.
- **World's Fair Block,** *Ladies Art Company,* 1897.

⓫ **Sunny Lanes,** Nancy Page, *Birmingham News,* Jun 4, 1935.

⓬ **Hither and Yon,** *Farm Journal and Farmer's Wife,* ca. 1941.

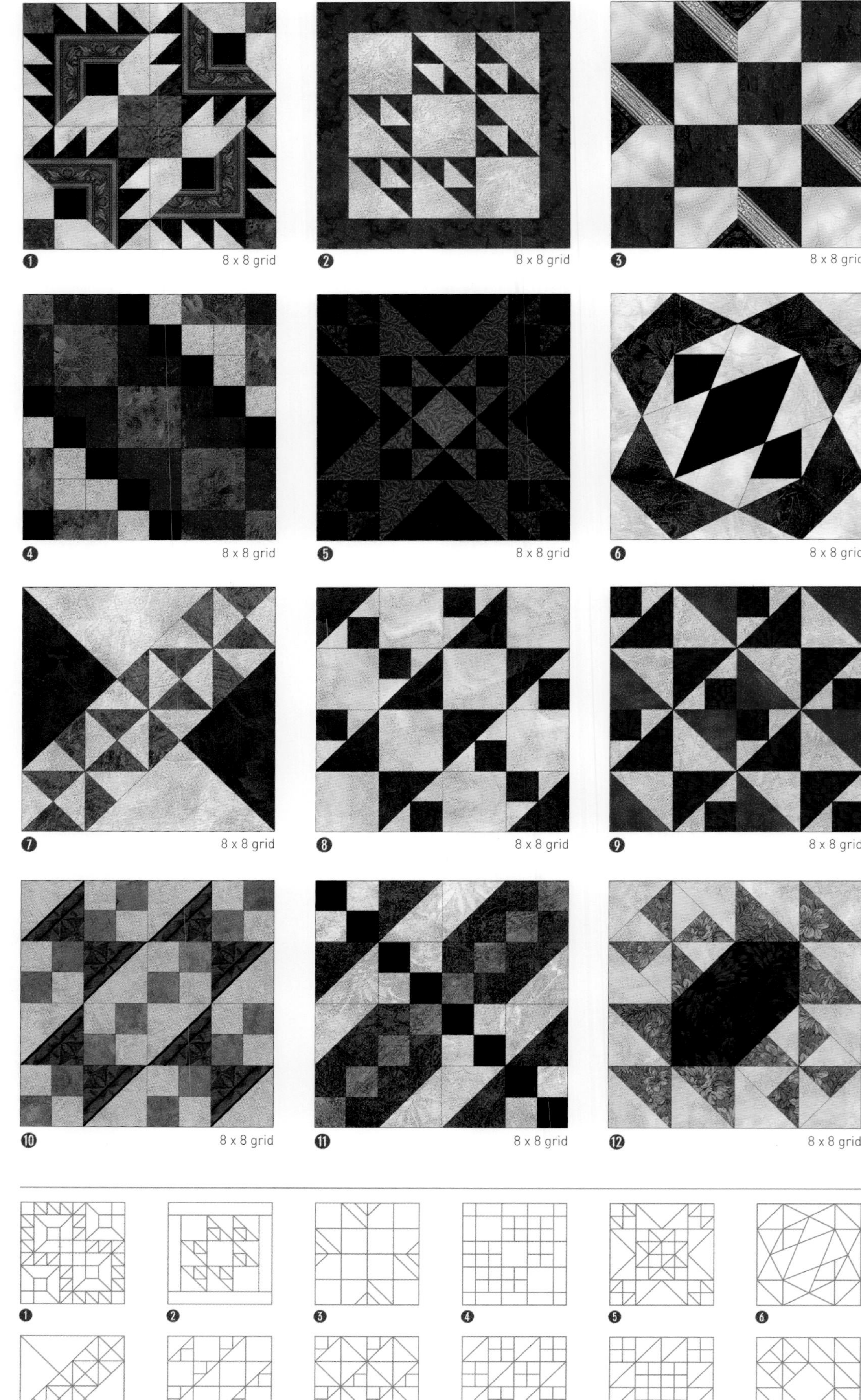

❶ **The Swallow,** Finley, 1929. Also known as:

- **Swallow,** Nancy Cabot, *Chicago Tribune,* May 16, 1933.

❷ **The Swallow,** Nancy Page, *Birmingham News,* Aug 31, 1937.

❸ **Garden Basket,** *Progressive Farmer,* 1892. Also known as:

- **Some Pretty Patchwork,** *Ladies Art Company,* 1897.

❹ **Potted Roses,** Nancy Cabot, *Chicago Tribune,* Oct 31, 1936.

❺ **Crazy Quilt Bouquet,** Nancy Cabot, *Chicago Tribune,* Oct 24, 1933.

❻ **Ships at Sea,** *Farmer's Advocate,* Mar 20, 1930. See 72-8.

❼ **Ships at Sea,** Nancy Cabot, *Chicago Tribune,* Aug 9, 1936. See 72-8.

❽ **Ships at Sea,** Nancy Cabot, *Chicago Tribune,* Mar 16, 1934. See 72-8.
"This nautical block has a salty tang that designates a point of origin on our eastern seaboard. As a matter of fact, the state of Maine may proudly claim the credit of creation." Nancy Cabot, *Chicago Tribune,* Mar 16, 1934

❾ **Ships a' Sea,** *Country Gentleman,* Mar 20, 1930.
"The ships are sailing a choppy sea—a new interpretation of the old-time design." *Country Gentleman,"* Jul 1930

❿ **Rocky Glen,** Nancy Cabot, *Chicago Tribune,* May 27, 1933.

⓫ **Rocky Glen,** Finley, 1929. Also known as:

- **Indian Meadow,** Hall, 1935.
- **Lend and Borrow,** Hall, 1935.
- **Little Saw Tooth,** Hall, 1935.
- **The Lost Ship,** Finley, 1929.
- **Lost Ship,** Hall, 1935.

⓬ **Flamingos in Flight,** Nancy Cabot, *Chicago Tribune,* Jan 24, 1938.

❶ **Lorna Doone,** *Farm Journal and Farmer's Wife* (Silver Anniversary issue), 1945.

❷ **Sheep Fold Quilt,** Eveline Foland, *Kansas City Star,* Jan 31, 1931. Also known as:
 Sheep Fold, Hall, 1935.

❸ **Steps to Glory,** Nancy Cabot, *Chicago Tribune,* May 1, 1937.

❹ **Four Squares,** Nancy Cabot, *Chicago Tribune,* Apr 23, 1936.

❺ **World's Fair Puzzle,** *Ladies Art Company,* 1897. Also known as:
 Lightning, Nancy Cabot, *Chicago Tribune,* Oct 3, 1934.

❻ **Round the Twist,** James, 1978.

❼ **Blazed Trail,** Nancy Cabot, *Chicago Tribune,* Jul 23, 1937.

❽ **Snail's Trail,** Nancy Cabot, *Chicago Tribune,* Mar 11, 1934. See 93-7 and 93-11.

❾ **Palm Leaf,** *Ladies Art Company,* 1922. Also known as:
 Hosanna, Finley, 1929.
 Hozanna, Hall, 1935.
 Palm, Laura Wheeler, *Indianapolis Star,* Jun 23, 1933.
 The Palm, Hall, 1935.
 The Palms, *Mountain Mist Blue Book of Quilts,* 1935.

❿ **Zig Zag,** *The Patchwork Book,* 1932.

⓫ **L Stripe,** ca. 1938, per Havig.

⓬ **Crazy Loons,** *Progressive Farmer,* 1922. Also known as:
 Crazy Loon, Nancy Cabot, *Chicago Tribune,* Apr 24, 1937.

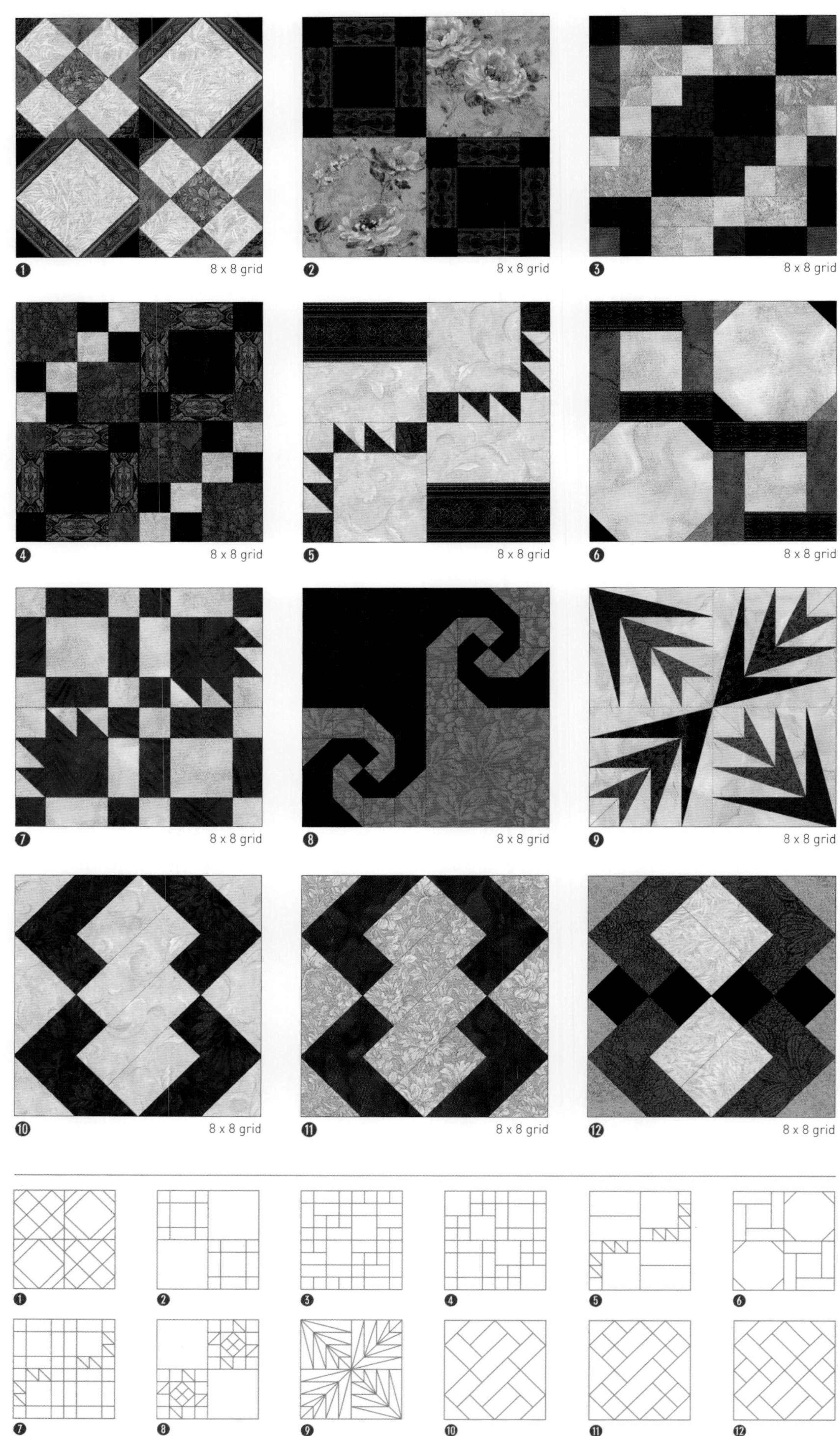

❶ **Rail Fence,** Ruby McKim, *Kansas City Star,* Jun 28, 1930.

❷ **Chinese Puzzle,** Nancy Page, *Birmingham News,* Oct 31, 1939.

❸ **A Block of Many Triangles,** *Kansas City Star,* Oct 3, 1951.

❹ **Chinese Puzzle,** *Grandmother Clark's Authentic Early American Quilts,* 1932.

❺ **Chain and Bar,** Clara Stone, *Practical Needlework,* ca. 1906

❻ **Tulip Lady Finger,** *Ladies Art Company,* 1897. See 226-1.

❼ **Ah' Teen,** ca. 1938, per Havig.

❽ **Navajo,** *Ladies Art Company,* 1928. Also known as:

Indian Mats, Nancy Cabot, *Chicago Tribune,* Oct 22, 1936.

❾ **Navajo,** Nancy Cabot, *Chicago Tribune,* Aug 30, 1934.

❿ **Memory's Chain,** *Farm Journal and Farmer's Wife,* ca. 1941

⓫ **Home Treasure,** *Ladies Art Company,* 1897.

⓬ **Hither and Yon,** Nancy Cabot, *Chicago Tribune,* Sep 10, 1936.

1 Diamonds and Shadow, Nancy Cabot, *Chicago Tribune,* Dec 22, 1933. Also known as:

Shaded Diamonds, Nancy Cabot, *Chicago Tribune,* Oct 27, 1937.

2 Red Peony Buds, Nancy Cabot, *Chicago Tribune,* Jun 15, 1936.
"For the quilt maker who dotes on intricate designs and difficult patterns, 'Red Peony Buds' affords grist for her mill . . . It is one of the most effective of the many all-over patterns because, when the quilt is completed there is a beautiful series of soft, red peonies rambling over the entire coverlet. *Chicago Tribune,* Jun 15, 1936

3 Improved Four Patch, date unknown, per Holstein.

4 Hawks in Flight, Nancy Cabot, *Chicago Tribune,* Dec 3, 1935.

5 Ozark Mountains, Nancy Cabot, *Chicago Tribune,* Jan 9, 1936.

6 Flying Geese, Nancy Cabot, *Chicago Tribune,* Nov 29, 1935.

7 Don Quixote's Mills, Nancy Cabot, *Chicago Tribune,* Jun 5, 1936.

8 Sailboat Quilt, Nancy Page, *Birmingham News,* Jul 7, 1934.

9 Basket of Diamonds, *Kansas City Star,* Aug 28, 1937.

10 The Chieftain, Nancy Cabot, *Chicago Tribune,* Oct 17, 1936.

11 Sea Pine, Jinny Beyer, Hilton Head Seminar design 1981; published in Beyer, Jinny, *Patchwork Portfolio.*

12 Cubist Rose, Nancy Cabot, *Chicago Tribune,* Oct 20, 1933.
"We have gone modernistic in art and everything else, so it was inevitable that quilt-dom go modern too." Nancy Cabot, *Chicago Tribune,* Oct 20, 1933

1. **Navajo,** *Detroit Free Press,* Book No. 6, May 26, 1933.
2. **Monastery Windows,** Nancy Cabot, *Chicago Tribune,* May 27, 1936.
3. **Century of Progress,** Nancy Cabot, *Chicago Tribune,* Jul 21, 1934.
   "'Century of Progress' is an unusual pieced block which, when combined with plain blocks, creates an illusion of the gorgeous panorama of the World's Fair. The Exposition colors have been successfully captured in cloth in the blue, green, chartreuse yellow, and rich mulberry shades. *Chicago Tribune,* Jul 21, 1934
4. **Interlaced Block,** Nancy Cabot, *Chicago Tribune,* Jun 11, 1934.
5. **Log Cabin,** date unknown, per Holstein.
6. **Straight Furrow,** Nancy Cabot, *Chicago Tribune,* Mar 30, 1934.
7. **Log Cabin,** Nancy Cabot, *Chicago Tribune,* Nov 17, 1934. Also known as:
   White House Steps, Hall, 1935.
8. **Bow Tie Quilt,** *Blue Ribbon Patterns, Vol. 2,* 1970.
9. **The Range's Pride,** *Farm Journal and Farmer's Wife* (Silver Anniversary issue), 1945.
10. **Farm Friendliness,** *Farm Journal and Farmer's Wife* (Silver Anniversary issue), 1945.
11. **Market Square,** Nancy Cabot, *Chicago Tribune,* Mar 14, 1936.
    "'Market Square' is named for the old market squares in the early colonial towns. Massachusetts is the state in which this quilt first was pieced in 1853. The original quilt was composed entirely of pieced blocks set together with half the blocks in reverse color and forming large Geneva crosses separating the market squares. White, red, and red and white print form one of the favorite combinations for this charmingly old fashioned quilt pattern." Nancy Cabot, *Chicago Tribune,* Mar 14, 1936
12. **Lone Star,** Alice Brooks, *Detroit Free Press,* Apr 7, 1934.

❶ **Yankee Charm,** Nancy Cabot, *Chicago Tribune,* Jul 29, 1933.

❷ **Aeroplane,** *The Patchwork Book,* 1932. See 184-2.

❸ **Twin Darts,** *Farm Journal and Farmer's Wife* (Silver Anniversary issue), 1945.

❹ **The Crow's Nest,** Eveline Foland, *Kansas City Star,* May 21, 1932.

❺ **Cross Within Cross,** *Ladies Art Company,* 1897. See 168-2, 212-11, and 184-3

❻ **4 Points,** ca. 1938, per Havig..

❼ **The Pride of Ohio,** *Kansas City Star,* Jun 28, 1939.

❽ **Philadelphia Pavement,** Alice Brooks, *Detroit Free Press,* Mar 23, 1934. Also known as:

> **Flying Geese,** Alice Brooks, unidentified newspaper clipping, date unknown.

❾ **Jack in the Pulpit,** *Kansas City Star,* Aug 26, 1933. See 94-8, 94-9, 96-5, 112-9, 167-10, 167-11, 167-12, and 217-10.

❿ **Aunt Anna's Album Block,** Clara Stone, *Practical Needlework,* ca. 1906.

⓫ **Subway Turnstile,** Nancy Page, *Birmingham News,* Nov 16, 1943.
"If your great-grandmother had been making this quilt she would have called it just plain 'Turnstile.' But today's quilt maker has little knowledge of the turnstiles which used to be put up at the entrance to roads or adjoining lots. The turnstiles which we know are found in subways. Whereas it used to cost nothing but physical energy to get over or through the turnstile, now it costs money. Times do change, as we all know." Nancy Page, *Birmingham News,* Nov 16, 1943

⓬ **Tiptop,** *Farm Journal and Farmer's Wife* (Silver Anniversary issue), 1945.

❶ ❷ ❸ ❹ ❺ ❻

❼ ❽ ❾ ❿ ⓫ ⓬

1 16 x 16 grid

2 16 x 16 grid

3 16 x 16 grid

4 16 x 16 grid

5 16 x 16 grid

6 16 x 16 grid

7 16 x 16 grid

8 16 x 16 grid

9 16 x 16 grid

10 16 x 16 grid

11 16 x 16 grid

12 16 x 16 grid

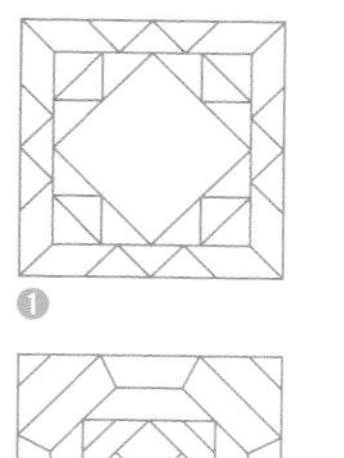

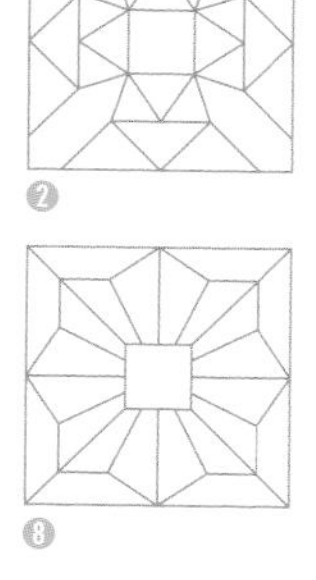

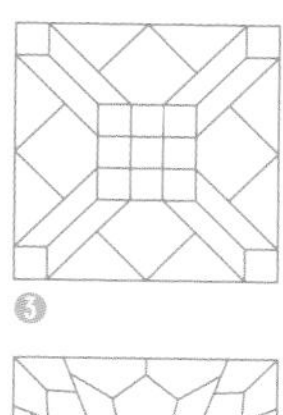

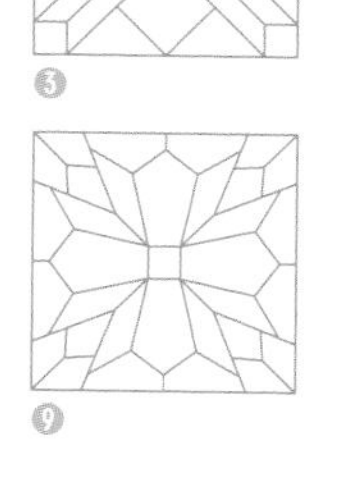

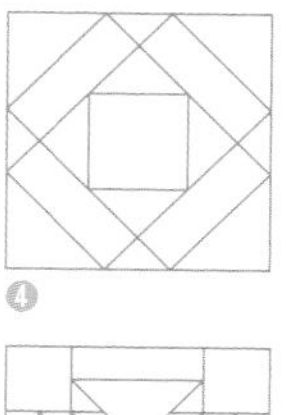

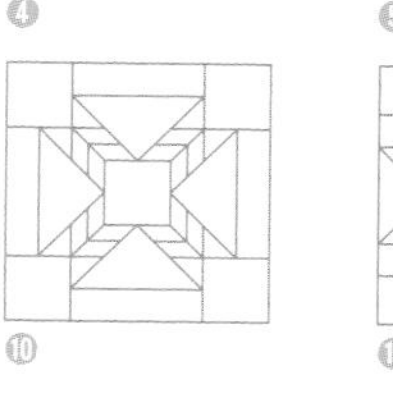

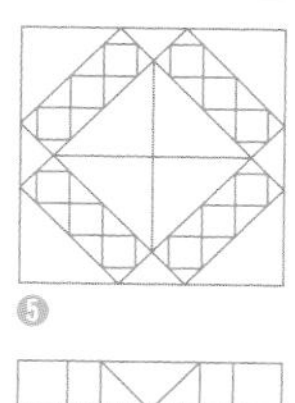

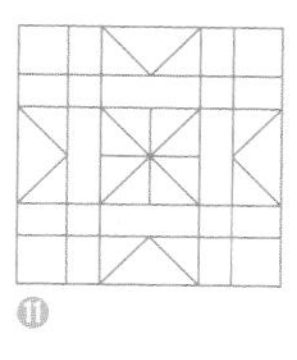

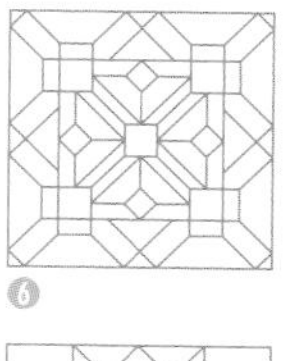

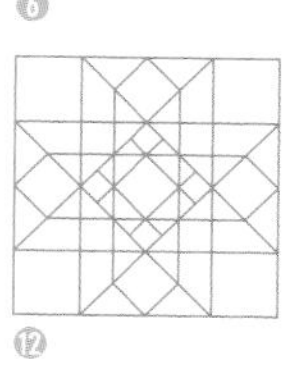

1 **An Odd Quilt Pattern,** *Farm and Home,* Mar 1, 1899.

2 **Annapolis Patch,** *Ladies Art Company,* 1922.

3 **Flowering Nine Patch,** *Kansas City Star,* May 19, 1934.

4 **Boy's Nonsense,** Nancy Cabot, *Chicago Tribune,* July 25, 1936. See 126-1.

5 **Blue Fields,** Nancy Cabot, *Chicago Tribune,* Oct 27, 1936.
"From Kentucky comes the interesting pieced pattern, 'Blue Fields.' Its inspiration is derived from the beautiful fields of blue grass." Nancy Cabot, *Chicago Tribune,* Oct 27, 1936

6 **Sky Rocket,** Virginia Snow, *Grandma Dexter New Appliqué and Patchwork Designs book 36b,* ca. 1932.

7 **Conventional Rose,** *Farm Journal and Farmer's Wife* (Silver Anniversary issue), 1945. See 203-2.

8 **Sunbeam,** Nancy Cabot, *Chicago Tribune,* Jul 31, 1933. See 300-3 and 300-4.

9 **Tiger Lily,** Laura Wheeler, *Cincinnati Enquirer,* Mar 4, 1934.

10 **The Air Port** *Kansas City Star,* Jul 11, 1936.
"Planes gliding to their destination inspired 14-year old Muriel Clift, Mammouth Springs, Ark., to design this block." Kansas City Star, Nov 11, 1936

11 **Starry Lane,** Hall, 1935.

12 **Seattle Sights,** Alice Newton, Beyer, *The Quilter's Album...,* 1980.

❶ **The Village Green,** *Country Gentleman,* Sep 1930.

❷ **The Army Star,** *Kansas City Star,* May 26, 1943.
"In appreciation of the many thoughtful deeds of American women for soldiers, two young men in an army training camp have sent The Weekly Star this pattern of their own origination. They are Eugene Aubuchan and Earl J. Faxton." *Kansas City Star,* May 26, 1943

❸ **Four Mills,** Nancy Cabot, *Chicago Tribune,* Jun 26, 1937.

❹ **Storm at Sea,** *Ladies Art Company,* 1897. See 98-11 and 171-11. Also known as:
Rolling Stone, Finley, 1929.

❺ **The V Block,** *Ladies Art Company,* 1922.

❻ **Gay Pinwheel,** Laura Wheeler, unidentified newspaper clipping, date unknown.

❼ **Spider Web,** Finley, 1929.

❽ **Arrow Head,** Virginia Snow, *Grandma Dexter New Appliqué and Patchwork Designs, Book 36b,* ca. 1932. See 162-2 and 328-2. Also known as:
Arrowheads, Nancy Cabot, *Chicago Tribune,* Mar 1, 1933.

❾ **Buckeye Beauty,** Nancy Cabot, *Chicago Tribune,* Dec 27, 1933. See 216-11. Also known as:
Rockingham Beauty, Nancy Cabot, *Chicago Tribune,* Dec 27, 1933.
Rockingham's Beauty, Nancy Cabot, *Chicago Tribune,* Sep 14, 1934.
"This attractive 'Buckeye Beauty' is an effective quilt design. It is also called the 'Rockingham Beauty,' but the title of 'Buckeye Beauty' is older, and, since the pattern is a native of Ohio, quilt historians quite naturally credit the latter name with being the original." Nancy Cabot, *Chicago Tribune,"* Dec 27, 1933

❿ **Prudence's Star,** Laura Wheeler, *Indianapolis Star,* Dec 16, 1937.
"At last you've found a use for all those bits of print you've hated to throw away! The gayer and more varied they are, the more striking this quilt, 'Prudence's Star,' will be." Laura Wheeler, *Indianapolis Star,* Dec 16, 1937

⓫ **Blazing Star,** Laura Wheeler, *Illinois State Register,* Jun 13, 1933.
"The star, as a decorative motif has probably lent itself to more quilt patterns than any other single motif. The Blazing Star is a popular old pattern. In this, the star has been developed quite differently than in the usual star pattern. A plastic effect is achieved by making the points of the star of two materials." Laura Wheeler, *Illinois State Register,* Jun 13, 1933

⓬ **Shooting Stars,** Jinny Beyer, Jinny Beyer Studio design, 2007.

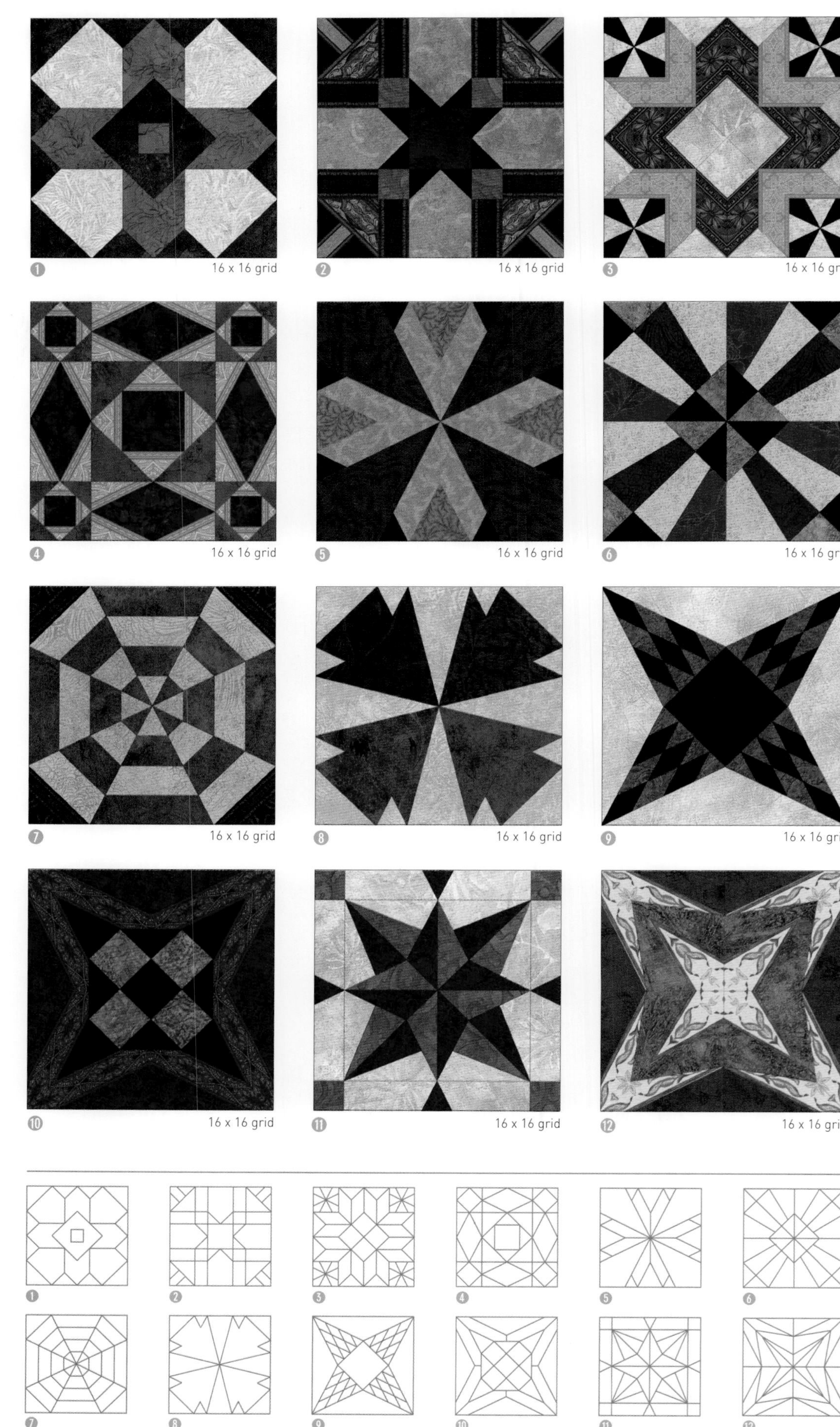

1 16 x 16 grid

2 16 x 16 grid

3 16 x 16 grid

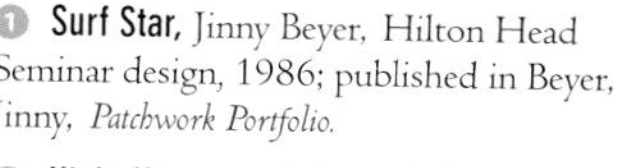

1 **Surf Star,** Jinny Beyer, Hilton Head Seminar design, 1986; published in Beyer, Jinny, *Patchwork Portfolio.*

2 **Night Heavens,** Nancy Cabot, *Chicago Tribune,* Mar 27, 1936.

3 **Century of Progress,** Virginia Snow, *Grandma Dexter Appliqué and Patchwork Designs, Book 36a,* ca. 1932.

4 **Beveled Glass,** Jinny Beyer, Beyer, Jinny, *Patchwork Portfolio,* 1989.

5 **Squares of Diamonds,** *Kansas City Star,* Jan 25, 1961.

6 **MacKenzie's Square,** Nancy Cabot, *Chicago Tribune,* Apr 7, 1936.

7 **Old Spanish Tile,** *Kansas City Star,* Jan 7, 1933.

8 **Quilt of 1000 Prints,** Aunt Martha series: *The Quilt Fair Comes to You,* ca. 1933. Also known as:

- **Paisley Shawl,** Nancy Page, *Lowell Sun,* Aug 6, 1934.
- **Postage Stamp,** Nancy Page, *Lowell Sun,* Aug 6, 1934.
- **Scrapbag,** Nancy Page, *Birmingham News,* Apr 31, 1934.
- **Steps to the White House,** Nancy Page, *Birmingham News,* Apr 31, 1934.

9 **Aunt Lucinda's Double Irish Chain,** Clara Stone, *Practical Needlework,* ca. 1906.

10 **Crib Quilt,** *Ladies Art Company,* 1901.

11 **Railroad Crossing,** *Ladies Art Company,* 1897.

12 **Twelve Crosses,** Nancy Cabot, *Chicago Tribune,* Aug 16, 1936.

13 **California Star,** Ickis, 1949.

4 16 x 16 grid

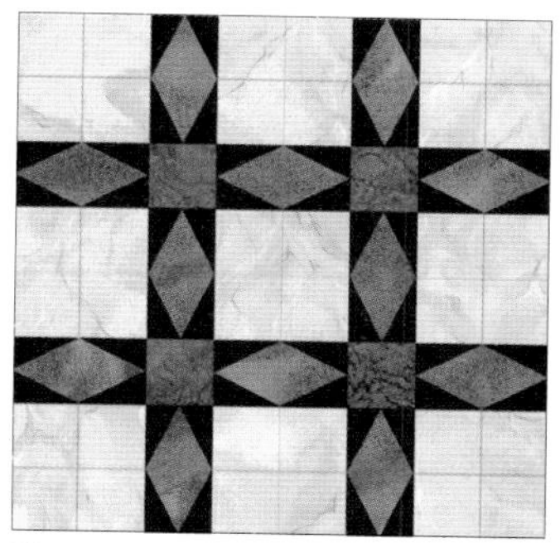

5 16 x 16 grid

6 16 x 16 grid

7 16 x 16 grid

8 16 x 16 grid

9 16 x 16 grid

10 16 x 16 grid

11 16 x 16 grid

12 16 x 16 grid

13 16 x 16 grid

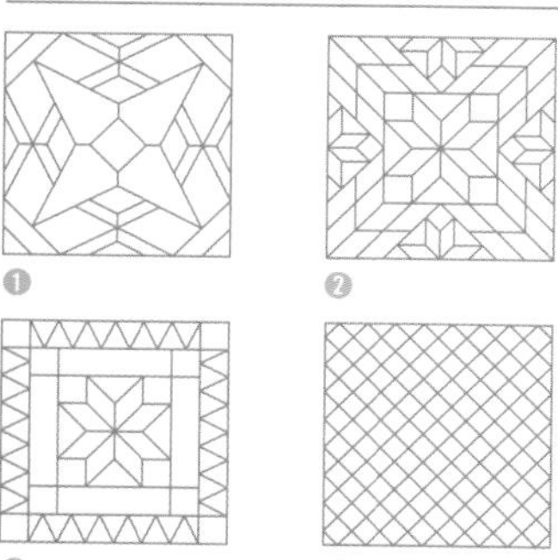
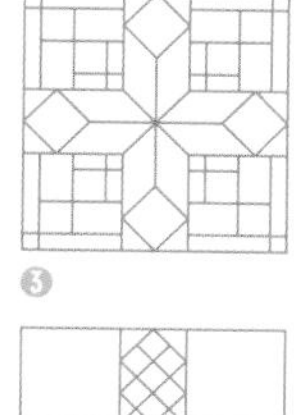
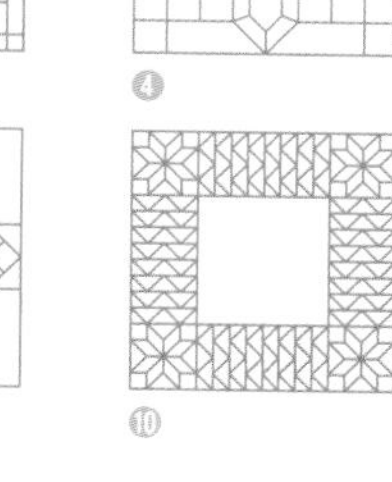
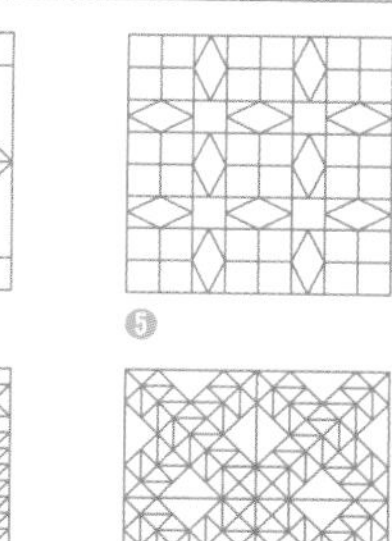
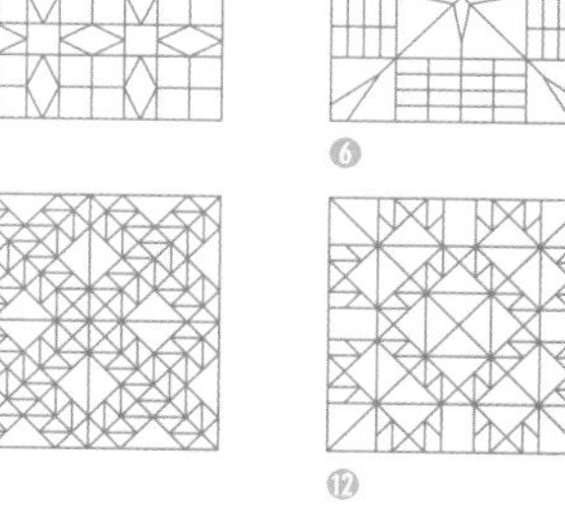
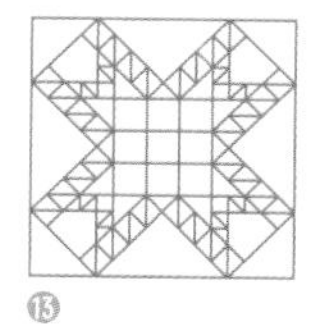

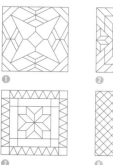

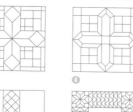

1 2 3 4 5 6

7 8 9 10 11 12 13

1 **Odd Fellow's Cross,** Finley, 1929. Also known as:

Ozark Trail, *Kansas City Star,* Nov 11, 1933.

2 **Wild Goose Chase,** Nancy Cabot, *Chicago Tribune,* May 21, 1933.

3 **Four Buds,** Nancy Cabot, *Chicago Tribune,* Oct 22, 1937.

4 **Chinese Square,** *Farm Journal and Farmer's Wife* (Silver Anniversary issue), 1945.

5 **Lehigh Maze,** Nancy Cabot, *Chicago Tribune,* Jun 7, 1937.

6 **Columbia Puzzle,** *Ladies Art Company,* 1897.

7 **Magnolia Bud,** Nancy Cabot, *Chicago Tribune,* Feb 19, 1934. See 104-8, 225-5, and 228-8.

8 **Sue's Delight,** *Farm Journal and Farmer's Wife,* 1941.

9 **Spirals,** Nancy Cabot, *Chicago Tribune,* Nov 21, 1936.

10 **Honeycomb,** *Ladies Art Company,* 1897.

11 **Riptide,** Jinny Beyer, *Hilton Head Seminar design,* 1987; published in Beyer, Jinny, *Patchwork Portfolio.*

12 **Pot of Gold,** Jinny Beyer, Beyer, Jinny, *Patchwork Portfolio,* 1989.

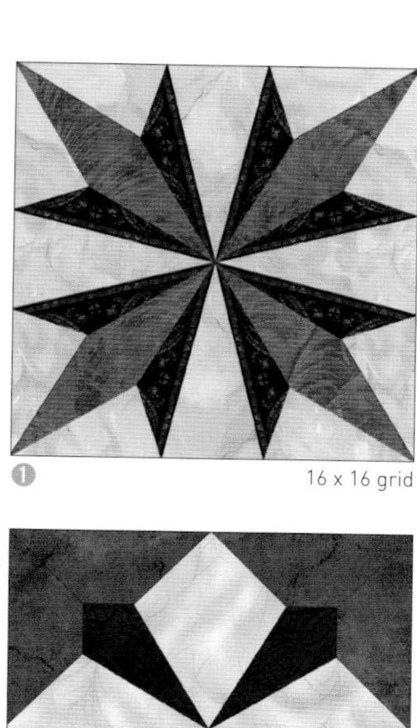

1 16 x 16 grid

2 16 x 16 grid

3 16 x 16 grid

4 16 x 16 grid

5 16 x 16 grid

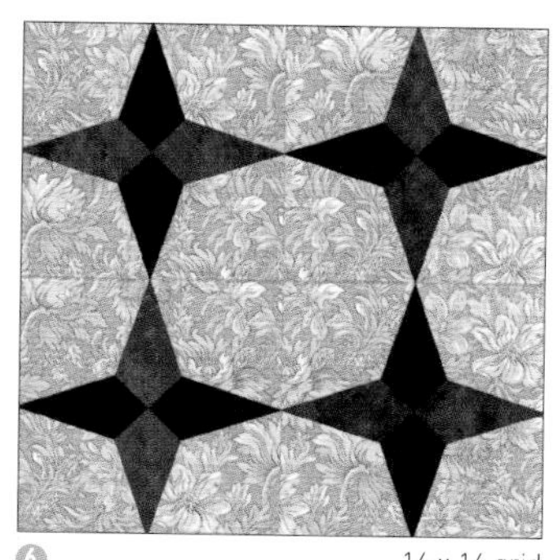

6 16 x 16 grid

7 16 x 16 grid

8 16 x 16 grid

9 16 x 16 grid

10 16 x 16 grid

11 16 x 16 grid

12 16 x 16 grid

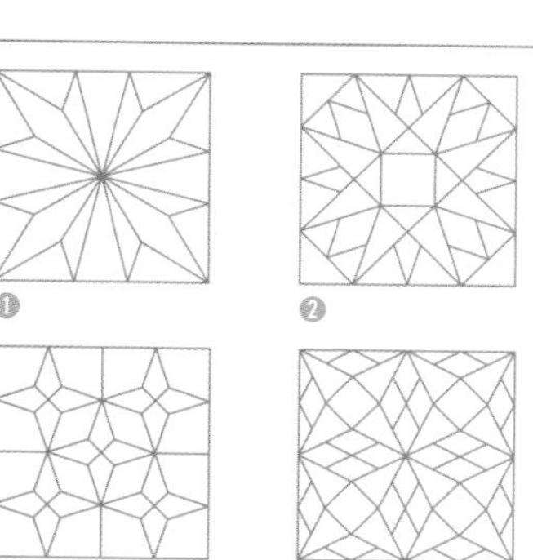

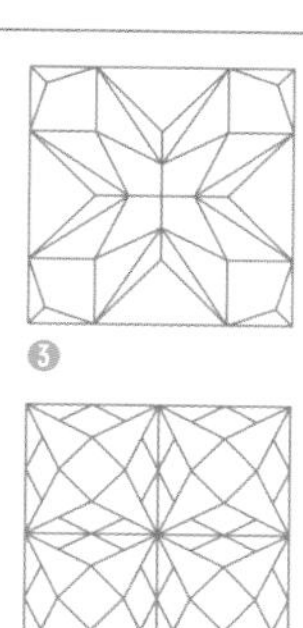

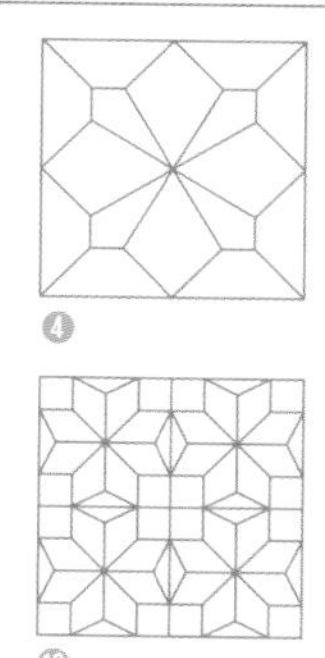

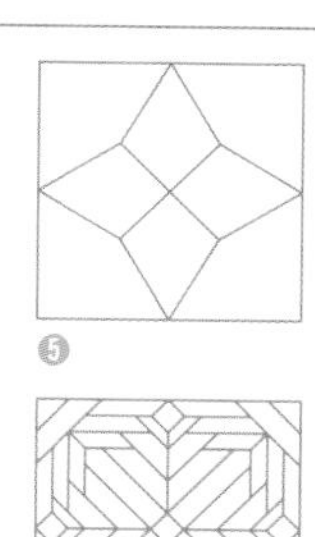

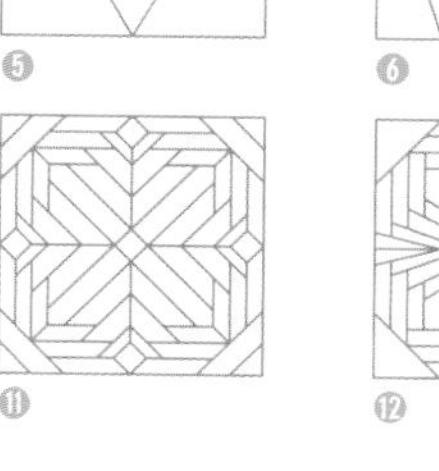

1 2 3 4 5 6

7 8 9 10 11 12

1 **Turnabout,** Alice Brooks, *Washington Post,* Dec 28, 1949.

2 **Eastern Sunrise,** Jinny Beyer, Hilton Head Seminar design, 1982; published in Beyer, Jinny, *Patchwork Portfolio.*

3 **Star Wonder,** Jinny Beyer, Beyer, Jinny, *Patchwork Portfolio,* 1989.

4 **Home Again,** *Farm Journal and Farmer's Wife* (Silver Anniversary issue), 1945.

5 **Arkansas Snow Flake,** *Kansas City Star,* Feb 9, 1935. Also known as:

- **Arkansas Star,** *Kansas City Star,* Feb 9, 1935.
- **Snow Flake,** *Kansas City Star,* Feb 9, 1935.

6 **Four Point,** *Prize Winning Designs,* ca. 1931. See 160-4. Also known as:

- **Job's Troubles,** Hall, 1935.
- **Kite,** Hall, 1935.
- **Snowball,** *Prize Winning Designs,* ca. 1931.

7 **Pontiac Star,** Hall, 1935.

8 **Geometrical Star,** Clara Stone, *Practical Needlework,* ca. 1906.

9 **Geometric Star,** *Prize Winning Designs,* ca. 1931.

10 **Twinkle, Twinkle Little Star,** *Kansas City Star,* May 15, 1935.

11 **Tavern Wall,** Jinny Beyer, published in Beyer, Jinny, *Patchwork Portfolio.*

12 **Bows and Arrows,** Jinny Beyer, Hilton Head Seminar design, 2006. Also known as:

- **Mardi Gras,** Jinny Beyer, RJR Patterns, 2006.

1 **Sea Mark,** Jinny Beyer, Hilton Head Seminar design, 1987; published in Beyer, Jinny, *Patchwork Portfolio.*

2 **Lacy Lattice Work,** *Farm Journal and Farmer's Wife* (Silver Anniversary issue), 1945.

3 **Windmill,** Alice Brooks, unidentified newspaper clipping, date unknown.

4 **Double Square,** Virginia Snow, *Grandma Dexter Appliqué and Patchwork Designs, Book 36a,* ca. 1932.

5 **Ring of Fortune,** Marcia Aasmundstad, Beyer, Jinny, *The Quilter's Album...,* 1980.

6 **Rainbow,** Laura Wheeler, *Sioux City Journal,* May 14, 1940.

7 **Shasta Daisy,** Laura Wheeler, *Sioux City Journal,* Dec 22, 1939.

8 **Colonial Pavement,** Alice Brooks, *Detroit Free Press,* Dec 24, 1935.
"Winter's the time for quilting and how fast the hours fly when one is engrossed in so profitable an occupation. 'Colonial Pavement' takes its inspiration from the rich mosaic pavements of Washington's time. It's an easy quilt to cut and piece, for with most patches the same width, the material can be cut in strips. Straight pieces are always easier to sew, too; with this quilt you start at the center." Alice Brooks, *Detroit Free Press,* Dec 24, 1935

9 **Lucky Knot,** Nancy Cabot, *Chicago Tribune,* Apr 26, 1937.
"'Lucky Knot' is one of the old knot patterns which have held popularity for generations. This is a large block set together with printed and plain materials to bring out the knot effect in the pattern. An entire coverlet composed of 'Lucky Knots' was supposed to be a good luck charm for the recipient if made and given by a close friend." Nancy Cabot, *Chicago Tribune,* Apr 26, 1937

10 **Lindy's Plane,** Nancy Cabot, *Chicago Tribune,* May 10, 1933.

11 **Hope of Hartford,** *Farm Journal and Farmer's Wife* (Silver Anniversary issue), 1945.

12 **Shooting Star,** Alice Brooks, *Detroit Free Press,* Feb 1, 1934.

1 16 x 16 grid

2 16 x 16 grid

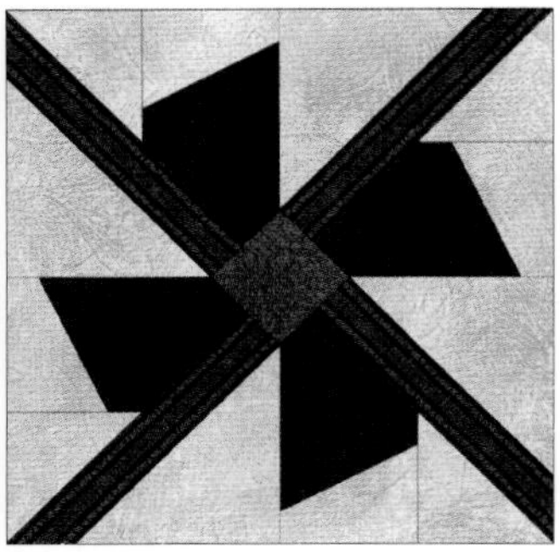

3 16 x 16 grid

4 16 x 16 grid

5 16 x 16 grid

6 16 x 16 grid

7 16 x 16 grid

8 16 x 16 grid

9 16 x 16 grid

10 16 x 16 grid

11 16 x 16 grid

12 16 x 16 grid

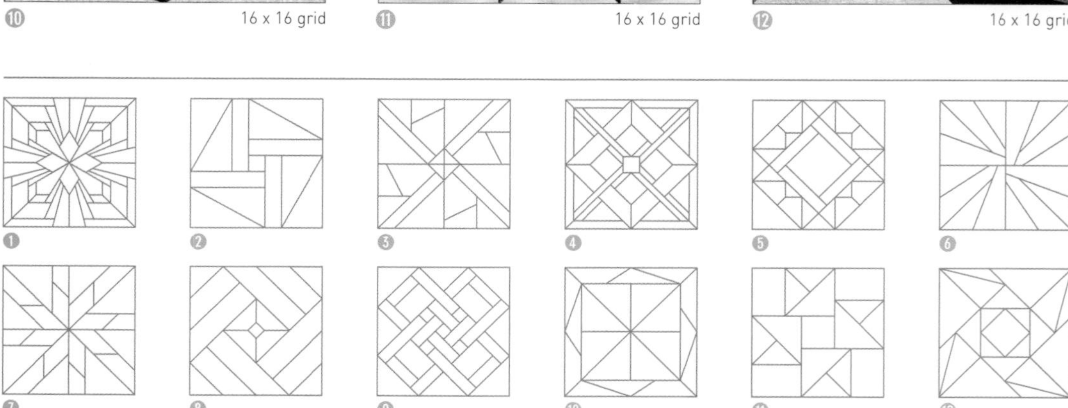

1. **Kansas Beauty,** Clara Stone, *Practical Needlework,* ca. 1906.
2. **T Quilt,** *Ladies Art Company,* 1897.
3. **The Big T Quilt,** *Grandmother Clark's Patchwork Quilt Designs, From Books 20-21-23,* 1932.
4. **The Century Quilt,** *Mrs. Danner's Fifth Quilt Book,* 1970.
5. **Conch Shells,** Nancy Cabot, *Chicago Tribune,* Mar 29, 1936.
6. **The Maple Leaf,** *Kansas City Star,* May 29, 1937.
7. **Broken Sash,** Nancy Cabot, *Chicago Tribune,* Jan 30, 1935. See 61-2, 233-12, and 253-5.
8. **Dad's Bow Tie,** *Grandmother's Patchwork Quilt Designs, Book 20,* 1931. Also known as:
   Neck Tie, *Mrs. Danner's Fifth Quilt Book,* 1970.
9. **Triangles and Squares,** *Kansas City Star,* Apr 26, 1950.
10. **Cross and Crown,** Finley, 1929. See 181-7.
11. **Norway Spruce,** Jinny Beyer, Quilter's Quest design, 2004.
12. **Red Maple,** Jinny Beyer, Quilter's Quest design, 2004.

1. **Evergreen Tree,** *Grandma Dexter New Appliqué and Patchwork Designs, Book 36b,* ca. 1932.
2. **Dresden Basket,** *Grandma Dexter New Appliqué and Patchwork Designs, Book 36b,* ca. 1932.
3. **Texas Cactus Basket,** Nancy Cabot, *Chicago Tribune,* Feb 3, 1936.
4. **Basket of Lilies,** Eveline Foland, *Kansas City Star,* Apr 4, 1931. Also known as:
   Basket of Tulips, Hall, 1935.
5. **Navajo Weaving,** Ca. 1938, per Havig.
6. **Century of Progress,** *Farm Journal and Farmer's Wife,* ca. 1941.
7. **A Design for Patriotism,** *Kansas City Star,* Aug 20, 1952.
8. **Homespun,** Nancy Cabot, *Chicago Tribune,* Dec 10, 1937.
9. **The Log Patch,** *Ladies Art Company,* 1897.
10. **American Patchwork,** Saward, *et al,* 1882. Also known as:
    Loghouse Quilting, Saward, *et al,* 1882.
11. **Monticello,** Jinny Beyer, RJR Patterns, 2003.
12. **Patagonia,** Jinny Beyer, RJR Patterns, 2006.

1 16 x 16 grid

2 16 x 16 grid

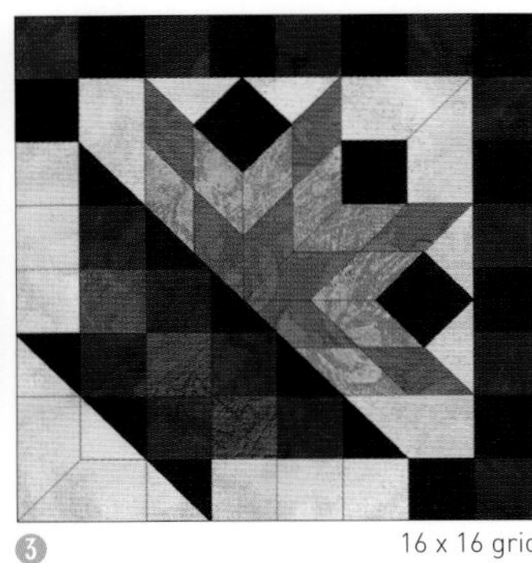
3 16 x 16 grid

4 16 x 16 grid

5 16 x 16 grid

6 16 x 16 grid

7 16 x 16 grid

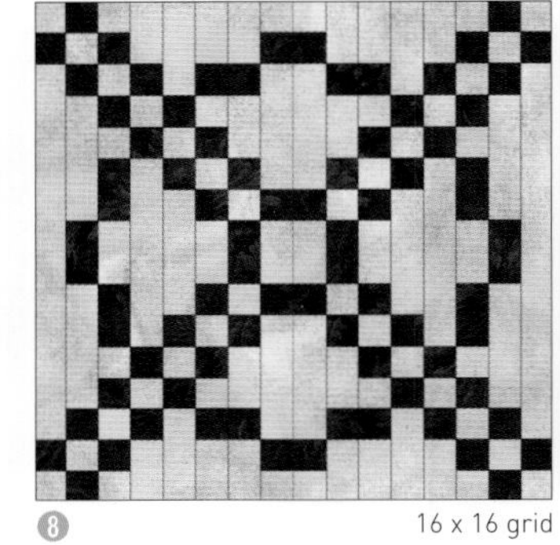
8 16 x 16 grid

9 16 x 16 grid

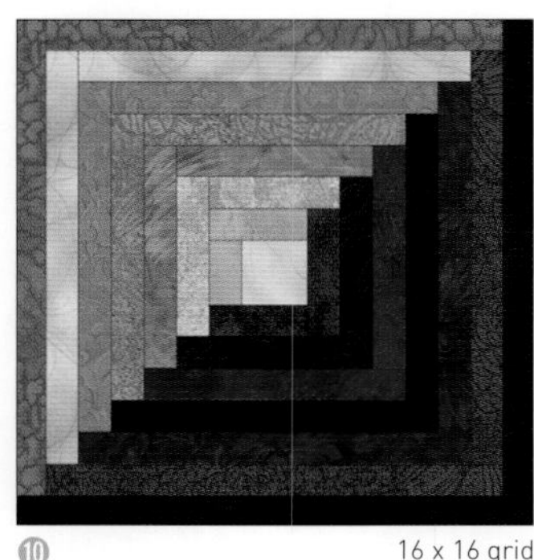
10 16 x 16 grid

11 16 x 16 grid

12 16 x 16 grid

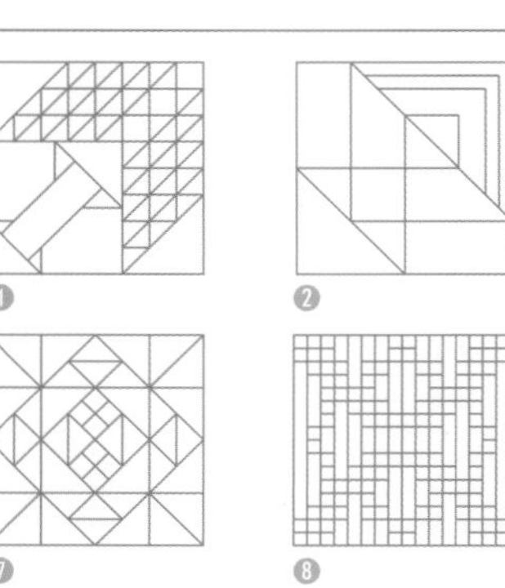

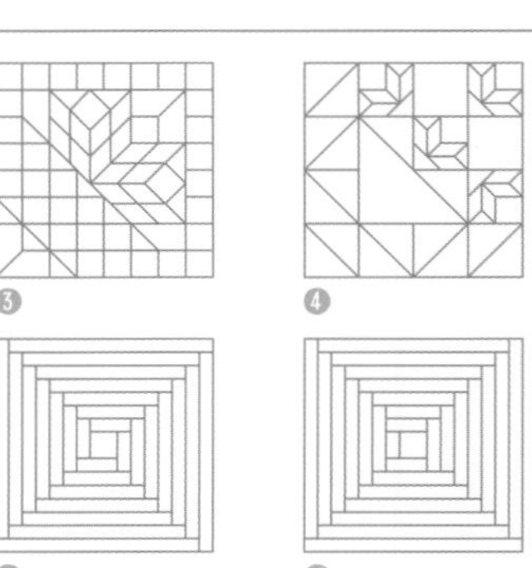

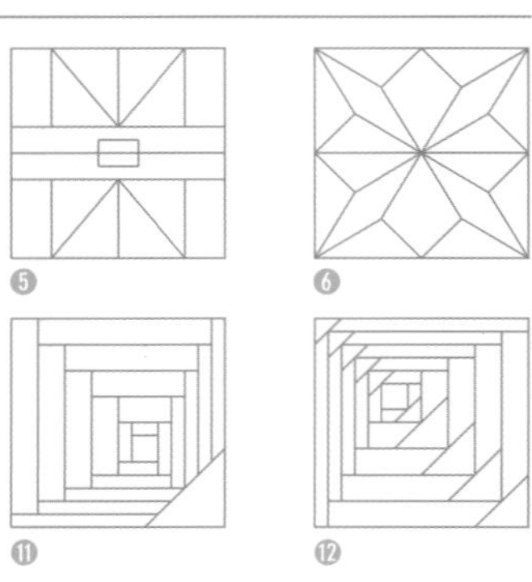

1 **Aztec Steps,** Jinny Beyer, Hilton Head Seminar design, 2006.

2 **Fox Glove,** Jinny Beyer, Quilter's Quest design, 2007.

3 **The Little Red Schoolhouse,** Nancy Cabot, *Chicago Tribune,* Jan 20, 1934.

4 **Linked Diamonds,** Nancy Cabot, *Chicago Tribune,* Jul 1, 1933. Also known as:
Diamond Chain, Nancy Cabot, *Chicago Tribune,* Oct 13, 1937.

5 **All Kinds,** Hall, 1935. See 199-11.

6 **Lover's Knot,** Alice Brooks, *Detroit Free Press,* Mar 21, 1936.

7 **Governor's Garden,** Nancy Cabot, *Chicago Tribune,* Jun 15, 1935.

8 **The Original,** Nancy Cabot, *Chicago Tribune,* Sep 17, 1933.
"With disconcerting simplicity this striking quilt pattern is named 'The Original.' A little venture into quilt history reveals the reason. Any number of quilt makers who have pieced this particular design have claimed it as an original execution of their own; the real title lost in the shuffle of false claims." Nancy Cabot, *Chicago Tribune,* Sep 17, 1933

9 **Blindman's Fancy,** *Ladies Art Company,* 1897. Also known as:
Blind Man's Fancy, Nancy Cabot, *Chicago Tribune,* Oct 14, 1934

10 **World's Fair,** Laura Wheeler, *Cincinnati Enquirer,* Aug 10, 1933.

11 **The Philippines,** Nancy Cabot, *Chicago Tribune,* Jan 13, 1935. See 256-1 and 269-4.
"Shortly after the treaty of Paris, whereby the Philippines were surrendered to the United States by Spain, a pioneer woman of southern California created and named this design for a coverlet. Before the spread was finished she sent one square to a sister in the east. From there and the west coast the pattern migrated in several directions." Nancy Cabot, *Chicago Tribune,* Jan 13, 1935

12 **Kite,** Clara Stone, *Practical Needlework,* ca. 1906.

❶ **Riviera,** Nancy Cabot, *Chicago Tribune,* Mar 12, 1938.

❷ **Pineapples,** *Grandmother Clark's Authentic Early American Patchwork Quilts, Book No. 21,* 1932.

❸ **Criss Cross,** Laura Wheeler, *Indianapolis Star,* May 13, 1934.

❹ **The Name Is Hesper,** *Kansas City Star,* Oct 31, 1951.

❺ **Criss Cross,** *Grandmother Clark's Authentic Early American Patchwork Quilts, Book No. 21,* 1932.

❻ **Star Flower Wreath,** Laura Wheeler, *Cincinnati Enquirer,* Jan 28, 1934.

❼ **The Bow Knot,** Finley, 1929. See 260-9 and 269-12. Also known as:

- **Bow Knot Quilt,** Nancy Page, *Detroit Free Press,* Sep 2, 1933.
- **The Farmer's Puzzle,** Finley, 1929.
- **Lover's Knot,** Nancy Page, *Birmingham News,* Aug 27, 1940.

❽ **Arrow Head,** *Kansas City Star,* Jan 18, 1936.

❾ **Dogwood,** Jinny Beyer, Quilter's Quest design, 2004.

❿ **Pine Tree,** Alice Brooks, *Detroit Free Press,* Aug 18, 1937.

⓫ **Field Cedar,** Jinny Beyer, Quilter's Quest design, 2004.

⓬ **Iris,** Laura Wheeler, *Cincinnati Enquirer,* Sep 3, 1933.

❶ ❷ ❸ ❹ ❺ ❻

❼ ❽ ❾ ❿ ⓫ ⓬

❶ **Friendship Lily,** Alice Brooks, *Detroit Free Press,* Jan 28, 1934.
"Friendship Lily' is a popular one of the group of Friendship quilts. It is, of course, a scrap quilt and can be made of different scraps throughout—a most colorful effect—or with the same scraps repeated in each block, if you prefer. It lends itself to many color arrangements." Alice Brooks, *Detroit Free Press,* Jan 28, 1934

❷ **Beech Basket,** Jinny Beyer, Quilter's Quest design, 2006.

❸ **Dove in the Window,** Home Art Studios, *Cincinnati Enquirer,* Apr 7, 1933.

❹ **Navajo,** Nancy Cabot, *Chicago Tribune,* Sep 10, 1935.

❺ **All Tangled Up,** *Ladies Art Company,* 1897.

❻ **Tea Leaf,** Nancy Cabot, *Chicago Tribune,* Mar 19, 1933. Also known as:
Tea Party, Nancy Cabot, *Chicago Tribune,* Mar 19, 1933.
"'Tea Leaf' is First in Quilt Series Commemorating Historic Events. Beginning today with the 'Tea Leaf' and continuing on forthcoming Sundays, a series of quilt patterns that have been chosen for their particular historical significance will be presented in this department. Each one will recall to readers an event in early American history. While 'Tea Leaf' may not bring up any historical association, you will react to the significance of another name by which the design sometimes is called 'Tea Party.' The pattern of course, commemorates the famous Boston tea party." Nancy Cabot, *Chicago Tribune,* Mar 19, 1933

❼ **Butterfly,** Alice Brooks, *Detroit Free Press,* Feb 19, 1934.
"Now that summer is practically here we enjoy not only the flowers in our gardens but also the butterflies that they attract. Here is a quilt 'Butterfly' that plainly shows its inspiration. Aside from its pictorial effectiveness it is popular with the quilt maker because it is easy to cut. The material can be cut in strips and the pattern pieces cut off as they are needed." Alice Brooks, *Detroit Free Press,* Jun 13, 1934

❽ **Swallow's Flight,** Nancy Cabot, *Chicago Tribune,* Dec 28, 1933.

❾ **Crazy Star,** *Grandma Dexter Appliqué and Patchwork Designs, Book 36a,* ca. 1932.

❿ **Arrant Red Birds,** Nancy Cabot, *Chicago Tribune,* Jan 2, 1936.

⓫ **Crazy Ann,** Hall, 1935. Also known as:
Follow the Leader, Hall, 1935.
Indian Hatchet, Hall, 1935.
Tree Everlasting, Hall, 1935.

⓬ **Tea Leaves,** Nancy Page, *Birmingham News,* Jul 4, 1939.

3 x 3 Base Grid Category

Includes ● *3 x 3,* ● *6 x 6,* ● *12 x 12,* ● *24 x 24,* ● *48 x 48, and* ● *96 x 96 grids*

❶ **Fred's Spool,** Clara Stone, *Practical Needlework,* ca. 1906. Also known as:
- **Empty Spools,** Nancy Cabot, *Chicago Tribune,* Aug 30, 1937.
- **Spool,** Ruby McKim, McKim, 1931

❷ **The Calico Puzzle,** Eveline Foland, *Kansas City Star,* Sep 13, 1930.

❸ **The Practical Orchard,** *Ladies Art Company,* 1897. Also known as:
- **Hour Glass #2,** Clara Stone, *Practical Needlework,* ca. 1906.

❹ **Practical Orchard,** Nancy Cabot, *Chicago Tribune,* Jun 5, 1934. Also known as:
- **Nine Patch,** Nancy Cabot, date unknown, per Alboum.

❺ **Shoo Fly,** *Ladies Art Company,* 1897. Also known as:
- **Fence Row,** Hall, 1935.

❻ **The Letter X,** *Ladies Art Company,* 1897.

❼ **Godey Design,** *Godey's Lady's Book,* 1862. Also known as:
- **Aunt Eliza's Star,** *Grandmother Clark's Patchwork Quilts, Book 19,* 1932.
- **Eastern Star,** Hinson, 1973.
- **Eight Point Design,** *Ladies Art Company,* 1897.
- **Eight Point Star,** Hinson, 1973.
- **Flying Crow,** *Farm Journal Quilt Patterns,* ca. 1935.
- **Flying Crows,** Nancy Cabot, *Chicago Tribune,* Aug 7, 1936.
- **Happy Home,** Clara Stone, *Practical Needlework,* ca. 1906.
- **Henry of the West,** Nancy Page, date unknown, per Alboum.
- **Lone Star,** Hall, 1935.
- **The Lone Star,** Finley, 1929.
- **Lucky Star,** Hinson, 1973.
- **Mosaic Patchwork,** Saward, 1882.
- **Mystery Flower Garden,** Hall, 1935.
- **Ohio Star,** *Capper's Farmer* 1927.
- **Shoo Fly,** Hinson, 1973.
- **Star Design,** *Patchwork Book,* 1932.
- **Star of Hope,** Nancy Page, *Detroit Free Press,* Jan 9, 1934.
- **Texas,** Finley, 1929.
- **Texas Star,** Hall, 1935.
- **Tippycanoe and Tyler Too,** Hinson, 1973.
- **Variable Star,** Finley, 1929.
- **Western Star,** Nancy Page, date unknown, per Alboum.

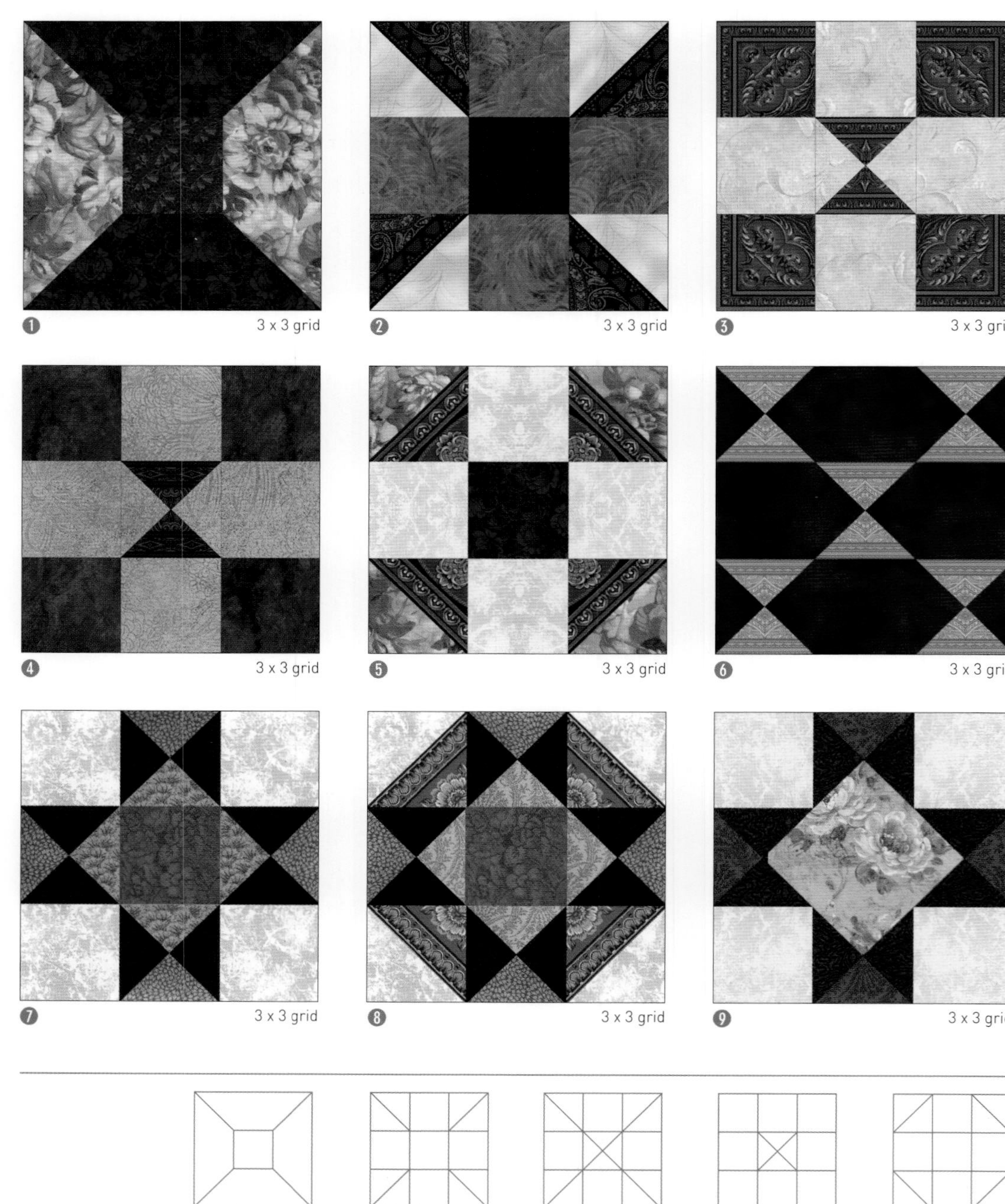

Album Quilts

Album quilts are in many respects similar to and often intertwined with friendship quilts and memory quilts, described on pages 129 to 135. All three feature names of special people among the blocks.

Album quilts might often be made up of repeats of the same block, or they might be a compilation of different blocks. Often, blocks intended for use in an album quilt were designed so as to leave open areas where the signature could be prominent. Usually names were inked or embroidered somewhere on the block. If the blocks were contributed to the quilter by friends, the quilt would generally be considered a friendship quilt. Often, album quilts would be used as fundraisers for worthy causes at fairs or churches. In these cases, people would typically pay a fee to have their names appear on the quilt. (See Women's Christian Temperance Movement on page 308). Other album quilts might celebrate a specific occasion, such as weddings, where the quilt would be presented to the person in whose honor it was made.

Thirty quilt blocks in this book have names that include the words *album, signature,* or *autograph.* At least two others were specifically designed for signatures—Lucy Hayes Quilt and W.C.T. Union. Various quilt columns of the 1930s and 1940s included comments about the history of the album quilt.

"The Album Quilt is a real old-timer. The original purpose was for a gift for a bride-to-be. A group of friends would get together and each would piece a block and embroider her name upon it. Then, of course, they would all come to the quilting bee, and the result, while not exactly a bride's shower, would be something in store for a rainy day ... be sure that the names on each block run in the same direction." Ruby McKim, *Kansas City Star,* Sep 26, 1928

"Today I have a variation of the 'album quilt.' You know, that's the one in which the centerpiece in the block is inscribed with the name of a person known to the quilt maker. Those quilts used to be money makers for churches and lodges. You paid a small sum, say 10 cents or 25 cents, to have your name embroidered in the space. Well, this idea is something like it, only in place of embroidering the name on a rectangular strip as one does in the album quilt, the names are embroidered in the center square block. And in addition to the name, the date of the birthday is embroidered, too. That's why I am calling this a 'birthday quilt.'" Nancy Page, *Birmingham News,* Nov 24, 1942

"The Album quilt was a very popular one hundred years ago. When an old lady brings out her collection of quilts, there invariably is one of these among it. The name embroidered in the center of a block was a lasting remembrance of the friend who probably had made it as her contribution to the quilt." Alice Brooks, *Detroit Free Press,* Apr 22, 1934

Album, *Kansas City Star.* **See 146-10.**

Happy Birthday, *Birmingham News.* **See 84-2.**

Lily Album, *Detroit Free Press.* **See 331-5.**

New Album. *Kansas City Star.* **See 149-5.**

The Ladies' Aid Album. *Kansas City Star.* **See 154-2.**

Lily Album. *Detroit Free Press.* **See 331-5.**

The Album. *Kansas City Star.* **See 91-10.**

Aunt Anna's Album Block. *Practical Needlework.* **See 112-10.**

New Album, *Ladies Art Company.* **See 57-7.**

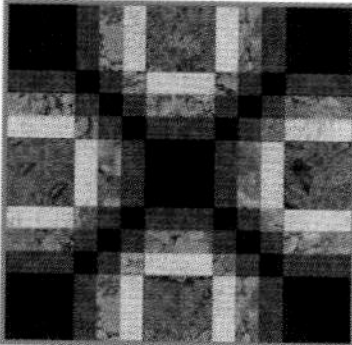
Album Quilt, *Ladies Art Company.* **See 263-2.**

W.C.T. Union, *Ladies Art Company.* **See 249-11**

The Lucy Hayes Quilt, *Q Book 124, White House Quilts.* **See 251-1.**

8 **Godey Design,** *Godey's Lady's Book,* 1858. Also known as:

- **The Four X Quilt,** *Mrs. Danner's Fifth Quilt Book,* 1970.
- **Mystery Flower Garden,** ca. 1938, per Havig.
- **Swamp Angel,** Nancy Cabot, *Chicago Tribune,* Jul 14, 1938.
- **Swamp Patch,** Beyer, Jinny, *The Quilter's Album...,* 1980.

9 **Aunt Eliza's Star,** *Ladies Art Company,* 1897. Also known as:

- **Aunt Lottie's Star,** Nancy Cabot, *Chicago Tribune,* Sep 4, 1936.
- **Lone Star,** Ickis, 1949.
- **Variable Star,** Nancy Page, *Birmingham News,* Jul 2, 1935.

❶ Boy's Nonsense, *Ladies Art Company,* 1897. See 113-4. Also known as:

- **Boy's Playmate,** Nancy Cabot, *Chicago Tribune,* Feb 23, 1935.
- **Forget Me Not,** Nancy Page, *Birmingham News,* Jan 7, 1941.
- **Nonsense,** *Ladies Art Company,* 1928.

"'Well, what do you know about this? Here is a new version of the old-fashioned 'album quilt!' 'I like that idea, Nancy.' I am glad you do. I thought that our youngsters might enjoy having a quilt with the names of their friends embroidered on it. The names may be embroidered in a darker color than is used for the blocks or they may be done in white." Nancy Page, *Birmingham News,* Jan 7, 1941

❷ Octagons, Nancy Page, *Birmingham News,* May 15, 1934.

❸ New Home, *Good Stories,* 1907, per Smith. Also known as:

- **Friendship Star,** Gutcheon, *The Perfect Patchwork Primer,* 1973.
- **The Lost Goslin',** *Kansas City Star,* Jun 7, 1939.
- **The Pin Wheel,** *Kansas City Star,* Aug 19, 1953.
- **Wings in a Whirl,** *Kansas City Star,* Jun 7, 1939.

"I have named this block from the fact that it was made and presented to me by some of my good neighbors at a 'housewarming' held when we moved into our new home after the old one was burned." *Good Stories,* 1907

❹ Formal Garden, *Farm Journal and Farmer's Wife* (Silver Anniversary issue), 1945. See 224-12 and 258-9. Also known as:

- **Box Quilt Pattern,** Beyer, Jinny, *The Quilter's Album...,* 1980.
- **Eccentric Star,** *Q Book 110, Star Quilts,* date unknown.

❺ Quartered Star, James, 1978.

❻ Nine Patch, Holstein, 1973.

❼ Double Hour Glass, Nancy Cabot, *Chicago Tribune,* May 3, 1933. Also known as:

- **Road to California,** Gutcheon, *Perfect Patchwork Primer,* 1973.
- **Contrary Wife Quilt,** *Kansas City Star,* Aug 27, 1941.

❽ Double X No. 1, *Ladies Art Company,* 1897. Also known as:

- **The Cat's Cradle,** *Kansas City Star,* Sep 21, 1960.
- **Double X,** Hall, 1935.
- **Hovering Hawks,** James, 1978.
- **Jack and Six,** Nancy Page, date unknown, per Alboum.
- **Needlework Basket,** *Progressive Farmer,* date unknown.
- **Nine Square,** *Farm Journal Quilt Patterns,* ca. 1935.
- **Tennessee,** Nancy Page, *Birmingham News,* Jul 24, 1934.
- **Three and Six,** Nancy Cabot, *Chicago Tribune,* Sep 21, 1936.

❾ Hour Glass, Finley, 1929.

❿ North Wind, Nancy Page, unidentified newspaper clipping, date unknown.

⓫ Split Nine-Patch, Hall, 1935.

⓬ Hour Glass, Laura Wheeler, *Cincinnati Enquirer,* Apr 15, 1934.

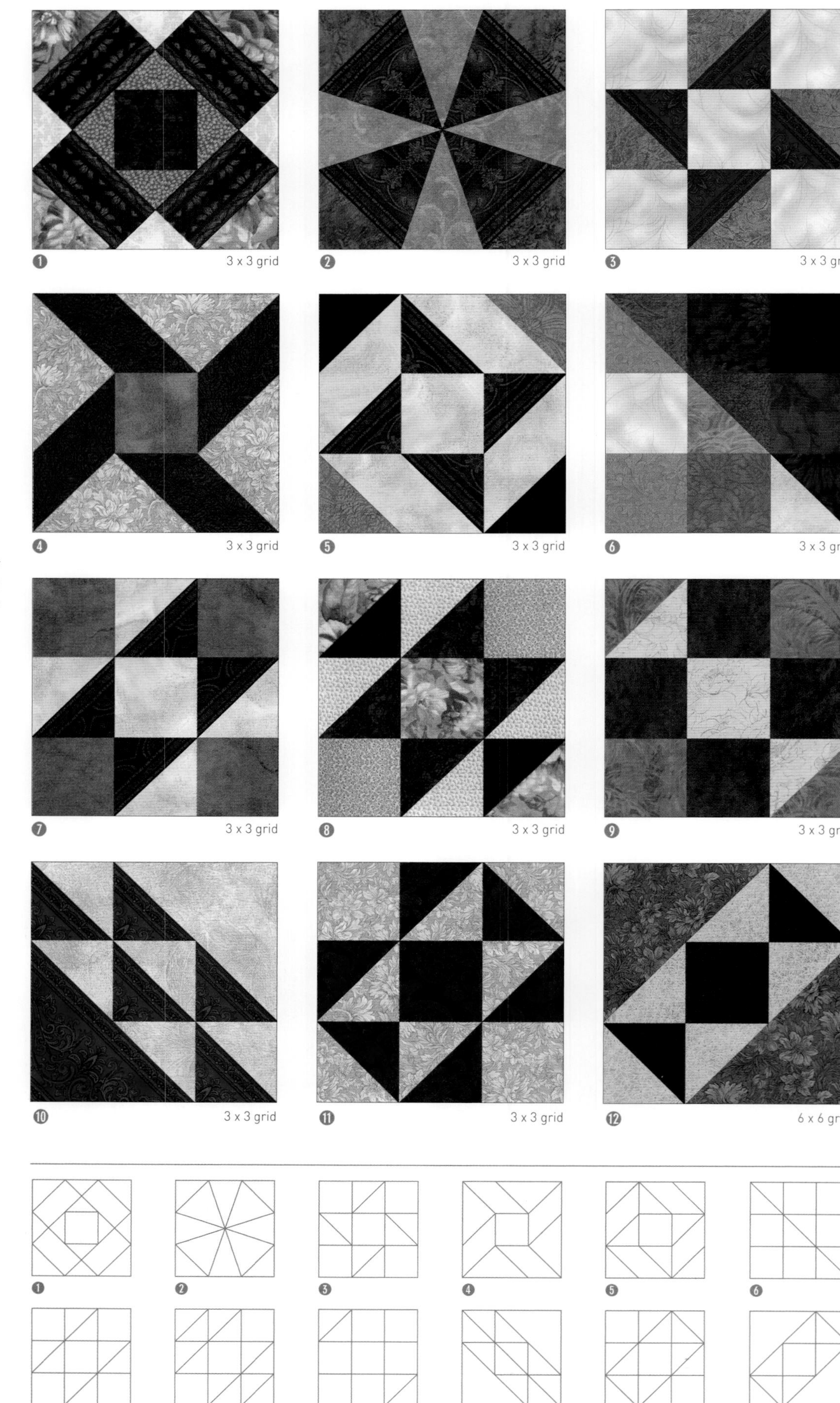

❶ **The Friendship Name Chain,** *Kansas City Star,* Apr 5, 1944.
"A much desired quilt block pattern is the Firendship Name Chain, frequently used by organizations of women ambitious to make money. A small charge is made to each person desiring to have his or her name appear on a block. After the quilt has been completed further gain may be realized by selling it at auction. Mrs. Dollie Veatch... is the contributor of the pattern." *Kansas City Star,* Apr 5, 1944

❷ **Golden Stairs,** Laura Wheeler, *Cincinnati Enquirer,* Aug 28, 1933.

❸ **Birds in the Air,** Finley, 1929. See 150-5. Also known as:
- **Birds of the Air,** *Mrs. Danner Presents Helen's Book of Basic Quiltmaking,* 1970.
- **Flock of Geese,** Finley, 1929.
- **Flying Birds,** Finley, 1929.
- **Flying X,** Alan, 1932.
- **Letter X,** Ickis, 1949.
- **White Cloud,** ca. 1938, per Havig.

❹ **Birds in the Air,** Holstein, 1973.

❺ **West Wind,** Nancy Page, *Birmingham News,* Aug 21, 1934. Also known as:
- **The Victory Boat,** *Kansas City Star,* Sep 27, 1944.

❻ **Sailboat,** Hall, 1935.

❼ **Triplet,** *Kansas City Star,* Aug 19, 1933.

❽ **Frank Leslie Design,** Frank Leslie, *Frank Leslie's Modewelt,* 1871. Also known as:
- **The Silent Star,** *Kansas City Star,* Apr 10, 1940.
- **Star X,** *Grandma Dexter Appliqué and Patchwork Designs, Book 36a,* ca. 1932.

❾ **Green River,** Nancy Page, *Birmingham News,* May 1, 1934.

❿ **Colonial Bow Tie,** *Virginia Snow Studio Art Needlework Creations,* 1932. Also known as:
- **Bow Tie,** *Modern Patchwork,* 1970.
- **Necktie,** Nancy Cabot, *Chicago Tribune,* Jul 23, 1936.
- **Necktie Pattern,** *Farm Journal Quilt Patterns,* ca. 1935.
- **The Necktie,** *Kansas City Star,* Dec 26, 1956.

⓫ **The Wishing Ring,** *Kansas City Star,* May 17, 1950

⓬ **Four Patch Variation,** Hall, 1935.

1 Pennsylvania, Nancy Page, *Birmingham News*, Jun 9, 1936. Also known as:

- **Easy Four Patch,** Laura Wheeler, *Women's Household Needlecraft Service*, 1967.
- **Four Patch,** Laura Wheeler, unidentified newspaper clipping, date unknown.
- **Friendship Quilt,** Alice Brooks, *Alice Brooks Designs.* date unknown.

2 Thrifty, *Kansas City Star*, Dec 27, 1939. "The idea for the 'Thrifty' design originated by Mrs. Clarence Welker, Millersville, Mo. She chose this name for the pattern because she went to her scrap bag for the three kinds of print and the 1-tone pieces required for it." *Kansas City Star*, Dec 27, 1939

3 Puss in the Corner, Eveline Foland, *Kansas City Star*, Nov 5, 1932. See 73-4.

4 Pussy in the Corner, *Grandmother Clark's Authentic Early American Patchwork Quilts, Book No. 21*, 1932.

5 Four Leaf Clover, *Farm Journal and Farmers Wife* (Silver Anniversary issue), 1945.

6 Flutter Wheel, *Ladies Art Company*, 1897. See 73-6, and 73-7. Also known as:

- **Clover Leaf,** *Dakota Farmer*, Feb 15, 1927.
- **Pin Wheels,** Ruby McKim, *Kansas City Star*, Apr 19, 1930.

7 Prairie Queen, Finley, 1929.

8 Grecian Designs, *Ladies Art Company*, 1897. Also known as:

- **Broken Plate,** date unknown, per Brackman.
- **Churn Dash,** Ruby McKim, McKim, 1931.
- **Churn Dasher,** Hall, 1935.
- **Double Monkey Wrench,** Finley, 1929.
- **Double Trouble,** Nancy Page, unidentified newspaper clipping, date unknown.
- **Grecian Design,** Nancy Cabot, *Chicago Tribune*, Jun 9, 1934.
- **Grecian Square,** Prairie Farmer Mar 24, 1928.
- **Greek Cross,** *Kansas City Star*, Ruby McKim, Nov 14, 1928.
- **Greek Square,** Nancy Cabot, *Chicago Tribune*, Oct 8, 1936.
- **Hens and Chickens,** *Wallace's Farmer*, 1928, per Brackman.
- **Hole in the Barn Door,** Hall, 1935.
- **Hubbard's Cupboard,** Nancy Page, unidentified newspaper clipping, date unknown.
- **Indian Hammer,** *Old Fashioned Quilts*, ca. 1931.
- **Joan's Doll Quilt,** Nancy Page, date unknown, per Alboum.
- **Lincoln's Platform,** Hall, 1935.
- **Love Knot,** Hall, 1935.
- **Monkey Wrench,** Ickis, 1949.
- **Puss in the Corner,** Hall, 1935.
- **Quail's Nest,** *Mrs. Danner's Fifth Quilt Book*, 1970.
- **Sherman's March,** Hall, 1935.

1 6 x 6 grid

2 6 x 6 grid

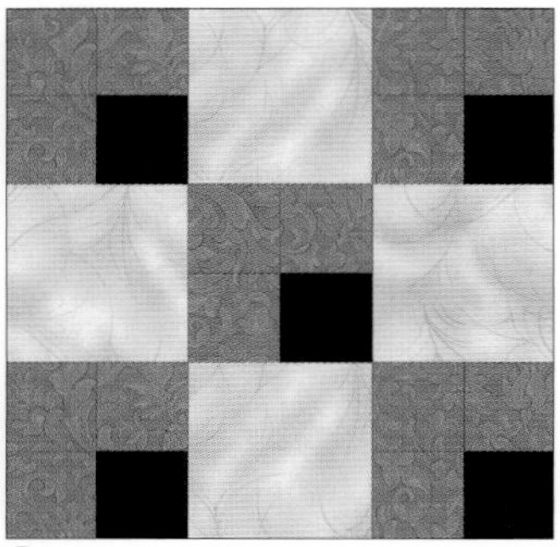

3 6 x 6 grid

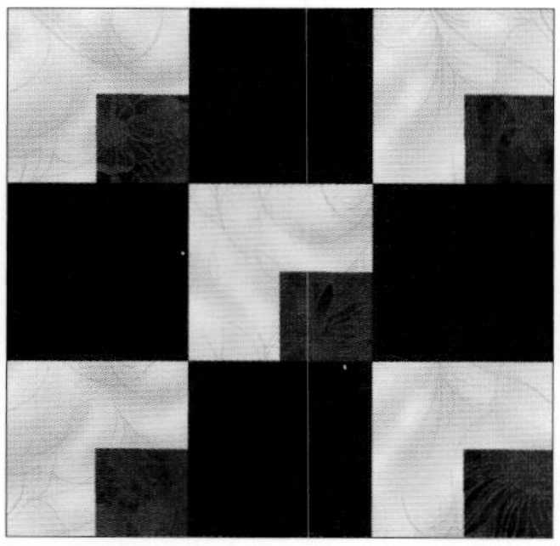

4 6 x 6 grid

5 6 x 6 grid

6 6 x 6 grid

7 6 x 6 grid

8 6 x 6 grid

9 6 x 6 grid

10 6 x 6 grid

11 6 x 6 grid

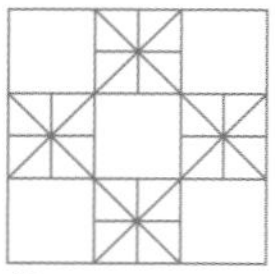

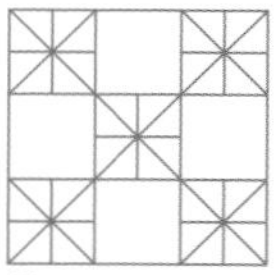

12 6 x 6 grid

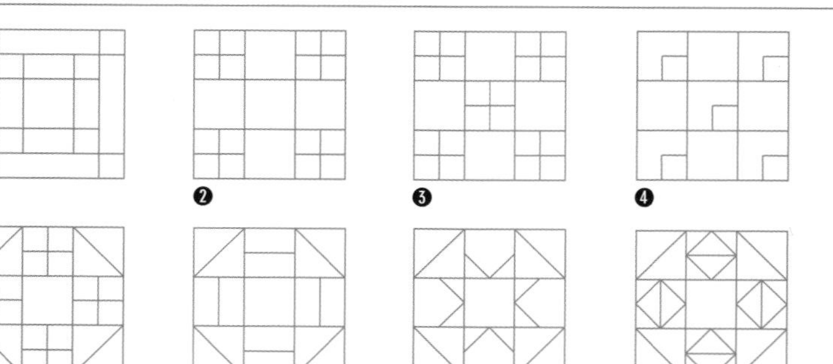

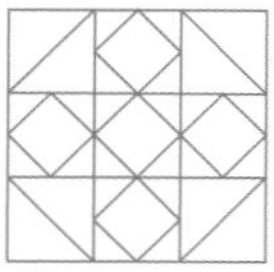

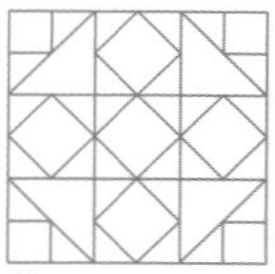

Friendship Quilts

I have found 73 quilt blocks that contain the word "friendship." Often, album quilts that were collections of signatures of friends were called friendship quilts. Sometimes friends would make their own block on which they signed their names; other times, they would sign a block that had already been made or they would sign a piece of fabric that would then be stitched into a block.

"Everything to be desired for a friendship signature quilt is included in this pattern. There is a long white strip for the name, there are print blocks and 1-tone pieces, with the choice of color left to the needlecrafter. The block was designed by Mrs. Clyde Offutt, Sleeper, Mo."

It seems that most friendship quilts were designed to be made with scraps of fabric donated by friends. Quilters would gather together, bringing their scraps. They would trade fabrics and put the pieces together into a block. Other friendship quilts would be made by friends, each making a block to contribute to the quilt. Quilt columnists from the 1930s and 1940s had patterns for a variety of friendship quilts, often accompanied by short explanations.

"'The Friendship Ring,' or 'Dresden Plate,' is a pattern which was created in Long Island, N.Y., about 1760. It derived the name 'Friendship Ring' from the fact that it was made at a time when materials were scarce and friends would contribute a petal each to form the ring." Nancy Cabot, *Chicago Tribune,* Mar 30, 1933

"Among the Friendship Quilts—those quilts that are made of materials contributed by friends, or quilts in which each friend makes a block—one of the most popular is the Friendship Knot." *Omaha Bee News,* date unknown

"An old-time pattern, the Friendship Fan is as popular today as a friendship quilt as it was in the early days of quilt making. It has all the qualities of the ideal quilt of this type. The parts of the fan are just the right size for scraps. A gathering of friends can quickly do a quantity of blocks for they are easily pieced." Laura Wheeler, *Cincinnati Enquirer,* Jun 16, 1933

"A scrap quilt that combines beauty, economy and sentiment is this one, Link of Friendship. Make it of scraps donated by your friends for remembrance--the old idea of a Friendship quilt." Laura Wheeler, *Columbus Evening Dispatch,* Sep 3, 1942

Signature Quilt, *Kansas City Star.* **See 105-5.**

The Fan, *The Dressmaking Book.* **See 385-12.**

Link of Friendship, *Columbus Evening Dispatch.* **See 316-7.**

Friendship Ring, *Quilt Booklet #1.* **See 375-4**

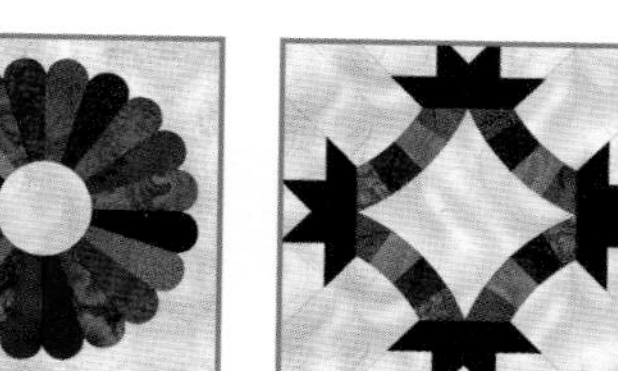

Friendship Knot, *Cincinnati Enquirer.* **See 346-2**

❾ **A Dandy,** Clara Stone, *Practical Needlework,* ca. 1906.

❿ **Pointed Star,** Marcia Aasmundstad, Beyer, Jinny, *The Quilter's Album...,* 1980.

⓫ **Sawtooth Patchwork,** *Ladies Art Company,* 1897. Also known as:
- **Five Diamonds,** ca. 1938, per Havig.
- **Sawtooth,** Nancy Page, *Birmingham News,* Dec 4, 1934.
- **Sawtooth Patch,** Nancy Cabot, *Chicago Tribune,* May 17, 1934.

⓬ **The Five Spot,** Nancy Cabot, *Chicago Tribune,* Sep 23, 1936.

❶ **State Fair,** Nancy Cabot, *Chicago Tribune,* Apr 14, 1938.

❷ **Summer Nights,** *Farm Journal and Farmer's Wife,* ca. 1941.

❸ **Broken Dish,** *Old Fashioned Quilts,* ca. 1931. Also known as:

> **The Chinese Block Quilt,** *Kansas City Star,* Jul 13, 1938.

❹ **Summer Winds,** Nancy Page, unidentified newspaper clipping, date unknown.

❺ **Double X, No.4,** *Ladies Art Company,* 1897. Also known as:

> **Double X,** ca. 1938, per Havig.

❻ **Double X's,** Nancy Cabot, *Chicago Tribune,* Apr 10, 1935.

❼ **Prairie Queen,** Aunt Martha series: *The Quilt Fair Comes to You,* ca. 1933.

❽ **Double X,** *The Patchwork Book,* 1932.

❾ **Corn and Beans,** *Ladies Art Company,* 1897.
"This was the pattern used for a quilt that was on the bed in the first 'Farm Demonstration Home' in Missouri, which attests its popularity," Hall, 1935

❿ **Corn and Beans,** Ruby McKim, *Kansas City Star,* Jan 11, 1930.

⓫ **Broken Window,** *Kansas City Star,* Sep 8, 1937. Also known as:

> **A Window of Triangles,** *Kansas City Star,* Dec 23, 1959.

⓬ **Union Square,** *Q Book 108, Centennial Quilts,* date unknown.

❶ **Puss in the Corner,** *Kansas City Star,* Nov 22, 1930. Also known as:
- **Puss in a Corner,** Aunt Martha series: *Quilt Designs,* ca. 1952.
- **Puss in Boots,** Hall, 1935.

❷ **Windmills All Around,** *Kansas City Star,* Sep 18, 1957.

❸ **Indian Puzzle,** Nancy Cabot, *Chicago Tribune,* Feb 18, 1936.

❹ **Lover's Lane,** *Kansas City Star,* Jun 9, 1934.

❺ **An Ocean Wave of Many Points,** *Kansas City Star,* Jun 25, 1958. See 93-3, 159-3, 159-4 and 409-11.

❻ **Rob Peter to Pay Paul,** Laura Wheeler, unidentified newspaper clipping, date unknown.

❼ **The Kitchen Woodbox,** *Kansas City Star,* Nov 26, 1941.

❽ **Signatures for Golden Memories,** *Kansas City Star,* Apr 5, 1961.

❾ **A Striped Plain Quilt,** *Kansas City Star,* Jan 12, 1944.

❿ **Hen and Chicks,** *Grandmother Clark's Patchwork Quilts, Book 19,* 1932. Also known as:
- **Duck and Ducklings,** Hall, 1935.
- **Handy Andy,** Hall, 1935.
- **Hen and Chickens,** Nancy Cabot, *Chicago Tribune,* Jan 15, 1934.
- **Mayflower,** Nancy Cabot, *Chicago Tribune,* Jul 27, 1934.
- **Shoo Fly,** Hall, 1935.

⓫ **Rolling Stone,** *Ladies Art Company,* 1897. Also known as:
- **Block Circle,** *Prize Winning Designs,* ca. 1931
- **Broken Wheel,** Clara Stone, *Practical Needlework,* ca. 1906.
- **Johnnie Round the Corner,** Hall, 1935.
- **Peekaboo,** Beyer, Jinny, *The Quilter's Album...,* 1980.
- **Single Wedding Ring,** Hall, 1935.
- **Squirrel in a Cage,** *Kansas City Star,* Nov 2, 1935.
- **Wheel,** Hall, 1935.

⓬ **The Queen's Favorite,** *Capper's Weekly,* June 21, 1930, per Brackman. Also known as:
- **Checkerboard,** Gutcheon, *The Perfect Patchwork Primer,* 1973.
- **Grandmother's Pride,** Home Art Studios, *Cincinnati Enquirer,* Feb 26, 1933.
- **Queen's Crown,** Nancy Page, unidentified newspaper clipping, date unknown.
- **Squares and Triangles,** *Q Book 130, Keepsake Quilts,* ca. 1970.

❶ **Kansas Star,** Eveline Foland, *Kansas City Star,* Jul 30, 1932. Also known as:
  Eight Point All Over, ca. 1938, per Havig.

❷ **Old Italian Block,** Nancy Cabot, *Chicago Tribune,* Jul 28, 1936.

❸ **Good Fortune,** Clara Stone, *Practical Needlework,* ca. 1906.

❹ **Betsy's Lattice,** Laura Wheeler, *Cincinnati Enquirer,* Aug 20, 1933.

❺ **Endless Squares,** Nancy Cabot, *Chicago Tribune,* Jun 4, 1938.

❻ **Cats and Mice,** *Ladies Art Company,* 1897. Also known as:
  Cat and Mice, Nancy Cabot, *Chicago Tribune,* Jul 25, 1934.

❼ **Symphony,** Jinny Beyer, RJR Patterns, 2004; published in Beyer, Jinny, *Quiltmaking by Hand.*

❽ **Repeat X,** *Farm Journal and Farmer's Wife,* ca. 1941.

❾ **Aurora Stars,** *Chicago Tribune,* Feb 26, 1936.

❿ **Linoleum,** Nancy Page, *Nashville Banner,* Mar 28, 1933.

⓫ **Prairie Flower,** Jane Alan, *Illinois State Register,* Apr 2, 1933.

⓬ **Sun Rays Quilt,** *Kansas City Star,* Apr 26, 1939. Also known as:
  Darting Minnows, Nancy Page, *Birmingham News,* Apr 27, 1943.

❶ **Judy in Arabia,** Gutcheon, *The Quilt Design Workbook*, 1976.

❷ **Border Print Star,** Jinny Beyer, Jinny Beyer Studio design, 1990.

❸ **Grandma's Star,** Clara Stone, *Practical Needlework*, ca. 1906. Also known as:

- **54 40 or Fight,** Aunt Martha series: *The Quilt Fair Comes to You*, ca. 1933.
- **Fifty Four Forty or Fight,** Finley, 1929.
- **Garden Patch,** *Grandma Dexter's New Appliqué and Patchwork Designs, Book 36b*, ca. 1932.
- **Garden Walk,** *Kansas City Star*, Apr 26, 1939.
- **Nine Patch Star,** *Kansas City Star*, Jan 4, 1956.
- **An Old Fashioned Pinwheel,** *Kansas City Star*, Feb 12, 1958.
- **Railroad,** Aunt Martha series: *The Quilt Fair Comes to You*, ca. 1933.
- **Texas,** Nancy Page, *Port Arthur News*, Jan 9, 1934.

❹ **Blue Meteors,** Nancy Cabot, *Chicago Tribune*, Feb 8, 1936.

❺ **Claws,** Gutcheon, *The Perfect Patchwork Primer*, 1973.

❻ **Union Square,** Nancy Cabot, *Chicago Tribune*, Jul 16, 1937.

❼ **Hail Storm,** Nancy Cabot, *Chicago Tribune*, Sep 5, 1935. Also known as:

- **Storm Signal,** Nancy Cabot, *Chicago Tribune*, Oct 16, 1937.

❽ **Mayor's Garden,** Nancy Cabot, *Chicago Tribune*, Jun 2, 1938.

"'Mayor's Garden' is southern in origin, coming from a town nesting at the foothills of the Cumberland mountains. His honor's garden was a riot of all shades of purple iris and rose bushes. The walk through the gardens was of light colored slate typical of the terrain in that section of the country." Nancy Cabot, *Chicago Tribune*, June 2, 1938

❾ **Diadem,** Clara Stone, *Practical Needlework*, ca. 1906. Also known as:

- **Star Premo,** Clara Stone, *Practical Needlework*, ca. 1906.

❿ **Sky Rocket,** Beyer, Jinny, *The Quilter's Album...*, 1980.

⓫ **Safe Harbour,** Jinny Beyer, Hilton Head Seminar design, 1982; published in Beyer, Jinny, *Patchwork Portfolio*.

⓬ **Ladies' Aid Block,** Nancy Cabot, *Chicago Tribune*, Apr 29, 1938.

❶ **Pinwheel and Squares,** Marcia Aasmundstad, 1980; published in Beyer, Jinny, *The Quilter's Album....*

❷ **Union Star,** Clara Stone, *Practical Needlework*, ca. 1906.

❸ **Cups and Saucers,** *Kansas City Star*, May 23, 1936.

❹ **Waste not Want not,** Nancy Page, *Birmingham News*, May 4, 1943.
"I have an ingenious pattern for you today. Its name is quite in keeping with the times. Too, its name smacks of New England where thrift has always been a virtue and where smart people have prided themselves upon being able to have to make do, and to do without. They believed that if one did not waste materials then one would not want or lack material. It's a good theory which is being put to practical uses in these wartime days." Nancy Page, *Birmingham News*, May 4, 1943

❺ **Mill and Stars,** Nancy Cabot, *Chicago Tribune*, Sep 26, 1936.

❻ **Maltese Cross,** *Ladies Art Company*, 1897. Also known as:
Iron Cross, Nancy Cabot, *Chicago Tribune*, May 10, 1935.

❼ **Nine Patch Kaleidoscope,** Jinny Beyer, Beyer, Jinny, *The Quilter's Album...*, 1980.

❽ **Treasure Box,** Nancy Page, *Birmingham News*, Jun 2, 1942.
"Perhaps it is the present trend toward saving that gave me this idea for a treasure box pattern. I can think of so many things that might be tucked away in treasure boxes. Yes, and we can make this quilt of treasured pieces taken from the piece box or bag." Nancy Page, *Birmingham News*, Jun 2, 1942

❾ **Lagoon Rose,** Jinny Beyer, Hilton Head Seminar design, 1983; published in Beyer, Jinny, *Patchwork Portfolio*.

❿ **Swing In The Center,** Laura Wheeler, *Illinois State Register*, Apr 24, 1933.
This was the first Laura Wheeler pattern that I found for the *Illinois State Register*. It was also the first one I found that appeared in the *Cincinnati Enquirer* on July 3, 1933

⓫ **T Block,** Laura Wheeler, *Illinois State Register*, May 27, 1933.

⓬ **Swing in the Center,** Finley, 1929. Also known as:
Eight Hands Around, Jane Alan, *Illinois State Register*, ca. 1932.
Ladies' Wreath, Nancy Page, *Birmingham News*, Jan 12, 1943.
"Remember the time when families kept small books with fancy bindings on the center table in the parlor? Usually these books were called 'Album of Thoughts' or 'Ladies' Wreath' or some such fancy name. The quilt pattern I have for you today is reminiscent of those books and so I am calling it 'Ladies' Wreath.'" Nancy Page, *Birmingham News*, Jan 12, 1943

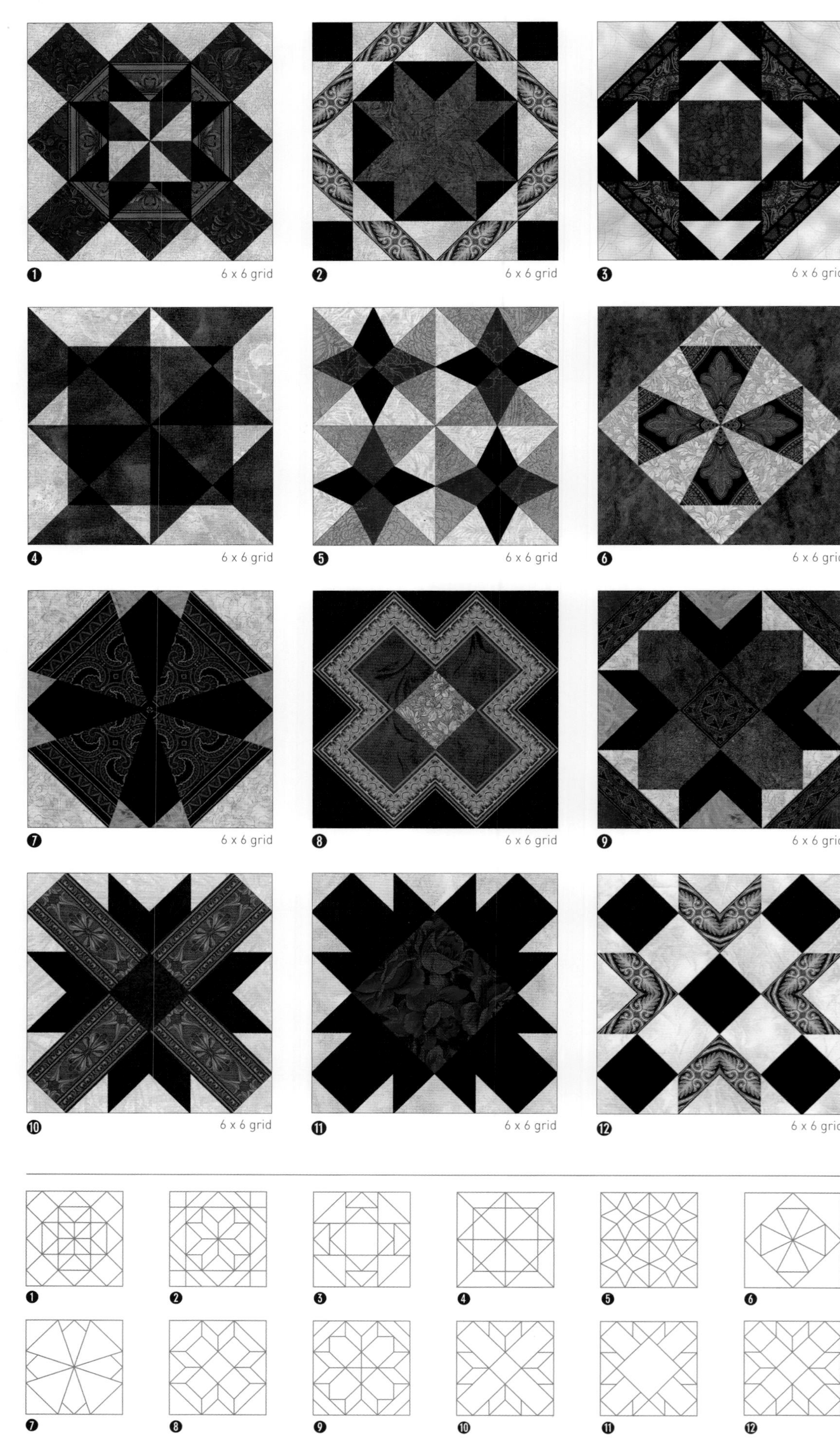

Memory Quilts

There are several different types of memory quilts. Some are Album quilts which contain signatures of friends, some are quilts made with fabrics from the clothing of a deceased person, and others are made with fabrics collected from friends as a remembrance of friendship. Memory quilts might also be made from the clothing of a child and then given to the child. There are 11 quilt blocks in this book which contain the word "memory".

"For those who know how to love, and how to feel the love of their children, quilt making has been a special joy. Thousands upon thousands of others have made these keepsakes for their children, as a labor of love, and well are they repaid, for the quilt made by other's own hands is their most prized possession. 'The Friendship Circle Quilt', with the entwined hearts quilting design, makes an admirable remembrance quilt." *World Herald*, Oct 14, 1933

"This block was made in 1870, and thus is not so old as many memory quilts made before that date. Early memory quilts customarily were made from the dresses of a mourned friend or relative. In 1870, however, they acquired a new significance. Pioneering relatives would receive pieces of a dress from the old home, and from these they would fashion a 'Memory Block.' Large families being what they were at that time, entire quilts were made from remnants traded back and forth among immediate relatives." Nancy Cabot, *Chicago Tribune*, Jul 19, 1934

"A scrap quilt that combines beauty, economy and sentiment is this one, Link of Friendship. Make it of scraps donated by your friends for remembrance—the old idea of a Friendship quilt." Laura Wheeler, *Columbus Evening Dispatch*, Sep 3, 1942. See 316-7

"When made of the dresses of a loved one who has passed on it is called 'Memory Wreath' and the name and date of death is embroidered in the center square." Hall, 1935. See 378-6

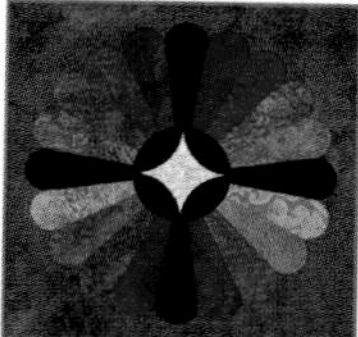

The Friendship Circle Quilt, *World Herald.* **See 375-8.**

Memory Blocks, *Chicago Tribune.* **See 204-12.**

Chips and Whetstones, *Kansas City Star.* **See 378-6.**

❶ 6 x 6 grid

❷ 6 x 6 grid

❸ 6 x 6 grid

❹ 6 x 6 grid

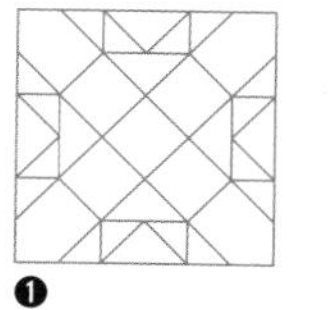

❶

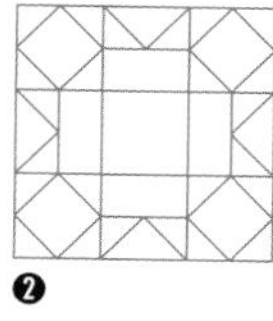

❷

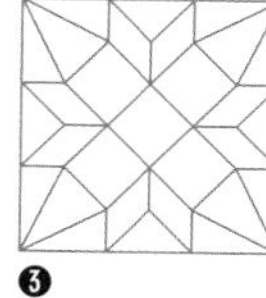

❸

❹

❶ **Swing in the Center,** *Ladies Art Company,* 1897. Also known as:

Mrs. Roosevelt's Favorite, Clara Stone, *Practical Needlework*, ca. 1906.

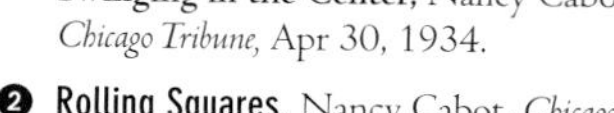

Roman Pavement, Nancy Cabot, *Chicago Tribune*, Mar 4, 1938.

Swinging in the Center, Nancy Cabot, *Chicago Tribune*, Apr 30, 1934.

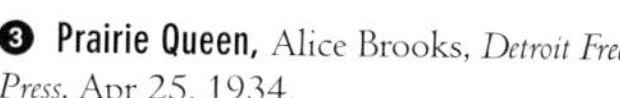

❷ **Rolling Squares,** Nancy Cabot, *Chicago Tribune*, Sep 19, 1936.

❸ **Prairie Queen,** Alice Brooks, *Detroit Free Press*, Apr 25, 1934.

"'Prairie Queen'—a scrap quilt that like the crazy quilt of olden times can be made of scraps sewn together, hit or miss. Unlike these old time quilts though, it makes a handsome pattern even with such hit or miss sewing. So here is a chance to be economical, for only the background and the one patch are of the same material throughout, and at the same time have a quilt that it certainly worth while." Alice Brooks, *Detroit Free Press*, Apr 25, 1934

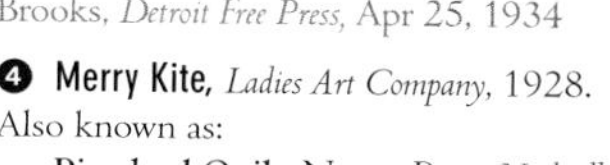

❹ **Merry Kite,** *Ladies Art Company*, 1928. Also known as:

Pinwheel Quilt, Nancy Page, *Nashville Banner*, Jul 5, 1932.

Quick Reference: Cactus Flowers

Cactus Flower is an example of how a very similar design changes over the years or from region to region.

Cactus Flower, *Kansas City Star.* **See 152-5.**

The Apple Leaf, *Kansas City Star.* **See 178-2.**

Cactus Flower, Hall. **See 181-4.**

Texas Flower, *Ladies Art Company.* **See 178-5.**

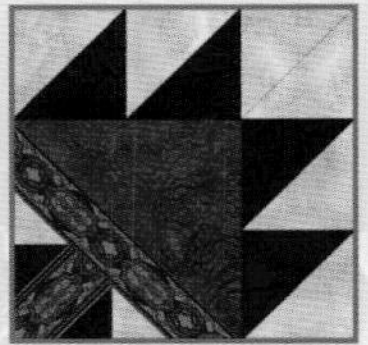

Texas Flower, *Chicago Tribune.* **See 178-4.**

The Texas Flower, *Kansas City Star.* **See 275-2.**

❶ **Wyoming Valley Block,** Nancy Cabot, *Chicago Tribune,* Feb 29, 1936.
"'Wyoming Valley Block' had its origin in the east, specifically Pennsylvania, to commemorate the terrible Wyoming Valley massacre, which took place many years before the piecing of this block. The story of the massacre was one which was told and retold to the Pennsylvania children." Nancy Cabot, *Chicago Tribune,* Feb 29, 1936

❷ **Wedding Bouquet,** Nancy Page, *Birmingham News,* Jan 5, 1943.

❸ **Barber Shop Quartet,** Jinny Beyer, Beyer, Jinny, *Patchwork Portfolio,* 1989.

❹ **Memory,** Clara Stone, *Practical Needlework,* ca. 1906.

❺ **Crow's Foot,** Nancy Page, *Nashville Banner,* Feb 6, 1934.

❻ **Mosaic Block,** *Old Fashioned Quilts,* ca. 1931. Also known as:
- **Delectable Mountains,** Alice Brooks, unidentified newspaper clipping, date unknown.
- **King's Crown,** Nancy Page, *Birmingham News,* Jun 19, 1934.
- **Sunshine,** *Old Fashioned Quilts,* ca. 1931.
- **Union Square,** Orlofsky, 1974.

❼ **Union,** *Ladies Art Company,* 1897. Also known as:
- **Centennial,** Nancy Page, *Birmingham News,* May 26, 1936.
- **An Effective Square,** *Ladies' Home Journal,* 1899, per Brackman.
- **Four Crowns,** Beyer, Jinny, *The Quilter's Album...,* 1980.
- **Union Square,** Hall, 1935.
- **Union Star,** Aunt Martha series: *Quilts: Heirlooms of Tomorrow,* ca. 1977.

❶ 6 x 6 grid

❷ 6 x 6 grid

❸ 6 x 6 grid

❹ 6 x 6 grid

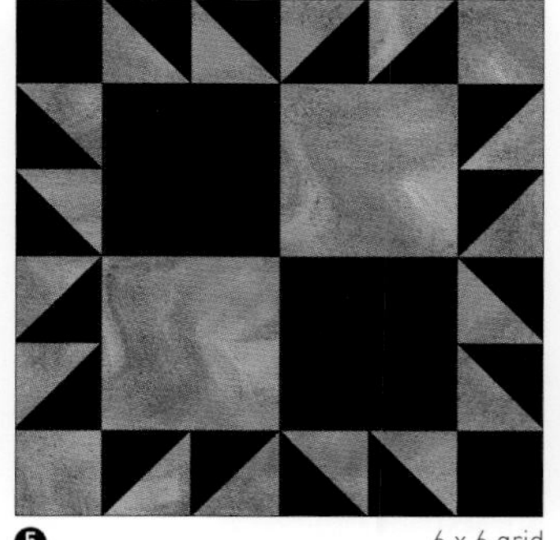

❺ 6 x 6 grid

❻ 6 x 6 grid

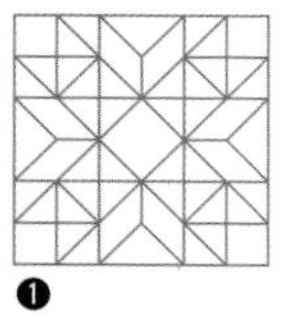

❶

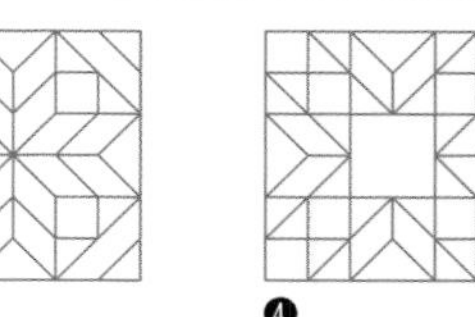

❷ ❸ ❹

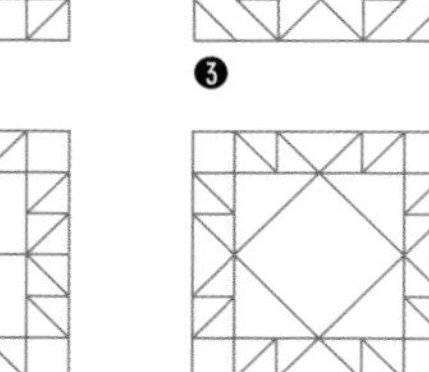

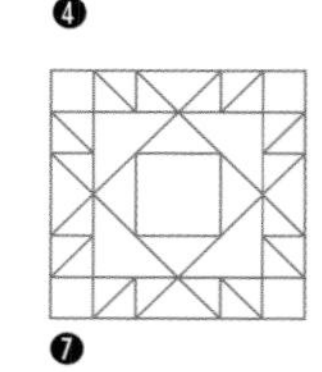

❺ ❻ ❼

❼ 6 x 6 grid

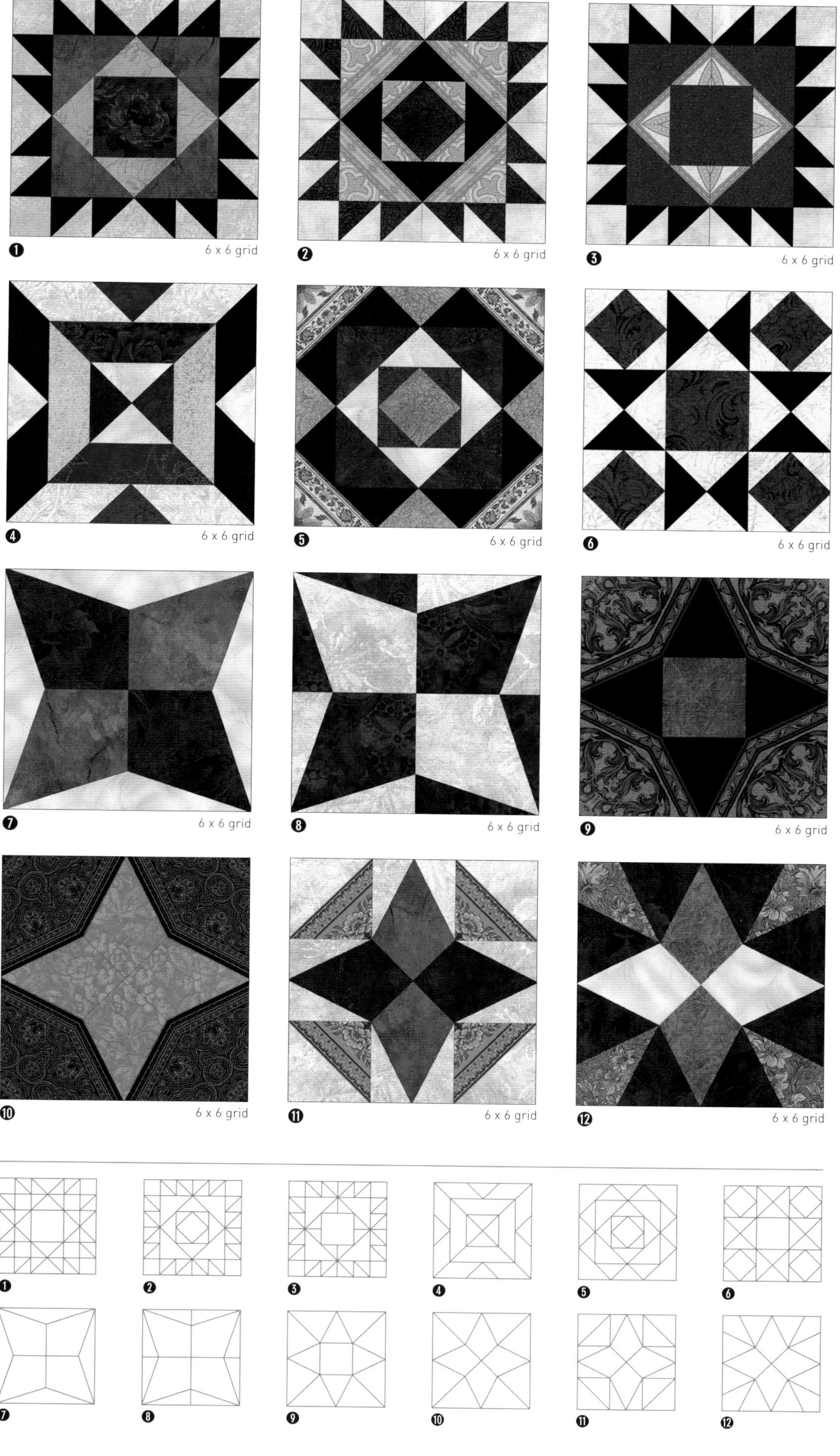

1 **Four Crowns,** *Kansas City Star,* Nov 18, 1933.

2 **Flaming Star,** Nancy Cabot, *Chicago Tribune,* Jan 13, 1938.

3 **Union Block,** Nancy Cabot, *Chicago Tribune,* Dec 17, 1934.
"Red, white, and blue were the accepted colors for all 'Union' quilts at the time they first were made. This Union Block, in fashion in 1840 is an example of the pieced block." Nancy Cabot, *Chicago Tribune,* Dec 17, 1934

4 **Just Scraps,** Laura Wheeler, unidentified newspaper clipping, date unknown.

5 **Pershing,** Nancy Page, *Nashville Banner,* Aug 22, 1933. Also known as:
- **Boxes,** Gutcheon, *The Perfect Patchwork Primer,* 1973.
- **Handy Andy,** Gutcheon, *The Perfect Patchwork Primer,* 1973.

6 **Combination Star,** *Ladies Art Company,* 1897. Also known as:
- **Ornate Star,** *Grandmother's Patchwork Quilt Designs, Book 20,* 1931.

7 **Humming Bird,** *Prairie Farmer,* 1928.

8 **Night and Day,** Laura Wheeler, *Columbus Evening Dispatch,* Aug 13, 1942.

9 **The Star of Alamo,** *Kansas City Star,* Nov 12, 1941.

10 **String Quilt,** ca. 1938, per Havig.

11 **Flying Triangles,** Nancy Page, *Birmingham News,* Nov 23, 1943.

12 **A Star of Four Points,** *Kansas City Star,* Jul 2, 1952. Also known as:
- **Time and Tide,** Aunt Martha series: *Bold and Beautiful Quilts,* ca. 1977.

❶ **Autumn Stars,** *Progressive Farmer,* ca. 1935. Also known as:
Golden Chains, Nancy Cabot, *Chicago Tribune,* Nov 20, 1937.

❷ **Optical Illusion,** *Farm Journal and Farmers Wife* (Silver Anniversary issue), 1945.

❸ **The Diamond Circle,** *Kansas City Star,* Aug 14, 1935.

❹ **Andromeda,** Jinny Beyer, Hilton Head Seminar design, 2000; published in Beyer, Jinny, *Quiltmaking by Hand.*

❺ **Emerald Block,** Nancy Cabot, *Chicago Tribune,* Apr 22, 1936.
"'Emerald Block' is a pieced pattern designed to illustrate in quilt form the beauty of that precious stone for which it was named. Varying shades of green are used for the several hues of the spectrum found when light strikes the stone." Nancy Cabot, *Chicago Tribune,* 1936

❻ **The Jewel Quilt,** *Kansas City Star,* May 3, 1950.

❼ **Sparkling Jewel,** Nancy Cabot, *Chicago Tribune,* Mar 11, 1937.

❽ **Vega,** Jinny Beyer, Hilton Head Seminar design, 2000.

❾ **Florentine Diamond,** Clara Stone, *Practical Needlework,* ca. 1906.

❿ **Three Patch Quilt,** Alice Brooks, *Alice Brooks Designs,* date unknown. Also known as:
Koala, Jinny Beyer, Beyer, Jinny, *Patchwork Portfolio,* 1989.

⓫ **Sand Dollar,** Jinny Beyer, Hilton Head Seminar design, 1989; published in Beyer, Jinny, *Patchwork Portfolio.*

⓬ **Crossed Canoes,** Ruby McKim, *Kansas City Star,* May 18, 1929. See 80-8 and 201-6. Also known as:
Indian Canoes, Nancy Cabot, *Chicago Tribune,* Oct 1, 1936.
Twinkling Star, Nancy Cabot, unidentified newspaper clipping, date unknown.
Two Canoes, Nancy Page, *Birmingham News,* Oct 29, 1940.

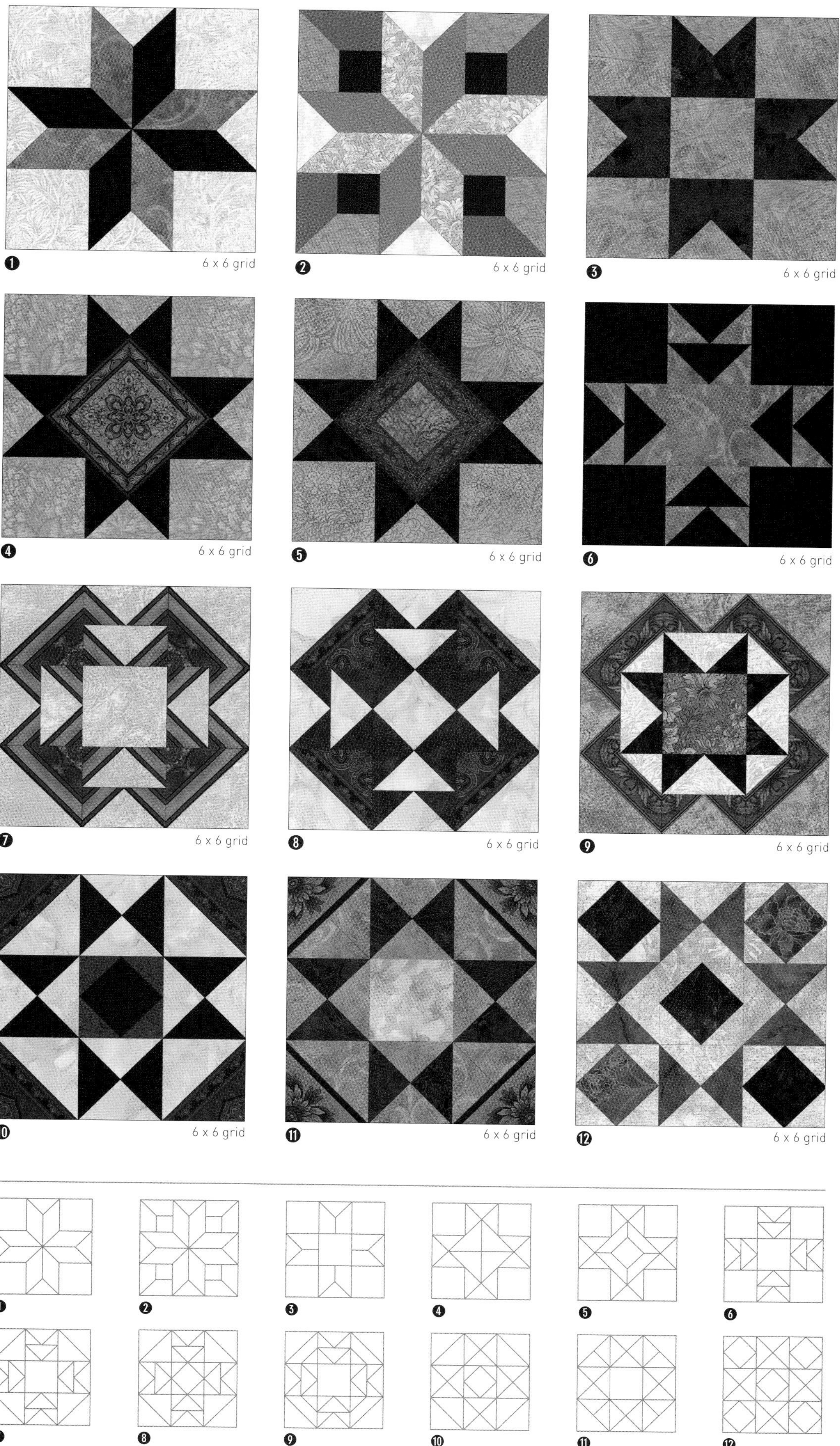

❶ **Godey Design,** *Godey's Lady's Book,* 1858.

❷ **Box Quilt,** Nancy Page, *Nashville Banner,* Mar 20, 1934.

❸ **Variable Star,** Home Art Studios, *World Herald,* Feb 15, 1934.

❹ **Right Hand of Fellowship,** *Kansas City Star,* Dec 5, 1936.

❺ **Braced Star,** *Ladies Art Company,* 1922.

❻ **Ohio Friendship Quilt,** *Anne Cabot's Fall and Winter Album,* ca. 1950. Also known as:

- **Eight Pointed Star,** Gutcheon, *The Perfect Patchwork Primer,* 1973.

❼ **Capital T,** *Louisville Farm and Fireside,* Feb 15, 1883. Also known as:

- **Capital Tee,** Nancy Page, *Birmingham News,* Feb 15, 1942.
- **Capitol T,** *Farmer's Wife,* Jan 1913.
- **Double T,** *Farmer's Wife Book of Quilts,* 1931.
- **The Double T,** *Kansas City Star,* Mar 27, 1937.
- **The Double T Quilt,** *Kansas City Star,* Dec 10, 1947.
- **Friendship Quilt,** *Q Book 102, Grandmother's Patchwork,* date unknown.
- **Imperial T,** Nancy Cabot, *Chicago Tribune,* Jun 26, 1934.
- **T Block,** Nancy Cabot, *Chicago Tribune,* Jun 26, 1934.
- **T' Quartette,** *Old Fashioned Quilts,* ca. 1931.

"The ingenuity of early America quilt makers is a constant marvel to those of us who study and analyze the patterns they evolve. They could do more things with triangles than seems possible. Triangles and squares appear as maple leaf, as duck track, as flight of wild geese, and in still another arrangement as something like what we have today—capital T. Of course, those women would never have thought of a 'tee' such as is used for a golf game. But the idea was there, nevertheless." Nancy Page, *Birmingham News,* Dec 29, 1942

"As the 'Imperial T,' or 'T Block,' this popular block was evolved from the old and effective nine patch known as 'Shoo Fly.' "Nancy Cabot, *Chicago Tribune,* Jun 26, 1934

❽ **Tea for Four,** Nancy Page, *Birmingham News,* Sep 5, 1937.

❾ **Rippling Star,** Marcia Aasmundstad, Beyer, Jinny *The Quilter's Album. . .,* 1980.

❿ **Mosaic,** Nancy Page, unidentified newspaper clipping date unknown.

⓫ **Mystery Flower Garden,** *Prize Winning Designs,* ca. 1931.

⓬ **Blocks and Stars,** Gutcheon, *The Perfect Patchwork Primer,* 1973.

❶ **Four Corners,** *Grandma Dexter Appliqué and Patchwork Designs, Book 36a,* ca. 1932.

❷ **Robbing Peter to Pay Paul,** *Ladies Art Company,* 1897. Also known as:
Arizona, Nancy Page, *Birmingham News,* Jul 7, 1936.

❸ **Talisman,** Jinny Beyer, Hilton Head Seminar design, 1998.

❹ **St. Gregory's Cross,** *Kansas City Star,* Apr 1, 1933.

❺ **Ocean Wave,** Nancy Page, *Nashville Banner,* Feb 20, 1934.

❻ **Gentleman's Fancy,** *Ladies Art Company,* 1897. Also known as:
Colonial Patchwork, Nancy Cabot, per Alboum, date unknown.
Mary's Block, Nancy Cabot *Chicago Tribune,* Jul 28, 1937.
Twenty Four Triangles, *Farm Journal and Farmer's Wife* (Silver Anniversary issue), 1945.

❼ **T Blocks,** Finley, 1929. Also known as:
Four T's, Nancy Cabot, *Chicago Tribune,* Jan 17, 1938.

❽ **Stars,** Nancy Cabot, *Chicago Tribune,* Jan 5, 1935. Also known as:
Eddystone Light, Nancy Cabot, *Chicago Tribune,* Jul 6, 1938.

❾ **Desert Sun,** Jinny Beyer, Hilton Head Seminar design, 1997.

❿ **Chain,** Gutcheon, *The Perfect Patchwork Primer,* 1973.

⓫ **Mrs. Bryan's Choice,** Clara Stone, *Practical Needlework,* ca. 1906.

⓬ **Lucky Clover Quilt,** Aunt Martha series: *Quilt Designs,* ca. 1952.

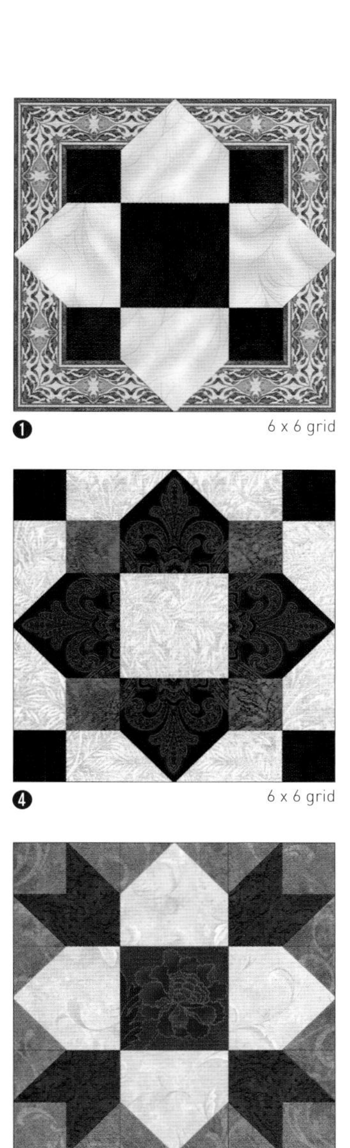

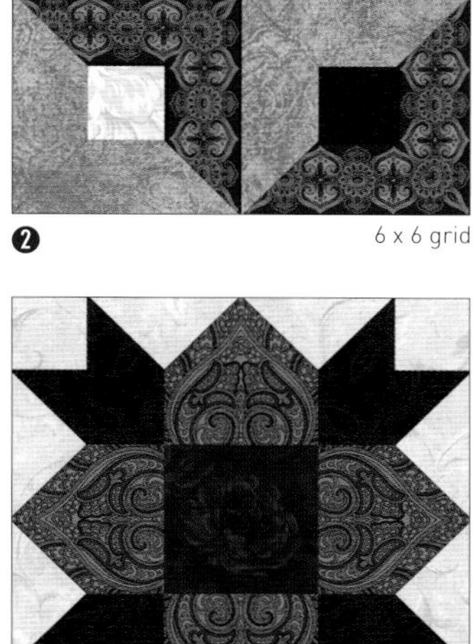

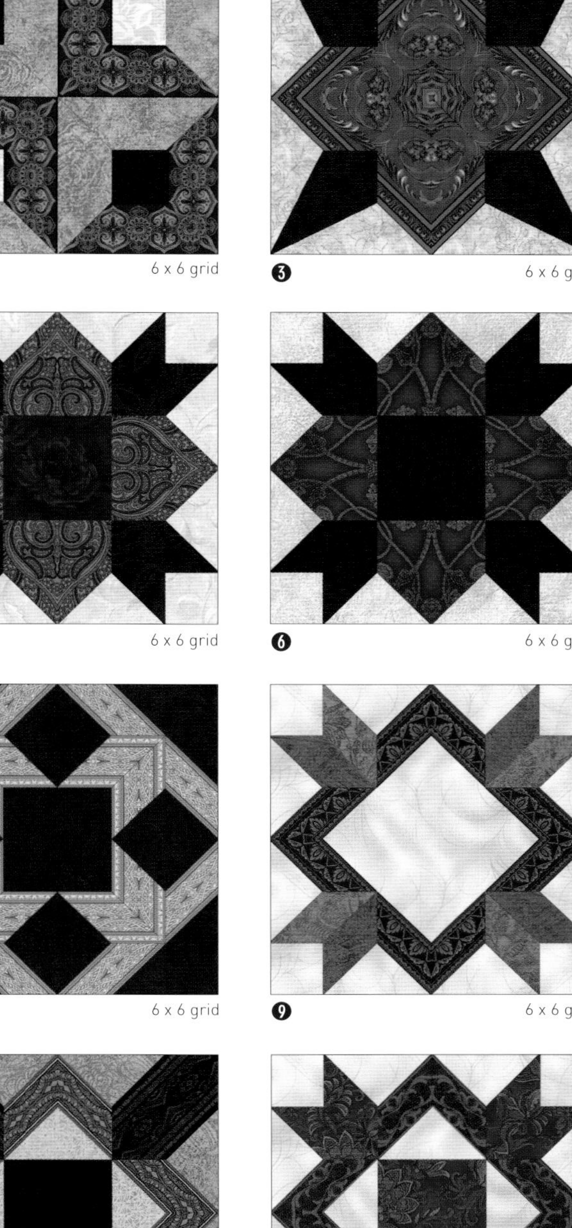

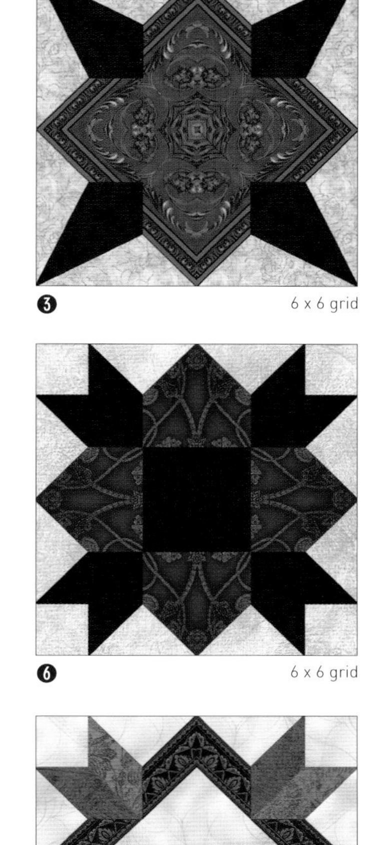

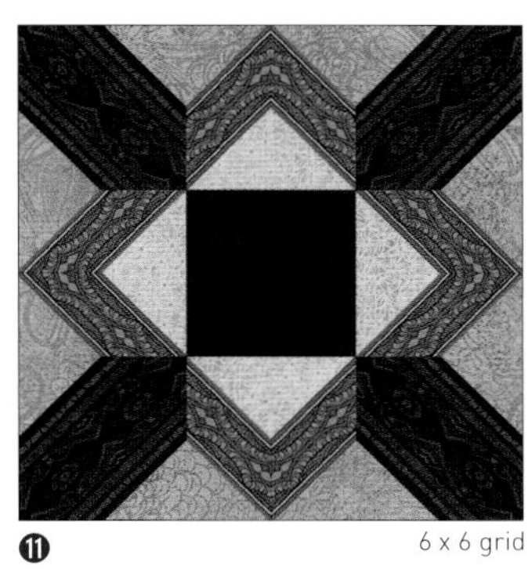

❶ 6 x 6 grid ❷ 6 x 6 grid ❸ 6 x 6 grid

❹ 6 x 6 grid ❺ 6 x 6 grid ❻ 6 x 6 grid

❼ 6 x 6 grid ❽ 6 x 6 grid ❾ 6 x 6 grid

❿ 6 x 6 grid ⓫ 6 x 6 grid ⓬ 6 x 6 grid

❶ **The Cornerstone,** *Kansas City Star,* Dec 23, 1942.

❷ **The Bat,** *Prize Winning Designs,* ca. 1931. Also known as:

- **The Bat's Block,** Nancy Cabot, *Chicago Tribune,* Feb 9, 1937.
- **Blue Bell Block,** *Progressive Farmer,* 1940.

❸ **Clam Bake,** Jinny Beyer, Hilton Head Seminar design, 1985; published in Beyer, Jinny, *Patchwork Portfolio.*

❹ **Quatrefoils,** Nancy Cabot, *Chicago Tribune,* Jun 29, 1936.

❺ **Weather Vane,** Ruby McKim, *Kansas City Star,* Jan 5, 1929. See 299-7. Also known as:

- **Weathervane,** Hall, 1935.

❻ **Weathervane,** *Old Fashioned Quilts,* ca. 1931. See 299-7.

❼ **Weathervane,** *The Patchwork Book,* 1932. See 299-7.

❽ **A Beauty,** Clara Stone, *Practical Needlework,* ca. 1906.

❾ **Modern Star,** *Virginia Snow Studio Art Needlework Creations,* 1932. Also known as:

- **David and Goliath,** Nancy Cabot, *Chicago Tribune,* Sep 6, 1936.
- **Doe and Darts,** Nancy Cabot, *Chicago Tribune,* Sep 6, 1936.
- **Four Darts,** Nancy Cabot, *Chicago Tribune,* Sep 6, 1936.
- **Star of Many Points,** Nancy Cabot, *Chicago Tribune,* Sep 6, 1936.

"'Star of Many Points' first was pieced in New England in 1782 under the name of 'David and Goliath.' It has been called variously 'Four Darts,' 'Doe and Darts,' and by its present title, depending upon the community in which it became popular. 'Star of Many Points' is the name under which the pieced pattern is known throughout the central states of the midwest." Nancy Cabot, *Chicago Tribune,* Sep 6, 1936

❿ **Welcome Hand,** Clara Stone, *Practical Needlework,* ca. 1906.

⓫ **Jim Dandy,** Nancy Cabot, *Chicago Tribune,* Jan 27, 1938.

⓬ **Laurel Wreath,** *Quilt Booklet No. 1,* ca. 1931. See 96-11 and 211-12. Also known as:

- **North Carolina,** Nancy Page, *Birmingham News,* Mar 15, 1938.

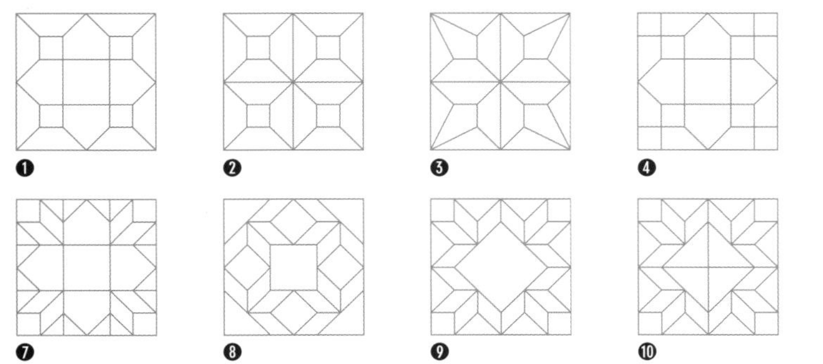

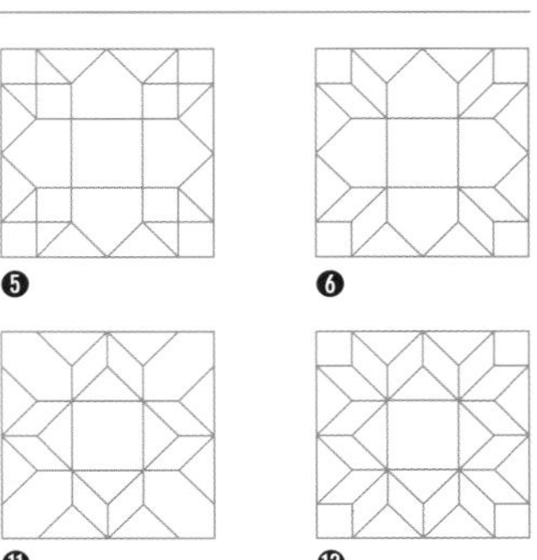

❶ ❷ ❸ ❹ ❺ ❻

❼ ❽ ❾ ❿ ⓫ ⓬

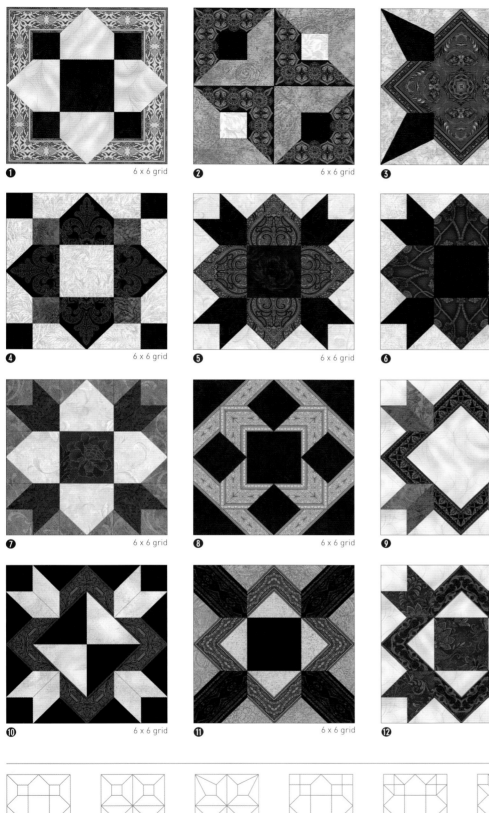

1 Aunt Sukey's Choice, Beyer, Jinny, *Patchwork Patterns,* 1979. See 228-11 and 259-4.

2 Puss in the Corner, Nancy Page, *Birmingham News,* Apr 30, 1940.

3 Bottleneck, Jinny Beyer, Beyer, Jinny, *Patchwork Portfolio,* 1989.

4 Love in a Mist, *Farm Journal and Farmer's Wife,* ca. 1941.

5 Moonstone, Jinny Beyer, Hilton Head Seminar design, 1989; published in Beyer, Jinny, *Patchwork Portfolio.*

6 Star of Erin, Nancy Cabot, *Chicago Tribune,* Apr 10, 1936.

7 Victory Garden, Nancy Page, *Birmingham News,* May 25, 1943.
"'Nancy... isn't this going to be quite a good deal of work?' I think it is. Perhaps that is why I called it a Victory Garden. Those gardens are going to be work too. If we don't waste the seeds which we sow we are going to have to put in many hours of work. But the results will justify the hard work we hope. And that's the way I feel about this pattern. The results when the quilt top is all pieced and set together ought to justify the time used in putting them together." Nancy Page, *Birmingham News,* May 25, 1943

8 Crisscross, *Farm Journal and Farmer's Wife* (Silver Anniversary issue), 1945.

9 Palace Parquet, Jinny Beyer, Hilton Head Seminar design, 2002.

10 Building Blocks, Virginia Snow, *Grandma Dexter Appliqué and Patchwork Designs, Book 36a,* ca. 1932. See 66-10 and 206-7.
Also known as:
- **Jerusalem Road,** Beyer, Jinny, *The Quilter's Album...,* 1980.
- **Pin Wheel,** Beyer, Jinny, *The Quilter's Album...,* 1980.
- **Whirl Around,** *Kansas City Star,* Jul 31, 1940.
- **Whirligig,** Aunt Martha series: *The Quilt Fair Comes to You,* ca. 1933.

11 Jig Saw, Jinny Beyer, Hilton Head Seminar design, 1993.

12 Windmill, *Prize Winning Designs,* ca. 1931.

❶ **Card Trick,** Jeffrey Gutcheon, Gutcheon, *The Perfect Patchwork Primer,* 1973.

❷ **Air Castle,** *Ladies Art Company,* 1897. Also known as:

- **Air Castles,** Nancy Page, *Birmingham News,* Jan 19, 1937.
- **Towers of Camelot,** Nancy Cabot, *Chicago Tribune,* Jul 14, 1937.

❸ **Castle in Air,** Gutcheon, *The Perfect Patchwork Primer,* 1973.

❹ **Indiana Puzzle,** Jane Alan, unidentified newspaper clipping, ca. 1932.

❺ **Star of Hope,** Marcia Aasmundstad, Beyer, Jinny, *The Quilter's Album...,* 1980.

❻ **Chinese Coin,** *Prize Winning Designs,* ca. 1931. Also known as:

- **Mill Wheel,** Nancy Cabot, *Chicago Tribune,* Mar 17, 1934.
- **Square and Half Square,** *Kansas City Star,* Oct 28, 1933.
- **Water Wheel,** Nancy Cabot, *Chicago Tribune,* Mar 11, 1934.
- **Waterwheel,** Nancy Cabot, *Chicago Tribune,* Sep 5, 1936.

❼ **Virginia Worm Fence,** Clara Stone, *Practical Needlework,* ca. 1906.

❽ **Pudding and Pie,** Alice Brooks, unidentified newspaper clipping, date unknown.

❾ **Good Luck,** Nancy Cabot, *Chicago Tribune,* Jul 16, 1936.

❿ **Wheel,** *Farm Journal Quilt Patterns,* ca. 1935.

⓫ **4 H,** Kansas City Star, Jan 24, 1940. Also known as:

- **A Quilt for a 4 H Club Room,** *Kansas City Star,* Apr 18, 1956.

"The 4-H club girl who is seeking a finishing touch for her own bedroom finds it in this quilt design coming from Mrs. Ollie Mae Rogers, Mount Vernon, Ark. One thinks immediately of green and white as colors of the block." *Kansas City Star,* Jan 24, 1940

⓬ **Toy Windmill,** *Detroit Free Press,* May 26, 1933.

Quick Reference: Garden of Eden or Broken Sash

Another testament of how blocks change over time are these six blocks all named either *Garden of Eden* or *Broken Sash* . They are very similar in design, yet each is drafted differently and none of them have any additional names.

Broken Sash, Khin. **See 61-2.**

Garden of Eden, *Chicago Tribune*, **See 183-3.**

Garden of Eden, *Ladies Art Company.* **See 183-2.**

Garden of Eden, *Chicago Tribune.* **See 243-4.**

Broken Sash, *Chicago Tribune.* **See 119-7.**

Broken Sash, *The Farm Journal Quilt Patterns.* **See 233-12.**

❶ **Arkansas Traveler,** *Ladies Art Company,* 1897.

❷ **The Box,** Nancy Page, *Nashville Banner,* Mar 20, 1934.
"From Welland Canada to Nancy Page quilt members all over the United States and Canada comes this new quilt block called 'The Box.' Mrs. E. Lemley is the generous person who shares the pattern with us. She says that her great-grandmother gave this pattern to her mother and Mrs. Lemley's mother in turn passed the pattern on to her daughter.
Nancy Page, *Nashville Banner,* Mar 20, 1934

❸ **Entertaining Motions,** Beth Gutcheon, Gutcheon, *The Perfect Patchwork Primer,* 1973.

❹ **Starry Path,** Alice Brooks, *Detroit Free Press,* Jan 23, 1936.

❺ **Windmill,** *Prize Winning Designs,* ca. 1931. Also known as:
- **The Radio Windmill,** *Kansas City Star,* Oct 22, 1941.
- **The Windmill of Amsterdam,** *Cincinnati Enquirer,* May 1, 1933.

❻ **Perpetual Motion,** Nancy Cabot, *Chicago Tribune,* Aug 29, 1936.

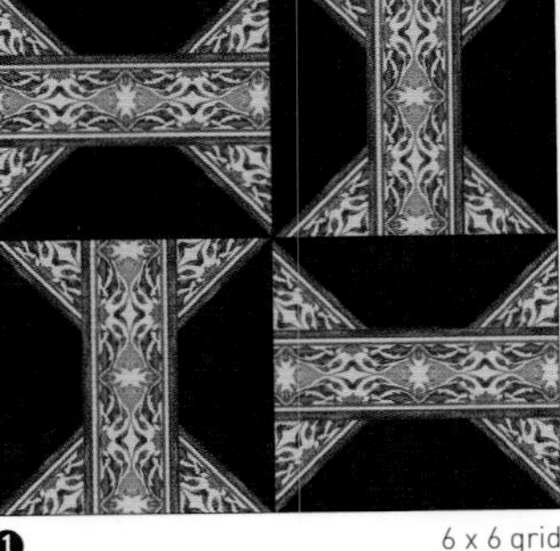

❶ 6 x 6 grid

❷ 6 x 6 grid

❸ 6 x 6 grid

❹ 6 x 6 grid

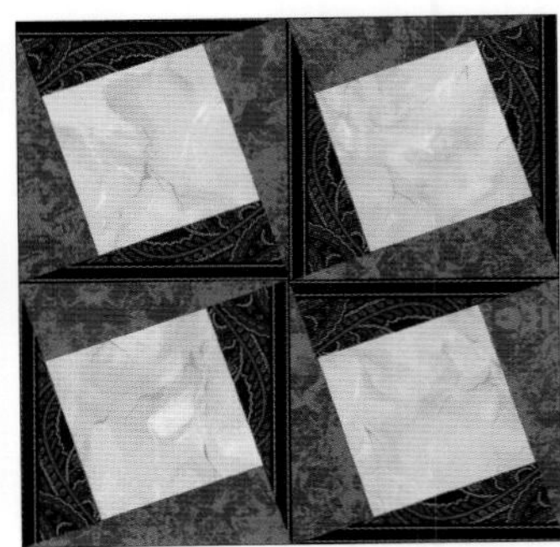

❺ 6 x 6 grid

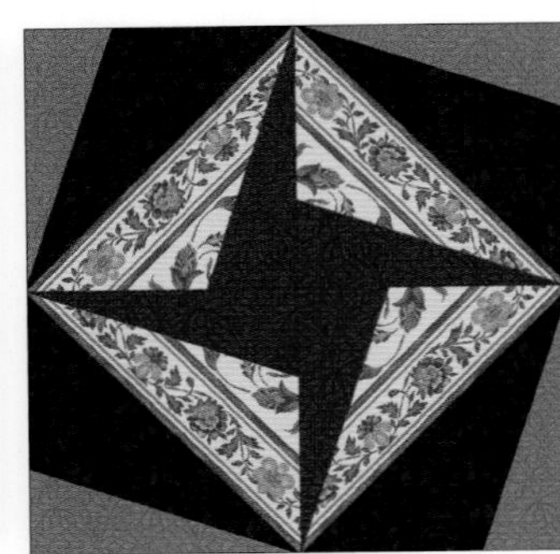

❻ 6 x 6 grid

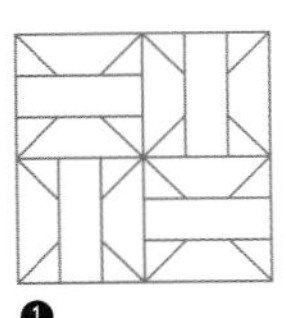

❶ ❷

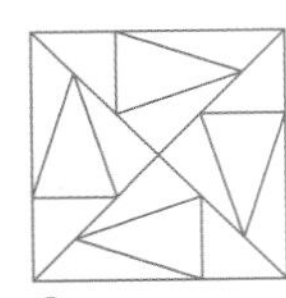

❸

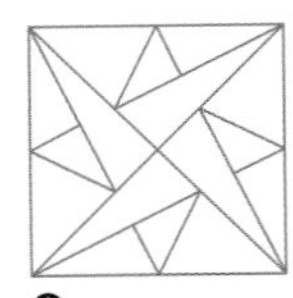

❹

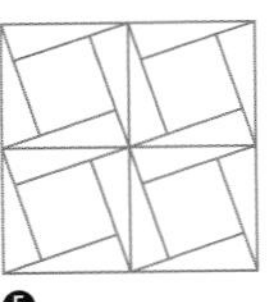

❺

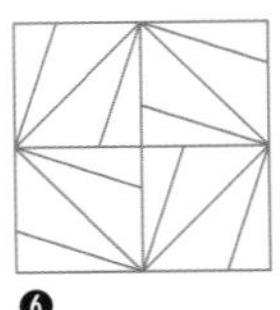

❻

❶ **Double Pinwheel,** Alice Brooks, *Bismark Tribune,* Dec 18, 1940.

❷ **Waterwheels,** Nancy Cabot, *Chicago Tribune,* Jun 24, 1936.

❸ **Mrs. Morgan's Choice,** Nancy Cabot, Chicago Tribune, Dec 25, 1934.
"The birthplace of this block, 'Mrs. Morgan's Choice,' is Alabama and the date 1862. It was made and named for the mother of Gen. John Hunt Morgan, the famous confederate raider." Nancy Cabot, *Chicago Tribune,* Dec 25, 1934

❹ **Mrs. Morgan's Choice,** Ladies Art Company, 1897. Also known as:
Paddle Wheel, *Prize Winning Designs,* ca. 1931.
Spinning Wheel, *Grandmother Clark's Patchwork Quilt Designs, From Books 20-21-23,* 1932.

❺ **Mrs. Morgan's Choice,** Nancy Cabot, *Chicago Tribune,* Nov 25, 1936.
"In various locales across the country, many a quilt block was designed which had no name, but which was so popular that its history passed by word of mouth with each pattern as it was traded and was referred to as 'Mrs. So-and-So's' block from 'Such-and-such.' 'Mrs. Morgan's Choice originated in Iowa." Nancy Cabot, *Chicago Tribune,* Nov 25, 1936

❻ **Rolling Pinwheel,** Gutcheon, *The Perfect Patchwork Primer,* 1973.
"The woman who invented the 'Paddle Wheel' block deserves merit for ingenuity and imagination. She originally was from Virginia, but moved to Vicksburg, Miss., where she had ample opportunity to see the paddle wheels of the old river boats." Nancy Cabot, Apr 9, 1937

❼ **Rolling Pinwheels,** Nancy Page, *Birmingham News,* Oct 15, 1940.

❽ **Whirling Pinwheel,** Nancy Cabot, *Chicago Tribune,* May 29, 1933.

❾ **Whirling Pin Wheel,** *Kansas City Star,* Sep 22, 1934.

❿ **Rolling Pinwheel,** *Ladies Art Company,* 1897. Also known as:
Pinwheel Star, *Old Fashioned Quilts,* ca. 1931.
Rolling Pin Wheel, Hall, 1935.

⓫ **Flying Darts,** Nancy Cabot, *Chicago Tribune,* Aug 17, 1934. Also known as:
Flying Dutchman, Nancy Cabot, *Chicago Tribune,* Aug 17, 1934.
"The quilt pattern, 'Flying Dutchman, also is known as 'Flying Darts.' This block was pieced first in 1861 in New York. From there, the pattern migrated to Boston, Philadelphia, and points west ... red and white have been the favorite color scheme of most of the quilts." Nancy Cabot, *Chicago Tribune,* Aug 17, 1934

⓬ **Beginner's Choice,** Laura Wheeler, *Sioux City Journal,* Nov 9, 1940.

❶ **Rumplestiltskin's Frolic,** Kathryn Kuhn, Beyer, Jinny, *The Quilter's Album ...*, 1980.

❷ **Flying Dutchman,** *Ladies Art Company*, 1897.

❸ **Star Light,** Marcia Aasmundstad, Beyer, Jinny, *The Quilter's Album ...*, 1980.

❹ **Lightning in the Hills,** Nancy Cabot, *Chicago Tribune*, May 19, 1936.

❺ **Spinning Arrows,** Nancy Cabot, *Chicago Tribune*, Feb 25, 1936.

❻ **Ribbon Quilt** Nancy Page, *Birmingham News*, Feb 26, 1935.

❼ **Four Winds,** Nancy Cabot, *Chicago Tribune*, Feb 20, 1936.

❽ **Hummingbird,** Clara Stone, *Practical Needlework*, ca. 1906. Also known as:
- **Bright Star,** Nancy Cabot, *Chicago Tribune*, Aug 29, 1934.
- **Budding Roses,** Nancy Page, *Birmingham News*, Nov 7, 1939.
- **Crow's Foot,** *Old Fashioned Quilts*, ca. 1931.
- **Maple Leaf,** Nancy Cabot, *Chicago Tribune*, Nov 30, 1936.
- **Rose Bud,** Hall, 1935.
- **Rosebud,** *Ladies Art Company*, 1928.

❾ **Straw Flowers,** Nancy Page, *Birmingham News*, Feb 21, 1939.

❿ **Album,** Ruby McKim, *Kansas City Star*, Sep 26, 1928. Also known as:
- **Arbor Window,** *Grandmother Clark's Authentic Early American Patchwork Quilts, Book No. 21*, 1932.
- Carrie Hall **Album,** ca. 1938, per Havig.
- **Courthouse Square,** Ickis, 1949.
- **Katie's Choice,** *Farm Journal and Farmer's Wife* (Silver Anniversary issue), 1945.

⓫ **Rocky Road to California,** *Ladies Art Company*, 1897. Also known as:
- **The Broken Sugar Bowl,** *Kansas City Star*, Jul 22, 1942.
- **Road to the White House,** *Farm Journal Quilt Patterns*, 1935.

⓬ **Steps to the Altar,** Jane Alan, *Illinois State Register*, Feb 12, 1933.

❶ 6 x 6 grid

❷ 6 x 6 grid

❸ 6 x 6 grid

❹ 6 x 6 grid

❺ 6 x 6 grid

❻ 6 x 6 grid

❼ 6 x 6 grid

❽ 6 x 6 grid

❾ 6 x 6 grid

❿ 6 x 6 grid

⓫ 6 x 6 grid

⓬ 6 x 6 grid

❶ ❷ ❸ ❹ ❺ ❻

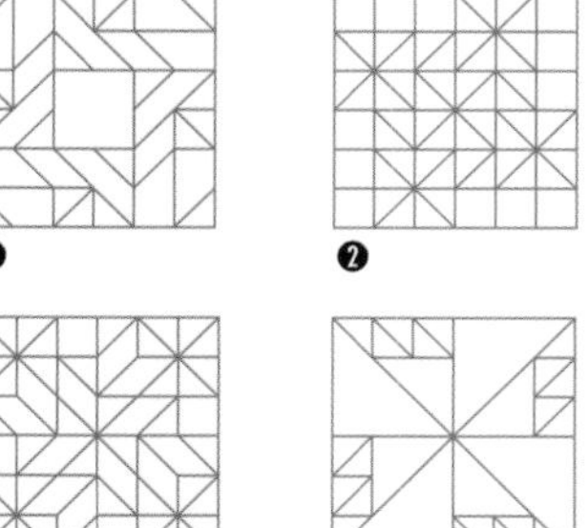

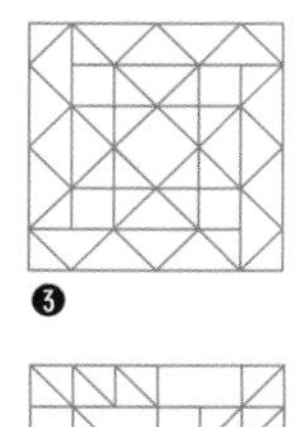

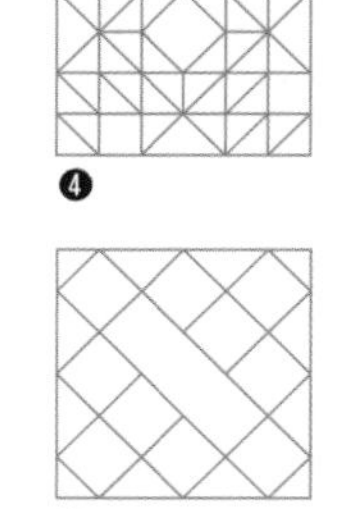

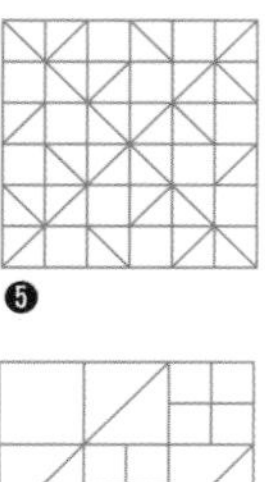

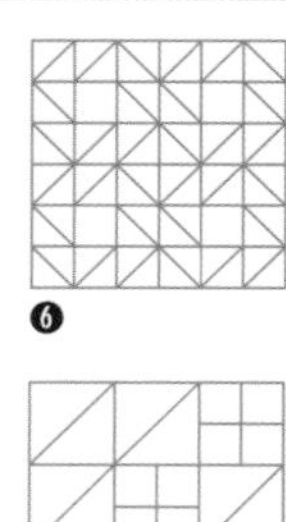

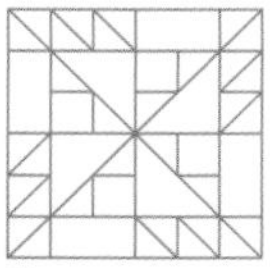

❼ ❽ ❾ ❿ ⓫ ⓬

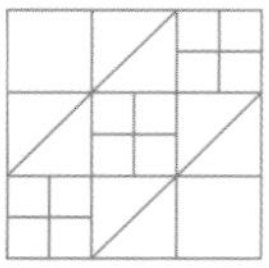

Quick Reference: Butterflies

Butterfly designs seemed to appear on the quilt scene in the early part of the 1900s. Here are ten butterfly patterns from several different categories in this book. The Evaline Foland block, which was published in the *Kansas City Star*, October 7, 1931, is the earliest butterfly design I found in print. Two blocks each are by Laura Wheeler and Alice Brooks and, as is the case with most of their designs, these blocks are more innovative in style than the other butterflies shown here.

A Butterfly in Angles, *Kansas City Star*. **See 438-9.**

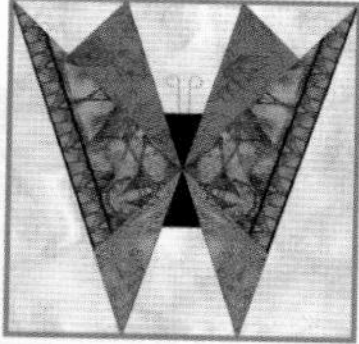

Pieced Butterfly, *Chicago Tribune*. **See 173-1.**

Butterfly, *Kansas City Star*. **245-10.**

Butterfly, *Cincinnati Enquirer*. **181-3.**

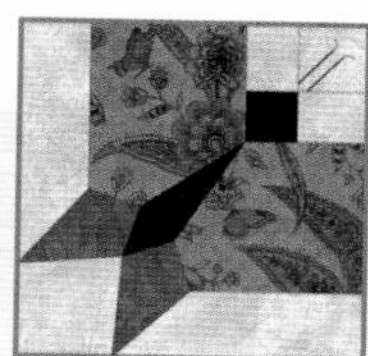

Butterfly, *Kansas City Star*. **See 220-4.**

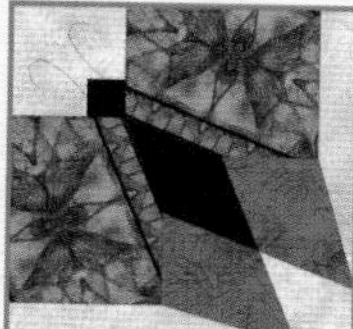

Fluttering Butterfly, *Cincinnati Enquirer*. **See 250-3.**

Butterfly, *Minneapolis Star, Freemont News Messenger*. **See 317-10.**

Butterfly, *Detroit Free Press*. **See 341-8.**

Butterfly, *Detroit Free Press*. **See 123-7.**

The Butterfly, *Des Moines Register*. **See 273-1.**

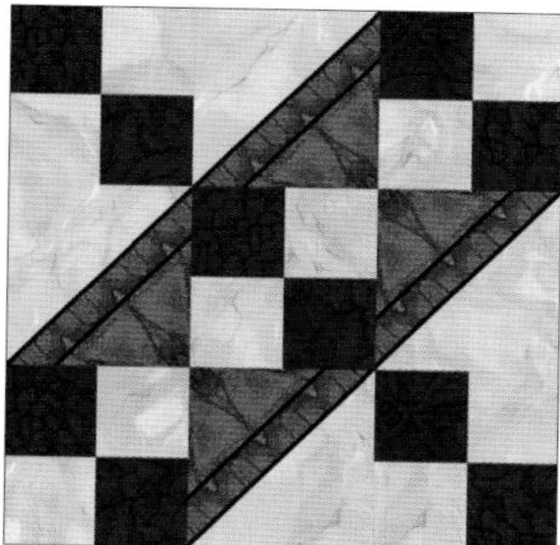

❶ 6 x 6 grid

❷ 6 x 6 grid

❸ 6 x 6 grid

❹ 6 x 6 grid

❺ 6 x 6 grid

❻ 6 x 6 grid

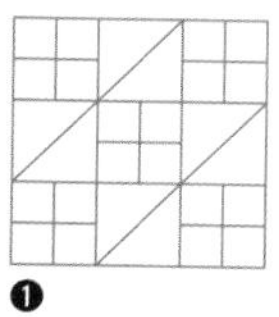

❶

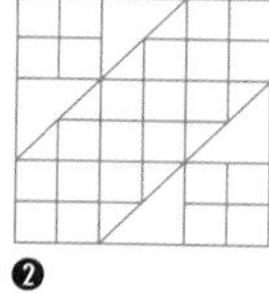

❷

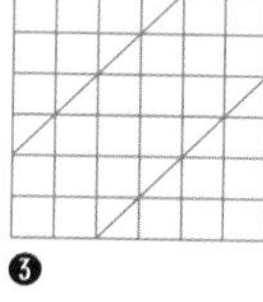

❸

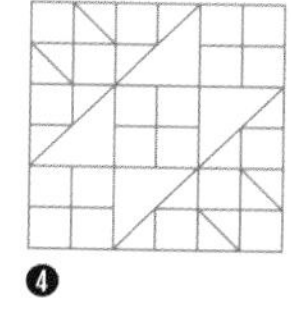

❹

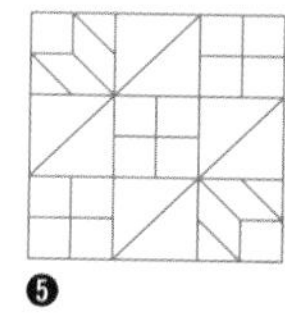

❺

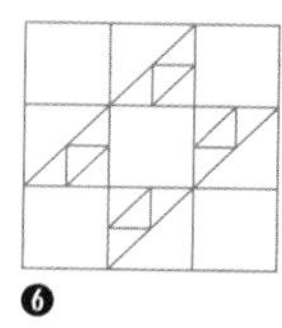

❻

❶ **The Railroad,** *Ladies Art Company*, 1897. Also known as:

- **Blue Chains,** Nancy Cabot, *Chicago Tribune*, Mar 7, 1936.
- **Double Hour Glass,** *Grandmother's Patchwork Quilt Designs, Book 20*, 1931.
- **Dublin Road Quilt,** Nancy Page, *Nashville Banner*, Jun 14, 1932.
- **Garden Walk,** *Farmer's Advocate*, Mar 16, 1933.
- **Golden Stairs,** Nancy Cabot, *Chicago Tribune*, Nov 14, 1936.
- **Jacob's Ladder,** Ruby McKim, *Kansas City Star*, Nov 7, 1928.
- **Off to San Francisco,** Nancy Page, *Birmingham News*, Apr 4, 1939.
- **Pacific Railroad,** Nancy Cabot, *Chicago Tribune*, Oct 9, 1936.
- **The Road to Arkansas,** *Kansas City Star*, Jun 6, 1956.
- **Road to California,** *The Patchwork Book*, 1932.
- **Rocky Road to California,** Home Art Studios, *Colonial Quilts*, 1932.
- **Stepping Stones,** Hall, 1935.
- **Tail of Benjamin Franklin's Kite,** Hall, 1935.
- **The Trail of the Covered Wagon,** Hall, 1935.
- **Underground Railroad,** Hall, 1935.
- **Wagon Tracks,** Hall, 1935.
- **Western Reserve,** Beyer, Jinny, *The Quilter's Album...*, 1980.

❷ **Jacob's Ladder,** Webster, 1915. Also known as:

- **Road to California,** *Old Fashioned Quilts*, ca. 1931.
- **Rocky Road to California,** Hinson, 1973.

❸ **Jacob's Ladder,** Finley, 1929. Also known as:

- **Stepping Stones,** Finley, 1929.
- **The Tail of Benjamin's Kite,** Finley, 1929.
- **The Trail of the Covered Wagon,** Finley, 1929.
- **The Underground Railroad,** Finley, 1929.
- **Wagon Tracks,** Finley, 1929.

❹ **Rocky Road to Dublin,** Nancy Cabot, *Chicago Tribune*, Aug 15, 1933.

❺ **Dublin Steps,** Virginia Snow, *Grandma Dexter Appliqué and Patchwork Designs, Book 36a*, ca. 1932.

❻ **Red White and Blue,** Nancy Page, *Birmingham News*, Aug 20, 1940.

Quick Reference: Leaves

The various "leaf" patterns have been collected here for easy reference.

The Maple Leaf, *Kansas City Star,* **See 236-5.**

Autumn Leaf, Finley, **See 333-1.**

Autumn Leaf, *Ladies Art Company.* **See 333-2.**

Tea Leaf, *Quilt Blocks from The Farmer's Wife.* **See 223-12.**

Autumn Leaf, Alboum, date unknown. **See 314-6.**

Maple Leaf, *Birmingham News.* **See 123-12.**

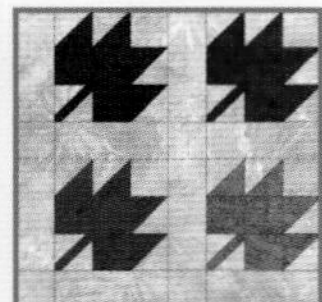
Maple Leaf, *Birmingham News.* **See 180-6 .**

Autumn Leaf, *Cincinnati Enquirer.* **See 335-7.**

Autumn Leaf, *Old Fashioned Quilts.* **See 170-4.**

The Oak Leaf, *Illinois State Register.* **See 275-8.**

Tree of Life, *Chicago Tribune.* **See 152-12.**

Autumn Leaves, *Chicago Tribune.* **See 178-6.**

Ohio Shade Tree, *Birmingham News.* **See 275-10.**

English Ivy, *Kansas City Star.* **See 178-7.**

Autumn Leaf, *Patchwork Book.* **See 178-6.**

Weeping Willow, *Old Fashioned Quilts.* **See 170-9.**

The Broken Branch, *Kansas City Star.* **See 218-3.**

Lily of the Field, Hall. **See 251-12.**

The Apple Leaf, *Kansas City Star.* **See 178-2.**

Maple Leaf, *Practical Needlework.* **See 178-3.**

Tea Leaves, *Chicago Tribune.* **See 153-7.**

Maple Leaf, *Old Fashioned Quilts.* **See 153-8.**

The Maple Leaf, *Kansas City Star.* **See 119-6.**

Flying Leaves, *Chicago Tribune.* **See 149-6.**

Maple Leaf Quilt, *Aunt Martha's Favorite Quilts.* **See 322-2.**

Tea Leaf, Gutcheon, *The Perfect Patchwork Primer.* **See 75-3.**

Tea Leaf, Finley. **See 316-5.**

Tea Leaf, *Chicago Tribune.* **See 123-6.**

Tea Leaf, Hall. **See 440-6.**

Tea Leaf, Ickis. **See 252-2.**

❶ **The 'Harrison' Design,** *Dakota Farmer,* Jun 1, 1929. Also known as:

- **The Cat's Cradle,** *Kansas City Star,* Feb 24, 1934.
- **Flying Bird,** Gutcheon, *The Perfect Patchwork Primer,* 1973
- **Flying Birds,** Nancy Page, *Birmingham News,* Sep 11, 1934.
- **Harrison,** *Old Fashioned Quilts,* ca. 1931.
- **The Harrison Quilt,** *Q Book 121, Bicentennial Quilts,* ca. 1976.
- **Hour Glass,** Nancy Page, unidentified newspaper clipping, 1934.

"It is interesting to note that of all the names attributed to this pattern, only one other has the word 'bird' as part of the name, given this quote from a Nancy Page column: "You are all well enough acquainted with the usual quilt design for birds to recognize this pattern. Whenever four triangles are put together to make a large triangle, and when the center triangle is different color from that of the other three you know the design will have the word 'bird' in the name somewhere." Nancy Page, *Birmingham News,* Sep 11, 1934

❷ **Cracker,** *The Patchwork Book,* 1932.

❸ **Letter H,** *Ladies Art Company,* 1897. Also known as:

- **H Quilt,** *Kansas City Star,* Jan 3, 1945.
- **The Gate,** *Kansas City Star,* Jan 3, 1945.

❹ **Indian Hatchet,** *Ladies Art Company,* 1897. "Warlike and treacherous as the name may sound, we guarantee this to be one of the most peacefully simple little blocks to put together of all the old-time pattrns. Many a little girl has learned to sew on Indian Hatchet blocks, although a mother perhaps supervised the cutting out." McKim

❺ **New Album,** *Kansas City Star,* Feb 3, 1934.

❻ **Flying Leaves,** Nancy Cabot, *Chicago Tribune,* May 2, 1936. "'Flying Leaves' comes from Wisconsin, where it was pieced one fall and winter 85 years ago. The original colors were brown and green." Nancy Cabot, *Chicago Tribune,* May 2, 1936

❼ **Double Tulip,** Aunt Martha series: *Bold and Beautiful Quilts,* ca. 1977.

❽ **Blue Boutonnieres,** Nancy Cabot, *Chicago Tribune,* Jun 26, 1936.

❾ **London Square,** Hall, 1935.

❾ **Framed Squares,** Nancy Page, *Birmingham News,* Oct 23, 1934. Also known as:

- **Waving Grain,** Nancy Page, *Birmingham News,* Aug 12, 1941.

⓫ **Attic Window,** *Farm Journal Quilt Patterns,* ca. 1935.

⓬ **Attic Windows,** Nancy Cabot, *Chicago Tribune,* Aug 31, 1936. Also known as:

- **Garret Windows,** Nancy Cabot, *Chicago Tribune,* Feb 16, 1938.

❶ Battle of Alamo, Nancy Cabot, *Chicago Tribune,* Mar 26, 1933.
"As a second contribution to the series of quilt patterns commemorating famous American historical events, which was inaugurated last Sunday, 'The Battle of the Alamo' is offered today. So long as American history is written the story of the siege of the Alamo and of the death of Crockett, far reaching events of 1836, will live. Not the least among evidences of its place in American annals are such mementos as the quilt named for the battle. The quilt pattern was created by a patriotic Texas woman in 1836." Nancy Cabot, *Chicago Tribune* , Mar 26, 1933

❷ Cut Glass Dish, *Ladies Art Company,* 1897. Also known as:
Golden Gates, Finley, 1929.
Winged Square, Nancy Cabot, *Chicago Tribune,* Sep 11, 1933.

❸ Cut Glass Dish, Hall, 1935.

❹ Lost Ship Pattern, *Ladies Art Company,* 1897. Also known as:
Lost Ship, Clara Stone, *Practical Needlework,* ca. 1906.

❺ Birds in the Air, Finley, 1929. See 127-3. Also known as:
Flight of Swallows, Nancy Cabot, *Chicago Tribune,* Jun 28, 1937.
Flock of Geese, Finley, 1935.
Flying Birds, Finley, 1929.

❻ Jacob's Ladder, Havig ca. 1938.

❼ Flying Shuttles, Nancy Cabot, *Chicago Tribune,* Mar 17, 1937.
"'Flying Shuttles' dates back to the early 19th century when weaving was a major household occupation in the New England states. The design is composed of two favorite patches of that period, the triangle and rectangle. The original pattern was made of turkey red, white, and a dark red printed material. The shuttles are apparent in a single block, and an entire quilt is one of the most strikingly beautiful examples of patchwork in existence." Nancy Cabot, *Chicago Tribune,* Mar 17, 1937

❽ Attic Window, Nancy Cabot, *Chicago Tribune,* Jan 2, 1935.

❾ Patience Corner, Ickis, 1949. See 408-10.

❿ Ozark Maple Leaf, Nancy Page, *Birmingham News,* Mar 5, 1935.

⓫ Tangled Briars, Laura Wheeler, *Cincinnati Enquirer,* Sep 10, 1933.

⓬ Grandma's Hop Scotch, *Kansas City Star,* Apr 5, 1950.

❶ 6 x 6 grid

❷ 6 x 6 grid

❸ 6 x 6 grid

❹ 6 x 6 grid

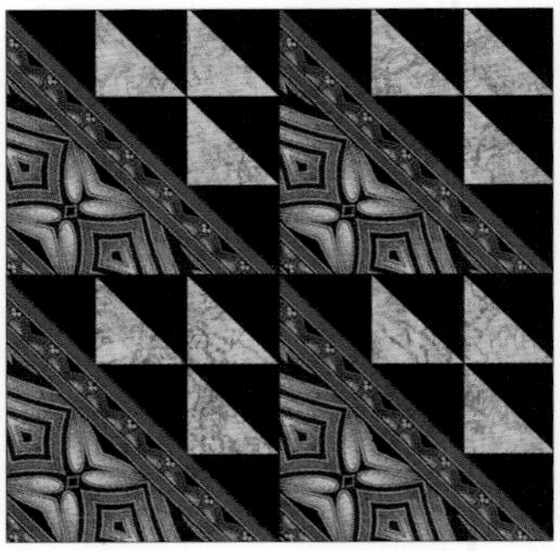

❺ 6 x 6 grid

❻ 6 x 6 grid

❼ 6 x 6 grid

❽ 6 x 6 grid

❾ 6 x 6 grid

❿ 6 x 6 grid

⓫ 6 x 6 grid

⓬ 6 x 6 grid

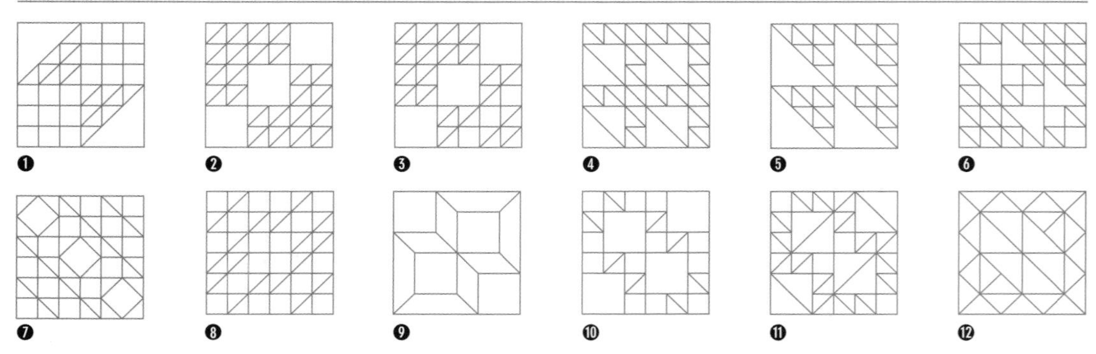

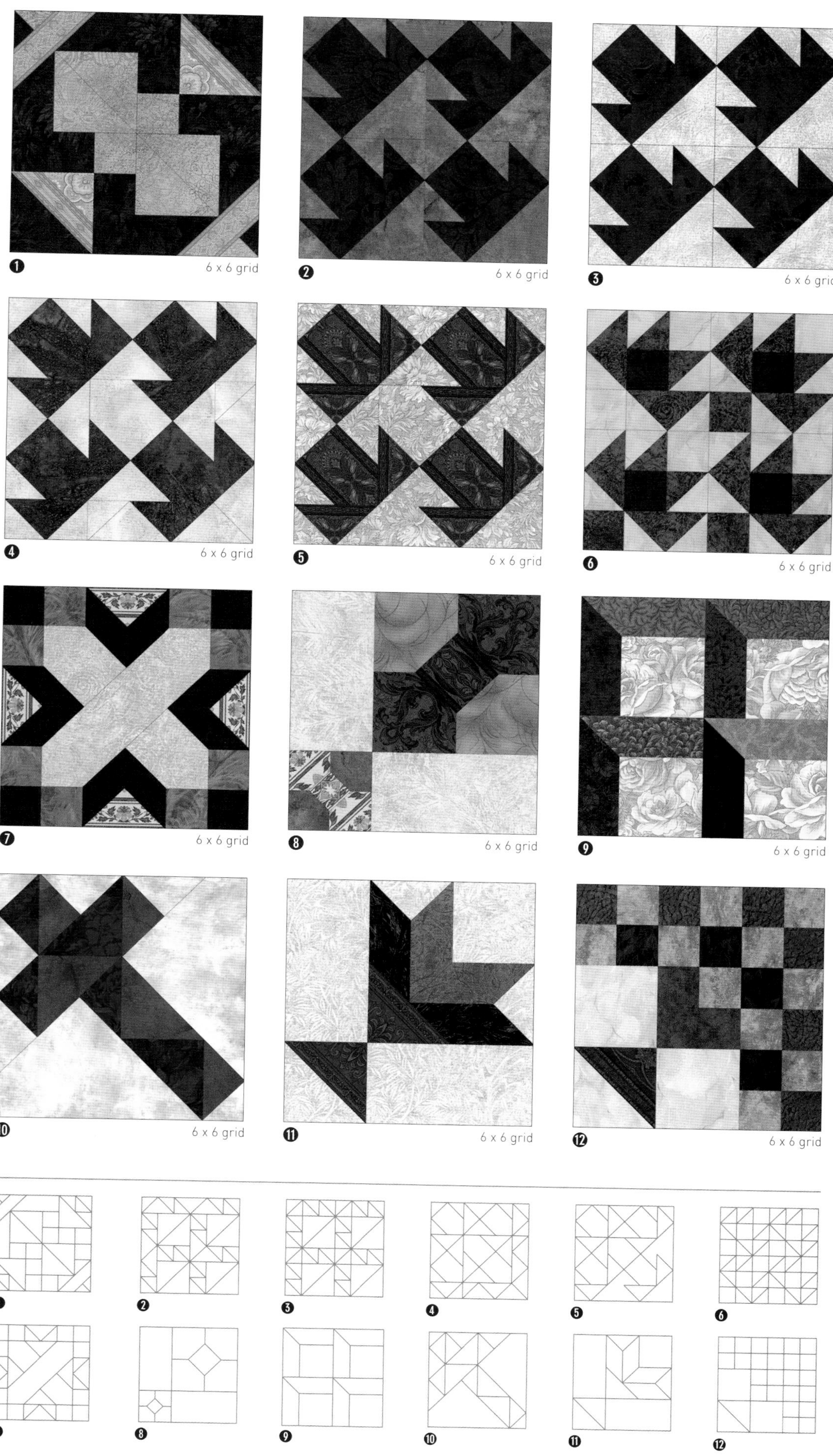

❶ **Indian Mat,** Nancy Cabot, *Chicago Tribune*, Apr 28, 1938.
"New Mexico was the source of inspiration for this beautiful 'Indian Mat.' It was adapted from a Zuni Indian mat and set together with blue and white materials. The Zunis are a tribe belonging to the Pueblos and are decidedly colorful in their regalia and habits. Their weaving is one of the outstanding examples of Indian art." Nancy Cabot, *Chicago Tribune*, Apr 28, 1938

❷ **Mixed T,** *Ladies Art Company*, 1897. Also known as:
  Mixed T Blocks, Nancy Cabot, *Chicago Tribune*, Mar 26, 1935.
"'Mixed T Blocks' is one of the ancient quilt patterns which almost always was made in blue and white. It has been most popular in New York and the New England states. Since the middle west adopted this design the color scheme has been varied." Nancy Cabot, *Chicago Tribune*, Mar. 26, 1935

❸ **The Letter T,** *Farm and Home*, Aug 1, 1891. Also known as:
  Mixed T, Nancy Page, *Nashville Banner*, Aug 15, 1933.

❹ **T Quartette,** Nancy Cabot, *Chicago Tribune*, Jul 17, 1934.
"'T Quartette' made its bow to the quilt world fifteen years ago in the hills of Tennessee. It is an unusual treatment of pieced blocks that is quite unintentionally modern. A clear Dutch blue and white formed the color scheme used in the original coverlet." Nancy Cabot, *Chicago Tribune*, Jul 17, 1934

❺ **T Quartette,** *Ladies Art Company*, 1897. Also known as:
  Four T's, Gutcheon, *The Perfect Patchwork Primer*, 1973.

❻ **Darting Birds,** Nancy Page, *Birmingham News*, Jul 9, 1935.

❼ **Friendship Quilt,** *Kansas City Star*, Jun 30, 1935.

❽ **Midget Necktie,** *Kansas City Star*, Jun 26, 1937. Also known as:
  Attic Windows, source unknown, date unknown.

❾ **New Pattern,** *Peterson's Magazine*, 1857. See 171-6, 171-7, 271-9, 407-10. Also known as:
  Cross, Hall, 1935.

❿ **The Cross,** *Ladies Art Company*, 1901.

⓫ **Basket of Scraps,** Hinson, 1973. Also known as:
  Cactus Basket, Hinson, 1973.
  Desert Rose, Hinson, 1973.
  Texas Rose, Hinson, 1973.
  Texas Treasure, Hinson, 1973.

⓬ **Bowl of Fruit,** Nancy Cabot, *Chicago Tribune*, May 6, 1938.

❶ **Steps to the Altar,** *Ladies Art Company,* 1897. Also known as:

Altar Steps, Nancy Cabot, *Chicago Tribune,* Sep 16, 1936.

Cake Stand, *Old Fashioned Quilts,* ca. 1931.

Fruit Dish, *Old Fashioned Quilts,* ca. 1931.

"Here is another of the blocks expressing a religious motif. Since ecclesiastical interpretations in quilting are characteristically picturesque, it is only natural that this quilt design should be striking as well as dignified. The arrangement of the completed blocks does much to create an illusion of 'Steps to the Altar.' " Nancy Cabot, *Chicago Tribune,* Apr 27, 1934

❷ **Strawberry Basket,** *Grandmother Clark's Old Fashioned Quilt Designs, Book 21,* 1931.

❸ **Grandmother's Basket,** Eveline Foland, *Kansas City Star,* Feb 27, 1932.

❹ **A Basket Quilt in Triangles,** *Kansas City Star,* Dec 16, 1942.

❺ **Cactus Flower,** Eveline Foland, *Kansas City Star,* Jul 4, 1931.

❻ **Magnolia,** Laura Wheeler, *Cincinnati Enquirer,* Nov 2, 1933. Also known as:

Magenta, Laura Wheeler, *Grit Patterns,* May 25, 1980.

"When a quiltmaker is looking for a quilt that is so lovely in design that she will be proud to claim it as her handiwork, and yet at the same time wants a pattern that is very simple to do, she selects the 'Magnolia.' With but one exception, all the pattern pieces are the same width, which to the quiltmaker means that the material can be cut in strips, and the patches cut off as needed—a saving of much time and labor. Not alone is the pattern an easy one to cut, but it is a very simple block to make." Laura Wheeler, *Cincinnati Enquirer,* Nov 2, 1933

❼ **Sycamore,** Jinny Beyer, Quilter's Quest design, 2004.

❽ **White Pine,** Jinny Beyer, Quilter's Quest design, 2004.

❾ **Juniper,** Jinny Beyer, Quilter's Quest design, 2004.

❿ **Centennial Tree,** Clara Stone, *Practical Needlework,* ca. 1906.

⓫ **Pine Tree,** Beyer, Jinny, *The Quilter's Album...,* 1980.

⓬ **Tree of Life,** Nancy Cabot, *Chicago Tribune,* Apr 27, 1938.

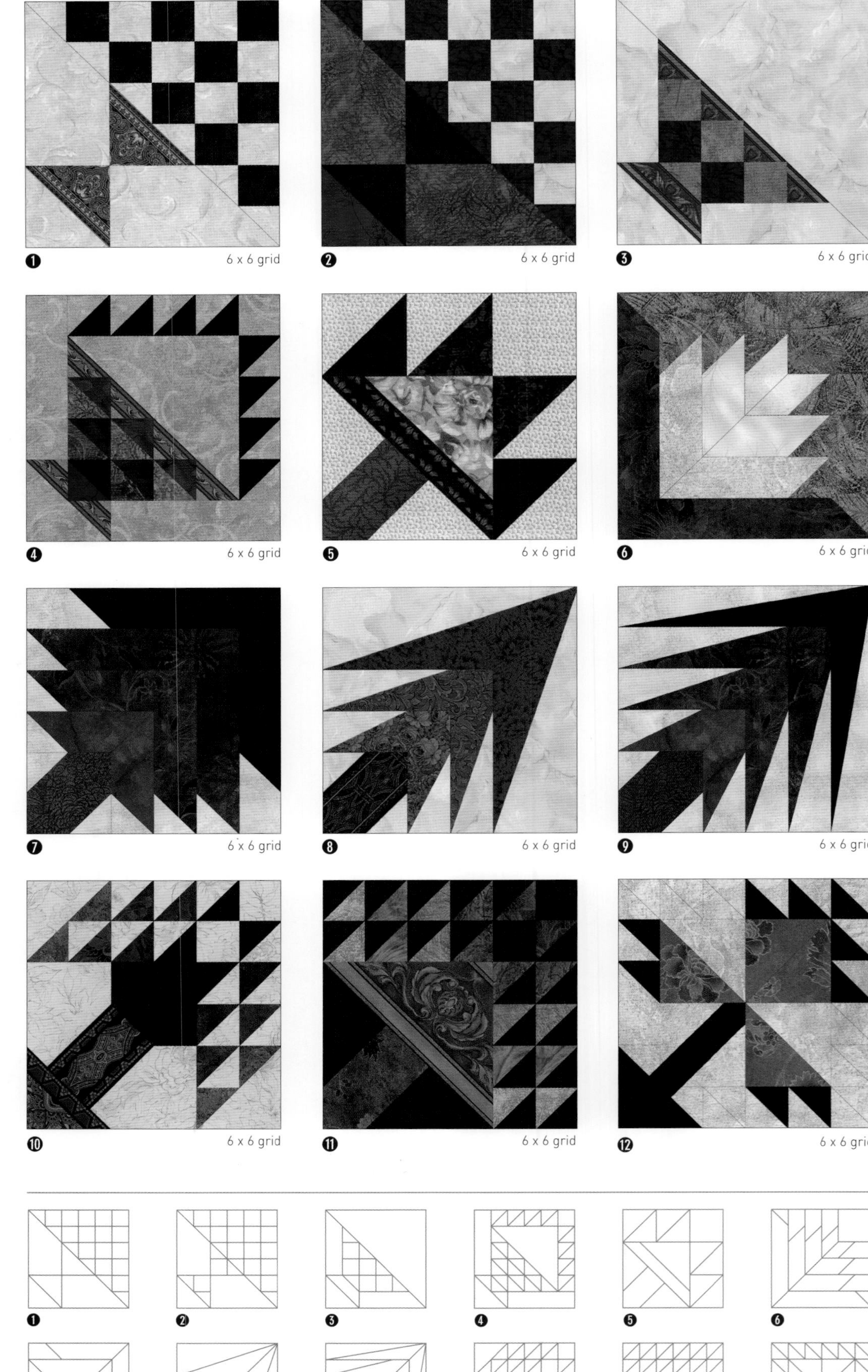

❶ **Domino Net,** Nancy Cabot, *Chicago Tribune,* Oct 28, 1937.

❷ **Linoleum Patch,** ca. 1938, per Havig.

❸ **Red Cross,** *Kansas City Star,* Jul 21, 1934. Also known as:

- **Baby 9 Patch,** *Mrs Danner Presents Quilt Book 7,* 1975.

❹ **Flagstones,** *Ladies Art Company,* 1928. Also known as:

- **Aunt Patsy's Pet,** Nancy Cabot, *Chicago Tribune,* Aug 25, 1936.
- **Aunt Patty's Favorite,** *Farm Journal and Farmer's Wife* (Silver Anniversary issue), 1945.
- **Federal Chain,** Nancy Cabot, *Chicago Tribune,* Aug 25, 1936.
- **Four and Nine Patch,** Nancy Cabot, *Chicago Tribune,* Feb 6, 1937.
- **Improved Nine Patch,** Hall, 1935.
- **The Mystery Snowball,** *Kansas City Star,* Jun 11, 1947.
- **Nine-Patch,** Hall, 1935.
- **Snow Ball,** Hall, 1935.
- **Snowball,** *Old Fashioned Quilts,* ca. 1931.
- **The Snowball and 9-Patch,** *Mrs. Danner's Fifth Quilt Book,* 1970.

❺ **Hayes Corner,** Gutcheon, *The Perfect Patchwork Primer,* 1973.

❻ **Tile Puzzle,** Hall, 1935. Also known as:

- **Tic Tac Toe,** Nancy Page, *Birmingham News,* Sep 17, 1935.

❼ **Tea Leaves,** Nancy Cabot, *Chicago Tribune,* Mar 1, 1937.

❽ **Maple Leaf,** *Old Fashioned Quilts,* ca. 1931.

❾ **Hayes Corner,** *Q Book 124, White House Quilts,* date unknown.

❿ **Domino,** *Ladies Art Company,* 1897. Also known as:

- **Chained Dominos,** Nancy Cabot, *Chicago Tribune,* Oct 10, 1933.
- **Enigma Square,** Nancy Cabot, *Chicago Tribune,* Sep 16, 1937.

⓫ **Wampum Block,** Nancy Cabot, *Chicago Tribune,* Apr 16, 1938.

⓬ **Whirlwind,** *The Patchwork Book,* 1932.

❶ **Double Z,** *Louisville Farm and Fireside,* 1883. See 269-7.

❷ **The Ladie's Aid Album,** *Kansas City Star,* Jan 22, 1938.

❸ **Antique Tile Block,** Nancy Cabot, *Chicago Tribune,* May 3, 1938.

❹ **The X,** *Kansas City Star,* Jul 10, 1940.

❺ **Jack's Delight,** Clara Stone, *Practical Needlework,* ca. 1906.

❻ **Sail Boat Block,** Ruby McKim, *Kansas City Star,* May 31, 1930.

❼ **Sail Boat,** Hall, 1935.

❽ **Buckwheat,** Nancy Cabot, *Chicago Tribune,* Mar 4, 1937.

❾ **Hour Glass,** *Ladies Art Company,* 1897.

❿ **Noon and Night,** Nancy Page, unidentified newspaper clipping, date unknown.

⓫ **Dancing Pinwheels,** Nancy Cabot, *Chicago Tribune,* Dec 19, 1935.
"The dazzling pinwheel provides the incentive for the design of this lovely 'Dancing Pinwheel' block. It is an old pattern, the first example of the block was pieced in red and white, portraying as realistically as possible the whirling, flaming sparks of a pyrotechnical wheel in motion." Nancy Cabot, *Chicago Tribune,* Dec 19, 1935

⓬ **Weathervane and Steeple,** Nancy Cabot, *Chicago Tribune,* Mar 24, 1936.
"As the title of this arresting pieced block might suggest, it is not of modern vintage. The original 'Weathervane and Steeple' block was pieced of turkey red and unbleached muslin. This combination still is retained although the material and shades of red have been varied slightly. It is easy to visualize a cupola of a barn with a double ended weathervane perched atop. Clever arrangement of pieced and plain blocks shows that the wind always is blowing in the right direction." Nancy Cabot, *Chicago Tribune,* Mar 24, 1936

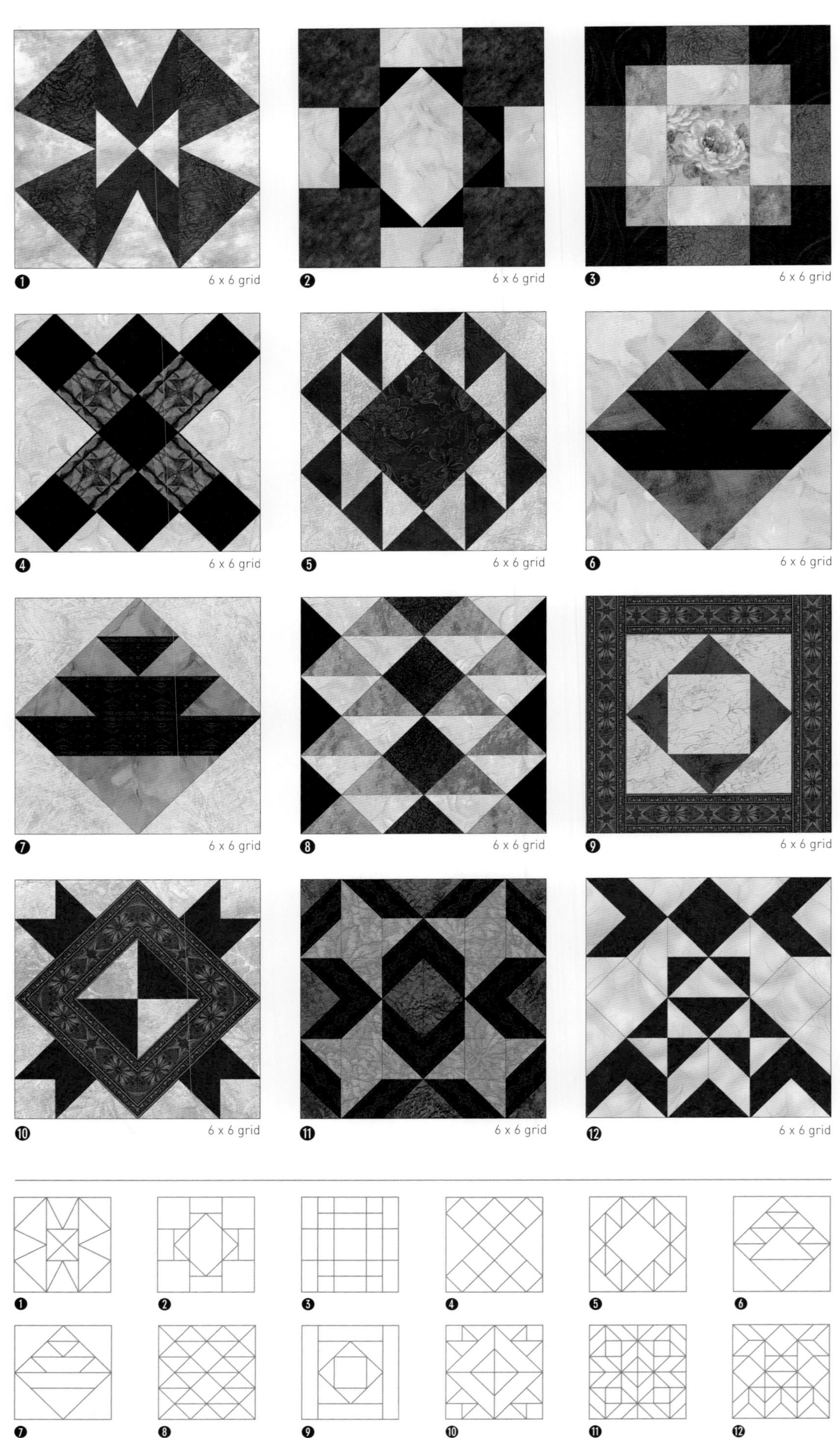

❶ **Hill and Valley,** unidentified newspaper clipping, date unknown.

❷ **Sunshine and Shadow,** Nancy Page, *Nashville Banner,* Mar 7, 1933.

❸ **Joseph's Necktie,** *Ladies Art Company,* 1897. Also known as:

> **Peter's Neckties,** Nancy Page, *Birmingham News,* Apr 14, 1942.

❹ **Economy 9 Patch,** *Mrs Danner Presents Quilt Book 7,* 1975.

❺ **The Owl Quilt,** *Kansas City Star,* May 1, 1937.

❻ **Squares and Diamonds,** *Kansas City Star,* Oct 21, 1959.

❼ **The Star of Bethlehem,** *Kansas City Star,* Apr 24, 1937.

❽ **Grandmother's Quilt,** *Kansas City Star,* Nov 3, 1948.

❾ **The Bridle Path,** *Kansas City Star,* Mar 9, 1935.

❿ **Illinois Road,** Nancy Cabot, *Chicago Tribune,* Feb 7, 1935. See 169-1.

⓫ **Counterpane,** Nancy Cabot, *Chicago Tribune,* Apr 4, 1934.

⓬ **King's Highway,** Nancy Page, *Birmingham News,* Sep 30, 1941.

1 **Puss in the Corner,** Webster, 1915. See 177-3.

2 **Kitty Corner,** Finley, 1929. Also known as:
- **Puss in the Corner,** Finley, 1929.
- **Tic Tac Toe,** Finley, 1929.

3 **The Double Arrow,** *Kansas City Star,* Jun 24, 1933.

4 **Chicago Star,** *Ladies Art Company,* 1897.

5 **Evening Star,** Laura Wheeler, *Indianapolis Star,* May 13, 1937.

6 **Columbian Star,** *Ladies Art Company,* 1897.
"The star Arcturus found its way to the quilt world during the 1933 Century of Progress, as the 'Columbian Star' did in the 1893 exposition." Nancy Cabot, *Chicago Tribune* , May 11, 1935

7 **Grandmother's Dream,** Nancy Cabot, *Chicago Tribune,* Aug 11, 1934. See 411-2.

8 **The Pin Wheel Quilt,** Eveline Foland, *Kansas City Star,* Oct 29, 1930. Also known as:
- **Aunt Vina's Favorite,** Aunt Martha series: *The Quilt Fair Comes to You,* ca. 1933.
- **Butterfly,** Nancy Cabot, *Chicago Tribune,* Sep 30, 1935.
- **Richmond,** *Hearth and Home,* date unknown, per Brackman.
- **Spinning Wheel,** ca. 1938, per Havig.

9 **Cross and Chains,** Nancy Cabot, *Chicago Tribune,* Feb 10, 1938.

10 **Goose Tracks,** Ickis, 1949.

11 **Sage Bud,** *Kansas City Star,* Nov 29, 1930. See 194-4, 223-8, 299-4, 299-5 . Also known as:
- **The Scrap Collector's Quilt,** *Kansas City Star,* May 13, 1958.
- **Turkey Tracks,** Ickis, 1949.

12 **Noon Day Lilies,** Nancy Page, *Birmingham News,* Jul 21, 1942.

1 12 x 12 grid

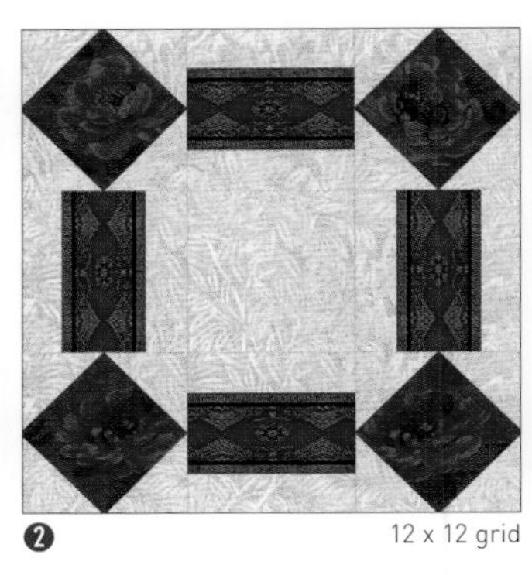

2 12 x 12 grid

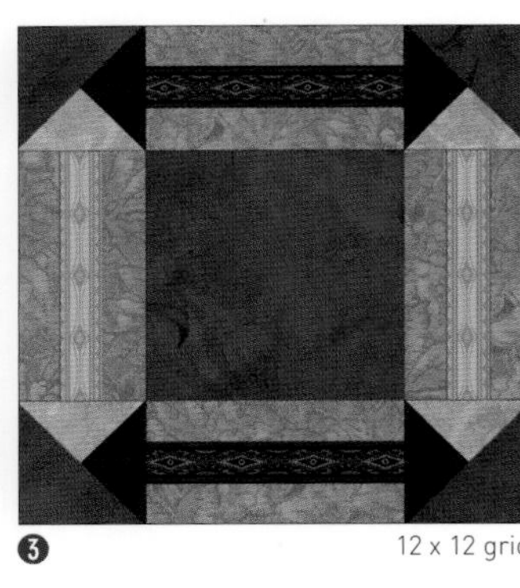

3 12 x 12 grid

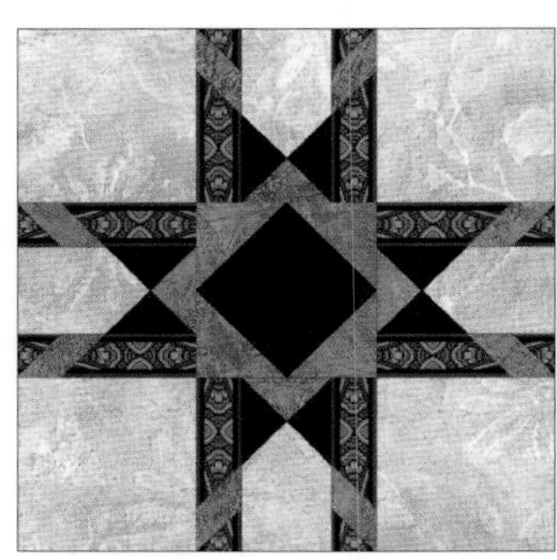

4 12 x 12 grid

5 12 x 12 grid

6 12 x 12 grid

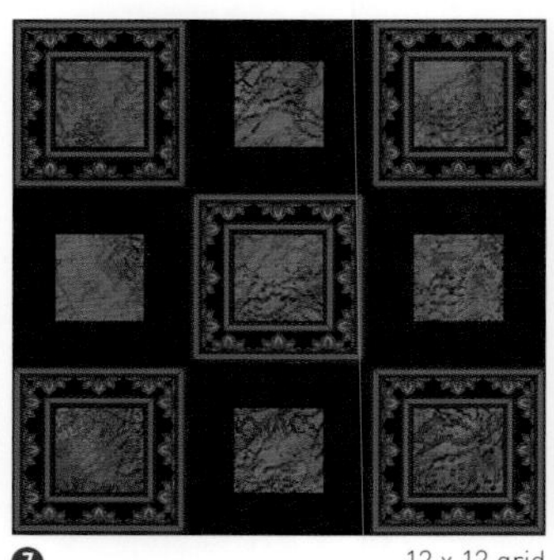

7 12 x 12 grid

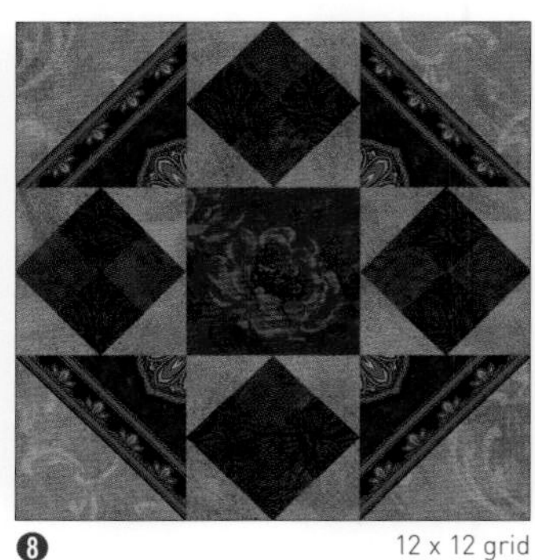

8 12 x 12 grid

9 12 x 12 grid

10 12 x 12 grid

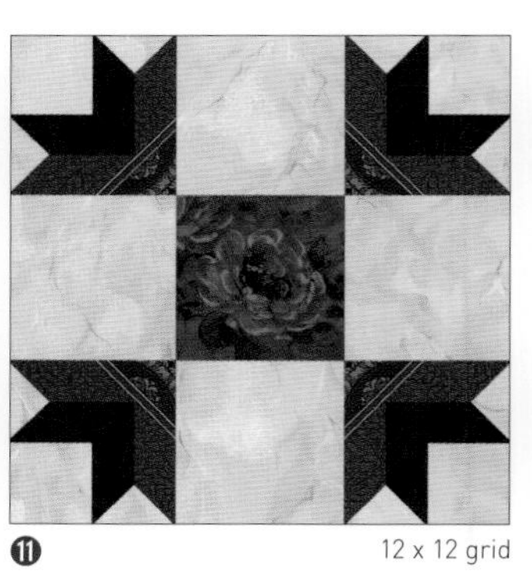

11 12 x 12 grid

12 12 x 12 grid

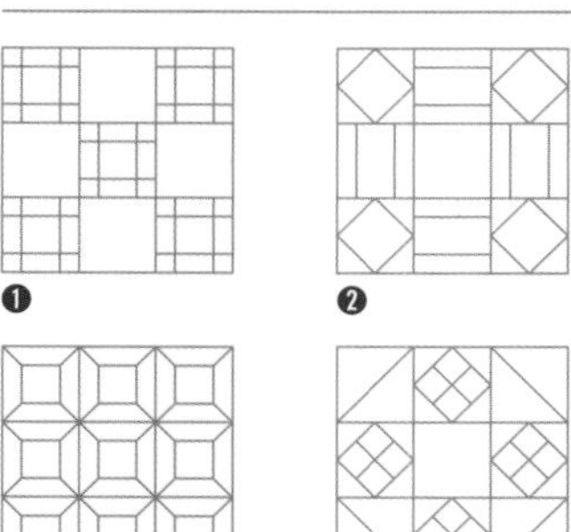

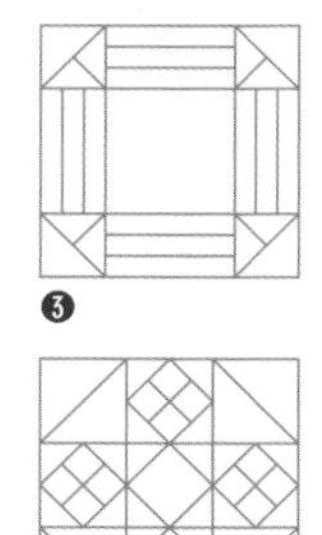

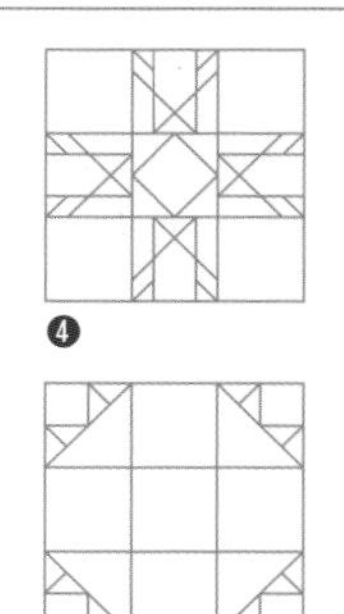

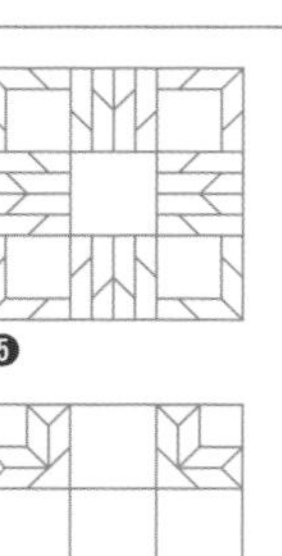

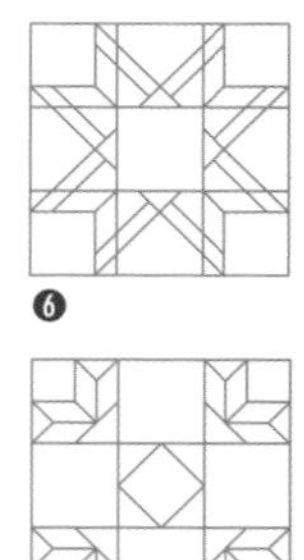

1 2 3 4 5 6

7 8 9 10 11 12

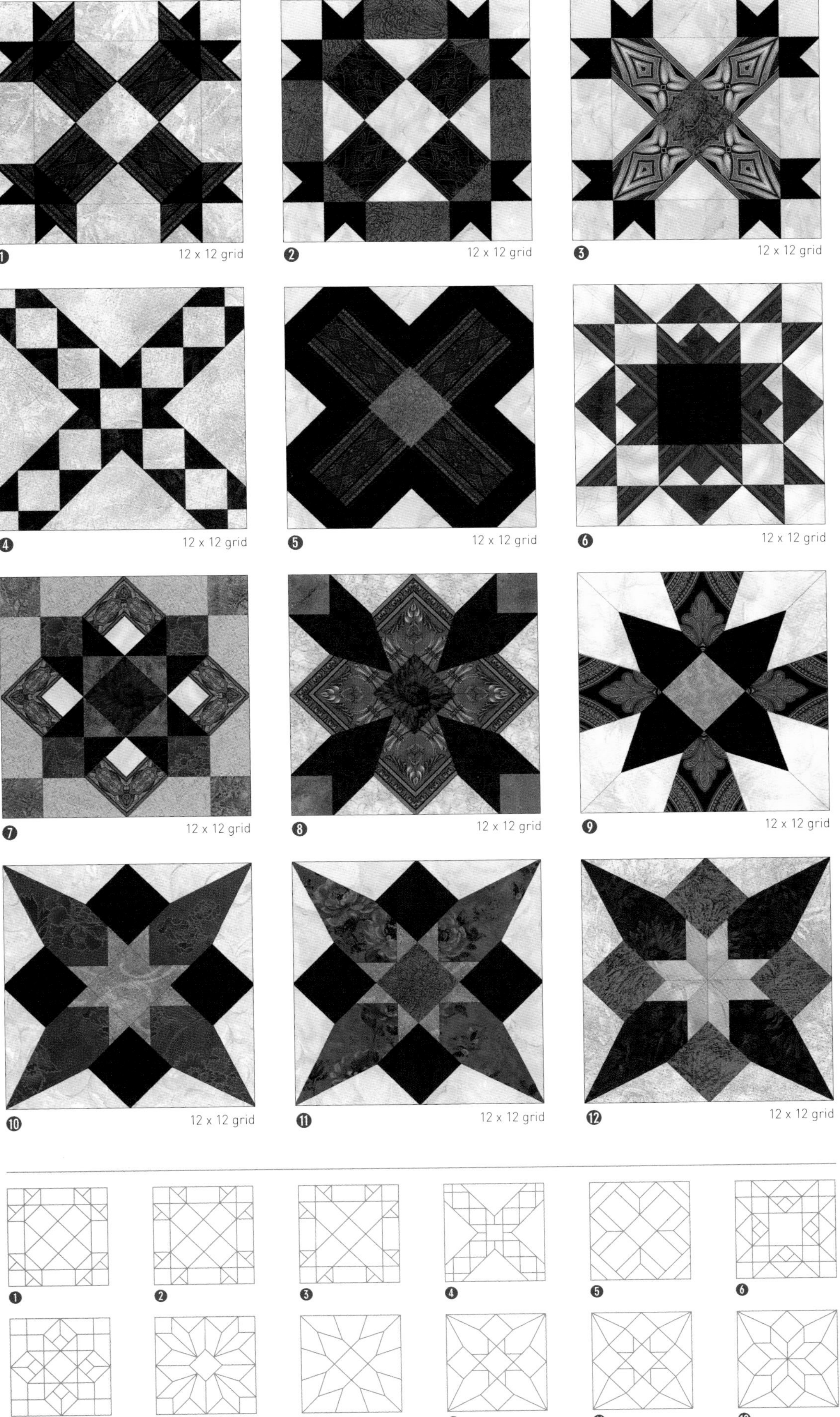

1 **New Mexico,** Nancy Page, *Birmingham News*, Mar 22, 1938.

2 **Cross upon Cross,** Finley, 1929. Also known as:
  Golgotha, Finley, 1929.
  The Three Crosses, Finley, 1929.

3 **Golgotha,** Nancy Cabot, *Chicago Tribune*, May 26, 1933. Also known as:
  The Crowned Cross, Nancy Cabot, *Chicago Tribune*, May 26, 1933.

4 **Variable Star,** Home Art Studios, *World Herald*, Feb 15, 1934.

5 **Cross of Geneva,** Nancy Cabot, *Chicago Tribune*, May 26, 1938.

6 **Best of All,** Clara Stone, *Practical Needlework*, ca. 1906. Also known as:
  Christmas Star, Hinson, 1973.

7 **Boxwood Hill,** Jinny Beyer, Beyer, Jinny, *Patchwork Portfolio*, 1989.

8 **Feathered Square,** Jinny Beyer, Hilton Head Seminar design, 1988; published in Beyer, Jinny, *Patchwork Portfolio*.

9 **Rocket Fire,** Jinny Beyer, Hilton Head Seminar design, 1997.

10 **Skyrocket,** *The Patchwork Book*, 1932. Also known as:
  Starlight, *The Patchwork Book*, 1932.

11 **Sky Rocket,** Ruby McKim, *Kansas City Star*, Nov 21, 1928. Also known as:
  The Album, *Kansas City Star*, Jun 5, 1937.
  Dogtooth Violet, Nancy Cabot, *Chicago Tribune*, Oct 15, 1936.
  Jewel Boxes, Nancy Page, *Birmingham News*, Aug 1, 1939.
  Skyrocket, Nancy Cabot, *Chicago Tribune*, Apr 24, 1933.

12 **Skyrocket,** Nancy Cabot, *Chicago Tribune*, Dec 17, 1936.

1 **Columbine,** Jinny Beyer, Beyer, Jinny, *Patchwork Portfolio,* 1989.

2 **Gunnell's Run,** Jinny Beyer, Beyer, Jinny, *Patchwork Portfolio,* 1989.

3 **Rain or Shine,** Nancy Page, unidentified newspaper clipping, date unknown.

4 **The Double Cross Quilt,** *Kansas City Star,* Sep 7, 1938.

5 **Cross,** Gutcheon, *The Perfect Patchwork Primer,* 1973.

6 **The Mayflower,** Beyer, Jinny, *The Quilter's Album ...,* 1980.

7 **Beginner's Delight,** Alice Brooks, unidentified newspaper clipping, date unknown.

8 **Emerald City,** Jinny Beyer, Hilton Head Seminar design, 1994.

9 **Fox Fire,** Jinny Beyer, Hilton Head Seminar design, 1994.

10 **Springtime Star,** Jinny Beyer, RJR Patterns, 1994.

11 **Pinwheel,** Alice Brooks, *Detroit Free Press,* Jul 13, 1935.

12 **Squares and Diamonds,** Laura Wheeler, unidentified newspaper clipping, date unknown.

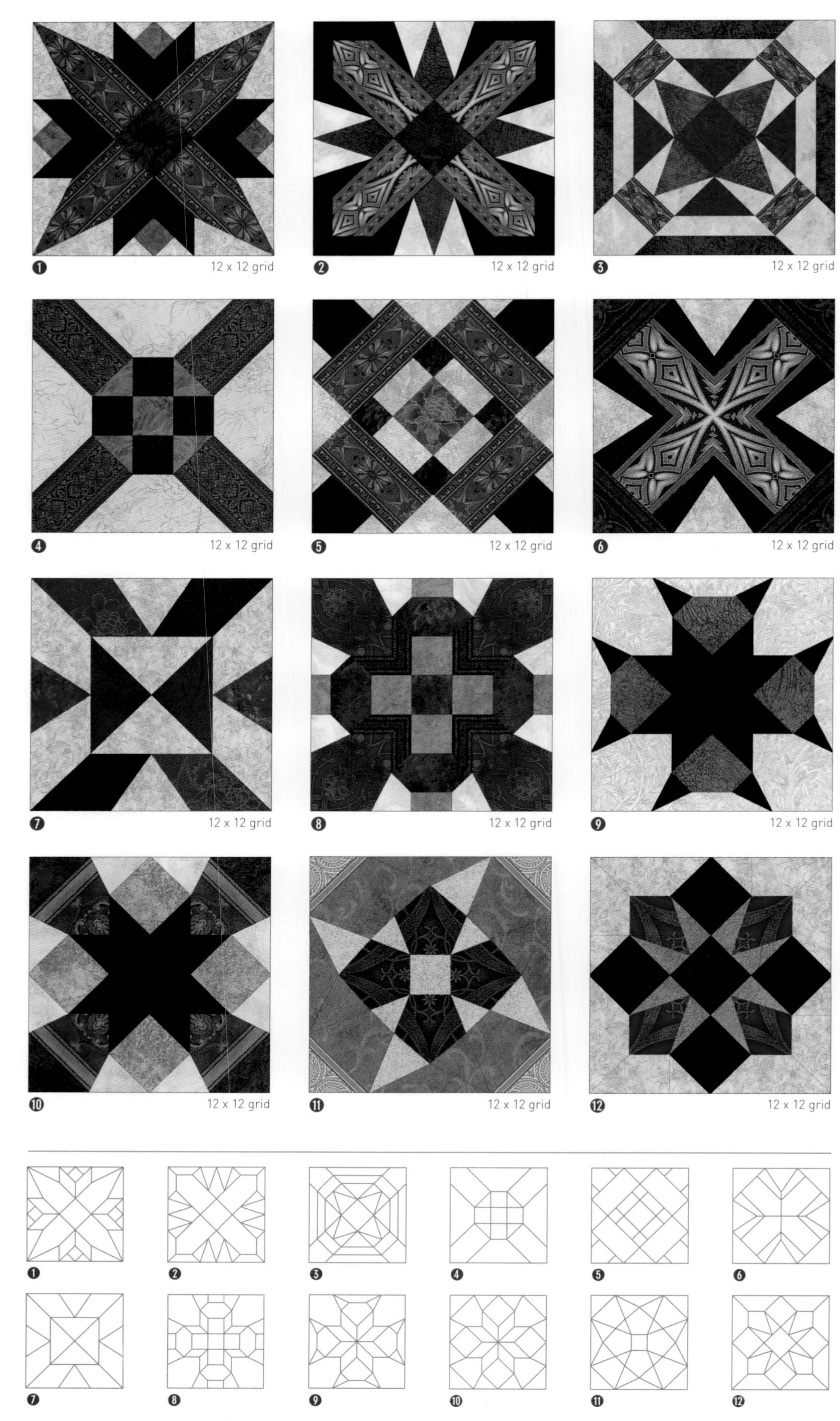

❶ **Danger Signal** Nancy Page, *Birmingham News,* Mar 5, 1940. See 91-3 and 200-6.

❷ **London Square,** *Q Book 111, 'Round the World Quilts,* date unknown.

❸ **Ocean Wave,** Ruby McKim, *Kansas City Star,* Dec 5, 1928. See 93-3, 131-5, and 409-11. Also known as:

- **The Ocean Wave,** *Kansas City Star,* Nov 4, 1942.
- **Sapphire Quilt Block,** *Kansas City Star,* Sep 2, 1953.
- **Waves of the Ocean,** date unknown, per Brackman.

❹ **Ocean Waves,** Nancy Cabot, *Chicago Tribune,* May 13, 1937. See 93-3, 131-5, and 409-11.

❺ **Signal Light,** Jinny Beyer, Hilton Head Seminar design, 1991; published in Beyer, Jinny. *Soft-Edge Piecing.*

❻ **Westward Ho,** Nancy Cabot, *Chicago Tribune,* Mar 21, 1936.

"The 'wild and wooly' west is represented by this strikingly beautiful pieced block, 'Westward Ho.' The original was made over one hundred years ago of white, red, blue, and purple, by a Kansas pioneer woman. A copy recently was made by the granddaughter of the creator, but the colors were decidedly pastel. She used orchid, lavender, violet, blue, and rose." Nancy Cabot, *Chicago Tribune,* Mar 21, 1936

❼ **Sentry's Pastime,** Nancy Cabot, *Chicago Tribune,* Jun 12, 1936.

❽ **Texas Treasure,** Nancy Page, *Birmingham News,* Jun 21, 1938. Also known as:

- **Rachel's Garden,** Nancy Page, *Birmingham News,* Sep 14, 1943.

❾ **Bride's Puzzle,** *Quilt Booklet No. 1,* ca. 1931. Also known as:

- **Twelve Crowns,** *Farm Journal and Farmer's Wife,* ca.1941.

❿ **Twenty Tees,** Nancy Page, *Birmingham News,* Oct 16, 1934.

"Today I have one of the prettiest blocks for you. It comes from Mrs. Myron Spaulding of Warners, New York. She says the block is at least 50 years old. It may be older for she has lost track of the origin." Nancy Page, *Birmingham News,* Oct 16, 1934

⓫ **Desert Rose,** Nancy Cabot, *Chicago Tribune,* Apr 4, 1936.

"One of those elaborate, modern pieced designs which have been adapted from an old quilt block is 'Desert Rose.' Noticeable in the sketch is the fact that the pattern has the good old four patch design as the fundamental motif." Nancy Cabot, *Chicago Tribune,* Apr 4, 1936

⓬ **The New Four Pointer,** *Kansas City Star,* May 31, 1944.

❶ **Night and Day,** Alice Brooks, *Detroit Free Press,* Mar 12, 1937.

❷ **Sheltered Cove,** Jinny Beyer, Hilton Head Seminar design, 1988; published in Beyer, Jinny, *Patchwork Portfolio.*

❸ **Facets,** Jinny Beyer, Hilton Head Seminar design, 1991; published in Beyer, Jinny, *Soft-Edge Piecing.*

❹ **Four Points,** *Ladies Art Company,* 1897. See 117-6 . Also known as:

- **Humming Bird,** *Prairie Farmer,* Mar 24, 1928.
- **The Kite Quilt,** Eveline Foland, *Kansas City Star,* Jun 27, 1931.
- **The Kite,** Nancy Cabot, *Chicago Tribune,* Jul 28, 1933.
- **Snowball,** Aunt Martha series: *Quilts: Modern-Colonial,* ca. 1954.
- **Star Kites,** Nancy Cabot, *Chicago Tribune,* Dec 25, 1937.

❺ **Eight Pointed Star,** Nancy Cabot, *Chicago Tribune,* Jan 29, 1935. See 202-2, 255-12, and 297-4.

❻ **Eight Pointed Stars,** *Ladies Art Company,* 1906. See 202-2, 255-12, and 297-4.

❼ **Star,** Gutcheon, *The Perfect Patchwork Primer,* 1973.

❽ **Geometric Star,** Ickis, 1949.

❾ **Geometric Star,** Hall, 1935.

❿ **Jewel of a Quilt,** Laura Wheeler, unidentified newspaper clipping, date unknown. Also known as:

- **Jewel Quilt,** Alice Brooks, unidentified newspaper clipping, date unknown.

⓫ **Scroll Work,** *Prize Winning Designs,* ca. 1931.

⓬ **Lost Children,** Clara Stone, *Practical Needlework,* ca. 1906.

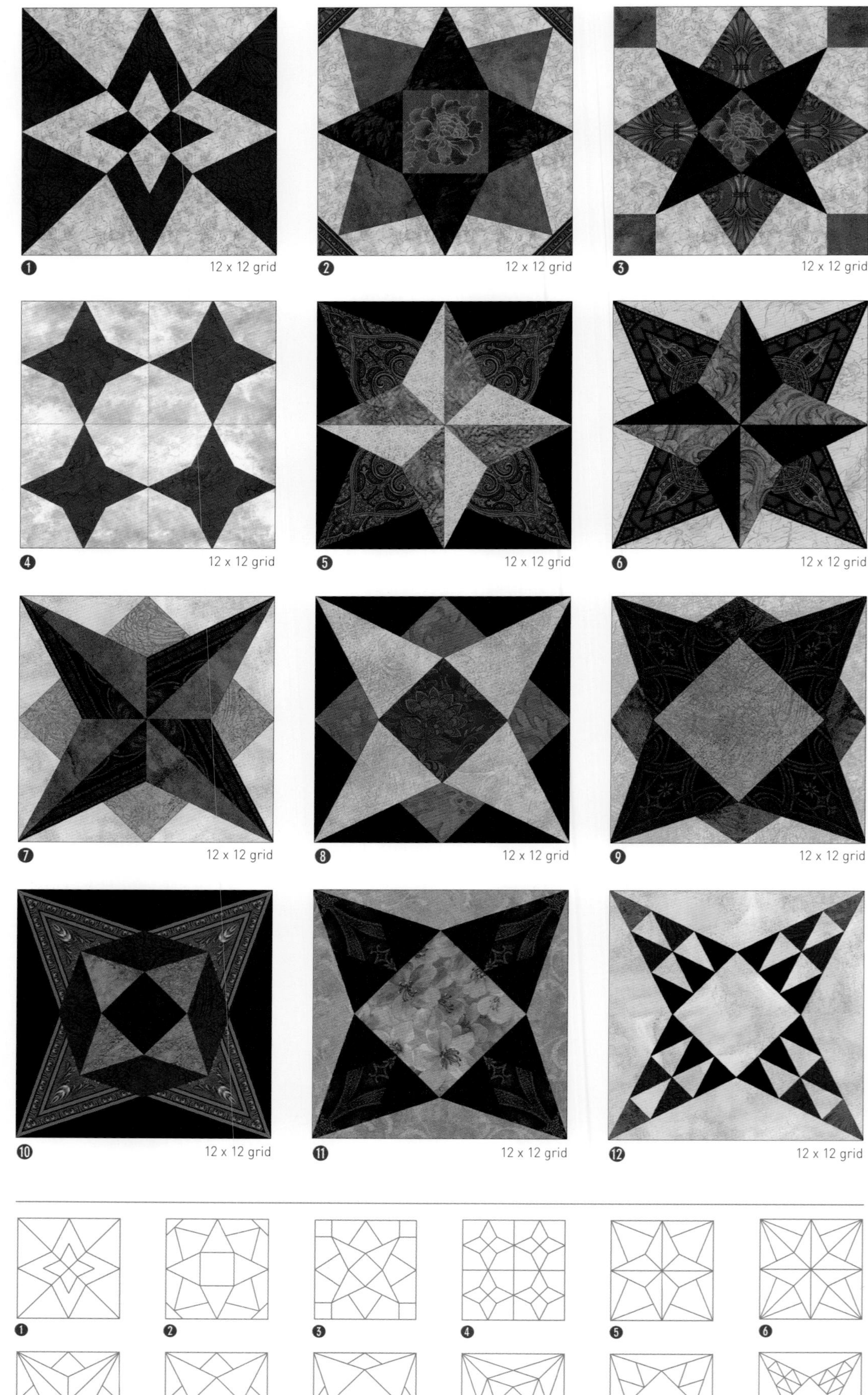

❶ **Cactus Flower,** Jinny Beyer, Beyer, Jinny, *Patchwork Portfolio,* 1989.

❷ **Four Star Block,** Nancy Cabot, *Chicago Tribune,* Jun 30, 1936.

❸ **Little Rock Block,** *Ladies Art Company,* 1922. Also known as:

> **Arkansas Star,** date unknown; published in Beyer, Jinny, *The Quilter's Album. . . .*
>
> **Butterfly Block,** Nancy Cabot, *Chicago Tribune,* Aug 12, 1937.
>
> **The Sea Star,** *Prairie Farmer, Book 1,* 1931.
>
> **Star of the Sea,** Nancy Cabot, *Chicago Tribune,* Mar 22, 1933.

❹ **David and Goliath,** Ickis, 1949.

❺ **My Country, For Loyalty,** *Kansas City Star,* Mar 23, 1955.

❻ **Economy,** *Kansas City Star,* Aug 12, 1933. See 183-2, 183-3, and 243-4.

❼ **Tete a Tete Block,** Nancy Cabot, *Chicago Tribune,* Apr 3, 1937.
"This clever pieced block has been virtually lost in the present day hustle and bustle. Many years ago this design was one of the ranking favorites but, for some unknown reason, it dropped from sight. Diligent research over a period of time brought this one time favorite to notice." Nancy Cabot, *Chicago Tribune,* Apr 3, 1937

❽ **Crow's Nest,** ca. 1938, per Havig.

❾ **The Scottish Cross,** *Kansas City Star,* Apr 4, 1945.

❿ **Morning Star,** Nancy Page, *Birmingham News,* Aug 22, 1939.

⓫ **Family Favorite,** Laura Wheeler, unidentified newspaper clipping, 1959.

⓬ **Calico Mosaic** Nancy Cabot, *Chicago Tribune,* Nov 5, 1935.
"The old and original 'Calico Mosaic' from which this pattern was taken contained several dozen different patches of figured prints of both light and dark materials. Trading patches was the method by which the designs for the original coverlet were obtained." Nancy Cabot, *Chicago Tribune,* Nov 5, 1935

❶ **Ann's Scrap Quilt,** Laura Wheeler, *Cincinnati Enquirer,* Nov 24, 1933. "When a quiltmaker chooses a pattern, she wants more than an economical and easy-to-make quilt. It must be attractive as well and one which she will always be proud to possess. Ann's Scrap Quilt is just such a quilt. Economical, in that left-over pieces of material form the flower, it is best to use the same scraps in one block. Simple, in that the patches grouping themselves into squares and triangles are easy to join. The illustration shows how lovely a design it is, thus fulfilling all the needlewoman's requirements." Laura Wheeler, *Cincinnati Enquirer,* Nov 24, 1933

❷ **Carolina Pinwheel,** Jinny Beyer, Hilton Head Seminar design, 1982; published in Beyer, Jinny, *Patchwork Portfolio.*

❸ **Diamond Star,** Nancy Cabot, *Chicago Tribune,* May 15, 1937.

❹ **Guiding Star,** *Kansas City Star,* Apr 8, 1933.

❺ **St. Louis Star,** Clara Stone, *Practical Needlework,* ca, 1906.

❻ **Irish Star,** Jinny Beyer, Hilton Head Seminar design, 1991; published in Beyer, Jinny, *Soft-Edge Piecing.*

❼ **Storm at Sea** Jinny Beyer, Beyer, Jinny, *The Quilter's Album...,* 1980.

❽ **California Sunset,** Jinny Beyer, Beyer, Jinny, *The Quilter's Album...,* 1980.

❾ **Calico Star,** Nancy Cabot, *Chicago Tribune,* Dec 5, 1933.

❿ **Star Flower,** Virginia Snow, *Grandma Dexter's New Appliqué and Patchwork Designs, Book 36b,* ca. 1932.

⓫ **St. Louis Star,** Gutcheon, *The Perfect Patchwork Primer,* 1973.

⓬ **Arrow Point,** *Quilt Booklet No. 1,* ca. 1931. See 114-8 and 328-2.

❶ **Godey Design** *Godey's Lady's Book*, 1859. Also known as:
Light and Shadow, *Kansas City Star*, Apr 15, 1933.

❷ **Mozart Star,** Jinny Beyer, Beyer, Jinny, *Patchwork Portfolio*, 1989.

❸ **Carnelian,** Jinny Beyer, Hilton Head Seminar design, 2008.

❹ **Double Star,** Laura Wheeler, unidentified newspaper clipping, date unknown.

❺ **Gyroscope,** Jinny Beyer, Beyer, *Patchwork Portfolio*, 1989.

❻ **Du Mont's Pride,** Home Art Studios, *Cincinnati Enquirer*, Apr 3, 1933.

❼ **Open Sesame,** Jinny Beyer, Beyer, Jinny, *Patchwork Portfolio*, 1989.

❽ **Print and Plain,** *Farm Journal and Farmer's Wife* (Silver Anniversary issue), 1945.

❾ **Springtime,** *Q Book 130*, *Keepsake Quilts*, ca. 1970.

❿ **Oriental Puzzle,** Nancy Cabot, *Chicago Tribune*, Jun 22, 1938.

⓫ **Star Flower,** *Progressive Farmer*, date unknown.

⓬ **Nora's Choice,** Nancy Cabot, *Chicago Tribune*, Jan 1, 1938.
"'Nora's Choice' comes from Massachusetts, the design created by a young girl brought from Ireland at the age of three and who lived with her parents in Lennox until she moved west to Albany, N.Y." Nancy Cabot, *Chicago Tribune*, Jan 1, 1938

1 **Blazing Star,** Hall, 1935. Also known as:
Flaming Star, Nancy Page, unidentified newspaper clipping date unknown.
Northern Lights, Nancy Page, *Birmingham News,* Jul 27, 1937.
Square Dance, Jinny Beyer, Beyer, Jinny, *Patchwork Portfolio,* 1989.
St. Louis, date unknown, per Brackman.

2 **Boxwood Hill,** Jinny Beyer, Beyer, Jinny, *Patchwork Portfolio,* 1989.

3 **Gladiator,** Jinny Beyer, Beyer, Jinny, *Patchwork Portfolio,* 1989.

4 **Mosaic Squares,** Nancy Cabot, *Chicago Tribune,* Jun 2, 1936.

5 **Victorian Cut-outs,** Nancy Page, *Birmingham News,* Feb 29, 1944.

6 **Mother's Choice,** Nancy Cabot, *Chicago Tribune,* Mar 25, 1938.

7 **Sunflower,** Nancy Page, *Birmingham News,* Oct 18, 1938. See 289-6.

8 **Easy Ways,** *Farm Journal and Farmer's Wife* (Silver Anniversary issue), 1945.

9 **Roman Courtyard,** Nancy Cabot, *Chicago Tribune, Apr 9, 1936.*

10 **Christmas Baubles,** Nancy Page, *Birmingham News,* Dec 14, 1943.

11 **Cluster of Stars,** *Ladies Art Company,* 1928. Also known as:
Star Cluster, Nancy Cabot, *Chicago Tribune,* Dec 21, 1934.

12 **The Kaleidoscope Quilt,** Eveline Foland, *Kansas City Star,* Aug 23, 1930. See 251-6. Also known as:
Kaleidoscope, Hall, 1935.

1 12 x 12 grid

2 12 x 12 grid

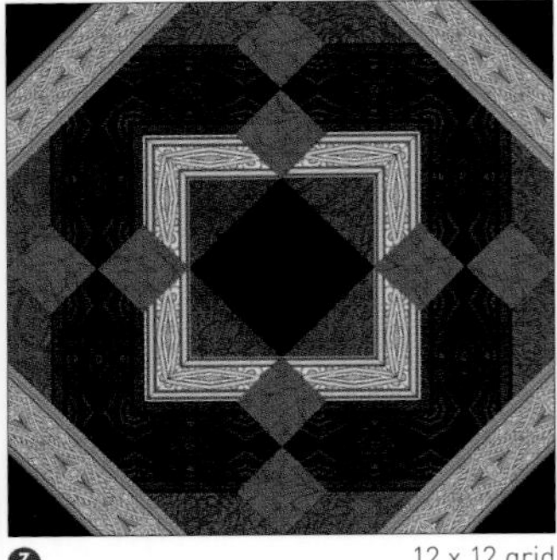

3 12 x 12 grid

4 12 x 12 grid

5 12 x 12 grid

6 12 x 12 grid

7 12 x 12 grid

8 12 x 12 grid

9 12 x 12 grid

10 12 x 12 grid

11 12 x 12 grid

12 12 x 12 grid

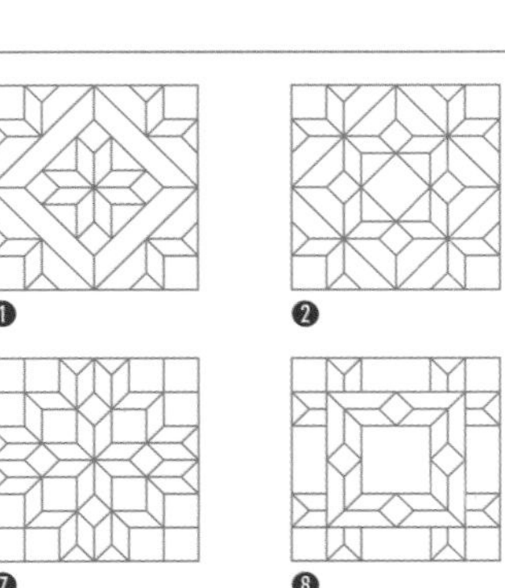
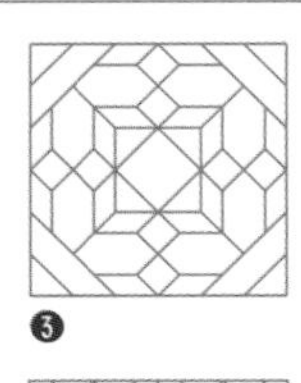
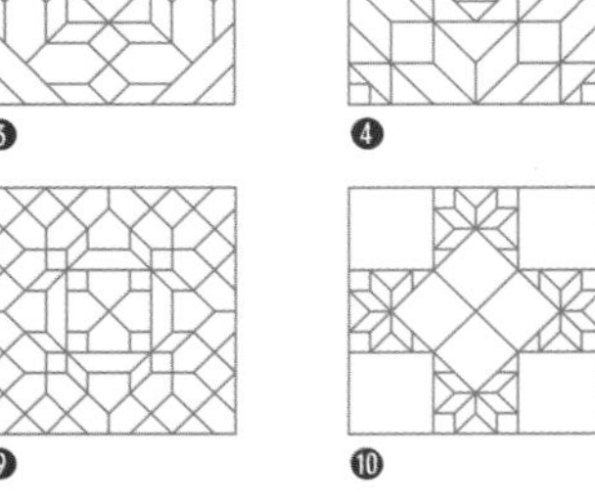
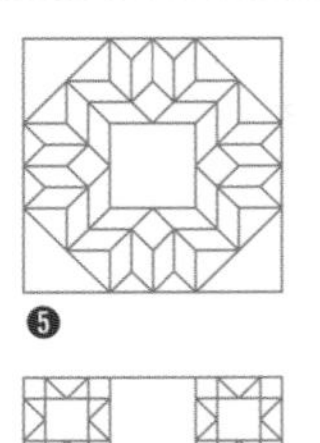
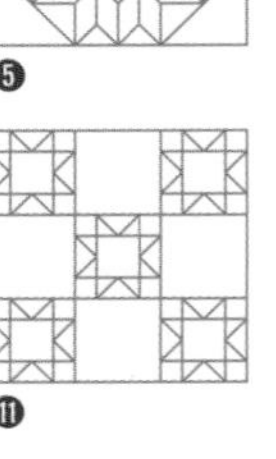
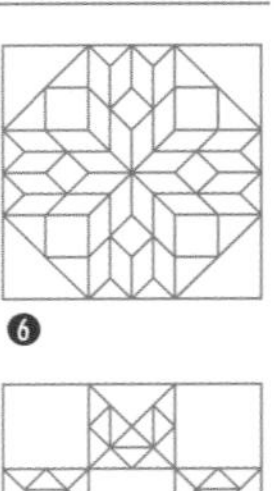

1 2 3 4 5 6

7 8 9 10 11 12

❶ **Blazing Star,** *Eight Star Quilt Designs,* ca. 1935.

❷ **Northumberland Star,** Clara Stone, *Practical Needlework,* ca. 1906.

❸ **The Brosius,** *Farm and Home,* Dec 1, 1899.

❹ **Baltimore Belle,** Clara Stone, *Practical Needlework,* ca. 1906.

❺ **Sanibel,** Jinny Beyer, RJR Patterns, 2004.

❻ **Spokane,** Nancy Page, *Birmingham News,* Aug 14, 1934.

❼ **Wild Goose Chase,** Ruby McKim, *Kansas City Star,* Dec 12, 1928.

❽ **Lady of the Lake,** Finley, 1929. See 201-2, 201-3.

"'Lady of the Lake', named after the poem by Sir Walter Scott, published in 1810... despite belligerent differences with the motherland, America during the early years of the nineteenth century imported with enthusiasm English Novels and writings of all kinds. The heroic tales of Scott were particularly pleasing ... and the women of the land honored the author in their most practiced method of artistic self-expression, patchwork. The 'Lady of the Lake' quilt appeared in a surprisingly short time after the publication of the poem, the one shown here having been made in Vermont before 1820... it is one of the few that seems never to have been known by other names." Finley, 1929

❾ **Lady of the Lake,** Aunt Martha series: *The Quilt Fair Comes to You,* ca.1933. Also known as:

- **Pennsylvania Pineapple,** Aunt Martha series: *The Quilt Fair Comes to You,* ca. 1933.

❿ **Flock of Birds,** Nancy Page, *Nashville Banner,* Apr 4, 1933.

⓫ **Chinese Holiday,** Nancy Cabot, *Chicago Tribune,* Feb 13, 1936.

⓬ **Cross Roads to Texas,** *Ladies Art Company,* 1897. See 180-5. Also known as:

- **Crossroads to Texas,** ca. 1938, per Havig.
- **Kentucky Cross Roads,** *Quilt Booklet No. 1, Prairie Farmer,* ca. 1931.
- **Kentucky Crossroads,** Nancy Cabot, *Chicago Tribune,* Jan 30, 1938.

"'Crossroads to Texas,' that's an interesing name. But I think it ought to be 'All Roads to Texas' because that is truer. Sooner or later everybody is going to take a road to Texas and see our wonderful state. Don't you think so?" Nancy Page, *Birmingham News,* Nov 26, 1940

❶ The House That Jack Built, *Ladies Art Company*, 1897. Also known as:
Triple Stripe, *Grandma Dexter's New Appliqué and Patchwork Designs, Book 36b*, ca. 1932.

❷ At The Depot Clara Stone, *Practical Needlework*, ca. 1906. Also known as:
Railroad Crossing, *Kansas City Star*, Aug 21, 1935.

❸ Chuck a Luck Block, Nancy Cabot, *Chicago Tribune*, Mar 29, 1937.

❹ 4 H Club Quilt, Eveline Foland, *Kansas City Star*, Apr 30, 1932. Also known as:
Four H Club Patch, Hall, 1935
The H Square Quilt, *Kansas City Star*, Jul 30, 1941.

"There are thousands upon thousands of members in this upstanding organization who would enjoy having a quilt made up in their own club colors. The quilt block pattern itself carries the lines of their club emblem and the quilt is worked up in green and white. The four-leaf clover—one of the symbols of this organization—is used as a quilting design." *World Herald*, Nov 16, 1933

❺ Cross and Crown, Finley, 1929. See 199-5 and 199-6. Also known as:
Crowned Cross, Finley, 1929.

❻ Texas Tears, *Ladies Art Company*, 1897. "In 1840 'Texas Tears' was first made and aptly titled by one of the many pioneed women who sorrowed over the early tribulations of the land." Nancy Cabot, *Chicago Tribune*, Jul 13, 1934

❼ Crowned Cross, Nancy Page, *Birmingham News*, May 31, 1938. 199-5 and 199-6. Also known as:
Four T's, Nancy Page, *Birmingham News*, May 31, 1938.

❽ Boxed T's, *Ladies Art Company*, 1897.
Original Double T, *Quilt Booklet No. 1, Prairie Farmer*, ca. 1931.

❾ Double T, *Farm Journal Quilt Patterns*, ca. 1935. Also known as:
Four T's, Nancy Cabot, *Chicago Tribune*, Aug 15, 1936.

❿ Star and Cross, *Ladies Art Company*, 1897. See 199-9 and 260-5. Also known as:
Shining Hour, *Farm Journal and Farmer's Wife* (Silver Anniversary issue), 1945.

⓫ Star and Cross, Nancy Cabot, *Chicago Tribune*, May 21, 1934. See 199-9 and 260-5.

"'Star and Cross,' like many other quilt blocks, takes its theme from religious symbolism. It enjoyed tremendous popularity during colonial times and its individuality makes it popular with present day quilters. It was made in New York, about 1840, of yellow, orange, brown and white." Nancy Cabot, *Chicago Tribune*, May 21, 1934

⓬ Railroad Crossing, Nancy Cabot, *Chicago Tribune*, Jan 1, 1937

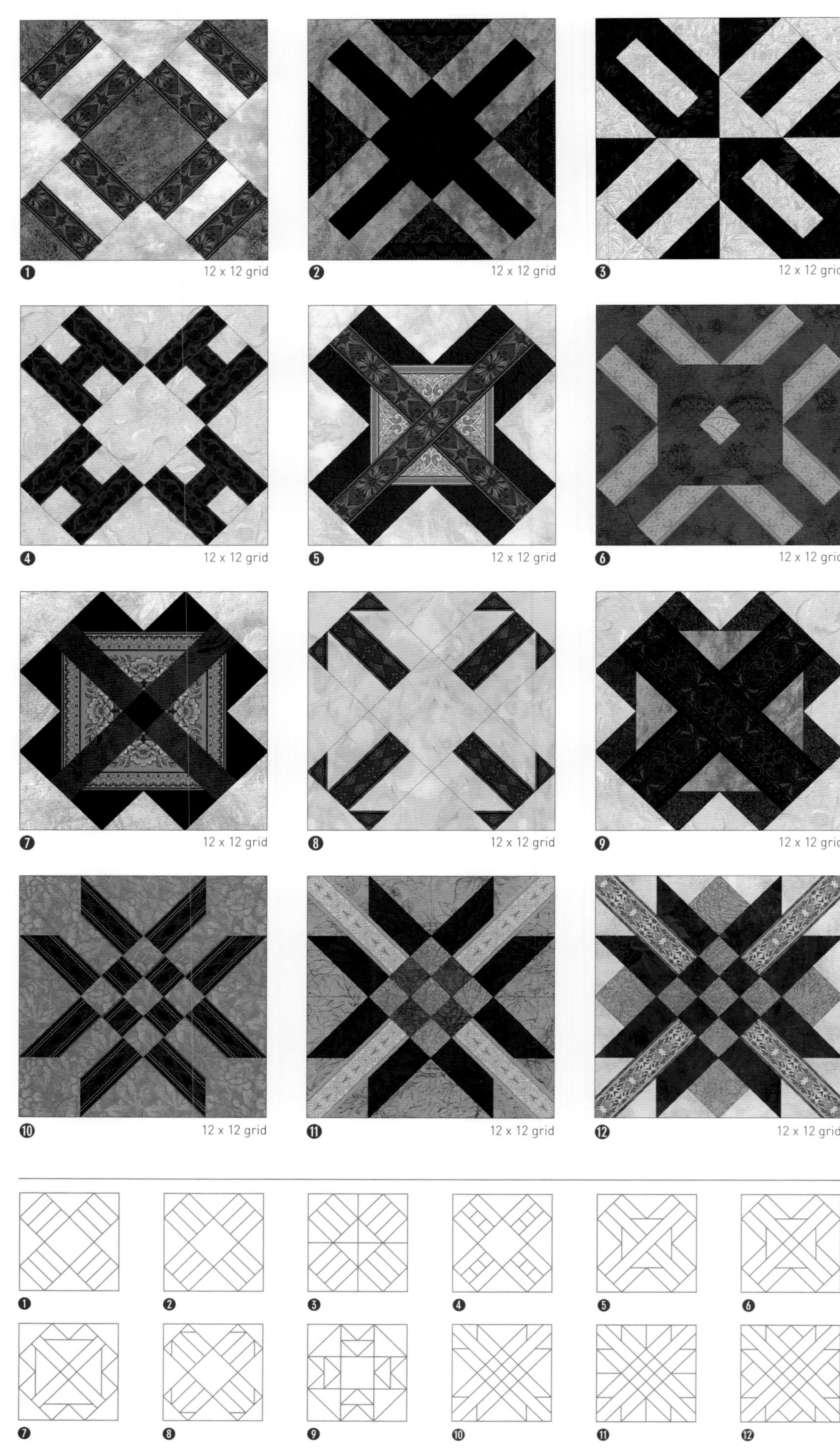

❶ **Ragged Robin,** Alice Brooks, *Detroit Free Press,* Jan 23, 1934.

❷ **The Spider Web,** *Kansas City Star,* Sep 25, 1940.

❸ **Washington Sidewalks,** *Q Book 124, White House Quilts,* date unknown.

❹ **Brick Pavement,** Nancy Cabot, *Chicago Tribune,* Jun 9, 1938.

❺ **Creole Puzzle,** Nancy Cabot, *Chicago Tribune,* Mar 24, 1938.

❻ **Palmetto,** Jinny Beyer, Hilton Head Seminar design, 1981; published in Beyer, Jinny, *Patchwork Portfolio.*

❼ **Tangled Garter,** Finley, 1929. See 173-9, 242-5, 258-8 and 274-4. Also known as:
- **Garden Maze,** Hall, 1935.
- **Sun Dial,** Hall, 1935.
- **Tirzah's Treasure,** Hall, 1935.

❽ **The Modern Broken Dish,** *Kansas City Star,* Dec 12, 1936.

❾ **Four Points,** *Ladies Art Company,* 1897. Also known as:
- **Lattice and Square,** Nancy Cabot, *Chicago Tribune,* Sep 8, 1937.

❿ **Jack in the Pulpit,** Clara Stone, *Practical Needlework,* ca. 1906. See 94-8, 94-9, and 112-9. Also known as:
- **Double Square,** Hall, 1935.

⓫ **The Dewey,** Nancy Page, *Nashville Banner,* Oct 31, 1933. See 94-8, 94-9, and 112-9.

⓬ **Jack in the Pulpit,** Finley, 1929. See 94-8, 94-9, and 112-9. Also known as:
- **Broken Dish,** Jane Alan, Alan, 1933.
- **Toad in the Puddle,** Finley, 1929.

❶ **The Friendship Quilt,** *Kansas City Star,* Aug 17, 1938.

❷ **Cross within a Cross,** Hall, 1935. See 112-5, 184-3, and 212-11.

❸ **Carolina Crown,** Jinny Beyer, Hilton Head Seminar design, 1988; published in Beyer, Jinny, *Patchwork Portfolio.*

❹ **Royal Star Quilt,** *Ladies Art Company,* 1922. Also known as:
- **Jungle Paths,** Nancy Page, *Birmingham News,* May 25, 1941.
- **Royal Star,** Hall, 1935.

❺ **Hopeful Star,** Nancy Page, *Birmingham News,* Feb 9, 1943.

❻ **Four Triangles,** *Farm Journal and Farmer's Wife,* ca. 1941.

❼ **Lady of the Lake,** *Quilt Booklet No. 1,* ca. 1931.

❽ **Vice President's Quilt** *Ladies Art Company,* 1897. Also known as:
- **Vice President's Block,** Nancy Cabot, *Chicago Tribune,* Jul 8, 1934.
- **Vice President's Star,** ca. 1938, per Havig.

"This old block was dedicated to Millard Fillmore and presented to him one year after he was elected to the vice presidency of the United States. Lavender, gold, and white were used in the block." Nancy Cabot, *Chicago Tribune,* Jul 8, 1934

❾ **The Long Nine Patch,** *Kansas City Star,* Jun 12, 1940. Also known as:
- **Nine Patch Star Quilt,** Aunt Martha series: *Favorite Quilts,* ca. 1953.
- **The Road to Oklahoma,** *Kansas City Star,* Jan 11, 1956.

❿ **Cabin Windows,** *Kansas City Star,* Apr 17, 1940.

⓫ **Four Square,** Nancy Cabot, *Chicago Tribune,* Mar 12, 1936,

⓬ **Lady of the Whitehouse,** Nancy Cabot, *Chicago Tribune,* Sep 6, 1933. Also known as:
- **Lady in the White House,** *Q Book 121, Bicentennial Quilts,* ca. 1976.
- **White House,** Nancy Cabot, *Chicago Tribune,* Oct 11, 1937.

"'Four Square' is one of the oldest quilt patterns and has been rescued only recently from oblivion. The quilt belongs to the 75 year old granddaughter of a woman in Kansas, whose son drew and cut all the patches." Nancy Cabot, *Chicago Tribune,* Mar 12, 1936

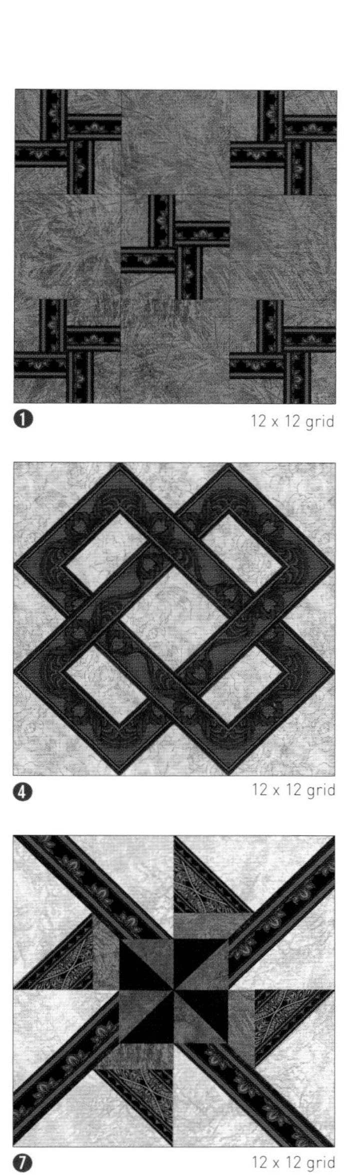

❶ 12 x 12 grid

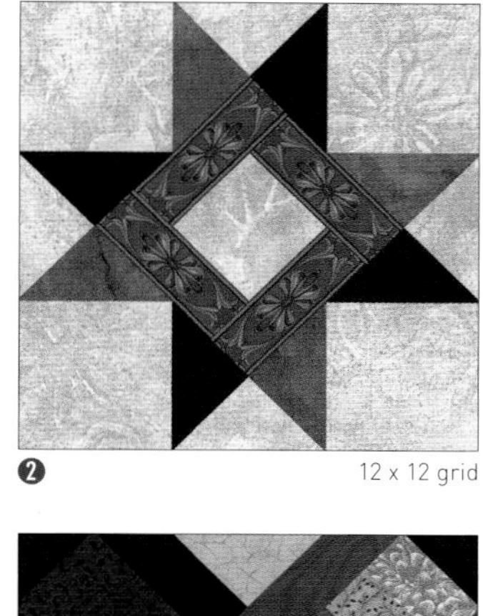

❷ 12 x 12 grid

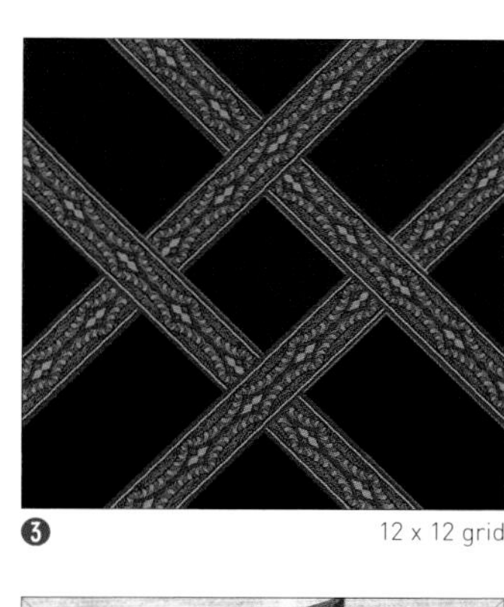

❸ 12 x 12 grid

❹ 12 x 12 grid

❺ 12 x 12 grid

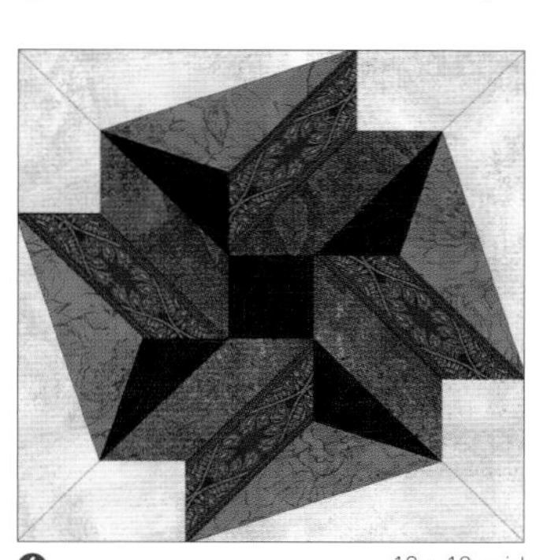

❻ 12 x 12 grid

❼ 12 x 12 grid

❽ 12 x 12 grid

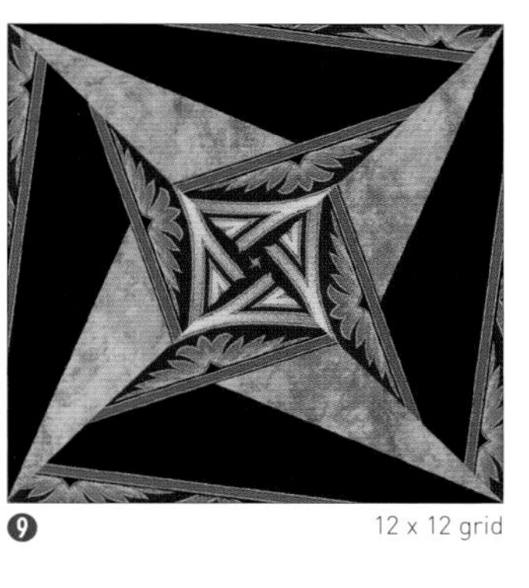

❾ 12 x 12 grid

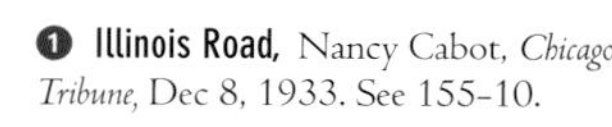

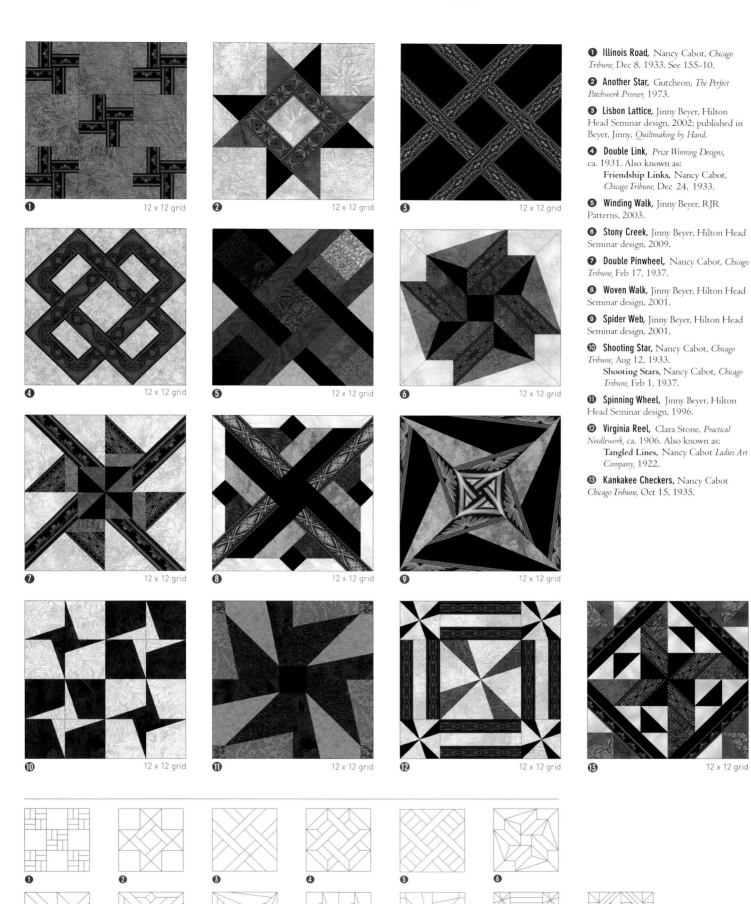

❶ **Illinois Road,** Nancy Cabot, *Chicago Tribune,* Dec 8, 1933. See 155-10.

❷ **Another Star,** Gutcheon, *The Perfect Patchwork Primer,* 1973.

❸ **Lisbon Lattice,** Jinny Beyer, Hilton Head Seminar design, 2002; published in Beyer, Jinny, *Quiltmaking by Hand.*

❹ **Double Link,** *Prize Winning Designs,* ca. 1931. Also known as:
- **Friendship Links,** Nancy Cabot, *Chicago Tribune,* Dec 24, 1933.

❺ **Winding Walk,** Jinny Beyer, RJR Patterns, 2003.

❻ **Stony Creek,** Jinny Beyer, Hilton Head Seminar design, 2009.

❼ **Double Pinwheel,** Nancy Cabot, *Chicago Tribune,* Feb 17, 1937.

❽ **Woven Walk,** Jinny Beyer, Hilton Head Seminar design, 2001.

❾ **Spider Web,** Jinny Beyer, Hilton Head Seminar design, 2001.

❿ **Shooting Star,** Nancy Cabot, *Chicago Tribune,* Aug 12, 1933.
- **Shooting Stars,** Nancy Cabot, *Chicago Tribune,* Feb 1, 1937.

⓫ **Spinning Wheel,** Jinny Beyer, Hilton Head Seminar design, 1996.

⓬ **Virginia Reel,** Clara Stone, *Practical Needlework,* ca. 1906. Also known as:
- **Tangled Lines,** Nancy Cabot *Ladies Art Company,* 1922.

⓭ **Kankakee Checkers,** Nancy Cabot *Chicago Tribune,* Oct 15, 1935.

❿ 12 x 12 grid

⓫ 12 x 12 grid

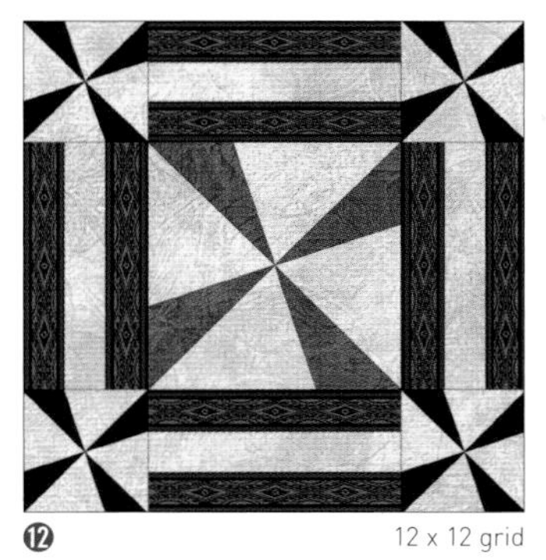

⓬ 12 x 12 grid

⓭ 12 x 12 grid

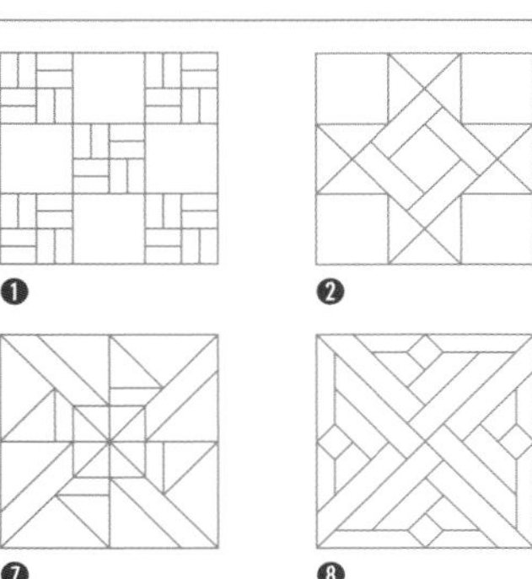

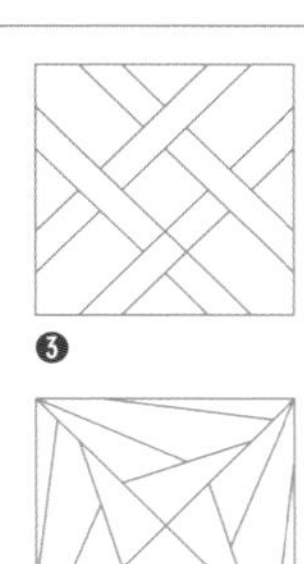

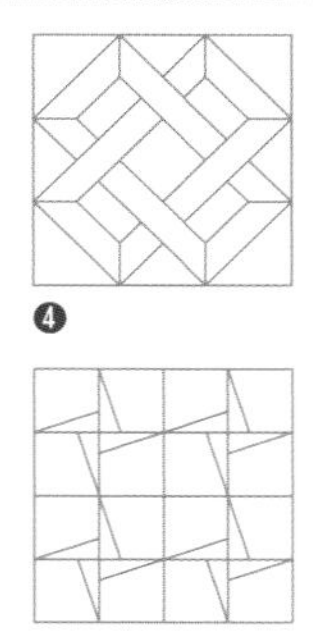

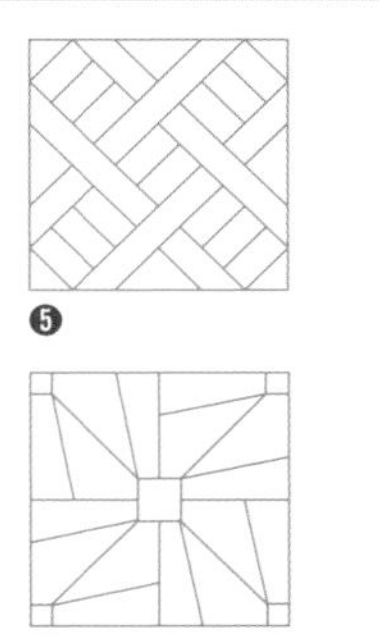

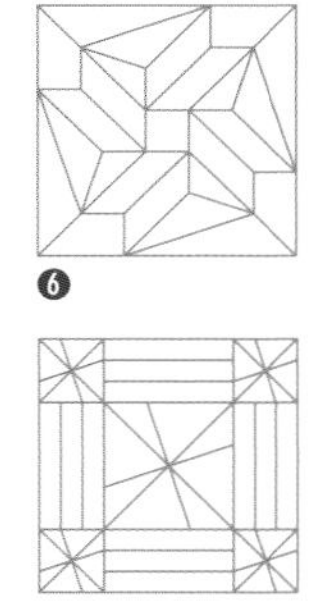

❶ ❷ ❸ ❹ ❺ ❻

❼ ❽ ❾ ❿ ⓫ ⓬ ⓭

❶ **Jaipur,** Jinny Beyer, RJR Patterns, 1999.

❷ **Christmas Package,** Nancy Page, *Birmingham News,* Nov 2, 1943.
"I can see where your mind was when you designed this quilt pattern, Nancy. You were thinking of all the servicemen away from home, and the packages their relatives were tying up to send them. You did a nice job of decorating the box, too."
Nancy Page, *Birmingham News,* Nov 2, 1943

❸ **Mission Stairs,** Jinny Beyer, Hilton Head design, 2006. Also known as:
Shimmering Sea, Jinny Beyer, *McCalls Quilting,* Feb 2009.
Synergy, Jinny Beyer, *McCalls Quilting,* Feb 2007.

❹ **Autumn Leaf,** *Old Fashioned Quilts,* ca. 1931.

❺ **Carrie Nation Quilt,** *Kansas City Star,* Dec 4, 1940. Also known as:
The Carrie Nation Quilt, *Kansas City Star,* Nov 12, 1947.

❻ **Double Pyramid,** Finley, 1929. Also known as:
Double Pyramids, Hall, 1935.

❼ **Maryland Beauty,** Hinson, 1973.

❽ **Crossed Chains,** Nancy Cabot, *Chicago Tribune,* May 12, 1938.

❾ **Pine Tree,** *Old Fashioned Quilts,* ca. 1931. Also known as:
Weeping Willow, *Old Fashioned Quilts,* ca. 1931.

❿ **American Holly,** Jinny Beyer, Quilter's Quest design, 2005.

⓫ **Lone Pine,** Jinny Beyer, Hilton Head Seminar design, 1997.

⓬ **Christmas Tree,** *Kansas City Star,* Jun 2, 1934. Also known as:
Pine Tree, *Kansas City Star,* Jun 2, 1934.

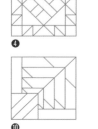

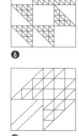

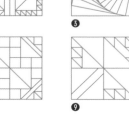

❶ ❷ ❸ ❹ ❺ ❻

❼ ❽ ❾ ❿ ⓫ ⓬

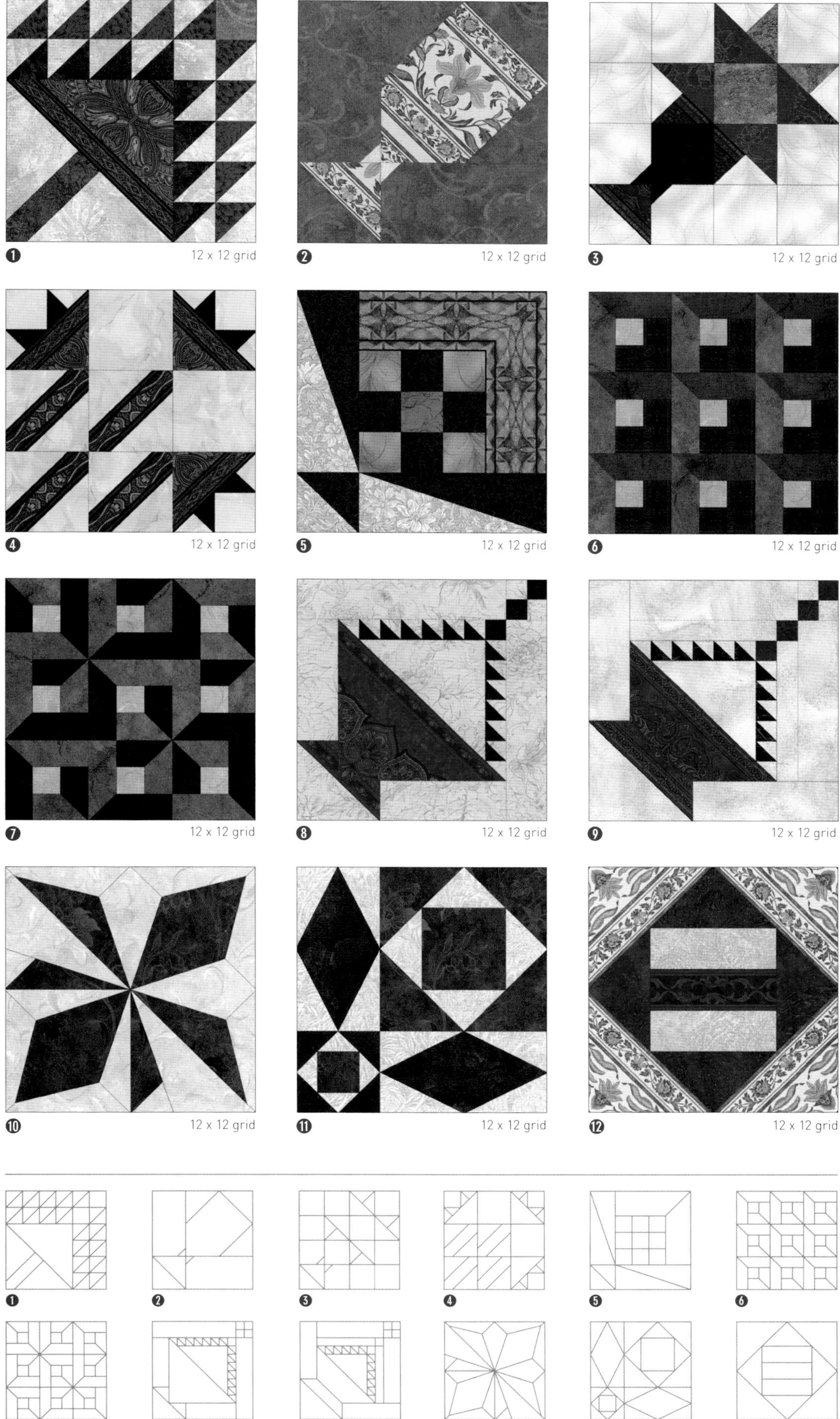

❶ **Christmas Tree,** Nancy Page, *Birmingham News,* Apr 20, 1943. Also known as:
- **Pine Tree,** Nancy Page, *Birmingham News,* Apr 20, 1943.
- **Tree of Paradise,** Nancy Page, *Birmingham News,* Apr 20, 1943.

❷ **The Old Fashioned Goblet,** *Kansas City Star,* Feb 27, 1937. See 274-12. Also known as:
- **An Old Fashioned Goblet,** *Kansas City Star,* Jan 7, 1955.

❸ **Vase of Flowers,** *Q Book 118: Grandmother's Flower Quilts,* date unknown.

❹ **Tassel Plant,** *Ladies Art Company,* 1897.

❺ **Pieced Bouquet,** Nancy Cabot, *Chicago Tribune,* Sep 21, 1933.

❻ **Shadow Box,** *Farm Journal and Farmer's Wife,* ca. 1957. See 151-9, 271-9 and 407-10.

❼ **Shadow Box,** *Farm Journal and Farmer's Wife,* ca. 1957. See 151-9, 271-9 and 407-10.

❽ **Baskets,** 1902, per Holstein. Also known as:
- **Hanging Basket,** *Kansas City Star,* Aug 14, 1937.

❾ **Mrs. Hardy's Hanging Basket,** Clara Stone, *Practical Needlework,* ca. 1906.

❿ **Leafy Basket,** *Americana Designs Quilts,* ca. 1954.

⓫ **Storm at Sea,** *Quilts,* 1945. See 98-11 and 114-4.

⓬ **The Double Anchor,** *Kansas City Star,* Nov 30, 1955.

1. **The Broken Path,** *Kansas City Star,* Oct 25, 1939. Also known as:
   End of the Road, *Kansas City Star,* Nov 9, 1955.
2. **Spools,** *Ladies Art Company,* 1897.
3. **Winged Squares,** Nancy Cabot, *Chicago Tribune,* Dec 26, 1935.
4. **Ceremonial Plaza,** ca. 1938, per Havig.
5. **Dove at the Window** *Kansas City Star,* Nov 29, 1945.
6. **Moss Rose,** Nancy Cabot, *Chicago Tribune,* Feb 27, 1936.
7. **Old Fashioned Pieced Block,** Nancy Cabot, *Chicago Tribune,* Apr 17, 1935. Also known as:
   Old Time Block, Nancy Cabot, *Chicago Tribune,* Jan 30, 1938.
   Pieced and Appliquéd Block, *Farm Journal and Farmer's Wife,* ca. 1941.
8. **New Hour Glass,** Clara Stone, *Practical Needlework,* ca. 1906.
9. **Hawks and Windmills** Nancy Cabot, *Chicago Tribune,* Oct 18, 1935.
10. **Pyramids,** Nancy Cabot, *Chicago Tribune,* Jun 18, 1936.
11. **Arrowhead,** Jinny Beyer, Hilton Head Seminar design, 1997.
12. **Magnolia Block,** Nancy Cabot, *Chicago Tribune,* Jan 28, 1936.
"'Magnolia Block' is one of the simple pieced blocks which feature floral motifs in what now is called the 'modern manner.' The block is not one of the moderns, yet it may not be numbered among the old quilts, since it is about 25 years old." Nancy Cabot, *Chicago Tribune,* Jan 28, 1936

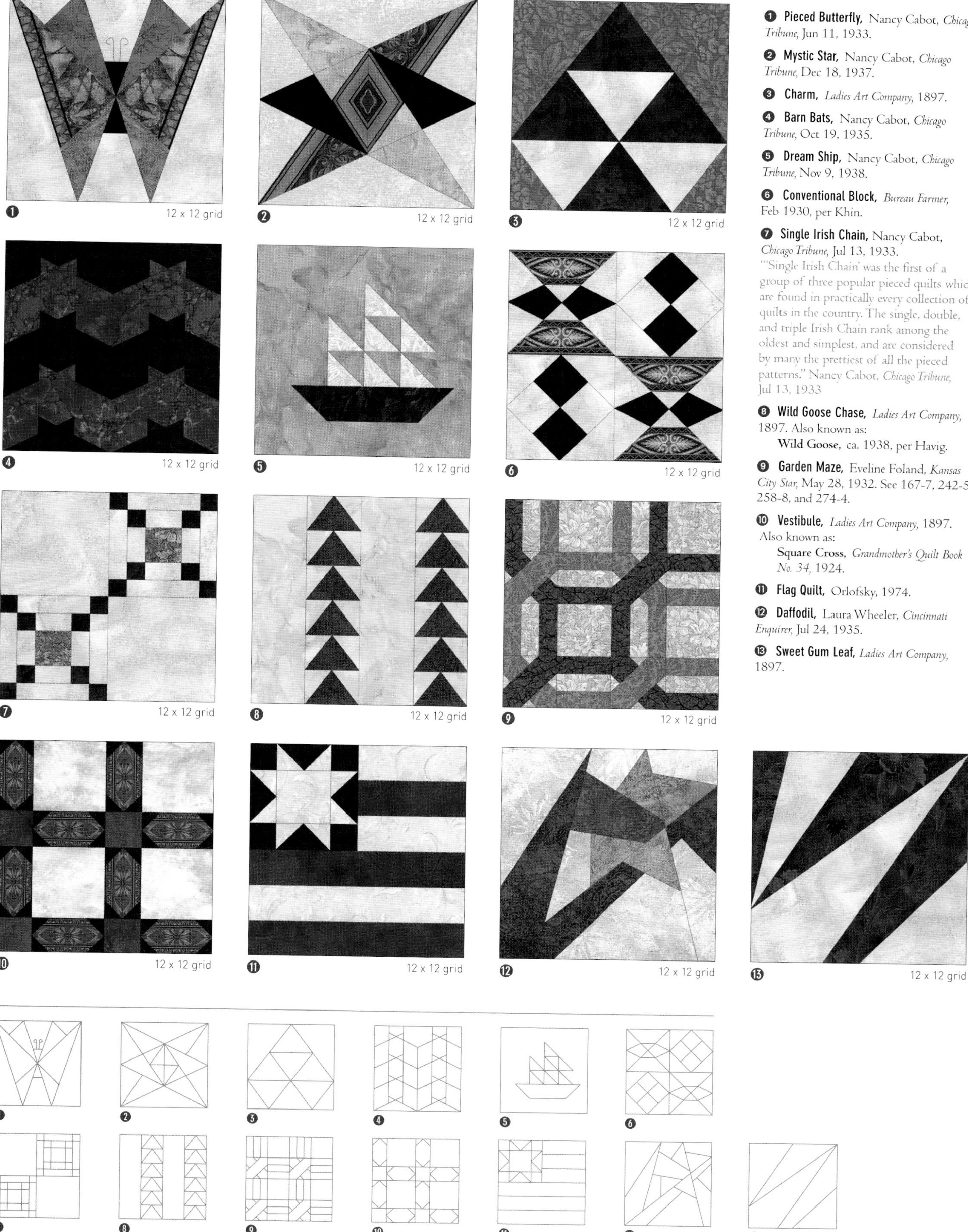

❶ **Pieced Butterfly,** Nancy Cabot, *Chicago Tribune,* Jun 11, 1933.

❷ **Mystic Star,** Nancy Cabot, *Chicago Tribune,* Dec 18, 1937.

❸ **Charm,** *Ladies Art Company,* 1897.

❹ **Barn Bats,** Nancy Cabot, *Chicago Tribune,* Oct 19, 1935.

❺ **Dream Ship,** Nancy Cabot, *Chicago Tribune,* Nov 9, 1938.

❻ **Conventional Block,** *Bureau Farmer,* Feb 1930, per Khin.

❼ **Single Irish Chain,** Nancy Cabot, *Chicago Tribune,* Jul 13, 1933.
"'Single Irish Chain' was the first of a group of three popular pieced quilts which are found in practically every collection of quilts in the country. The single, double, and triple Irish Chain rank among the oldest and simplest, and are considered by many the prettiest of all the pieced patterns." Nancy Cabot, *Chicago Tribune,* Jul 13, 1933

❽ **Wild Goose Chase,** *Ladies Art Company,* 1897. Also known as:
Wild Goose, ca. 1938, per Havig.

❾ **Garden Maze,** Eveline Foland, *Kansas City Star,* May 28, 1932. See 167-7, 242-5, 258-8, and 274-4.

❿ **Vestibule,** *Ladies Art Company,* 1897. Also known as:
Square Cross, *Grandmother's Quilt Book No. 34,* 1924.

⓫ **Flag Quilt,** Orlofsky, 1974.

⓬ **Daffodil,** Laura Wheeler, *Cincinnati Enquirer,* Jul 24, 1935.

⓭ **Sweet Gum Leaf,** *Ladies Art Company,* 1897.

❶ **Day Lily,** Jinny Beyer, Jinny Beyer Studio design, 2006.

❷ **Maple Leaf,** Clara Stone, *Practical Needlework,* ca. 1906. Also known as:
- **Broad Arrow,** Nancy Cabot, *Chicago Tribune,* Jul 21, 1936.

❸ **Cabin in the Woods,** Nancy Cabot, *Chicago Tribune,* Mar 15, 1937.

❹ **Log Cabin,** *Grandmother Clark's Old Fashioned Quilt Designs, Book 21,* 1931.

❺ **Old Fashioned Log Cabin,** *Mrs. Danner's Fifth Quilt Book,* 1970.

❻ **Pineapple,** *Farmer's Wife Book of New Designs and Patterns,* 1934.

❼ **Pineapple,** *The Patchwork Book,* 1932.

❽ **Pineapple Quilt,** Eveline Foland, *Kansas City Star,* Aug 22, 1931. Also known as:
- **Church Steps,** Hall, 1935.
- **Log Cabin Variation,** Hall, 1935.

❾ **The Comfort Quilt,** *Kansas City Star,* May 8, 1940.

❿ **Duck and Ducklings,** *Kansas City Star,* May 4, 1929. See 184-4, 273-3, and 269-10. Also known as:
- **Corn and Beans,** Hall, 1935.
- **Handy Andy,** Hall, 1935.
- **Hen and Chickens,** Hall, 1935.
- **Shoo Fly,** Hall, 1935.

⓫ **The Evening Star,** *Kansas City Star,* Mar 29, 1944.

⓬ **Mrs. Lloyd's Favorite,** Clara Stone, *Practical Needlework,* ca. 1906.

❶ 12 x 12 grid ❷ 12 x 12 grid ❸ 12 x 12 grid

❹ 12 x 12 grid

❺ 12 x 12 grid

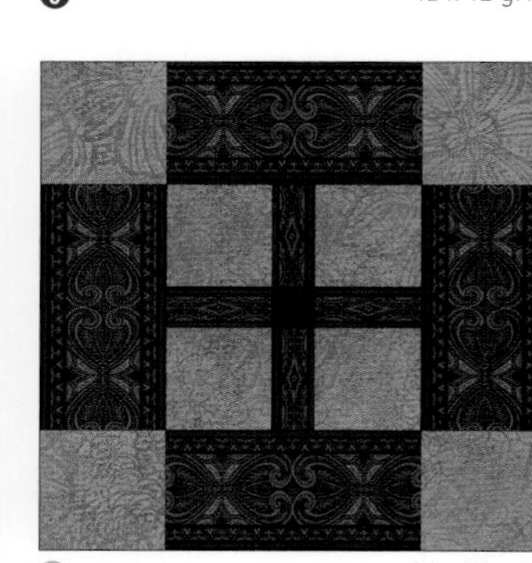

❻ 12 x 12 grid

❼ 12 x 12 grid

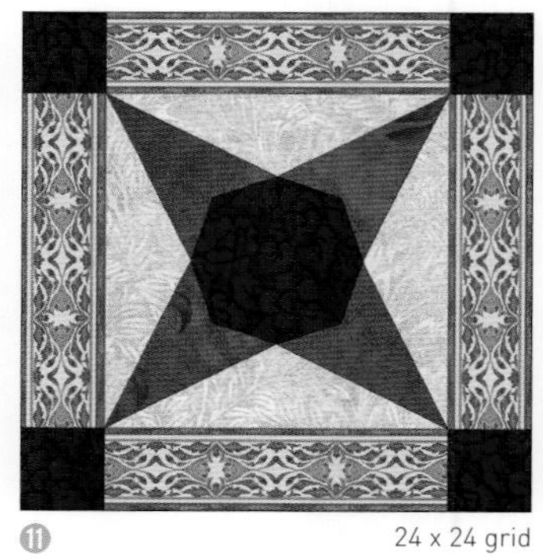

❽ 12 x 12 grid

❾ 24 x 24 grid

❿ 24 x 24 grid ⓫ 24 x 24 grid ⓬ 24 x 24 grid

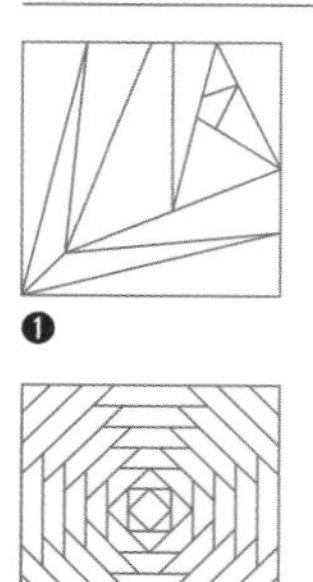
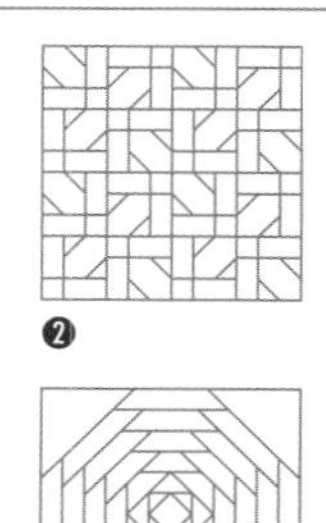
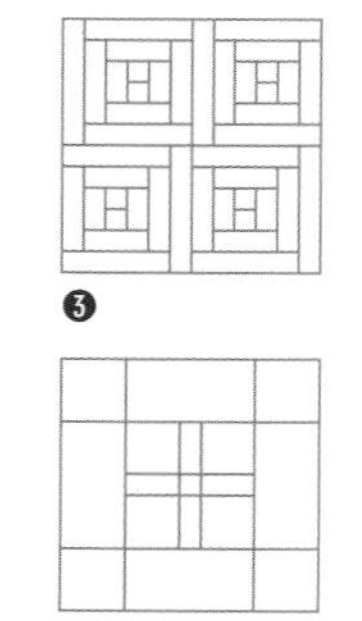
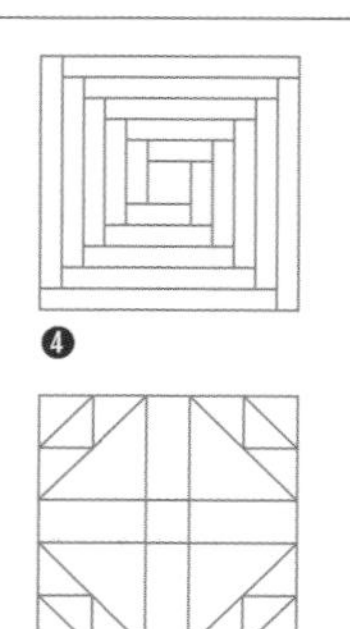
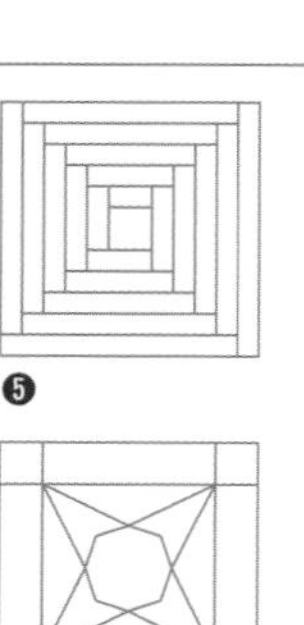
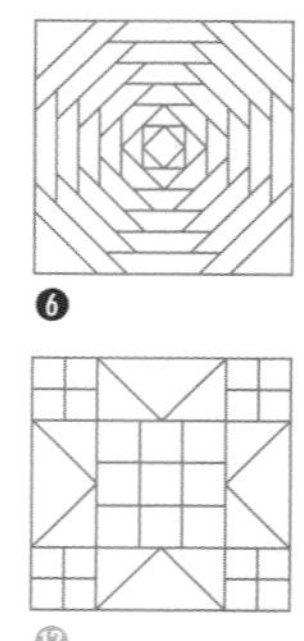

❶ ❷ ❸ ❹ ❺ ❻ ❼ ❽ ❾ ❿ ⓫ ⓬

1 **Album Block,** Nancy Cabot, *Chicago Tribune,* Jun 5, 1935. Also known as:
- **Token of Affection,** Nancy Cabot, *Chicago Tribune,* Jun 5, 1935.
- **Tricolor Star,** Nancy Cabot, *Chicago Tribune,* Jul 31, 1937.

"A direct descendant of the old 'Autograph' quilt, this 'Album Block' was the last of that type of coverlet to be made before the introduction of the present day guest book. This 'Token of Affection' quilt as it was called a few generations ago, contains 36 pieced blocks, alike in design and color. These are alternated with plain blocks of white or a harmonizing color." Nancy Cabot, *Chicago Tribune,* Jun 5, 1935

2 **Album Blocks,** *Ladies Art Company,* 1897. Also known as:
- **Folded Stars,** Nancy Page, *Birmingham News,* Nov 17, 1942.

3 **Christmas Star,** Nancy Page, *Birmingham News,* Dec 25, 1934.

4 **Bethlehem Star,** Nancy Page, *Birmingham News,* Dec 12, 1939.

5 **Three Cheers,** *Farm Journal and Farmer's Wife,* ca. 1941.

6 **Advisor's Block,** Hazel Carter, Beyer, Jinny, *The Quilter's Album...,* 1980.

7 **Star of the West,** Alice Brooks, *Detroit Free Press,* Apr 2, 1934.

8 **Lena's Choice,** Clara Stone, *Practical Needlework,* ca. 1906.

9 **Sunflower,** Laura Wheeler, *Cincinnati Enquirer,* Jul 19, 1933.

10 **Summer's Dream,** Orange Judd and Company, Aug 2, 1902.

11 **Winged Square,** Laura Wheeler, *Cincinnati Enquirer,* Jan 26, 1934.

12 **Mrs. Cleveland's Choice,** Nancy Cabot, *Chicago Tribune,* May 8, 1933. See 249-9.

1 **Meadowlark,** Jinny Beyer, Beyer, Jinny, *Patchwork Portfolio,* 1989.

2 **Grape Vine,** Jinny Beyer, Beyer, Jinny, *Patchwork Portfolio,* 1989.

3 **The Four Pointed Star,** *Kansas City Star,* Feb 13, 1937.

4 **Star A,** *Ladies Art Company,* 1897.
Also known as:
An 'A' Star, Nancy Cabot, *Chicago Tribune,* Feb 11, 1935.

5 **Crazy Quilt Star,** Nancy Cabot, *Chicago Tribune,* Aug 3, 1933.

6 **A Modern Version of the String Quilt,** *Kansas City Star,* Nov 18, 1942.

7 **Greek Puzzle,** Quilt Blocks from The Farmer's Wife, 1932.

8 **Burnham Square,** *Ladies Art Company,* 1897. See 198-8.

9 **Children of Israel,** Hall, 1935.

10 **Missouri Puzzle,** Ladies Art Company, 1928. See 258-5.
"You may want to call this design by some other name, but Missouri Puzzle is what my great-grandmother called it, and so Missouri Puzzle it stays with me." Nancy Page, *Birmingham News,* Nov 11, 1941

11 **Mother's Fancy,** *Ladies Art Company,* 1897. Also known as:
Mother's Fancy Star, Hall, 1935.
"'Mother's Fancy' is another of the many 'fancies' in the quilt world. When early quilters created original designs and were at a loss for a suitable name, the result usually was 'somebody's fancy.'" Nancy Cabot, *Chicago Tribune,* Dec 10, 1934

12 **Ribbon Square,** Nancy Cabot, *Chicago Tribune,* May 8, 1935.

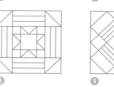

1 24 x 24 grid

2 24 x 24 grid

3 24 x 24 grid

4 24 x 24 grid

5 24 x 24 grid

6 24 x 24 grid

7 24 x 24 grid

8 24 x 24 grid

9 24 x 24 grid

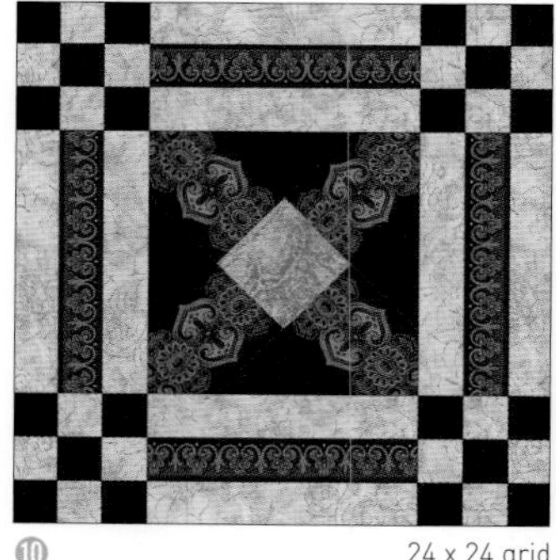
10 24 x 24 grid

11 24 x 24 grid

12 24 x 24 grid

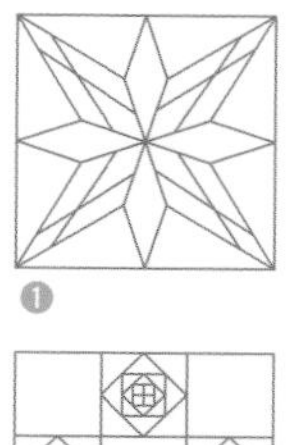
1

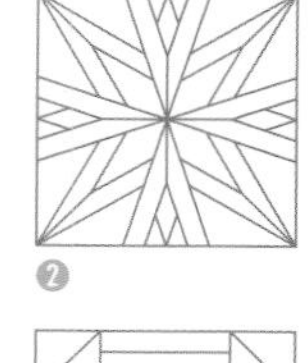
2

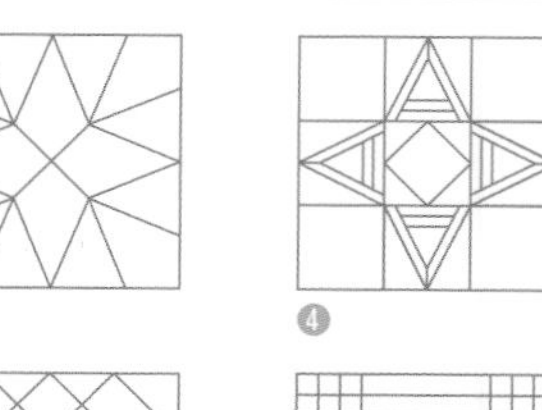
3 4

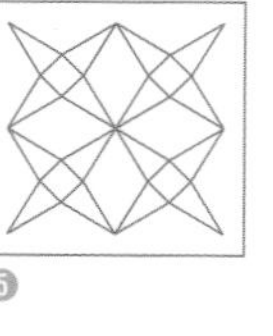
5

6

7

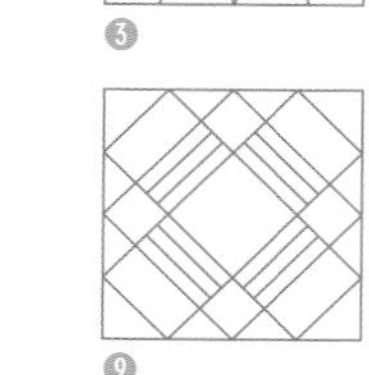
8

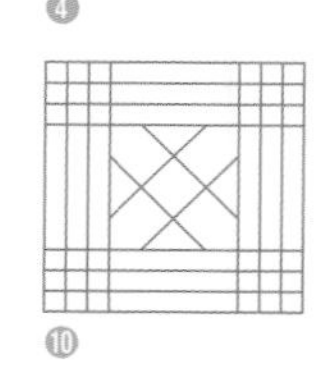
9 10

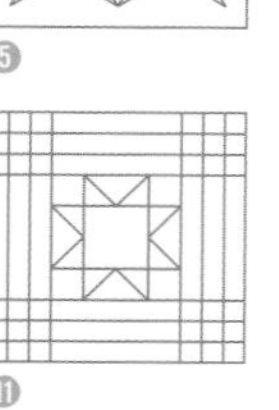
11

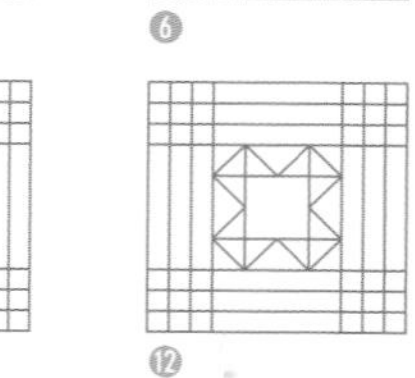
12

1 24 x 24 grid

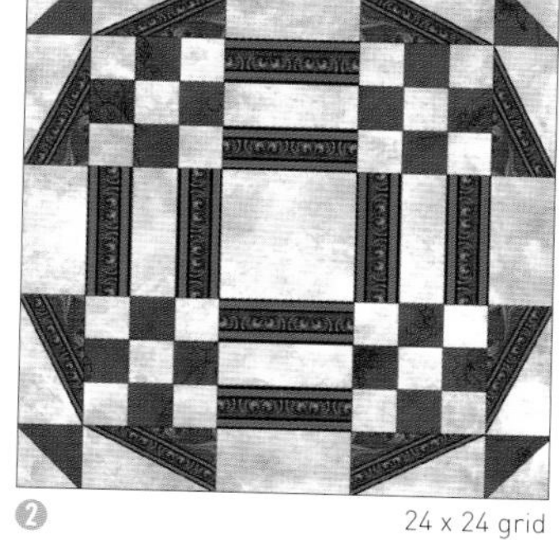

2 24 x 24 grid

3 24 x 24 grid

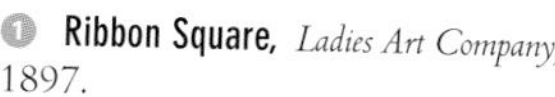

4 24 x 24 grid

5 24 x 24 grid

6 24 x 24 grid

7 24 x 24 grid

8 24 x 24 grid

9 24 x 24 grid

10 24 x 24 grid

11 24 x 24 grid

12 24 x 24 grid

1. **Ribbon Square,** *Ladies Art Company,* 1897.
2. **Spider's Den,** *Ladies Art Company,* 1897.
3. **Puss in the Corner,** Alan, ca. 1932. See 156-1.
4. **One Dozen Napkins,** Nancy Cabot, *Chicago Tribune,* May 22, 1937.
5. **Nine Patch Plaid,** Aunt Martha series: *Patchwork Simplicity,* ca. 1977.
6. **Crossroads,** Aunt Martha series: *Bold and Beautiful Quilts,* ca. 1977.
7. **Nine Patch,** Virginia Snow, *Grandma Dexter Appliqué and Patchwork Designs, Book 36a,* ca. 1932.
8. **Cubes and Bars,** Aunt Martha series: *The Quilt Fair Comes to You,* ca. 1933.
9. **Solomon's Temple,** Nancy Cabot, *Chicago Tribune,* Sep 23, 1934. See 265-11.
10. **Delectable Mountains,** *Antique Quilts,* 1974.
11. **Apache Trail,** Nancy Cabot, *Chicago Tribune,* Jan 5, 1938.
12. **Whirlwind,** Nancy Cabot, *Chicago Tribune,* Mar 28, 1938.

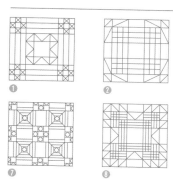

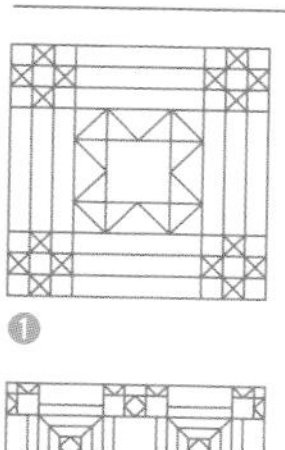
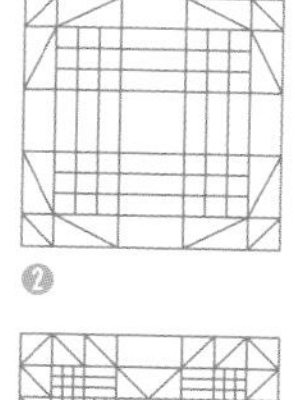
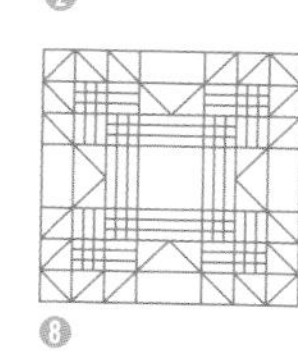
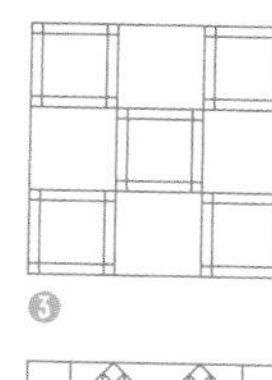
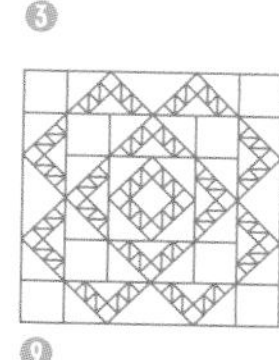
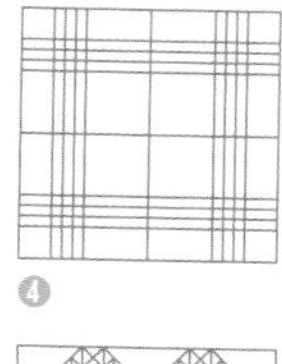
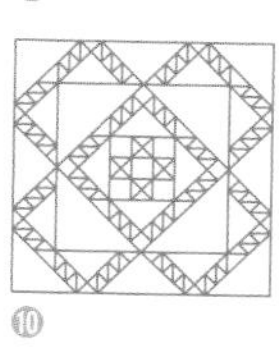
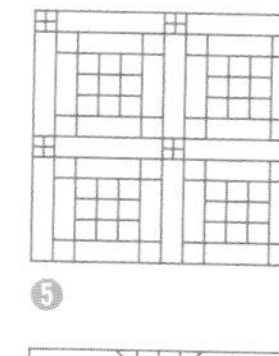
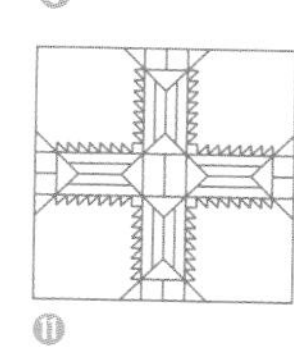
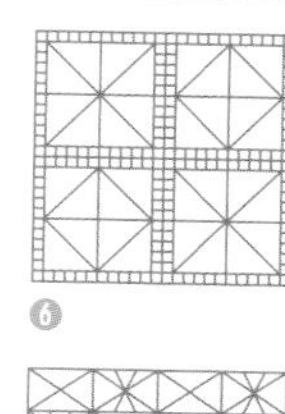
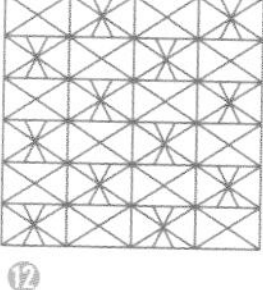

1 2 3 4 5 6

7 8 9 10 11 12

1 **Merrie England,** Nancy Cabot, *Chicago Tribune,* Oct 4, 1935.
"The history surrounding 'Merrie England' is unusual. The block was designed by a man, for the purpose of cheering a homesick young English woman. She had been in this country for some time and felt she never would be able to return to her beloved England. Being an ardent needleworker, this woman had a wide collection of quilts, but nothing she had brought from home. To appease her loneliness, 'Merrie England' was designed to occupy her time, and with the idea that she would take her quilt, completed, back home." Nancy Cabot, *Chicago Tribune,* Oct 4, 1935

2 **The Apple Leaf,** *Kansas City Star,* Sep 14, 1935.

3 **Maple Leaf,** Clara Stone, *Practical Needlework,* ca. 1906. Also known as:
- **Magnolia Leaf,** *Practical Needlework,* ca. 1906.
- **Palm Leaf,** Gutcheon, *The Perfect Patchwork Primer,* 1973.
- **Tea Leaves,** Webster, 1915.

4 **Texas Flower,** Nancy Cabot, *Chicago Tribune,* Sep 15, 1935. Also known as:
- **Cactus Flower,** Beyer, *The Quilter's Album...,* 1980.

5 **Texas Flower,** *Ladies Art Company,* 1897.

6 **Autumn Leaf,** *The Patchwork Book,* 1932.

7 **English Ivy,** Eveline Foland, *Kansas City Star,* May 9, 1931. Also known as:
- **The Clover Blossom,** *Mrs. Danner's Quilts, Books 1 & 2,* 1934.

8 **Crocus,** Jinny Beyer, Quilter's Quest design, 2007.

9 **Spring Garden,** Nancy Page, *Birmingham News,* Apr 29, 1941.

10 **Modernistic Pansy,** Nancy Cabot, *Chicago Tribune,* Sep 30, 1933.

11 **Pine Needle Basket,** Jinny Beyer, Quilters' Quest design, 2006.

12 **Virginia Basket,** Jinny Beyer, Quilters' Quest design, 2006.

1 **Swallow's Flight,** *Prize Winning Designs,* ca. 1931.

2 **Tiny Pine,** Nancy Page, *Birmingham News,* May 16, 1939.

3 **Balsam Fir,** Nancy Cabot, *Chicago Tribune,* Feb 17, 1938.

4 **Pine Tree,** *Ladies Art Company,* 1901. Also known as:

> **The Christmas Tree,** Eveline Foland, *Kansas City Star,* Dec 24, 1932.
>
> **Pine Forest,** *Quilt Book No. 6,* Jul 29, 1933.

5 **Pine Tree,** Nancy Cabot, *Chicago Tribune,* Nov 4, 1934.

6 **The Log Cabin,** *Kansas City Star,* Jun 13, 1945. Also known as:

> **The Log Cabin Quilt,** *Kansas City Star,* Sep 29, 1948.

7 **Golden Stairs,** *Prize Winning Designs,* ca. 1931.

8 **Iowa Star Block,** *Ladies Art Company,* 1922. See 80-4.

9 **Southern Star,** *Grandma Dexter's New Appliqué and Patchwork Designs, Book 36b,* ca. 1932.

10 **King David's Crown,** Hall, 1935. See 204-8.

11 **Crystal Flower,** Jinny Beyer Hilton Head Seminar design, 1985; published in Beyer, Jinny, *Patchwork Portfolio.*

12 **Goldenrod,** Jinny Beyer Beyer, Jinny, *Patchwork Portfolio,* 1989.

❶ **No Name Quilt,** *Ladies Art Company,* 1897.

❷ **Starry Path,** Alice Brooks, *Alice Brooks Designs,* ca. 1950.

❸ **Small Business,** Gutcheon, *Perfect Patchwork Primer,* 1973.

❹ **Larkspur,** Jinny Beyer, Beyer, Jinny, *Patchwork Portfolio,* 1989.

❺ **Kentucky Cross Roads,** Nancy Cabot *Chicago Tribune,* Jan 29, 1933. See 165-12. "There is romance in the history of every patchwork quilt and in the history of the pattern from which it was fashioned. The stories of some may be longer and more entrancing than others, it is true, but they all have charm. Years ago, in the early days of Kentucky, the rough clay roads of that section would hardly have been considered romantic. Nevertheless, the rutty, sticky roads were the inspiration for the quilt block 'Kentucky Cross Roads.' The 'Kentucky Cross Roads' pattern, by the way, is one of a very, very few that have been inherited from our ancestresses through many generations without a change of name; though there have been, in most cases variations in the pattern itself as it has been handed from one to another, from mother to daughter, or perhaps even copied from memory. There may have been a scarcity of materials, too, to necessitate slight changes in the details, since all the pieces, of course were cut from the materials in scrap bags or from remnants of well worn aprons or housedresses. Mrs. A.H. Roberts of 4951 North Leavitt Street, has an antique quilt of the 'Kentucky Cross Roads' design made in 1842 by her grandmother, from whom she inherited it. The materials were hand woven, the thread for quilting spun by hand. It is a highly prized heirloom." Nancy Cabot, *Chicago Tribune,* Jan 29, 1933

❻ **Maple Leaf,** Nancy Page, *Birmingham News,* Oct 30, 1934.

❼ **Burgoyne's Surrender,** Nancy Cabot, *Chicago Tribune,* Nov 24, 1933.

❽ **Save All,** Aunt Martha series: *Easy Quilts,* ca. 1958.

❾ **Feather Star,** Hall, 1935.

❿ **Unknown,** *Prize Winning Designs,* ca. 1931.

⓫ **Five Lilies,** Nancy Cabot, *Chicago Tribune,* Sep 30, 1936.

⓬ **Butterfly Bush,** Nancy Cabot, *Chicago Tribune,* Oct 8, 1934. "'Rhode Island' claims the distinction of producing a prize winning addition to quilt ranks, in the form of a block named 'Butterfly Bush.' It is popular along the eastern seaboard, and is gradually becoming a prime favorite among middle westerners." Nancy Cabot, *Chicago Tribune,* Oct 8, 1934

❶ 48 x 48 grid

❷ 48 x 48 grid

❸ 48 x 48 grid

❹ 48 x 48 grid

❺ 48 x 48 grid

❻ 48 x 48 grid

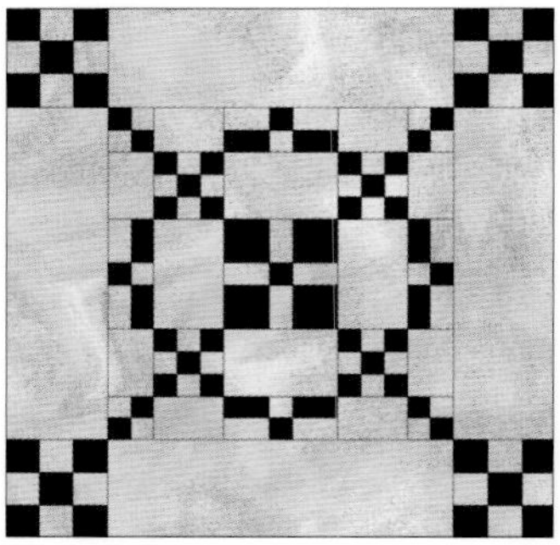

❼ 48 x 48 grid

❽ 48 x 48 grid

❾ 48 x 48 grid

❿ 48 x 48 grid

⓫ 48 x 48 grid

⓬ 48 x 48 grid

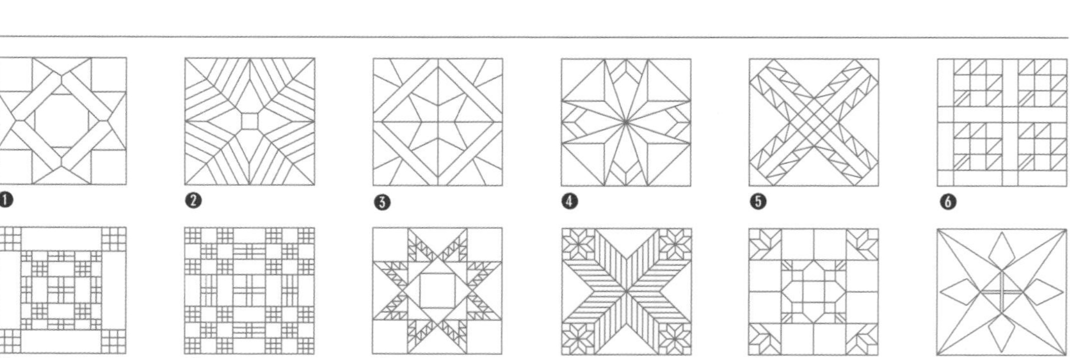

❶ 48 x 48 grid

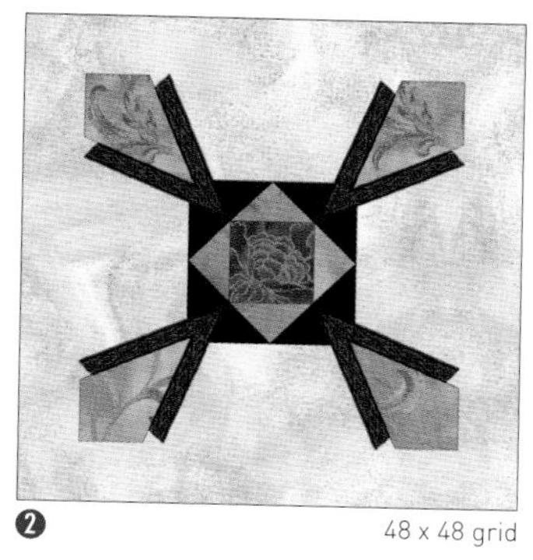

❷ 48 x 48 grid

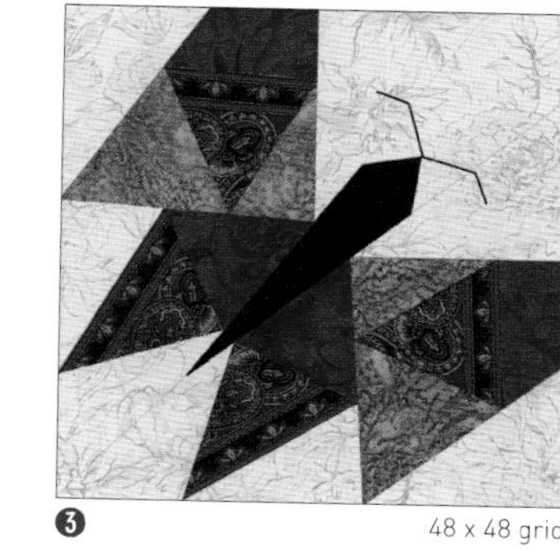

❸ 48 x 48 grid

❹ 48 x 48 grid

❺ 48 x 48 grid

❻ 48 x 48 grid

❼ 48 x 48 grid

❽ 48 x 48 grid

❾ 48 x 48 grid

❿ 48 x 48 grid

⓫ 48 x 48 grid

⓬ 96 x 96 grid

❶ **Four Vases,** *Kansas City Star,* Mar 28, 1951.

❷ **Modern Corsage,** Nancy Cabot, *Chicago Tribune,* Oct 10, 1936.

❸ **Butterfly,** Laura Wheeler, *Cincinnati Enquirer,* Nov 4, 1934.

❹ **Cactus Flower,** Hall, 1935.

❺ **Autumn Leaves,** Nancy Cabot, *Chicago Tribune,* Jun 8, 1936.

❻ **Floral Bouquet,** Nancy Cabot, *Chicago Tribune,* Aug 31, 1934.
"Quilt history records that the designer of this dainty block met her husband at an entertainment at which she sang. It was a case of love at first sight. The dress she wore on that memorable occasion was of a dainty figured material, and when it became worn she decided to preserve it by incorporating it in a quilt." Nancy Cabot, *Chicago Tribune,* Aug 31, 1934

❼ **Cross and Crown,** Hall, 1935. See 119-10.

❽ **Colonial Basket,** Hall, 1935.

❾ **Dahlia,** Jinny Beyer Quilter's Quest design, 2007.

❿ **The Star's Exhibition Home Quilt Block Pattern,** Ruby McKim, *Kansas City Star,* May 11, 1929. Also known as:

- **House on the Hill,** Ruby McKim, McKim, 1929.
- **Little White House on the Hill,** Nancy Cabot, *Chicago Tribune,* Nov 23, 1933.

⓫ **Log Cabin,** Nancy Cabot, *Chicago Tribune,* Feb 8, 1935.

⓬ **Kite,** Laura Wheeler, *Tulsa Tribune,* Jun 3, 1981. Also known as:

- **Pinwheel,** Laura Wheeler, *Tulsa Tribune,* Jun 3, 1981.
- **Quilt of Patches,** Laura Wheeler, *Tulsa Tribune,* Jun 3, 1981.

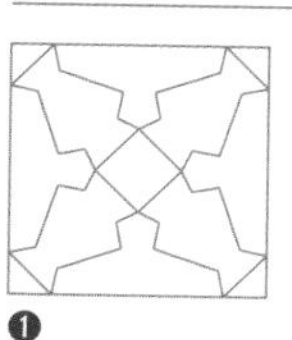

❶

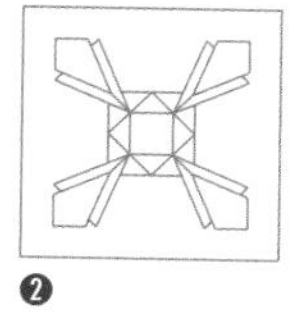

❷

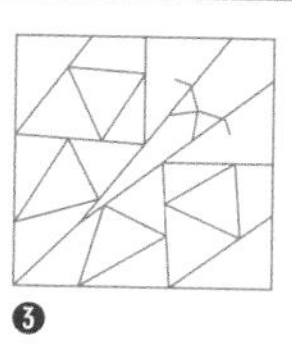

❸

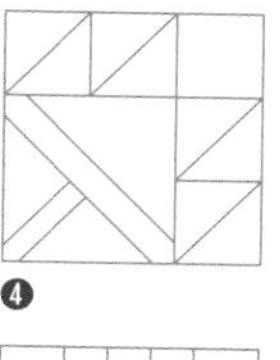

❹

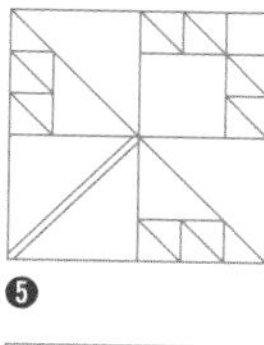

❺

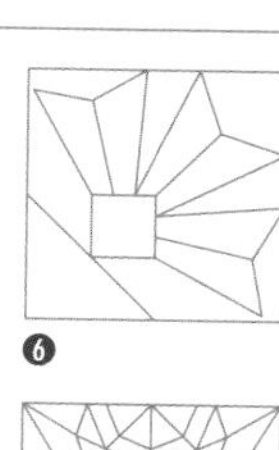

❻

❼

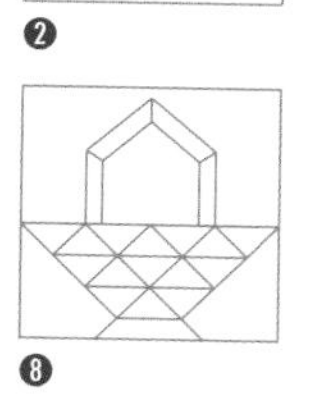

❽

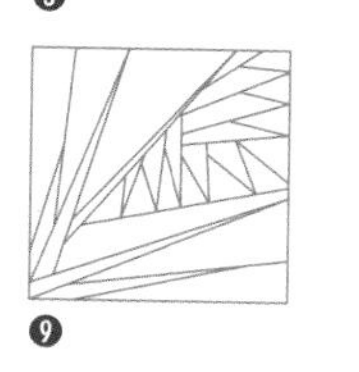

❾

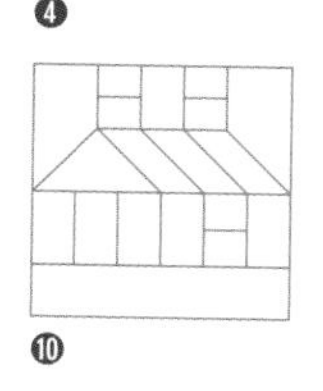

❿

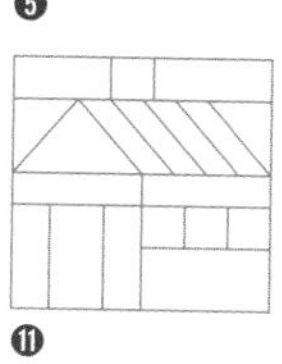

⓫

⓬

5 x 5 Base Grid Category

Includes ● 5 x 5, ● 10 x 10, ● 20 x 20, ● 40 x 40, and ● 80 x 80 grids

❶ **Electric Fan, No. 2,** Clara Stone, *Practical Needlework,* ca. 1906.

❷ **The Diversion Quilt,** *Kansas City Star,* Jul 11, 1945.

❸ **Puss in the Corner,** *Ladies Art Company,* 1897.

❹ **Multiple Square Quilt,** *Kansas City Star,* May 6, 1953.

❺ **Criss Cross,** Nancy Page, *Detroit Free Press,* Oct 27, 1933. Also known as: **Single Irish Chain,** Nancy Page, *Birmingham News,* Feb 28, 1939.

❻ **Red Cross,** Nancy Page, *Birmingham News,* Jul 13, 1937.

❼ **Whirling Square,** Nancy Cabot, *Chicago Tribune,* Dec 23, 1937.

❽ **Forest Paths,** *Farm Journal and Farmer's Wife* (Silver Anniversary issue), 1945.

❾ **Squares and Square,** Nancy Page, unidentified newspaper clipping, date unknown.

❶ ❷ ❸ ❹ ❺

❻ ❼ ❽ ❾

1 **Philadelphia Pavement,** Finley, 1929. See 84-4 and 253-3.

2 **Garden of Eden,** *Ladies Art Company,* 1897. See 161-6 and 243-4.

3 **Garden of Eden,** Nancy Cabot, *Chicago Tribune,* Jun 23, 1934. See 161-6 and 243-4.

4 **Mrs. Anderson's Quilt,** *Mrs. Danner's Fourth Quilt Book,* 1958.

5 **Red Cross,** *Ladies Art Company,* 1897.

6 **Jack in the Box,** James, 1978.

7 **Bright Jewel,** *Kansas City Star,* Sep 28, 1949.

8 **Handy Andy,** *Ladies Art Company,* 1897. Also known as:
Foot Stool, date unknown; published in Beyer, Jinny, *The Quilter's Album ....*
Maine Woods, Nancy Page, *Birmingham News,* Mar 3, 1936.

9 **Clowns,** Nancy Cabot, *Chicago Tribune,* Nov 13, 1934. Also known as:
Clown's Choice, Hall, 1935.

10 **Clown's Choice,** Finley, 1929.

11 **Baton Rouge Square,** Nancy Cabot, *Chicago Tribune,* May 22, 1936.

12 **Wishing Ring,** *Mrs. Danner's Quilts, Books 1 & 2,* 1934.

1. **Grandmother's Choice,** *Mrs. Danner Presents Quilt Book 7,* 1975.

2. **A Wrench,** *Louisville, Farm and Fireside,* Feb 15, 1883. See 112-2. Also known as:
   - **Beginner's Quilt,** Alice Brooks, unidentified newspaper clipping, date unknown.
   - **Chinese Coin,** Nancy Cabot, *Chicago Tribune,* Aug 19, 1936.
   - **Churn Dash,** Eveline Foland, *Kansas City Star,* Jan 4, 1930.
   - **Churn Dasher,** ca. 1938, per Havig.
   - **Double Wrench,** *Ladies Art Company,* 1897.
   - **French 4's,** Nancy Page, *Nashville Banner,* Dec 19, 1933.
   - **Monkey Wrench,** ca. 1938, per Havig.
   - **Pioneer Block,** date unknown; published in Beyer, Jinny, *The Quilter's Album....*
   - **Pioneer Patch,** *Q Book 103, All Year Quilts,* date unknown.

3. **Grandmother's Choice,** *Ladies Art Company,* 1897. See 112-5, 168-2 and 212-11. Also known as:
   - **Memory Quilt,** *Farm and Home,* Mar 1, 1899.
   - **T Quilt,** *Farm and Home,* Mar 1, 1899.

4. **Ducks and Ducklings,** Finley, 1929. See 174-10, 273-3 and 269-10. Also known as:
   - **Corn and Beans,** Finley, 1929.
   - **Ducklings,** *Kansas City Star,* Jun 11, 1949.
   - **Ducklings for Friendship,** *Kansas City Star,* Oct 19, 1949.
   - **Hen and Chickens,** Finley, 1929.
   - **Wild Goose Chase,** *Farmer's Wife,* Jan 1913.

5. **Chinese Coin,** Nancy Cabot, *Chicago Tribune,* Apr 7, 1934.

6. **Duck and Ducklings,** *Ladies Art Company,* 1897. Also known as:
   - **Monkey Wrench,** *Farm Journal Quilt Patterns,* ca. 1935.

7. **Red Cross,** Clara Stone, *Practical Needlework,* ca. 1906.

8. **Square Dance,** James, 1978.

9. **Handy Andy,** Finley, 1929.

10. **Handy Andy (2),** Gutcheon, *The Perfect Patchwork Primer,* 1973.

11. **Wedding Ring,** *Ladies Art Company,* 1897. Also known as:
    - **Crown and Thorns,** Ickis, 1949. **Crown of Thorns,** Hall, 1935.
    - **English Wedding Ring,** Nancy Page, unidentified newspaper clipping, date unknown.
    - **Georgetown Circle,** Hall, 1935.
    - **Memory Wreath,** Hall, 1935.
    - **Mill Wheel,** Nancy Page, *Birmingham News,* Aug 4, 1936.
    - **Nest and Fledgeling,** *Kansas City Star,* Mar 25, 1933.
    - **Odd Scraps Patchwork,** *Ladies Art Company,* 1897.
    - **Old English Wedding Ring,** *Kansas City Star,* Dec 28, 1955.
    - **Rolling Stone,** *Farmer's Wife,* 1920, per Brackman.
    - **Single Wedding Ring,** Eveline Foland, *Kansas City Star,* Apr 12, 1930.
    - **Thrift Block,** Nancy Cabot, *Chicago Tribune,* Jun 16, 1934.
    - **Wedding Knot,** *Farmer's Advocate,* Mar 16, 1933.

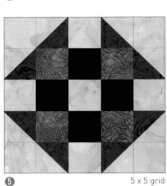

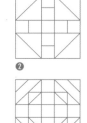

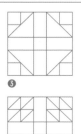

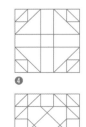

12. **Mrs. Keller's Nine Patch,** Hall, 1935.

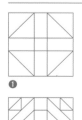

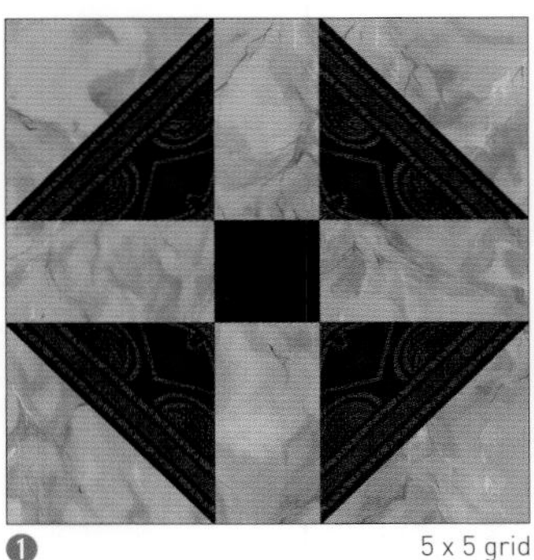

1 5 x 5 grid

2 5 x 5 grid

3 5 x 5 grid

4 5 x 5 grid

5 5 x 5 grid

6 5 x 5 grid

7 5 x 5 grid

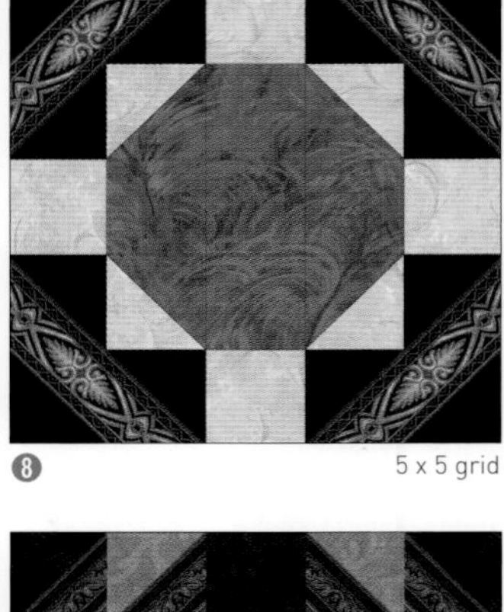

8 5 x 5 grid

9 5 x 5 grid

10 5 x 5 grid

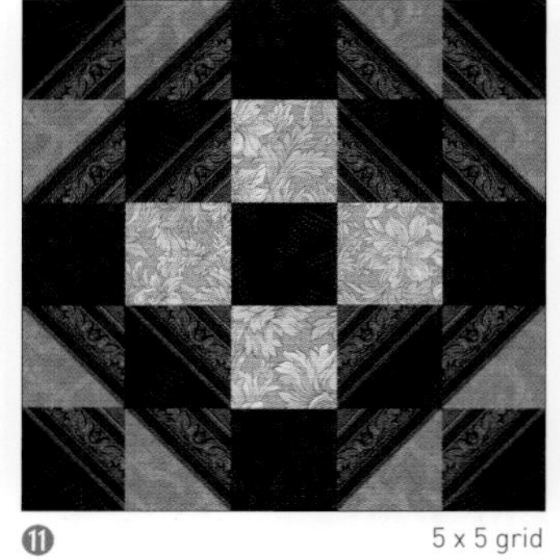

11 5 x 5 grid

12 5 x 5 grid

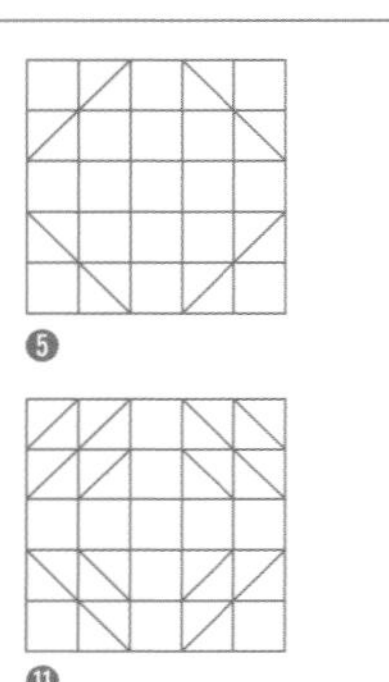

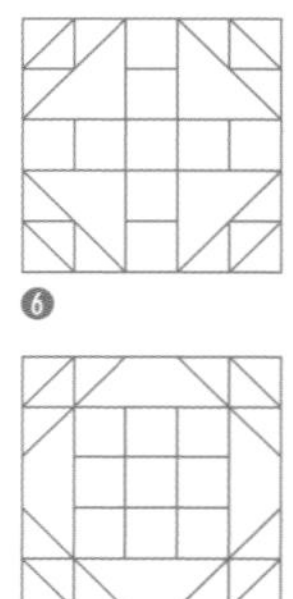

1 2 3 4 5 6

7 8 9 10 11 12

❶ **Johnny Round the Corner,** Nancy Page, *Birmingham News,* Sep 4, 1934. Also known as:
  Round the Corner, Nancy Page, *Birmingham News,* Sep 4, 1934.

❷ **Country Lanes,** *Mountain Mist Blue Book of Quilts,* 1938. Also known as:
  Cross in the Square, *Quilt Engagement Calendar Treasury,* 1982.

❸ **Grandma's Favorite,** Clara Stone, *Practical Needlework,* ca. 1906. Also known as:
  Grandma's Choice, Nancy Cabot, *Chicago Tribune,* Nov 26, 1936.

❹ **Propeller,** *Ladies Art Company,* 1928.

❺ **Butterfly at the Cross,** Clara Stone, *Practical Needlework,* ca. 1906. Also known as:
  Algonquin Charm, *Progressive Farmer,* 1936.
  Butterfly at the Crossroads, *Hearth and Home,* 1928.

❻ **Oregon,** Nancy Page, *Birmingham News,* Nov 24, 1936. Also known as:
  Miller's Daughter, Nancy Cabot, *Chicago Tribune,* Sep 9, 1937.

❼ **Farmer's Daughter,** *Ladies Art Company,* 1901. Also known as:
  Corner Posts, Eveline Foland, *Kansas City Star,* Dec 3, 1932.
  Flying Birds, Nancy Cabot, *Chicago Tribune,* May 10, 1938.
  Jack's Blocks, *Grandmother's Patchwork Quilt Designs, Book 20,* 1931.
  Rolling Star, date unknown; published in Beyer, Jinny, *The Quilter's Album....*
  Two Crosses, Nancy Cabot, *Chicago Tribune,* Sep 28, 1936.

"In a prim little town in Ohio, during the circumspect fifties, the wife of one of the esteemed members of the Methodist church pieced 'The Farmer's Daughter.' It made a beautiful coverlet pieced in colors of soft lavender, gold, and white; all colors most expressive of a quiet sensitive person." Nancy Cabot, *Chicago Tribune,* Nov 21, 1934

❽ **Gold Brick,** *Prize Winning Designs,* ca. 1931.

❾ **Fool's Square,** Nancy Cabot, *Chicago Tribune,* Sep 2, 1934.

❿ **Sister's Choice,** *Ladies Art Company,* 1897. Also known as:
  Star and Cross, *Museum Quilts,* date unknown.

⓫ **The Greek Cross,** *Kansas City Star,* Jul 7, 1954. Also known as:
  Friendship Block, *Kansas City Star,* Oct 10, 1956.

"When called 'Memory Wreath', it was made of pieces of dresses worn by the dear departed, the name and date of death being embroidered in the white center square." Hall, 1935

⓬ **Four X Star,** *Ladies Art Company,* 1897. Also known as:
  Double X Star, Aunt Martha series: *The Quilt Fair Comes to You,* ca. 1933.
  Father's Choice, James, 1978.
  Five Patch Star, Gutcheon, *The Perfect Patchwork Primer,* 1973.
  Jack's Blocks, Nancy Cabot, *Chicago Tribune,* Jan 17, 1935.
  Sister's Choice, Nancy Page, *Birmingham News,* Nov 6, 1934.

❶ **Fool's Square,** *Ladies Art Company,* 1897.

❷ **Spool Block,** Nancy Cabot, *Chicago Tribune,* Apr 1, 1938.

❸ **Thistle,** Jinny Beyer, Jinny Beyer Studio design, 2005.

❹ **Potomac Pride,** Jinny Beyer, Jinny Beyer Studio design, 2005.

❺ **Garden Gate,** Jinny Beyer, Jinny Beyer Studio design, 2005.

❻ **Noon Day Sun,** Nancy Page, *Birmingham News,* May 20, 1941.

❼ **Memory Blocks,** date unknown; published in Beyer, Jinny, *The Quilter's Album....*

❽ **Square and a Half,** *Ladies Art Company,* 1897.

❾ **Southern Pride,** Jinny Beyer, Jinny Beyer Studio design, 2005.

❿ **Stepping Stones,** Jinny Beyer, Jinny Beyer Studio design, 2005.

⓫ **Falls Landing,** Jinny Beyer Studio design, 2005.

⓬ **Providence Quilt Block,** *Ladies Art Company,* 1928. Also known as:
 North Dakota, Nancy Page, *Birmingham News,* Dec 22, 1936.
 Providence, Nancy Cabot, *Chicago Tribune,* Jul 3, 1933.

"In our parade of the states as shown in their quilt patterns we have not had North Dakota. Here is the design I have selected for that state." Nancy Page, *Birmingham News,* Dec 22, 1936

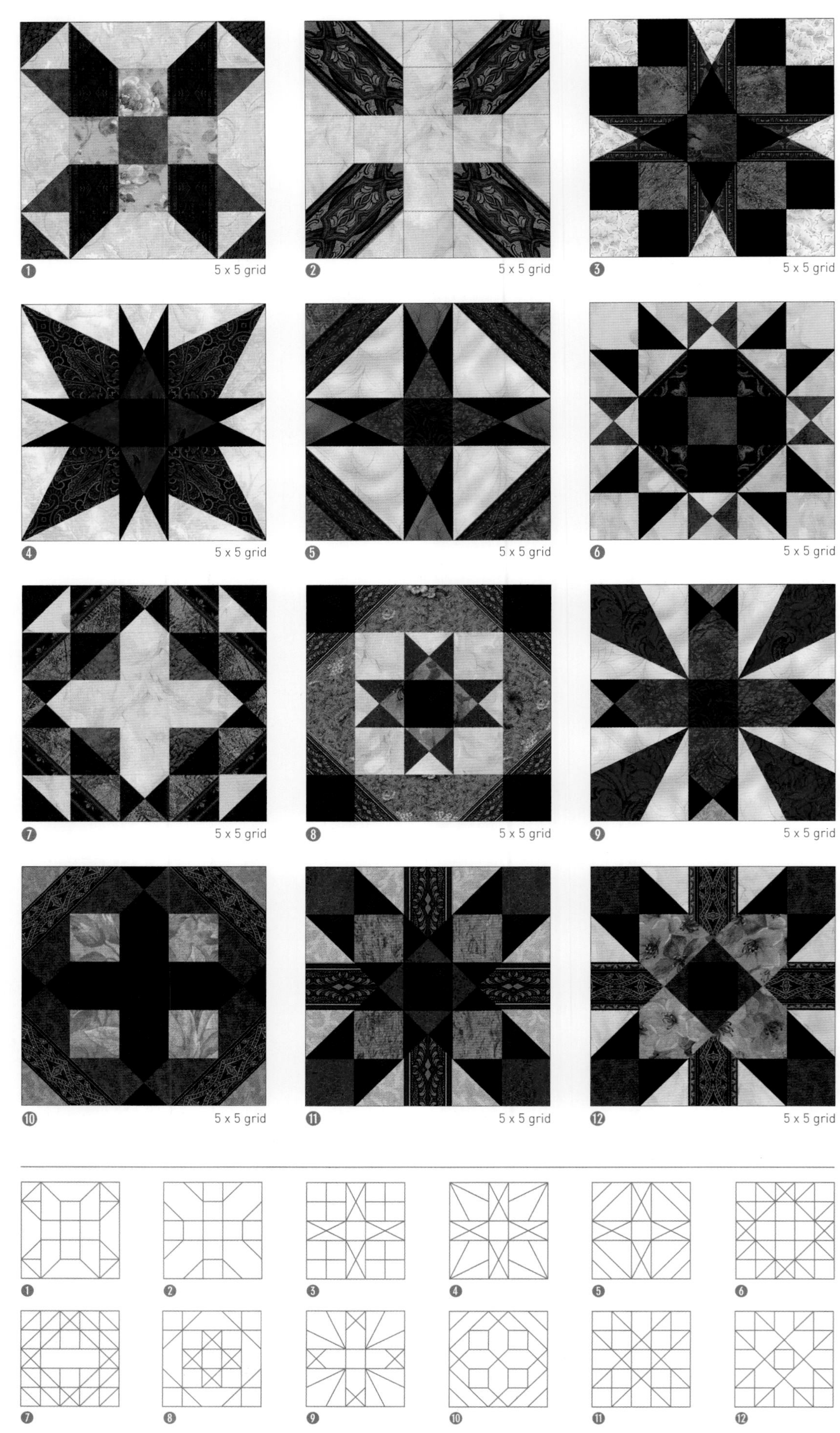

1. **Parfait,** Jinny Beyer, Jinny Beyer Studio design, 2005.
2. **Wayside Inn,** Jinny Beyer, Jinny Beyer Studio design, 2005.
3. **Virginia Crossroads,** Jinny Beyer, Jinny Beyer Studio design, 2005.
4. **Courtyard Square,** Jinny Beyer, Jinny Beyer Studio design, 2005.
5. **Wildwood,** Jinny Beyer, Jinny Beyer Studio design, 2005.
6. **Cross Bow,** Jinny Beyer, Jinny Beyer Studio design, 2005.
7. **Sienna,** Jinny Beyer, Jinny Beyer Studio design, 2005.
8. **Melody** 1, Jinny Beyer, Jinny Beyer Studio design, 2005.
9. **Melody 2,** Jinny Beyer, Jinny Beyer Studio design, 2005.
10. **Melody** 3, Jinny Beyer, Jinny Beyer Studio design, 2005.
11. **Country Crossroads,** Jinny Beyer, Jinny Beyer Studio design, 2005.
12. **Pleated Star,** Jinny Beyer, Jinny Beyer Studio design, 2005.

1 **Crossed Stars,** Jinny Beyer, Jinny Beyer Studio design, 2005.

2 **Flying Squares,** *Ladies Art Company,* 1897. Also known as:
- **Flying Square,** Nancy Cabot, *Chicago Tribune,* Jul 7, 1933.

3 **Brock House,** Nancy Page, *Birmingham News,* Mar 26, 1935.

4 **Swastika,** *Dakota Farmer,* Feb 16, 1926.

5 **Crazy House,** *Ladies Art Company,* 1928. Also known as:
- **Z Cross,** Gutcheon, *The Perfect Patchwork Primer,* 1973.

6 **Crazy Ann,** Finley, 1929. Also known as:
- **Crazy Anne,** *Kansas City Star,* Oct 15, 1932.
- **Follow the Leader,** Finley, 1929.
- **Twist and Turn,** Finley, 1929.

7 **Pinwheel Square,** *Ladies Art Company,* 1897. Also known as:
- **Follow the Leader,** Home Art Studios, unidentified newspaper clipping, date unknown.

8 **Jack in the Box,** Ruby McKim, *Kansas City Star,* Jul 6, 1929. Also known as:
- **Wheel of Chance,** Nancy Cabot, *Chicago Tribune,* Mar 20, 1935.
- **Wheel of Fortune,** *Farm Journal Quilt Patterns,* ca. 1935.
- **Whirligig,** Hall, 1935.

9 **Wheel of Fortune,** Nancy Cabot, *Chicago Tribune,* Sep 2, 1936.

10 **Mosaic # 14,** ca. 1938, per Havig.

11 **Flying Geese,** James, 1978.

12 **Pinwheel Skew,** Gutcheon, *The Perfect Patchwork Primer,* 1973.

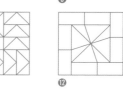

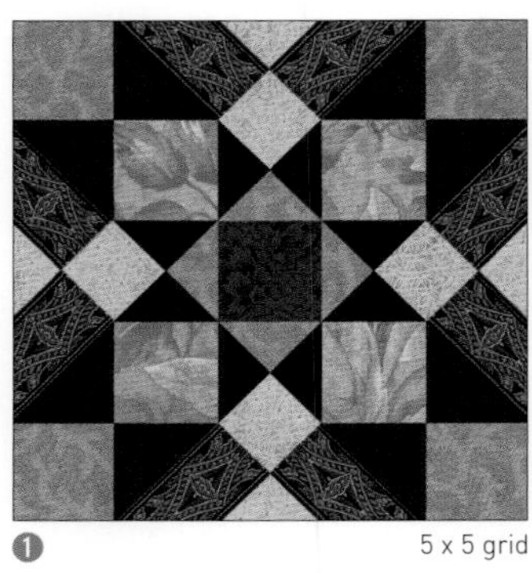
1 5 x 5 grid

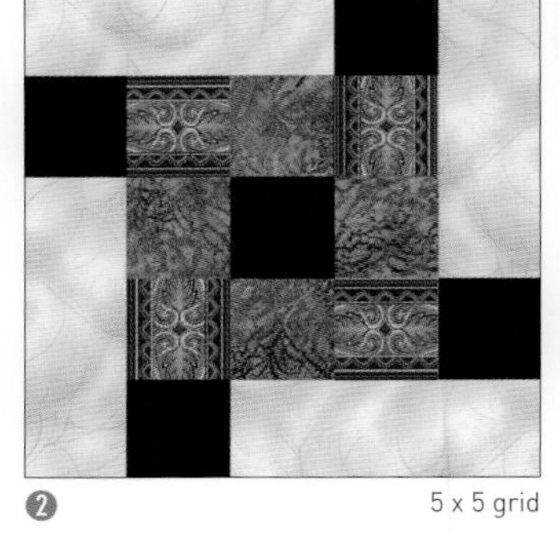
2 5 x 5 grid

3 5 x 5 grid

4 5 x 5 grid

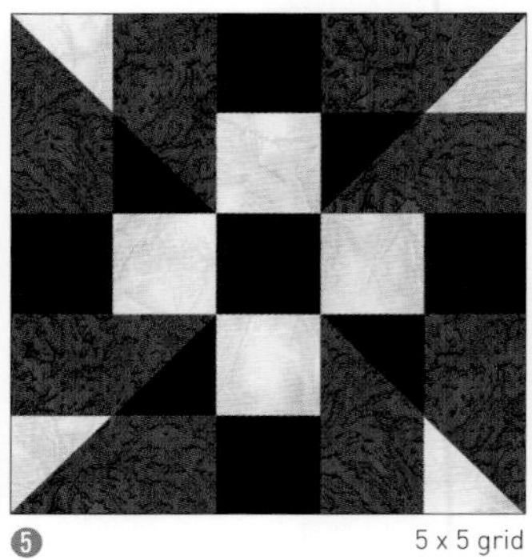
5 5 x 5 grid

6 5 x 5 grid

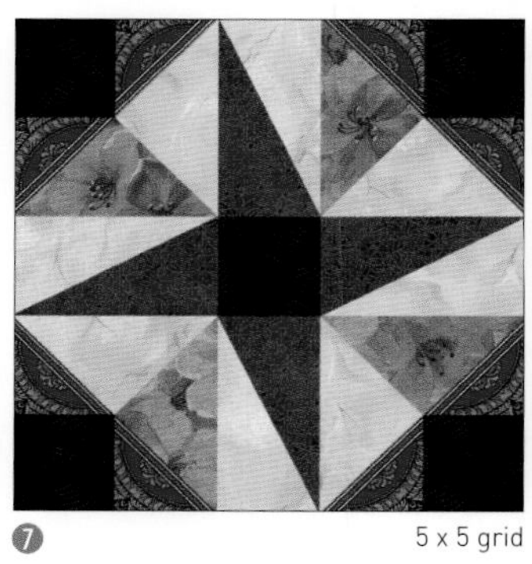
7 5 x 5 grid

8 5 x 5 grid

9 5 x 5 grid

10 5 x 5 grid

11 5 x 5 grid

12 5 x 5 grid

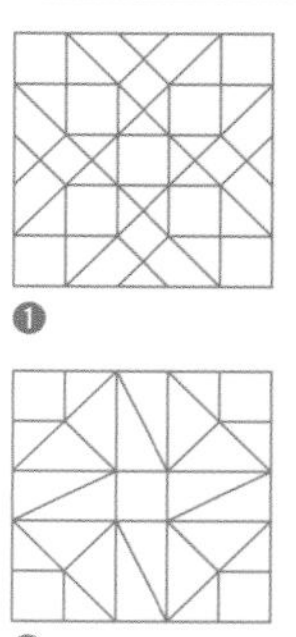
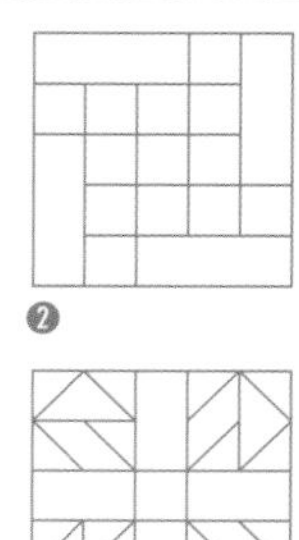
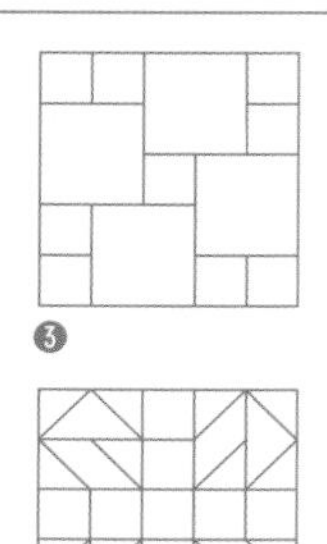
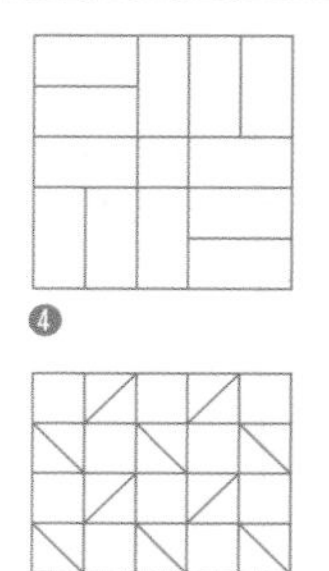
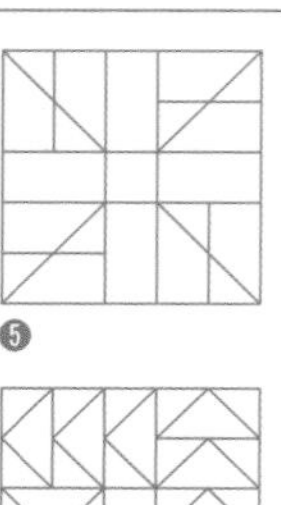
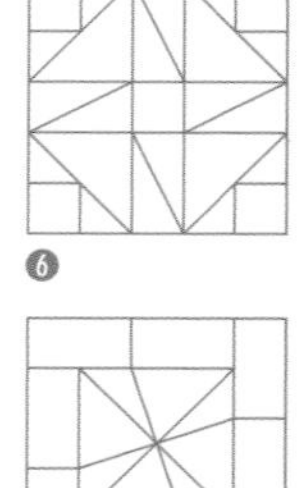

1 2 3 4 5 6

7 8 9 10 11 12

❶ Captain's Wheel, Gutcheon, *The Perfect Patchwork Primer,* 1973.

❷ Jack in the Pulpit, Jinny Beyer, Hilton Head Seminar design, 2001.

❸ Pathfinder, Nancy Cabot, *Chicago Tribune,* Jul 13, 1935. Also known as:
- **Pioneer Block,** Nancy Cabot, *Chicago Tribune,* Jan 20, 1938.

❹ Delaware Crosspatch, Nancy Cabot, *Chicago Tribune,* Sep 18, 1937.

❺ King's Crown, *Ladies Art Company,* 1897. Also known as:
- **Greek Cross,** Ickis, 1949.
- **John's Favorite,** Clara Stone, *Practical Needlework,* ca. 1906.
- **Old King Cole's Crown,** Ruby McKim, *Kansas City Star,* Nov 30, 1929.

"A Virginian honored George III by naming her favorite quilt block 'King's Crown' for him. The beauty of the block is more apparent in the completed spread, since four pieced blocks are arranged to fashion a crown." Nancy Cabot, *Chicago Tribune,* Aug 4, 1934

❻ King's Crown, Nancy Cabot, *Chicago Tribune,* Apr 15, 1937.

❼ The Delectable Mountains, Aunt Martha series: *The Quilt Fair Comes to You,* ca. 1933.

"When the pioneers came to these shores, they brought with them the tried and tested volumes of treasured literature that had been their closest friends in the homeland. 'Pilgrim's Progress' was one of these and the 'Delectaable Mountains' of which Bunyan writes were significant of the promise of peace and plenty. It is only natural that a name so symbolical should be perpetuated in a quilt made by early American needlewomen." Aunt Martha series: *The Quilt Fair Comes to You,* ca. 1933

❽ Quilting Party, Alice Brooks, unidentified newspaper clipping, date unknown.

❾ Star of Hope, *Ladies Art Company,* 1928.

❿ Lend and Borrow, *The Patchwork Book,* 1932. See 208-11. Also known as:
- **Maryland Beauty,** *Detroit Free Press,* Apr 19, 1933.
- **Rocky Glen,** date unknown, per Brackman.
- **Saw Tooth,** Ickis, 1949.

⓫ Edgemoore, Jinny Beyer, RJR Patterns, 2001.

⓬ Birthday Cake, Nancy Page, *Birmingham News,* Feb 4, 1936. Also known as:
- **Birthday Parties,** Nancy Page, *Birmingham News,* Jun 4, 1942.

1 Southern Pine, Alice Brooks, *Detroit Free Press,* Sep 14, 1935.

2 Tulip Time, Nancy Page, *Birmingham News,* Mar 28, 1939.

3 Bouquet, Aunt Martha series: *The Quilt Fair Comes to You,* ca. 1933.

4 Nosegay, Alice Brooks, unidentified newspaper clipping, date unknown.

5 The Basket Quilt, *Wallace's Farmer,* Jul 27, 1928, per Brackman. Also known as:
- **Basket of Triangles,** *Mrs. Danner's Quilts, Books 1 & 2,* 1934.
- **The Broken Dish,** *Wallace's Farmer,* Jul 27, 1928, per Brackman.
- **The Broken Sugar Bowl,** *Wallace's Farmer,* Jul 27, 1928, per Brackman.
- **May Basket,** *The Farmer's Wife Book of Quilts,* 1931.
- **Pieced Basket,** Aunt Martha series: *The Quilt Fair Comes to You,* ca. 1933.

6 Cake Stand, *Ladies Art Company,* 1897. Also known as:
- **Altar Candles,** Nancy Page, *Birmingham News,* Jul 14, 1942.
- **Basket,** Laura Wheeler, *Cincinnati Enquirer,* Dec 29, 1933.
- **Baskets,** date unknown, per Holstein.

7 Flower Pot, Hall, 1935. Also known as:
- **Anna's Basket,** *Mrs. Danner's Fifth Quilt Book,* 1970.
- **Basket of Flowers,** *Quilts,* 1945.
- **Chip Basket,** *Farm Journal* and *Farmer's Wife Quilt Patterns,* date unknown.
- **Flower Basket,** unidentified newspaper clipping, date unknown.

8 Mrs. Young's Basket, Nancy Page, *Birmingham News,* Sep 1, 1942.

9 Grandmother's Basket, *Q Book 118, Grandmother's Flower Quilts,* date unknown.

10 Fruit Basket, McKim, 1931.

11 The Flower Pot, *Kansas City Star,* Jan 16, 1937.

12 Flower Basket, Clara Stone, *Practical Needlework,* ca. 1906. Also known as:
- **A May Basket in Floral Tones,** Alice Brooks, *Kansas City Star,* Sep 17, 1947.
- **Basket,** *Detroit Free Press,* Jan 5, 1934.

"From the earliest days of quiltmaking, baskets were among the favorite designs used. Here is one found in Pennsylvania and popular there for generations. It has many possibilities as far as arrangement goes. It can be done in three materials as shown; in two materials and also in alternating patchwork and plain blocks." Alice Brooks, *Detroit Free Press,* Mar 18, 1934

1 — 5 x 5 grid

2 — 5 x 5 grid

3 — 5 x 5 grid

4 — 5 x 5 grid

5 — 5 x 5 grid

6 — 5 x 5 grid

7 — 5 x 5 grid

8 — 5 x 5 grid

9 — 5 x 5 grid

10 — 5 x 5 grid

11 — 5 x 5 grid

12 — 5 x 5 grid

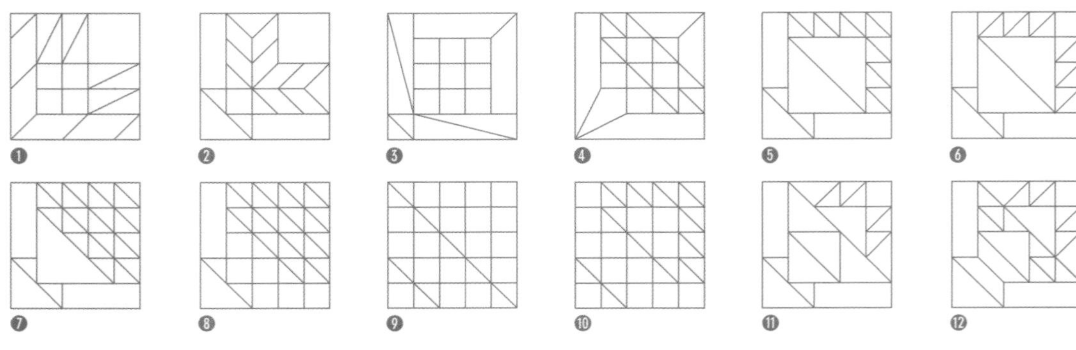

❶ **Cake Stand,** Nancy Cabot, *Chicago Tribune,* Nov 18, 1933.

❷ **Basket of Blueberries,** Jinny Beyer, Jinny Beyer Studio design, 2006.

❸ **Grape Basket,** *Ladies Art Company,* 1897. Also known as:
- **Peach Basket,** Nancy Page, *Birmingham News,* Feb 15, 1938.
- **Picnic Basket,** Nancy Page, *Birmingham News,* Jul 25, 1939.

❹ **Grape Basket,** Nancy Cabot, *Chicago Tribune,* Sep 20, 1934.

❺ **May Basket,** *Q Book 103, All Year Quilts,* date unknown.

❻ **Strength in Union,** Nancy Cabot, *Chicago Tribune,* Jan 8, 1938.

❼ **Sawtooth,** James, 1978.

❽ **Double Saw Tooth,** Nancy Page, *Birmingham News,* Jul 16, 1940.

❾ **Lady of the Lake,** *Ladies Art Company,* 1897. Also known as:
- **Hills of Vermont,** Nancy Page, *Birmingham News,* Aug 9, 1938.

❿ **Zig Zag,** *The Mountain Mist Blue Book of Quilts,* 1935.

⓫ **Twister,** James, 1978.

⓬ **Indian Meadow,** Finley, 1929. See 192-1. Also known as:
- **Queen Charlotte's Crown,** Nancy Cabot, *Chicago Tribune,* Apr 17, 1933.
- **Queen's Crown,** Nancy Page, *Detroit Free Press,* Aug 14, 1933.

❶ **Queen Charlotte's Crown,** Gutcheon, *The Perfect Patchwork Primer,* 1973. See 191-12.

❷ **Spinning Tops,** Nancy Cabot, *Chicago Tribune,* Dec 7, 1937.

❸ **The Letter T,** date unknown, per Waldvogel, *Childhood Treasures.*

❹ **Children's Delight,** *Ladies Art Company,* 1897.

❺ **The Double V,** *Kansas City Star,* Jul 24, 1940.

❻ **Sugar Loaf,** *Ladies Art Company,* 1897. See 409-4.

❼ **Clown Block,** Nancy Cabot, *Chicago Tribune,* Jun 2, 1937.

❽ **Clown,** *Ladies Art Company,* 1928.

❾ **Many Stars,** *Farm Journal and Farmer's Wife* (Silver Anniversary issue), 1945.

❿ **The Triangle Puzzle,** *Ladies Art Company,* 1897. Also known as:
 Triangle Puzzles, Nancy Cabot, *Chicago Tribune,* Oct 5, 1933.

⓫ **Triangle Trails,** Nancy Cabot, *Chicago Tribune,* Aug 25, 1937.

⓬ **Six Pointed Star,** Nancy Cabot, *Chicago Tribune,* Oct 26, 1934.

⓭ **Necktie,** Aunt Martha series: *Quilts: Modern-Colonial,* ca. 1954.

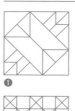

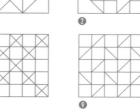

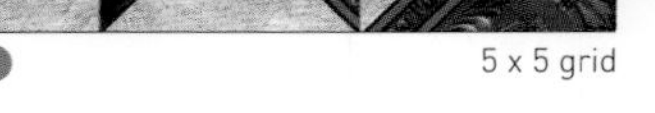

❶ 5 x 5 grid

❷ 5 x 5 grid

❸ 5 x 5 grid

❹ 5 x 5 grid

❺ 5 x 5 grid

❻ 5 x 5 grid

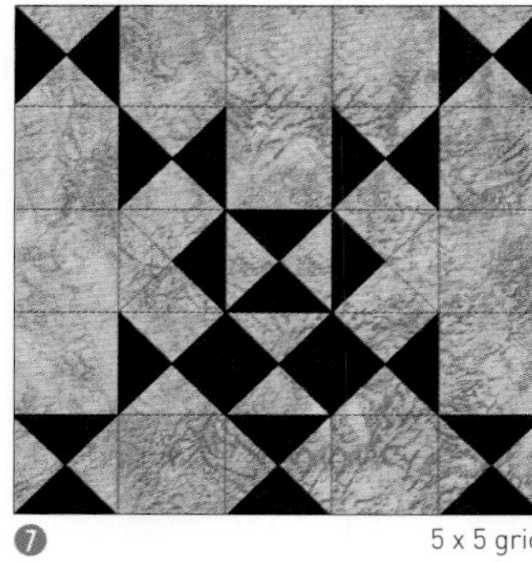

❼ 5 x 5 grid

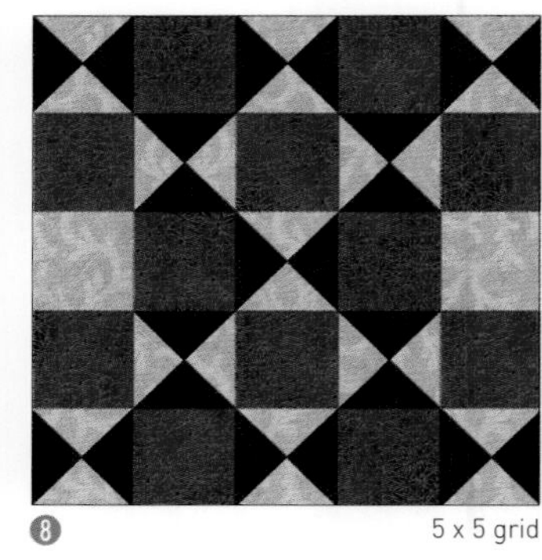

❽ 5 x 5 grid

❾ 5 x 5 grid

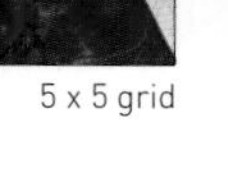

❿ 5 x 5 grid

⓫ 5 x 5 grid

⓬ 5 x 5 grid

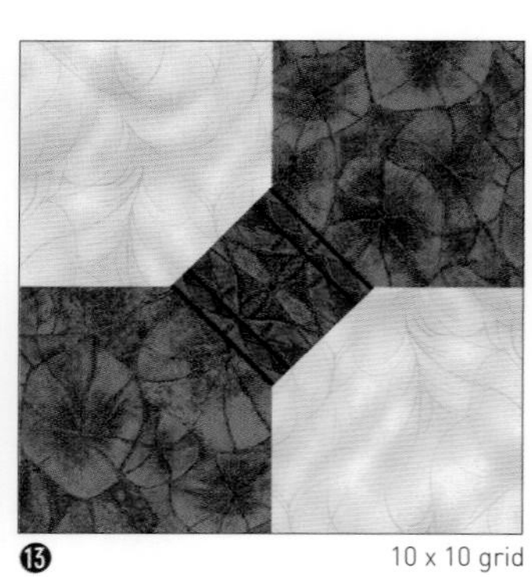

⓭ 10 x 10 grid

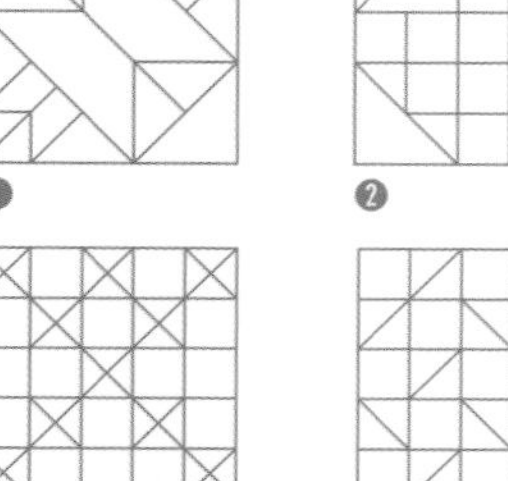
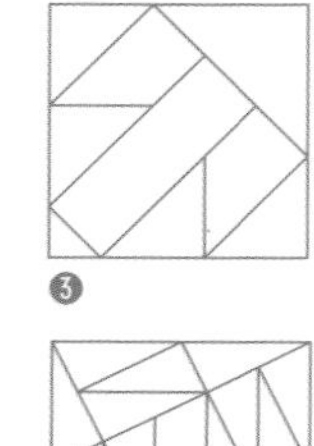
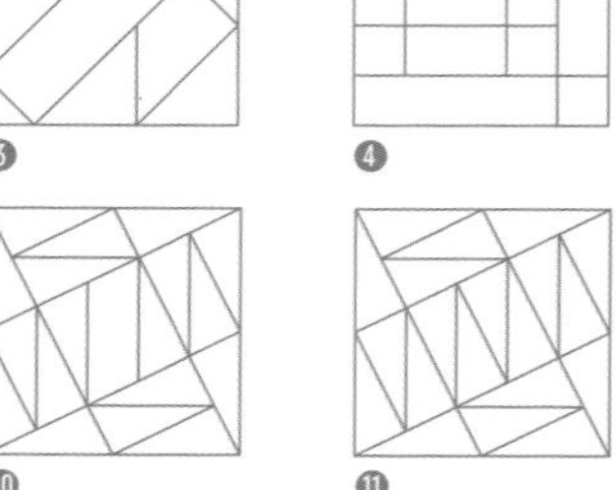
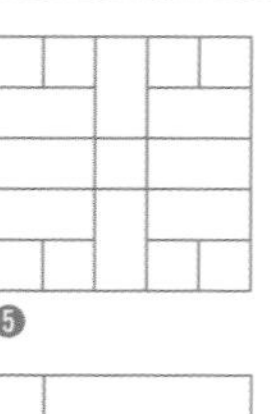
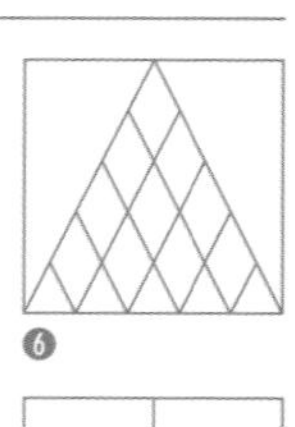

❶ ❷ ❸ ❹ ❺ ❻

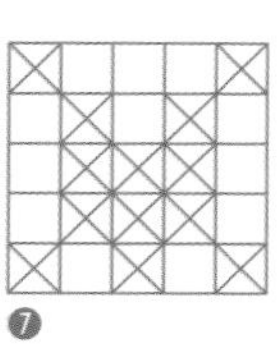
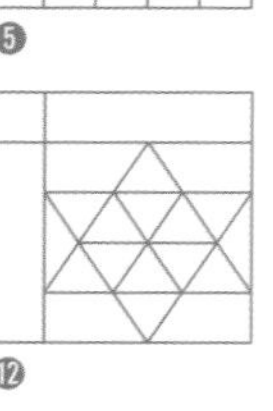
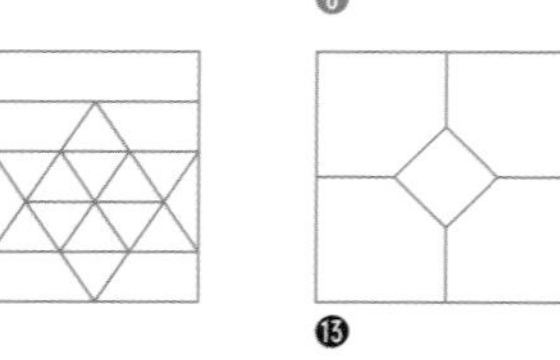

❼ ❽ ❾ ❿ ⓫ ⓬ ⓭

1 **Cross Is Mother's Choice,** *Kansas City Star,* Jan 8, 1958.

2 **Cross Bars,** Nancy Page, *Birmingham News,* Apr 23, 1935.

3 **Danish Stars,** *Kansas City Star,* Jun 10, 1942.

"Simple and effective is the 'Danish Stars' design created by Mrs. Addie Nielsen, Charleston, Ark. The scissors with which she cut the pattern were hand forged in Glasgow, Scotland, in April, 1874, where her husband's family was stormbound on their way to America from their home in Denmark. Mrs. Nielsen says her then future mother-in-law was a very industrious little woman, so during her stay in Glasgow she wanted to use scissors. As all her baggage was in the hold of the ship at the docks, she persuaded a blacksmith living near their hotel to make her a pair." *Kansas City Star,* Jun 10, 1942

4 **Turnabout,** Alice Brooks, *Detroit Free Press,* Feb 18, 1937.

5 **Bachelor's Puzzle,** *Ladies Art Company,* 1897. See 236-4 and 270-2.

6 **Bachelor's Puzzle,** *Old Fashioned Quilts,* ca. 1931.

7 **Domino,** *The Patchwork Book,* 1932.

8 **Crosses and Star,** *Ladies Art Company,* 1897. See 274-3. Also known as:

2 Crosses and a Star, Nancy Page, *Birmingham News,* Nov 10, 1942.

9 **Cross and Panel,** Nancy Cabot, *Chicago Tribune,* Dec 23, 1936.

10 **Ladies' Delight,** *Ladies Art Company,* 1897. Also known as:

Quilter's Delight, Nancy Cabot, *Chicago Tribune,* Dec 21, 1936.

Stars within Stars, Nancy Cabot, *Chicago Tribune,* Jul 4, 1934.

11 **Mona and Monette,** Nancy Page, unidentified newspaper clipping, date unknown.

12 **Premium Star,** *Ladies Art Company,* 1897. See 85-10, 223-9, 223-11, 243-6, and 262-7.

❶ **Pilot's Wheel,** Jinny Beyer, Hilton Head Seminar design 1986; published in Beyer, Jinny, *Patchwork Portfolio.*

❷ **Harmony Square,** Nancy Cabot, *Chicago Tribune,* May 7, 1937.

❸ **Cross and Crown,** *Ladies Art Company,* 1897. See 271-3. Also known as:
- **Goose Tracks,** Hall, 1935.
- **Signal,** *The Patchwork Book,* 1932.
- **Signal Design,** *Prairie Farmer,* Mar 24, 1928.

❹ **Cross and Crown,** Eveline Foland, *Kansas City Star,* Aug 10, 1929. Also known as:
- **Crown and Cross,** Nancy Page, *Birmingham News,* Aug 5, 1941.
- **David and Goliath,** Hinson, 1973.
- **Point and Feather,** date unknown; published in Beyer, Jinny, *The Quilter's Album ....*

❺ **Fanny's Fan,** Nancy Page, *Birmingham News,* Nov 5, 1935. Also known as:
- **Point and Feather,** Nancy Cabot, *Chicago Tribune,* Oct 13, 1936. See 156-11, 223-8, 299-4, and 299-5.

❻ **Bull's Eye,** Finley, 1929.Also known as:
- **David and Goliath,** Nancy Page, *Birmingham News,* Jul 30, 1935.
- **Doe and Darts,** Hinson, 1973.
- **Flying Darts,** Finley, 1929.
- **Four Darts,** Finley, 1929.
- **Katie's Favorite,** Nancy Page, *Birmingham News,* Oct 5, 1943.

❼ **Nosegays,** Nancy Page, *Birmingham News,* Jul 28, 1936.

❽ **Goshen Star,** Clara Stone, *Practical Needlework,* ca. 1906.

❾ **Bird's Nest,** *Ladies Art Company,* 1897.

❿ **A 4 Square Block with Diamonds,** *Kansas City Star,* Jul 11, 1951.

⓫ **Signal Bars,** Nancy Page, *Birmingham News,* Oct 8, 1940.

⓬ **Bird's Nest,** Ruby McKim, *Kansas City Star,* Jun 15, 1929.

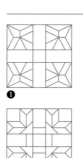

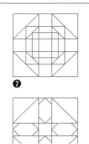

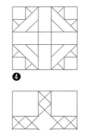

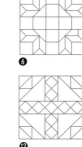

❶ **Coronation Block,** Nancy Cabot, *Chicago Tribune,* Mar 19, 1937.

❷ **Woodland Path,** Nancy Cabot, *Chicago Tribune,* Apr 21, 1934.
"In Philadelphia, in the year 1907 this dainty 'Woodland Path' was first pieced. It is composed entirely of triangles in white, red, green, and yellow. The block is extremely attractive; and the whole spread of the pieced block alternated with some plain blocks, makes one of the most striking quilts seen in any collection." Nancy Cabot, *Chicago Tribune,* Apr 21, 1934

❸ **Seminole Block,** Nancy Cabot, *Chicago Tribune,* Dec 9, 1937.

❹ **Moonstone,** Jinny Beyer, Hilton Head Seminar design, 1998. Also known as:

❺ **Shepherd's Crossing,** *Kansas City Star,* Jun 24, 1942.

❻ **Mystery Rose,** Jinny Beyer, Hilton Head Seminar design 1995; published in Beyer, Jinny, *Soft-Edge Piecing.*

❼ **Poinsettia,** Jinny Beyer, Hilton Head Seminar design, 1992.

❽ **Night and Day,** Nancy Cabot, *Chicago Tribune,* Apr 2, 1934.
"'Night and Day' is another of those geometric quilt designs that are most mystifying to the beholder. Only two patterns are used in cutting the block, but it is the color arrangement that created such bewilderment, when your friends attempt to figure out the pattern from the completed coverlet." Nancy Cabot, *Chicago Tribune,* Apr 2, 1934

❾ **Fair and Square,** *Kansas City Star,* Mar 16, 1938.

❿ **Charlotte's Webb,** Jinny Beyer, Hilton Head Seminar design 1995; published in Beyer, Jinny, *Soft-Edge Piecing.*

⓫ **Bluebell Block,** Nancy Cabot, *Chicago Tribune,* Nov 28, 1935.

⓬ **Palace Walk,** Jinny Beyer, Beyer, Jinny, *Patchwork Portfolio,* 1989.

❶ Old Antique, Nancy Cabot, *Chicago Tribune,* Apr 28, 1933.
"Though this pattern is not quite so antique as the title and the general feeling of the design itself would lead you to believe, it has lived through several generations since its origin 90 years ago. The correct name—that is, the one bestowed on it by the designer—never has been ferreted out. So it simply has been labeled the 'Old Antique' by its present owner, a nephew of the designer." Nancy Cabot, *Chicago Tribune,* Apr 28, 1933

❷ Four Knaves, Nancy Cabot, *Chicago Tribune,* Jan 21, 1938.

❸ Shasta Daisy, Alice Brooks, *Detroit Free Press,* Mar 5, 1934.
"Though Shasta daisies are still a long way from blooming, you can have them in this quilt. It's the quiltmaker's favorite for, in it, the cutting of the patches is so simple. Many of them are the same width and you know that means that you can cut the material in strips and then snip off the patches as you want them." Alice Brooks, *Detroit Free Press,* Jun 21, 1935

❹ Old Fashioned Daisy, Nancy Cabot, *Chicago Tribune,* Jul 29, 1934. Also known as:

Granny's Favorite, Nancy Cabot, *Chicago Tribune,* Aug 8, 1937.

❺ Camelia, Jinny Beyer, Jinny Beyer Studio design, 2005.

❻ White Water, Jinny Beyer, Beyer, Jinny, *Patchwork Portfolio,* 1989.

❼ Tudor Rose, Nancy Cabot, *Chicago Tribune,* Nov 20, 1936.

❽ Uncle Sam's Favorite, Clara Stone, *Practical Needlework,* ca. 1906.

❾ Pine Burr, Hall, 1935. Also known as:

The Urn, Nancy Page, *Birmingham News,* Aug 13, 1940.

❿ Star Wedge, *Grandma Dexter Appliqué and Patchwork Designs, Book 36a,* ca. 1932.

⓫ Arrow Crossing, Jinny Beyer Hilton Head Seminar design 1988; published in Beyer, Jinny, *Patchwork Portfolio.*

⓬ Beacon, Jinny Beyer Hilton Head Seminar design 1986; published in Beyer, Jinny, *Patchwork Portfolio.*

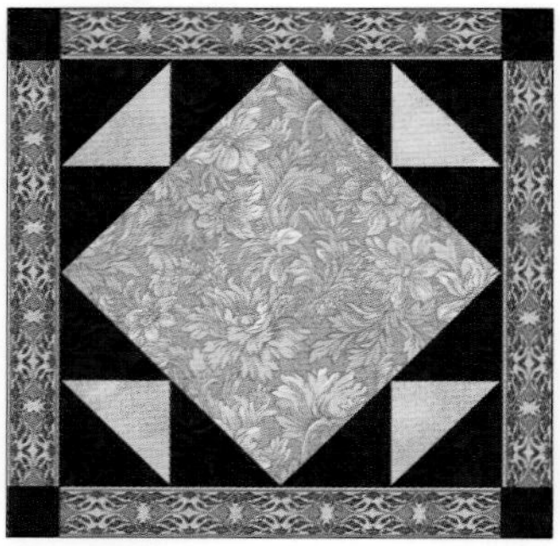

❶ 10 x 10 grid

❷ 10 x 10 grid

❸ 10 x 10 grid

❹ 10 x 10 grid

❺ 10 x 10 grid

❻ 10 x 10 grid

❼ 10 x 10 grid

❽ 10 x 10 grid

❾ 10 x 10 grid

❿ 10 x 10 grid

⓫ 10 x 10 grid

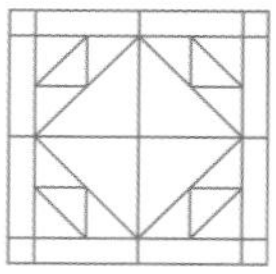

⓬ 10 x 10 grid

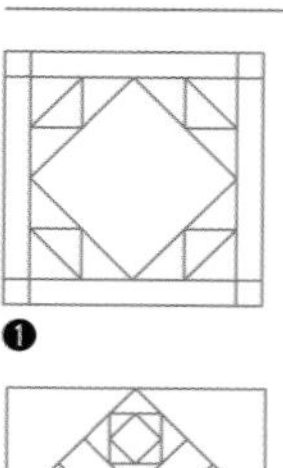

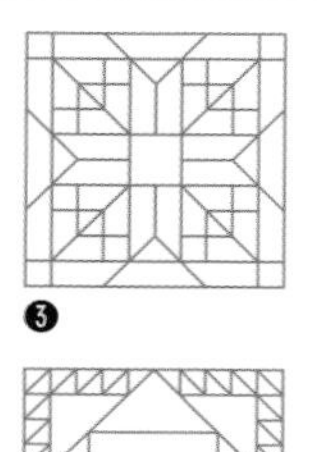

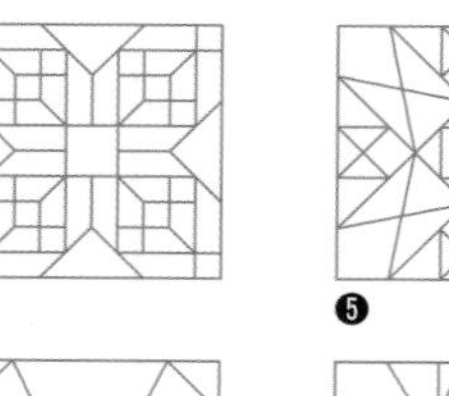

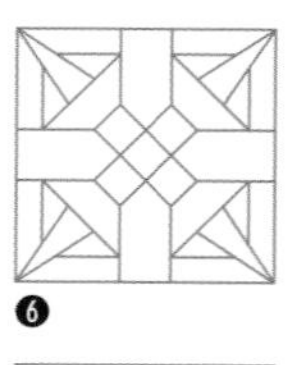

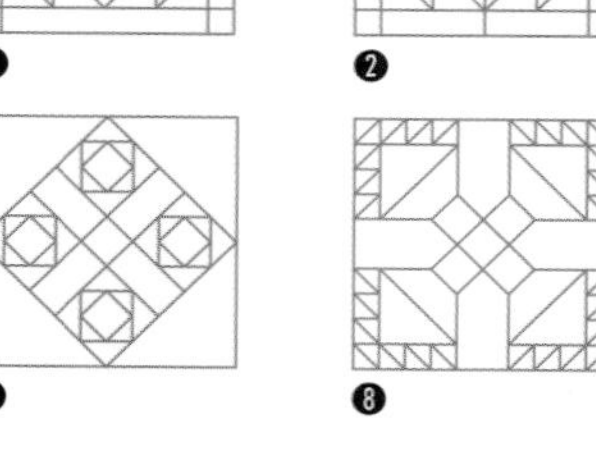

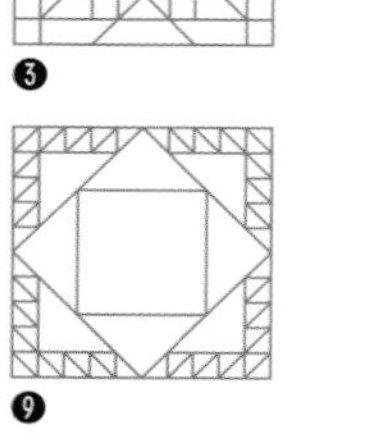

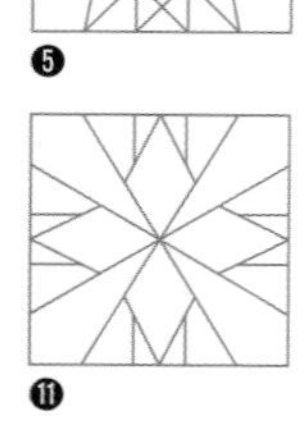

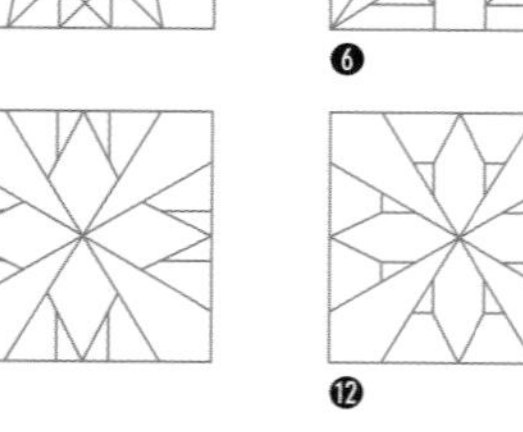

❶ **Surprise Package,** Jinny Beyer, Beyer, *Patchwork Portfolio,* 1989.

❷ **Middleburg,** Jinny Beyer, RJR Patterns, 2005.

❸ **Blue Ridge Star,** Jinny Beyer, Jinny Beyer Studio design, 2005.

❹ **Bird of Paradise,** Jinny Beyer, Beyer, Jinny, *Patchwork Portfolio,* 1989.

❺ **English Garden,** Jinny Beyer, RJR fabric collection design, 2005.

❻ **Prairie Points,** Hilton Head Seminar design 1995; published in Beyer, Jinny, *Soft-Edge Piecing.*

❼ **Grandmother's Cross,** Ruby McKim, McKim, 1931.

❽ **Single Chain and Knot,** Nancy Cabot, *Chicago Tribune,* Mar 25, 1937.

❾ **Triangle Puzzle,** *Grandma Dexter Appliqué and Patchwork Designs, Book 36a,* ca. 1932.

❿ **Pigeon Toes,** Beth Gutcheon, Gutcheon, *The Perfect Patchwork Primer,* 1973.

⓫ **Star I,** Marcia Aasmundstad, Beyer, Jinny, *The Quilter's Album. . .,* 1980.

⓬ **Star II,** Marcia Aasmundstad, Beyer, Jinny, *The Quilter's Album. . .,* 1980.

❶ **Japanese Poppy,** Nancy Cabot, *Chicago Tribune,* Mar 28, 1936.

❷ **Hill and Crag,** Nancy Cabot, *Chicago Tribune,* Jun 27, 1936.

❸ **Heirloom Quilt,** Alice Brooks, *Modesto Bee,* Apr 4, 1942.

❹ **Game Cocks,** Nancy Cabot, *Chicago Tribune,* Feb 14, 1936.

❺ **Building Blocks,** Home Art Studios, *Cincinnati Enquirer,* Mar 1, 1933. See 258-2. Also known as:

Tic Tac Toe, Nancy Cabot, *Chicago Tribune,* Aug 18, 1947.

❻ **True Lover's Knot,** *The Dressmaking Book,* 1929.

❼ **The Hen and Her Chicks,** *Kansas City Star,* Jun 18, 1947.

❽ **Burnham Square,** Hall, 1935. See 176-8. Also known as:

Hole in the Barn Door, date unknown, per Brackman.

❾ **Blue Heather,** Nancy Cabot, *Chicago Tribune,* Feb 10, 1936.

Cobblestones, Nancy Cabot, *Chicago Tribune,* Jun 30, 1937.

❿ **Doors and Windows,** Nancy Cabot, *Chicago Tribune,* Jun 17, 1935. Also known as:

New Double Irish Chain, Nancy Cabot, *Chicago Tribune,* Sep 15, 1936.

Windows and Doors, Nancy Cabot, *Chicago Tribune,* Jun 17, 1935.

⓫ **Yreka Square,** Nancy Cabot, *Chicago Tribune,* Apr 30, 1936.

"Most of the older quilt patterns have migrated from east to west, but 'Yreka Square' reverses the tradition and comes from a famous mining town of Yreka, California, in the days of the Forty-niners. The original coverlet was used as an all-over design, with the small prints set in the block on the diagonal, and the solid colors in contrasting color forming pairs of squares." Nancy Cabot, Apr 30, 1936

⓬ **Cathedral Tile,** Jinny Beyer, Jinny Beyer Studio design, 2008.

❶ 10 x 10 grid

❷ 10 x 10 grid

❸ 10 x 10 grid

❹ 10 x 10 grid

❺ 10 x 10 grid

❻ 10 x 10 grid

❼ 10 x 10 grid

❽ 10 x 10 grid

❾ 10 x 10 grid

❿ 10 x 10 grid

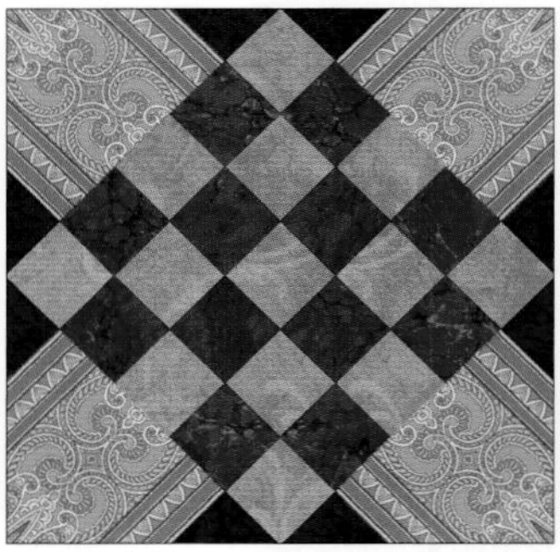

⓫ 10 x 10 grid

⓬ 10 x 10 grid

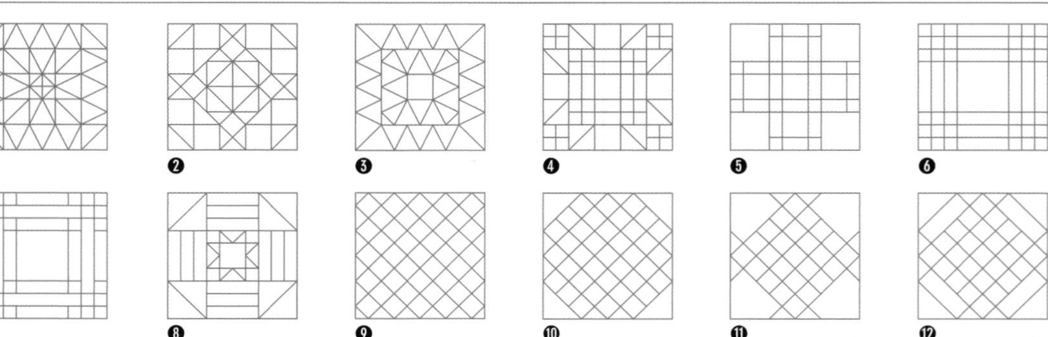

❶ **Flying Geese,** Alice Brooks, unidentified newspaper clipping, date unknown. Also known as:
- **Quilter's Choice,** Laura Wheeler, unidentified newspaper clipping, date unknown.

❷ **Depression,** Nancy Page, *Birmingham News,* Jun 12, 1934. Also known as:
- **Minnesota,** Nancy Page, *Birmingham News,* Jun 12, 1934.

❸ **Friendship Quilt,** *Kansas City Star,* Sep 21, 1938.

❹ **Pennsylvania Cross Roads,** Clara Stone, *Practical Needlework,* ca. 1906.

❺ **Cross and Crown,** Hall, 1935. See 166-5, 166-6, and 166-7. Also known as:
- **Crown and Cross,** Ickis, 1949.
- **Crowned Cross,** Hall, 1935.

❻ **Texas Cheers,** Nancy Page, *Birmingham News,* Aug 25, 1942. See 166-5, 166-6, and 166-7.

❼ **My Star,** Lesly-Claire Greenberg, Beyer, Jinny, *The Quilter's Album...,* 1980.

❽ **Garden Paths,** Nancy Cabot, *Chicago Tribune,* May 5, 1937.

❾ **The Mexican Star,** Ruby McKim, *Kansas City Star,* Jul 5, 1930. See 166-10, 166-11, and 260-5. Also known as:
- **Dallas Star,** Nancy Page, *Nashville Banner,* Jan 7, 1936.
- **Mexican Rose,** Ickis, 1949.
- **Mexican Star,** Hall, 1935.
- **Panama Block,** Nancy Cabot, *Chicago Tribune,* Aug 3, 1937.
- **Star and Cross,** Nancy Page, *Birmingham News,* Nov 3, 1936.

❿ **Grape Vines,** Nancy Cabot, *Chicago Tribune,* Oct 24, 1936.

⓫ **All Kinds,** *Ladies Art Company,* 1897. See 121-5. Also known as:
- **Beggar's Blocks,** Hall, 1935.
- **Cats and Mice,** Hall, 1935.
- **Turnstile,** Nancy Page, *Birmingham News,* Nov 29, 1938.

⓬ **Star and Cross,** Nancy Cabot, *Chicago Tribune,* Apr 27, 1936.

"'Star and Cross' is another of the old pieced quilts inspired by biblical literature. It is the second oldest quilt of that name, the first being pieced in 1840 in New York. The pattern illustrated today was pieced in 1869 in a small town seven or eight miles outside of Clinton, Ia." Nancy Cabot, Apr 27, 1936

❶ **Old Hollow,** Jinny Beyer, Jinny Beyer Studio design, 2005.

❷ **Butterfly Bush,** Jinny Beyer, Jinny Beyer Studio design, 2005.

❸ **Santa Maria,** Jinny Beyer, Hilton Head Seminar design, 1992.

❹ **Manor Steps,** Jinny Beyer, Jinny Beyer Studio design, 2005.

❺ **Millstone,** Jinny Beyer, Beyer, Jinny, *Patchwork Portfolio,* 1989.

❻ **Hill and Hollow,** Nancy Cabot, *Chicago Tribune,* Jul 7, 1937. See 91-3 and 159-1.

❼ **Linton,** *Ladies Art Company,* 1897. Also known as:

- **Path Through the Woods,** Miall, 1937.
- **Sun and Shade,** Nancy Page, *Birmingham News,* Aug 16, 1938.

❽ **Dumbarton Oaks,** Jinny Beyer, RJR Patterns, 2007.

❾ **Godey Design,** *Godey's Lady's Book,* 1858.

❿ **Odd Fellows,** *Ladies Art Company,* 1897. See 116-1. Also known as:

- **Odd Fellow's Cross,** Nancy Cabot, *Chicago Tribune,* Feb 3, 1933.
- **Odd Fellow's Patch,** Hall, 1935.
- **Wild Goose Flight,** *Quilts: Heirlooms of Tomorrow,* ca. 1977.

⓫ **Flying Geese,** Martens, 1970.

⓬ **Whirlwind,** *The Farmer's Advocate,* Mar 16, 1933.

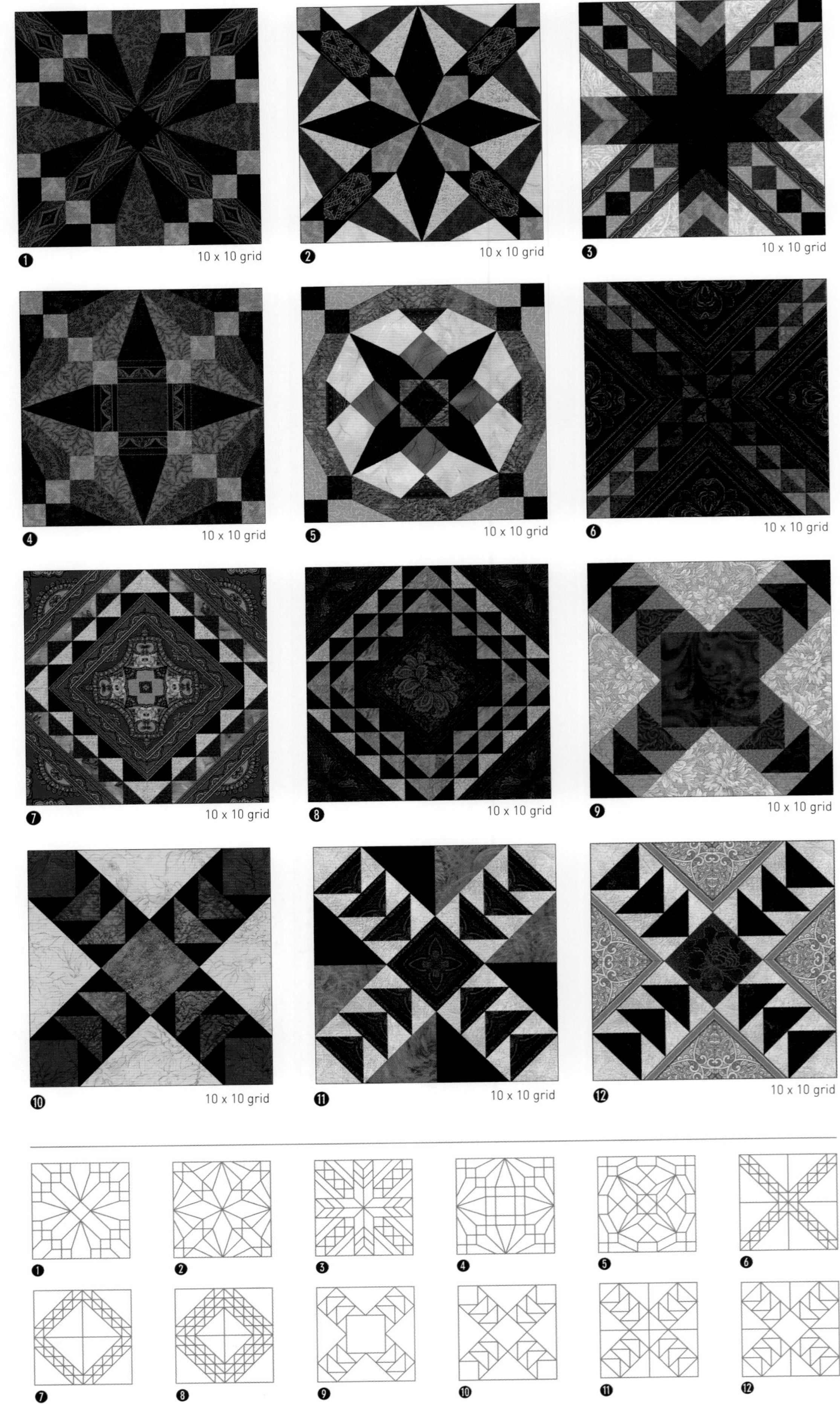

1 **An Effective Square,** *Ladies' Home Journal* 1896.

2 **Lady of the Lake,** Hall, 1935. See 165-8.

3 **Lady of the Lake,** Nancy Page, *Nashville Banner,* Dec 5, 1933. See 165-8, 165-9 and 165-10.

4 **Coat of Arms,** Jinny Beyer, Beyer, Jinny, *Patchwork Portfolio,* 1989.

5 **Young Man's Fancy,** Laura Wheeler, *Illinois State Register,* May 20, 1933.

6 **Indian Canoes,** *Kansas City Star,* Jul 22, 1933. See 80-8 and 138-12.

7 **Hobby Nook,** *Kansas City Star,* Sep 21, 1955.

8 **The Dragon Fly,** *Kansas City Star,* Oct 24, 1936.

9 **Sea Crest,** Jinny Beyer, Hilton Head Seminar design, 1983; published in Beyer, Jinny, *Patchwork Portfolio.*

10 **Guiding Star,** Aunt Martha series: *Bold and Beautiful Quilts,* ca. 1977.

11 **Atlantic Star,** Jinny Beyer, Hilton Head Seminar design, 1982; published in Beyer, Jinny, *Patchwork Portfolio.*

12 **Crow's Nest,** Jinny Beyer, Hilton Head Seminar design, 1984; published in Beyer, Jinny, *Patchwork Portfolio.*

❶ **Star of Mystery,** Linda L. Lowe, *Quilter's Newsletter Magazine,* Oct 1974. Also known as:

- **Here Is the Steeple,** Beth Gutcheon, Gutcheon, *The Quilt Design Workbook,* 1976.

❷ **Blazing Star,** Nancy Cabot, *Chicago Tribune,* Feb 25, 1933. See 160-6, 255-12, and 297-4.

❸ **Cynthia Ann Dancing,** Beth Gutcheon, Gutcheon, *The Quilt Design Workbook,* 1976.

❹ **Rolling Stars,** Nancy Page, *Nashville Banner,* Sep 12, 1933. Also known as:

- **Golden Wedding,** Nancy Page, *Detroit Free Press,* Jan 1, 1934.
- **Golden Wedding Quilt,** *Detroit Free Press,* Oct 17, 1933.

❺ **Five Patch,** Alice Brooks, unidentified newspaper clipping, date unknown. Also known as:

- **Prized Possession,** Laura Wheeler, unidentified newspaper clipping, date unknown.

❻ **Tulip Tree,** Jinny Beyer, Beyer, Jinny, *Patchwork Portfolio,* 1989.

❼ **Blue Heaven,** Nancy Cabot, *Chicago Tribune,* Jun 23, 1936.

❽ **Mariner's Star,** Alice Brooks, unidentified newspaper clipping, date unknown.

❾ **The String Quilt,** Ruby McKim, McKim, 1931.

❿ **Lotus Star,** Virginia Snow, *Grandma Dexter New Appliqué and Patchwork Designs, Book 36b,* ca. 1932.

⓫ **Great Falls,** Jinny Beyer, Beyer, Jinny, *Patchwork Portfolio,* 1989.

⓬ **Magnolia,** Jinny Beyer, Beyer, Jinny, *Patchwork Portfolio,* 1989.

❶ **Broken Dishes,** Nancy Cabot, *Chicago Tribune,* Jan 29, 1937.

❷ **Confederate Rose,** Nancy Cabot, *Chicago Tribune,* 1936. See 113-7.

❸ **Lighthouse,** Nancy Cabot, *Chicago Tribune,* Feb 17, 1936.

❹ **Uncle Sam's Hour Glass,** Clara Stone, *Practical Needlework,* ca. 1906.

❺ **Indian Squares,** Nancy Cabot, *Chicago Tribune,* Mar 23, 1937.
"This Block Ideal for Quilt Maker Who Has Patience." Nancy Cabot, *Chicago Tribune,* Mar 23, 1937

❻ **Star Net,** Nancy Cabot, *Chicago Tribune,* Apr 2, 1937.

❼ **Star Lane,** *Ladies Art Company,* 1901. Also known as:
 Starry Lane, *Q Book 110, Star Quilts,* date unknown.

❽ **Checkered Star,** Marcia Aasmundstad Beyer, Jinny, *The Quilter's Album . . .*,1980.

❾ **Monarch,** Jinny Beyer, Beyer, Jinny, *Patchwork Portfolio,* 1989.

❿ **Domino and Square,** *Ladies Art Company,* 1897. Also known as:
 Domino and Squares, Nancy Cabot, *Chicago Tribune,* May 3, 1934.

⓫ **Broken Irish Chain,** Nancy Cabot, *Chicago Tribune,* Mar 9, 1938.

⓬ **Crossed Squares,** Nancy Cabot, *Chicago Tribune,* Dec 24, 1936.

❶ **Dolly's Favorite,** Nancy Page, *Birmingham News,* Jan 2, 1941.

❷ **Bursting Star,** Nancy Cabot, *Chicago Tribune,* Apr 30, 1937. See 287-12.

❸ **Sherwood Forest,** Jinny Beyer, Hilton Head Seminar design, 1989; published in Beyer, Jinny, *Patchwork Portfolio.*

❹ **Simple Design,** *Ladies Art Company,* 1897. Also known as:

> **Flower Bed,** Nancy Cabot, *Chicago Tribune,* Jun 17, 1938.
>
> **Happy New Year,** Nancy Page, *Birmingham News,* Jan 3, 1939.

"A talented young New England girl with a sense of humor called this quilt block a 'Simple Design.' It probably is one of the most complicated and difficult blocks to make, but it also is one of the most beautiful." Nancy Cabot, *Chicago Tribune,* Jul 28, 1934

❺ **The White Square Quilt,** *Kansas City Star,* Jan 11, 1939.

❻ **Ravello,** Jinny Beyer, RJR Patterns, 2004.

❼ **Arrow Head,** Jinny Beyer, Hilton Head Seminar design 1989; published in Beyer, Jinny, *Patchwork Portfolio.*

❽ **King David's Crown,** Nancy Page, *Illinois State Register,* Aug 13, 1935. See 179-10.

❾ **St. Louis Star,** *Ladies Art Company,* 1897. Also known as:

> **Star of St. Louis,** Nancy Cabot, *Chicago Tribune,* Mar 2, 1938.
>
> **Variable Star,** Nancy Cabot, *Chicago Tribune,* Aug 27, 1933.

❿ **Joseph's Coat,** *Ladies Art Company,* 1897. Also known as:

> **Lewis and Clark,** Clara Stone, *Practical Needlework,* ca. 1906.
>
> **Mrs. Thomas,** Nancy Page, *Birmingham News,* Jul 11, 1939.
>
> **Scrap Bag,** Hall, 1935.

⓫ **Memory Blocks,** Nancy Page, *Birmingham News,* Jan 28, 1935.

⓬ **Memory Blocks,** *Ladies Art Company,* 1897. Also known as:

> **Album Quilt,** *Mrs. Danner's Fifth Quilt Book,* 1970.
>
> **Memory Block,** Hall, 1935.

"'Memory Block,' often made of pieces of different dresses of a child or of some other loved member of the family, as a 'keepsake' and in after years each piece was pointed to with pride." Hall, 1935

❶ 10 x 10 grid

❷ 10 x 10 grid

❸ 10 x 10 grid

❹ 10 x 10 grid

❺ 10 x 10 grid

❻ 10 x 10 grid

❼ 10 x 10 grid

❽ 10 x 10 grid

❾ 10 x 10 grid

❿ 10 x 10 grid

⓫ 10 x 10 grid

⓬ 10 x 10 grid

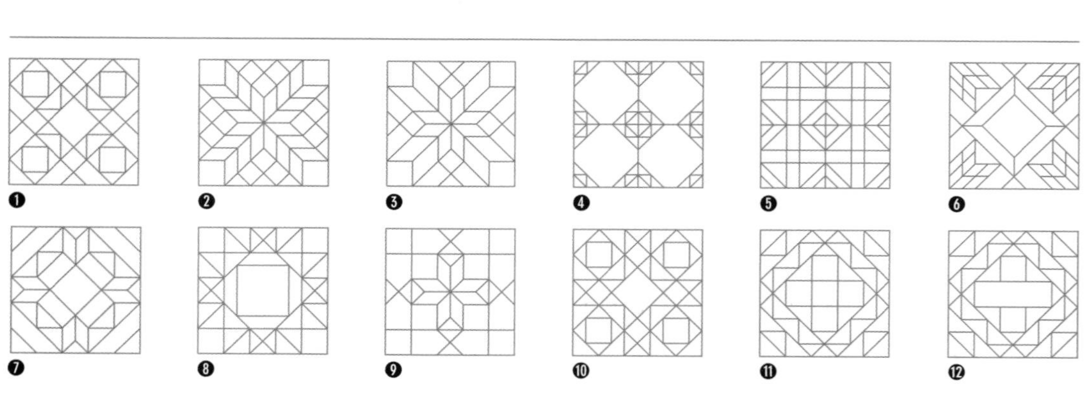

❶ **Chimney Sweep,** Hall, 1935.

❷ **Album,** *Ladies Art Company,* 1897.

❸ **Ellen's Dream,** Jinny Beyer, Hilton Head Seminar design, 1987; published in Beyer, Jinny, *Patchwork Portfolio.*

❹ **Godey Design,** *Godey's Lady's Book,* 1851.

❺ **Jig Saw Puzzle,** Home Art Studios, *World Herald,* Aug 19, 1933.

❻ **Church Windows,** *Quilt Booklet No. 1,* 1931. Also known as:

> **Cathedral Window,** Nancy Cabot, *Chicago Tribune,* Apr 13, 1933.
>
> **Mystic Maize,** *Grandma Dexter New Appliqué and Patchwork Designs, Book 36b,* ca. 1932.

❼ **Church Windows,** Nancy Cabot, *Chicago Tribune,* May 31, 1938.

"The inspiration for this beautiful pieced design is an old cathedral in Bardstown, Ky., which is over 140 years old and today has every appearance of a modern structure. So faithfully has this structure been preserved that one feels it possesses immortality. The beautiful stained glass windows in the cathedral were imported from Europe and, as far as is known, never have been repaired. 'Church Windows' is an artistic interpretation of a peaceful religious scene and employs colors almost identical to those used for the panes." Nancy Cabot, *Chicago Tribune,* May 31, 1938

❽ **Star Patchwork,** *Farm and Home,* Feb 15, 1890. See 292-2 and 292-3. Also known as:

> **Snow Crystals,** *Q Book 109, Early American Quilts,* date unknown.

❾ **Formal Garden,** Nancy Page, *Birmingham News,* Mar 30, 1937.

❿ **County Farm,** Nancy Cabot, *Chicago Tribune,* Oct 7, 1934. Also known as:

> **County Fair,** Nancy Cabot, *Chicago Tribune,* Oct 2, 1937.

⓫ **Cathedral Windows,** Nancy Cabot, *Chicago Tribune,* Dec 12, 1934.

⓬ **Climbing Roses,** Nancy Cabot, *Chicago Tribune,* Dec 5, 1935.

"This interesting block was designed by an architect because his wife wanted an original design for her newly decorated bedroom. It is distinctly individual because of its thoroughly modern interpretation of climbing roses." Nancy Cabot, *Chicago Tribune,* Dec 5, 1935

1 Star and Corona, Nancy Cabot, *Chicago Tribune,* Jun 24, 1938.

2 Railroad Crossing, Finley, 1929.

3 Five Crosses, Nancy Cabot, *Chicago Tribune,* Nov 15, 1935.

4 Prudence's Choice, Alice Brooks, unidentified newspaper clipping, date unknown.

5 Rose Trellis, Nancy Cabot, *Chicago Tribune,* May 14, 1936.

6 Friendly Hand, *Comfort,* ca. 1920, per Brackman. See 102-12. Also known as:

- **Chinese Coin,** Nancy Page, *Nashville Banner,* Aug 30, 1932.
- **Crosses and Losses,** Nancy Page, *Nashville Banner,* Aug 30, 1932.
- **Indian Puzzle,** Aunt Martha series: *Quilt Lover's Delights,* ca. 1960.
- **Indiana Puzzle,** Hall, 1935.
- **Milky Way,** *Ladies Art Company,* 1928.
- **Monkey Wrench,** *Nashville Banner,* Aug 30, 1932.
- **Pinwheels,** Nancy Cabot, *Chicago Tribune,* Jan 30, 1933.

7 Bachelor's Puzzle, Eveline Foland, *Kansas City Star,* Aug 8, 1931. See 66-10 and 142-10. Also known as:

- **The Pin Wheel,** *Kansas City Star,* Apr 23, 1938.

8 Beginner's Joy, Alice Brooks, unidentified newspaper clipping, date unknown.

9 Flying Geese, Alice Brooks, unidentified newspaper clipping, date unknown.

10 California, Nancy Page, *Birmingham News,* Jan 29, 1935.

11 4 E Block, *Ladies Art Company,* 1897.

12 Prize Possession, Laura Wheeler, unidentified newspaper clipping, date unknown.

1 10 x 10 grid

2 10 x 10 grid

3 10 x 10 grid

4 10 x 10 grid

5 10 x 10 grid

6 10 x 10 grid

7 10 x 10 grid

8 10 x 10 grid

9 10 x 10 grid

10 10 x 10 grid

11 10 x 10 grid

12 10 x 10 grid

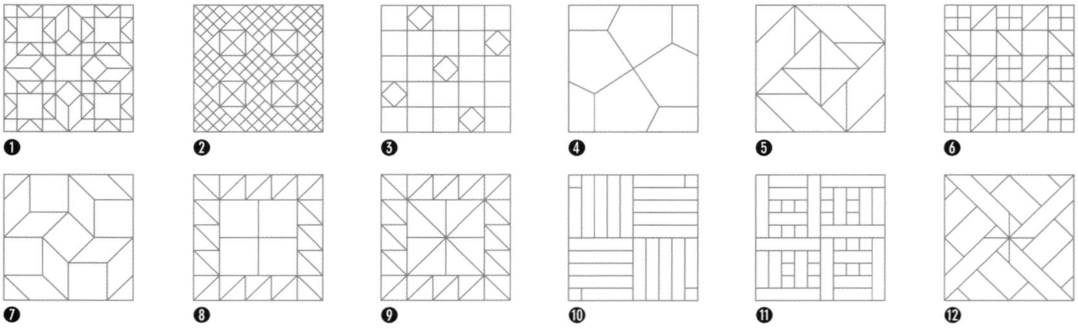

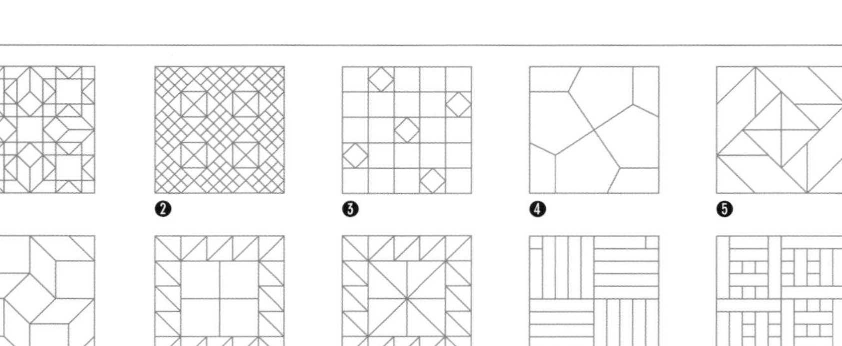

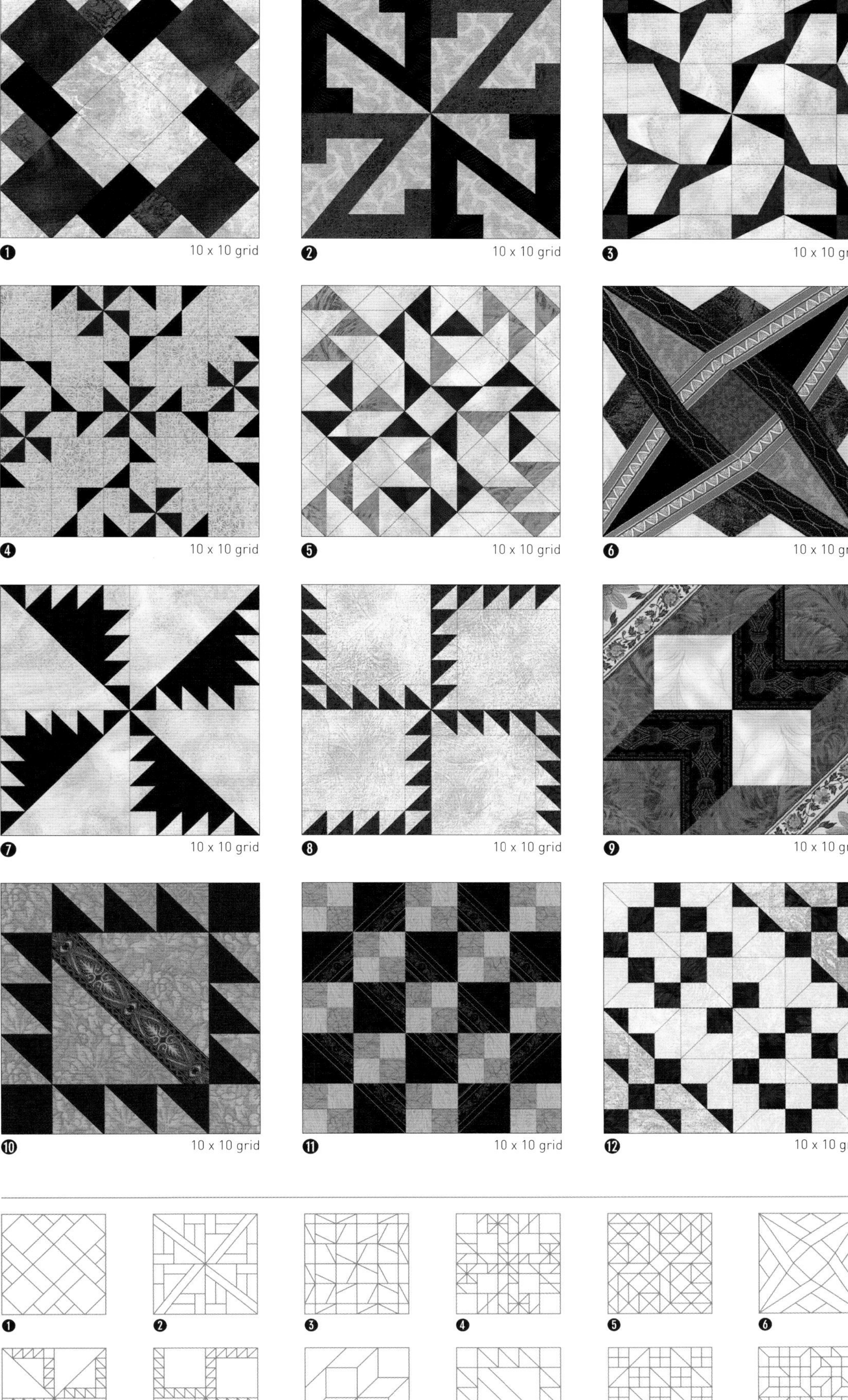

❶ **Chimney Sweep,** Nancy Page, *Birmingham News,* Jun 7, 1938.

❷ **Four Z Patch,** *Ladies Art Company,* 1897.

❸ **Star and Mill Block,** Nancy Cabot, *Chicago Tribune,* Jul 3, 1936.
"During the week preceding Independence Day, patriotic quilt designs have come to our attention quite unexpectedly. They are most appropriate. 'Star and Mill' is a combination of windmills, pinwheels, and stars, all symbolic of Fourth of July celebrations." Nancy Cabot, *Chicago Tribune,* Jul 3, 1936

❹ **Pinwheel and Vine,** Nancy Cabot, *Chicago Tribune,* May 28, 1938.

❺ **Yellow Clover,** Nancy Cabot, *Chicago Tribune,* Mar 19, 1936.
"Yellow, green, and white form one of the most popular of present day quilt color combinations. 'Yellow Clover' is one of the newer pieced blocks which allow the quilt maker to use these colors in a most appropriate pattern." Nancy Cabot, *Chicago Tribune,* Mar 19, 1936

❻ **Devonshire,** Jinny Beyer, RJR Patterns, 1999.

❼ **Kansas Troubles,** *Q Book 116, Blue Ribbon Quilts,* date unknown. See 100-12 and 101-2.

❽ **Grandmother's Pinwheel,** *Mrs. Danner's Fifth Quilt Book,* 1970.

❾ **The Builder's Block Quilt,** *Kansas City Star,* Mar 31, 1943.

❿ **The Old Indian Trail,** *Kansas City Star,* Jun 4, 1958.

⓫ **The Ozark Trail,** *Kansas City Star,* Apr 17, 1935.

⓬ **Spanish Squares,** Nancy Cabot, *Chicago Tribune,* Dec 1, 1937.

1. **Pine Cones,** Nancy Page, *Birmingham News,* Feb 6, 1940.
2. **Somerset,** Jinny Beyer, RJR Patterns, 2004.
3. **Rocky Glen,** *Ladies Art Company,* 1897.
4. **Sky Rocket,** *Grandma Dexter Appliqué and Patchwork Designs, Book 36a,* ca. 1932.
5. **Pine Tree,** Laura Wheeler, *Illinois State Register,* May 3, 1933. Also known as:
   - **Canadian Pine,** Nancy Page, *Birmingham News,* May 11, 1943.
   - **Norway Pine,** Nancy Cabot, *Chicago Tribune,* Aug 27, 1936.
   - **Wye Oak,** Jinny Beyer, Quilters's Quest design, 2004.
6. **Pine Tree,** Aunt Martha series: *Patchwork Simplicity,* ca. 1977.
7. **Pine Tree,** *Grandmother Clark's Authentic Early American Quilts,* 1932.
8. **Pine Tree,** *Prairie Farmer,* Mar 24, 1928. Also known as:
   - **Temperance Tree,** Hall, 1935.
9. **Pine Tree,** *Kansas City Star,* Sep 19, 1928. Also known as:
   - **Pine Tree Design,** *Book of Quilts, Farmer's Wife,* 1980.
   - **Tree of Paradise,** Hall, 1935.
10. **Pine Tree Design,** *The Farmer's Wife Book of Quilts,* 1931.
11. **Lend and Borrow,** Eveline Foland, *Kansas City Star,* Jun 18, 1932. See 189-10. Also known as:
    - **Indian Meadow,** Hall, 1935.
    - **Little Saw Tooth,** Hall, 1935.
    - **Lost Ship,** Hall, 1935.
    - **Rocky Glen,** Hall, 1935.
12. **Indian Plume,** Aunt Martha series: *Quilts,* ca. 1963.

❶ **King Solomon's Temple,** Clara Stone, *Practical Needlework,* ca. 1906. Also known as:

  Solomon's Temple, *Kansas City Star,* Nov 7, 1936.

❷ **Double Irish Chain,** Jane Alan, *Illinois State Register,* May 1, 1932.

❸ **Triple Irish Chain,** Aunt Martha series: *Bold and Beautiful Quilts,* ca. 1977.

❹ **Country Lanes,** *The Mountain Mist Blue Book of Quilts,* 1935.

❺ **Double Irish Chain,** *Ladies Art Company,* 1897. Also known as:

  Chained Five Patch, Hall, 1935.
  Cube Lattice, *Farm Journal Quilt Patterns,* ca. 1935.
  Double Irish Cross, Ruby McKim, *Kansas City Star,* Jun 7, 1930.
  Irish Chain, *Farm Journal Quilt Patterns,* ca. 1935.

❻ **Love Chain,** *Quilt Booklet No. 1,* ca. 1931.

❼ **Federal Chain,** Nancy Cabot, *Chicago Tribune,* Jun 9, 1933.

❽ **Grandmother's Irish Chain,** Clara Stone, *Practical Needlework,* ca. 1906.

❾ **Widower's Choice,** *Ladies Art Company,* 1897.

❿ **Leap Frog,** Nancy Cabot, *Chicago Tribune,* Dec 29, 1936.

⓫ **Leap Frog,** *Ladies Art Company,* 1897.

⓬ **Leap Frog,** Nancy Cabot, *Chicago Tribune,* Jan 1, 1935.

❶ **The Four Diamonds,** *Kansas City Star,* Aug 1, 1945.

❷ **Noon and Night,** Laura Wheeler, *Kansas City Star,* Feb 2, 1934. See 154-10. Also known as:

- **Five Patch,** Alice Brooks, unidentified newspaper clipping, date unknown.

❸ **Vineyard,** Nancy Cabot, *Chicago Tribune,* May 25, 1937.

❹ **Arabic Lattice,** *Ladies Art Company,* 1901. See 218-8.

❺ **Tree of Paradise,** Nancy Cabot, *Chicago Tribune,* Aug 11, 1936.

❻ **Monday's Block,** Nancy Cabot, *Chicago Tribune,* Jun 1, 1936.

"'Monday's Block' is a pattern first made about 45 years ago, it was set together with other designs indicating the activities of the week. The laundry tree expresses in an unusual fashion the duties of every Monday. A combination of printed and plain materials may be used, and many of the pieces in the scrap bag may be utilized, since all 'Monday's Blocks' need not necessarily be alike." Nancy Cabot, *Chicago Tribune,* Jun 1, 1936

❼ **Straight Furrow,** Finley, 1929. Also known as:

- **American Log Cabin,** Home Art Studios, *The New Barbara Taylor Book on Quilting* ca. 1977.
- **Barn Raising,** date unknown.
- **Log Cabin,** Home Art Studios, *Colonial Quilts,* 1932.

❽ **Log Cabin,** ca. 1875, per Holstein.

❾ **Pineapple Quilt,** *Antique Quilts,* 1974.

❿ **True Lover's Knot,** Aunt Martha series: *Quilts: Modern-Colonial,* ca. 1954.

⓫ **The Yellow Square,** *Kansas City Star,* Aug 30, 1950.

⓬ **Endless Chain,** *Old Fashioned Quilts,* 1931.

❶ 10 x 10 grid

❷ 10 x 10 grid

❸ 10 x 10 grid

❹ 10 x 10 grid

❺ 10 x 10 grid

❻ 10 x 10 grid

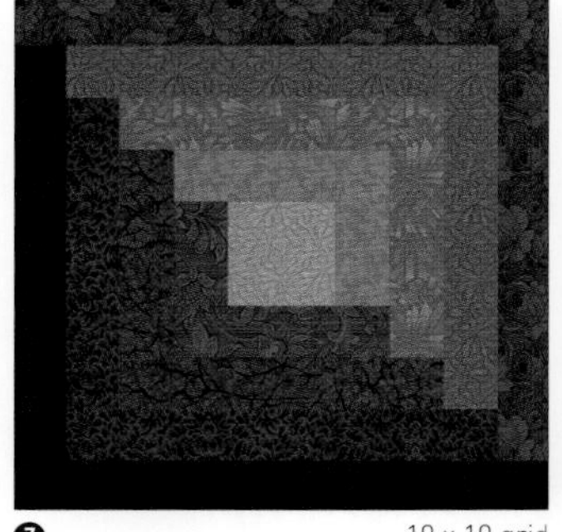

❼ 10 x 10 grid

❽ 10 x 10 grid

❾ 10 x 10 grid

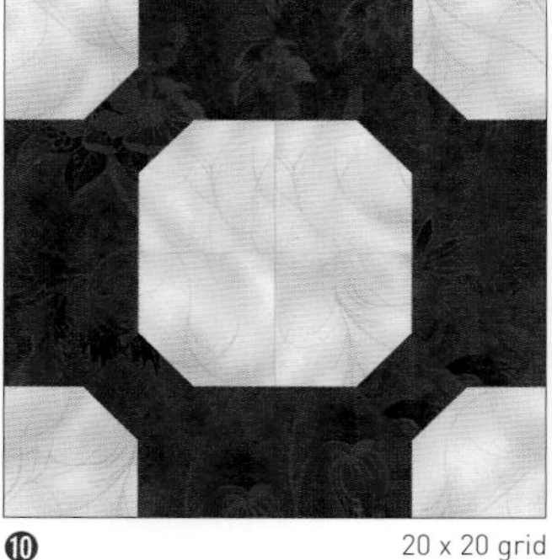

❿ 20 x 20 grid

⓫ 20 x 20 grid

⓬ 20 x 20 grid

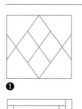

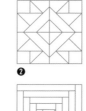

❶ ❷

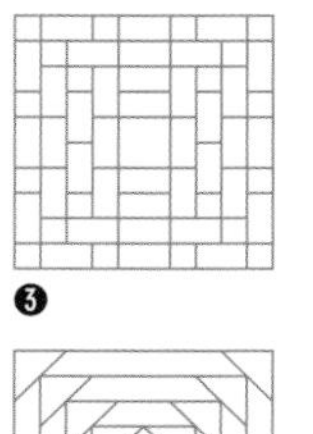

❸ ❹

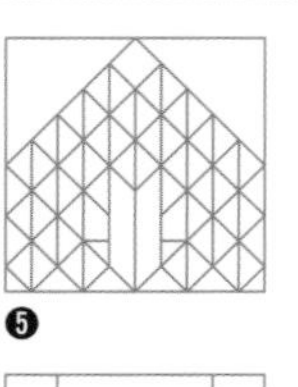

❺

❻

❼

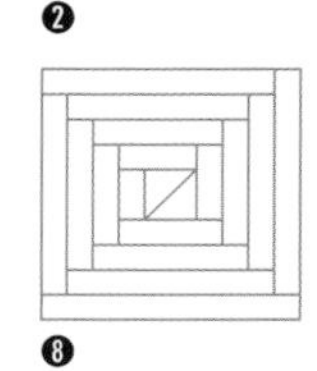

❽

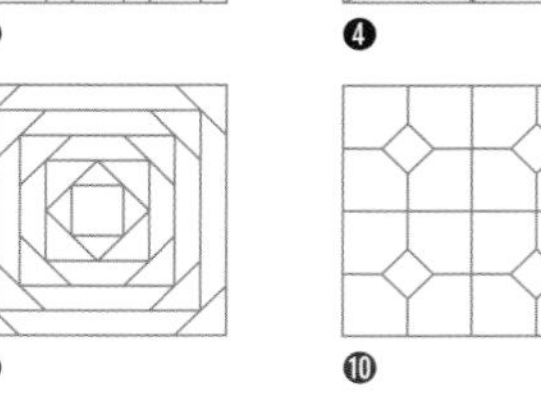

❾ ❿

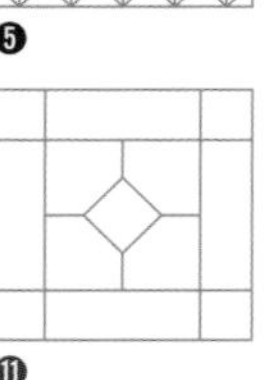

⓫

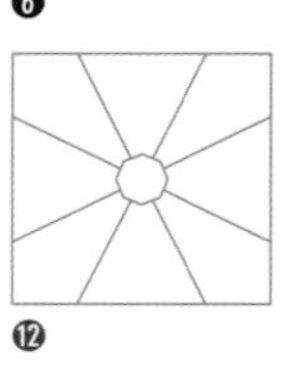

⓬

❶ **Eight-Pointed Star,** Miall, 1937.

❷ **Mosaic No. 2,** ca. 1938, per Havig.

❸ **Friendship Chain,** Alice Brooks, *Alice Brooks Collection of Needlecraft Masterpieces,* ca. 1958.

❹ **Orion,** Jinny Beyer, Hilton Head Seminar design, 2000.

❺ **Her Sparkling Jewels,** *Kansas City Star,* Dec 30, 1959.

❻ **Star of North Carolina,** *Old Fashioned Quilts,* ca. 1931. See 284-12 and 285-1. Also known as:

New Star of North Carolina, Nancy Cabot, *Chicago Tribune,* Apr 2, 1938.

❼ **Carnival,** Nancy Cabot, *Chicago Tribune,* Mar 18, 1938.

❽ **Star of the East,** Laura Wheeler, *Souix City Journal,* Apr 14, 1939.

❾ **Gyro,** Jinny Beyer, Hilton Head Seminar design, 2001.

❿ **Shaded Stars,** *Birmingham News,* May 17, 1938.

⓫ **Corona,** Jinny Beyer, Jinny Beyer Studio design, 2005.

⓬ **Fringed Square,** Nancy Cabot, *Chicago Tribune,* Sep 9, 1936. See 96-11. Also known as:

A Quilt Mosaic, *Kansas City Star,* Sep 5, 1945.

❶ **Tapestry,** Jinny Beyer, RJR Patterns, 2001.

❷ **Sapphire Net,** Nancy Cabot, *Chicago Tribune,* May 12, 1937.

❸ **Pot of Gold,** Jinny Beyer Studio design, 2007.

❹ **Sunshiny Day,** *Farm Journal and Farmer's Wife* (Silver Anniversary issue), 1945.

❺ **Cosmos,** Jinny Beyer Studio design, 2005.

❻ **Gretchen,** Eveline Foland, *Kansas City Star,* Jul 16, 1932. Also known as:
  A Feather Bone Block, *Kansas City Star,* Nov 15, 1950.

❼ **Sunbeam Crossroad,** Nancy Cabot, *Chicago Tribune,* Dec 25, 1935.
"One of the oldest of the middle western patterns is this delightful little pieced block with such a cheerful name. 'Sunbeam Crossroad' first was made in Ohio about 1854." Nancy Cabot, *Chicago Tribune,* Dec 25, 1935

❽ **Alice's Favorite,** *Mrs. Danner's Quilts, Books 1 & 2,* 1934.

❾ **Eastertide,** Women's Club of the Air, *Topeka Daily Capital,* Apr 1, 1934.

❿ **Simple Stars,** Jinny Beyer, Jinny Beyer Studio design, 2005.

⓫ **Cross within Cross,** Nancy Page, *Birmingham News,* Sep 8, 1936. See 112-5, 168-2, and 184-3.

⓬ **Inverted 'T',** *Old Fashioned Quilts,* ca. 1931. Also known as:
  T Quartette, *Old Fashioned Quilts,* ca. 1931.

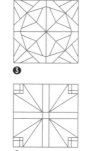

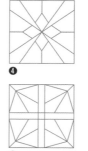

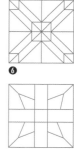

❶ ❷ ❸ ❹ ❺ ❻ ❼ ❽ ❾ ❿ ⓫ ⓬

❶ **Odd Star,** *Ladies Art Company,* 1897.
Also known as:
Roman Roads, Nancy Cabot, *Chicago Tribune,* Jul 23, 1935.

❷ **New Star,** *Ladies Art Company,* 1897.
Also known as:
Heavenly Problem, Nancy Cabot, *Chicago Tribune,* Apr 9, 1935.

❸ **Fanny's Fan,** *Ladies Art Company,* 1897.

❹ **Calico Bouquets,** Nancy Cabot, *Chicago Tribune,* Apr 27, 1937.

❺ **Broken Heart,** *Quilt Booklet No. 1,* ca. 1931.

❻ **Galaxy,** Jinny Beyer, Hilton Head Seminar design, 1999.

❼ **Galileo,** Jinny Beyer, Jinny Beyer Studio design, 2005.

❽ **Peony,** Jinny Beyer, Jinny Beyer Studio design, 2005.

❾ **Falling Star,** Jinny Beyer, Beyer, Jinny, *Patchwork Portfolio,* 1989.

❿ **Old Indian Trails,** *Kansas City Star,* Mar 10, 1943.

⓫ **Starstruck,** Jinny Beyer, Jinny Beyer Studio design, 2005.

⓬ **Northern Lights,** Jinny Beyer, Hilton Head Seminar design, 1994; published in Beyer, Jinny, *Soft-Edge Piecing.*

Quick Reference: Flowers *(without Curved Elements)*

In this quick reference section are all the flowers without curved lines. (Those with curved lines appear together on pages 360 to 370). Flower designs that are part of a basket or vase are not shown here; you will find them on page 319. There are many floral blocks that are reminiscent of bouquets or nosegays and those are grouped together here.

Forget Me Not, Aunt Martha series: *Aunt Martha's Favorite Quilts.* **See 296-8.**

Meadow Flower, *Cincinnati Enquirer.* **See 222-1.**

Colonial Garden, Aunt Martha series: *Aunt Martha's Favorite Quilts.* **See 411-10.**

Calico Bouquets, *Chicago Tribune.* **See 213-4.**

Modern Daisies, *Chicago Tribune.* **See 362-9.**

Pink Magnolias, *Chicago Tribune.* **See 228-5.**

Magnolia Bud, *Chicago Tribune.* **See 116-7.**

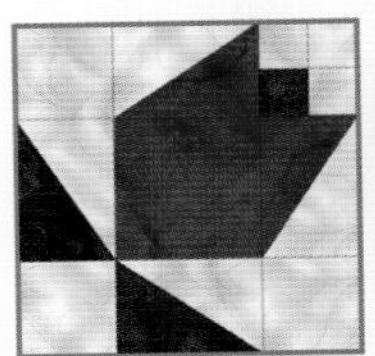
Magnolia Bud, Hall. **See 225-8.**

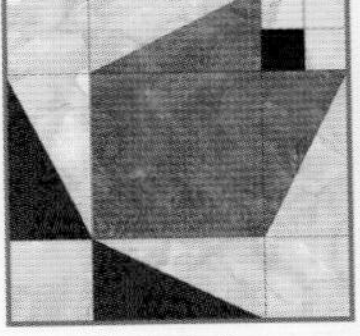
Magnolia Bud, *Kansas City Star.* **See 104-8.**

Cornucopia, Ickis. **See 307-3.**

Old Fashioned Nosegay, *Pioneer Press.* **See 307-5.**

Cockscomb, *World Herald.* **See 307-4.**

Nosegay, unidentified newspaper clipping. **See 190-4.**

Friendship Bouquet, *Detroit Free Press.* **See 225-9.**

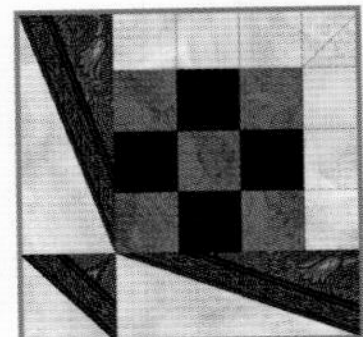
Nosegay, *Chicago Tribune.* **See 255-1.**

Nose Gay, *Kansas City Star.* **See 275-4.**

Pieced Bouquet, *Chicago Tribune.* **See 171-5.**

Bouquet, Aunt Martha series: *The Quilt Fair Comes to You.* **See 190-3.**

Cubist Rose, *Chicago Tribune.* **See 110-12.**

Pansy, McKim. **See 104-10.**

Modernistic Pansy, *Chicago Tribune.* **See 178-10.**

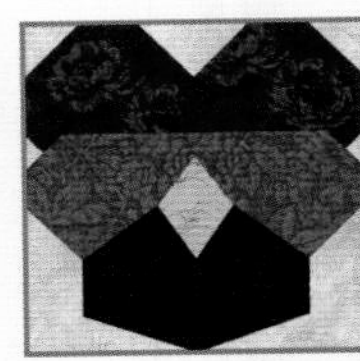
Pansy Quilt, *Cincinnati Enquirer.* **See 250-9.**

Grandmother's Pride, *Indianapolis Star.* **See 256-10.**

Magnolia, *Detroit Free Press.* **See 257-8.**

Magnolia, *Cincinnati Enquirer.* **See 152-6.**

Lotus Blossom, *Detroit Free Press.* **See 232-4.**

Nosegay, *Detroit Free Press.* **See 250-2.**

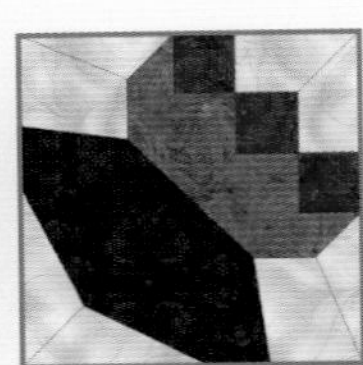
Water Beauty, *Cincinnati Enquirer.* **See 255-5.**

Pine Cone, *Cincinnati Enquirer.* **See 218-5.**

Fringed Aster, Hinson. **See 365-4.**

Orange Bud, Aunt Martha series: *The Quilt Fair Comes to You.* **See 220-6.**

Dresden Rose, Aunt Martha series: *The Quilt Fair Comes to You.* **See 245-11.**

Modernistic Acorn, Hall. **See 271-8.**

Iris, *Cincinnati Enquirer.* **See 122-12.**

Trumpet Vine, McKim. **See 245-6.**

Mountain Pink, *Indianapolis Star.* **See 264-1.**

Chrysanthemum, *Detroit Free Press.* **See 261-4.**

Daffodil, *Cincinnati Enquirer.* **See 173-12.**

Old Fashioned Garland, *Cincinnati Enquirer.* **See 265-7.**

Purple Cone Flower, Quilter's Quest design. **See 218-4.**

Dahlia, Quilter's Quest design. **See 181-9.**

Harlequin Flower, Jinny Beyer Studio design. **See 270-9.**

Crocus, Quilter's Quest design. **See 178-8.**

Tulip, Quilter's Quest design. **See 220-5.**

Day Lily, Jinny Beyer Studio design. **See 174-1.**

Daffodil, Quilter's Quest design. **See 220-7.**

Fox Glove, Quilter's Quest design. **See 121-2.**

Spring Garden, *Birmingham News*. **See 178-9.**

Tulip, *Cincinnati Enquirer*. **See 307-9.**

Victorian Rose, *Chicago Tribune*. **See 263-11.**

Iris Quilt, McKim. **See 440-9.**

Magnolia Block, *Chicago Tribune*. **See 172-12.**

Oriental Tulip, *Chicago Tribune*. **See 440-7.**

Tulip, McKim. **See 440-8.**

Floral Sampler, Jinny Beyer, 2007. Designed for the 2007 Quilter's Quest. The quilt was pieced by Carole Nicholas and quilted by Leslie Sevigney.

❶ Mackinac, Jinny Beyer, Beyer, *Patchwork Portfolio,* 1989.

❷ Dutch Windmill, *Grandma Dexter New Appliqué and Patchwork Designs, Book 36b,* ca. 1932.

❸ New Star, *Grandmother's Quilt Book, No. 34,* 1924.
"There are at least fifty known star patterns and 'New Star,' one of this number was first pieced in northern New York in 1825, about the time the glorious 'Rising Star' made its debut." Nancy Cabot, *Chicago Tribune,* May 15, 1934.

❹ Hemisphere, Jinny Beyer, Jinny Beyer Studio design, 2005.

❺ The Quint Five Quilt, *Kansas City Star,* Jul 23, 1941.

❻ Fort Sumpter, Nancy Cabot, *Chicago Tribune,* Jul 2, 1937.

❼ In Red and White, Clara Stone, *Practical Needlework,* ca. 1906.

❽ Blocks and Bars, *Farm Journal and Farmer's Wife* (Silver Anniversary issue), 1945.

❾ New Jersey, Nancy Page, *Birmingham News,* Aug 15, 1939.

❿ Delectable Mountains, Nancy Cabot, *Chicago Tribune,* Nov 12, 1933.
"'Delectable Mountains,' one of trhe most noteworthy patterns presented in these columns, recently won three prizes in a nation-wide quilt contest. The design was created long ago in New Jersey by the invalid wife of a clergyman; during her long years of confinement to bed and chair she designed and made many quilts, but considered this her masterpiece." Nancy Cabot, *Chicago Tribune,* Nov 12, 1933

⓫ Rockingham's Beauty, *Ladies Art Company,* 1897. See 114-9.

⓬ Flying Fish, Nancy Cabot, *Chicago Tribune,* Jul 18, 1936. Also known as:
Swallows, Nancy Cabot, *Chicago Tribune,* Jul 18, 1936.
"'Flying Fish' also has been known as 'Swallows.' The first title is probably the best known, becaise that was the original name given the block. A small village on the coast of Maine was the home of the block, and the original design was made of two shades of red and blue print materials set together and Appliquéd on a white ground." Nancy Cabot, *Chicago Tribune,* Jul 18, 1936

❶ **Unknown,** Kate Marchbanks, *Capper's Weekly,* May 27, 1986.

❷ **Poinsettia,** Faye Goldey, Beyer, Jinny, *The Quilter's Album ...,*1980.

❸ **Wild Goose Chase,** Aunt Martha series: *Easy Quilts,* ca, 1958.

❹ **The Four Corners,** Nancy Cabot, *Chicago Tribune,* Jan 13, 1936.

❺ **Whirligig,** *Prize Winning Designs,* ca. 1931. See 102-2 Also known as:
  Flora's Favorite, Clara Stone, *Practical Needlework,* ca. 1906.

❻ **Letter F,** Clara Stone, *Practical Needlework,* ca. 1906.

❼ **Golden Puzzle,** Jinny Beyer, Hilton Head Seminar design, 2004.

❽ **Diamond Link,** Nancy Cabot, *Chicago Tribune,* Sep 25, 1936.

❾ **The Thorny Thicket,** *Kansas City Star,* Aug 5, 1942.
"The much desired 'Thorny Thicket' is supplied by Mrs. M. Dees, Coldwater, Mo., who found it among a pattern collection made during her childhood. She says when the youngsters of her day were learning to piece quilts they were first required to use their small scraps in this pattern before they were allowed to have large new pieces. Sometimes each thorn would be of a different color." *Kansas City Star,* Aug 5, 1942

❿ **Double Squares,** *Ladies Art Company,* 1897. See 94-9, 112-9, 167-10, 167-11 and 167-12. Also known as:
  Double Square, Nancy Cabot, *Chicago Tribune,* Nov 16, 1934.

⓫ **Ash Basket,** Jinny Beyer, Quilters's Quest design, 2006.

⓬ **Pine Tree,** Nancy Page, *Birmingham News,* Dec 11, 1934. Also known as:
  Patch Blossom, Aunt Martha series: *Quilts,* ca. 1963.

❶ **Tree of Paradise,** Webster, 1915. Also known as:
Tree of Life, Ickis, 1949.

❷ **Pine Tree,** Nancy Page, *Birmingham News,* Dec 11, 1934.

❸ **The Broken Branch,** *Kansas City Star,* Nov 30, 1935.

❹ **Purple Cone Flower,** Jinny Beyer, Quilters's Quest design, 2007.

❺ **Pine Cone,** Laura Wheeler, *Cincinnati Enquirer,* Aug 19, 1934.

❻ **The Road to California,** Finley, 1929. Also known as:
The Wheel of Fortune, Finley, 1929.

❼ **A Japanese Garden,** *Kansas City Star,* Aug 4, 1934.

❽ **Kaleidoscope,** *Farm Journal and Farmers Wife,* ca. 1941. See 210-4.

❾ **Star Points,** *Farm Journal and Farmers Wife,* ca. 1957.

❿ **Garfield's Monument,** *Ladies Art Company,* 1897.

⓫ **Winding Trail,** Nancy Cabot, *Chicago Tribune,* Aug 10, 1935.

⓬ **The Old Homestead,,** *Ladies Art Company,* 1897.

⓭ **Work Box,** *Ladies Art Company,* 1897.

❶ 20 x 20 grid

❷ 20 x 20 grid

❸ 20 x 20 grid

❹ 20 x 20 grid

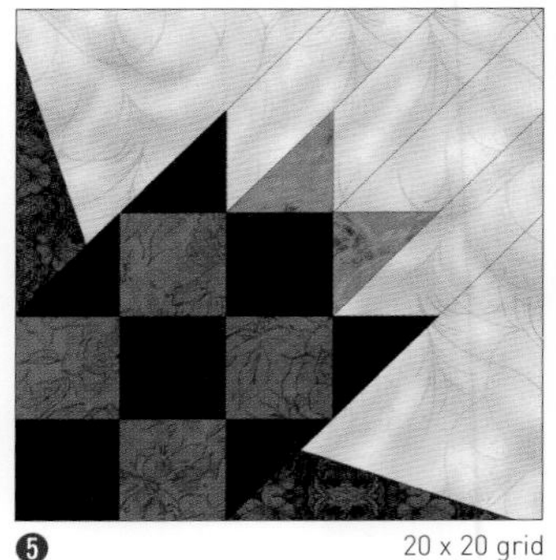

❺ 20 x 20 grid

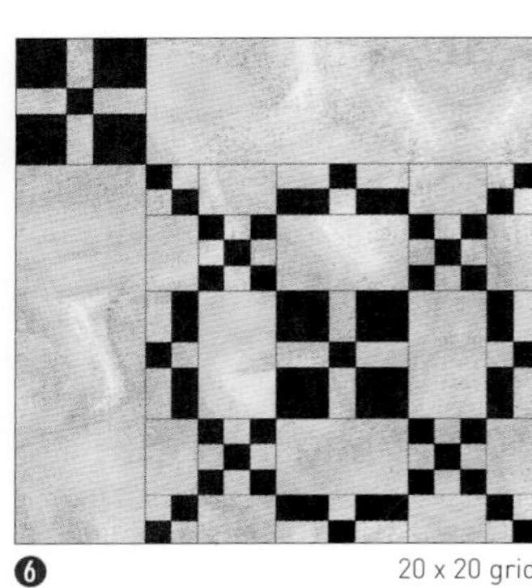

❻ 20 x 20 grid

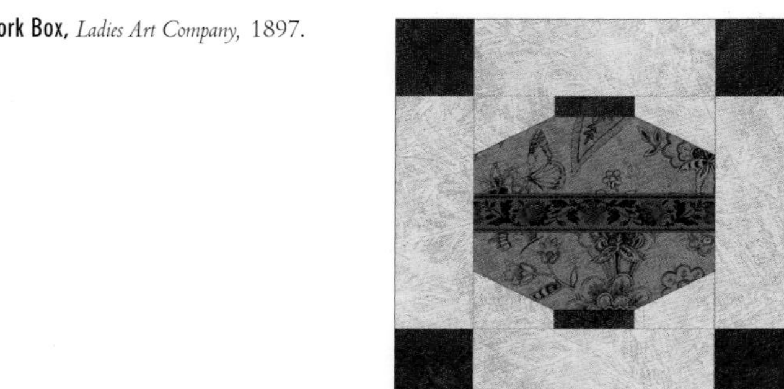

❼ 20 x 20 grid

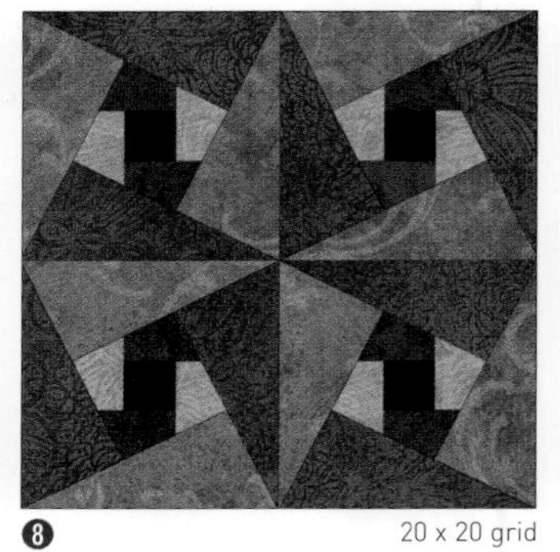

❽ 20 x 20 grid

❾ 20 x 20 grid

❿ 20 x 20 grid

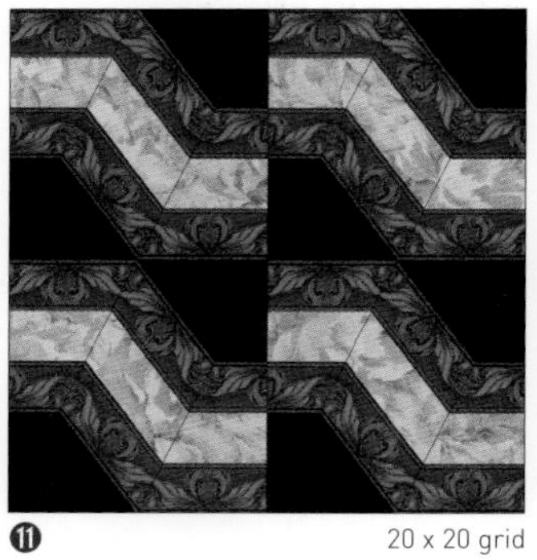

⓫ 20 x 20 grid

⓬ 20 x 20 grid

⓭ 20 x 20 grid

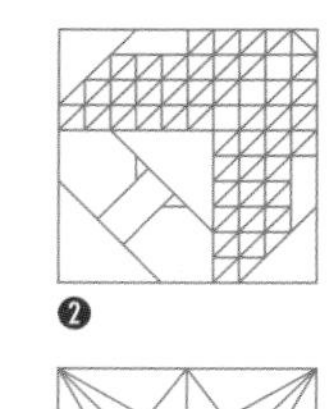

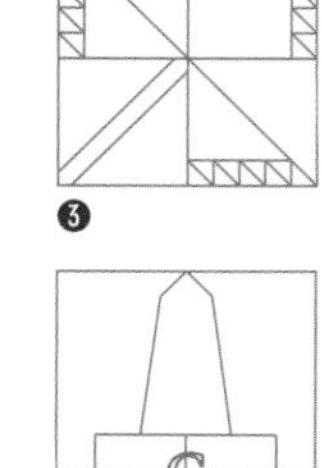

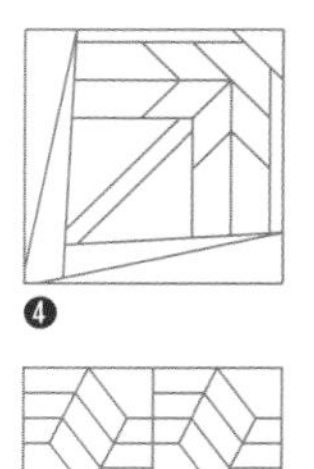

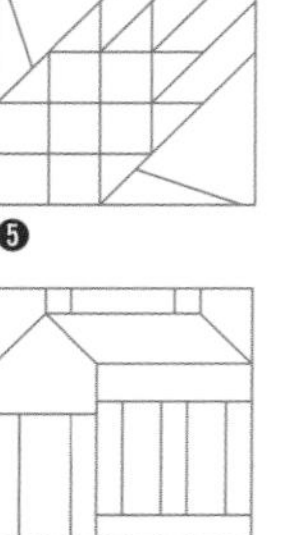

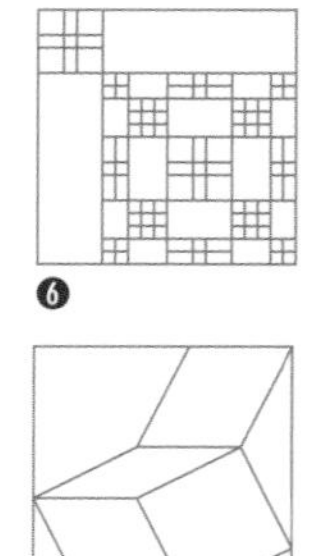

❶ ❷ ❸ ❹ ❺ ❻

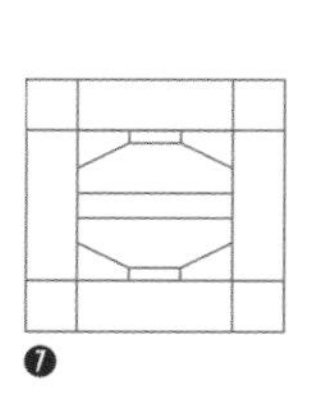

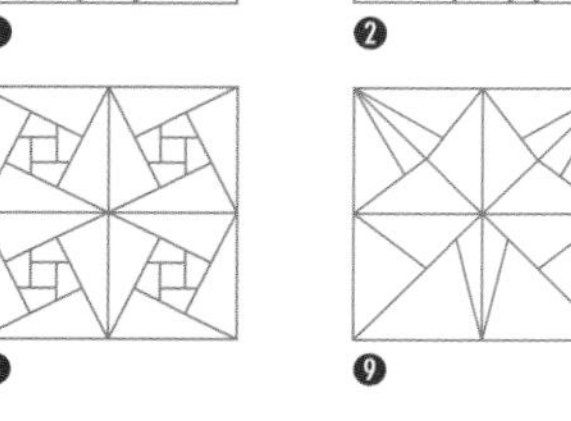

❼ ❽ ❾ ❿ ⓫ ⓬ ⓭

❶ **Jasper,** Jinny Beyer, Hilton Head Seminar design, 2008.

❷ **Exploding Stars,** Aunt Martha series: *Patchwork Simplicity,* ca. 1977.

❸ **The Pine Burr Quilt,,** *Kansas City Star,* Aug 2, 1939.

❹ **Adaptation of the Indian Trail,** *Kansas City Star,* Mar 10, 1943.

❺ **Alexandrite,** Jinny Beyer, Hilton Head Seminar design, 2008.

❻ **Charleston,** Jinny Beyer, Beyer Studio design, 2000.

❼ **Friendship Chain,** *Kansas City Star,* Aug 13, 1941.

❽ **Happiness,** *Farm Journal and Farmers Wife,* ca. 1941.

❾ **Pattern Lacking Name,** Nancy Cabot, *Chicago Tribune,* Sep 9, 1935.

❿ **Five Square,** *Farm Journal and Farmers Wife,* ca. 1941.

⓫ **Star of Spring,** Laura Wheeler, *Indianapolis Star,* Mar 12, 1936.

⓬ **Duck Creek Puzzle,** Nancy Cabot, *Chicago Tribune,* Jul 17, 1937.

1 **Letter E,** ca. 1938, per Havig.

2 **Tree of Paradise,** *Ladies Art Company,* 1897. Also known as:
  Pine Tree Quilt, Orlofsky, 1974.

3 **Leafy Basket,** Laura Wheeler, *Cincinnati Enquirer,* Sep 22, 1934.

4 **Butterfly,** *Kansas City Star,* Apr 4, 1936.
  The Butterfly, *Mrs. Danner's Fifth Quilt Book,* 1970.

5 **Tulip,** Jinny Beyer, Quilter's Quest design, 2007.

6 **Orange Bud,** Aunt Martha series: *The Quilt Fair Comes to You,* ca. 1933.

7 **Daffodil,** Jinny Beyer, Quilter's Quest design, 2007.

8 **Swallows in Flight,** Beyer, Alice, *Quilting,* 1934. Also known as:
  Swallow's Flight, Nancy Cabot, *Chicago Tribune,* Feb 21, 1938.

9 **Work Box,** ca. 1938, per Havig.

10 **Jack's House,** *Ladies Art Company,* 1897.

11 **White House Steps,** Laura Wheeler, *Paris News,* Sep 4, 1933.

12 **Tree of Temptation,** *Grandmother Clark's Patchwork Designs, Book No. 22,* 1932.

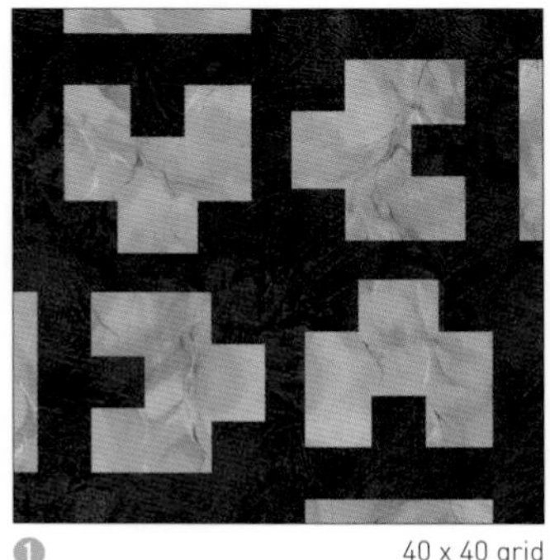

1 40 x 40 grid

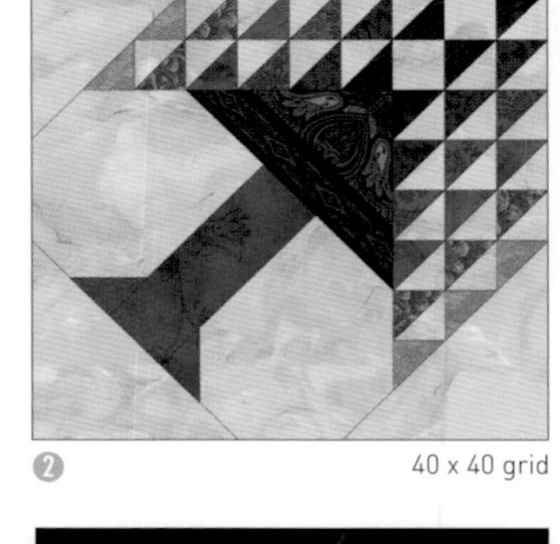

2 40 x 40 grid

3 40 x 40 grid

4 40 x 40 grid

5 40 x 40 grid

6 40 x 40 grid

7 40 x 40 grid

8 40 x 40 grid

9 40 x 40 grid

10 40 x 40 grid

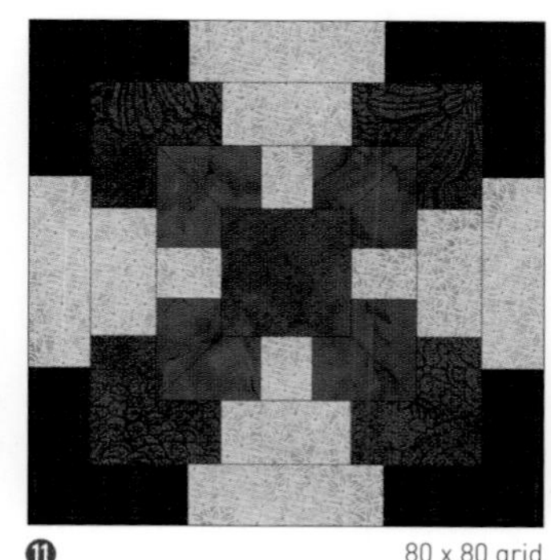

11 80 x 80 grid

12 80 x 80 grid

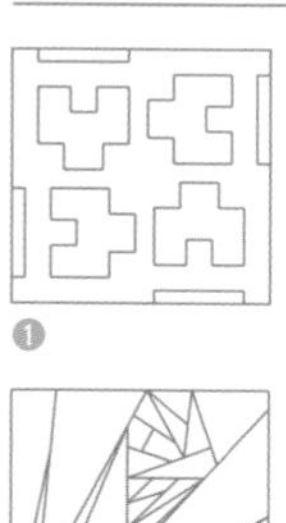

1

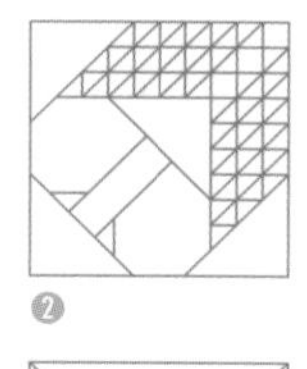

2

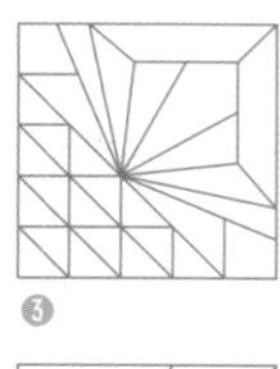

3

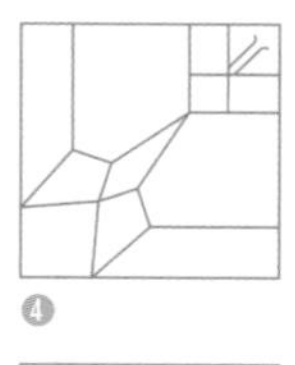

4

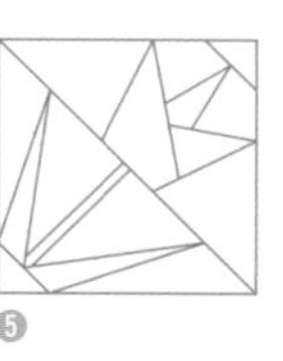

5

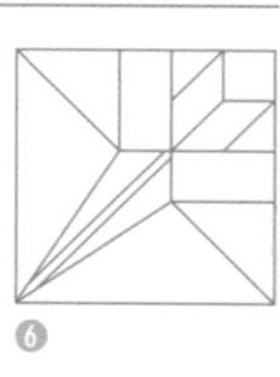

6

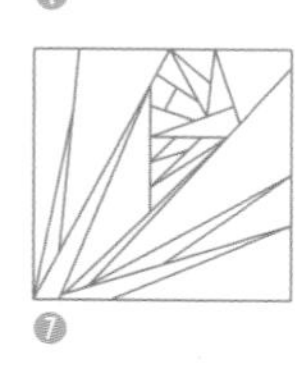

7

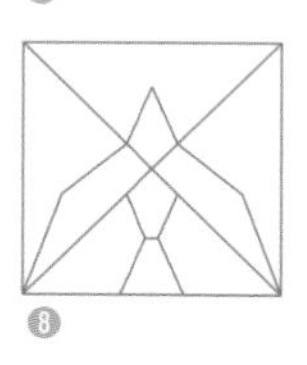

8

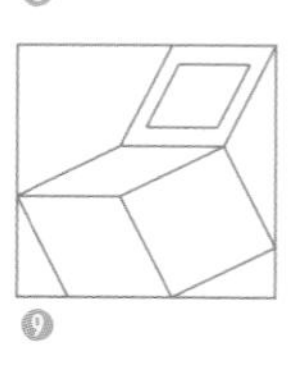

9

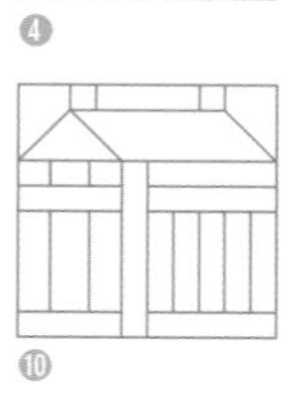

10

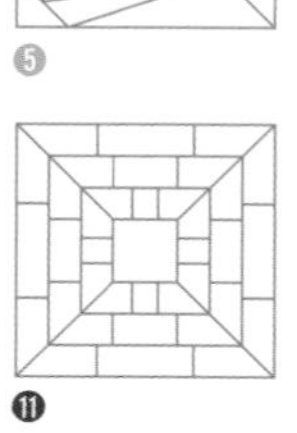

11

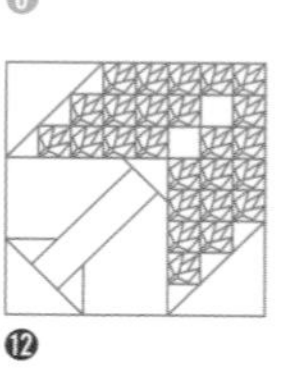

12

Quick Reference: Irish Chain

On October 27, 1933, the pattern *Criss Cross* appeared in the Nancy Page column in the *Detroit Free Press.* More than five years later, Nancy Page offered the pattern again on February 28, 1939, this time calling it *Single Irish Chain.* She had this to say:

> "The Irish chain patterns have a long and honorable history. There are three of them—a single, a double and a triple. The single one is a nine-patch with a square block at each of the four corners of the nine patch and a rectangle joining these squares. The double Irish Chain has a center block with 25 small squares and then outer corner squares and rectangles. The triple chain has 49 small squares with corner squares and rectangles besides." Nancy Page, *Birmingham News,* Feb 28, 1939

While this fairly simple explanation holds true with many Irish Chain patterns, it is not universal, as you will see in the grouping of the blocks here. Quilters through the years have devised a number of variations of the pattern to achieve more or less the same results.

Single Irish Chain, *Birmingham News.* **See 182-5.**

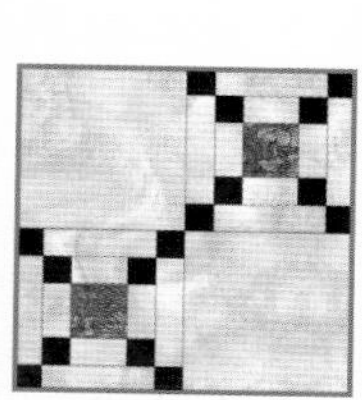

Single Irish Chain, *Chicago Tribune.* **See 173-7.**

An Irish Chain Hint, *Kansas City Star.* **See 438-8.**

Double Irish Chain, *Cincinnati Enquirer.* **See 425-3.**

Triple Irish Chain, *Chicago Tribune.* **See 425-8.**

Irish Chain, *The Patchwork Book.* **See 424-8.**

Double Irish Chain, *Quilts.* **See 253-9.**

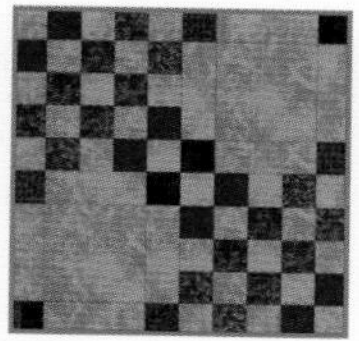

Double Irish Chain, *Ladies Art Company.* **See 209-5.**

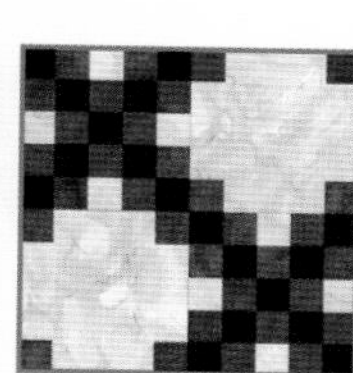

Double Irish Chain, *Illinois State Register.* **See 209-2.**

Grandmother's Irish Chain, *Practical Needlework.* **See 209-8.**

Double Irish Chain, *Kansas City Star.* **See 233-3.**

The Irish Chain Quilt, *Kansas City Star.* **See 425-9.**

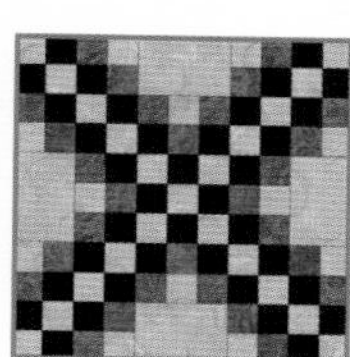

Triple Irish Chain, Hall. **See 254-1.**

Madam X, Hall, 1935. **See 233-11.**

Irish Chain, *Kansas City Star.* **See 250-7.**

Triple Irish Chain, Aunt Martha series: *Bold and Beautiful Quilts.* **See 209-3.**

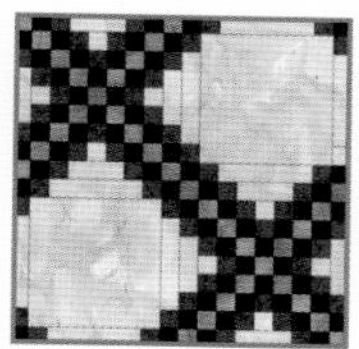

Triple Irish Chain, *Chicago Tribune.* **See 250-5.**

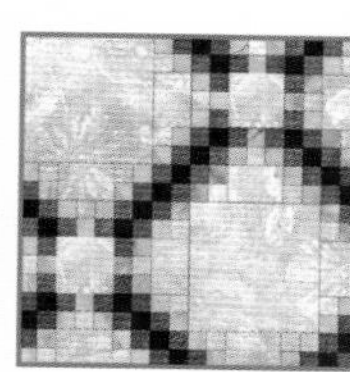

Triple Irish Chain (Large), *Birmingham News.* **See 250-6.**

Aunt Lucinda's Double Irish Chain, *Practical Needlework.* **See 115-9.**

Doors and Windows, *Chicago Tribune.* **See 198-10.**

Mrs. Noel's Quilt, *Mrs. Danner's Fifth Quilt Book.* **See 254-3.**

Triple Irish Chain, Finley, 1929. **See 233-02.**

7 x 7 Base Grid Category

Includes ● 7 x 7, ● 14 x 14, ● 28 x 28, and ● 56 x 56 grids

❶ **Meadow Flower,** Laura Wheeler, *Cincinnati Enquirer,* Oct 15, 1933.

❷ **Batswings,** Aunt Martha series: *The Quilt Fair Comes to You,* ca. 1933.

❸ **Greek Column,** Jinny Beyer, Beyer, Jinny, *Patchwork Portfolio,* 1989.

❹ **Nine Patch,** *Ladies Art Company,* 1897. Also known as:
  Checkers, Nancy Cabot, *Chicago Tribune,* Nov 15, 1934.
  Nine Patch Variation, Hall, 1935.

❺ **Lincoln's Platform,** *Q Book 108, Centennial Quilts,* date unknown.

❻ **Keystone,** Jinny Beyer, Jinny Beyer Studio design, 2009.

❼ **Greek Cross,** *Kansas City Star,* Jan 24, 1931. Also known as:
  The Greek Cross, *Kansas City Star,* Oct 5, 1949.

❽ **Lincoln's Platform,** *Ladies Art Company,* 1897.
"That even quilt lore reflected the heat of the controversies of the Lincoln era, considering the fierceness with which popular passions raged, is not to be wondered at. 'Lincoln's Platform' was an example, carrying into quilt nomenclature the issues of the day. First made in 1860, by the wife of an ardent co-worker of Lincoln, the quilt was patriotically pieced in red, white and blue." Nancy Cabot, *Chicago Tribune,* May 27, 1934

❾ **Leavenworth Nine-Patch,** Hall, 1935. Also known as:
  Tonganoxie Nine-Patch, Hall, 1935.

❶ **Greek Cross,** Clara Stone, *Practical Needlework,* ca. 1906.

❷ **Bouquet,** Laura Wheeler, unidentified newspaper clipping, date unknown.

❸ **Stone Mason's Puzzle,** *Ladies Art Company,* 1922. Also known as:
- **Chained 5 Patch,** ca. 1938, per Havig.
- **City Streets,** Nancy Page, *Birmingham News,* Apr 12, 1938.
- **Double Irish Chain,** ca. 1938, per Havig.

❹ **Stone Mason's Puzzle,** Nancy Cabot, *Chicago Tribune,* Apr 18, 1934.

❺ **Diamond Panes,** Nancy Cabot, *Chicago Tribune,* Feb 12, 1938.

❻ **Flying Geese,** Laura Wheeler, unidentified newspaper clipping, date unknown.

❼ **Harbour Lights,** Jinny Beyer, Hilton Head Seminar design, 1987; published in Beyer, Jinny, *Patchwork Portfolio.* Also known as:
- **Around the World,** Jinny Beyer, Beyer, Jinny, *Patchwork Portfolio,* 1989.

❽ **Dove at the Crossroads,** Clara Stone, *Practical Needlework,* ca. 1906. See 156-11, 194-5, 299-4 and 299-5. Also known as:
- **Cross and Crown,** *Q Book 102, Grandmother's Patchwork Quilts,* date unknown.
- **Lily Pond,** Nancy Cabot, *Chicago Tribune,* Apr 7, 1938.

❾ **Bear's Foot,** *Ladies Art Company,* 1897. See 85-10 and 262-7. Also known as:
- **Bear's Paw,** Laura Wheeler, *Illinois State Register,* Jun 5, 1933.
- **The Bear's Paw,** Finley, 1929.
- **Bear's Paws,** *Old Fashioned Quilts,* ca. 1932.
- **Bear's Track,** Ickis, 1949.
- **Bear's Tracks,** James, 1978.
- **Big Bear Paw,** *Progressive Farmer* (issue 1416), ca. 1932.
- **The Big Bear's Paw,** *Kansas City Star,* Jun 15, 1960.
- **Cat's Paw,** Nancy Page, *Birmingham News,* May 29, 1934.
- **Duck's Foot,** *Farm Journal and Farmers Wife:* ca. 1941.
- **Hand of Friendship,** Finley, 1929.
- **Illinois Turkey Track,** *Mrs. Danner's Fourth Quilt Book,* 1958.
- **Pieced Bear Paw,** *Mrs. Danner Presents Quilt Book 7,* 1975.

❿ **Bear's Paw,** Nancy Cabot, *Chicago Tribune,* Mar 23, 1933. See 85-10 and 262-7.

⓫ **Bear's Paw,** *Grandmother Clark's Authentic Early American Quilts, Book No. 23,* 1932. See 85-10 and 262-7. Also known as:
- **American Rose Bud,** Alice Brooks, *Detroit Free Press,* Jan 31, 1933.
- **The Best Friend,** date unknown, per Brackman.
- **Doves in the Window,** Nancy Cabot, *Chicago Tribune,* Mar 14, 1935.
- **Duck's Foot in the Mud,** Nancy Cabot, *Chicago Tribune,* Mar 12, 1934.
- **Rosebud,** Aunt Martha series: *The Quilt Fair Comes to You,* ca. 1933.
- **Tea Rose,** *Q Book 125, Rose Quilts,* date unknown.

⓬ **Tea Leaf,** *Quilt Blocks from The Farmer's Wife,* 1932.

1 **Rosebuds,** Nancy Page, *Birmingham News,* Mar 12, 1934.

2 **Dove in the Window,** *Ladies Art Company,* 1897. Also known as:

> **Doves in the Window,** Nancy Page, *Birmingham News,* Dec 5, 1939.

3 **Hen and Chickens,** *Ladies Art Company,* 1897. Also known as:

> **Surprise Package,** James, 1978.

4 **Cactus Flower,** Jinny Beyer, Beyer, Jinny, *Patchwork Portfolio,* 1989.

5 **Dragon Fly,** Jinny Beyer, Hilton Head Seminar design 1984; published in Beyer, Jinny, *Patchwork Portfolio.*

6 **Schoenrock Cross,** Nancy Cabot, *Chicago Tribune,* Jun 24, 1937.

7 **Breakwater,** Jinny Beyer, Hilton Head Seminar design 1986; published in Beyer, Jinny, *Patchwork Portfolio.*

8 **Dutch Tulips,** Laura Wheeler, *Cincinnati Enquirer,* Sep 17, 1933.
"The tulip was one of the favorite flowers of the early Dutch settlers and it was they who first introduced them to this country. It is no wonder then that we find it used in such a variety of ways in quilt patterns. Dutch Tulips though has more than just beauty of form to recommend it for it is composed to a great part of scraps of material. This gives the thrifty quiltmaker an opportunity to make a charming quilt most economically." Laura Wheeler, *Cincinnati Enquirer,* Sep 17, 1933

9 **Montana Maze,** Nancy Cabot, *Chicago Tribune,* Jun 21, 1938.

10 **St. Elmo's Cross,** Nancy Cabot, *Chicago Tribune,* Apr 30, 1938.

11 **Boston Commons,** Nancy Cabot, *Chicago Tribune,* Feb 5, 1935.

12 **Box Quilt Pattern,** *Ladies Art Company,* 1897. See 126-4 and 258-9. Also known as:

> **Box Car Patch,** Nancy Cabot, *Chicago Tribune,* Nov 10, 1934.
> **Box Quilt,** Hall, 1935.
> **Churn Dash,** ca. 1938, per Havig.
> **Contrary Husband Quilt,** *Kansas City Star,* Nov 9, 1938.
> **Eccentric Star,** Hall, 1935.

1 2 3 4 5 6

7 8 9 10 11 12

❶ **Prairie Points,** Jinny Beyer, Hilton Head Seminar design, 1996.

❷ **Swastika,** *The Patchwork Book,* 1932.

❸ **Chain Link Quilt,** Nancy Page, *Nashville Banner,* Sep 6, 1932.

❹ **Whirling Squares,** Nancy Cabot, *Chicago Tribune,* Dec 23, 1937.

❺ **Prickly Pear,** Eveline Foland, *Kansas City Star,* Oct 3, 1931.

❻ **Allentown,** Nancy Page, *Birmingham News,* Jan 22, 1935.

❼ **Lady Slipper,** *Quilt Book No. 6,* May 26, 1933. Also known as:

Slipper Bow, *Quilt Book No. 6,* Jul 29, 1933.

❽ **Magnolia Bud,** Hall, 1935. See 104-8, 116-7 and 228-5.

❾ **Friendship Bouquet,** Alice Brooks, *Detroit Free Press,* Mar 20, 1934.

"Here is another friendship quilt and what quiltmaker will not welcome it! Simple to do; gay in the scraps used to form the flowers; it would be a pleasure to friends to make a single block as their contribution and an interesting pastime for the needlewoman who plans to make it all herself." Alice Brooks, *Detroit Free Press, Mar 20,* 1934

❿ **Pine Tree,** Laura Wheeler, *Indianapolis Star,* Jan 20, 1937.

⓫ **Tree of Heaven,** Nancy Page, *Birmingham News,* Jun 1, 1943.

⓬ **The Alta Plane,** ca. 1938, per Havig.

❶ **Tulip Lady Fingers,** Hall, 1935. See 109-6.

❷ **Bowknot,** Laura Wheeler, *Indianapolis Star,* Aug 21, 1933.

❸ **The Weaving House,** Jinny Beyer, Jinny Beyer Studio design, 2009.

❹ **Three Patch,** Laura Wheeler, unidentified newspaper clipping, date unknown.

❺ **Log Cabin 'Light and Dark',** *Q Book 102, Grandmother's Patchwork Quilts,* date unknown.

❻ **Parquetry for a Quilt Block,** *Kansas City Star,* Oct 4, 1950.

❼ **The Mayflower,** *Ladies World Mgazine,* May 1893. Also known as:
  Mayflower Quilt, Nancy Page, *Detroit Free Press,* Sep 22, 1933.

❽ **Endless Chain,** Laura Wheeler, *Cincinnati Enquirer,* Aug 14, 1933.

❾ **Endless Chain,** Laura Wheeler, *Cincinnati Enquirer,* Jun 12, 1936.

❿ **The V Block,** Nancy Cabot, *Chicago Tribune,* Jan 15, 1935.

⓫ **Northern Lights,** Nancy Cabot, *Chicago Tribune,* Jul 12, 1938.

⓬ **The Priscilla,** *Ladies World Mgazine,* May 1893. See page 65. Also known as:
  Golden Wedding, Nancy Page, *Nashville Banner,* Aug 16, 1932.
  Golden Wedding Quilt, Nancy Page, *Nashville Banner,* Aug 16, 1932.
  World Without End, Finley, 1929.

"When Mrs. Lacey's mother and father celebrated their golden wedding anniversary the whole day had been one of delight. Guests spoke of the table with its beautiful color arrangement of white and gold. At the time Mrs. Lacey had said grandmother planned to use that white and gold sateen for a quilt. She thought that each of the daughters would cherish such a gift... she chose a pattern in many of the old families, 'World Without End'... the effect when the blocks are pieced side by side... is a curious one of encircling worlds that go on and on 'without end.' Mrs. Lacey called her pattern 'Golden Wedding,' becase she was using the white and gold sateen and becase as she said, 'the influence of her father's and mother's life would go on 'world without end.'" Nancy Page, *Nashville Banner,* Aug 16, 1932

❶ 7 x 7 grid

❷ 7 x 7 grid

❸ 7 x 7 grid

❹ 7 x 7 grid

❺ 7 x 7 grid

❻ 14 x 14 grid

❼ 14 x 14 grid

❽ 14 x 14 grid

❾ 14 x 14 grid

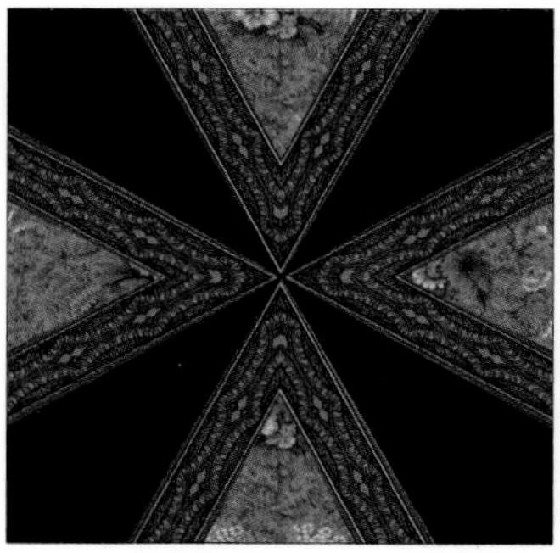

❿ 14 x 14 grid

⓫ 14 x 14 grid

⓬ 14 x 14 grid

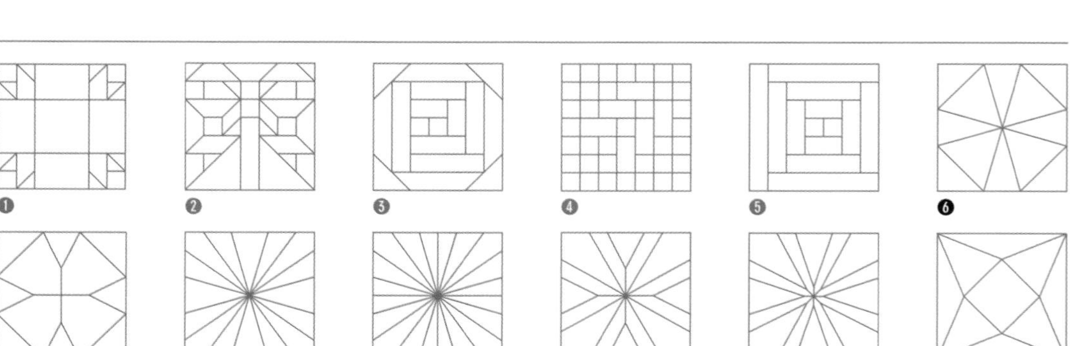

❶ World Without End, Nancy Cabot, *Chicago Tribune,* Feb 11, 1933. Also known as:
Kaleidoscope, ca. 1938, per Havig.

❷ Cross and Star, *Prize Winning Designs,* ca. 1931. Also known as:
King David's Crown, Hall, 1935.

❸ Walls of Jericho, Nancy Cabot, *Chicago Tribune,* Oct 28, 1935.

❹ Fox and Geese, Nancy Cabot, *Chicago Tribune,* Feb 20, 1933. Also known as:
The Whirling Five Patch, *Kansas City Star,* Dec 17, 1941.

❺ Cross and Crown, Nancy Cabot, *Chicago Tribune,* Dec 8, 1934.

❻ The Diamond Cross, *Kansas City Star,* May 22, 1937. Also known as:
The Ratchet Wheel, *Kansas City Star,* Mar 5, 1947.

❼ Our Country, *Kansas City Star,* Oct 4, 1939.

❽ Rubic's Cube, Jinny Beyer, Hilton Head Seminar design, 2001.

❾ Cave Crystal, Jinny Beyer, Hilton Head Seminar design, 1984; published in Beyer, Jinny, *Patchwork Portfolio.*

❿ South of the Border, Jinny Beyer, Hilton Head Seminar design, 1985; published in Beyer, Jinny, *Patchwork Portfolio.*

⓫ New Horizon, Jinny Beyer, Hilton Head Seminar design, 1999.

⓬ Cypress, *Kansas City Star,* Sep 9, 1933. Also known as:
The Cypress, *Kansas City Star,* Mar 9, 1960.

1 Girl's Joy, *Ladies Art Company,* 1897. See 250-11. Also known as:
Maiden's Delight, Nancy Cabot, *Chicago Tribune,* Oct 30, 1937.

2 Dutch Mill, Nancy Cabot, *Chicago Tribune,* Dec 28, 1934.
Holland Mill, Nancy Cabot, *Chicago Tribune,* Sep 14, 1937.

3 California Oak Leaf, Hall, 1935. Also known as:
The Hand, Hall, 1935.
Sassafras Leaf, Hall, 1935.
True Lover's Knot, Hall, 1935.

4 Yankee Charm, Nancy Cabot, *Chicago Tribune,* Nov 5, 1937.

5 Pink Magnolias, Nancy Cabot, *Chicago Tribune,* Jul 26, 1936. See 104-8, 116-7 and 225-8.
"'Pink Magnolia' is a pieced block of southern origin, made for the first time in New Orleans. The completed block is really made up of four magnolias with the stems set together and with the blossoms radiating from the center." Nancy Cabot, *Chicago Tribune,* Jul 26, 1936

6 Yellow Lilies, Nancy Cabot, *Chicago Tribune,* Dec 30, 1936.

7 Friday 13th, *Kansas City Star,* Feb 16, 1935.

8 Vines at the Window, Nancy Cabot, *Chicago Tribune,* Dec 4, 1937.

9 Devil's Claw, Nancy Cabot, *Chicago Tribune,* Oct 23, 1936.
"'Devil's Claw' is one of the old quilt patterns and was christened a long time ago when women raised geese for feathers and the children stayed away from these hissing, biting creatures of the barnyard on account of their dispositions. One clever mother appropriately named them 'Devil's Claws' as any person once chased by geese may understand. She then pieced a quilt block and bestowed this name upon the pattern because of the clawlike effect at the edge." Nancy Cabot, *Chicago Tribune,* Oct 23, 1936

10 Old Fashioned String Quilt, *Kansas City Star,* Feb 2, 1935.

11 Aunt Sukey's Choice, Ickis, 1949. See 259-4.

12 Lone Star, Laura Wheeler, *Indianapolis Star,* Mar 13, 1934.

1 14 x 14 grid

2 14 x 14 grid

3 14 x 14 grid

4 14 x 14 grid

5 14 x 14 grid

6 14 x 14 grid

7 14 x 14 grid

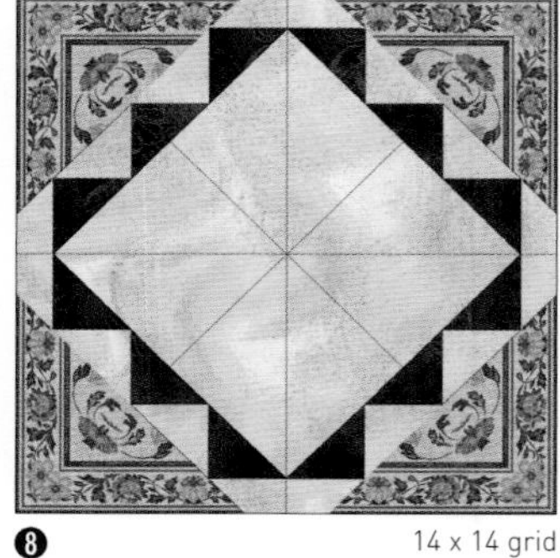
8 14 x 14 grid

9 14 x 14 grid

10 14 x 14 grid

11 14 x 14 grid

12 14 x 14 grid

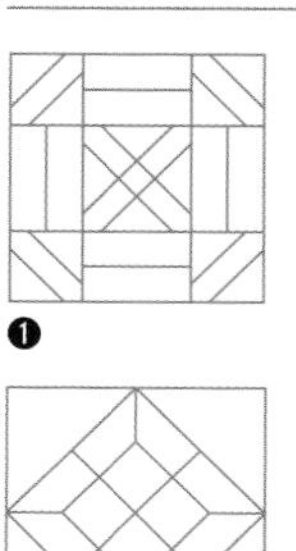
1 7

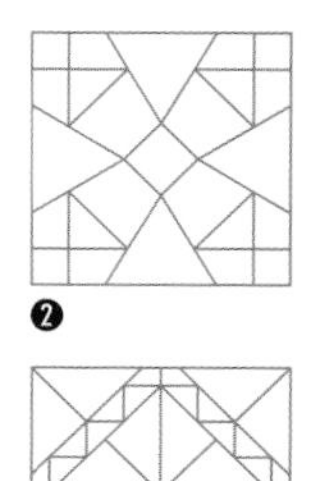
2 8

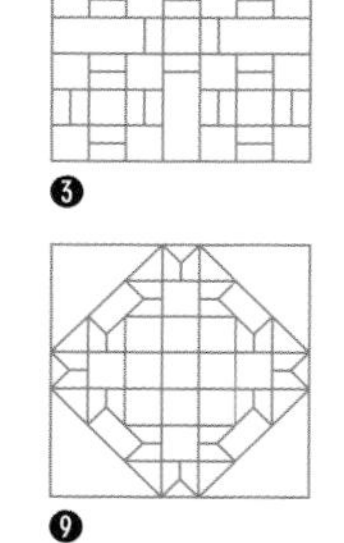
3 9

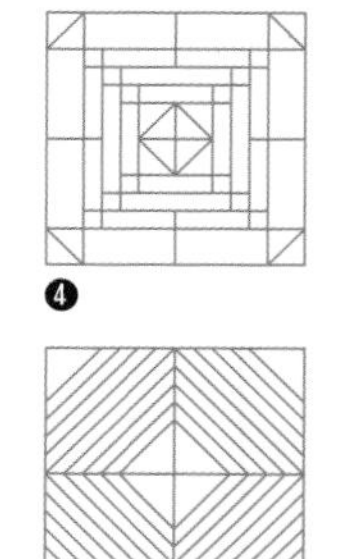
4 10

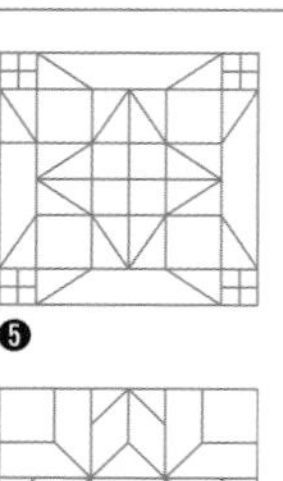
5 11

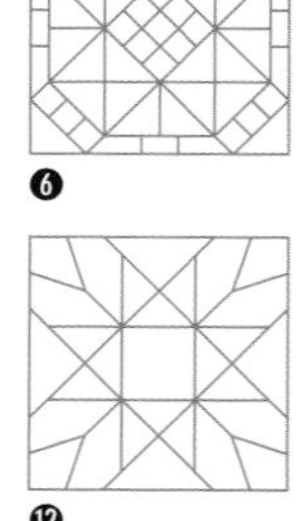
6 12

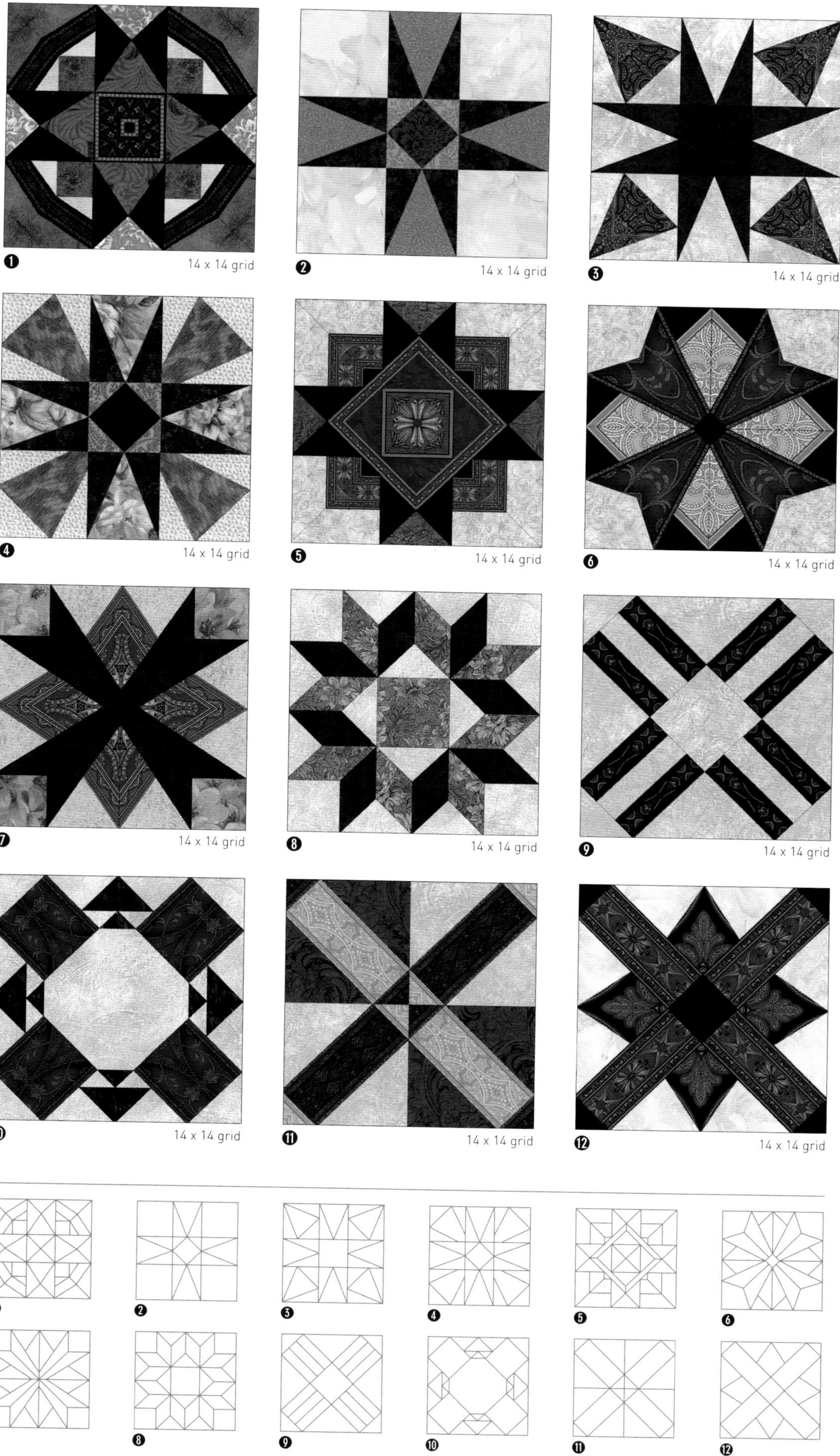

❶ **Spectre Star,** Jinny Beyer, Beyer, Jinny, *Patchwork Portfolio,* 1989.

❷ **Rosewood,** Jinny Beyer, RJR Patterns, 2000.

❸ **Prairie Queen,** Laura Wheeler, *Sioux City Journal,* Jun 10, 1938.

❹ **Starflower,** Jinny Beyer, Jinny Beyer Studio design, 2003.

❺ **Tavern Steps,** Jinny Beyer, Beyer, Jinny, *Patchwork Portfolio,* 1989.

❻ **Square Knot,** Jinny Beyer, Beyer, Jinny, *Patchwork Portfolio,* 1989.

❼ **North Star,** Laura Wheeler, *Sioux City Journal,* Mar 8, 1940.

❽ **Dove at the Window,** *Mrs. Danner's Quilts, Books 1 & 2* , 1934.

❾ **Autograph Quilt,** Eveline Foland, *Kansas City Star,* Feb 6, 1932. Also known as:

> **Autograph,** *The New Barbara Taylor Book on Quilting,* ca. 1977.
> **Autograph Patch,** Hall, 1935.
> **The Autograph Quilt,** *Kansas City Star,* Mar 2, 1949.

❿ **Ladies' Chain,** Clara Stone, *Practical Needlework,* ca. 1906.

⓫ **Devil's Puzzle,** Hall, 1935. See 90-8 and 90-9. Also known as:

> **Fly Foot,** Hall, 1935.

⓬ **Tiger Eye,** Jinny Beyer, Hilton Head Seminar design, 1984.

1. **Clematis,** Jinny Beyer, Hilton Head Seminar design, 1996; published in Beyer, Jinny, *Quiltmaking by Hand*.
2. **Sticky Wicket,** Jinny Beyer, Beyer, Jinny, *Patchwork Portfolio,* 1989.
3. **Sixpence,** Jinny Beyer, Beyer, Jinny, *Patchwork Portfolio,* 1989.
4. **Our Country,** Beyer, Jinny, *The Quilter's Album...,* 1980.
5. **Cove Cross,** Jinny Beyer, Hilton Head Seminar design, 1987; Beyer, Jinny, *Patchwork Portfolio*.
6. **Halley's Comet,** Jinny Beyer, Beyer, Jinny, *Patchwork Portfolio,* 1989.
7. **Persian,** *Ladies Art Company,* 1928. Also known as:
   Persian Squares, Nancy Page, *Birmingham News,* Jul 28, 1942.
   Persian Star, Hall, 1935.
8. **T Square #1,** Holice Turnbow, 1980; published in Beyer, Jinny, *The Quilter's Album . . . .*
9. **T Square #2,** Holice Turnbow, 1980; published in Beyer, Jinny, *The Quilter's Album . . . .*
10. **Rolling Road,** Jinny Beyer, Hilton Head Seminar design; 2001, Beyer, Jinny, *Quiltmaking by Hand*.
11. **Nova,** Jinny Beyer, Hilton Head Seminar design, 2000.
12. **Big Bang,** Jinny Beyer, Beyer, Jinny, *Patchwork Portfolio,* 1989.

1 14 x 14 grid

2 14 x 14 grid

3 14 x 14 grid

4 14 x 14 grid

5 14 x 14 grid

6 14 x 14 grid

7 14 x 14 grid

8 14 x 14 grid

9 14 x 14 grid

10 14 x 14 grid

11 14 x 14 grid

12 14 x 14 grid

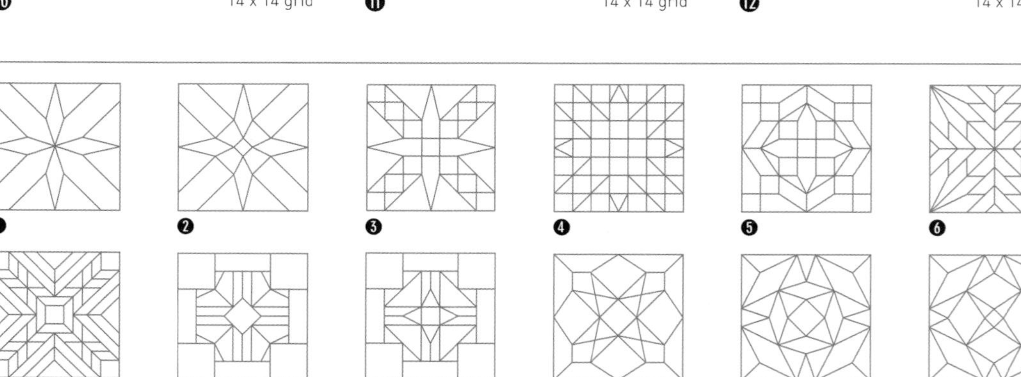

❶ **A Coverlet in Jewel Tones,** *Kansas City Star,* Jan 14, 1959.

❷ **Arrowhead,** *Prize Winning Designs,* ca. 1931.

❸ **Topaz,** Jinny Beyer, Hilton Head Seminar design, 1994.

❹ **Crown of Stars,** Nancy Cabot, *Chicago Tribune,* Dec 10, 1935.

❺ **Star of '49,** Nancy Cabot, *Chicago Tribune,* Apr 22, 1937.

❻ **Four Queens,** Nancy Cabot, *Chicago Tribune,* Feb 7, 1936.
"The bridge fan may think it was the love of that game which is responsible for the title of this block, but 'Four Queens' was bestowed upon this block by an elderly whist player, whose wife designed a pieced quilt composed of these blocks, the arrangement of which called to his mind the crowns of four queens with yellow caps surrounding a purple and yellow throne." Nancy Cabot, *Chicago Tribune,* Feb 7, 1936

❼ **Ruth's Favorite,** Nancy Page, *Birmingham News,* Sep 16, 1941.

❽ **Yankee Pride,** *Quilt Booklet No. 1,* ca. 1931.

❾ **Feather Star,** Nancy Cabot, *Chicago Tribune,* Aug 14, 1935.
"'Feather Star' always has been among the favorites in star patterns. It is classified as one of the older blocks and always has been outstanding in the field of elaborate quilt designs. The first 'Feather Star' was pieced as early as 1825 and the favorite colors, at that time, were red, green and white, while modern colors are more varied." Nancy Cabot, *Chicago Tribune,* Aug 14, 1935

❿ **Birds in Air,** Ickis, 1949.

⓫ **Pulsar,** Jinny Beyer, Hilton Head Seminar design, 2000.

⓬ **Pin Wheel,** *Grandmother Clark's Authentic Early America Quilts, Book No. 21,* 1932. Also known as:

Flying Kite, *Kansas City Star,* Jul 7, 1937.

❶ **Eccentric Star,** *Grandmother's Patchwork Quilt Designs, Book 20,* 1931. Also known as:
Mill Blade, Jane Alan, *Illinois State Register,* Jan 22, 1933.

❷ **Flag In, Flag Out,** Letha McBroom, *Kansas City Star,* Nov 8, 1939.

❸ **A Name on Each Line,** *Kansas City Star,* Sep 7, 1955.

❹ **Lotus Blossom,** Alice Brooks, *Detroit Free Press,* Aug 10, 1934. Also known as:
Lotus Block, Nancy Cabot, *Chicago Tribune,* May 18, 1938.

❺ **Tree of Temptation,** *Hall,* 1935.
"Note the branches hang very low and the flowers are within easy reach." Hall, 1935

❻ **Chestnut,** Jinny Beyer, Quilter's Quest design, 2004.

❼ **Redbud,** Jinny Beyer, Quilter's Quest design, 2005.

❽ **Tree of Paradise,** Hall, 1935.

❾ **Tree of Paradise,** *The Dressmaking Book,* 1929.

❿ **Tree of Paradise,** Beyer, Alice, *Quilting,* 1934.

⓫ **Cone Tree,** Nancy Cabot, *Chicago Tribune,* Jun 12, 1937.

⓬ **Hour Glass,** ca. 1938, per Havig.

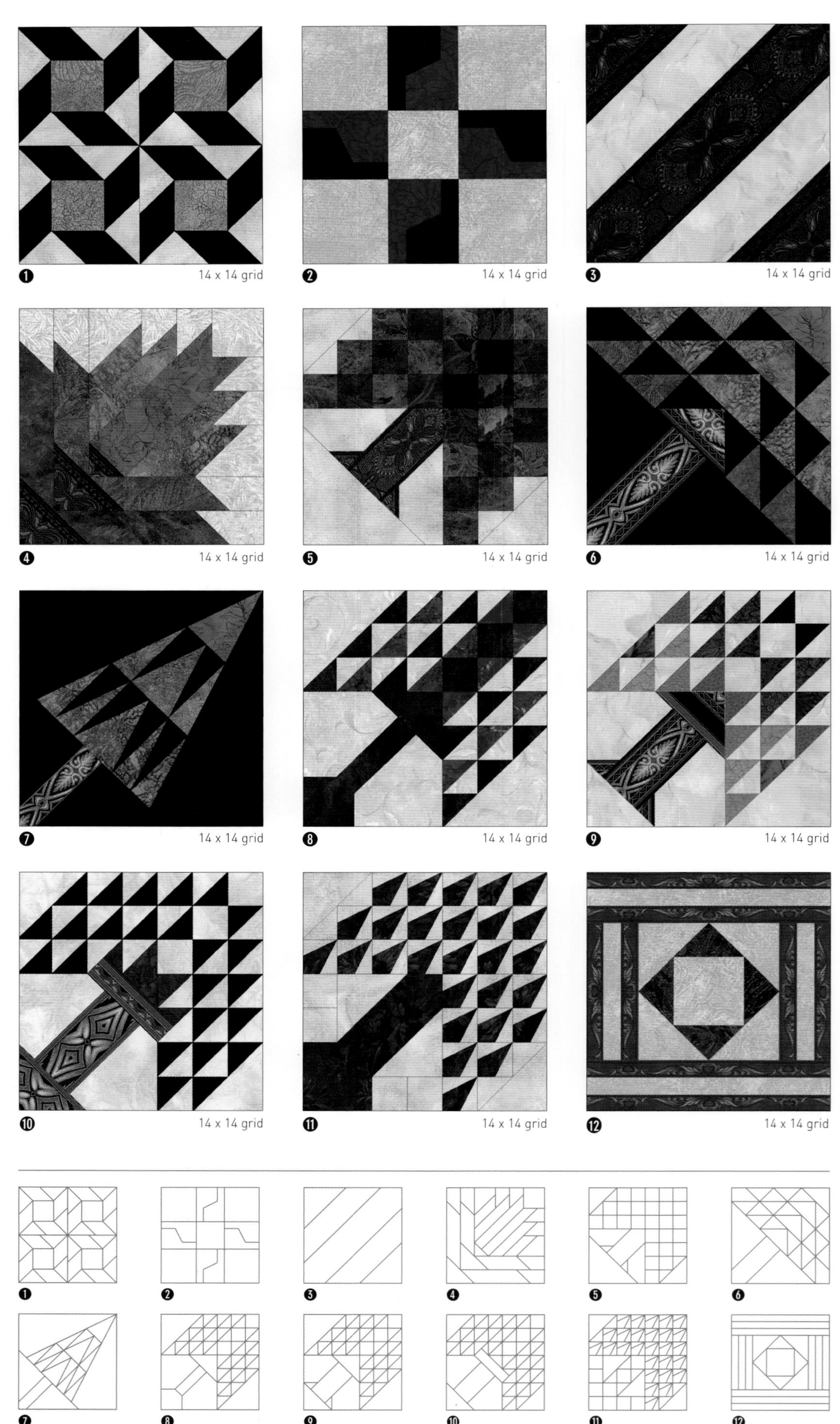

❶ V for Victory, Nancy Page, *Birmingham News,* Aug 11, 1942.
"Every war brings forth a crop of military quilts and this war is no exception. From one of the Southern states I received this pattern which I am passing on to you with many thanks." Nancy Page, *Birmingham News,* Aug 11, 1942

❷ Triple Irish Chain, Finley, 1929.

❸ Double Irish Chain, *Kansas City Star,* Jan 13, 1934. Also known as:
  The Double Irish Chain, *Kansas City Star,* Jul 14, 1948.

❹ Interlaced Ribbons, Nancy Cabot, *Chicago Tribune,* Apr 11, 1936.

❺ Discovery, Jinny Beyer, Hilton Head Seminar design, 1997.

❻ Spring and Fall, Nancy Cabot, *Chicago Tribune,* Sep 23, 1937.

❼ Log Cabin, ca. 1860, per Holstein. Also known as:
  Log Patch, Hall, 1935.

❽ Log Cabin, Eveline Foland, *Kansas City Star,* Jul 9, 1932.

❾ New Log Cabin, Nancy Cabot, *Chicago Tribune,* Jul 18, 1935.

❿ Kissing Lanes, Nancy Cabot, *Chicago Tribune,* Nov 12, 1935.

⓫ Madam X, Hall, 1935.

⓬ Broken Sash, *Farm Journal Quilt Patterns,* ca. 1935. See 61-2, 119-7 and 253-5.

❶ A, *Ladies Art Company*, 1906.
❷ B, *Ladies Art Company*, 1906.
❸ C, *Ladies Art Company*, 1906.
❹ D, *Ladies Art Company*, 1906.
❺ E, *Ladies Art Company*, 1906.
❻ F, *Ladies Art Company*, 1906.
❼ G, *Ladies Art Company*, 1906.
❽ H, *Ladies Art Company*, 1906.
❾ I, *Ladies Art Company*, 1906.
❿ J, *Ladies Art Company*, 1906.
⓫ K, *Ladies Art Company*, 1906.
⓬ L, *Ladies Art Company*, 1906.
⓭ M, *Ladies Art Company*, 1906.

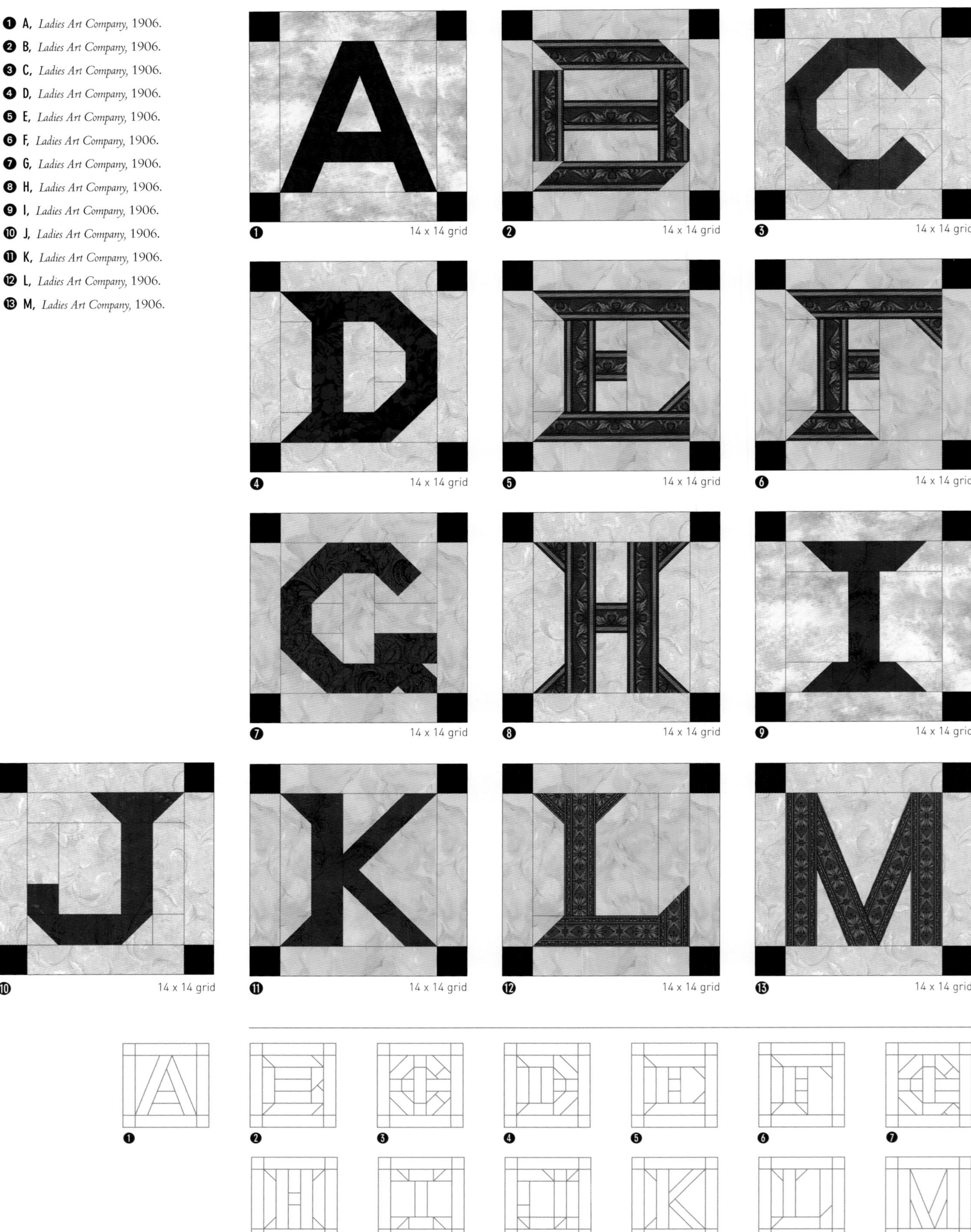

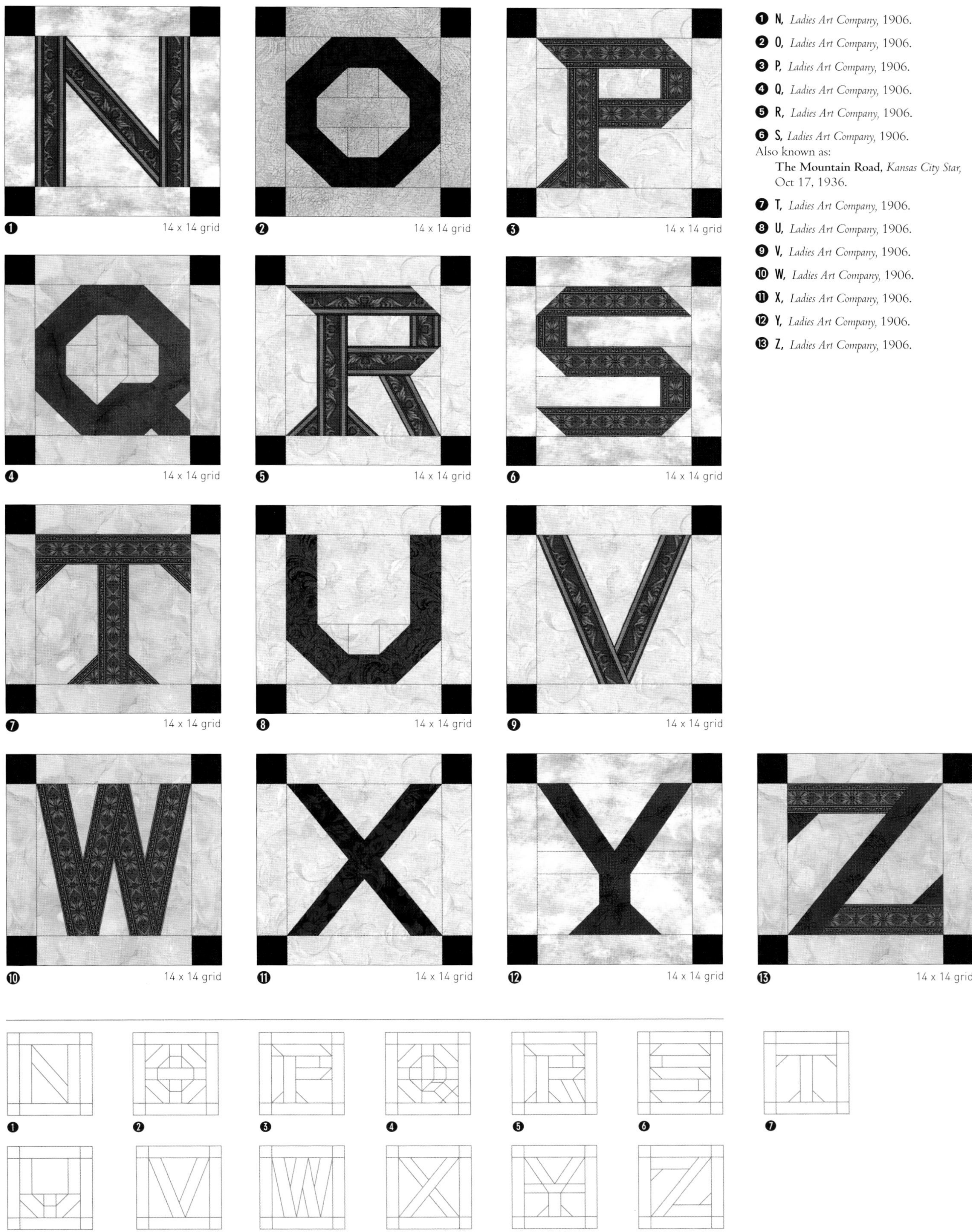

❶ N, *Ladies Art Company,* 1906.
❷ O, *Ladies Art Company,* 1906.
❸ P, *Ladies Art Company,* 1906.
❹ Q, *Ladies Art Company,* 1906.
❺ R, *Ladies Art Company,* 1906.
❻ S, *Ladies Art Company,* 1906.
Also known as:
The Mountain Road, *Kansas City Star,* Oct 17, 1936.
❼ T, *Ladies Art Company,* 1906.
❽ U, *Ladies Art Company,* 1906.
❾ V, *Ladies Art Company,* 1906.
❿ W, *Ladies Art Company,* 1906.
⓫ X, *Ladies Art Company,* 1906.
⓬ Y, *Ladies Art Company,* 1906.
⓭ Z, *Ladies Art Company,* 1906.

1. **Little Boy's Britches,** *Kansas City Star,* Sep 6, 1939. See 275-7, 338-3 and 342-2.
2. **Morning Patch,** *Ladies Art Company,* 1922.
3. **The E Z Quilt,** *Kansas City Star,* Aug 7, 1940.
4. **Bachelor's Puzzle,** *Hall,* 1935. See 270-2 and 193-5.
5. **The Maple Leaf,** Eveline Foland, *Kansas City Star,* Aug 2, 1930. Also known as:
   - **Autumn Leaf,** Hall, 1935.
   - **Autumn Leaves,** Alice Brooks, *Detroit Free Press,* Mar 30, 1934.
   - **Maple Leaf,** Hall, 1935.
   - **Peony,** Ickis, 1949.
6. **Eight Hands Around,** Laura Wheeler, *Cincinnati Enquirer,* Sep 11, 1933. "'Eight Hands Around'—quaint in name, striking in pattern, simple to make—is an old-time favorite. The square dances of olden days gave this quilt its name, eight-hands-around being a figure of a dance popular in the early days of quiltmaking. The eight patches, meeting to form the lovely starlike figure, gave the quiltmaker this idea." Laura Wheeler, *Cincinnati Enquirer,* Sep 11, 1933
7. **Picnic Basket,** Jinny Beyer, Beyer, Jinny, *Patchwork Portfolio,* 1989.
8. **Illinois Star,** Nancy Cabot, *Chicago Tribune,* Aug 13, 1933.
9. **Midnight Oil,** Jinny Beyer, Beyer, Jinny, *Patchwork Portfolio,* 1989.
10. **Bachelor Bouquet,** Jinny Beyer, Hilton Head Seminar design 1991; published in Beyer, Jinny, *Soft-Edge Piecing.*
11. **Double Star,** Clara Stone, *Practical Needlework,* ca. 1906.
12. **Chateau,** Jinny Beyer, Beyer, Jinny, *Soft-Edge Piecing,* 1995.

1 28 x 28 grid

2 28 x 28 grid

3 28 x 28 grid

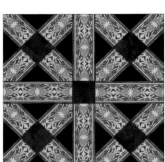

4 28 x 28 grid

5 28 x 28 grid

6 28 x 28 grid

7 28 x 28 grid

8 28 x 28 grid

9 28 x 28 grid

10 28 x 28 grid

11 28 x 28 grid

12 28 x 28 grid

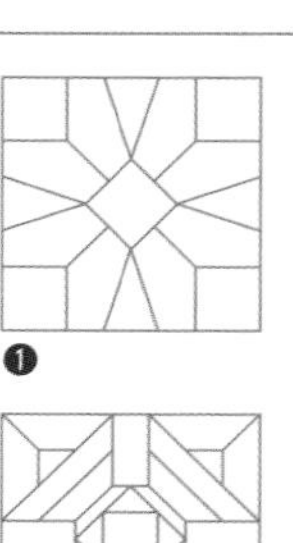

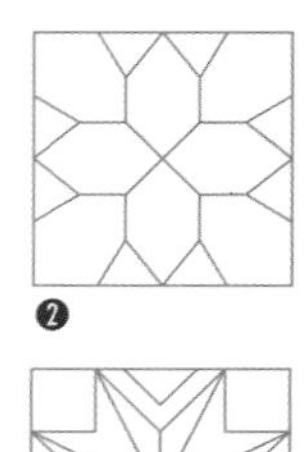

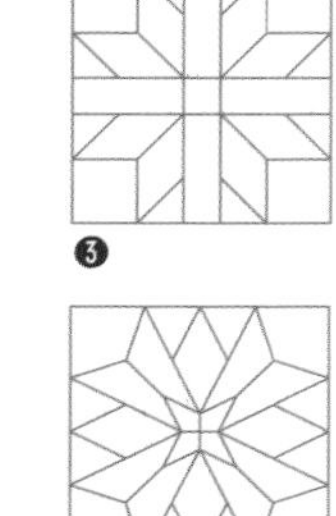

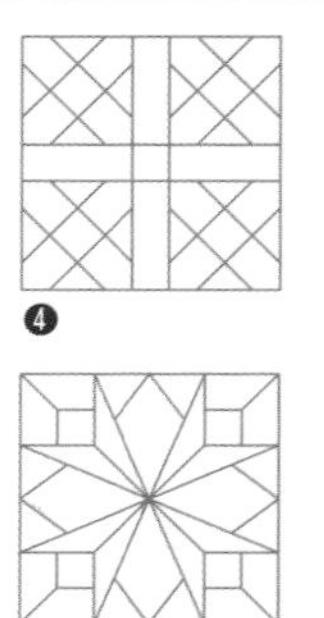

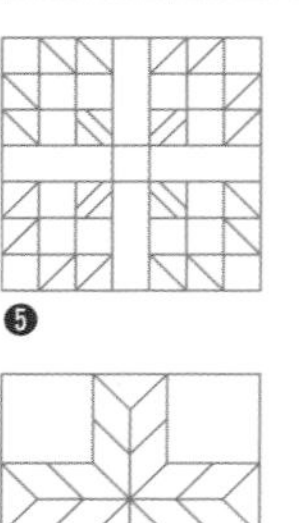

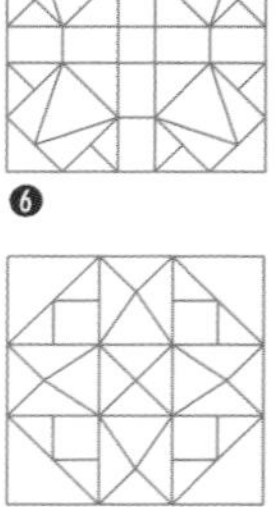

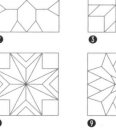

1 2 3 4 5 6

7 8 9 10 11 12

❶ **Shenandoah,** Jinny Beyer, Jinny Beyer Studio design, 2007.

❷ **Chevrons,** Nancy Page, *Birmingham News*, Aug 4, 1942.

❸ **Fern,** ca.1938, per Havig.

❹ **The North Star,** *Kansas City Star*, Mar 9, 1949.

❺ **Sandy's Star,** Jinny Beyer, Hilton Head Seminar design, 1984; published in Beyer, Jinny, *Patchwork Portfolio*.

❻ **Prism,** Jinny Beyer, Hilton Head Seminar design, 1994.

❼ **Dutch Mill,** Jinny Beyer, Beyer, Jinny, *Patchwork Portfolio*, 1989.

❽ **The Wandering Flower,** *Kansas City Star*, Mar 15, 1939. See 82-4 and 413-9.

❾ **Exea's Star,** Clara Stone, *Practical Needlework*, ca. 1906.

❿ **Grandma's Scraps,** Laura Wheeler, unidentified newspaper clipping, date unknown.

⓫ **River Bend,** Jinny Beyer, Jinny Beyer Studio design, 2007.

⓬ **Casino,** Jinny Beyer, RJR Patterns, 1995.

1 **Pontiac Star,** Clara Stone, *Practical Needlework,* ca. 1906.

2 **Arrowheads,** Nancy Cabot, *Chicago Tribune,* Sep 30, 1937. See 114-8 and 162-12.

3 **Wheel of Fortune,** *Quilt Book, Collection 1* ca. 1965.

4 **State of Ohio,** Hall, 1935.

5 **Birch Basket,** Jinny Beyer, Quilter's Quest design, 2006.

6 **Autumn Tints,** *Hall,* 1935.

7 **Manor House,** Jinny Beyer, RJR Patterns, 2007.

8 **North Carolina Star,** Nancy Cabot, *Chicago Tribune,* Dec 21, 1933.
"Today's design is one of the loveliest of all the variations of the star pattern. It is the authentic state star pattern of North Carolina and, of course, quite old." Nancy Cabot, *Chicago Tribune,* Dec 21, 1933

9 **Highland Trail,** Jinny Beyer, Beyer, Jinny, *Patchwork Portfolio,* 1989.

1 28 x 28 grid

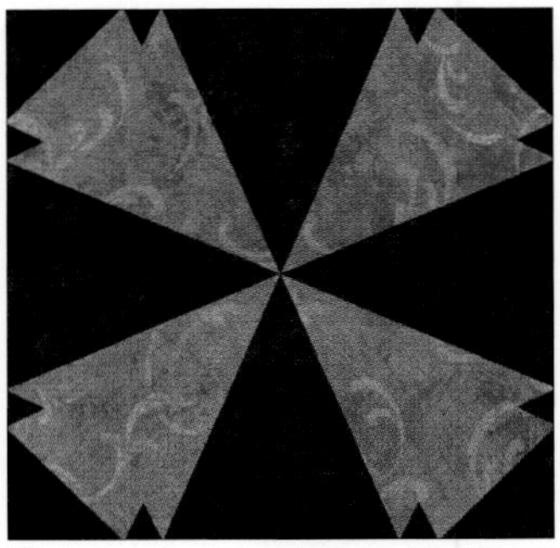

2 28 x 28 grid

3 28 x 28 grid

4 28 x 28 grid

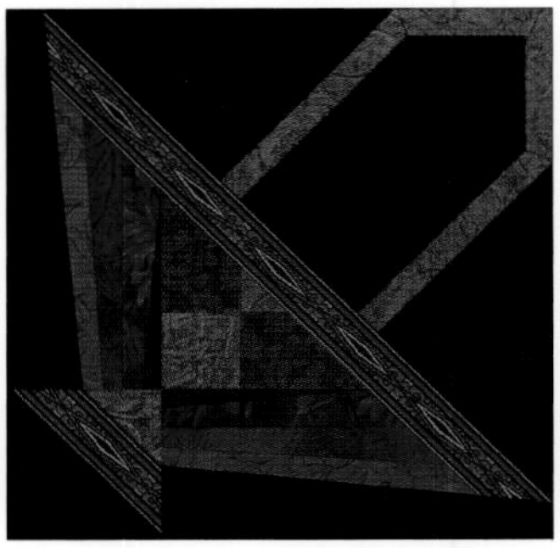

5 28 x 28 grid

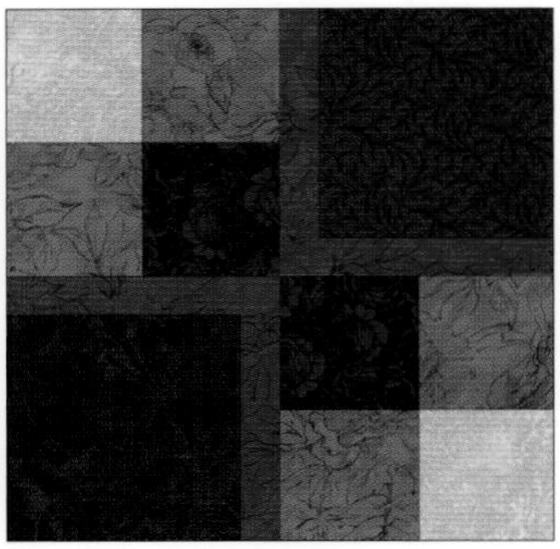

6 28 x 28 grid

7 56 x 56 grid

8 56 x 56 grid

9 56 x 56 grid

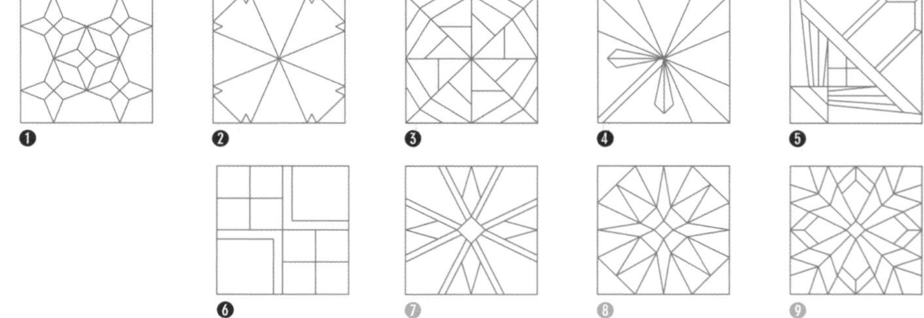

Quick Reference: T Blocks

While searching my data base for blocks depicting letters, I was surprised to find 28 T blocks and more than 42 names associated with them—that is more than any other letter of the alphabet. Upon questioning quilters about why there are so many T blocks, some suggested that they were designed for the temperance movement and that *Capital T* has an alternate name, *Temperance T.* Others suggested that T blocks represented the Boston Tea Party, while some quilters in Tennessee and Texas thought the block might reflect the names of their states. It is possible that all of these answers apply to one or more of these blocks, but it is difficult to verify.

Of all the descriptions of blocks I have found in the newspapers and in books by Webster, Finley and Hall, none reference any of the T blocks as being part of the temperance movement. I have not seen any of the T blocks referred to as *Temperance T.* There is speculation, however, that the popularity of quilts made with a T in the late 1800s and early 1900s may be due to the fact that when people signed their names on the roll books of temperance meetings they would put a T by their name if they practiced total abstinence. (Brackman et al, *Kansas Quilts and Quilters*, p 33-34)

Several of the T blocks—*Imperial T, Tea for Four, T Blocks* and *Capital T*—look very similar after they are colored, even though there are differences in how they are drawn. The earliest date I have found for a T block so far was sent to me by Merikay Waldvogel. It is *Capital T* and appeared in *The Louisville Farm and Fireside* on February 15, 1883. This block also appeared as a full block and several partial blocks in an Album Presentation Quilt labeled, "Presented by your scholars at Sunnyside, Ohio, 1894". (Cummings, *Album Quilts of Ohio's Miami Valley)*.

The Letter T, another early block, was sent to me by Wilene Smith. It appeared in *Farm and Home* on August 1, 1883 and is very similar to *Mixed T*, which appeared in the first *Ladies Art Company* catalog in 1897.

As for the Boston Tea Party, I found only two T blocks named for "tea"— *Tea Time* and *Tea for Four.* These names suggest an afternoon ritual rather than a violent event.

Some could have been named for the states, such as *Texas Cheers.* When *T Quartette* appeared in a Nancy Cabot column, the following blurb accompanied the design:

"T Quartette made its bow to the quilt world fifteen years ago in the hills of Tennessee. It is an unusual treatment of pieced blocks that is quite unintentionally modern. A clear Dutch blue and white formed the color scheme used in the original coverlet." Nancy Cabot, *Chicago Tribune*, Jul 17, 1934

T blocks may also be popular because there are so many surnames that begin with T. Two of the blocks shown here, *T Square 1* and *T Square 2,* were designed by Holice Turnbow for his last name.

Imperial T, *Ladies Art Company.* **See 264-9.**

Tea for Four, *Birmingham News.* **See 139-8.**

T Blocks, Finley. **See 140-7.**

Capital T, *Farm and Fireside.* **See 139-7.**

Boxed T's, *Ladies Art Company.* **See 166-8.**

T Square, *Practical Needlework.* **See 90-5.**

T Block, *Illinois State Register.* **See 134-11.**

Twenty Tees, *Birmingham News.* **See 159-10.**

T Square #1, *The Quilter's Album.* **See 230-8.**

T Square #2, *The Quilter's Album.* **See 230-9.**

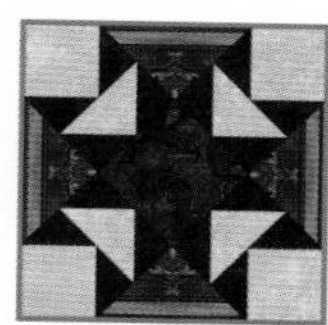
Double T, *Kansas City Star.* **See 78-7.**

9 Patch 'T', *Mrs. Danner's Quilt Presents Book Seven.* **See 244-8.**

Turnabout T, *Kansas City Star.* **See 270-4.**

Texas Cheers, *Birmingham News.* **See 199-6.**

Double T, *The Farm Journal Quilt Patterns.* **See 166-9.**

T Quilt, *Farm and Home.* **See 184-3.**

T Block, Hall. **See 248-12.**

T Quilt, *Ladies Art Company.* **See 119-2.**

The Big T Quilt, *Grandmother Clark's Patchwork Designs.* **See 119-3.**

The Letter T, *Waldvogel.* **See 192-3.**

T Quilt, *Farm and Home.* **See 72-6.**

T Quartette, *Ladies Art Company.* **See 151-5.**

T Quartette, *Chicago Tribune.* **See 151-4.**

The 'T' Quilt Pattern, *Kansas City Star.* **See 72-7.**

The Letter T, *Farm and Home,.* **See 151-3.**

Mixed T, *Ladies Art Company.* **See 151-2.**

T, *Ladies Art Company.* **See 235-7.**

Tea Time, *Chicago Tribune.* **See 266-5.**

9 x 9 Base Grid Category

Includes ● 9 x 9, ● 18 x 18, and ● 36 x 36 grids

❶ **Kitten in the Corner,** Nancy Cabot, *Chicago Tribune,* Jun 25, 1934. Also known as:
- **Kitty Corner,** Hall, 1935.
- **Puss in the Corner,** Hall, 1935.
- **Tic Tac Toe,** Hall, 1935.

❷ **Puss in Corner,** Nancy Cabot, *Chicago Tribune,* Dec 20, 1937.

❸ **The Mountain Peak,** *Kansas City Star,* Jul 7, 1943.

❹ **Granny's Choice,** *Kansas City Star,* Dec 29, 1948.

❺ **Double Nine Patch,** Ruby McKim, *Kansas City Star,* Feb 16, 1929.

❻ **Bradford 9-Patch,** Nancy Page, *Birmingham News,* Jul 1, 1941.

❼ **Five Patch,** *Ladies Art Company,* 1897. Also known as:
- **New Nine-Patch,** Jinny Beyer, Beyer, Jinny, *The Quilter's Album . . .,* 1980.
- **Puss in the Corner,** Gutcheon, *The Perfect Patchwork Primer,* 1973.

❽ **Double Nine Patch,** Webster, 1915. Also known as:
- **Golden Steps,** *Museum Quilts,* date unknown.
- **Green Springs,** Nancy Page, *Birmingham News,* Mar 19, 1935.
- **Nine Patch Variation,** *Early American Quilts,* date unknown.

❾ **Child's Crib Quilt,** Nancy Page, *Birmingham News,* May 6, 1941.

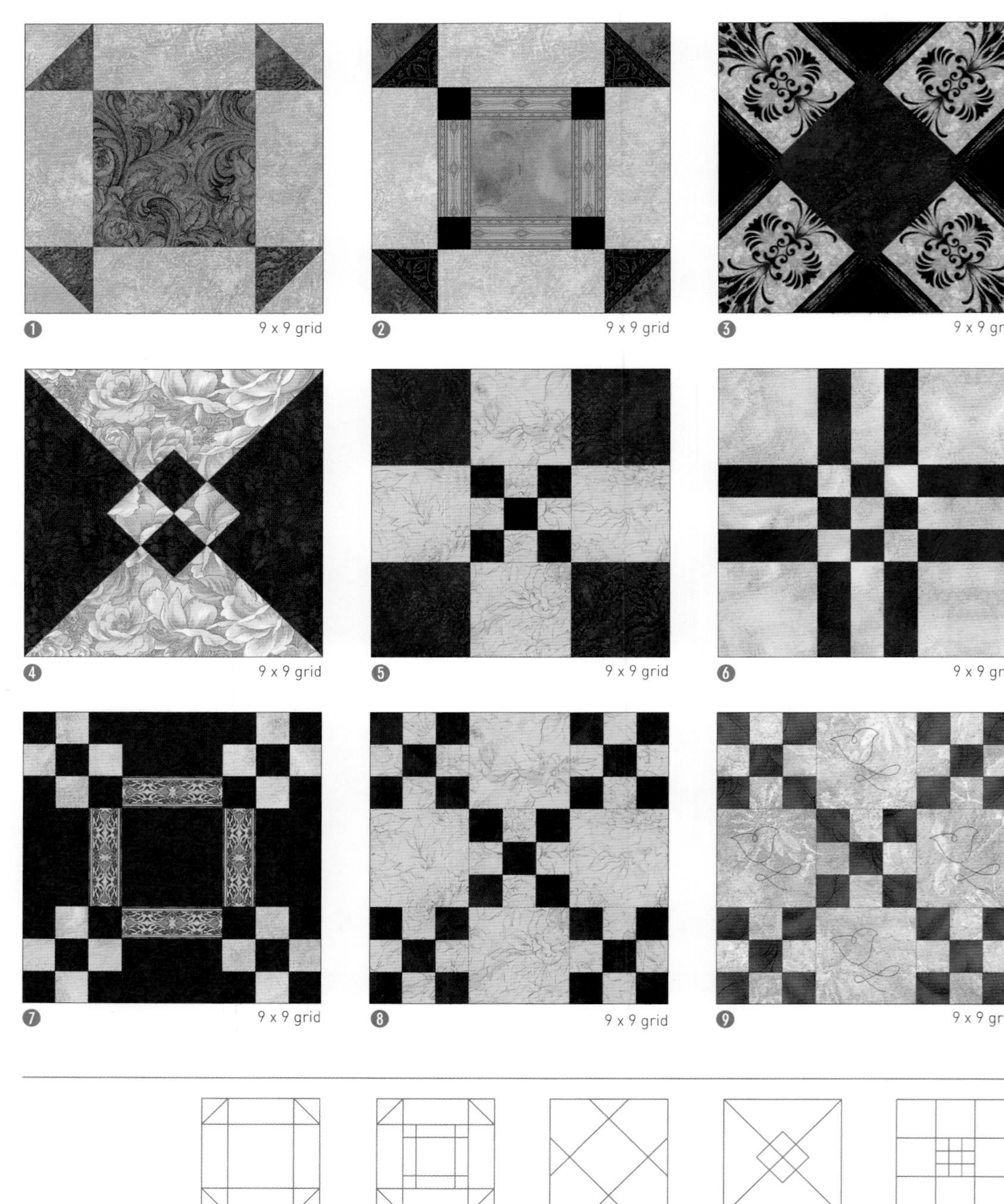

❶ ❷ ❸ ❹ ❺

❻ ❼ ❽ ❾

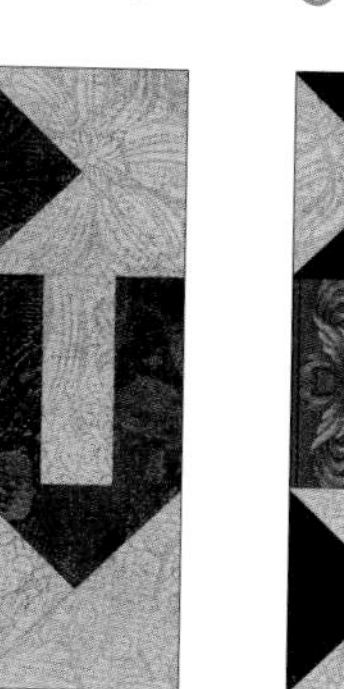

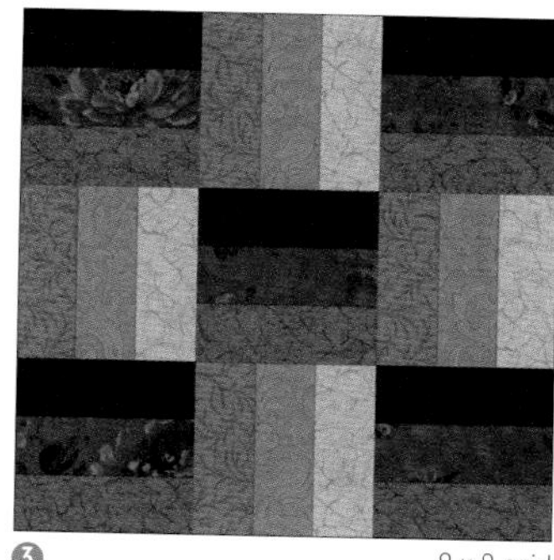
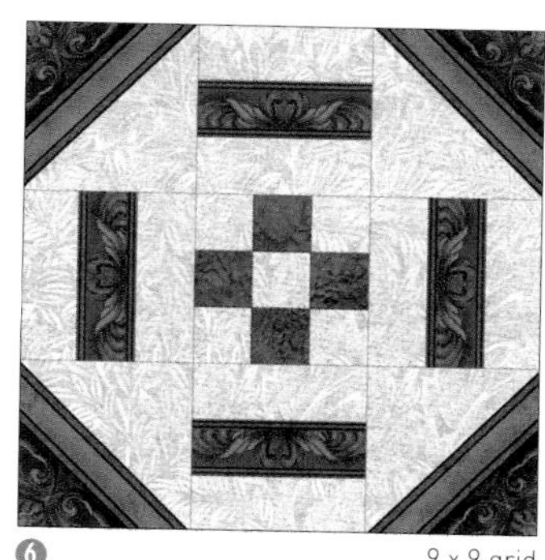

1 9 x 9 grid

2 9 x 9 grid

3 9 x 9 grid

4 9 x 9 grid

5 9 x 9 grid

6 9 x 9 grid

7 9 x 9 grid

8 9 x 9 grid

9 9 x 9 grid

10 9 x 9 grid

11 9 x 9 grid

12 9 x 9 grid

1 **Nine Patch Chain,** Gutcheon, *The Perfect Patchwork Primer,* 1973.

2 **Beggar's Blocks,** Finley, 1929. Also known as:
- Cats and Mice, Finley, 1929.

3 **The Roman Stripe,** *Kansas City Star,* Dec 21, 1955.

4 **Independence Square,** Nancy Cabot, *Chicago Tribune,* Jun 10, 1938.

5 **Attic Window,** Nancy Page, *Nashville Banner,* Jun 27, 1933. Also known as:
- Crow's Nest, *Kansas City Star,* Nov 25, 1933.

6 **New Waterwheel,** Nancy Cabot, *Chicago Tribune,* Apr 8, 1938.

7 **Mosaic No. 8,** *Ladies Art Company,* 1897. Also known as:
- London Roads, Nancy Page, date unknown, per Brackman.

8 **London Roads,** *Ladies Art Company,* 1897. Also known as:
- The Arrow, *Prize Winning Designs,* ca. 1931.
- At the Square, Nancy Page, *Nashville Banner,* Jun 28, 1932.
- The Broken Dish, *Kansas City Star,* Aug 21, 1937.
- Fireside Visitor, Clara Stone, *Practical Needlework,* ca. 1906.
- The Rope and Anchor, *Kansas City Star,* May 11, 1960.

9 **Friendship Quilt,** *Kansas City Star,* Oct 27, 1934.
"Here is another version of the Album quilt which is again popular as those made a generation ago." *Kansas City Star,* Oct 27, 1934

10 **Chain and Hourglass,** Nancy Page, *Birmingham News,* Apr 24, 1934.

11 **Path and Stiles,** Nancy Cabot, *Chicago Tribune,* Apr 17, 1937. Also known as:
- Far West, *Progressive Farmer,* date unknown.

12 **Hand Weave,** *Ladies Art Company,* 1928. Also known as:
- City Streets, Nancy Cabot, *Chicago Tribune,* Dec 21, 1937.
- Handcraft, Nancy Cabot, *Chicago Tribune,* Oct 24, 1934.
- Interwoven, Nancy Page, *Birmingham News,* Feb 8, 1939.
- Over and Under, Nancy Page, *Detroit Free Press,* Jan 30, 1934.

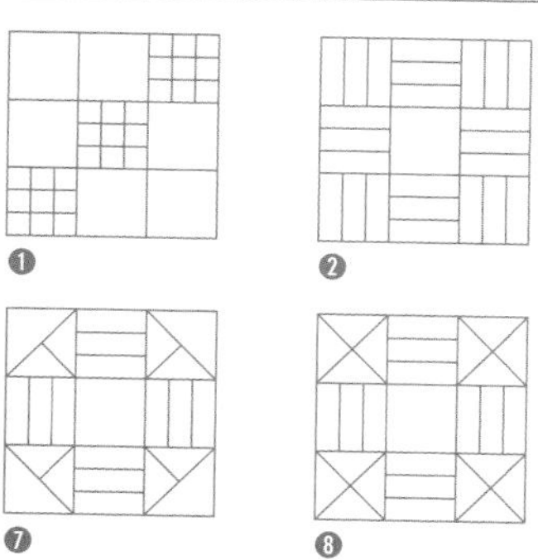
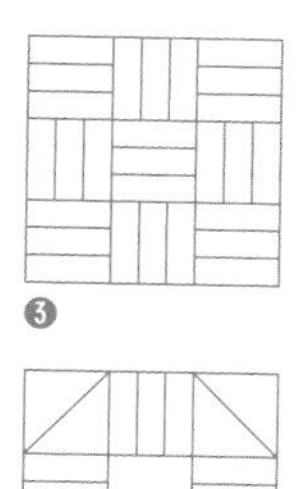
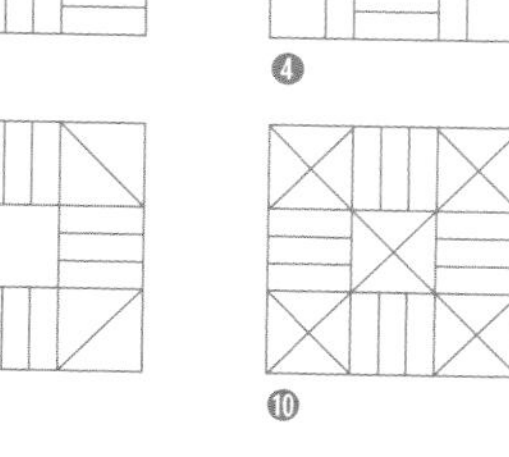
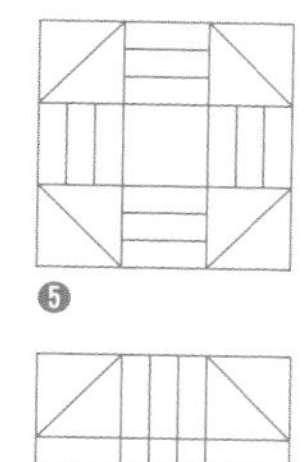
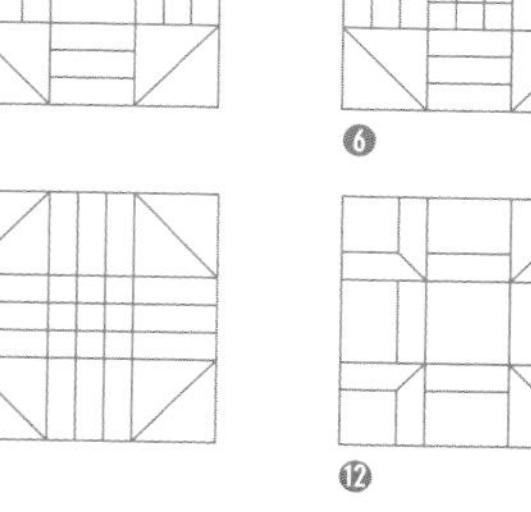

1 2 3 4 5 6

7 8 9 10 11 12

❶ **Beggar Blocks,** *Ladies Art Company,* 1897. Also known as:

- **Beggar Block,** Ruby McKim, *Kansas City Star,* Mar 30, 1929.
- **Beggar's Block,** Nancy Cabot, *Chicago Tribune,* Jun 30, 1933.
- **Cats and Mice,** Jane Alan, *Illinois State Register,* Jun 4, 1933.
- **Homespun,** Nancy Page, *Birmingham News,* Jun 13, 1939.
- **Over and Under Quilt,** Nancy Page, *Detroit Free Press,* Jan 30, 1934.
- **Spool and Bobbin,** Nancy Cabot, *Chicago Tribune,* Dec 9, 1936.
- **Spools and Bobbins,** Nancy Cabot, *Chicago Tribune,* Dec 9, 1936.

"This interesting block harks back to the neighborly custom of begging one's friends for scraps of their frocks, or for the men's old neckties to put into a quilt." McKim, 1931

❷ **Beggar's Blocks,** Nancy Page, *Birmingham News,* Aug 7, 1934. Also known as:

- **Beggar's Choice,** Nancy Page, *Birmingham News,* Aug 7, 1934.
- **Under and Over,** Nancy Page, *Birmingham News,* Dec 30, 1941.

❸ **Mollie's Choice,** *Ladies Art Company,* 1897.

"Since housekeeping was the goal of every girl's ambition in the good old days, her 'setting out' was planned several years before an eligible young man appeared. However, the original of this block bears the name of the young woman who designed and made this for her first pieced quilt." Nancy Cabot, *Chicago Tribune,* Apr 25, 1934

❹ **Mona's Choice,** *Kansas City Star,* Jun 5, 1940.

❺ **Tangled Garter,** *Ladies Art Company,* 1897. See 167-7, 173-9, 258-8, and 274-4. Also known as:

- **Crossroads,** Nancy Page, *Birmingham News,* Jun 25, 1935.
- **Queen of May,** Clara Stone, *Practical Needlework,* ca. 1906.

❻ **Village Green,** Nancy Page, *Birmingham News,* Jun 6, 1939.

❼ **Garden Paths,** Nancy Page, *Birmingham News,* Mar 10, 1936.

❽ **Cross Patch,** Aunt Martha series: *Patchwork Simplicity,* ca. 1977.

❾ **Five Crosses,** Jane Alan, *Illinois State Register,* Jan 15, 1933.

❿ **Dublin Chain,** Nancy Cabot, *Chicago Tribune,* Jun 14, 1938. Also known as:

- **Dublin Square,** Nancy Cabot, *Chicago Tribune,* Jun 14, 1938.
- **Rocky Road to Dublin,** Nancy Cabot, *Chicago Tribune,* Jun 14, 1938.

⓫ **Amethyst Chains,** Nancy Cabot, *Chicago Tribune,* Apr 17, 1936.

⓬ **Meeting House Square,** Nancy Cabot, *Chicago Tribune,* Dec 31, 1935.

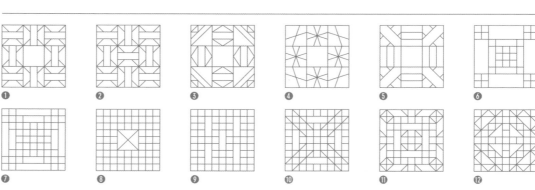

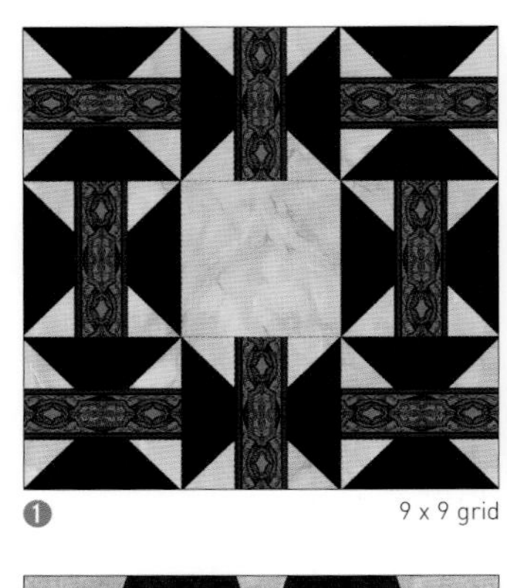
❶ 9 x 9 grid

❷ 9 x 9 grid

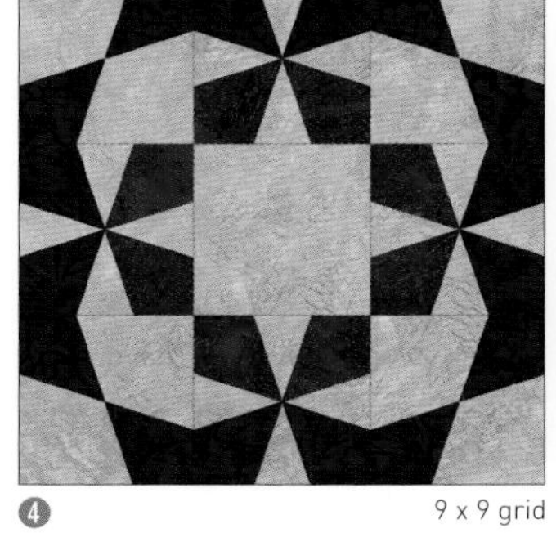
❸ 9 x 9 grid

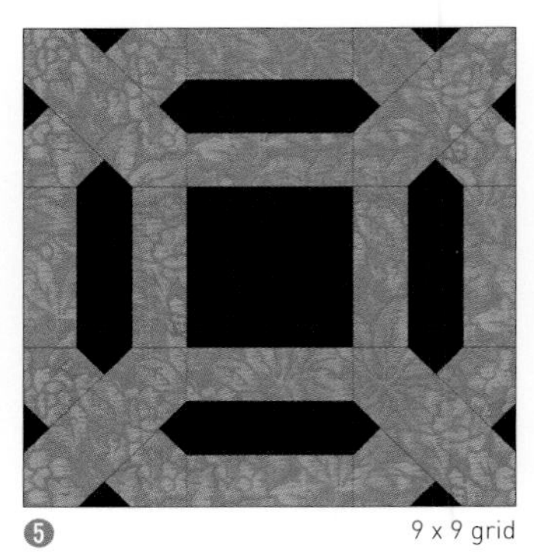
❹ 9 x 9 grid

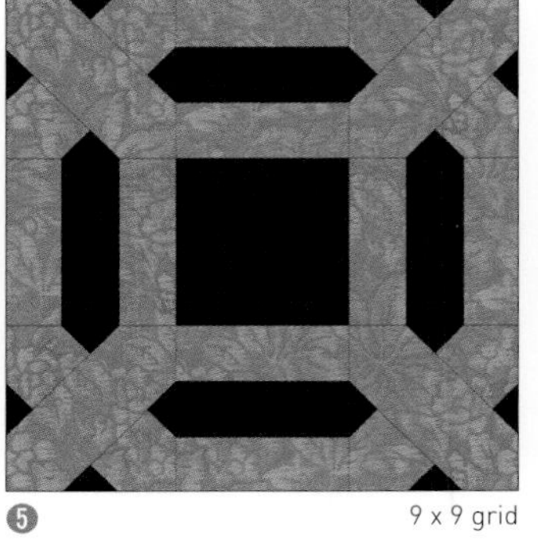
❺ 9 x 9 grid

❻ 9 x 9 grid

❼ 9 x 9 grid

❽ 9 x 9 grid

❾ 9 x 9 grid

❿ 9 x 9 grid

⓫ 9 x 9 grid

⓬ 9 x 9 grid

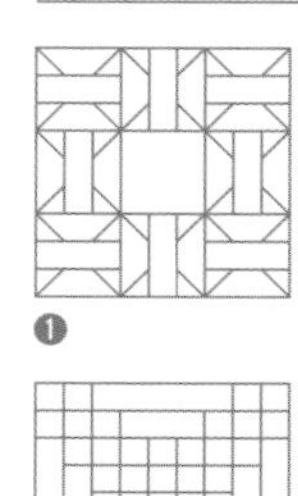
❶

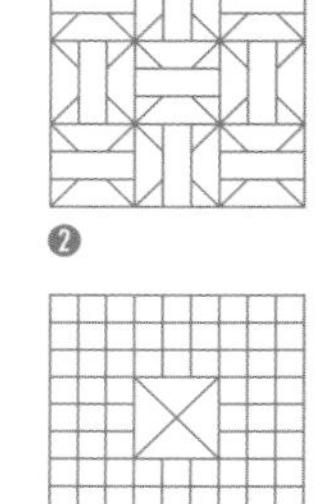
❷

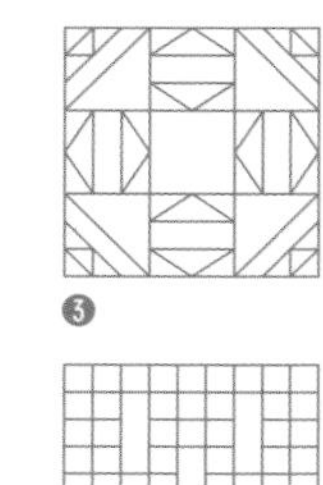
❸

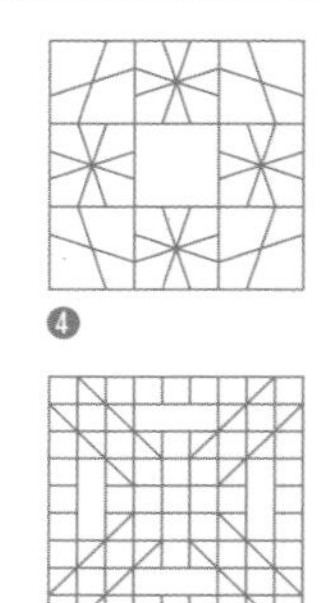
❹

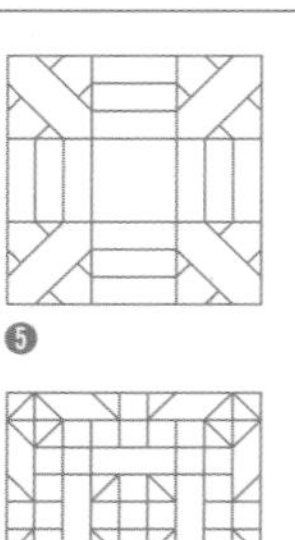
❺

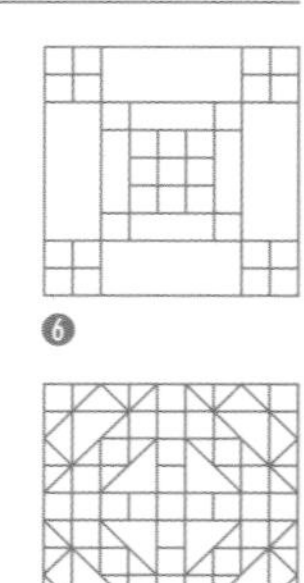
❻

❼ ❽ ❾ ❿ ⓫ ⓬

❶ **Medieval Mosaic,** Nancy Cabot, *Chicago Tribune,* Mar 30, 1936. Also known as:
Medieval Walls, Nancy Cabot, *Chicago Tribune,* Mar 30, 1936.

❷ **Field of Stars,** Nancy Page, *Birmingham News,* Sep 23, 1941.

❸ **Scotch Heather,** Nancy Cabot, *Chicago Tribune,* Apr 24, 1936.

❹ **Garden of Eden,** Nancy Cabot, *Chicago Tribune,* Dec 20, 1933. See 183-2 and 183-3.

❺ **The Seasons,** Nancy Cabot, *Chicago Tribune,* Mar 7, 1938.

❻ **Premium Star,** Hall, 1935. See 85-10, 193-12, 223-9, 223-10, 223-11 and 262-7.

❼ **Cross and Star,** Clara Stone, *Practical Needlework,* ca. 1906.

❽ **Far West,** Nancy Cabot, *Chicago Tribune,* Mar 31, 1937.

❾ **Bear's Paw,** Martens, 1970.

❿ **Four Clowns,** Nancy Cabot, *Chicago Tribune,* Nov 16, 1937.

⓫ **Diamond Plaid Block,** Nancy Cabot, *Chicago Tribune,* Apr 20, 1936.

⓬ **String Quilt,** Jane Alan, *Commercial News,* Jan 28, 1932.
"Women of fifty and seventy-five years ago looked in the scrapbag to furnish quilt material, so that fact accounts for the dozens of old patterns which are designed with the idea of using a big variety of goods. String quilt pattern, published today, is of such origin. There is a quaint charm about a quilt made from many kinds of material so if you do have any scraps from other quilts or from summer dresses, I suggest you use them." Jane Alan, *Commercial News,* Jan 28, 1932

❶ **The Prosperity Block,** *Quilt Booklet No. 1,* 1922. See 295-1 and 295-2.

❷ **Miss Jackson,** *Ladies Art Company,* 1922. See 295-1 and 295-2. Also known as:
- **Empty Spools,** Nancy Page, *Birmingham News,* Jun 15, 1937.
- **Walled Garden,** Nancy Page, *Birmingham News,* Sep 21, 1943.

❸ **New Star in the Heavens,** Laura Wheeler, unidentified newspaper clipping, date unknown.

❹ **Dolley Madison's Star,** *Q Book 124, White House Quilts,* date unknown.

❺ **Blazing Arrow Point,** Clara Stone, *Practical Needlework,* ca. 1906.

❻ **Jeffrey's Nine Patch,** Gutcheon, *The Perfect Patchwork Primer,* 1973.

❼ **Rustic Wheel,** Nancy Cabot, *Chicago Tribune,* Jul 2, 1936.
"From the delightfully historical state of Virginia comes an old and complicated pieced quilt pattern. From the illustration of the single block it readily may be seen that the pattern was adapted from woodwork made of limbs and roots of trees and arranged in a wheel design." Nancy Cabot, *Chicago Tribune,* Jul 2, 1936

❽ **9 Patch T,** *Mrs Danner Presents Quilt Book 7,* 1975.

❾ **Aquarius,** Jinny Beyer, Hilton Head Seminar design, 2000.

❿ **Four H Quilt,** Nancy Page, *Birmingham News,* Dec 28, 1937.
"I knew a number of girls who are enthusiastic members of the 4-H clubs and I thought it would be nice to give them a quilt all their own. So here I am with a 4-H pattern. It's easy to make, nothing but straight lines. And the colors used are only two. Those colors May vary with the color in the girl's room." Nancy Page, *Birmingham News,* Nov 30, 1937

⓫ **Turkey Tracks,** *Ladies Art Company,* 1897. See 266-4. Also known as:
- **Resolutions,** Nancy Page, *Birmingham News,* Jan 1, 1935.

⓬ **Adaptation of The Chimney Sweep,** *Quilts,* 1945.

❶ 9 x 9 grid ❷ 9 x 9 grid ❹ 9 x 9 grid ❺ 9 x 9 grid

❸ 9 x 9 grid

❻ 9 x 9 grid

❼ 9 x 9 grid

❽ 9 x 9 grid

❾ 9 x 9 grid

❿ 9 x 9 grid

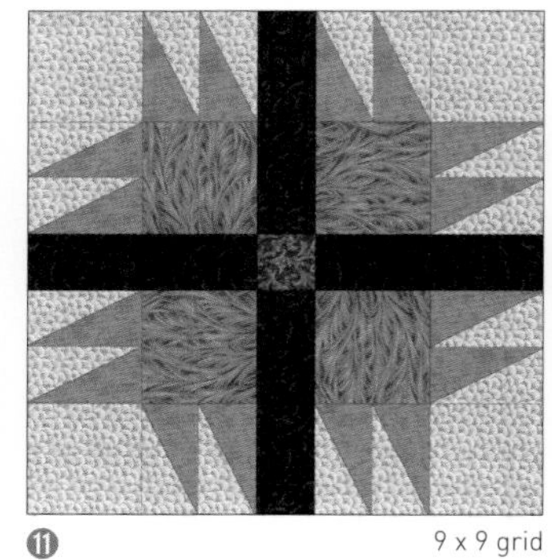

⓫ 9 x 9 grid

⓬ 9 x 9 grid

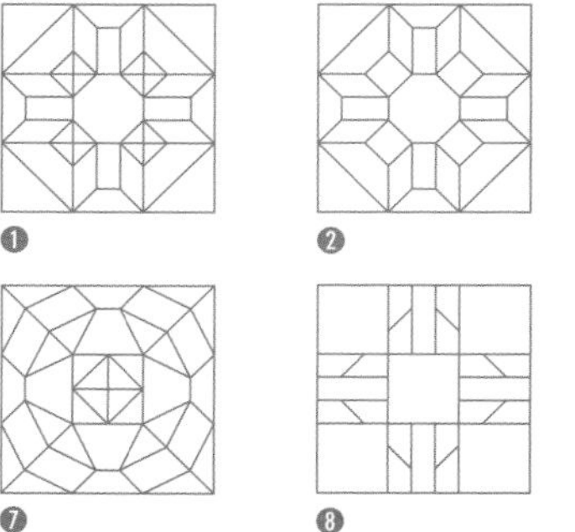

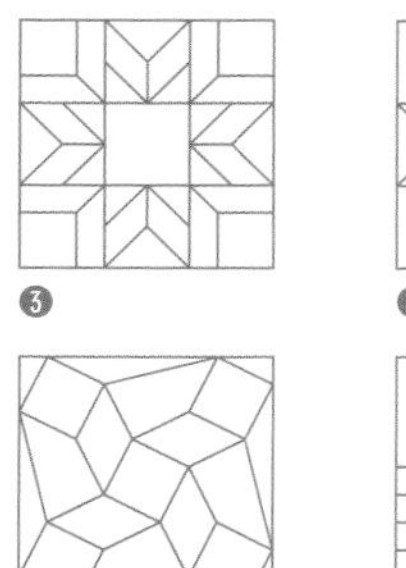

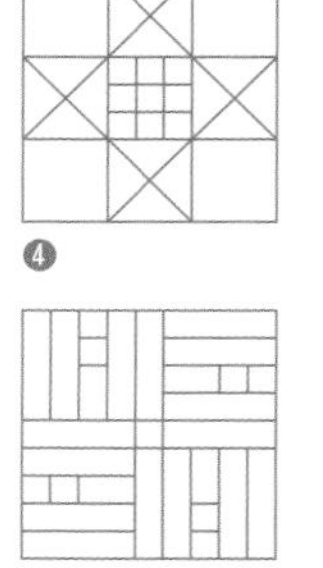

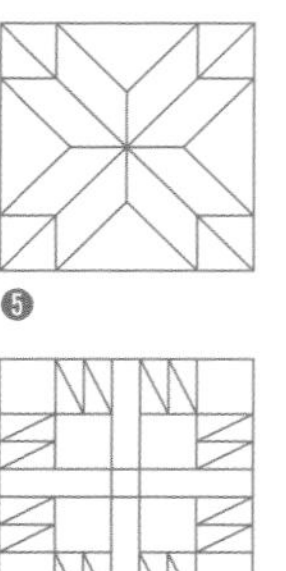

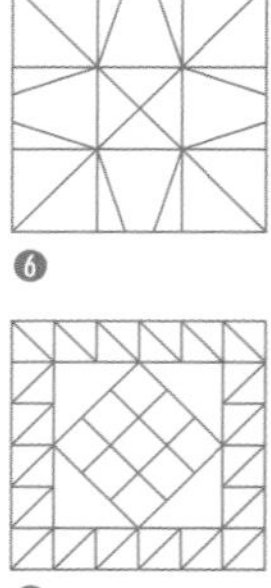

❶ ❷ ❸ ❹ ❺ ❻ ❼ ❽ ❾ ❿ ⓫ ⓬

1. **The Cross Patch,** *Kansas City Star,* Nov 16, 1955. See 72-1.
2. **The Spool Quilt,** *Kansas City Star,* Mar 13, 1937.
3. **Odds and Ends,** *Ladies Art Company,* 1897.
4. **Double Hour Glass,** *Prize Winning Designs,* ca. 1931.
5. **Floral Centerpiece,** Nancy Cabot, *Chicago Tribune,* Mar 15, 1936.
6. **Trumpet Vine,** McKim, 1931. Also known as:
   Modernistic Trumpet Vine, Hall, 1935.
7. **Pine Tree,** Nancy Cabot, *Chicago Tribune,* May 10, 1937.
8. **Independence Square,** *Q Book 121, Bicentennial Quilts,* date unknown.
9. **Sumatra,** Jinny Beyer, RJR Patterns, 1999.
10. **Butterfly,** Eveline Foland, *Kansas City Star,* Oct 17, 1931.
11. **Dresden Rose,** Aunt Martha series: *The Quilt Fair Comes to You,* ca. 1933.
12. **Log Cabin Straight Furrow,** ca. 1925, per Holstein.

❶ **Barn Raising,** Finley, 1929. Also known as:
  Log Cabin, Hall, 1935.

❷ **Border Block,** Alice Brooks, *Detroit Free Press,* Mar 18, 1934.
This is the border of Alice Brooks' serial quilt, Bowl of Flowers

❸ **White House Steps,** *Ladies Art Company,* 1897.

❹ **Swastika Patch,** *Ladies Art Company,* 1922. Also known as:
  The Battle Ax of Thor, Hall, 1935.
  Catch Me if You Can, Hall, 1935.
  Chinese 10,000 Perfections, Hall, 1935.
  Favorite of the Peruvians, Hall, 1935.
  Heart's Seal, Hall, 1935.
  Mound Builders, Hall, 1935.
  Swastika, Hall, 1935.
  The Pure Symbol of Right Doctrine, Hall, 1935.
  Wind Power of the Osages, Hall, 1935.

❺ **Double Windmill,** Alice Brooks, *Detroit Free Press,* Mar 25, 1934.
"'Windmills'—in the days of the early settlers they were a common part of the landscape. Today most of us are only familiar with them in pictures and in quilts. And though you must say they're just triangles, they do look like a windmill, a most popular quilt motif. Here is a double one—a big one of scraps and a small one inside of it. Though the same scraps are shown repeated throughout, it's a very effective quilt if they are just sewn on higgeldy-piggeldy. It's best to make the small windmill of the same material throughout—it seems to hold all the other gay colors together most harmoniously." Alice Brooks, *Detroit Free Press,* Mar 25, 1934

❻ **Nine Patch,** Hall, 1935.

❼ **The Coverlet,** *Prize Winning Designs,* ca. 1931.

❽ **1941 Nine Patch,** *Kansas City Star,* Sep 17, 1941.

❾ **Klondike Star,** *Practical Needlework,* ca. 1906.

❿ **Peaceful Hours,** *Farm Journal and Farmer's Wife* (Silver Anniversary issue), 1945.

⓫ **Distant Star,** Jinny Beyer, Hilton Head Seminar design, 2001.

⓬ **Morning Star,** *Ladies Art Company,* 1897. Also known as:
  Virginia, *Hearth and Home,* 1897, per Brackman.
"This is block 5 of the Star of Many Points Quilt Series by Nancy Page." *The Lowell Sun,* Jun 18, 1934

❶ **Rosebud,** Nancy Cabot, *Chicago Tribune,* Aug 27, 1934.

❷ **Chicago Star,** Hall, 1935.

❸ **Penny Lane,** Jinny Beyer, Beyer, Jinny, *Patchwork Portfolio,* 1989.

❹ **Joseph's Coat,** Finley, 1929. Also known as:
  Scrapbag, Finley, 1929.

❺ **Goose Creek,** Nancy Page, *Birmingham News,* Nov 2, 1937.

❻ **Mrs. Dewey's Choice,** Clara Stone, *Practical Needlework,* ca. 1906. Also known as:
  Widow's Mite, ca. 1938, per Havig.

❼ **Blockhouse,** Nancy Cabot, *Chicago Tribune,* Dec 22, 1936.

❽ **Peekaboo,** *The Patchwork Book,* 1932.

❾ **Polly's Puzzle,** Jinny Beyer, Jinny Beyer Studio design, 2009.

❿ **Mother's Dream,** *Prize Winning Designs,* ca. 1931. Also known as:
  Turkey in the Straw, *Farm Journal and Farmer's Wife* (Silver Anniversary issue), 1945.

⓫ **Columbian Puzzle,** Clara Stone, *Practical Needlework,* ca. 1906.

⓬ **Many Roads to the White House,** *Kansas City Star,* Aug 17, 1955.

❶ **Sonnie's Play House,** *Kansas City Star,* Jul 10, 1935.

❷ **Thousand Islands,** Nancy Cabot, *Chicago Tribune,* Apr 9, 1938.

❸ **Star of Many Points,** Nancy Cabot, *Chicago Tribune,* Jul 4, 1933.

❹ **Star Struck,** Jinny Beyer, Beyer, Jinny, *Patchwork Portfolio,* 1989.

❺ **Grandma's Scrap Quilt,** Laura Wheeler, *Sioux City Journal,* Sep 21, 1940. Also known as:

  Grandma's Scraps, Kate Marchbanks, *Capper's Weekly,* date unknown.

❻ **Farmer's Fields,** *Kansas City Star,* Apr 5, 1939.

❼ **Blue Diamond,** *Detroit Free Press,* Mar 5, 1933.

❽ **Checkered Star,** Laura Wheeler, *Cincinnati Enquirer,* Jan 16, 1934.

❾ **Golden Gates,** *Ladies Art Company,* 1897. Also known as:

  Golden Gate, *Old Fashioned Quilts,* ca. 1932.

  Winged Square, *Old Fashioned Quilts,* ca. 1932.

❿ **An Odd Patchwork,** Nancy Cabot, *Chicago Tribune,* Dec 23, 1934.

⓫ **The North Star,** *Kansas City Star,* May 14, 1938.

⓬ **T Block,** Hall, 1935.

1. **4 H Block,** Aunt Martha series: *The Quilt Fair Comes to You,* ca. 1933.
2. **Sergeant's Chevron,** *Farm Journal and Farmer's Wife* (Silver Anniversary issue), 1945.
3. **World's Fair,** *Farmer's Wife Book of New Designs and Patterns,* 1934.
4. **Checkerboards,** Nancy Page, *Birmingham News,* Jun 11, 1935.
5. **The Pine Tree,** Finley, 1929.
6. **Pine Tree Quilt,** Home Art Studios, *Cincinnati Enquirer,* Feb 28, 1933.
7. **Tree of Life,** *Mrs. Danner's Fourth Quilt Book,* 1958.
8. **Tree of Life,** Ickis, 1949.
9. **Mrs. Cleveland's Choice,** *Ladies Art Company,* 1897. See 175-12. Also known as:
   - **County Fair,** Hall, 1935.
   - **Square within Square,** *Kansas City Star,* May 13, 1933.
10. **Four Patch,** Alice Brooks, unidentified newspaper clipping, date unknown. Also known as:
    - **Friendship,** Laura Wheeler, unidentified newspaper clipping, date unknown.
11. **W.C.T. Union,** *Ladies Art Company,* 1897. Also known as:
    - **Celestial Problem,** Nancy Cabot, *Chicago Tribune,* May 4, 1935.
    - **W. C. T. U. Patch,** Hall, 1935.
12. **A Patchwork Cushion Top,** *Kansas City Star,* Dec 8, 1943.

❶ **The Basket,** *Kansas City Star,* Apr 16, 1938.

❷ **Nosegay,** Alice Brooks, *Detroit Free Press,* Aug 22, 1935.

❸ **Fluttering Butterfly,** Home Art Studios, *Cincinnati Enquirer,* May 3, 1933.

❹ **Big and Little Spools,** Nancy Page, *Birmingham News,* Oct 27, 1942.

❺ **Triple Irish Chain,** Nancy Cabot, *Chicago Tribune,* Dec 3, 1933.

❻ **Triple Irish Chain (Large),** Nancy Page, *Birmingham News,* May 21, 1935.

❼ **Irish Chain,** Ruby McKim, *Kansas City Star,* Jan 26, 1929. Also known as:
Triple Irish Chain (Small), Nancy Page, *Birmingham News,* May 14, 1935.

❽ **House That Jack Built,** *Grandmother Clark's Patchwork Designs, Book No. 22,* 1932.

❾ **Pansy Quilt,** Home Art Studios, *Cincinnati Enquirer,* Mar 20, 1933.
"After the first few warm days have passed, bright flowers start nodding in the breeze, bringing forth the beauty of nature. You will find in the pansy quilt an ideal way of re-creating the lovely colors that mother nature uses so profusely during the spring and summer months."
World Herald, Mar 20, 1933

❿ **American Log Patchwork,** *Ladies Art Company,* 1897.

⓫ **Girl's Joy,** Hall, 1935. See 228-1.

⓬ **Test Tube,** Jinny Beyer, Beyer, Jinny, *Patchwork Portfolio,* 1989.

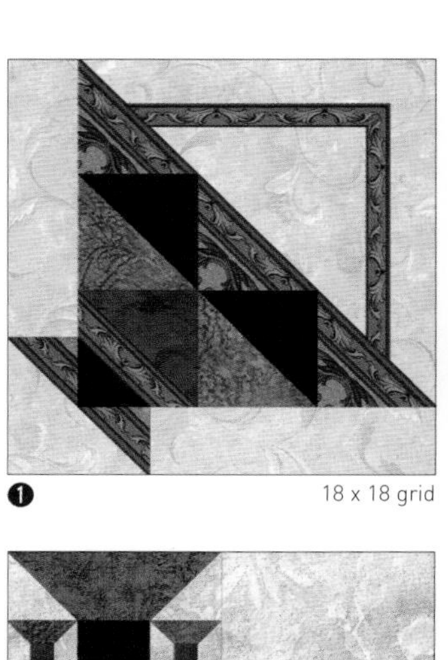

❶ 18 x 18 grid

❷ 18 x 18 grid

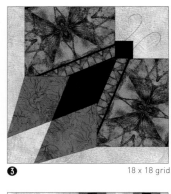

❸ 18 x 18 grid

❹ 18 x 18 grid

❺ 18 x 18 grid

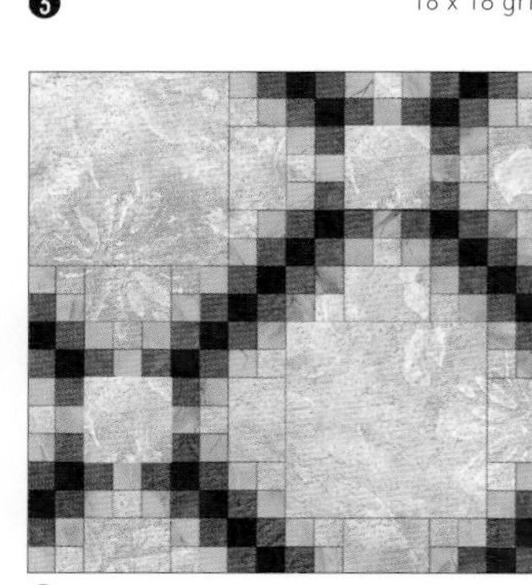

❻ 18 x 18 grid

❼ 18 x 18 grid

❽ 18 x 18 grid

❾ 18 x 18 grid

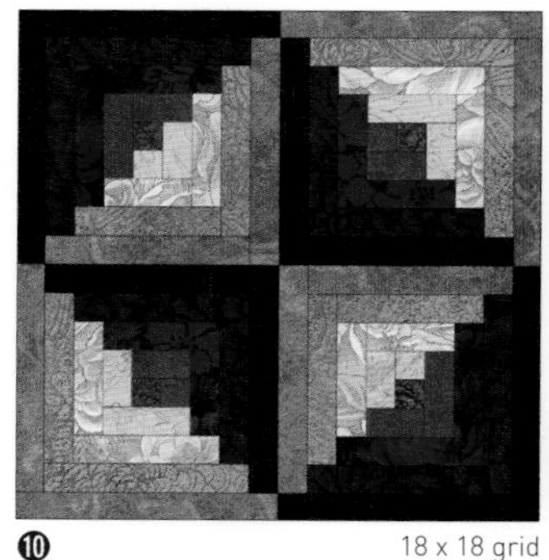

❿ 18 x 18 grid

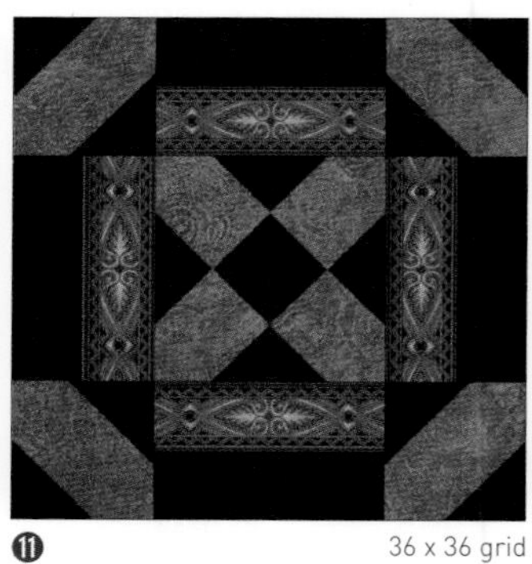

⓫ 36 x 36 grid

⓬ 36 x 36 grid

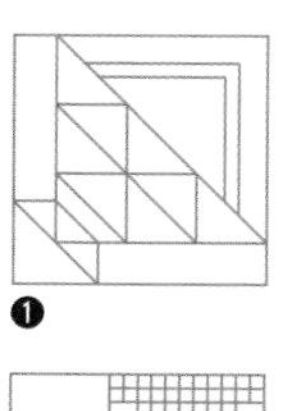

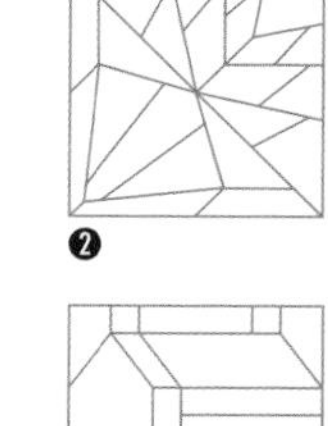

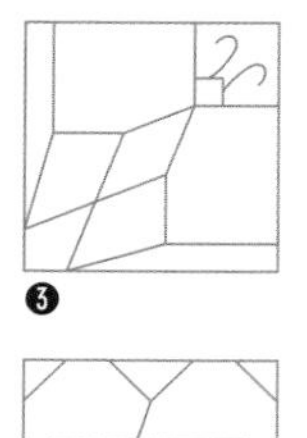

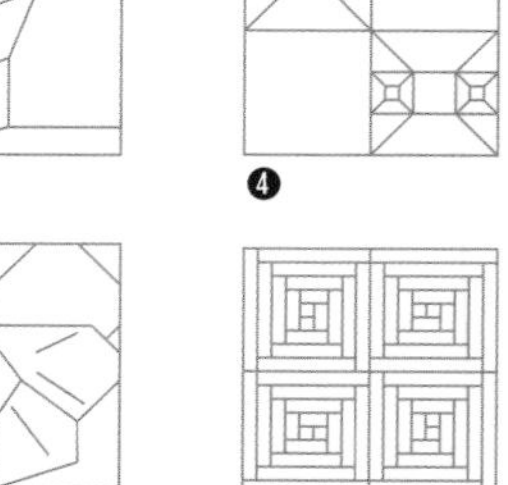

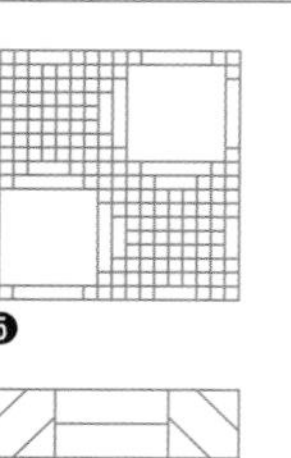

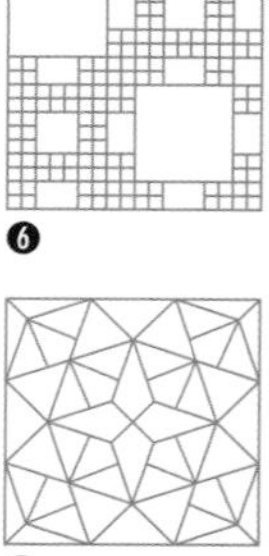

❶ ❷ ❸ ❹ ❺ ❻

❼ ❽ ❾ ❿ ⓫ ⓬

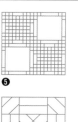

❶ **Morning Star,** Laura Wheeler, *Sioux City Journal,* Aug 5, 1939.

❷ **Chrysanthemum,** Laura Wheeler, *Cincinnati Enquirer,* Dec 12, 1933.

❸ **Santa Fe Trail,** Nancy Cabot, *Chicago Tribune,* Feb 17, 1934. Also known as:

Old Fashioned Garden, Nancy Page, *Birmingham News,* Mar 23, 1943.

"When pioneer women trekked across the country, their quilts were part and parcel of their household goods. Over the Santa Fe and Oregon trails these sturdy women pushed forward, undaunted by hardships. Their destination reached, they found utterance for the beauties of the trail in new quilt blocks made from worn calicoes." Nancy Cabot, *Chicago Tribune,* Feb 17, 1934

❹ **The Star Spangled Banner,** *Kansas City Star,* Sep 10, 1941.

❺ **Arkansas,** Nancy Page, *Birmingham News,* Jul 20, 1939.

❻ **Dolly Madison Star,** Finley, 1929. See 164-12. Also known as:

Dolly Madison's Star, Hall, 1935.

President's Block, Nancy Cabot, *Chicago Tribune,* Sep 19, 1937.

"Dolly Madison was the first 'Mistress of the White House' with social consciousness and the only one who held that title for sixteen years. The design of Virginia origin in the early nineteenth century, developed in red, white, and blue, was very appropriate, signifying the new Republic." Finley, 1929

❼ **Santa Fe Block,** *Ladies Art Company,* 1922.

❽ **Boston Star,** Nancy Page, *Birmingham News,* Mar 16, 1943.

❾ **House That Jack Built,** ca. 1938, per Havig.

❿ **The Kite,** *Kansas City Star,* Jan 2, 1937.

⓫ **The Lucy Hayes Quilt,** *Q Book 124, White House Quilts,* date unknown.

⓬ **Lily of the Field,** Hall, 1935.

❶ **Flower Vase,** Nancy Cabot, *Chicago Tribune,* Nov 6, 1936.
"From the time 'Flower Vase' first was pieced it was the favorite of virtually every quilt maker. When it was the custom to have fifteen or twenty quilts for a small family, as many as two or three quilts of this same pattern were found in one household." Nancy Cabot, *Chicago Tribune,* Nov 6, 1936

❷ **Tea Leaf,** Ickis, 1949.

❸ **Vine Block,** Nancy Cabot, *Chicago Tribune,* May 14, 1938.

❹ **Our Country,** *Kansas City Star,* Sep 10, 1941. Also known as:
Squares and Stripes, Aunt Martha series: *Bold and Beautiful Quilts,* ca. 1977.

❶ 36 x 36 grid

❷ 36 x 36 grid

❸ 36 x 36 grid

❹ 36 x 36 grid

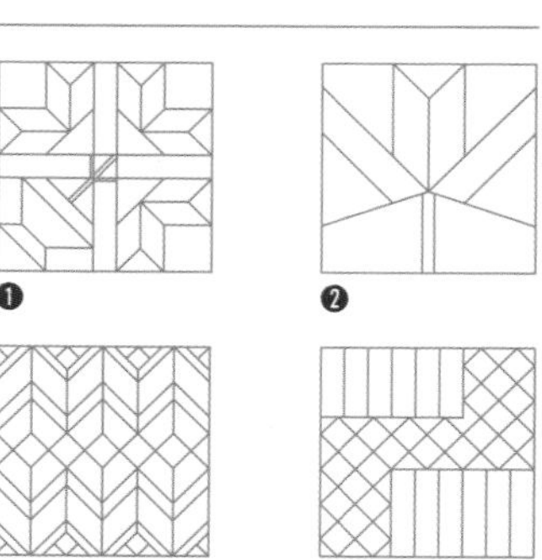
❶ ❷ ❸ ❹

Quick Reference: Houses

House blocks have long been a favorite with quilters. The ones I have found are shown here.

Village Church, *Ladies Art Company.* **See 337-2.**

Village Church, Havig. **See 439-12.**

Little Red Schoolhouse, Aunt Martha' series: *Bold and Beautiful Quilts.* **See 439-8.**

Log Cabin, *Chicago Tribune.* **See 181-11.**

KC Star Exhibition Home, Havig. **See 274-2.**

The Star's Exhibition Home Quilt Block Pattern, *Kansas City Star.* **See 181-10.**

The Little Red Schoolhouse, *Chicago Tribune.* **See 121-3.**

The Old Homestead, *Ladies Art Company.* **See 218-12.**

Little Red House, *Ladies Art Company.* **See 257-3.**

Jack's House, *Ladies Art Company.* **See 220-10.**

House That Jack Built, *Grandmother Clark's Patchwork Quilt Designs, From Books 20-21-23.* **See 250-8.**

Little Red Schoolhouse, *Birmingham News.* **See 265-9.**

Log Cabin, *The Patchwork Book.* **See 273-10.**

Early Colonial Cottage, Havig. **See 439-9.**

Log Cabin Quilt, *Ladies Art Company.* **See 439-10.**

Honeymoon Cottage, Hall. **See 439-11.**

11 x 11 Base Grid Category

Includes ● 11 x 11, ● 22 x 22, and ● 44 x 44 grids

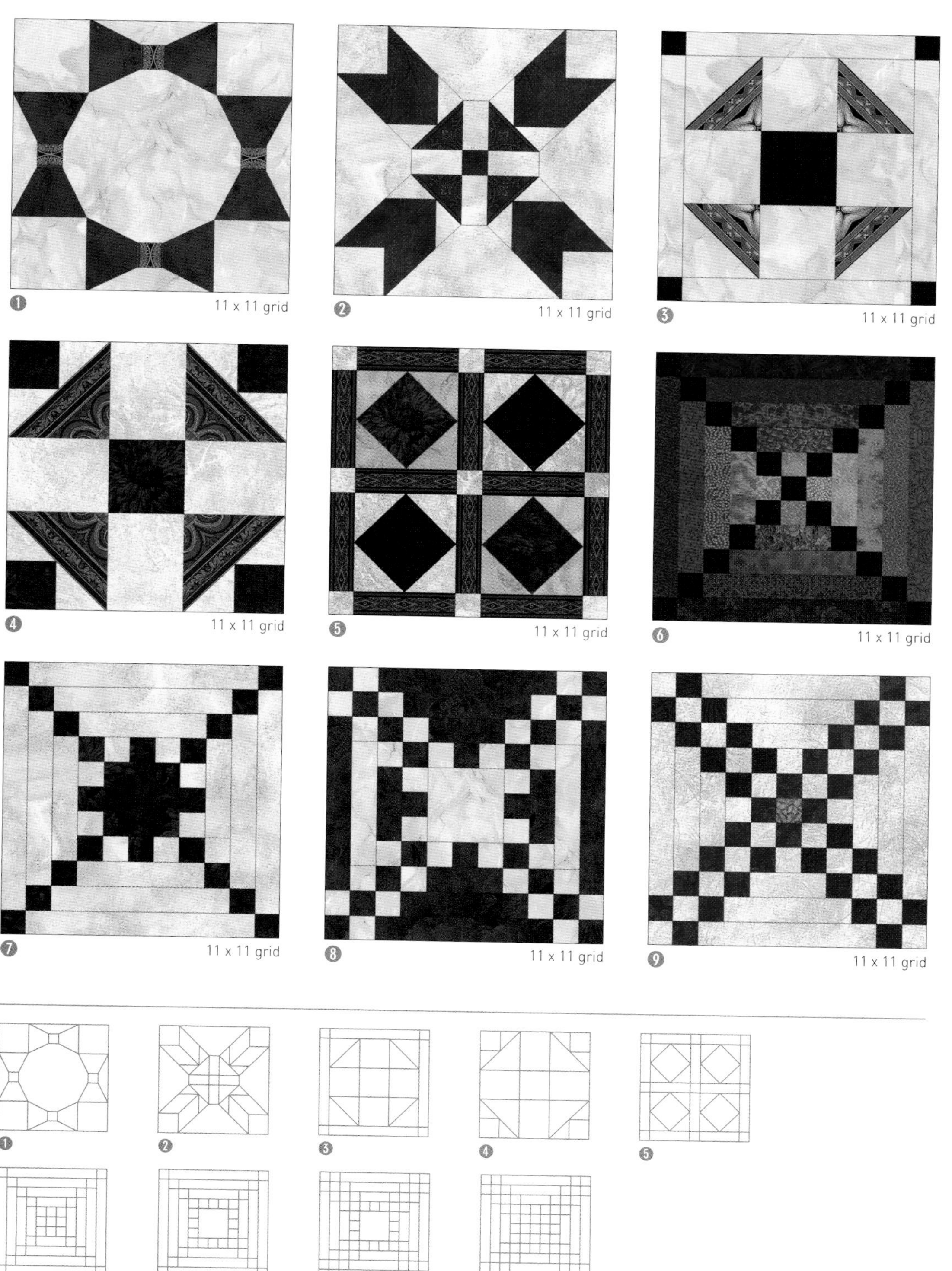

1. **Bow Tie Quilt,** Aunt Martha series: *Quilts: Modern-Colonial,* ca. 1954.
2. **Darts and Square,** *Farm Journal & Farmers Wife,* ca. 1941.
3. **Philadelphia Pavement,** Nancy Cabot, *Chicago Tribune,* Mar 7, 1933. See 84-4 and 183-1.
4. **Flower and Leaf Block,** *Farm and Home,* Feb 15, 1915.
5. **Dutch Tile,** Nancy Cabot, *Chicago Tribune,* Dec 19, 1936. See 61-2, 119-7, and 233-12.
6. **The Border Sea,** Jinny Beyer, RJR Patterns, 1999.
7. **Stepping Stones,** *The Farmer's Wife Book of New Designs and Patterns,* 1934.
8. **Steps to the Light House,** Nancy Page, *Nashville Banner,* Jan 16, 1934. Also known as:
   White House Steps, Nancy Cabot, date unknown, per Alboum and Brackman.
9. **Double Irish Chain,** *Quilts,* 1945.

❶ **Triple Irish Chain,** Hall, 1935.

❷ **Cross of Tennessee,** Nancy Cabot, *Chicago Tribune,* Jun 22, 1935. Also known as:
Tennessee Puzzle, Nancy Cabot, *Chicago Tribune,* Jun 22, 1935.

❸ **Mrs. Noel's Quilt,** *Mrs. Danner's Fifth Quilt Book,* 1970.

❹ **Mary Tenny Grey Travel Patch Club,** Hall, 1935.

❺ **Broken Windmills,** Nancy Cabot, *Chicago Tribune,* Feb 5, 1936.

❻ **Log Cabin,** Jinny Beyer Studio design, 2009.

❼ **Courthouse Steps,** Hall, 1935. Also known as:
Log Cabin, Hall, 1935.

❽ **Log Cabin,** Laura Wheeler, *Illinois State Register,* May 15, 1933. Also known as:
Lincoln, Laura Wheeler, unidentified newspaper clipping, date inknown.
Pioneer Days, Laura Wheeler, unidentified newspaper clipping, date unknown.

❾ **Interlaced Blocks,** *Ladies' Art Company,* 1898. Also known as:
True Lover's Knot, *Capper's Weekly,* Feb 27, 1931.

❿ **Carpenter's Square,** *Ladies' Art Company,* 1897.
"Early colonists often incorporated the names or tools of their professions into quilt blocks. This one boasts a pre-revolution birth date." Nancy Cabot, *Chicago Tribune,* Feb 12, 1935

⓫ **White Nights,** Jinny Beyer, *RJR Patterns,* 2008.
A visit to St. Petersburg, Russia, one July was the inspiration for a Jinny Beyer fabric collection and the quilt block White Nights. Russian nights in July are known as white nights because the sun barely sets. It is light well into the late hours of the day, with spectacular colors when the sun finally goes down and quickly rises again. See quilt on page 12

⓬ **Fields and Fences,** Nancy Cabot, *Chicago Tribune,* Jul 5, 1938.

❶ 11 x 11 grid

❷ 11 x 11 grid

❸ 11 x 11 grid

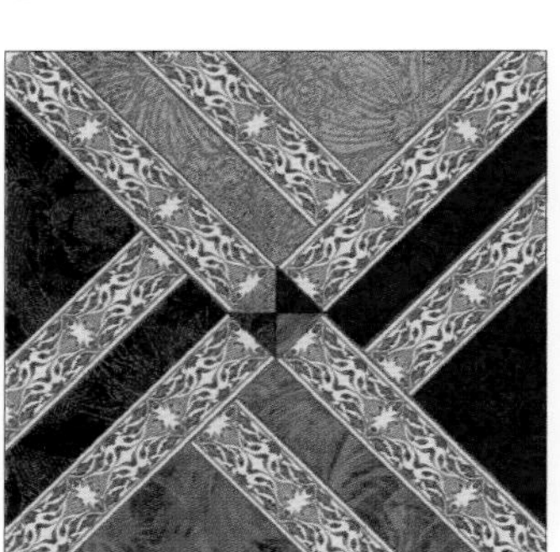

❹ 11 x 11 grid

❺ 11 x 11 grid

❻ 11 x 11 grid

❼ 11 x 11 grid

❽ 11 x 11 grid

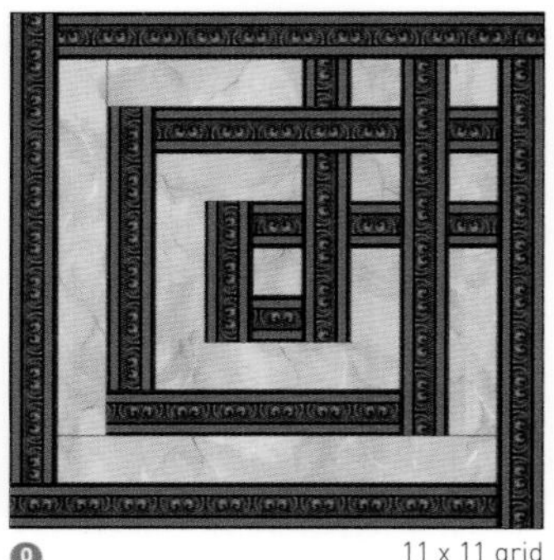

❾ 11 x 11 grid

❿ 11 x 11 grid

⓫ 11 x 11 grid

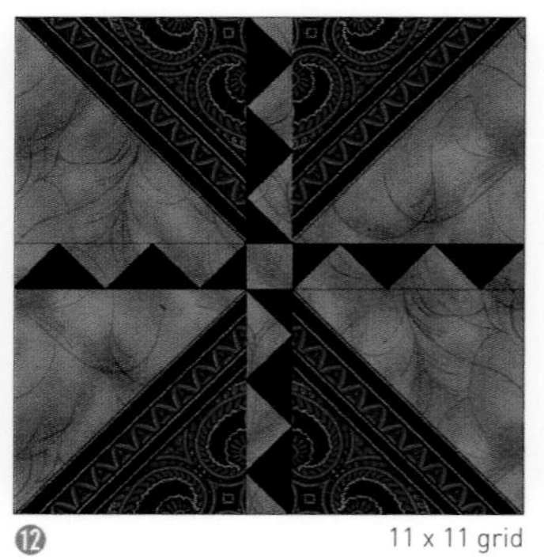

⓬ 11 x 11 grid

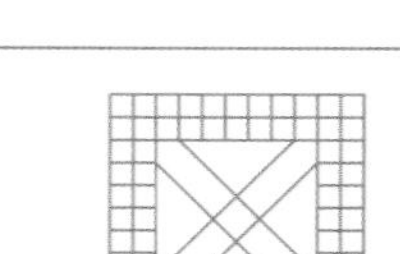

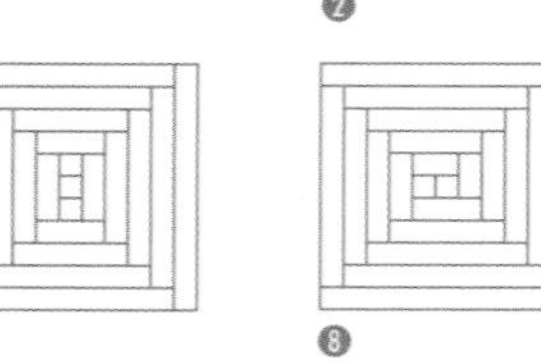

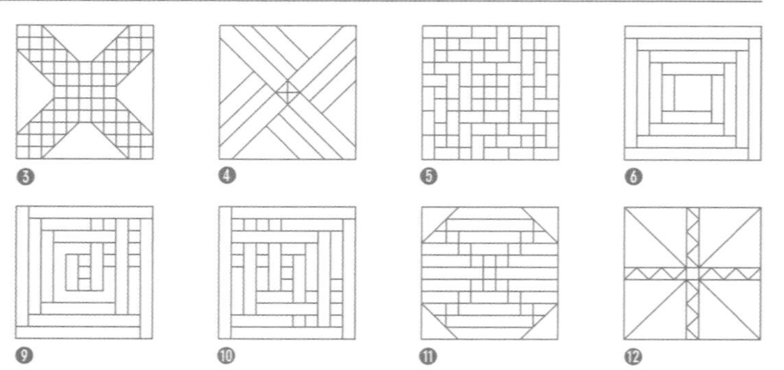

❶ ❷ ❸ ❹ ❺ ❻

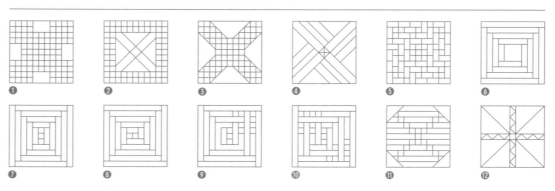

❼ ❽ ❾ ❿ ⓫ ⓬

1 **Nosegay,** Nancy Cabot, *Chicago Tribune,* Mar 19, 1934.
"Young colonial girls would make quilts for their hope chests, and the dainty Nosegay pattern was one of the first to be pieced. Since it is a simple pattern, its completion meant the young bride-to-be was ready to work on more elaborate blocks." Nancy Cabot, *Chicago Tribune,* Mar 19, 1934

2 **Pine Tree,** Nancy Cabot, *Chicago Tribune,* Jan 22, 1933. Also known as:
 Tree of Life, Nancy Cabot, *Chicago Tribune,* Jan 26, 1933.
The Pine Tree block was the first design to be featured in a Nancy Cabot column. "The splendid example of the Pine Tree portrayed is owned by Mrs. C.C. Lively whose grandmother patiently stitched it 90 years ago. The Pine Tree made its appearance in Massachusetts, along with the pine tree shilling, in 1652. It was in that year that the colony's first mint began turning out the historic pine tree coin. The quilt also is known as the Tree of Life, but its richest associations cluster about the pine tree, that colonial emblem blazoned upon the Pine Tree flag, the historical symbolism of which is preserved on the state seals of Maine, Vermont, and Indiana." Nancy Cabot, *Chicago Tribune,* Jan 22, 1933

3 **Christmas Tree,** Hall, 1935. Also known as:
 Tree of Life, Hall, 1935.

4 **Weaving Paths,** Nancy Cabot, *Chicago Tribune,* Feb 21, 1936.

5 **Water Beauty,** Laura Wheeler, *Cincinnati Enquirer,* Sep 14, 1934.

6 **Bishop Hill,** Nancy Cabot, *Chicago Tribune,* Oct 7, 1935.

7 **The Quilt Without a Name,** *Kansas City Star,* Apr 3, 1937.

8 **Nosegay,** Nancy Cabot, *Chicago Tribune,* Jul 22, 1936.

9 **Cross and Crown,** *The Country Gentleman,* Jul 1930.

10 **Poinsettia,** Laura Wheeler, *Sioux City Journal,* Jun 18, 1940.

11 **Primrose Path,** Laura Wheeler, *Cincinnati Enquirer,* Nov 26, 1933.

12 **Blazing Star,** Jane Alan, *Quilt Designs,* 1933. See 160-6, 202-2, and 297-4.

❶ **Philippines,** Hall, 1935. Also known as:
Philopena, ca. 1938, per Havig. See 121-11 and 269-4.

❷ **Star and Triangles,** *Grandma Dexter New Appliqué and Patchwork Designs, Book 36b,* ca. 1932.

❸ **Star of the West,** Laura Wheeler, *Indianapolis Star,* Jul 18, 1936.

❹ **Tuscan Tile,** Jinny Beyer, Hilton Head Seminar, 2002. Also known as:
Lisbon Lattice 2, Jinny Beyer, Jinny Beyer Studio design, 2002.

❺ **Whirling Square,** Alice Brooks, *Detroit Free Press,* Dec 19, 1933.

❻ **Inspiration Quilt,** *Prize Winning Designs,* ca. 1931. Also known as:
Inspiration, Nancy Cabot, *Chicago Tribune,* Feb 19, 1937.

❼ **Glory Vine,** Nancy Cabot, *Chicago Tribune,* Feb 11, 1936.

❽ **Top Hat,** Nancy Cabot, *Chicago Tribune,* Mar 1, 1936.
Even the movies have inspired quilt block designs. Top Hat is a grand example of one young mother's ingenuity. The pattern appears to simulate four wise owls with their beaks pointed to the center. Each one wears a top hat!

❾ **Bouquet in a Fan,** Edna Marie Dunn, *Kansas City Star,* Mar 18, 1933.

❿ **Grandmother's Pride,** Laura Wheeler, *Indianapolis Star,* Jan 5, 1937.

⓫ **Airplane,** ca. 1938, per Havig.

⓬ **Queen's Favorite,** *Quilt Book 130: Keepsake Quilts,* ca. 1970.

❶ 22 x 22 grid

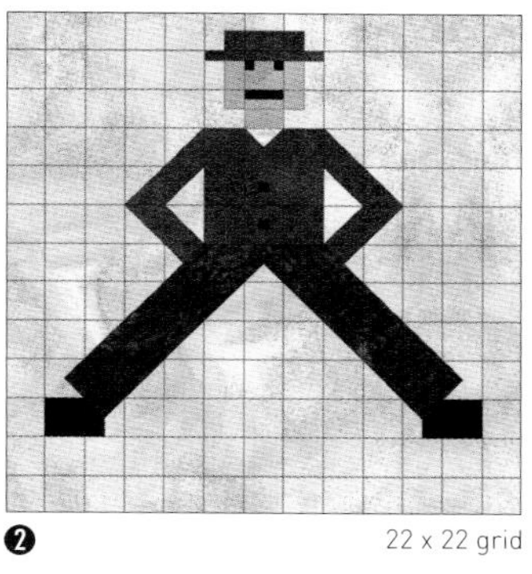

❷ 22 x 22 grid

❸ 22 x 22 grid

❹ 44 x 44 grid

❺ 44 x 44 grid

❻ 44 x 44 grid

❼ 44 x 44 grid

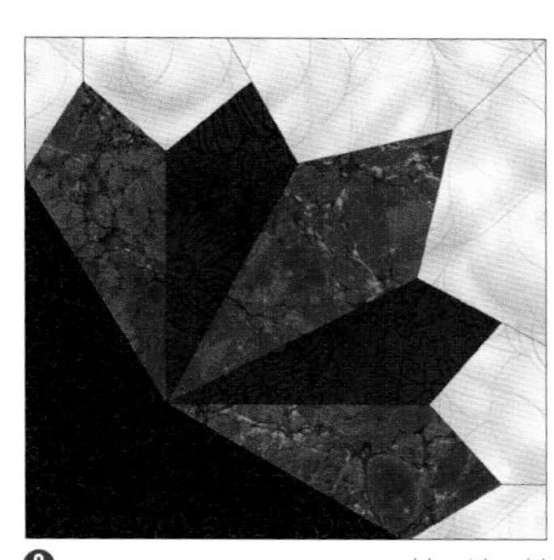

❽ 44 x 44 grid

❶ **Double Link,** Nancy Cabot, *Chicago Tribune,* Oct 7, 1933.

❷ **Long Pants,** Nancy Cabot, *Chicago Tribune,* Feb 12, 1936.

❸ **Little Red House,** Ladies Art Company, 1898.

❹ **Oriental Star,** Nancy Cabot, *Chicago Tribune,* Aug 10, 1933.

❺ **Star of the Orient,** Nancy Cabot, *Chicago Tribune,* Jan 11, 1938.

❻ **Modern Tulip,** Virginia Snow Studio, *Art Needlework Creations,* 1932.

❼ **Pine Cone,** *Kansas City Star,* Oct 23, 1935.

❽ **Magnolia,** *Detroit Free Press,* Apr 1, 1934.

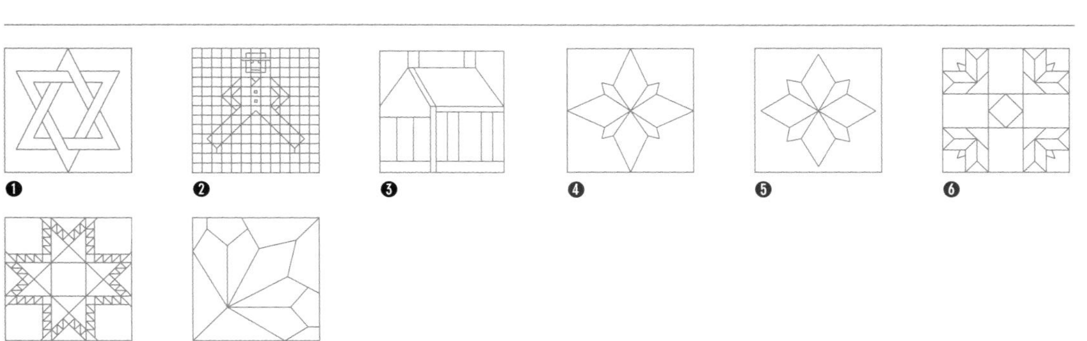

❶ ❷ ❸ ❹ ❺ ❻

❼ ❽

13 x 13 Base Grid Category

Includes ● 13 x 13, ● 26 x 26, and ● 52 x 52 grids

❶ **Oklahoma's Square Dance,** *Kansas City Star,* Oct 30, 1957

❷ **Tick Tack Toe,** *Ladies Art Company,* 1897. See 198-5. Also known as:
- **Tic Tac Toe,** Nancy Cabot, *Chicago Tribune,* Aug 18, 1934.

❸ **Strip Squares,** *Ladies Art Company,* 1897. Also known as:
- **Interlocked Squares,** Nancy Cabot, *Chicago Tribune,* Apr 24, 1934.
- **Stripes and Squares,** Nancy Cabot, *Chicago Tribune,* Apr 24, 1934.
- **Strips and Squares,** Hall, 1935.

❹ **Crossword Puzzle,** Nancy Page, *Birmingham News,* Jun 10, 1941.

❺ **Missouri Puzzle,** Nancy Cabot, *Chicago Tribune,* Jan 21, 1935. See 176-10.
"'Missouri Puzzle,' a block as attractive as its name is intriguing, is a lovely design the history of which has been obscured by antiquity. Pieced in 1818, it ranks among the favorites of the oldest of quilt patterns. The primary colors—red, blue, and yellow—were used in the original coverlet." Nancy Cabot, *Chicago Tribune,* Jan 21, 1935

❻ **Homespun Block,** Nancy Cabot, *Chicago Tribune,* Dec 10, 1937.
"Most of the quilt patterns adapted from homespun patterns are done in blue and white; tan, red and black or red and white with an occasional dash of black. This 'Homespun Block' is to be pieced in blue and white. It was successfully copied from an old homespun coverlet made in Tennessee." Nancy Cabot, *Chicago Tribune,* Dec 10, 1937

❼ **Gnadhutten Cross,** Nancy Cabot, *Chicago Tribune,* Nov 21, 1935.
"This 'Gnadhutten Cross' first was made in Ohio in imitation of one of the homespun coverlets created by the well-to-do families in the Moravian settlement there. This was one of the first settlements in the state of Ohio, which general date gives one a vague idea of the age of the quilt." Nancy Cabot, *Chicago Tribune,* Nov 21, 1935

❽ **Dutch Puzzle,** *Prize Winning Designs,* ca. 1931. See 167-7, 173-9, 242-5, and 274-4.

❾ **Box Quilt,** Hall, 1935. See 126-4 and 224-12.

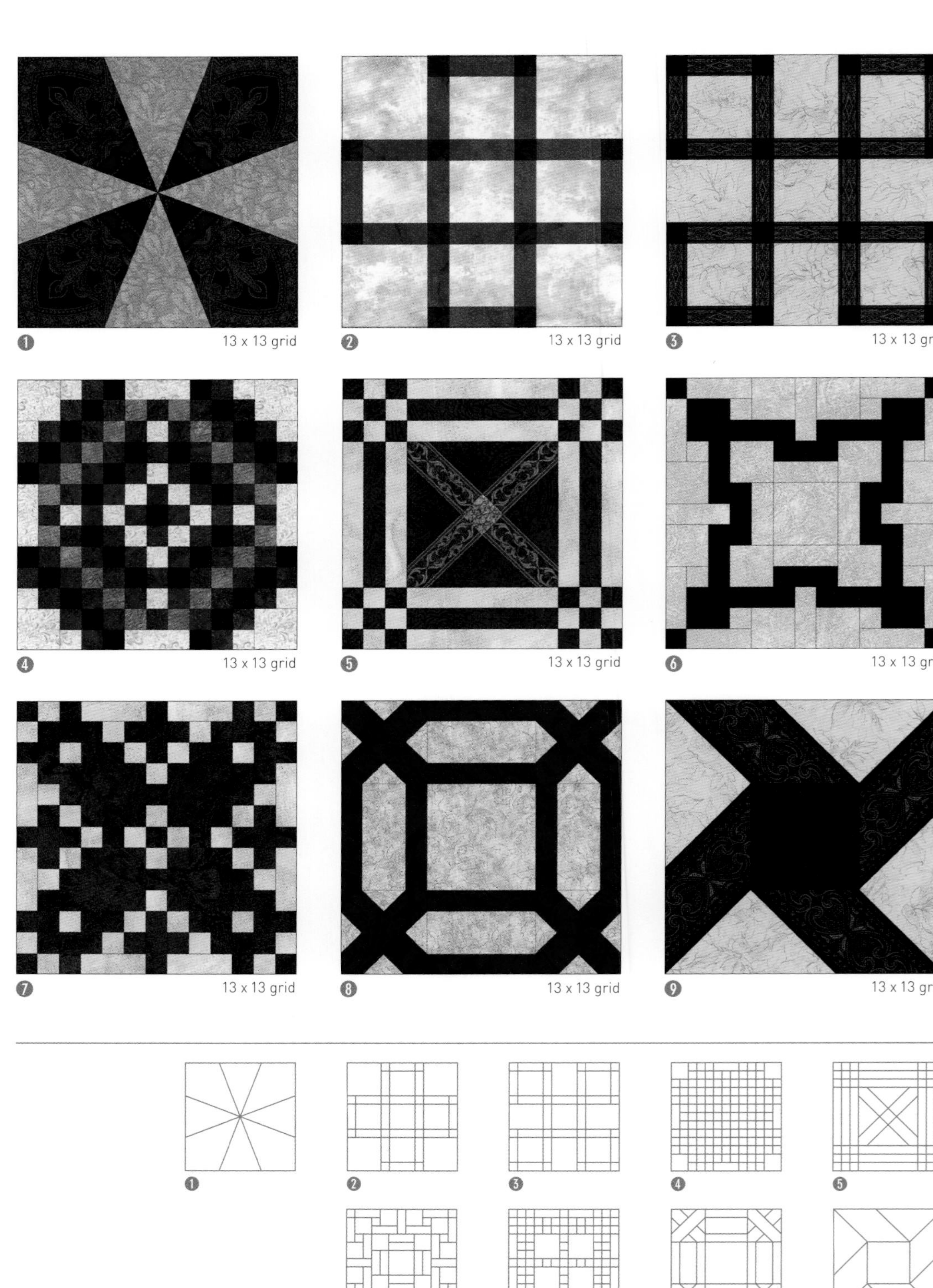

1. **Log Cabin,** *Ten Piecework Quilts for Southern Homes,* ca 1936. Also known as: **Courthouse Steps,** source unknown, date unknown.
2. **Log Cabin,** Ruby McKim, *Kansas City Star,* Oct 10, 1928.
3. **Doris' Delight,** *Farm Journal and Farmers Wife,* ca. 1941.
4. **Aunt Sukey's Choice,** Hall, 1935. See 228-11.
5. **Spider Web,** Alice Brooks, *Detroit Free Press,* Apr 29, 1934.
6. **Fish Tails,** Nancy Page, *Nashville Banner,* May 9, 1933.
7. **Fairfax Station,** Jinny Beyer, Jinny Beyer Studio design, 2007.
8. **Virginia Crossroads,** Jinny Beyer, Jinny Beyer Studio design, 2007.
9. **Ice Crystals,** Jinny Beyer, Jinny Beyer Studio design, 2007.
10. **Hermitage,** Jinny Beyer, Jinny Beyer Studio design, 2007.
11. **Emporia,** Jinny Beyer, Hilton Head Seminar design, 2009.
12. **Santee,** Jinny Beyer, Hilton Head Seminar design, 2009.

1 Coosawhatchie, Jinny Beyer, Hilton Head Seminar design, 2009.

2 Selma, Jinny Beyer, Hilton Head Seminar design, 2009.

3 Marion, Jinny Beyer, Hilton Head Seminar design, 2009.

4 Double Friendship Knot, Laura Wheeler, *Sioux City Journal,* Jun 29, 1940.

5 Mexican Cross, Ickis, 1949. See 166-11 and 199-9.

6 Jacob's Ladder, *Kansas City Star,* Jul 3, 1935.

7 Morning Star, Nancy Cabot, *Chicago Tribune,* Jun 17, 1937.

8 A Maltese Cross, *Ladies Art Company,* 1897.

9 Bow Knot, Hall, 1935. See 122-7 and 269-12. Also known as:
- **Farmer's Puzzle,** Hall, 1935.

10 Road to Fortune, Laura Wheeler, *Indianapolis Star,* Mar 10, 1937. Also known as:
- **Pinwheel Quilt,** *Antique Quilts,* date unknown.

"In and out winds the 'Road to Fortune,' but you can easily follow it every step of the way in this simple patchwork quilt. Quickly, gaily you'll piece out the identical 11-inch blocks with bits of scraps that are anything but identical—variety's your keynote here!" Laura Wheeler, Indianapolis Star, Mar 10, 1937

11 Cardinal Points, ca. 1938, per Havig.

12 Exit 8, Jinny Beyer, Hilton Head Seminar design, 2009.

13 Rocky Mount, Jinny Beyer, Hilton Head Seminar design, 2009.

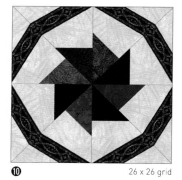

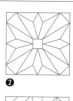

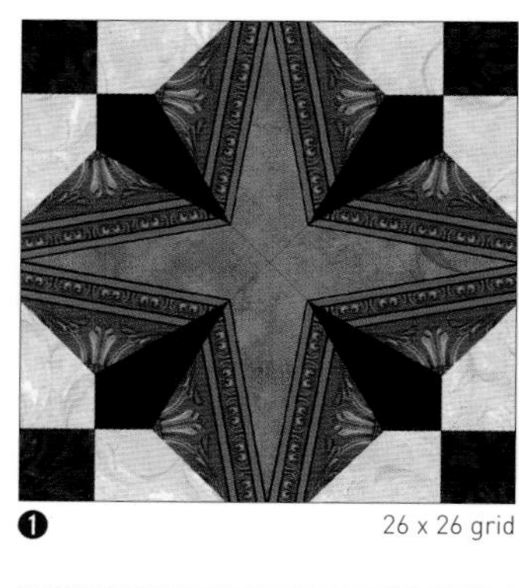

1 26 x 26 grid

2 26 x 26 grid

3 26 x 26 grid

4 26 x 26 grid

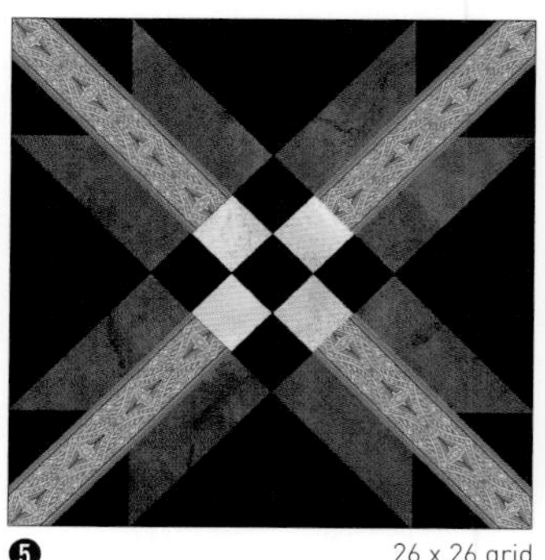

5 26 x 26 grid

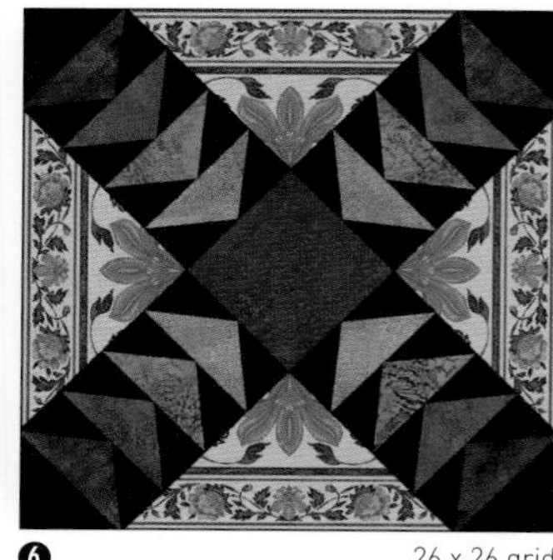

6 26 x 26 grid

7 26 x 26 grid

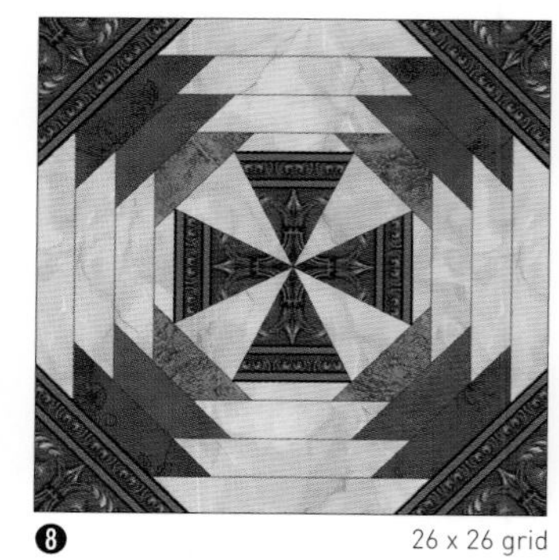

8 26 x 26 grid

9 26 x 26 grid

10 26 x 26 grid

11 26 x 26 grid

12 26 x 26 grid

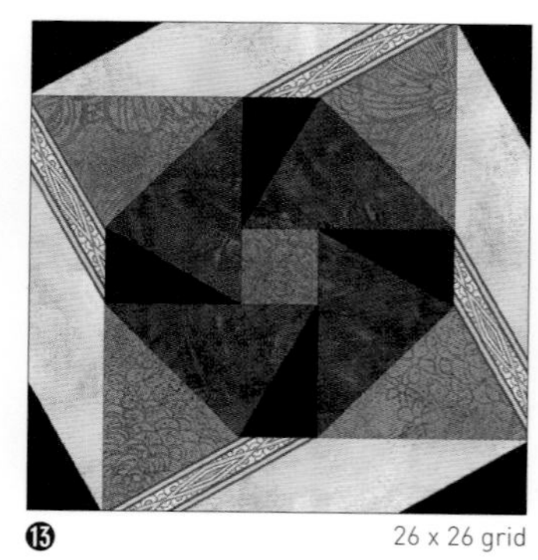

13 26 x 26 grid

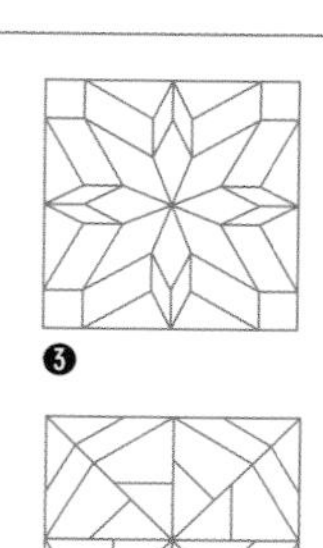

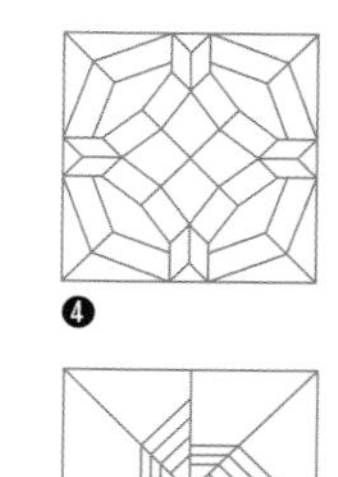

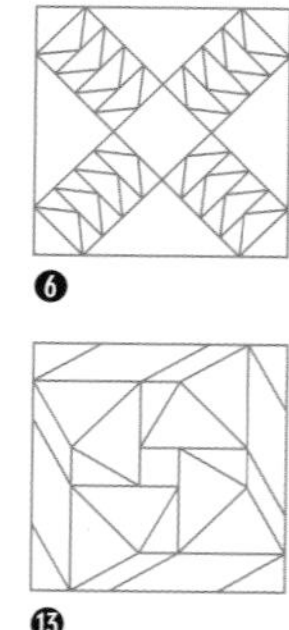

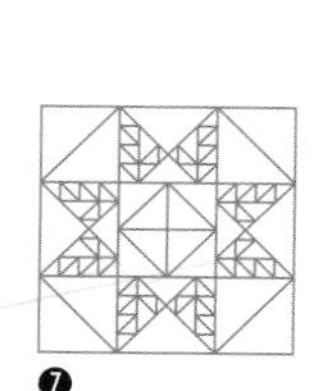

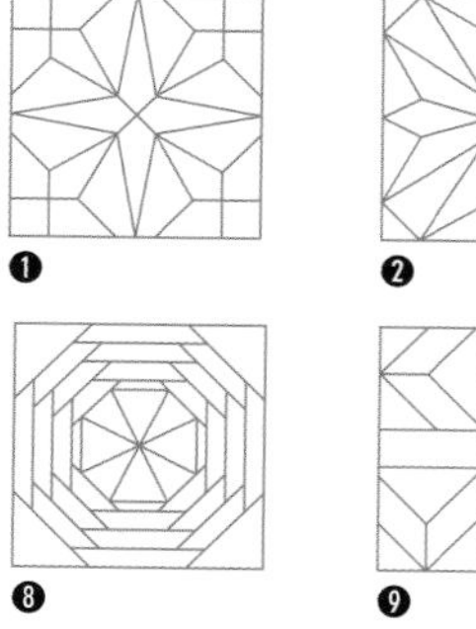

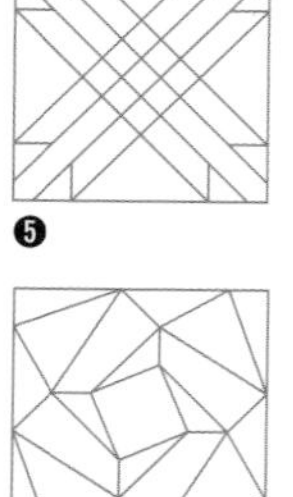

1 2 3 4 5 6 7 8 9 10 11 12 13

Quick Reference: Pineapples

Pineapple quilt blocks are in the *Log Cabin* family. The difference is that there are eight sets of logs going around the central square, rather than four. *Pineapple* is one of the older patterns, and has many variations.

"Have you ever seen a Pineapple Quilt all done, and burned with envy because it didn't belong to you? Here is your opportunity to gratify your wish and own this handsome quilt. It is one of the oldest Colonial patterns—you know the pineapple was the Colonial symbol for hospitality. What is more, this quilt design is very easy to make. Nearly all the patch pieces are the same width so you can cut your material into strips and then just snip it off to the right size. Then when the pieces are cut, you just start at the center patch and keep sewing round and round and before you know it the block is done!" Alice Brooks, *Detroit Free Press*, March 11, 1934

Washington Pavement, *Birmingham News.* **See 302-10.**

Washington Pavement, *Indianapolis Star.* **See 302-11.**

Pineapple, Hall. **See 303-2.**

Pineapple, *The Farmer's Wife, Book of New Designs and Patterns.* **See 174-6.**

Pineapple Block, *Chicago Tribune.* **See 271-2.**

Pineapple Quilt, *Kansas City Star.* **See 174-8.**

Pineapple, *Detroit Free Press.* **See 302-12.**

Pineapple Quilt, *McCalls Needlework & Crafts Antique Quilts.* **See 210-9.**

Pineapple, *The Patchwork Book,* 1932. **See 174-7.**

Pineapple, *Des Moines Register.* **See 303-3.**

Pineapple No. 1, *Ladies Art Company.* **See 303-4.**

Pineapple, *Illinois State Register.* **See 271-1.**

Pineapples, *Grandmother Clark's Authentic Early American Quilts, Book 21.* **See 122-2.**

Maltese Cross, Hall. **See 303-1.**

A Maltese Cross, *Ladies Art Company.* **See 260-8.**

Cactus Flower, *RJR Patterns.* **See 302-8.**

The Pineapple, *Grandmother Clark's Patchwork Designs, Book 22.* **See 303-5.**

❶ 26 x 26 grid

❷ 26 x 26 grid

❸ 52 x 52 grid

❹ 52 x 52 grid

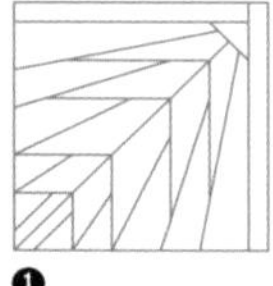

❶

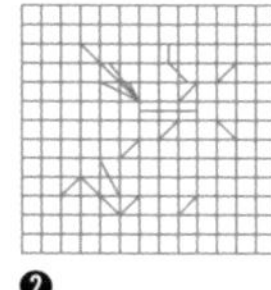

❷

❸

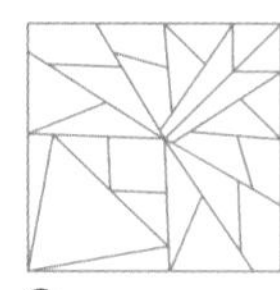

❹

❶ **Four Seasons,** Jinny Beyer, RJR Patterns, 2005.

❷ **Balloon Girl,** *Farm Journal and Farmers Wife,* ca. 1941.

❸ **Shining Star,** *Prize Winning Designs,* ca. 1931.

❹ **Chrysanthemum,** Alice Brooks, *Detroit Free Press,* Aug 13, 1934.

15 x 15 Base Grid Category

Includes ● 15 x 15, ● 30 x 30, and ● 60 x 60 grids

❶ **Dragon's Head,** *The Patchwork Book,* 1932.

❷ **Greek Cross,** *Grandmother Clark's Patchwork Quilt Designs, From Books 20-21-23,* 1932.

❸ **Carrie's Choice,** Clara Stone, *Practical Needlework,* ca. 1906.

❹ **Toganoxie Nine-Patch,** Hall, 1935.

❺ **Pink Magnolia,** *Farm Journal and Farmers Wife,* ca. 1941.

❻ **A Block of Many Triangles,** *Kansas City Star,* Sep 17, 1952.

❼ **Bear's Paw,** *Grandmother Clark's Patchwork Quilt Designs, From Books 20-21-23,* 1932. See 85-10, 223-9, 223-10, and 223-11 Also known as:

The Best Friend, *Grandmother Clark's Authentic Early American Patchwork Quilts, Book No. 23,* 1932.

❽ **The Bull's Eye,** Finley, 1929. Also known as:

Bull's Eye, Nancy Cabot, *Chicago Tribune,* Feb 17, 1933.
David and Goliath, Finley, 1929.
Doe and Darts, Finley, 1929.
Flying Darts, Finley, 1929.
Four Darts, Finley, 1929.

"David and Goliath has several other names... all having similar association of the hunt or archery. The older the pattern the more likely it is to have many names, showing that it has migrated from one community to another and has taken its successive names from association with various incidents in the history and development of home life in America." Finley, 1929

❾ **Confetti,** Jinny Beyer, Jinny Beyer Studio design, 2005.

❶ ❷ ❸ ❹ ❺ ❻ ❼ ❽ ❾

1 15 x 15 grid

2 15 x 15 grid

3 15 x 15 grid

4 15 x 15 grid

5 15 x 15 grid

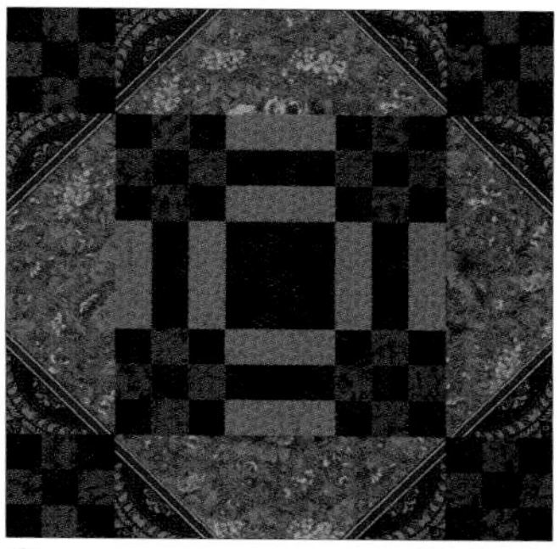

6 15 x 15 grid

7 15 x 15 grid

8 15 x 15 grid

9 15 x 15 grid

10 15 x 15 grid

11 15 x 15 grid

12 15 x 15 grid

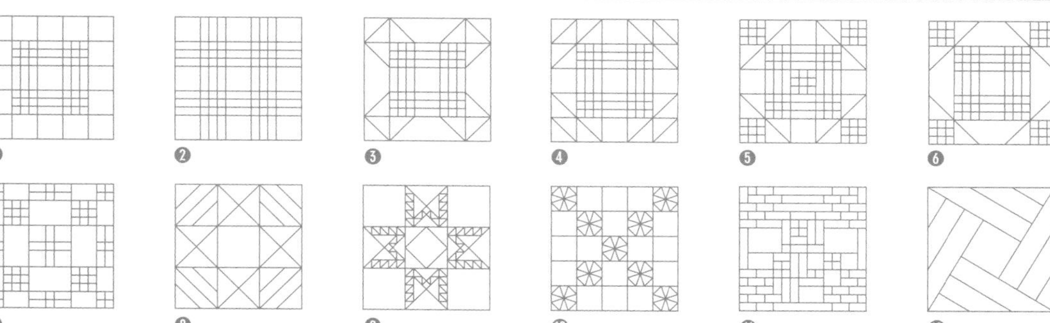

1 **Album Patch,** Hall, 1935.

2 **Album Quilt,** *Ladies Art Company,* 1897. Also known as:

- **Child's Album,** Nancy Page, *Birmingham News,* May 9, 1939.

3 **The Missouri Puzzle,** Eveline Foland, *Kansas City Star,* May 3, 1930. Also known as:

- **Balance,** Nancy Page, *Birmingham News,* Jun 8, 1943.
- **Missouri Puzzle,** Hall, 1935.
- **Rose for Elsa's Pride,** *Kansas City Star,* Jul 23, 1952.

4 **Goose in the Pond,** *Ladies Art Company,* 1897. Also known as:

- **Geometric Garden,** *Grandma Dexter New Appliqué and Patchwork Designs, Book 36b,* ca. 1932.
- **Goose in Pond,** Nancy Cabot, *Chicago Tribune,* Dec 29, 1934.
- **Missouri Puzzle,** Clara Stone, *Practical Needlework,* ca. 1906.
- **Mrs. Wolf's Red Beauty,** *Mrs. Danner's Fifth Quilt Book,* 1970.
- **The Scrap Bag,** *Kansas City Star,* Oct 16, 1935.
- **Young Man's Fancy,** Finley, 1929.

5 **Queen's Crown,** Nancy Cabot, *Chicago Tribune,* Jun 18, 1933.

6 **Bouquets,** source unknown, date unknown. Also known as:

- **Goose Tracks,** source unknown, date unknown.
- **Signal,** source unknown, date unknown.
- **Tulip Wreath,** source unknown, date unknown.

7 **An Odd Patchwork,** *Ladies Art Company,* 1897. Also known as:

- **Burgoyne Surrounded,** Hall, 1935.
- **Burgoyne's Quilt,** Ruby McKim, McKim, 1931.
- **Coverlet Quilt,** *Q Book 116, Blue Ribbon Quilts,* date unknown.
- **Road to California,** Nancy Page, *Birmingham News,* Nov 23, 1937.
- **Wheel of Fortune,** Finley, 1929.

8 **Treasure Chest,** Alice Brooks, *Detroit Free Press,* Mar 8, 1934.

9 **Joining Star,** *Ladies Art Company,* 1897.

10 **Blue Blades Flying,** *Kansas City Star,* Jul 19, 1944.

11 **Victorian Rose,** Nancy Cabot, *Chicago Tribune,* May 5, 1936.

12 **Quebec,** Nancy Cabot, *Chicago Tribune,* May 21, 1938.

"'Quebec,' the lovely and unusual pieced design presented today, is the contribution of Mrs. John Graveile of Deadwood, S.D. The coverlet made from this pattern was brought from Quebec by her mother and was made many years ago when she lived in the province. The pattern was a general favorite among the Canadians, but the exact historical background of the block is obscure." Nancy Cabot, *Chicago Tribune,* May 21, 1938

❶ **Mountain Pink,** Laura Wheeler, *Indianapolis Star,* Jun 24, 1934.

❷ **Log Cabin Straight Furrow,** Holstein, 1973.

❸ **Stars and Stripes,** Nancy Cabot, *Chicago Tribune,* Jul 4, 1936.

❹ **Kaleidoscope,** Ruby McKim, *Kansas City Star,* Mar 22, 1930.

❺ **Pine Burr,** Nancy Page, *Nashville Banner,* Mar 13, 1934.

❻ **Friendship Chain,** Laura Wheeler, *Seattle Star,* Jan 21, 1939.

❼ **Periwinkle,** *Grandmother Clark's Patchwork Quilts, Book No.* 19, 1932.

❽ **The Square Diamond,** *Kansas City Star,* Jan 23, 1937.

❾ **Imperial T,** *Ladies Art Company,* 1897.

❿ **Letter A,** ca. 1938, per Havig.

⓫ **Idle Hours,** *Farm Journal and Farmer's Wife* (Silver Anniversary issue), 1945.

⓬ **Chosen Children,** *Prize Winning Designs,* ca. 1931. Also known as:
Children of Israel, Nancy Cabot, *Chicago Tribune,* Dec 16, 1933.

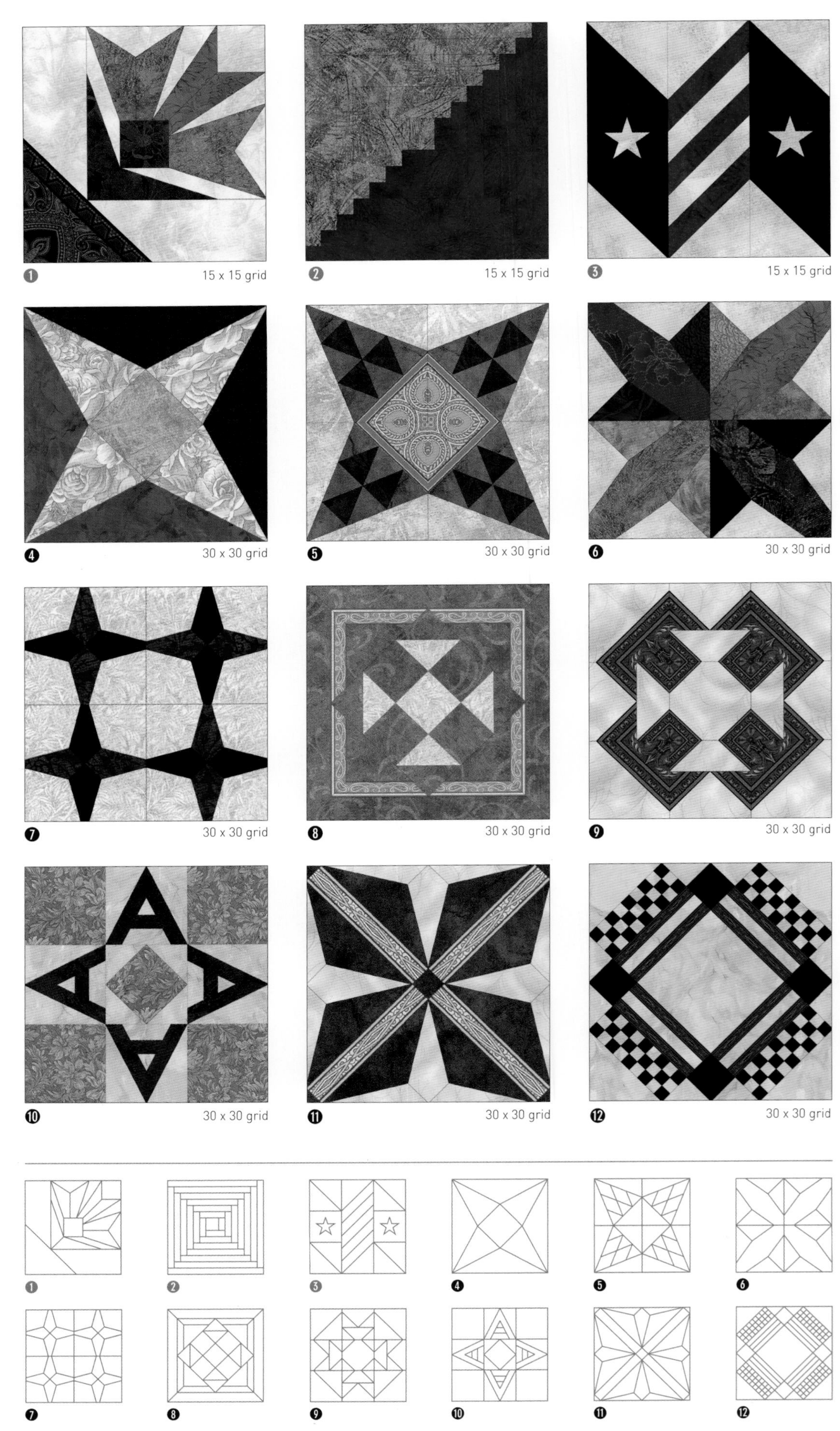

❶ **Joined Star,** Nancy Cabot, *Chicago Tribune,* Apr 1, 1935.

❷ **Puss in Corner,** Nancy Cabot, *Chicago Tribune,* Sep 3, 1935.
"When early American quilt makers created a simple design, and were unable to bestow a suitable title upon the block, they frequently chose names of popular pastimes. 'Puss in Corner' was a favorite game among the youngsters, and the simplicity of the game is charmingly recalled in the quilt block illustrated today." Nancy Cabot, *Chicago Tribune,* Sep 3, 1935

❸ **North Carolina Beauty,** Nancy Cabot, *Chicago Tribune,* Jul 10, 1935.

❹ **Crazy Anne,** *Kansas City Star,* Jun 15, 1949.

❺ **The Air Plane,** *Kansas City Star,* Jul 28, 1934.

❻ **Anchors Aweigh,** Alice Brooks, *Washington Post,* Oct 29, 1942.

❼ **Old Fashioned Garland,** Laura Wheeler, *Cincinnati Enquirer,* Jul 31, 1933.

❽ **Old Indian Trail,** *Kansas City Star,* Dec 24, 1941.

❾ **Little Red Schoolhouse,** Nancy Page, *Birmingham News,* Dec 20, 1938.

❿ **Washington's Puzzle,** *Ladies Art Company,* 1897. See 56-2. Also known as:
 Checkerboard Skew, Gutcheon, *The Quilt Design Workbook,* 1976.

⓫ **Solomon's Temple,** *Ladies Art Company,* 1897. See 177-9.

⓬ **Rose Garden,** Nancy Cabot, *Chicago Tribune,* Jun 22, 1936.

Jack in the Pulpit

A classic example of how designs change over time is evidenced in the ones shown here. Several are called *Jack in the Pulpit*; two have the alternate name of *Toad in the Puddle.* The line drawings show what perhaps could have originated as the same design. Even when colored in their original form, they look similar except for Mosaic No. 7. The way that block is colored sets it apart. Of the seven designs, only two are from the same source. To draft the seven designs, five different grids are used.

Broken Dishes, *Michigan Farmer.* **See 94-9.**

Jack in the Pulpit, *Practical Needlework.* **See 167-10.**

Jack in the Pulpit, *Kansas City Star.* **See 112-9.**

Jack in the Pulpit. Finley. **See 167-12.**

Hour Glass, *Nashville Banner.* 1934. **See 60-9.**

Double Squares, *Ladies Art Company.* **See 217-10.**

Mosaic No. 7, *Ladies Art Company.* **See 94-8.**

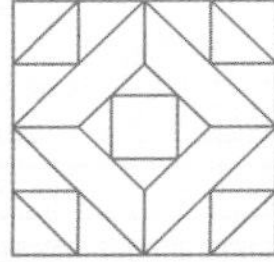
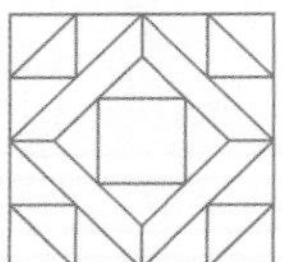
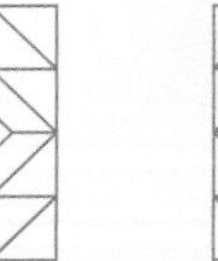
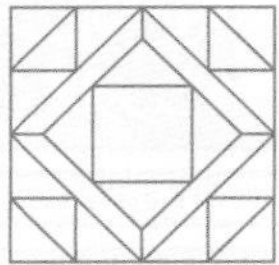
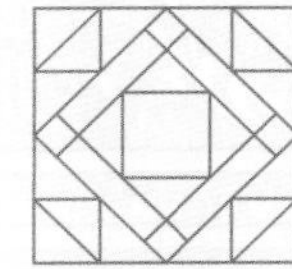
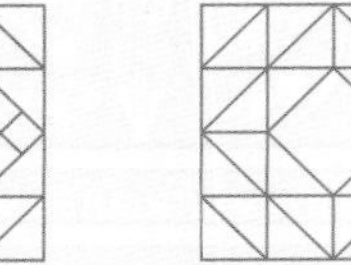
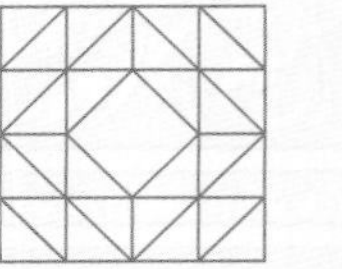

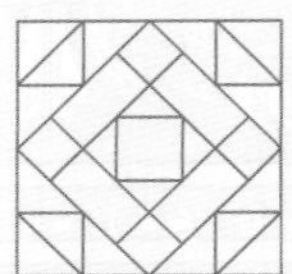

❶ **Blazing Star,** Laura Wheeler, *Sioux City Journal,* Aug 2, 1941.

❷ **Maltese Cross Block,** Nancy Cabot, *Chicago Tribune,* Dec 26, 1936.

❸ **California Star Pattern,** *Ladies Art Company,* 1897. Also known as:
California Star, Nancy Cabot, *Chicago Tribune,* Mar 21, 1935.

❹ **Turkey Tracks,** Nancy Cabot, *Chicago Tribune,* Aug 20, 1934. See 244-11.
"'Turkey Tracks' is an interesting block which was developed by a quaint little woman from Maine, who ventured into the middle west with her husband in 1849. There are other turkey track patterns, but this one has enjoyed wide popularity because of its simplicity and effective design." Nancy Cabot, *Chicago Tribune,* Aug 20, 1934

❺ **Tea Time,** Nancy Cabot, *Chicago Tribune,* Jul 8, 1937.

❶ 60 x 60 grid

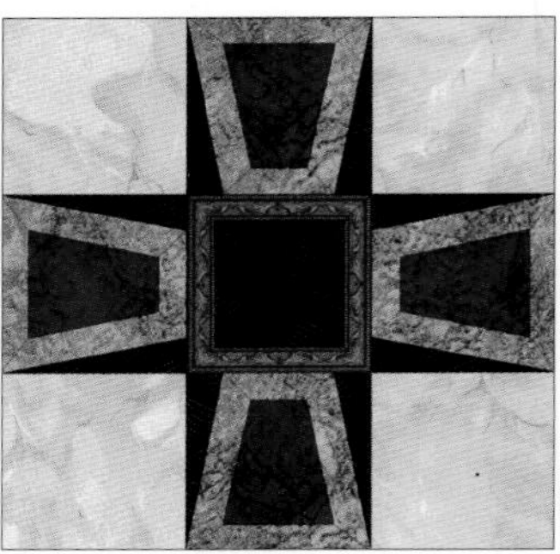

❷ 60 x 60 grid

❸ 60 x 60 grid

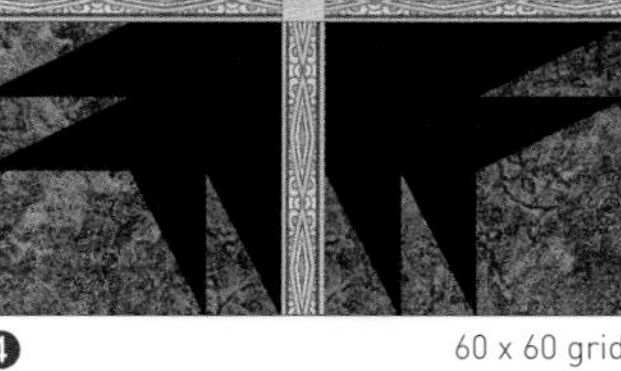

❹ 60 x 60 grid

❺ 60 x 60 grid

❶

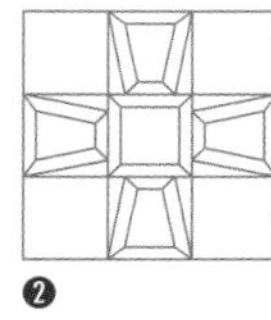

❷

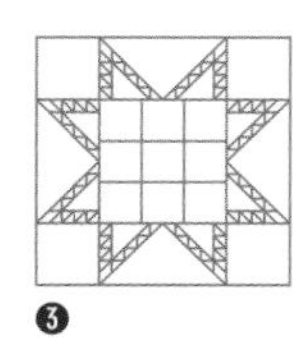

❸

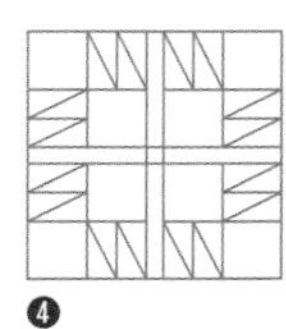

❹

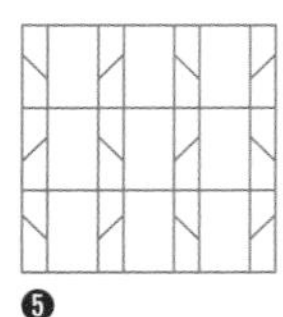

❺

Quick Reference: Patriotic Blocks

When events in history wear heavy on our hearts, quiltmakers usually work through their worries by making quilts. World War II was no exception. Many quilt blocks with patriotic themes cropped up in the early 1940s. Some were completely new designs and others were older patterns that were given new names.

PATRIOTIC STAR "As an alternate for 'Whirling Star,' the creator of the design, Mrs. Willard Herrick, suggests 'Patriotic Star.' To be consistent with its second title, the star should be built of red, white and blue blocks. Mrs. Herrick developed the pattern at her home at Hazel Valley, Ark., during one of the late winter cold snaps." *Kansas City Star,* Apr 16, 1941

ANCHORS AWEIGH "Anchors Aweigh! You're in the Navy, now! Snip, go your scissors, as you cut out the pieces in easy strips. Be first to make this patriotic Anchor Quilt. Alice Brooks, *Washington Post,* Oct 29, 1942

The Red, the White, the Blue, *Kansas City Star.* **See 268-1.**

Union Block, *Chicago Tribune.* **See 137-3.**

The Star Spangled Banner, *Kansas City Sta.* **See 251-4.**

The Liberty Star, *Kansas City Star.* **See 303-8.**

Liberty Star, Havig. **See 303-7.**

Patriotic Star, *Kansas City Star.* **See 300-2.**

Patriotic Star, *Kansas City Star.* **See 277-7.**

A Design for Patriotism, *Kansas City Star.* **See 120-7.**

The Army Star, *Kansas City Star.* **See 114-2.**

A Salute to the Colors, *Kansas City Star.* **See 79-10.**

July Fourth, *Birmingham News.* **See 68-3.**

July Fourth, *Birmingham News.* **See 68-2.**

Unknown, *Prize Winning Designs.* **See 180-10.**

Flag Quilt, Orlofsky. **See 173-11.**

Soldier Boy, *Kansas City Star.* **See 440-1.**

Victory Quilt, *Kansas City Star.* **See 439-13.**

V for Victory, *Birmingham News.* **See 233-1.**

Stars and Stripes, *Chicago Tribune.* **See 264-3.**

Sergeant's Chevron, *Farm Journal and Farmer's Wife* (Silver Anniversary issue). **See 249-2.**

Red, White and Blue, *Farm Journal and Farmer's Wife* (Silver Anniversary issue). **See 104-9.**

Salute to Loyalty, *Kansas City Star.* **See 437-12.**

The Twentieth Century Star, *Practical Needlework.* **See , 436-8.**

Anchors Aweigh, *Washington Post.* **See 265-6.**

More Square Design Categories

Includes ● 17 x 17 (34 x 34, 68 x 68), ● 19 x 19 (38 x 38), ● 21 x 21 (42 x 42), ● 23 x 23 (46 x 46), ● 25 x 25 (50 x 50) ● 27 x 27 (54 x 54), ● 29 x 29, ● 31 x 31 (62 x 62), ● 33 x 33, ● 41 x 41, ● 51 x 51, and ● 70 x 70 grids

1. **The Red, the White, the Blue,** *Kansas City Star,* Dec 14, 1955.
2. **Michigan Favorite,** *Farm Journal and Farmers Wife,* ca. 1941.
3. **Chariot Wheel,** Nancy Cabot, *Chicago Tribune,* May 31, 1935. Also known as:
   Quilter's Delight, Nancy Cabot, *Chicago Tribune,* Jul 10, 1937.
4. **Friendship,** *Q Book 130, Keepsake Quilts* ca. 1970.
5. **Hemlock,** Jinny Beyer, Jinny Beyer Studio design, 2007.
6. **Bright Star,** Laura Wheeler, unidentified newspaper clipping, date unknown.
7. **Airport,** ca. 1938, per Havig.
8. **Fortune's Fancy,** Alice Brooks, *Detroit Free Press,* Dec 14, 1933.
9. **Firecracker and Rockets,** *Farm Journal and Farmers Wife,* ca. 1941.

1 17 x 17 grid

2 17 x 17 grid

3 17 x 17 grid

4 17 x 17 grid

5 17 x 17 grid

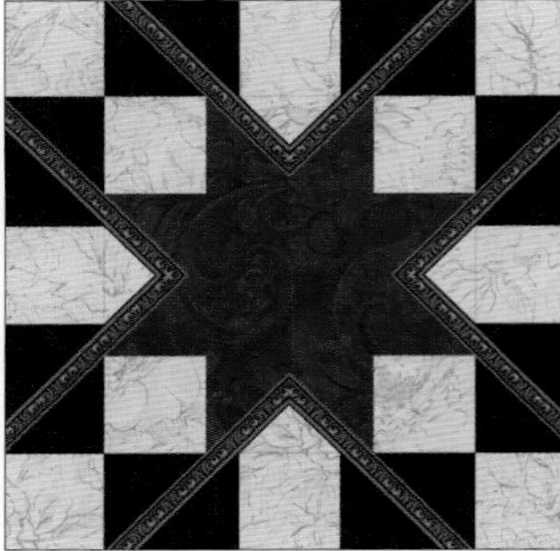
6 34 x 34 grid

7 34 x 34 grid

8 34 x 34 grid

9 34 x 34 grid

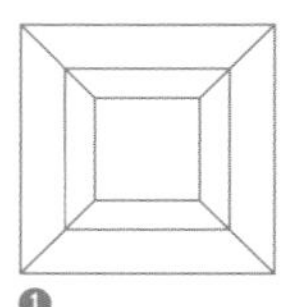
1

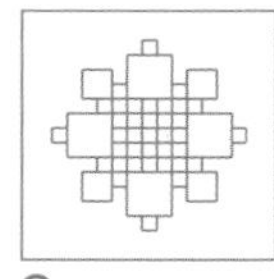
2

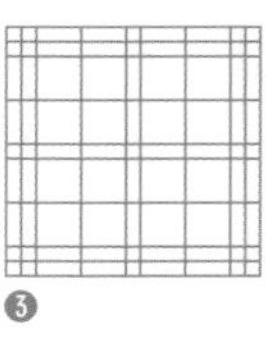
3

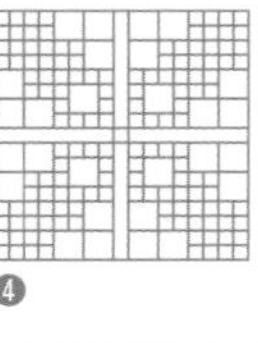
4

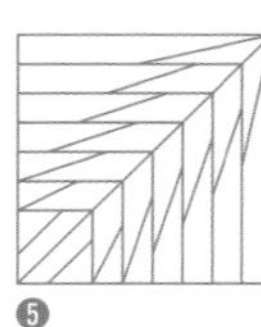
5

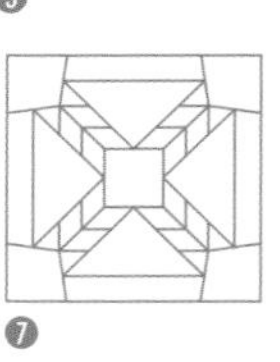
6

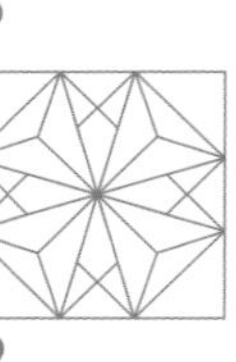
7

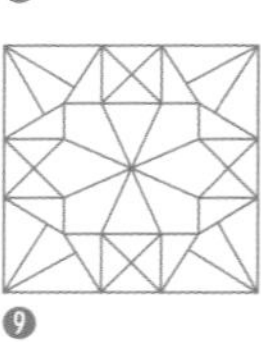
8

9

1 **Glove Design,** *Prize Winning Designs,* ca. 1931.

2 **Summer Flowers,** *Farm Journal and Farmers Wife,* ca. 1941.

3 **Tulips,** Aunt Martha series: *The Quilt Fair Comes to You,* ca. 1933.

4 **The Philippines,** *Ladies Art Company,* 1901. See 121-11 and 256-1.

5 **Twinkling Star,** *Ladies Art Company,* 1897.

6 **Marietta Blockhouse,** Nancy Cabot, *Chicago Tribune,* Nov 14, 1935.

"'Marietta Blockhouse' is a variation of the old octagon and eight pointed star design. In this pattern neither the octagon nor the star is strikingly apparent when the patches are set together. As the name implies the design represents a square blockhouse typical in western and southern United States with bastions at the corners gateways at the center of each side and sloping earth work or ramparts all around." Nancy Cabot, *Chicago Tribune,* Nov 14, 1935

7 **Double Z,** Hall 1935. See 154-1.

8 **The Aircraft Quilt,** Eveline Foland, *Kansas City Star,* Jul 13, 1929. Also known as:

- **Aeroplane,** Nancy Page, *Nashville Banner,* Oct 10, 1933.
- **Air Plane,** Hall 1935.
- **Aircraft,** Hall 1935.
- **Airplane,** ca. 1938, per Havig.

"Here is modern design in pieced quilts. Mrs. Otto Prell, Miami, Ok. sent The Star this design just as two transcontinental airplane lines are being inaugurated in their flight through Kansas City from coast to coast. May it have its place in the history of the world as emblematic of this age just as our great-grandmothers designed the saw-tooth and the churn dash and the log cabin patterns which were symbolic of the time in which they lived." *Kansas City Star,* Jul 13, 1929

9 **Ice Cream Bowl,** *Ladies Art Company,* 1897.

10 **Wild Goose Chase,** Laura Wheeler, *Illinois State Register,* May 22, 1933. See 174-10, 184-4, and 273-3.

"Triangular patterns are one of the most common forms in quilts. When they form the design as they do in the Wild Goose Chase they are more than just a patch—they are the symbol for birds. In this pattern we have the large geese and the small in flight together. This old pattern is found under different names but it always refers to birds." Laura Wheeler, *Illinois State Register,* May 22, 1933

11 **Whirligig,** Hall, 1935. Also known as:

- **Alpine Cross,** Nancy Cabot, *Chicago Tribune,* Sep 11, 1936.

12 **Bowknot,** Nancy Cabot, *Chicago Tribune,* May 19, 1933. See 122-7 and 260-9.

1 Lancelot, Jinny Beyer, Jinny Beyer Studio design, 2007.

2 Bachelor's Puzzle, ca. 1938, per Havig. See 193-5 and 236-4.

3 Patricia's Patch, ca. 1938, per Havig.

4 Turnabout T, Eveline Foland, *Kansas City Star,* Dec 6, 1930.

5 Lily, Havig, ca. 1938.

6 Midnight Sun, Jinny Beyer, Jinny Beyer Studio design, 2007.

7 Burgoyne's Quilt, *Grandmother Clark's Patchwork Quilt Designs, From Books 20-21-23,* 1932. Also known as:

- **Burgoyne's Puzzle,** Home Art Studios, *Cincinnati Enquirer,* Jan 25, 1933.
- **Homespun,** *The Mountain Mist Blue Book of Quilts,* 1935.
- **The Road to California,** Hall, 1935.
- **Wheel of Fortune,** Hall, 1935.

8 Log Cabin, Nancy Cabot, *Chicago Tribune,* Feb 22, 1933.

9 Harlequin Flower, Jinny Beyer, Jinny Beyer Studio design, 2007.

10 Ships in the Night, Nancy Cabot, *Chicago Tribune,* Oct 21, 1934.

11 Etoile de Chamblie, *Prize Winning Designs,* ca. 1931. Also known as:

- **Star of Chamblie,** Hall, 1935.

12 Sawtooth, Nancy Cabot, *Chicago Tribune,* Jul 25, 1935. See 288-9, 288-10, 414-11, and 414-12.

"Woman's familiarity with trades and occupations of the civil war period is recognizable in the 'Sawtooth' quilt block. When this quilt first was pieced the colors were turkey red, green and white." Nancy Cabot, *Chicago Tribune,* Jul 25, 1935

1 38 x 38 grid

2 38 x 38 grid

3 21 x 21 grid

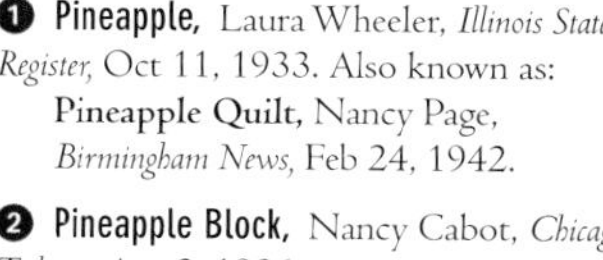

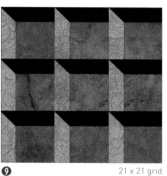

1 Pineapple, Laura Wheeler, *Illinois State Register,* Oct 11, 1933. Also known as:
  Pineapple Quilt, Nancy Page, *Birmingham News,* Feb 24, 1942.

2 Pineapple Block, Nancy Cabot, *Chicago Tribune,* Apr 2, 1936.

3 Bouquets, Nancy Page, *Nashville Banner,* Jul 26, 1932. See 194-3.

4 Facets, Jinny Beyer, Hilton Head Seminar design, 2004.

5 Old Snowflake, Nancy Cabot, *Chicago Tribune,* Mar 12, 1937.

6 Cactus Star, Jinny Beyer, Hilton Head Seminar design, 2004.

7 Nonsuch, *Ladies Art Company,* 1897. Also known as:
  Nonesuch, ca. 1938, per Havig.

8 Modernistic Acorn, Hall, 1935.

9 Shadow Box, Aunt Martha series: *Patchwork Simplicity,* ca. 1977. See 151-9, 171-7 and 407-10.

10 Nebraska, Nancy Cabot, *Chicago Tribune,* Jul 22, 1933.

11 Gordian Knot, Nancy Cabot, *Chicago Tribune,* Sep 16, 1934.
"Ancient mythology has familiarized us with the intricate knot tied by Gordius king of Phrygia in the thong which connected the pole of his chariot with the yoke and the declaration of the oracle that he who should untie it would be master of Asia. This indissoluble knot has been transferred to the quilt realm." Nancy Cabot, *Chicago Tribune,* Sep 16, 1934

12 The Gordian Knot, *Kansas City Star,* Jul 14, 1934. Also known as:
  The Mystic Maze, *Kansas City Star,* Jul 14, 1934.

13 Columbian Chain, *Chicago Tribune,* May 27, 1935.

4 21 x 21 grid

5 21 x 21 grid

6 21 x 21 grid

7 21 x 21 grid

8 21 x 21 grid

9 21 x 21 grid

10 21 x 21 grid

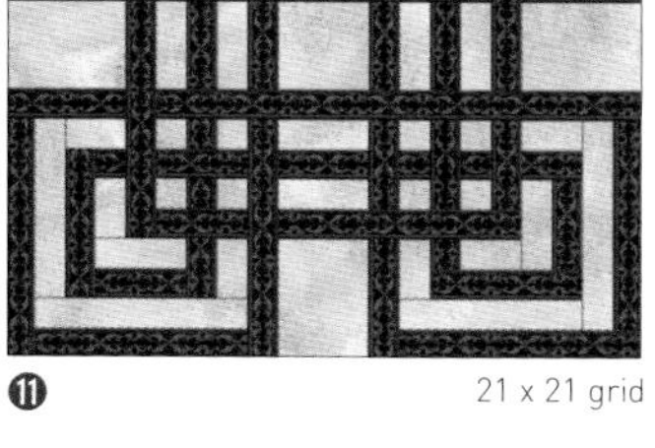
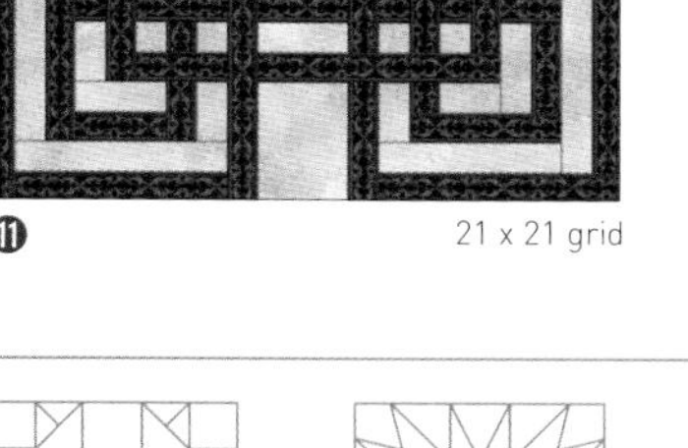

11 21 x 21 grid

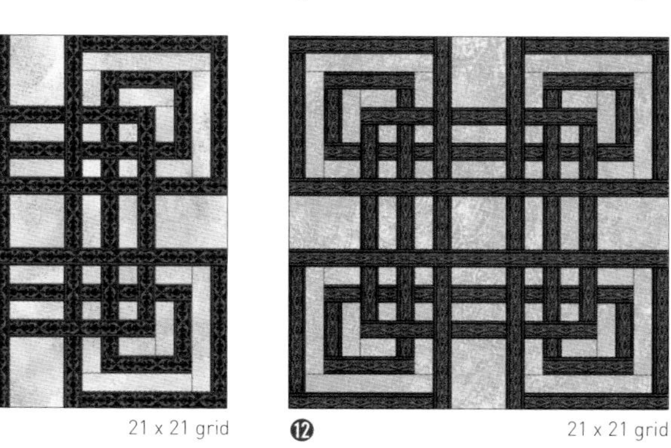

12 21 x 21 grid

13 12 x 12 grid

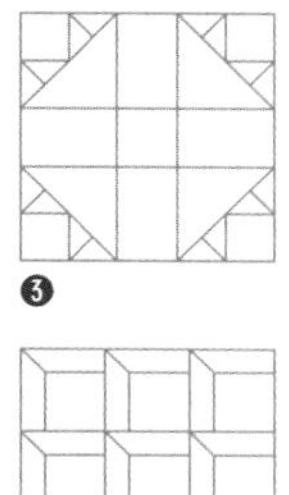
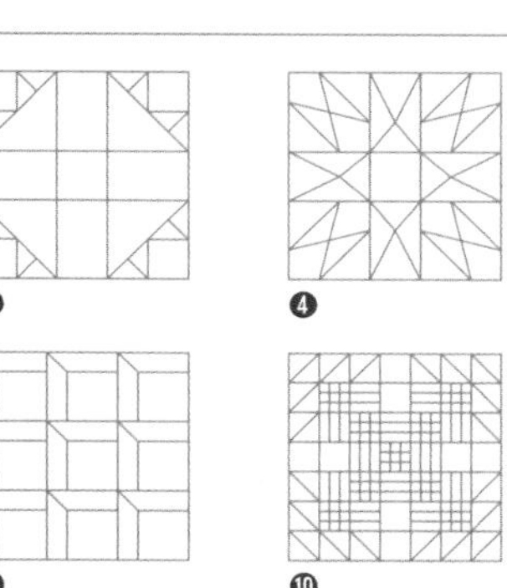
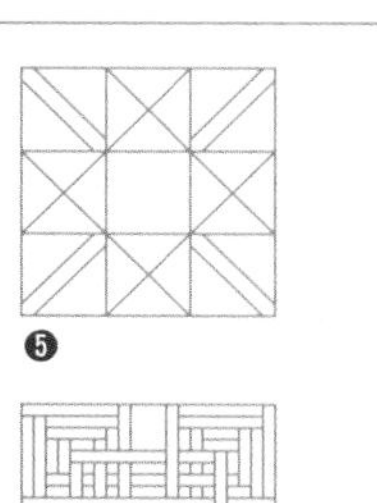
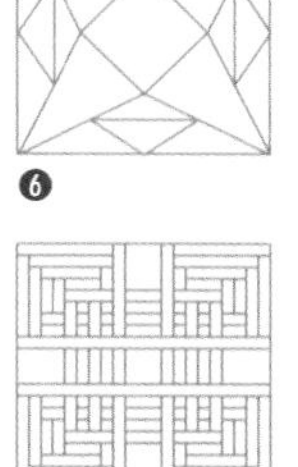
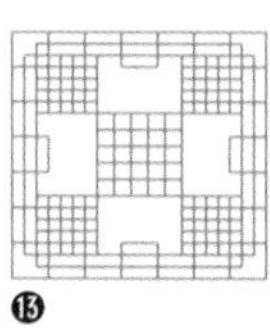
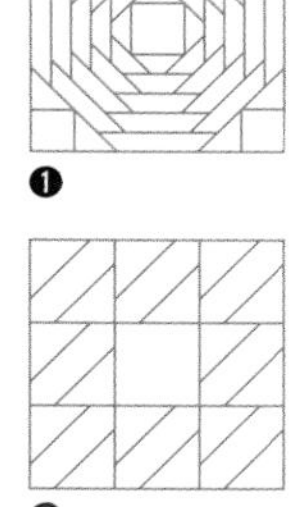
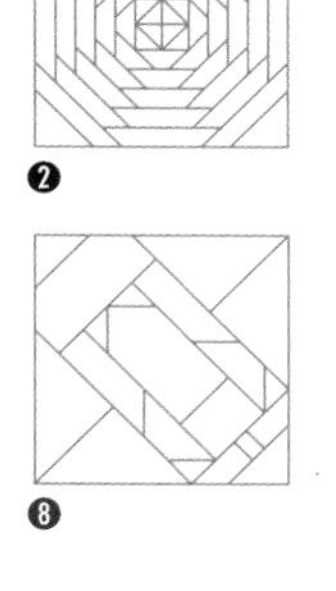
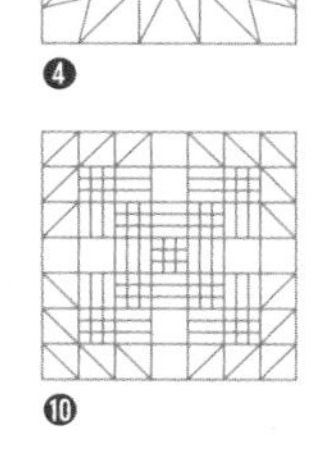

1 2 3 4 5 6

7 8 9 10 11 12 13

❶ **Log Cabin,** Orlofsky, 1947.

❷ **A Frame with Diamonds,** *Kansas City Star,* Oct 1, 1947.

❸ **Four H Club,** ca. 1938, per Havig.

❹ **Cluster of Lillies** [sic], *Kansas City Star,* Dec 22, 1934. See 0-0.
"This cluster of lilies name quilt may be made in the colors of natural lilies. Old-time quilters used to begin a name quilt early in the new year and finish it before the next one." *Kansas City Star,* Dec 22, 1934

❺ **Lover's Knot,** Laura Wheeler, *Cincinnati Enquirer,* Oct 13, 1933.

❻ **Feather Star,** *Ladies Art Company,* 1897. Also known as:
Saw Tooth, Eveline Foland, *Kansas City Star,* Aug 3, 1929.

❼ **Feather Star,** Webster, 1915.

❽ **Halley's Comet,** Nancy Cabot, *Chicago Tribune,* Aug 4, 1935.

❾ **Squares and Oblongs,** *Grandmother Clark's Authentic Early American Patchwork Quilts, Book No. 23,* 1932.

❿ **Mountain Homespun,** Nancy Cabot, *Chicago Tribune,* Jun 7, 1935.

⓫ **Feathered Square,** Laura Wheeler, *Cincinnati Enquirer,* Mar 18, 1934.

⓬ **Evergreen Tree,** Nancy Cabot, *Chicago Tribune,* May 26, 1937.

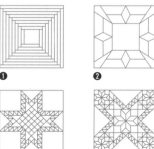

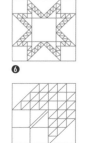

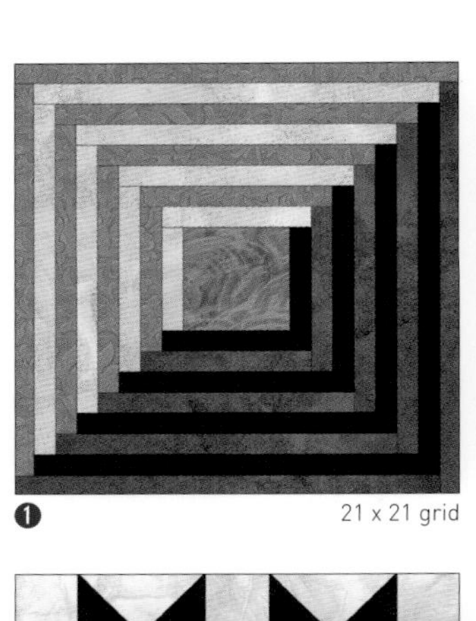
❶ 21 x 21 grid

❷ 42 x 42 grid

❸ 42 x 42 grid

❹ 42 x 42 grid

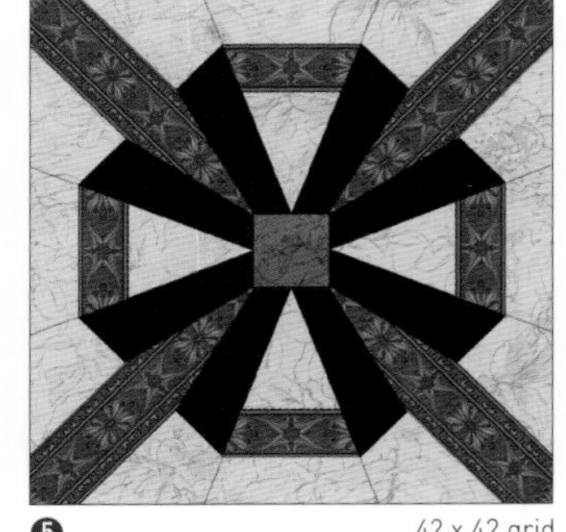
❺ 42 x 42 grid

❻ 42 x 42 grid

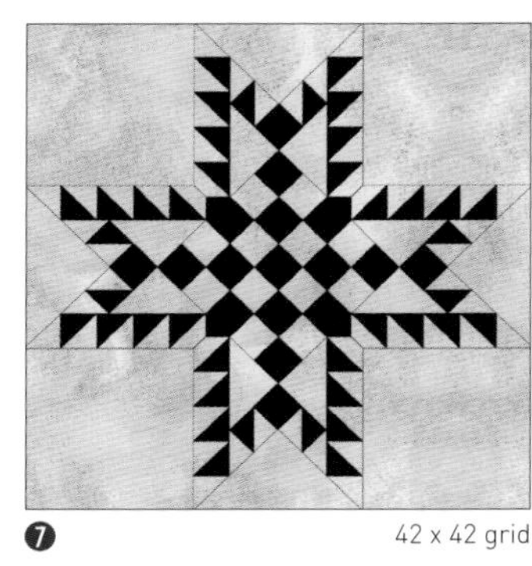
❼ 42 x 42 grid

❽ 42 x 42 grid

❾ 42 x 42 grid

❿ 42 x 42 grid

⓫ 42 x 42 grid

⓬ 42 x 42 grid

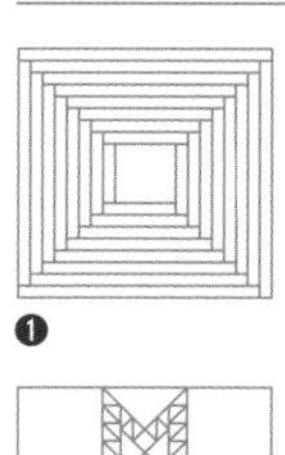
❶

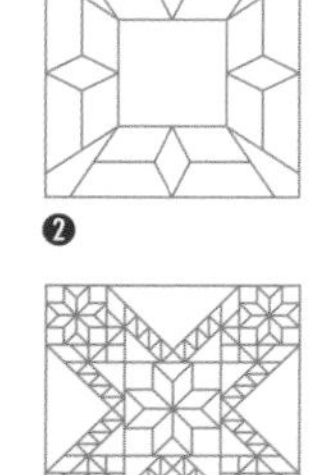
❷ ❸

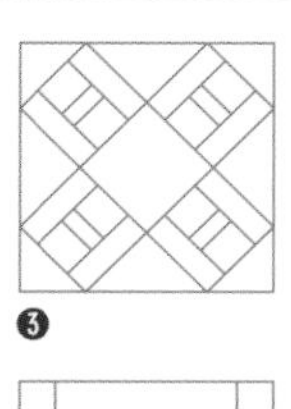
❹ ❺

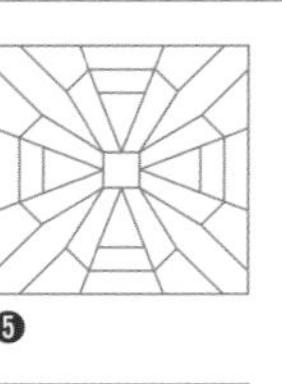
❻

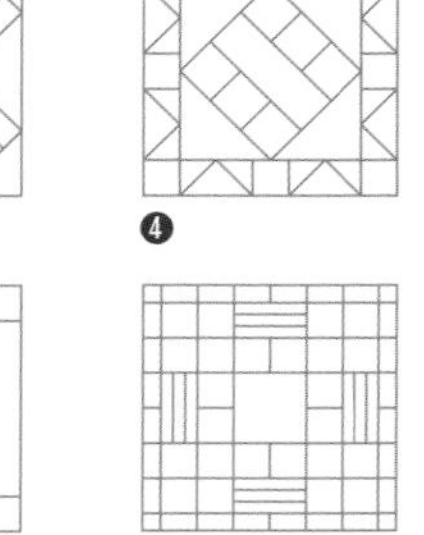
❼ ❽ ❾ ❿

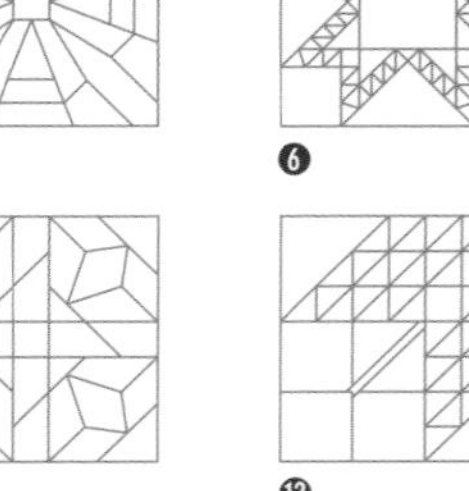
⓫ ⓬

❶ **The Butterfly,** Home Art Studios, Bettina, *Des Moines Register,* Nov 6, 1932.

❷ **The Farmer's Daughter,** Nancy Cabot, *Chicago Tribune,* Nov 21, 1934.
"In a prim little town in Ohio during the circumspect fifties, the wife of one of the esteemed members of the Methodist church pieced 'The Farmer's Daughter.' It made a beautiful coverlet pieced in colors of soft lavender gold and white; all colors most expressive of a quiet sensitive person." Nancy Cabot, *Chicago Tribune,* Nov 21, 1934

❸ **Wild Goose Chase,** Miall, 1937. See 174-10, 184-4, and 269-10.

❹ **Watermill,** *Grandmother Clark's Authentic Early American Quilts, Book No. 21,* 1932.

❺ **Gilbert's Corner,** Jinny Beyer, Jinny Beyer Studio design, 2007.

❻ **Reflections,** Jinny Beyer, Jinny Beyer Studio design, 2007.

❼ **Pineapple,** *The Patchwork Book,* 1932.

❽ **Pineapple Squares,** Nancy Cabot, *Chicago Tribune,* Jan 26, 1937.

❾ **White House Steps,** ca. 1938, per Havig. Also known as:
Widower's Choice, ca. 1938, per Havig.

❿ **Log Cabin,** *The Patchwork Book,* 1929.

⓫ **Happy Days,** *Farm Journal and Farmers Wife,* ca. 1941.

⓬ **Twister,** Jinny Beyer, Jinny Beyer Studio design, 2007.

❶ **Lightning,** Nancy Cabot, *Chicago Tribune,* May 20, 1935.

❷ **KC Star Exhibition Home,** ca. 1938, per Havig.

❸ **Star and Cross,** Finley, 1929. See 193-8

❹ **Garden Maze,** Nancy Cabot,*Chicago Tribune,* Mar 3, 1934. See 167-6, 173-9, 242-5, and 258-8 Also known as:

Sun Dial, Nancy Cabot, *Chicago Tribune,* Mar 3, 1934.

Tangled Garter, Nancy Cabot, *Chicago Tribune,* Mar 3, 1934.

Tirzah's Treasure, Nancy Cabot, *Chicago Tribune,* Mar 3, 1934.

❺ **The Red Cross Quilt,** *Kansas City Star,* Jan 22, 1941.

❻ **Framed Cross,** Nancy Cabot, *Chicago Tribune,* Mar 29, 1935.

❼ **Star of the Night,** Laura Wheeler, *Cincinnati Enquirer,* Apr 29, 1934.

❽ **Little Giant,** Nancy Cabot, *Chicago Tribune,* Apr 16, 1933.

❾ **Feather Edge Star,** *Kansas City Star,* Aug 11, 1934.

❿ **Hour Glass,** Nancy Cabot, *Chicago Tribune,* Jan 18, 1934.

⓫ **Tree of Life,** Laura Wheeler, *Cincinnati Enquirer,* Nov 9, 1933.

"This beautiful design, one of the very oldest in the art of quiltmaking, comes from Vermont. It is one of the numerous 'Tree of Life' patterns which were originally inspired by the 'Tree of Life' motifs so recurrent in Oriental rugs. At the present time, quilts of this design are very rare and to make one would be to create a priceless heirloom. Since this quilt is simple to make, there is as much enjoyment in making it as there is in being the proud possessor of so lovely a piece of handicraft." Laura Wheeler, *Cincinnati Enquirer,* Jan 9, 1933

⓬ **The Goblet Quilt,** Eveline Foland, *Kansas City Star,* Sep 6, 1930. See 171-2. Also known as:

Water Glass, *Kansas City Star,* Mar 10, 1934.

"In the days of Carrie Nation and Frances E. Willard this was a popular block among quilters of the W.C.T.U. Often women embroidered the date of their pledge card in the triangles or on the print." *Kansas City Star,* Mar 10, 1934

❶ 46 x 46 grid

❷ 46 x 46 grid

❸ 25 x 25 grid

❹ 25 x 25 grid

❺ 25 x 25 grid

❻ 25 x 25 grid

❼ 50 x 50 grid

❽ 50 x 50 grid

❾ 50 x 50 grid

❿ 50 x 50 grid

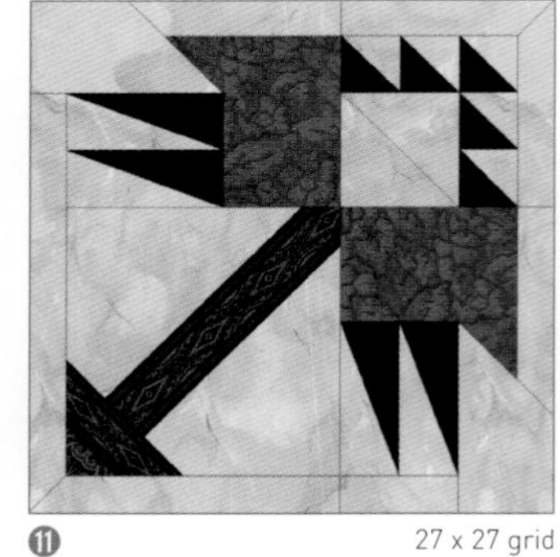
⓫ 27 x 27 grid

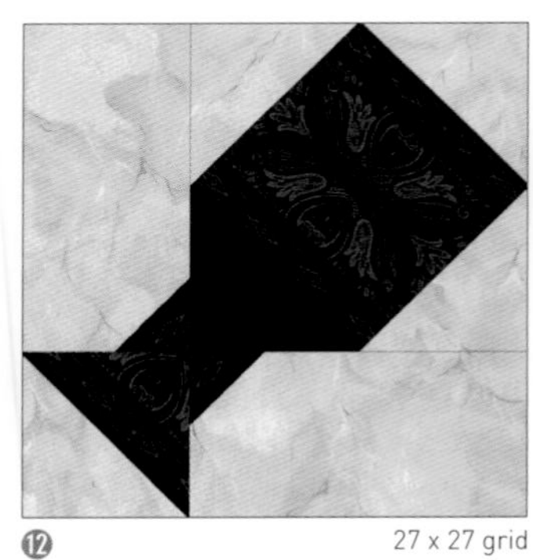
⓬ 27 x 27 grid

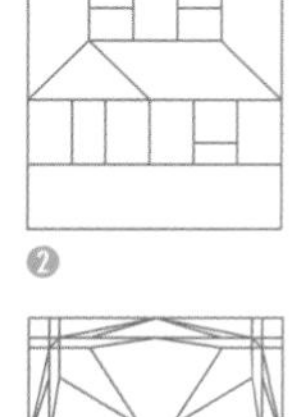
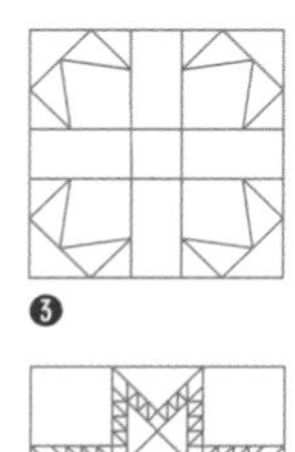
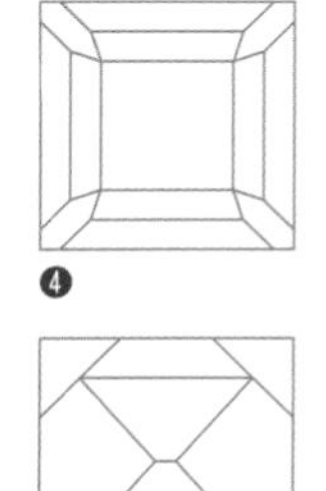
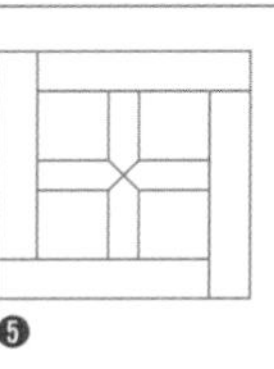
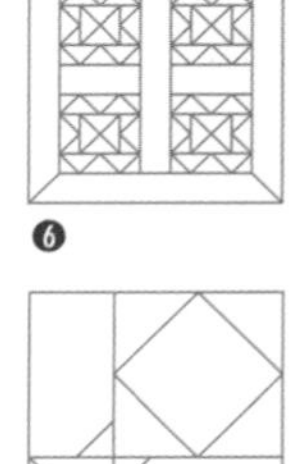
❶ ❷ ❸ ❹ ❺ ❻

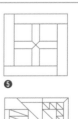

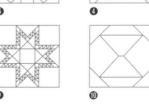

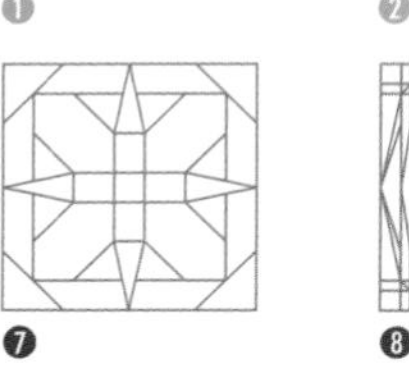
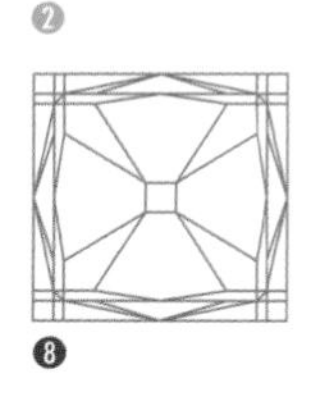
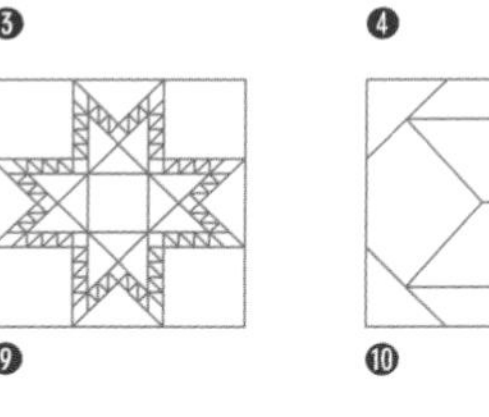
❼ ❽ ❾ ❿ ⓫ ⓬

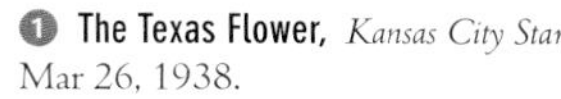

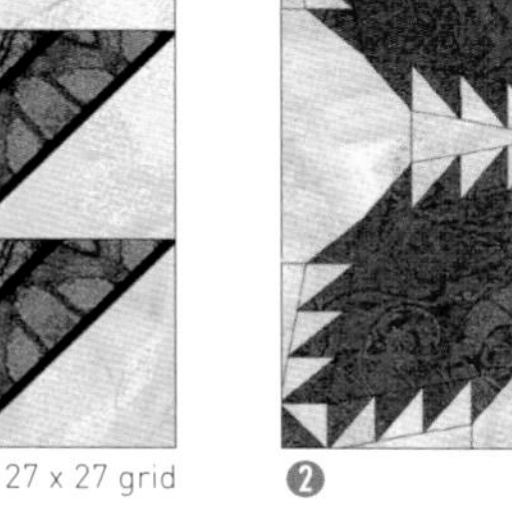

1 27 x 27 grid

2 54 x 54 grid

3 29 x 29 grid

4 58 x 58 grid

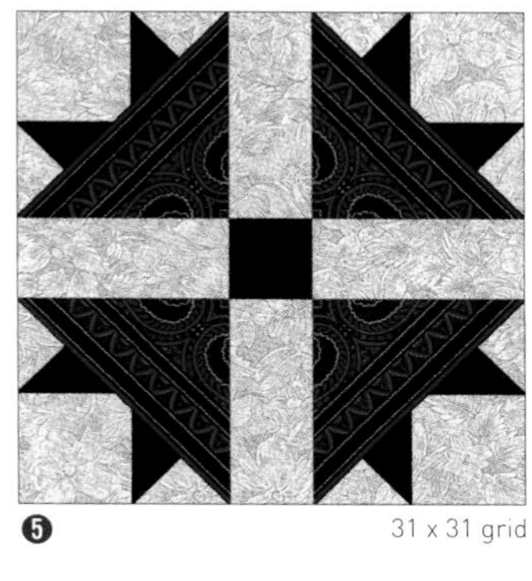

5 31 x 31 grid

6 62 x 62 grid

7 33 x 33 grid

8 41 x 41 grid

9 51 x 51 grid

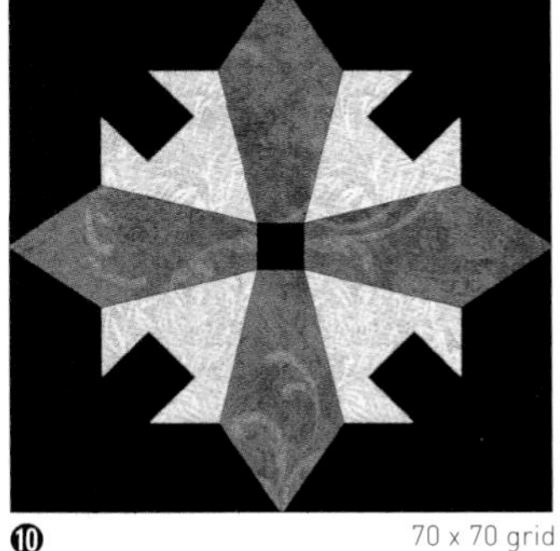

10 70 x 70 grid

1. **The Texas Flower,** *Kansas City Star,* Mar 26, 1938.
2. **The Fish in the Dish,** *Mrs. Danner's Third Quilt Book,* 1954.
3. **Nose Gay,** Eveline Foland, *Kansas City Star,* Apr 2, 1932.
4. **Chestnut Burr,** Hall, 1935.
   Feather Star, Hall, 1935.
   Saw Tooth, Hall, 1935.
   Star of Bethlehem, Hall, 1935.
   Twinkling Star, Hall, 1935.
5. **Tulip Wreath,** ca. 1938, per Havig.
6. **Little Boy's Breeches,** *Kansas City Star,* Jul 16, 1938. See 236-1, 338-3, and 342-2.
7. **The Oak Leaf,** Jane Alan, *Illinois State Register,* Apr 10, 1932.
8. **California Star,** Hall, 1935.
9. **Ohio Shade Tree,** Nancy Page, *Birmingham News,* Apr 11, 1933. Also known as:
   The Historic Oak Leaf, *Kansas City Star,* Jan 4, 1961.
10. **Swords and Plowshares,** *Kansas City Star,* Jan 21, 1953.

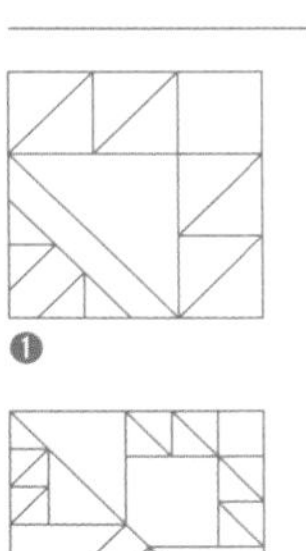
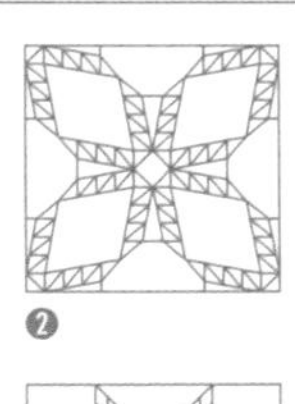

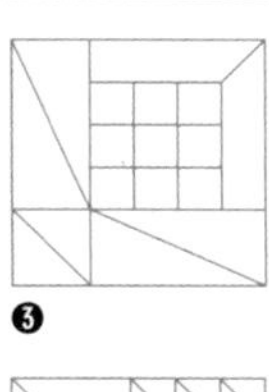
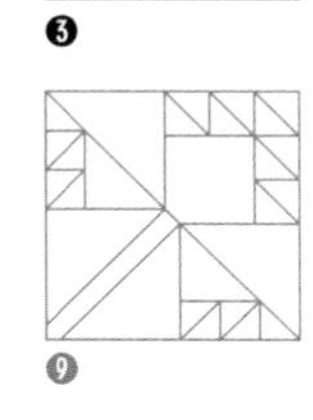
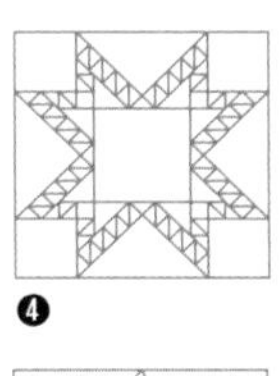
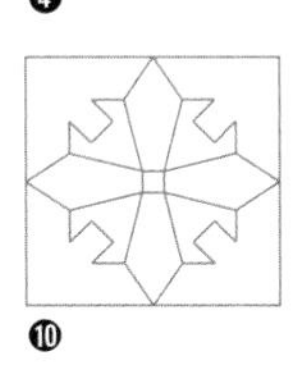
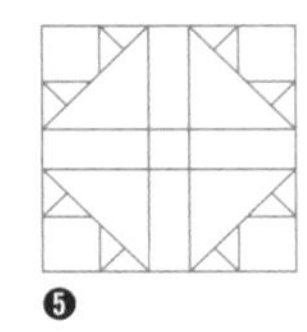
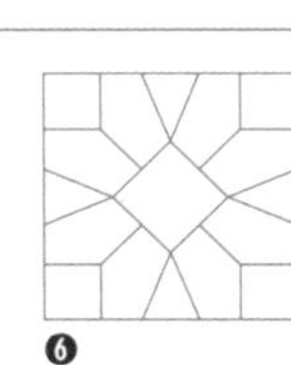

1 2 3 4 5 6 7 8 9 10

8-Pointed Star Category

Includes ● *multi-grid designs*

❶ **Star,** *Ohio Farmer,* Nov 29, 1894. See 64-5 and 139-1. Also known as:
- **Diamond,** *The Dressmaking Book,* 1929.
- **Diamond Star,** *Q Book 103, All Year Quilts,* date unknown.
- **Eastern Star,** date unknown, per Brackman.
- **Eight Point Star,** *Colonial Quilts,* 1932.
- **Eight Pointed Star,** *Ladies Art Company,* 1897.
- **Hanging Diamonds,** date unknown, per Brackman.
- **Lemon Star,** Finley, 1929.
- **Lone Star,** Nancy Cabot, *Chicago Tribune,* Oct 25, 1936.
- **Simple Star,** date unknown, per Brackman.
- **A Star of Diamond Points,** *Kansas City Star,* Apr 17, 1957.
- **Star of Lemoyne,** Hall, 1935.
- **Star of the East,** Home Art Studios, *Cincinnati Enquirer* Mar 11, 1933.
- **Sunlight and Shadows,** *Kansas City Star,* Jan 7, 1942.
- **The Star,** *Kansas City Star,* Aug 8, 1936.
- **Two Star Quilt,** *Farm and Home,* Jul 15, 1899.
- **Variable Star,** date unknown, per Brackman.

❷ **Polk Ohio,** Nancy Page, *Birmingham News,* Oct 13, 1936.

❸ **The North Star,** Home Art Studios, *Cincinnati Enquirer,* Mar 4, 1943. Also known as:
- **The Divided Star,** *Mrs. Danner's Fourth Quilt Book,* 1958.
- **Le Moyne Star,** Ickis, 1949.
- **Star of Le Moine,** Hinson, 1973.

❹ **Silver and Gold,** Eveline Foland, *Kansas City Star,* Jan 3, 1931. Also known as:
- **Gold and Silver,** Nancy Cabot, *Chicago Tribune,* Jun 29, 1935.
- **Star of the East,** Hall, 1935.
- **Winter Stars,** Nancy Cabot, *Chicago Tribune,* May 7, 1938.

❺ **Prosperity,** Nancy Cabot, *Chicago Tribune,* Jul 20, 1938.

❻ **St. Louis Block,** Nancy Cabot, *Chicago Tribune,* Oct 22, 1934. Also known as:
- **Star of St. Louis,** Nancy Cabot, *Chicago Tribune,* Aug 9, 1937.

❼ **Enigma Star,** See 283-8. Hall, 1935.

❽ **St. Louis Block,** *Ladies Art Company,* 1922. See 276-8 and 283-9. Also known as:
- **St. Louis Star,** Hall, 1935.

❾ **Kaleidostar,** Virginia Tolston, Beyer, Jinny, *The Quilter's Album...,* 1980.

❶ 8-pointed star grid 1

❷ 8-pointed star grid 1

❸ 8-pointed star grid 1

❹ 8-pointed star grid 1

❺ 8-pointed star grid 1

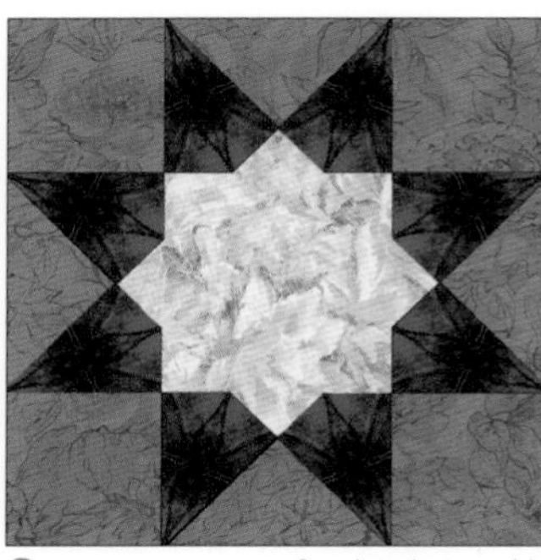

❻ 8-pointed star grid 1

❼ 8-pointed star grid 1

❽ 8-pointed star grid 1

❾ 8-pointed star grid 1

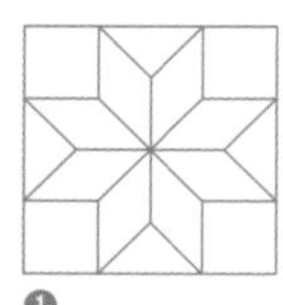

❶

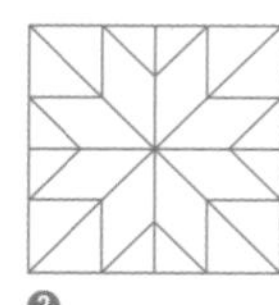

❷

❸

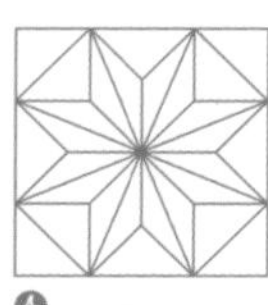

❹

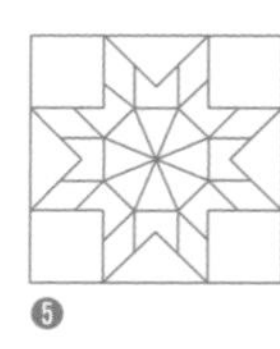

❺

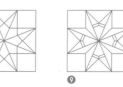

❻

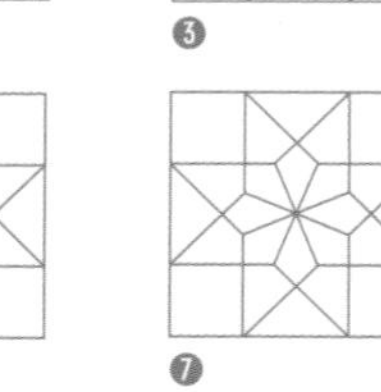

❼

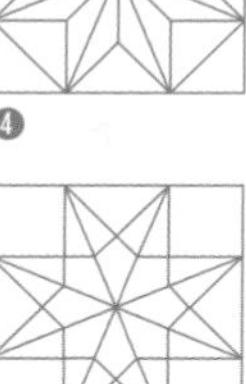

❽

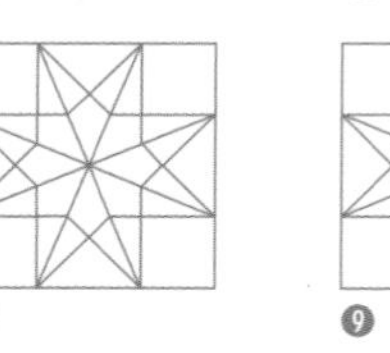

❾

❶ 8-pointed star grid 1 and 4

❷ 8-pointed star grid 1

❸ 8-pointed star grid 1

❹ 8-pointed star grid 1

❺ 8-pointed star grid 1

❻ 8-pointed star grid 1

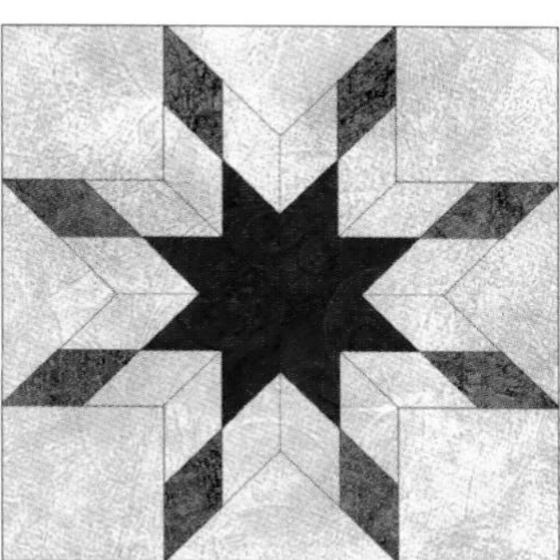
❼ 8-pointed star grid 1

❽ 8-pointed star grid 1

❾ 8-pointed star grid 1

❿ 8-pointed star grid 1

⓫ 8-pointed star grid 1

⓬ 8-pointed star grid 1

❶ **Castle Keep,** Jinny Beyer, Beyer, Jinny *The Quilter's Album ...,* 1980.

❷ **Friendship Star,** *Kansas City Star,* Apr 29, 1933.

❸ **The Missouri Daisy,** *Kansas City Star,* Mar 12, 1958. Also known as:

- **Missouri Daisy,** Aunt Martha series: *Quilt Designs,* ca. 1952.

❹ **Charm Star,** *Prize Winning Designs,* ca. 1931.

❺ **The Sunflower,** *The Country Gentleman,* Jul 1930.

❻ **Shadow Star,** Aunt Martha' series: *Quilts: Modern-Colonial,* ca. 1954.

❼ **Star of Le Moyne,** ca. 1850, per Holstein. See 283-3. Also known as:

- **Blazing Star,** Ruby McKim, McKim, 1931.
- **The Bright Morning Star,** *Kansas City Star,* Sep 14, 1960.
- **Eastern Star,** Gutcheon, *The Perfect Patchwork Primer,* 1973.
- **Eight Pointed Star,** Beyer, Alice, *Quilting,* 1934.
- **Little Stars,** *Antique Quilts,* 1974.
- **Morning Star,** *Old Fashioned Quilts,* ca. 1931.
- **Patriotic Star,** *Kansas City Star,* May 9, 1936.
- **Pierced Star,** *Stearns and Foster Catalog of Quilt Patterns Designs,* date unknown.
- **Quilt of the Century,** *Q Book 116, Blue Ribbon Quilts,* date unknown.
- **Rising Star,** Nancy Page, *Nashville Banner,* Jun 21, 1932.
- **Star of the Bluegrass,** *The Mountain Mist Blue Book of Quilts,* date unknown.
- **Star of the East,** date unknown, per Brackman.
- **Star upon Stars,** Hall, 1935.
- **Twinkling Star,** Nancy Cabot, *Chicago Tribune,* Apr 22, 1935.
- **Virginia Star,** Hall, 1935.

❽ **Blazing Star,** *Ladies Art Company,* 1897. "This is block 3 of the Star of Many Points Series quilt by Nancy Page." *The Lowell Sun,* Jun 4, 1934

❾ **Unknown Star,** Clara Stone, *Practical Needlework,* ca. 1906.

❿ **All American Star,** Aunt Martha series: *Quilt Designs,* ca. 1952.

⓫ **Witch's Star,** Nancy Cabot, *Chicago Tribune,* Jan 29, 1938.

⓬ **Formosa Tea Leaf,** Eveline Foland, *Kansas City Star,* Nov 14, 1931.

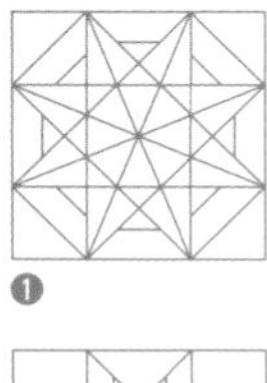
❶

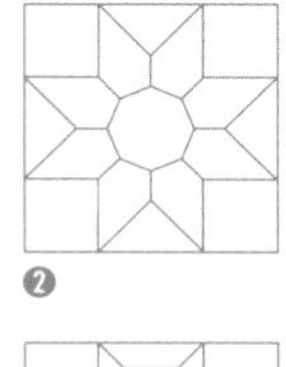
❷

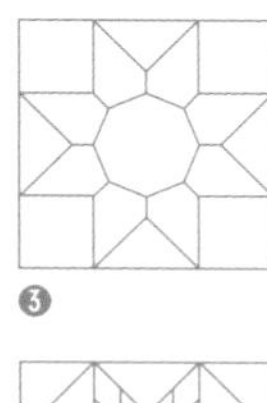
❸

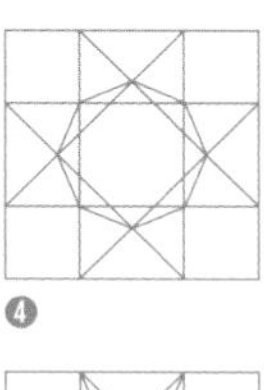
❹

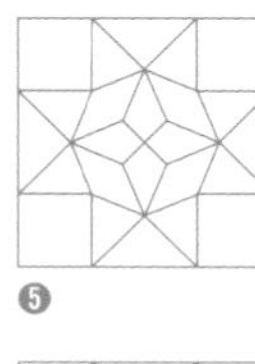
❺

❻

❼

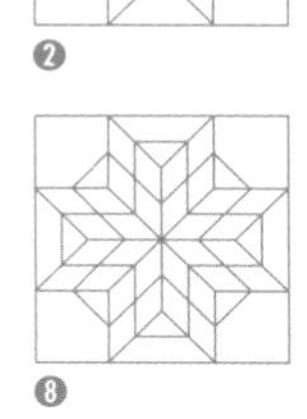
❽

❾

❿

⓫

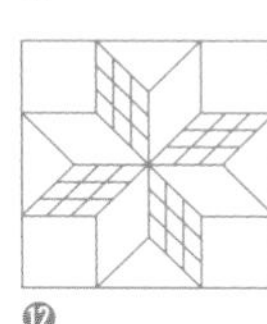
⓬

❶ **Connecticut Star,** *Farm Journal and Farmer's Wife* (Silver Anniversary issue), 1945.

❷ **Flying Bat,** *Ladies Art Company,* 1897. Also known as:

- **Airplanes,** *Farm Journal and Farmers Wife,* ca. 1941.
- **Dove at the Window,** *Kansas City Star,* Jun 6, 1936.
- **Dove in the Window,** Ruby McKim, *Kansas City Star,* Mar 9, 1929.
- **Doves,** *Colonial Quilts,* 1932.
- **Doves at the Window,** *Old Fashioned Quilts,* ca. 1931.
- **Flying Bats,** Nancy Cabot, *Chicago Tribune,* Mar 12, 1935.
- **Flying Star,** *Colonial Quilts,* 1932.
- **Formosa Tea Leaf,** Hall, 1935.
- **Four Birds,** *The Dressmaking Book,* 1929.
- **Four Doves,** Nancy Page, *Nashville Banner,* Sep 5, 1933.
- **Four Swallows,** *Old Fashioned Quilts,* ca. 1931.
- **Morning Star,** Nancy Cabot, *Chicago Tribune,* Jul 5, 1937.
- **Polaris Star,** Hall, 1935.

❸ **Doves in the Window,** Nancy Cabot, *Chicago Tribune,* Jul 8, 1933.

❹ **Star of Hope,** Clara Stone, *Practical Needlework,* ca. 1906. Also known as:

- **Harvest Sun,** Finley, 1929.
- **Patty's Star,** Hall, 1935.
- **Prairie Star,** Hall, 1935.
- **Ship's Wheel,** Hall, 1935.
- **The Ship's Wheel,** Finley, 1929.
- **Shower of Stars,** Orlofsky, 1974.
- **Star Bouquet,** Virginia Snow, *Grandma Dexter's Appliqué and Patchwork Designs, Book 36a,* ca. 1932.
- **Stars of Alabama,** *The Mountain Mist Blue Book of Quilts,* 1935.
- **Triple Star,** *Prairie Farmer,* Mar 24, 1928.
- **Virginia Star,** Ruby McKim, *Kansas City Star,* Jul 8, 1933.
- **Virginia's Star,** Ickis, 1949.

❺ **Stars upon Stars,** *Ladies Art Company,* 1897. Also known as:

- **Star of Bethlehem,** Ickis, 1949.

❻ **Glittering Star,** *Grandmother Clark's Patchwork Quilt Designs, From Books 20-21-23,* 1932.
Also known as:

- **Star upon Star Quilt,** Home Art Studios, *Des Moines Register,* Feb 5, 1933.
- **Stonewall Jackson,** Nancy Cabot, *Chicago Tribune,* Apr 23, 1933.
- **Sunburst Star,** Laura Wheeler, *Illinois State Register,* May 24, 1933.

"The confederate general, Thomas Jonathan Jackson, received his historic sobriquet, 'Stonewall,' from the rallying cry of Bee at the first battle of Bull Run on July 21, 1881. Bee's brigade broke under the federal charge and was threatened with defeat when Jackson hurried to the rescue with five Virginia regiments and put up an indomitable resistance. Bee made a dramatic appeal to his soldiers, pointing to Jackson 'standing like a stone wall' and taking up the refrain, his men remobilized to stem the charge. Representing the powerful courage of Jackson, the accompanying quilt pattern shows the points of the star being joined together to make a solid wall." Nancy Cabot, *Chicago Tribune,* Apr 23, 1933

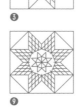

❶ 8-pointed star grid 1

❷ 8-pointed star grid 1

❸ 8-pointed star grid 1

❹ 8-pointed star grid 1

❺ 8-pointed star grid 1

❻ 8-pointed star grid 1

❼ 8-pointed star grid 1

❽ 8-pointed star grid 1

❾ 8-pointed star grid 1

❿ 8-pointed star grid 1

⓫ 8-pointed star grid 4

⓬ 8-pointed star grid 1

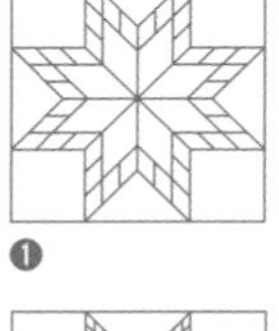
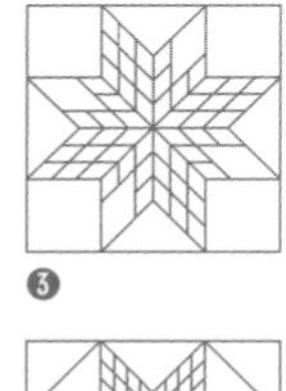

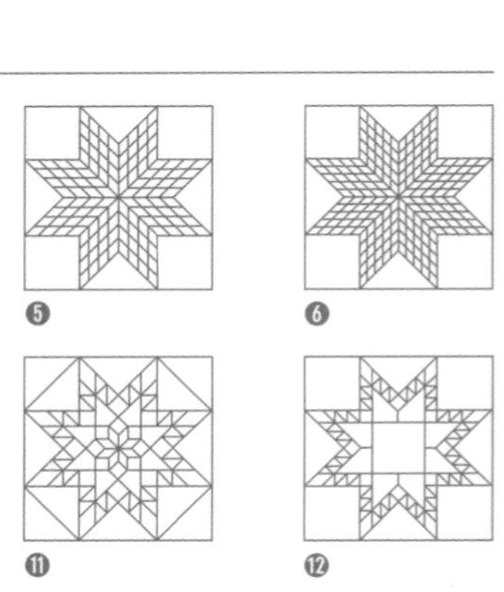
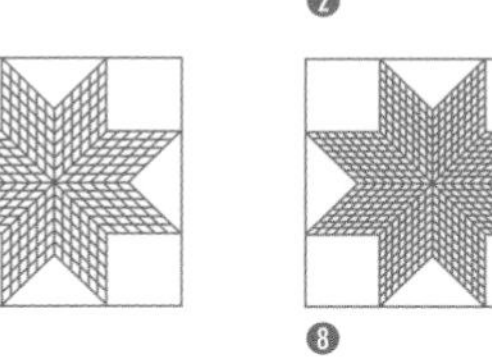
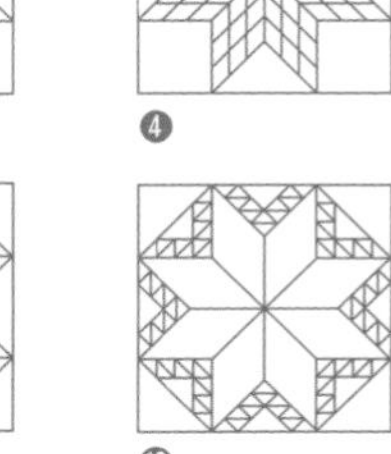

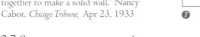

❶ ❷ ❸ ❹ ❺ ❻ ❼ ❽ ❾ ❿ ⓫ ⓬

Quick Reference: Feathered Stars

"'Feather star' always has been among the favorites in star patterns. It is classified as one of the older blocks and always has been outstanding in the field of elaborate quilt designs. The first "Feather Star" was pieced as early as 1825, and the favorite colors, at that time, were red, green, and white, while modern colors are more varied." Nancy Cabot, *Chicago Tribune*, August 14, 1935

Feather Star, Hall. **See : 275-5.**

Feather Star, *Ladies Art Company.* **See 272-6.**

Twinkling Star, *Ladies Art Company.* **See 269-5.**

Star of Chamblie, Hall. **See 270-11.**

Star of Bethlehem, *Old Fashioned Quilts.* **See 278-12 .**

Feather Star, Hall. **See 180-9.**

Feather Edge Star, *Kansas City Star.* **See 274-9.**

The Feather Edged Star, McKim. **See 281-7.**

Feathered Star, *Colonial Quilts.* **See 281-13.**

Star of Bethlehem, *Topeka Daily Capital.* **See 281-2.**

Golden Splendor, *Mrs. Danner's Third Quilt Book.* **See 346-10.**

Radiant Star, *Prize Winning Designs.* **See 281-1.**

Discovery Bay, *Patchwork Portfolio.* **See 281-3.**

Starfish, *Patchwork Portfolio.* **See 303-11.**

Lucinda's Star, Hall. **See 278-10.**

Summer Sun, *Chicago Tribune.* **See 278-11.**

Constellation, *Patchwork Portfolio.* **See 281-4.**

Ferris Wheel, *Patchwork Portfolio.* **See 281-9.**

Pigeon Toes, *Patchwork Portfolio.* **See 281-5.**

Sparkler, *Patchwork Portfolio.* **See 281-8.**

California Star, Ickis. **See : 115-13.**

California Star Pattern, *Ladies Art Company.* **See : 266-3.**

Joining Star, *Ladies Art Company.* **See 263-9.**

Feather Star, *Webster.* **See 272-7.**

Joined Star, *Chicago Tribune.* **See 265-1.**

Feather Star, *Chicago Tribune.* **See 231-9.**

Morning Star, *Chicago Tribune.* **See 260-7.**

Halley's Comet, *Chicago Tribune.* **See 272-8.**

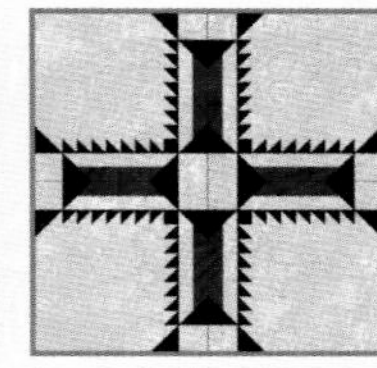

Apache Trail, *Chicago Tribune.* **See 177-11.**

The Pine Burr Quilt, *Kansas City Star.* **See 219-3.**

"Mysterious—beautiful—the stars have held a fascination for man since earliest times. The quiltmaker of olden times, too, found them a practical and decorative motif to use in her quilt patterns. Probably the loveliest of all her star patterns is the 'Sunburst Star,' known under other names, too, but always developed from a diamond patch that starts out as a small eight-pointed star and grows, sometimes in shaded colors, sometimes in contrasting patches, to a beautiful large star." Laura Wheeler, *Charleston Gazette,* May 24, 1933

❼ **Lone Star,** *Ladies Art Company,* 1928. Also known as:
  Bethlehem Star, *Quilt Blocks from The Farmer's Wife,* 1932.

❽ **Texas Star,** *Grandmother's Patchwork Quilt Designs, From Books 20, 21 and 22,* 1932.

❾ **Olde World Star,** Jinny Beyer, Beyer, Jinny, *Soft-Edge Piecing,* 1989.

❿ **Lucinda's Star,** Hall, 1935.

⓫ **Summer Sun,** Nancy Cabot, *Chicago Tribune,* Mar 22, 1936.

⓬ **Blazing Star,** *Old Fashioned Quilts,* ca. 1931. Also known as:
  Diadem Star, *Old Fashioned Quilts,* ca. 1931.
  Star of Bethlehem, *Old Fashioned Quilts,* ca. 1931.

(continued next page)

Cocklebur, Aunt Martha series: *The Quilt Fair Comes to You.* **See 317-3.**

Pineapple Cactus, *Kansas City Star.* **See 317-4.**

Philadelphia Patch, *Ladies Art Company.* **See 337-6.**

Pine Cones, *Chicago Tribune.* **See 340-8.**

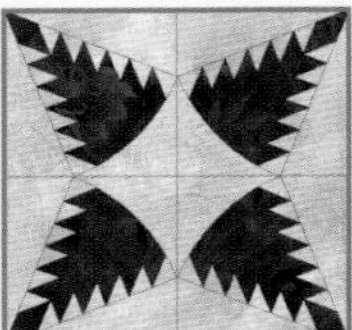

Evergreen, *The Farmer's Wife Book of New Designs and Patterns.* **See 340-9.**

The Mayflower Quilt, *Mrs. Danner's Fifth Quilt Book.* **See 324-9.**

The Philippines, *Ladies Art Company.* **See 269-4.**

Philippines, Hall. **See 256-1.**

The Philippines, *Chicago Tribune.* **See 121-11.**

Cocklebur, *Chicago Tribune.* **See 331-11.**

Cockelburr, *Ladies Art Company.* **See , 336-10.**

The Fish in the Dish, *Mrs. Danner's Third Quilt Book.* **See 275-3.**

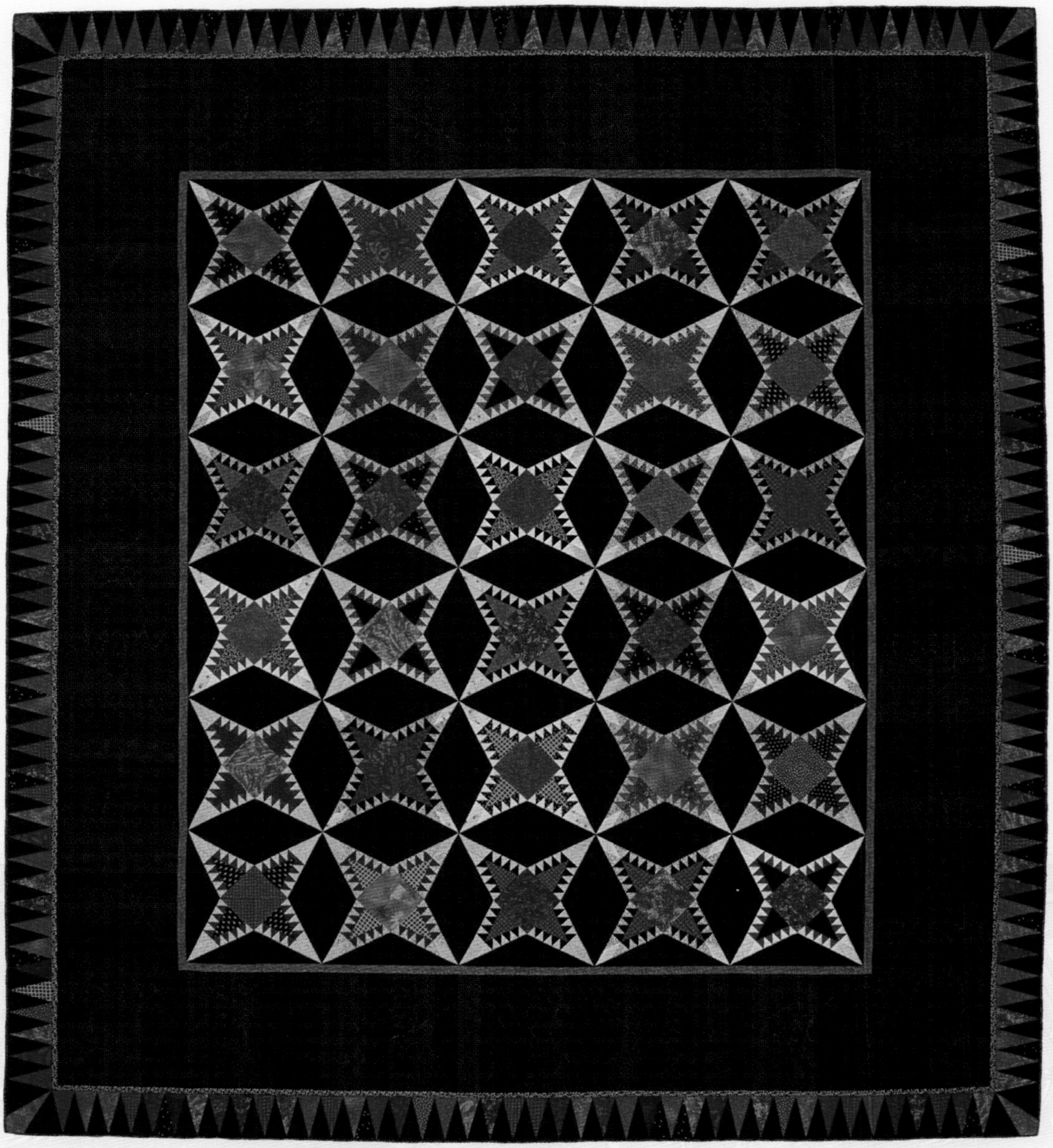

Hearts Design, Karen Luman, 2004. An adaptation of **Pine Burr** block.

❶ 8-pointed star grid 1

❷ 8-pointed star grid 1

❸ 8-pointed star grid 1

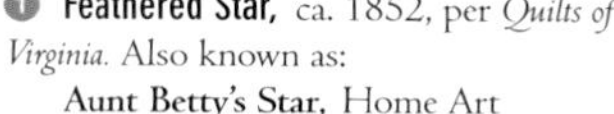

❶ **Feathered Star,** ca. 1852, per *Quilts of Virginia.* Also known as:
- **Aunt Betty's Star,** Home Art Studios, *World Herald,* Nov 6, 1933.
- **Chestnut Burr,** *Prize Winning Designs,* ca. 1931.
- **Radiant Star,** *Prize Winning Designs,* ca. 1931.
- **Snowflake,** *Farmer's Wife Book of New Designs and Patterns,* 1934.

❷ **Star of Bethlehem,** *Topeka Daily Capital,* Apr 15, 1934. Also known as:
- **Feathered Star,** *Mrs. Danner's Third Quilt Book,* 1954.

❸ **Discovery Bay,** Jinny Beyer, Beyer, Jinny, *Patchwork Portfolio,* 1989.

❹ **Constellation,** Jinny Beyer, Beyer, Jinny, *Patchwork Portfolio,* 1989.

❺ **Pigeon Toes,** Jinny Beyer, Beyer, Jinny, *Patchwork Portfolio,* 1989.

❻ **Feathered Star,** *Grandmother Clark's Patchwork Quilt Designs, From Books 20-21-23,* 1932.

❼ **The Feather Edged Star,** McKim, 1931.

❽ **Sparkler,** Jinny Beyer, Beyer, Jinny, *Patchwork Portfolio,* 1989.

❾ **Ferris Wheel,** Jinny Beyer, Beyer, Jinny, *Patchwork Portfolio,* 1989.

❿ **Knight's Star,** Nancy Cabot, *Chicago Tribune,* Feb 11, 1937.

⓫ **Gift Box,** Jinny Beyer, Hilton Head Seminar design, 2005.

⓬ **Crossed Star,** Jinny Beyer, Beyer, Jinny, *Patchwork Portfolio,* 1989.

⓭ **Feathered Star,** Home Art Studios, *Colonial Quilts,* 1932.

❹ 8-pointed star grid 1

❺ 8-pointed star grid 1

❻ 4 x 4 grid/8-pointed star grid 4

❼ 4 x 4 grid/8-pointed star grid

❽ 8-pointed star grid 4

❾ 8-pointed star grid 1

❿ 8-pointed star grid 3

⓫ 8-pointed star grid 3

⓬ 8-pointed star grid 3

⓭ multiple grids

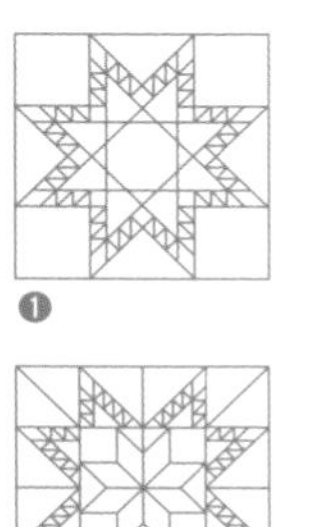

❶ ❼

❷

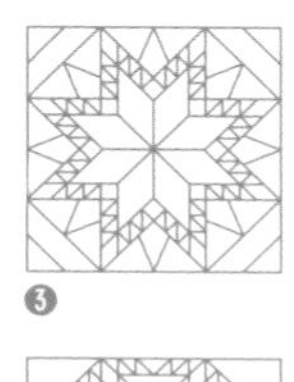

❸

❹

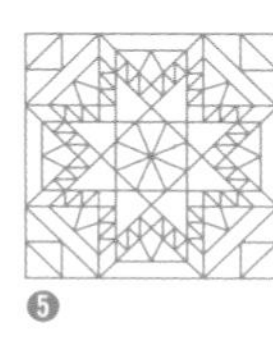

❺

❻

❽

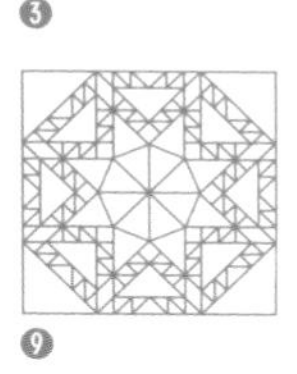

❾

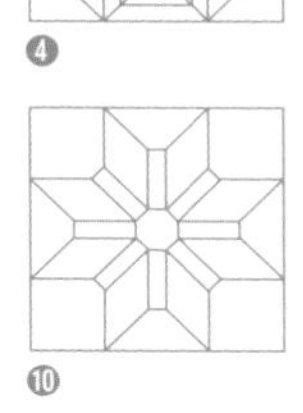

❿

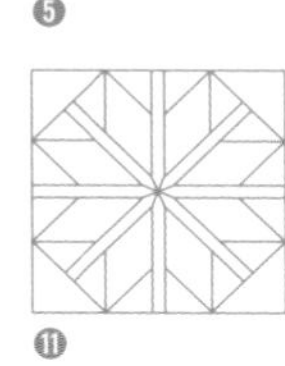

⓫

⓬

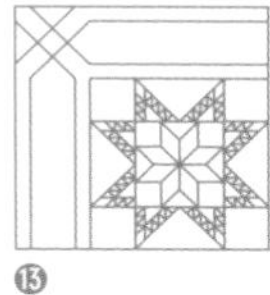

⓭

1 **River Bend,** Jinny Beyer, Beyer, Jinny, *Patchwork Portfolio,* 1989.

2 **Chateau,** Jinny Beyer, RJR Patterns, 2000. Also known as:
Shady Garden I, Jinny Beyer, RJR Patterns, 2000.

3 **May Apple,** Jinny Beyer, Beyer, Jinny, *Patchwork Portfolio,* 1989.

4 **Reef Rose,** Jinny Beyer, Hilton Head Seminar design, 1987; published in Beyer, Jinny, *Patchwork Portfolio.*

5 **Sydney Star,** Jinny Beyer, Beyer, Jinny, *Patchwork Portfolio,* 1989.

6 **Ramsey Rose,** Jinny Beyer, Beyer, Jinny, *Patchwork Portfolio,* 1989.

7 **Sand Dollar,** Jinny Beyer, Hilton Head Seminar design, 1986; published in Beyer, Jinny, *Patchwork Portfolio.*

8 **Mariner's Delight,** Jinny Beyer, Hilton Head Seminar design, 1987; published in Beyer, Jinny, *Patchwork Portfolio.*

9 **Starflower,** *Farmer's Wife Book of New Designs and Patterns,* 1934. Also known as:
Eight Point Star, unidentified newspaper clipping, date unknown.
Log Cabin Star, Hall, 1935.

10 **Star Bright,** Jinny Beyer, Beyer, Jinny, *The Quilter's Album ...,* 1980.

11 **Tennessee Star,** Eveline Foland, *Kansas City Star,* Jan 10, 1931.
"If the fondness for patchwork goes on presently there will be a star design for every state that has a star in Old Glory!"
Kansas City Star, Jan 10, 1931

12 **Star of the East,** *Grandmother Clark's Old Fashioned Quilt Designs, Book 21,* 1931.

1 8-pointed star grid 1

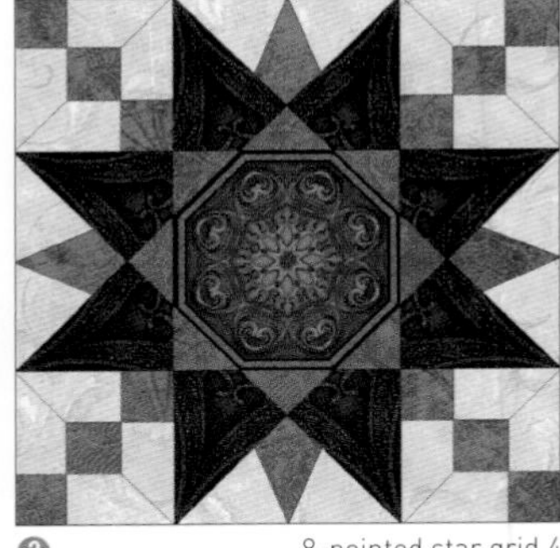

2 8-pointed star grid 4

3 8-pointed star grid 3

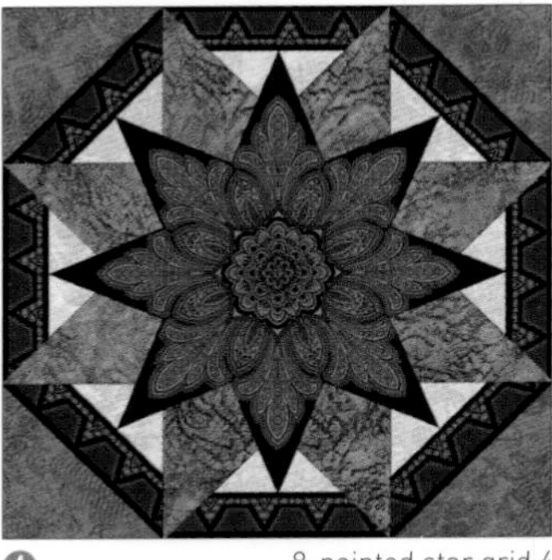

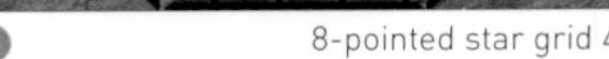

4 8-pointed star grid 4

5 8-pointed star grid 4

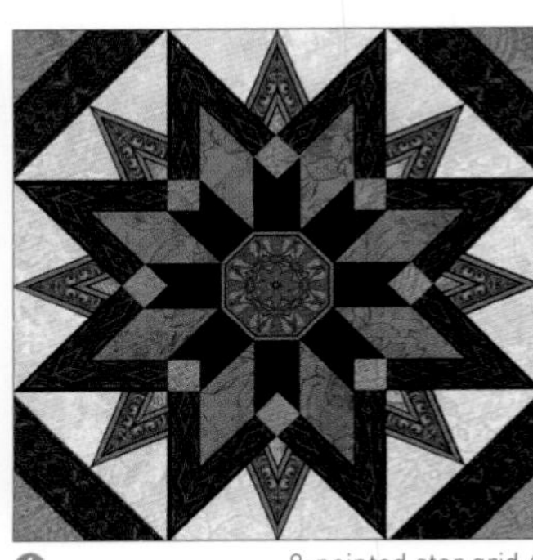

6 8-pointed star grid 4

7 8-pointed star grid 2

8 8-pointed star grid 4

9 8-pointed star grid 2

10 8-pointed star grid 2

11 8-pointed star grid 2

12 8-pointed star grid 2

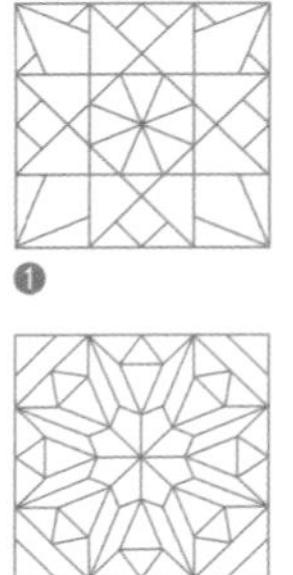

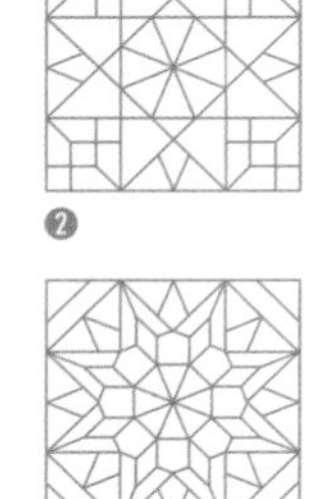

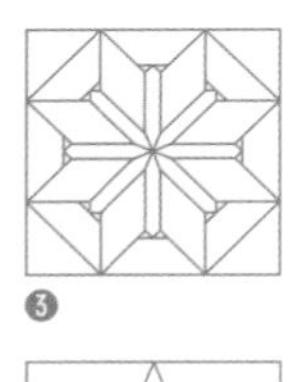

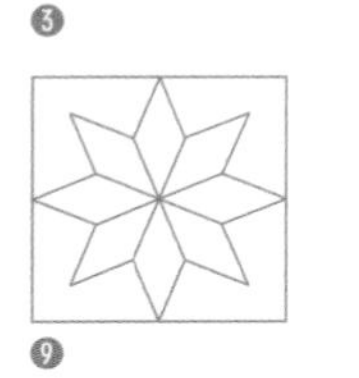

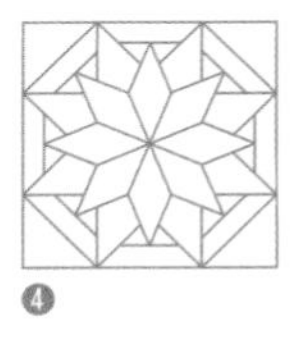

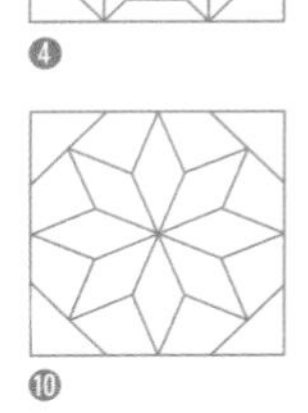

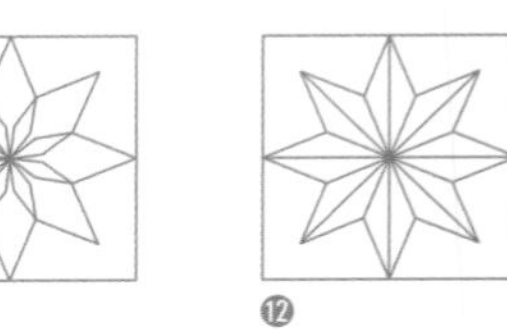

1 2 3 4 5 6

7 8 9 10 11 12

1 8-pointed star grid 2

2 8-pointed star grid 2

3 8-pointed star grid 2

4 8-pointed star grid 1

5 8-pointed star grid 2

6 8-pointed star grid 2

7 8-pointed star grid 2

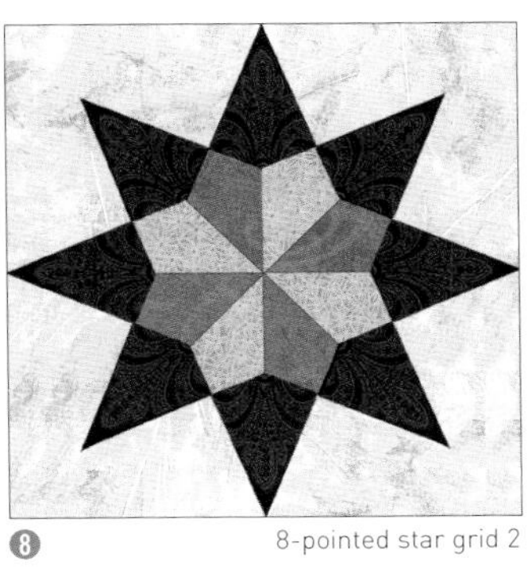
8 8-pointed star grid 2

9 8-pointed star grid 2

10 8-pointed star grid 2

11 8-pointed star grid 2

12 8-pointed star grid 2

1 **Star Flower,** *Q Book 102, Grandmother's Patchwork Quilts,* date unknown.

2 **Grandmother's Star,** *Anne Cabot's Album,* ca. 1952. Also known as:
Star Flower, *Capper's Weekly,* ca. 1960.

3 **Pieced Eight Point Star,** Nancy Cabot, *Chicago Tribune,* Dec 11, 1933. See 277-7.

4 **Jupiter Star,** *Kansas City Star,* Jun 20, 1956. Also known as:
Jupiter of Many Points, *Kansas City Star,* May 30, 1956.

5 **Morning Star,** Eveline Foland, *Kansas City Star,* Aug 15, 1931. Also known as:
Evening Star, Eveline Foland, *Kansas City Star,* Nov 28, 1931.
Kaleidoscope, *Q Book 130, Keepsake Quilts,* ca. 1970.
Spider Web, *Kansas City Star,* Apr 14, 1948.
A Spider Web Gone Awry, *Kansas City Star,* Jun 17, 1959.

6 **Bordered Star,** Jinny Beyer Studio design, 2008.

7 **Verna Belle's Favorite,** *Kansas City Star,* Sep 4, 1937.

8 **Star Puzzle,** Nancy Cabot, *Chicago Tribune,* Sep 15, 1937.

9 **Enigma,** *Ladies Art Company,* 1897. See 276-7 and 276-8. Also known as:
North Star, Nancy Page, *Birmingham News,* Sep 19, 1939.

10 **Seville,** Jinny Beyer, Hilton Head Seminar design, 1993; published in Beyer, Jinny, *Soft-Edge Piecing.*

11 **Bellflower,** Jinny Beyer, Hilton Head Seminar design, 1995; published in Beyer, Jinny, *Soft-Edge Piecing.*

12 **Inlay Star,** ca. 1938, per Havig.

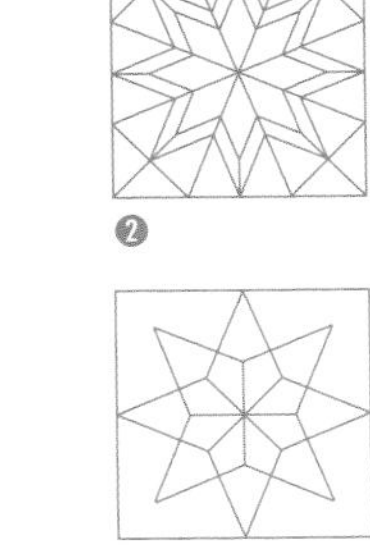
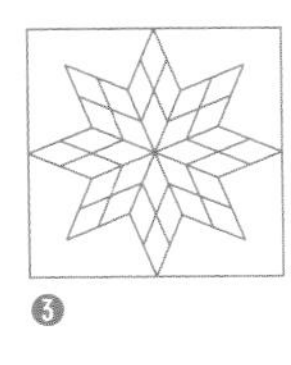
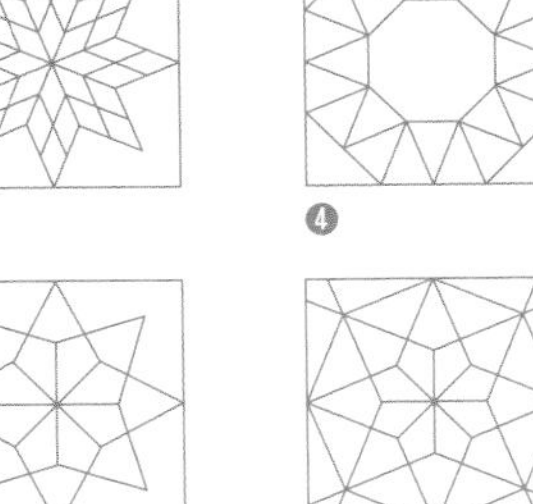
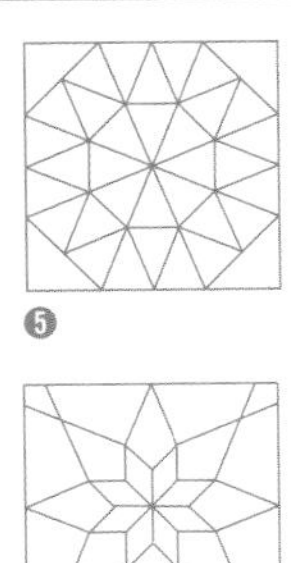
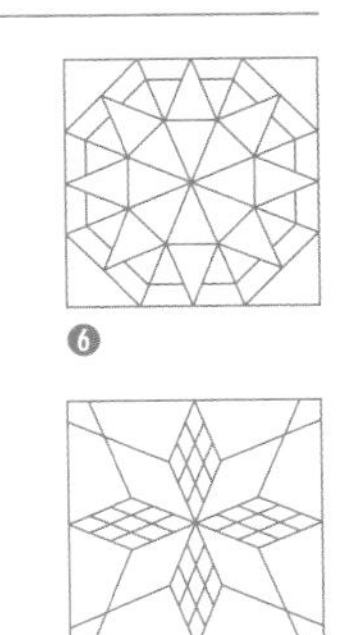

1 2 3 4 5 6

7 8 9 10 11 12

1 **Octagon Star,** *Farm Journal and Farmers Wife,* ca. 1941. Also known as:
  Cart Wheel, Jinny Beyer, Hilton Head Seminar design, 2005.

2 **Pinwheel Star,** Home Art Studios, *World Herald,* Mar 13, 1934.

3 **Morning Star,** Laura Wheeler, *Cincinnati Enquirer,* Sep 18, 1933.

4 **Beach Rose,** Jinny Beyer, Hilton Head Seminar design, 1985; published in Beyer, Jinny, *Patchwork Portfolio.*

5 **Ribbon Star,** Jinny Beyer, Hilton Head Seminar design, 2005.

6 **Planet Earth Star,** Jinny Beyer, RJR Patterns, 1993.

7 **Seaside Star,** Jinny Beyer, Jinny Beyer Studio design, 1989.

8 **Queen Anne's Lace,** Jinny Beyer, RJR fabric collection design, 1997.

9 **Your Lucky Star,** Laura Wheeler, unidentified newspaper clipping, date unknown.

10 **Sea Lily,** Jinny Beyer, Hilton Head Seminar design, 1986; published in Beyer, Jinny, *Patchwork Portfolio.*

11 **Rising Sun,** Laura Wheeler, *Sioux City Journal,* Apr 4, 1938.

12 **Star of North Carolina,** Hall, 1935. See 211-6.

❶ 8-pointed star grid 1

❷ 8-pointed star grid 3

❸ 8-pointed star grid 3

❹ 8-pointed star grid 1

❺ 8-pointed star grid 3

❻ 8-pointed star grid 1

❼ 8-pointed star grid 1

❽ 8-pointed star grid 1

❾ 8-pointed star grid 4

❿ 8-pointed star grid 4

⓫ 8-pointed star grid 4

⓬ 8-pointed star grid 4

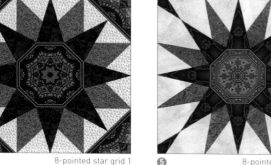

❶ **Star of North Carolina,** *Ladies Art Company,* 1922. See 211-6.

❷ **North Carolina Star,** Nancy Cabot, *Chicago Tribune,* Feb 18, 1938.

❸ **Victoria's Crown,** Jinny Beyer, Jinny Beyer Studio design, 1995.

❹ **Atlantic Jewel,** Jinny Beyer, Hilton Head Seminar design, 1984; Beyer, Jinny *Patchwork Portfolio.*

❺ **White Nights,** Jinny Beyer, Jinny Beyer Studio design, 2007.

❻ **Silver Star,** Jinny Beyer, Jinny Beyer Studio design, 1999.

❼ **Shooting Star,** Jinny Beyer, Hilton Head Seminar design, 1999.

❽ **New Millennium,** Jinny Beyer, Hilton Head Seminar design, 1999.

❾ **Garden Star,** Jinny Beyer, Hilton Head Seminar design, 1999.

❿ **Sea Pines Star,** Jinny Beyer, Hilton Head Seminar design, 1983; published in Beyer, Jinny, *Patchwork Portfolio.*

⓫ **Star Sapphire,** Jinny Beyer, Hilton Head Seminar design, 1981; published in Beyer, Jinny, *Patchwork Portfolio.*

⓬ **Diamond Cluster in a Frame,** *Kansas City Star,* Mar 21, 1956.

❶

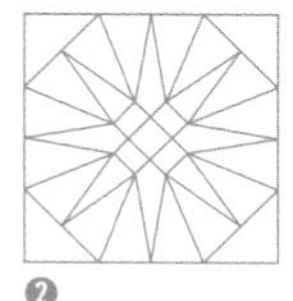

❷

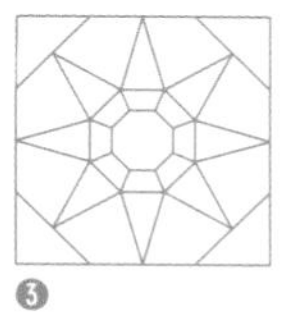

❸

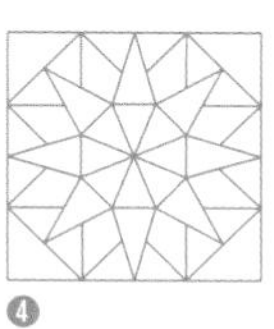

❹

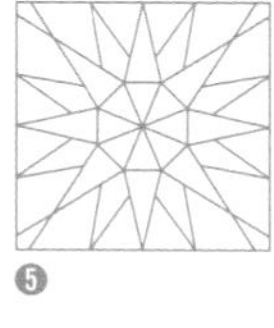

❺

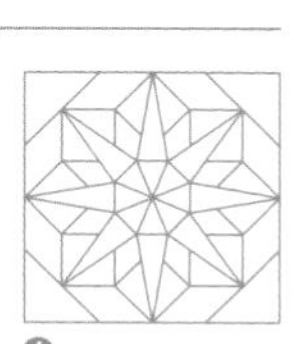

❻

❼

❽

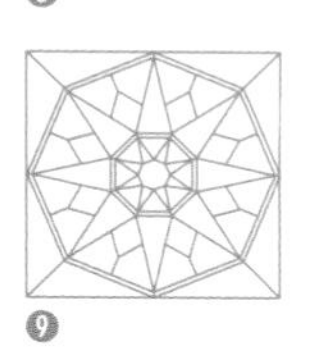

❾

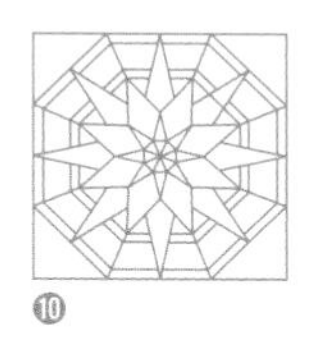

❿

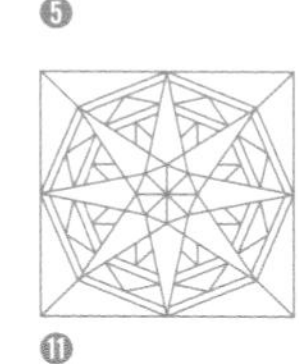

⓫

⓬

1 Brunswick Star, Laura Wheeler, *Illinois State Register,* Apr 20, 1933.

2 Rolling Star, *Ladies Art Company,* 1897. Also known as:
- **Brunswick Star,** Finley, 1929.
- **Chained Star,** Finley, 1929.
- **Eight Pointed Star,** Ruby McKim, *Kansas City Star,* Feb 23, 1929.
- **Mother's Favorite Star,** *Kansas City Star,* May 1, 1940.
- **The Parallelogram Block,** *Kansas City Star,* May 30, 1945.
- **Rolling Stone,** *Grandma Dexter New Appliqué and Patchwork Designs, Book 36b,* ca. 1932
- **Starry Field,** Alice Brooks, *Detroit Free Press,* date unknown.
- **The Virginia Reel,** *Mrs. Danner's Quilts, Books 1 & 2,* 1934.

"This is block 8 of the Quilt of Many Stars series quilt by Nancy Page." *Lowell Sun,* Jul 2, 1934

3 The Blazing Star, Eveline Foland, *Kansas City Star,* Feb 15, 1930. Also known as:
- **Blazing Star,** Hall, 1935.

4 Starlight, *Ladies Art Company,* 1928.

5 Diamond Star, Aunt Martha series: *Quilt Lover's Delights,* ca. 1960.

6 Pinwheel Star, *The Patchwork Book,* 1932.

7 Missouri Star Quilt, Eveline Foland, *Kansas City Star,* May 24, 1930. Also known as:
- **Missouri Star,** Hall, 1935.
- **Shining Star,** Hall, 1935.
- **Star and Arrow,** Nancy Cabot, *Chicago Tribune,* Feb 20, 1937.

8 Pinwheel Star, *Ladies Art Company,* 1897. Also known as:
- **Star and Wreath,** Nancy Cabot, *Chicago Tribune,* May 24, 1938.

9 Turnabout, Jinny Beyer, Hilton Head Seminar design, 1995; published in Beyer, Jinny, *Soft-Edge Piecing.*

10 Boxed Star, Jinny Beyer, Beyer, Jinny, *Patchwork Portfolio,* 1989.

11 Kansas City Star, Hall, 1935. Also known as:
- **Kansas Dust Storm,** Hall, 1935.
- **The Kansas Dust Storm,** *Kansas City Star,* Dec 28, 1935.

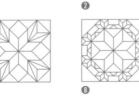

12 Grandma's Brooch, *Kansas City Star,* Jul 24, 1935.

1 8-pointed star grid 1

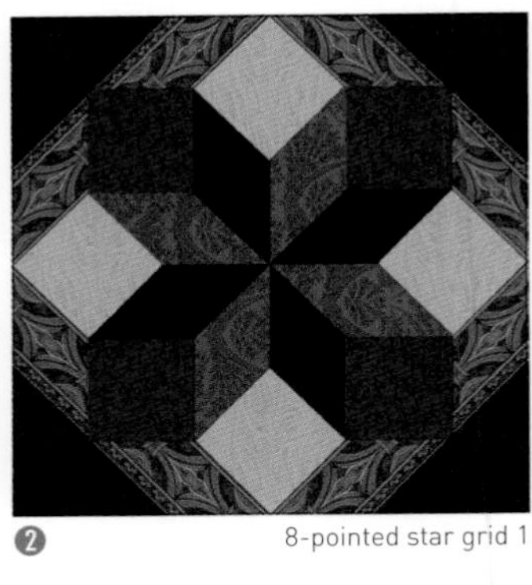
2 8-pointed star grid 1

3 8-pointed star grid 4

4 8-pointed star grid 1

5 8-pointed star grid 4

6 8-pointed star grid 1

7 8-pointed star grid 1

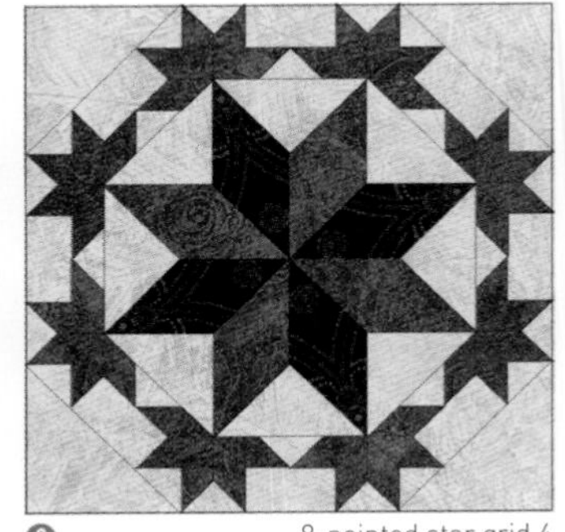
8 8-pointed star grid 4

9 8-pointed star grid 1

10 8-pointed star grid 1

11 8-pointed star grid 1

12 8-pointed star grid 1

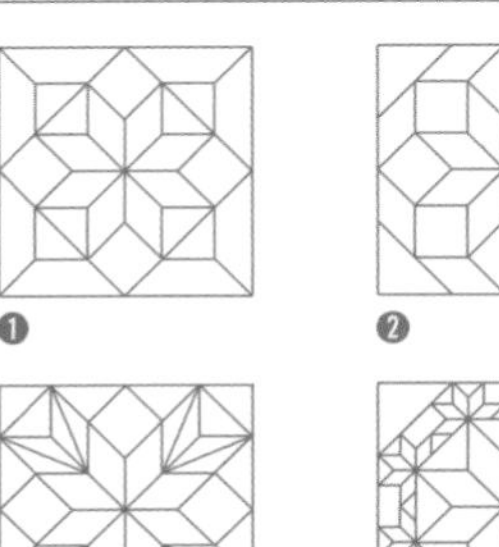
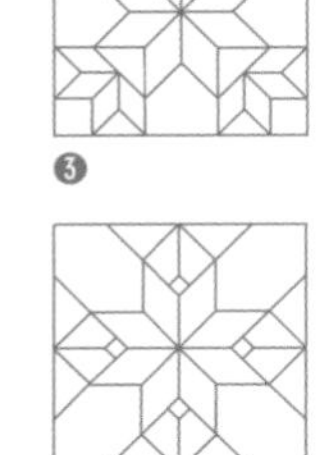
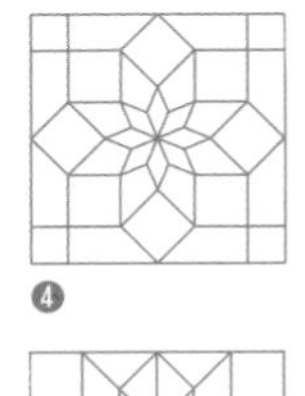
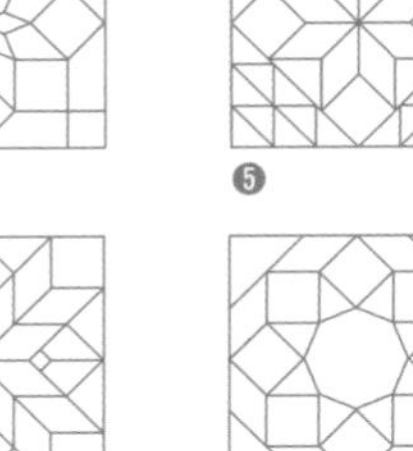
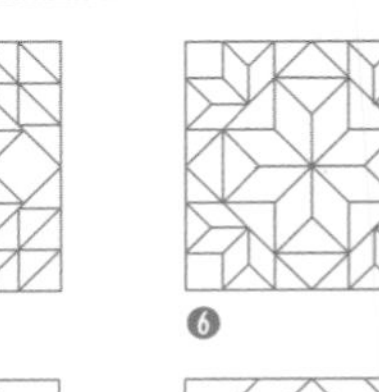
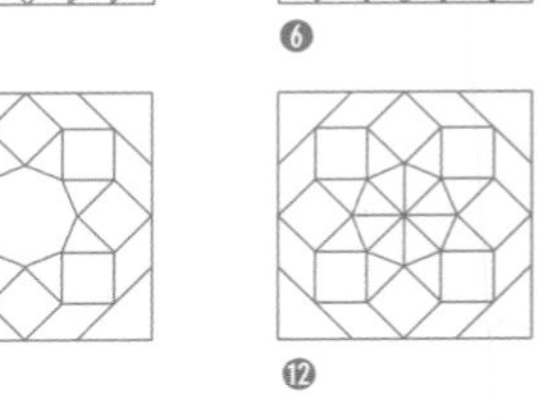

1 2 3 4 5 6

7 8 9 10 11 12

1 8-pointed star grid 1

2 8-pointed star grid 1

3 8-pointed star grid 1

4 8-pointed star grid 4

5 8-pointed star grid 1

6 8-pointed star grid 1

7 8-pointed star grid 1

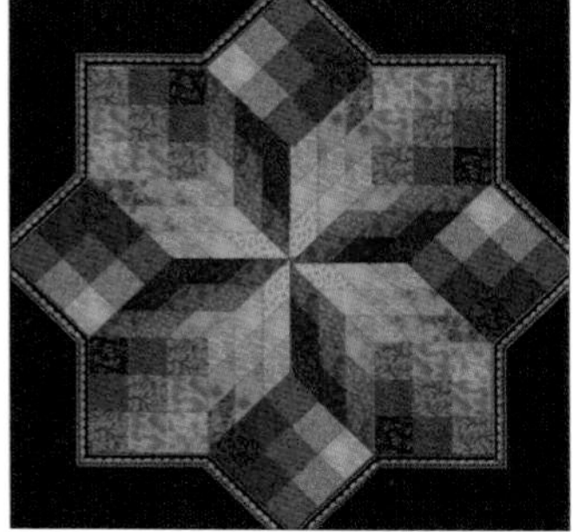

8 8-pointed star grid 1

9 8-pointed star grid 3

10 8-pointed star grid 1

11 8-pointed star grid 3

12 8-pointed star grid 1

13 8-pointed star grid 3

1 **Fortress,** Jinny Beyer, Beyer, Jinny, *Patchwork Portfolio,* 1989.

2 **Sunset Star,** Jinny Beyer, Hilton Head Seminar design, 1991; published in Beyer, Jinny, *Soft-Edge Piecing.*

3 **Stars,** Alice Brooks, unidentified newspaper clipping, date unknown.

4 **Shady Garden II,** Jinny Beyer, Beyer, Jinny, *Patchwork Portfolio,* 1989.

5 **Horizon,** Jinny Beyer, Hilton Head Seminar design, 1992.

6 **Ring Around the Star,** *Prize Winning Designs,* ca. 1931.

7 **Pennsylvania Hex,** Nancy Cabot, *Chicago Tribune,* Nov 1, 1935.

8 **Stained Glass Star,** Jinny Beyer, Jinny Beyer Studio design, 1999.

9 **Patch As Patch Can,** Aunt Martha series: *Quilt Designs,* ca. 1952.

10 **Starry Heavens,** *Kansas City Star,* Aug 6, 1941.

11 **Wandering Jew,** Clara Stone, *Practical Needlework,* ca. 1906. Also known as:
- **The Winding Blade,** *Kansas City Star,* Nov 19, 1941.

12 **Moorish Mosaic,** Nancy Cabot, *Chicago Tribune,* Aug 26, 1936. See 204-2. Also known as:
- **Mosaic,** *Farm Journal and Farmers Wife,* ca. 1941.

13 **Desert Star,** Jinny Beyer, Hilton Head Seminar design, 2005.

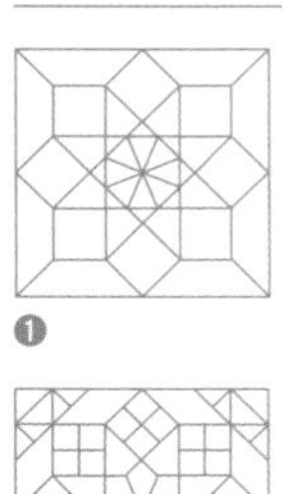
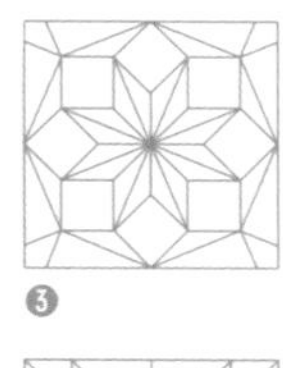

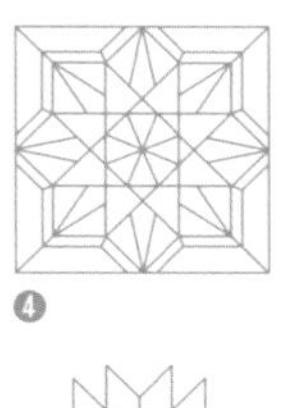
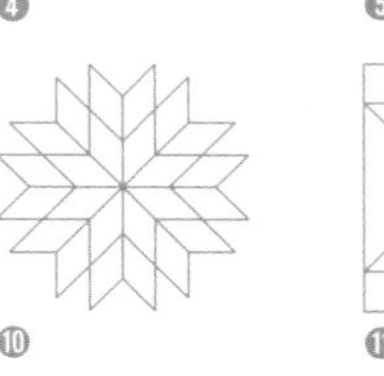
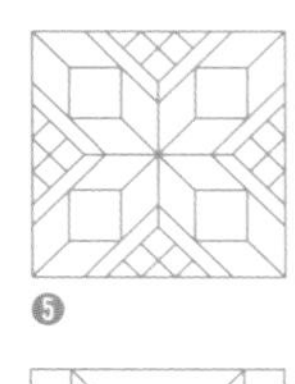
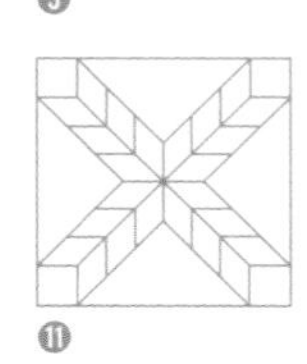
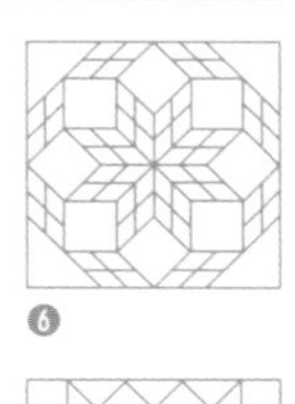
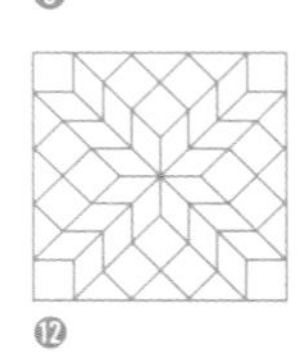
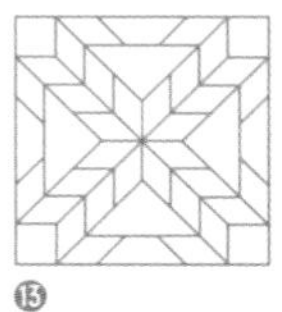

1 2 3 4 5 6

7 8 9 10 11 12 13

1 **Indian Head,** *Kansas City Star,* Mar 7, 1936. Also known as:
- **St. Elmo's Fire,** Nancy Cabot, *Chicago Tribune,* Apr 14, 1936.
- **Wood Lily,** *Kansas City Star,* Mar 7, 1936.

2 **Quasar,** Jinny Beyer, Beyer, Jinny, *Patchwork Portfolio,* 1989.

3 **Garden Path,** Jinny Beyer, Beyer, Jinny, *Patchwork Portfolio,* 1989.

4 **Snow Flake,** Jinny Beyer, Hilton Head Seminar design, 2005.

5 **Christmas Star,** Eveline Foland, *Kansas City Star,* Dec 19, 1931.

6 **Rising Sun,** *Dakota Farmer,* Sep 15, 1926.

7 **Aunt Dinah's Star,** Home Art Studios, *Cincinnati Enquirer,* Feb 23, 1933.

8 **The Spider Web,** *Kansas City Star,* Jun 16, 1943.

9 **Tangled Cobwebs,** Home Art Studios, *Cincinnati Enquirer,* Apr 19, 1933.

10 **Saw Teeth,** *The Patchwork Book,* 1932. See 270-12, 414-11, and 414-12.

11 **Fish,** Clara Stone, *Practical Needlework,* ca. 1906. See 270-12, 414-11, and 414-12. Also known as:
- **Airplane Motif,** *Kansas City Star,* Apr 2, 1947.
- **Dove in the Window,** date unknown, per Brackman.
- **Fish Block,** Ruby McKim, *Kansas City Star,* Sep 21, 1929.
- **Fish Quilt,** Nancy Page, *Birmingham News,* Jan 15,
- **The Fish Quilt,** *Kansas City Star,* Jun 11, 1941.
- **Gold Fish,** Hall, 1935.
- **Goldfish,** Eveline Foland, *Kansas City Star,* Dec 12, 1931.
- **Trout and Bass Block,** Nancy Cabot, *Chicago Tribune,* Oct 1, 1937.
- **Whirligig,** Clara Stone, *Practical Needlework,* ca. 1906.

12 **Dutch Rose,** Clara Stone, *Practical Needlework,* ca. 1906.

1 8-pointed star grid 1

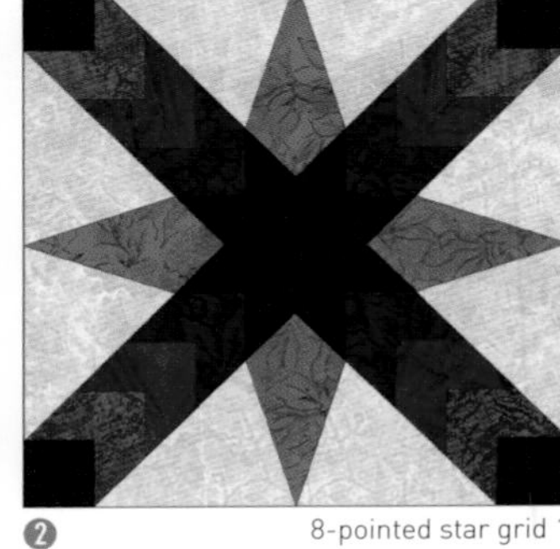
2 8-pointed star grid 1

3 8-pointed star grid 1

4 8-pointed star grid 2

5 8-pointed star grid 2

6 8-pointed star grid 3

7 8-pointed star grid 1

8 58 x 58 grid

9 8-pointed star grid 1

10 8-pointed star grid 3

11 8-pointed star grid 4

12 8-pointed star grid 1

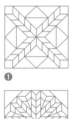

1

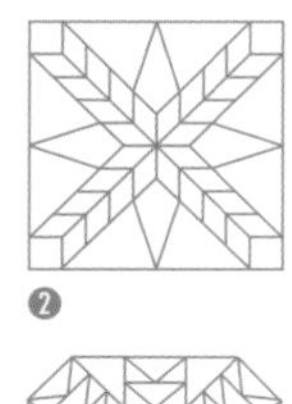
2

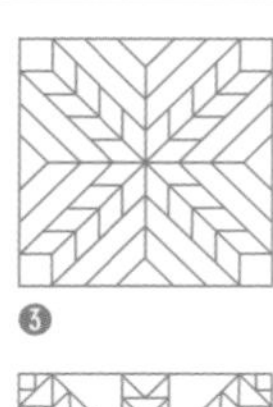
3

4

5

6

7

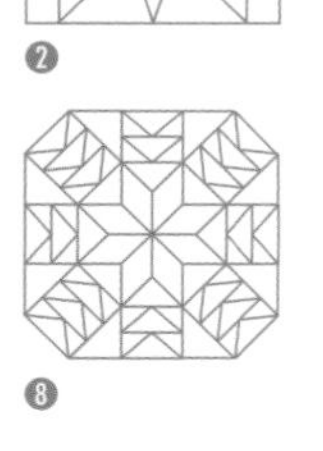
8

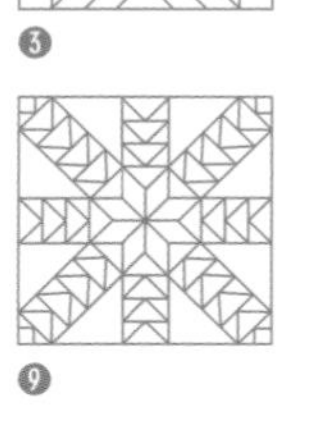
9

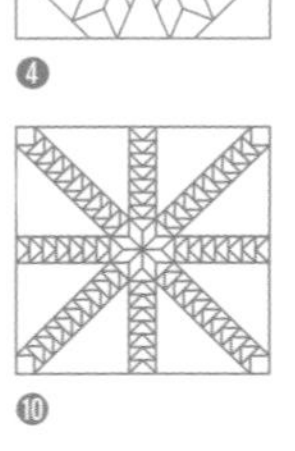
10

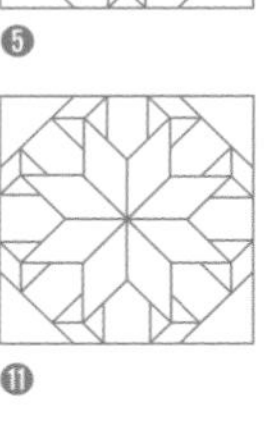
11

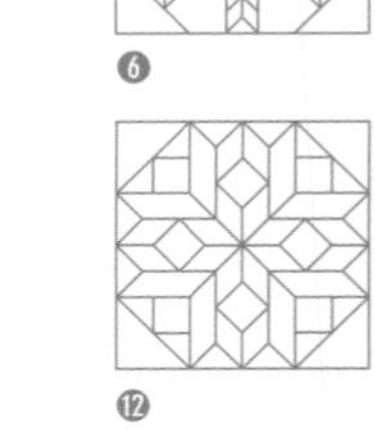
12

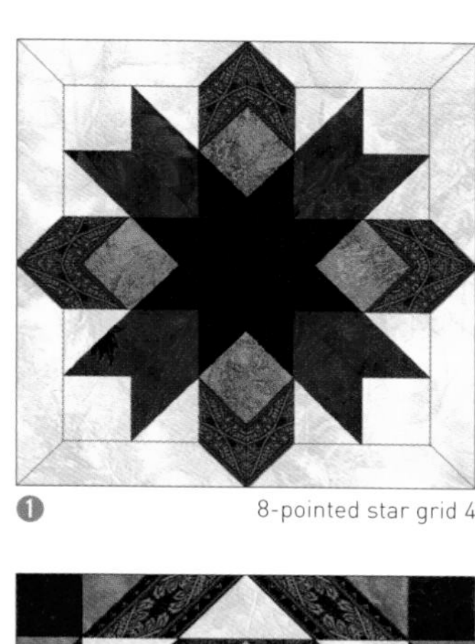

1 8-pointed star grid 4

2 8-pointed star grid 1

3 8-pointed star grid 1

4 8-pointed star grid 1

5 8-pointed star grid 1

6 8-pointed star grid 1

7 8-pointed star grid 1

8 8-pointed star grid 4

9 8-pointed star grid 1

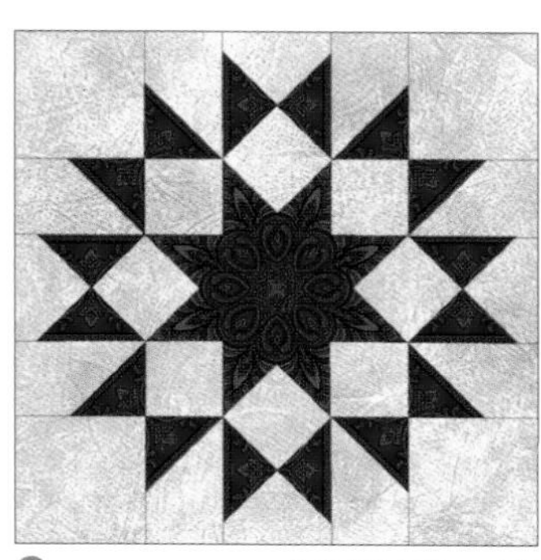

10 8-pointed star grid 1

11 8-pointed star grid 4

12 8-pointed star grid 1

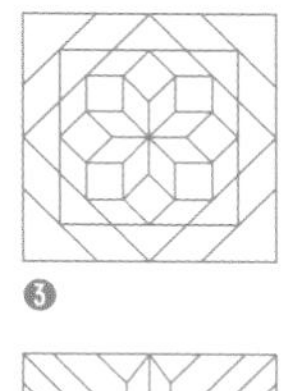

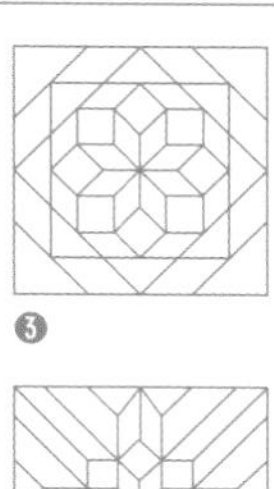

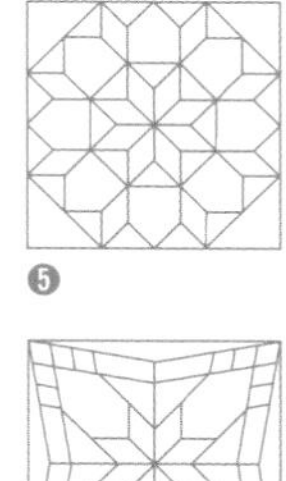

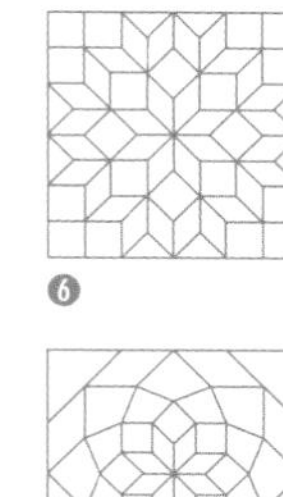

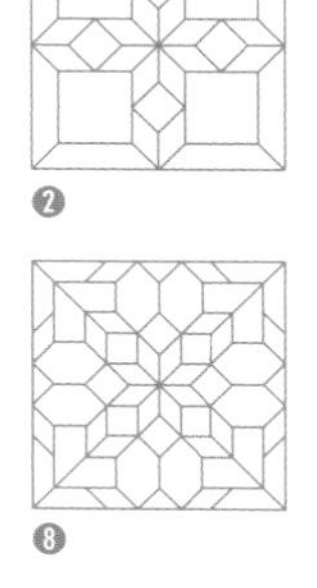

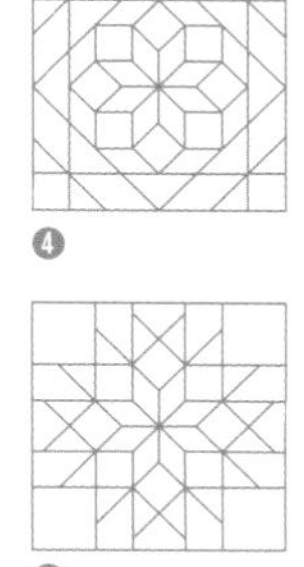

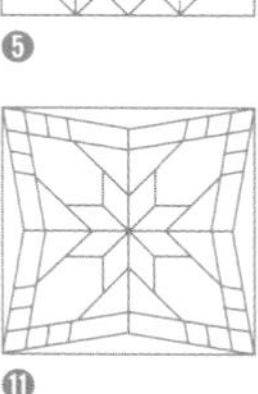

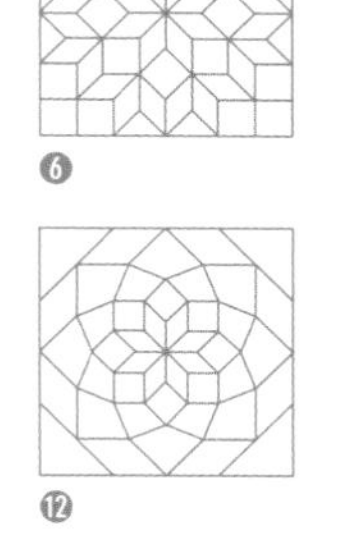

1 2 3 4 5 6

7 8 9 10 11 12

1 **Robert Mourning's Centennial Star,** Jinny Beyer, Hilton Head Seminar design, 1992.

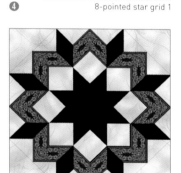

2 **Centennial Star,** Jinny Beyer, Hilton Head Seminar design, 1995; published in Beyer, Jinny, *Soft-Edge Piecing.*

3 **Star and Chains,** *Ladies Art Company,* 1897. Also known as:

- **Ring Around the Star,** Hall, 1935.
- **Rolling Star,** Hall, 1935.

4 **Chained Star,** Nancy Cabot, *Chicago Tribune,* Nov 28, 1934.

5 **Star of Bethlehem,** *Prize Winning Designs,* ca. 1931. Also known as:

- **Bethlehem Star,** *Kansas City Star,* Apr 30, 1938.
- **Jewels in a Frame,** *Kansas City Star,* Feb 27, 1957.
- **Star of Magi,** Nancy Cabot, *Chicago Tribune,* Feb 24, 1937.

6 **Square A,** Hearth and Home, 1880. See 164-7. Also known as:

- **Black Diamond,** Clara Stone, *Practical Needlework,* ca. 1906.
- **Broken Star,** Holstein, 1973.
- **Carpenter's Star,** Hall, 1935.
- **Carpenter's Wheel,** Finley, 1929.
- **Circle Saw,** *Kansas City Star,* Jan 25, 1936.
- **The Double Star Quilt,** Eveline Foland, *Kansas City Star,* Jun 29, 1929.
- **Dutch Rose,** Hall, 1935.
- **Eccentric Star,** *Virginia Snow Studio Art Needlework Creations,* 1932.
- **The Lone Star of Paradise,** *Kansas City Star,* Mar 11, 1933.
- **Morning Star,** Khin, date unknown.
- **Octagonal Star,** Hall, 1935.
- **Star and Diamond,** date unknown, per Brackman.
- **Star within a Star,** Hall, 1935.
- **Twin Star,** Patty Shannon, *Kentucky Farmer's Home Journal,* Dec 1941, per Waldvogel.
- **Twinkling Stars,** Nancy Page, *Birmingham News,* Jun 5, 1934.

7 **Dutch Rose,** *Ladies Art Company,* 1897. See 164-6. Also known as:

- **Feathered Star,** Home Art Studios, unidentified newspaper clipping, date unknown.
- **Star of the East,** *Mrs. Danner's Quilts, Books 1 & 2,* 1934.
- **Star with Diamonds,** *Grandmother's Patchwork Quilt Designs,* 1931.
- **Unknown Star,** Webster, 1915.

8 **Diamond Facet,** Jinny Beyer, Hilton Head Seminar design, 1994.

9 **Cassiopeia,** Jinny Beyer, Beyer, Jinny, *Patchwork Portfolio,* 1989.

10 **Aunt Mary's Star,** Clara Stone, *Practical Needlework,* ca. 1906. Also known as:

- **Green Mountain Star,** Clara Stone, *Practical Needlework,* ca. 1906.

11 **Peggy Anne's Special,** *Kansas City Star,* Oct 3, 1936.

12 **Wishing Star,** Nancy Cabot, *Chicago Tribune,* Jun 30, 1938.

"'Wishing Star' received its name from the reflection of an exceedingly bright star in a romantic old wishing well. On the outskirts of a quaint New England village, Lowell's Wishing Well was a popular summer gathering place, and it was in this town that the quilt first was pieced." Nancy Cabot, *Chicago Tribune,* Jun 30, 1938

❶ New Star, *Ladies Art Company,* 1897. Also known as:
: **Leavenworth Star,** Hall, 1935.

❷ Corsican Crystal, Jinny Beyer, Hilton Head Seminar design, 2002.

❸ Path to Happiness, Home Art Studios, *World Herald,* Dec 6, 1933.

❹ Crystals, Jinny Beyer, Hilton Head Seminar design, 2007.

❺ Golden Dahlia Quilt, Home Art Studios, *Des Moines Register,* Mar 5, 1933. "Here is a modern design for the woman of today who wants to create a quilt that is new and different and will go down in quilt history as one of the new designs for 1933. You will enjoy making this treasured heirloom for the years to come." *World Herald,* Jul 19, 1933

❻ Silver Star, Jinny Beyer, Hilton Head Seminar design, 2005.

❼ Western Spy, Clara Stone, *Practical Needlework,* ca. 1906.

❽ Wagon Wheel, Jinny Beyer, Beyer, *Patchwork Portfolio,* 1989.

❾ Calliope, Jinny Beyer, Beyer, Jinny *Patchwork Portfolio,* 1989.

❿ Brilliant Star, Laura Wheeler, unidentified newspaper clipping, date unknown.

⓫ Diamond Star, Nancy Cabot, *Chicago Tribune,* Feb 13, 1937. Also known as:
: **Economy Quilt Block,** Nancy Cabot, *Chicago Tribune,* Feb 13, 1937.

⓬ Addie's Star, Jinny Beyer, Jinny Beyer Studio design, 2005.

⓭ Delectable Mountains, Hall, 1935.

❶ 8-pointed star grid 1

❷ 8-pointed star grid 4

❸ 8-pointed star grid 4

❹ 8-pointed star grid 4

❺ 8-pointed star grid 4

❻ 8-pointed star grid 2

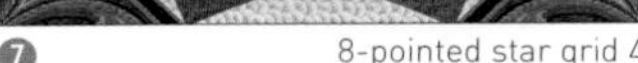
❼ 8-pointed star grid 4

❽ 8-pointed star grid 4

❾ 8-pointed star grid 4

❿ 8-pointed star grid 4

⓫ 8-pointed star grid 2

⓬ 8-pointed star grid 2

⓭ multiple grids

❶

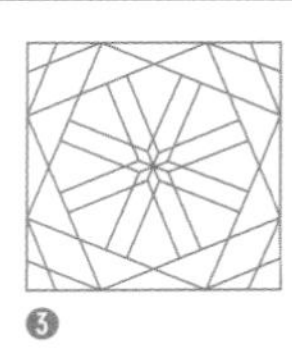
❷

❸

❹

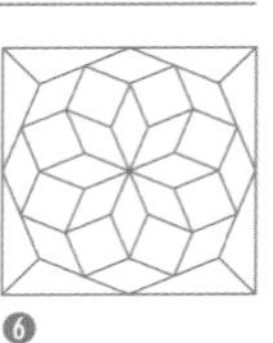
❺

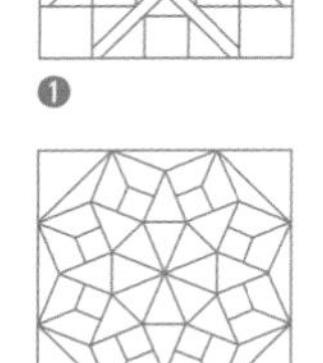
❻

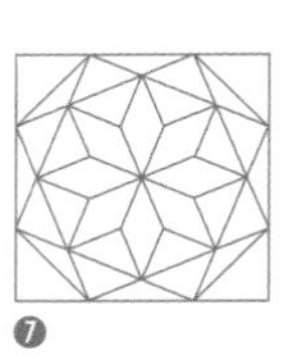
❼

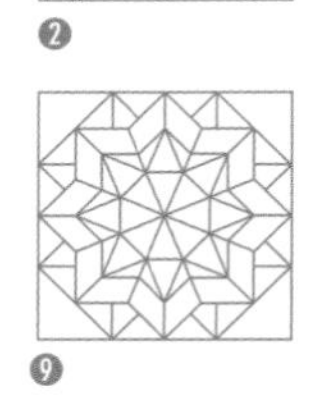
❽

❾

❿

⓫

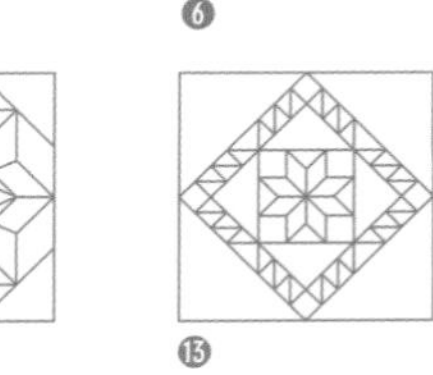
⓬

⓭

❶ 8-pointed star grid 2

❷ 8-pointed star grid 1

❸ 8-pointed star grid 4

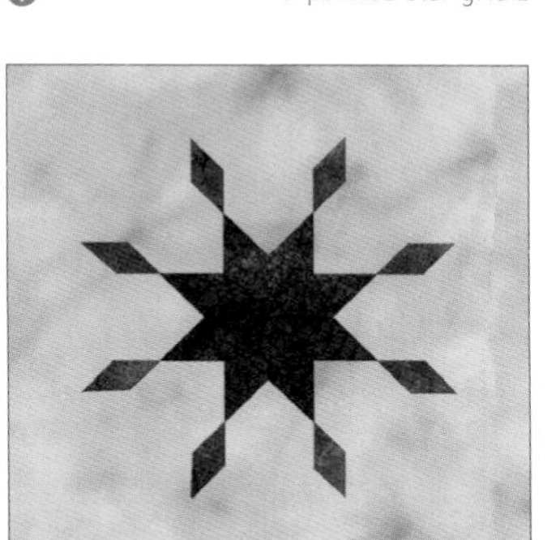

❹ 8-pointed star grid 1

❺ 8-pointed star grid 4

❻ 8-pointed star grid 4

❼ 8-pointed star grid 4

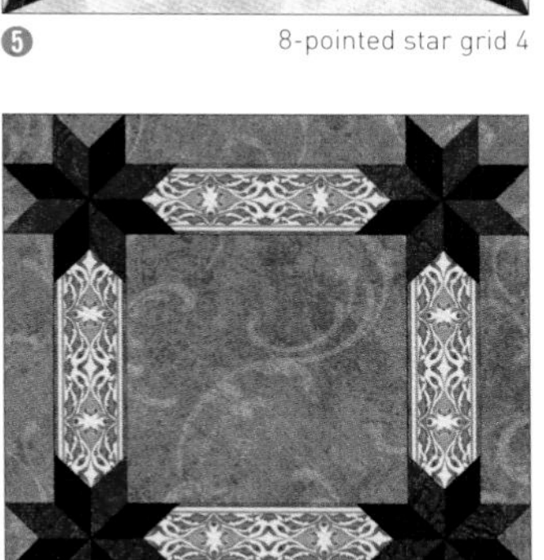

❽ 8-pointed star grid 4

❾ 8-pointed star grid 4

❿ 8-pointed star grid 4

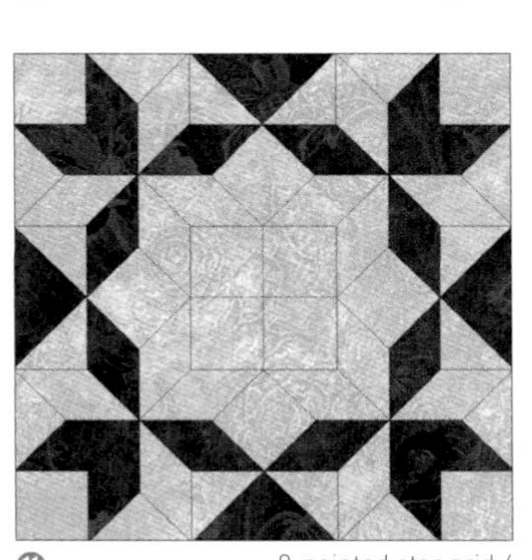

⓫ 8-pointed star grid 4

⓬ 8-pointed star grid 4

⓭ multiple grids

❶ **Hunter's Star,** Hall, 1935.

❷ **Hunter Star,** Aunt Martha series: *Quilt Lover's Delights,* ca. 1960. Also known as:
- **Indian Arrowhead,** Aunt Martha series: *Quilt Lover's Delights,* ca. 1960.

❸ **Shooting Star,** *Farm Journal and Farmer's Wife,* (Silver Anniversary issue), 1945.

❹ **Snow Crystal,** Nancy Cabot, *Chicago Tribune,* Aug 3, 1936.

❺ **Evening Star,** Nancy Cabot, *Chicago Tribune,* Oct 23, 1933.

❻ **Starlight,** Nancy Cabot, *Chicago Tribune,* Jul 12, 1935.

❼ **Fireworks,** Nancy Cabot, *Chicago Tribune,* Aug 13, 1935. Also known as:
- **Midnight Sky,** Nancy Cabot, *Chicago Tribune,* Feb 1, 1938.

❽ **Diamonds in the Corners,** *Kansas City Star,* Sep 5, 1956.

❾ **Snowbound,** *The Mountain Mist Blue Book of Quilts,* date unknown.

❿ **Four Stars Patchwork,** *Ladies Art Company,* 1897. See 97-9. Also known as:
- **Four Stars,** Nancy Page, *Lowell Sun,* Jun 25, 1932.
- **The Four Stars,** *Grandmother Clark's Patchwork Quilt Designs, From Books 20-21-23,* 1932.
- **Jackson Star,** Eveline Foland, *Kansas City Star,* May 16, 1931.
- **Jackson's Star,** *Colonial Quilts,* 1932.

"This is Block 6 of the Quilt of Many Stars Series Quilt by Nancy Page." *Lowell Sun,* Jun 25, 1934

⓫ **Diamond Wedding Ring,** Nancy Cabot, *Chicago Tribune,* Apr 23, 1938. See 97-10.

⓬ **Flash of Diamonds,** *Kansas City Star,* Apr 6, 1949.

⓭ **Modern Star,** Hall, 1935.

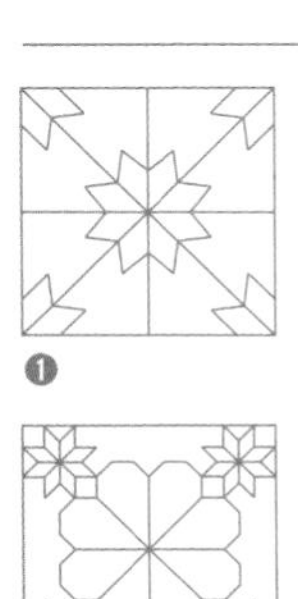

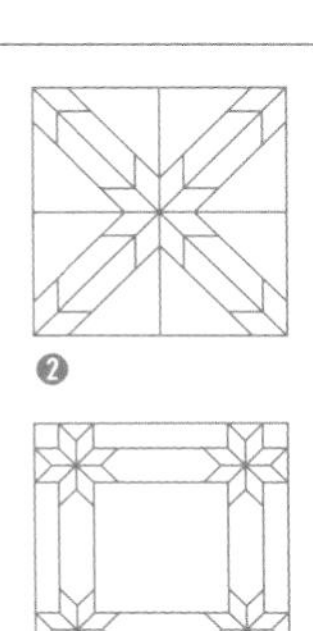

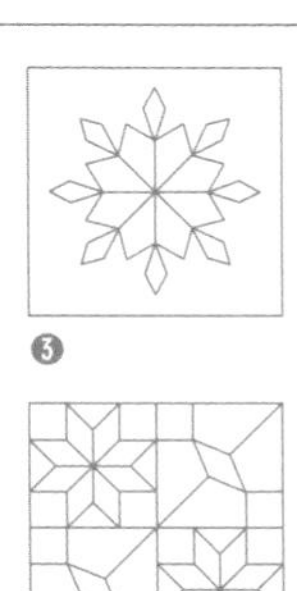

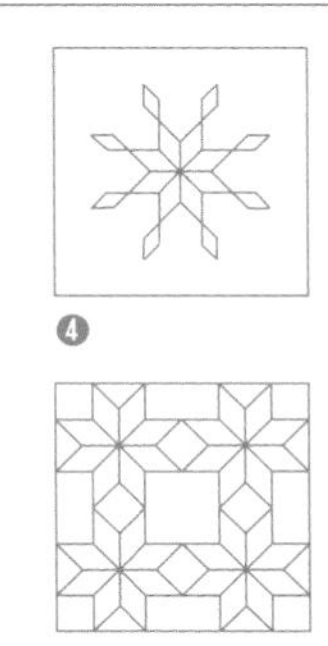

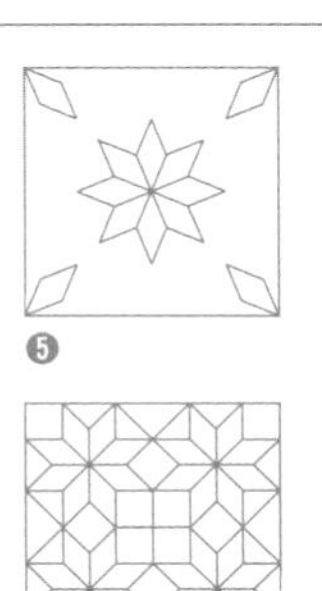

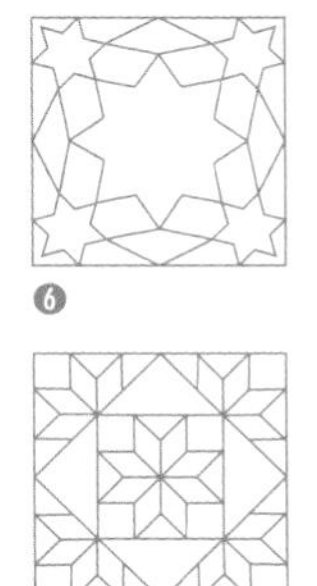

❶ ❷ ❸ ❹ ❺ ❻

❼ ❽ ❾ ❿ ⓫ ⓬ ⓭

❶ **Snow Crystals,** Eveline Foland, *Kansas City Star,* Dec 13, 1930. See 97-8. Also known as:

- **All Hands Around,** date unknown, per Brackman.
- **Captive Beauty,** Aunt Martha series: *Quilt Designs,* ca. 1952.
- **Heavenly Stars,** *Mrs. Danner's Quilts, Books 1 & 2,* 1934.
- **Yankee Pride,** Hall, 1935.

❷ **Stars Patchwork,** *Farm and Home,* Feb 15, 1890. See 97-8. Also known as:

- **Double Star,** *Hearth and Home,* per Brackman, date unknown.
- **Maple Leaf,** Hall, 1935.
- **Stars and Cubes,** *Ladies Art Company,* 1897.
- **Victory Star,** Clara Stone, *Practical Needlework,* ca. 1906.
- **Yankee Pride,** Finley, 1929.

❸ **Cubes and Tile,** Nancy Cabot, *Chicago Tribune,* Sep 7, 1936. Also known as:

- **Stars and Cubes,** Martens, 1970.

❹ **Heavenly Star,** Laura Wheeler, unidentified newspaper clipping, date unknown.

❺ **Flaming Star,** Nancy Cabot, *Chicago Tribune,* Jan 17, 1936.

❻ **Evening Star,** Nancy Cabot, *Chicago Tribune,* Jun 25, 1938.

❼ **Job's Troubles,** Clara Stone, *Practical Needlework,* ca. 1906. Also known as:

- **Melon Patch,** Holstein, 1973.

❽ **Propeller,** Jinny Beyer, Beyer, Jinny, *The Quilter's Album ...,* 1980.

❾ **Merry Go Round,** Nancy Cabot, *Chicago Tribune,* Oct 2, 1935. Also known as:

- **Amazing Windmill,** Nancy Cabot, *Chicago Tribune,* Sep 29, 1936.
- **Mystic Maze,** Nancy Cabot, *Chicago Tribune,* Sep 29, 1936.

❿ **Godey Design,** *Godey's Lady's Book,* 1852 Also known as:

- **Autumn Leaves,** *Q Book 116, Blue Ribbon Quilts,* ca. 1970.
- **Spider Web,** *Kansas City Star,* Jan 19, 1929.
- **Spider's Web,** *Ladies Art Company,* 1897.

⓫ **Spider Web,** Finley, 1929.
"An early picture of the little room Martha Washington occupied after the death of General Washington possesses the 'Spider Web' quilt upon her bed. It was here that she spent her last days gazing out upon the broad Potomac and you, too, will delight in reproducing this beautiful quilt with this historic significance." Home Arts, Apr 30, 1933

⓬ **Merry Go Round,** *Quilt Blocks from Grandma Dexter,* ca. 1933. Also known as:

- **Mystic Maze,** Nancy Cabot, *Chicago Tribune,* Mar 15, 1933.
- **Spider's Web,** Virginia Snow, *Grandma Dexter Appliqué and Patchwork Designs, Book 36a,* ca. 1932.

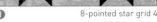

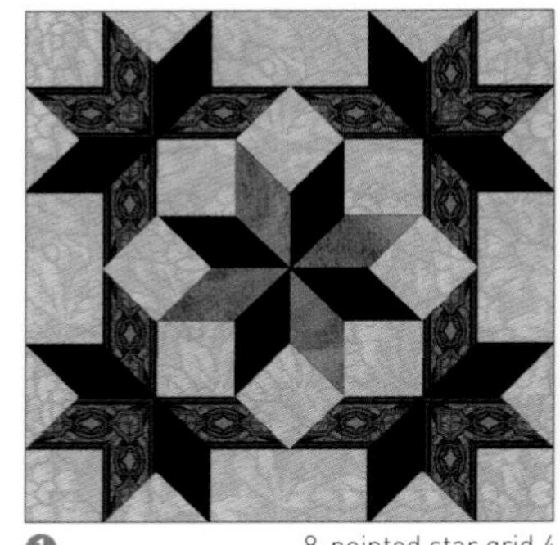

❶ 8-pointed star grid 4

❷ 8-pointed star grid 1

❸ 8-pointed star grid 1

❹ 8-pointed star grid 4

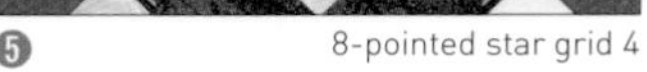

❺ 8-pointed star grid 4

❻ 8-pointed star grid 4

❼ 8-pointed star grid 1

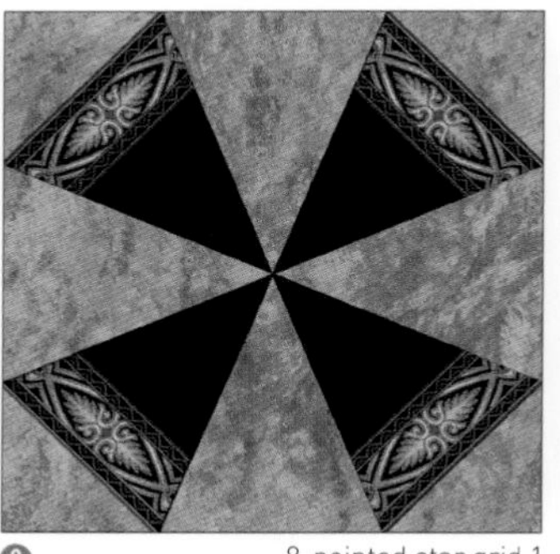

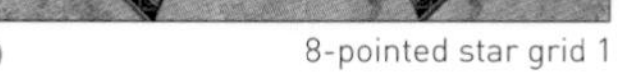

❽ 8-pointed star grid 1

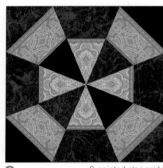

❾ 8-pointed star grid 2

❿ 8-pointed star grid 1

⓫ 8 x 8 grid/8-pointed star grid 1

⓬ 12 x 12 grid/8-pointed star grid 1

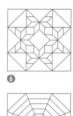

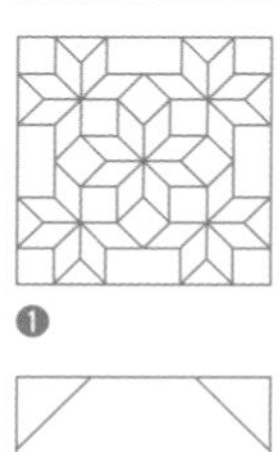
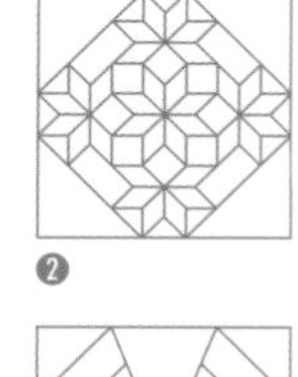

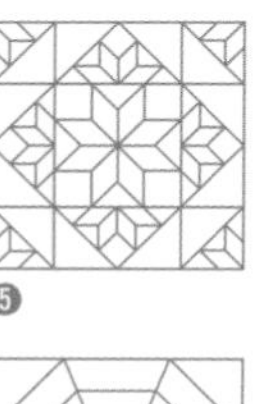

❶ ❷ ❸ ❹ ❺ ❻

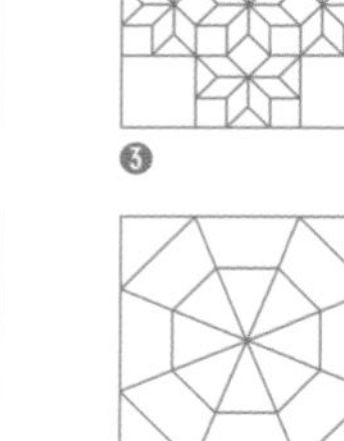
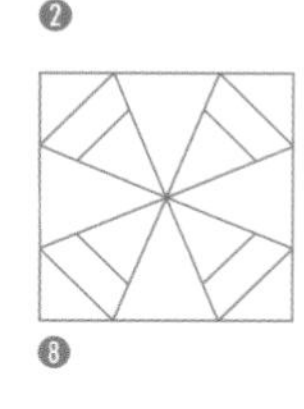
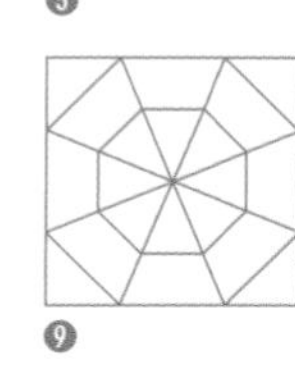
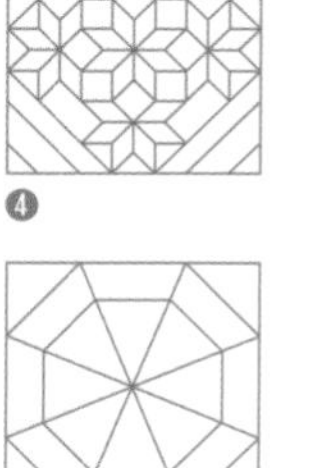

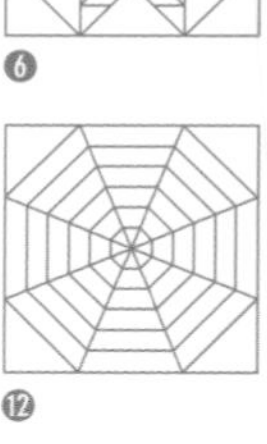

❼ ❽ ❾ ❿ ⓫ ⓬

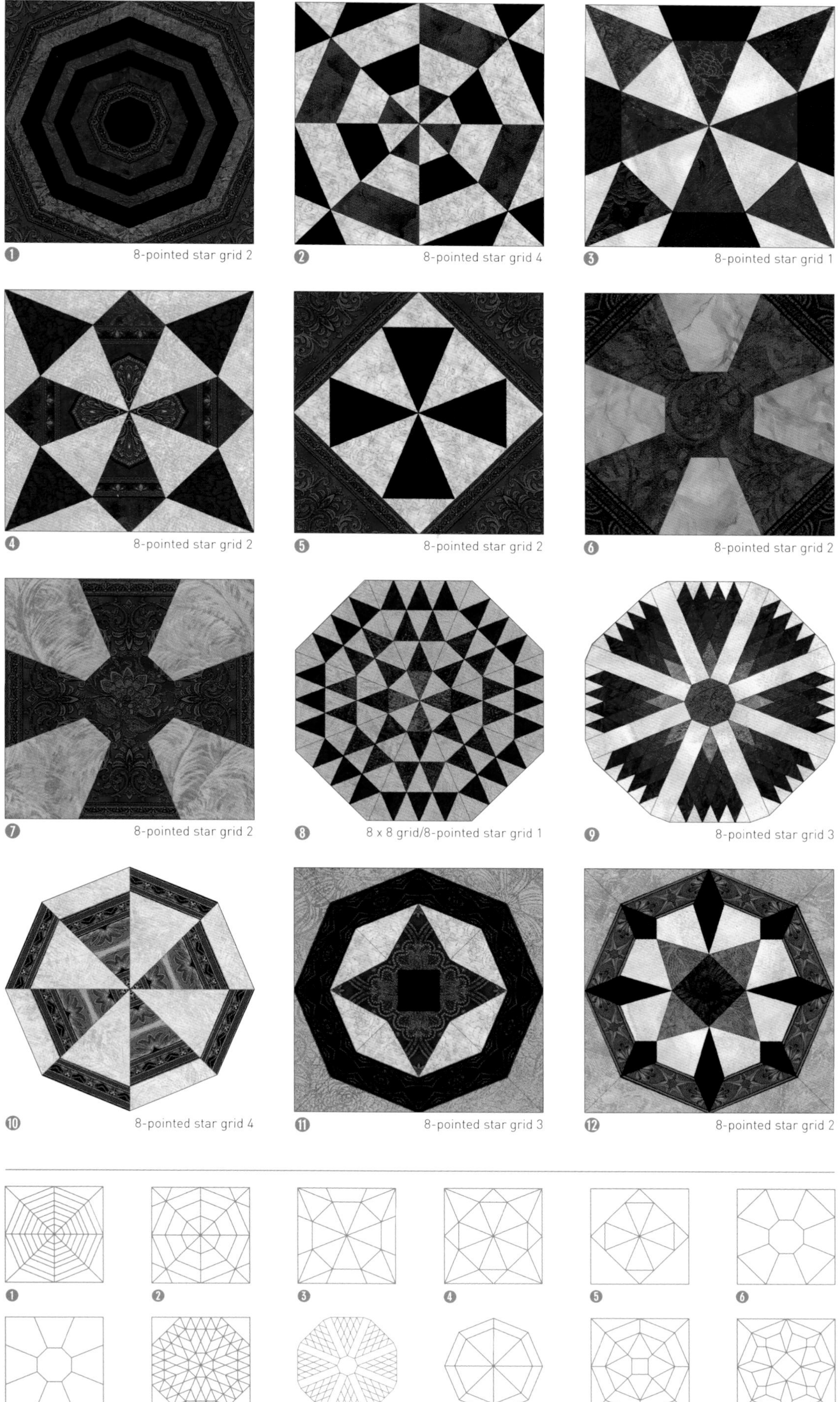

1. **String Quilt,** Home Art Studios, *Cincinnati Enquirer,* Mar 3, 1933.
2. **Spider Web,** Laura Wheeler, *Cincinnati Enquirer,* Aug 8, 1933.
3. **Joseph's Coat,** Laura Wheeler, *Women's Circle,* 1966
4. **Whirling Star,** *Grandma Dexter Appliqué and Patchwork Designs, Book 36a,* ca. 1932.
5. **Maltese Cross,** Ickis, 1949.
6. **The Wind Mill,** *Kansas City Star,* Aug 7, 1935.
7. **Wedge and Circle,** Clara Stone, *Practical Needlework,* ca. 1906.
8. **Spinning Triangles,** Hall, 1935.
9. **Pinks,** Aunt Martha series: *The Quilt Fair Comes to You,* ca. 1933.
10. **Hexagon Beauty Quilt Block,** *Kansas City Star,* Jun 14, 1939.
11. **Star and Crown,** Laura Wheeler, *Sioux City Journal,* Mar 31, 1938.
12. **Ocean Star,** Jinny Beyer, Hilton Head Seminar design, 1985; published in Beyer, Jinny, *Patchwork Portfolio.*

❶ **Nine Patch Star,** Home Art Studios, *World Herald,* Nov 17, 1933.
"The nine-patch quilt is a favored pattern for all beginners. When combined with the star it makes a very unusual quilt when completed. Each nine-patch star can be of a different color combination of different prints, and this gives a very beautiful effect when the quilt is made up in the various pastel shades." *World Herald,* Nov 17, 1933

❷ **Jewel,** *Grandmother Clark's Authentic Early American Quilts, Book No. 21,* 1932.

❸ **Turkey Giblets,** Nancy Cabot, *Chicago Tribune,* Feb 8, 1938.

❹ **Kaleidoscope,** *Grandma Dexter Appliqué and Patchwork Designs, Book 36a,* ca. 1932.

❺ **Starry Crown,** Alice Brooks, *Detroit Free Press,* Sep 7, 1934.
"Starry Crown is a scrap quilt that is a special joy to make. Get out the scrap bag and sew the patches in hit or miss and before you know it your block is done. It's really that easy! The one material that is repeated throughout gives the joined quilt its lovely continuous pattern." Alice Brooks, *Detroit Free Press,* Sep 7, 1934

❻ **Venetian Design,** *Ladies Art Company,* 1897. Also known as:
  Mosaic, *Grandmother's Patchwork Quilt Designs, Book 20,* 1931.

❼ **Brown Eyed Susan,** *Needlecraft,* Feb, 1935.

❽ **Midsummer Night,** Nancy Cabot, *Chicago Tribune,* May 13, 1935.

❾ **Wagonwheel,** Laura Wheeler, *Sioux City Journal,* Nov 29, 1940.

❿ **Shamrock,** Jinny Beyer, Beyer, Jinny, *Patchwork Portfolio,* 1989.

⓫ **Wheel of Fortune,** *Ladies Art Company,* 1897. Also known as:
  Buttons and Bows, *Mrs. Danner's Fifth Quilt Book,* 1970.
  Rising Sun, *The Patchwork Book,* 1932.
  Wheel of Luck, Nancy Cabot, *Chicago Tribune,* Dec 5, 1934.

⓬ **Rising Sun,** Nancy Cabot, *Chicago Tribune,* Jan 30, 1937.

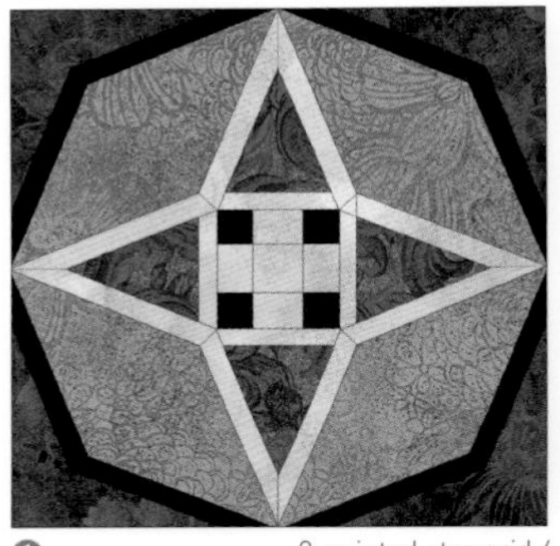

❶ 8-pointed star grid 4

❷ 8-pointed star grid 1

❸ 8-pointed star grid 1

❹ 8-pointed star grid 3

❺ 8-pointed star grid 2

❻ 8-pointed star grid 1

❼ 8-pointed star grid 4

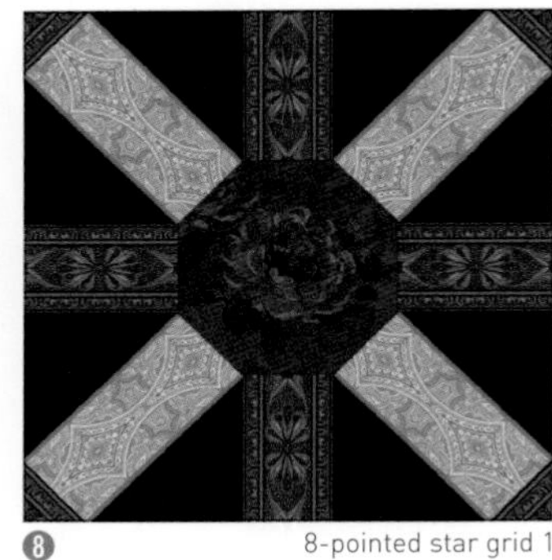
❽ 8-pointed star grid 1

❾ 8-pointed star grid 4

❿ 8-pointed star grid 1

⓫ 8-pointed star grid 4

⓬ 8-pointed star grid 4

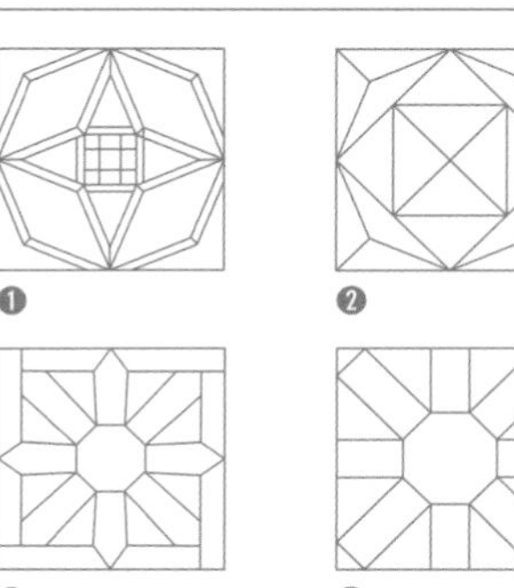
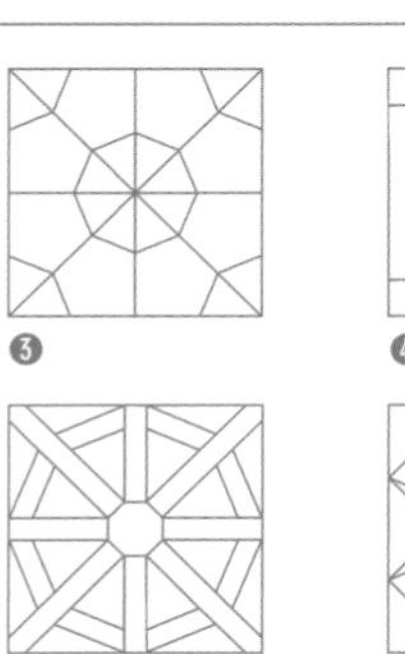
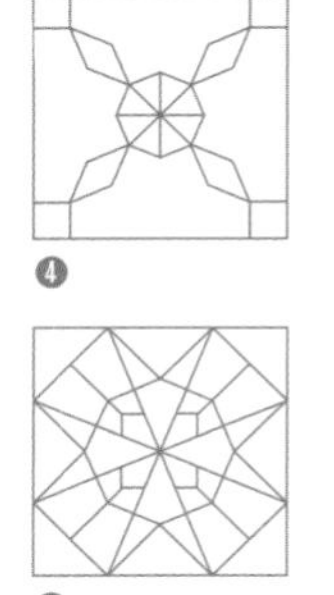
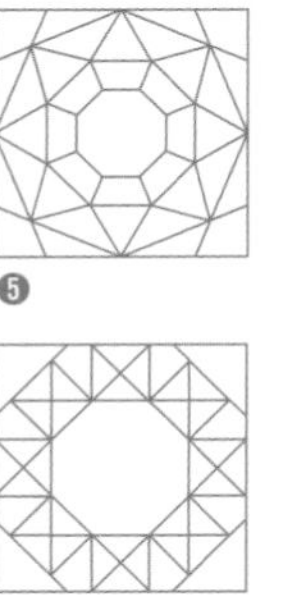
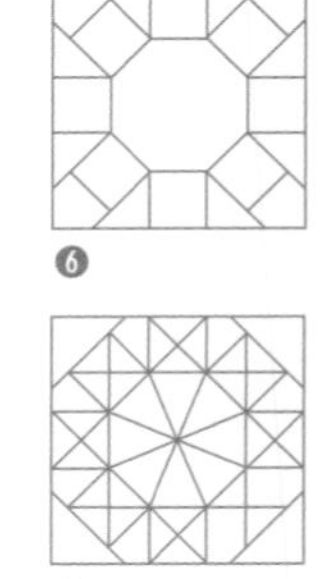
❶ ❷ ❸ ❹ ❺ ❻

❼ ❽ ❾ ❿ ⓫ ⓬

1 8-pointed star grid 1

2 8-pointed star grid 1

3 8-pointed star grid 4

4 8-pointed star grid 1

5 8-pointed star grid 1

6 8-pointed star grid 1

7 8-pointed star grid 1

8 8-pointed star grid 1

9 8-pointed star grid 1

10 8-pointed star grid 1

11 8-pointed star grid 3

12 8-pointed star grid 2

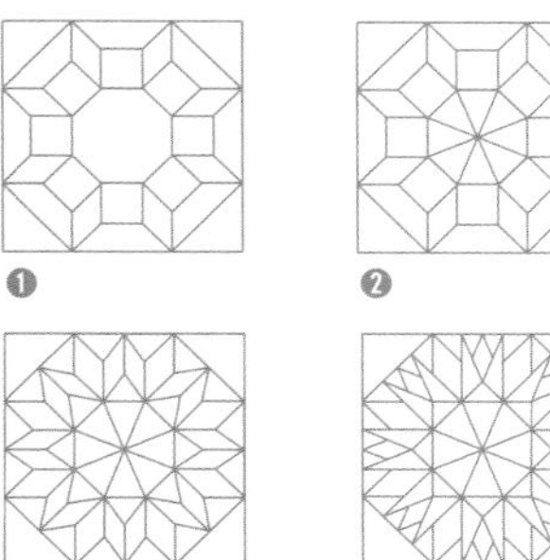
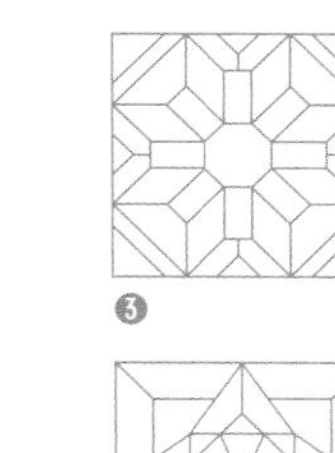
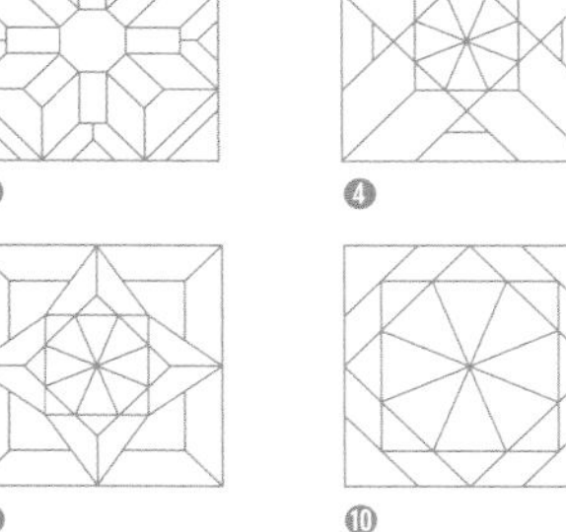
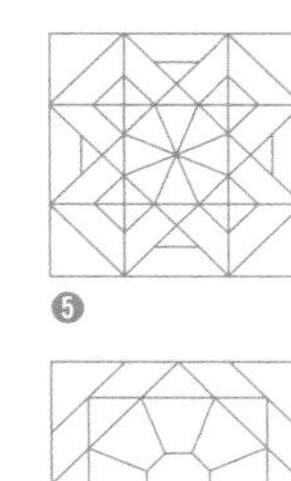
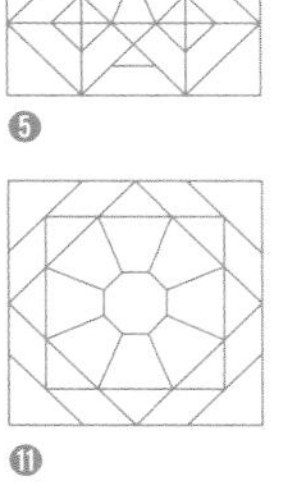
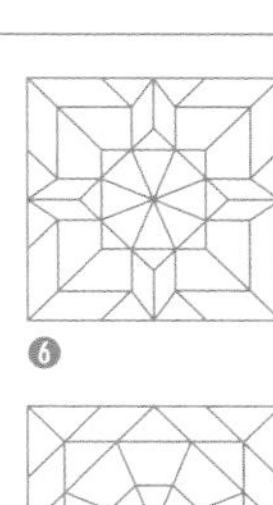

1 2 3 4 5 6

7 8 9 10 11 12

1 **The Castle Wall,** Eveline Foland, *Kansas City Star,* Oct 10, 1931. See 244-1 and 244-2. Also known as:
Castle Wall, Hall, 1935.

2 **Godey Design,** *Godey's Lady's Book,* 1851. See 244-1 and 244-2. Also known as:
Castle Wall, Ickis, 1949.

3 **Spring Glory,** Laura Wheeler, *Laura Wheeler Catalog,* ca. 1954.

4 **Courtyard Square,** Jinny Beyer, Beyer, Jinny, *Patchwork Portfolio,* 1989.

5 **Harlequin,** Jinny Beyer, Beyer, Jinny, *Patchwork Portfolio,* 1989.

6 **Lighthouse Tower,** Jinny Beyer, Hilton Head Seminar design, 1981; published in Beyer, Jinny, *Patchwork Portfolio.*

7 **Water Lily,** Jinny Beyer, Hilton Head Seminar design, 1983; published in Beyer, Jinny, *Patchwork Portfolio.*

8 **Cabaret,** Jinny Beyer, Beyer, Jinny, *Patchwork Portfolio,* 1989.

9 **Kiran's Choice,** Jinny Beyer, Hilton Head Seminar design, 1983; published in Beyer, Jinny, *Patchwork Portfolio.*

10 **Circling Swallows,** Laura Wheeler, *Indianapolis Star,* Sep 24, 1933.
"Quiltmaking is an art, and like all arts it uses symbols to express things that in reality are far more complicated in appearance. So we find birds—every sort of birds—shown as triangles and it really is not hard to imagine the bird with outspread wings in this form. In this pattern the swallows are very gay, for they are made of all variety of scraps. Each block can be made in the same scraps or different ones used throughout as illustrated." Laura Wheeler, *Cincinnati Enquirer,* Sep 24, 1933

11 **Eight Diamonds and a Star,** Aunt Martha series: *Quilts: Modern-Colonial,* ca. 1954.

12 **Oriental Star,** Nancy Cabot, *Chicago Tribune,* Mar 26, 1936.
"Perhaps one of the simplest of the older pieced patterns which are suitable for the beginning quilt maker to attempt is 'Oriental Star.'" Nancy Cabot, *Chicago Tribune,* Mar 26, 1936

❶ **Sagebrush,** Jinny Beyer, Beyer, Jinny, *Patchwork Portfolio,* 1989.

❷ **Star within Star,** Nancy Cabot, *Chicago Tribune,* Mar 13, 1937.

❸ **The Double Star,** Home Art Studios, *Cincinnati Enquirer,* Mar 15, 1933.

❹ **Unknown,** *Prize Winning Designs,* ca. 1931.

❺ **Ring Around Rosy,** *Happy Hours,* Jun 1899, per Smith.

❻ **Corn Flower,** Home Art Studios, *World Herald,* Oct 18, 1933.

❼ **Four Leaf Clover,** *Kansas City Star,* Oct 29, 1941.

❽ **Forget Me Not,** Aunt Martha series: *Favorite Quilts,* ca. 1953.

❾ **Patchwork Sofa Quilt,** *Ladies Art Company,* 1897.

❿ **Catalpa Flower,** Nancy Cabot, *Chicago Tribune,* May 25, 1935.

⓫ **Old Staffordshire,** Nancy Cabot, *Chicago Tribune,* Apr 21, 1937.
"'Old Staffordshire' is an ancient pieced block which was made in Massachusetts in 1852. It was copied from an old plate which was brought to this country from England by the mother of the designer." Nancy Cabot, *Chicago Tribune,* Apr 21, 1937

⓬ **Nine Snowballs,** Nancy Cabot, *Chicago Tribune,* Aug 20, 1935.

❶ 8-pointed star grid 2

❷ 8-pointed star grid 1

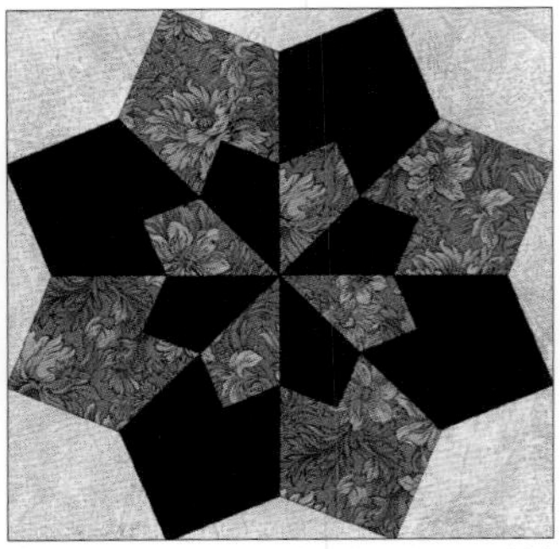

❸ 8-pointed star grid 4

❹ 8-pointed star grid 3

❺ 8-pointed star grid 1 and 3

❻ 8-pointed star grid 4

❼ 8-pointed star grid 1

❽ 8-pointed star grid 1

❾ 8-pointed star grid 1

❿ 8-pointed star grid 4

⓫ 8-pointed star grid 1

⓬ 8-pointed star grid 4

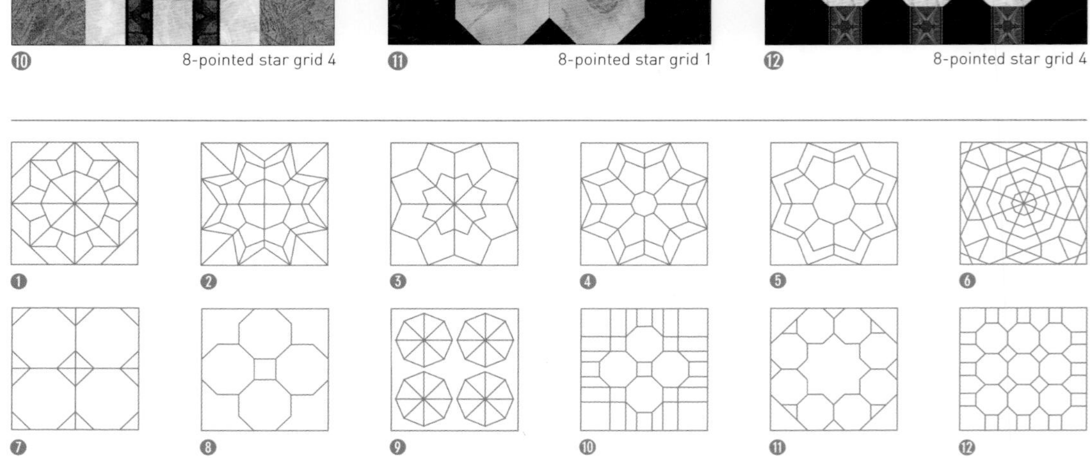

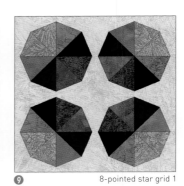

1 8-pointed star grid 1

2 8-pointed star grid 1

3 4 x 4 grid/8-pointed star grid 1

4 8-pointed star grid 1

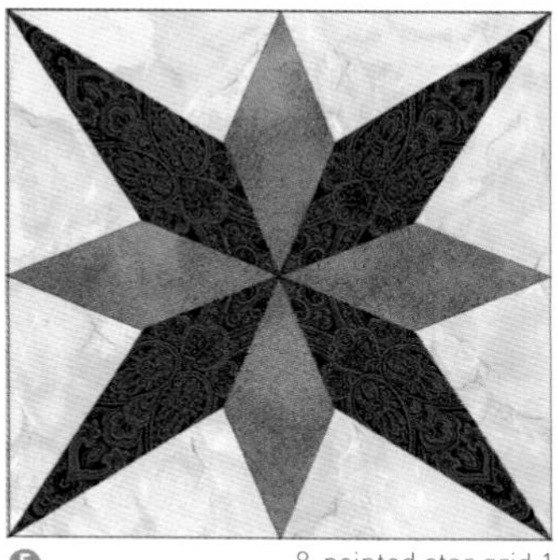
5 8-pointed star grid 1

6 8-pointed star grid 1

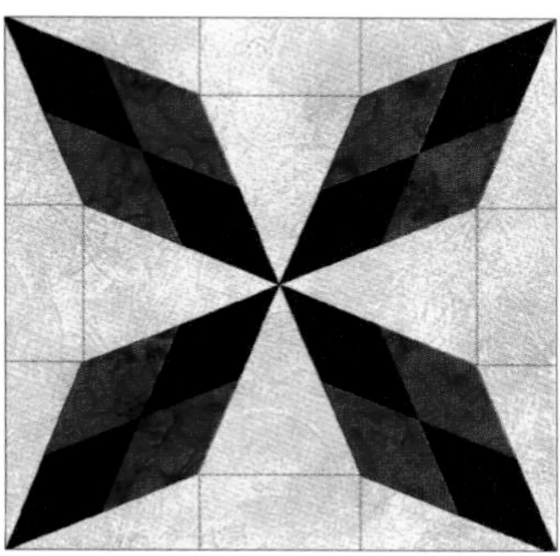
7 8-pointed star grid 2

8 8-pointed star grid 1

9 8-pointed star grid 1

10 8-pointed star grid 1

11 8-pointed star grid 4

12 8-pointed star grid 1

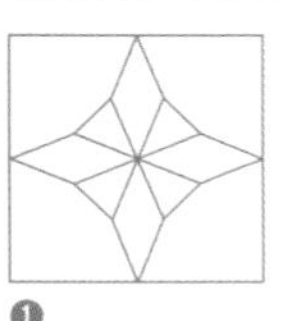
1

2

3

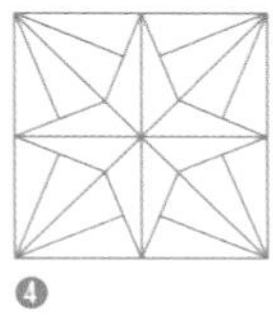
4

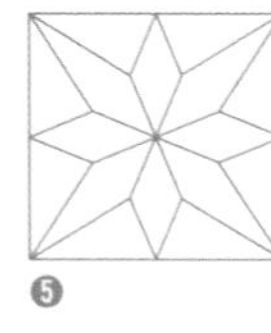
5

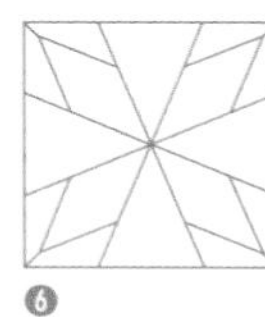
6

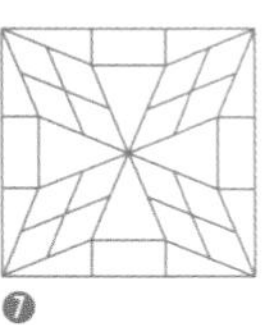
7

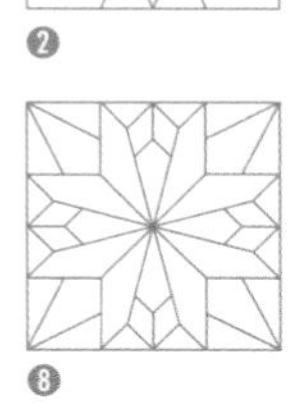
8

9

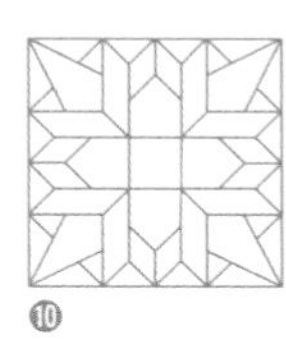
10

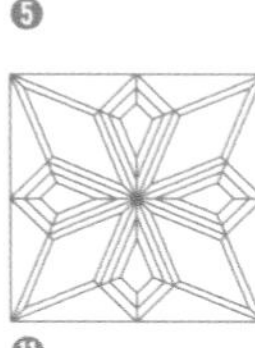
11

12

1 **Beautiful Star,** *Ladies Art Company,* 1897. Also known as:
- **Fancy Star,** *Grandmother's Patchwork Quilt Designs,* 1931.

2 **Beacon Star,** Jinny Beyer, Hilton Head Seminar design, 2005.

3 **Broken Spider Web,** Nancy Cabot, *Chicago Tribune,* Aug 3, 1935.

4 **Patchwork Design,** *The Ladies' Friend,* 1866. See 160-6, 202-2, and 255-12. Also known as:
- **Blazing Star,** Finley, 1929.
- **Four-Pointed Star,** Hall, 1935.
- **Mother's Delight,** Clara Stone, *Practical Needlework,* ca. 1906.
- **Western Star,** James, 1978.

5 **The Long Pointed Star,** *Kansas City Star,* Apr 1, 1942.

6 **Illusions,** Jinny Beyer, Hilton Head Seminar design, 2005.

7 **Teddy's Choice,** Clara Stone, *Practical Needlework,* ca. 1906. Also known as:
- **Arkansas Traveler,** Finley, 1929.
- **Cowboy's Star,** Finley, 1929.
- **Travel Star,** Finley, 1929.

8 **Snapdragon,** Jinny Beyer, Beyer, Jinny, *Patchwork Portfolio,* 1989.

9 **Magnolia,** Jinny Beyer, Beyer, Jinny, *Patchwork Portfolio,* 1989.

10 **Treasure Chest,** Jinny Beyer, Hilton Head Seminar design, 1984; published in Beyer, Jinny *Patchwork Portfolio.*

11 **Star of Empire,** Clara Stone, *Practical Needlework,* ca. 1906.

12 **Facets,** Jinny Beyer, Hilton Head Seminar design, 1985; published in Beyer, Jinny, *Patchwork Portfolio.*

❶ **Sea Crystal,** Jinny Beyer, Hilton Head Seminar design, 1982; published in Beyer, Jinny, *Patchwork Portfolio.*

❷ **Dahlia,** Jinny Beyer, Beyer, Jinny, *Patchwork Portfolio,* 1989.

❸ **Sunburst Quilt,** Laura Wheeler, *Stockman's Journal,* date unknown.

❹ **Captain's Wheel,** Jinny Beyer, Hilton Head Seminar design, 1983; published in Beyer, Jinny, *Patchwork Portfolio.*

❺ **Lover's Knot,** *Grandma Dexter New Appliqué and Patchwork Designs, Book 36b,* ca. 1932.

❻ **Ice Crystals,** Nancy Cabot, *Chicago Tribune,* Dec 27, 1934.

❼ **Hidden Star,** Jinny Beyer, Beyer, Jinny, *Patchwork Portfolio,* 1989.

❽ **Dutch Blades,** Jinny Beyer, Beyer, Jinny, *Patchwork Portfolio,* 1989.

❾ **Court Jester,** Jinny Beyer, Beyer, Jinny, *Patchwork Portfolio,* 1989.

❿ **Aerial Beacon,** *Quilt Booklet No.* 1, ca. 1931.

⓫ **Aerial Beacon,** Nancy Cabot, *Chicago Tribune,* Apr 18, 1938. Also known as:
Lighthouse Block, Nancy Cabot, *Chicago Tribune,* Apr 18, 1938.

⓬ **V Block,** date unknown; published in Beyer, Jinny, *The Quilter's Album. . . .*

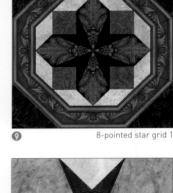

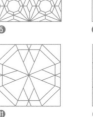

❶ 8-pointed star grid 4

❷ 8-pointed star grid 4

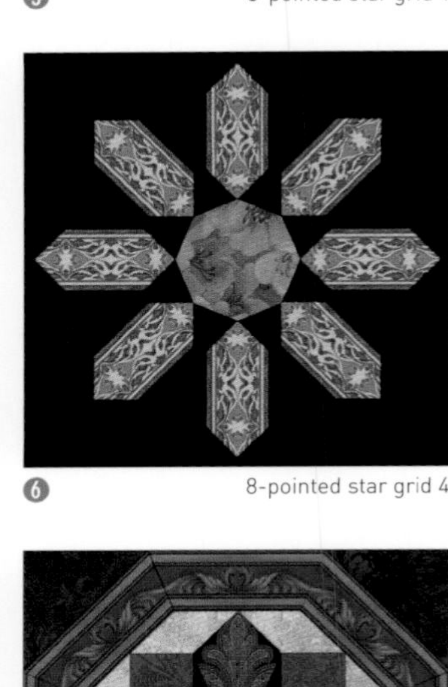

❸ 8-pointed star grid 1

❹ 8-pointed star grid 1

❺ 8-pointed star grid 4

❻ 8-pointed star grid 4

❼ 8-pointed star grid 4

❽ 8-pointed star grid 3

❾ 8-pointed star grid 1

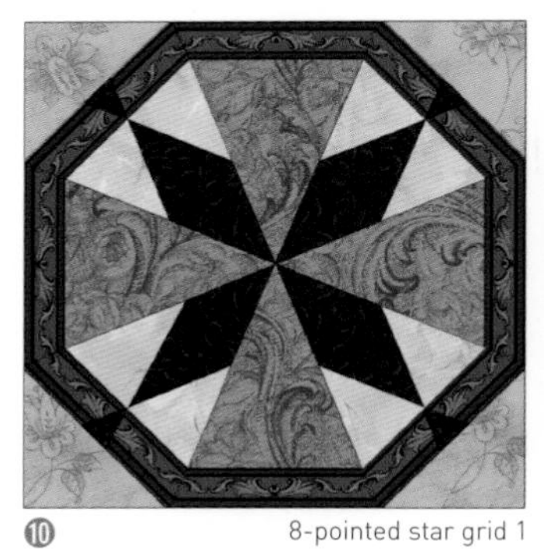

❿ 8-pointed star grid 1

⓫ 8-pointed star grid 1

⓬ 8-pointed star grid 1

❶ ❷ ❸ ❹ ❺ ❻

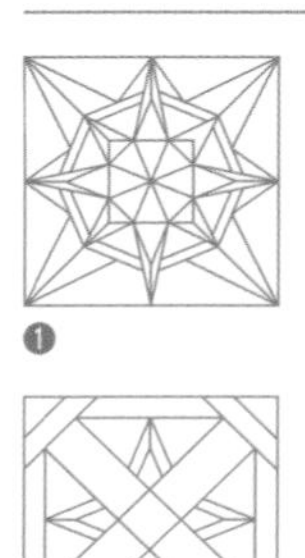

❼

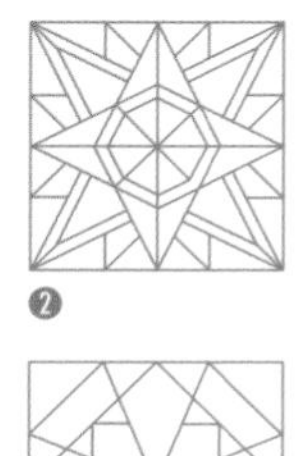

❽

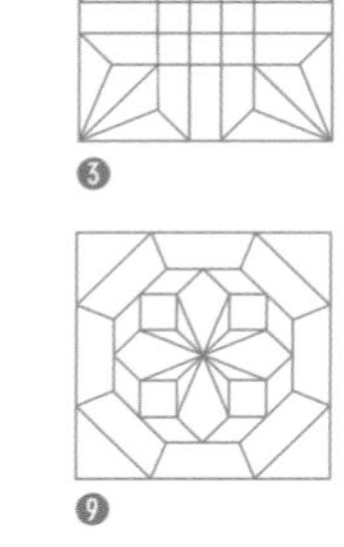

❾

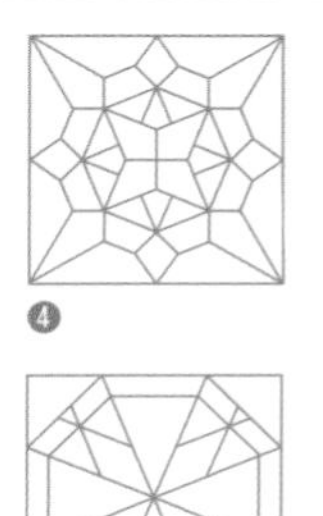

❿

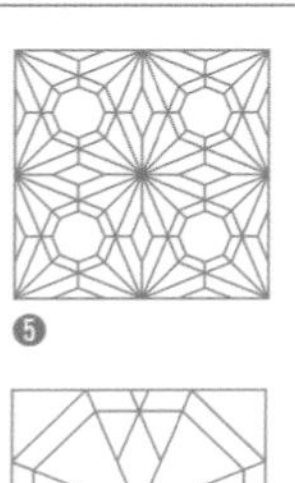

⓫

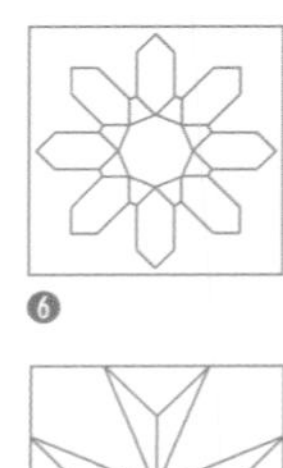

⓬

1 8-pointed star grid 1

2 8-pointed star grid 4

3 8-pointed star grid 1

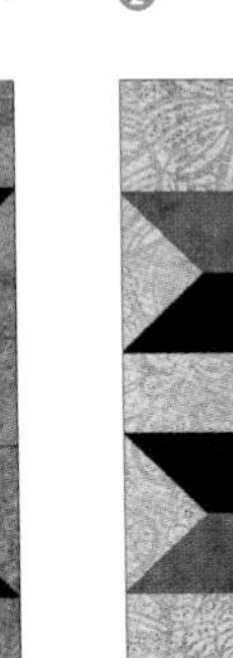

4 8-pointed star grid 1

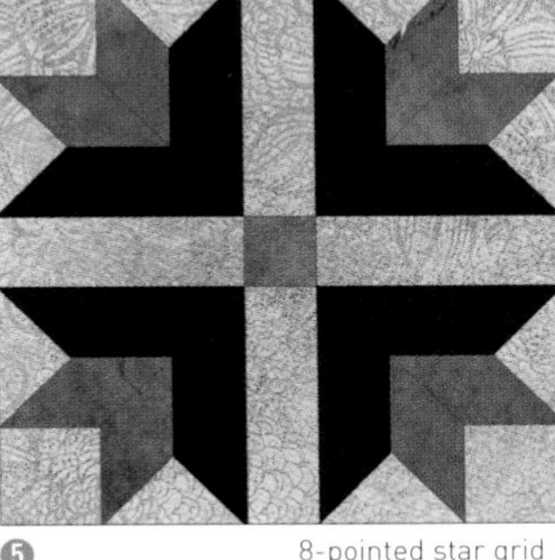

5 8-pointed star grid 1

6 8-pointed star grid 4

7 8-pointed star grid 1

8 8-pointed star grid 4

9 8-pointed star grid 2

10 8-pointed star grid 1

11 8-pointed star grid 1

12 8-pointed star grid 1

1 Variation IV, Jinny Beyer, Hilton Head Seminar design, 1989; published in Beyer, Jinny, *Patchwork Portfolio.*

2 Royal Star, *Grandmother Clark's Old Fashioned Quilt Designs, Book 21,* 1931. Also known as:

- **Maltese Cross,** Alice Brooks, *Detroit Free Press,* Jan 1, 1934.

3 Pineapple, Hall, 1935. Also known as:

- **Alhambra,** Jinny Beyer, Hilton Head Seminar design, 1993.

4 Goose Tracks, *Ladies Art Company,* 1897. See 156-11, 194-5, and 223-8. Also known as:

- **Duck Paddle,** Hall, 1935.
- **Fancy Flowers,** *Grandmother's Patchwork Quilt Designs, Book 20,* 1931.
- **Fanny's Fan,** Hall, 1935.
- **Lily Corners,** *One Dozen Quilt Patterns,* ca. 1936.
- **Pride of Italy,** McKim, 1931.

5 Crossroads, *The Farmer's Wife Book of Quilts,* 1931. See 156-11, 194-5, and 223-8. Also known as:

- **Dove at the Window,** *Kansas City Star,* Apr 11, 1936.

6 Star of Many Points, *Ladies Art Company,* 1897. Also known as:

- **Arrow Head Star,** Eveline Foland, *Kansas City Star,* Jul 11, 1931.
- **Arrowhead Star,** Hall, 1935.
- **Laurel Leaf,** *Grandmother Clark's Patchwork Quilts, Book No. 19,* 1932.

"This is Block 2 in the Nancy Page Star of Many Points Series Quilt." *Lowell Sun,* May 28, 1934

7 Weathervane, Nancy Cabot, *Chicago Tribune,* Jan 20, 1937. See 141-5, 141-6, and 141-7.

8 Lotus Star, source unknown, ca. 1933.

9 Swallows in the Window, Eveline Foland, *Kansas City Star,* Sep 27, 1930.

10 Queen's Crown, Jinny Beyer, Beyer, Jinny, *Patchwork Portfolio,* 1989.

11 Friendship Star, Laura Wheeler, *Cincinnati Enquirer,* Aug 2, 1933.

12 Leaves and Flowers, *Kansas City Star,* Aug 24, 1935.

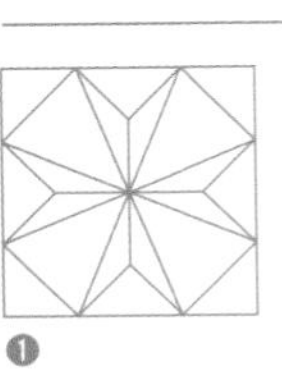

1

2

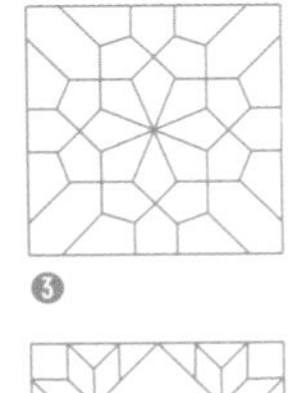

3

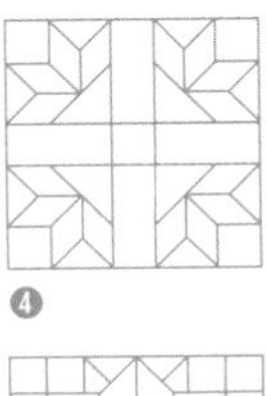

4

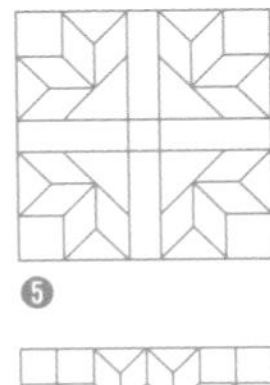

5

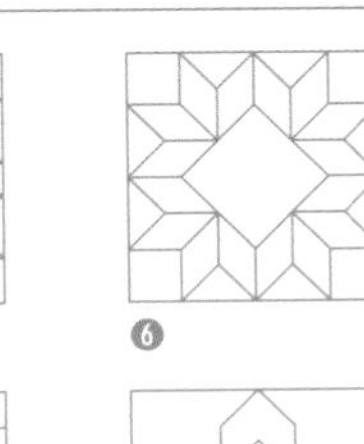

6

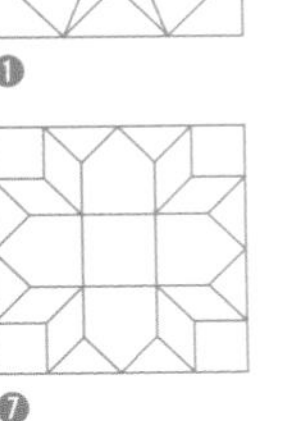

7

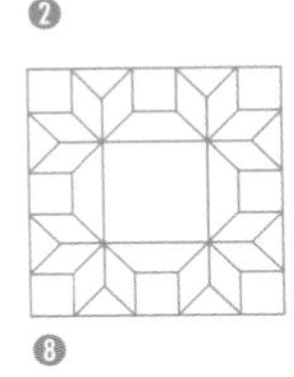

8

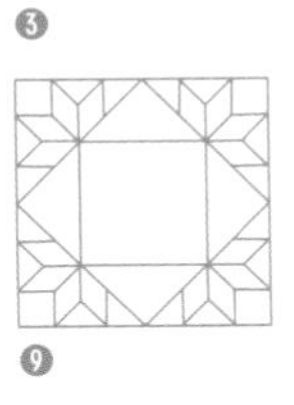

9

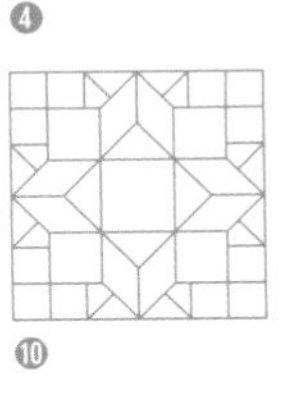

10

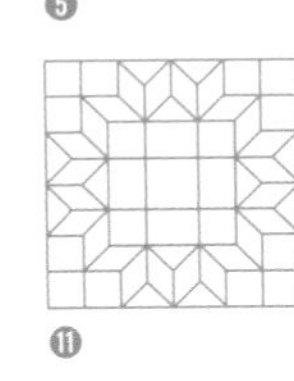

11

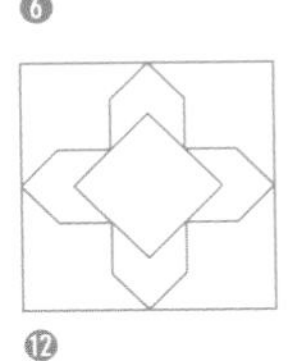

12

❶ **Shaded Trail,** Laura Wheeler, *Kansas City Star,* Oct 2, 1933. Also known as:
- **Four Patch,** Alice Brooks, unidentified newspaper clipping, date unknown.

❷ **The Whirling Star,** *Kansas City Star,* Apr 16, 1941. Also known as:
- **Patriotic Star,** *Kansas City Star,* Apr 16, 1941.

❸ **Sunbeam,** *The Patchwork Book,* 1932. See 113-8.

❹ **Sunbeam,** Ruby McKim, *Kansas City Star,* Jul 27, 1929. See 113-8. Also known as:
- **Squared Star,** Home Art Studios, *World Herald,* Mar 6, 1934.

❺ **Double Square,** *Kansas City Star,* Jul 10, 1937.

❻ **The 8 Point Snowflake,** *Kansas City Star,* Apr 8, 1953.

❼ **Album Flower,** Laura Wheeler, *Cincinnati Enquirer,* Sep 23, 1933. Also known as:
- **Patchwork Quilt,** Alice Brooks, *Wichita Eagle,* date unknown.

❽ **Peach Blow,** Clara Stone, *Practical Needlework,* ca. 1906.

❾ **Aberdeen,** Jinny Beyer, RJR Patterns, 2001.

❿ **Granada Star,** Jinny Beyer, Hilton Head Seminar design, 2002.

⓫ **Sea of Ingenuity,** Jinny Beyer, RJR Patterns, 1999.

⓬ **Sea of Tranquility,** Jinny Beyer, RJR Patterns, 1999.

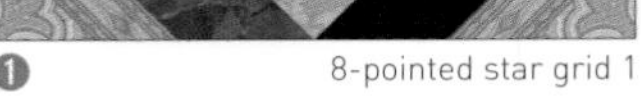

❶ 8-pointed star grid 1

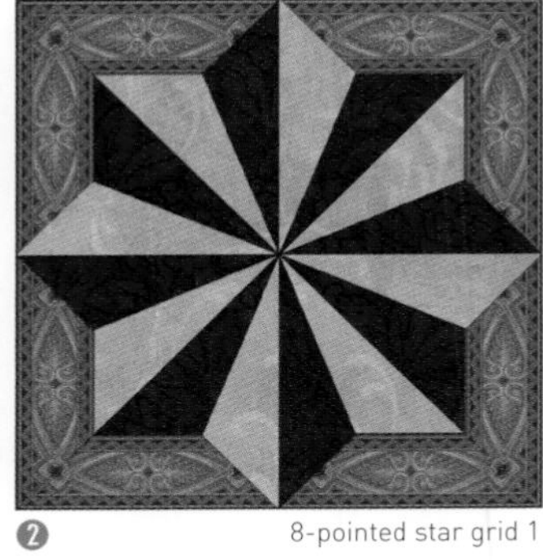

❷ 8-pointed star grid 1

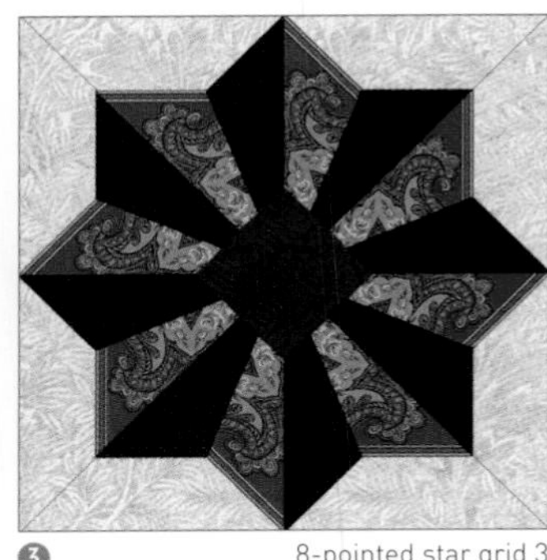

❸ 8-pointed star grid 3

❹ 8-pointed star grid 2

❺ 8-pointed star grid 1

❻ 8-pointed star grid 3

❼ 8-pointed star grid 4

❽ 8-pointed star grid 3

❾ 8-pointed star grid 1

❿ 8-pointed star grid 1

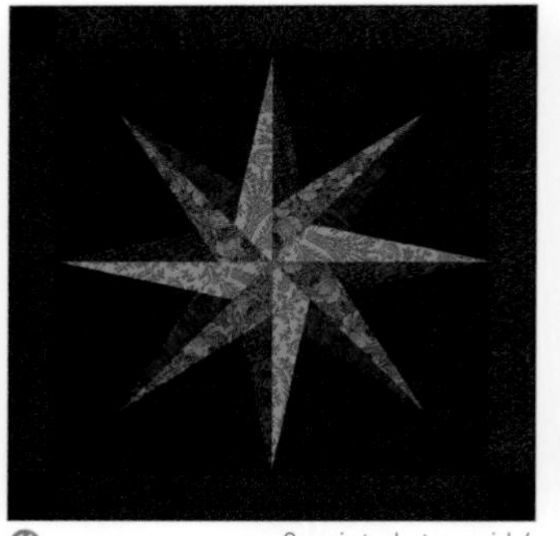

⓫ 8-pointed star grid 4

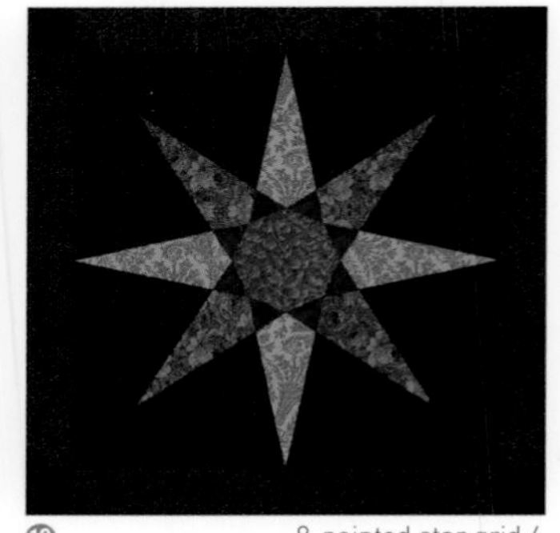

⓬ 8-pointed star grid 4

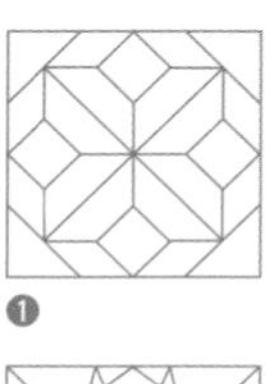

❶

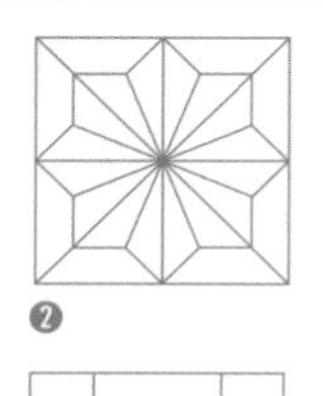

❷

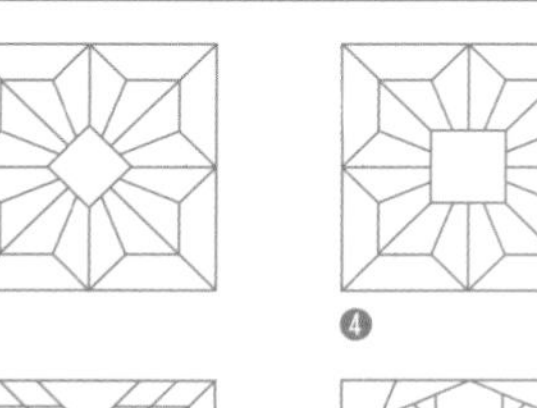

❸ ❹

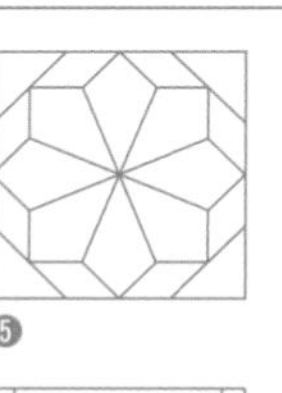

❺

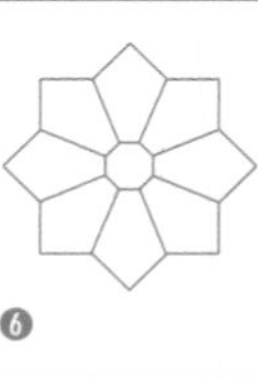

❻

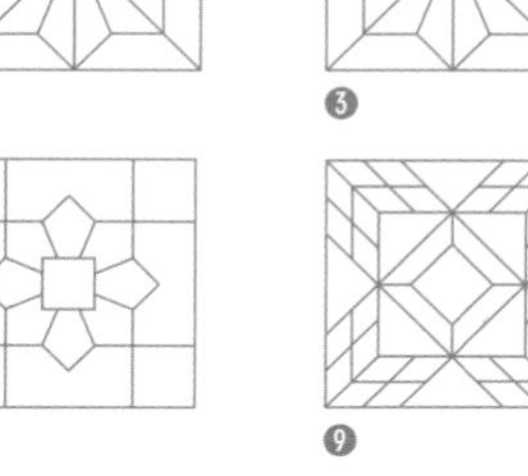

❼ ❽

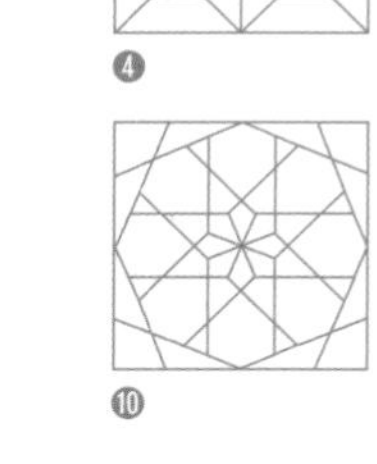

❾ ❿

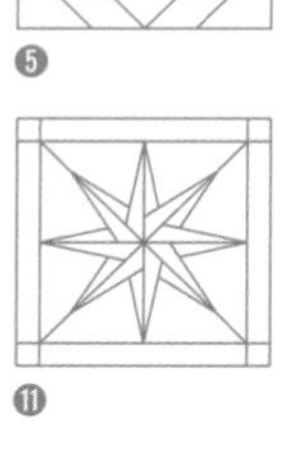

⓫

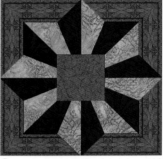

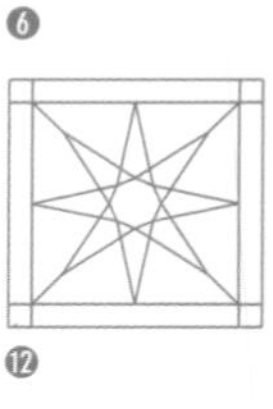

⓬

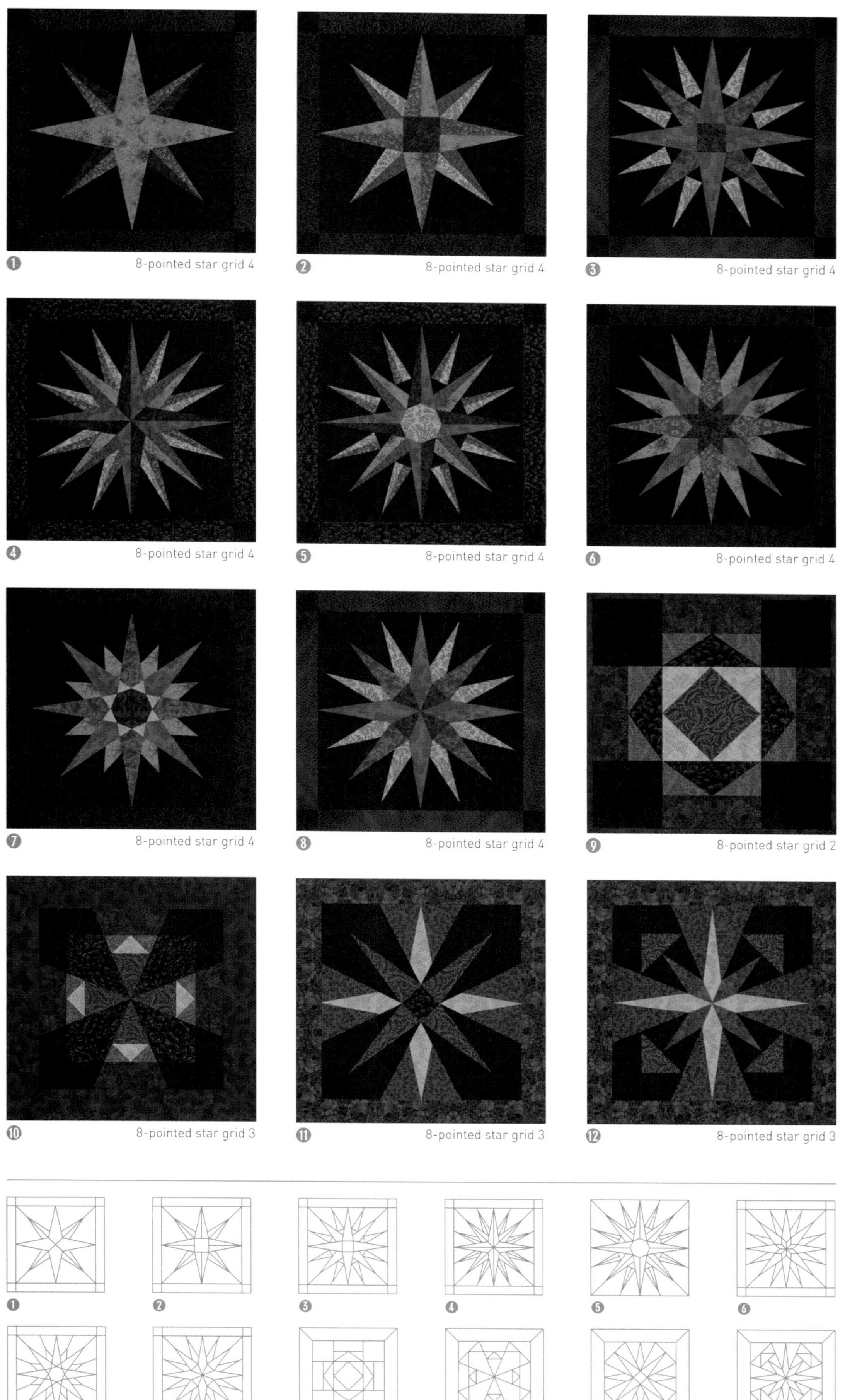

1. **Sea of Nectar,** Jinny Beyer, RJR Patterns, 1999.
2. **Sea of Moisture,** Jinny Beyer, RJR Patterns, 1999.
3. **Sea of Clouds,** Jinny Beyer, RJR Patterns, 1999.
4. **Sea of Crisis,** Jinny Beyer, RJR Patterns, 1999.
5. **Sea of Serenity,** Jinny Beyer, RJR Patterns, 1999.
6. **Sea of Fertility,** Jinny Beyer, RJR Patterns, 1999.
7. **Sea of Vapor,** Jinny Beyer, RJR Patterns, 1999.
8. **Sea of Rains,** Jinny Beyer, RJR Patterns, 1999.
9. **Castle Dome,** Jinny Beyer, RJR Patterns, 2000.
10. **Crystal Cave,** Jinny Beyer, RJR Patterns, 2000.
11. **Sedona Sunrise,** Jinny Beyer, RJR Patterns, 2000.
12. **Sonora Sunset,** Jinny Beyer, RJR Patterns, 2000.

❶ **Phoenix Star,** Jinny Beyer, RJR Patterns, 2000.

❷ **Painted Desert,** Jinny Beyer, RJR Patterns, 2000.

❸ **Mesa Verde,** Jinny Beyer, RJR Patterns, 2000.

❹ **Desert Rose,** Jinny Beyer, RJR Patterns, 2000.

❺ **Mojave Morning,** Jinny Beyer, RJR Patterns, 2000.

❻ **Tuscon Trail,** Jinny Beyer, RJR Patterns, 2000.

❼ **Santa Fe Sky,** Jinny Beyer, RJR Patterns, 2000.

❽ **Cactus Flower,** Jinny Beyer, RJR Patterns, 2000.

❾ **Log Star,** Jinny Beyer, Jinny Beyer Studio design, 1999.

❿ **Washington Pavement,** Nancy Page, *Birmingham News,* May 12, 1936. Also known as:

Hamilton Gardens, Nancy Page, *Birmingham News,* Jul 27, 1943.

⓫ **Washington Pavement,** Laura Wheeler, *Indianapolis Star,* Aug 11, 1933. Also known as:

Priscilla, Nancy Page, *Indianapolis Star,* Aug 11, 1933.

⓬ **Pineapple,** Alice Brooks, *Detroit Free Press,* Jan 1, 1934.

❶ 8-pointed star grid 3

❷ 8-pointed star grid 1

❸ 8-pointed star grid 1

❹ 8-pointed star grid 1

❺ 8-pointed star grid 1

❻ 8-pointed star grid 1

❼ 8-pointed star grid 3

❽ 8-pointed star grid 3

❾ 8-pointed star grid 3

❿ 9 x 9 grid/8-pointed star grid 3

⓫ 9 x 9 grid/8-pointed star grid 1

⓬ 8-pointed star grid 3

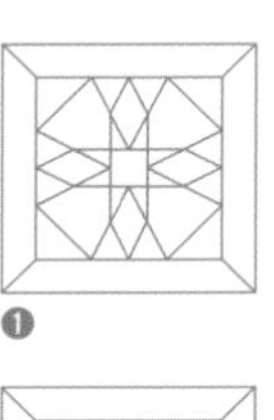

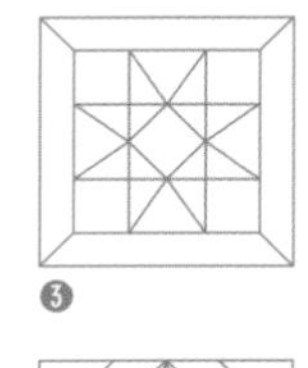

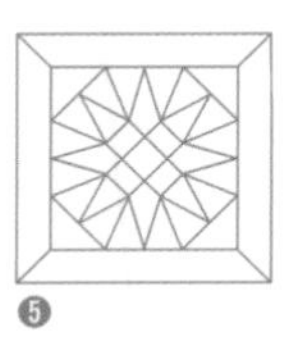

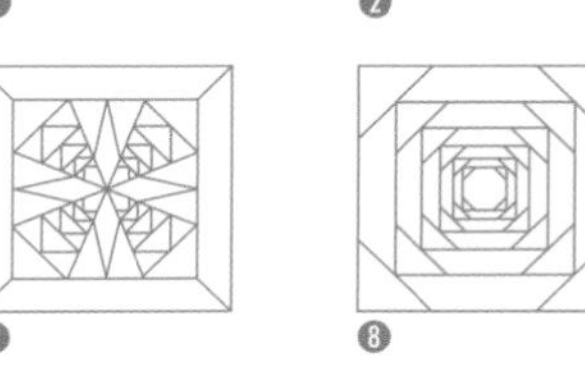

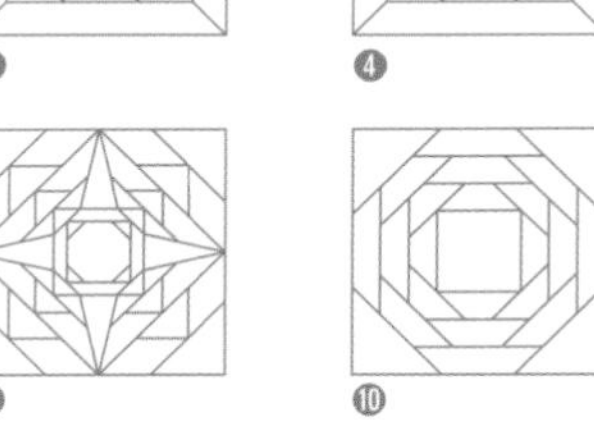

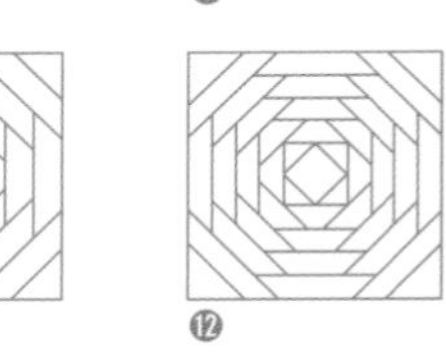

❶ ❷ ❸ ❹ ❺ ❻

❼ ❽ ❾ ❿ ⓫ ⓬

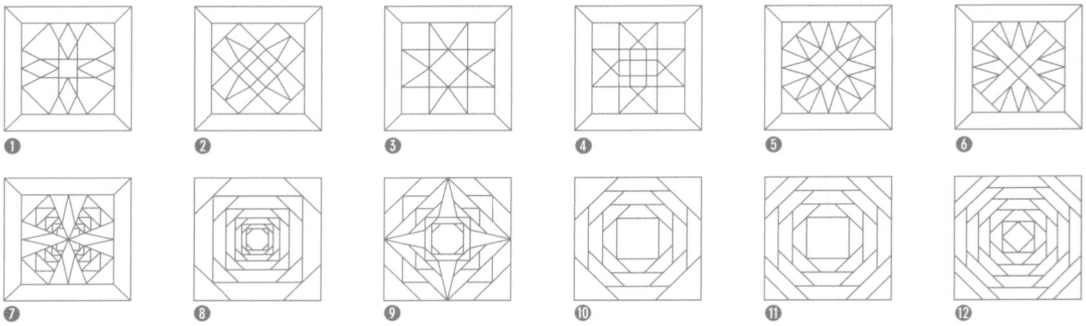

1 8-pointed star grid 3

2 8-pointed star grid 1

3 14 x 14 grid/8-pointed star grid 1

4 8-pointed star grid 1

5 8-pointed star grid 3

6 8-pointed star grid 1

7 8-pointed star grid 4

8 8-pointed star grid 4

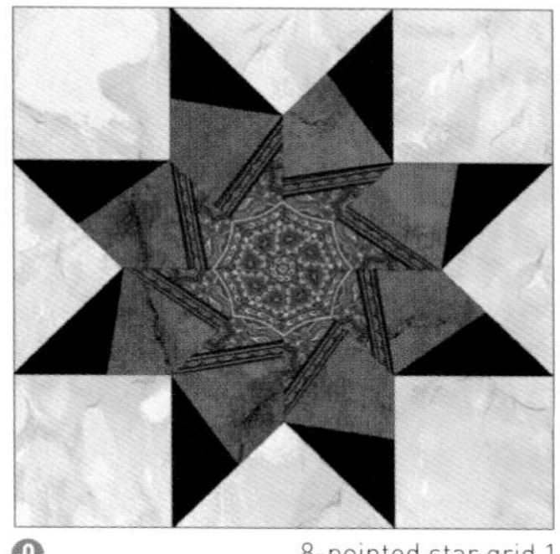
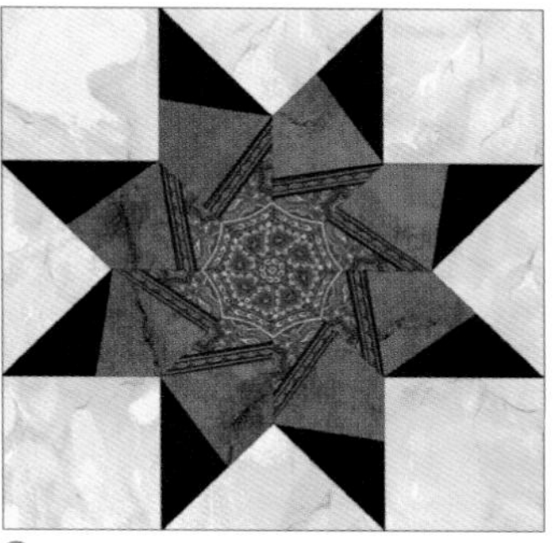

9 8-pointed star grid 1

10 8-pointed star grid 4

11 8-pointed star grid 4

12 8-pointed star grid 1

1 **Maltese Cross,** Hall, 1935.

2 **Maltese Cross,** Hall, 1935. Also known as:

Pineapple, Hall, 1935.

3 **Pineapples,** ca. 1875, per Holstein. Also known as:

Pineapple, Home Art Studios, *Des Moines Register,* Dec 4, 1932.

"Old fashioned quilts are popular again. Women of the Colonial days would not feel that their bedrooms were complete without a patchwork quilt on each bed. The Pineapple, illustrated above, is a striking example of the popular handwork which was enjoyed so much during the Colonial days. You, too, will find it interesting as pick-up work, and you will be surprised how much you can accomplish during spare moments. Many afternoon gatherings are now spent in making patchwork quilts. Your friends and neighbors will be delighted when you invite them to an old-fashioned quilting bee." *World Herald,* Sep 14, 1933

4 **Pineapple No. 1,** *Ladies Art Company,* 1897. Also known as:

Colonial Pineapple Block, Nancy Cabot, *Chicago Tribune,* Jun 2, 1933.

Washington Pavement, Ruby McKim, McKim, 1931.

5 **The Pineapple,** *Grandmother Clark's Patchwork Quilt Designs, From Books 20-21-23,* 1932.

6 **Star of Stripes,** Aunt Martha series: *Bold and Beautiful Quilts,* ca. 1977.

7 **Liberty Star,** ca. 1938, per Havig.

8 **Liberty Star,** Eveline Foland, *Kansas City Star,* Aug 10, 1932. Also known as:

The Liberty Star, *Kansas City Star,* Apr 21, 1948.

9 **Rosette of Points,** *Kansas City Star,* Aug 29, 1956.

10 **Circling Swallows,** Finley, 1929. Also known as:

Falling Star, Finley, 1929.

Flying Barn Swallows, Nancy Cabot, *Chicago Tribune,* Feb 27, 1935.

Flying Star, Finley, 1929.

Flying Swallow, Hall, 1935.

Flying Swallows, *Ladies Art Company,* 1928.

Whirling Star, *Kansas City Star,* Jan 30, 1937.

Wreath, Laura Wheeler, *Sioux City Journal,* Jul 2, 1933.

11 **Starfish,** Jinny Beyer, Beyer, Jinny, *Patchwork Portfolio,* 1989.

12 **Fancy's Favorite,** Alice Brooks, *Detroit Free Press,* Mar 22, 1938.

1

2

3

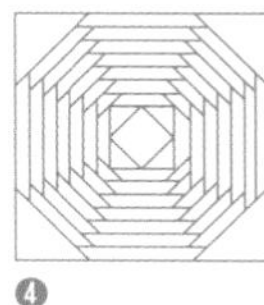

4

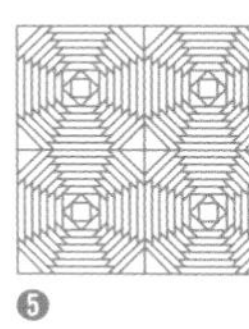

5

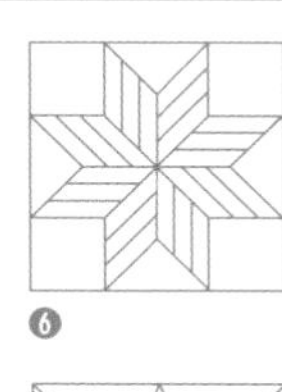

6

7

8

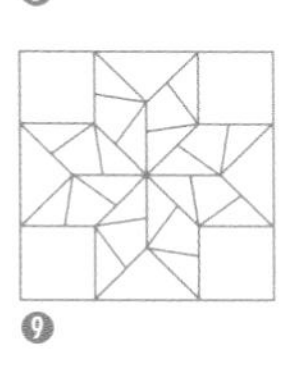

9

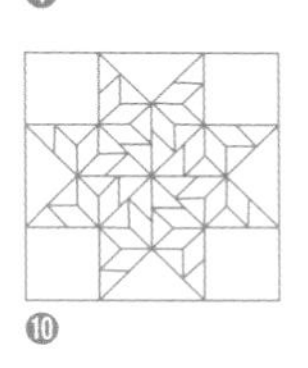

10

11

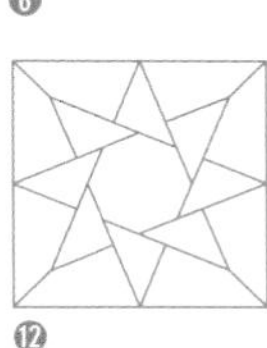

12

❶ **Lucky Star Quilt,** Alice Brooks, unidentified newspaper clipping, date unknown.

❷ **Whirling Star,** Laura Wheeler, *Cincinnati Enquirer,* Aug 31, 1933.

❸ **Interlocked Squares,** Eveline Foland, *Kansas City Star,* Oct 1, 1932.

❹ **Pattern 564,** unidentified newspaper clipping, Sep 13, 1983.

❺ **Paddle Wheel,** Jinny Beyer, Beyer, Jinny, *Patchwork Portfolio,* 1989.

❻ **Interlacing Squares,** Home Art Studios, *Cincinnati Enquirer,* Apr 23, 1933. "Here's a new patchwork design which is exceptionally easy to make. This is an all-over pattern combining both plain colors and prints with white." *World Herald,* Sep 9, 1933

❼ **Star Puzzle,** Jinny Beyer, Beyer, Jinny, *Patchwork Portfolio,* 1989.

❽ **Majorca Maze,** Jinny Beyer, Hilton Head Seminar design, 2002.

❾ **Roman Road,** Jinny Beyer, Hilton Head Seminar design, 2002.

❿ **Milky Way,** Jinny Beyer, Beyer, Jinny, *Patchwork Portfolio,* 1989.

⓫ **Sunburst and Mills,** Nancy Cabot, *Chicago Tribune,* Feb 22, 1936.

⓬ **Friendship Circle,** Laura Wheeler, *Sioux City Journal,* Dec 31, 1940.

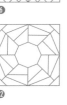

❶ 8-pointed star grid 1

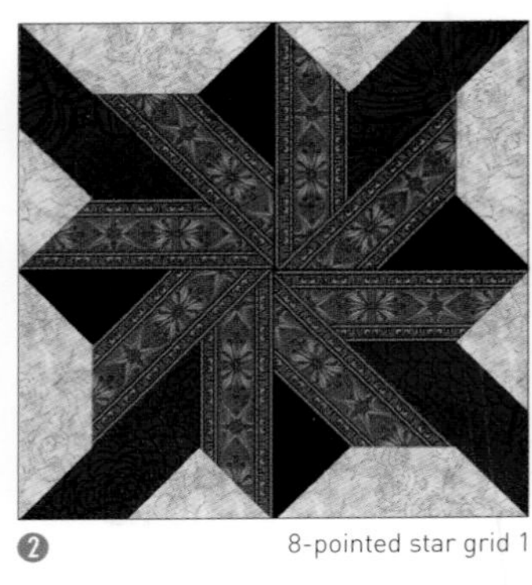

❷ 8-pointed star grid 1

❸ 8-pointed star grid 3

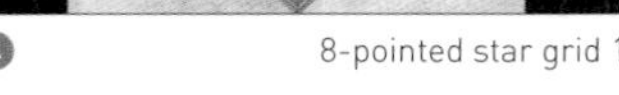

❹ 8-pointed star grid 1

❺ 8-pointed star grid 3

❻ 8-pointed star grid 3

❼ 8-pointed star grid 2

❽ 8-pointed star grid 1

❾ 8-pointed star grid 4

❿ 8-pointed star grid 1

⓫ 8-pointed star grid 1

⓬ 8-pointed star grid 2

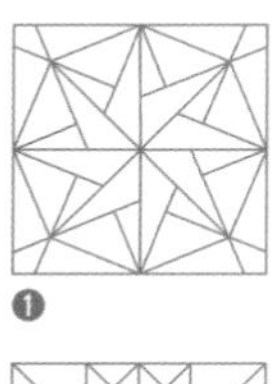

❶

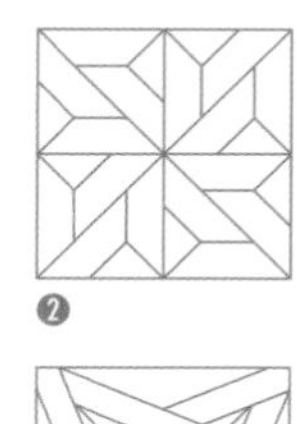

❷

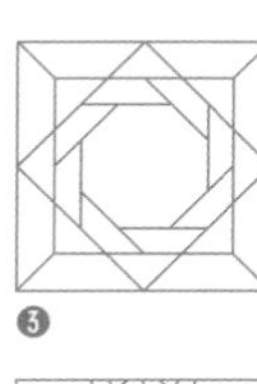

❸

❹

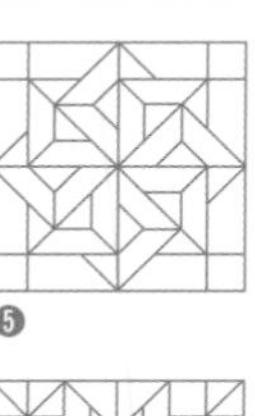

❺

❻

❼

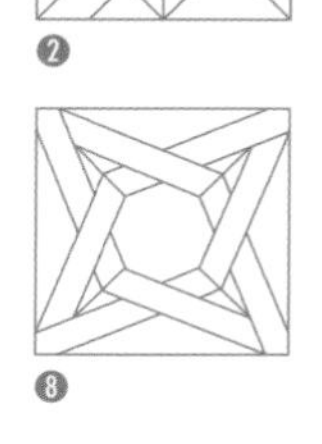

❽

❾

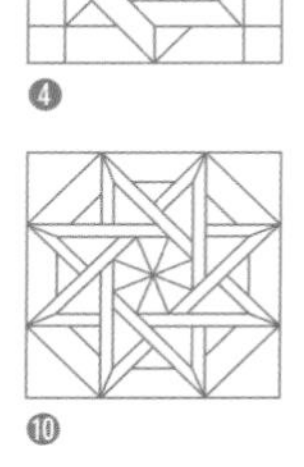

❿

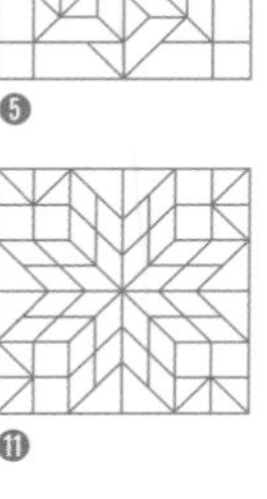

⓫

⓬

1 8-pointed star grid 1

2 8-pointed star grid 1

3 8-pointed star grid 4

4 8-pointed star grid 3

5 8-pointed star grid 3

6 8-pointed star grid 4

7 8-pointed star grid 1

8 8-pointed star grid 1

9 8-pointed star grid 1

10 8-pointed star grid 1

11 8-pointed star grid 1

12 8-pointed star grid 1

1 **Morning Star,** Alice Brooks, unidentified newspaper clipping, date unknown.

2 **Water Wheel,** Laura Wheeler, *Illinois State Register,* May 1, 1933.

3 **Waterwheel,** *Farmer's Wife Book of New Designs and Patterns,* 1934.

4 **Carnival Time,** *Kansas City Star,* Sep 9, 1959.

5 **Carnival Time Quilt,** Aunt Martha series: *Favorite Quilts,* ca. 1953.

6 **Unfolding Star,** Nancy Cabot, *Chicago Tribune,* Apr 1, 1936.

7 **Terrazzo,** Jinny Beyer, Hilton Head Seminar design, 2002; published in Beyer, Jinny, *Quiltmaking by Hand.*

8 **Flower Pot,** Ruby McKim, *Kansas City Star,* Aug 31, 1929. Also known as:
- **Cactus Basket,** Nancy Cabot, *Chicago Tribune,* Jan 23, 1933.
- **Desert Rose,** Hall, 1935.

9 **Flower Basket,** *Kansas City Star,* Jul 31, 1935. Also known as:
- **Basket of Diamonds,** *Kansas City Star,* Sep 5, 1936.
- **Basket of Scraps,** Holstein, 1973.

10 **Cactus Basket,** Alice Brooks, *Detroit Free Press,* Sep 29, 1934.

11 **May Basket,** *Farm Journal Quilt Patterns,* ca. 1935.

12 **Flower Pot,** Clara Stone, *Practical Needlework,* ca. 1906. Also known as:
- **The Great Circle Quilt,** *Kansas City Star,* Apr 11, 1956.
- **Tulip Basket,** *Ladies Art Company,* 1928.

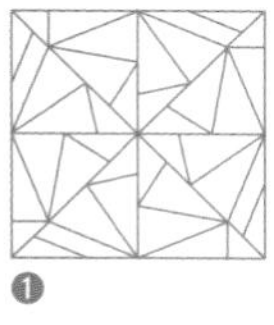
1

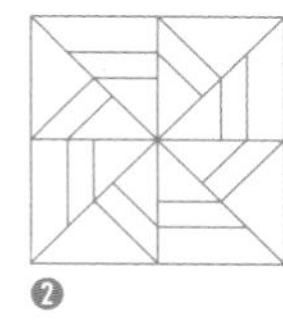
2

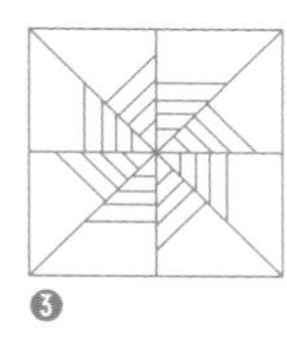
3

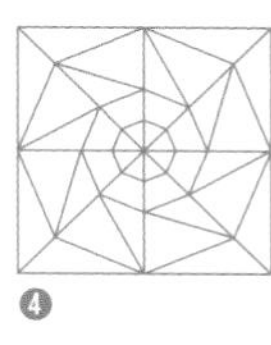
4

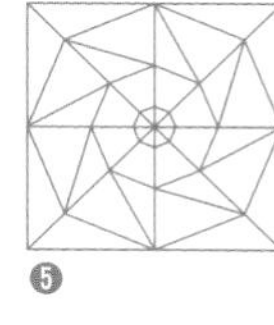
5

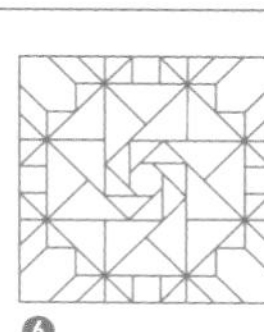
6

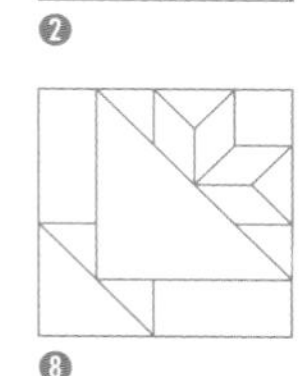
7

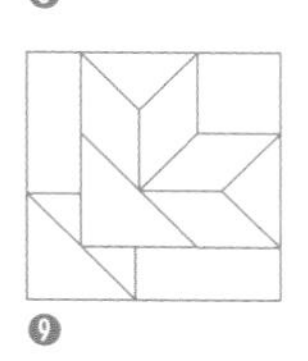
8

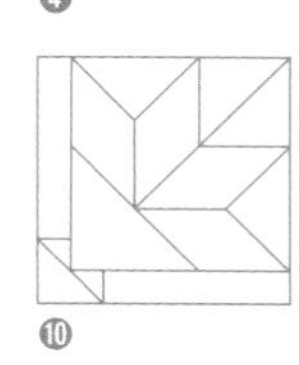
9

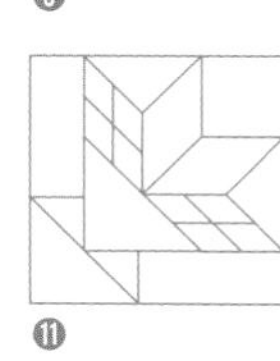
10

11

12

❶ **Flower Pot,** Clara Stone, *Practical Needlework,* ca. 1906. Also known as:
- **Hicks Basket,** *Kansas City Star,* Mar 13, 1940.
- **May Basket,** Nancy Cabot, *Chicago Tribune,* Aug 21, 1936.
- **A Section of Parquetry,** *Kansas City Star,* Mar 13, 1940.

❷ **Calico Bush,** Nancy Cabot, *Chicago Tribune,* Nov 27, 1933. Also known as:
- **Tulip Basket,** Aunt Martha series: *Favorite Quilts,* ca. 1953.

❸ **Flowers in a Basket,** *Kansas City Star,* Aug 20, 1941.

❹ **Hicks Flower Basket,** *Kansas City Star,* May 14, 1958.

❺ **Friendship Basket,** Laura Wheeler, *Indianapolis Star,* Aug 23, 1933.
"Friendship quilts are as popular today as they were in the early days of quiltmaking. And rightly so. Aside from the sentiment attached to each quilt, the variety of the scraps of material adds new interest to each block. This 'Friendship Basket' is one of the choice friendship quilts for besides being made of scraps, each block alone makes a handsome motif. So, if each friend is making a block, as was formerly the custom, the work would be especially interesting." Laura Wheeler, *Indianapolis Star,* Aug 23, 1933

❻ **White Oak Basket,** Jinny Beyer, Quilter's Quest design, 2006.

❼ **Cane Basket,** Jinny Beyer, Quilter's Quest design, 2006.

❽ **Cactus Basket,** Laura Wheeler, *Illinois State Register,* May 4, 1933.

❾ **Tulip in Vase,** Aunt Martha series: *The Quilt Fair Comes to You,* ca. 1933. Also known as:
- **Basket of Daffodils,** Jinny Beyer, Quilter's Quest design, 2006.

❿ **Double Peony,** *Grandmother Clark's Patchwork Quilt Designs, From Books 20-21-23,* 1932.

⓫ **Peonies,** Jinny Beyer, Quilter's Quest design, 2007.

⓬ **Black Eyed Susan,** Jinny Beyer, Quilter's Quest design, 2007.

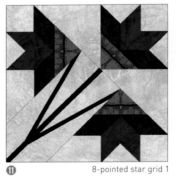

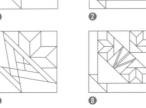

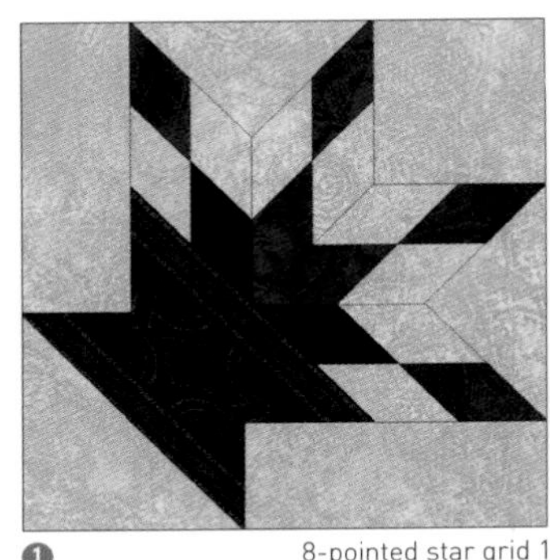

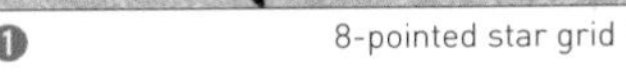

❶ 8-pointed star grid 1

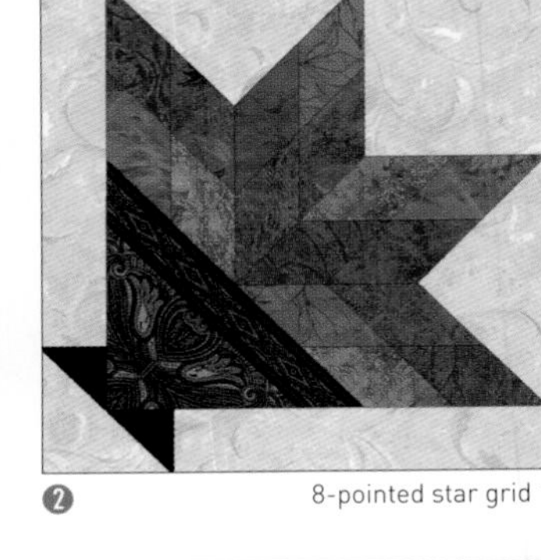

❷ 8-pointed star grid 1

❸ 8-pointed star grid 1

❹ 8-pointed star grid 1

❺ 8-pointed star grid 1

❻ 8-pointed star grid 1

❼ 8-pointed star grid 1

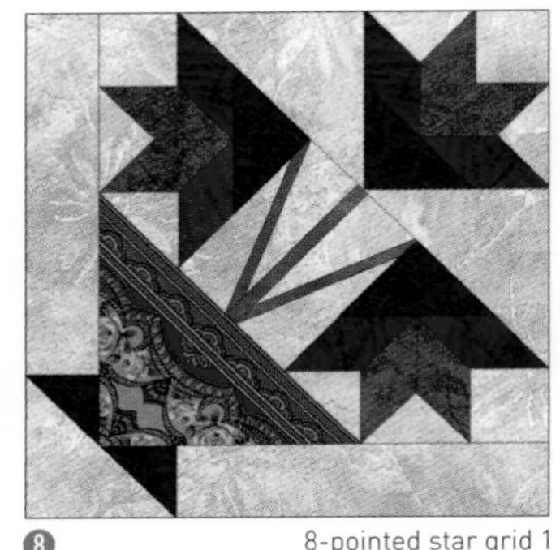

❽ 8-pointed star grid 1

❾ 8-pointed star grid 1

❿ 8-pointed star grid 1

⓫ 8-pointed star grid 1

⓬ 8-pointed star grid 4

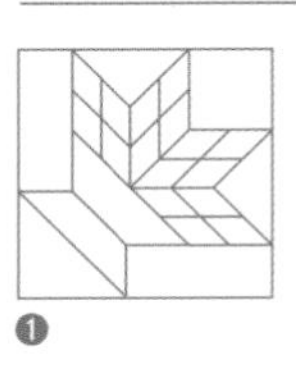

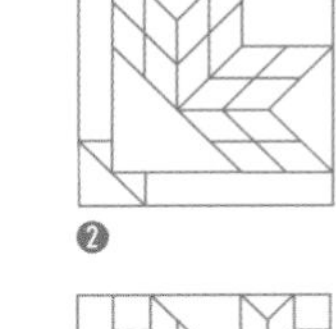

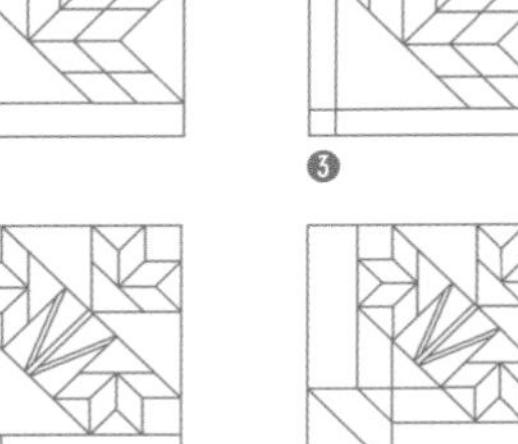

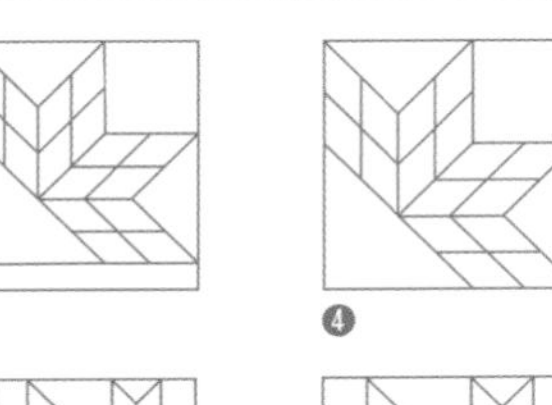

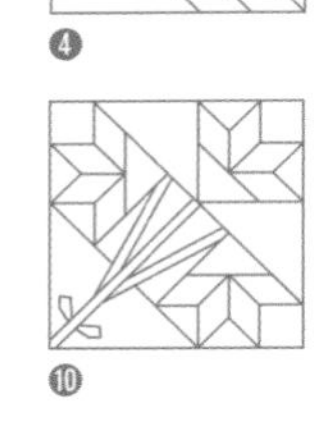

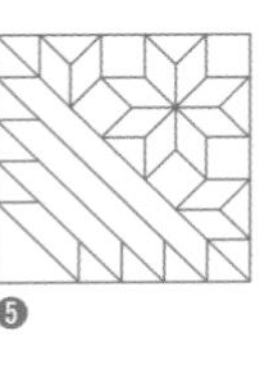

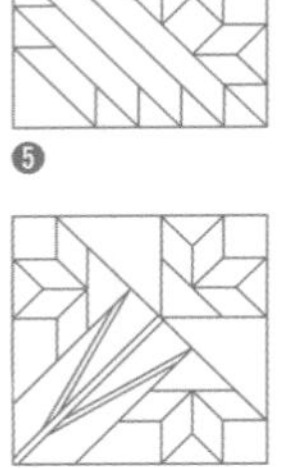

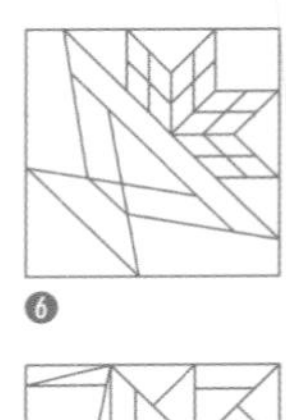

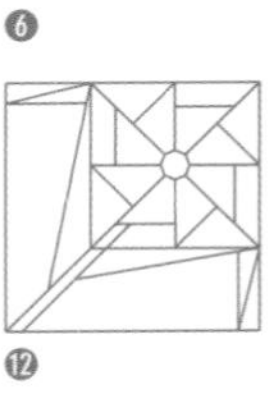

❶ ❷ ❸ ❹ ❺ ❻

❼ ❽ ❾ ❿ ⓫ ⓬

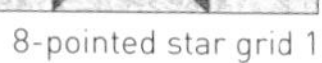

1 8-pointed star grid 1

2 8-pointed star grid 1

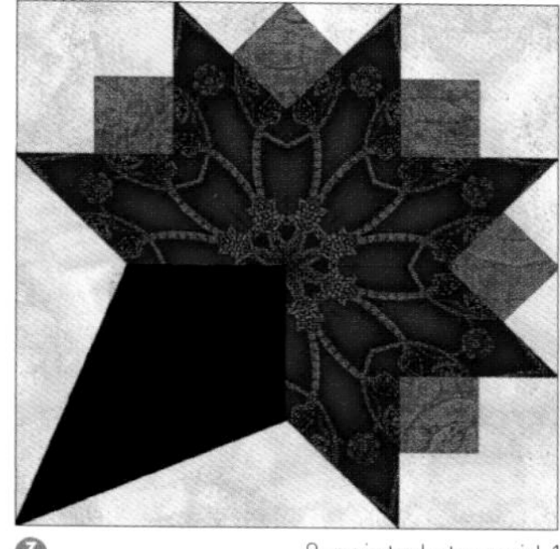

3 8-pointed star grid 1

4 8-pointed star grid 1

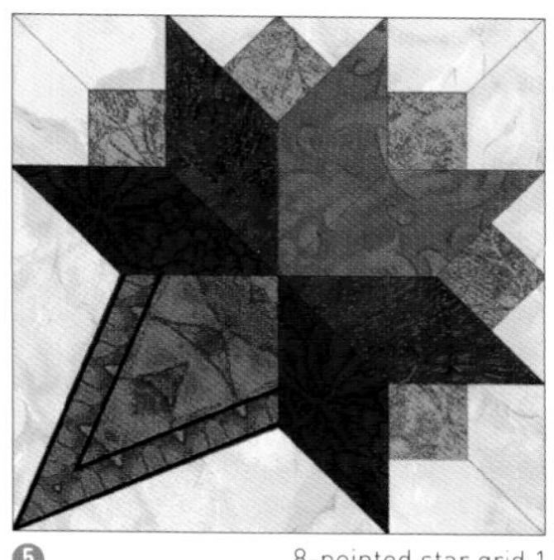

5 8-pointed star grid 1

6 8-pointed star grid 1

7 8-pointed star grid 4

8 8-pointed star grid 1

9 8-pointed star grid 4

10 8-pointed star grid 1

11 8-pointed star grid 1

12 8-pointed star grid 1

13 8-pointed star grid 1

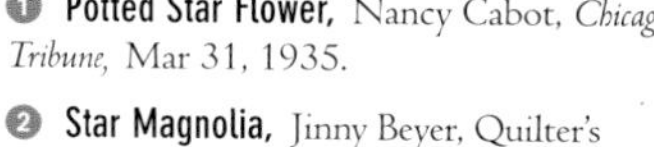

1 **Potted Star Flower,** Nancy Cabot, *Chicago Tribune,* Mar 31, 1935.

2 **Star Magnolia,** Jinny Beyer, Quilter's Quest design, 2004.

3 **Cornucopia,** Ickis, 1949.

4 **Cockscomb,** Home Art Studios, *World Herald,* Oct 21, 1933.

5 **Old Fashioned Nosegay,** Laura Wheeler, Pioneer Press Jul 11, 1933. Also known as:
- **Bride's Bouquet,** Nancy Cabot, *Chicago Tribune,* Jan 11, 1945.
- **Nosegay,** Laura Wheeler, *Cincinnati Enquirer,* Dec 7, 1933.
- **The Nosegays,** *Kansas City Star,* Feb 6, 1937.

6 **Cactus Basket,** Finley, 1929. Also known as:
- **Desert Rose,** Finley, 1929.
- **Texas Rose,** Finley, 1929.
- **Texas Treasure,** Finley, 1929.

7 **Flower Basket,** Alice Brooks, *Household Arts,* Dec 2, 1934.

8 **Flower Basket,** Jinny Beyer, Jinny Beyer Studio design, 2006.

9 **Tulip,** Laura Wheeler, *Cincinnati Enquirer,* Aug 12, 1933.

10 **Forbidden Fruit Tree,** Nancy Cabot, *Chicago Tribune,* May 7, 1935.

11 **Forbidden Fruit Tree,** *Ladies Art Company,* 1897.

12 **Lozenge Tree,** Nancy Cabot, *Chicago Tribune,* Sep 17, 1936.

13 **Forbidden Fruit Tree,** Hall, 1935.

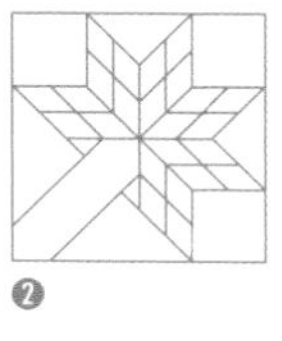

1

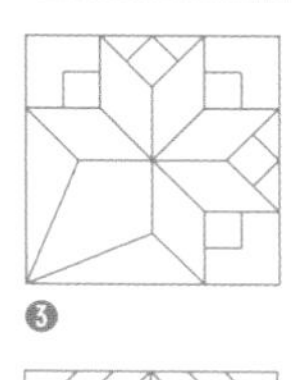

2

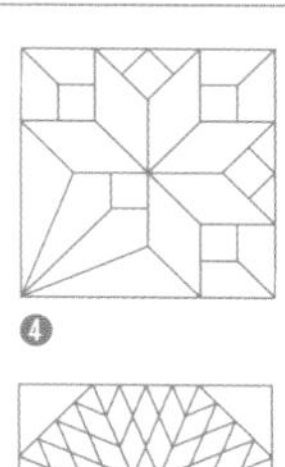

3

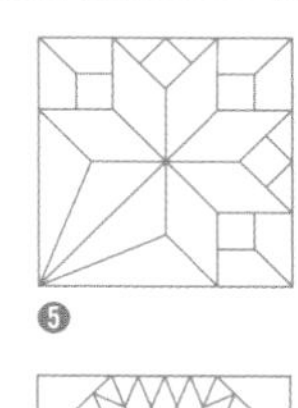

4

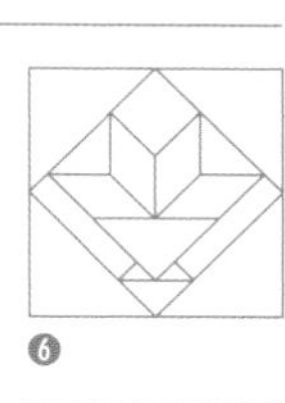

5

6

7

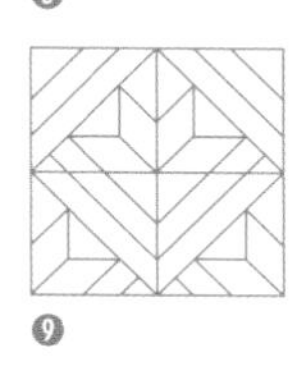

8

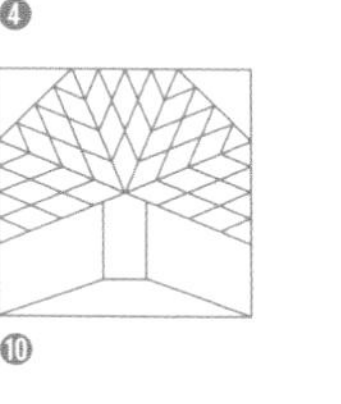

9

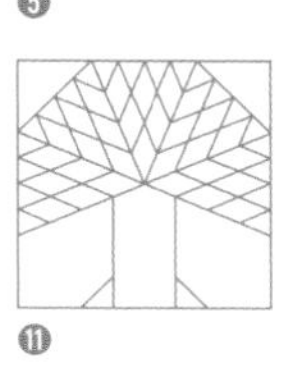

10

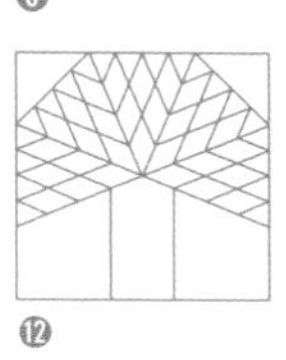

11

12

13

Women's Christian Temperance Union

The WCTU was founded in Ohio in 1874 by a group of women who were angry at the effects of alcohol abuse on their families. The Union also addressed issues such as women's suffrage, childcare, training, and prison reform. As the organization grew nationwide, Frances Willard, the second president (1879-1898), became one of the most prominent women in the United States. The prohibition of alcohol was initially one of the main focuses of the group. Bands of women would go into saloons and urge the owners to stop selling alcohol. They would drop to their knees and pray. If they were banned from entering the bar, they sat on the front steps and prayed. (www.wctu.com)

Notorious crusader Carrie Nation was so worked up by what alcohol had done to her first marriage and by what she saw around her as the evils of alcohol, that she vandalized bars, rather than silently protesting as most members did. She marched into saloons, sometimes alone and sometimes with other women, at first smashing items in the bar with rocks. Soon, she began using hatchets to do her damage. Newspapers around the nation gave accounts of her actions. Here are excerpts from two:

"Smashed an Oil Painting with Rock: WCTU Leader Makes a Rough House in a Kansas Saloon
"Wichita, Kan., Dec 27—Mrs. Carrie Nation, president of the Barber County WCTU, entered the Carey Hotel barroom and with a stone smashed a $200 painting of Cleopatra at her bath and a mirror valued at $100. She is under arrest.... She appealed to Governor Stanley, who is in the city, and he refused to act in any way. She broke mirrors at Kiowa, Kan., in two saloons some months ago. She declares there is no law under which she can be prosecuted and she threatens to continue her violent opposition to saloons.... She has been taken to the county jail." *Oakland Tribune,* December 27, 1900

"Mrs. Nation Begins Her Crusade Anew
"Mrs. Carrie Nation came back to Wichita today after her recent incarceration ... and the net result of ten minutes of work by her this afternoon are two wrecked saloons ... Mrs. Nation was assisted by Mrs. Julia Evans, Mrs. Lucy Wilholt, and Mrs. Lydia Muntz, all of the local Women's Christian Temperance Union ... with hatchets concealed under their cloaks the women entered the saloon ... and did not leave a complete piece of glass or a working slot machine in the place. All showcases, both for liquors and cigars, as well as the plate-glass windows and doors were broken into smithereens." *New York Times,* January 22, 1901

To earn money for the causes of the WCTU, booths were set up at fairs and meetings; very often quilts would be used as fundraisers. The 10-cent signature quilts became popular. These raised money in two ways. First people made a donation to have their signature appear on the quilt. Some would pay more to have it in a prominent position. After the quilt was finished it would be raffled off. (Kiracofe) Signature or album quilt blocks were designed and colored in such a way that names could be signed or embroidered on the blocks. W.C.T. Union block is an example. Sometimes, as in a quilt published in Kiracofe's *The American Quilt,* contributed blocks would be set with alternate plain blocks. This quilt has a block of Emory Chapel, a small Methodist church near Hopewell, New York. Other assorted blocks are in the quilt, and all are set with blocks of muslin that contain signatures. One of the blocks has dates showing that the quilt was "commenced" on Mar 28, 1896 and finished on September 22, 1896. It also has the words: "amount of money raised $104" and "Rev S A Brown Pastor." (Kiracofe)

Drunkard's Path and *Double T* are two other patterns that some say were used for the WCTU cause. So far, I have not been able to find a reference to support that claim, although those two patterns were very popular during the late 1800s and early 1900s.

I found some interesting instructions from the Victorian era on how to set a proper table. The household should have "three dozen wine glasses, two dozen champagne glasses, two dozen claret glasses, three dozen goblets ... " *(The New Cyclopaedia of Domestic Economy, 1873)* Once temperance gained popularity, women supporters would order only water goblets. *Domesticating Drink, Women, Men, and Alcohol in America, 1870-1940*. Thus such quilt blocks as *The Old Fashioned Goblet* and *Water Glass* became symbols of the movement as well. When the pattern for *Water Glass* appeared in the *Kansas City Star* on March 3, 1934, it was accompanied by this description:

"In the days of Carrie Nation and Frances E. Willard this was a popular block among quilters of the WCTU. Often women embroidered the date of their pledge card in the triangles or on the print." *Kansas City Star,* Mar 3, 1934

The temperance movement even reached the White House. Rutherford B. Hayes, 19th President of the United States, serving from 1877 to 1881, married Lucy Ware Webb of Chillicothe, Ohio, in 1852. An alumnus of Cincinnati's Wesleyan Women's College, she was the first wife of a president to graduate from college. She and Rutherford had eight children. Once in the White House, Lucy Hayes was considered the most popular hostess since Dolley Madison. She was a supporter of Temperance, though she resisted the urgings of the WCTU to lend her name to the cause. Still, no alcohol was served in the White House during the Hayes administration, prompting some to dub Mrs. Hayes as "Lemonade Lucy." It is interesting to note that the Lucy Hayes Quilt block is identical to the *W.C.T. Union* block, except for the width of the strip in the center square. (www.whitehouse.gov/-history/firstladies/lh19.html)

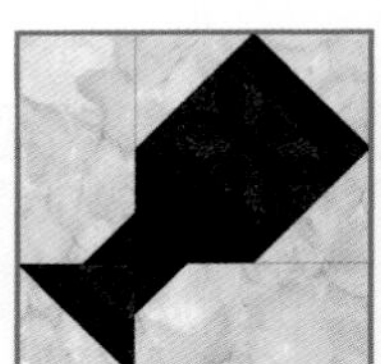

Water Glass, *Kansas City Star.* **See 275-1.**

The Old Fashioned Goblet, *Kansas City Star.* **See 171-2.**

W.C.T. Union, *Ladies Art Company.* **See 249-11.**

The Lucy Hayes Quilt, *Q Book 124, White House Quilts.* **See 251-11.**

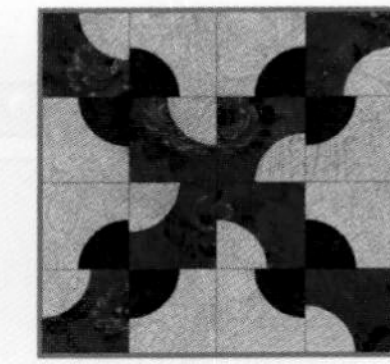

Drunkard's Path, Finley. **See 352-6.**

T Blocks, Finley. **See 140-7.**

2 x 2 Base Grid Category (with Curved Elements)

Includes ● 2 x 2, ● 4 x 4, ● 8 x 8, ● 16 x 16, ● 32 x 32, and ● 64 x 64 grids

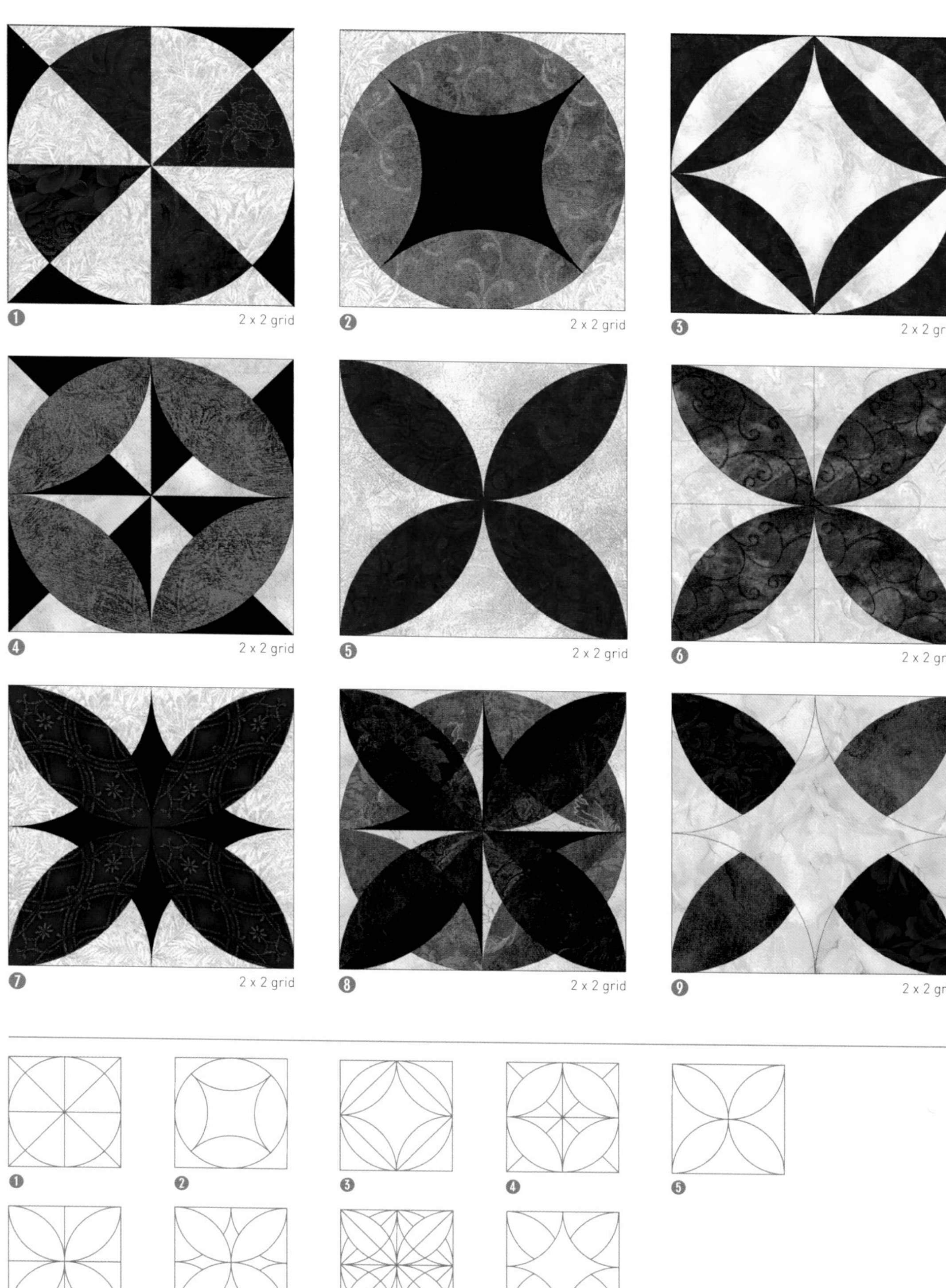

❶ **Scrap Happy,** Laura Wheeler, unidentified newspaper clipping, date unknown.

❷ **Reminiscent of the Wedding Ring,** *Kansas City Star,* Aug 11, 1943.

❸ **Orange Peel,** Alice Brooks, unidentified newspaper clipping, date unknown.

❹ **Grist Mill,** Nancy Cabot, *Chicago Tribune,* May 21, 1937.

❺ **Lafayette Orange Peel,** Home Art Studios, *Cincinnati Enquirer,* Apr 8, 1933. Also known as:

> **Joseph's Coat,** Alice Brooks, *Detroit Free Press,* Jun 20, 1934.

"Joseph's Coat—a quilt that has come by its name deservedly. Like the coat of Biblical fame, it, too, is made of many gay-hued scraps of material. Formed of but two pattern pieces, it has long been a favorite with the quiltmaker. So now all you need to do is get out the scrap-bag, pick out your favorite scraps and put them together!" Alice Brooks, *Detroit Free Press,* Jun 20, 1934

"History recounts how the gay Marquise Lafayette, while attending a social function used precision in paring an orange, by quartering the peel. Colonial women were always on the lookout for new designs and upon seeing the novel effect the orange peel made, called the pattern the 'Lafayette Orange Peel Quilt.'" *World Herald,* Jul 27, 1933

❻ **Orange Peel,** *Ladies Art Company,* 1897. Also known as:

> **Lafayette Orange Peel,** Ruby McKim, *Kansas City Star,* Apr 20, 1929.
> **Melon Patch,** Nancy Cabot, *Chicago Tribune,* Aug 2, 1933.
> **An Orange Peel Quilt,** *Kansas City Star,* Aug 1, 1956.

❼ **Alabama Beauty,** Nancy Cabot, *Chicago Tribune,* Jun 6, 1933.

❽ **Bay Leaf,** Home Art Studios, *World Herald,* Oct 26, 1933.

❾ **The Kansas Beauty,** *Kansas City Star,* Feb 22, 1936.

❶ Orange Peel, Nancy Cabot, *Chicago Tribune,* Mar 29, 1934. Also known as:
 Melon Patch, Nancy Cabot, *Chicago Tribune,* Mar 29, 1934.

"Quilt historians maintain that some of the most interesting quilt designs have been lost. 'Orange Peel,' however, is one of the oldest of the southern quilts. It is equally well known as 'Melon Patch,'... orange, green and white form the striking color combination." Nancy Cabot, *Chicago Tribune,* Mar 29, 1934

❷ The Four Leaf Clover, *Kansas City Star,* Jul 2, 1947.

❸ Lillian's Favorite, Clara Stone, *Practical Needlework,* ca. 1906. Also known as:
 Monkey Puzzle, *Prize Winning Designs,* ca. 1931.

❹ The Ice Cream Cone, *Kansas City Star,* Jan 14, 1942

❺ Round Robin, Clara Stone, *Practical Needlework,* ca. 1906.

❻ The Monkey Wrench, *Kansas City Star,* Mar 7, 1956.

❼ Magic Circle, Laura Wheeler, *Cincinnati Enquirer,* Sep 14, 1933.

❽ Home Maker, Clara Stone, *Practical Needlework,* ca. 1906.

❾ Four Patch, Laura Wheeler, *Daily Republic,* Jan 1, 1936. Also known as:
 Southern Moon, Laura Wheeler, unidentified newspaper clipping, date unknown.

❿ The Star Sapphire, *Kansas City Star,* Mar 14, 1936.

⓫ Fore and Aft, Nancy Cabot, *Chicago Tribune,* Apr 5, 1936. See 315-5, 329-5, and 338-2.

⓬ French Star, Nancy Cabot, *Chicago Tribune,* Oct 31, 1933. See 343-3.

⓭ Winding Walk, *Ladies Art Company,* 1901.

❶ 2 x 2 grid

❷ 2 x 2 grid

❸ 2 x 2 grid

❹ 4 x 4 grid

❺ 4 x 4 grid

❻ 4 x 4 grid

❼ 4 x 4 grid

❽ 4 x 4 grid

❾ 4 x 4 grid

❿ 4 x 4 grid

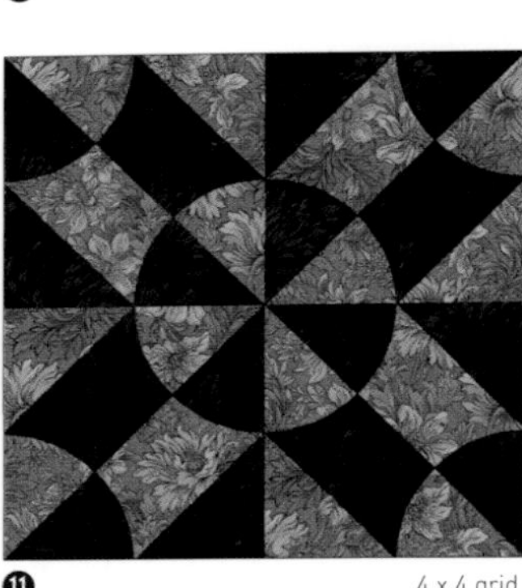

⓫ 4 x 4 grid

⓬ 4 x 4 grid

⓭ 4 x 4 grid

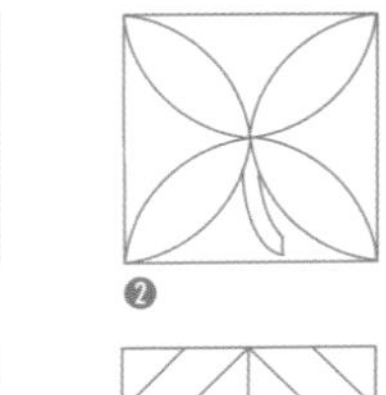

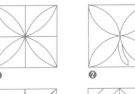

❶ ❷

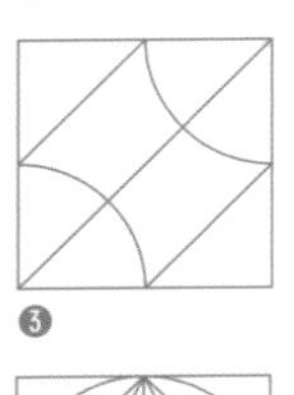

❸

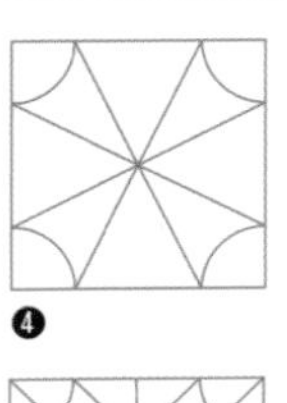

❹

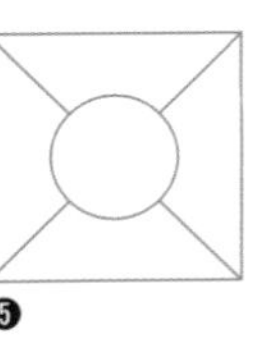

❺

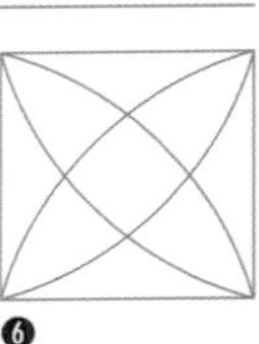

❻

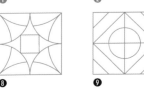

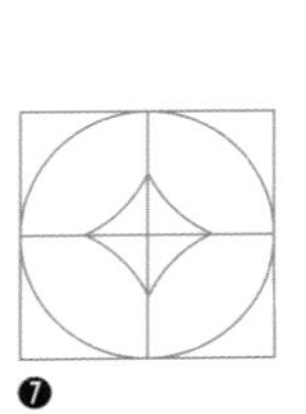

❼ ❽

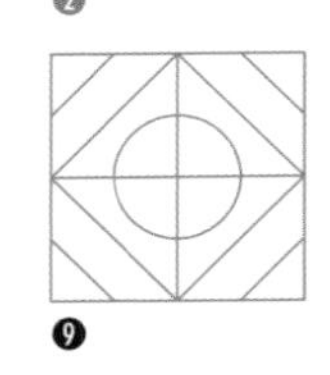

❾

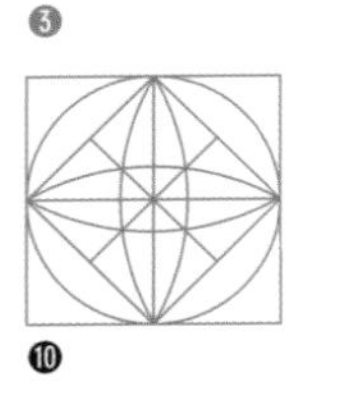

❿

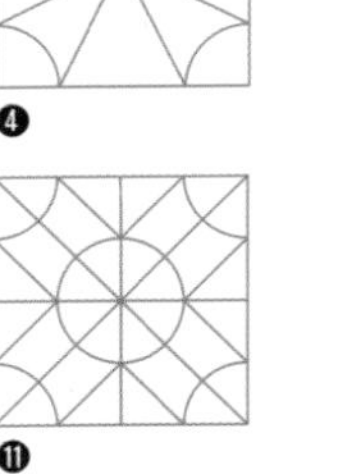

⓫

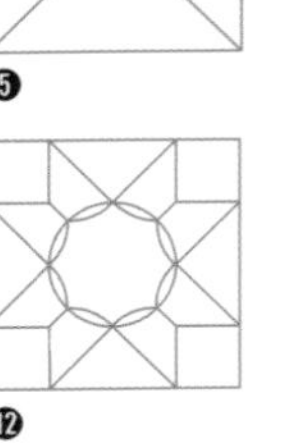

⓬

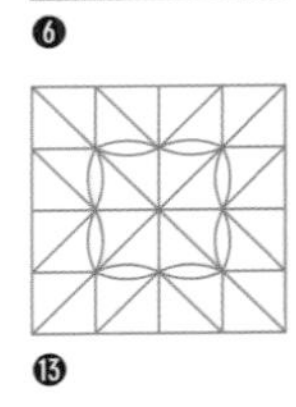

⓭

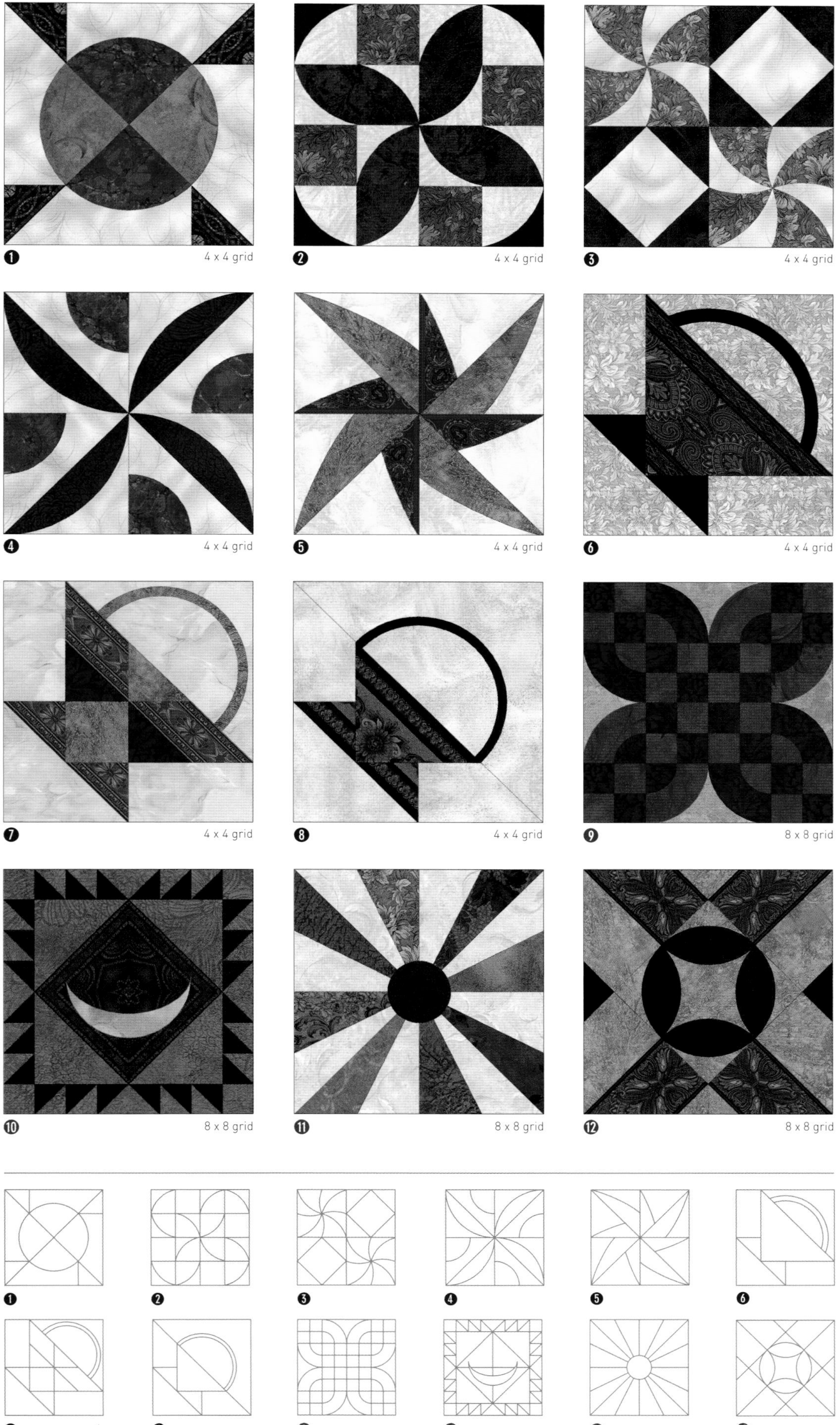

❶ **Three Patch,** Alice Brooks, *Detroit Free Press,* May 20, 1937.

❷ **Windflower,** Laura Wheeler, *Cincinnati Enquirer,* Sep 28, 1933.

❸ **Pinwheel,** Aunt Martha series: *Quilts: Modern-Colonial,* ca. 1954.

❹ **Waving Plumes,** Laura Wheeler, *Cincinnati Enquirer,* May 3, 1934.

❺ **Dahlia,** Laura Wheeler, *Sioux City Journal,* Mar 21, 1940. Also known as:
Double Pinwheel, Alice Brooks, unidentified newspaper clipping, date unknown.

❻ **Tiny Basket,** Hall, 1935.

❼ **Basket Quilt,** *Ladies Art Company,* 1897. Also known as:
Bread Basket, Hall, 1935.

❽ **Decorated Basket,** Nancy Cabot, *Chicago Tribune,* Nov 22, 1933.

❾ **A Dogwood Blossom,** *Kansas City Star,* Sep 17, 1958.

❿ **New Moon,** Nancy Cabot, *Chicago Tribune,* Apr 13, 1938.

⓫ **The Thrifty Wife,** *Kansas City Star,* May 10, 1939.

⓬ **Dover Quilt Block,** *Ladies Art Company,* 1922.

❶ **Herald Square,** Nancy Cabot, *Chicago Tribune,* Mar 1, 1938.

❷ **Pullman Puzzle,** Nancy Cabot, *Chicago Tribune,* Nov 27, 1934.

❸ **Pullman Puzzle,** *Ladies Art Company,* 1897. Also known as:
- **Baseball,** Hall, 1935.
- **Roman Pavements,** Nancy Cabot, *Chicago Tribune,* Nov 27, 1934.
- **Snowball,** Hall, 1935.

❹ **Wedgwood Tiles,** Nancy Cabot, *Chicago Tribune,* May 31, 1937.

❺ **Endless Chain,** Nancy Cabot, *Chicago Tribune,* May 4, 1933. See 338-12, 329-6, and 341-6. Also known as:
- **The Broken Square,** *Kansas City Star,* Apr 9, 1938.
- **Lover's Knot,** *Quilt Book 130, Keepsake Quilts,* ca. 1990.
- **True Lover's Knot,** Nancy Cabot, *Chicago Tribune,* Jan 22, 1937.
- **Cactus Rose,** Nancy Page, unidentified newspaper clipping, 1937.

❻ **Snowball Wreath,** Laura Wheeler, *Cincinnati Enquirer,* Nov 19, 1933.

❼ **Elsie's Favorite,** Clara Stone, *Practical Needlework,* ca. 1906.

❽ **Papa's Delight,** Clara Stone, *Practical Needlework,* ca. 1906. See 322-1, 322-6, 329-7 and 335-5.

❾ **Friendship Circle,** Laura Wheeler, *Indianapolis Star,* Jul 6, 1935.
"Get out your scrap bag—select your pet pieces and then just add the rest hit or miss for this gay scrap quilt, Friendship Circle. Its interlocking rings make a lovely covered pattern. It is indeed a Friendship quilt for following the old-time custom, you can let your friends contribute the patches for one block or even let them piece it and you will still have a very harmonious quilt." Laura Wheeler, *Indianapolis Star,* Jul 6, 1935

❿ **Summer and Winter,** Alice Brooks, *Detroit Free Press,* Jun 3, 1937.

⓫ **Rainbow Square,** Laura Wheeler, *Cincinnati Enquirer,* Mar 6, 1934.

⓬ **Caps for Witches and Dunces,** *Kansas City Star,* Aug 15, 1956.

❶ 8 x 8 grid

❷ 8 x 8 grid

❸ 8 x 8 grid

❹ 8 x 8 grid

❺ 8 x 8 grid

❻ 8 x 8 grid

❼ 8 x 8 grid

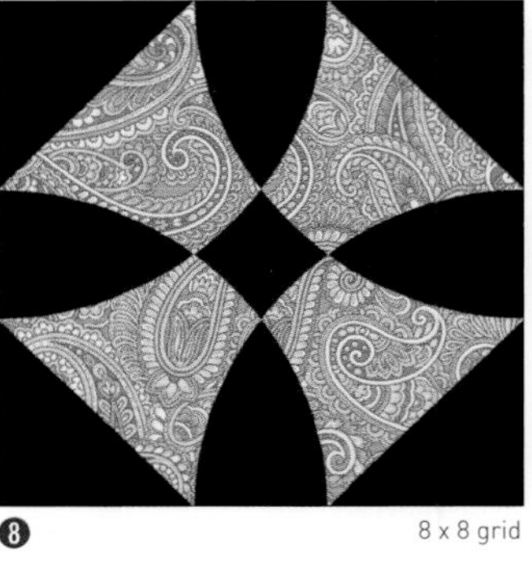
❽ 8 x 8 grid

❾ 8 x 8 grid

❿ 8 x 8 grid

⓫ 8 x 8 grid

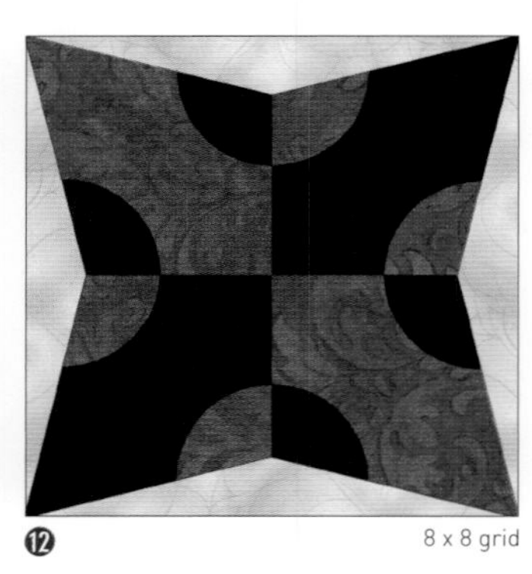
⓬ 8 x 8 grid

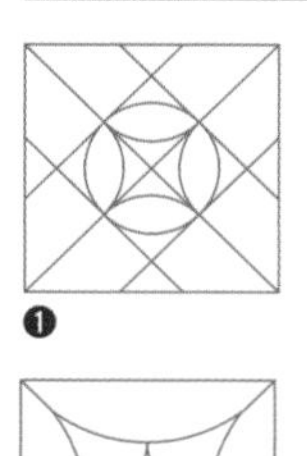
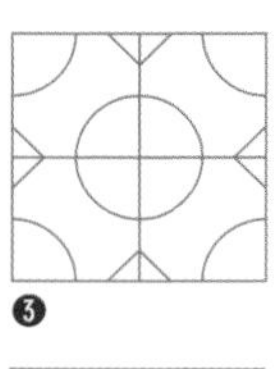
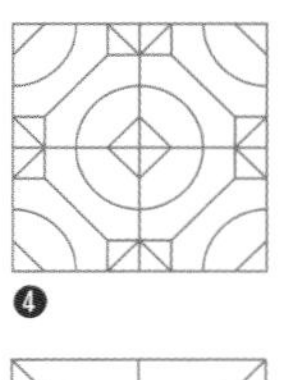
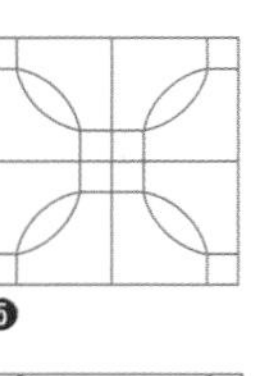
❶ ❷ ❸ ❹ ❺ ❻

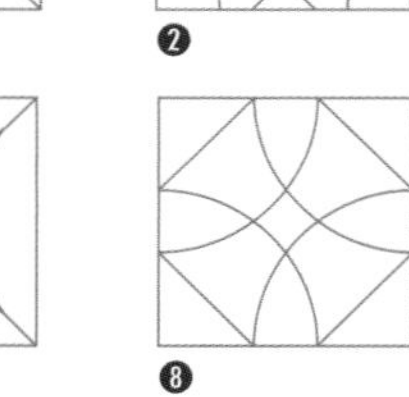
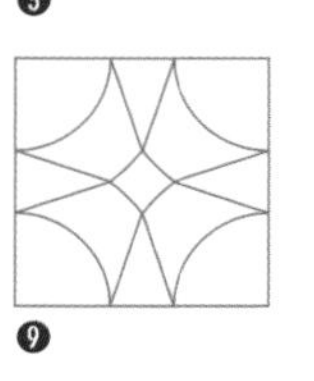
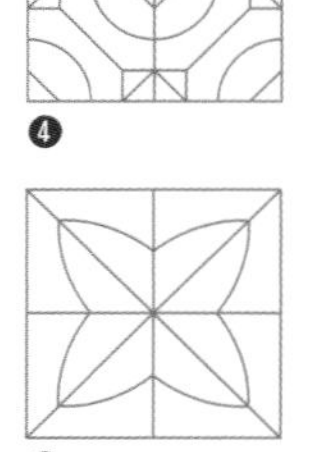
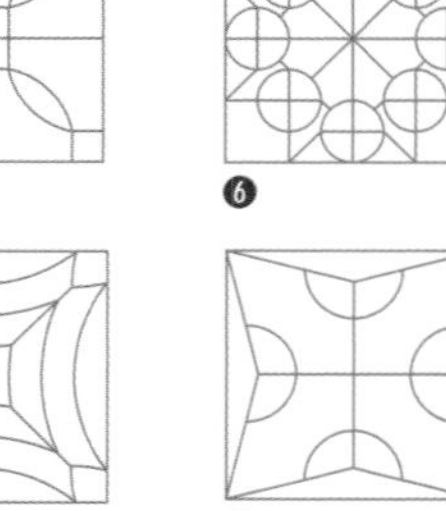
❼ ❽ ❾ ❿ ⓫ ⓬

Realistic Blocks

The majority of quilt blocks depicting realistic objects are appliquéd, but now and then the creative quilter designed such patterns that could be pieced. The ones I found are grouped here. Please note that some *Cross* patterns have already been shown on page 69. Other realistic patchwork patterns such as fans, baskets, trees, hearts, flowers, houses and airplanes have their own group.

Long Pants, *Chicago Tribune.* **See 257-2.**

Soldier Boy, *Kansas City Star.* **See 440-1.**

Oklahoma Bloomer, *Ladies Art Company.* **See 440-2**

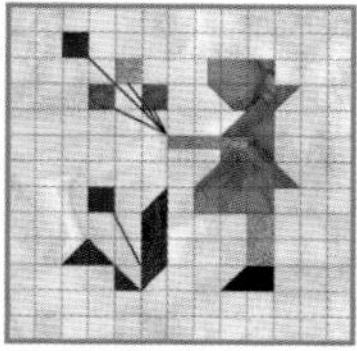

Balloon Girl, *Farm Journal and Farmer's Wife.* **See 261-2.**

Sunbonnet Girl, *Indianapolis Star.* **See 338-11.**

Top Hat, *Chicago Tribune.* **See 256-8.**

A Japanese Garden, *Kansas City Star.* **See 218-7.**

Japanese Lantern, Hall. **See 440-11.**

Japanese Lantern, *Prize Winning Designs.* **See 339-4.**

Japanese Lantern, *Chicago Tribune.* **See 342-3.**

Four Vases, *Kansas City Star.* **See 181-1.**

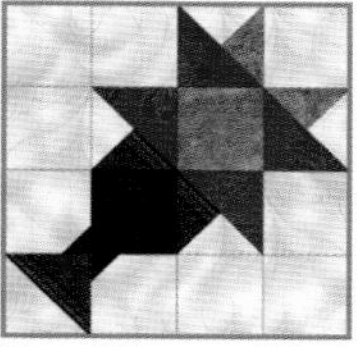

Vase of Flowers, *Q Book 118, Grandmother's Flower Quilts.* **See 171-3.**

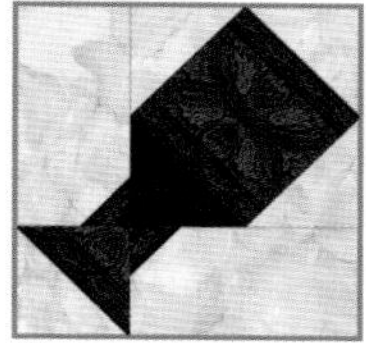

The Goblet Quilt, *Kansas City Star.* **See 275-1.**

The Old Fashioned Goblet, *Kansas City Star.* **See 171-2.**

Coffee Cups, *Kansas City Star.* **See 341-5.**

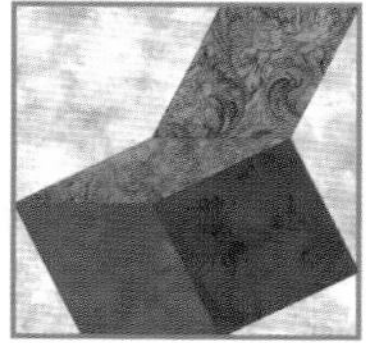

Work Box, *Ladies Art Company.* **See 218-13.**

Work Box, Havig. **See 220-9.**

The Ice Cream Cone, *Kansas City Star.* **See 310-4.**

The Ice Cream Cone, *Kansas City Star.* **See 332-4.**

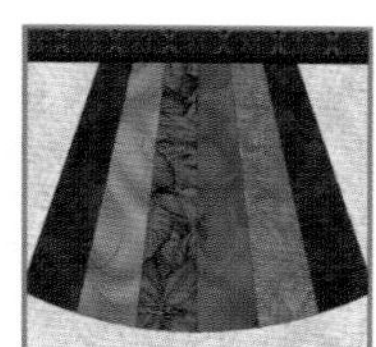

My Mother's Apron, *Kansas City Star.* **See 335-9.**

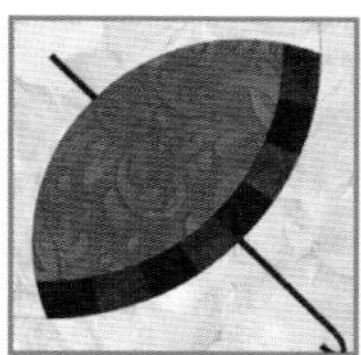

Patty's Summer Parasol, *Kansas City Star.* **See 355-8.**

Garfield's Monument, *Ladies Art Company.* **See 218-10.**

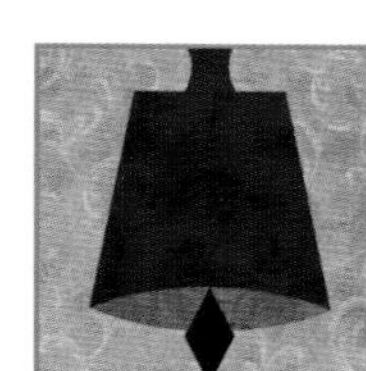

Bell, *Kansas City Star.* **See 335-7.**

The White Cross, *Kansas City Star.* **See 438-7.**

The Cross, *Ladies Art Company.* **See 151-10.**

Cross and Crown, Hall. **See 181-7.**

Cross and Crown, Finley. **See 119-10.**

The Dog Quilt, *Kansas City Star.* **See 440-3.**

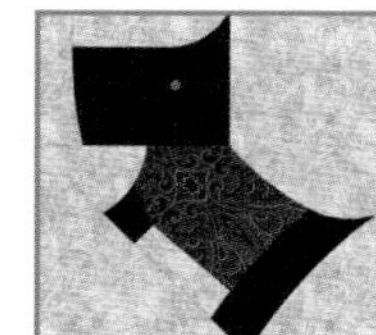

Scottie Quilt, *Detroit Free Press.* **See 335-4.**

Scottie Quilt, *Indianapolis Star.* **See 339-6.**

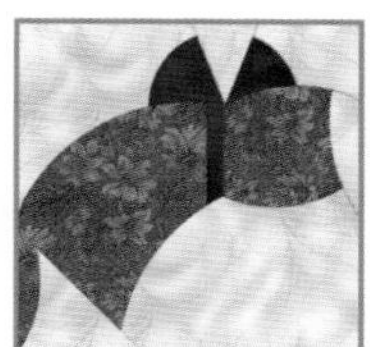

Calico Cat, *Detroit Free Press.* **See 332-3.**

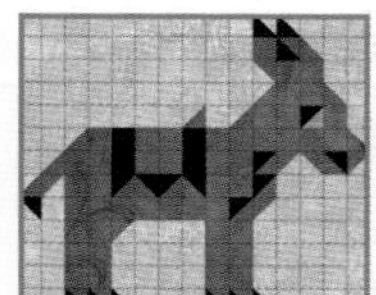

Giddap, *Kansas City Star.* **See 440-4.**

Elephant Ararat, *Kansas City Star.* **See 440-5.**

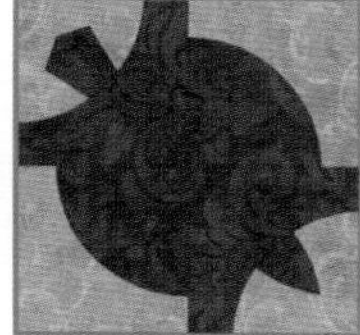

The Terrapin, *Kansas City Star.* **See 314-12.**

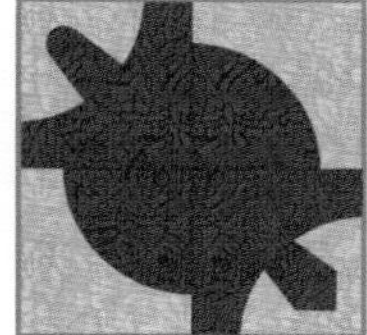

Turtle on a Quilt, *Kansas City Star.* **See 338-10**

The Turtle Quilt, *Kansas City Star.* **See 338-9.**

Windmill, *Detroit Free Press.* **See 339-5.**

❶ **Rose Point,** Aunt Martha series: *The Quilt Fair Comes to You,* ca. 1933.

❷ **Diamond Head,** Nancy Cabot, *Chicago Tribune,* Mar 6, 1936.
"'Diamond Head' is one of the quilt patterns which should be attempted by only the expert quilt makers endowed with a superabundance of patience and exactitude. The many faceted surface of 'Diamond Head' will be completely destroyed if the patches are carelessly cut or set together." Nancy Cabot, *Chicago Tribune,* Mar 6, 1936

❸ **Fairy Star,** Nancy Cabot, *Chicago Tribune,* Nov 16, 1933.

❹ **Palm Leaf Block,** Nancy Cabot, *Chicago Tribune,* Jun 27, 1937.

❺ **A Century Old Tulip Pattern,** *Kansas City Star,* Sep 24, 1947.

❻ **Autumn Leaf,** Nancy Cabot, date unknown, per Alboum.

❼ **Two in One,** Laura Wheeler, *Laura Wheeler Catalog,* 1959.

❽ **Double Pinwheel,** Laura Wheeler, *Cincinnati Enquirer,* Oct 10, 1935.
"'Double Pinwheel' is an easy block to make and one that will look unusually effective when the quilt is pieced. As the blocks are joined, the second pinwheel is formed. And they do, indeed, look like the colorful ones that the youngsters love to make twirl in the wind!" Laura Wheeler, *Cincinnati Enquirer,* Oct 10, 1935

❾ **Pointed Ovals,** *Kansas City Star,* Apr 27, 1955.

❿ **Tangled Trails,** Nancy Cabot, *Chicago Tribune,* Jun 11, 1936.
"In Philadelphia, in 1907, this attractive pieced block, 'Tangled Trails,' first was made. The quilt is composed entirely of pieced blocks, which, when set together form an over-all design of interlacing bands of two colors, and apparently is further complicated by knots in the bands where block is set to block." Nancy Cabot, *Chicago Tribune,* Jun 11, 1936

⓫ **Beech Tree,** Nancy Cabot, *Chicago Tribune,* Mar 25, 1935.
"Certain types of old quilts become identified with the regions in which they have been most popular. Thus the 'Beech Tree' pattern is typical of New England." Nancy Cabot, *Chicago Tribune,* Mar 25, 1935

⓬ **The Terrapin,** *Kansas City Star,* Apr 13, 1949. See 338-9 and 338-10.

1 **Melon Patch,** Laura Wheeler, *Sioux City Journal,* Nov 8, 1941.

2 **Arkansas Centennial,** *Kansas City Star,* Jan 9, 1937.

3 **Four Leaf Clover,** Laura Wheeler, *Lansing State Journal,* Apr 3, 1934.

4 **Whale Block,** *Ladies Art Company,* 1922.

5 **Square and Compass,** Ruby McKim, McKim, 1931. See 310-11, 329-5, and 338-2.

"The Square and Compass quilt is one of the delightful old New England patterns that has lived for generations, and it takes it (sic)name from the sea faring activities of the New England people... this quilt is usually made up in a combination of green and white or blue and white." *World Herald,* Sep 18, 1933

6 **Hazel Valley Cross Roads,** *Kansas City Star,* Oct 6, 1934.

7 **Penelope's Favorite,** Nancy Cabot, *Chicago Tribune,* Sep 3, 1934.

"All quilters have favorite patterns, seemingly suited to their personalities. 'Penelope's Favorite' charmingly expresses the personality of a young woman of the '70s for whom the block was named. It is not the easiest of patterns to piece, since patience is required in setting the pieces together neatly, but the completed coverlet is an achievement." Nancy Cabot, *Chicago Tribune,* Sep 3, 1934

8 **Rose Point,** Home Art Studios, *World Herald,* Oct 2, 1933.

9 **Rolling Star,** *Quilt Booklet No. 1,* ca. 1931. See 340-6, 346-8, and 346-9.

10 **Moon and Star,** Clara Stone, *Practical Needlework,* ca. 1906.

11 **Queen's Pride,** Laura Wheeler, *Topeka State Journal,* Apr 17, 1934.

12 **The Southside Star Quilt,** *Kansas City Star,* Nov 13, 1940.

"Because 'Southside Star' is the name of the school she attends, Miss Ona Lee Jones, R.R. 1, Damscus, Ark., gave that title to this quilt she designed." *Kansas City Star,* Nov 13, 1940

1 **Friendship Medley,** Laura Wheeler, *Indianapolis Star,* Sep 29, 1936.

2 **Bird of Paradise,** Laura Wheeler, unidentified newspaper clipping, date unknown.

3 **Pictures in the Stairwell,** *Kansas City Star,* Oct 3, 1956.

4 **Basket,** *The Patchwork Book,* 1932. Also known as:
Colonial Basket, *The Patchwork Book,* 1932.

5 **Tea Leaf,** Finley, 1929.

6 **Hour Glass,** Nancy Cabot, *Chicago Tribune,* May 22, 1935.

7 **Link of Friendship,** Laura Wheeler, *Columbus Evening Dispatch,* Sep 3, 1942. "A scrap quilt that combines beauty, economy and sentiment is this one, 'Link of Friendship.' Make it of scraps donated by your friends for remembrance—the old idea of a Friendship quilt." Laura Wheeler, *Columbus Evening Dispatch,* Sep 3, 1942

8 **Four Leaf Clover,** Nancy Cabot, *Chicago Tribune,* Aug 29, 1935.

9 **Job's Tears,** Nancy Cabot, *Chicago Tribune,* Apr 22, 1933. Also known as:
Endless Chain, Nancy Cabot, *Chicago Tribune,* Oct 29, 1937.

10 **Flower of the Plains,** Laura Wheeler, *Sioux City Journal,* Aug 27, 1938.

11 **Grandmother's Choice,** Laura Wheeler, *Kansas City Star,* Jan 11, 1934.

12 **Bachelor's Puzzle,** Virginia Snow, *Quilt Blocks from Grandma Dexter,* ca. 1933.

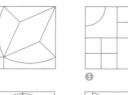

1 16 x 16 grid

2 16 x 16 grid

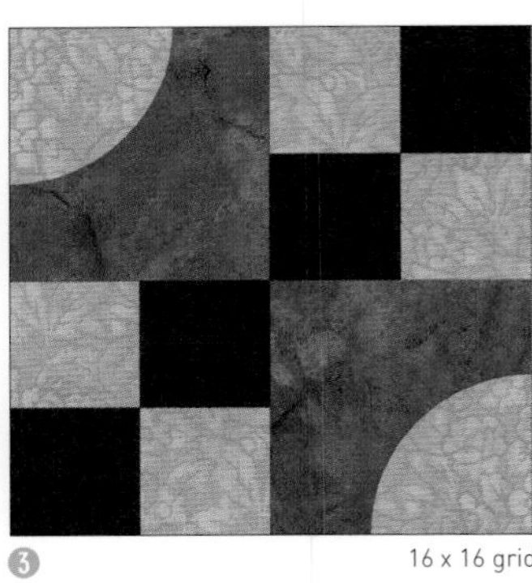

3 16 x 16 grid

4 16 x 16 grid

5 16 x 16 grid

6 16 x 16 grid

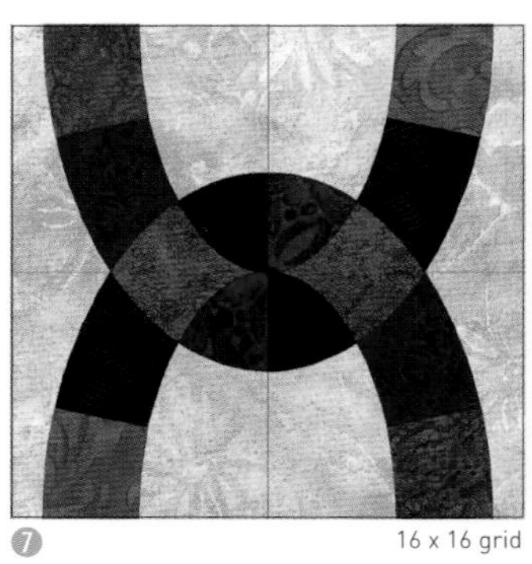

7 16 x 16 grid

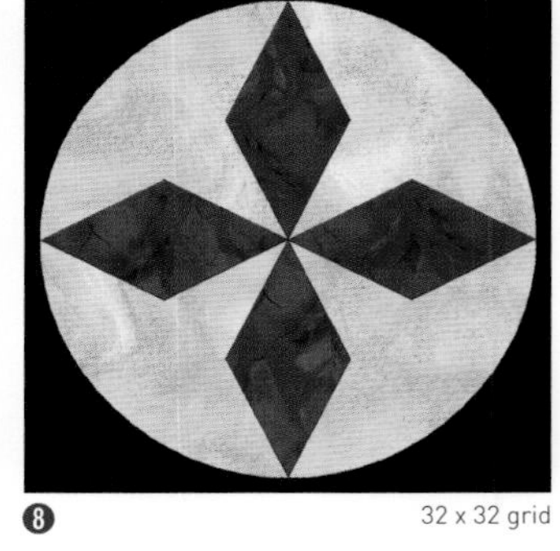

8 32 x 32 grid

9 32 x 32 grid

10 32 x 32 grid

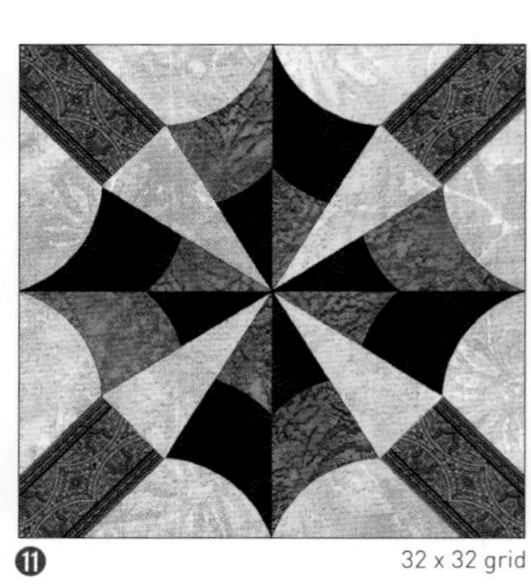

11 32 x 32 grid

12 32 x 32 grid

1

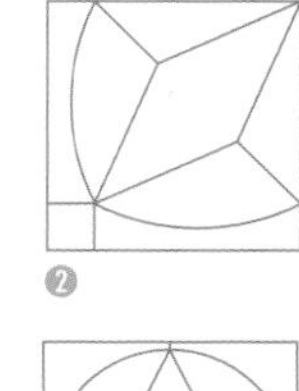

2

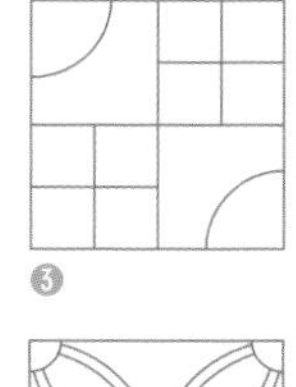

3

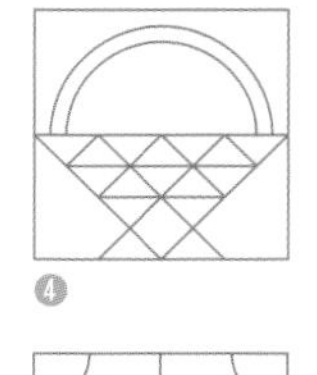

4

5

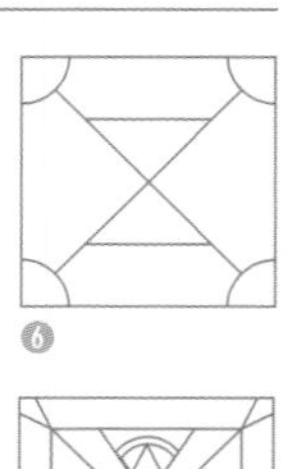

6

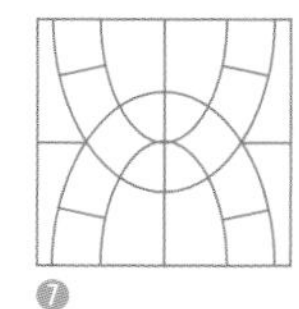

7

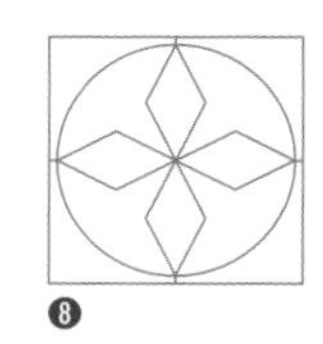

8

9

10

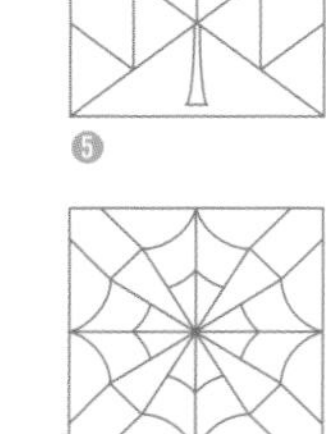

11

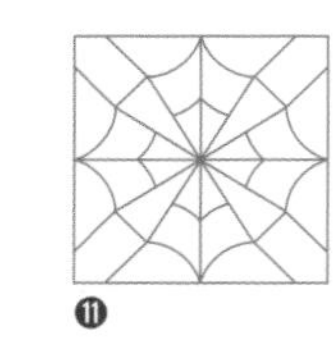

12

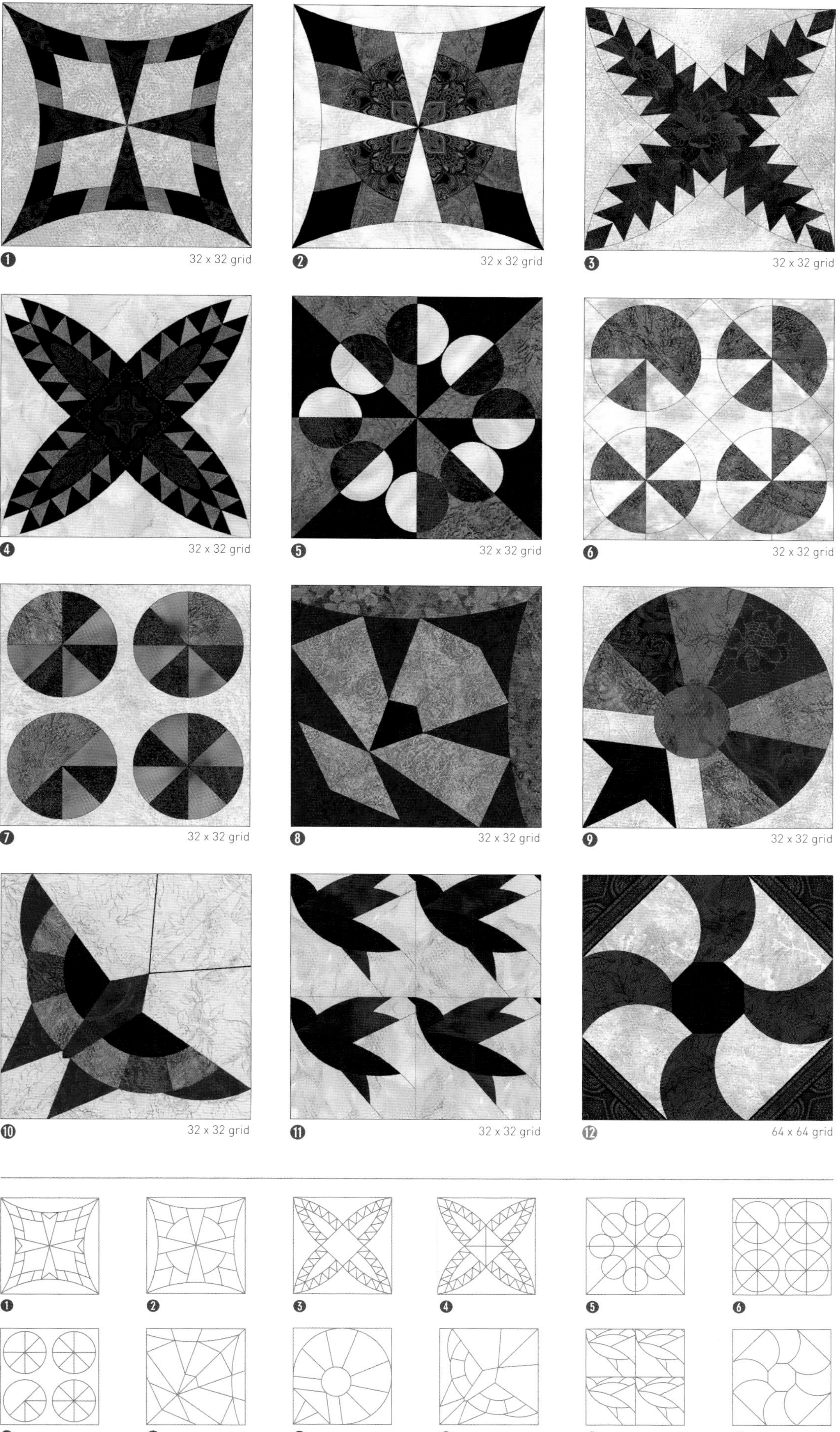

❶ **Chimney Swallows,** Hall, 1935. See 326-6, 336-6, 346-5, and 346-6.

❷ **Cowboy Star,** Laura Wheeler, *Cincinnati Enquirer,* Sep 30, 1933.

❸ **Cocklebur,** Aunt Martha series: *The Quilt Fair Comes to You,* ca. 1933.

❹ **Pineapple Cactus,** Eveline Foland, *Kansas City Star,* Oct 8, 1932.

❺ **Wonder of the World,** Nancy Cabot, *Chicago Tribune,* Sep 7, 1935. Also known as:

Sunshine and Shadow, Nancy Cabot, *Chicago Tribune,* Dec 27, 1937.

❻ **Moon and Stars,** *Ladies Art Company,* 1897.

❼ **Moon and Stars,** Hall, 1935.

❽ **Queen's Treasure,** Laura Wheeler, *Cincinnati Enquirer,* May 31, 1935.

❾ **Sweet Sultan,** Alice Brooks, *Dayton News,* Jul 1, 1934.

❿ **Butterfly,** Laura Wheeler, *Minneapolis Star,* Feb 10, 1937.

⓫ **Spring,** Alice Brooks, *Detroit Free Press,* Apr 29, 1936.

⓬ **Whirlaway,** Laura Wheeler, *Columbus Evening Dispatch,* Aug 19, 1942.

"Women today are turning to quilt-making as handiwork that fascinates and is so serviceable, too. This three patch quilt, Whirlaway, is easy even for a beginner." Laura Wheeler, *Columbus Evening Dispatch,* Aug 19, 1942

3 x 3 Base Grid Category
(with Curved Elements)

Includes ● 3 x 3, ● 6 x 6, ● 12 x 12, ● 24 x 24, and ● 48 x 48 grids

❶ **The Broken Stone,** *Kansas City Star,* Jan 4, 1950.

❷ **Tea Leaf,** *Ladies Art Company,* 1897. See 329-5 and 389-5. Also known as:
- **Bay Leaf,** *Virginia Snow Studio Art Needlework Creations,* 1932.
- **Circle upon Circle,** *Mrs. Danner's Quilts, Books 1 & 2,* 1934.
- **Linked Petals,** Nancy Page, *Birmingham News,* Nov 3, 1942.
- **Lover's Knot,** *Grandmother Clark's Patchwork Quilts, Book No. 19,* 1932.
- **Tea Leaves,** Hall, 1935.
- **Tealeaf,** *Grandmother Clark's Patchwork Quilts, Book No. 19,* 1932.
- **True Lover's Knot,** Nancy Cabot, *Chicago Tribune,* Jun 1, 1933.

❸ **Pin Cushion,** Nancy Cabot, *Chicago Tribune,* Jul 15, 1934.
"The old 'Pin Cushion' quilt, dating from 1840, is more complicated than the usual all over pieced designs, necessitating proficiency in needlework." Nancy Cabot, *Chicago Tribune,* Jul 15, 1934

❹ **Pin Cushion,** *Ladies Art Company,* 1897. Also known as:
- **Attic Window,** Alice Brooks, unidentified newspaper clipping, date unknown.
- **Cushion Design,** *Grandmother's Patchwork Quilt Designs, Book 20,* 1931.
- **Dolly Madison's Workbox,** Ruby McKim, McKim, 1931.
- **Lafayette Orange Peel,** Bacon, 1973.
- **Lemon Peels,** Nancy Page, *Birmingham News,* Jun 27, 1939.
- **Love Ring,** Eveline Foland, *Kansas City Star,* May 30, 1931.
- **Orange Peel,** Ruby McKim, McKim, 1931.
- **Rob Peter and Pay Paul,** Ruby McKim, *Kansas City Star,* Oct 17, 1928.
- **Rob Peter to Pay Paul,** Nancy Cabot, *Chicago Tribune,* Feb 4, 1933.
- **Robbing Peter to Pay Paul,** Hall, 1935.
- **Sugar Bowl,** Nancy Page, *Nashville Banner,* Apr 25, 1933.
- **Turnabout,** Alice Brooks, unidentified newspaper clipping, date unknown.

❺ **Lock and Chain,** *Ladies Art Company,* 1928.

❻ **Heirloom Quilt,** Alice Brooks, unidentified newspaper clipping, date unknown.

❼ **Double L,** Dec 1907, per Smith, "Happy Hours,"; published in Horton.

❽ **Moon and Swastika,** Nancy Cabot, *Chicago Tribune,* May 2, 1935.

❾ **Greek Square,** *Ladies Art Company,* 1897.

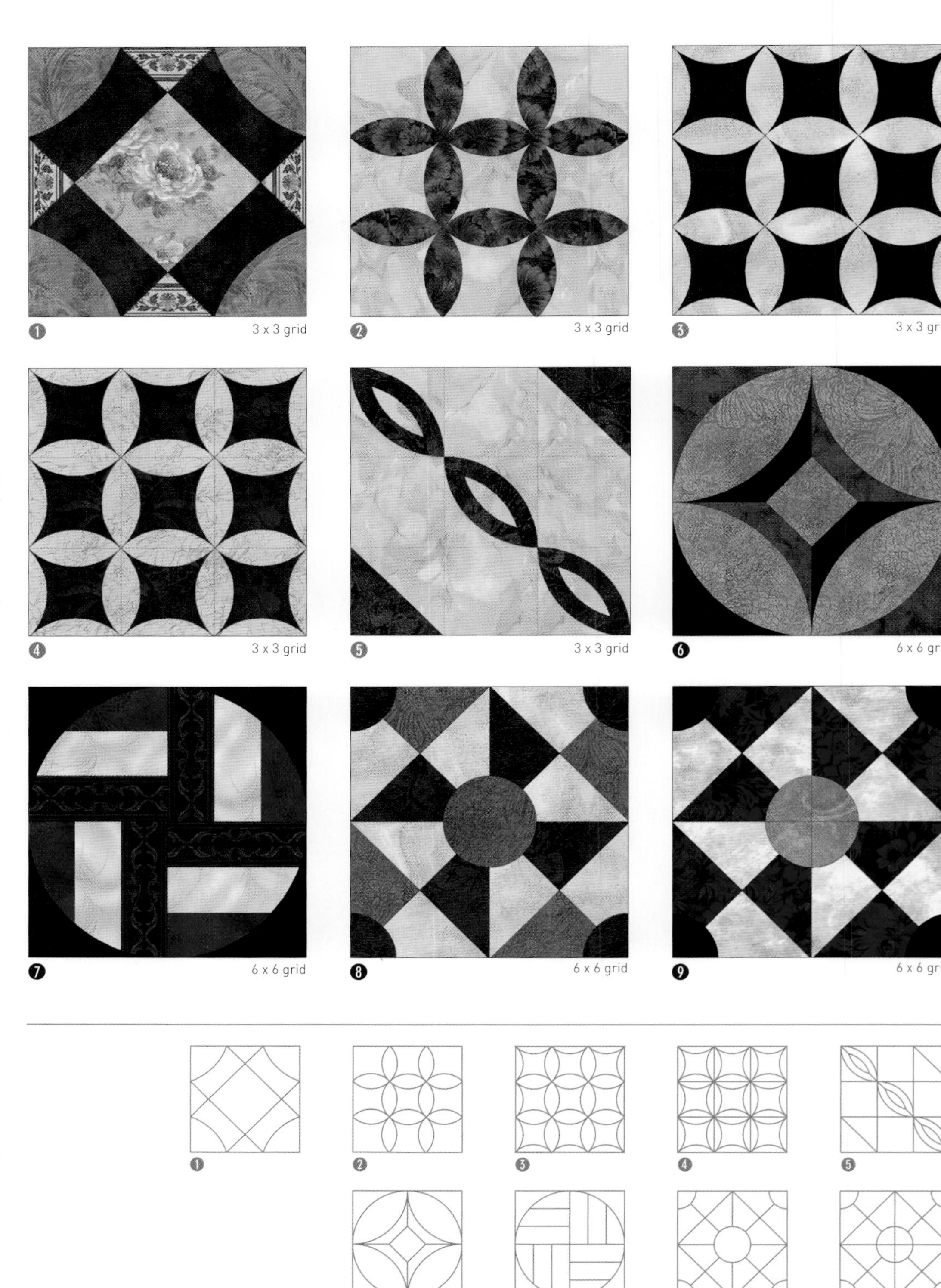

Quick Reference: Baskets

"Basket quilts are always popular.... that was why I was glad to get this pattern from Mrs. Sullivan of Baltimore, Maryland. She says that her mother pieced one like this over eighty years ago."
Nancy Page, *Nashville Banner*, Jan 2, 1934

Basket patterns have been a long-time favorite of quiltmakers. They have been drafted on a variety of grids, with and without curved lines. Sometimes it is hard to distinguish whether a basket is, instead, a vase or bowl, so those have all been included in this quick reference section. Here are all the ones I have found.

Four Little Baskets, *Ladies Art Company.* **See 339-1.**

May Basket, *Patchwork Portfolio.* **See 333-9.**

Four Little Baskets, *Chicago Tribune.* **See 326-5.**

Four Little Baskets, Hall. **See 336-9.**

Picnic Basket, *Patchwork Portfolio.* **See 236-7.**

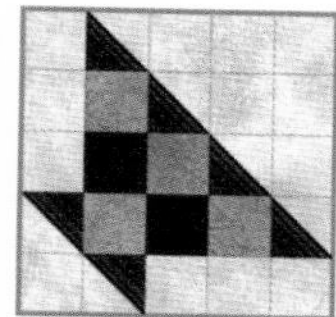
Grandmother's Basket, *Q Book 118, Grandmother's Flower Quilts.* **See 190-9.**

Grandmother's Basket, *Kansas City Star.* **See 152-3.**

Steps to the Altar, *Ladies Art Company.* **See 225-13.**

Bowl of Fruit, *Chicago Tribune.* **See 151-12.**

Strawberry Basket, *Grandmother Clark's Authentic Early American Quilts, Book 21.* **See 152-2.**

Sky Rocket, *Grandma Dexter Applique and Patchwork Designs, Book 36a.* **See 208-4.**

Tulip Time, *Birmingham News.* **See 190-2.**

The Disk, *Ladies Art Company.* **See 74-8.**

Cactus Basket, Hinson. **See 151-11.**

Sugar Bowl, *The Farm Journal Quilt Patterns.* **See 74-11.**

May Basket, unidentified newspaper clipping. **See 74-12.**

Flower Basket, *Ladies Art Company.* **See 74-10.**

Flower Basket, *Chicago Tribune.* **See 75-1.**

Basket, *Nashville Banner.* **See 74-9.**

Mrs. Young's Basket, *Birmingham News.* **See 190-8.**

Flower Pot, Hall. **See 190-7.**

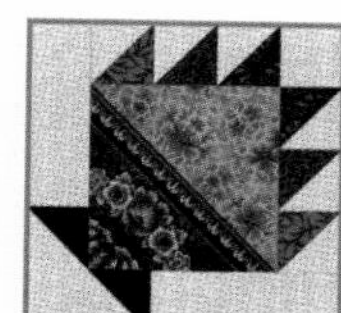
Cake Stand, *Ladies Art Company.* **See 190-6.**

Grape Basket, *Chicago Tribune.* **See 191-4.**

May Basket, *Q Book 103, All Year Quilts.* **See 191-5.**

Basket of Blueberries, *Jinny Beyer Studio design.* **See 191-2.**

Grape Basket, *Ladies Art Company.* **See 191-3.**

Cake Stand, *Chicago Tribune.* **See 191-1.**

Flower Basket, *Practical Needlework.* **See 190-12.**

The Flower Pot, *Kansas City Star.* **See 190-11.**

May Basket, *The Farmer's Wife Book of Quilts.* **See 190-5.**

Fruit Basket, McKim . **See 190-10.**

Ash Basket, Quilter's Quest design. **See 217-11.**

A Basket Quilt in Triangles, *Kansas City Star.* **See 152-4.**

Hanging Basket, *Kansas City Star.* **See 171-8.**

Mrs. Hardy's Hanging Basket, *Practical Needlework.* **See 171-9.**

(continued next page)

Basket of Diamonds, *Kansas City Star*. **See 305-9.**

Cactus Basket, *Detroit Free Press*. **See 305-10.**

The Flower Pot, *Kansas City Star*. **See 190-11.**

Cane Basket, Quilter's Quest design. **See 306-7.**

May Basket, *The Farm Journal Quilt Patterns*. **See 305-11.**

Flowers in a Basket, *Kansas City Star*. **See 306-3.**

Calico Bush, *Chicago Tribune*. **See 306-2.**

Floral Centerpiece, *Chicago Tribune*. **See 245-5.**

Tulip Basket, *Ladies Art Company*. **See 305-12.**

Flower Pot, *Practical Needlework*. **See 306-1.**

Hicks Flower Basket, *Kansas City Star*. **See 306-4.**

White Oak Basket, Quilter's Quest design. **See 306-6.**

Texas Cactus Basket, *Chicago Tribune*. **See 120-3.**

Tiny Basket, Hall. **See 311-6.**

The May Basket Quilt, *Kansas City Star*. **See 332-8.**

Decorated Basket, *Chicago Tribune*. **See 311-8.**

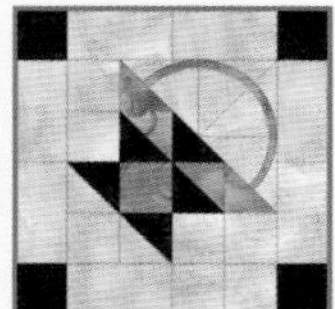
Framed Basket, *Chicago Tribune*. **See 325-2.**

Basket Quilt, *Ladies Art Company*. **See 311-7.**

Pieced Baskets, Webster. **See 328-3.**

An Old Favorite, *Grandmother Clark's Patchwork Designs, Book 22*. **See 323-1.**

Cherry Basket, *Ladies Art Company*. **See 322-11.**

Flower Basket. See 322-10.

Basket, *Grandmother's Patchwork Quilt Designs, Book 20*. **See 322-12.**

Flower Basket, *Virginia Snow Studio Art Needlework Creations*. **See 334-8.**

Basket, The, *Kansas City Star*. **See 250-1.**

Dresden Basket, *Grandma Dexter Appliqué and Patchwork Designs, Book 36a*. **See 120-2.**

Colonial Basket, *Detroit Free Press*. **See 325-3.**

Birch Basket, Quilter's Quest design. **See 238-5.**

Beech Basket, Quilter's Quest design. **See 123-2.**

Pine Needle Basket, Quilter's Quest design. **See 178-11.**

Virginia Basket, Quilter's Quest design. **See 178-12.**

Vase of Flowers, *Detroit Free Press*. **See 369-1.**

Tea Basket, *Mrs. Danner's Quilts Books 1 & 2*. **See 369-5.**

Colonial Basket, *Detroit Free Press*. **See 369-6.**

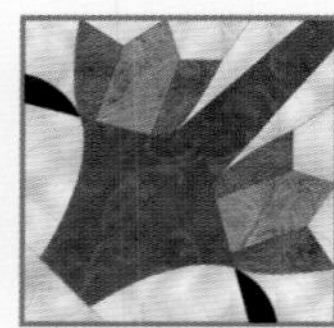
Basket of Lilies, *Detroit Free Press*. **See 369-4.**

Floral Bouquet, *Chicago Tribune*. **See 181-6.**

Mountain Pink, *Indianapolis Star*. **See 264-1.**

Garden of Friendship, *Detroit Free Press*. **See 369-3.**

Chrysanthemum, *Detroit Free Press*. **See 261-4 .**

Vase of Flowers, *Indianapolis Star*. **See 369-2.**

Friendship Basket, *Indianapolis Star*. **See 306-5.**

Leafy Basket, *Cincinnati Enquirer*. **See 220-3.**

Basket of Lilies, *Kansas City Star*. **See 120-4.**

Basket of Lilies, *Ladies Art Company*. **See 367-11.**

Cactus Basket, *Illinois State Register*. **See 306-8.**

Basket of Daffodils, Quilter's Quest design. **See 306-9.**

Basket of Flowers, *Kansas City Star*. **See 367-12.**

Tuip in Vase [sic], *Ladies Art Company*. **See 368-3.**

Royal Japanese Vase, *Ladies Art Company*. **See 368-4.**

Potted Star Flower, *Chicago Tribune.* **See 307-1.**

Potted Star Flower, *The Farm Journal Quilt Patterns.* **See 368-1.**

Potted Star Flower, *Chicago Tribune.* **See 368-2.**

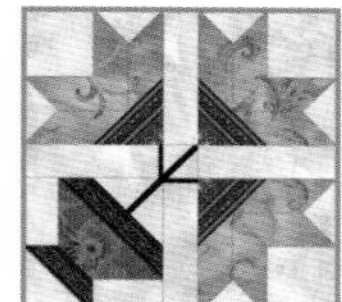

Flower Vase, *Chicago Tribune.* **See 252-1.**

Snowdrop, *Detroit Free Press.* **See 367-5.**

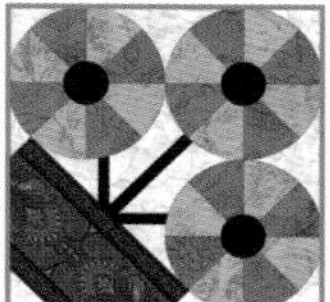

Aster, *Detroit Free Press.* **See 367-9.**

Tulip, *Detroit Free Press.* **See 367-8.**

Rose, *Detroit Free Press.* **See 367-10.**

Lily, *Detroit Free Press.* **See 367-7.**

Poppy, *Detroit Free Press.* **See 367-6.**

Basket of Diamonds, *Kansas City Star.* **See 110-9.**

Cactus Basket, Finley. **See 307-6.**

Flower Basket, unidentified newspaper clipping. **See 307-7.**

Flower Basket, *Jinny Beyer Studio Design.* **See 307-8.**

Basket Quilt, *Farmer's Wife.* **See 323-2.**

Basket, *The Patchwork Book.* **See 316-4.**

Colonial Basket, Hall. **See 181-8.**

Arkansas Meadow Rose, *Kansas City Star.* **See 370-11.**

Baskets, Jinny Beyer, 2006. Quilter's Quest sampler quilt, pieced by Carole Nicholas and quilted by Judy Hendrickson.

1 **Greek Cross,** *Ladies Art Company,* 1897. See 312-8, 329-7 and 335-5. Also known as:

Maltese Cross, Nancy Cabot, *Chicago Tribune,* Jun 11, 1938.

2 **Maple Leaf Quilt,** Aunt Martha series: *Favorite Quilts,* ca. 1953.

3 **Sweet Gum Leaf,** Clara Stone, *Practical Needlework,* ca. 1906.

4 **Biloxi,** Clara Stone, *Practical Needlework,* ca. 1906. Also known as:

Fox Chase, Clara Stone, *Practical Needlework,* ca. 1906.

5 **Lady of the Lake,** Nancy Cabot, *Chicago Tribune,* Jun 17, 1933. Also known as:

Galahad's Shield, Nancy Cabot, *Chicago Tribune,* Oct 23, 1937.

6 **The Royal,** *Ladies Art Company,* 1897. See 312-8, 329-7, and 335-5. Also known as:

Regal Cross, Nancy Cabot, *Chicago Tribune,* Sep 2, 1937.

Royal Cross, Nancy Cabot, *Chicago Tribune,* Jul 15, 1934.

Tennessee Circle, Beyer, Alice, *Quilting,* 1934.

Tennessee Circles, *Quilt Booklet No. 1,* ca. 1931.

7 **Quatrefoils,** Nancy Cabot, *Chicago Tribune,* Jun 14, 1937.

8 **Colonial Rose,** Laura Wheeler, *Cincinnati Enquirer,* Oct 1, 1933.

9 **Trenton Quilt Block,** *Ladies Art Company,* 1928. Also known as:

Trenton Patch, Nancy Cabot, *Chicago Tribune,* Jan 31, 1934.

"Here is another of those interesting historical quilt blocks which owe their designing to the famous Battle of Trenton. The oft repeated story of Washington's famous defeat of the Hessians, in December of 1776 and January of 1777, is the inspiration of the 'Trenton Patch.'" Nancy Cabot, *Chicago Tribune,* Jan 31, 1934

10 **Flower Basket,** Laura Wheeler unidentified newspaper clipping, date unknown.

11 **Cherry Basket,** *Ladies Art Company,* 1897. Also known as:

Pieced Basket, date unknown; published in Beyer, Jinny, *The Quilter's Album ....*

12 **Basket,** *Grandmother's Patchwork Quilt Designs, Book* 20, 1931.

1 6 x 6 grid

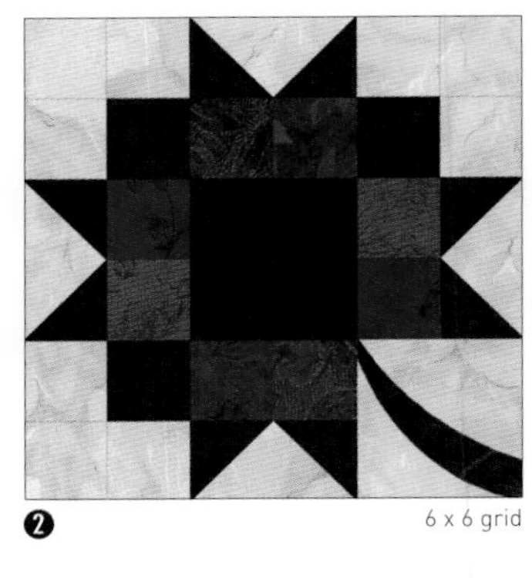

2 6 x 6 grid

3 6 x 6 grid

4 6 x 6 grid

5 6 x 6 grid

6 6 x 6 grid

7 6 x 6 grid

8 6 x 6 grid

9 6 x 6 grid

10 6 x 6 grid

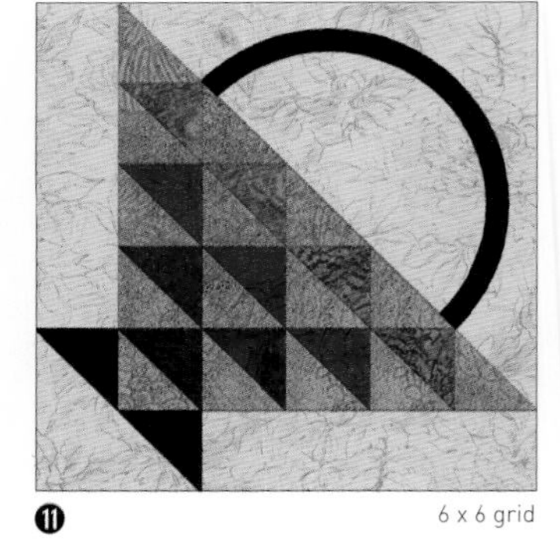

11 6 x 6 grid

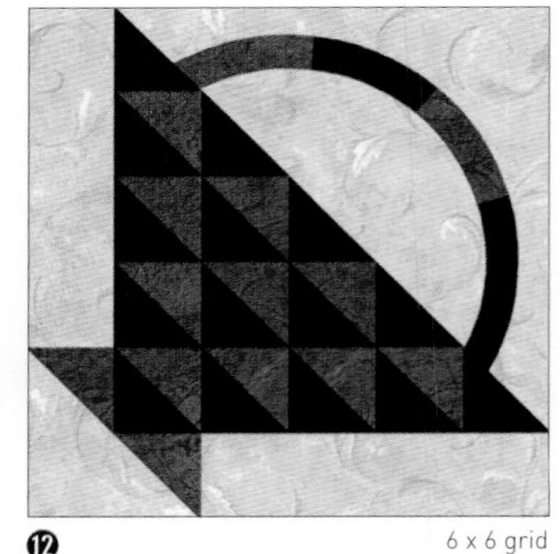

12 6 x 6 grid

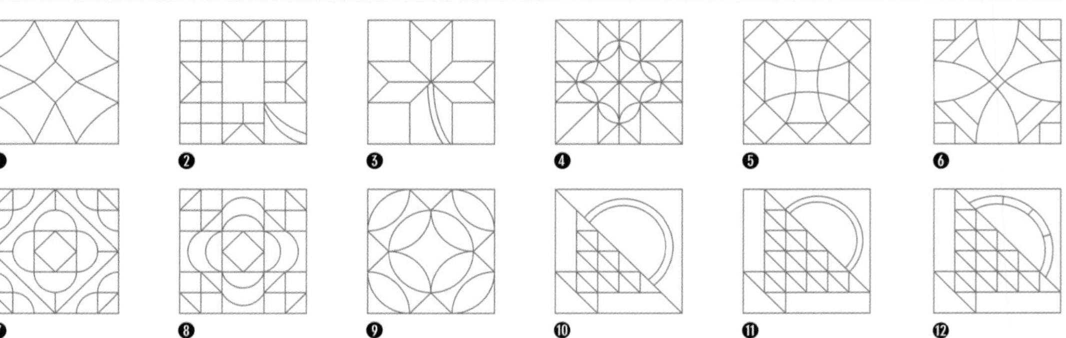

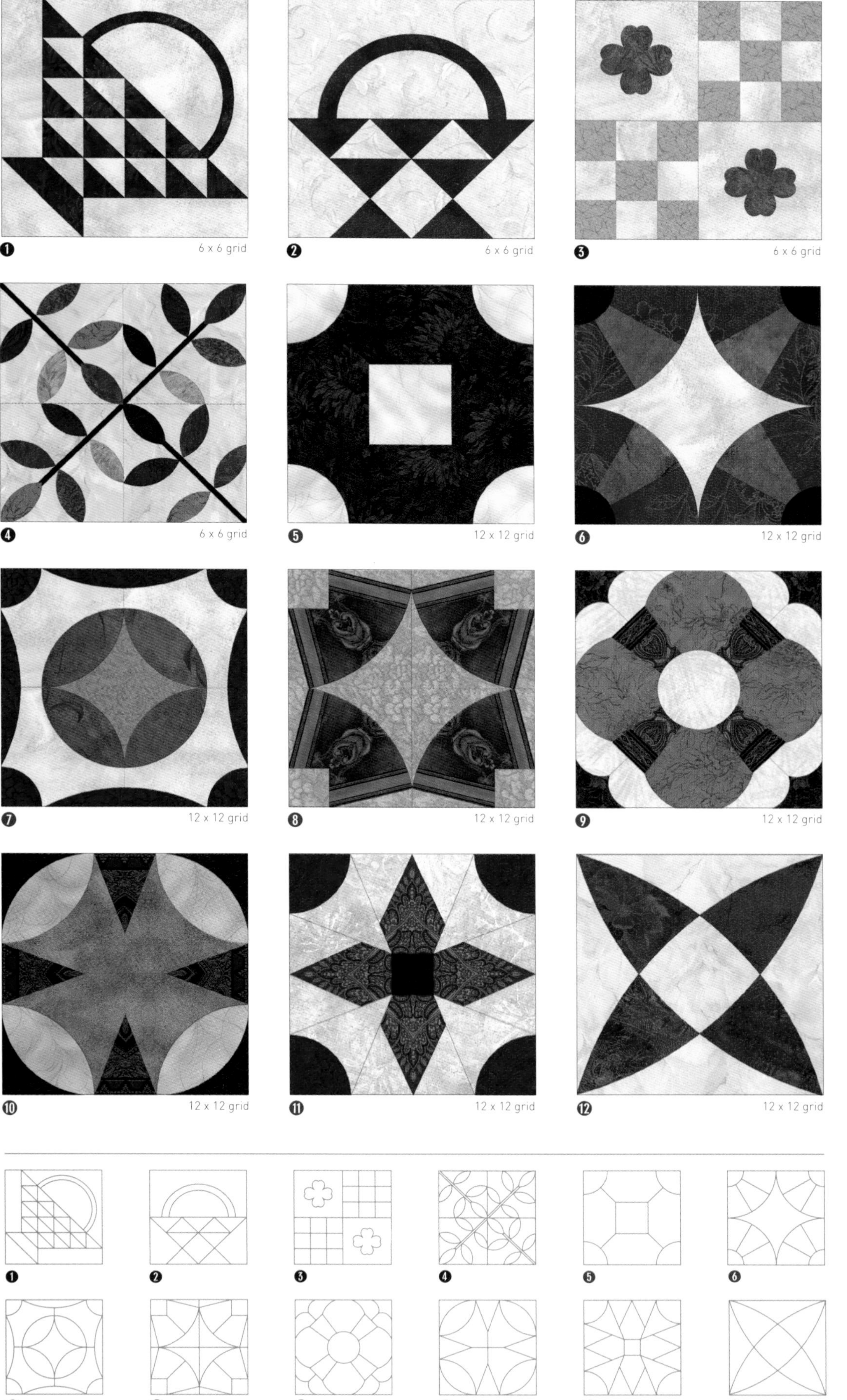

❶ **An Old Favorite,** *to Grandmother Clark's Patchwork Quilt Designs, From Books 20-21-23,* 1932.

❷ **Basket Quilt,** *Farmer's Wife,* Jan 1913.

❸ **Good Luck Block,** Nancy Cabot, *Chicago Tribune,* Sep 14, 1933. Also known as:
- **Clover Patch,** Nancy Page, *Birmingham News,* Sep 12, 1939.
- **Lucky Block,** Nancy Cabot, *Chicago Tribune,* Oct 14, 1937.

❹ **Indian Summer,** Laura Wheeler, *Cincinnati Enquirer,* Nov 7, 1933.
"What an appropriate time of year to start on this lovely quilt so aptly named Indian Summer! Suggestive of autumn leaves with all their gay colors, this patchwork quilt affords an excellent opportunity for using up scraps—an opportunity which the quiltmaker is not likely to miss. The leaves can be done in all sorts of gay scraps, each leaf being a different material as shown. Though designed entirely for patchwork, the leaves could be done in appliqué if desired." Laura Wheeler, *Cincinnati Enquirer,* Nov 7, 1933

❺ **Circuit Rider,** Home Art Studios, unidentified newspaper clipping, date unknown.

❻ **Patchwork Quilt,** Alice Brooks, unidentified newspaper clipping, date unknown.

❼ **Paneled Roses,** Nancy Cabot, *Chicago Tribune,* Jun 11, 1937.

❽ **Lost Paradise,** *Kansas City Star,* Oct 11, 1939.

❾ **Noon Day Splendor,** Laura Wheeler, *Cincinnati Enquirer,* May 20, 1934.

❿ **Oklahoma's Semi-Centennial,** *Kansas City Star,* Apr 24, 1957.

⓫ **Sunset Star,** Laura Wheeler, *Indianapolis Star,* Aug 6, 1937.
"With true quiltmaker's license sun and stars mingle proudly in this pieced quilt, 'Sunset Star.' It allows you to mix favorite scraps of fabric—as many different ones as you wish. Or keep each block uniform in color arrangement. A single block is fun to work up and would make a pillow that would be a grand fair donation." Laura Wheeler, *Indianapolis Star,* Aug 6, 1937

⓬ **The Great Circle Quilt,** Aunt Martha series: *Aunt Martha's Favorite Quilts,* ca. 1953.

1 Honey Bee, Ruby McKim, *Kansas City Star,* Aug 24, 1929. Also known as:
Blue Blazes, Hall, 1935.
Honey Bees, Nancy Cabot, *Chicago Tribune,* Feb 2, 1938.

2 Bordered 9 Patch, Nancy Page, *Birmingham News,* Aug 3, 1943.

3 Flying Birds, Alice Brooks, *Detroit Free Press,* Apr 30, 1934.

4 Penn's Puzzle, Nancy Cabot, *Chicago Tribune,* Feb 11, 1938.

5 Linked Squares, Laura Wheeler, *Cincinnati Enquirer,* May 6, 1934.

6 Starry Pavement, Laura Wheeler, *Cincinnati Enquirer,* Jan 21, 1934.

7 Star Tulip, Nancy Cabot, *Chicago Tribune,* May 2, 1938.

8 Wings, Nancy Cabot, *Chicago Tribune,* Oct 3, 1935.

9 The Mayflower Quilt, *Mrs. Danner's Fifth Quilt Book,* 1970.
"This is one of the prettiest quilts I ever saw and Mrs. Ericson whose hobby is historical quilts, found a picture just like it listed as a pattern that came over on the Mayflower in 1620." *Mrs. Danner's Fifth Quilt Book,* 1970

10 Twist and Turn, Laura Wheeler, *Cincinnati Enquirer,* May 23, 1936.

11 Cubic Measure, Nancy Cabot, *Chicago Tribune,* Jan 23, 1936.

12 Lively Quilt, Laura Wheeler, *Columbus Evening Dispatch,* Aug 6, 1944.

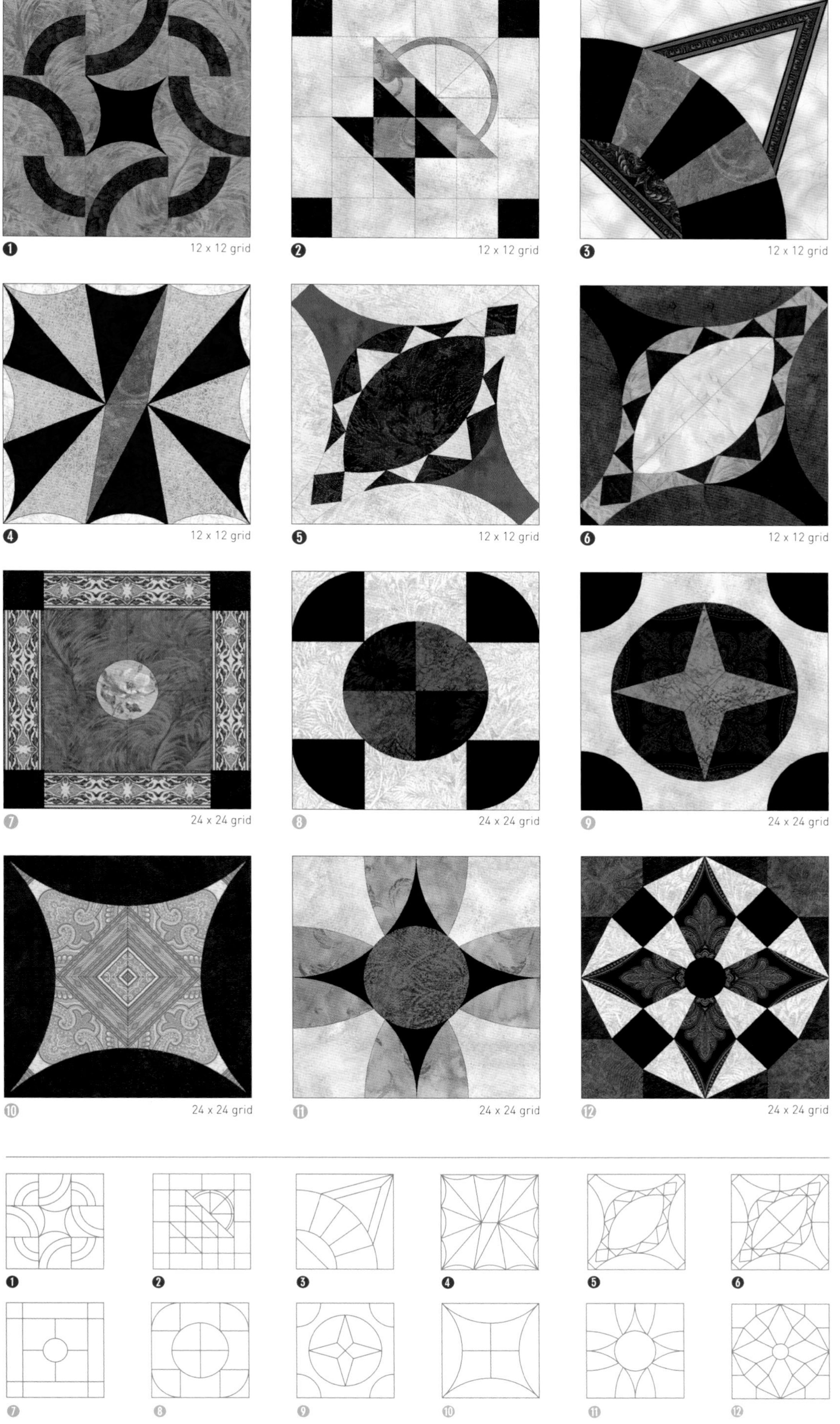

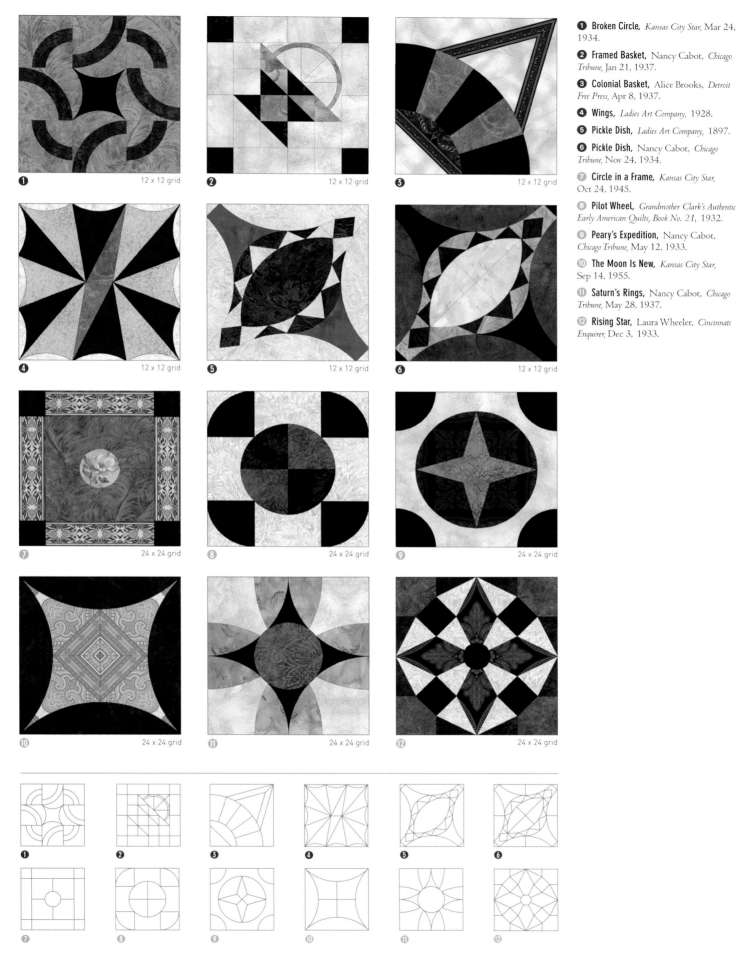

1. **Broken Circle,** *Kansas City Star,* Mar 24, 1934.
2. **Framed Basket,** Nancy Cabot, *Chicago Tribune,* Jan 21, 1937.
3. **Colonial Basket,** Alice Brooks, *Detroit Free Press,* Apr 8, 1937.
4. **Wings,** *Ladies Art Company,* 1928.
5. **Pickle Dish,** *Ladies Art Company,* 1897.
6. **Pickle Dish,** Nancy Cabot, *Chicago Tribune,* Nov 24, 1934.
7. **Circle in a Frame,** *Kansas City Star,* Oct 24, 1945.
8. **Pilot Wheel,** *Grandmother Clark's Authentic Early American Quilts, Book No. 21,* 1932.
9. **Peary's Expedition,** Nancy Cabot, *Chicago Tribune,* May 12, 1933.
10. **The Moon Is New,** *Kansas City Star,* Sep 14, 1955.
11. **Saturn's Rings,** Nancy Cabot, *Chicago Tribune,* May 28, 1937.
12. **Rising Star,** Laura Wheeler, *Cincinnati Enquirer,* Dec 3, 1933.

❶ **Bull's Eye,** Nancy Page, *Detroit Free Press,* Apr 11, 1933.

❷ **America's Pride,** Laura Wheeler, *Indianapolis Star,* Jul 1, 1934.

❸ **Peony,** Alice Brooks, *Detroit Free Press,* Sep 23, 1934.

❹ **The World's Fair,** *Ladies Art Company,* 1897.

❺ **Four Little Baskets,** Nancy Cabot, *Chicago Tribune,* Feb 18, 1935.

❻ **Chimney Swallows,** *Ladies Art Company,* 1897. See 317-1, 336-6, 346-5, and 346-6.

❼ **Winding Ways,** *Ladies Art Company,* 1922. See 341-12. Also known as:

- **Four Leaf Clover,** Nancy Cabot, *Chicago Tribune,* Nov 12, 1943.
- **Rob Peter to Pay Paul,** Home Art Studios, *Colonial Quilts,* 1932.
- **Robbing Peter to Pay Paul,** *Mrs. Danner's Quilts, Books 1 & 2,* 1934.
- **Ways of the World,** Aunt Martha series: *The Quilt Fair Comes to You,* ca. 1933.
- **Wheel of Mysterie,** Hall, 1935.
- **Wheel of Mystery,** Eveline Foland, *Kansas City Star,* Feb 14, 1931.
- **Winding Way,** *Michigan Farmer,* date unknown.
- **Wondrous Ways,** Aunt Martha series: *The Quilt Fair Comes to You,* ca. 1933.
- **Yours for Luck,** *Kansas City Star,* Nov 19, 1959.

❽ **Three Patch,** Alice Brooks, *Detroit Free Press,* Apr 2, 1936.

❾ **Pinwheel,** Alice Brooks, *Washington Post,* Sep 22, 1943. Also known as:

- **The Whirling Pinwheel,** *Kansas City Star,* Sep 22, 1943.

❿ **Twist and Turn,** *Quilt Book, Collection 1,* ca. 1965

⓫ **Cart Wheel,** *Grandmother Clark's Authentic Early American Quilts,* 1932.

⓬ **Springtime,** Laura Wheeler, *Cincinnati Enquirer,* Apr 5, 1934.

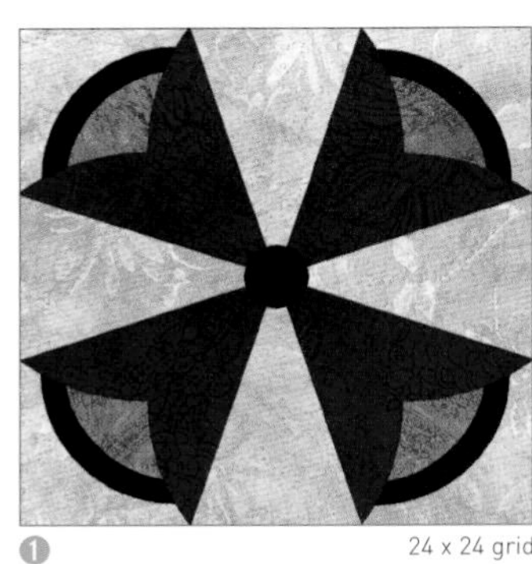

❶ 24 x 24 grid

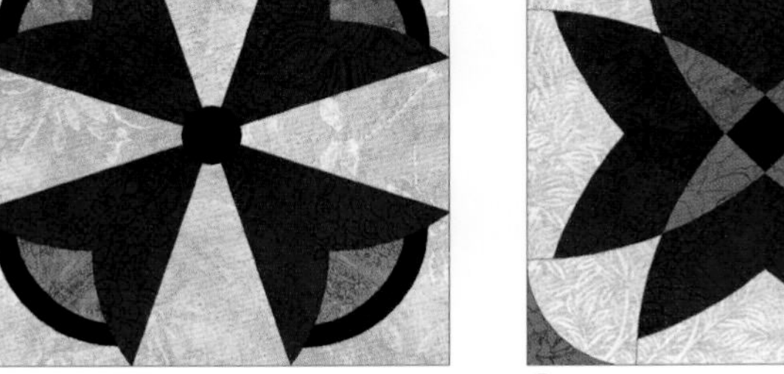

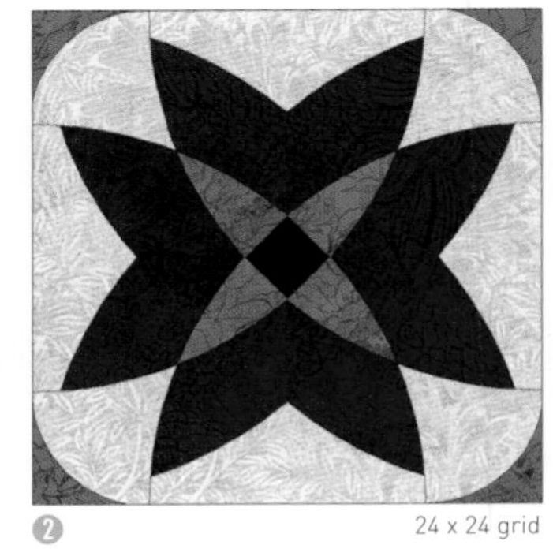

❷ 24 x 24 grid

❸ 24 x 24 grid

❹ 24 x 24 grid

❺ 24 x 24 grid

❻ 24 x 24 grid

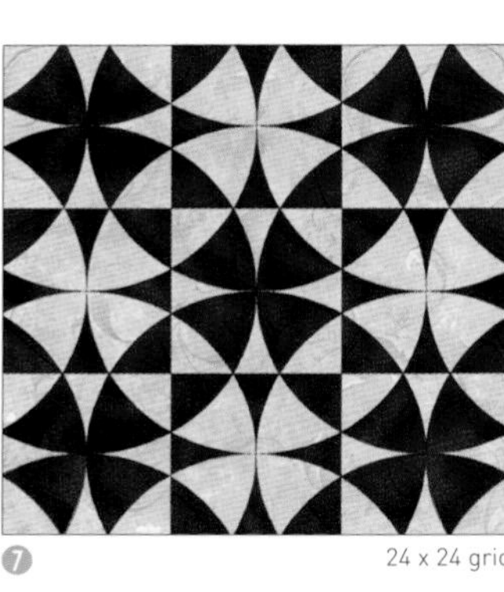

❼ 24 x 24 grid

❽ 24 x 24 grid

❾ 24 x 24 grid

❿ 48 x 48 grid

⓫ 48 x 48 grid

⓬ 48 x 48 grid

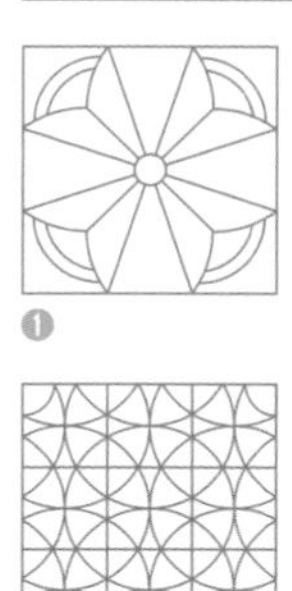

❶ ❼

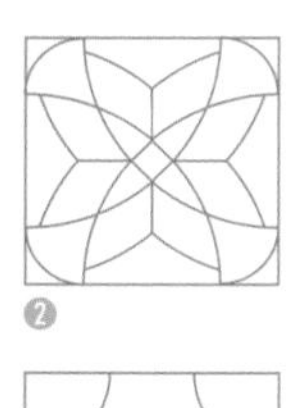

❷

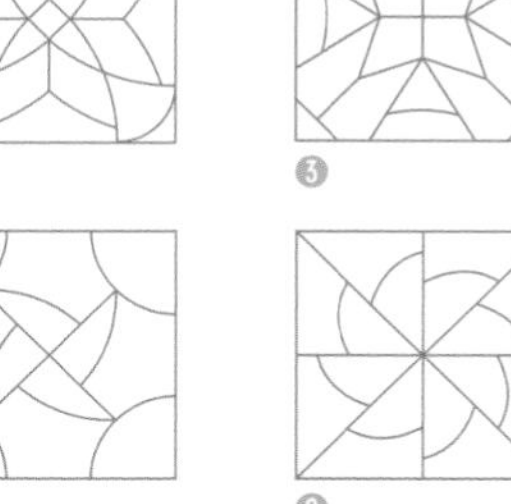

❸ ❽ ❾

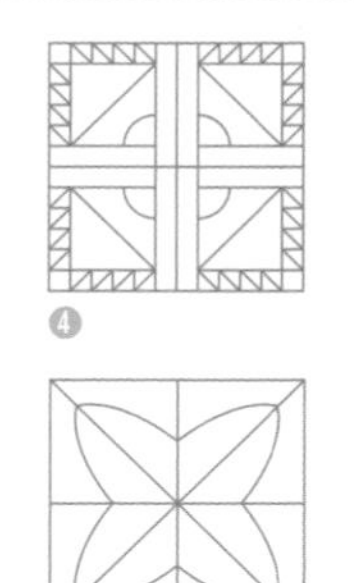

❹ ❿

❺ ⓫

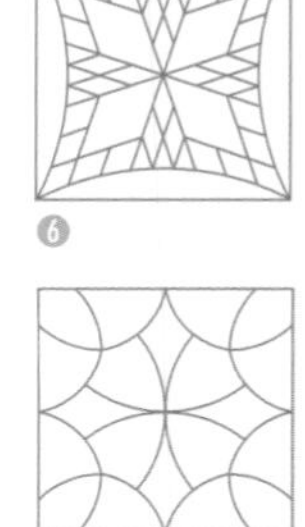

❻ ⓬

Quick Reference: H Blocks

Letters of the alphabet show up again and again in early quilt blocks, with some letters appearing more often than others. I found seven unique H designs in researching this book. Two blocks feature a single letter H. The first is from a *Ladies' Art Company* catalog dated 1897; the other is from a 1928 issue of the same catalog and is shown there along with all of the other letters of the alphabet. The other five designs each have four letter H's. As their name suggests, they were likely designed for a youth organization, the Four H Club. All were found in periodicals dated after the formation of the club in the early 1900s. They depict the Four H symbols that stand for Head, Heart, Hands, and Health.

Letter H, *Ladies Art Company.* **See 149-3.**

H, *Ladies Art Company.* **See 234-8.**

4 H Block, Aunt Martha series: *The Quilt Fair Comes to You.* **See 249-1.**

4H Club Quilt, *Kansas City Star.* **See 166-4.**

4 H, *Kansas City Star.* **See 143-11.**

Four H Club, Havig. **See 272-3.**

Four H Quilt, *Birmingham News.* **See 244-10.**

❶ 48 x 48 grid

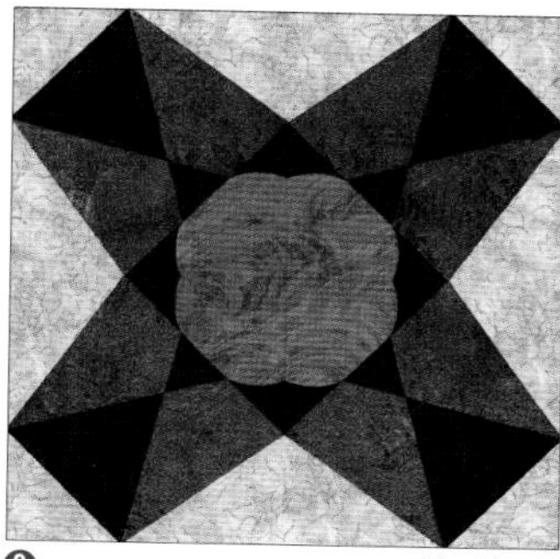

❷ 48 x 48 grid

❸ 48 x 48 grid

❹ 48 x 48 grid

❶ **Coronation,** Laura Wheeler, *Illinois State Register,* Jun 7, 1933.
"Even though the women of the early 19th century scorned crowned heads, Coronation patterns were popular for quilts and so today they still are favorites. This graceful variation makes a charming pattern that is easy to do. Another attractive feature of this quilt is that scraps of material can be used to form the rounded patches at the sides of the blocks. This feature makes it especially popular as a Friendship quilt, for it offers the opportunity of using a variety of material harmoniously." Laura Wheeler, *Illinois State Register,* Jun 7, 1933

❷ **Rose Windows,** Laura Wheeler, *Omaha Bee News,* Aug 12, 1934.

❸ **Rosebuds of Spring,** *Kansas City Star,* May 19, 1954.

❹ **Double Bowknot,** Nancy Cabot, *Chicago Tribune,* Jul 8, 1935.

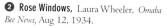

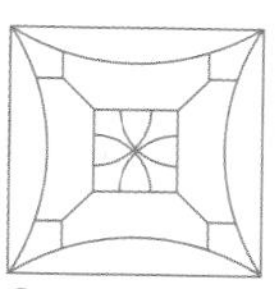

❶

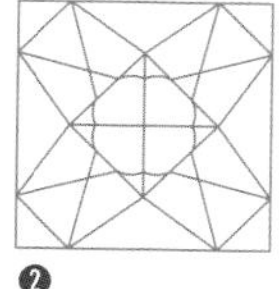

❷

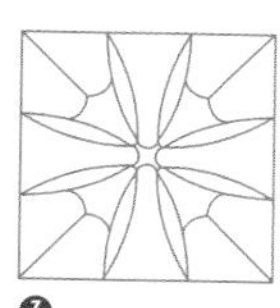

❸

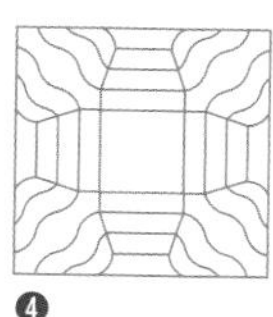

❹

5 x 5 Base Grid Category
(with Curved Elements)

Includes • 5 x 5, • 10 x 10, • 20 x 20, • 40 x 40, and • 80 x 80 grids

❶ **Nocturne,** Nancy Cabot, *Chicago Tribune,* Jun 28, 1934.

❷ **Sacramento City,** Nancy Cabot, *Chicago Tribune,* Jul 28, 1938. See 114-8 and 162-12.

❸ **Pieced Baskets,** Webster, 1915. Also known as:

Grape Basket, Aunt Martha series: *The Quilt Fair Comes to You,* ca.1933.
Little Red Riding Hood's Basket, *Michigan Farmer,* May 27, 1926.

❹ **Friendship Chain,** Alice Brooks, *Detroit Free Press,* Feb 28, 1934.

❺ **Puritan Maiden,** Nancy Cabot, *Chicago Tribune,* Jun 3, 1935.
"When our forebears designed a quilt pattern requiring circles, semi-circles, etc., they had no draftsman's compass at hand. They resorted to cups, saucers, pie plates, or whatever fitted their needs. 'Puritan Maiden' was first designed during that era, in 1840, in a village near Plymouth, Mass. Red, printed lavender, and brown formed a lovely color arrangement at that time, but modern tastes would find it scarcely suitable, preferring gay prints or delicate pastels." Nancy Cabot, *Chicago Tribune,* Jun 3, 1935

❻ **Grandmother's Quilt,** *Prize Winning Designs,* ca. 1931.

❼ **The Rosebud,** *Kansas City Star,* May 3, 1944.

❽ **Day and Night,** Laura Wheeler, *Cincinnati Enquirer,* Oct 29, 1937.

❾ **Friendship Ring,** *Kansas City Star,* Dec 3, 1941. Also known as:

Night and Day, Alice Brooks, *Alice Brooks Collection of Needlecraft Masterpieces,* ca. 1958.

❶ ❷ ❸ ❹ ❺ ❻ ❼ ❽ ❾

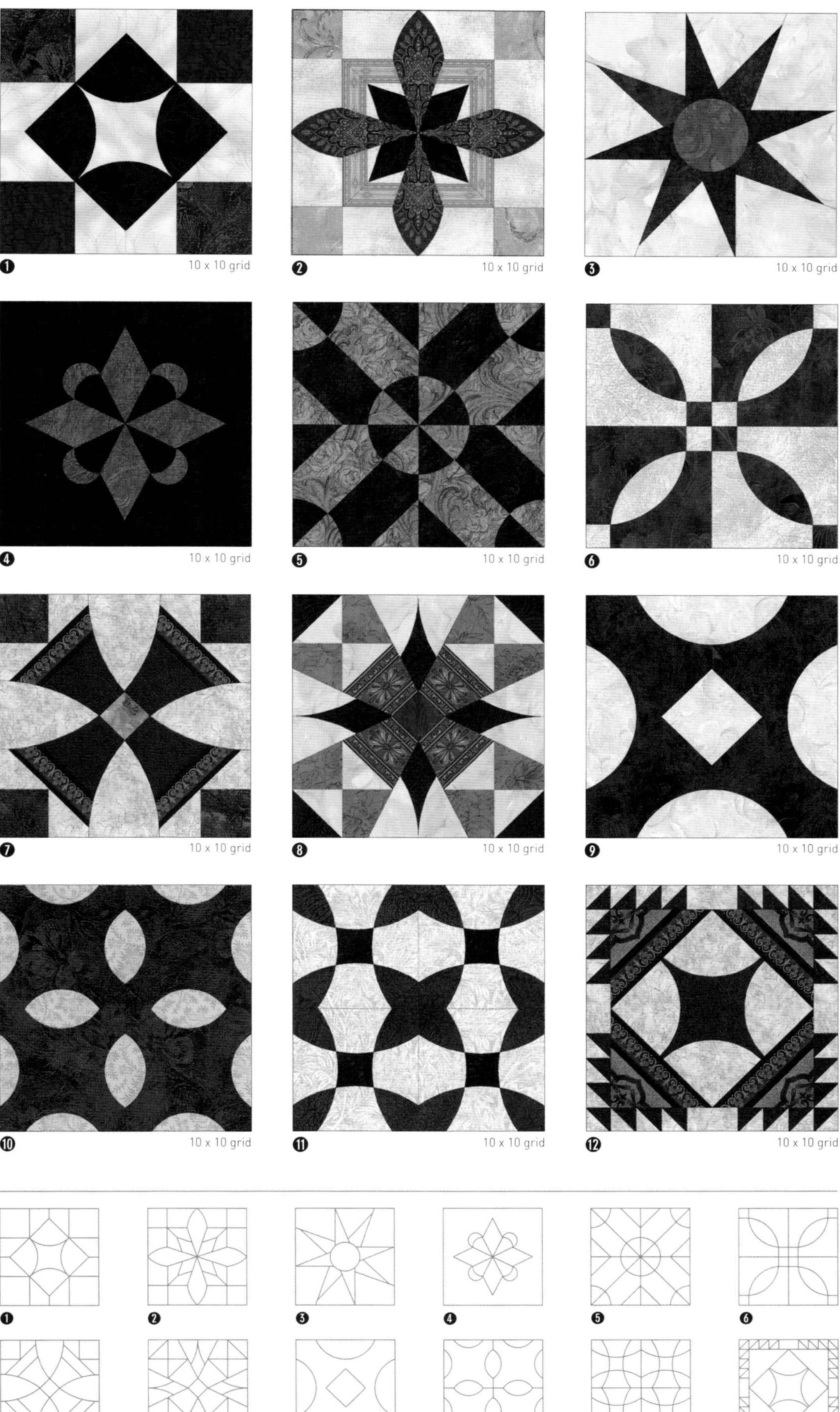

❶ **Window Squares,** *Grandmother Clark's Authentic Early American Patchwork Quilts,* 1932.

❷ **Paducah Peony,** Nancy Cabot, *Chicago Tribune,* Mar 24, 1937.
"'Paducah Peony' is an old pieced block first made in Kentucky in 1849. For a while it enjoyed great popularity, but it's star began to wane and it was relegated to dim and dusty corners. Recently an old coverlet was brought to light in Indiana and recognized by a great grandmother as one of her mother's favorite patterns. Since its return to circulation it has been the same favorite it was when it first was pieced." Nancy Cabot, *Chicago Tribune,* Mar 24, 1937

❸ **The Oak Grove Star Quilt Block,** *Kansas City Star,* Jun 21, 1939.

❹ **King's Crown,** *The Dressmaking Book,* 1929. See 243-8, 343-9, and 344-1. Also known as:
Four Winds, Hall, 1935.
Star of the Four Winds, Ickis, 1949.

❺ **Old Maid Combination,** *Ladies Art Company,* 1897. See 310-11, 315-5 and 338-2.

❻ **Rose Dream,** Eveline Foland, *Kansas City Star,* Dec 27, 1930. See 312-5, 338-12 and 341-6. Also known as:
Hollows and Squares, *Kansas City Star,* Sep 7, 1949.
True Lover's Knot, Home Art Studios, *Colonial Quilts,* 1932.
"The American woman's ingenuity in furnishing her home artistically and at low cost with the products of her own handicraft is strikingly demonstrated during the present times. The amount of interest shown in patchwork quilts is amazing, and because of the many inquiries we have received on quilts and needlework, we are featuring this True Lover's Knot design which is an old favorite with needleworkers of today." *World Herald,* Sep 4, 1933

❼ **Grecian Cross,** *Old Fashioned Quilts,* ca. 1931. See 312-8, 322-1, 322-6 and 335-5.

❽ **Dogwood,** Laura Wheeler, *Cincinnati Enquirer,* Feb 4, 1934.

❾ **Saddlebag,** *The Patchwork Book,* 1932.

❿ **Corn and Beans,** Nancy Cabot, *Chicago Tribune,* Oct 16, 1934.

⓫ **Spirit of 1849,** Nancy Cabot, *Chicago Tribune,* Jan 29, 1936.
"The approximate age of this quilt is determined by the title of the design, 'Spirit of 1849.' The original quilt was made in colors most closely approximating the gold nugget, which were brown, red, and tan. Today the quilt is pieced in gold, yellow, and orange, which is a vast improvement, thanks to dye manufacturers." Nancy Cabot, *Chicago Tribune,* Jan 29, 1936

⓬ **Old Maid's Puzzle,** *Prize Winning Designs,* ca. 1931.

❶ **Jupiter's Moons,** Nancy Cabot, *Chicago Tribune,* Mar 6, 1937.

❷ **Scrap Bag Tree,** Nancy Cabot, *Chicago Tribune,* Mar 14, 1933.

❸ **Little Beech Tree,** Nancy Cabot, *Chicago Tribune,* Mar 14, 1933. Also known as:
 Pine Tree, *Detroit Free Press,* Apr 5, 1933.
 Tree of Life, Nelson, 1982.

❹ **Cluster of Stars,** Nancy Cabot, *Chicago Tribune,* Oct 26, 1933.

❺ **Kaleidoscope,** Nancy Cabot, *Chicago Tribune,* Jan 15, 1936.

❻ **Dogwood Blossoms,** Hall, 1935.

❼ **Chinese Gongs,** Nancy Cabot, *Chicago Tribune,* Jan 7, 1937.

❽ **Pride of the South,** Laura Wheeler, *Sioux City Journal,* Jun 15, 1938.

❾ **Chained Star,** Laura Wheeler, *Cincinnati Enquirer,* Jan 7, 1934.

❿ **The Full Moon,** *Kansas City Star,* Oct 14, 1942.

⓫ **Southern Rose,** Alice Brooks, *Detroit Free Press,* Dec 20, 1933.
"Every quiltmaker loves the scrap-quilt. And why shouldn't she? It's economical; it's delightful in color when done; it certainly lends plenty of variety to the work of making it. In 'Southern Rose' there not only is the beauty of a scrap-quilt but that added feature found only occasionally in quilts. The design has the effect of two patterns one laid on top of the other. and isn't it a lovely effect?" Alice Brooks, *Detroit Free Press,* Dec 20, 1933

⓬ **Lucky Clover,** Alice Brooks, *Detroit Free Press,* May 9, 1934.

❶ **Everglades,** Nancy Cabot, *Chicago Tribune,* May 10, 1936.

❷ **Cowboy's Star Quilt,** Laura Wheeler, *Columbus Evening Dispatch,* Dec 11, 1942.

❸ **Heart's Desire,** Eveline Foland, *Kansas City Star,* Jan 16, 1932. See 339-10 and 339-11.

❹ **Radiant Star,** Laura Wheeler, *Cincinnati Enquirer,* Oct 21, 1933.

❺ **Lily Album,** Alice Brooks, *Detroit Free Press,* Apr 22, 1934.

❻ **Dawn,** Laura Wheeler, *Cincinnati Enquirer,* Feb 25, 1934.

❼ **Star Flower,** Alice Brooks, *Detroit Free Press,* Jan 4, 1934.

❽ **The Compass Quilt,** Eveline Foland, *Kansas City Star,* Aug 16, 1930. Also known as:

Compass, Hall, 1935.
Maltese Cross, Hall, 1935.

❾ **Round Robin Scrap Quilt,** Alice Brooks, *Detroit Free Press,* Apr 10, 1934.
"Here is a quilt that has come by its name fairly. 'Round Robin Scrap Quilt'—as its name—implies, it is just like a Round Robin letter that passes from one to the other endlessly. So this—in true Friendship Quilt style could be made of the contributions of many scraps. As you can imagine, it is a very gay quilt. When the scraps shown dark in the illustration are made of darker or stronger colored scraps, they tie up in an interesting design." Alice Brooks, *Detroit Free Press,* Apr 10, 1934

❿ **Rainbow and Sunshine,** *Prize Winning Designs,* ca. 1931.

⓫ **Cocklebur,** Nancy Cabot, *Chicago Tribune,* Aug 28, 1935.

⓬ **Little Beech Tree,** Ruby McKim, *Kansas City Star,* Oct 26, 1929.

❶ Little Beech Tree, *Ladies Art Company,* 1897.

❷ Tree of Paradise, *Prize Winning Designs,* ca. 1931.

❸ Calico Cat, Alice Brooks, *Detroit Free Press,* Oct 16, 1936.
"'Pretty Pussy' may be just a Calico Cat, but he certainly makes a bright and amusing quilt motif! Make him a 'calico' cat. Indeed, by using up your scraps, it will lend variety to the work and a gayness to your finished quilt. Dark floss outlines the features." Alice Brooks, *Detroit Free Press,* Oct 16, 1936

❹ The Ice Cream Cone, *Kansas City Star,* Sep 15, 1943.

❺ Rose in Summer, Alice Brooks, *Detroit Free Press,* Jan 25, 1934.

❻ Tulip Wheel, Nancy Cabot, *Chicago Tribune,* May 23, 1935.

❼ Red Buds, Nancy Cabot, *Chicago Tribune,* Dec 22, 1935.

❽ The May Basket Quilt, *Kansas City Star,* Jul 2, 1941.

❾ Dusty Miller, Finley, 1929. See 345-6.
Also known as:
The Dusty Miller Quilt, Home Art Studios, *Cincinnati Enquirer,* Mar 6, 1933.

❶ 20 x 20 grid

❷ 20 x 20 grid

❸ 20 x 20 grid

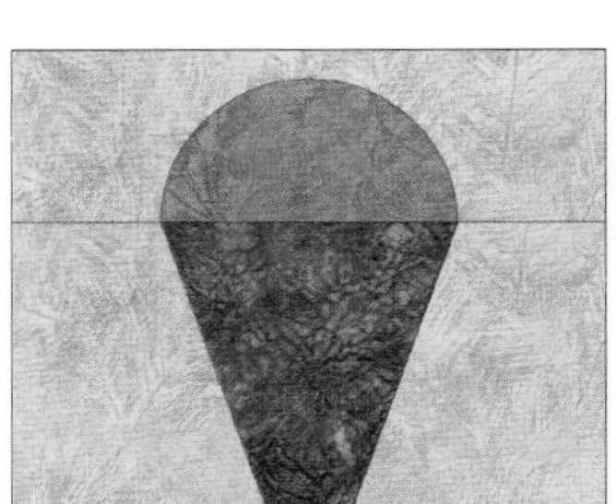
❹ 20 x 20 grid

❺ 40 x 40 grid

❻ 40 x 40 grid

❼ 40 x 40 grid

❽ 40 x 40 grid

❾ 80 x 80 grid

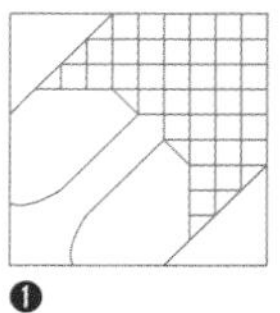
❶

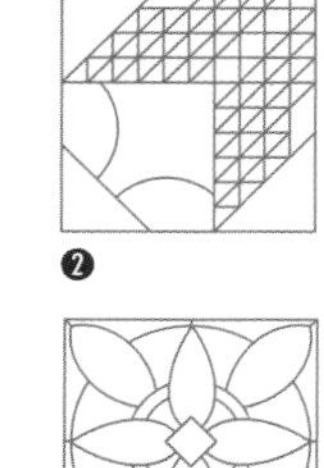
❷ ❻

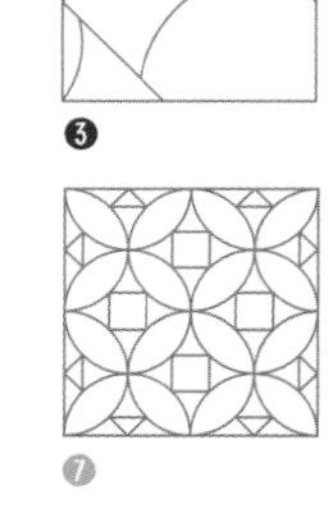
❸ ❼

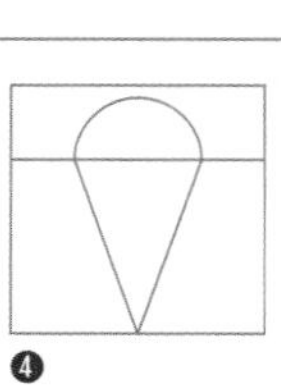
❹

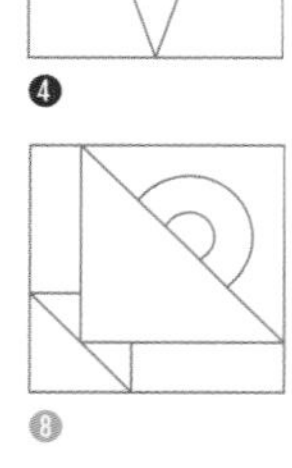
❽

❺

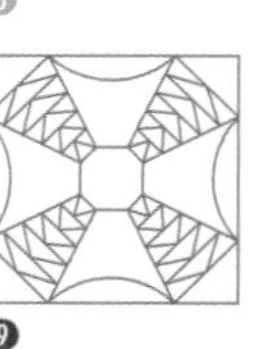
❾

More Categories Based on Grids of Squares (with Curved Elements)

Includes ● *7 x 7 (14 x 14, 28 x 28, 56 x 56),* ● *9 x 9 (18 x 18, 36 x 36, 72 x 72),* ● *11 x 11 (22 x 22, 44 x 44),* ● *13 x 13 (26 x 26, 52 x 52),* ● *15 x 15 (30 x 30, 60 x 60),* ● *17 x 17 (34 x 34),* ● *19 x 19 (76 x 76), and* ● *21 x 21 (42 x 42)* ● *25 x 25 (50 x 50),* ● *29 x 29,* ● *33 x 33 (66 x 66)* ● *35 x 35 grids*

❶ 7 x 7 grid

❷ 7 x 7 grid

❸ 7 x 7 grid

❹ 7 x 7 grid

❺ 7 x 7 grid

❻ 7 x 7 grid

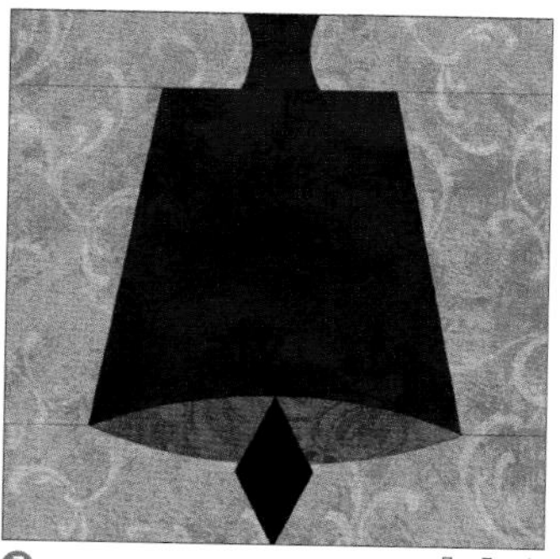

❼ 7 x 7 grid

❽ 14 x 14 grid

❾ 14 x 14 grid

❶ **Autumn Leaf,** Finley, ca. 1929.

❷ **Autumn Leaf,** *Ladies Art Company,* 1928. See 335-7. Also known as:

Autumn Leaves, Nancy Cabot, *Chicago Tribune*, Feb 13, 1933.

Tea Leaves, *The Dressmaking Book*, ca. 1932.

❸ **Mayflower,** Laura Wheeler, *Cincinnati Enquirer*, Oct 17, 1933.

❹ **The Snowball Quilt,** *Kansas City Star*, May 5, 1934.

❺ **Ola's Quilt,** *Kansas City Star*, May 13, 1942.

❻ **Daisy Chain,** Laura Wheeler, *Cincinnati Enquirer*, Feb 11, 1934.

"A favorite in the earliest days of quiltmaking, the scrap quilt today still holds that place with the needlewomen. In 'Daisy Chain' the quiltmaker will find a design that is as graceful as it is practical. The squares are of scraps; all different materials can be used higgledy-piggledy as they come to hand, and what a gay quilt that makes. The daisies are done in the same material throughout. Of course this arrangement can be varied and the flowers made in scraps as well as the squares. Needless to say this quilt lends itself to a great variety of color schemes. Laura Wheeler, *Cincinnati Enquirer*, Feb 11, 1934

❼ **Bell,** *Kansas City Star*, Mar 15, 1961.

❽ **Compass Star,** Laura Wheeler, unidentified newspaper clipping, date unknown.

❾ **May Basket,** Jinny Beyer, Beyer, Jinny, *Patchwork Portfolio*, 1989.

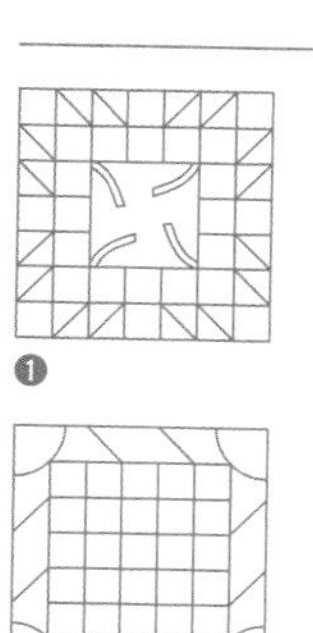

❶

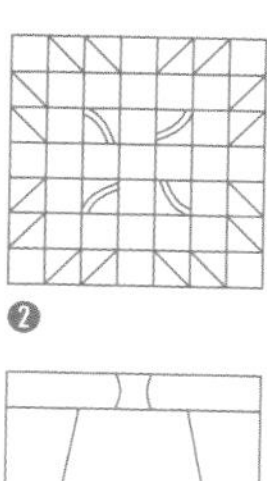

❷

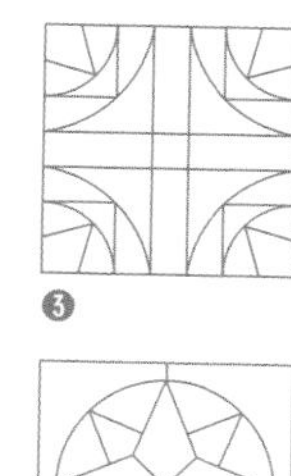

❸

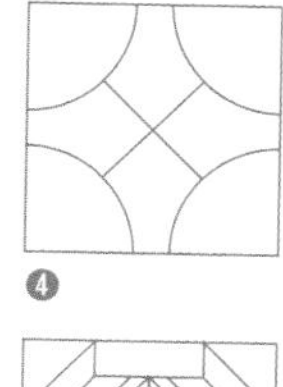

❹

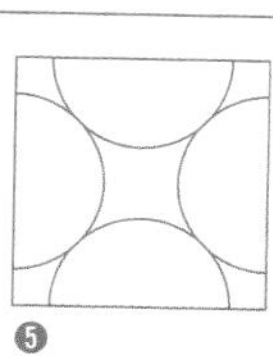

❺

❻

❼

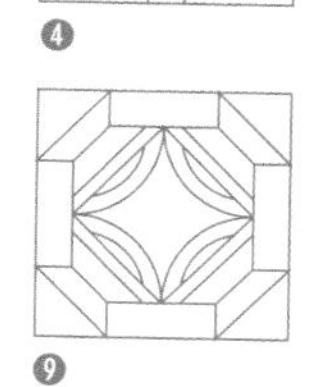

❽

❾

❶ **Space for Many Names,** *Kansas City Star,* Nov 4, 1959.

❷ **Robbing Peter to Pay Paul,** Hall, 1935. Also known as:

> **Dolly Madison's Workbasket,** *Q Book 124, White House Quilts,* date unknown.

❸ **Star and Cross,** Nancy Cabot, *Chicago Tribune,* Feb 7, 1933.

❹ **Dresden Plate,** *Grandma Dexter Appliqué and Patchwork Designs, Book 36a,* ca. 1932.

❺ **Love in a Tangle,** *Kansas City Star,* Feb 1, 1950. See 389-6 and 389-7.

❻ **Broken Squares,** *Grandmother Clark's Authentic Early American Quilts, Book No. 21,* 1932.

❼ **Pride of the Prairie,** *Topeka State Journal,* Sep 28, 1935.

❽ **Flower Basket,** Virginia Snow, *Virginia Snow Studio Art Needlework Creations,* ca. 1932.

❾ **Merry Go Round,** *Quilt Book, Collection 1,* ca. 1965

❿ **Full Blown Tulip,** Laura Wheeler, *Illinois State Register,* Jul 16, 1933.

⓫ **Peony,** Laura Wheeler, *Cincinnati Enquirer,* Mar 11, 1934.

⓬ **Starry Chain,** Alice Brooks, *Detroit Free Press,* May 6, 1934.

❶ 14 x 14 grid

❷ 14 x 14 grid

❸ 14 x 14 grid

❹ 14 x 14 grid

❺ 14 x 14 grid

❻ 14 x 14 grid

❼ 14 x 14 grid

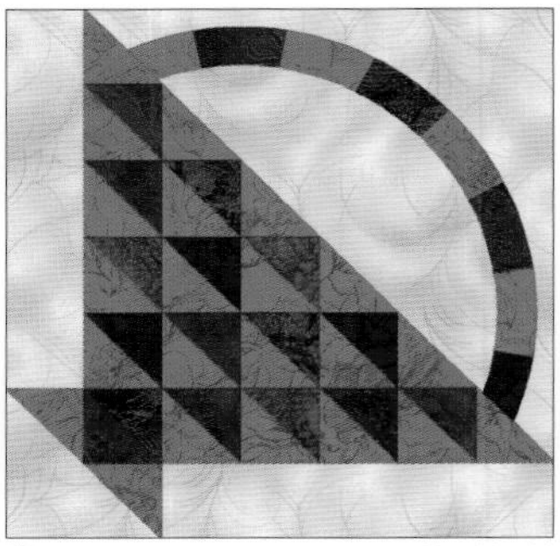

❽ 14 x 14 grid

❾ 28 x 28 grid

❿ 28 x 28 grid

⓫ 28 x 28 grid

⓬ 28 x 28 grid

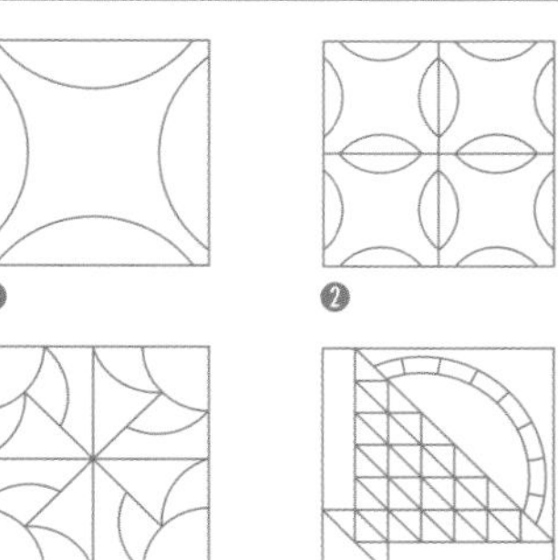

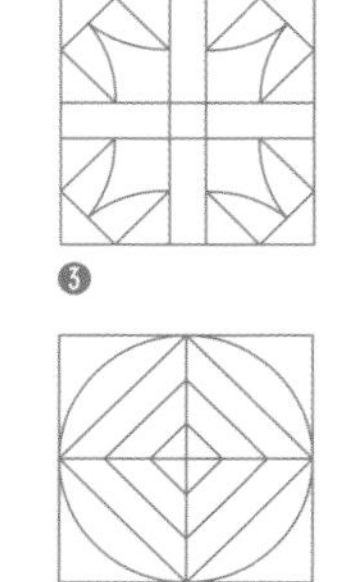

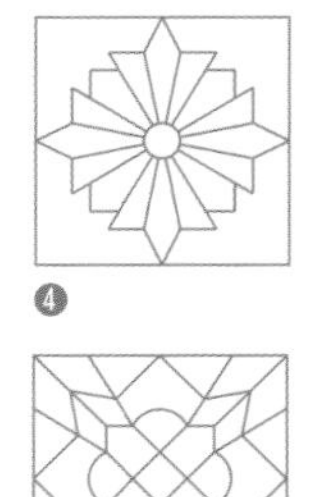

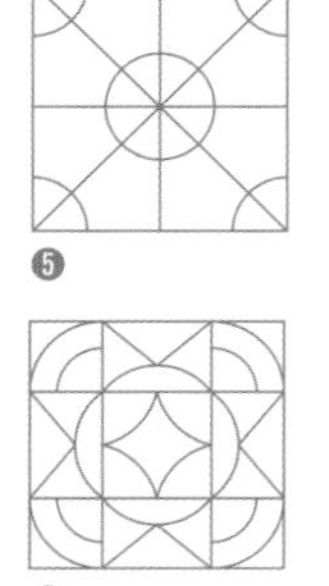

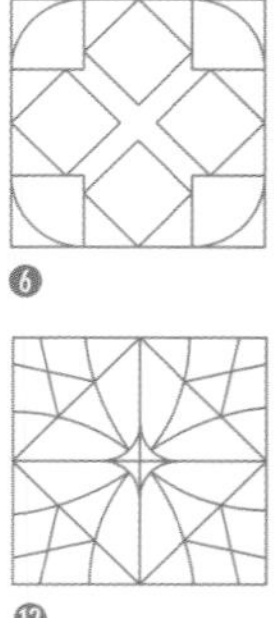

❶ ❷ ❸ ❹ ❺ ❻

❼ ❽ ❾ ❿ ⓫ ⓬

1 **Melon Patch,** Laura Wheeler, *Illinois State Register*, May 13, 1933.

2 **Peony**, Alice Brooks, *Detroit Free Press*, Jul 20, 1935.

3 **Aeroplane**, Aunt Martha series: *The Quilt Fair Comes to You*, ca. 1933.

4 **Scottie Quilt**, Alice Brooks, *Detroit Free Press*, Aug 5, 1936.
"Scotties to right of you, Scotties to left of you, and each one fun to piece for this amusing and colorful quilt. Here at last, your chance to use up scrap after scrap of gay cotton in the contrasting blankets, being sure to keep Scottie's squarish head and legs in a dark, uniform color. It's a world of fun to piece and the pattern may also be used for a patchwork pillow." Alice Brooks, *Detroit Free Press*, Aug 5, 1936

5 **Royal Cross**, Ickis, 1949. See 312-8, 322-1, 322-6, 329-7 and 338-12.

6 **Full Blown Tulip**, *Quilt Book, Collection 1*, ca. 1965.

7 **Autumn Leaf**, Laura Wheeler, *Cincinnati Enquirer*, Dec 15, 1933. See 333-1 and 333-2.

8 **Patty's Summer Parasol**, *Kansas City Star*, Apr 1, 1953.

9 **My Mother's Apron**, *Kansas City Star*, Aug 27, 1952.

10 **The Missouri Morning Star**, *Kansas City Star*, Feb 15, 1950.

11 **Cartwheel**, Nancy Cabot, *Chicago Tribune*, Jan 25, 1935.
"Dusty gold, blue and lavender are typically pioneer colors, as is this pattern in which they were used. 'Cartwheel' was pieced in Nebraska in 1847. It is a simple design which includes the most fundamental patches. The original quilt was composed entirely of pieced blocks and set together with bands of blue." Nancy Cabot, *Chicago Tribune*, Jan 25, 1935

12 **Byrd at the South Pole**, Nancy Cabot, *Chicago Tribune*, Nov 14, 1934.
"Byrd's flight over the south pole, the epoch-making event which climaxed his explorations in Little America, is marked in quilting history by the creation of the design presented today. Rose, ice blue, and white are the colors combined to symbolize the polar region. The coverlet is composed entirely of pieced blocks which make a most unusual pattern in the spread." Nancy Cabot, *Chicago Tribune*, Nov 14, 1934

1 **Moon and Stars,** Laura Wheeler, *Cincinnati Enquirer,* Sep 6, 1934.

2 **Friendship Knot,** Alice Brooks, *Detroit Free Press,* May 4, 1934.
"'Friendship Knot,' that popular old-time quilt, earned its name from the custom of friends contributing scraps to form a block thus making this a lasting remembrance of their friendship. You'll find the variety of the scraps used adds fascination to the work." Alice Brooks, *Detroit Free Press,* Jun 27, 1936

3 **Carolina Favorite,** Laura Wheeler, *Cincinnati Enquirer,* Feb 15, 1934.

4 **Stars and Stars,** Aunt Martha series: *Quilt Designs,* ca 1952.

5 **Anna's Pride,** *Kansas City Star,* Aug 1, 1936.

6 **Chimney Swallows,** Finley, 1929. See 317-1, 326-6, 346-5, and 346-6.

7 **Mexican Siesta,** Nancy Cabot, *Chicago Tribune,* Apr 18, 1936.
"'Mexican Siesta' was cleverly designed by a young Texas woman with a sense of humor. Visiting her neighboring country she was much amused by dozing Mexicans whose sombreros gathered cobwebs while the indifferent owners slept." Nancy Cabot, *Chicago Tribune,* Apr 18, 1936

8 **Thelma's Choice,** Hall, 1935.

9 **Four Little Baskets,** Hall, 1935.

10 **Cockelburr,** *Ladies Art Company,* 1928.

11 **Whirling Star,** Alice Brooks, *Detroit Free Press,* Feb 26, 1936.

12 **Rising Sun,** Alice Brooks, *Detroit Free Press,* May 16, 1935.

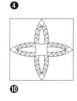

1 18 x 18 grid

2 18 x 18 grid

3 18 x 18 grid

4 18 x 18 grid

5 18 x 18 grid

6 18 x 18 grid

7 18 x 18 grid

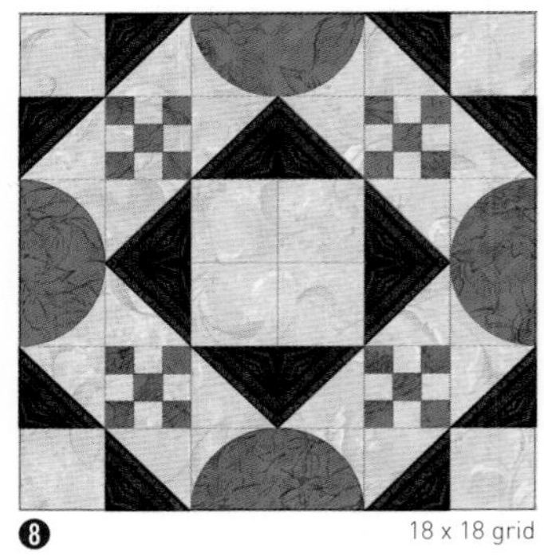
8 18 x 18 grid

9 18 x 18 grid

10 18 x 18 grid

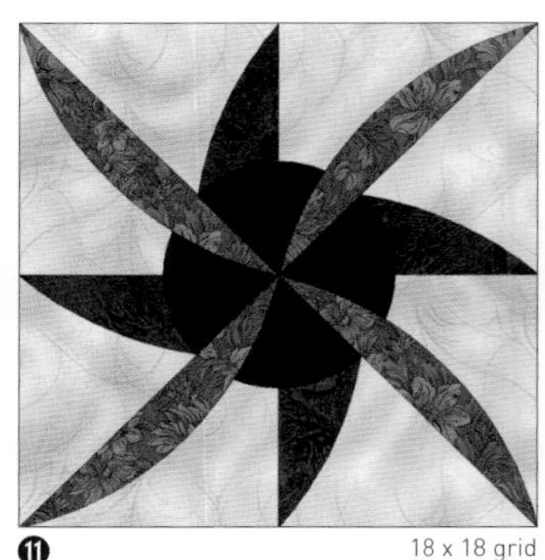
11 18 x 18 grid

12 18 x 18 grid

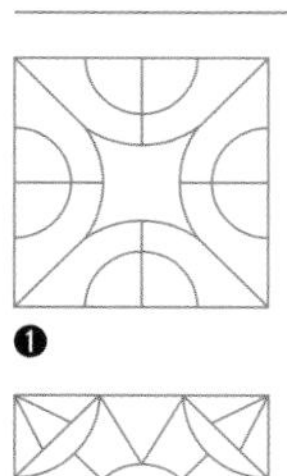
1

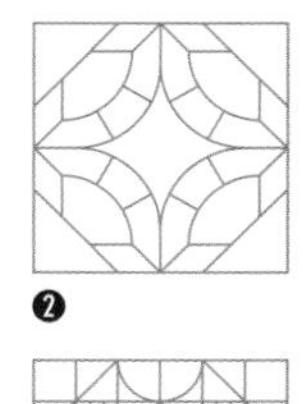
2

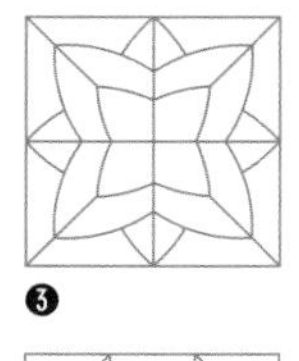
3

4

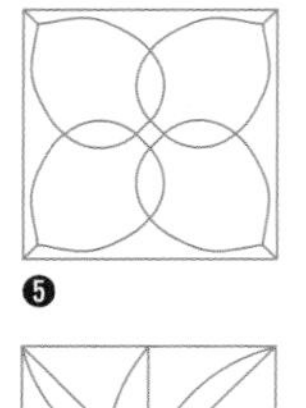
5

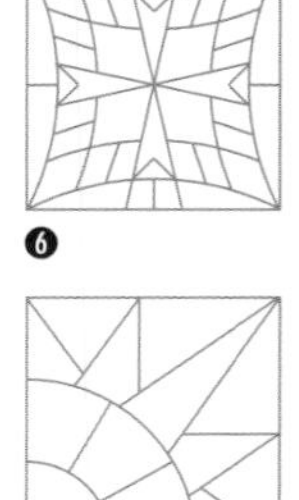
6

7

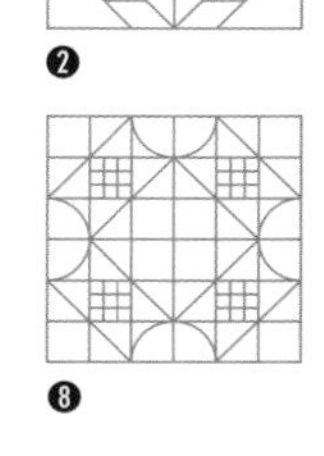
8

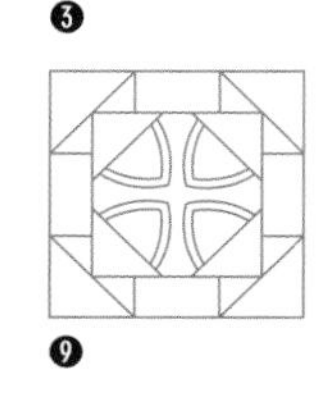
9

10

11

12

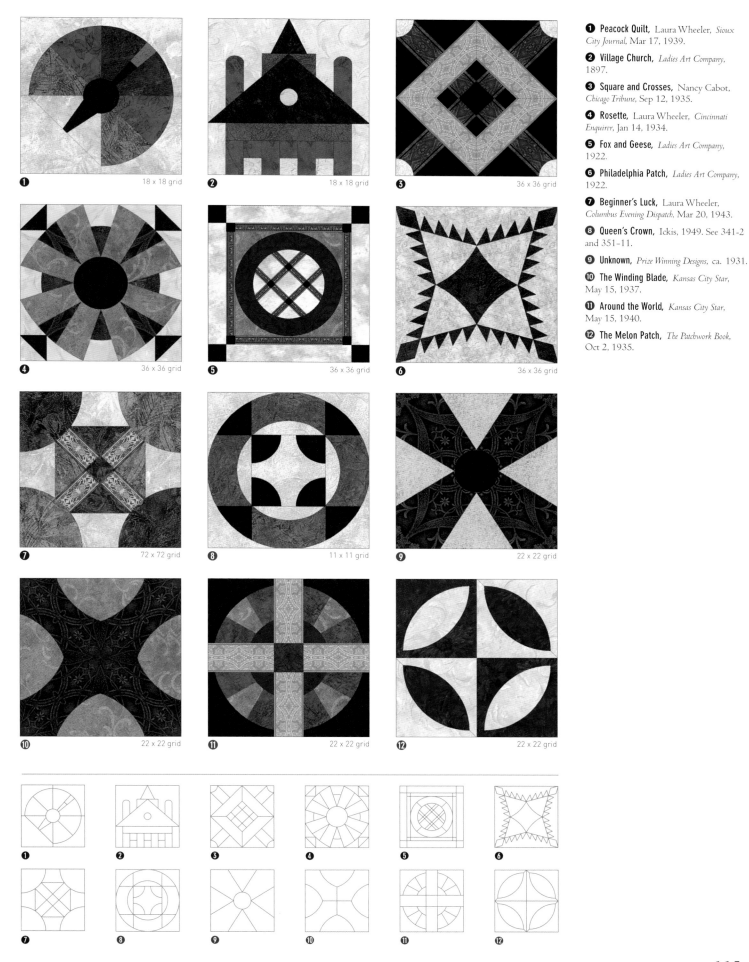

1. **Peacock Quilt,** Laura Wheeler, *Sioux City Journal,* Mar 17, 1939.
2. **Village Church,** *Ladies Art Company,* 1897.
3. **Square and Crosses,** Nancy Cabot, *Chicago Tribune,* Sep 12, 1935.
4. **Rosette,** Laura Wheeler, *Cincinnati Enquirer,* Jan 14, 1934.
5. **Fox and Geese,** *Ladies Art Company,* 1922.
6. **Philadelphia Patch,** *Ladies Art Company,* 1922.
7. **Beginner's Luck,** Laura Wheeler, *Columbus Evening Dispatch,* Mar 20, 1943.
8. **Queen's Crown,** Ickis, 1949. See 341-2 and 351-11.
9. **Unknown,** *Prize Winning Designs,* ca. 1931.
10. **The Winding Blade,** *Kansas City Star,* May 15, 1937.
11. **Around the World,** *Kansas City Star,* May 15, 1940.
12. **The Melon Patch,** *The Patchwork Book,* Oct 2, 1935.

1 Work Basket, Jane Alan, Alan, 1933.

2 Square and Compass, Nancy Cabot, *Chicago Tribune,* Mar 4, 1933. See 310-11, 315-5 and 329-5.

3 Dutchman's Breeches, Nancy Cabot, *Chicago Tribune,* Feb 27, 1937. See 236-1, 275-7, and 342-2.
"'Dutchman's Breeches' is an amusing and attractive pieced block usually done in blues and white. The block was so named because of the resemblance of the white patches to the wild flower known as 'Dutchman's Breeches.'" Nancy Cabot, *Chicago Tribune,* Feb 27, 1937

4 The Spider Web, *Kansas City Star,* Jul 15, 1942.

5 Flower of Spring, Laura Wheeler, *Cincinnati Enquirer,* Mar 25, 1934.
"This quilt is Easy to Do." Laura Wheeler, *Cincinnati Enquirer,* Mar 25, 1934

6 Wedding Ring Bouquet, Aunt Martha series: *Easy Quilts,* ca. 1958.

7 Hummingbirds, Nancy Cabot, *Chicago Tribune,* Jan 11, 1937.

8 Friendship Knot, Finley, 1929. Also known as:
 Starry Crown, Finley, 1929.

9 The Turtle Quilt, *Kansas City Star,* Feb 17, 1960. See 314-12.

10 Turtle on a Quilt, *Kansas City Star,* Jan 6, 1943. See 314-12.

11 Sunbonnet Girl, Laura Wheeler, *Indianapolis Star,* Jul 29, 1936.

12 True Lovers' Link, Home Art Studios, *Cincinnati Enquirer,* Apr 15, 1933. See 312-5, 329-6, and 341-6.

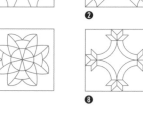

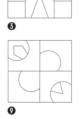

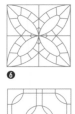

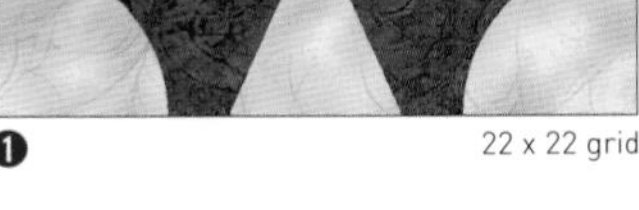

1 22 x 22 grid

2 22 x 22 grid

3 22 x 22 grid

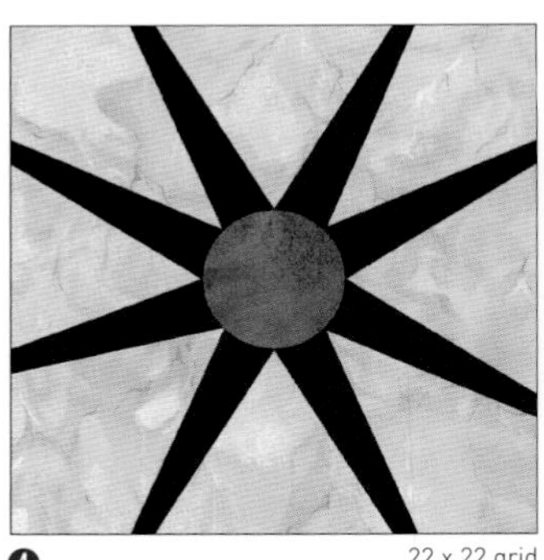

4 22 x 22 grid

5 22 x 22 grid

6 22 x 22 grid

7 22 x 22 grid

8 22 x 22 grid

9 22 x 22 grid

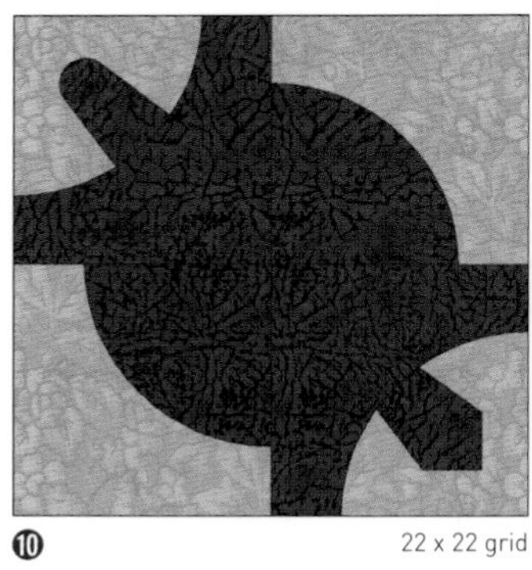

10 22 x 22 grid

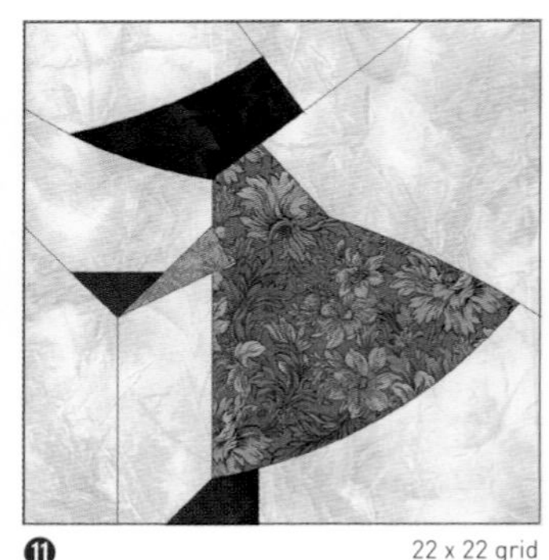

11 22 x 22 grid

12 44 x 44 grid

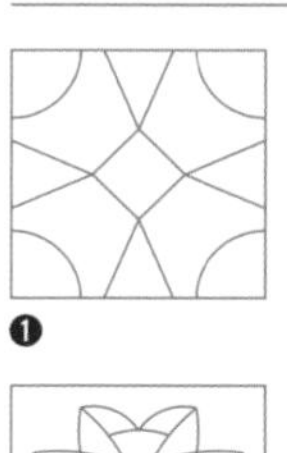

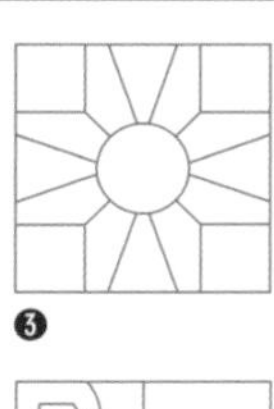
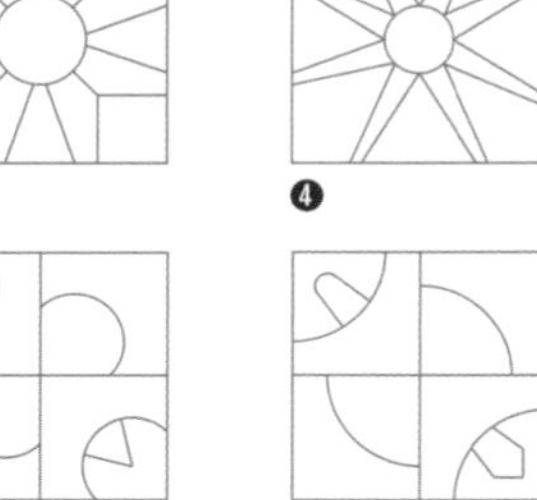
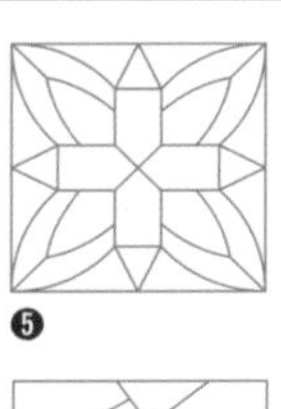
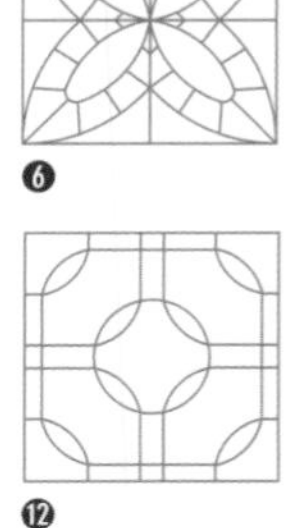

1 2 3 4 5 6

7 8 9 10 11 12

1. **Four Little Baskets,** *Ladies Art Company,* 1897.
2. **Hidden Flower,** Laura Wheeler, *Cincinnati Enquirer,* Sep 21, 1933.
3. **Quilter's Pride,** Alice Brooks, *Detroit Free Press,* Nov 1, 1935.
4. **Japanese Lantern,** *Prize Winning Designs,* ca. 1931. See 342-3 and 440-11.
5. **Windmill,** Alice Brooks, *Detroit Free Press,* Jul 21, 1937.
6. **Scottie Quilt,** Laura Wheeler, *Indianapolis Star,* Oct 19, 1936.
7. **Half Moon Patch,** Nancy Cabot, *Chicago Tribune,* Nov 3, 1934. Also known as:
   Moon Block, Nancy Cabot, *Chicago Tribune,* Oct 12, 1937.
8. **Biloxi,** ca.1938, per Havig.
9. **Old Missouri,** Eveline Foland, *Kansas City Star,* Oct 22, 1932.
10. **Little Giant,** Finley, 1929. See 331-3. Also known as:
    Heart's Desire, Hall, 1935.
11. **The Little Giant Quilt,** Home Art Studios, *Cincinnati Enquirer,* Mar 26, 1933. See 331-3. Also known as:
    Little Giant, *Kansas City Star,* Jun 10, 1933.
12. **Sailboat,** Laura Wheeler, *Indianapolis Star,* Aug 11, 1937.

❶ **Oriole Window,** Hall, 1935.
Also known as:
  Circular Saw, Hall, 1935.
  Four Leaf Clover, Nancy Cabot, *Chicago Tribune*, May 18, 1935.
  Four Little Fans, Hall, 1935.

❷ **Four Leaf Clover,** *Needlecraft*, Feb 1935

❸ **The Circular Saw,** Eveline Foland, *Kansas City Star*, Jan 9, 1932.

❹ **Rainbow,** Alice Brooks, *Detroit Free Press*, Jan 5, 1934.

❺ **Buckeye,** *Prize Winning Designs*, ca. 1931. Also known as:
  Buckeye Block, *Prize Winning Designs*, ca. 1931.

❻ **Farmer's Wife,** Nancy Cabot, *Chicago Tribune*, Jan 11, 1935. See 315-9, 346-8, and 346-9.

❼ **Arkansas,** *Kansas City Star*, Dec 9, 1933.

❽ **Pine Cones,** Nancy Cabot, *Chicago Tribune*, Apr 19, 1938.

❾ **Evergreen,** *Farmer's Wife Book of New Designs and Patterns*, 1934.

❿ **Green Cross,** Nancy Cabot, *Chicago Tribune*, Apr 6, 1936.

⓫ **Missouri Daisy,** Nancy Cabot, *Chicago Tribune*, Jun 4, 1933.

⓬ **President Roosevelt,** *Kansas City Star*, May 17, 1944.

❶ 15 x 15 grid

❷ 15 x 15 grid

❸ 15 x 15 grid

❹ 30 x 30 grid

❺ 30 x 30 grid

❻ 30 x 30 grid

❼ 30 x 30 grid

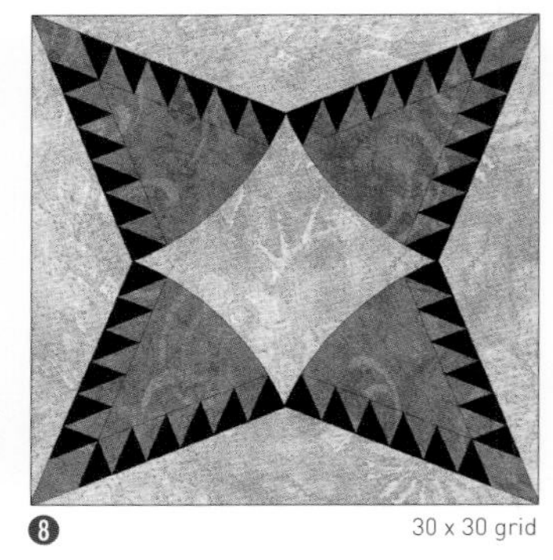
❽ 30 x 30 grid

❾ 30 x 30 grid

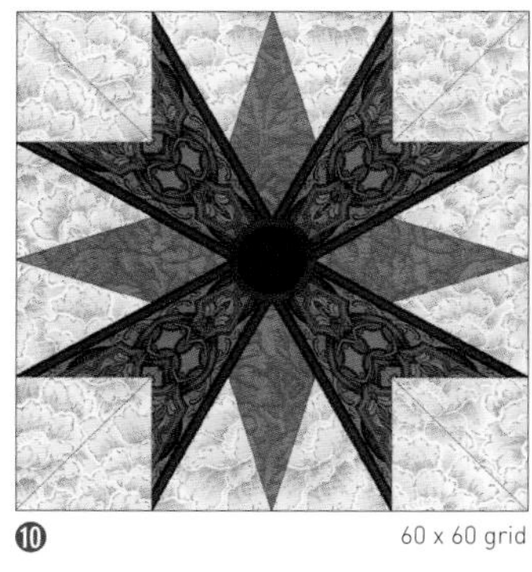
❿ 60 x 60 grid

⓫ 60 x 60 grid

⓬ 34 x 34 grid

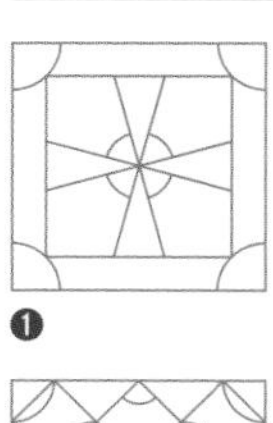
❶

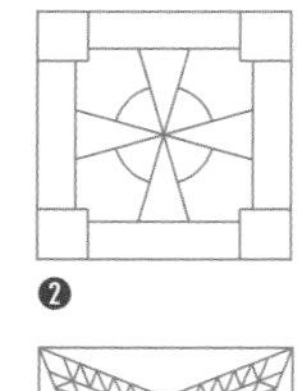
❷

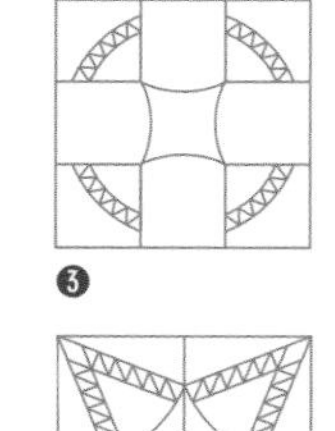
❸

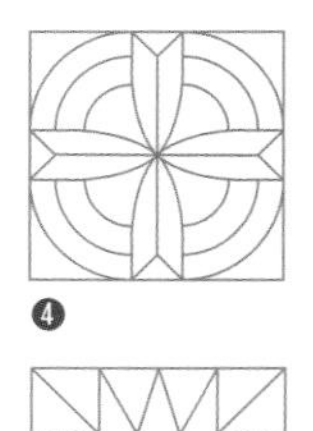
❹

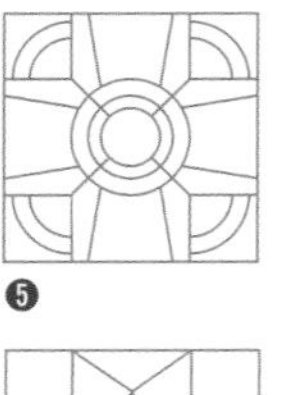
❺

❻

❼

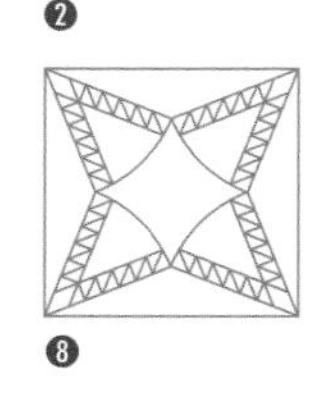
❽

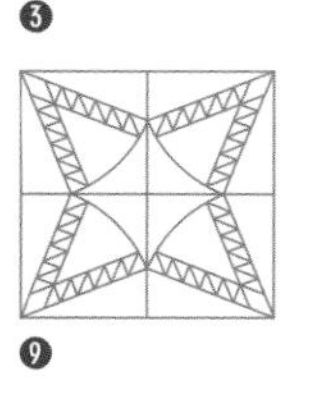
❾

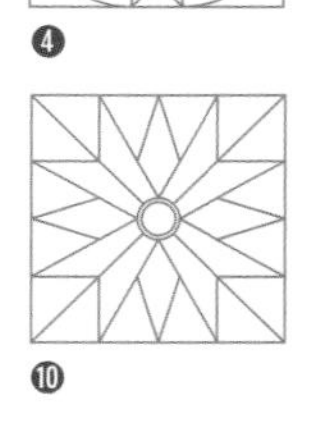
❿

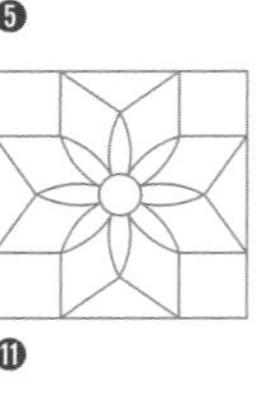
⓫

⓬

❶ 34 x 34 grid

❷ 34 x 34 grid

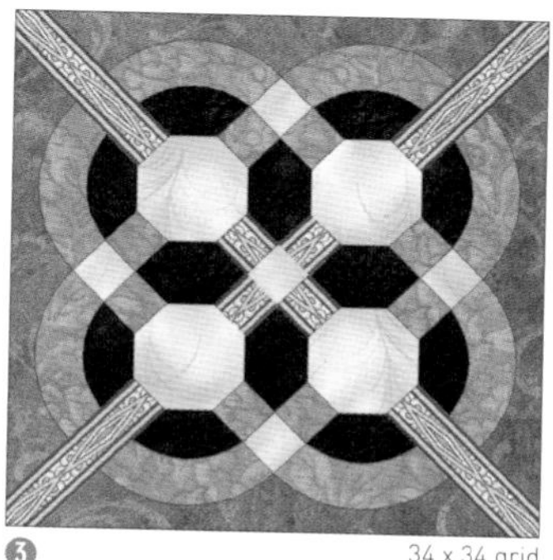

❸ 34 x 34 grid

❹ 34 x 34 grid

❺ 34 x 34 grid

❻ 19 x 19 grid

❼ 19 x 19 grid

❽ 19 x 19 grid

❾ 19 x 19 grid

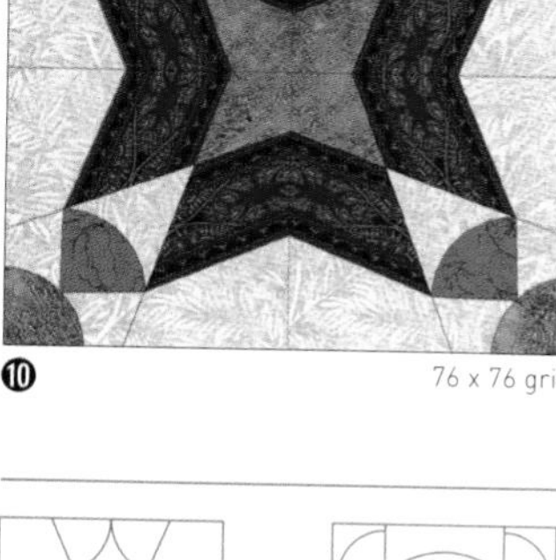

❿ 76 x 76 grid

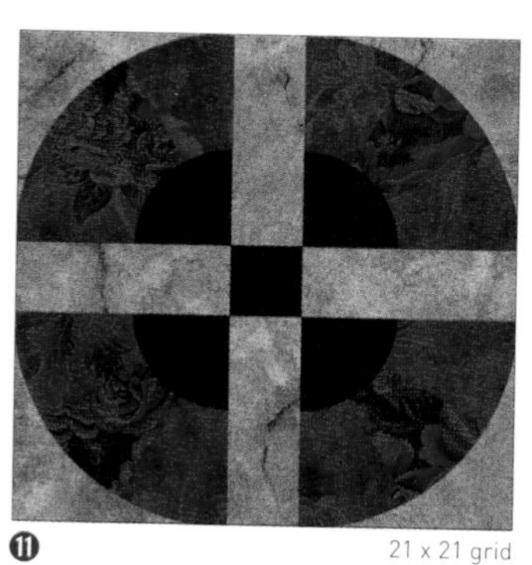

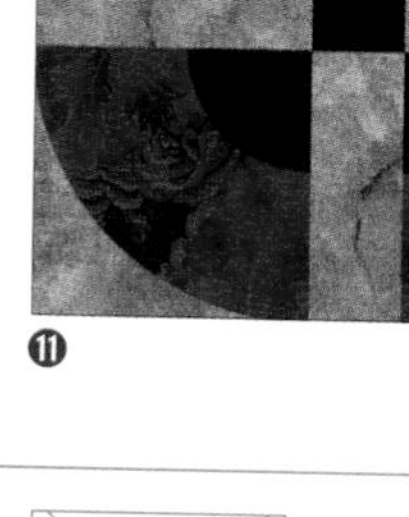

⓫ 21 x 21 grid

⓬ 42 x 42 grid

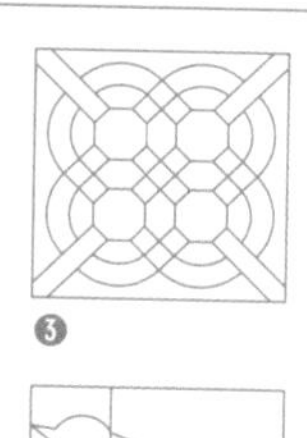

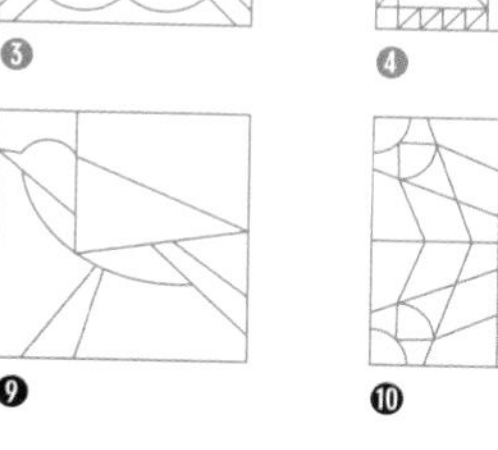

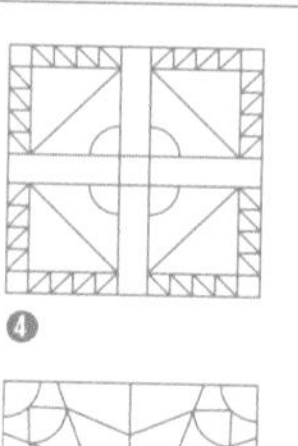

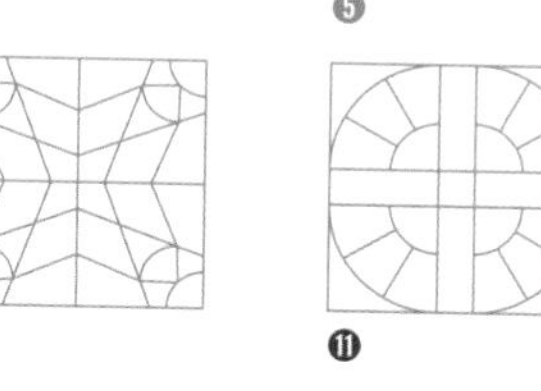

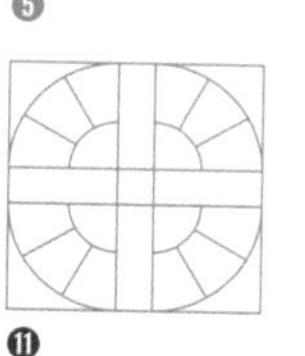

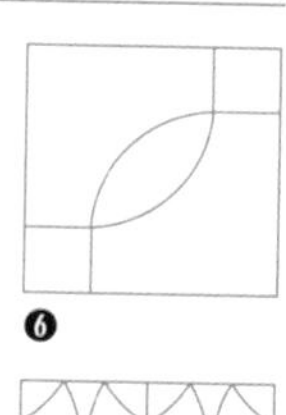

❶ **Priscilla's Prize,** Laura Wheeler, *Cincinnati Enquirer,* Jul 29, 1934.

❷ **Queen's Crown,** Hall, 1935. See 337-8 and 351-11.

❸ **Missouri Trouble,** Nancy Cabot, *Chicago Tribune,* Jun 26, 1935.
"'Missouri Trouble,' like 'Kansas Trouble,' 'Nebraska Troubles,' or 'Rocky Mountain Troubles,' dates back to the pioneer days of the covered wagoneers. It was pieced of blue, yellow and white, in southern Missouri in 1850." Nancy Cabot, *Chicago Tribune,* Jun 26, 1935

❹ **World's Fair,** Hall, 1935.

❺ **Coffee Cups,** *Kansas City Star,* Jan 12, 1935. Also known as:
- **Coffee Cup,** ca. 1938, per Havig.
- **The Cup and Saucer,** *Kansas City Star,* Feb 27, 1946.

❻ **The Rain Drop Quilt Block,** *Kansas City Star,* Mar 16, 1960. See 312-5, 329-6, and 338-12.

❼ **Rainbow,** *Prize Winning Designs,* ca. 1931.

❽ **Butterfly,** Alice Brooks, *Detroit Free Press,* Jul 25, 1936.

❾ **Red Robin,** Laura Wheeler, *Indianapolis Star,* Jul 2, 1936.

❿ **Garden Bloom,** Laura Wheeler, *Cincinnati Enquirer,* Apr 24, 1934.

⓫ **Around the World,** Laura Wheeler, *Sioux City Journal,* Jan 10, 1938.

⓬ **Wheel of Mystery,** *Grandmother Clark's Patchwork Quilts, Book No. 19,* 1932. See 326-7. Also known as:
- **Peter and Paul,** *Grandmother Clark's Patchwork Quilt Designs, From Books 20-21-23,* 1932.
- **Robbing Peter to Pay Paul,** *Mrs. Danner's Third Quilt Book,* 1954.

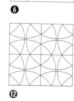

Quick Reference: Snail Trails

Snail Trail, *Monkey Wrench*, *Indiana Puzzle*, and many more names accompany these designs which are very similar when colored. Many of the line drawings of the blocks are quite different, but when colored, the similarities become apparent. Multiple blocks put side by side create an all-over tessellating pattern (see page 49).

Monkey Wrench, per Havig. **See 93-7.**

Nautilus, *Practical Needlework.* **See 93-12.**

Snail Trail, *Ladies Art Company.* **See 93-11.**

Indiana Puzzle, *Kansas City Star.* **See 102-12.**

Greek Puzzle, *Quilt Blocks from The Farmer's Wife.* **See 176-7.**

Conch Shells, *Chicago Tribune* **See 119-5.**

Spirals, *Chicago Tribune.* **See 116-9.**

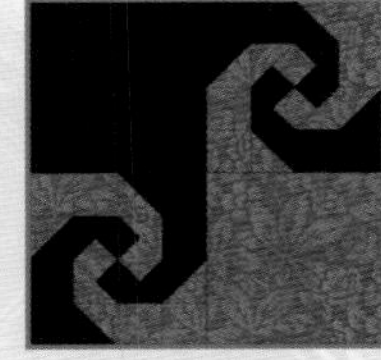
Snail's Trail, *Chicago Tribune.* **See 108-8.**

❶ **Thunder Clouds,** ca. 1938, per Havig.

❷ **Lone Eagle,** ca. 1938, per Havig.

❸ **Breeches Quilt,** *Prize Winning Designs,* ca. 1931. See 236-1, 315-5, and 375-7.

❹ **Japanese Lantern,** Nancy Cabot, *Chicago Tribune,* Jun 20, 1933. See 339-4 and 440-11.

❺ **Road to the West,** Laura Wheeler, *Sioux City Journal,* Sep 19, 1938.

❶ 42 x 42 grid

❷ (25 x 25) 50 x 50

❸ 29 x 29 grid

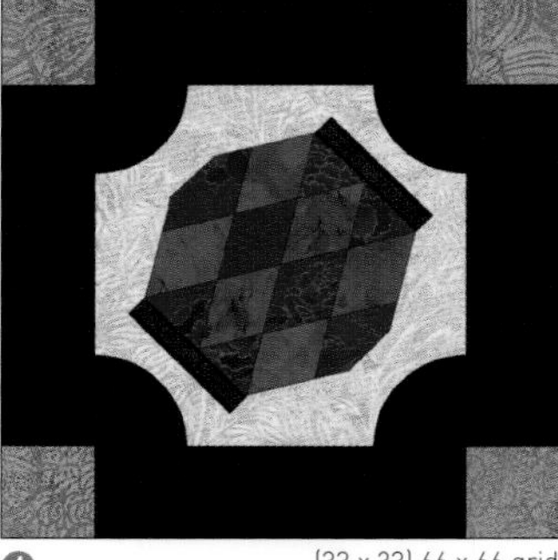
❹ (33 x 33) 66 x 66 grid

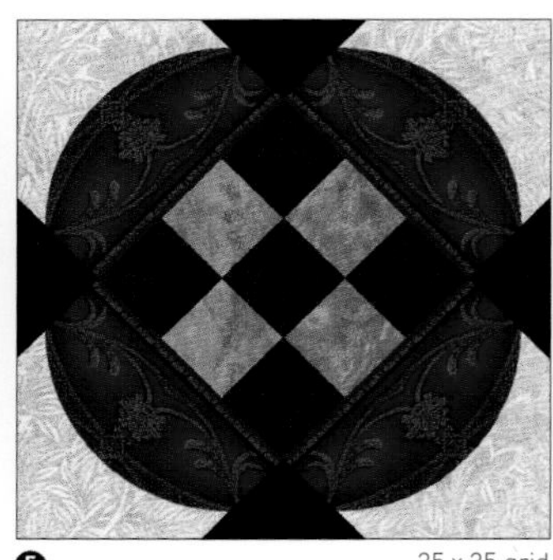
❺ 35 x 35 grid

❶

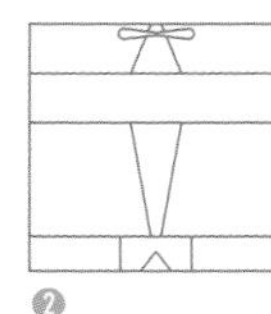
❷

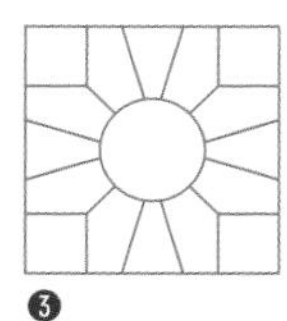
❸

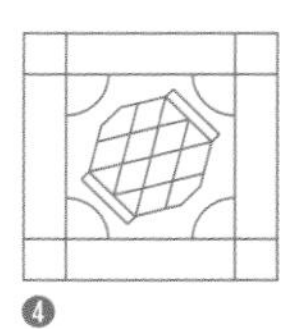
❹

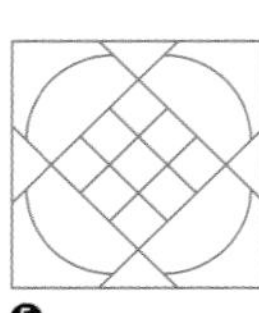
❺

8-Pointed Star Grid Category
(with Curved Elements)

Includes ● multi-grid designs

1 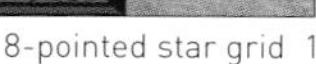
8-pointed star grid 1

2 8-pointed star grid 1

3 8-pointed star grid 1

4 8-pointed star grid 1

5 8-pointed star grid 1

6 8-pointed star grid 1

7 8-pointed star grid 1

8 8-pointed star grid 1

9 8-pointed star grid 2

1 **The Arkansas Star,** *Kansas City Star,* Jan 14, 1933. Also known as:
 Bursting Star, Home Art Studios, *World Herald,* Nov 20, 1933.
 The Morning Sun, *Kansas City Star,* Mar 7, 1945.

2 **Sailor's Joy,** Clara Stone, *Practical Needlework,* ca. 1906.

3 **French Star,** Ruby McKim, *Kansas City Star,* Oct 3, 1928. See 310-12. Also known as:
 Flaming Sun, Nancy Cabot, *Chicago Tribune,* Oct 19, 1936.

4 **Missouri Daisy,** *Prize Winning Designs,* ca. 1931. Also known as:
 Golden Glow, Eveline Foland, *Kansas City Star,* Aug 13, 1932.
 Star Flower, *Prize Winning Designs,* ca. 1931.

5 **King's Star,** Hall, 1935.

6 **The King's Crown,** *Ladies Art Company,* 1897. Also known as:
 King's Crown, *Colonial Quilts,* 1932.

7 **King's Star,** Nancy Cabot, *Chicago Tribune,* Oct 31, 1937.
"King's Star' is by far one of the most unusual of all the star designs, and also is one of the oldest. It was pieced in Boston, Mass., by a young Irish girl just before she and her husband went west to Albany, New York." Nancy Cabot, *Chicago Tribune,* Oct 31, 1937

8 **King's Star,** Ickis, 1949. See 329-4 and 344-1.

9 **Star and Crescent,** Finley, 1929. See 329-4 and 344-1. Also known as:
 Compass, Hall, 1935.
 Star of the West, Hall, 1935.

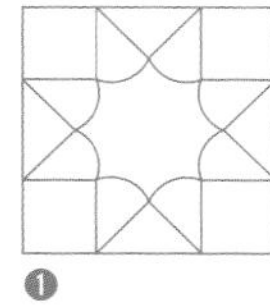

1

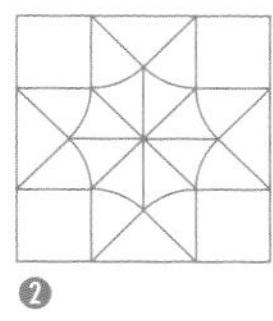

2

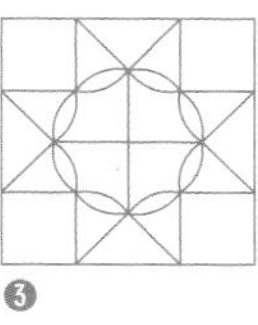

3

4

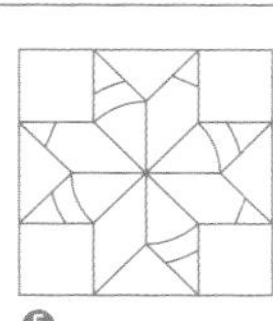

5

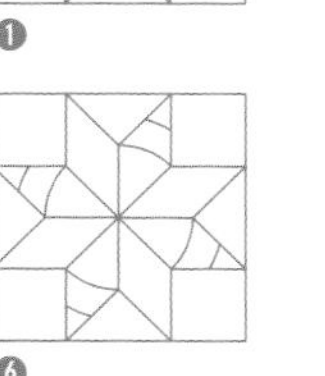

6

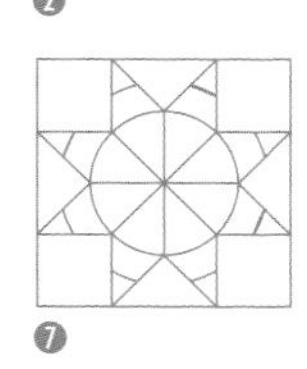

7

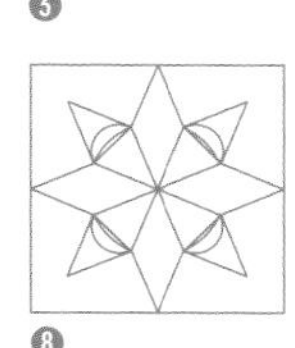

8

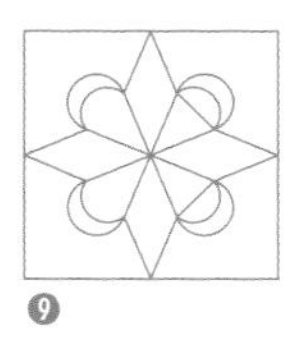

9

1 The Four Winds, Eveline Foland. *Kansas City Star,* Nov 26, 1932. Also known as:

> **Four Winds,** Nancy Page, *Nashville Banner,* Dec 26, 1933.
>
> **Lucky Star,** Nancy Page, *Nashville Banner,* Dec 26, 1933.

"'We really ought to call this quilt design by some hilly or mountainous name, I think,' said Nancy to her group of quilt club women. The design was sent to me by Mrs. Hill who lives in Mount Pleasant, Tenn. Now if that doesn't make the design a rocky one, I miss my guess. But instead we are calling it the 'Lucky Star'. Miss Hill says she calls it the Four Winds. But as I worked with it and chose the colors I could see a four leaf clover lurking in the background. So lucky star it is." Nancy Page, *Nashville Banner,* Dec 26, 1933

2 Rose Point, Nancy Cabot, *Chicago Tribune,* Apr 21, 1938.

3 Twinkling Stars, *Ladies Art Company,* 1901. Also known as:

> **Celestial Sphere,** Nancy Cabot, *Chicago Tribune,* Jun 19, 1935.
>
> **Twinkling Star,** *Quilt Blocks from The Farmer's Wife,* date unknown.

4 Star of Hope, Eveline Foland, *Kansas City Star,* Dec 31, 1932.

5 Tennessee Star, Clara Stone, *Practical Needlework,* ca. 1906.

6 Ozark Sunflower, *Kansas City Star,* Aug 4, 1937. Also known as:

> **The Pieced Sunflower,** *Kansas City Star,* Apr 2, 1947.

7 Pride of the Garden, Alice Brooks, *Detroit Free Press,* Mar 2, 1934.

8 The Car Wheel Quilt, *Kansas City Star,* Sep 4, 1940.

9 The Purple Cross, Eveline Foland, *Kansas City Star,* Aug 27, 1932. Also known as:

> **Royal Diamonds,** Eveline Foland, *Kansas City Star,* Jun 30, 1948.

10 Cather Robinson Star, date unknown, per *Quilts of Virginia.*

11 Eight Points in a Square, *Kansas City Star,* Sep 29, 1954.

12 Eight Pointed Star, *Kansas City Star,* Mar 17, 1934.

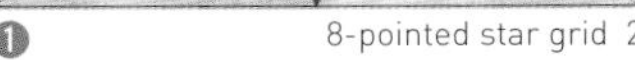

1 8-pointed star grid 2

2 8-pointed star grid 4

3 8-pointed star grid 2

4 8-pointed star grid 2

5 8-pointed star grid 2

6 8-pointed star grid 3

7 8-pointed star grid 4

8 8-pointed star grid 1

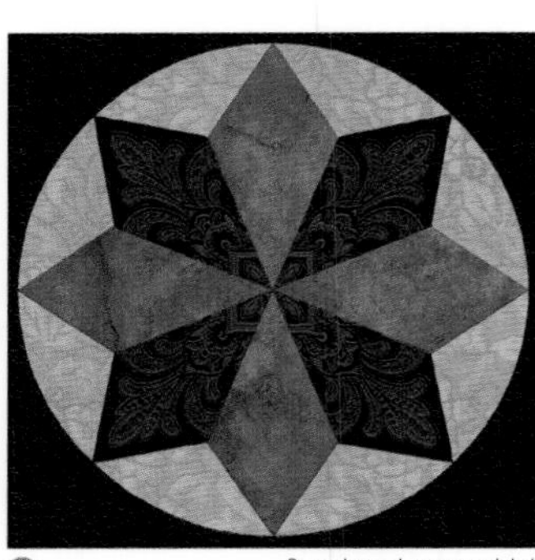

9 8-pointed star grid 4

10 8-pointed star grid 4

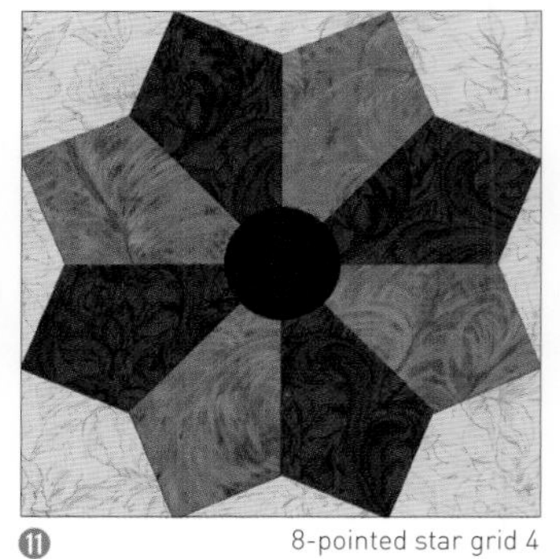

11 8-pointed star grid 4

12 8-pointed star grid 4

1

2

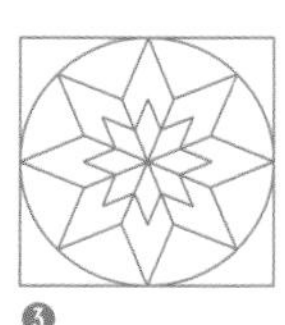

3

4

5

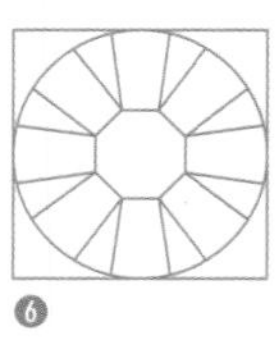

6

7

8

9

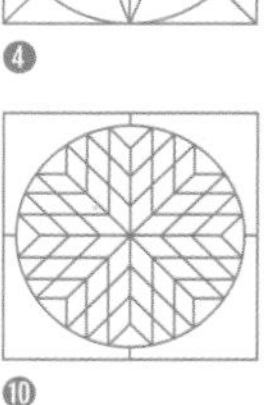

10

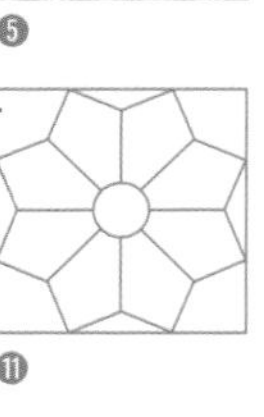

11

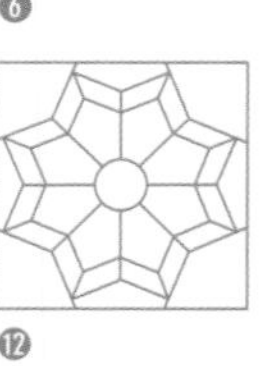

12

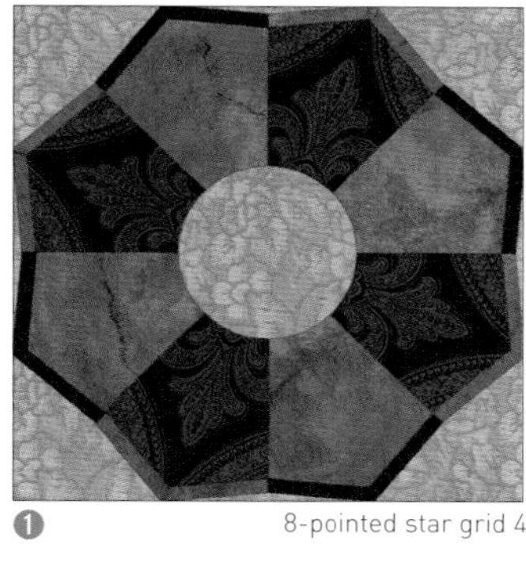

1 8-pointed star grid 4

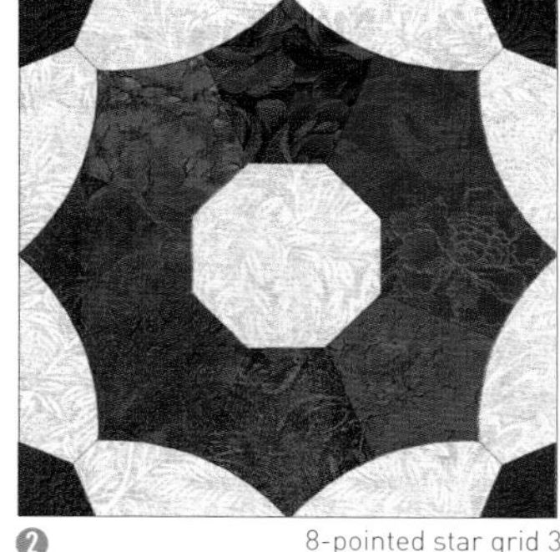

2 8-pointed star grid 3

3 8-pointed star grid 4

4 8-pointed star grid 3

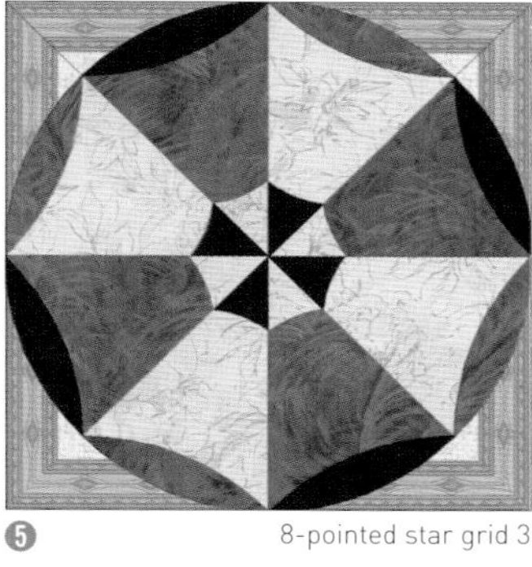

5 8-pointed star grid 3

6 8-pointed star grid 1

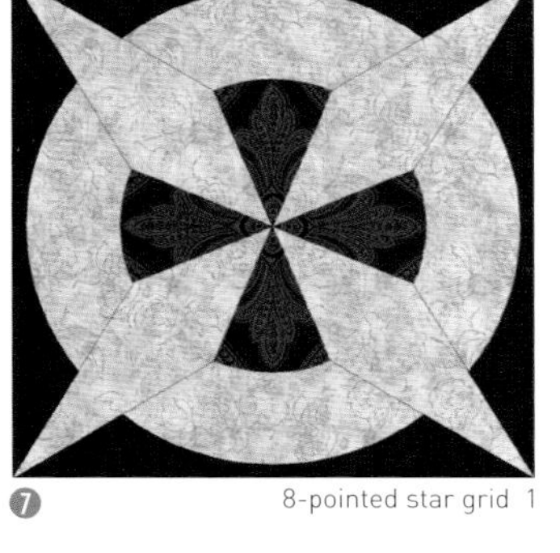

7 8-pointed star grid 1

8 8-pointed star grid 1

9 8-pointed star grid 1

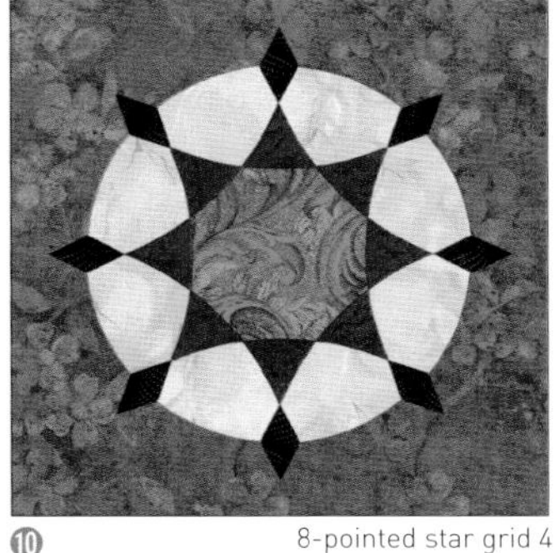

10 8-pointed star grid 4

11 8-pointed star grid 1

12 8-pointed star grid 3

13 8-pointed star grid 3

1 **Mother's Choice Quilt,** *Kansas City Star,* Feb 5, 1941.

2 **Friendship Garden,** Laura Wheeler, *Sioux City Journal,* Jan 12, 1940.

3 **Queen's Crown,** Laura Wheeler, *Cincinnati Enquirer,* Oct 24, 1933.

4 **My Graduation Class Ring,** *Kansas City Star,* Apr 3, 1935.

5 **The Electric Fan,** *Kansas City Star,* Feb 5, 1938.

6 **Dusty Miller,** Hall, 1935. See 332-9.

7 **Wheel of Fate,** Clara Stone, *Practical Needlework,* ca. 1906.

8 **Nouveau Rose,** Jinny Beyer, Hilton Head Seminar design, 1991; published in Beyer, Jinny, *Soft-Edge Piecing.*

9 **Flower Star,** Hall, 1935.

10 **Mace Head,** Nancy Cabot, *Chicago Tribune,* Nov 8, 1936.

11 **Hands All Round,** *Ladies Art Company,* 1901. Also known as:
  Hands All Around, Home Art Studios, *Colonial Quilts,* 1932.
  An Old Fashioned Star Quilt, *Kansas City Star,* Dec 12, 1956.

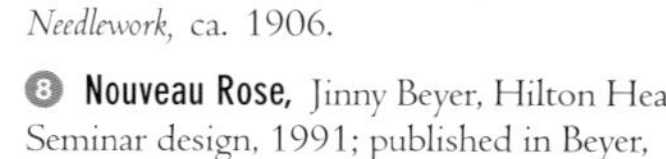

12 **Star Flowers,** Laura Wheeler, *Illinois State Register,* May 5, 1933.

13 **Genesis,** Jinny Beyer, *Mystery Quilt Guide,* 2004.

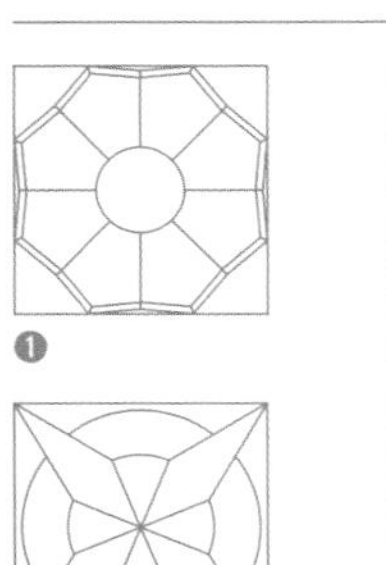

1

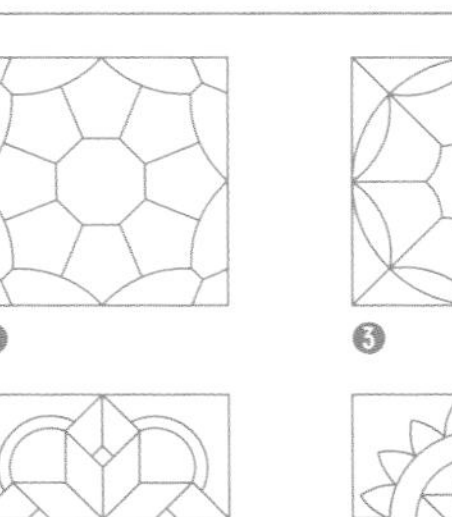

2

3

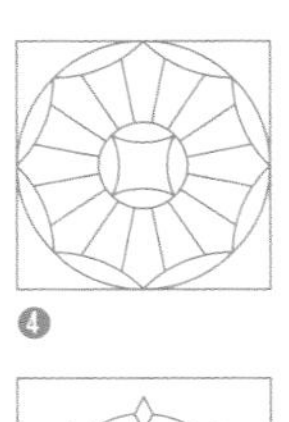

4

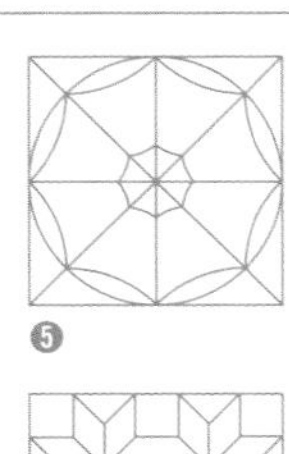

5

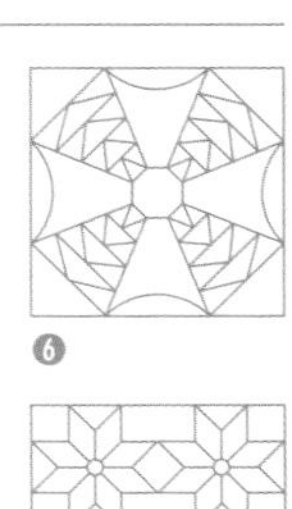

6

7

8

9

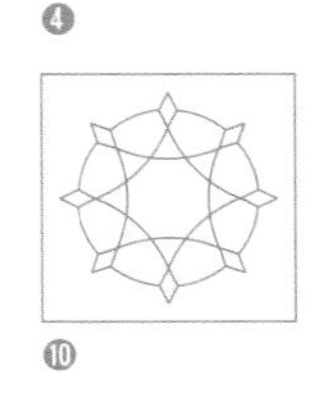

10

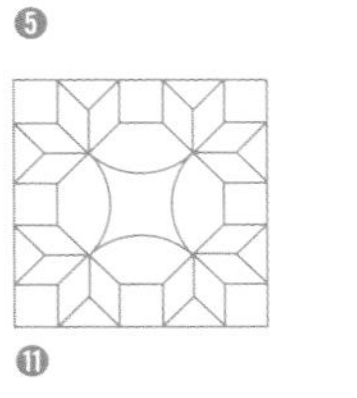

11

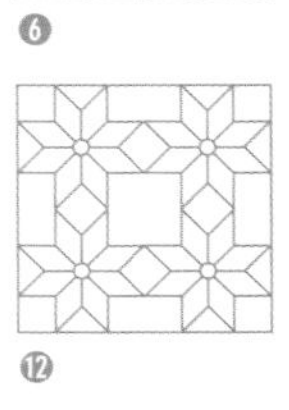

12

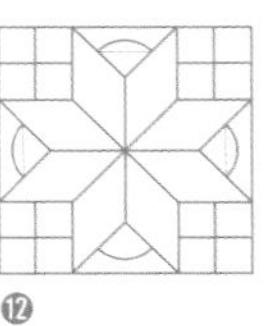

12

❶ **Friendship Knot,** Hall, 1935. Also known as:
  Starry Crown, Hall, 1935.

❷ **Friendship Knot,** Laura Wheeler, *Cincinnati Enquirer,* Aug 7, 1933. "Among the Friendship Quilts—those quilts that are made of materials contributed by friends, or quilts in which each friend makes a block—one of the most popular is the Friendship Knot." *Omaha Bee News,* date unknown

❸ **Job's Tears,** Eveline Foland, *Kansas City Star,* Jan 23, 1932.

❹ **Endless Chain,** Finley, 1929. Also known as:
  Job's Tears, Finley, 1929.
  Kansas Troubles, Finley, 1929.
  The Rocky Road to Kansas, Finley, 1929.
  Slave Chain, Hall, 1935.
  The Slave Chain, Finley, 1929.
  Texas Tears, Finley, 1929.

"'Job's Tears' in 1800, in 1825 it became the 'Slave Chain,' showing the tendency of the times, when slavery and not religion was the paramount issue of the day. In 1840, when Texas was the topic in everyone's thought, this pattern became 'Texas Tears.' After the Civil War it was called 'The Rocky Road to Kansas' or 'Kansas Troubles,' and finally it became the 'Endless Chain.'" Hall, 1935

❺ **Chimney Swallow,** Nancy Cabot, *Chicago Tribune,* Feb 16, 1933. See 317-1, 317-2, 326-6, and 336-6. Also known as:
  Arab Tent, Nancy Cabot, *Chicago Tribune,* Nov 2, 1937.

❻ **Chimney Swallows,** Finley, 1929. See 317-1, 317-2, 326-6, and 336-6. Also known as:
  Coronation, Finley, 1929.
  King's Crown, Hall, 1935.
  The King's Crown, Finley, 1929.
  Potomac Pride, Finley, 1929.
  President's Quilt, Hall, 1935.
  The President's Quilt, Finley, 1929.
  The Coronation Quilt, Home Art Studios, *Cincinnati Enquirer,* Apr 9, 1933.
  Washington's Own, Finley, 1929.
  Washington's Quilt, Hall, 1935.

❼ **The Jewel,** *Prize Winning Designs,* ca. 1931. Also known as:
  Jewel, ca. 1938, per Havig.

❽ **The Farmer's Wife,** *The Farmer's Wife,* Jan 1913. See 315-9 and 340-6. Also known as:
  Farmer's Wife, Eveline Foland, *Kansas City Star,* Sep 3, 1932.

❾ **Farmer's Wife,** Hall, 1935. See 315-9 and 340-6.

❿ **Golden Splendor,** *Mrs. Danner's Third Quilt Book,* 1954.

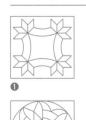

⓫ **Live Oak Tree,** *Ladies Art Company,* 1897.

⓬ **Weeping Willow,** *Quilt Booklet No. 1,* ca. 1931.

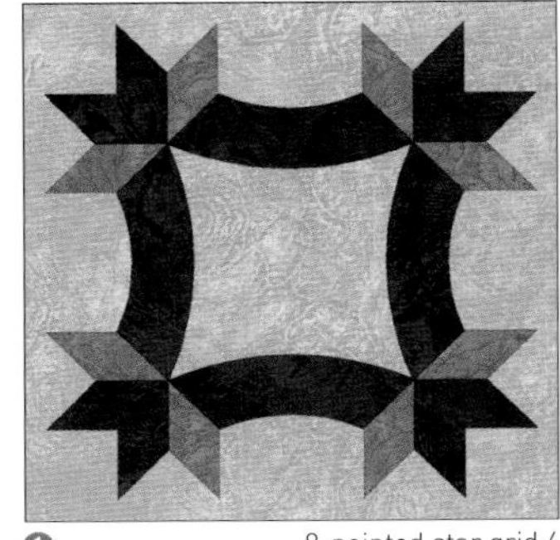

❶ 8-pointed star grid 4

❷ 8-pointed star grid 4

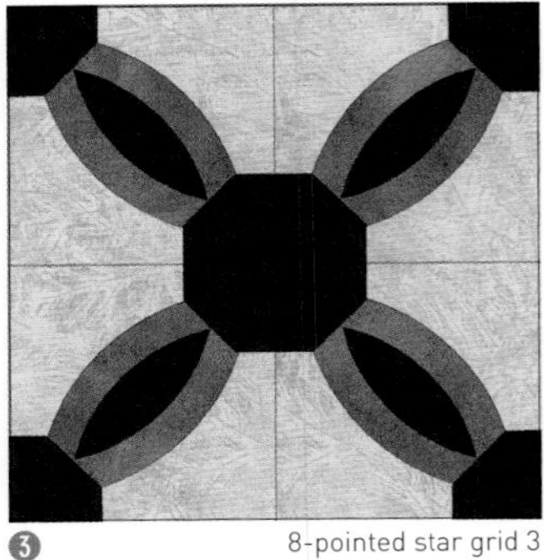

❸ 8-pointed star grid 3

❹ 8-pointed star grid 3

❺ 8-pointed star grid 3

❻ 8-pointed star grid 4

❼ 8-pointed star grid 1

❽ 8-pointed star grid 4

❾ 8-pointed star grid 4

❿ 8-pointed star grid 4

⓫ 8-pointed star grid 4

⓬ 8-pointed star grid 1

❶

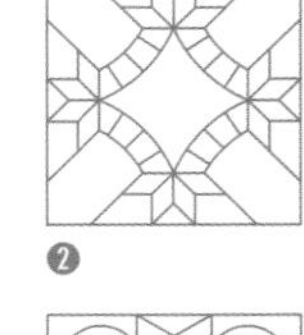

❷

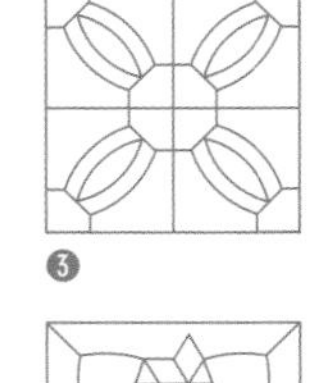

❸

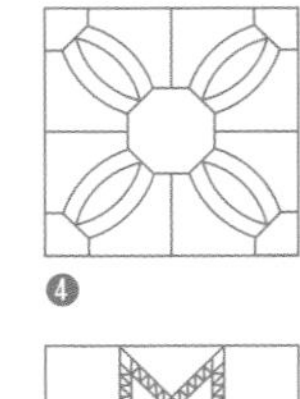

❹

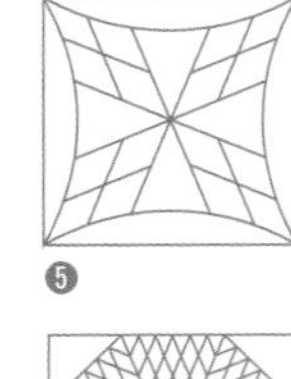

❺

❻

❼

❽

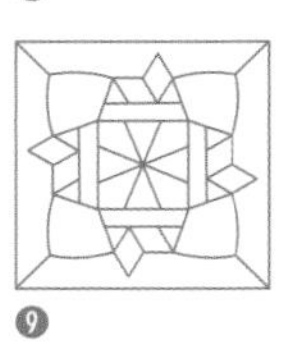

❾

❿

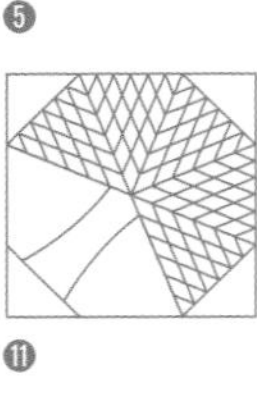

⓫

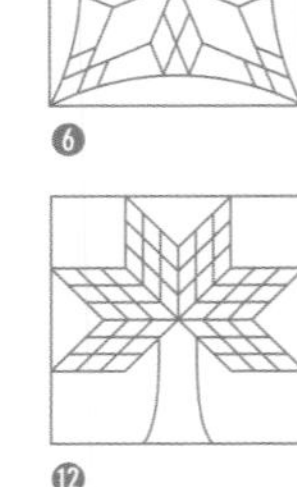

⓬

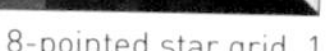

1 8-pointed star grid 1

2 8-pointed star grid 1

3 8-pointed star grid 1

1. **Modern Peony,** Nancy Cabot, *Chicago Tribune,* Apr 20, 1935.
2. **Paeony Block,** *Ladies Art Company,* 1897.
   Also known as:
   Peony Patch, Hall, 1935.
   Piney, Hall, 1935.
3. **Forbidden Fruit,** Ickis, 1949.
4. **Live Oak Tree,** Ickis, 1949.

4 8-pointed star grid 1

Trees Sampler, Jinny Beyer, 2004. This quilt was designed for the 2004 Quilter's Quest Shop Hop (see page 11). The blocks were made by participating shops and assembled by Carole Nicholas. The quilting was done by Leslie Sevigney.

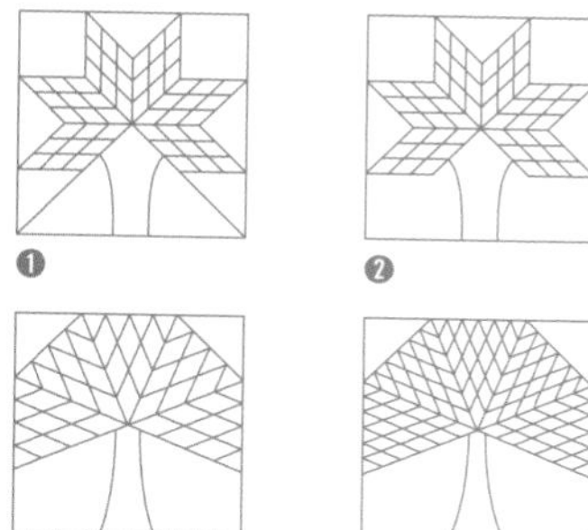

Quick Reference: Trees

After baskets, tree blocks seems to be the next most popular of quilt motifs. Of the 75 tree blocks that I have found, 24 of them have Pine Tree in their names. A pine tree block was the first one to inaugurate at least two newspaper columns, Kansas City Star and Nancy Cabot's column in *Chicago Tribune*. The blocks have been organized here according to similarities.

Lone Pine, Hilton Head Seminar design. **See 170-11.**

Tree of Life, *Chicago Tribune*. **See 152-12.**

Ohio Shade Tree, *Birmingham News*. **See 275-10.**

Tree of Life, *Cincinnati Enquirer*. **See 274-12.**

Southern Pine, *Detroit Free Press*. **See 190-1.**

Pine Tree, *Indianapolis Star*. **See 225-10.**

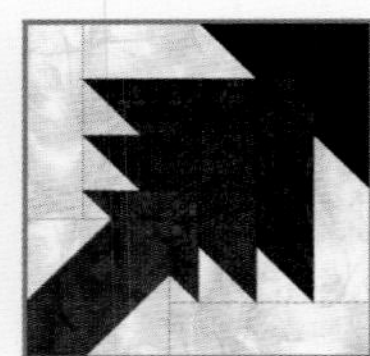
American Holly, Quilter's Quest design. **See 170-10.**

Pine Tree Quilt, *Indianapolis Star*. **See 104-7.**

Sycamore, Quilter's Quest design. **See 152-7.**

Dogwood, Quilter's Quest design. **See 122-9.**

Pine Tree, *Detroit Free Press*. **See 122-10.**

Norway Spruce, Quilter's Quest design. **See 119-11.**

White Pine, Quilter's Quest design. **See 152-8.**

Four Seasons, *RJR Patterns*. **See 261-1.**

Hemlock, *Jinny Beyer Studio design*. **See 268-5.**

Juniper, Quilter's Quest design. **See 152-9.**

Pine Tree, *The Detroit Free Press*. **See 330-3.**

Little Beech Tree, *Kansas City Star*. **See 331-12.**

Little Beech Tree, *Ladies Art Company*. **See 332-1.**

Beech Tree, *Chicago Tribune*. **See 314-11.**

Tree of Temptation, Hall. **See 232-5.**

Little Beech Tree, *Chicago Tribune*. **See 330-2.**

Field Cedar, Quilter's Quest design. **See 122-11.**

Redbud, Quilter's Quest design. **See 232-7.**

Copper Beech, Quilter's Quest design. **See 104-6.**

Patch Blossom, *Aunt Martha's Quilts*. **See 217-12.**

Pine Tree, *Aunt Martha's Patchwork Simplicity*. **See 208-6.**

Pine Tree, *Prairie Farmer*. **See 208-8.**

Pine Tree, *Illinois State Register*. **See 208-5.**

Pine Tree, *Grandmother Clark's Authentic Early American Quilts*, **See 208-7.**

Centennial Tree, *Practical Needlework*. **See 152-10.**

Tree of Paradise, Nancy Page, *Birmingham News*. **See 171-1.**

Pine Tree, *The Quilter's Album ....* **See 152-11.**

Tree of Paradise, Hall. **See 232-8.**

Red Maple, Quilter's Quest design. **See 119-12.**

Tree of Paradise, *The Dressmaking Book.* **See 232-9.**

Tree of Paradise, *Quilting.* **See 232-10.**

Tree of Heaven, *Birmingham News.* **See 225-11.**

Evergreen Tree, *Chicago Tribune.* **See 272-12.**

Christmas Tree, *Kansas City Star.* **See 170-12.**

Evergreen Tree, *Grandma Dexter New Applique and Patchwork Designs, Book 36b.* **See 120-1.**

Pine Tree, *Chicago Tribune.* **See 245-7.**

Pine Tree Quilt, *Cincinnati Enquirer.* **See 249-6.**

Tree of Life, *Mrs. Danner's Fourth Quilt Book.* **See 249-7.**

Pine Tree, The, Finley. **See 249-5.**

Pine Tree Design, *The Farmer's Wife Book of Quilts.* **See 208-10.**

Pine Tree, *Kansas City Star.* **See 208-9.**

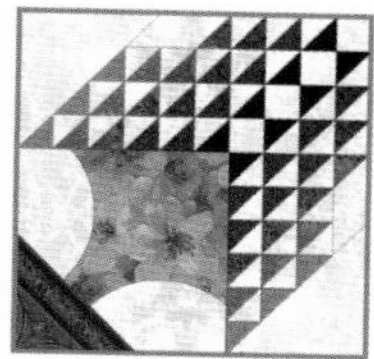
Tree of Paradise, *Prize Winning Designs.* **See 322-2.**

Tree of Paradise, *Ladies Art Company.* **See 220-2.**

Tree of Life, Ickis. **See 249-8.**

Pine Tree, *Chicago Tribune.* **See 255-2.**

Christmas Tree, Hall. **See 255-3.**

Pine Tree, *Birmingham News.* **See 218-2.**

Tree of Paradise, Webster. **See 218-1.**

Cone Tree, *Chicago Tribune.* **See 232-11.**

Tree of Temptation, *Grandmother Clark's Patchwork Designs, Book 22.* **See 220-12.**

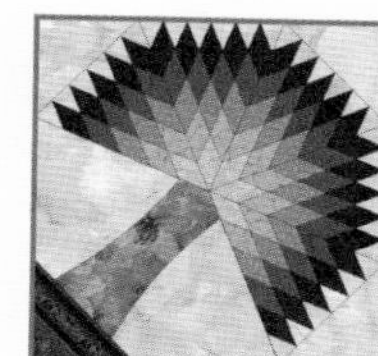
Live Oak Tree, *Ladies Art Company.* **See 346-11.**

Star Magnolia, Quilter's Quest design. **See 307-2.**

Lozenge Tree, *Chicago Tribune.* **See 307-12.**

Forbidden Fruit Tree, Hall. **See 307-13.**

Forbidden Fruit Tree, *Chicago Tribune.* **See 307-10.**

Forbidden Fruit Tree, *Ladies Art Company.* **See 307-11.**

Modern Peony, *Chicago Tribune.* **See 347-1.**

Weeping Willow, *Quilt Booklet No. 1, Prairie Farmer.* **See 346-12.**

Paeony Block, *Ladies Art Company.* **See 347-2.**

Forbidden Fruit, Ickis. **See 347-3.**

Live Oak Tree, Ickis. **See 347-4.**

Tree of Paradise, *The Farm Journal Quilt Patterns.* **See 439-5.**

Tree of Paradise, *Chicago Tribune.* **See 210-5.**

Sea Pine, Hilton Head Seminar design. **See 110-11.**

Tiny Pine, *Birmingham News.* **See 179-2.**

Balsam Fir, *Chicago Tribune.* **See 179-3.**

Pine Tree, *Ladies Art Company.* **See 179-4.**

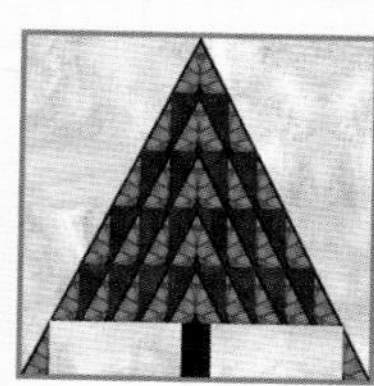
Pine Tree, *Chicago Tribune.* **See 179-5.**

Tall Pine Tree, Hall. **See 410-6.**

Distinct Pattern Category
(with Curved Elements)

Includes ● Drunkard's Path, ● Reel, ● Strawberry, ● Tulip, ● Flower, ● Wheel, ● Dresden Plate, ● Compass, ● Crossroads, ● Fan, and ● Hearts

❶ **Snowball,** Laura Wheeler, *Cincinnati Enquirer,* Aug 4, 1933. Also known as:
- **Rob Peter to Pay Paul,** Hall, 1935.

❷ **Polka Dot,** Clara Stone, *Practical Needlework,* ca. 1906.

❸ **Base Ball,** *Ladies Art Company,* 1897. Also known as:
- **Baseball,** ca. 1935, per Havig.
- **Bows and Arrows,** Nancy Cabot, *Chicago Tribune,* Mar 6, 1934.
- **Circle Design,** *Grandmother's Patchwork Quilt Designs, Book 20,* 1931.
- **Double Snowball,** Laura Wheeler, unidentified newspaper clipping, date unknown.
- **Marble Quilt,** *Kansas City Star,* Jul 18, 1936.
- **The Marble Quilt,** *Kansas City Star,* Dec 1, 1934.
- **Robbing Peter to Pay Paul,** Clara Stone, *Practical Needlework,* ca. 1906.
- **Steeple Chase,** Finley, 1929.
- **Steeplechase,** Nancy Cabot, *Chicago Tribune,* Mar 6, 1934.

❹ **Snowball,** Alice Brooks, *Detroit Free Press,* Nov 7, 1933.
This is the first Alice Brooks design to appear in *Detroit Free Press.* "It is no longer necessary to gaze with longing eyes on a colonial quilt that some fortunate friend has inherited. The American needlewoman today is producing quilts as beautiful, and ones that will be as greatly prized as those of long ago. Outstanding among designs popular for generations is the Snowball. Simple to do, it is made of two contrasting materials, and has that beauty that is the result of good design. The large and small snowballs give a touch of variety that is most pleasing." *Detroit Free Press,* Nov 7, 1933

❺ **Snow Ball,** *Ladies Art Company,* 1897.

❻ **Snowball,** Nancy Cabot, *Chicago Tribune,* Feb 2, 1933. Also known as:
- **Mill Wheel,** Ickis, 1949.
- **Robbing Peter to Pay Paul,** Hall, 1935.

❼ **The Mill Wheel,** Ruby McKim, *Kansas City Star,* Nov 16, 1929. Also known as:
- **Mill Wheel,** Hall, 1935.
- **Millwheel,** Gutcheon, *The Perfect Patchwork Primer,* 1973.

❽ **The Oklahoma Wonder,** *Kansas City Star,* Jul 18, 1956.

❾ **Boston Puzzle,** *Ladies Art Company,* 1897. Also known as:
- **Baseball,** Nancy Page, *Nashville Banner,* Sep 27, 1932.
- **Circle Design,** *Grandmother's Patchwork Quilt Designs, Book 20,* 1931.
- **Polka Dots,** Nancy Page, *Nashville Banner,* Sep 27, 1932.

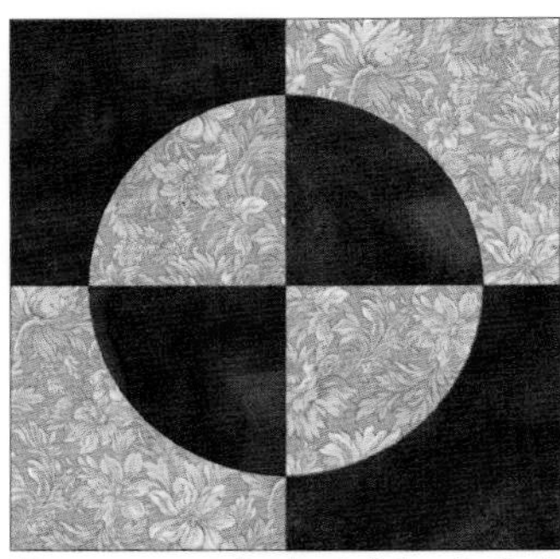

❶ Drunkard's Path on 7 x 7 grid

❷ Drunkard's Path on 18 x 18 grid

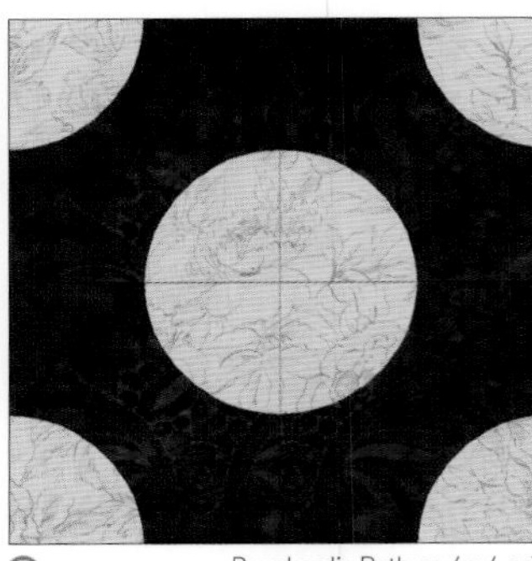
❸ Drunkard's Path on 4 x 4 grid

❹ Drunkard's Path on 20 x 20 grid

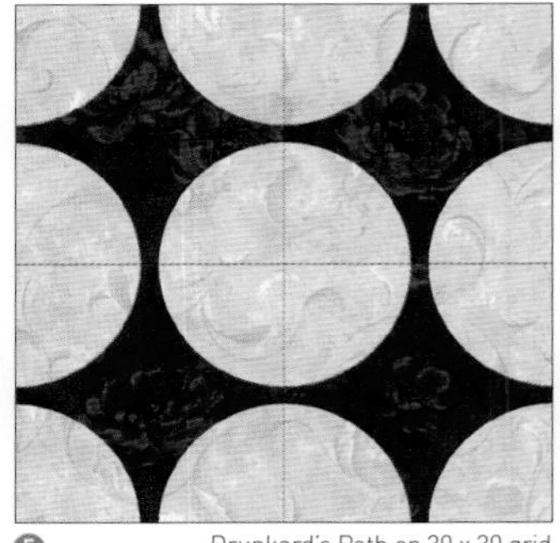
❺ Drunkard's Path on 30 x 30 grid

❻ Drunkard's Path on 14 x 14 grid

❼ Drunkard's Path on 16 x 16 grid

❽ Drunkard's Path on 8 x 8 grid

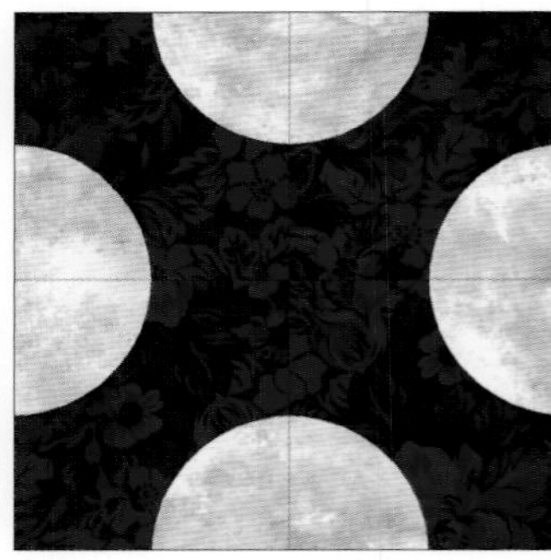
❾ Drunkard's Path on 4 x 4 grid

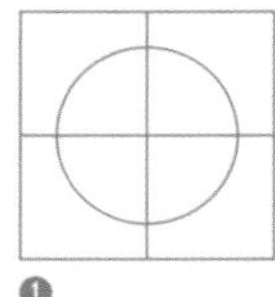
❶

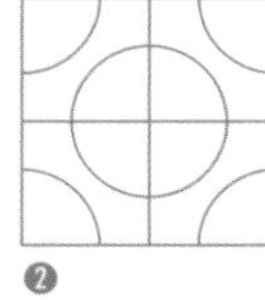
❷

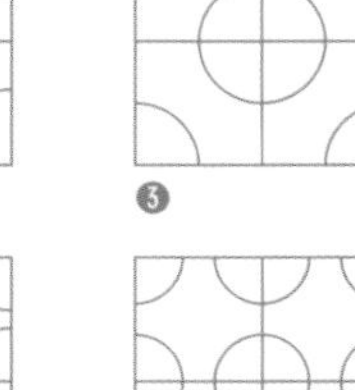
❸

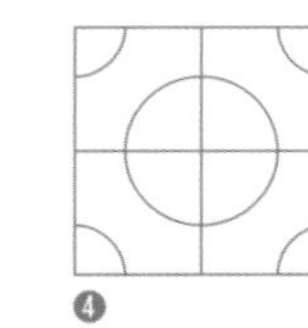
❹

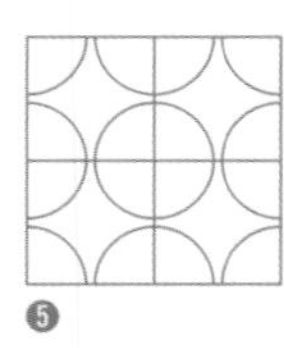
❺

❻

❼

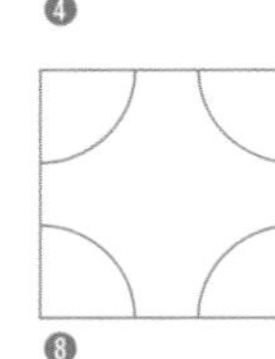
❽

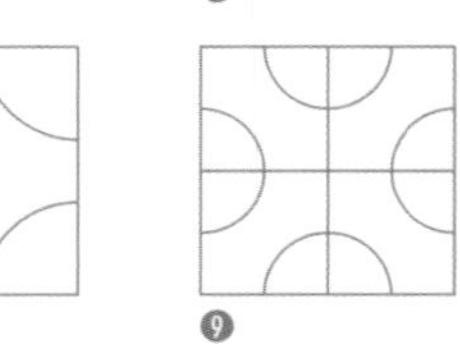
❾

❶ Drunkard's Path on 8 x 8 grid

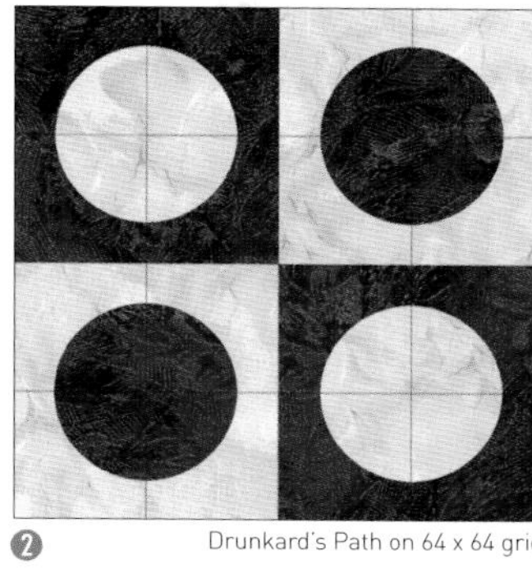

❷ Drunkard's Path on 64 x 64 grid

❸ Drunkard's Path on 4 x 4 grid

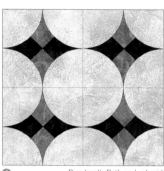

❹ Drunkard's Path on 4 x 4 grid

❺ Drunkard's Path on 4 x 4 grid

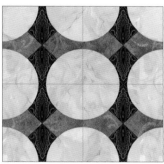

❻ Drunkard's Path on 4 x 4 grid

❼ Drunkard's Path on 22 x 22 grid

❽ Drunkard's Path on 64 x 64 grid

❾ Drunkard's Path on 16 x 16 grid

❿ Drunkard's Path on 24 x 24 grid

⓫ Drunkard's Path on 7 x 7 grid

⓬ Drunkard's Path on 16 x 16 grid

❶ **Indiana Puzzle,** *Quilt Booklet No. 1,* ca. 1931.

❷ **Polka Dots,** Aunt Martha series: *Easy Quilts,* ca. 1958. Also known as:
  Mill Wheel, Martens, 1970.

❸ **Give and Take,** Clara Stone, *Practical Needlework,* ca. 1906.

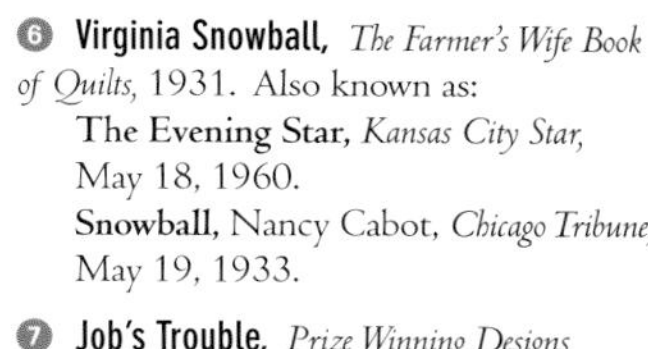

❹ **The Jinx Star,** *Kansas City Star,* Apr 14, 1934.

❺ **Washington Snowball,** Clara Stone, *Practical Needlework,* ca. 1906.

❻ **Virginia Snowball,** *The Farmer's Wife Book of Quilts,* 1931. Also known as:
  The Evening Star, *Kansas City Star,* May 18, 1960.
  Snowball, Nancy Cabot, *Chicago Tribune,* May 19, 1933.

❼ **Job's Trouble,** *Prize Winning Designs,* ca. 1931.

❽ **Cleopatra's Puzzle,** Nancy Cabot, *Chicago Tribune,* Jun 5, 1933.

❾ **King Tut's Crown,** *Quilt Booklet No. 1,* ca. 1931.

❿ **Mohawk Trail,** Nancy Cabot, *Chicago Tribune,* Aug 9, 1933. Also known as:
  Path of Fans, Nancy Cabot, *Chicago Tribune,* Aug 26, 1937.

⓫ **Queen's Crown,** *Ladies Art Company,* 1922. See 337-8 and 341-2.

⓬ **Around the World,** Hall, 1935.

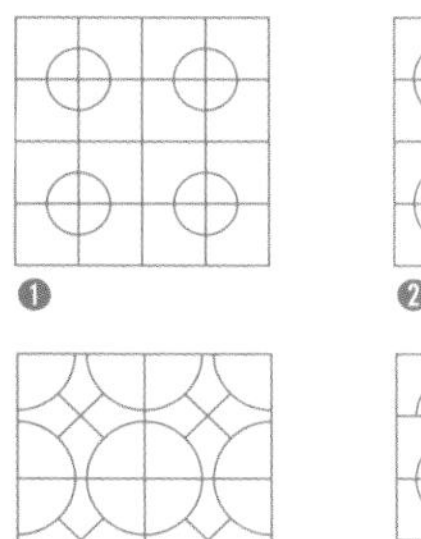

❶

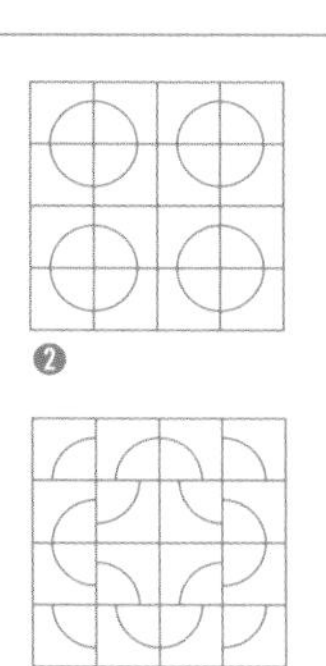

❷

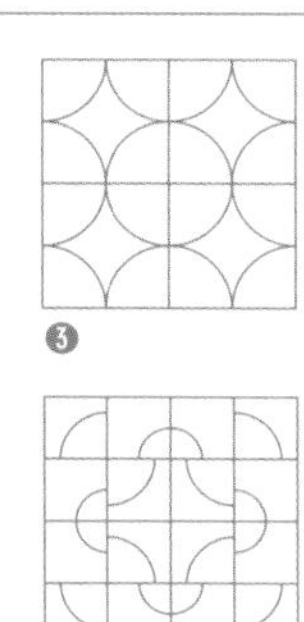

❸

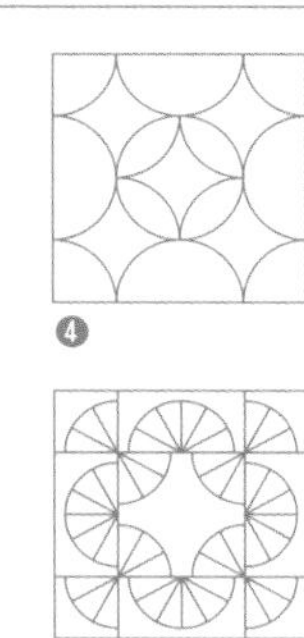

❹

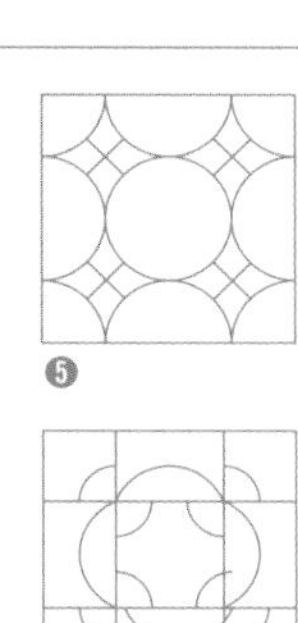

❺

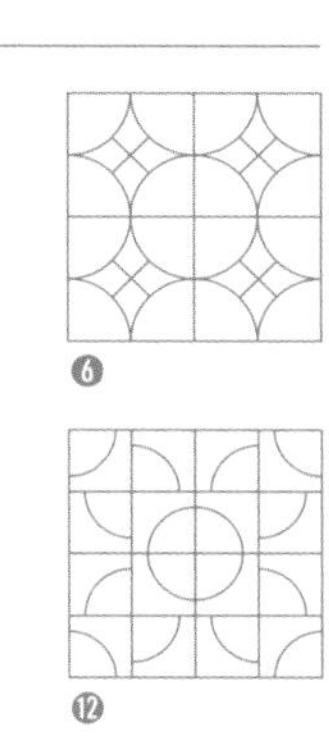

❻

❼ ❽ ❾ ❿ ⓫ ⓬

❶ **Love Ring,** Hall, 1935. Also known as:
- **The Jig Saw Puzzle,** *Kansas City Star,* Aug 14, 1940.
- **Nonesuch,** Hall, 1935.

❷ **Around the World,** Holstein, 1973.

❸ **Chainlinks,** Aunt Martha series: *Easy Quilts,* ca. 1958.

❹ **Aunt Polly's Puzzle,** Nancy Cabot, *Chicago Tribune,* Feb 9, 1936.

❺ **Solomon's Puzzle,** Nancy Cabot, *Chicago Tribune,* May 24, 1933.

❻ **Drunkard's Path,** Finley, 1929. Also known as:
- **Country Husband,** Hall, 1935.
- **Robbing Peter to Pay Paul,** Finley, 1929.
- **Rocky Road to California,** Hall, 1935.
- **Rocky Road to Dublin,** Hall, 1935.

❼ **Drunkard's Path,** *Ladies Art Company,* 1897. Also known as:
- **Rocky Road to Dublin,** Martens, 1970.

❽ **Drunkard's Trail,** Nancy Cabot, *Chicago Tribune,* Feb 10, 1933. Also known as:
- **Drunkard's Path,** Aunt Martha series: *Easy Quilts,* ca. 1958.
- **Road to California,** Aunt Martha series: *Easy Quilts,* ca. 1958.

❾ **Drunkard's Trail,** *The Dressmaking Book,* 1929. Also known as:
- **Old Maid's Puzzle,** *Rural New Yorker,* ca. 1932.
- **Rocky Road to Dublin,** *Grandmother Clark's Patchwork Quilts, Book No.* 19, 1932.
- **Solomon's Puzzle,** Eveline Foland, *Kansas City Star,* Apr 23, 1932.
- **Wonder of the World,** *Capper's Weekly,* ca. 1960.

❿ **Solomon Puzzle,** Nancy Cabot, *Chicago Tribune,* Jan 7, 1934. Also known as:
- **Old Maid's Puzzle,** *Kansas City Star,* Jun 23, 1937.

⓫ **Way of the World,** ca. 1938, per Havig.

⓬ **Drunkard's Path,** Nancy Page, *Birmingham News,* Apr 28, 1936.

❶ Drunkard's Path on 18 x 18 grid

❷ Drunkard's Path on 36 x 36 grid

❸ Drunkard's Path on 96 x 96 grid

❹ Drunkard's Path on 24 x 24 grid

❺ Drunkard's Path on 16 x 16 grid

❻ Drunkard's Path on 28 x 28 grid

❼ Drunkard's Path on 20 x 20 grid

❽ Drunkard's Path on 16 x 16 grid

❾ Drunkard's Path on 12 x 12 grid

❿ Drunkard's Path on 32 x 32 grid

⓫ Drunkard's Path on 16 x 16 grid

⓬ Drunkard's Path on 12 x 12 grid

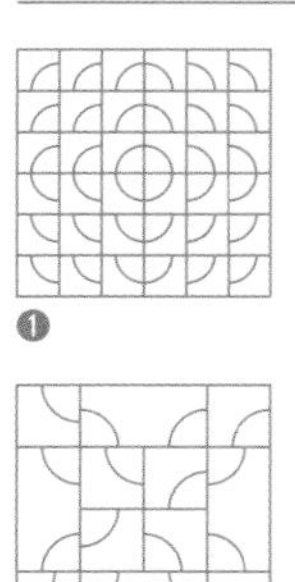
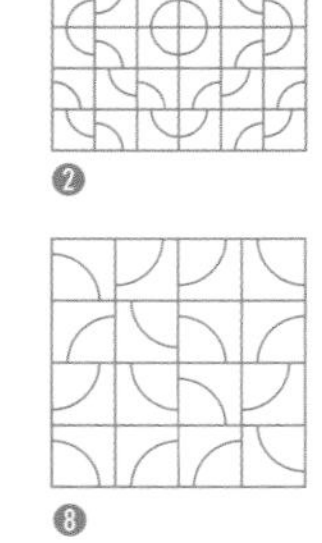
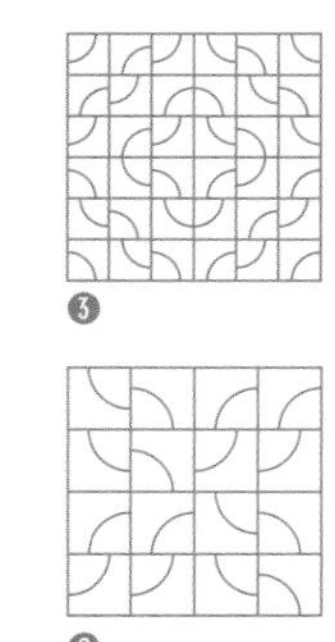
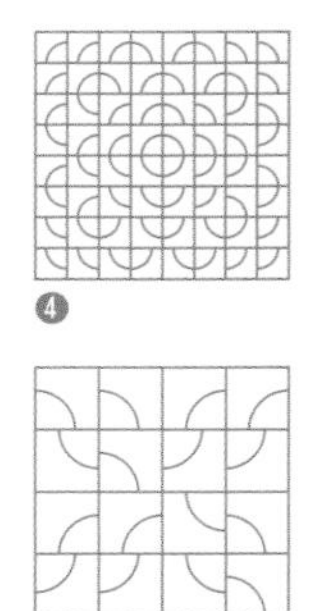
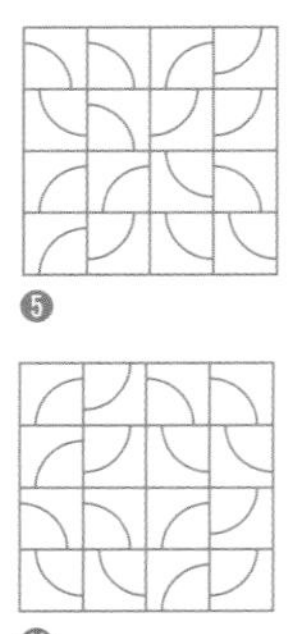
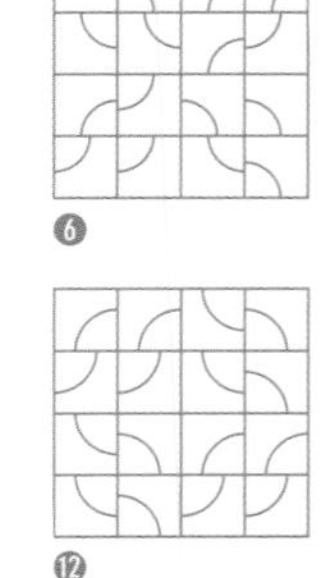

❶ ❷ ❸ ❹ ❺ ❻

❼ ❽ ❾ ❿ ⓫ ⓬

❶ Drunkard's Path on 12 x 12 grid

❷ Drunkard's Path on 16 x 16 grid

❸ Drunkard's Path on 16 x 16 grid

❹ Drunkard's Path on 20 x 20 grid

❺ Drunkard's Path on 12 x 12 grid

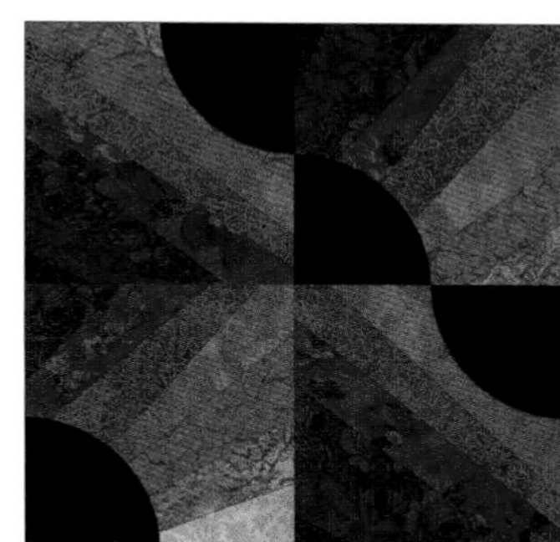

❻ Drunkard's Path on 4 x 4 grid

❼ Drunkard's Path on 64 x 64 grid

❽ Drunkard's Path on 64 x 64 grid

❾ Drunkard's Path on 21 x 21 grid

❿ Drunkard's Path on 56 x 56 grid

⓫ Drunkard's Path on 32 x 32 grid

⓬ Drunkard's Path on 36 x 36 grid

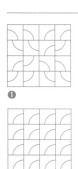

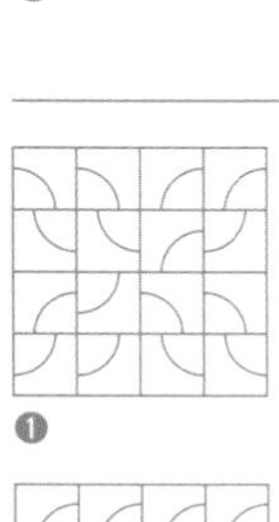

❶

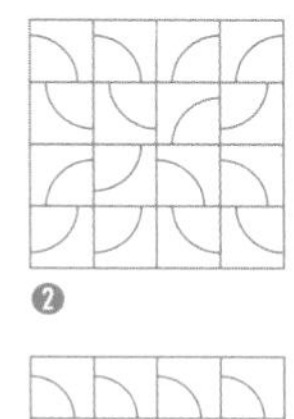

❷

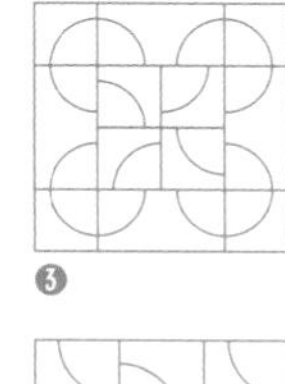

❸

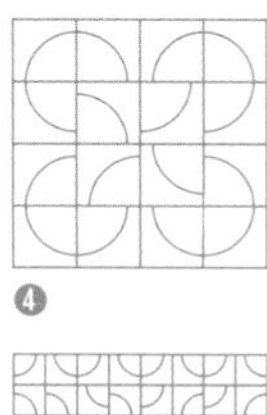

❹

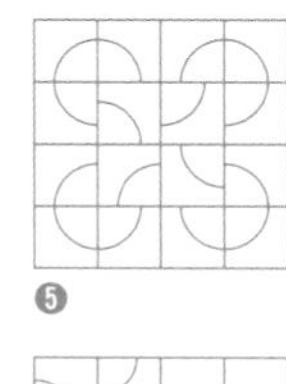

❺

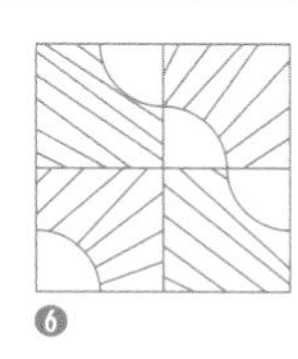

❻

❼

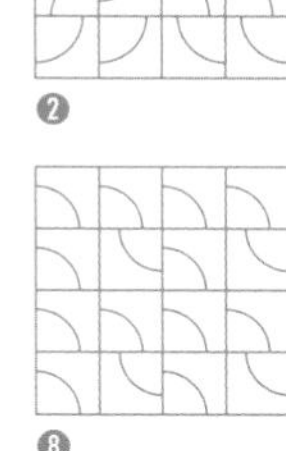

❽

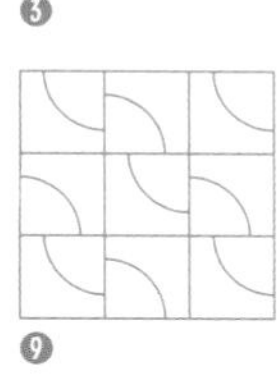

❾

❿

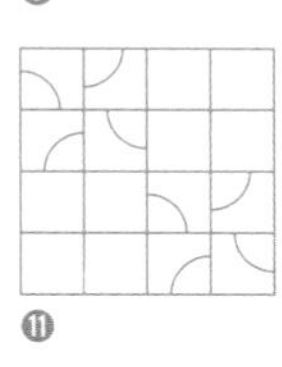

⓫

⓬

❶ **Crooked Path,** Nancy Page, *Birmingham News*, Jun 26, 1934.

❷ **Drunkard's Path,** Laura Wheeler, *Cincinnati Enquirer*, Jul 14, 1933. Also known as:

Wonder of the World, Alice Brooks, *Detroit Free Press*, Nov 16, 1934.

"The drunkard's path has always been pictured as most thorny and one to be avoided. It is rather astonishing then that the old-time quiltmaker chose to call something so choice as this lovely pattern, the Drunkard's Path. It does indeed shift from side to side, but, in doing this achieves a most decorative design." Laura Wheeler, *Cincinnati Enquirer*, Jul 14, 1933

❸ **Fool's Puzzle,** *Ladies Art Company*, 1897. Also known as:

Wonder of the World, Hall, 1935.

"This design was first quilted in Ohio about 1850, and is reminiscent of 'The Drunkard's Trail,' 'Solomon's Puzzle,' and 'Robbing Peter to Pay Paul.' Pieced with a dark center and light background, 'Fool's Puzzle' makes one of quiltdom's most striking coverlets." Nancy Cabot, *Chicago Tribune*, Aug 26, 1934

❹ **Robbing Peter to Pay Paul,** Nancy Page, *Birmingham News*, Aug 18, 1942. Also known as:

Canadian Puzzle, Nancy Page, *Birmingham News*, Aug 18, 1942.

"Well, here I am with that old-time pattern which has almost as many names as makers. It uses just two pieces. One of them looks as if it had been bitten or cut from the other. That is why the design is sometimes called 'Robbing Peter to Pay Paul.' Nancy Page, *Birmingham News*, Aug 18, 1942

❺ **Fool's Puzzle,** Hall, 1935.

"Here I am back with that quilt pattern which has about as many names as a centipede has legs. It seems quite incredible that a pattern which uses just two shapes for pieces can be put together in so many different ways." Nancy Page, *Birmingham News*, Jun 17, 1941

❻ **String Quilt in a Sea Shell Motif,** *Kansas City Star*, Sep 26, 1956.

"This design is made by sewing strips of fabric together and then cutting the pieces from the sewn strips." *Kansas City Star*, Sep 26, 1965

❼ **Diagonal Stripes,** Aunt Martha series: *Easy Quilts*, ca. 1958.

❽ **Vine of Friendship,** Hall, 1935.

❾ **Chain Quilt,** *Kansas City Star*, Feb 25, 1942.

❿ **Quilter's Delight,** Nancy Cabot, *Chicago Tribune*, Apr 12, 1936.

"One glance at this design, 'Quilter's Delight,' and one says: 'Ah, I know, it's 'Drunkard's Trail' or 'Solomon's Puzzle' with printed and plain materials.' It is just that, with the original crazy quilt furnishing the inspiration. Careful study and inspection will reveal that each block in the quilt consists of a nine patch block with a frame around it. This allows much ingenuity for the quilter because all may be different. The border of half circles around the individual squares forms an interesting frame for each nine patch." Nancy Cabot, *Chicago Tribune*, Apr 12, 1936

⓫ **Indian Patch,** Martens, 1970.

⓬ **Wonder of the World,** Nancy Cabot, *Chicago Tribune*, Nov 12, 1934.

❶ **World's Wonder,** Nancy Cabot, *Chicago Tribune,* Sep 22, 1936. Also known as:
Drunkard's Path, Martens, 1970.
Rocky Road, Martens, 1970.

❷ **Wonder of the World,** *Ladies Art Company,* 1897.

❸ **Snowball,** Aunt Martha series: *The Quilt Fair Comes to You,* ca. 1933.

❹ **Mushrooms,** Martens, 1970.

❺ **Falling Timber,** Hall, 1935.

❻ **Nautilus,** Jinny Beyer, Hilton Head Seminar design, 2004.

❼ **The Road Home,** Nancy Cabot, *Chicago Tribune,* Sep 25, 1937.

❽ **Drunkard's Patchwork,** *Ladies Art Company,* 1897.

❾ **Drunkard's Patchwork,** Nancy Cabot, *Chicago Tribune,* Apr 26, 1935.

❿ **Poplar Leaf,** ca. 1938, per Havig.

⓫ **The Texas Pointer,** *Kansas City Star,* Apr 28, 1934.

⓬ **Reel,** Nancy Cabot, *Chicago Tribune,* May 11, 1933.

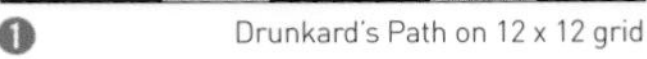

❶ Drunkard's Path on 12 x 12 grid

❷ Drunkard's Path on 48 x 48 grid

❸ Drunkard's Path on 24 x 24 grid

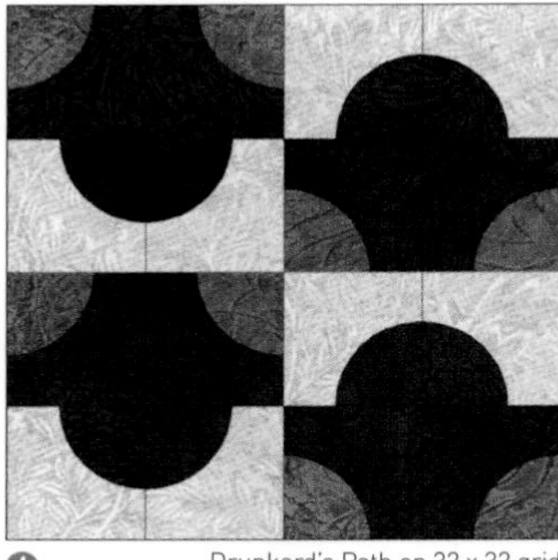

❹ Drunkard's Path on 32 x 32 grid

❺ Drunkard's Path on 16 x 16 grid

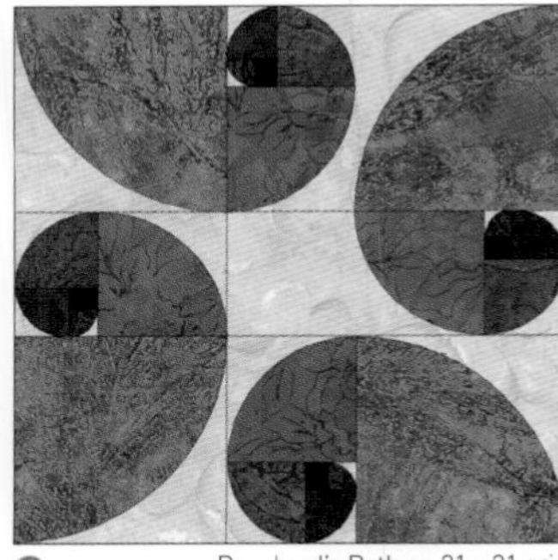

❻ Drunkard's Path on 21 x 21 grid

❼ Drunkard's Path on 12 x 12 grid

❽ Drunkard's Path on 12 x 12 grid

❾ Drunkard's Path on 12 x 12 grid

❿ Reel on 18 x 18 grid

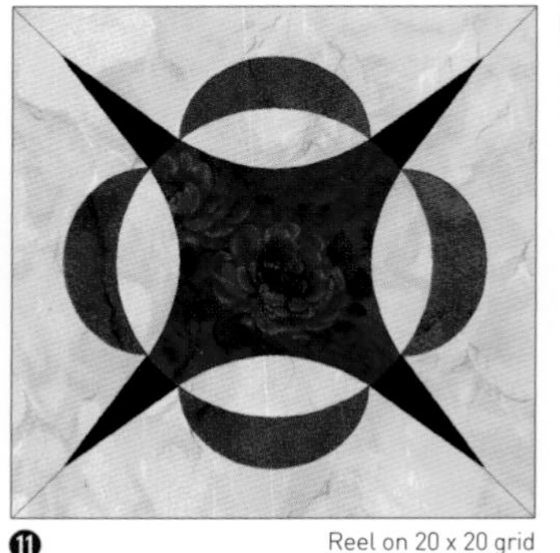

⓫ Reel on 20 x 20 grid

⓬ Reel on 4 x 4 grid

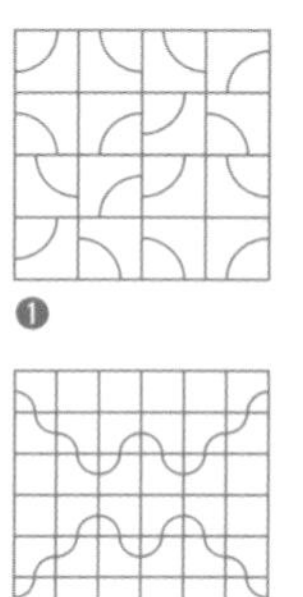
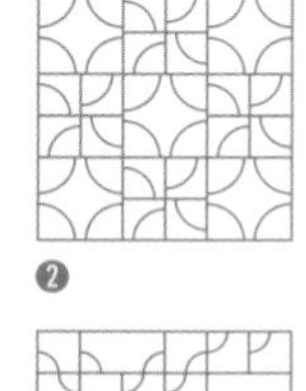
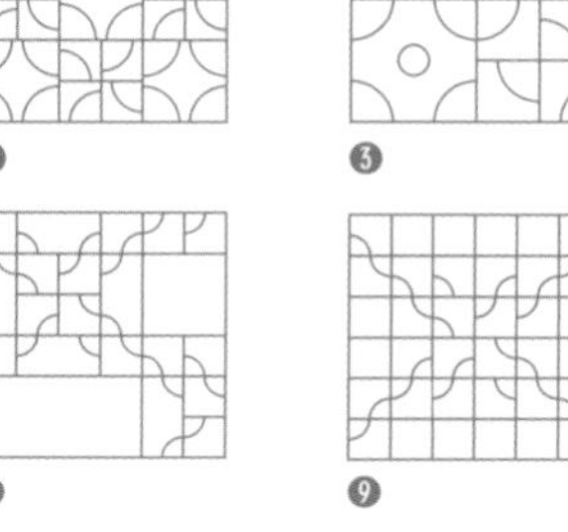
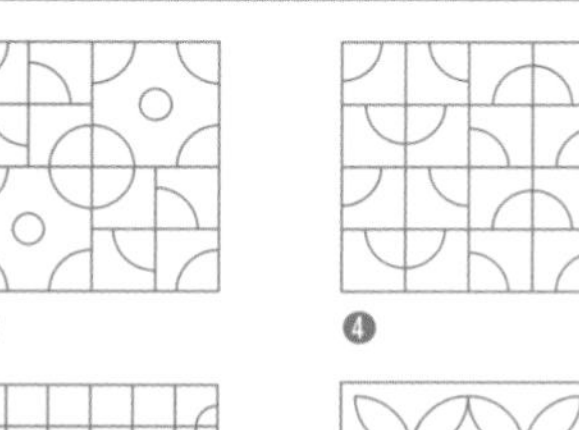
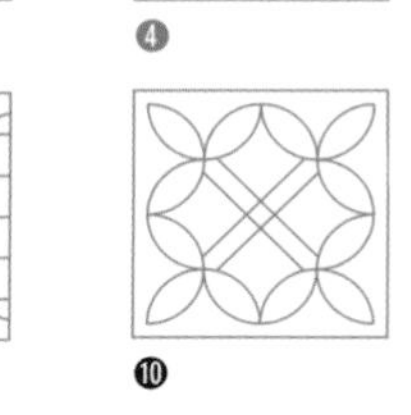
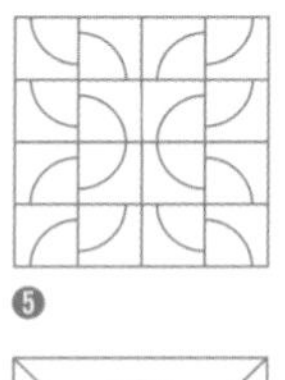
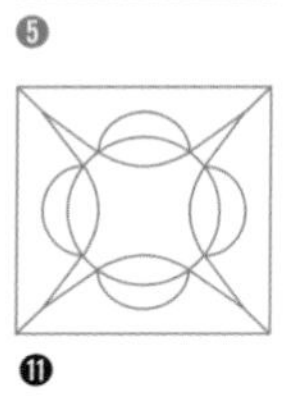
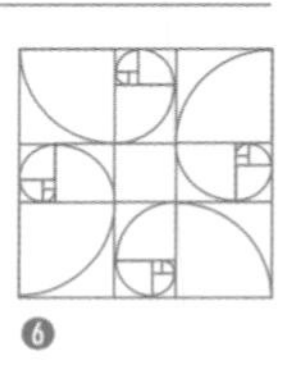

❶ ❷ ❸ ❹ ❺ ❻

❼ ❽ ❾ ❿ ⓫ ⓬

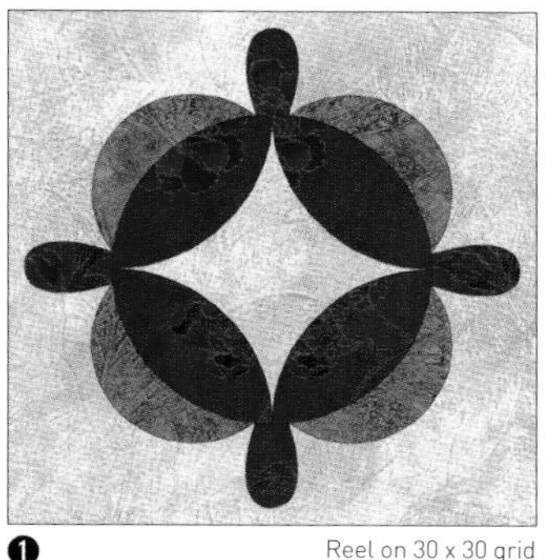

1 Reel on 30 x 30 grid

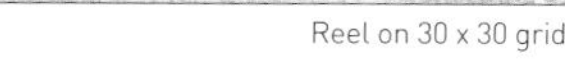

2 Reel on 14 x 14 grid

3 Reel on 4 x 4 grid

4 Strawberry on 8-pointed star grid 4

5 Strawberry on 8-pointed star grid 1

6 Strawberry on 7 x 7 grid

7 Strawberry on 27 x 27 grid

8 Strawberry on 8-pointed star grid 1

9 Strawberry on 8-pointed star grid 1

10 Strawberry on 8-pointed star grid 1

11 Strawberry on 8-pointed star grid 1

12 Strawberry on 18 x 18 grid

1 **Harvest Moon,** Home Art Studios, *Cincinnati Enquirer,* Feb 3, 1933.

2 **Hickory Leaf,** *Ladies Art Company,* 1897. Also known as:
  The Reel, Hall, 1935.

3 **Circle and Square,** *Kansas City Star,* Nov 21, 1936. Also known as:
  The Oil Fields of Oklahoma, *Kansas City Star,* Aug 7, 1957.

4 **The Gardener's Prize,** Aunt Martha series: *Favorite Quilts,* ca. 1953.

5 **Rose Album,** Ruby McKim, *Kansas City Star,* Jul 19, 1930.

6 **Nelly Bly,** *Farm Journal and Farmers Wife,* ca. 1941.

7 **The Rising Sun,** *Kansas City Star,* Feb 1, 1956.

8 **Rose Album,** *Ladies Art Company,* 1897. Also known as:
  California Rose, Nancy Cabot, *Chicago Tribune,* Jun 26, 1933.
  Full Blown Tulip, Hall, 1935.

9 **California Rose,** *Ladies Art Company,* 1928. Also known as:
  Rose Album, Nancy Cabot, *Chicago Tribune,* Jul 11, 1935.
  Strawberry, Aunt Martha series: *The Quilt Fair Comes to You,* ca. 1933.

10 **The Crown of Thorns,** *Kansas City Star,* Nov 1, 1939.

11 **King David's Crown,** Clara Stone, *Practical Needlework,* ca. 1906.

12 **Chinese Star,** Hall, 1935.

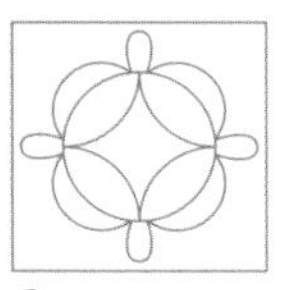

1

2

3

4

5

6

7

8

9

10

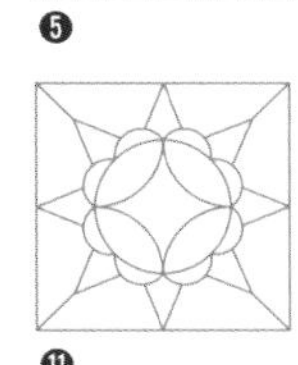

11

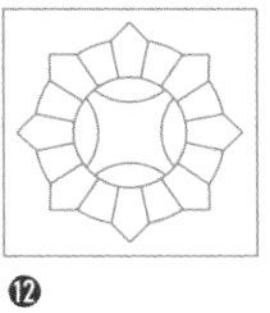

12

1 Grecian Star, *Grandmother's Patchwork Quilt Designs, Book 20,* 1931. Also known as:
- **Strawberry Patch,** *Grandmother's Patchwork Quilt Designs, Book 20,* 1931.

2 The Sunflower, *Ladies Art Company,* 1897. Also known as:
- **Chinese Star,** *Virginia Snow Studio Art Needlework Creations,* 1932.

3 Caesar's Crown, Hall, 1935.

4 Friendship Ring, Laura Wheeler, *Cincinnati Enquirer,* Jul 6, 1933.
"The Friendship Ring is an old-time favorite that enjoys great popularity today. It is made of scraps of material; there are old quilts in which each block was made of different scraps, making a most attractive quilt, if the pieces used in each block were harmonious. In this way, the pattern affords an excellent opportunity for using up small pieces of material or for the popular Friendship quilt, devoting each block to the materials given by one friend." Laura Wheeler, *Cincinnati Enquirer,* Jul 6, 1933

5 Kentucky Beauty, Hall, 1935. Also known as:
- **Strawberrie,** Hall, 1935.

6 The Strawberry, Ruby McKim, *Kansas City Star,* Dec 7, 1929. Also known as:
- **Full Blown Tulip,** *Grandmother Clark's Patchwork Quilts, Book No. 19,* 1932.
- **Pilot's Wheel,** Eveline Foland, *Kansas City Star,* Dec 17, 1932.

7 Strawberry, *Ladies Art Company,* 1897.

8 Oriental Star, Hall, 1935.

9 Oriental Star, *Grandma Dexter Appliqué and Patchwork Designs, Book 36a,* ca. 1932.

10 Full Blown Tulip, *Grandmother Clark's Patchwork Quilts, Book No.* 19, 1932. Also known as:
- **Strawberry,** *Grandmother Clark's Patchwork Quilts, Book No.* 19, 1932.

11 Stars and Stirrups, Nancy Cabot, *Chicago Tribune,* May 6, 1937.

12 Queen Anne's Crown, Nancy Cabot, *Chicago Tribune,* Feb 3, 1937.
"'Crown' quilt patterns have been named for people as ancient as Julius Caesar, 'Queen Anne's Crown,' illustrated today, and another block, 'Victoria's Crown,' are well known patterns, but hardly worthy of the antique rating of a design such as 'Caesar's Crown.' Despite the comparative youth of the pattern, which first was made in 1878, it has all the grace and charm of the woman for whom it was named." Laura Wheeler, *Cincinnati Enquirer,* Jul 6, 1933

1 Strawberry on 18 x 18 grid

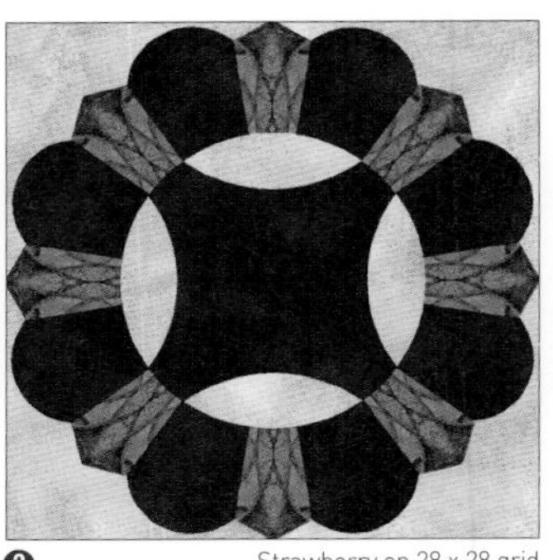

2 Strawberry on 28 x 28 grid

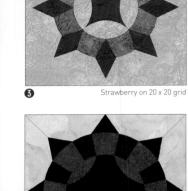

3 Strawberry on 20 x 20 grid

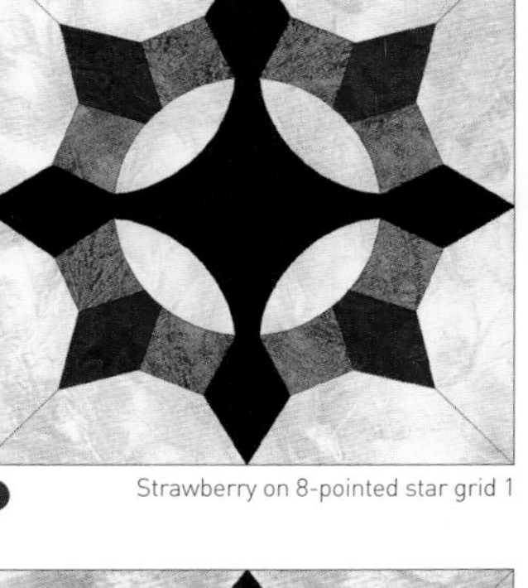

4 Strawberry on 8-pointed star grid 1

5 Strawberry on 15 x 15 grid

6 Strawberry on 8-pointed star grid 1

7 Strawberry on 8 x 8 grid

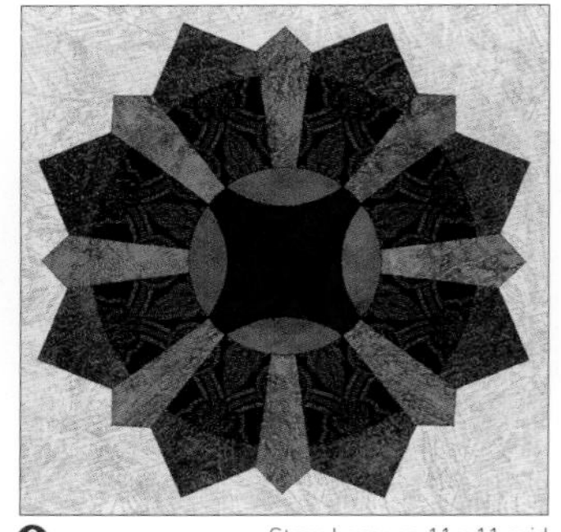

8 Strawberry on 11 x 11 grid

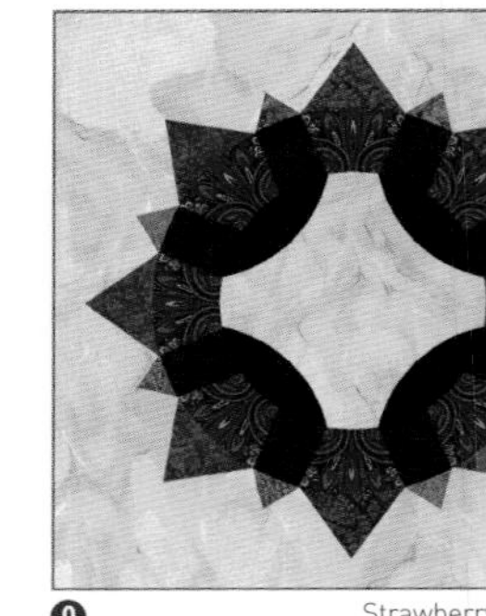

9 Strawberry on 9 x 9 grid

10 Strawberry on 18 x 18 grid

11 Strawberry on 48 x 48 grid

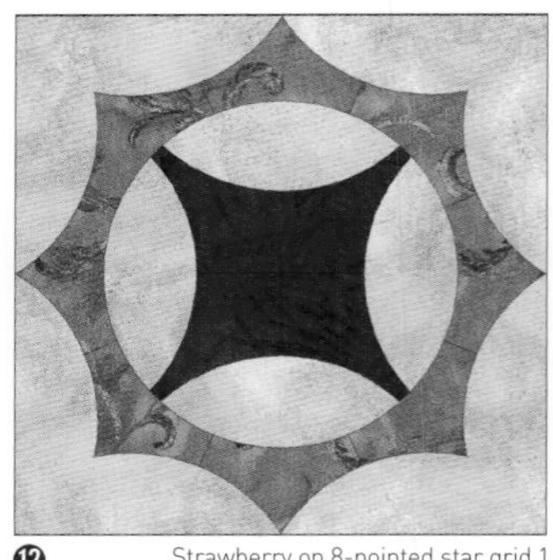

12 Strawberry on 8-pointed star grid 1

1
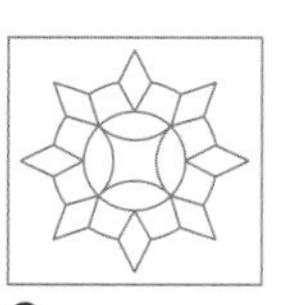
2
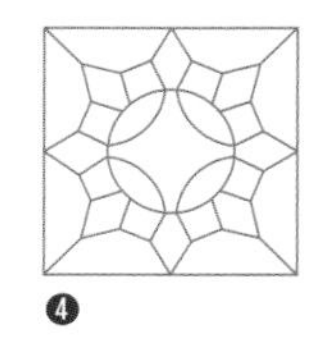
3
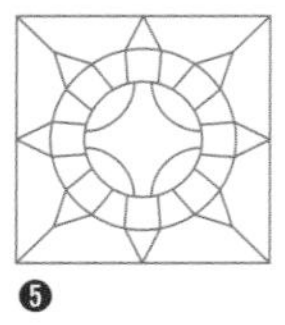
4

5
6

7
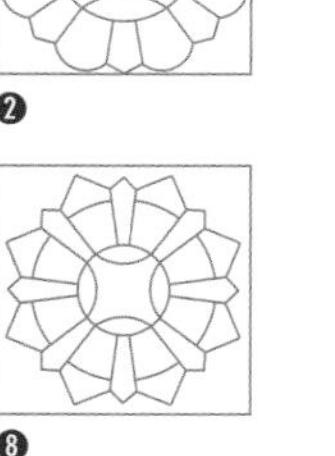
8
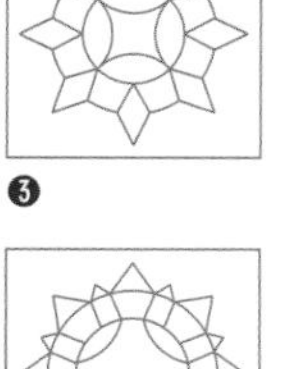
9
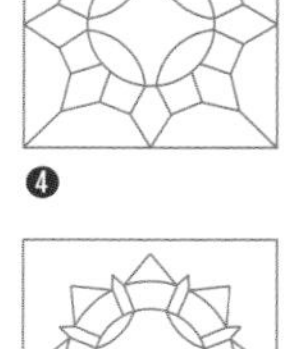
10
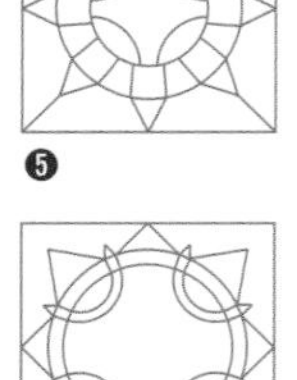

11

12

1 Strawberry on 32 x 32 grid

2 Strawberry on 24 x 24 grid

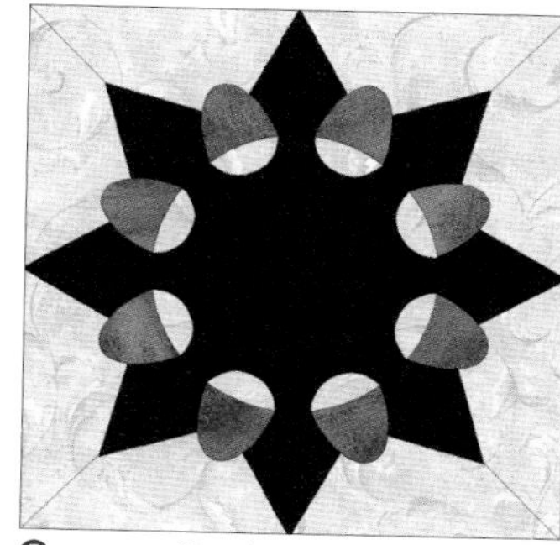

3 Strawberry on 8-pointed star grid 1

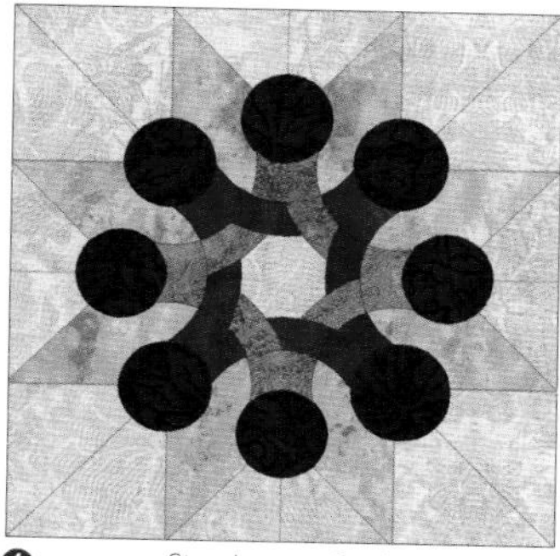

4 Strawberry on 8-pointed star grid 1

5 Tulip on 10 x 10 grid

6 Tulip on 22 x 22 grid

7 Tulip on 36 x 36 grid

8 Tulip on 8 x 8 grid

9 Tulip on 8 x 8 grid

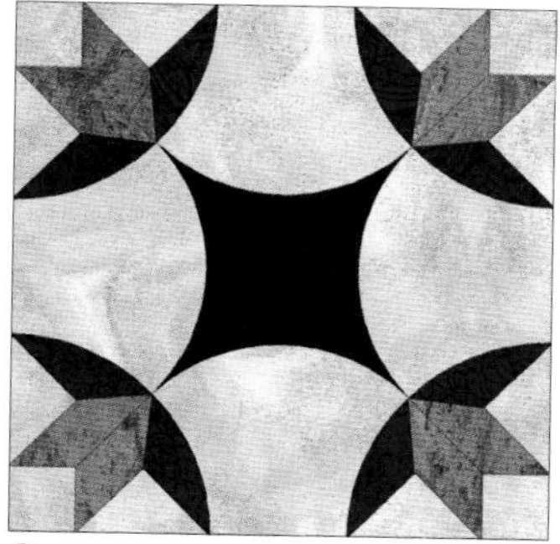

10 Tulip on 8 x 8 grid

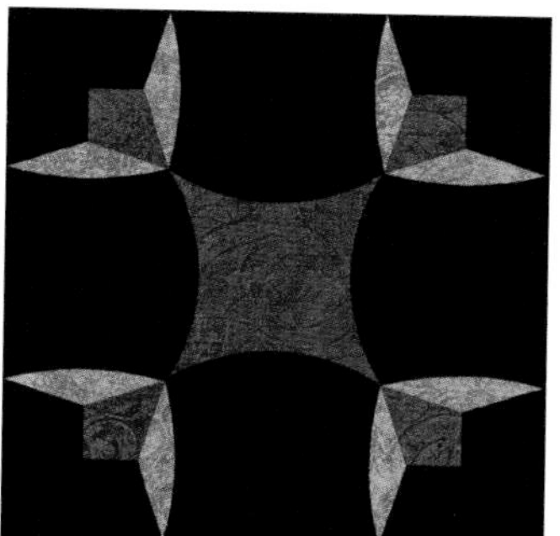

11 Tulip on 20 x 20 grid

12 Tulip on 13 x 13 grid

1 **Victoria's Crown,** *Grandmother's Patchwork Quilt Designs, Book 20,* 1931.

2 **Petal Circle in a Square,** *Kansas City Star,* Aug 24, 1955.

3 **A Young Man's Invention,** *Kansas City Star,* Feb 29, 1936. Also known as:

Alcazar, Nancy Cabot, *Chicago Tribune,* Jun 1, 1938.

Young Man's Invention, Nancy Cabot, *Chicago Tribune,* Jun 1, 1938.

4 **Starry Crown,** Nancy Cabot, *Chicago Tribune,* Apr 19, 1936.

"'Starry Crown' is a strikingly beautiful quilt design. It is difficult to piece accurately, but the completed quilted coverlet is an object to be marveled at." Nancy Cabot, *Chicago Tribune,* Apr 19, 1936

5 **Orange Peel,** *Grandma Dexter Appliqué and Patchwork Designs, Book 36a,* ca. 1932.

6 **Painted Snowball,** Nancy Cabot, *Chicago Tribune,* Jul 25, 1933.

7 **Dutch Tulip,** Hall, 1935.

8 **Dutch Tulip,** Eveline Foland, *Kansas City Star,* May 23, 1931.

9 **Dutch Tulip,** Finley, 1929.

10 **Eight Hands Around,** Nancy Cabot, *Chicago Tribune,* Sep 25, 1933.

11 **Square and Lily,** *The Dressmaking Book,* 1929.

12 **Wandering Foot,** Nancy Cabot, *Chicago Tribune,* Feb 5, 1933.

1

3

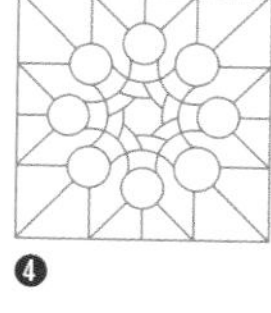

4

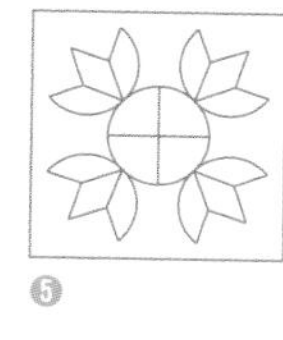

5

6

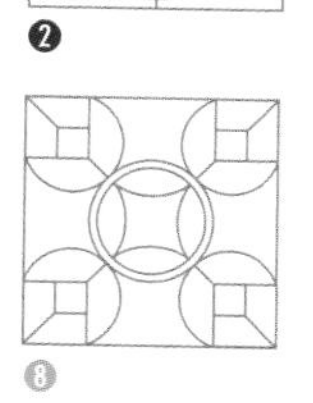

8

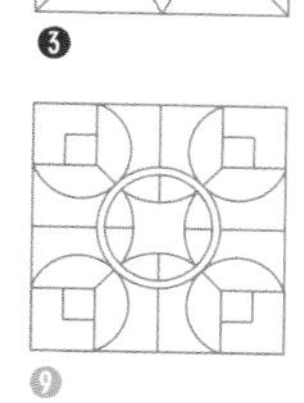

9

10

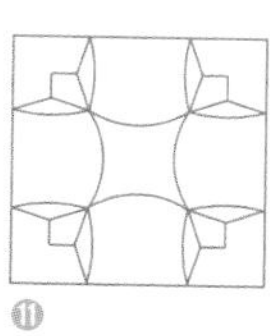

11

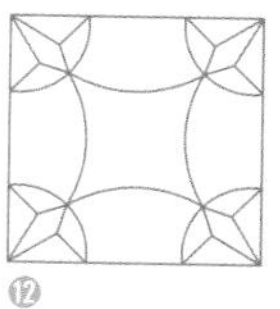

12

1 **Duck Pond,** Aunt Martha series: *The Quilt Fair Comes to You,* ca. 1933.

2 **Cottage Tulips,** Eveline Foland, *Kansas City Star,* Nov 7, 1931. Also known as:
  Olive's Yellow Tulip, *Mrs. Danner's Fourth Quilt Book,* 1958.

3 **Turkey Tracks,** *Kansas City Star,* Jun 13, 1936.
"This pattern was the inspiration for the quilt series in The Star. It was the first pattern offered in this series sketched from a quilt at The Star's Better Homes Show in 1928. There are many variations of the Turkey Track block and here is one that is pieced differently from the usual pattern. It was contributed by Ollie Wainwright, French, Ark." *Kansas City Star,* Jun 13, 1936

4 **Square and Swallow,** *The Patchwork Book,* 1932.

5 **Tulip,** *Prize Winning Designs,* ca. 1931.

6 **Pond Lily,** Jane Alan, *St. Louis Post-Dispatch,* Nov 12, 1932.

7 **Turkey Tracks,** Eveline Foland, *Kansas City Star,* May 25, 1929.

8 **Flying Swallows,** Nancy Cabot, *Chicago Tribune,* Jan 22, 1935.

9 **Swinging Corners,** *Ladies Art Company,* 1901. Also known as:
  Dutch Tulips, *Grandma Dexter New Appliqué and Patchwork Designs, Book 36b,* ca. 1932.
  Flying Swallows, *Kansas City Star,* Jul 29, 1933.
  Pond Lily, unidentified newspaper clipping, Nov 12, 1932.
  Swallow's Nest, Clara Stone, *Practical Needlework,* ca. 1906.
  Turkey Tracks, *Colonial Quilts,* 1932.

10 **Flying Swallows,** Nancy Cabot, *Chicago Tribune,* Jun 16, 1933.

11 **Turkey Tracks,** Alice Brooks, *Detroit Free Press,* Nov 2, 1933.
"With Thanksgiving only a short time off, it is natural that the turkey should begin to be a most popular bird. The old-time quilt maker was inspired in her design and in their quaint names, too, by the things of her every day life. The footprints of the turkey gave her the idea for this lovely pattern. Simple to do it has the grace of line that results in a quilt that any needlewoman is proud to show. Only three materials are needed for it, and the simplicity of the block makes it quick to complete." Alice Brooks, *Detroit Free Press,* Nov 2, 1933

12 **Chimney Swallows,** Nancy Page, *Birmingham News,* May 22, 1934. Also known as:
  Turkey Tracks, Hall, 1934.
  Wandering Foot, Hall, 1934.

1 Tulip on 8-pointed star grid 1

2 Tulip on 8-pointed star grid 1

3 Tulip on 12 x 12 grid

4 Tulip on 5 x 5 grid

5 Tulip on 12 x 12 grid

6 Tulip on 8 x 8 grid

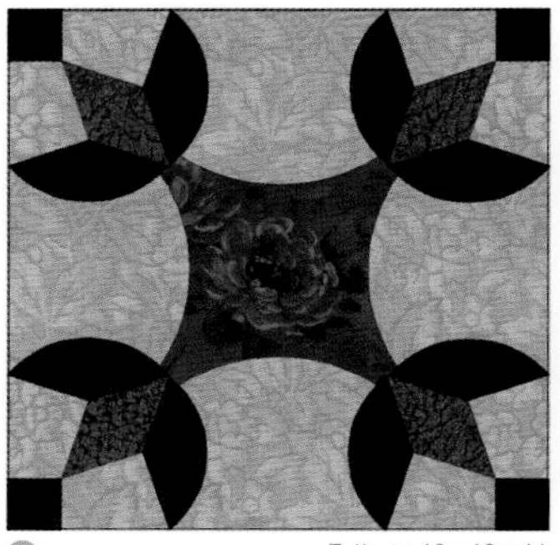
7 Tulip on 10 x 10 grid

8 Tulip on 23 x 23 grid

9 Tulip on 14 x 14 grid

10 Tulip on 10 x 10 grid

11 Tulip on 48 x 48 grid

12 Tulip on 50 x 50 grid

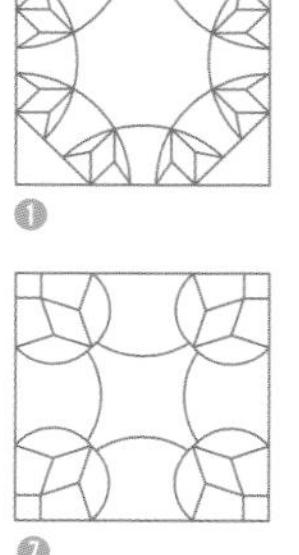
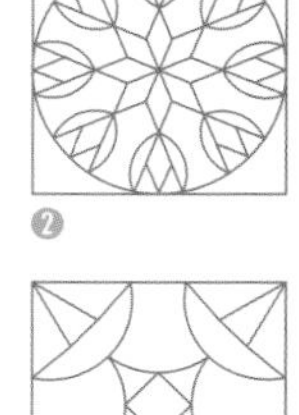

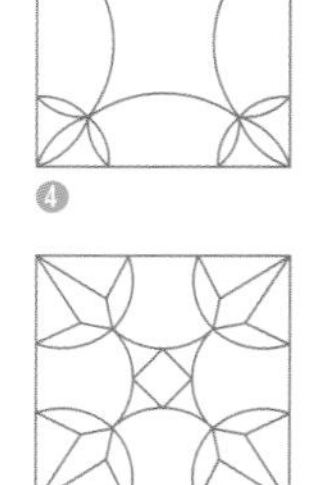
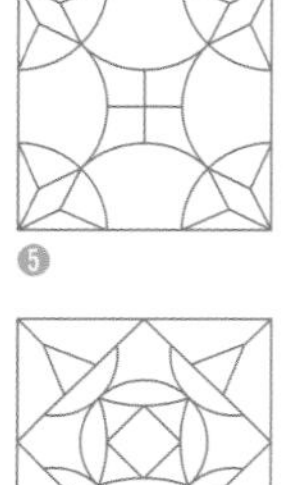
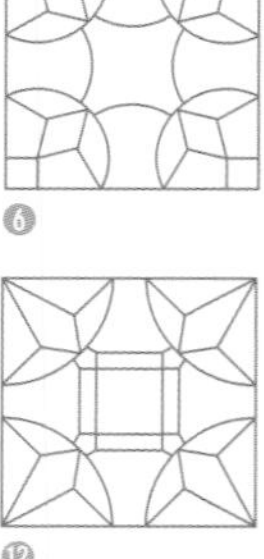

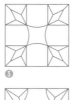

1 2 3 4 5 6

7 8 9 10 11 12

1 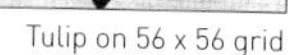 Tulip on 56 x 56 grid

2 Tulip on 13 x 13 grid

3 Tulip on 13 x 13 grid

4 Tulip on 28 x 28 grid

5 Tulip on 3 x 3 grid

6 Tulip on 26 x 26 grid

7 Tulip on 4 x 4 grid

8 Tulip on 48 x 48 grid

9 Tulip on 18 x 18 grid

10 Tulip on 18 x 18 grid

11 Tulip on 51 x 51 grid

12 Tulip on 24 x 24 grid

1 **Orange Peel,** Nancy Cabot, *Chicago Tribune,* Jan 10, 1937.

2 **Aunt Dinah's Hunt,** Nancy Cabot, *Chicago Tribune,* Jul 17, 1938. Also known as:

Devil's Footprints, Nancy Cabot, *Chicago Tribune,* Jul 17, 1938.

Turkey Tracks, Nancy Cabot, *Chicago Tribune,* Jul 17, 1938.

"In its simplest form, 'Devil's Footprints' was done in two colors and called 'Wandering Foot.' This original and early colonial name was bound up with the quaint old superstition that if any boy was allowed to sleep under a 'Wandering Foot' coverlet he became afflicted with the wanderlust, so it was changed to 'Devil's Footprints.' Later on it became 'Turkey Tracks' and 'Aunt Dinah's Hunt,' but it never lost its two earlier names." Nancy Cabot, *Chicago Tribune,* Jul 17, 1938

3 **Western Rose,** Laura Wheeler, *Kansas City Star,* Nov 15, 1933

4 **Hickory Leaf,** Nancy Cabot, *Chicago Tribune,* Feb 3, 1934.

"The tree family is well represented in quilt lore, and this 'Hickory Leaf' design is an outstanding example. It is an old quilt, with a background dating as far back as 1830." Nancy Cabot, *Chicago Tribune,* Feb 3, 1934

5 **Iris Leaf,** Eveline Foland, *Kansas City Star,* Jan 13, 1931.

"As the 'Wandering Foot' was supposed to have a malign influence, no child was allowed to sleep under one, else he would grow up discontented, unstable, and of a roving disposition. No bride would have one in her dower-chest. Later the name was changed to 'Turkey Tracks' to break the curse. Developed in green on a white foundation it is called 'Iris Leaf.' Hall, 1935

6 **Milwaukee's Own,** *Ladies Art Company,* 1922. Also known as:

Milwaukee's Pride, Nancy Cabot, *Chicago Tribune,* Dec 3, 1936.

7 **Mississippi Oak Leaves,** Nancy Cabot, *Chicago Tribune,* Jan 28, 1942.

8 **The Tulip Quilt,** *Kansas City Star,* Apr 17, 1935.

9 **Dutch Tulip,** Home Art Studios, *Colonial Quilts,* 1932.

10 **Bird of Paradise,** Hall, 1935.

11 **The Four Buds Quilt,** *Kansas City Star,* Oct 1, 1941.

12 **Lily of the Valley,** *Ladies Art Company,* 1928.

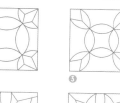

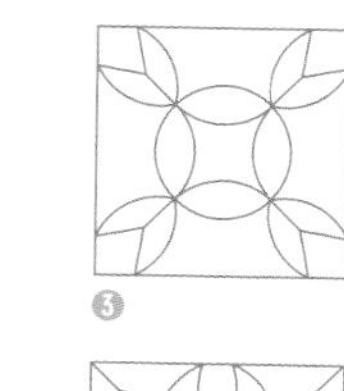

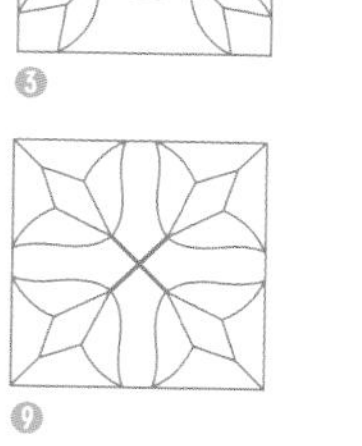

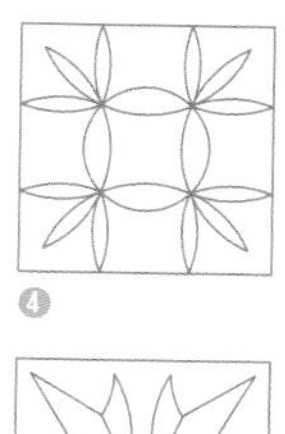

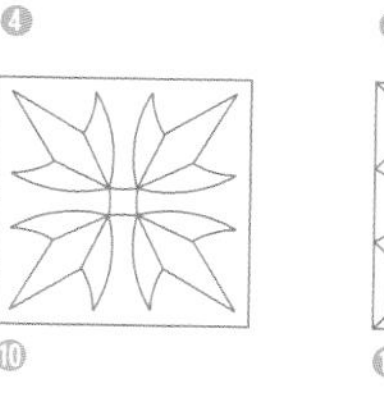

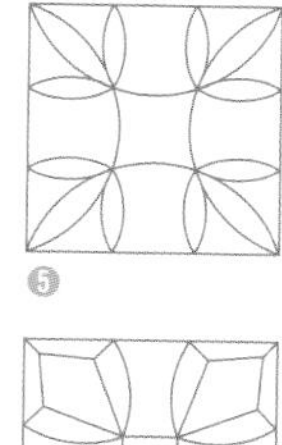

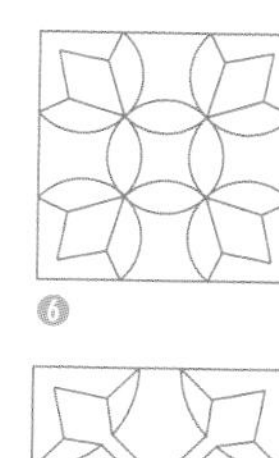

❶ **Lily of the Valley,** Nancy Cabot, *Chicago Tribune,* Jan 30, 1934.

❷ **Bleeding Heart,** *Ladies Art Company,* 1928.

❸ **Bleeding Heart,** Hall, 1935. Also known as:
Violet Blossoms, Nancy Cabot, *Chicago Tribune,* Jun 9, 1937.

❹ **Snowball Flower,** Laura Wheeler, *Cincinnati Enquirer,* Sep 7, 1935.

❺ **Rose and Trellis,** Laura Wheeler, *Cincinnati Enquirer,* Oct 6, 1933.

❻ **Gold Bloom,** *Kansas City Star,* Sep 4, 1935.

❼ **Molly's Rose Garden,** *Kansas City Star,* ca. Jan 28, 1942.

❽ **Rose,** Laura Wheeler, *Indianapolis Star,* Aug 21, 1933.

❾ **Full Blown Rose,** Nancy Cabot, *Chicago Tribune,* Oct 26, 1937.

❿ **Rose in Bloom,** Laura Wheeler, *Cincinnati Enquirer,* Apr 1, 1934. Also known as:
Full Blown Rose, Nancy Cabot, *Chicago Tribune,* Jul 12, 1934.
"'Full Blown Rose' dates back to 1853, and the original coverlet was composed entirely of gay figured material in combinations of reds and blues." Nancy Cabot, *Chicago Tribune,* Jul 12, 1934

⓫ **Moonflower,** Alice Brooks, *Detroit Free Press,* Apr 16, 1934.

⓬ **Radiant Star Flower,** *Grandmother Clark's Old Fashioned Quilt Designs, Book* 21, 1931. Also known as:
Star Flower, *Grandmother Clark's Old Fashioned Quilt Designs, Book* 21, 1931.

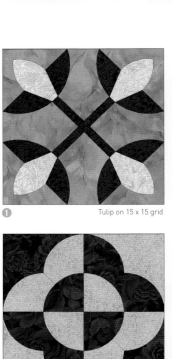

❶ Tulip on 15 x 15 grid

❷ Tulip on 6 x 6 grid

❸ Tulip on 15 x 15 grid

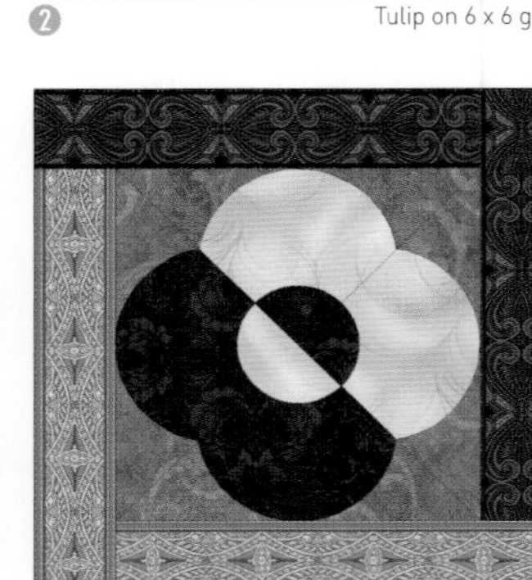

❹ Flower on 4 x 4 grid

❺ Flower on 13 x 13 grid

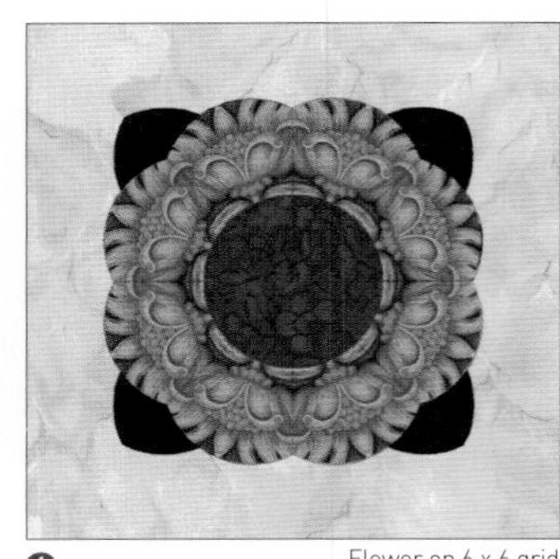

❻ Flower on 6 x 6 grid

❼ Flower on 7 x 7 grid

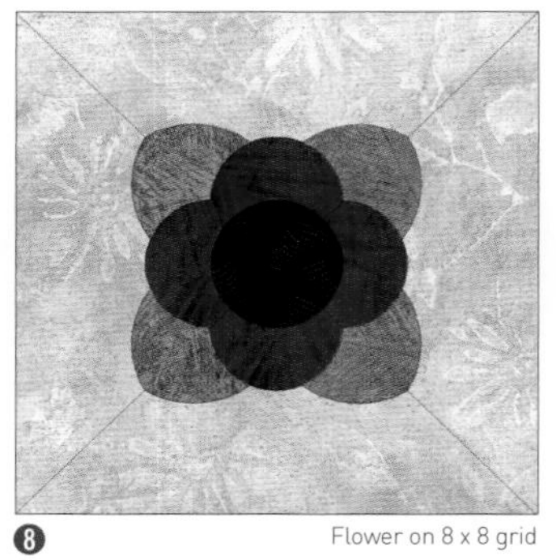

❽ Flower on 8 x 8 grid

❾ Flower on 23 x 23 grid

❿ Flower on 23 x 23 grid

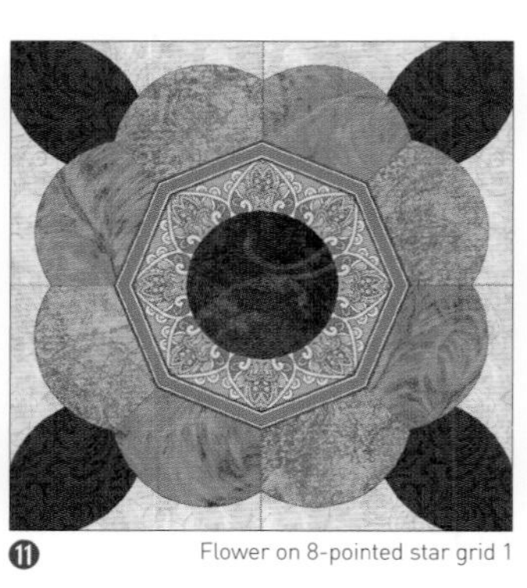

⓫ Flower on 8-pointed star grid 1

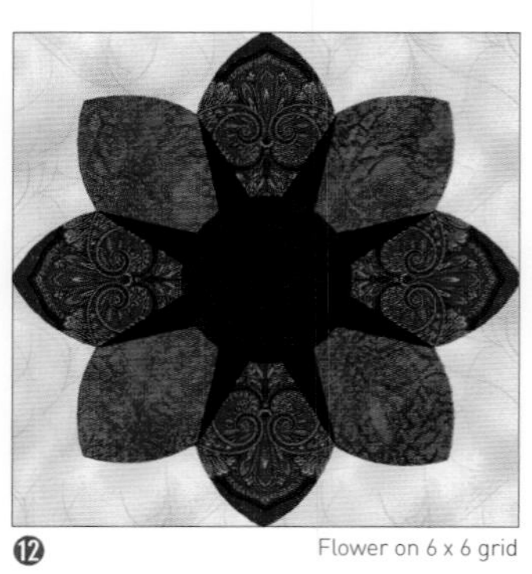

⓬ Flower on 6 x 6 grid

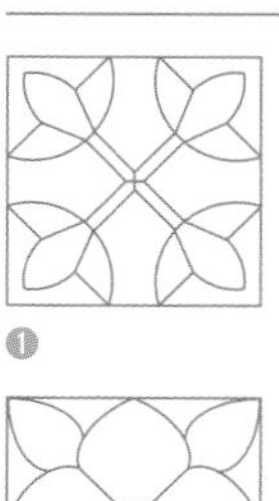

❶

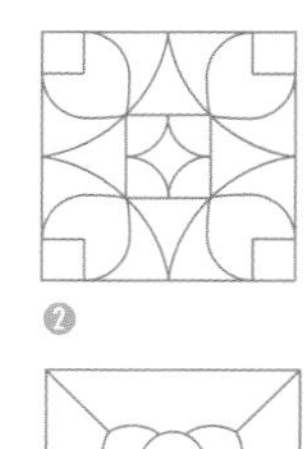

❷

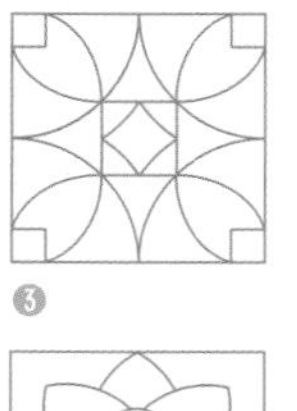

❸

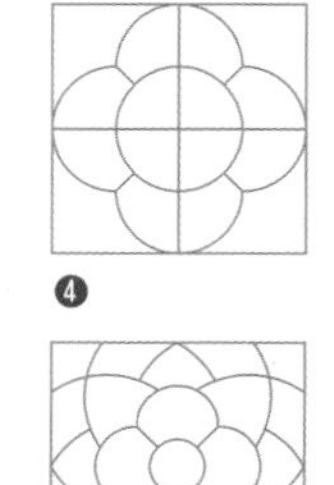

❹

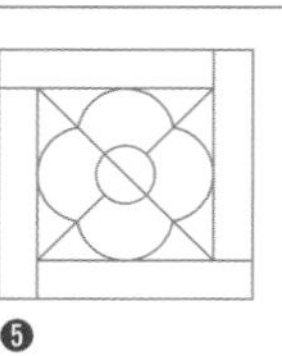

❺

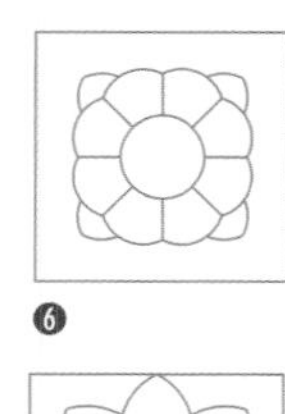

❻

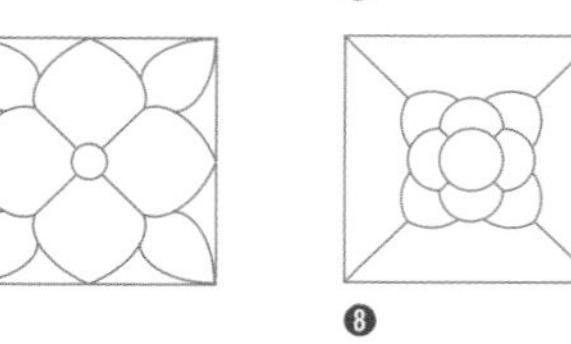

❼ ❽

❾

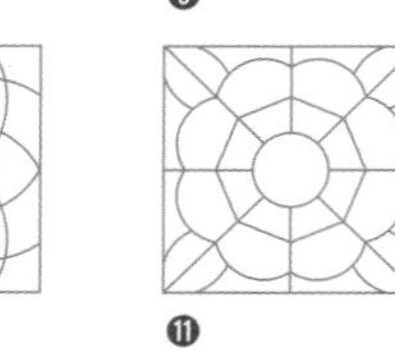

❿ ⓫ ⓬

1 Flower on 8-pointed star grid 2

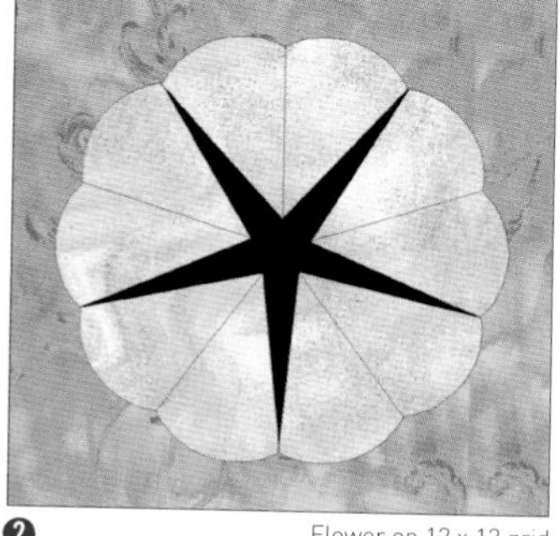

2 Flower on 12 x 12 grid

3 Flower on 26 x 26 grid

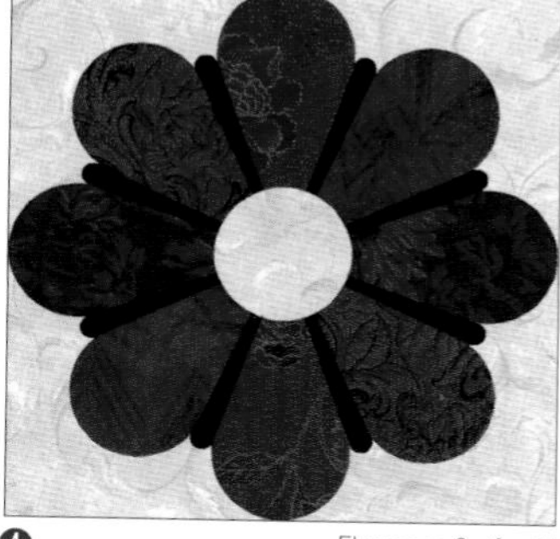

4 Flower on 8 x 8 grid

5 Flower on 40 x 40 grid

6 Flower on 16 x 16 grid

7 Flower on 16 x 16 grid

8 Flower on 22 x 22 grid

9 Flower on 10 x 10 grid

10 Flower on 12 x 12 grid

11 Flower on 24 x 24 grid

12 Flower on 48 x 48 grid

1

2

3

4

5

6

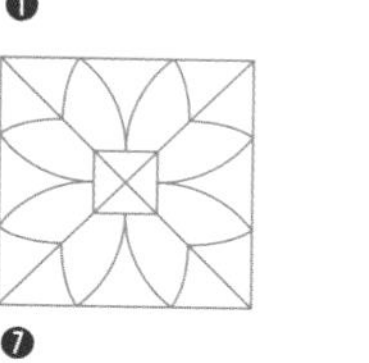

7

8

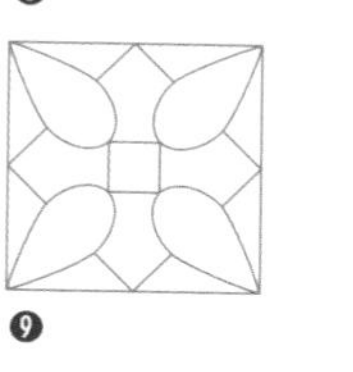

9

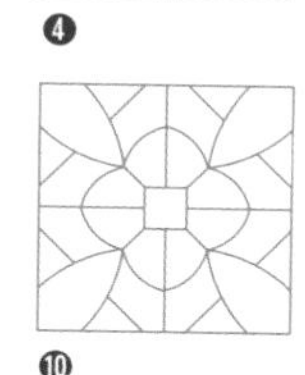

10

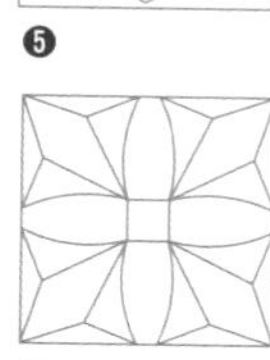

11

12

1 **Golden Glow,** Hall, 1935. Also known as:
  Star Flower, Hall, 1935.

2 **Moon Flower,** *Farm Journal and Farmers Wife*, ca. 1941.

3 **Star Flower,** Nancy Cabot, *Chicago Tribune*, Oct 14, 1933.
"Not really old, but quaintly old fashioned in spirit is the 'Star Flower'... It is extremely simple to piece." Nancy Cabot, *Chicago Tribune*," Oct 14, 1933

4 **Mother's Favorite,** *Grandma Dexter's New Appliqué and Patchwork Designs, Book 36b*, ca. 1932.

5 **Sunflower,** Nancy Cabot, *Chicago Tribune*, Jul 9, 1933. Also known as:
  Kansas Sunflower, Nancy Cabot, *Chicago Tribune*, Mar 6, 1938.
"Only a woman with the soul of an artist and one familiar with plant life could have designed this pattern. when the sunflower has attained full-bloom, the petals become lighter in color. And the Designer shows that in this pattern." Nancy Cabot, *Chicago Tribune*, Jul 9, 1933

6 **Dream Garden,** Alice Brooks, *Detroit Free Press*, Aug 5, 1934.
"'Dream Garden'—an alluring name for a quilt. and the quilt is every bit as alluring as its name! The simple flower form that makes the blocks is quickly pieced and can be done different materials in each block, if desired. this would make the finished quilt look exactly like a colorful flower garden. the block is of a good size for a cushion, too, and cushions are going to be a most popular item with the college-goers very shortly!" Alice Brooks, *Detroit Free Press*, Aug 5, 1934

7 **Charming Patchwork,** *Washington Post*, Jul 4, 1943.

8 **Garden Beauty,** Laura Wheeler, *Cincinnati Enquirer*, Dec 1, 1933.

9 **Full Blown Flower,** Laura Wheeler, *Indianapolis Star*, Jul 16, 1933.

10 **Friendship Rose,** Alice Brooks, *Detroit Free Press*, Jan 29, 1934.

11 **Lily,** Alice Brooks, *Detroit Free Press*, Jan 13, 1934.
"One look at this quilt design, and the name needs no explanation. The lily forms make a dainty block that is as lovely on a pillow as on a quilt. you know it is very much the vogue now to have patchwork pillows about! Of course, in the quilt the joined blocks form another lovely pattern." Alice Brooks, *Detroit Free Press*, Jan 13, 1934

12 **Bed of Tulips,** Alice Brooks, *Detroit Free Press*, May 20, 1934.

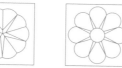

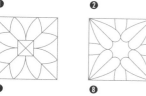

❶ **Morning Glory,** Laura Wheeler, *Cincinnati Enquirer,* Oct 2, 1933.

❷ **Cosmos,** Laura Wheeler, *Cincinnati Enquirer,* Sep 29, 1934.

❸ **Modernized Poppy,** Nancy Cabot, *Chicago Tribune,* Nov 8, 1934.
"Quilt patches continue to reflect the prevalent tendency toward modernization witnessed in every phase of decorative art. The color arrangement of 'Modernized Poppy' is an example. This design is a favorite with many quilts because it is delightfully easy to piece and the variety of colors creates an interesting problem in color harmony. The richly beautiful shades of blue, purple, red and white are used for the petals of the flower with white and gold as an interesting background." Nancy Cabot, *Chicago Tribune,* Nov 8, 1934

❹ **Bluebell,** *Kansas City Star,* Jan 24, 1940.

❺ **The Rosebud Quilt,** *Kansas City Star,* Sep 13, 1939. Also known as:
 A Panel of Roses, *Kansas City Star,* Sep 5, 1951

❻ **Grandmother's Tulip,** *Kansas City Star,* Nov 28, 1936.

❼ **Grandma's Tulip,** *Prize Winning Designs,* ca. 1931.

❽ **Texas Tulip,** Nancy Cabot, *Chicago Tribune,* Jun 8, 1933.

❾ **Modern Daisies,** Nancy Cabot, *Chicago Tribune,* Sep 17, 1935. Also known as:
 Modern Daisy, Nancy Cabot, *Chicago Tribune,* Jul 27, 1937.

❿ **Patchwork and Quilting for Your Chamber,** *Modern Priscilla,* Aug 1927.

⓫ **Friendship Dahlia,** Hall, 1935.

⓬ **Friendship Dahlia,** *Prize Winning Designs,* ca. 1931.

❶ Flower on 48 x 48 grid

❷ Flower on 12 x 12 grid

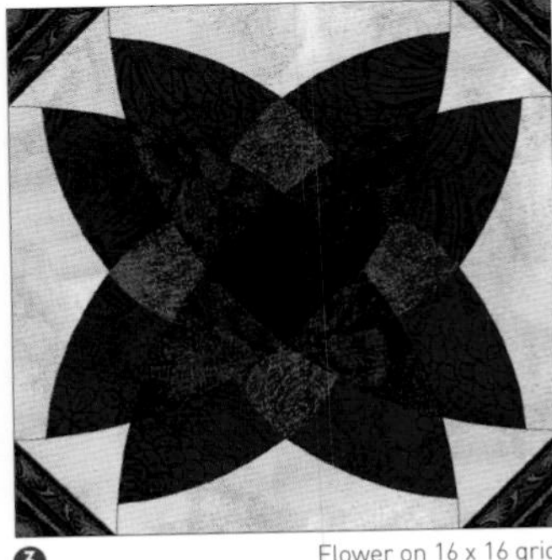

❸ Flower on 16 x 16 grid

❹ Flower on 24 x 24 grid

❺ Flower on 15 x 15 grid

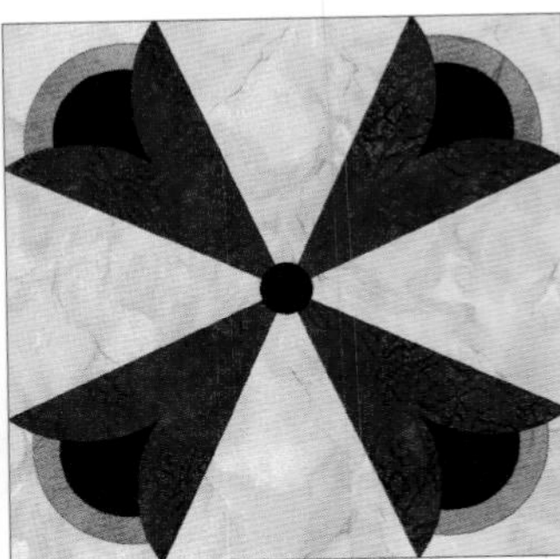

❻ Flower on 22 x 22 grid

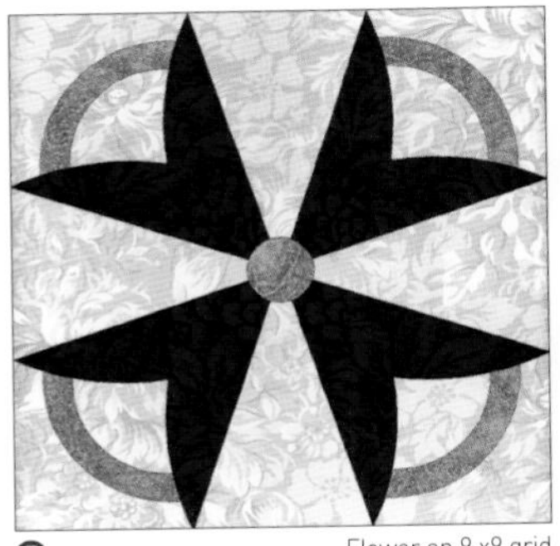

❼ Flower on 9 x9 grid

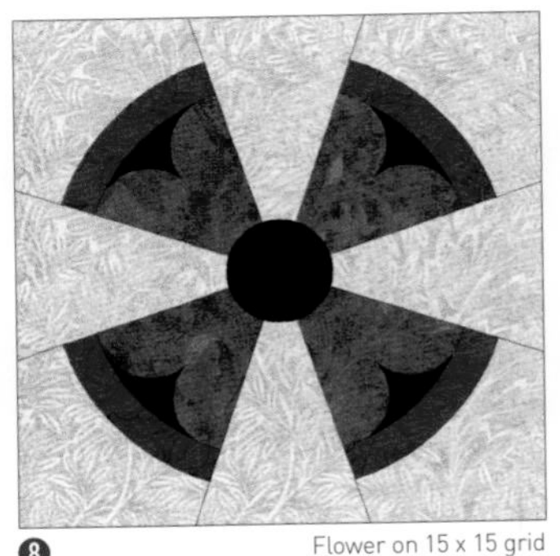

❽ Flower on 15 x 15 grid

❾ Flower on 20 x 20 grid

❿ Flower on 38 x 38 grid

⓫ Flower on 7 x 7 grid

⓬ Flower on 7 x 7 grid

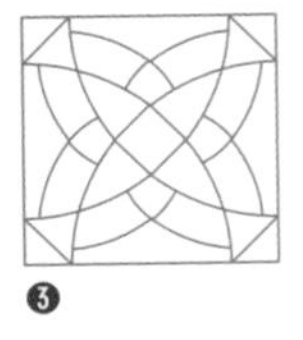

❸

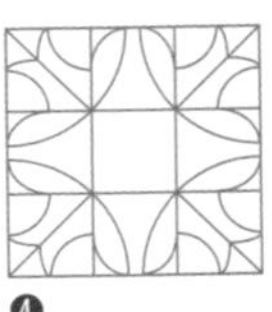

❹

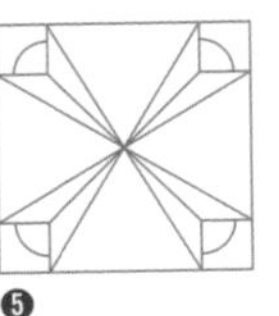

❺

❻

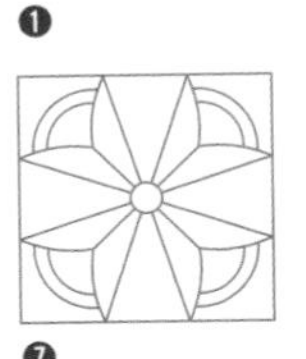

❼

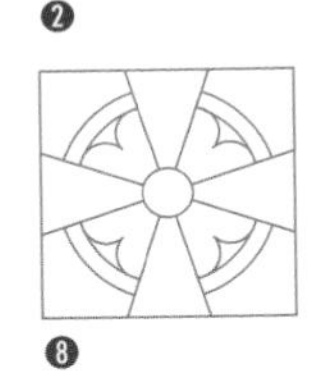

❽

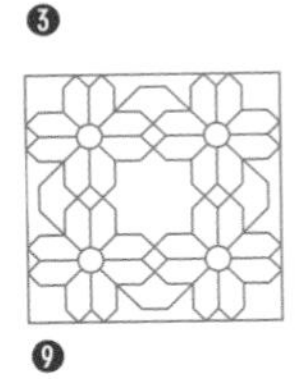

❾

❿

⓫

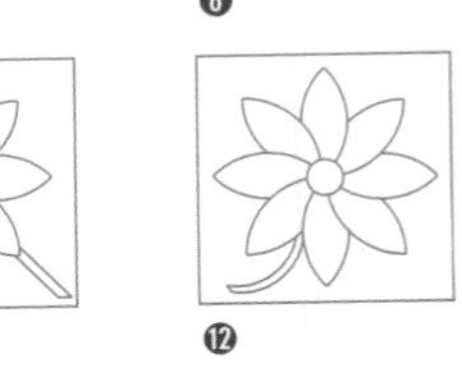

⓬

1 Flower on 7 x 7 grid

2 Flower on 14 x 14 grid

3 Flower on 48 x 48 grid

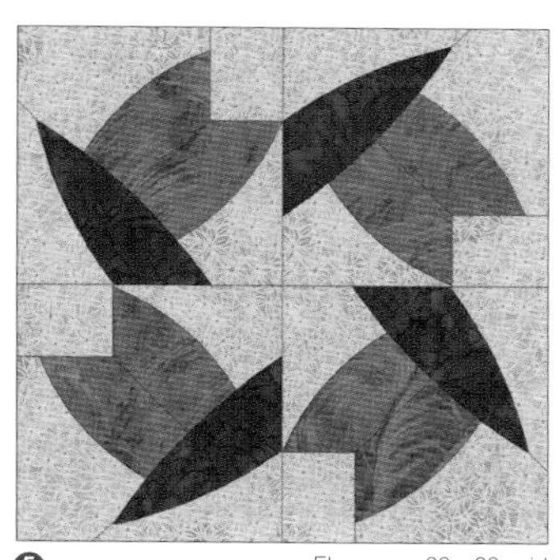

4 Flower on 8-pointed star grid 1

5 Flower on 22 x 22 grid

6 Flower on 18 x 18 grid

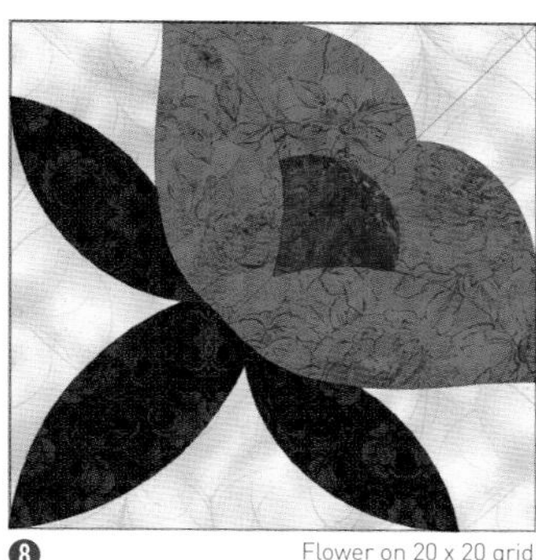
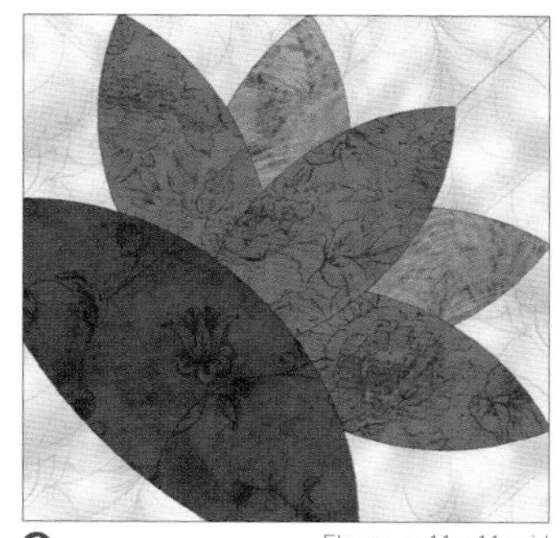

7 Flower on 21 x 21 grid

8 Flower on 20 x 20 grid

9 Flower on11 x 11 grid

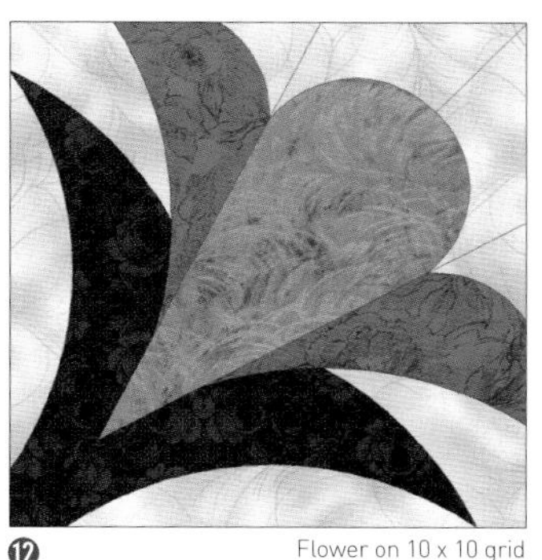

10 Flower on 11 x 11 grid

11 Flower on 7 x 7 grid

12 Flower on 10 x 10 grid

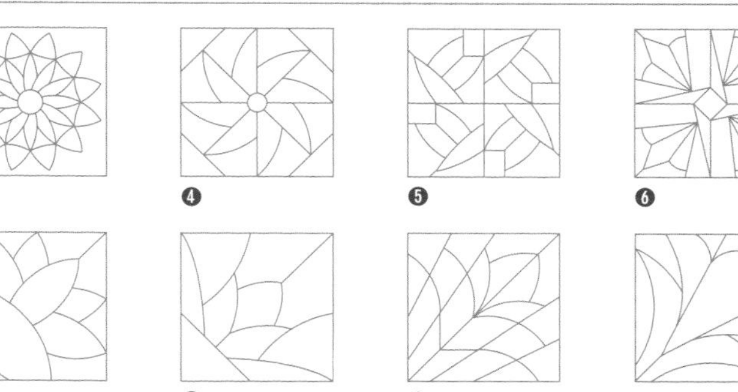

1 **Friendship Dahlia,** Nancy Cabot, *Chicago Tribune,* Feb 10, 1937.

2 **Dahlia,** Alice Brooks, *Detroit Free Press,* Apr 8, 1934.

3 **Double Poppy,** Nancy Cabot, *Chicago Tribune,* Apr 26, 1936.

4 **Black-Eyed Susan,** *Q Book 102, Grandmother's Patchwork Quilts,* date unknown.

5 **Flower Wreath,** Laura Wheeler, *Cincinnati Enquirer,* Aug 26, 1934.

6 **Canterbury Bells,** Alice Brooks, *Detroit Free Press,* Aug 26, 1934.

7 **Regal Lily,** Alice Brooks, *Detroit Free Press,* Apr 18, 1934.

8 **Flower of Spring,** Alice Brooks, *Detroit Free Press,* Feb 7, 1935.

"'How fresh and lovely!' would be your instant comment, if you saw this quilt, 'Flower of Spring', in color. The flower that inspired the design is the anemone, and though it may grow in our garden in spring, still we cherish its beauty all year round." Alice Brooks, *Detroit Free Press,* Aug 30, 1935

9 **Water Lily,** Laura Wheeler, *Cincinnati Enquirer,* May 8, 1934.

10 **Tulip Patch,** Alice Brooks, *Detroit Free Press,* Mar 20, 1935.

11 **Cleopatra's Fan,** Laura Wheeler, *Cincinnati Enquirer,* Oct 5, 1934.

12 **Pride of the West,** Alice Brooks, *Detroit Free Press,* May 15, 1936.

❶ **Wild Rose,** Laura Wheeler, *Pasadena Post,* Sep 17, 1936.

❷ **Friendship Flowers,** Laura Wheeler, *Cincinnati Enquirer,* Sep 16, 1933.

❸ **Evening Flower,** Alice Brooks, *Detroit Free Press,* Jul 18, 1934.

❹ **Calico Plant,** Nancy Cabot, *Chicago Tribune,* Jun 3, 1938.

❺ **Crocus,** Laura Wheeler, *Cincinnati Enquirer,* Apr 19, 1934.

❻ **Garden Favorite,** Alice Brooks, *Detroit Free Press,* Jul 9, 1934.

❼ **Old Fashioned Garden,** Alice Brooks, *Detroit Free Press,* Jul 3, 1934.

❽ **Flower of the Woods,** Laura Wheeler, *Cincinnati Enquirer,* Aug 2, 1934.

❾ **Prairie Flower,** Alice Brooks, *Detroit Free Press,* Apr 25, 1936.

❿ **Pond Lily,** Laura Wheeler, *Topeka State Journal,* Aug 15, 1935.

⓫ **Rose,** Alice Brooks, *Detroit Free Press,* Sep 26, 1936.

⓬ **Field of Daisies,** Laura Wheeler, *Daily Republic,* Mar 21, 1935. Also known as:
Field of Pansies, Laura Wheeler, *Grit Patterns,* 1980.

❶ Flower on 20 x 20 grid

❷ Flower on 20 x 20 grid

❸ Flower on 18 x 18 grid

❹ Flower on 36 x 36 grid

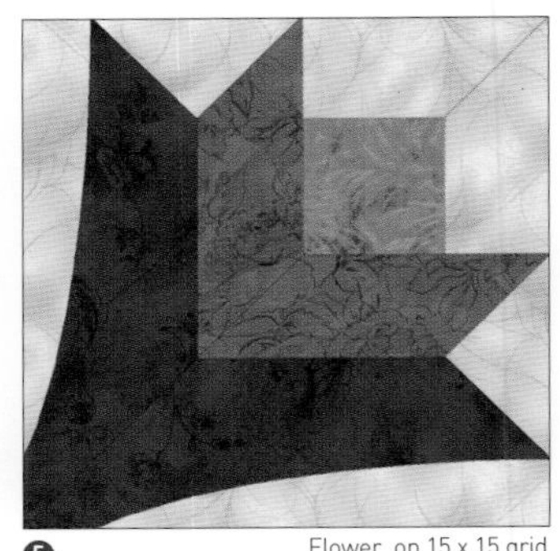

❺ Flower on 15 x 15 grid

❻ Flower on 18 x 18 grid

❼ Flower on 11 x 11 grid

❽ Flower on 14 x 14 grid

❾ Flower on 8 x 8 grid

❿ Flower on 17 x 17 grid

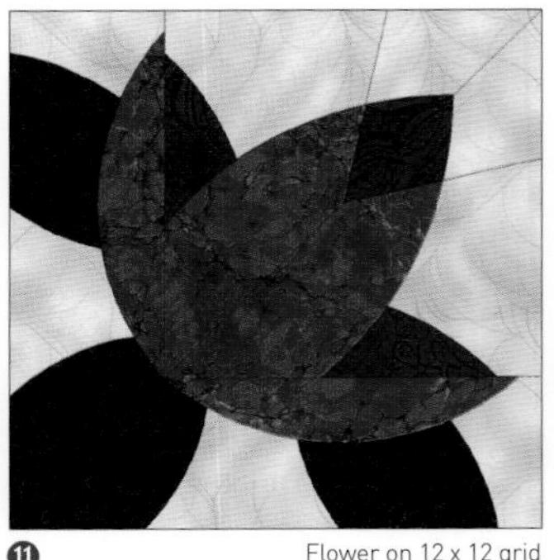

⓫ Flower on 12 x 12 grid

⓬ Flower on 16 x 16 grid

❶

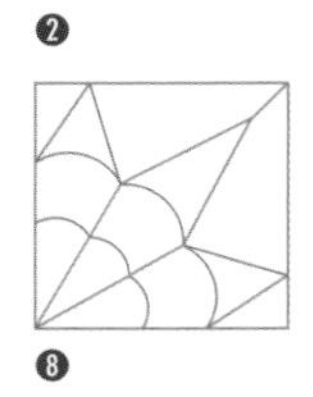

❷ ❽

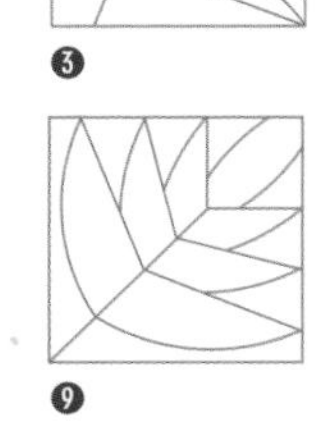

❸ ❾

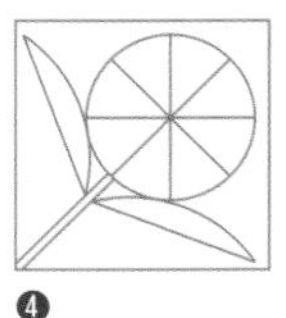

❹

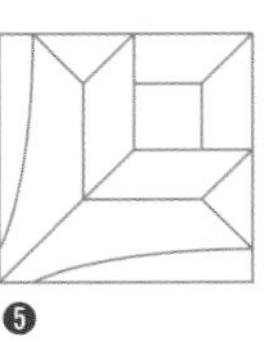

❺

❻

❼

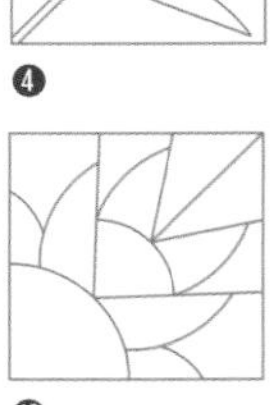

❿

⓫

⓬

❶ Flower on 22 x 22 grid

❷ Flower on 16 x 16 grid

❸ Flower on 36 x 36 grid

❹ Flower on 29 x 29 grid

❺ Flower on 21 x 21 grid

❻ Flower on 27 x 27 grid

❼ Flower on hexagon grid

❽ Flower on 12 x 12 grid

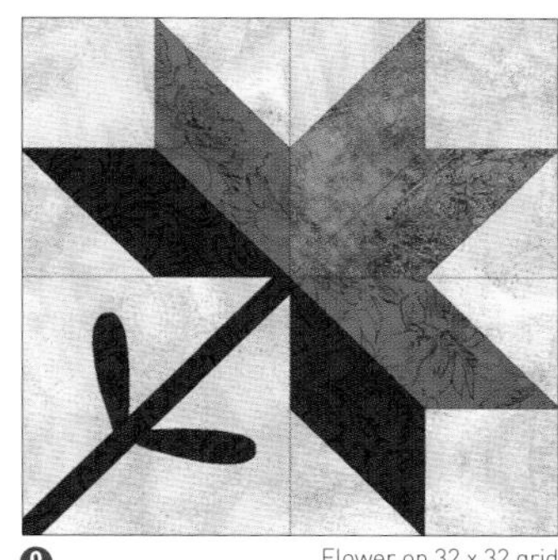
❾ Flower on 32 x 32 grid

❿ Flower on 18 x 18 grid

⓫ Flower on 48 x 48 grid

⓬ Flower on 18 x 18 grid

❶

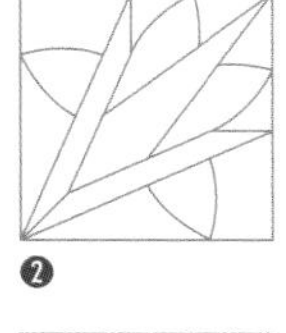
❷

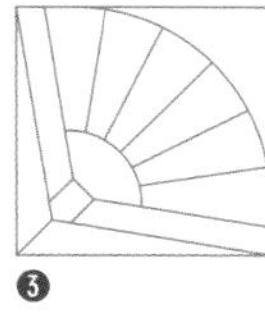
❸

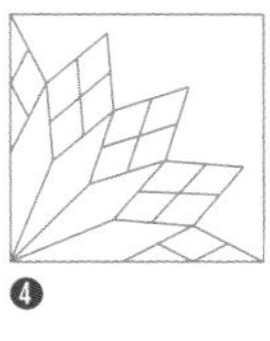
❹

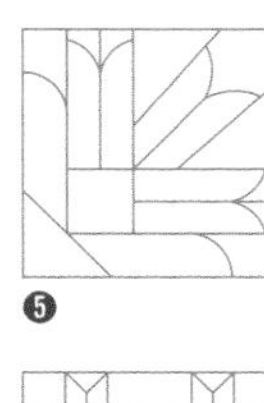
❺

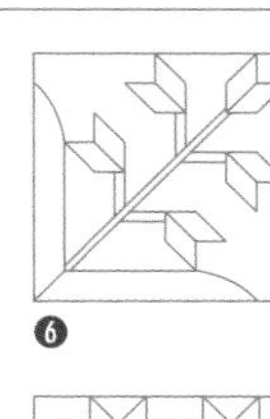
❻

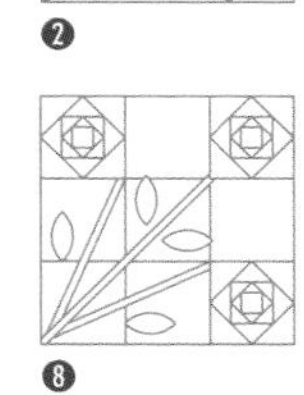
❼

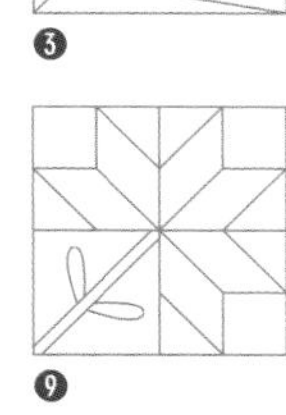
❽

❾

❿

⓫

⓬

❶ **Spring Fancy,** Laura Wheeler, *Cincinnati Enquirer,* Apr 19, 1935.

❷ **Fleur De Lis,** Laura Wheeler, *Cincinnati Enquirer,* Jul 10, 1934.

❸ **Flower in Scraps,** Laura Wheeler, *Cincinnati Enquirer,* Nov 14, 1933.
"This quilt—so colorful—so economical—such fun to make, is one of those charming quilts that every quiltmaker loves—a scrap quilt. It is ideal as a 'Friendship Quilt,' in which each friend contributes her own patches for a block, each block can be off different scraps and still make a most effective quilt. The flower, somewhat the shape of a fan, is as easy to make as the popular Fan Quilt and is enhanced by the leaves and stems." Laura Wheeler, *Cincinnati Enquirer,* Nov 14, 1933

❹ **Fringed Aster,** Hinson, 1973.

❺ **Flowery Field,** Alice Brooks, *Detroit Free Press,* Feb 16, 1935.

❻ **Bell Flower,** Laura Wheeler, *Cincinnati Enquirer,* Feb 18, 1934.
"What garden is complete without bell flowers of some sort? What flowers are more decorative in form? In this quilt they have been translated into gay scraps and the quiltmaker can make the colors just as varied as are the bell flowers in her garden. Simple in making, the resulting quilt will have that same firmness in design that the bell flowers have in the garden." Laura Wheeler, *Cincinnati Enquirer,* Feb 18, 1934

❼ **Flower of the Woods,** Alice Brooks, *Detroit Free Press,* May 22, 1935.
"'Flower of the Woods'—and that's the starry anemone, of course—will make a quilt that any quiltmaker would be proud to show. The flower—made in a plain material—is set off by the figured material of the background. You could do the flowers in the same material throughout, or in a different color in each block." Alice Brooks, *Detroit Free Press,* May 22, 1935

❽ **Triple Rose,** Aunt Martha series: *Quilts,* ca. 1963.

❾ **Single Lily,** Nancy Cabot, *Chicago Tribune,* Aug 16, 1963.

❿ **President's Quilt,** Hall, 1935.

⓫ **Square and Swallow,** *The Patchwork Book,* 1932.

⓬ **President's Quilt,** *Ladies Art Company,* 1897.

❶ **Triple Sunflower,** Nancy Cabot, *Chicago Tribune,* Mar 24, 1933.

❷ **Album Presentation Quilt,** Orlofsky, 1974.

❸ **Double Peony,** *Ladies Art Company,* 1897.

❹ **Cleveland Tulip,** Hall, 1935.

❺ **Peony,** Hall, 1935.

❻ **Triple Sunflower,** Clara Stone, *Practical Needlework,* ca. 1906.

❼ **Three Flowered Sunflower,** *Ladies Art Company,* 1897.

❽ **Tulip,** *Old Fashioned Quilts,* ca. 1932.

❾ **Noon Day Lily,** *Ladies Art Company,* 1897. Also known as:
- **Fire Lily,** Hall, 1935.
- **Mariposa Lily,** Hall, 1935.
- **Meadow Lily,** Hall, 1935.
- **Mountain Lily,** Hall, 1935.
- **North Carolina Lily,** Hall, 1935.
- **Prairie Lily,** Hall, 1935.
- **Wood Lily,** Hall, 1935.

❿ **North Carolina Lily,** *The Patchwork Book,* 1932.

⓫ **Triangle Flower,** *Virginia Snow Studio Art Needlework Creations,* 1932. Also known as:
- **Triangular Flower,** Beyer, Alice, *Quilting,* 1934.

⓬ **Pot of Flowers,** *Grandmother's Patchwork Quilt Design,* 1932.

❶ Flower on 8 x 8 grid

❷ Flower on 8-pointed star grid 3

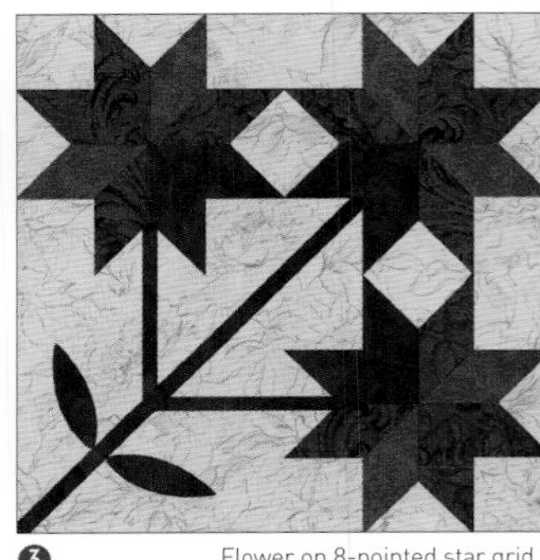

❸ Flower on 8-pointed star grid 3

❹ Flower on 8-pointed star grid 3

❺ Flower on 8-pointed star grid 3

❻ Flower on 8-pointed star grid 3

❼ Flower on 8-pointed star grid 3

❽ Flower on 8-pointed star grid 3

❾ Flower on 8-pointed star grid 3

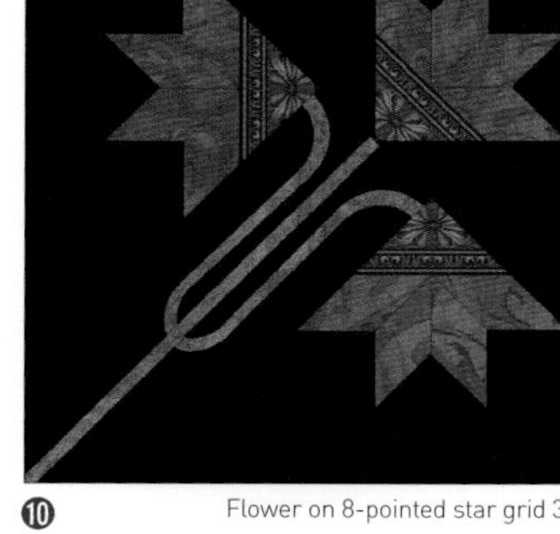

❿ Flower on 8-pointed star grid 3

⓫ Flower on 8-pointed star grid 3

⓬ Flower on 8-pointed star grid

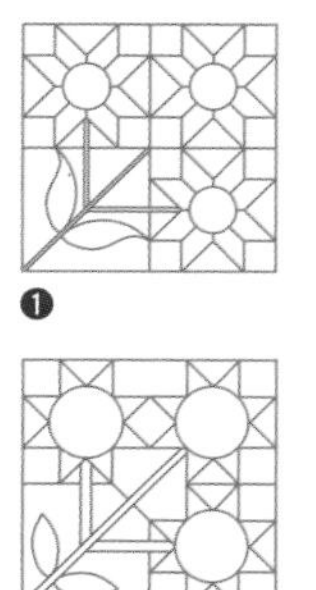

❶ ❼

❷

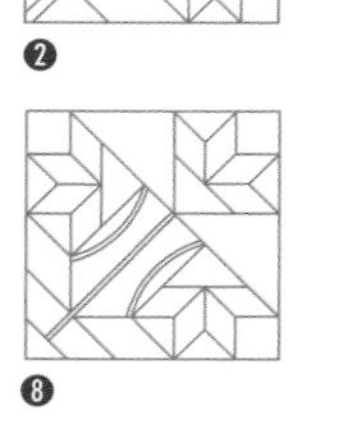

❽

❸

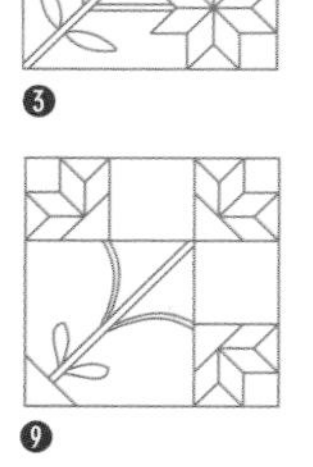

❾

❹

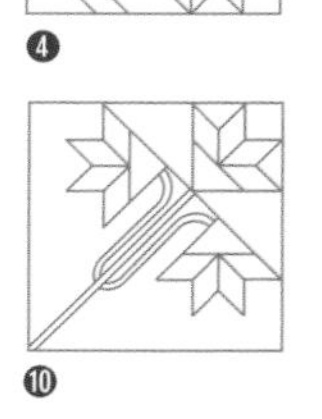

❿

❺

⓫

❻

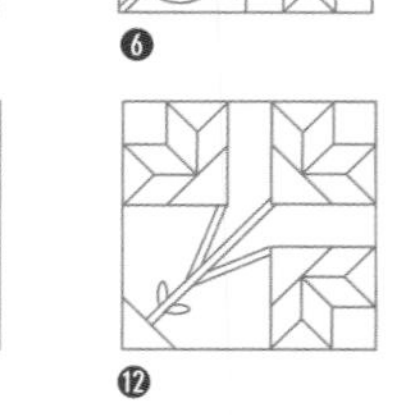

⓬

❶ Flower on 8-pointed star grid 3

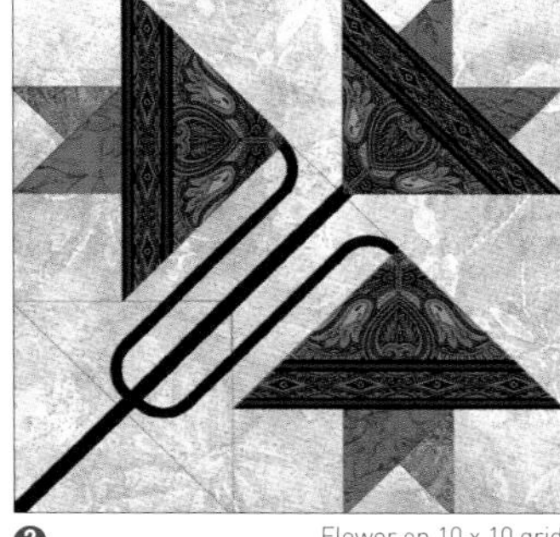

❷ Flower on 10 x 10 grid

❸ Flower on 7 x7 grid

❹ Flower on 6 x6 grid

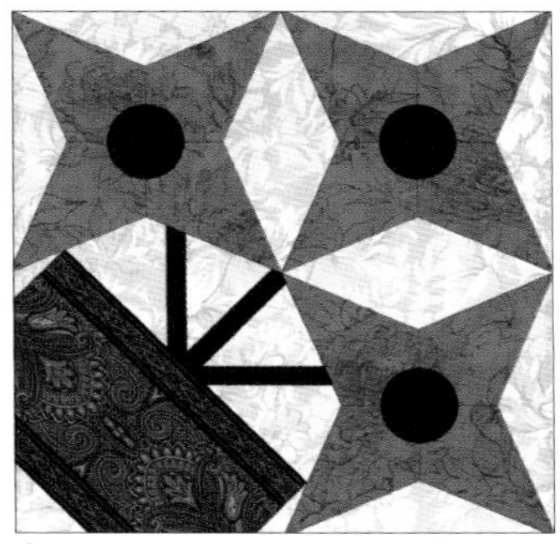

❺ Flower on 28 x 28 grid

❻ Flower on 56 x 56 grid

❼ Flower on 28 x 28 grid

❽ Flower on 28 x 28 grid

❾ Flower on 28 x 28 grid

❿ Flower on 28 x 28 grid

⓫ Flower on 8-pointed star grid 3

⓬ Flower on 8-pointed star grid 3

❶

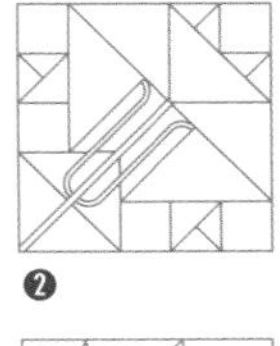

❷

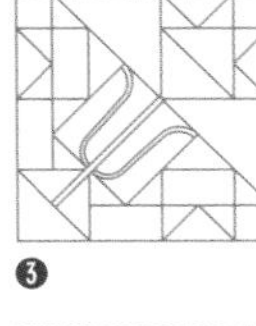

❸

❹

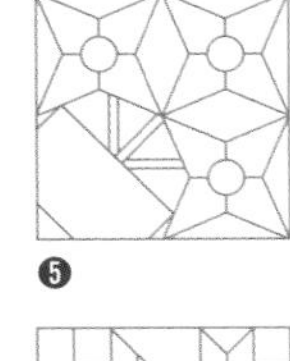

❺

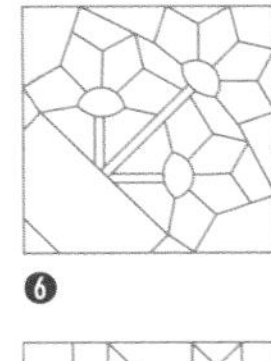

❻

❼

❽

❾

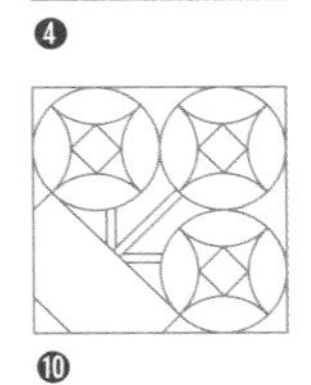

❿

⓫

⓬

❶ **Cleveland Lilies,** *Ladies Art Company,* 1897.

❷ **Mariposa Lily,** Nancy Page, *Birmingham News,* Jan 5, 1937.

❸ **North Carolina Lily,** Nancy Page, *Birmingham News,* Aug 26, 1941.

❹ **Mariposa Lily,** Nancy Cabot, *Chicago Tribune,* Feb 23, 1933. Also known as:

- **Noon Day Lily,** Nancy Cabot, *Chicago Tribune,* Feb 23, 1933.
- **North Carolina Lily,** Nancy Cabot, *Chicago Tribune,* Feb 23, 1933.

"'Mariposa-Lily,' 'North Carolina Lily,' or 'Noon Day Lily,' in any case, it is a lily. We shall call it by the first name. The lilies which grow so abundantly throughout the Carolina states provided the inspiration. Originally the block was made of white flowers on a green background, and that still seems an appropriate color combination. Present day quilt makers, however, have changed all that the 'Mariposa Lily' is cultivated in different colors to suit individual favorite color schemes." Nancy Cabot, *Chicago Tribune,* Feb 23, 1933

❺ **Snowdrop,** Alice Brooks, *Detroit Free Press,* Feb 4, 1934.

"'Bowl of Flowers'—an unusual patchwork quilt—striking in design—made of scraps—each block in a different design and each block carefully planned to be not only beautiful when used alone but to make a harmonious whole—is a serial quilt. The various blocks will appear on seven consecutive Sundays, starting today with block 1, 'Snowdrop.' There are six different bowls of flowers, each of which would also make a lovely cushion, for the block is 12½ inches square. Plain blocks alternate with these and can be enhanced with the quilting motif which is available in a perforated pattern. When all the flower blocks have appeared, the border will be given." *Detroit Free Press,* Feb 4, 1934

❻ **Poppy,** Alice Brooks, *Detroit Free Press,* Mar 11, 1934.

❼ **Lily,** Alice Brooks, *Detroit Free Press,* Mar 4, 1934.

❽ **Tulip,** Alice Brooks, *Detroit Free Press,* Feb 18, 1934.

❾ **Aster,** Alice Brooks, *Detroit Free Press,* Feb 11, 1934.

❿ **Rose,** Alice Brooks, *Detroit Free Press,* Feb 25, 1934.

⓫ **Basket of Lilies,** *Ladies Art Company,* 1897. Also known as:

- **Basket of Tulips,** Hinson, 1973.
- **Royal Dutch Tulip and Vase,** Home Art Studios, *Cincinnati Enquirer,* Mar 8, 1933.

⓬ **Basket of Flowers,** *Kansas City Star,* Dec 14, 1935. Also known as:

- **A Basket of Bright Flowers,** *Kansas City Star,* Apr 24, 1946.

❶ **Potted Star Flower,** *Farm Journal Quilt Patterns,* ca. 1935.

❷ **Potted Star Flower,** Nancy Cabot, *Chicago Tribune,* Aug 18, 1936.

❸ **Tuip in Vase** [sic], *Ladies Art Company,* 1897. Also known as:

- **Basket of Tulips,** Nancy Cabot, *Chicago Tribune,* Jun 3, 1934.
- **Royal Dutch Tulip and Vase,** Home Art Studios, *Cincinnati Enquirer,* Mar 8, 1933.
- **Royal Japanese Vase,** Hall, 1935.
- **Tulip in a Vase,** *Grandmother Clark's Patchwork Quilt Designs, From Books 20-21-23,* 1932.
- **Tulips and Vase,** *Colonial Quilts,* 1932.
- **Tulips in a Vase,** Hall, 1935.

"A quilt block of almost universal popularity is 'Tulip in Vase.' It is an all pieced quilt which was made first in 1839 in Philadelphia, where it was called 'A Basket of Tulips.'" Nancy Cabot, *Chicago Tribune,* Jun 3, 1934

❹ **Royal Japanese Vase,** *Ladies Art Company,* 1897.

❶ Flower on 8-pointed star grid 3

❷ Flower on 8-pointed star grid 3

❸ Flower on 8-pointed star grid 3

❹ Flower on 8-pointed star grid 3

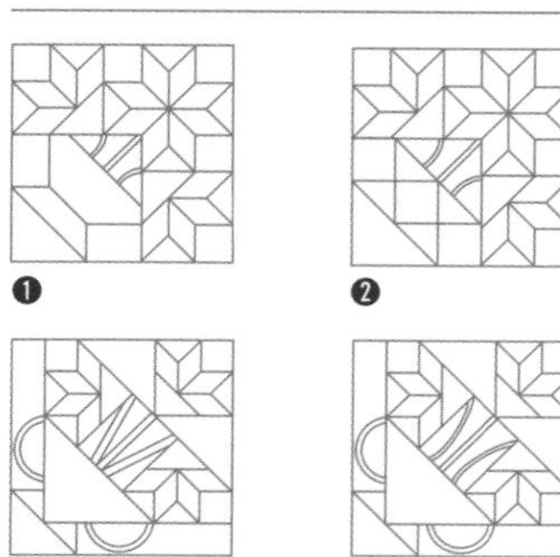

Quick Reference: Lilies *(without Curved Elements)*

There are many lily patterns and many names that go along with them. Nancy Page talks about the lily in her column:

"The lily is a flower that has been used in quilt making since women first pieced bits of cloth together and made a block for a quilt. And oddly enough, the lily design has been given a characteristic name in each locality. For instance, this design, or slight modification of it, was known as the 'Wood Lily' in New England, as the 'Meadow Lily' in Southern New England, as 'Tiger Lily' in Pennsylvania and parts of Ohio as 'Fire Lily' in other parts of Ohio, Indiana, and Illinois, and 'North Carolina Lily' in all of the South except Tennessee and Kentucky where it was known as 'Mountain Lily' and then when the pattern traveled West of the Mississippi but east of the Rockies it was the 'Prairie Lily'. Once it had crossed the Great Divide it was called 'Mariposa Lily'. It is that name which I have chosen for the flower today." Nancy Page, *Birmingham News,* Jan 5, 1937

The majority of lily patterns contain curved elements and have been shown among the flower designs. The lily designs shown here have no curved elements.

Peonies, Quilter's Quest design. **See 306-11.**

Double Peony, *Grandmother Clark's Patchwork Designs, Book 22.* **See 306-10.**

Friendship Lily, *Detroit Free Press.* **See 123-1.**

Flower Vase, *Chicago Tribune.* **See , 252-1.**

Cactus Basket, *Illinois State Register.* **See 306-8.**

Basket of Daffodils, Jinny Beyer, Quilter's Quest design. **See 306-9.**

Potted Star Flower, *Chicago Tribune.* **See 307-1.**

Basket of Lilies, *Kansas City Star.* **See 120-4.**

Tassel Plant, *Ladies Art Company.* **See 171-4.**

❶ **Vase of Flowers,** Alice Brooks, *Detroit Free Press,* Sep 12, 1934.

❷ **Vase of Flowers,** Laura Wheeler, *Indianapolis Star,* Feb 20, 1934.

❸ **Garden of Friendship,** Alice Brooks, *Detroit Free Press,* Feb 11, 1937.

❹ **Basket of Lilies,** Alice Brooks, *Detroit Free Press,* Sep 26, 1934.

❺ **Tea Basket,** *Mrs. Danner's Quilts, Books 1 & 2,* 1934.

❻ **Colonial Basket,** Alice Brooks, *Detroit Free Press,* Jan 8, 1934.

❼ **Oriental Rose,** Nancy Cabot, *Chicago Tribune,* Oct 13, 1933.

❽ **Rose,** McKim, 1931. Also known as:
Modern Pieced Rose, ca. 1938, per Havig.
Modernistic Rose, Hall, 1935.

❾ **Flower of Friendship,** Laura Wheeler, *Cincinnati Enquirer,* Jul 25, 1934.

❿ **Sunflower,** Laura Wheeler, *Cincinnati Enquirer,* Dec 7, 1935.

⓫ **Grandmother's Favorite,** Laura Wheeler, *Cincinnati Enquirer,* Aug 31, 1935.

⓬ **Star Flower,** Laura Wheeler, *Cincinnati Enquirer,* Sep 2, 1934.

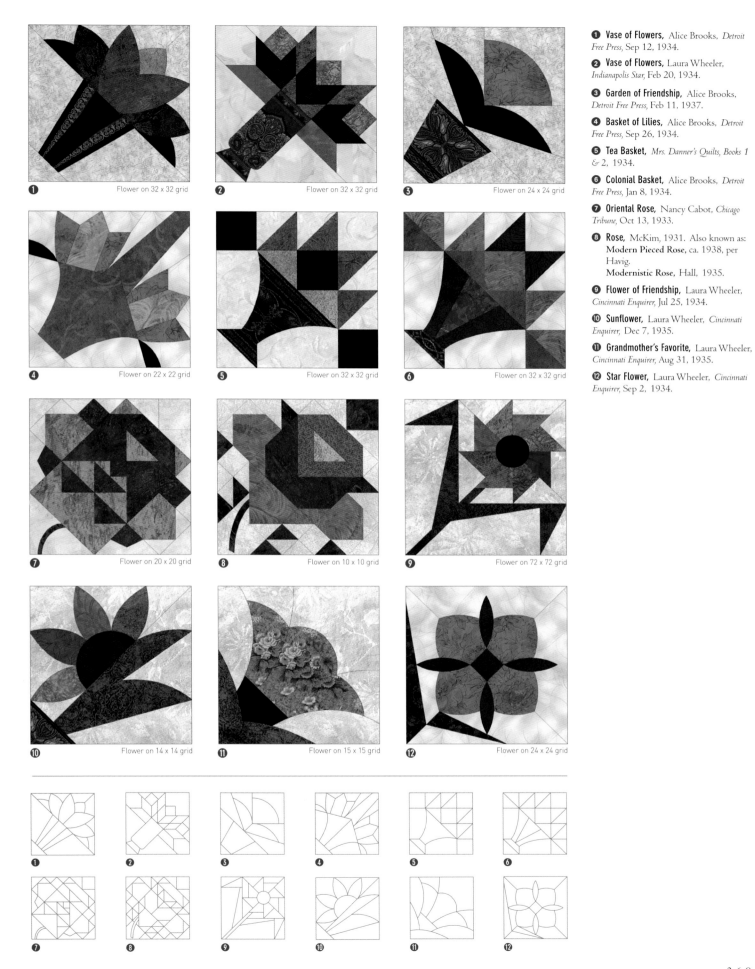

❶ **Tulip Garden,** Alice Brooks, *Detroit Free Press,* Sep 7, 1936.

❷ **Morning Glory,** Alice Brooks, *Detroit Free Press,* Aug 30, 1934.

❸ **Japanese Morning Glory,** Laura Wheeler, *Cincinnati Enquirer,* Jul 17, 1934.

❹ **Garden Treasure,** Alice Brooks, *Detroit Free Press,* Oct 2, 1935.

❺ **Calla Lily,** Laura Wheeler, *Cincinnati Enquirer,* May 7, 1935.

❻ **Tulip Garden,** Laura Wheeler, *Cincinnati Enquirer,* Feb 9, 1935. Also known as:
Tulip in Patchwork, Alice Brooks, Alice Brooks *Designs,* 1935.

❼ **Dogwood,** Alice Brooks, *Detroit Free Press,* Jun 13, 1935.

❽ **Priscilla's Choice,** Laura Wheeler, *Cincinnati Enquirer,* May 23, 1935.

❾ **White Lilies,** Nancy Cabot, *Chicago Tribune,* Oct 16, 1936.

❿ **The White Lily,** *Kansas City Star,* Feb 8, 1936.

⓫ **Arkansas Meadow Rose,** *Kansas City Star,* Oct 9, 1935.

⓬ **My Little Girl's Skirt,** *Kansas City Star,* Apr 23, 1952.
"A twofold purpose inspired Mrs. Bertha Capps, Sallisaw, Ok., to create this design. One was to make an interesting use of scraps left from frocks made for her little daughter and the other was to have a memory quilt top. She chose leftovers from plaids and small prints for the larger pie-shaped pieces, and solids for the fillers." *Kansas City Star,* Apr 23, 1952

⓭ **Round Table,** Clara Stone, *Practical Needlework,* ca. 1906.

❶ Flower on 40 x 40 grid

❷ Flower on 18 x 18 grid

❸ Flower on 17 x 17 grid

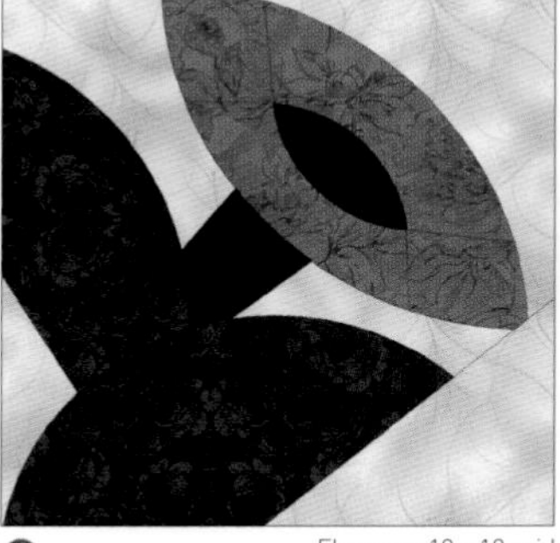

❹ Flower on19 x 19 grid

❺ Flower on 20 x 20 grid

❻ Flower on 32 x 32 grid

❼ Flower on 20 x 20 grid

❽ Flower on 22 x 22 grid

❾ Flower on 8-pointed star grid 1

❿ Flower on 4 x 4 grid

⓫ Flower on 8 x 8 grid

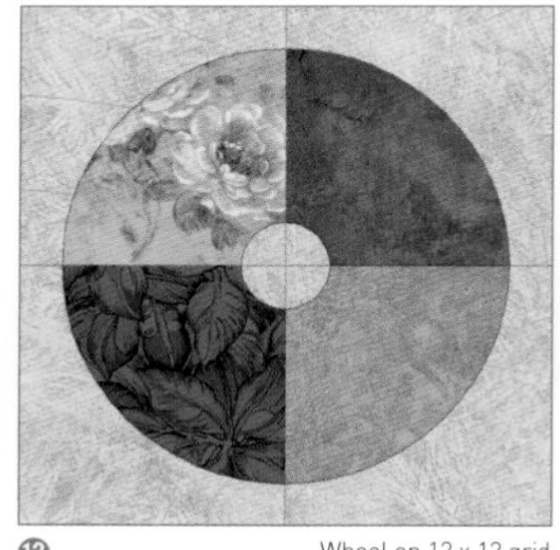

⓬ Wheel on 12 x 12 grid

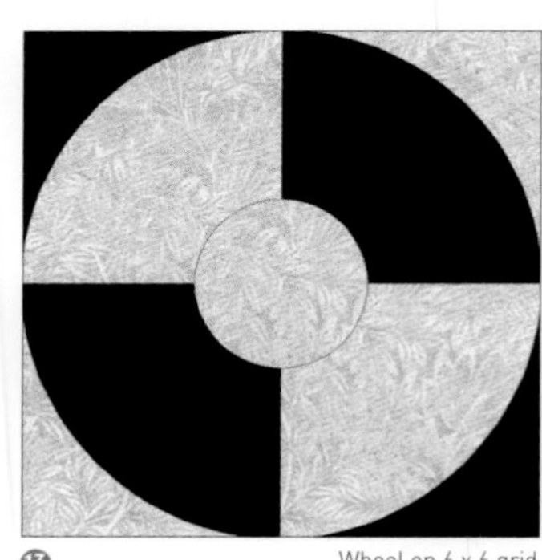

⓭ Wheel on 6 x 6 grid

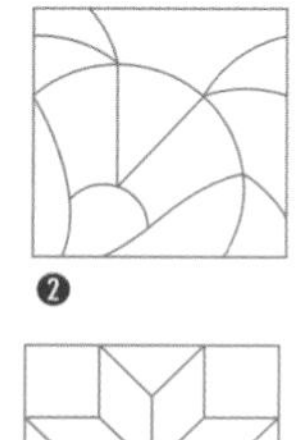
❶

❷

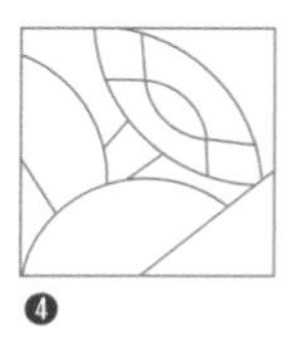
❸

❹

❺ ❻

❼

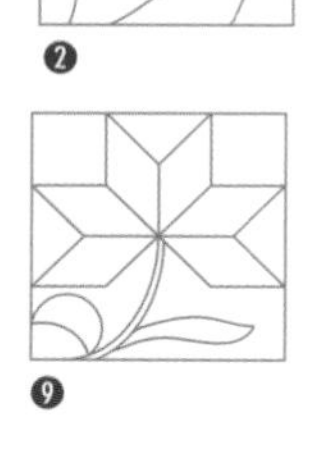
❽

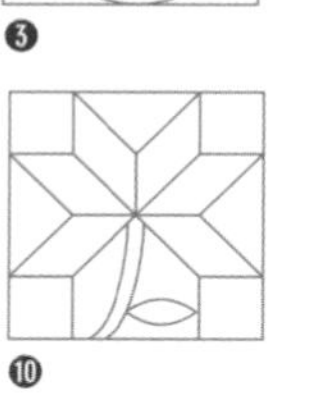
❾

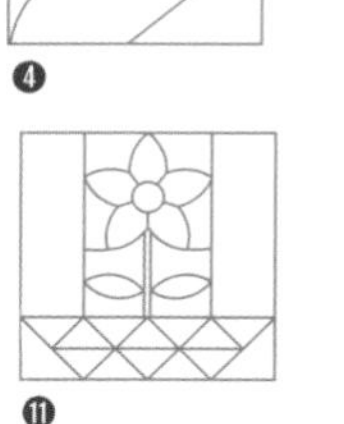
❿

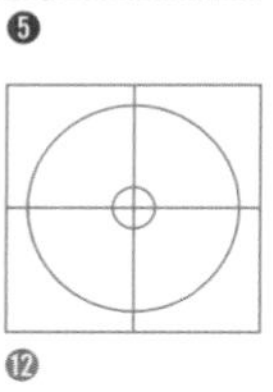
⓫

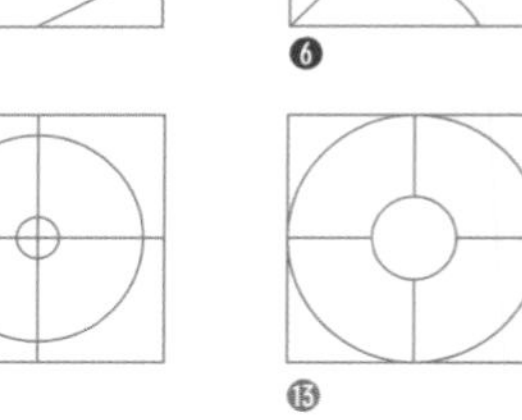
⓬ ⓭

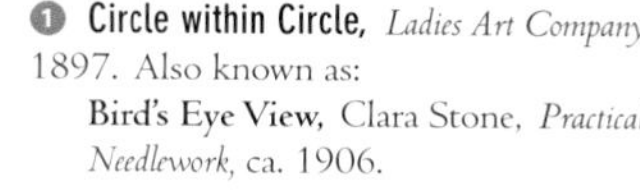

❶ **Circle within Circle,** *Ladies Art Company,* 1897. Also known as:

- **Bird's Eye View,** Clara Stone, *Practical Needlework,* ca. 1906.

❷ **Baby Aster,** *Prize Winning Designs,* ca. 1931.

❸ **Wagon Wheels Carry Me Home,** *Kansas City Star,* Jun 4, 1952.

❹ **The Old Fashioned Wagon Wheel,** *Kansas City Star,* Jul 20, 1955.

❺ **Circle within Circle,** Nancy Cabot, *Chicago Tribune,* Jan 8, 1935.

❻ **Three Patch,** Alice Brooks, *Detroit Free Press,* Jul 1, 1934.

❼ **True Lover's Buggy Wheel,** Eveline Foland, *Kansas City Star,* Feb 1, 1930. Also known as:

- **Wheel of Chance,** Eveline Foland, *Kansas City Star,* Feb 1, 1930.

❽ **Golden Wedding Ring,** *Kansas City Star,* Mar 12, 1952.

❾ **Fair Play,** *Dakota Farmer,* Feb 15, 1927

❿ **The Pig Pen,** *Kansas City Star,* Mar 22, 1939.

⓫ **Millwheel,** Laura Wheeler, *Sioux City Journal,* Apr 28, 1938.

⓬ **Wheel of Fortune,** Eveline Foland, *Kansas City Star,* Jun 25, 1932.

⓭ **The Formal Flower Bed,** *Kansas City Star,* Dec 1, 1943.

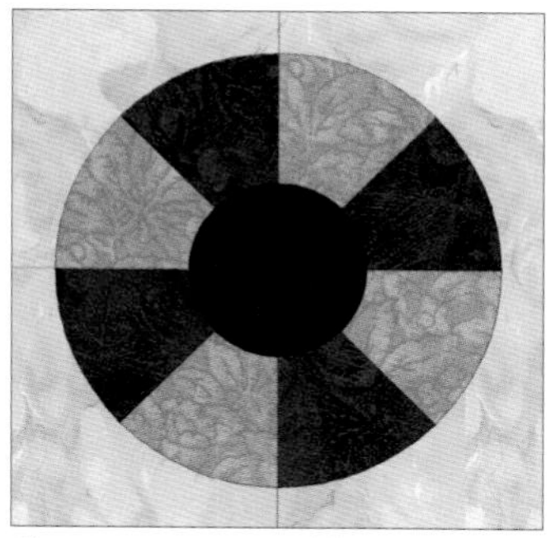

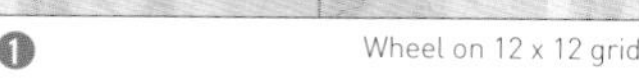

❶ Wheel on 12 x 12 grid

❷ Wheel on 11 x 11 grid

❸ Wheel on 3 x 3 grid

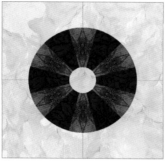

❹ Wheel on 12 x 12 grid

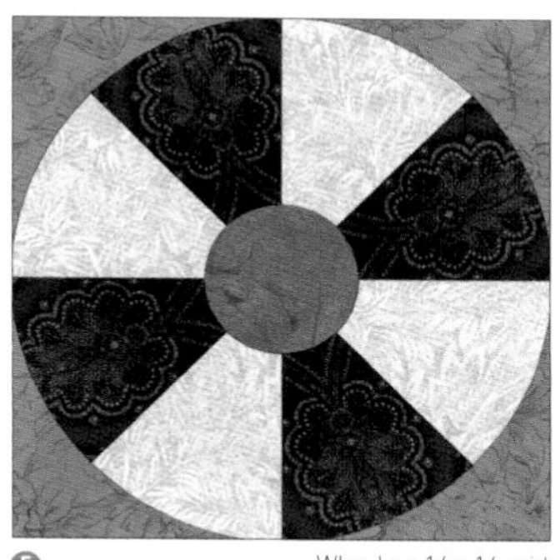

❺ Wheel on 14 x 14 grid

❻ Wheel on 8-pointed star grid 1

❼ Wheel on 16 x 16 grid

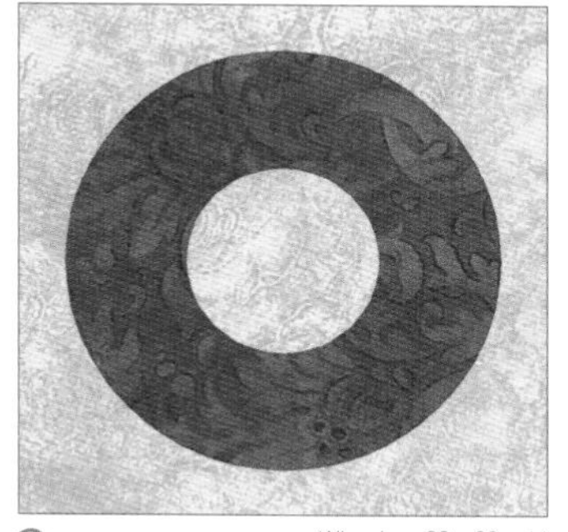

❽ Wheel on 22 x 22 grid

❾ Wheel on 8 x 8 grid

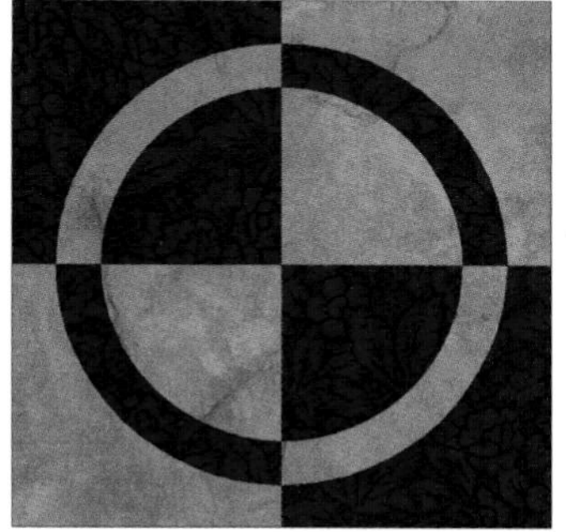

❿ Wheel on 12 x 12 grid

⓫ Wheel on 16 x 16 grid

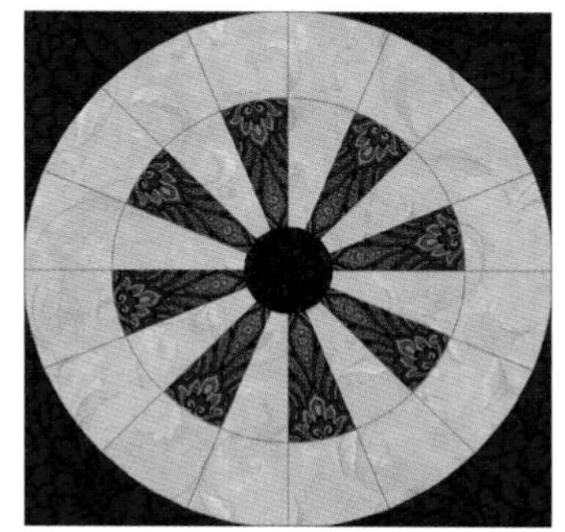

⓬ Wheel on 12 x 12 grid

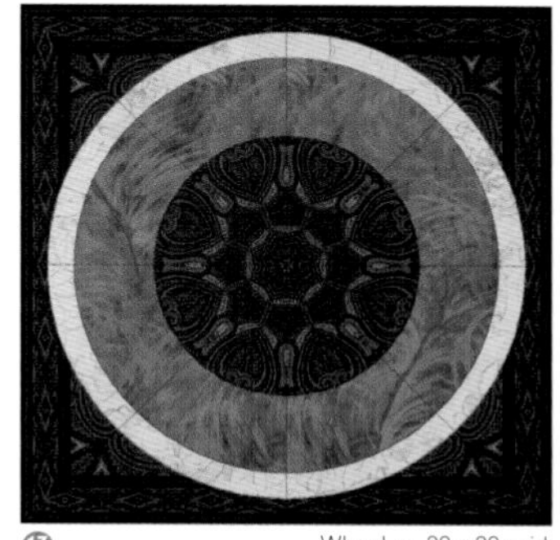

⓭ Wheel on 20 x 20 grid

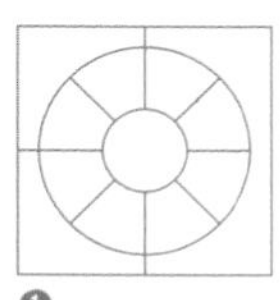

❶

❷

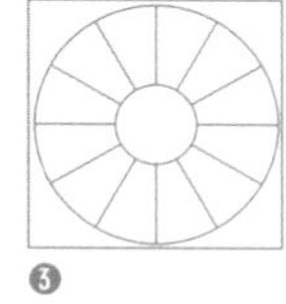

❸

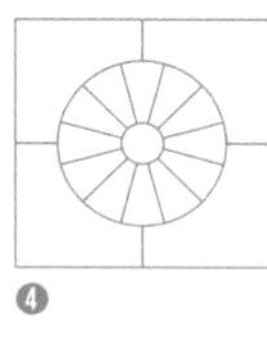

❹

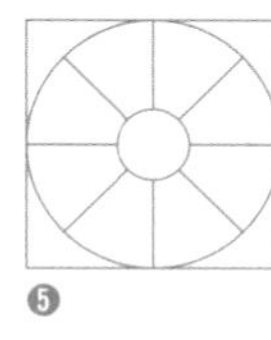

❺

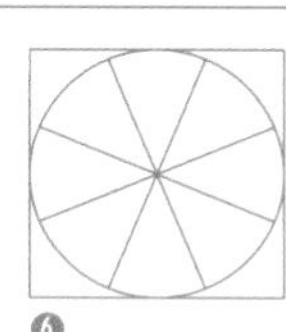

❻

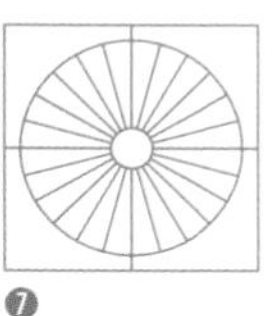

❼

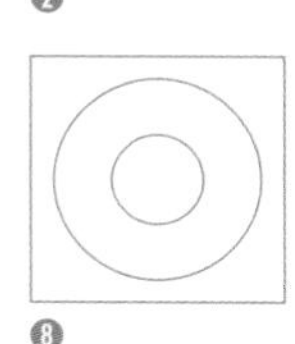

❽

❾

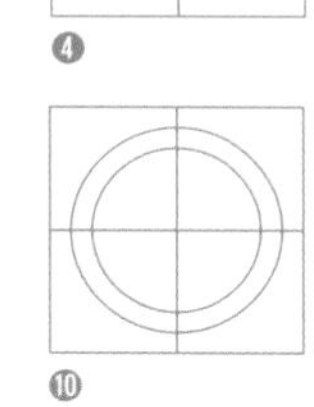

❿

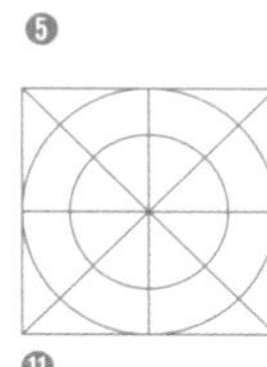

⓫

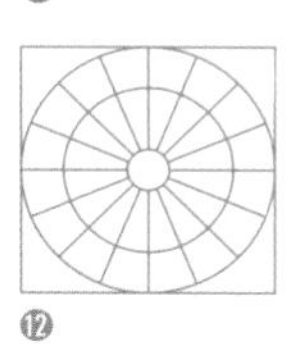

⓬

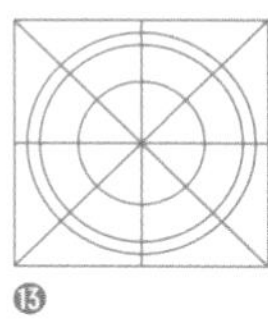

⓭

1 **The Wagon Wheel,** Nancy Cabot, *Chicago Tribune,* Sep 26, 1937. Also known as:
 The Wheel, Nancy Cabot, *Chicago Tribune,* Sep 26, 1937.

2 **Wheel of Fortune,** Webster, 1915.

3 **Gene's Pride,** Home Art Studios, *Evening World Herald,* Nov 9, 1933.

4 **Fortune's Wheel,** Nancy Cabot, *Chicago Tribune,* Oct 28, 1934.
"'Fortune's Wheel' is a variation of the original wheel of fortune created in 1850, which was a combination pieced and appliqué block. 'Fortune's Wheel' is an entirely pieced pattern. Each pattern follows the wheel idea, however, and each dates back to the time when circles, conical patches, and pie shaped pieces were cut with bowls or plates serving as patterns for the sizes desired." Nancy Cabot, *Chicago Tribune,* Oct 28, 1934

5 **Queen of the May,** Laura Wheeler, *Topeka State Journal,* Mar 29, 1934.

6 **Aster,** Laura Wheeler, *Kansas City Star,* Nov 13, 1933.

7 **Wheel of Fortune,** Alice Brooks, *Detroit Free Press,* Mar 16, 1934.

8 **Air Ship Propeller,** *Kansas City Star,* Jul 8, 1933.

9 **Double Rainbow,** Laura Wheeler, *Columbus Evening Dispatch,* Feb 6, 1943.

10 **Dogwood Bloom,** Clara Stone, *Practical Needlework,* ca. 1906.

11 **Mountain Pink,** *Prize Winning Designs,* ca. 1931.

12 **The Broken Crown,** *Kansas City Star,* May 6, 1933.

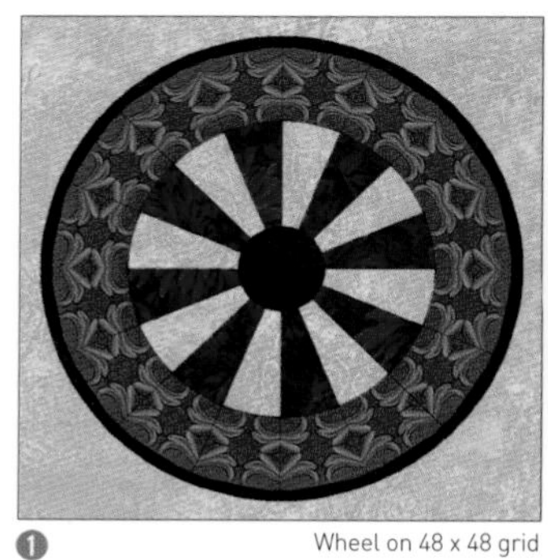

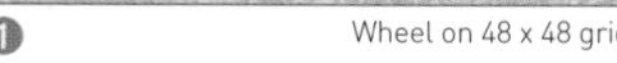

1 Wheel on 48 x 48 grid

2 Wheel on 18 x 18 grid

3 Wheel on 24 x 24 grid

4 Wheel on 32 x 32 grid

5 Wheel on 6 x 6 grid

6 Wheel on 40 x 40 grid

7 Wheel on 14 x 14 grid

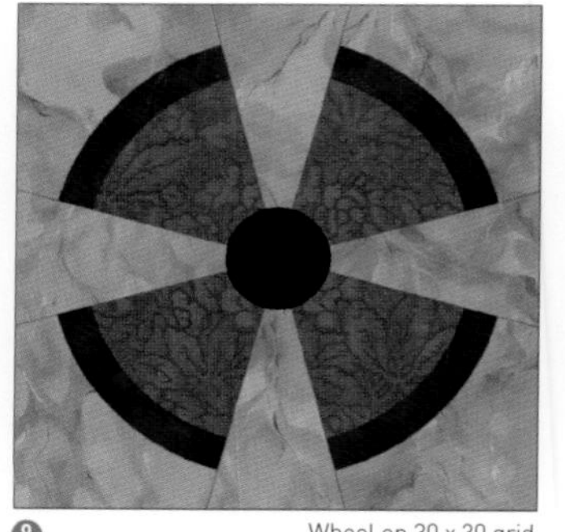

8 Wheel on 30 x 30 grid

9 Wheel on 13 x 13 grid

10 Wheel on 15 x 15 grid

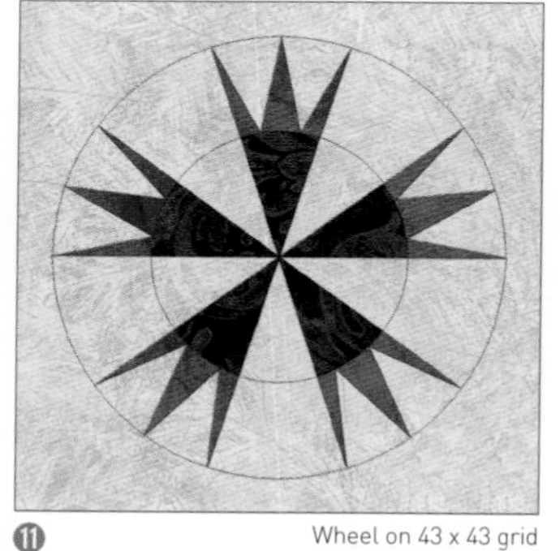

11 Wheel on 43 x 43 grid

12 Wheel on 20 x 20 grid

1

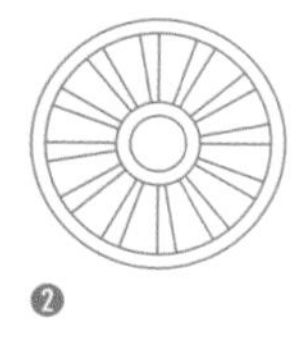

2

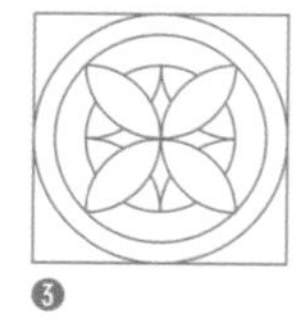

3

4

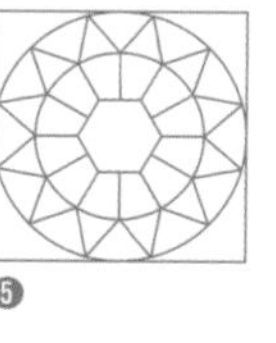

5

6

7

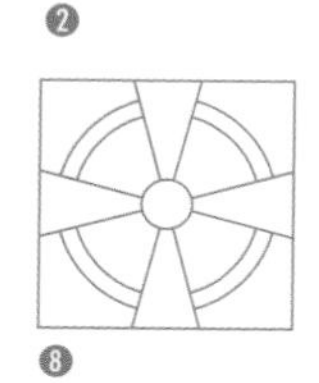

8

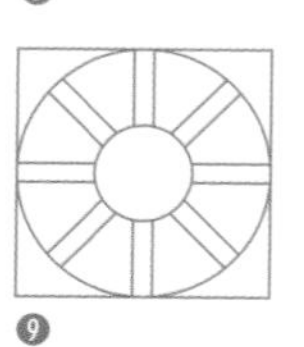

9

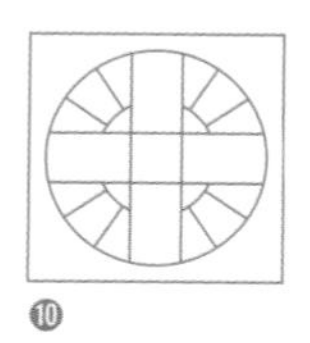

10

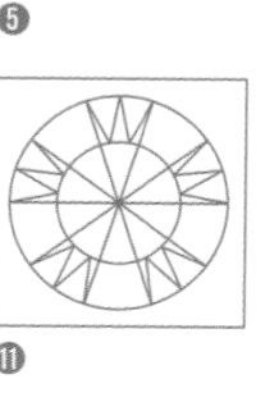

11

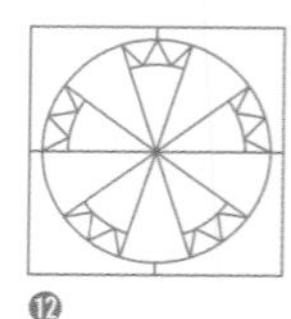

12

❶ **Mountain Pink,** Nancy Cabot, *Chicago Tribune,* Jun 3, 1933.

❷ **The Compass,** *Prize Winning Designs,* ca. 1931.

❸ **Compass,** Nancy Cabot, *Chicago Tribune,* Jun 27, 1933. Also known as:

- **Calico Compass,** Nancy Cabot, *Chicago Tribune,* Nov 17, 1937.

❹ **Flower Star,** Nancy Cabot, *Chicago Tribune,* Jun 18, 1937.

❺ **Fortune's Wheel,** *Ladies Art Company,* 1928.

❻ **Cogwheel,** *Grandmother's Patchwork Quilt Designs, Book 20,* 1931.

❼ **Morning Glory,** Aunt Martha series: *The Quilt Fair Comes to You,* ca. 1933. Also known as:

- **Wheel,** *Farmer's Wife Book of New Designs and Patterns,* 1934.

❽ **Pyrotechnics,** *Ladies Art Company,* 1897. Also known as:

- **Wheel,** *Farm Journal Quilt Patterns,* ca. 1935.

❾ **Pyrotechnics,** Hall, 1935.

❿ **Georgetown Circle,** *Ladies Art Company,* 1897.

⓫ **Georgetown Circle,** *Prize Winning Designs,* ca. 1931.

⓬ **Georgetown Circle,** Hall, 1935.

❶ Wheel on 32 x 32 grid

❷ Wheel on 8-pointed star grid 4

❸ Wheel on 8-pointed star grid 1

❹ Wheel on 24 x 24 grid

❺ Wheel on 56 x 56 grid

❻ Wheel on 40 x 40 grid

❼ Wheel on 30 x 30 grid

❽ Wheel on 13 x 13 grid

❾ Wheel on 13 x 13 grid

❿ Wheel on 8-pointed star grid 4

⓫ Wheel on 56 x 56 grid

⓬ Wheel on 64 x 64 grid

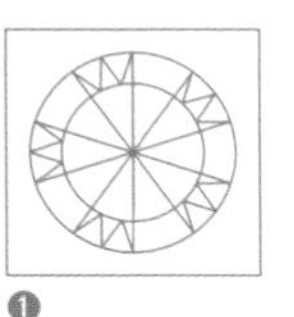

❶

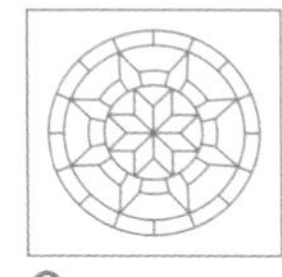

❷

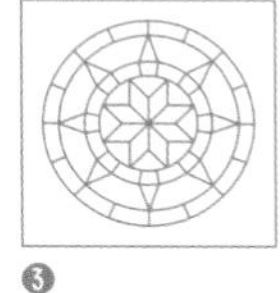

❸

❹

❺

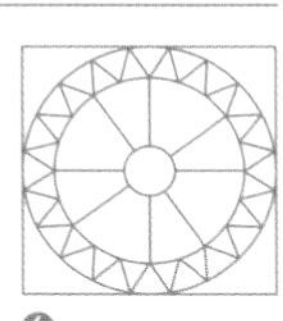

❻

❼

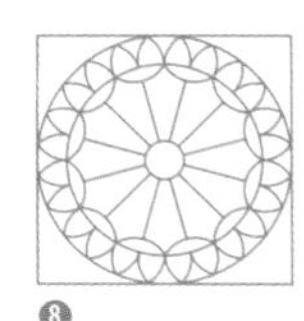

❽

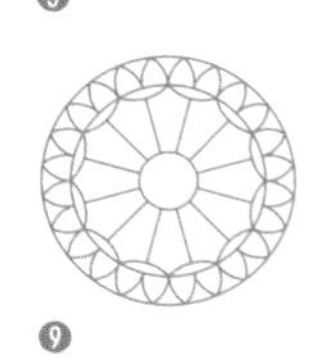

❾

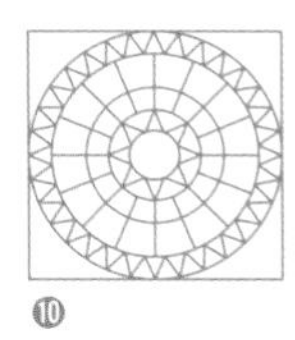

❿

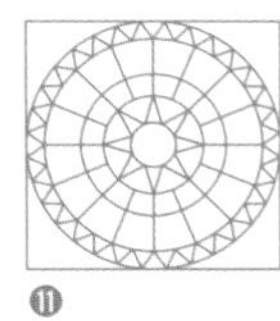

⓫

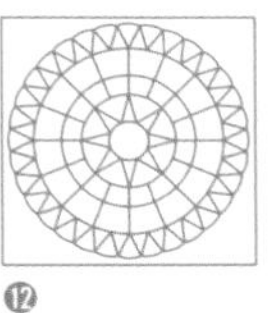

⓬

1 Feathered Star, Laura Wheeler, *Kansas City Star*, Oct 13, 1933.

2 Rising Sun, *Ladies Art Company*, 1897. Also known as:

- **The Rising Sun,** *Q Book 130, Keepsake Quilts*, ca. 1990.
- **The Wheel of Life,** Home Art Studios, *Cincinnati Enquirer*, Feb 1, 1933

3 Rising Sun, *Kansas City Star*, Feb 2, 1929. Also known as:

- **The Circle Saw,** *Kansas City Star*, Jun 30, 1954.
- **Flywheel,** *Grandmother's Patchwork Quilt Designs, Book 20*, 1931.

4 The Wheel of Fortune, *Kansas City Star*, Nov 12, 1952.

5 Whirlwind, *The Patchwork Book*, 1932. Also known as:

- **Reacting Wheel,** Aunt Martha series: *The Quilt Fair Comes to You*, 1933.
- **Whirling Wheel,** *The Patchwork Book*, 1932.

6 Wheel of Time, *The Dressmaking Book*, ca. 1932.

7 Parasol Block, Nancy Cabot, *Chicago Tribune*, Feb 5, 1937.

8 Dresden Plate, Home Art Studios, *Cincinnati Enquirer*, Jan 26, 1933.

"If you have ever wondered how to make an old shabby bedroom cheerful, colorful, modern—your answer is quilts!

Look again at the fascinating patchwork design illustrated above. This Dresden plate quilt design is one that your great-grandmother delighted in making, and nothing at the present time is more modern." *World Herald*, Jan 26, 1933

9 Daisy Patchwork, Laura Wheeler, *Minneapolis Star*, date unknown.

10 Dessert Plate, *Kansas City Star*, Jun 23, 1954.

11 Missouri Sunflower, *Kansas City Star*, May 7, 1941.

12 Dresden Plate, Home Art Studios, *World Herald*, Jan 30, 1934.

1 Wheel on 7 x 7 grid

2 Wheel on 7 x 7 grid

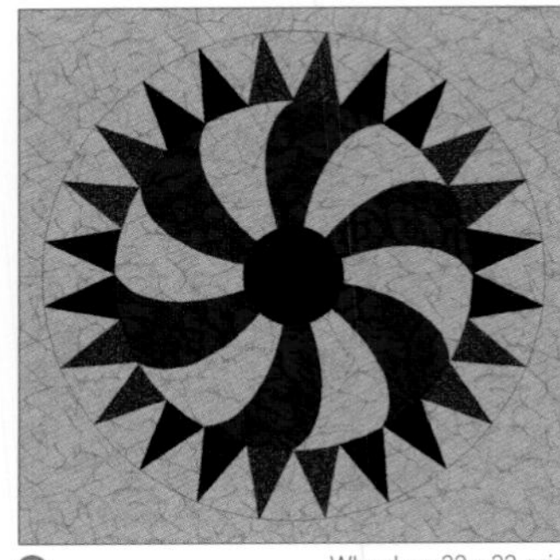
3 Wheel on 22 x 22 grid

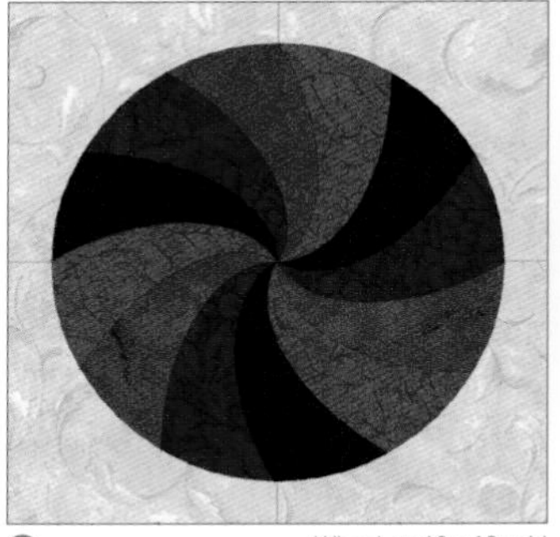
4 Wheel on 12 x 12 grid

5 Wheel on pentagon grid

6 Wheel on 7 x 7 grid

7 Wheel on 20 x 20 grid

8 Dresden Plate on 8 x 8 grid

9 Dresden Plate on 20 x 20 grid

10 Dresden Plate on 12 x 12 grid

11 Dresden Plate on 17 x17 grid

12 Dresden Plate on 8 x 8 grid

1

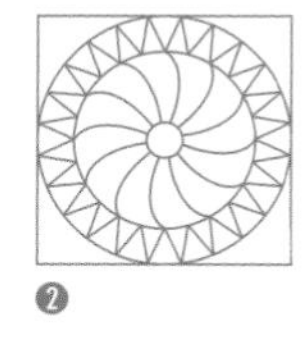
2

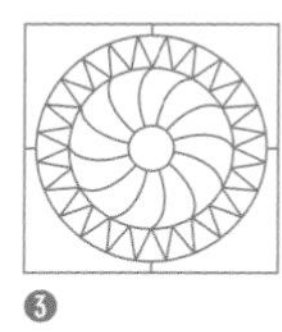
3

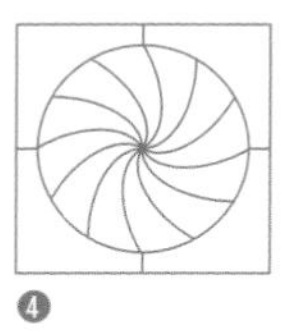
4

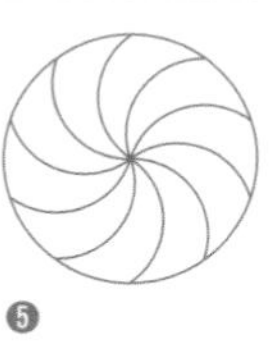
5

6

7

8

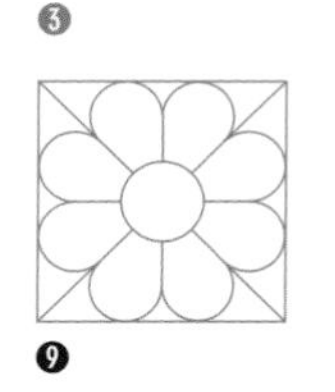
9

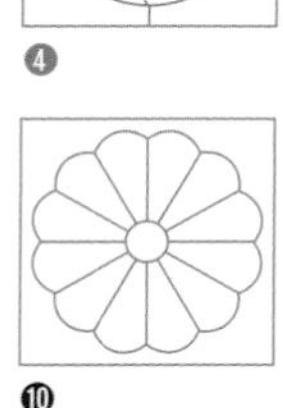
10

11

12

1 Dresden Plate on 26 x 26 grid

2 Dresden Plate on 18 x 18 grid

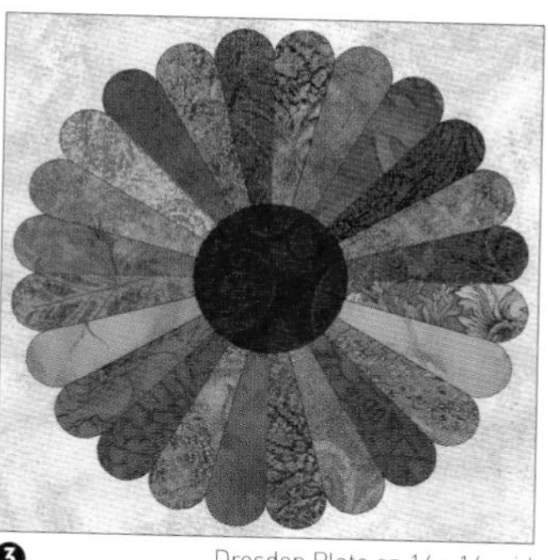

3 Dresden Plate on 14 x 14 grid

4 Dresden Plate on 18 x 18 grid

5 Dresden Plate on 18 x 18 grid

6 Dresden Plate on 6 x 6 grid

7 Dresden Plate on 26 x 26 grid

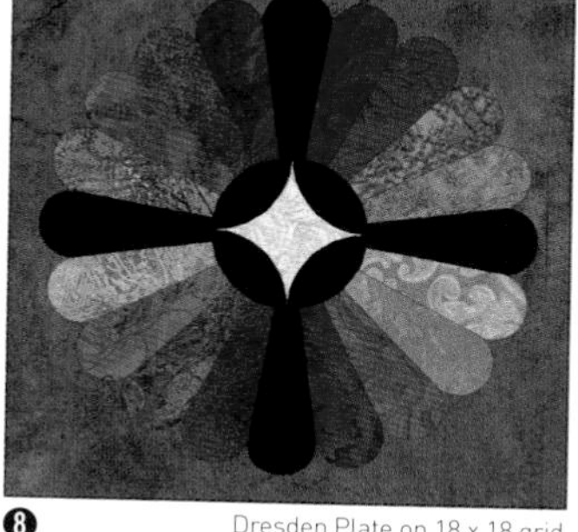

8 Dresden Plate on 18 x 18 grid

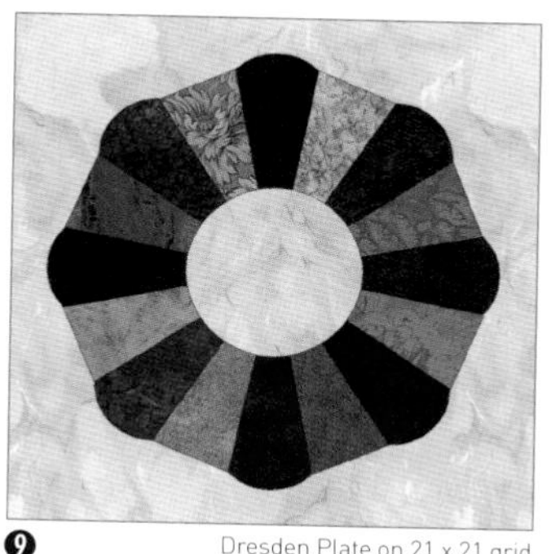

9 Dresden Plate on 21 x 21 grid

10 Dresden Plate on 21 x 21 grid

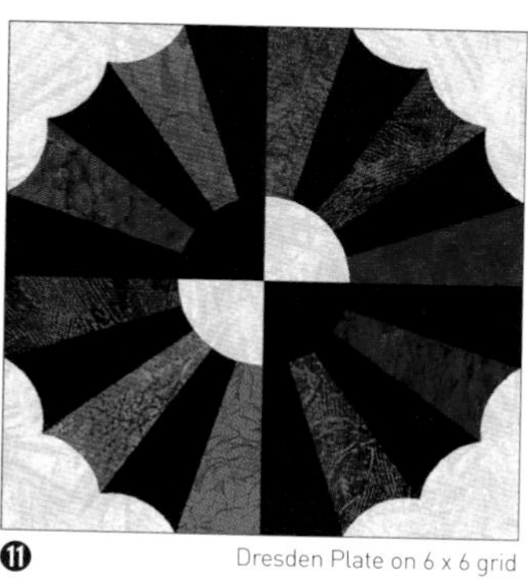

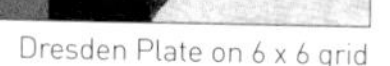

11 Dresden Plate on 6 x 6 grid

12 Dresden Plate on 30 x 30 grid

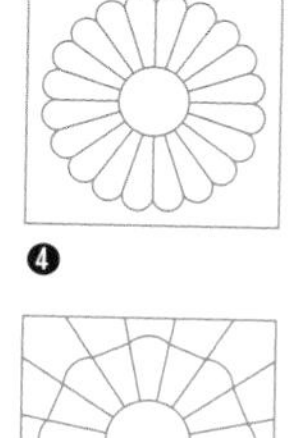

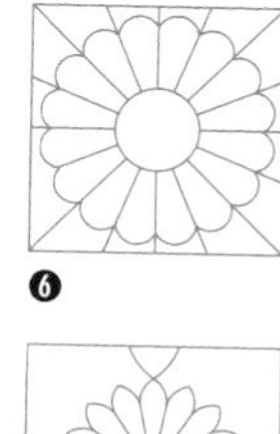

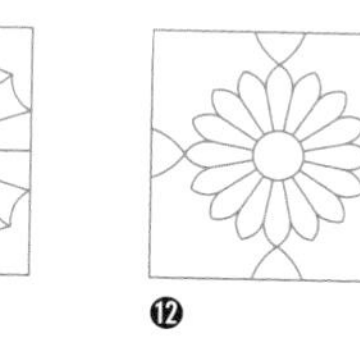

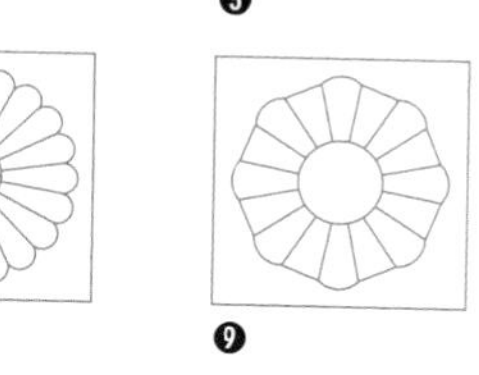

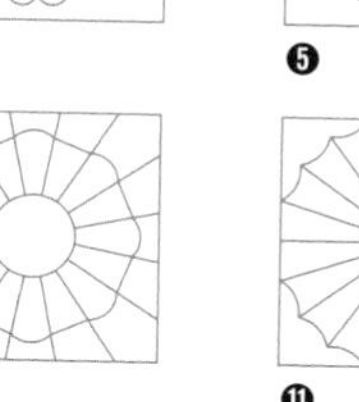

1 2 3 4 5 6

7 8 9 10 11 12

1 **Dresden Plate,** *Grandmother Clark's Patchwork Quilts, Book No.* 19, 1932.

2 **Friendship,** *Old Fashioned Quilts,* ca. 1931.

3 **The Aster,** Jane Alan, Alan, 1933. Also known as:

Friendship Ring, Jane Alan, Alan, 1933.

4 **Grandmother's Sunbonnet,** *Quilt Booklet No.* 1, ca. 1931. Also known as:

Dresden Plate, Nancy Cabot, *Chicago Tribune,* Mar 30, 1933.

Friendship Ring, Nancy Cabot, *Chicago Tribune,* Mar 30, 1933.

5 **The Aster Quilt,** Eveline Foland, *Kansas City Star,* Feb 22, 1930. Also known as:

Dresden Plate, Ruby McKim, *Kansas City Star,* Aug 29, 1931.

Friendship Ring, Eveline Foland, *Kansas City Star,* Feb 22, 1930.

6 **Dresden Plate,** Laura Wheeler, *Cincinnati Enquirer,* Jul 26, 1933.

7 **Dresden Plate,** Aunt Martha series: *Bold and Beautiful Quilts,* ca. 1977.

8 **The Friendship Circle Quilt,** Home Art Studios, *World Herald,* Jul 22, 1933.

"For those who know how to love, and how to feel the love of their children, quilt making has been a special joy. Thousands upon thousands of others have made these keepsakes for their children, as a labor of love, and well are they repaid, for the quilt made by other's own hands is their most prized possession. 'The Friendship Circle' quilt, with the entwined hearts quilting design makes an admirable remembrance quilt." *World Herald,* Oct 14, 1933

9 **Dresden Plate,** Alice Brooks, *Detroit Free Press,* May 11, 1940.

10 **Friendship Plate,** Alice Brooks, *Detroit Free Press,* Nov 9, 1933.

11 **Setting Sun,** Laura Wheeler, *Cincinnati Enquirer,* Sep 26, 1933.

"The old-time quiltmaker, whose day often started with the rising sun, was so taken with the beauty of the sunrise and sunset, that she was inspired to capture it in her quilts. There are many 'Rising Sun' and 'Setting Sun' patterns, but probably the loveliest is the 'Setting Sun.' Here is not only the sun in all its glory, but the tiny clouds that so often accompany the sunset are also scattered throughout the quilt. The rays of the sun can be done in scraps, as shown here, or the dark patches can all be done in one material, the light, figured ones in a second one. Pattern 549 comes to you with complete, simple instructions for cutting, sewing and finishing, together with yardage chart, diagram of quilt to help arrange the blocks for single and double bed size, and a diagram of the block which serves as a guide for placing the patches in suggests contrasting materials. Send 10c for this pattern to The Cincinnati Enquirer Needlecraft Department, 83 Eighth Avenue, New York City." Laura Wheeler, *Cincinnati Enquirer,* Sep 26, 1933

12 **African Daisy,** Nancy Cabot, *Chicago Tribune,* Jun 4, 1935.

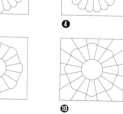

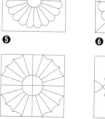

1 **Lenox Plate,** Nancy Page, *Birmingham News,* May 28, 1935.

2 **Nosegay,** Home Art Studios, *Cincinnati Enquirer,* Mar 29, 1933.

3 **Ferris Wheel Quilt,** Aunt Martha series: *Quilt Designs,* ca. 1952. Also known as:
- **Ferris Wheel,** *Kansas City Star,* Jul 29, 1959.

4 **Sunflowers,** Aunt Martha series: *The Quilt Fair Comes to You,* ca. 1933.

5 **China Aster,** *Old Fashioned Quilts,* ca. 1932.

6 **Landon Sunflower,** *Kansas City Star,* Sep 12, 1936.
"Alf Landon, Governor of Kansas, was the GOP candidate against Franklin D. Roosevelt in the 1936 presidential campaign. Kansas City Star, offered a pattern in his name on Sep 12, 1936. From the beginning of American quilt-making, patterns have been named for candidates and campaigns. Mrs. H.E. Meyers, Cherokee, Kas., sends this one to mark the important campaign in Kansas. *Kansas City Star,* Sep 12, 1936

7 **The Sunflower,** Home Art Studios, *Des Moines Register,* Dec 18, 1932.

8 **Sun Flower,** *Grandmother Clark's Patchwork Quilts, Book No.* 19, 1932. Also known as:
- **Aster,** Nancy Cabot, *Chicago Tribune,* Jun 21, 1933.
- **Asters,** Nancy Cabot, *Chicago Tribune,* Oct 29, 1935.

"Called Friendship Ring or Dresden Plate when ends of petals are rounded instead of pointed." *Grandmother Clark's Patchwork Quilts, Book No.* 19,1932

9 **Design 2467,** *Virginia Snow Studio Art Needlework Creations,* 1932. Also known as:
- **Aster,** Hall, 1935.
- **Dresden Plate,** Hall, 1935.
- **Friendship Ring,** Hall, 1935.
- **Sunflower,** *Grandma Dexter's Appliqué and Patchwork Designs, Book 36a,* ca. 1932.

10 **Friendship Daisy,** Nancy Cabot, *Chicago Tribune,* Jan 27, 1936.
"Like 'Friendship Ring,' 'Friendship Dahlia,' and various other friendship blocks, 'Friendship Daisy' is composed of a variety of prints. In days of old, the prints were exchanged, hence the name 'friendship' given to the block. Modern quilt makers do not depend upon their neighbors but rather upon their shopkeepers for the entire selection of prints." Nancy Cabot, *Chicago Tribune,* Jan 27, 1936

11 **The Buzz Saw,** *Kansas City Star,* Nov 5, 1941.

12 **Dresden Plate,** Hinson, 1973.

1 Dresden Plate on 48 x 48 grid

2 Dresden Plate on 10 x 10 grid

3 Dresden Plate on 32 x 32 grid

4 Dresden Plate on 8-pointed star grid 3

5 Dresden Plate on 8-pointed star grid 3

6 Dresden Plate on 8-pointed star grid 1

7 Dresden Plate on 14 X 14 grid

8 Dresden Plate on 5 X 5 grid

9 Dresden Plate on 12 X 12 grid

10 Dresden Plate on 22 X 22 grid

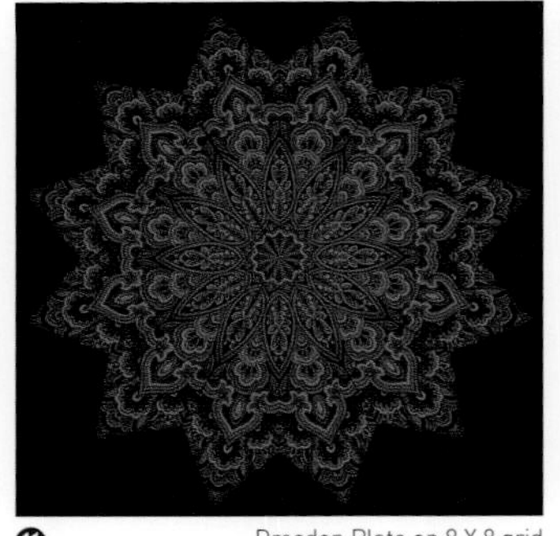
11 Dresden Plate on 8 X 8 grid

12 Dresden Plate on 10 X 10 grid

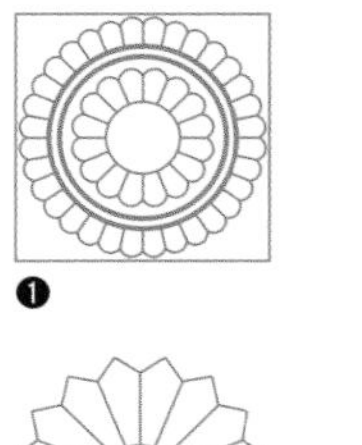

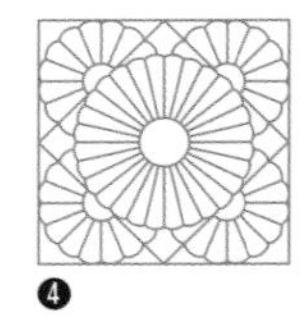

1 2 3 4 5 6

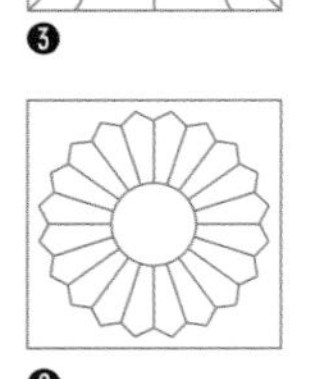
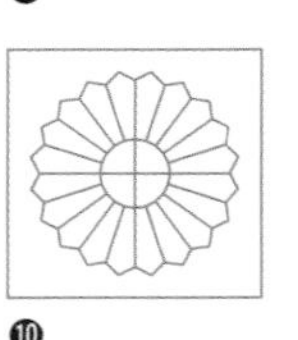
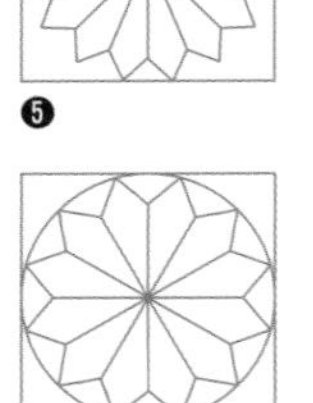

7 8 9 10 11 12

1 Dresden Plate on 8-pointed star grid

2 Dresden Plate on 12 x 12 grid

3 Dresden Plate on 12 x 12 grid

4 Dresden Plate on 16 x 16 grid

5 Dresden Plate on 26 x 26 grid

6 Dresden Plate on 11 x11 grid

7 Dresden Plate on 14 x 14 grid

8 Dresden Plate on 8-pointed star grid 1

9 Dresden Plate on 8-pointed star grid 1

10 Dresden Plate on 20 x 20 grid

11 Dresden Plate on 16 x 16 grid

12 Dresden Plate on 30 x 30 grid

1 **Pinwheel,** *Grandma Dexter New Appliqué and Patchwork Designs, Book 36b,* ca. 1932.

2 **Farmer's Delight,** ca. 1842, per *Quilts of Virginia.* Also known as:
  Farmer's Fancy, ca. 1842, per *Quilts of Virginia.*

3 **Farmer's Delight,** ca. 1842, per *Quilts of Virginia.*

4 **The Yellow Gaillardia Quilt,** Home Art Studios, *World Herald,* Nov 14, 1933.

5 **Priscilla Alden,** Nancy Cabot, *Chicago Tribune,* Mar 12, 1933.

"Just the name of this quilt pattern, 'Priscilla Alden,' connotates all that is prim and dainty, simple and charming. The pattern is the epitomization of all these associations. The name, too, placed the credit for its origin unmistakably with the Pilgrims. And though the design is an old one, it is not old fashioned but one that is becoming increasingly popular with the young moderns of this generation." Nancy Cabot, *Chicago Tribune,* Mar 12, 1933

6 **Turk's Cap Lily,** Nancy Cabot, *Chicago Tribune,* Apr 16, 1936.

7 **Daisy Swirl,** Nancy Cabot, *Chicago Tribune,* Apr 25, 1933. Also known as:
  Friendship Dahlia, Nancy Cabot, *Chicago Tribune,* Sep 7, 1937.
  Friendship Flower, Nancy Cabot, *Chicago Tribune,* Sep 7, 1937.

"A youngster in quiltdom to have attained such a high position on the popularity platform, the 'Daisy Swirl,' is scarcely two years old; yet it has superseded many older and more historically important patterns in favor and May soon compete with 'Double Wedding' and 'Grandma's Garden.'" Nancy Cabot, *Chicago Tribune,* Apr 25, 1933

8 **Chinese Waterwheel,** Nancy Cabot, *Chicago Tribune,* Oct 5, 1936.

9 **Merry Go Round,** Laura Wheeler, *Sioux City Journal,* Mar 28, 1941.

10 **Wheel of Fortune,** Laura Wheeler, *Cincinnati Enquirer,* Aug 16, 1933.

11 **Pinwheel,** Alice Brooks, *Washington Post,* Mar 16, 1947.

12 **Evelyne's Whirling Dust Storm,** *Kansas City Star,* May 5, 1943.

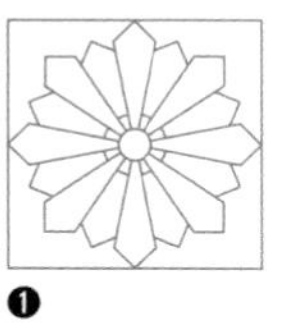

1

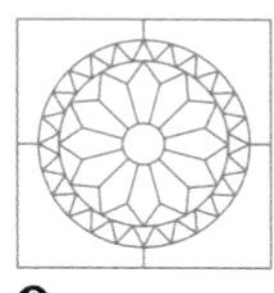

2

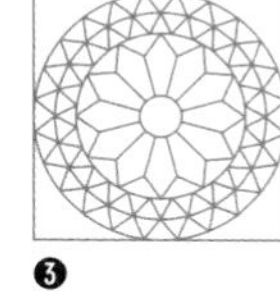

3

4

5

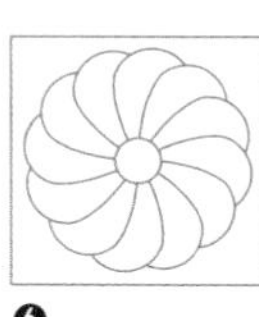

6

7

8

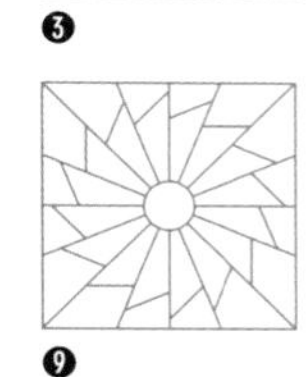

9

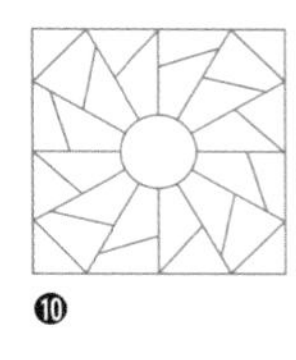

10

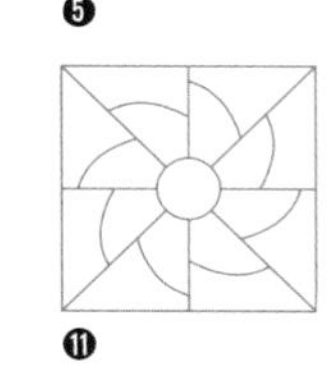

11

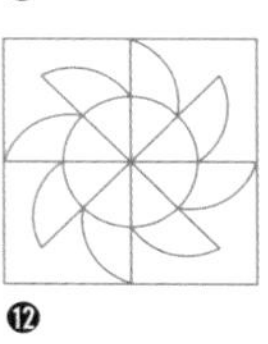

12

1 **Four and Four,** *Farm Journal and Farmers Wife,* ca. 1941.

2 **Circle Star,** ca. 1840, per *Quilts of Virginia.*

3 **Cather Robinson Compass,** 1848, per *Quilts of Virginia.*

4 **Sunburst,** *Farmer's Wife Book of New Designs and Patterns,* 1934.

5 **Chips and Whetstones,** ca. 1840, per *Quilts of Virginia.* Also known as:
- **Sun Burst,** Ickis, 1949.

6 **Chips and Whetstones,** Eveline Foland, *Kansas City Star,* Sep 19, 1931. Also known as:
- **Crown of Thorns,** Hall, 1935.
- **Georgetown Circle,** Hall, 1935.
- **Memory Wreath,** Hall, 1935.
- **Single Wedding Ring,** Hall, 1935.

"When made of the dresses of a loved one who has passed on it is called 'Memory Wreath' and the name and date of death is embroidered in the center square." Hall, 1935

7 **Blazing Sun,** Hall, 1935. Also known as:
- **Blazing Star,** date unknown; published in Beyer, Jinny, *The Quilter's Album ....*
- **Chips and Whetstones,** date unknown; published in Beyer, Jinny, *The Quilter's Album ....*
- **Mariner's Compass,** date unknown, published in Beyer, Jinny, *The Quilter's Album ....*
- **Sunflower,** Hall, 1935.

8 **Slashed Star,** Hall, 1935.

9 **Sea of Knowledge,** Jinny Beyer, RJR Patterns, 2000.

10 **Slashed Star,** *Ladies Art Company,* 1897. Also known as:
- **Rising Sun,** Nancy Cabot, *Chicago Tribune,* Aug 31, 1937.
- **Sunburst,** Nancy Cabot, *Chicago Tribune,* Aug 31, 1937.
- **Twinkling Star,** Nancy Cabot, *Chicago Tribune,* Aug 31, 1937.

"The 'Slashed Star' design offered today appears at first glance to be too complicated for the amateur or even the experienced quilter. As a matter of fact it is quite easy to piece and the finished quilt is sufficiently beautiful to be well worth the effort." Nancy Cabot, *Chicago Tribune,* Dec 23, 1933

11 **The Rising Sun,** Home Art Studios, *Cincinnati Enquirer,* Jan 29, 1933.

12 **Compass Rose,** Jinny Beyer, Beyer, Jinny, *Quiltmaking by Hand,* 2004.

1 Dresden Plate on 20 x 20 grid

2 Compass on 32 x 32 grid

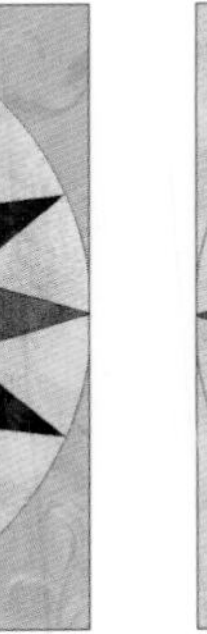

3 Compass on 8-pointed star grid 3

4 Compass on 8-pointed star grid 1

5 Compass on 32 x 32 grid

6 Compass on 8-pointed star grid 1

7 Compass on 8-pointed star grid 1

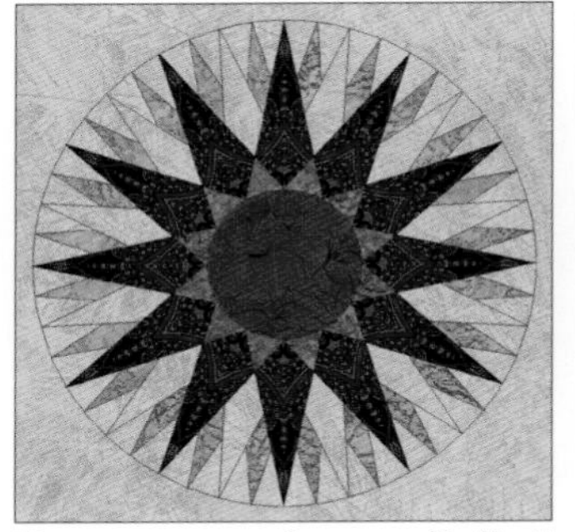

8 Compass on 28 x 28 grid

9 Compass on 8-pointed star grid 1

10 Compass on 13 x 13 grid

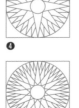

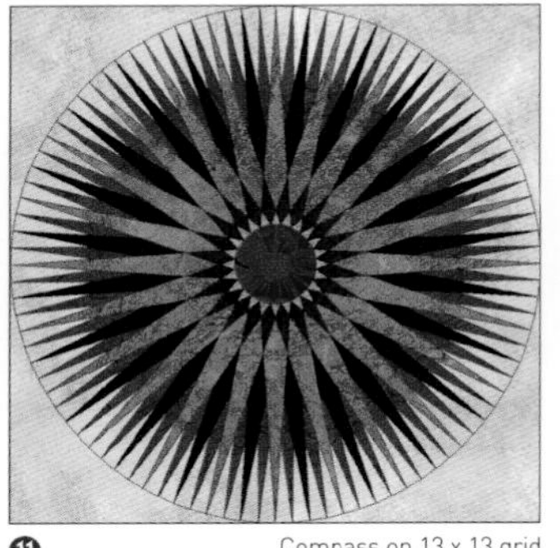

11 Compass on 13 x 13 grid

12 Compass on 8-pointed star grid 1

1

2

3

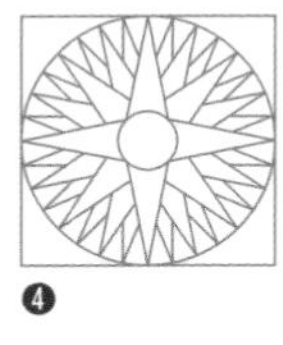

4

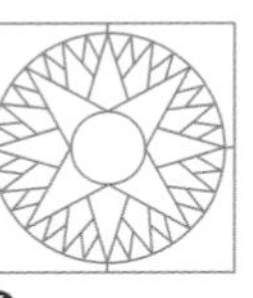

5

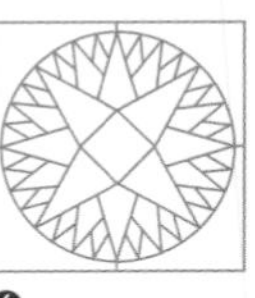

6

7

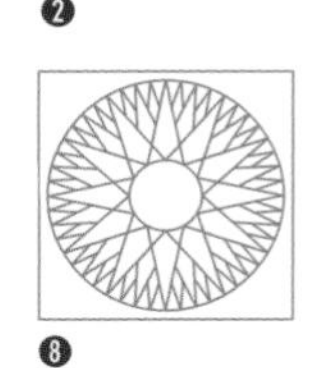

8

9

10

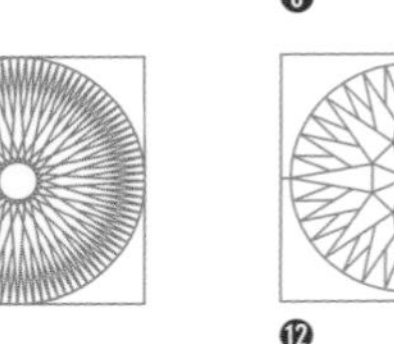

11

12

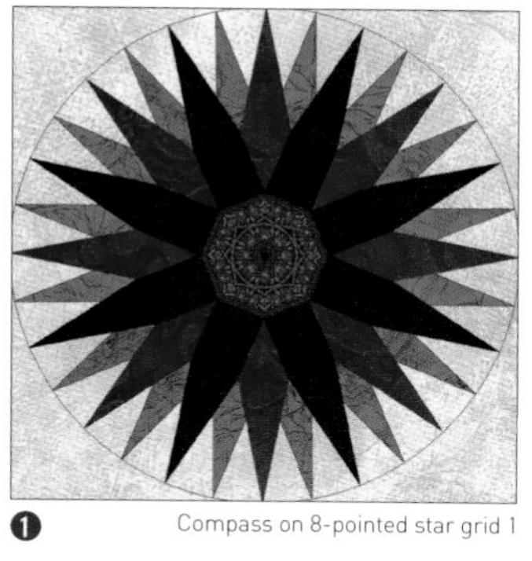

❶ Compass on 8-pointed star grid 1

❷ Compass on 8-pointed star grid 1

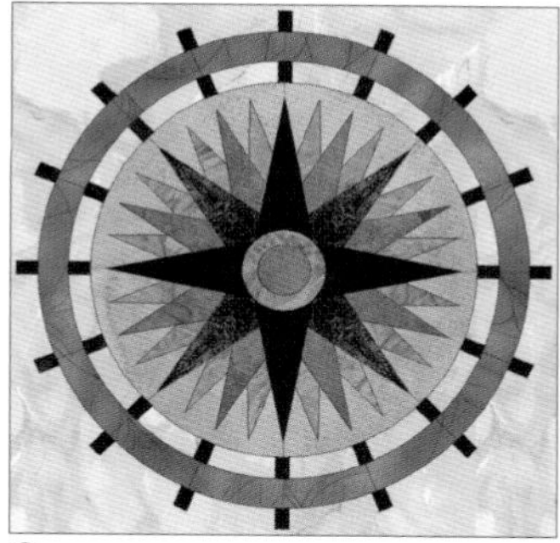

❸ Compass on 8-pointed star grid 1

❹ Compass on 8-pointed star grid 1

❺ Compass on 8-pointed star grid 1

❻ Compass on 8-pointed star grid 1

❼ Compass on 30 x 30 grid

❽ Compass on hexagon grid

❾ Compass on 14 x 14 grid

❿ Compass on 8-pointed star grid 1

⓫ Compass on 8-pointed star grid 1

⓬ Compass on 6 x 6 grid

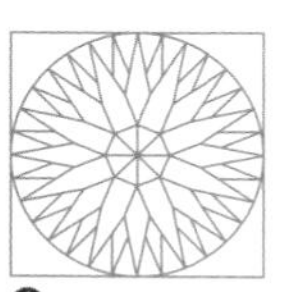
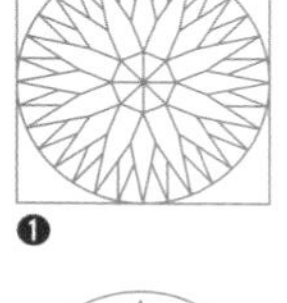

❶

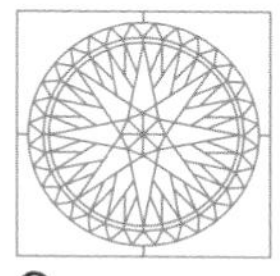

❷

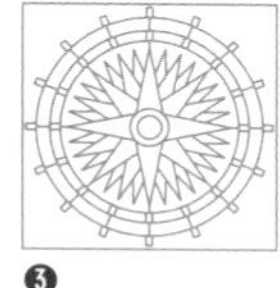

❸

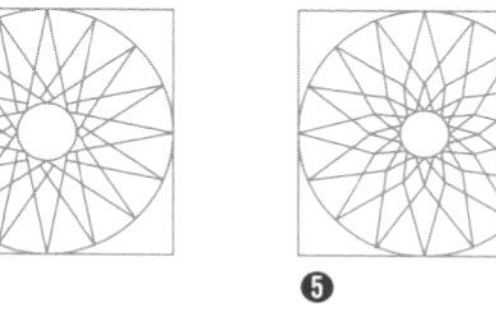
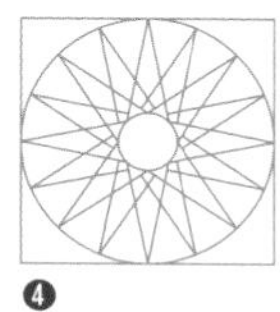

❹

❺

❻

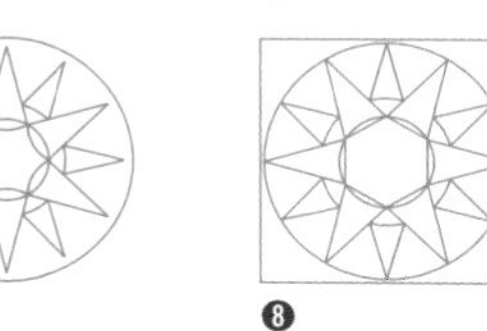

❼

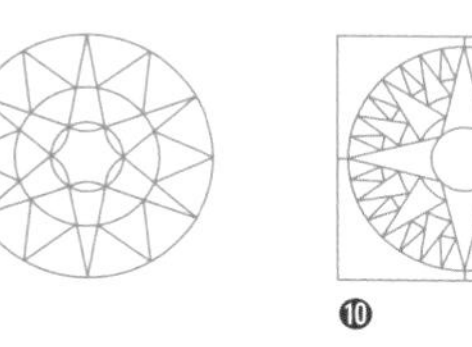

❽

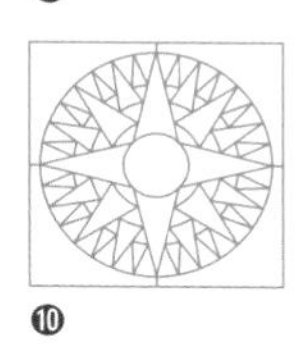

❾

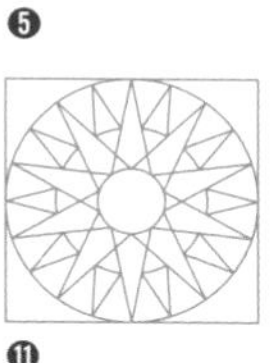
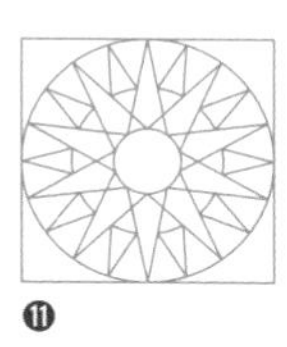

❿

⓫

⓬

❶ **Mariner's Beacon,** Jinny Beyer, Hilton Head Seminar design, 1990.

❷ **Mariner's Compass,** Jinny Beyer, Jinny Beyer Studio design, 1995.

❸ **Mariner's Block,** Nancy Cabot, *Chicago Tribune,* Mar 2, 1936.
"While 'Mariner's Block' is one of the old quilt patterns, it is not listed among the seafaring titled ancients which date back to 1820. This design first was created in Massachusetts in 1863, when the original pattern was entirely pieced. As the design was traded back and forth changes occurred in its makeup, and today it is not the difficult pattern originally created. Now it is a combination pieced and appliqué block." Nancy Cabot, *Chicago Tribune,* Mar 2, 1936

❹ **Golden Compass,** Jinny Beyer, Hilton Head Seminar design, 2004.

❺ **Sunburst,** Jinny Beyer, Hilton Head Seminar design, 1999.

❻ **Himalayan Sun,** Jinny Beyer, Beyer, Jinny, *Patchwork Portfolio,* 1989.

❼ **Setting Sun,** Hall, 1935.

❽ **Rolling Pin Wheel,** Ickis, 1949.

❾ **Grandma's Favorite Compass,** *Prize Winning Designs,* ca. 1931.

❿ **Sunburst,** Webster, 1915.

⓫ **Sunburst,** *Museum Quilts,* date unknown.

⓬ **Merry Go Round,** *Colonial Quilts,* 1932.
Also known as:
Mery Go Round (sic), *Grandmother Clark's Patchwork Quilt Designs, From Books 20-21-23.* 1932.

1 Sunrise, *Grandma Dexter Appliqué and Patchwork Designs, Book 36a,* ca. 1932. Also known as:
Sunburst, Hall, 1935.

2 Rising Sun, Miall, 1937. Also known as:
Sunburst, Miall, 1937.

3 Sunburst, Nancy Cabot, *Chicago Tribune,* Mar 20, 1933.

4 Tropical Sun, Home Art Studios, *World Herald,* Mar 31, 1933.

5 Cogwheels, Nancy Cabot, *Chicago Tribune,* Aug 24, 1935.

6 Cog Wheels, *Ladies Art Company,* 1897.

7 Sunburst, Nancy Cabot, *Chicago Tribune,* Sep 18, 1935.

8 Mariner's Wheel, Jinny Beyer, Hilton Head Seminar design, 1981; published in Beyer, Jinny, *Patchwork Portfolio.*

9 Mariner's Rose, Jinny Beyer, Hilton Head Seminar design, 1982; published in Beyer, Jinny, *Patchwork Portfolio.*

10 Atlantic Aster, Jinny Beyer, Hilton Head Seminar design, 1985; published in Beyer, Jinny, *Patchwork Portfolio.*

11 Island Compass, Jinny Beyer, Hilton Head Seminar design, 1983; published in Beyer, Jinny, *Patchwork Portfolio.*

12 Rolling Compass, Jinny Beyer, Hilton Head Seminar design, 1982; published in Beyer, Jinny, *Patchwork Portfolio.*

1 Compass on 17 x 17 grid

2 Compass on 25 x 25 grid

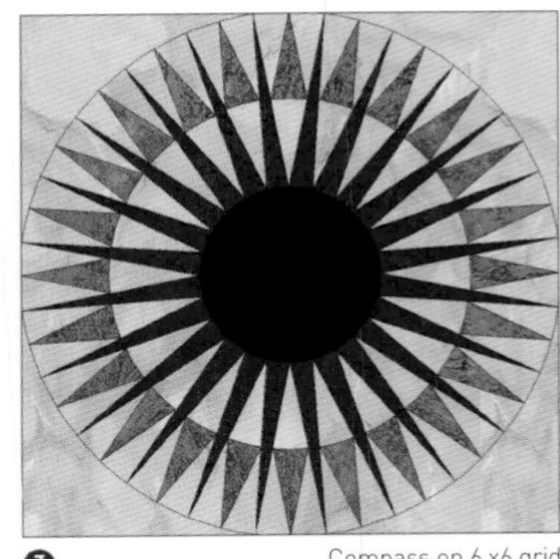

3 Compass on 6 x6 grid

4 Compass on 16 x 16 grid

5 Compass on 8-pointed star grid 4

6 Compass on 20 x 20 grid

7 Compass on 10 x 10 grid

8 Compass on 8-pointed star grid 1

9 Compass on 8-pointed star grid 1

10 Compass on 8-pointed star grid 1

11 Compass on 8-pointed star grid 1

12 Compass on 8-pointed star grid 1

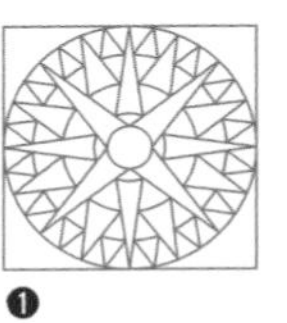

1

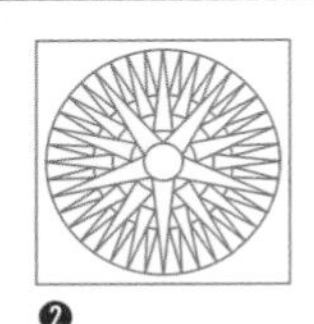

2

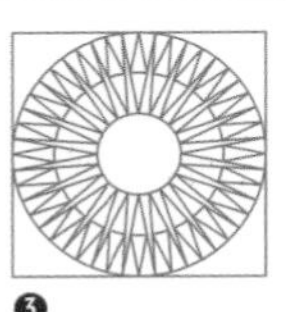

3

4

5

6

7

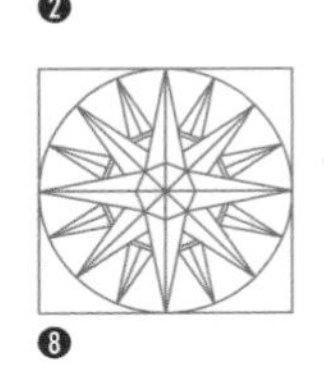

8

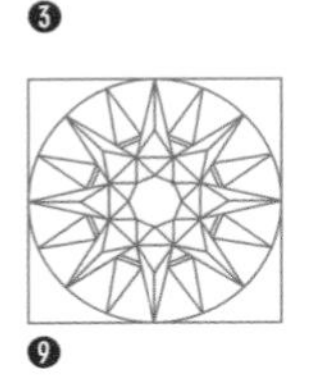

9

10

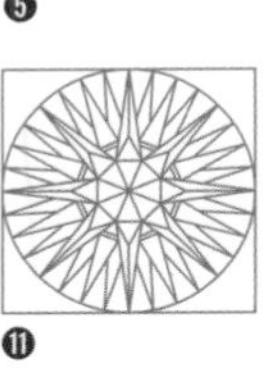

11

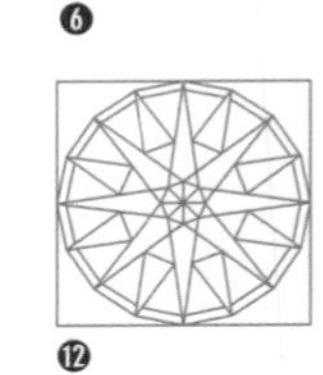

12

1 Compass on 8-pointed star grid 1

2 Compass on 8-pointed star grid 1

3 Compass on 8-pointed star grid 1

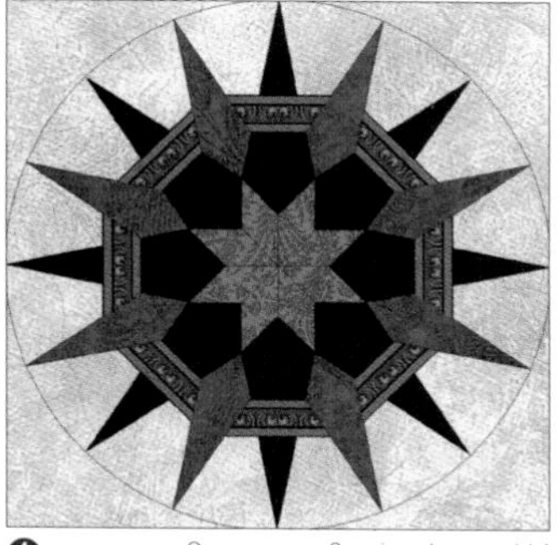

4 Compass on 8-pointed star grid 1

5 Compass on 8-pointed star grid 2

6 Compass on 40 x 40 grid

7 Compass on 14 x 14 grid

8 Compass on 20 x 20 grid

9 Compass on 22 x 22 grid

10 Compass on 20 x 20 grid

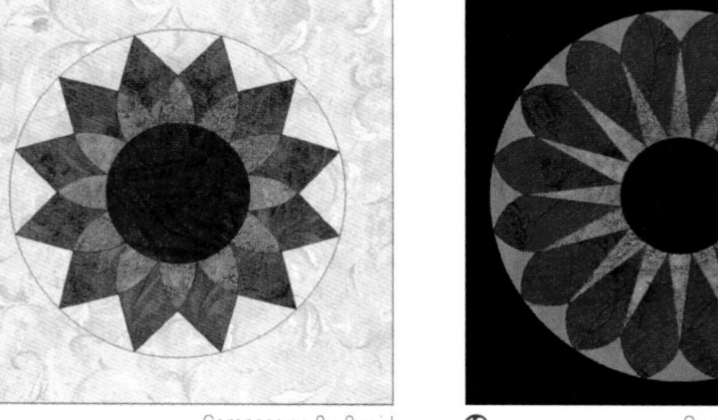

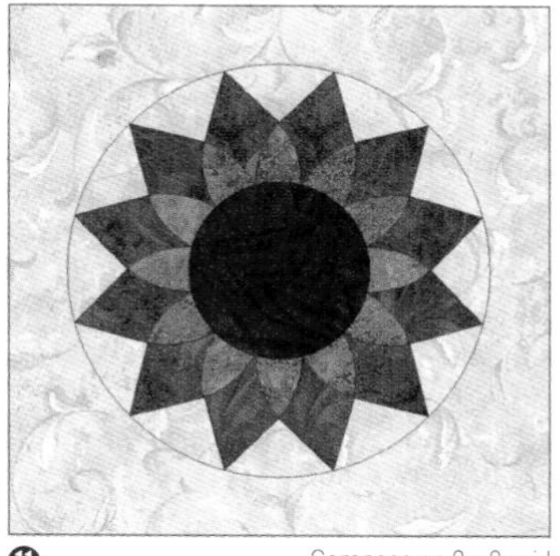

11 Compass on 9 x 9 grid

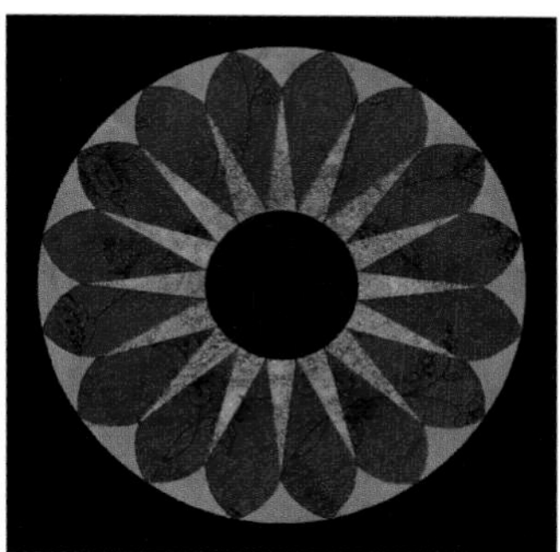

12 Compass on 18 x 18 grid

1 Carolina Compass, Jinny Beyer, Hilton Head Seminar design, 1984; published in Beyer, Jinny, *Patchwork Portfolio*.

2 Compass Rose, Jinny Beyer, Hilton Head Seminar design, 1981; published in Beyer, Jinny, *Patchwork Portfolio*.

3 Diamond Radiants, Jinny Beyer, Hilton Head Seminar design, 1990.

4 Star Illusion, Jinny Beyer, Hilton Head Seminar design, 1990.

5 Sunflower, Ruby McKim, *Kansas City Star*, Mar 1, 1930.

6 Kansas Sunflower, Hall, 1935.

7 The Zinnia Quilt, Home Art Studios, *World Herald*, Apr 28, 1933. Also known as:
- **Noonday,** Jane Alan, Alan, 1933.
- **Sunflower,** Jane Alan, Alan, 1933.

"The Zinnia, a gay colorful flower that blooms forth in reds, yellows and oranges, makes up this lovely quilt design. Each flower May be a different color, and by skillfully blending your combinations, you will have a lovely quilt when completed." *World Herald*, Oct 23, 1933

8 Rising Sun, Clara Stone, *Practical Needlework*, ca. 1906. Also known as:
- **A Brave Sunflower,** *Kansas City Star*, Dec 26, 1951.
- **Oklahoma Sunburst,** *Kansas City Star*, May 20, 1933.
- **Russian Sunflower,** Eveline Foland, *Kansas City Star*, May 7, 1932.
- **The Sunflower,** *Q Book 126, All Time Quilt Favorites*, date unknown.

9 Single Sunflower, *Ladies Art Company*, 1897. Also known as:
- **Blazing Sun,** Ickis, 1949.

10 Seaflower, Jinny Beyer, Hilton Head Seminar design, 1990.

11 Kansas Sunflower, *Detroit Free Press*, Jul 29, 1933.

12 Sunflower, *Ladies Art Company*, 1928.

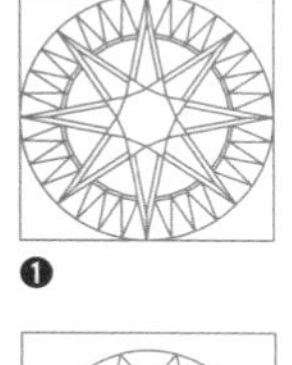

1

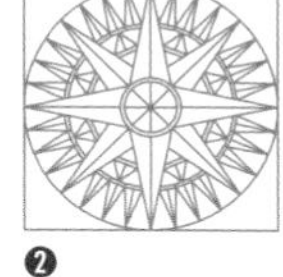

2

3

4

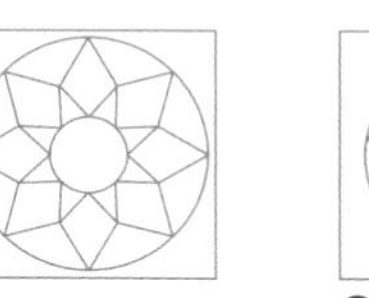

5

6

7

8

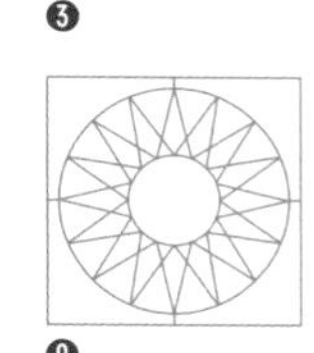

9

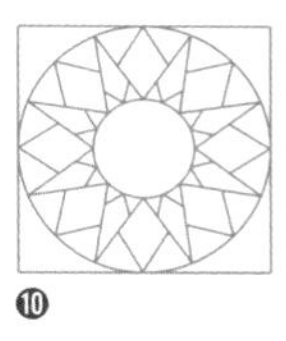

10

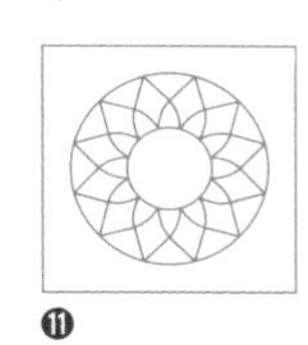

11

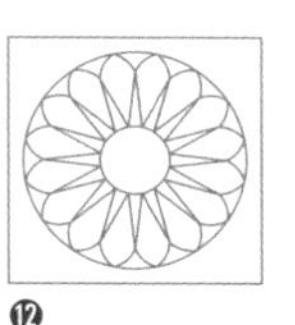

12

1 Sunflower, *is Grandmother Clark's Patchwork Quilt Designs, From Books 20-21-23* 1932. Also known as:

Kansas Sunflower, Home Art Studios, *World Herald,* Jan 19, 1934.

Sunflower Quilt, Home Art Studios, *Cincinnati Enquirer,* Mar 10, 1933.

"The Sunflower quilt makes a beautiful patchwork design when worked up in three shades of yellow. You will enjoy working this fascinating pattern, and it will make a lovely addition to your bedroom. When combined with walnut furniture, the shades of yellow give a very pleasing combination and will add both warmth and charm to your room." *World Herald,* Aug 3, 1933

2 Cone Flower, Jinny Beyer, Jinny Beyer Studio design, 1999.

3 Sunburst, Jane Alan, *Saint Louis Post Dispatch,* Nov 24, 1932. Also known as:

Sunflower Motif, *Kansas City Star,* Feb 1, 1961.

4 Sunburst, date unknown, published in *Quilts of Virginia.*

5 Virginia Compass, Jinny Beyer, Jinny Beyer Studio design, 2007.

6 Wyoming Patch, *Ladies Art Company,* 1928.

7 Noonday, Nancy Cabot, *Chicago Tribune,* Feb 26, 1934.

"Connecticut was the place of the origin of the 'Noonday' quilt, and the date was about 1825 . . . The completed coverlet is an object of great beauty and charm, and one that is not difficult to piece." Nancy Cabot, *Chicago Tribune,* Feb 26, 1934

8 Alabama Beauty, *Prize Winning Designs,* ca. 1931.

9 Chips and Whetstones, Ickis, 1949.

10 The Sunburst Quilt, *Kansas City Star,* Jan 13, 1931.

11 Explosion, Nancy Cabot, *Chicago Tribune,* Jan 15, 1937.

12 Mariner's Whirl, Jinny Beyer, Hilton Head Seminar design, 1990.

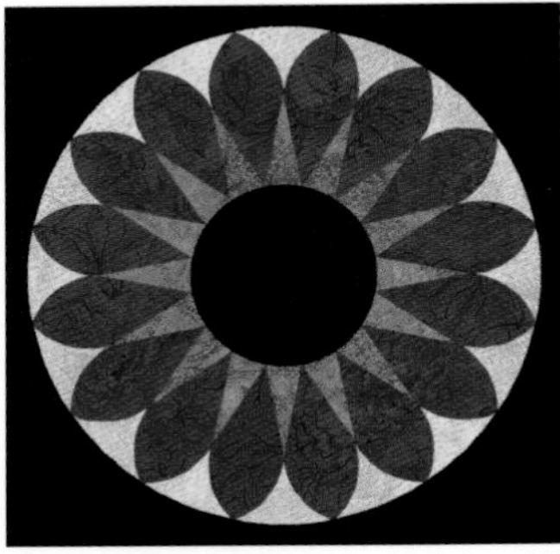

1 Compass on 8-pointed star grid 1

2 Compass on 8-pointed star grid 1

3 Compass on 4 x 4 grid

4 Compass on 4 x 4 grid

5 Compass on hexagon grid 2

6 Compass on 19 x 19 grid

7 Compass on 19 x 19 grid

8 Compass on 15 x 15 grid

9 Compass on 26 x 26 grid

10 Compass on hexagon grid 2

11 Compass on 10 x 10 grid

12 Compass on 8-pointed star grid 1

1

2 3 4

5

6

7

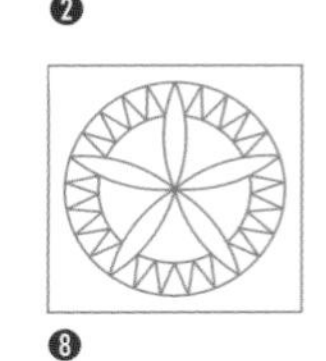

8

9

10

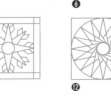

11

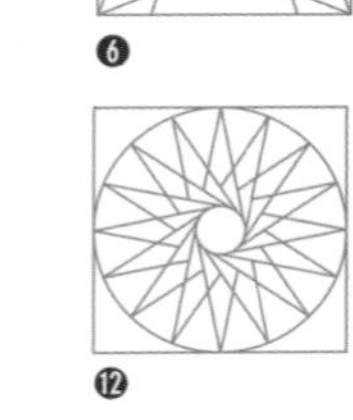

12

1 **Nautilus,** Jinny Beyer, Hilton Head Seminar design, 1990.

2 **Friendship,** Laura Wheeler, unidentified newspaper clipping, date unknown.

3 **The Rainbow Quilt,** *Kansas City Star,* Sep 20, 1950. Also known as:
Spearheads and Quarter Circles, *Kansas City Star,* Jun 13, 1956.

4 **The Drunkard's Trail,** *Kansas City Star,* Sep 16, 1942.

5 **The Broken Stone,** *Kansas City Star,* Sep 2, 1933.

6 **Block and Ring Quilt,** Nancy Page, *Detroit Free Press,* May 2, 1933. Also known as:
A Friendship Quilt, *Kansas City Star,* May 2, 1945.

7 **Cross Roads,** Home Art Studios, *Cincinnati Enquirer,* Jan 21, 1933.

8 **Cross Roads to Bachelor's Hall,** Clara Stone, *Practical Needlework,* ca. 1906. Also known as:
The Broken Circle, *Kansas City Star,* Dec 17, 1952
Cross Roads, Eveline Foland, *Kansas City Star,* Aug 1, 1931.
Wagon Wheels, *Kansas City Star,* May 28, 1941.

9 **Crossroads,** *Q Book 130, Keepsake Quilts,* ca. 1990.

10 **Cross Roads,** *Prize Winning Designs,* ca. 1931.

11 **Summer Fancy,** Laura Wheeler, *Indianapolis Star,* Jul 8, 1934. Also known as:
Pot of Gold, Nancy Cabot, *Chicago Tribune,* Aug 10, 1937.
Rainbow Block, Nancy Cabot, *Chicago Tribune,* Sep 7, 1934.

12 **Indian Summer,** Nancy Cabot, *Chicago Tribune,* Apr 15, 1933.

1 **Indian Summer,** Finley, 1929. Also known as:

Setting Sun, Finley, 1929.

2 **Broken Circle,** Clara Stone, *Practical Needlework,* ca. 1906. Also known as:

Sunflower, Ruby McKim *Kansas City Star,* Mar 23, 1929.

3 **Broken Circle,** Hall, 1935. Also known as:

Indian Summer, Hall, 1935.
Sunflower, Hall, 1935.

4 **Suspension Bridge,** *Ladies Art Company,* 1922.

5 **Suspension Bridge,** Aunt Martha series: *The Quilt Fair Comes to You,* ca. 1933.

6 **Buggy Wheel,** Hall, 1935. Also known as:

Wheel of Fortune, Hall, 1935.

7 **Sunflower,** *Prize Winning Designs,* ca. 1931.

8 **Sunrise,** Nancy Cabot, *Chicago Tribune,* Dec 9, 1934.
"Early colonists and pioneer women, conscious of the beauties of sunrise, evolved many and varied interpretations of 'Sunrise.' The pattern today is one of the youngest, being a combination pieced and appliqué block made during the late nineteenth century. The colors used in this pattern are yellow, soft orange, rose and light blue." Nancy Cabot, *Chicago Tribune,* Dec 9, 1934

9 **Baby Bunting,** *Ladies Art Company,* 1922. Also known as:

Broken Saw, *The Patchwork Book,* 1932.

10 **Dogwood Blossom,** *Grandmother Clark's Patchwork Quilt Designs, From Books 20-21-23,* 1932. Also known as:

Oklahoma Dogwood, *Kansas City Star,* Feb 17, 1934.

11 **Chinese Fan,** *Old Fashioned Quilts,* ca. 1931.

12 **New York Beauty,** Home Art Studios, *Cincinnati Enquirer,* Apr 2, 1933. Also known as:

Crown of Thorns, Hall, 1935.
Rocky Mountain Road, Hall, 1935.
"This is only one fourth of the finished block." Hall, 1935

1 Crossroads on 20 x 20 grid

2 Crossroads on 7 x 7 grid

3 Crossroads on 20 x 20 grid

4 Crossroads on 32 x 32 grid

5 Crossroads on 24 x 24 grid

6 Crossroads on 27 x 27 grid

7 Crossroads on 18 x 18 grid

8 Crossroads on 28 x 28 grid

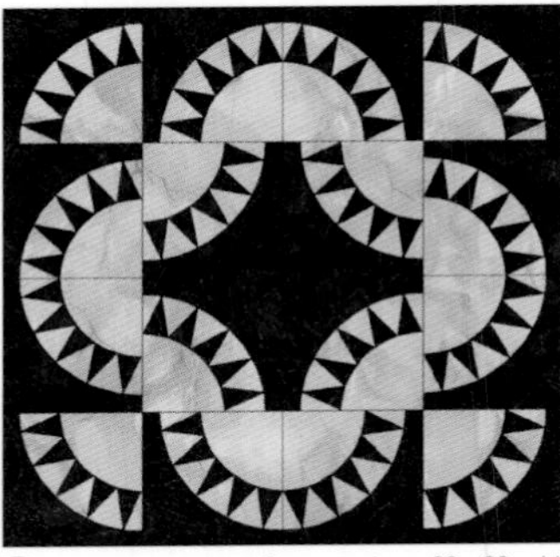

9 Crossroads on 28 x 28 grid

10 Crossroads on 8 x 8 grid

11 Crossroads on 10 x 10 grid

12 Crossroads on multiple grids

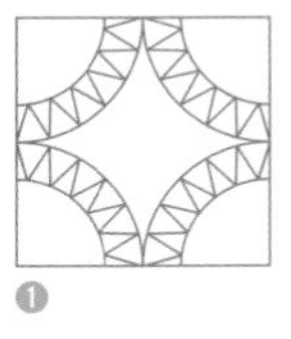

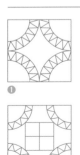

1

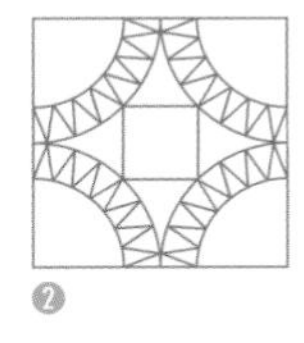

2

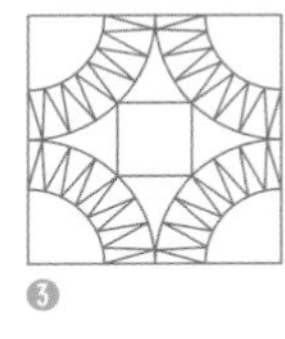

3

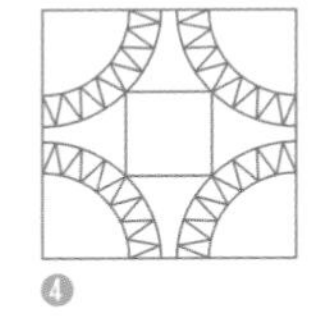

4

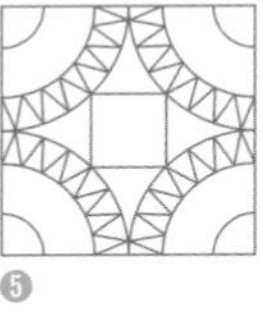

5

6

7

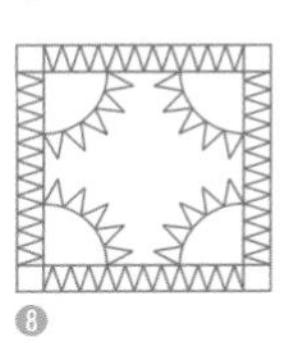

8

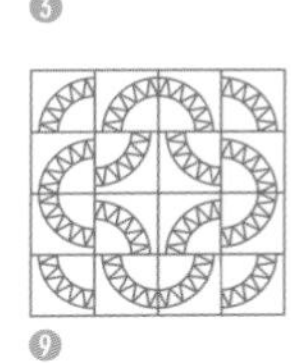

9

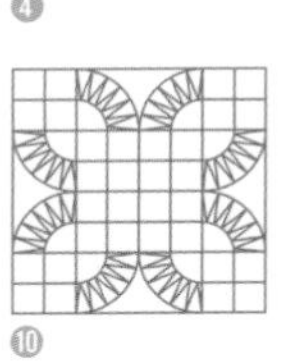

10

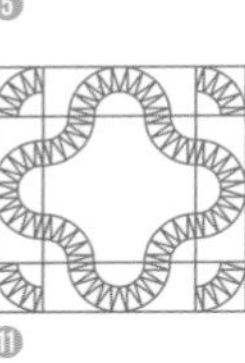

11

12

1 Crossroads on 4 x 4 grid

2 Crossroads on 32 x 32 grid

3 Crossroads on 30 x 30 grid

4 Crossroads on 14 x 14 grid

5 Fan on 26 x 26 grid

6 Fan on 18 x 18 grid

7 Fan on 28 x 28 grid

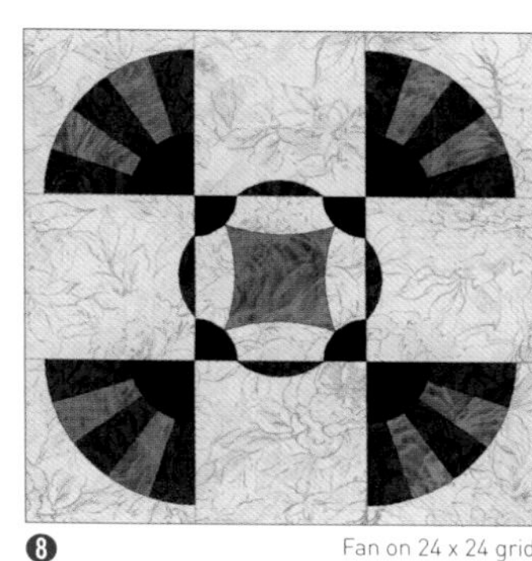

8 Fan on 24 x 24 grid

9 Fan on 12 x 12 grid

10 Fan on 7 x 7 grid

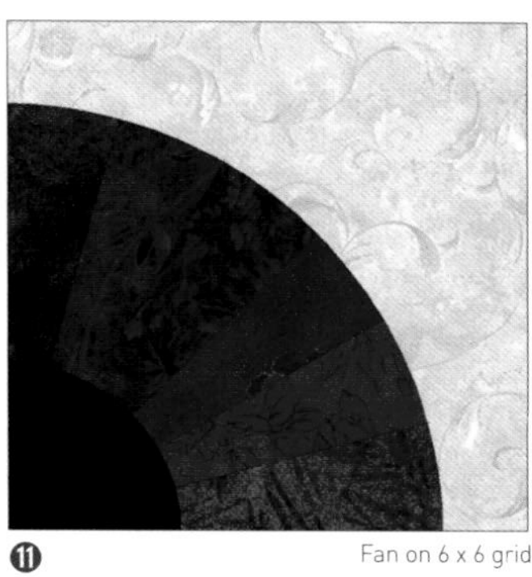

11 Fan on 6 x 6 grid

12 Fan on 9 x 9 grid

1 **Constellation,** *Quilt Blocks from Grandma Dexter,* ca. 1930.

2 **Wagon Wheels,** *Kansas City Star,* Jun 23, 1934.

3 **Fanny's Favorite,** Hall, 1935.

4 **Baby Bunting,** Hall, 1935.

5 **Ladies' Fancy,** *Kansas City Star,* Jan 31, 1940.

6 **Ladies' Fancy,** *Ladies Art Company,* 1897.

7 **Rebecca's Fan,** Eveline Foland, *Kansas City Star,* Mar 14, 1931.
"The 'fan' as a motif for quilt patterns was very popular in our grandmothers' day. No lady was properly gowned for a social function unless the ensemble included a fan." Hall, 1935

8 **Fan and Ring,** *Kansas City Star,* Mar 27, 1940. Also known as:
Fans and a Ring, *Kansas City Star,* Aug 11, 1948.

9 **Letha's Electric Fan,** *Kansas City Star,* Apr 2, 1938.

10 **Fan,** Laura Wheeler, *Kansas City Star,* Nov 13, 1933. Also known as:
Flirtation, Miall, 1937.

11 **Grandmother's Fan,** *Ten Piecework Quilts for Southern Homes,* ca. 1936.

12 **The Fan,** *The Dressmaking Book,* 1929. Also known as:
Fannie's Fan, Holstein, 1973.
Friendship Fan, Laura Wheeler, *Indianapolis Star,* Jun 16, 1933.
"An old-time pattern, the Friendship Fan is as popular today as a friendship quilt as it was in the early days of quilt making. It has all the qualities of the ideal quilt of this type. The parts of the fan are just the right size for scraps. A gathering of friends can quickly do a quantity of blocks for they are easily pieced. Each block of course, could be made in the same scraps, as illustrated." Laura Wheeler, *Cincinnati Enquirer,* Jun 16, 1933

"In the days when quiltmaking first became the American handicraft there not only were certain favorite patterns but also special types of quilts. The friendship quilt was one of them. It varied in style. Some friendship quilts were made of materials donated by one's many friends; to make others, friends congregated of an evening and each sewed a block. This fan pattern lends itself well to the friendship quilt for the fan may be formed by the patches donated by friends.' *Charleston Gazette,* Aug 9, 1933

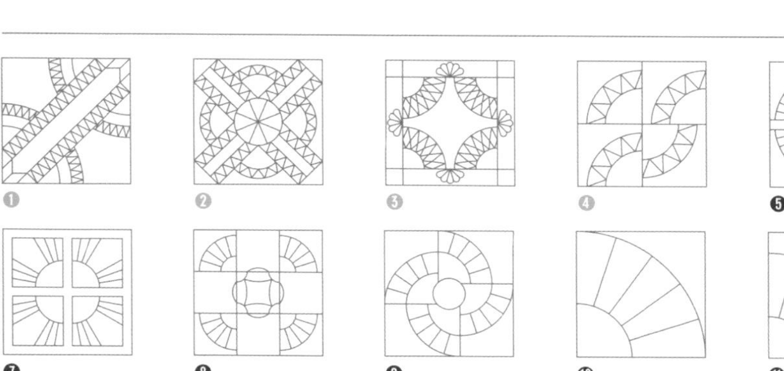

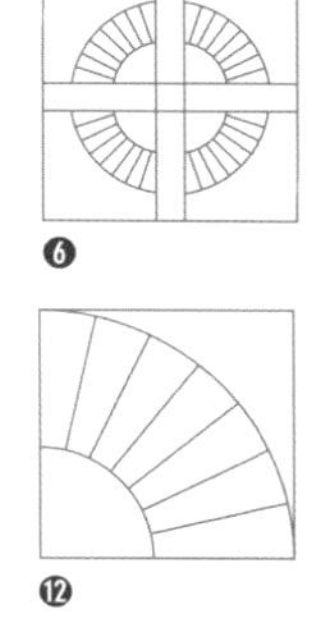

❶ **Grandmother's Fan,** *Old Fashioned Quilts,* ca. 1931. Also known as:

Fan, *Farm Journal Quilt Patterns,* ca. 1935.

❷ **Formosa Fan,** Nancy Cabot, *Chicago Tribune,* Aug 20, 1936.

❸ **Fan Patchwork,** *Ladies Art Company,* 1897. Also known as:

A Fan of Many Colors, *Kansas City Star,* May 24, 1961.

Fan Piecework, *The New Barbara Taylor Book on Quilting,* ca. 1977.

❹ **Fans,** *Antique Quilts,* 1974.

❺ **Grandmother's Fan,** Hall, 1935.

❻ **Grandmother's Fan,** Alice Brooks, *Detroit Free Press,* Jan 10, 1934. Also known as:

Art Deco Fans, date unknown, per Holstein.

"Grandmother's fan—what could be lovelier in a quilt? Patch after patch of gay scraps and the lovely fan results. You could, of course, repeat the same scraps in every block, or just take them as they come to hand. This quilt, just because it is made of scraps, is as economical as it is beautiful. It is the type of quilt that any needlewoman will be proud to give to her children as an example of her handiwork." Alice Brooks, *Detroit Free Press,* Mar 4, 1934

❼ **Grandmother's Fan,** Laura Wheeler, unidentified newspaper clipping, ca. 1932. Also known as:

Grandmother's Scrap Quilt, Alice Brooks, *Detroit Free Press,* Jun 25, 1937.

❽ **Heirloom Block,** Nancy Cabot, *Chicago Tribune,* May 16, 1938.

❾ **Calico Fan,** Nancy Cabot, *Chicago Tribune,* Mar 8, 1936.

"It is hardly necessary to state that 'Calico Fan' is a member of the old guard in the quilt realm. It radiates an authentic charm of quaintness having first been pieced in the early colonial times. The exact date when the quilt was made is obscure, but the state which claims to be its birthplace is Virginia." Nancy Cabot, *Chicago Tribune,* Mar 8, 1936

❿ **Grandmother's Fan,** *Mrs. Danner's Fifth Quilt Book,* 1970.

⓫ **Imperial Fan,** Laura Wheeler, *Daily Republic,* Mar 22, 1934.

⓬ **Mary's Fan,** *Grandma Dexter New Appliqué and Patchwork Designs, Book 36b,* ca. 1932. Also known as:

Mary's Star, *Virginia Snow Studio Art Needlework Creations,* 1932.

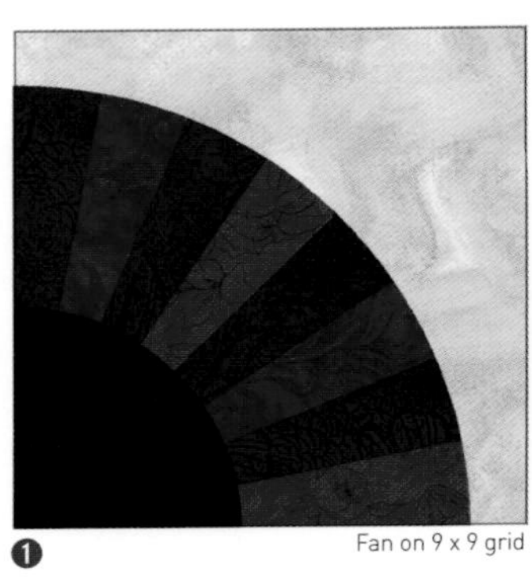
❶ Fan on 9 x 9 grid

❷ Fan on 11 x 11 grid

❸ Fan on 14 x 14 grid

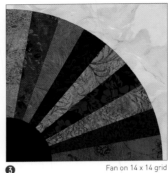

❹ Fan on 16 x 16 grid

❺ Fan on 15 x 15 grid

❻ Fan on 8 x 8 grid

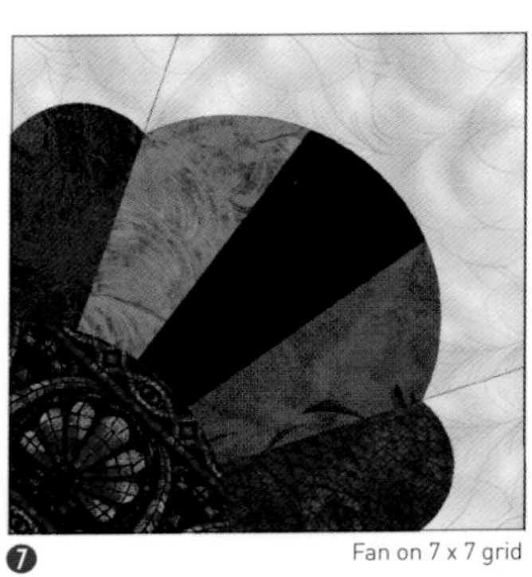
❼ Fan on 7 x 7 grid

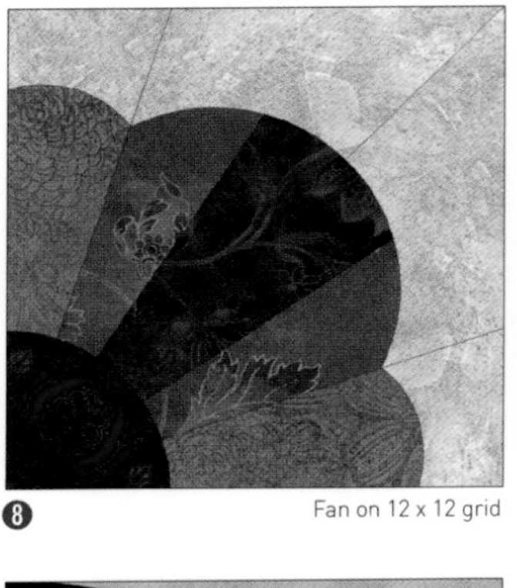
❽ Fan on 12 x 12 grid

❾ Fan on 17 x 17 grid

❿ Fan on 10 x 10 grid

⓫ Fan on 12 x 12 grid

⓬ Fan on 9 x 9 grid

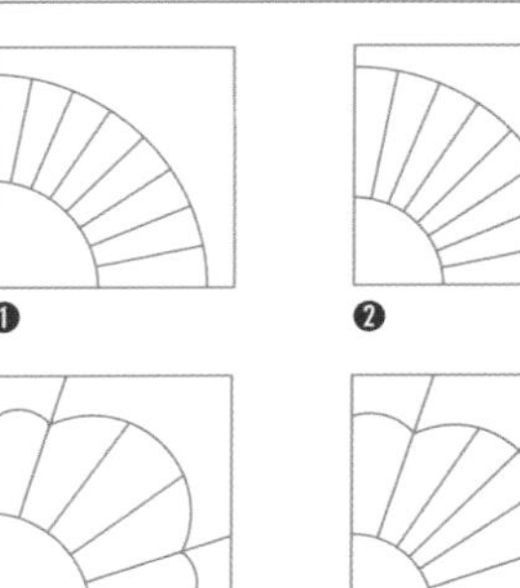
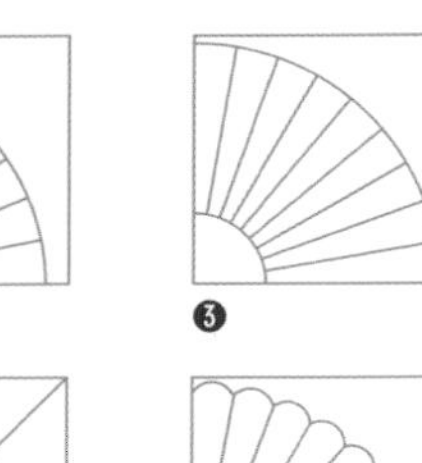
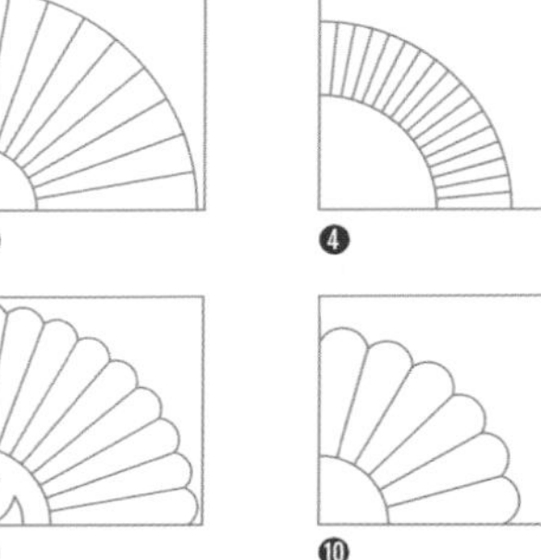
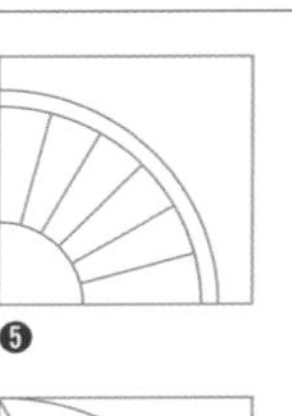

❶ ❷ ❸ ❹ ❺ ❻

❼ ❽ ❾ ❿ ⓫ ⓬

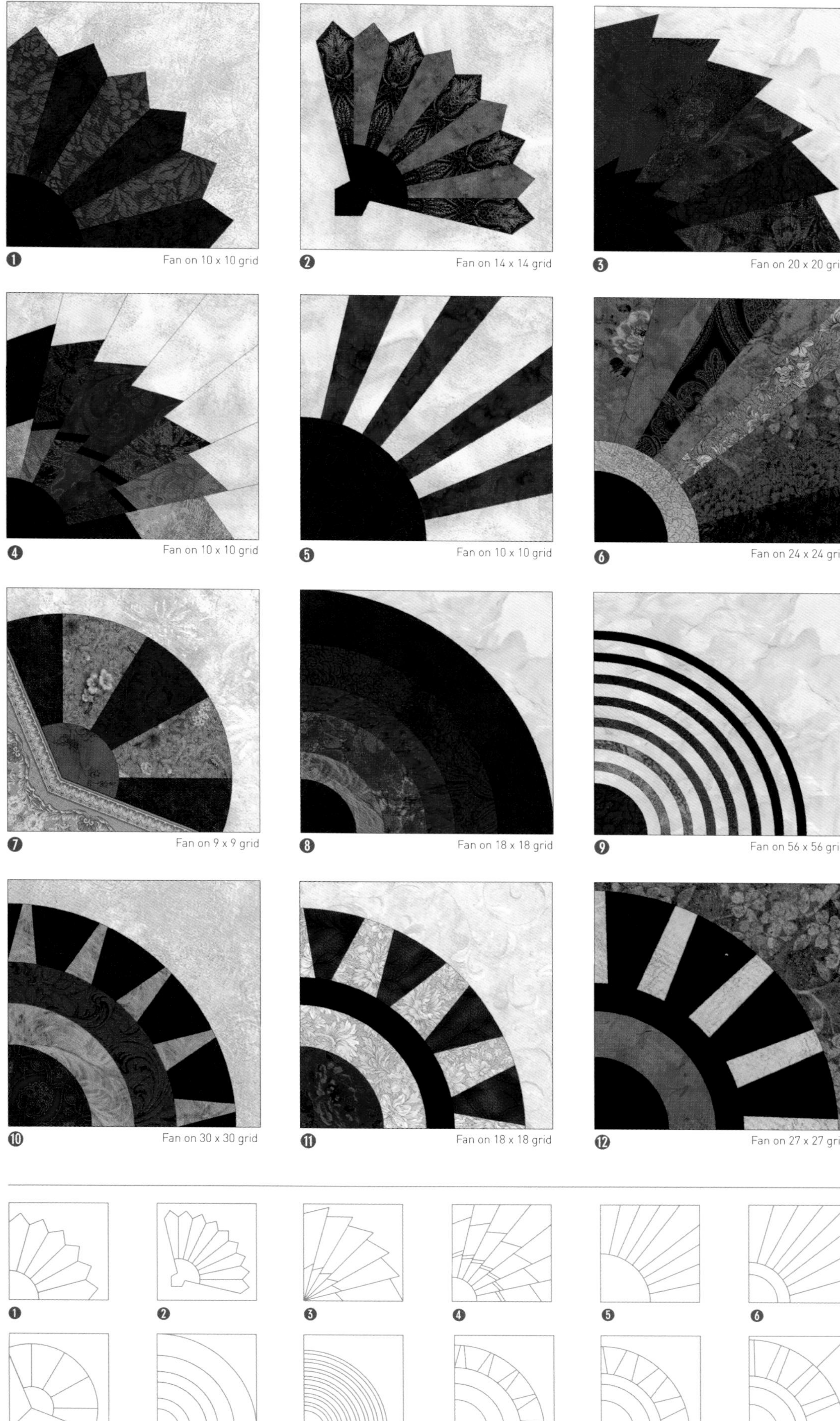

❶ **Grandmother's Fan,** *Grandmother's Patchwork Quilt Designs, Book 20,* 1931.

❷ **Milady's Fan,** Nancy Cabot, *Chicago Tribune,* Nov 7, 1934.
"'Miladay's Fan' takes its place beside the other fan inspired patterns, delightful design without which any quilt collection would be incomplete. In its early days in Massachusetts the pattern usually was pieced in quaint old fashioned prints, with a plain handle, and appliquéd to a white block." Nancy Cabot, *Chicago Tribune,* Nov 7, 1934

❸ **Milady's Fan,** Aunt Martha series: *Easy Quilts,* ca. 1958.

❹ **Great Falls Fan,** Jinny Beyer, Quilter's Quest design, 2008.

❺ **Sunshine,** Clara Stone, *Practical Needlework,* ca. 1906.

❻ **Friendship Fan,** Nancy Cabot, *Chicago Tribune,* Sep 13, 1933.

❼ **Pride of the North,** Laura Wheeler, *Indianapolis Star,* May 17, 1937.
"'Pride of the North'—and well this quilt May be the pride of the quiltmaker of today. Colorful and economical in its scraps arranged successfully." Laura Wheeler, *Indianapolis Star,* May 17, 1937

❽ **Rainbow Scrap Quilt,** Alice Brooks, *Alice Brooks Designs,* date unknown.

❾ **Caroline's Fan,** Hall, 1935.

❿ **Flo's Fan,** Hall, 1935.

⓫ **Fanny's Fan,** *Ladies Art Company,* 1897.
Also known as:
Fan, *Ladies Art Company,* 1928.

⓬ **Fan,** Nancy Cabot, *Chicago Tribune,* Jun 12, 1935.

1 Potomac Fan, Jinny Beyer, Quilter's Quest design, 2008.

2 Whirling Fans, Alice Brooks, *Detroit Free Press,* Apr 4, 1934.
"Whirling Fans—and don't they really look as if they were whirling? And what fun they are to put together gay scrap next to gay scrap—just as they come to hand. It takes no time to get this quilt done and it's one that gets attention wherever it is shown." Alice Brooks, *Detroit Free Press,* Apr 4, 1934

3 Grandma's Fan, Nancy Cabot, *Chicago Tribune,* Jan 12, 1935.

4 Gypsy Trail, Alice Brooks, *Detroit Free Press,* Nov 2, 1934.

5 Baby Fan Appliqué, *Kansas City Star,* Oct 3, 1945. Also known as:
A Wee Fan, *Kansas City Star,* Apr 10, 1946.

6 Fan Quilt, *Kansas City Star,* Jan 26, 1935.

7 Japanese Fan, Laura Wheeler, *Cincinnati Enquirer,* Mar 27, 1934.

8 Grandmother's Choice, Laura Wheeler, *Sioux City Journal,* May 9, 1941.

9 The Valentine Quilt, *Kansas City Star,* Feb 10, 1934.

10 Bride's Quilt, Laura Wheeler, *State Journal,* Apr 9, 1934.

11 Square and Circle, Hall, 1935.
"Square in Circle. Insignia of the Presidents and Past President's General Assembly. The colors, red, purple, crimson and white." Hall, 1935

12 Bride's Quilt, Alice Brooks, *Detroit Free Press,* Apr 22, 1937.

1 Fan on 10 x 10 grid

2 Fan on 13 x 13 grid

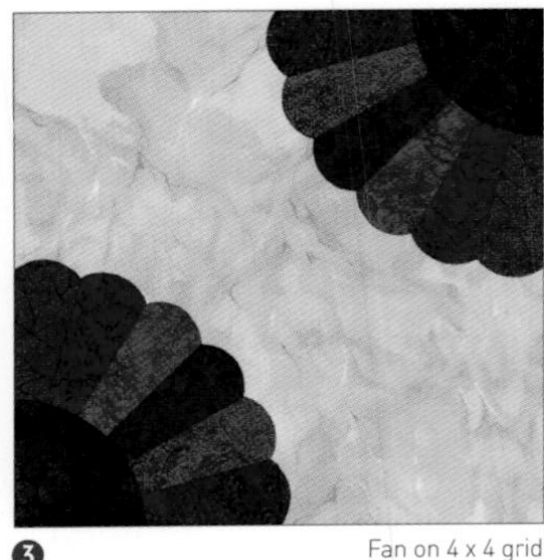

3 Fan on 4 x 4 grid

4 Fan on 25 x 25 grid

5 Fan on 14 x 14 grid

6 Fan on 22 x 22 grid

7 Fan on 14 x 14 grid

8 Fan on 8 x 8 grid

9 Hearts on 12 x 12 grid

10 Hearts on 32 x 32 grid

11 Hearts on 10 x 10 grid

12 Hearts on 18 x 18 grid

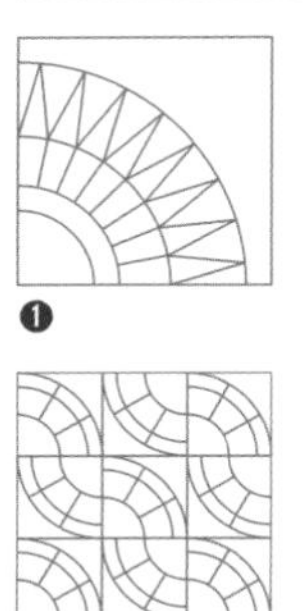
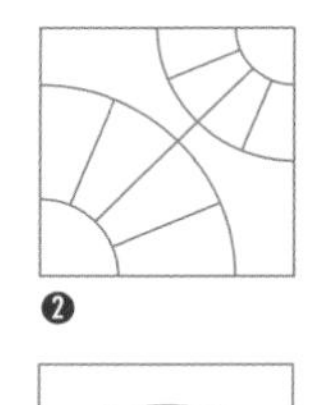
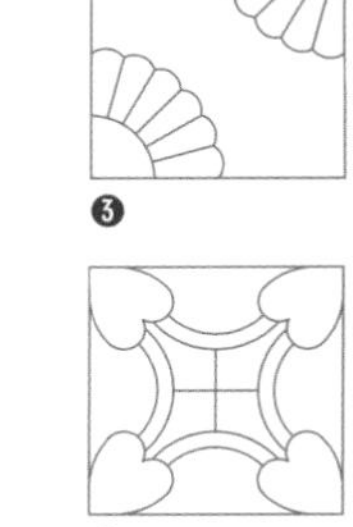
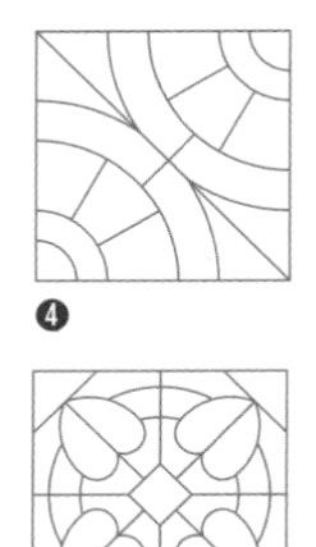
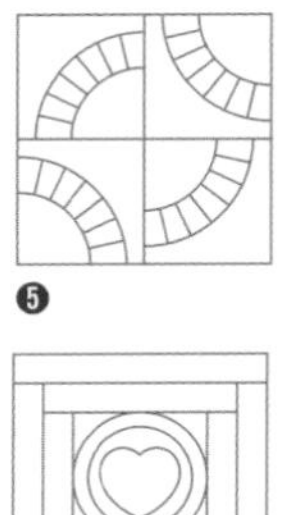
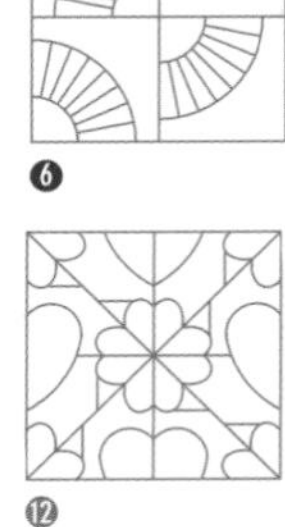

1 2 3 4 5 6

7 8 9 10 11 12

1 Hearts on 18 x 18 grid

2 Hearts on 5 x 5 grid

3 Hearts on 2 x 2 grid

4 Hearts on 17 x 17 grid

5 Hearts on 6 x 6 grid

6 Hearts on 10 x 10 grid

7 Hearts on 6 x 6 grid

8 Hearts on 8 x 8 grid

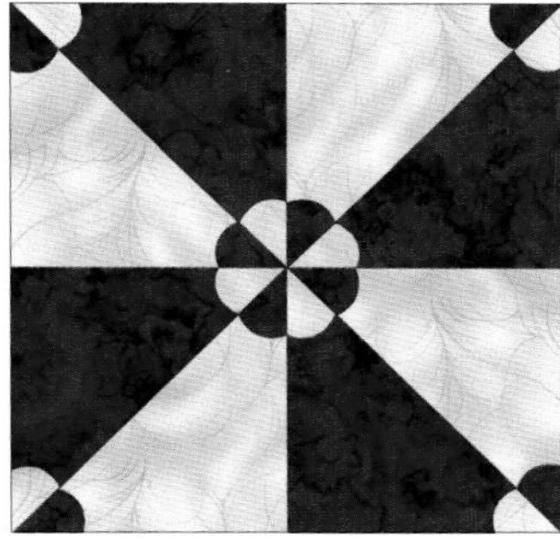

9 Hearts on 8 x 8 grid

10 Hearts on 12 x 12 grid

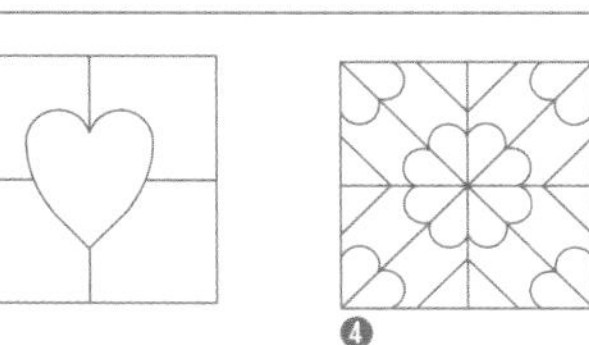
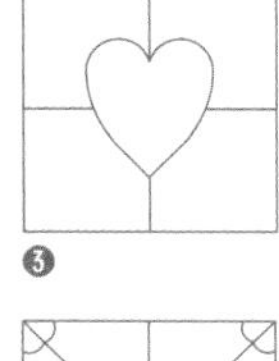
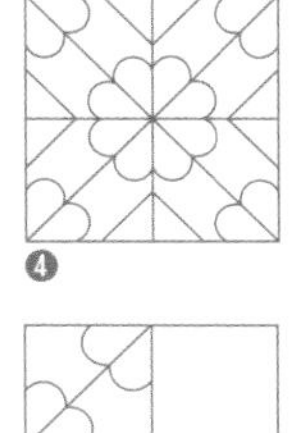
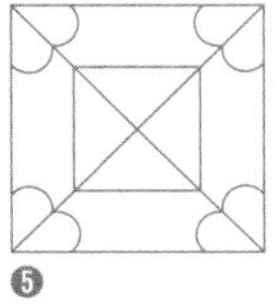
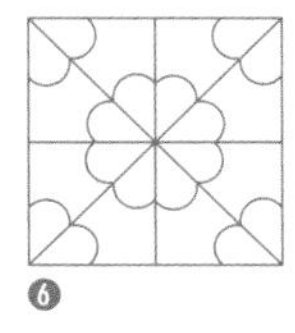

1 2 3 4 5 6

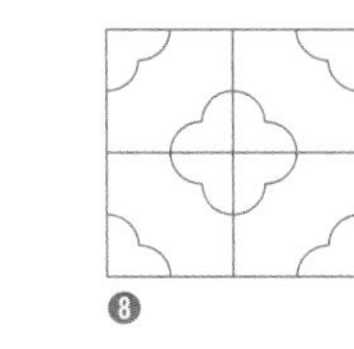
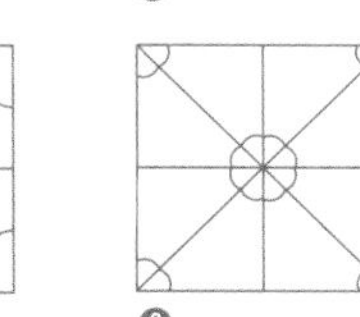
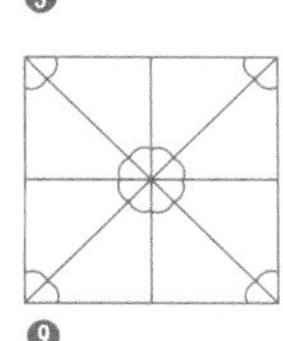
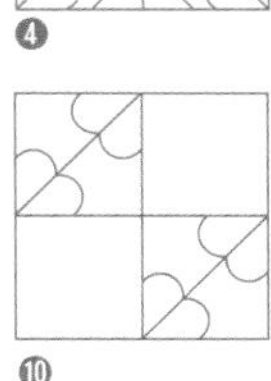
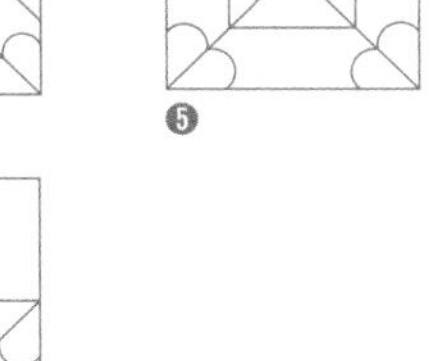

7 8 9 10

1 **Bride's Prize,** Laura Wheeler, *Indianapolis Star,* Jun 10, 1937.
"'Good luck's assured the proud possessor of this striking quilt for what else could be foretold by its colorful, romantic hearts? Prized by the bride and more experienced homemaker alike, this colorful coverlet is a joy to behold made of gay scraps." Laura Wheeler, *Indianapolis Star,* Jun 10, 1937

2 **Pride of the Bride,** Alice Brooks, *Detroit Free Press,* Oct 6, 1937.

3 **The Heart of the Home,** *Kansas City Star,* Jul 27, 1938.

4 **Virginia's Choice,** Nancy Cabot, *Chicago Tribune,* Nov 11, 1937. See 329-5 and 389-6. Also known as:

- **Martha's Choice,** Nancy Cabot, Nov 11, 1937.

5 **Martha's Choice,** Nancy Cabot, *Chicago Tribune,* Aug 19, 1934.
"Martha's Choice is a variation of the old patterns, Dutch rose and hearts and gizzards. It was pieced in 1882 by Mrs. E. Maxon of Belvedere, Ill. At the age of 69, with years of quilt making to her credit, she created a quilt that proved to be a prize winner every time it was exhibited. A friend of Mrs. Maxons, a Mrs. Ellick, quilted the coverlet in 1899. The quilt is made of light red figured material, combined with a dainty white print. 'Martha's Choice is still in the Maxom family, the property of Mrs. Leora Maxon of Chicago." Nancy Cabot, *Chicago Tribune,* Aug 19, 1934

6 **Lover's Knot,** Clara Stone, *Practical Needlework,* ca. 1906. See 334-5. Also known as:

- **Dutch Rose,** Nancy Cabot, *Chicago Tribune,* Mar 8, 1934.
- **The Dutch Rose,** Home Art Studios, Oct 30, 1932.
- **Dutch Windmill,** *Grandmother Clark's Patchwork Designs, Book 22,* 1932.
- **Hearts and Gizzards,** Finley, 1929.
- **Lazy Daisy,** Hall, 1935.
- **Martha's Choice,** Nancy Cabot, *Chicago Tribune,* Dec 28, 1936.
- **Mill Wheel,** *Old Fashioned Quilts,* ca. 1931.
- **Petal Quilt,** Hall, 1935.
- **The Petal Quilt,** Eveline Foland, *Kansas City Star,* Jul 20, 1929.
- **Pierrot's Pom Pom,** Finley, 1929.
- **Spring Blossoms,** Nancy Cabot, *Chicago Tribune,* Dec 28, 1936.
- **Springtime Blossoms,** Eveline Foland, *Kansas City Star,* Jul 20, 1929.
- **Tennessee Snowball,** *The Patchwork Book,* 1932.
- **Wheel of Fortune,** Eveline Foland, *Kansas City Star,* Jul 20, 1929.
- **Windmill,** *American Heritage Quilt Book,* date unknown.

7 **Lover's Knot,** Nancy Page, unidentified newspaper clipping, date unknown. See 334-5.

8 **Hearts and Gizzards,** *Ladies Art Company,* 1898. Also known as:

- **Pierrot's Pom Pom,** Hall, 1935.

9 **Wheel of Fortune,** Ickis, 1949.

10 **Borrow & Return,** *Quilts,* 1945.

Sampler Quilt, Carole Nicholas, 2003. The quilt uses these hexagon blocks: *North Star, Block Party, Cubicle, Hollow Cube, Starburst, Venetian Star,* and *Command Star.*

PART 3

Hexagon Blocks

"There are many things to induce women to piece quilts. The desire for a handsome bed furnishing, or the wish to make a gift of one to a dear friend, have inspired some women to make quilts. With others, quiltmaking is a recreation, a diversion, a means of occupying restless fingers. However, the real inducement is love of the work; because the desire to make a quilt exceeds all other desires. In such a case it is worked on persistently, laid aside reluctantly, and taken up each time with renewed interest and pleasure. It is this intense interest in the work which produces the most beautiful quilts."

MARIE D. WEBSTER, *QUILTS: THEIR STORY & HOW TO MAKE THEM*, 1915

Hexagon Base Grid Category

Includes ● multi-grid hexagons

❶ **Brilliant Star,** Nancy Page, *Nashville Banner,* Jan 23, 1934. Also known as:
- **Pointing Star,** *Kansas City Star,* Mar 21, 1936.

❷ **Poinsettia,** Home Art Studios, *World Herald,* Oct 30, 1933.

❸ **A Hexagon,** *Ladies Art Company,* 1897. Also known as:
- **Hexagon Beauty,** *Farm Journal and Farmer's Wife,* ca. 1941.
- **Hexagons,** Nancy Page, *Nashville Banner,* Oct 24, 1933.
- **An Old Fashioned Wheel Quilt,** *Kansas City Star,* Jan 8, 1938.
- **Spider Web,** Hall, 1935.

❹ **Spider Web,** *Grandmother Clark's Patchwork Quilts, Book No. 19,* 1932.

❺ **Spider Web,** *Old Fashioned Quilts,* ca. 1931.

❻ **Spider Web,** Eveline Foland, *Kansas City Star,* Oct 11, 1930.

❼ **The Hexagon Star,** *Kansas City Star,* Oct 9, 1940.

❽ **Diamonds and Arrow Points,** *Kansas City Star,* Feb 21, 1945.

❾ **Dolly Madison Pattern,** *Kansas City Star,* Apr 10, 1937. Also known as:
- **6 Point Flower Garden,** *Kansas City Star,* Jul 22, 1959.
- **Box and Star,** Miall, 1937.
- **The Flower Garden,** *Kansas City Star,* May 30, 1951.
- **The Flower Garden Block,** *Kansas City Star,* May 8, 1937.
- **Garden of Flowers,** *Kansas City Star,* Aug 10, 1955.
- **Star Bouquet,** *Q Book 116, Blue Ribbon Quilts,* date unknown.

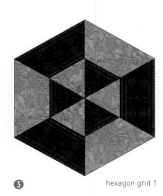

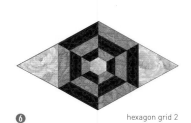

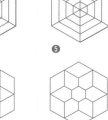

❶ hexagon grid 1 ❷ hexagon grid 1 ❸ hexagon grid 1

❹ hexagon grid 2 ❺ hexagon grid 2 ❻ hexagon grid 2

❼ hexagon grid 1

❽ hexagon grid 1

❾ hexagon grid 2

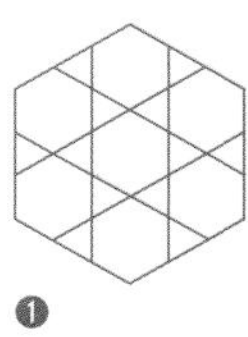

❶

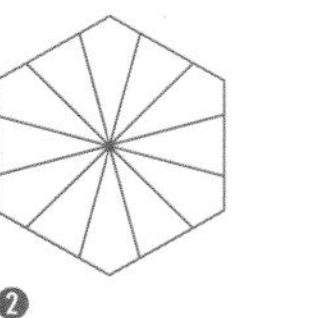

❷

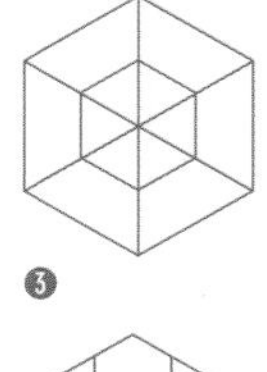

❸

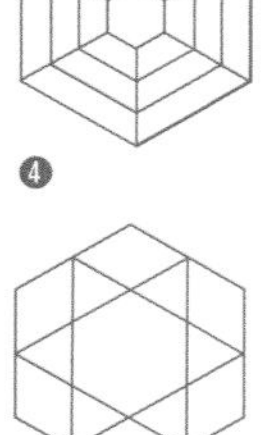

❹

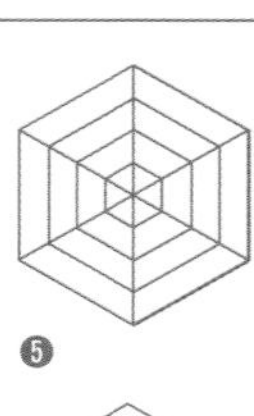

❺

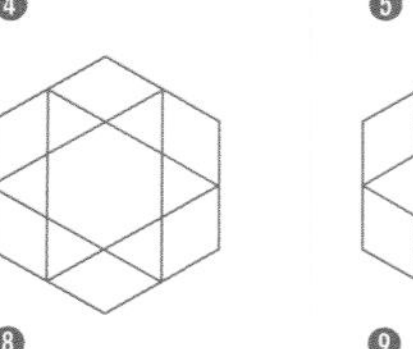

❻ ❼ ❽ ❾

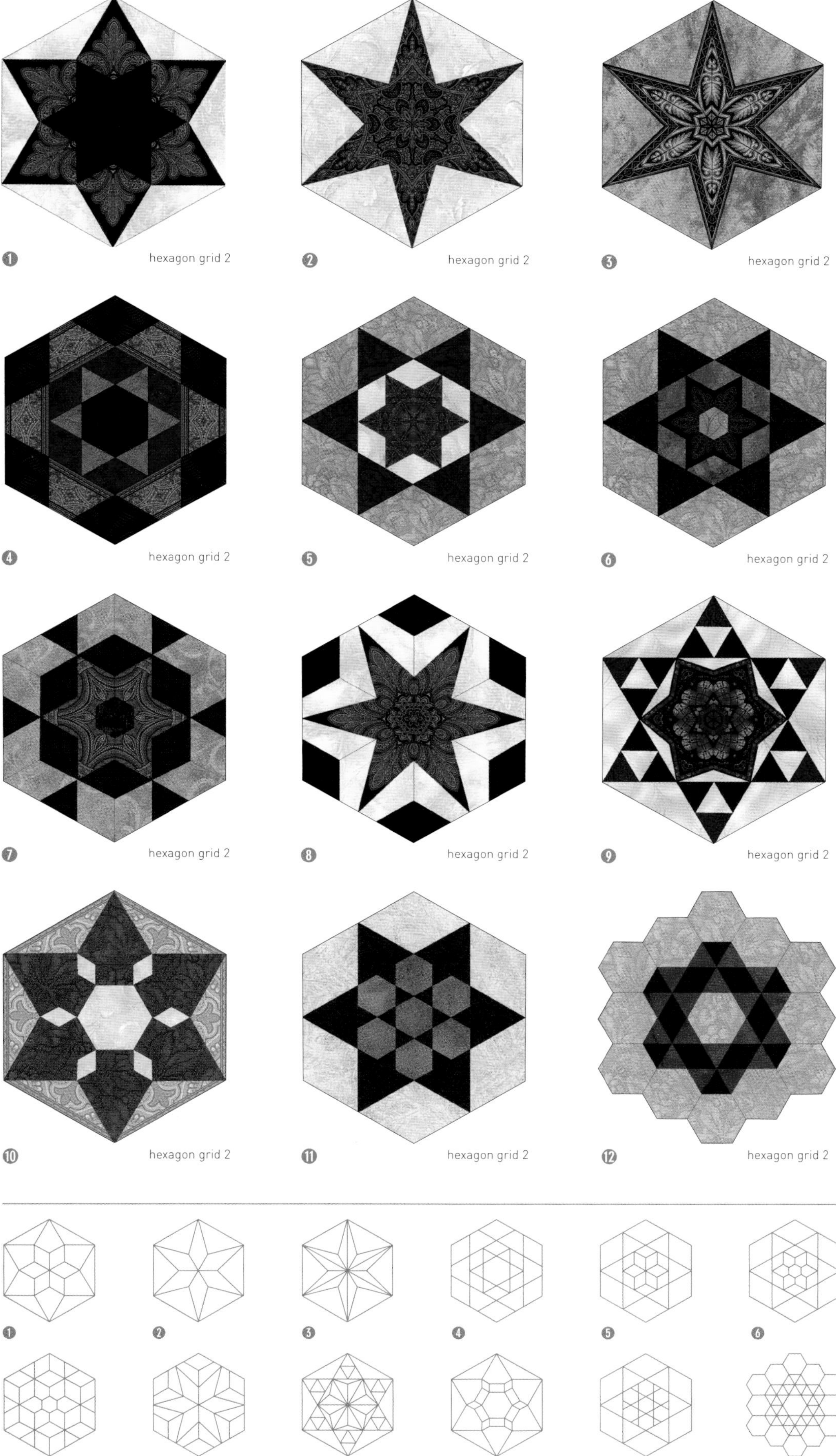

❶ **New World,** Jinny Beyer, Hilton Head Seminar design, 1992.

❷ **Hexagon Star,** Home Art Studios, date unknown.

❸ **North Star,** Jinny Beyer, Hilton Head Seminar design, 2003.

❹ **Star Studded Beauty,** Laura Wheeler, *Laura Wheeler Collection of Needlecraft Masterpieces.* ca. 1958.

❺ **The Oklahoma Star,** *Kansas City Star,* Jan 17, 1945.

❻ **Ozark Star,** *Kansas City Star,* Dec 21, 1935. Also known as:
: **True America,** *Kansas City Star,* Feb 8, 1956.

❼ **Boutonnière,** Eveline Foland, *Kansas City Star,* Sep 26, 1931.

❽ **España,** Jinny Beyer, Hilton Head Seminar design, 1992.

❾ **Eastern Star,** Alice Brooks, *Detroit Free Press,* Dec 15, 1933.

❿ **Arrow Heads,** *Kansas City Star,* Jan 21, 1942.

⓫ **Hidden Star,** *Kansas City Star,* 1936.

⓬ **Snow Crystal,** Edna Marie Dunn, *Kansas City Star,* Dec 10, 1932. Also known as:
: **Star Center on French Bouquet,** *Kansas City Star,* Jan 6, 1934.

"Here is a favorite among our English sisters as well as among American women. In early New England days the diamond was used in making 'best quilts,' and the combination of diamond and hexagons makes a good looking quilt that is used only for 'state occasions.' " Nancy Cabot, *Chicago Tribune,* Mar 20, 1934

1. **Hollow Cube,** Jinny Beyer, Hilton Head Seminar design, 2003.
2. **Cubicle,** Jinny Beyer, Hilton Head Seminar design, 2003.
3. **Three Patch,** Laura Wheeler, *Cincinnati Enquirer,* Dec 15, 1936.
4. **Morning Star,** *Kansas City Star,* Feb 1, 1936.
5. **Ozark Diamond,** Eveline Foland, *Kansas City Star,* Jun 20, 1931. Also known as:
   Ozark Star, Hall, 1935.
   Star and Diamonds, *Aunt Martha series: The Quilt Fair Comes to You,* ca. 1933.
6. **Glory Design,** *The Patchwork Book,* 1932. Also known as:
   Glory Block, *Kansas City Star,* Sep 30, 1933.
   Old Glory, Nancy Cabot, *Chicago Tribune,* Jan 23, 1937.
   One Patch Star, Laura Wheeler, unidentified newspaper clipping, date unknown.
   Tumbling Blocks, Alice Brooks, unidentified newspaper clipping, date unknown.
7. **Roman Mosaic,** Jinny Beyer, Hilton Head Seminar design, 1993.
8. **Glistening Star,** *The Country Gentleman,* Jul, 1930
9. **Ma Perkin's Flower Garden,** *Kansas City Star,* May 16, 1936.
10. **Octagon,** *Farm Journal and Farmers Wife,* ca. 1941.
11. **A Little Girl's Star,** *Kansas City Star,* Aug 16, 1950.
12. **Seven Sisters,** Nancy Cabot, *Chicago Tribune,* Mar 13, 1933. Also known as:
   Seven Stars, *Kansas City Star,* Feb 15, 1936.
   The Seven Stars Quilt, *Kansas City Star,* Aug 16, 1944.
   Rolling Star, *Kansas City Star,* Feb 15, 1936.

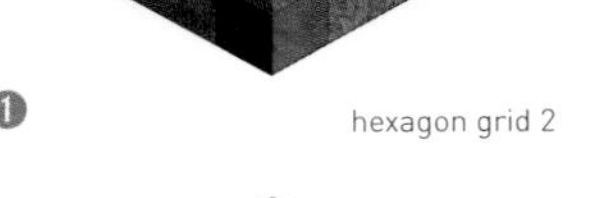
1 hexagon grid 2

2 hexagon grid 2

3 hexagon grid 2

4 hexagon grid 2

5 hexagon grid 2

6 hexagon grid 2

7 hexagon grid 2

8 hexagon grid 2

9 hexagon grid 2

10 hexagon grid 2

11 hexagon grid 2

12 hexagon grid 2

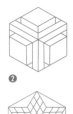

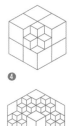

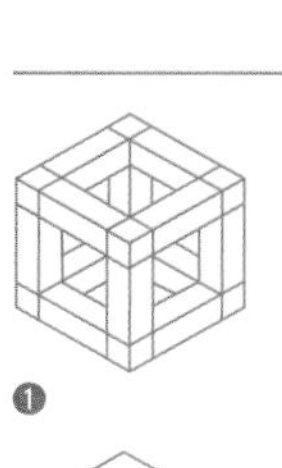
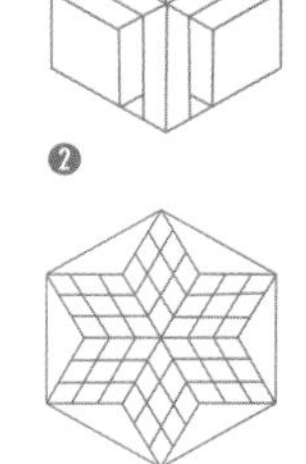
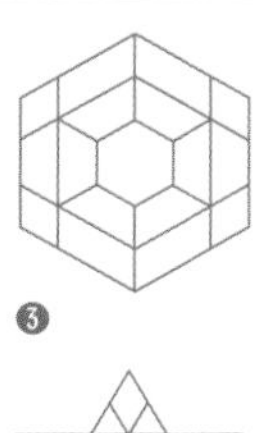
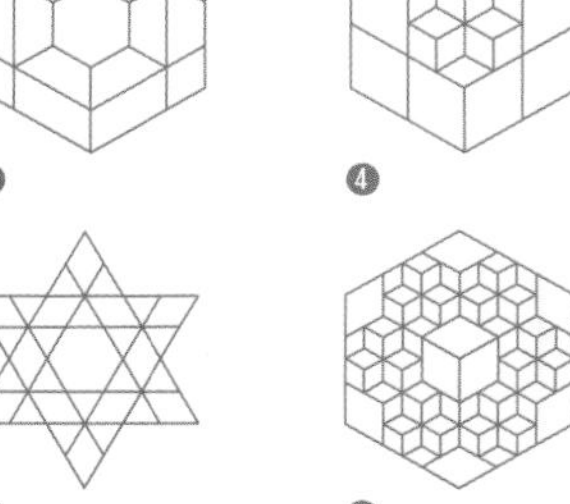
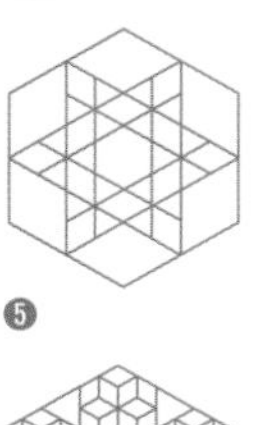
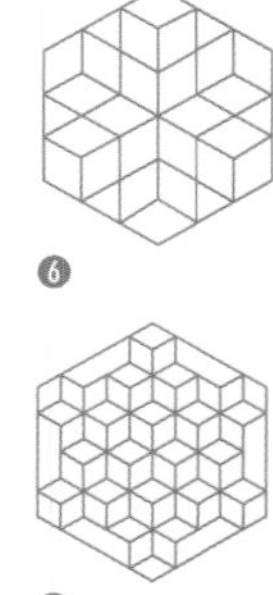
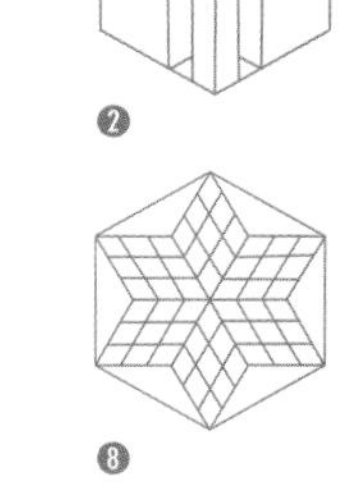

1 2 3 4 5 6

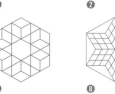

7 8 9 10 11 12

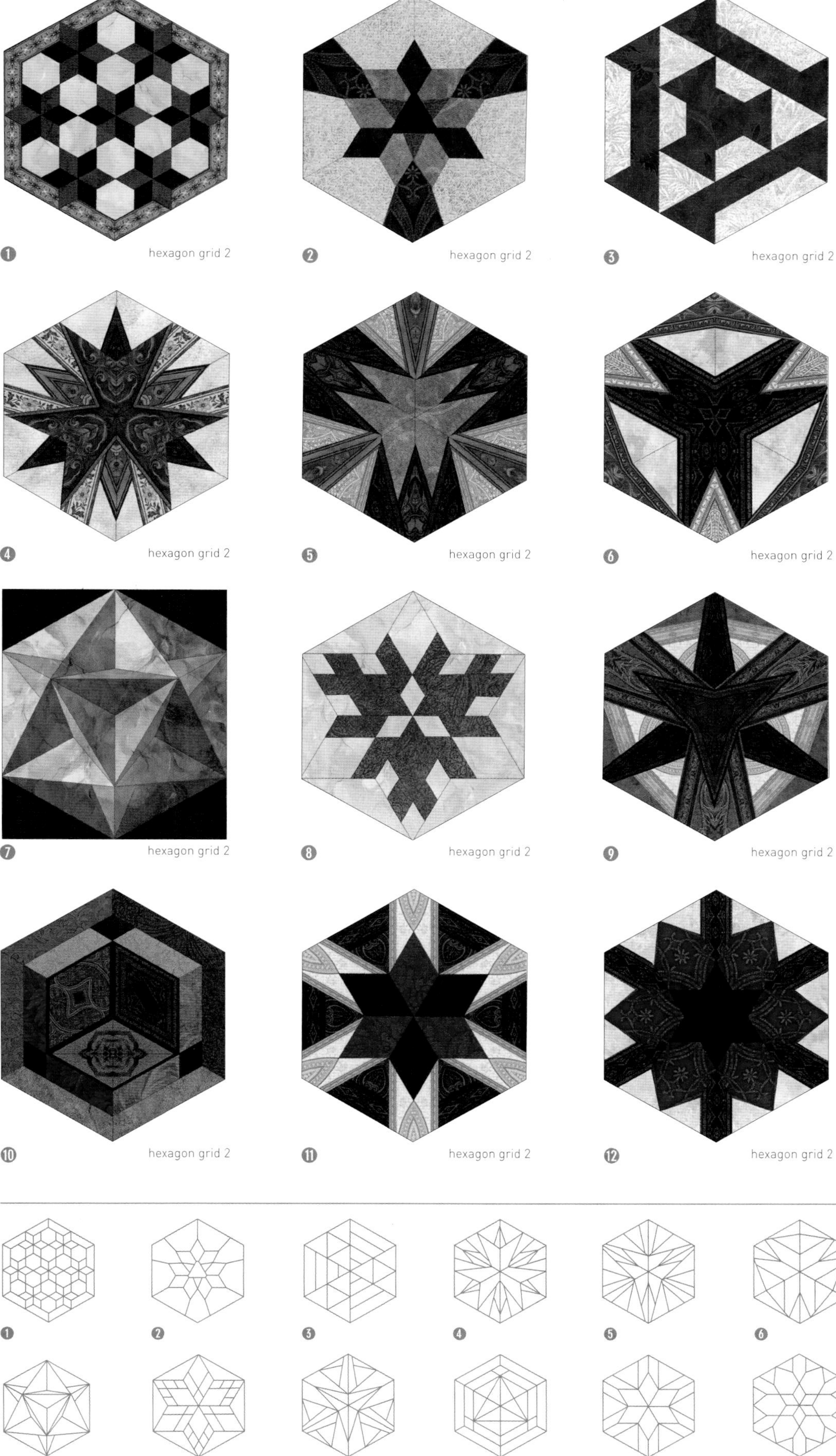

1 Seven Stars, *Grandmother Clark's Patchwork Quilt Designs, From Books 20-21-23.* ca. 1932. Also known as:

Seven Great Lights, Nancy Page, *Birmingham News,* Nov 28, 1933.

"Mrs. John Evans of Pueblo, Colo., is the donor of this old-time favorite. She says that her mother received it recently from the grandmother who made it when she lived in Arkansas. The grandmother called it 'Seven Stars' but Mrs. Evans would like to rechristen it and call it 'Seven Great Lights.'" Nancy Page, *Birmingham News,* Nov 28, 1933

2 Jacob's Coat, *Prize Winning Designs,* ca. 1931.

3 Trials and Troubles, *Old Fashioned Quilts,* ca. 1931.

4 Trilogy, Jinny Beyer, Jinny Beyer Studio design, 2007.

5 Refractions, Jinny Beyer, Jinny Beyer Studio design, 2007.

6 Lapis, Jinny Beyer, Hilton Head Seminar design, 2008.

7 Command Star, Jinny Beyer, Hilton Head Seminar design, 2003.

8 Blue Birds, Hall, 1935.

9 Malachite, Jinny Beyer, Hilton Head Seminar design, 2008.

10 Triple Play, Jinny Beyer, Beyer, Jinny, *Quiltmaking by Hand,* 2004.

11 From a Grandmother's Collection, *Kansas City Star,* Aug 19, 1959.

12 Moroccan Garden, Jinny Beyer, Hilton Head Seminar design, 1993.

❶ **Morning Star,** Laura Wheeler, *Sioux City Journal,* May 9, 1940.

❷ **Tsunami,** Jinny Beyer, Hilton Head Seminar design, 1993.

❸ **Florida Star,** Eveline Foland, *Kansas City Star,* Sep 24, 1932.

❹ **Crystal Star,** Jinny Beyer, Hilton Head Seminar design, 1999.

❺ **Alhambra Star,** *Weldon's Practical Patchwork,* ca. 1890.

❻ **Citrine,** Jinny Beyer, Hilton Head Seminar design, 2008.

❼ **Shattered Star,** Jinny Beyer, Hilton Head Seminar design, 2007.

❽ **Winter Fantasy,** Jinny Beyer, Hilton Head Seminar design, 2007.

❾ **Brewster's Choice,** Jinny Beyer, Hilton Head Seminar design, 2007.

❿ **Modernistic Star,** *Prize Winning Designs,* ca. 1931.

⓫ **Shasta Daisy,** Jinny Beyer, Jinny Beyer Studio design, 2007.

⓬ **Garnet,** Jinny Beyer, Hilton Head Seminar design, 2008.

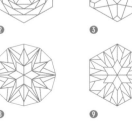

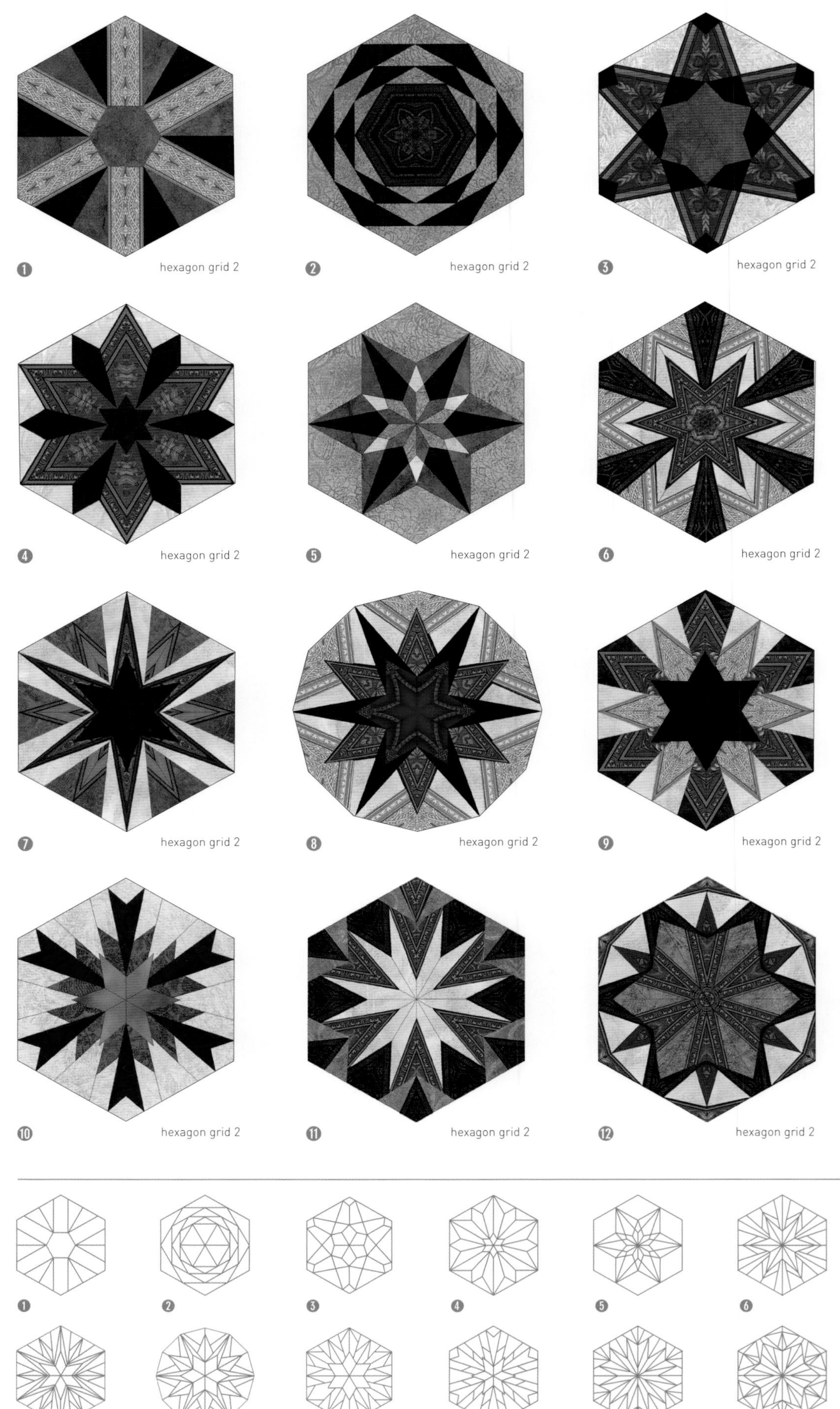

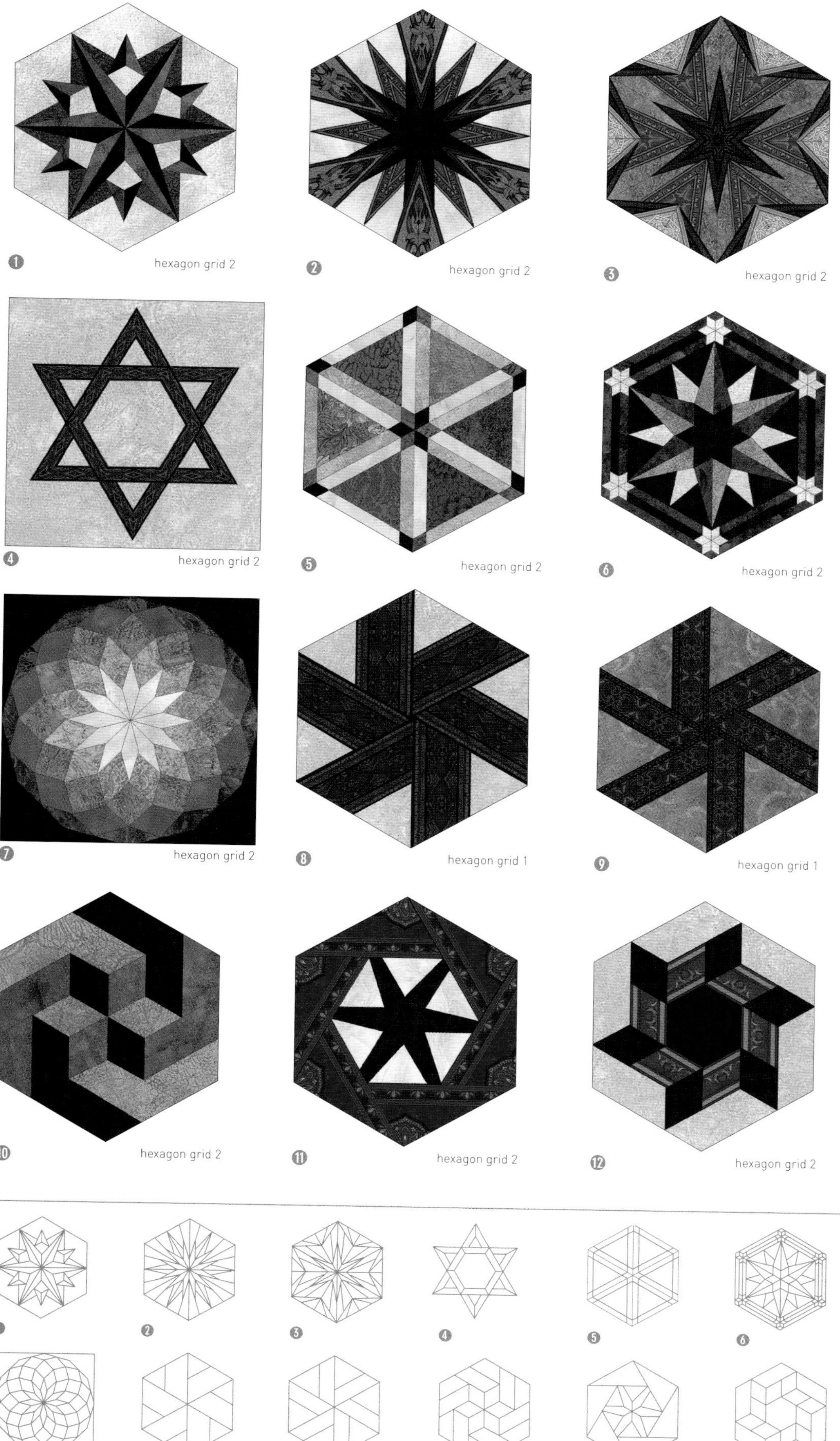

1. **Star Pattern,** *Weldon's Practical Patchwork,* ca. 1890.
2. **Heliotrope,** Jinny Beyer, Hilton Head Seminar design, 2008.
3. **Icicles,** Jinny Beyer, Jinny Beyer Studio design, 2007.
4. **Solomon's Seal,** Nancy Cabot, *Chicago Tribune,* Oct 25, 1937.
5. **Diamond String,** Nancy Page, *Nashville Banner,* Mar 6, 1934. Also known as:
   Star Rays, Nancy Page, *Nashville Banner,* Mar 6, 1934.
6. **Dutch Tile,** Home Art Studios, *World Herald,* Jan 4, 1934.
7. **Global Star,** Jinny Beyer, Hilton Head Seminar design, 2003.
8. **Whirligig Hexagon,** *Kansas City Star,* Jul 25, 1936.
9. **The Texas Trellis,** *Kansas City Star,* Jul 28, 1943.
10. **Mediterranean Puzzle,** Jinny Beyer, Hilton Head Seminar design, 1993.
11. **Water Wheel,** Jinny Beyer, Hilton Head Seminar design, 1996.
12. **The Pin Wheel,** *Kansas City Star,* Jul 7, 1934.

❶ **Origami,** Jinny Beyer, Hilton Head Seminar design, 1997.

❷ **Spinning Sunflower,** Jinny Beyer, Hilton Head Seminar design, 1997.

❸ **Sport,** Jinny Beyer, Hilton Head Seminar design, 1996.

❹ **Forget Me Not,** Jinny Beyer, Hilton Head Seminar design, 1996.

❺ **Double Twisted Hexagon,** *Weldon's Practical Patchwork,* ca. 1890.

❻ **Twister,** Jinny Beyer, Hilton Head Seminar design, 2006.

❼ **Morning Star,** Nancy Cabot, *Chicago Tribune,* Feb 26, 1937.

❽ **Madison Quilt Block,** *Ladies Art Company,* 1922. Also known as:
- **Madison Block,** Nancy Cabot, *Chicago Tribune,* Oct 6, 1937.
- **Madison's Patch,** Hall, 1935.

❾ **Cube Work,** *Ladies Art Company,* 1897. Also known as:
- **Baby Blocks,** Hall, 1935.

❿ **Star and Diamonds,** Nancy Cabot, *Chicago Tribune,* Jul 24, 1937.

⓫ **Block Star,** *Grandma Dexter Appliqué and Patchwork Designs, Book 36a* ca. 1932.

⓬ **Solomon's Garden,** Nancy Cabot, *Chicago Tribune,* May 31, 1936.

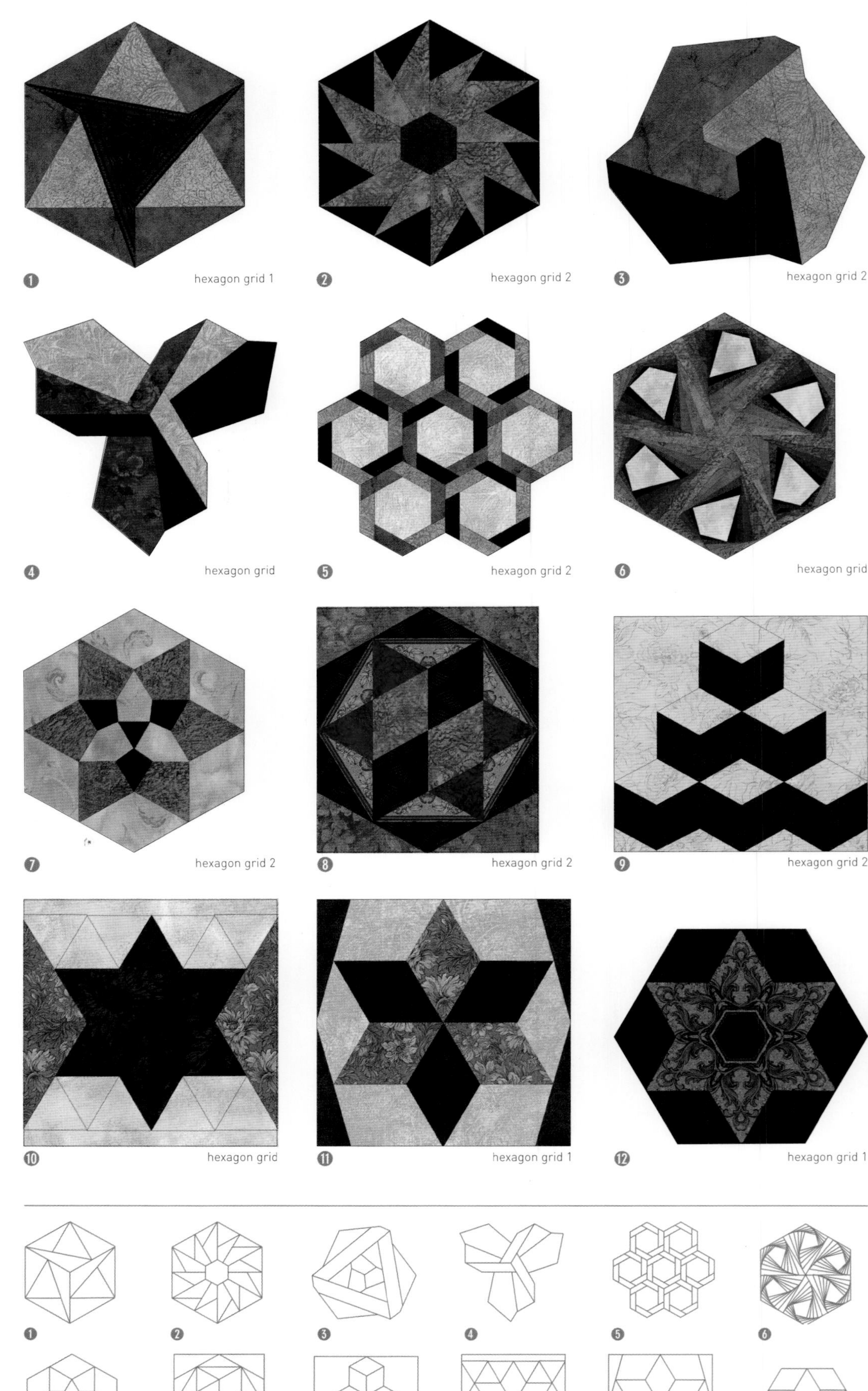

1 hexagon grid 1

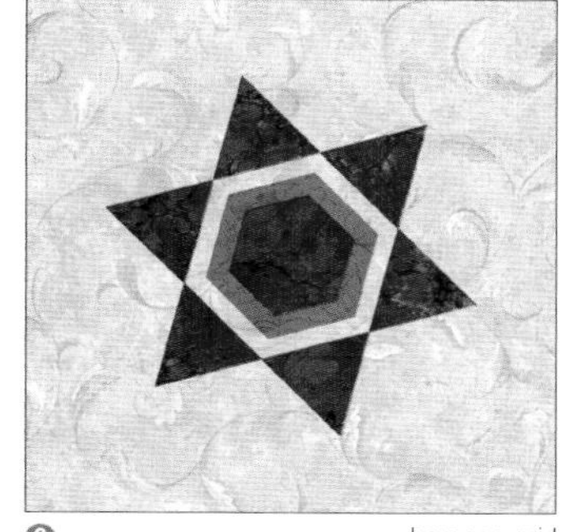

2 hexagon grid

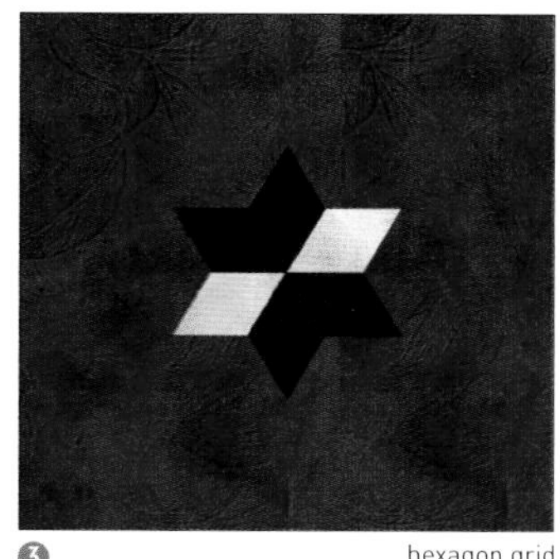

3 hexagon grid

4 hexagon grid

5 hexagon grid

6 hexagon grid

7 hexagon grid 1

8 hexagon grid 1

9 hexagon grid 1

10 hexagon grid 2

11 hexagon grid 2

12 hexagon grid 1

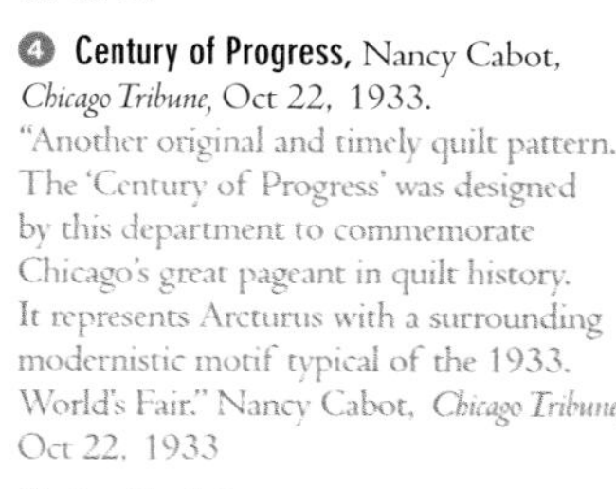

1. **Star of Bethlehem,** Ickis, 1949.
2. **Star of Bethlehem,** Hall, 1935.
3. **Liberty,** *Farm Journal and Farmers Wife,* ca. 1941.
4. **Century of Progress,** Nancy Cabot, *Chicago Tribune,* Oct 22, 1933.
   "Another original and timely quilt pattern. The 'Century of Progress' was designed by this department to commemorate Chicago's great pageant in quilt history. It represents Arcturus with a surrounding modernistic motif typical of the 1933 World's Fair." Nancy Cabot, *Chicago Tribune,* Oct 22, 1933
5. **Saw Tooth Pattern,** *Kansas City Star,* Aug 18, 1934.
6. **Star of the West,** *Kansas City Star,* Aug 22, 1956.
7. **Wonder of Egypt,** Nancy Cabot, *Chicago Tribune,* May 24, 1937.
8. **Star of Bethlehem,** *Ladies Art Company,* 1897. Also known as:
   A Pattern of Chinese Origin, *Kansas City Star,* Dec 30, 1942.
9. **Hexagonal,** *Ladies Art Company,* 1897. Also known as:
   Six Pointed Star, Clara Stone, *Practical Needlework,* ca. 1906.
10. **Novel Star,** *Ladies Art Company,* 1922.
11. **Texas Star,** *Ladies Art Company,* 1922. Also known as:
    Friendship Hexagon, Nancy Page, unidentified newspaper clipping, date unknown.
    Hexagon Stars, Nancy Page, *Birmingham News,* Apr 17, 1934.
12. **Little Girl's Star,** *Kansas City Star,* Aug 16, 1950.

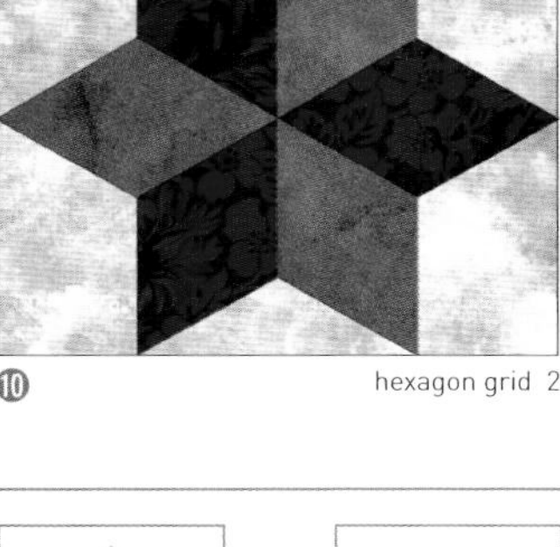

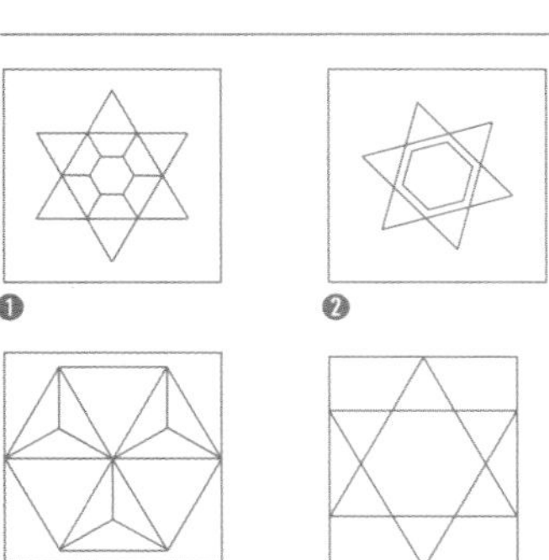

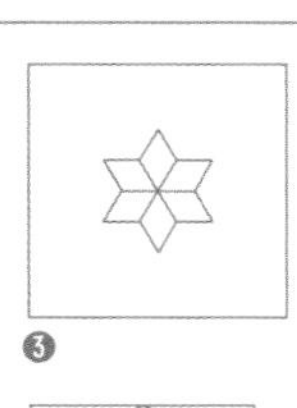

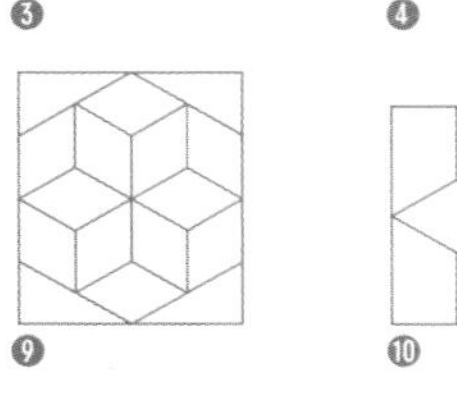

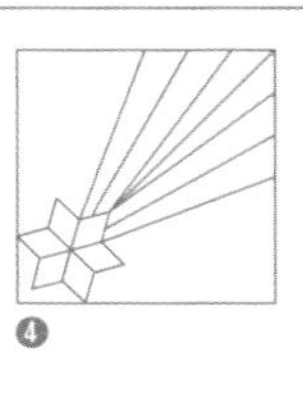

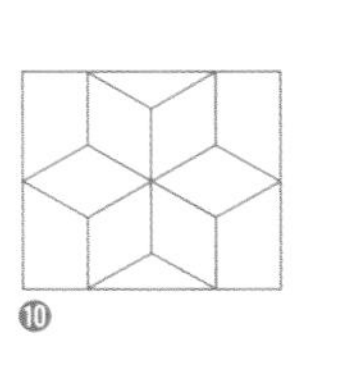

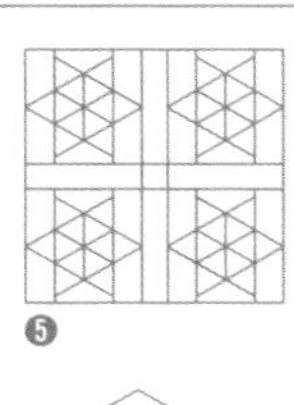

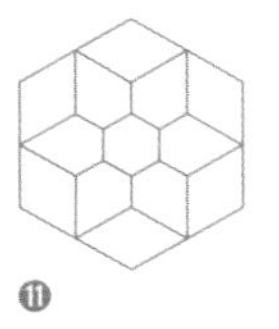

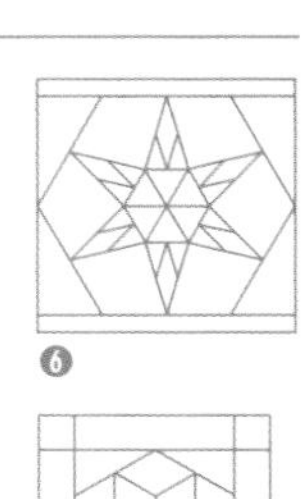

1 2 3 4 5 6

7 8 9 10 11 12

❶ **Sam's Quilt,** Clara Stone, *Practical Needlework,* ca. 1906.

❷ **Star of the East,** Hall, 1935.

❸ **The Columbia,** *Ladies World Magazine,* May 1893 Also known as:
 Columbia Star, Hall, 1935.

❹ **Double Star,** Hall, 1935.

❺ **Charm,** Hall, 1935.

❻ **Six Point String Quilt,** *Kansas City Star,* Feb 21, 1940.

❼ **Eternity,** Jinny Beyer, Hilton Head Seminar design, 2006.

❽ **Triangle Maze,** Jinny Beyer, Hilton Head Seminar design, 2006.

❶ hexagon grid 2

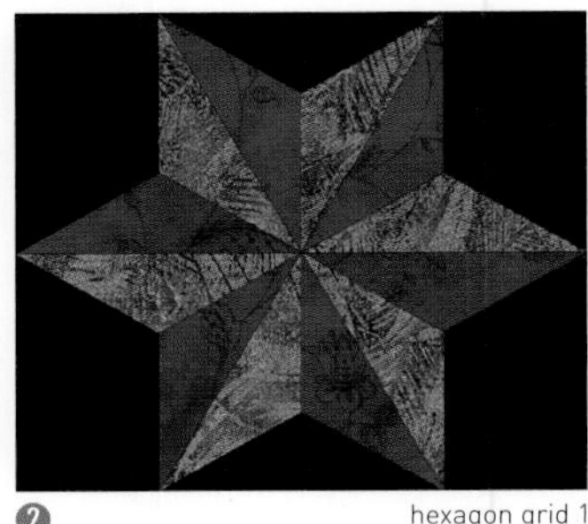

❷ hexagon grid 1

❸ hexagon grid 2

❹ hexagon grid 2

❺ hexagon grid

❻ hexagon grid 1

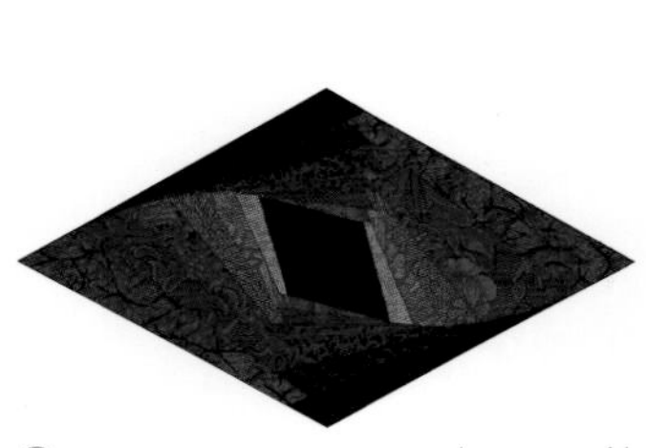
❼ hexagon grid

❽ hexagon grid

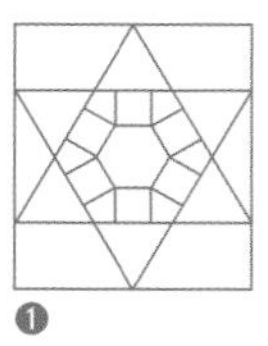
❶

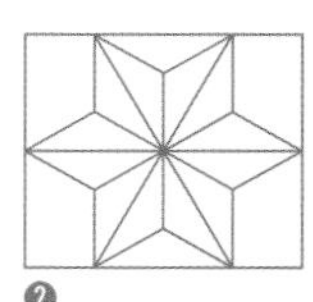
❷

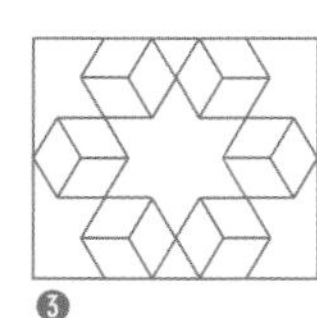
❸

❹

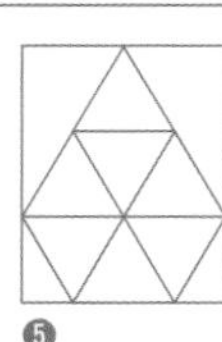
❺

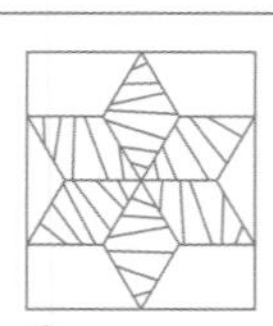
❻

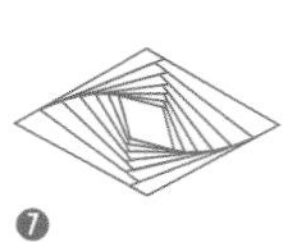
❼

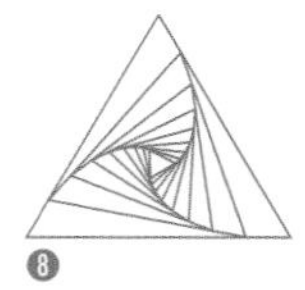
❽

Hexagon Base Grid Category
(with Curved Elements)

Includes ● *multi-grid hexagons*

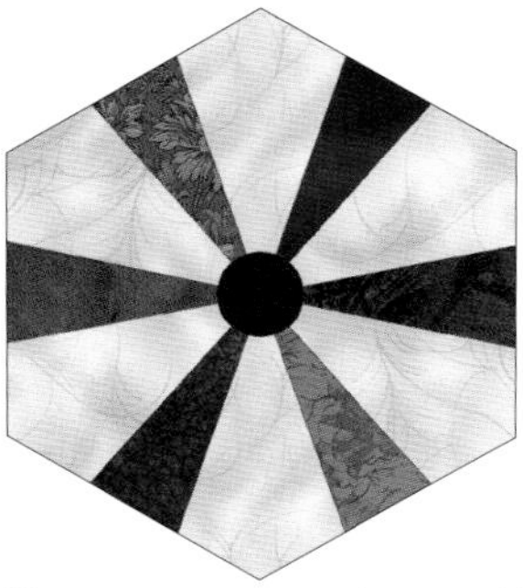

❶ hexagon grid 2

❷ hexagon grid 2

❸ hexagon grid 2

❹ hexagon grid 2

❺ hexagon grid 2

❻ hexagon grid 2

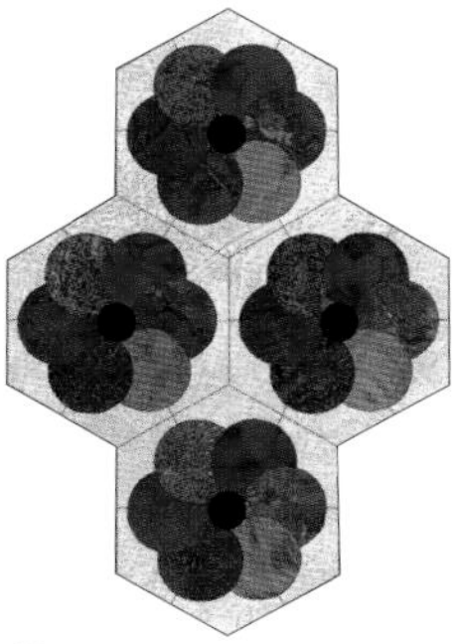

❼ hexagon grid 2

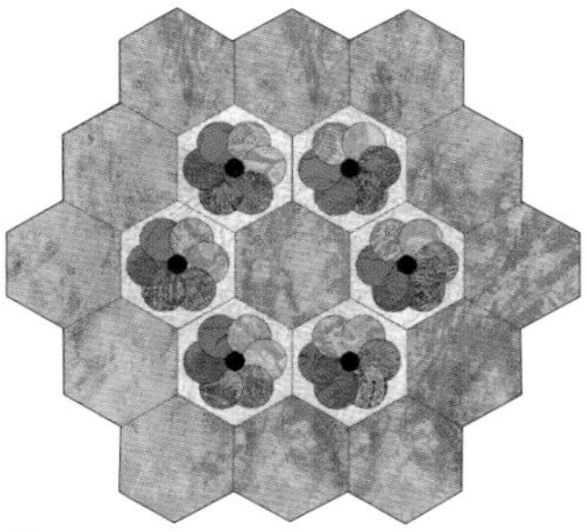

❽ hexagon grid 2

❾ hexagon grid 2

❶ **Endless Chain,** Alice Brooks, *Detroit Free Press,* Jun 5, 1940. Also known as:
Economical Chain, Laura Wheeler, *Americana Designs Quilts,* ca. 1940.
"In the early days of quiltmaking, the scrap quilt was an outstanding favorite. Not only did it appeal because of the economy of using up odds and ends of material, but it had its social and sentimental side, too. Many scrap quilts were friendship quilts—each friend invited to the quilting bee brought her scraps and made a block—her donation to the quilt. Endless Chain, a prize scrap quilt, would have been a leading favorite then." Alice Brooks, *Detroit Free Press,* Jun 5, 1940

❷ **Daisy Chain,** *Prize Winning Designs,* ca. 1931.

❸ **Flower Star,** Ickis, 1949.

❹ **Star and Crescent,** Hall, 1935. Also known as:
Twinkling Star, Hall, 1935.

❺ **Sparkling Dew,** Nancy Cabot, *Chicago Tribune,* Feb 23, 1937.

❻ **Rose Star,** Home Art Studios, *World Herald,* Nov 8, 1933.

❼ **Roses of Picardy,** Home Art Studios, *World Herald,* Oct 31, 1933.
"The Roses of Picardy is a lovely new pattern that offers you the opportunity of using any or all of the gay colored prints that repose in your scrap bag. Each rose can be of a different color combination. The design is patchwork or can also be used as an appliqué." *World Herald,* Oct 31, 1933

❽ **Garden of Roses,** Home Art Studios, *World Herald,* Dec 12, 1933.

❾ **Spring Fancy,** Jinny Beyer, Hilton Head Seminar design, 2007.

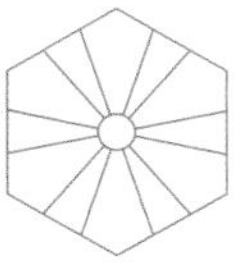

❶ ❷

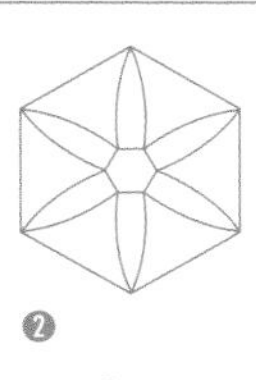

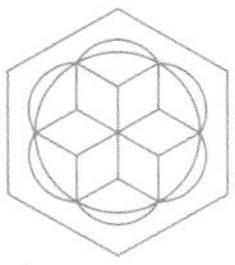

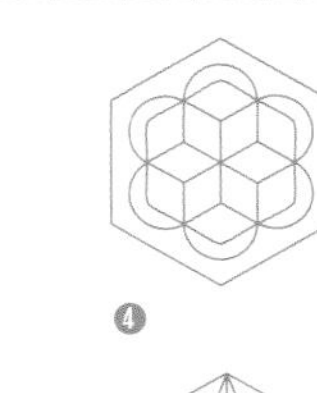

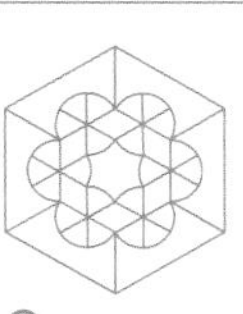

❸ ❹ ❺

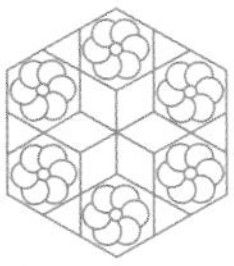

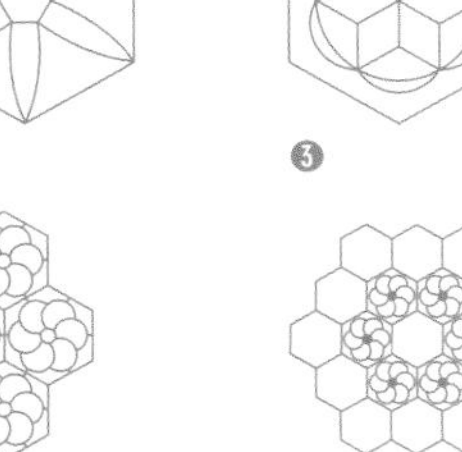

❻ ❼ ❽ ❾

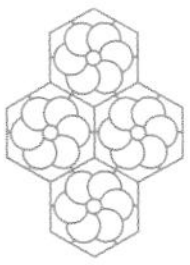

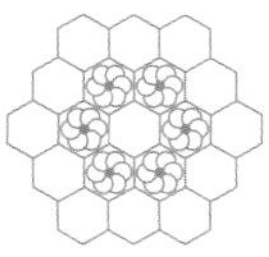

❶ **Dahlia,** Jinny Beyer, Hilton Head Seminar design, 2007.

❷ **Six Pointed Star,** *Kansas City Star,* Oct 5, 1938.

❸ **Savannah Beautiful Star,** Nancy Cabot, *Chicago Tribune,* Jan 19, 1935.

❹ **Savannah Beautiful Star,** *Ladies Art Company,* 1922.

❺ **Star and Planets,** Ickis, 1949.

❻ **Four O'Clock Quilt,** *Kansas City Star,* Mar 18, 1942.

❼ **Triangle Friendship,** Home Art Studios, *World Herald,* Jan 3, 1934.

❽ **Rainbow Star,** Home Art Studios, *World Herald,* Nov 10, 1933.

❾ **Elephant Foot,** *Prize Winning Designs,* ca. 1931.

❿ **Savannah Beautiful Star,** Hall, 1935.

⓫ **Stars and Planets,** *Grandmother Clark's Old Fashioned Quilt Designs, Book* 21, 1931.

⓬ **Solar System,** Nancy Cabot, *Chicago Tribune,* Jan 25, 1938.

⓭ **Circle and Saw,** *The Patchwork Book,* 1932.

❶ hexagon grid 2

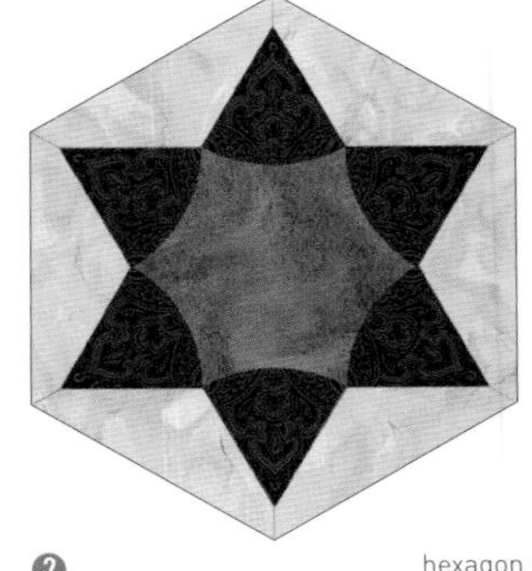
❷ hexagon grid 2

❸ hexagon grid 2

❹ hexagon grid 2

❺ hexagon grid 2

❻ hexagon grid 2

❼ hexagon grid 2

❽ hexagon grid 2

❾ hexagon grid 2

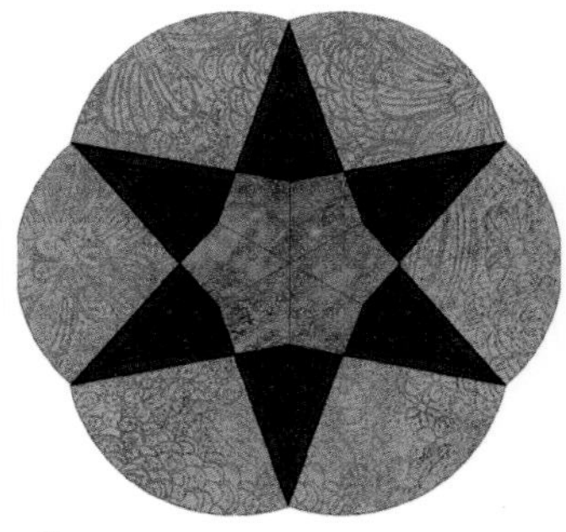
❿ hexagon grid 2

⓫ hexagon grid 2

⓬ hexagon grid 2

⓭ hexagon grid 2

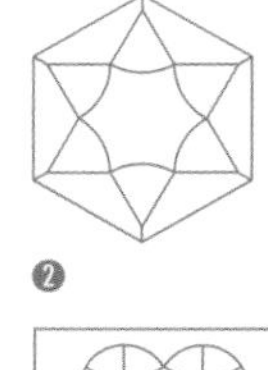
❶

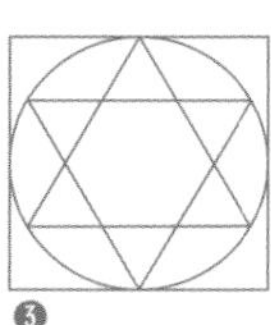
❷

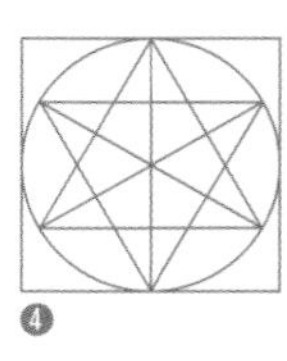
❸

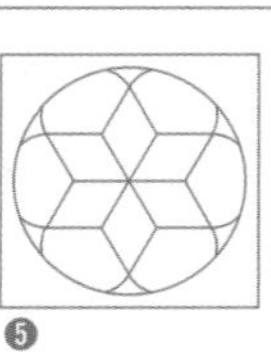
❹

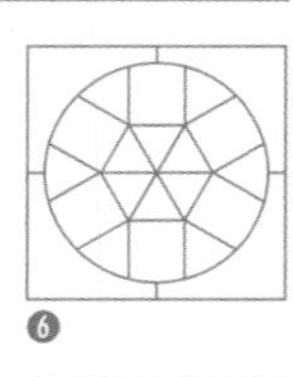
❺ ❻

❼

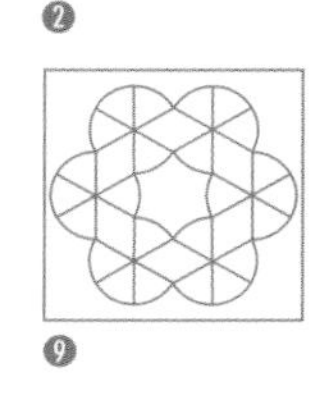
❽

❾

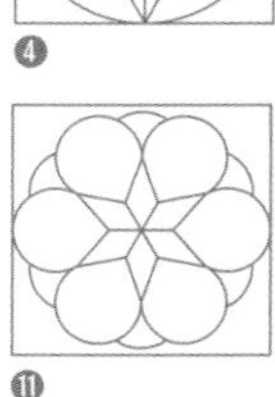
❿

⓫

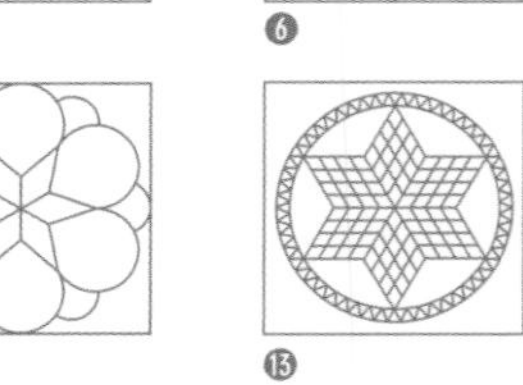
⓬ ⓭

The Swastika

The Swastika, a symbol of good luck, was used in ancient cultures and religions for thousands of years before it was adopted as the emblem of the Nazi flag. The name comes from the Sanskrit *svastika,* "su" meaning good and "asti" to be; in other words—good luck. It is a sacred symbol in the Buddhist, Hindu and many other religions and can be seen as design motifs in many cultures including Turkish, Tibetan and Navajo rugs. It is a shame that such a sacred symbol of well-being, has become so hated because of its use by Nazi Germany.

The Swastika was also a popular quilt design, and several blocks depict the symbol in various ways. *Whirligig* appeared in the *Michigan Farmer* in 1926 and Ruth Finley had the same design in her book and called it *Devil's Puzzle, Swastika* or *Fly Foot*:

"These blocks set together without intervening bands or squares of solid color produce a 'Puzzling' effect indeed. 'Fly Foot' was the earlier name for this pattern, a designation difficult to account for until a single block was isolated. Then the design was seen to resemble a swastika. But what had fly's foot to do with that symbol of luck? In fact, the pattern is much older than the popularizing of the swastika in this country. Webster's Dictionary defines the swastika as a "symbol or ornament of great antiquity" and goes on to state: Many modified forms exist, while various decorative designs, as the Greek fret, are derived from or closely associated with it. Called also 'flyfot'."

Ruby McKim, in *101 Patchwork Patterns,* has a pattern for a *Swastika* block:

"Our frontier mothers ingeniously converted this ancient symbol of good luck into a quilt pattern which is made simply from two triangles."

The latest date I have for any of the Swastika blocks I found was in June 2, 1935, when *Moon and Swastika* appeared in the Nancy Cabot column. For obvious reasons after that time, quiltmakers no longer considered this symbol one of good luck.

Patch Me If You Can, *Dakota Farmer.* **See 68-9.**

Whirligig, *Michigan Farmer.* **See 428-4.**

Dutchman's Puzzle, *Ladies Art Company.* **See 68-10.**

Pin Wheel, *The Farm Journal Quilt Patterns.* **See 99-9.**

Flyfoot, *Illinois State Register.* **See 100-1.**

Swastika, *Dakota Farmer.* **See 188-4.**

Swastika, *The Patchwork Book.* **See 225-2.**

Swastika Patch, *Ladies Art Company.* **See 246-4.**

Swastika, *Grandmother Clark's Authentic Early American Quilts, Book 21.* **See 99-2.**

Moon and Swastika, *Chicago Tribune.* **See 318-8.**

Indian Mats, *Chicago Tribune.* **See 410-8.**

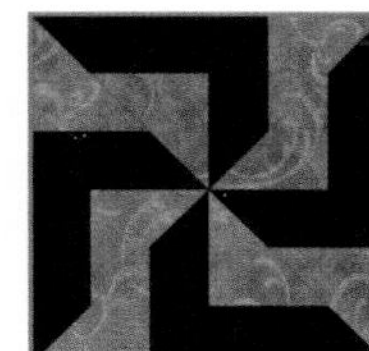

Wheel, *Farm Journal Quilt Patterns.* **See 143-9.**

Good Luck, *Chicago Tribune.* **See 143-10.**

County Clare, Jinny Beyer, 2006. Designed for the County Clare fabric collection by RJR Fabrics. This quilt is a "fragmented" variation (see page 45) of the continuous pattern design *Cube Lattice*.

PART

Continuous Pattern Blocks

"Let's get out the scrap bag and take stock of its contents. Materials for many quilts repose blissfully in obscure places for the want of hands to make them into lasting treasures. Pleasure and companionship go hand in hand when once you have started a quilt, and you will lay it aside with reluctance, so why not join the happy throng of women who are enjoying quilt making...

World Herald, Oct 27, 1933

Continuous Pattern Category

Includes ● multi-grid straight-line designs and ● hexagon straight-line designs

❶ **Elongated Box Pattern,** *Weldon's Practical Patchwork,* ca. 1890.

❷ **Tumbling Blocks,** *Quilts,* 1945.

❸ **Brick Pile,** *Ladies Art Company,* 1928.

❹ **Magic Squares,** Aunt Martha series: *Patchwork Simplicity,* ca. 1977.

❺ **Variegated Diamonds,** Nancy Cabot, *Chicago Tribune,* Mar 13, 1935. Also known as:
 Golden Cubes, Nancy Cabot, *Chicago Tribune,* May 13, 1936.
"Here is a quilt pattern that will make up beautifully in striped materials. Many of us have scraps that simply beg to be made up into such pieced blocks." Nancy Cabot, *Chicago Tribune,* Mar 13, 1935

❻ **Box Quilt,** Finley, 1929. Also known as:
 The Heavenly Steps, Finley, 1929.
 Pandora's Box, Finley, 1929.

❼ **Cube Lattice,** *Ladies Art Company,* 1901. Also known as:
 Cubes and Tile, Nancy Cabot, *Chicago Tribune,* Dec 15, 1933.
 Idle Moments, Nancy Cabot, *Chicago Tribune,* Jun 4, 1937.
 Lattice, Nancy Cabot, *Chicago Tribune,* Mar 23, 1935.

❽ **Country Farm,** *Ladies Art Company,* 1897.

❾ **Sultan's Block,** Nancy Cabot, *Chicago Tribune,* Dec 3, 1937.

❶ continuous pattern on 9 x 9 grid

❷ continuous pattern

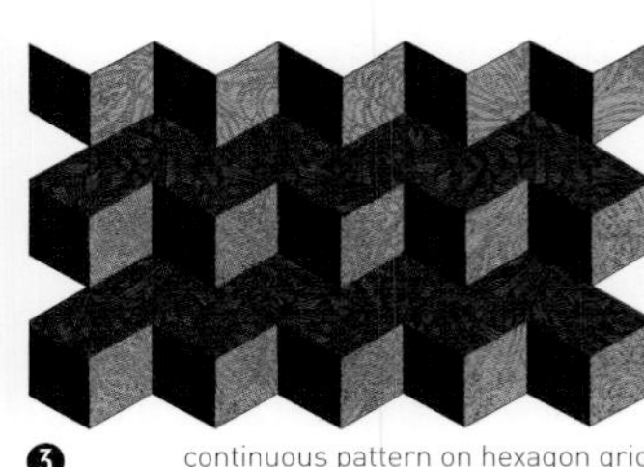
❸ continuous pattern on hexagon grid

❹ continuous pattern

❺ continuous pattern 12 x 12 grid

❻ continuous pattern

❼ continuous pattern 8 x 8 grid

❽ continuous pattern 10 x 10 grid

❾ continuous pattern 12 x 12 grid

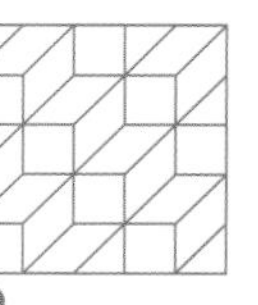
❶

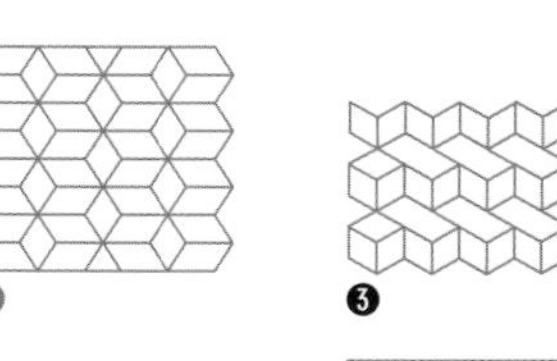
❷ ❸

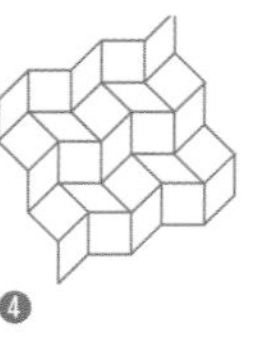
❹

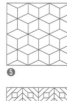

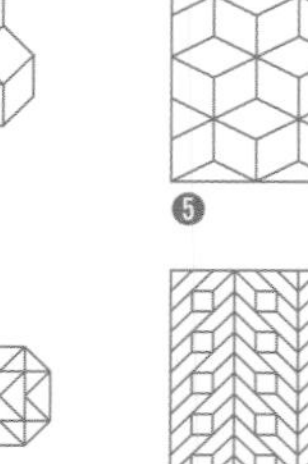
❺

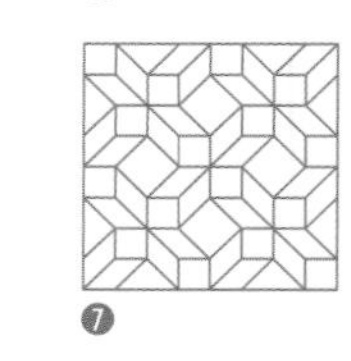
❻ ❼ ❽ ❾

1 continuous pattern on 8 x 10 grid

2 continuous pattern on 8 x 8 grid

3 continuous pattern on 10 x 10 grid

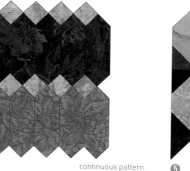

4 continuous pattern

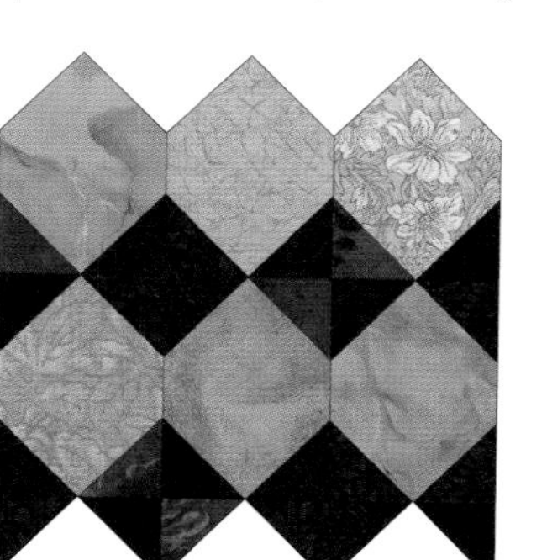

5 continuous pattern

6 continuous pattern

7 continuous pattern on hexagon grid

8 continuous pattern on 12 x12 grid

9 continuous pattern

10 continuous pattern on 12 x12 grid

11 continuous pattern on 11 x11 grid

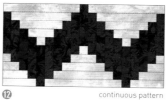

12 continuous pattern

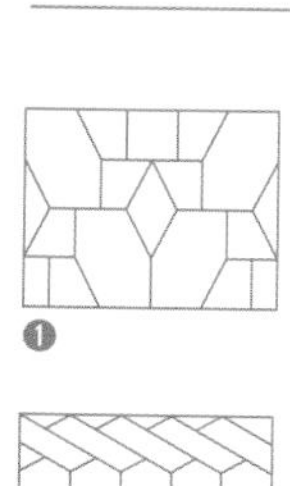
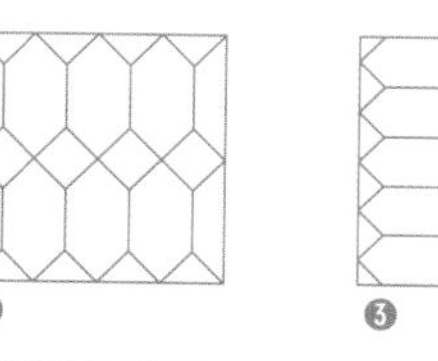
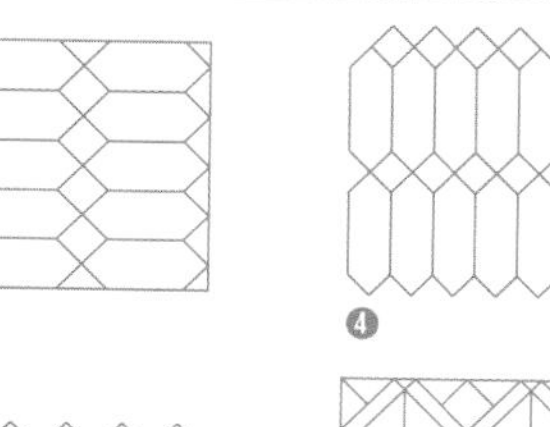
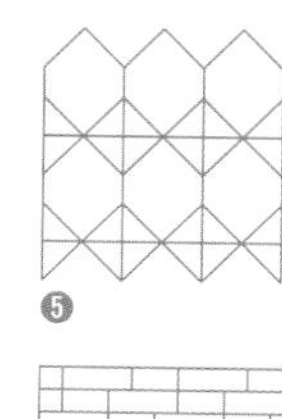
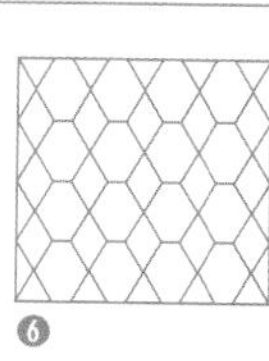
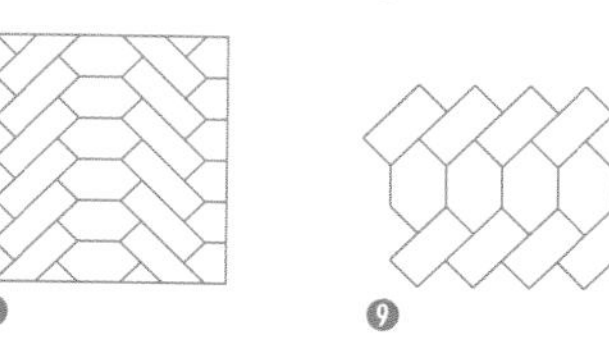
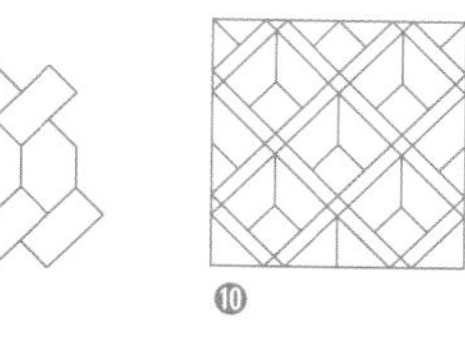

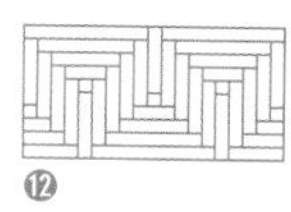

1 2 3 4 5 6 7 8 9 10 11 12

1 **Topaz Trail,** Nancy Cabot, *Chicago Tribune,* Nov 9, 1935.

2 **Rail Fences,** Nancy Cabot, *Chicago Tribune,* Jan 3, 1936.

3 **Fantastic Patchwork,** *Ladies Art Company,* 1897.

4 **Quintettes,** Nancy Page, *Birmingham News,* Nov 8, 1938.

5 **The World Fair Quilt,** *Kansas City Star,* Oct 27, 1943.

6 **Diamond Rows,** *Farm Journal and Farmer's Wife* (Silver Anniversary issue), 1945.

7 **Cable Blocks,** *The Patchwork Book,* 1932.

8 **Rope Block,** Nancy Cabot, *Chicago Tribune,* Mar 9, 1937.

9 **The Rope Strands,** *Kansas City Star,* Apr 20, 1960.

10 **Cellular Pattern,** *Weldon's Practical Patchwork,* ca. 1890. See 151-9, 171-6, 171-7, and 271-9.

11 **Aunt Sukey's Patch,** *Ladies Art Company,* 1897.

12 **Coarse Woven Patchwork,** *Ladies Art Company,* 1897. Also known as:
- **Coarse Patchwork,** Nancy Cabot, *Chicago Tribune,* Nov 30, 1934.
- **Coarse Woven,** Hall, 1935.
- **Fine Woven,** Hall, 1935.

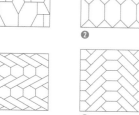

1 **Bridal Stairway Patchwork Block,** *Kansas City Star,* Jul 1, 1933. Also known as:
   Bridal Stairway, Hall, 1935.

2 **Pleasant Paths,** *Farm Journal and Farmers Wife,* ca. 1941.

3 **Zigzag Blocks,** *Grandmother Clark's Old Fashioned Quilt Designs, Book* 21, 1931.

4 **Pieced Pyramids,** Hall, 1935.

5 **Pyramids,** *Ladies Art Company,* 1901.

6 **Basket Weave,** *Farm Journal and Farmers Wife,* ca. 1941.

7 **Basket Lattice,** *Ladies Art Company,* 1901.

8 **Chevron,** Beyer, Jinny, *The Quilter's Album . . .",* 1980.

9 **Dancing Cubes,** Nancy Cabot, *Chicago Tribune,* May 8, 1937.

10 **Patience Corners,** *Ladies Art Company,* 1897. See 150-9.

11 **Nothing Wasted,** *Farm Journal and Farmers Wife* (Silver Anniversary edition), 1945.

12 **Tree Everlasting,** Finley, 1929. Also known as:
   Herringbone, Finley, 1929.
   The Prickly Path, Finley, 1929.
   The Path of Thorns, Finley, 1929.
   Arrowheads, Finley, 1929.

13 **Tree Everlasting,** Havig, ca. 1938.

1 continuous pattern

2 continuous pattern

3 continuous pattern on 60 x 60 grid

4 continuous pattern on 21 x 21 grid

5 continuous pattern on 48 x 48 grid

6 continuous pattern 12 x 12 grid

7 continuous pattern on 12 x 12 grid

8 continuous pattern on 4 x 4 grid

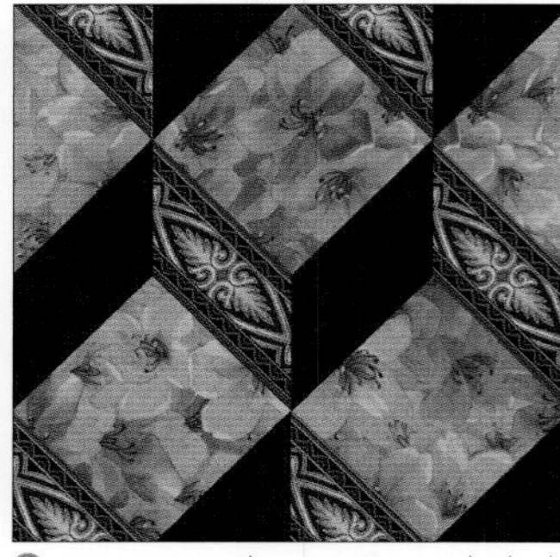

9 continuous pattern on 4 x 4 grid

10 continuous pattern on 4 x 4 grid

11 continuous pattern grid

12 continuous pattern

13 continuous pattern

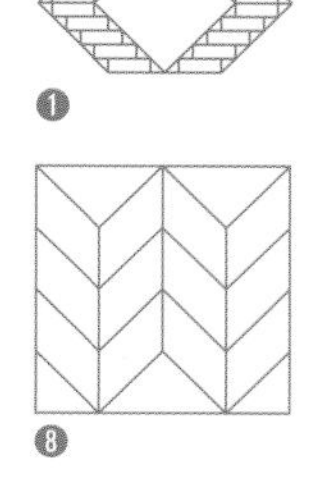
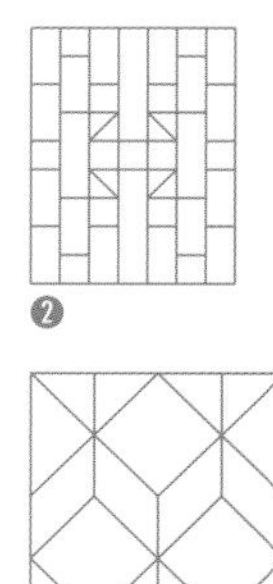
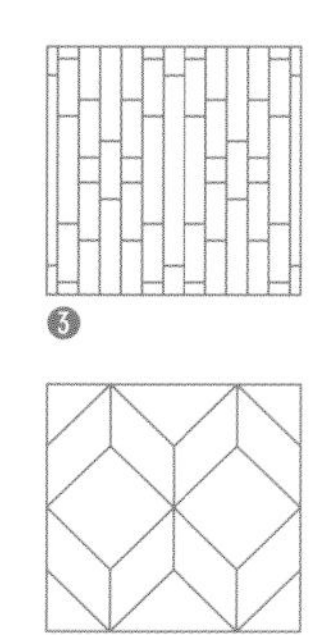
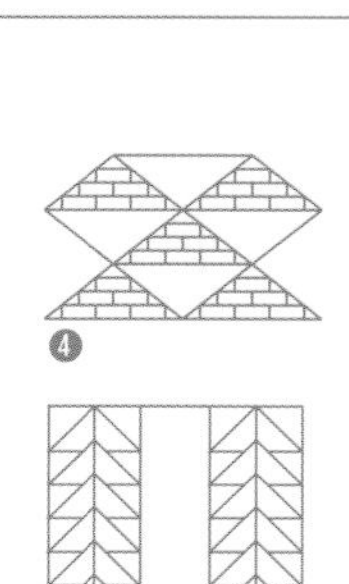
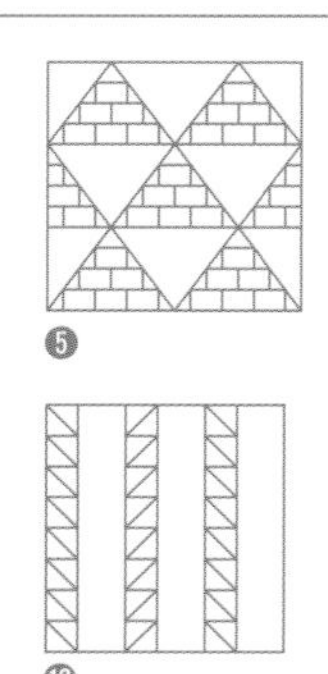
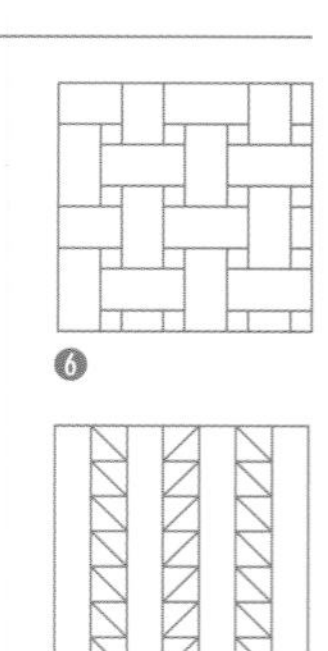

1 2 3 4 5 6

7 8 9 10 11 12 13

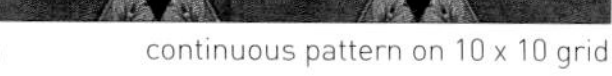

1 continuous pattern on 10 x 10 grid

2 continuous pattern on 8 x 8 grid

3 continuous pattern on 8 x 8 grid

4 continuous pattern on hexagon grid

5 continuous pattern on 10 x 10 grid

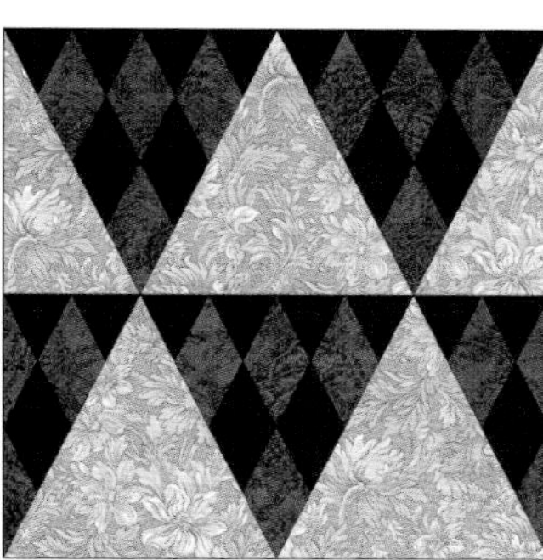

6 continuous pattern on 8 x 8 grid

7 continuous pattern on 32 x 32 grid

8 continuous pattern on 12 x 12 grid

9 continuous pattern 12 x 12 grid

10 continuous pattern on 16 x 16 grid

11 continuous pattern on 18 x 18 grid

12 continuous pattern on 6 x 6 grid

13 continuous pattern on 6 x 6 grid

1 **Trellis Quilt,** Nancy Page, *Birmingham News,* Sep 20, 1938.

2 **Diamonds,** Nancy Page, *Nashville Banner,* May 16, 1933.

3 **Walk Around,** *Ladies Art Company,* 1928. Also known as:
- **Boston Corners,** Nancy Cabot, *Chicago Tribune,* Feb 10, 1934.
- **Double X's,** Nancy Cabot, *Chicago Tribune,* Mar 5, 1938.
- **Web of Diamonds,** Nancy Cabot, *Chicago Tribune,* Jun 8, 1937.

4 **Diamond 9 Patch,** Mrs. Danner Presents Quilt Book 7, 1975. See 192-6.

5 **Sugar Loaf,** Nancy Page, *Birmingham News,* Apr 10, 1934.

6 **Flatiron,** Nancy Cabot, *Chicago Tribune,* Aug 6, 1933.

7 **Triangular Triangle,** *Ladies Art Company,* 1897. Also known as:
- **Triangular Triangles,** Hall, 1935.

8 **Triangular Triangle,** *Prize Winning Designs,* ca. 1931.

9 **Flying Geese,** Ickis, 1949.

10 **Wild Geese,** Nancy Page, *Birmingham News,* Apr 20, 1937.

11 **Ocean Wave,** *Farmer's Wife Book of New Designs and Patterns,* 1934. See 93-2, 93-3, 159-2 , 159-3, 159-4, and 131-5.

12 **Bow Knots,** Nancy Cabot, *Chicago Tribune,* May 30, 1936.

13 **Four Windmills,** Nancy Cabot, *Chicago Tribune,* Jun 20, 1936.

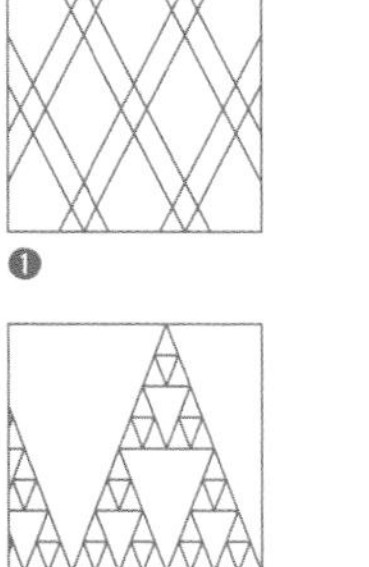
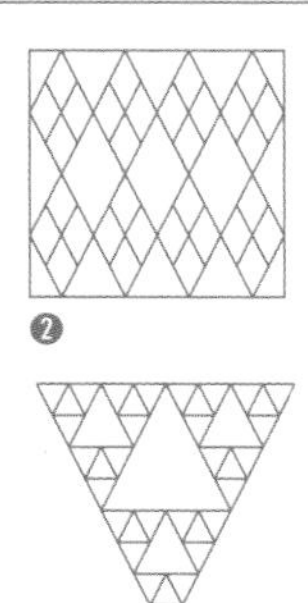
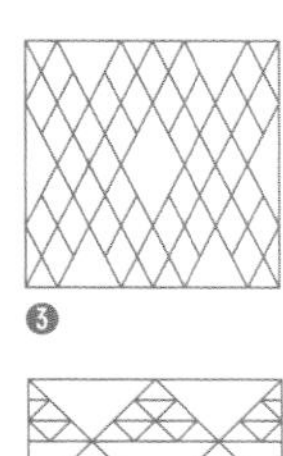
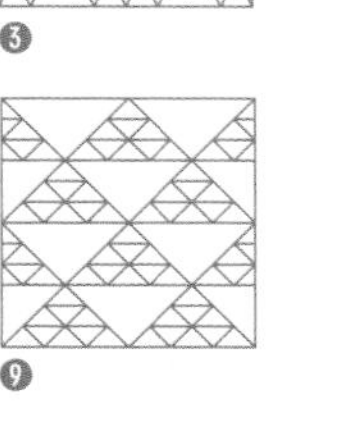
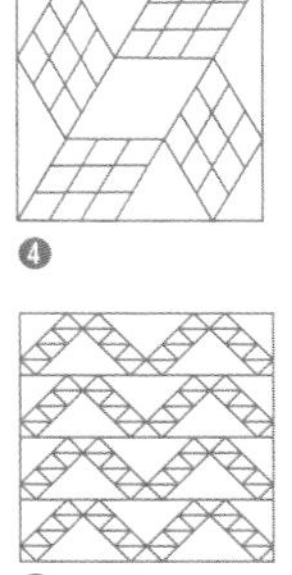
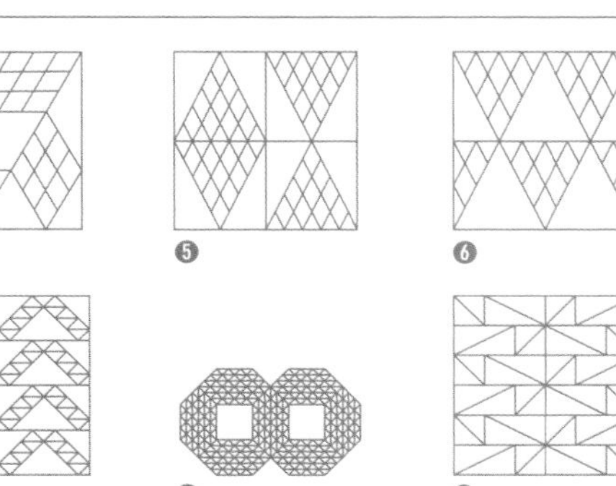
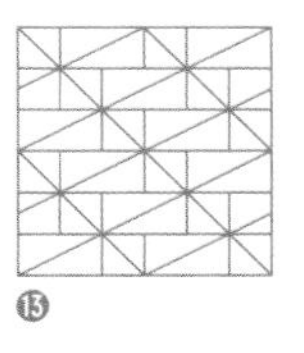

1 2 3 4 5 6

7 8 9 10 11 12 13

1 **Cumberland Gap,** Nancy Cabot, *Chicago Tribune,* Dec 7, 1935.

2 **Star Fish Pattern,** Home Art Studios, *World Herald,* Jan 23, 1933. See 438-10.

3 **Aunt Mary's Squares,** *Grandmother Clark's Old Fashioned Quilt Designs, Book* 21, 1931.

4 **Irish Plaid,** Nancy Cabot, *Chicago Tribune,* Nov 3, 1935.
"The original 'Irish Plaid' quilt was made by an Irish woman for her Scotch husband when he demanded a quilt with a plaid design. She probably was one of the mathematical geniuses of the quilt world." Nancy Cabot, Chicago Tribune, Nov 3, 1935

5 **Tangled Squares,** Nancy Cabot, *Chicago Tribune,* Dec 17, 1935.

6 **Lonesome Pine,** Home Arts Studio, *Cincinnati Enquirer,* Mar 22, 1933. Also known as:
- **Tall Pine Tree,** Hall, 1935.
- **Tall Pines,** Nancy Page, *Birmingham News,* Jun 4, 1940.

7 **Thousand Stars Quilt,** *Kansas City Star,* Jul 28, 1954

8 **Indian Mats,** Nancy Cabot, *Chicago Tribune,* Oct 17, 1935.

9 **Summer Trellis,** Miall, 1937.

10 **Memory Chain,** Aunt Martha series: *Quilts,* ca. 1963.

11 **Tallahassee Quilt Block,** *Ladies Art Company,* 1922. Also known as:
- **Tallahassee Block,** Nancy Cabot, *Chicago Tribune,* Sep 4, 1937.

12 **Octagon Tile,** *Ladies Art Company,* 1897.

1 continuous pattern on 12 x 12 grid

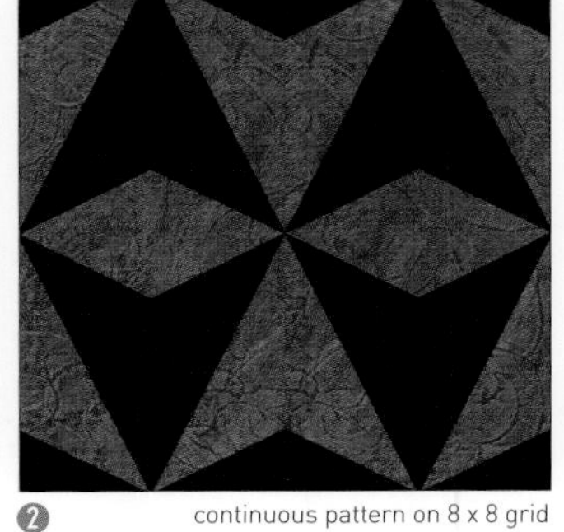

2 continuous pattern on 8 x 8 grid

3 continuous pattern on 21 x 21 grid

4 continuous pattern on 20 x 20 grid

5 continuous pattern on 16 x 16 grid

6 continuous pattern

7 continuous pattern on 18 x 18 grid

8 continuous pattern on 8 x 8 grid

9 continuous pattern

10 continuous pattern

11 continuous pattern on 16 x 16 grid

12 continuous pattern on 12 x 12 grid

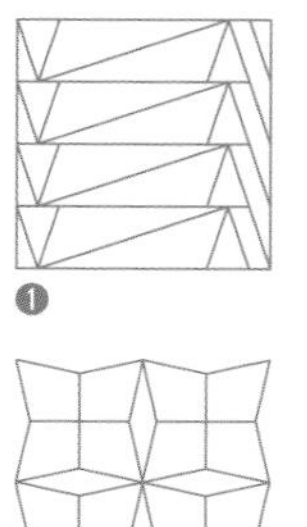
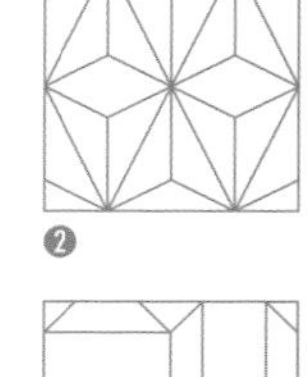
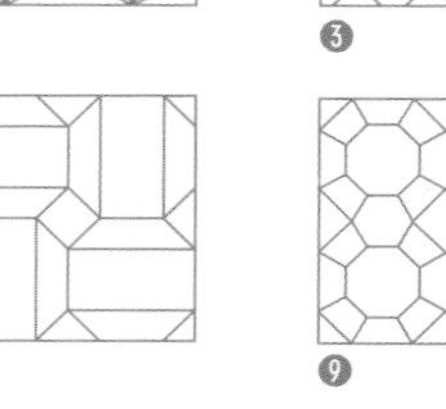
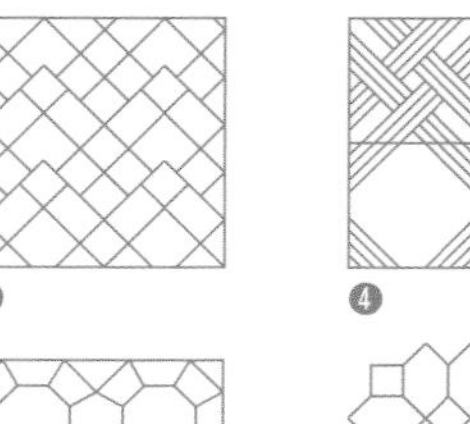
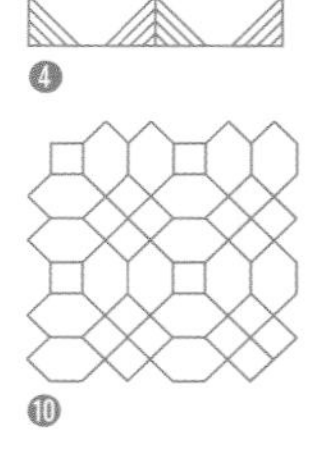

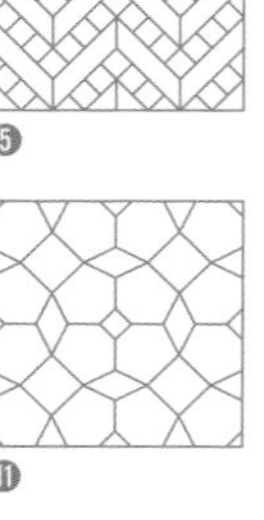
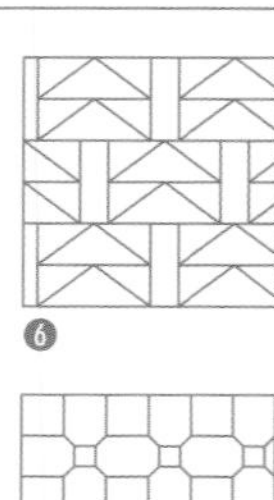

1 2 3 4 5 6

7 8 9 10 11 12

❶ continuous pattern on 8-pointed star grid

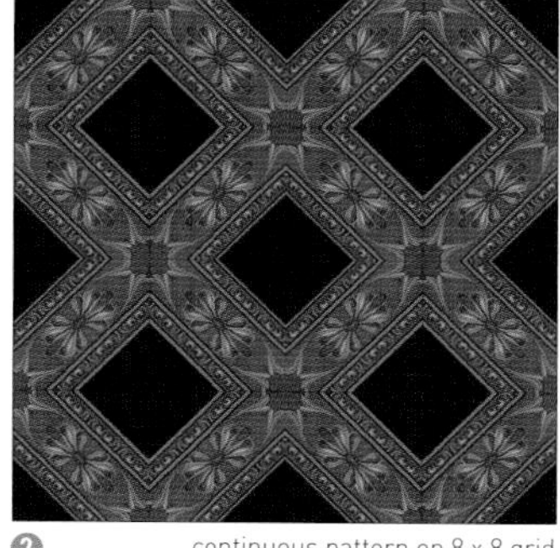

❷ continuous pattern on 8 x 8 grid

❸ continuous pattern on 12 x 12 grid

❹ continuous pattern on 9 x 9 grid

❺ continuous pattern on 12 x 12 grid

❻ continuous pattern on 12 x 12 grid

❼ continuous pattern on 12 x 12 grid

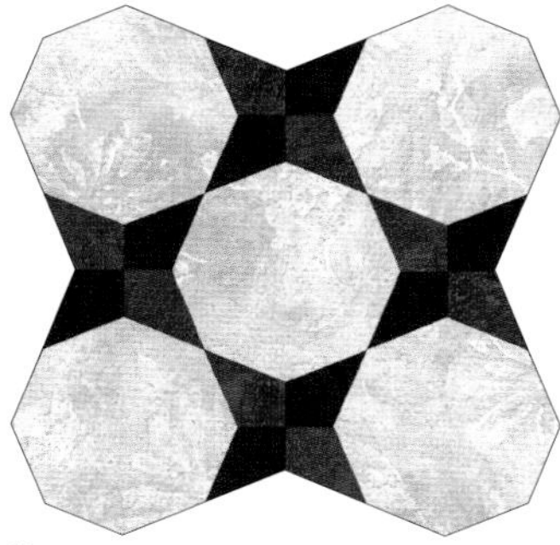

❽ continuous pattern on 8-pointed star grid

❾ continuous pattern on 8-pointed star grid

❿ continuous pattern on 8-pointed star grid

⓫ 8-pointed star grid

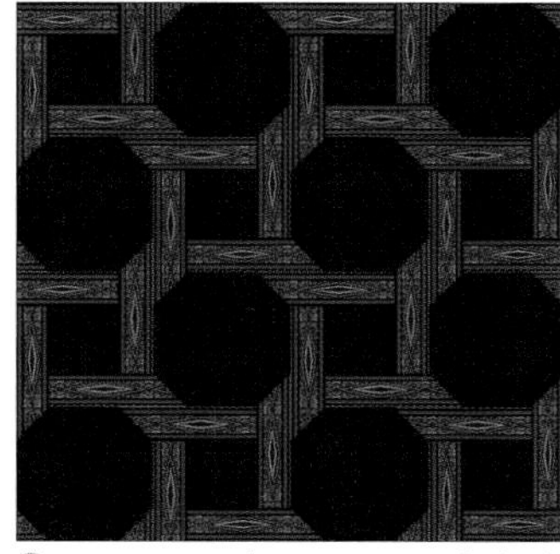

⓬ continuous pattern on 8 x 8 grid

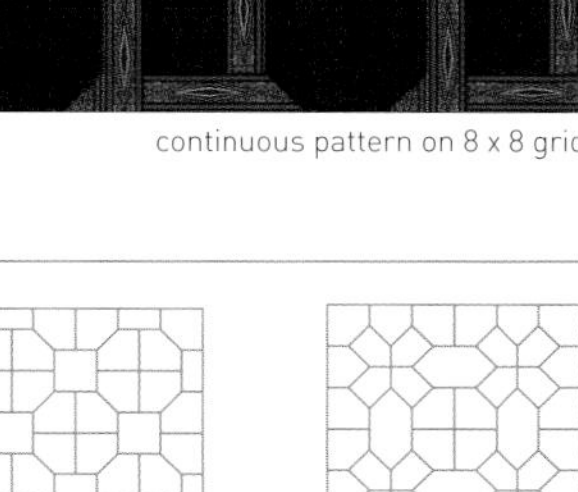
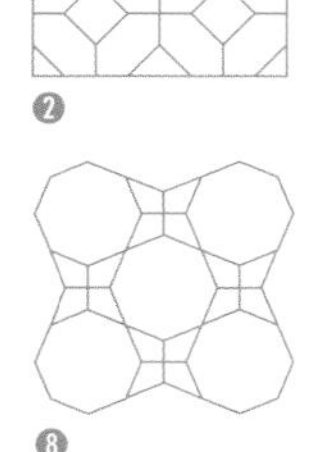
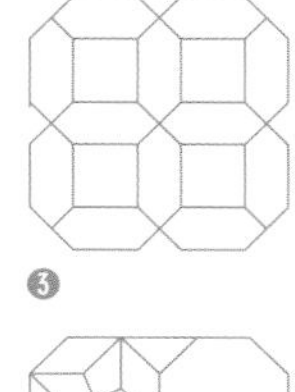
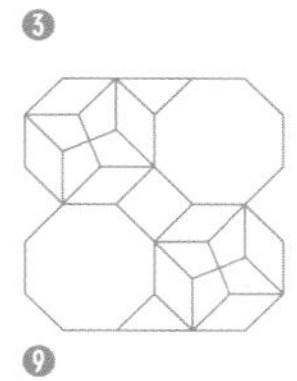
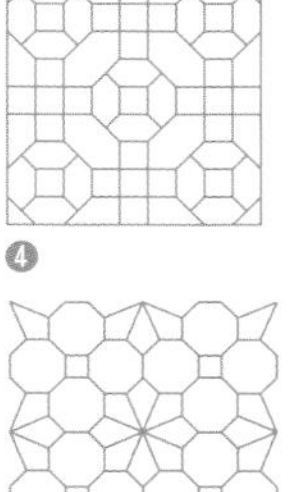
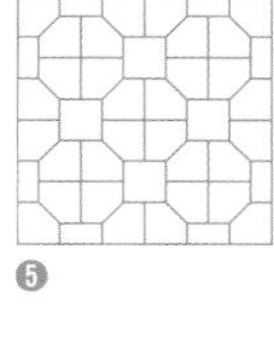
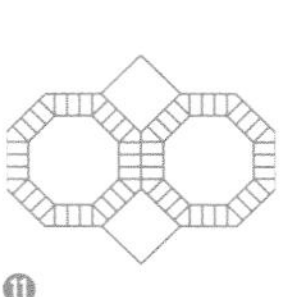
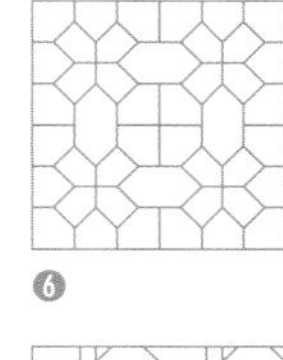
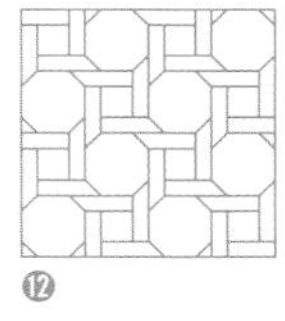

❶ ❷ ❸ ❹ ❺ ❻

❼ ❽ ❾ ❿ ⓫ ⓬

❶ **Octagon,** *Ladies Art Company,* 1897. Also known as:

- **Cobblestones,** Nancy Page, *Birmingham News,* Oct 26, 1937.
- **Octagonal Block,** Nancy Cabot, *Chicago Tribune,* Aug 6, 1934.
- **An All-Over Pattern of Octagons,** *Kansas City Star,* Sep 23, 1942.
- **Octagons and Squares,** *Kansas City Star,* Apr 21, 1943.
- **Ozark Cobble Stone,** *Kansas City Star,* Aug 22, 1936.

❷ **Godey Design,** *Godey's Lady's Book* 1851. See 156-7. Also known as:

- **Church Window Quilt,** Nancy Page, *Detroit Free Press,* Aug 2, 1932.
- **Five Cross,** Clara Stone, *Practical Needlework,* ca. 1906.
- **Going Home,** *Farm Journal and Farmers Wife,* ca. 1941.
- **Grandmother's Dream,** *Ladies Art Company,* 1897.
- **Kansas Dugout,** *Prize Winning Designs,* ca. 1931.
- **Lattice Block,** Nancy Cabot, *Chicago Tribune,* Aug 5, 1934.
- **Lovely Patchwork,** date unknown, per Brackman.
- **Old Fashioned Quilt,** *Kansas City Star,* Sep 11, 1937.
- **The Ozark Tile Pattern,** *Kansas City Star,* Apr 17, 1937.
- **Puss in the Corner,** *Kansas City Star,* Jan 18, 1956.
- **Road to Tennessee,** Nancy Page, *Birmingham News,* Jul 21, 1936.

❸ **Jewel Box,** Hall, 1935.

❹ **Mosaic No. 4,** Saward, 1882 Also known as:

- **Tile Puzzle,** Hall, 1935.
- **Puzzle Tile,** *Ladies Art Company,* 1897.

❺ **Squares upon Squares,** Nancy Cabot, *Chicago Tribune,* May 27, 1937.

❻ **Victorian Maze,** Nancy Cabot, *Chicago Tribune,* May 19, 1937.

❼ **Nauvoo Lattice,** Nancy Cabot, *Chicago Tribune,* Apr 19, 1937.

❽ **Periwinkle,** Home Art Studios, *World Herald,* Aug 5, 1933. Also known as:

- **Bluet,** Nancy Page, *Birmingham News,* Mar 12, 1935.

❾ **The Missouri Wonder,** *Kansas City Star,* Jan 4, 1936.

❿ **Colonial Garden,** Aunt Martha series: *Favorite Quilts,* ca. 1963.

⓫ **Wedding Ring Tile,** Aunt Martha series: *Bold and Beautiful Quilts,* ca. 1977.

⓬ **Godey Design,** *Godey's Lady's Book* 1851. Also known as:

- **Fishnets,** Nancy Page, *Birmingham News,* Apr 13, 1943.
- **Plaited Block,** Nancy Cabot, *Chicago Tribune,* Feb 12, 1937.
- **Ribbon Twist,** Nancy Page, *Birmingham News,* Apr 13, 1943.
- **Twist Patchwork,** Saward, 1882.
- **Twist Pattern Patchwork,** *Weldon's Practical Patchwork,* ca. 1890.

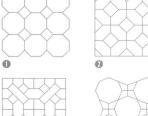

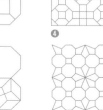

❶ **Chinese Puzzle,** *Kansas City Star,* Sep 19, 1936.

❷ **Tile Patchwork,** *Ladies Art Company,* 1897.

❸ **Cupid's Arrow Point,** Eveline Foland, *Kansas City Star,* Apr 6, 1929.

❹ **White Mountains,** Nancy Cabot, *Chicago Tribune,* Jun 21, 1935. Also known as:
Octagon Block, Nancy Cabot, *Chicago Tribune,* Dec 14, 1937.

❺ **Pointed Tile,** Aunt Martha series: *Quilts: Modern-Colonial,* ca. 1954.

❻ **Hard Times Block,** Nancy Cabot, *Chicago Tribune,* Nov 22, 1937.

❼ **Happy Hunting Grounds,** *Kansas City Star,* Oct 21, 1936.

❽ **The Red Cross,** *Kansas City Star,* Sep 27, 1939.

❾ **Red Cross Quilt,** *Kansas City Star,* Apr 16, 1932. Also known as:
A Red White Blue Color Scheme, *Kansas City Star,* Jan 13, 1943.

❿ **Fence Row Quilt,** Eveline Foland, *Kansas City Star,* Apr 25, 1931.

⓫ **Attic Stairs,** Nancy Cabot, *Chicago Tribune,* Nov 13, 1937.

⓬ **Locked Squares,** Nancy Cabot, *Chicago Tribune,* Oct 21, 1937.

⓭ **Little Foxes,** Nancy Cabot, *Chicago Tribune,* Oct 8, 1935.
"'Little Foxes' is a pattern which rates among the most intriguing and beautiful of the many pieced quilt blocks. It is not one of the simple patterns, but rather one which must be pieced with extreme care and caution in order to achieve the effect of 'Little Foxes.'" Nancy Cabot, *Chicago Tribune,* Oct 8, 1935

❶ continuous pattern on 12 x 12 grid

❷ continuous pattern on 16 x 16 grid

❸ continuous pattern on 16 x 16 grid

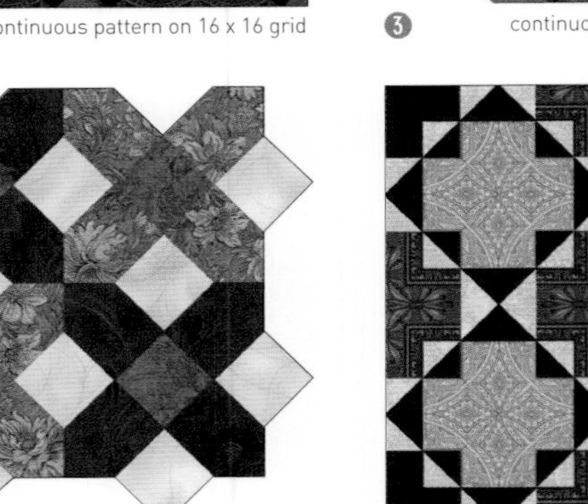

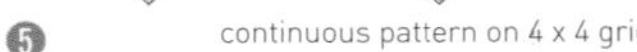

❹ continuous pattern on 16 x 16 grid

❺ continuous pattern on 4 x 4 grid

❻ continuous pattern on 12 x 12 grid

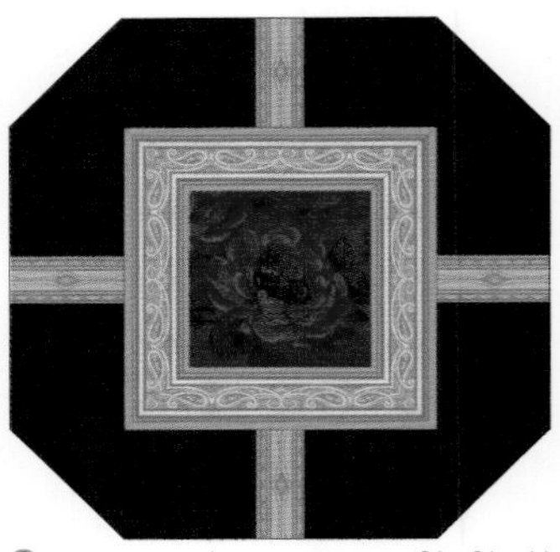

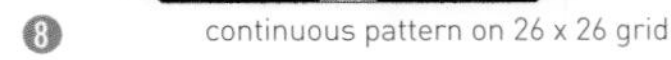

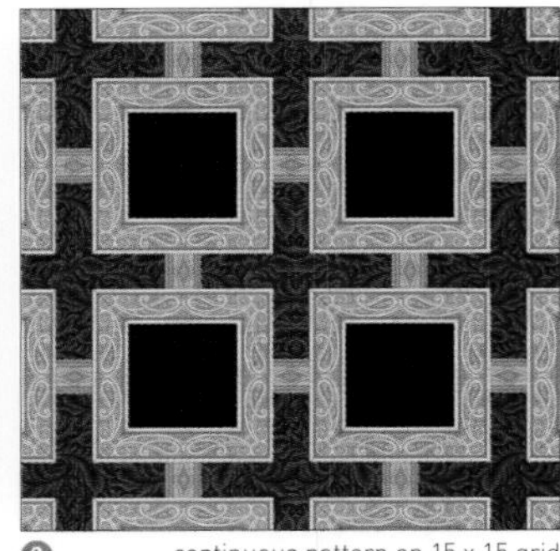

❼ continuous pattern on 28 x 28 grid

❽ continuous pattern on 26 x 26 grid

❾ continuous pattern on 15 x 15 grid

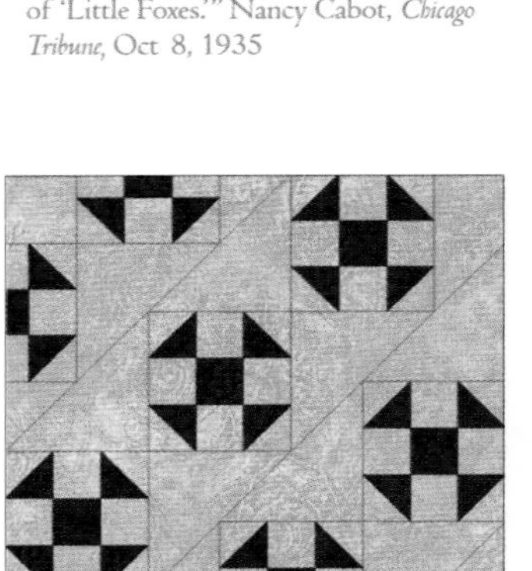

❿ continuous pattern

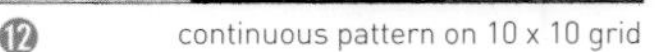

⓫ continuous pattern on 10 x 10 grid

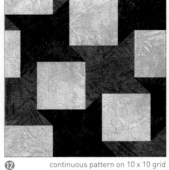

⓬ continuous pattern on 10 x 10 grid

⓭ continuous pattern on 12 x 12 grid

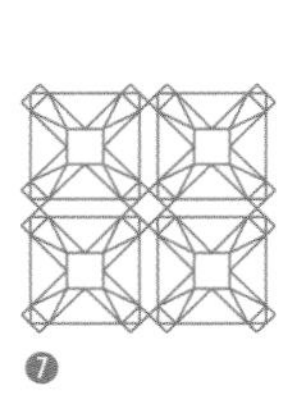

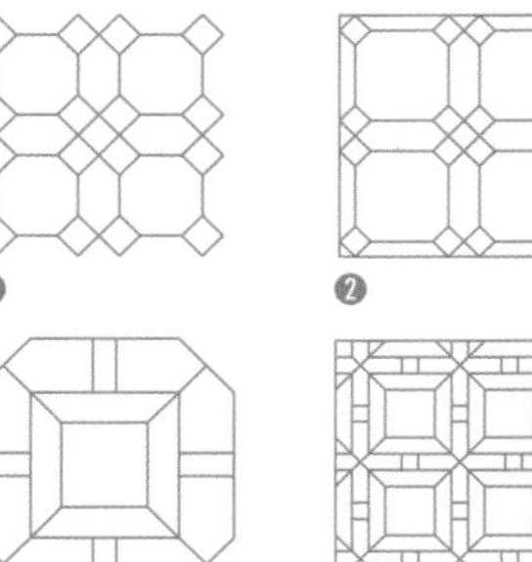

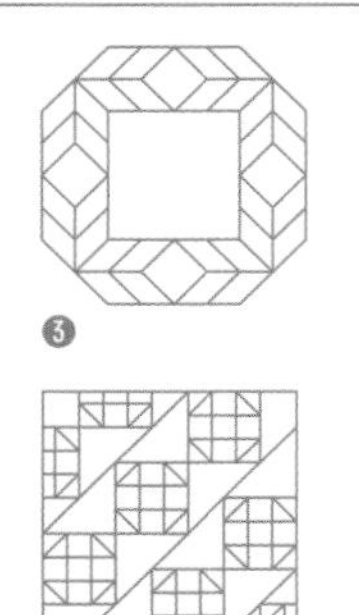

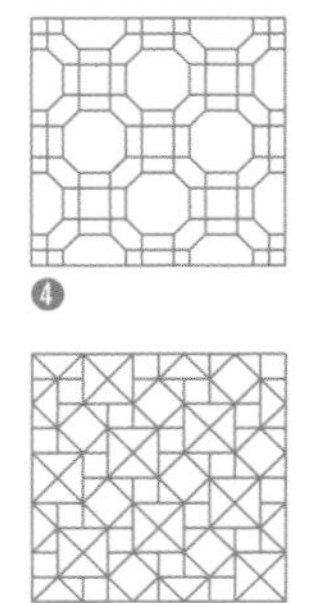

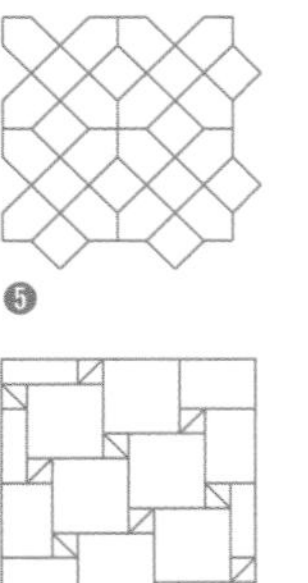

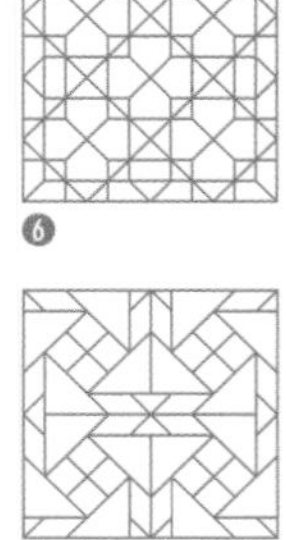

❶ ❷ ❸ ❹ ❺ ❻ ❼ ❽ ❾ ❿ ⓫ ⓬ ⓭

❶ continuous pattern on 12 x 12 grid

❷ continuous pattern on 93 x 93 grid

❸ continuous pattern on 8 x 8 grid

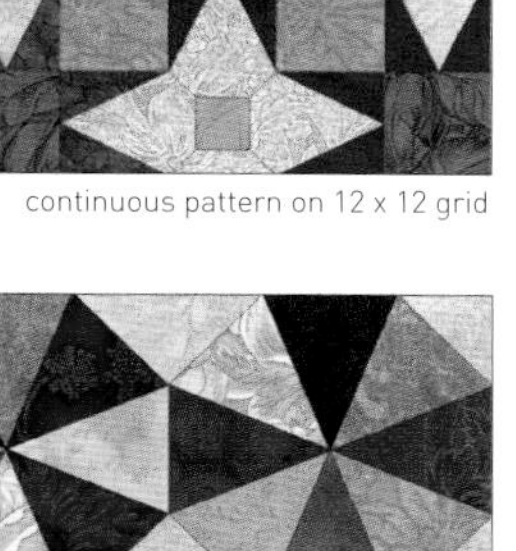

❹ continuous pattern on 12 x 12 grid

❺ continuous pattern on 10 x 10 grid

❻ continuous pattern on 12 x 12 grid

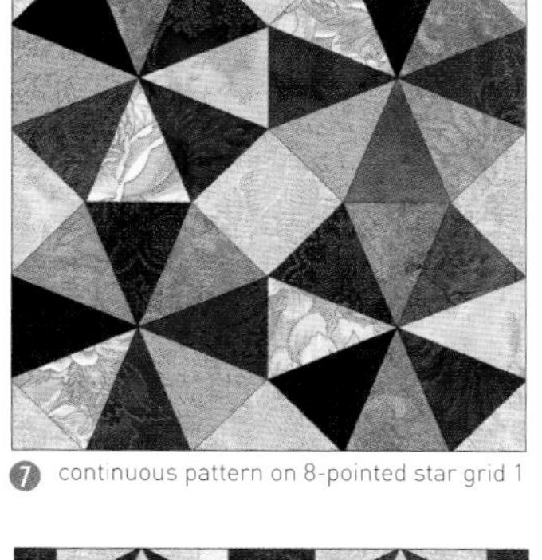

❼ continuous pattern on 8-pointed star grid 1

❽ continuous pattern on 4 x 4 grid

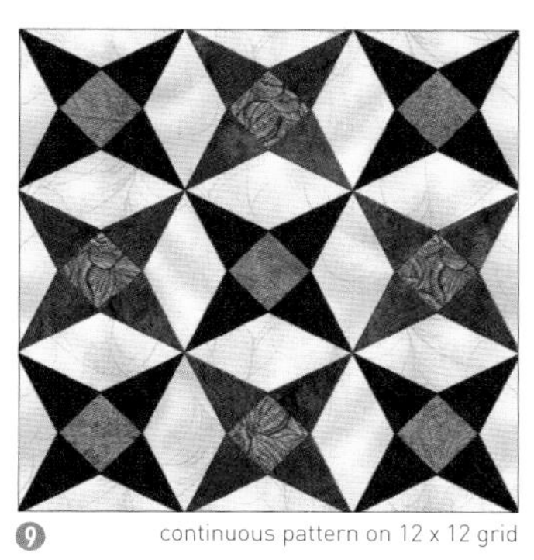

❾ continuous pattern on 12 x 12 grid

❿ continuous pattern on 12 x 12 grid

⓫ continuous pattern on 8-pointed star grid

⓬ continuous pattern on 10 x 10 grid

⓭ continuous pattern on 24 x 24 grid

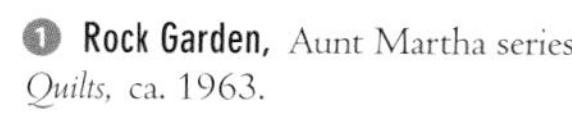

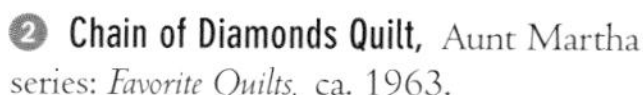

❶ **Rock Garden,** Aunt Martha series: *Quilts,* ca. 1963.

❷ **Chain of Diamonds Quilt,** Aunt Martha series: *Favorite Quilts,* ca. 1963.

❸ **Boston Streets,** Nancy Cabot, *Chicago Tribune,* Mar 16, 1936.

❹ **Narcissus Motif,** *Kansas City Star,* Apr 6, 1960.

❺ **Twisted Ribbons,** Nancy Cabot, *Chicago Tribune,* Nov 4, 1937.

❻ **The Periwinkle,** *Kansas City Star,* Jul 9, 1941.

❼ **Kaleidoscope,** date unknown, per Holstein.

❽ **Ribbon Border,** *Ladies Art Company,* 1897. Also known as:
- **Beach and Boats,** Nancy Cabot, *Chicago Tribune,* Aug 21, 1937.

❾ **Kaleidoscopic Patch,** Nancy Cabot, *Chicago Tribune,* Sep 21, 1934. See page 65.

❿ **Priscilla,** Home Art Studios, *World Herald,* Nov 7, 1933.

⓫ **Diamond and Star,** *Ladies Art Company,* 1922. Also known as:
- **Frontier Fiesta,** Nancy Page, *Birmingham News,* Aug 17, 1937.

⓬ **Kaleidoscope Patch,** *Ladies Art Company,* 1897.

⓭ **Starry Night,** Nancy Cabot, *Chicago Tribune,* Dec 14, 1935.

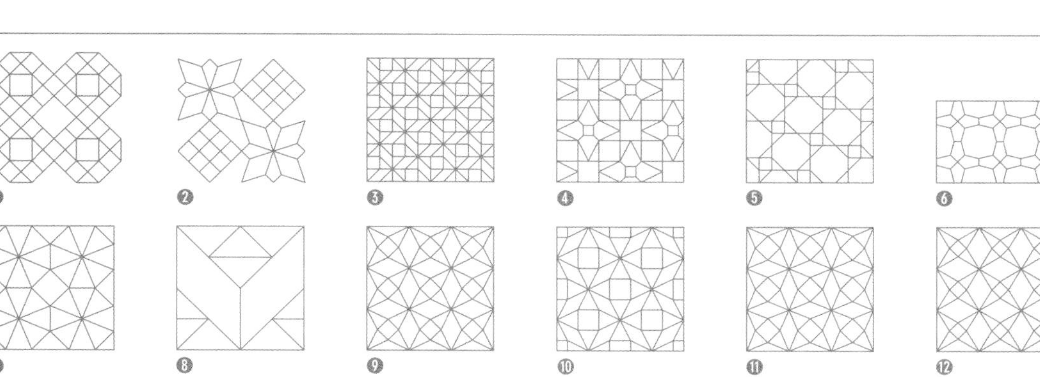

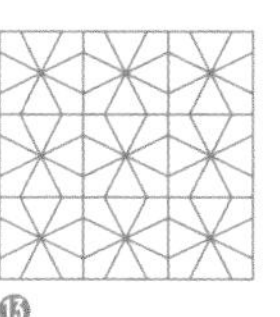

❶ **Kansas Star,** Hall, 1935.

❷ **Castor and Pollux,** Nancy Cabot, *Chicago Tribune,* Nov 30, 1935.
"A most erudite young woman made this unusual pieced block and instead of calling it 'the heavenly twins,' since that evidently was what she determined to name the pattern, she called it 'Castor and Pollux,' its correct astronomical appellation. The pattern is simple, containing only three patches from which pieces for the entire block are cut. It May be made in celestial colors—two shades of blue and white, or in patriotic shades of red, white and blue." Nancy Cabot, *Chicago Tribune,* Nov 30, 1935

❸ **Southern Cross,** Nancy Cabot, *Chicago Tribune,* Dec 4, 1935.

❹ **The Compass and Chain,** *Kansas City Star,* Nov 23, 1935.

❺ **A Three in One Quilt Pattern,** *Kansas City Star,* Dec 15, 1948.

❻ **Continuous Star,** Clara Stone, *Practical Needlework,* ca. 1906. Also known as:
  Star and Cross, Home Art Studios, *World Herald,* Nov 2, 1933.

❼ **Wandering Diamond,** Aunt Martha series: *Patchwork Simplicity,* ca. 1977.

❽ **Net of Stars,** Nancy Cabot, *Chicago Tribune,* May 9, 1936.

❾ **Lazy Daisy,** Eveline Foland, *Kansas City Star,* Dec 26, 1931.

❿ **George B.,** Nancy Page, *Birmingham News,* Jun 28, 1938.

⓫ **Spiderweb,** *Mrs. Danner's Quilts, Books 1 & 2,* 1934. Also known as:
  Wild Goose Chase, date unknown, per Holstein. See 270-12, 288-10 and 414-11.

⓬ **Rising Sun,** Miall, 1937. See 270-12 , 288-9 and 288-10. Also known as:
  Wild Geese, Miall, 1937.

❶ continuous pattern on 24 x 24 grid

❷ continuous pattern on 10 x 10 grid

❸ continuous pattern on 24 x 24 grid

❹ continuous pattern on 8-pointed star grid

❺ continuous pattern on 8-pointed star grid

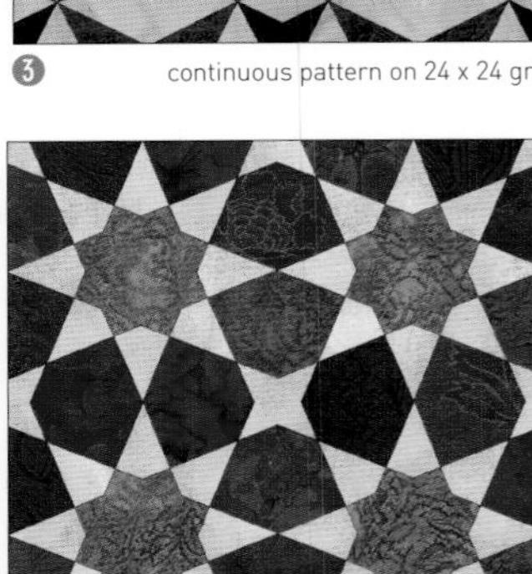

❻ continuous pattern on 8-pointed star grid

❼ continuous pattern on 8-pointed star grid

❽ continuous pattern on 8-pointed star grid

❾ continuous pattern on 32 x 32 grid

❿ continuous pattern on 8-pointed star grid

⓫ continuous pattern on 8-pointed star grid

⓬ continuous pattern on 8-pointed star grid

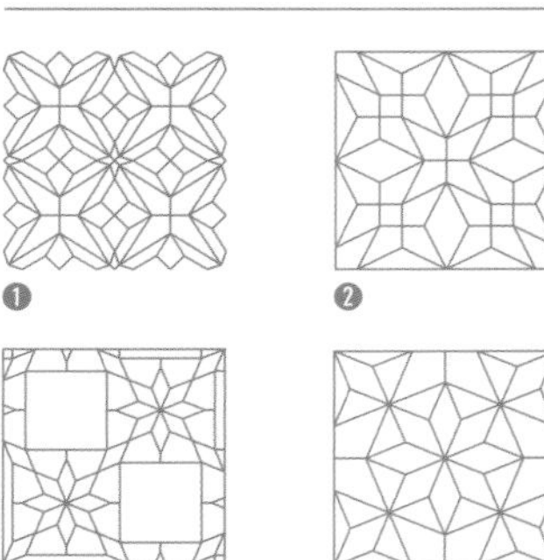

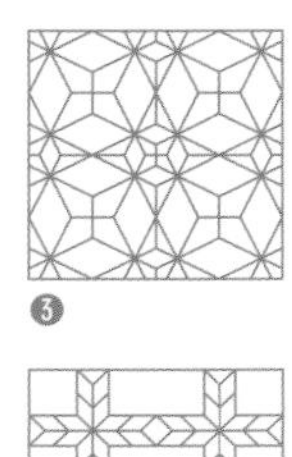

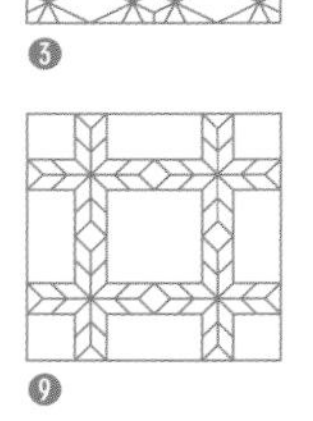

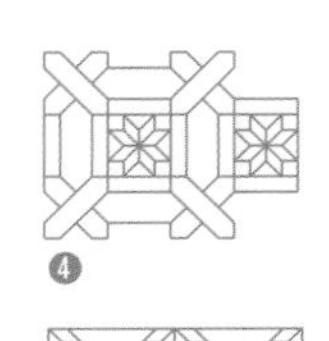

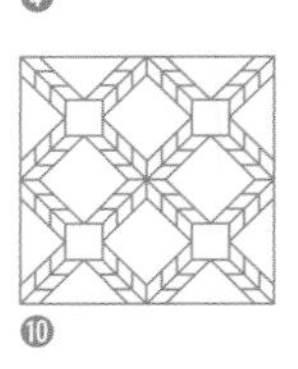

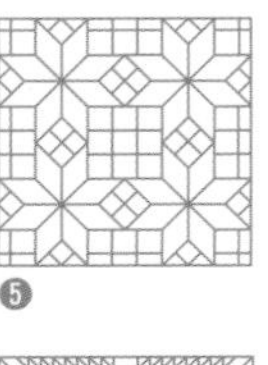

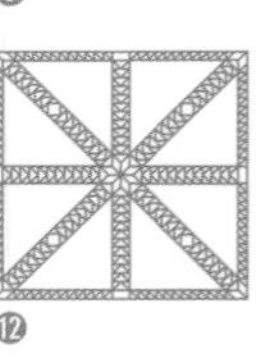

❶ ❷ ❸ ❹ ❺ ❻

❼ ❽ ❾ ❿ ⓫ ⓬

❶ continuous pattern on hexagon grid

❷ continuous pattern on hexagon grid

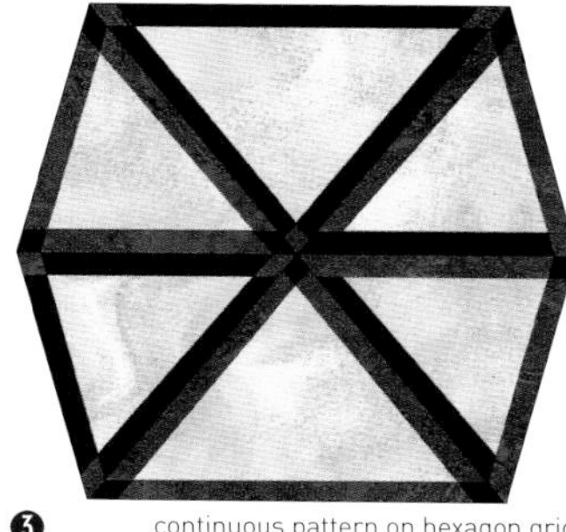

❸ continuous pattern on hexagon grid

❹ continuous pattern on hexagon grid

❺ continuous pattern on hexagon grid

❻ continuous pattern on hexagon grid

❼ continuous pattern on hexagon grid

❽ continuous pattern on hexagon grid

❾ continuous pattern on hexagon grid

❿ continuous pattern on hexagon grid

⓫ continuous pattern on hexagon grid

⓬ continuous pattern on hexagon grid

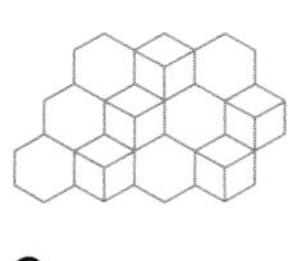
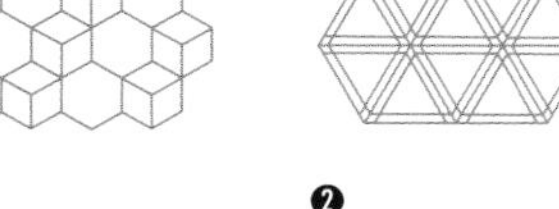

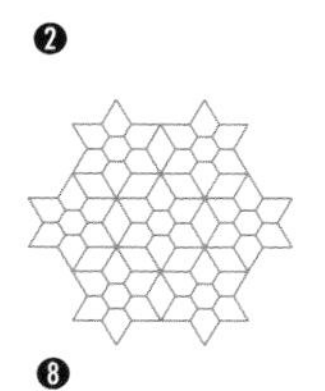
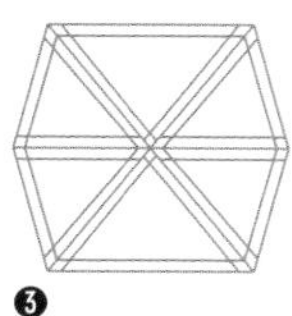
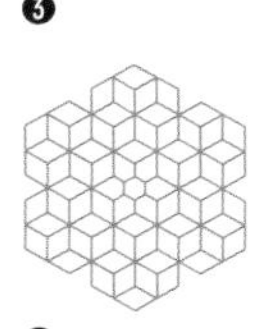
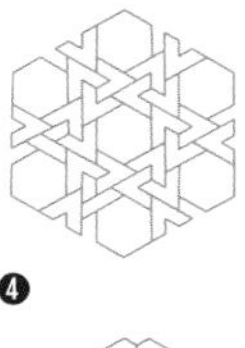
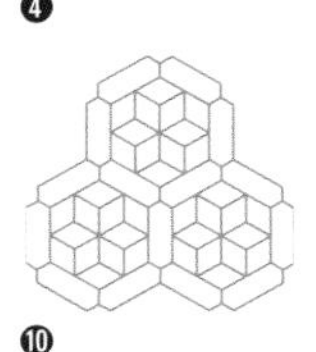
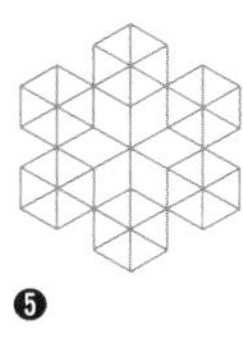
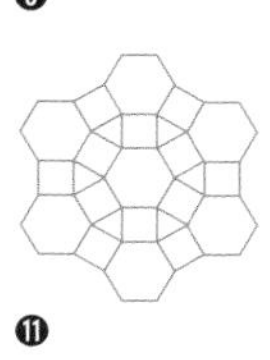
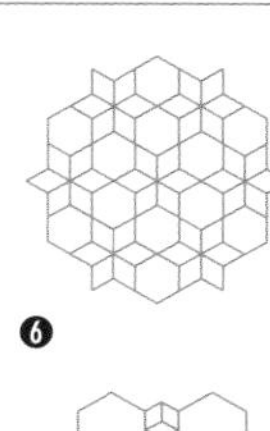
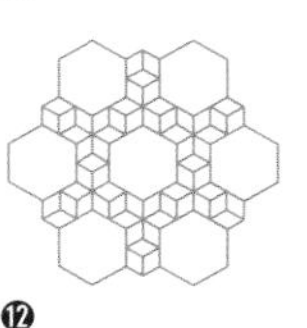

❶ ❷ ❸ ❹ ❺ ❻

❼ ❽ ❾ ❿ ⓫ ⓬

❶ **Diamond Hexagon Quilt,** Nancy Page, unidentified newspaper clipping, date unknown.

❷ **Oriental Splendor,** Home Art Studios, *Des Moines Register,* Feb 19, 1933.

❸ **Many Paths,** Nancy Cabot, *Chicago Tribune,* Dec 18, 1933. Also known as:
- **Oriental Splendor,** Nancy Cabot, *Chicago Tribune,* Dec 18, 1933.

❹ **Check and Double Check,** Home Art Studios, *World Herald,* Jan 5, 1934.

❺ **Lone Star,** Nancy Page, *Birmingham News,* Jul 10, 1934. Also known as:
- **Blazing Star,** Nancy Page, unidentified newspaper clipping, 1934.
- **Sunburst,** Nancy Page, unidentified newspaper clipping, 1934.

❻ **Star Bouquet,** Home Art Studios, *World Herald,* Nov 3, 1933.

"A never ending variety of gay colored prints set together in an unusual way, makes this beautiful quilt. You may utilize all of the scraps you may have in your scrap bag to the best advantage." *World Herald,* Nov 3, 1933

❼ **The Triple Star,** *Kansas City Star,* Jul 7, 1934.

❽ **Dolly Madison Stars,** Home Art Studios, *Des Moines Register,* Dec 25, 1932. Also known as:
- **The Star Garden,** *Kansas City Star,* Jan 27, 1954.
- **Texas Star,** Aunt Martha series: *The Quilt Fair Comes to You,* ca. 1933.

❾ **Boutonniere,** Eveline Foland, *Kansas City Star,* Sep 19, 1931. Also known as:
- **A Boutonniere,** *Kansas City Star,* Mar 10, 1948.

❿ **Brunswick Star,** *Ladies Art Company,* 1897. Also known as:
- **Chained Star,** Hall, 1935.
- **Heirloom Jewel,** *Kansas City Star,* Apr 11, 1951.
- **Rolling Star,** Hall, 1935.
- **The Golden Circle Star,** *Kansas City Star,* Feb 20, 1937.

⓫ **Joseph's Coat,** Laura Wheeler, unidentified newspaper clipping, date unknown. Also known as:
- **Patchwork Quilt,** Alice Brooks, unidentified newspaper clipping, date unknown.

⓬ **Box Quilt,** Nancy Page, *Birmingham News,* Jul 23, 1935.

❶ **Block Patchwork,** *Ladies Art Company,* 1897. Also known as:
- **Building Blocks,** Nancy Cabot, *Chicago Tribune,* Oct 31, 1934.
- **Ferris Wheel,** Hall, 1935.
- **The Ferris Wheel,** *Prize Winning Designs,* ca. 1931.
- **Hexagon,** Hall, 1935.
- **Morning Glory,** Edna Marie Dunn, *Kansas City Star,* Dec 23, 1933.
- **Wandering Paths,** Nancy Cabot, *Chicago Tribune,* Jul 30, 1937.

❷ **Rosalia Flower Garden,** *Kansas City Star,* Dec 3, 1939.

❸ **Faithful Circle,** Aunt Martha series: *Quilts,* ca. 1963.

❹ **Aunt Martha's Rose,** Aunt Martha series: *Quilts: Modern-Colonial,* ca. 1954.

❺ **Diamond Field Star,** Home Art Studios, *World Herald,* Oct 27, 1933.

❻ **Diamond Beauty,** Aunt Martha series: *Bold and Beautiful Quilts,* ca. 1977.

❼ **Zodiac Stars,** Home Art Studios, *Cincinnati Enquirer,* Apr 20, 1933.

❽ **Geometric Star,** Home Art Studios, *World Herald,* Nov 28, 1933.

❾ **Floating Clouds,** *Kansas City Star,* Nov 23, 1938.

❿ **Star Chain,** Home Art Studios, *World Herald,* Nov 9, 1933.

⓫ **Man in the Moon,** Aunt Martha series: *Easy Quilts,* ca. 1958.

⓬ **Glimmering Star,** Home Art Studios, *World Herald,* Dec 18, 1933.

⓭ **Milky Way,** Alice Brooks, *Detroit Free Press,* Feb 17, 1934.

❶ continuous pattern on hexagon grid

❷ continuous pattern on hexagon grid

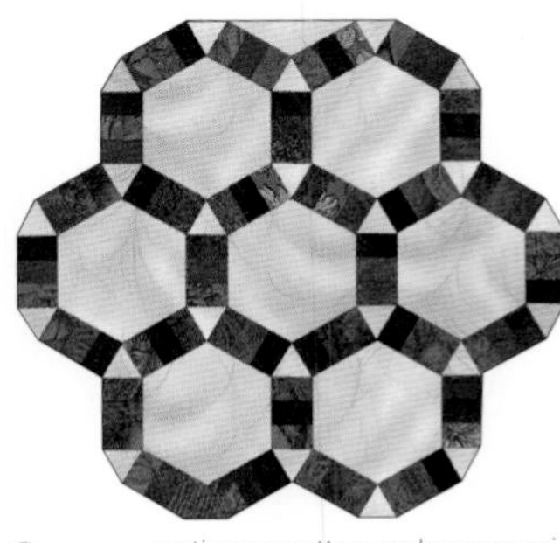
❸ continuous pattern on hexagon grid

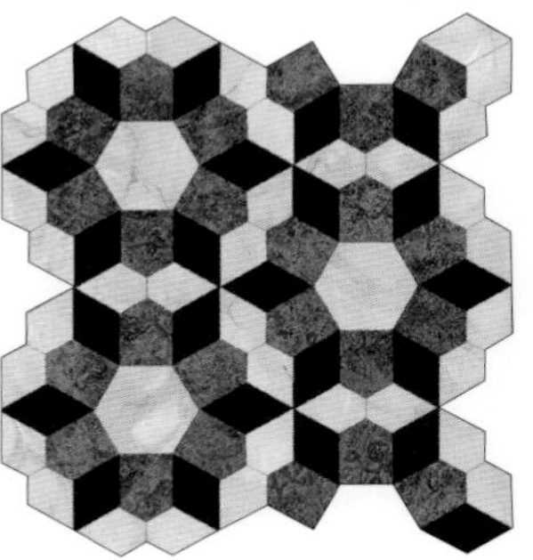
❹ continuous pattern on hexagon grid

❺ continuous pattern on hexagon grid

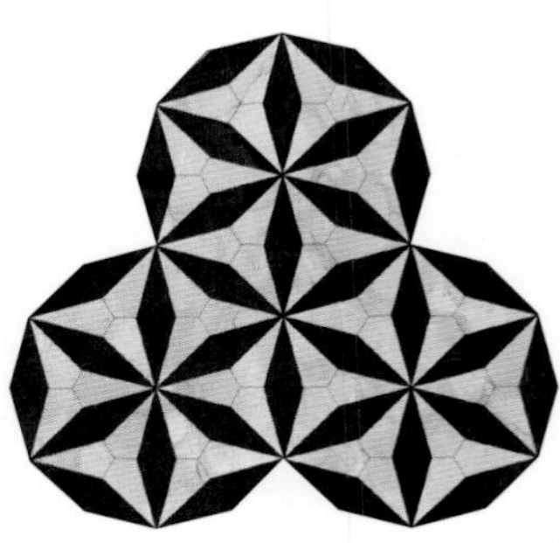
❻ continuous pattern on hexagon grid

❼ continuous pattern on hexagon grid

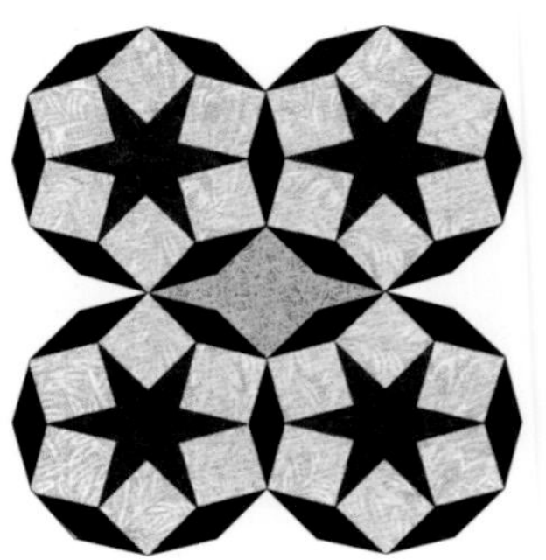
❽ continuous pattern on hexagon grid

❾ continuous pattern on hexagon grid

❿ continuous pattern on hexagon grid

⓫ continuous pattern on hexagon grid

⓬ continuous pattern on hexagon grid

⓭ continuous pattern on hexagon grid

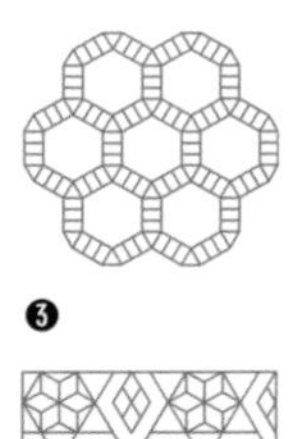
❶

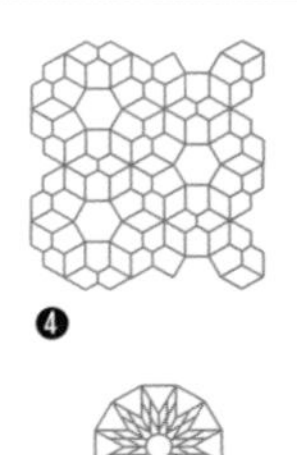
❷

❸

❹

❺

❻

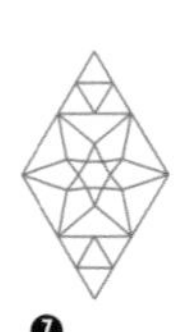
❼

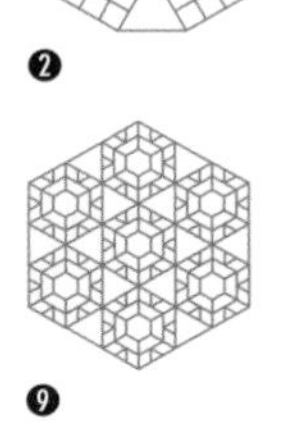
❽

❾

❿

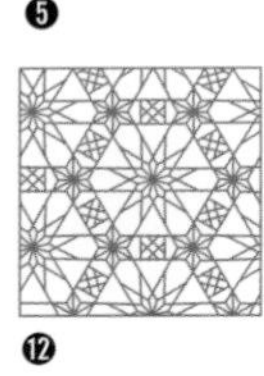
⓫

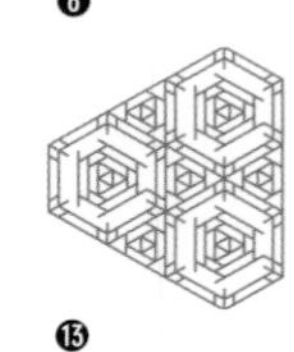
⓬

⓭

Scrap Quilts

As a child, growing up in the 1940s and '50s, I learned to sew by making my own clothes. This is just something we did, and we always ended up with scraps of leftover fabric that went into a scrap bag or box. My mother cut the buttons off worn shirts and saved the good parts of used clothing. Chicken feed came in bags decorated with calico or floral designs, and my mother would carefully wash and save them. Even though I was not quilting then, I took great pleasure in hunting through the scrap bag to find interesting fabric to make doll clothes. Today, with so many women working, with home economics no longer a requirement in schools, and with the easy access to inexpensive clothing through chain stores and foreign imports, it is now more economical to purchase clothes than to make them. The scrap bag is no longer a standard household item. However, in times past, scraps of fabrics were saved and quilts were made with little bits of cloth that were either left over from cutting other items, or from the good parts of used clothing. That does not mean that new fabrics were not purchased for quilts as well. They certainly were, but "scrap quilts" held a special place in the hearts of quiltmakers.

Scrap Quilts and *Friendship Quilts* are certainly intertwined. Many a scrap quilt was made with fabrics traded with or "begged" from friends. I have found seven blocks with "beggar" in the name, 24 with "scrap," six with "thrift" or "thrifty," and five with "economy." More than 60 of the blocks had descriptions that indicated the block was well suited to a scrap quilt. With the economic hard times from 1929 through the 1930s, it is no wonder that scrap quilts were so popular. It seems that the Alice Brooks and Laura Wheeler columns presented more designs for scrap quilts than any of the others. In fact of the 60 descriptions I found that indicated the block was perfect for scraps, 21 were from Alice Brooks and 25 were from Laura Wheeler. Headlines such as these accompanied some of the Laura Wheeler blocks: "Scraps Make Handsome Quilt", "Colorful Scrap Quilt", "Quilt in Light and Dark Scraps," "Simple Scrap Quilt," "Nosegay is Favorite Scrap Quilt," "Delve into Your Scrap Bag to Make New Laura Wheeler Quilt," "Flower in Scraps Is Easy to Make," "Leaves in Gay Colored Scraps."

Alice Brooks Patterns had similar headlines: "Scraps Form Quaint Flowers," "Charming Scrap Quilt," "Simple Scraps Make Friendship Quilt," "Scraps Form Effective Quilt."

ENDLESS CHAIN "In the early days of quiltmaking, the scrap quilt was an outstanding favorite. Not only did it appeal because of the economy of using up odds and ends of material, but it had its social and sentimental side, too. Many scrap quilts were friendship quilts—each friend invited to the quilting bee brought her scraps and made a block—her donation to the quilt. Endless Chain, a prize scrap quilt, would have been a leading favorite then." Alice Brooks, *Detroit Free Press*, Jun 5, 1940

BEGGAR'S BLOCKS "This interesting block harks back to the neighborly custom of begging one's friends for scraps of their frocks, or for the men's old neckties to put into a quilt." McKim

ODD SCRAPS PATCHWORK "'Odd Scraps Patchwork' is a grand block in which to utilize all the pretty scraps in the bag that are too small for other purposes, and each block may be in a different color arrangement.....It was known throughout the early Dutch colonies as the 'Thrift Block.'" Nancy Cabot, *Chicago Tribune*, Sep 5, 1934

DOUBLE WEDDING RING "'Double Wedding Ring'—one of those old-time patterns that has been handed down from generation to generation! It is easy to imagine its popularity with the old-time quiltmaker for she was obliged to save every scrap of precious material, and she certainly could do it with this pattern. The modern quiltmaker, too, feels that economy is an item to be considered; she has also found that piecing scraps together gives greater variety and therefore interest, than using the same material. So 'Double Wedding Ring'-oh-so effective when done—meets all of her needs." Alice Brooks, *Detroit Free Press*, Jul 27, 1934

ROAD TO FORTUNE "In and out winds the 'Road to Fortune,' but you can easily follow it every step of the way in this simple patchwork quilt. Quickly, gaily you'll piece out the identical 11-inch blocks with bits of scraps that are anything but identical—variety's your keynote here!" Laura Wheeler, *Indianapolis Star*, Mar 10, 1937

JOSEPH'S COAT "The family Bible was an essential possession of every American family times past, its stories being the inspiration for many of the old quilt names. Here, most aptly named, is 'Joseph's Coat', inspired by the Biblical story of Joseph's coat of many colors that moved his brothers to envy, this quilt, too, is made of many-hued scraps of material, and like the coat, will arouse envy in those who do not possess it." Laura Wheeler, *Charleston Gazette*, May 29, 1933

Endless Chain, *Detroit Free Press.* **See 401-1.**

Beggar Blocks, *Ladies Art Company.* **See 242-1.**

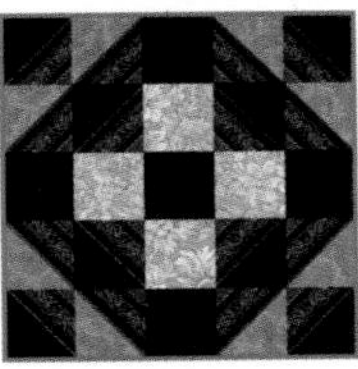

Odd Scraps Patchwork, *Ladies Art Company.* **See 184-11.**

Double Wedding Ring, *Detroit Free Press.* **See 419-10.**

Road to Fortune, *Indianapolis Star.* **See 260-10.**

Joseph's Coat, *World Herald.* **See 421-2.**

Continuous Pattern Category
(with Curved Elements)

Includes ● multi-grid designs with curves and ● hexagons with curves

❶ **Improved Nine-Patch,** Nancy Cabot, *Chicago Tribune,* Feb 28, 1933. Also known as:
- **Bailey Ninepatch,** *Mrs. Danner's Fourth Quilt Book,* 1958.
- **Circle Upon Circle,** *Kansas City Star,* Dec 2, 1933.
- **Four Leaf Clover,** *Kansas City Star,* Sep 25, 1935.
- **Nine Patch,** Hall, 1935.

❷ **Hearts and Diamonds,** Home Art Studios, *Cincinnati Enquirer,* Apr 6, 1933.

❸ **Remnant Ovals,** *Kansas City Star,* Mar 14, 1951.

❹ **Black Beauty,** Clara Stone, *Practical Needlework,* ca. 1906.

❺ **Wonder of the World,** *Prize Winning Designs,* ca. 1931.

❻ **White Rose,** Hall, 1935.

❼ **Broken Stave,** *Prize Winning Designs,* ca. 1931. Also known as:
- **Lovers' Quarrel,** *Prize Winning Designs,* ca. 1931.

❽ **True Lovers' Link,** *Prize Winning Designs,* ca. 1931.

❾ **Lover's Links,** *Ladies Art Company,* 1897.

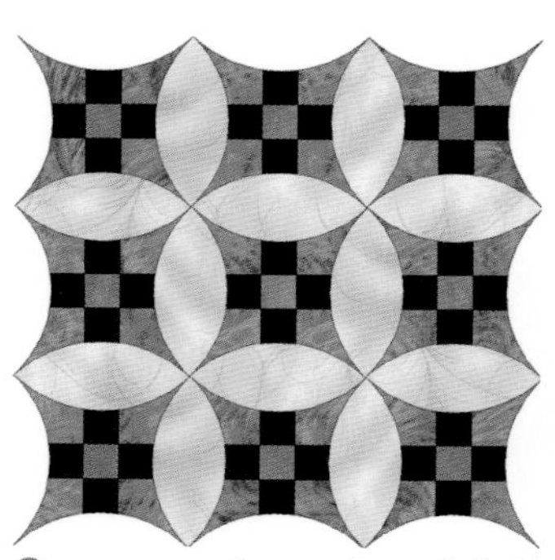
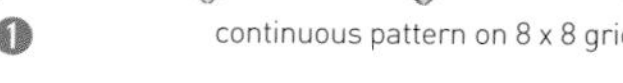

❶ continuous pattern on 8 x 8 grid

❷ continuous pattern

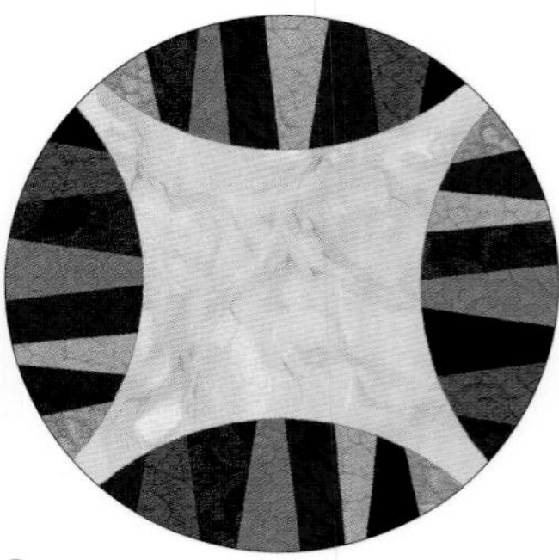

❸ continuous pattern on 8 x 8 grid

❹ continuous pattern on 4 x 4 grid

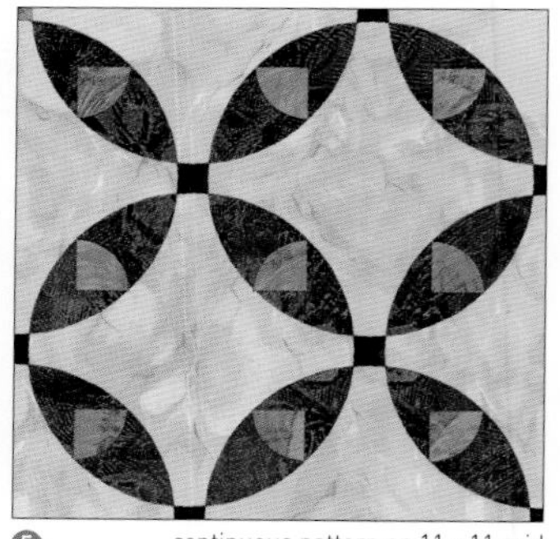

❺ continuous pattern on 11 x 11 grid

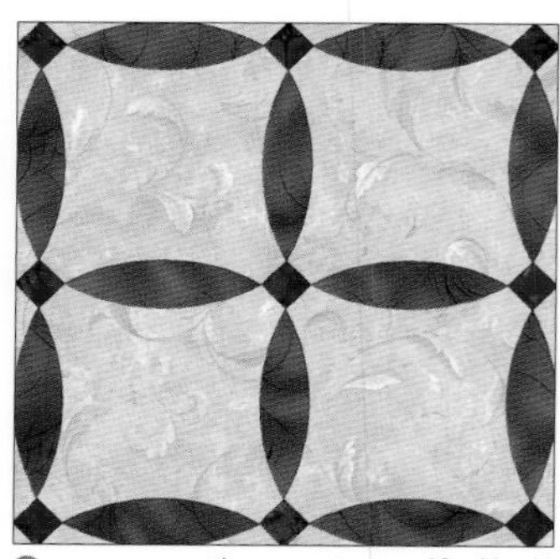

❻ continuous pattern on 12 x 12 grid

❼ continuous pattern on 12 x 12 grid

❽ continuous pattern on 14 x 14 grid

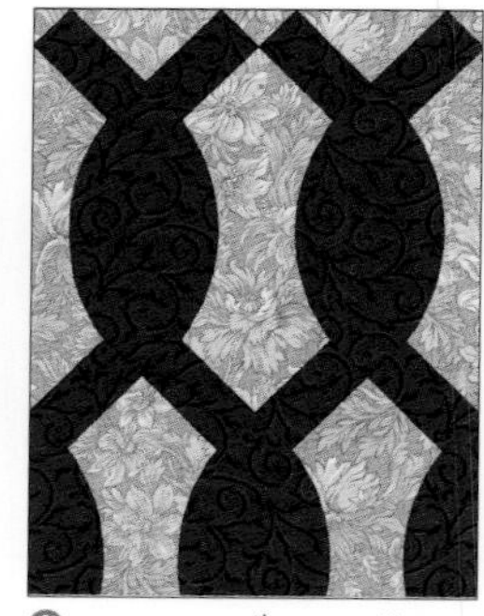

❾ continuous pattern on 12 x 12 grid

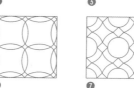

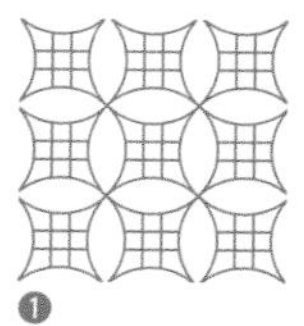
❶
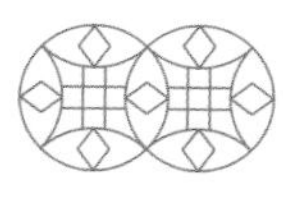

❷
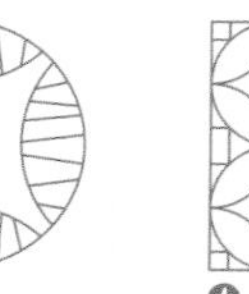
❸
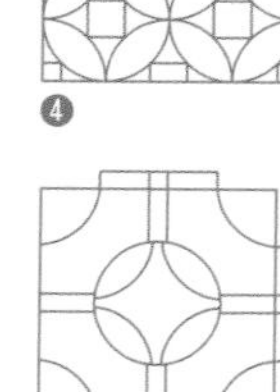
❹
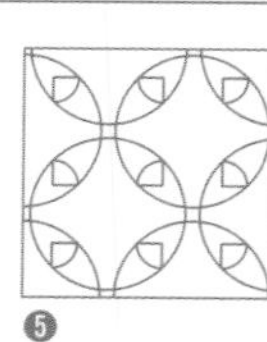
❺
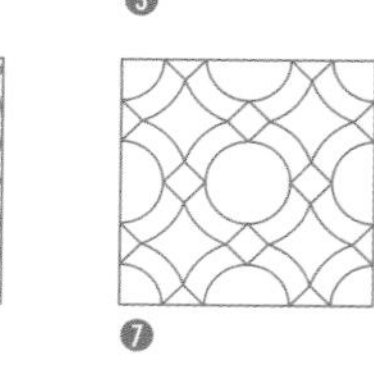
❻ ❼
❽

❾

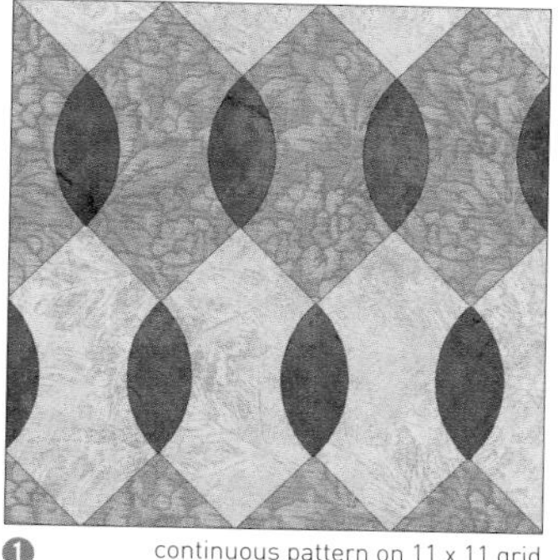

1 continuous pattern on 11 x 11 grid

2 continuous pattern on 14 x 14 grid

3 continuous pattern on 11 x 11 grid

4 continuous pattern on 14 x 14 grid

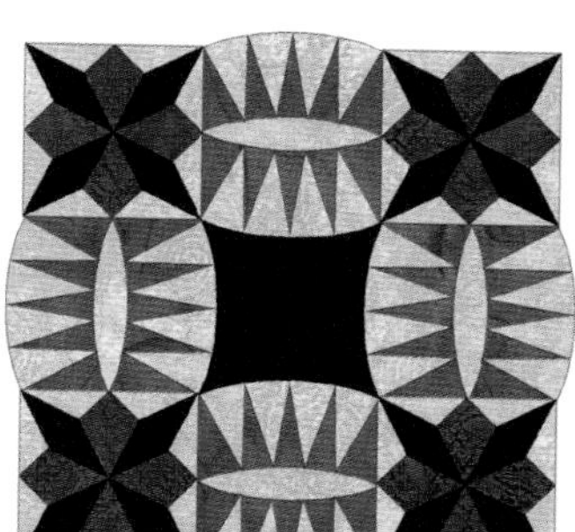

5 continuous pattern on 18 x 18 grid

6 continuous pattern on 32 x 32 grid

7 continuous pattern on 12 x 12 grid

8 continuous pattern on 16 x 16 grid

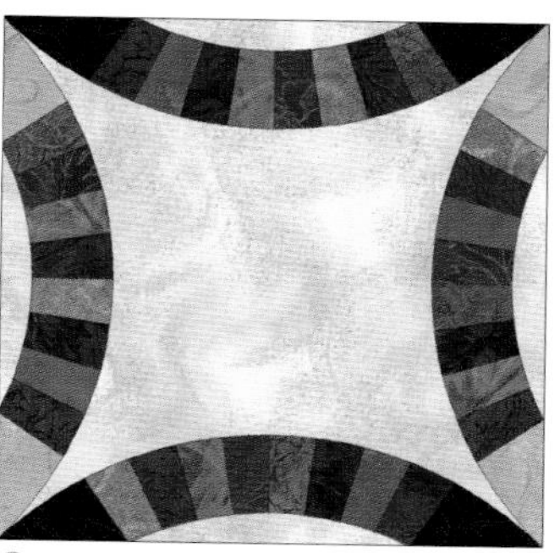

9 continuous pattern on 4 x 4 grid

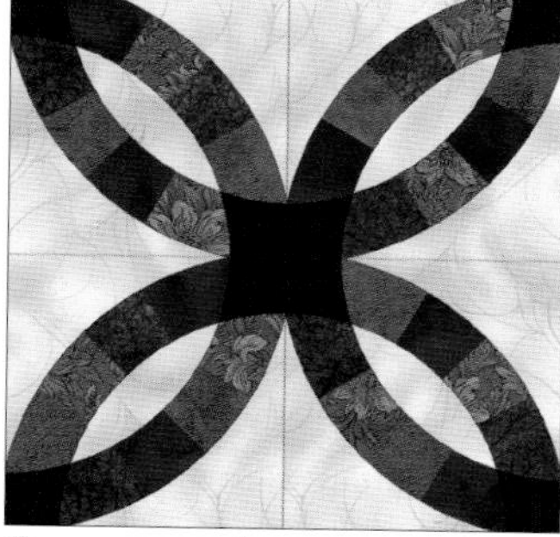

10 continuous pattern on 2 x 2 grid

11 continuous pattern on 30 x 30 grid

12 continuous pattern on 8 x 8 grid

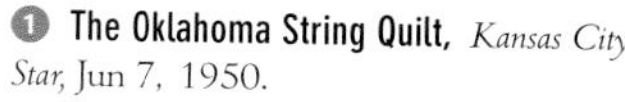

1 **The Oklahoma String Quilt,** *Kansas City Star,* Jun 7, 1950.

2 **Compass,** *Ladies Art Company,* 1897.

3 **The Snowball,** *Kansas City Star,* Mar 8, 1950.

4 **Rainbows,** Nancy Page, *Birmingham News,* May 26, 1942.

5 **The Flower Ring,** *Kansas City Star,* May 29, 1940.

6 **Yule Vine,** Nancy Cabot, *Chicago Tribune,* May 7, 1936.

7 **Flowing Ribbons,** Nancy Cabot, *Chicago Tribune,* Nov 2, 1935.

8 **Double Wedding Ring,** Laura Wheeler, *Illinois State Register,* May 24, 1933.

9 **Large Double Wedding Ring,** *Virginia Snow Studio Art Needlework Creations,* 1932.

10 **Double Wedding Ring,** Alice Brooks, *Detroit Free Press,* Mar 26, 1934.

11 **New Wedding Ring,** *Old Fashioned Quilts,* ca. 1931.

12 **Wedding Ring Chain,** Virginia Snow, *Grandma Dexter Appliqué and Patchwork Designs, Book 36a,* ca. 1932.

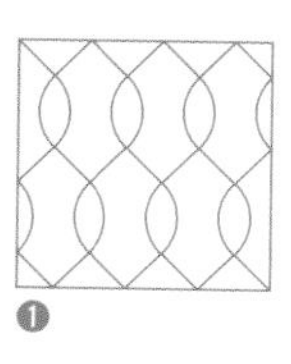

1

2

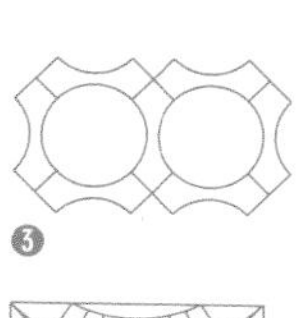

3

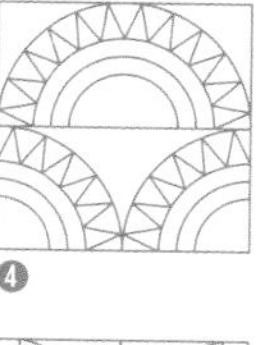

4

5

6

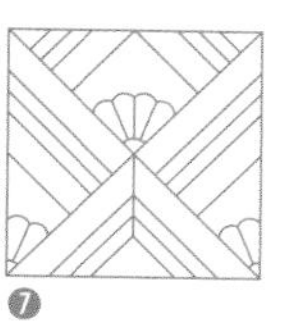

7

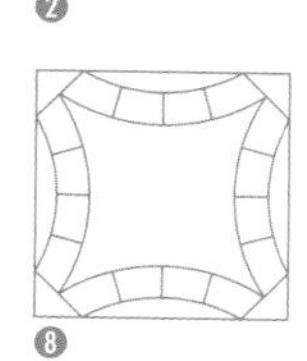

8

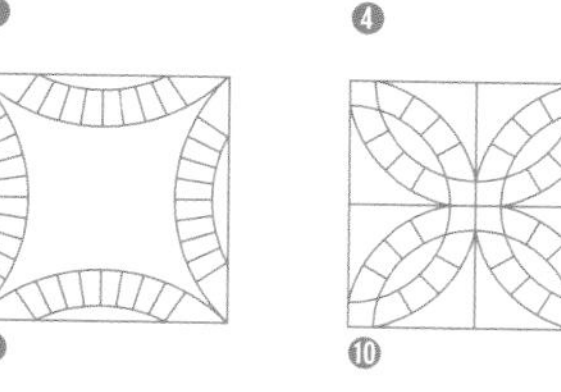

9

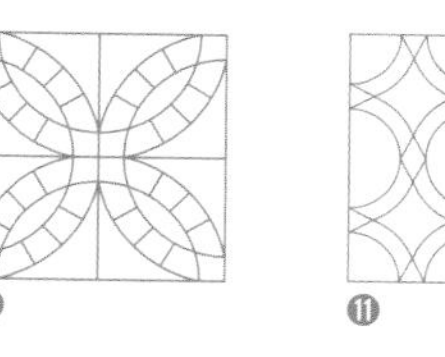

10

11

12

❶ **Double Wedding Ring,** Hall, 1935.

❷ **Double Wedding Ring,** Nancy Cabot, *Chicago Tribune,* Mar 14, 1937.

❸ **Small Wedding Ring Quilt,** *Kansas City Star,* Feb 15, 1939.

❹ **Wedding Ring,** Ruby McKim, *Kansas City Star,* Oct 3, 1928. Also known as:

The Little Wedding Ring, *Kansas City Star,* Jul 4, 1945.

Small Double Wedding Ring, *Grandmother Clark's Patchwork Quilts, Book No. 19,* 1932.

Double Wedding Ring, Home Art Studios, *Des Moines Register,* Nov 13, 1932.

The Wedding Ring, *Kansas City Star,* Feb 23, 1955.

"This double Wedding Ring quilt should not be attempted by anyone except a real quilt enthusiast. Believe it or not, the friend from whom we got this pattern boasts 720 small blocks in her counterpane, mighty nearly all different. That is the unique idea here--no two of the wedge-shaped blocks alike, in close proximity at least. Such a variegated scheme suggests 'married life' rather than just the wedding ring, and yet when you see the melon-shaped blocks set together, forming four-patches where they join, you also see large perfect circles overlapping regularly into a really lovely design—wedding rings it seems." McKim

❺ **Pickle Dish,** Eveline Foland, *Kansas City Star,* Oct 24, 1931. Also known as:

Burr, Nancy Cabot, *Chicago Tribune,* Nov 27, 1935.

Indian Wedding Ring, Home Art Studios, *Kansas City Star,* Apr 4, 1933.

The Pickle Dish Quilt, Home Art Studios, *Cincinnati Enquirer,* Mar 30, 1933.

"A little more than a century ago this lovely pieced pattern was designed in Long Island, on the eastern seaboard. It was then called the 'Burr,' and it is assumed that it was named after the famous Aaron. As the design became known across the country in its trek westward with the pioneer women, the name was changed, through some mysterious evolution, to 'Indian Wedding Ring.' " Nancy Cabot, *Chicago Tribune,* Nov 27, 1935

❻ **Pickle Dish,** *Quilt Booklet No. 1,* ca. 1931.

❼ **Double Wedding Ring,** *Ladies Art Company,* 1928.

❽ **Double Wedding Ring,** *Grandmother Clark's Patchwork Quilt Designs, From Books 20-21-23,* 1932.

❾ **Golden Wedding Ring,** Home Art Studios, *World Herald,* Nov 27, 1934.

❿ **Toy Balloon,** Home Art Studios, *World Herald,* Feb 24, 1934.

⓫ **Orange Peel,** Laura Wheeler, *Cincinnati Enquirer,* Jan 11, 1934.

⓬ **Rainbow Flower,** Laura Wheeler, *Illinois State Register,* Aug 3, 1933.

"Just as the rainbow runs the gamut of all colors, so this Rainbow Flower quilt incorporates every color and every scrap of material to form this pattern. It is a design that does not fall into blocks, but just goes on and on, one flower form interlocking with the next. Like Joseph's Coat, it is made entirely of scraps joined on just as they come to hand." Laura Wheeler, *Illinois State Register,* Aug 13, 1933

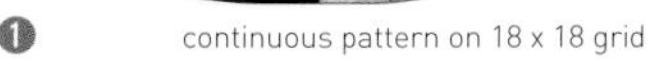
❶ continuous pattern on 18 x 18 grid

❷ continuous pattern on 6 x 6 grid

❸ continuous pattern on 6 x 6 grid

❹ continuous pattern on 2 x 2 grid

❺ continuous pattern on 10 x 10 grid

❻ continuous pattern on 8 x 8 grid

❼ continuous pattern on 40 x 40 grid

❽ continuous pattern on 44 x 44 grid

❾ continuous pattern on hexagon grid

❿ continuous pattern on hexagon grid

⓫ continuous pattern on hexagon grid

⓬ continuous pattern on hexagon grid

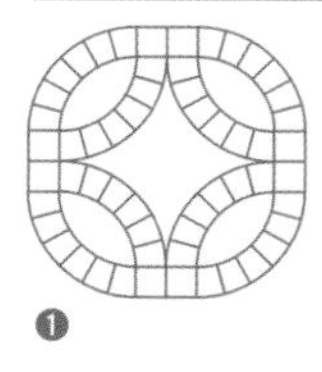
❶

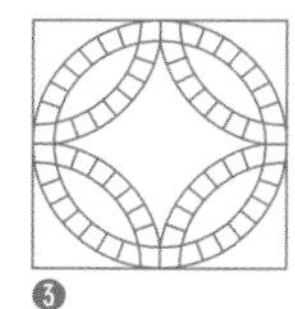
❷

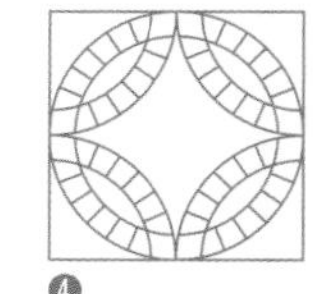
❸

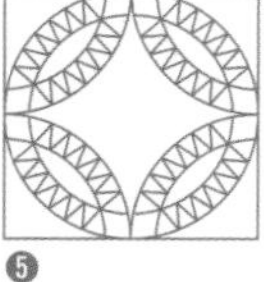
❹

❺

❻

❼

❽

❾

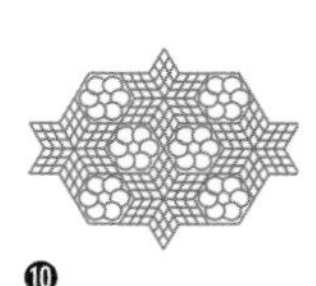
❿

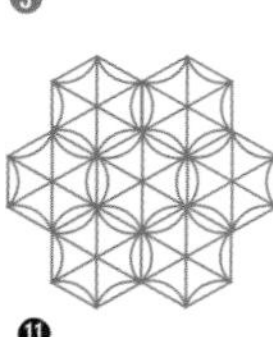
⓫

⓬

❶ continuous pattern on hexagon grid

❷ continuous pattern on hexagon grid

❸ continuous pattern on hexagon grid

❹ continuous pattern on hexagon grid

❺ continuous pattern on hexagon grid

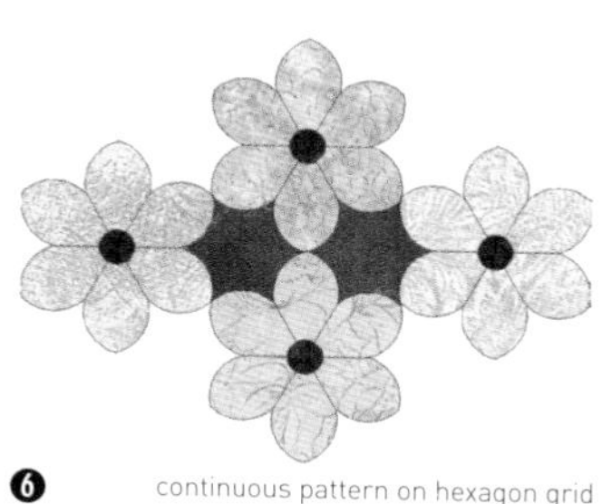

❻ continuous pattern on hexagon grid

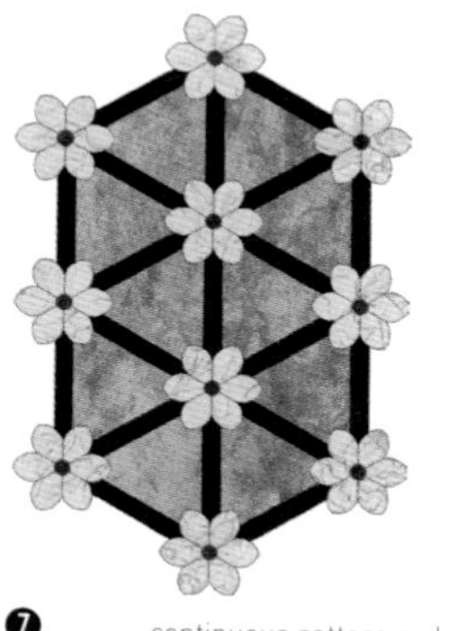

❼ continuous pattern on hexagon grid

❽ continuous pattern on hexagon grid

❶ **The Gay Cosmos,** Home Art Studios, *World Herald,* Mar 20, 1934.

❷ **Joseph's Coat,** Home Art Studios, *World Herald,* Mar 17, 1933. Also known as:

Ace of Diamonds, Home Art Studios, *World Herald,* Jan 31, 1934.

Banana, Aunt Martha series: *The Quilt Fair Comes to You,* ca. 1933.

Orange Ring, Aunt Martha series: *The Quilt Fair Comes to You,* ca. 1933.

Peeled Orange, Nancy Cabot, *Chicago Tribune,* May 8, 1936.

Queen's Choice, Aunt Martha series: *The Quilt Fair Comes to You,* ca. 1933.

"'Joseph's Coat' is a fascinating patchwork pattern that lends itself beautifully in utilizing any bright colored scraps that you may have in your rag bag. 'Joseph's Coat' had many colors, and this quilt will accommodate as wide a variety of prints as you can assemble in one quilt." *World Herald,* Aug 8, 1933

"The family Bible was an essential possession of every American family times past, its stories being the inspiration for many of the old quilt names. Here, most aptly named, is 'Joseph's Coat,' inspired by the Biblical story of Joseph's coat of many colors that moved his brothers to envy, this quilt, too, is made of many-hued scraps of material, and like the coat, will arouse envy in those who do not possess it." *Charleston Gazette,* May 29, 1933

❸ **Morning Glory,** Home Art Studios, *World Herald,* Oct 19, 1933.

❹ **Purple Clematis,** Home Art Studios, *World Herald,* Dec 13, 1933.

❺ **The Star Chain,** *Kansas City Star,* Dec 22, 1948.

❻ **The Easter Lily,** Home Art Studios, *World Herald,* Mar 22, 1934.

❼ **Rose Arbor,** Home Art Studios, *Cincinnati Enquirer,* Mar 16, 1933.

❽ **The Painted Daisy,** Home Art Studios, *World Herald,* Mar 8, 1934.

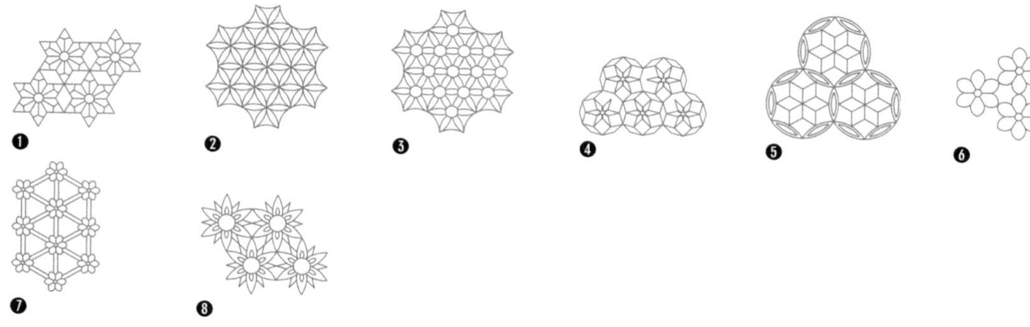

Hexagon Star Charm Quilt, ca. 1875, collection of Jinny Beyer.

PART 5

One-Patch Blocks

Memories of My Keepsake Quilt

As you so calmly view my quilts,
Of red and green and blue.
They seem a jumbled lot of goods
And tangled floss to you.

But when I fondly gaze at them
Through smiles, or maybe tears,
They tell me many a thrilling tale
Of all the bygone years.

This piece of bright red calico
To you means nothing more.
To me–it's my first day at school,
I'm six years old once more.

I see again that old schoolhouse
I see the home-nest, too,
My father, mother, brother Jim,
My gentle sister Sue.

This tiny piece of yellowed white,
To me has much to say,
For I'm a blushing bride once more,
And this–my wedding day.

I see the little, brown stone church,
The faces of my friends,
I hear "Until death do you part,"
And then the service ends.

And we go forth on unknown seas,
Our niche in life to fill,
And all the world is at our feet
To conquer as we will.

This dainty piece of pink and white
Bids all past years depart,
My first-born baby once more likes
Close to my mother-heart.

And I again live o'er those days,
And thrill again with joy
O'er that wee mite–just his and mine–
Our own first baby boy!

With reverence–this dainty blue
I see through blinding tears
The little girl God beckoned to
Back through the bygone years.

And so all woven through my quilts,
Are woven days of life,
The high days and the holidays,
The days of joy and strife.

And when I leave God's footstool here
To cross death's narrow sea,
I'll wrap these memories round my soul
And take them Home with me.

MAUDE WILLIAMSON ENGLISH, *THE PATCHWORK BOOK, WOMAN'S WORLD SERVICE LIBRARY*, 1932

One-Patch Category

Includes ● *single-shape pieces without curves and* ● *singe-shape pieces with curves*

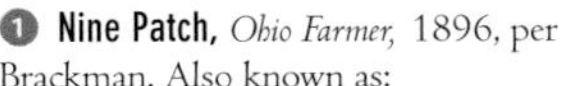

❶ **Nine Patch,** *Ohio Farmer,* 1896, per Brackman. Also known as:

Checkerboard, *The Patchwork Book,* 1932.
Greek Cross, Miall, 1937.
Fundamental Nine Patch, Finley, 1929.
Patience Nine Patch, Gutcheon, *The Perfect Patchwork Primer,* 1973.

"The 'Nine-patch' in its simplest form was the next step in the use of the square patch and the one oftenest used for the child's first lesson in quilt-making." Hall, 1935

❷ **Mosaic No. 20,** *Ladies Art Company,* 1897. Also known as:

Four Patch Variation, Orlofsky, 1974.

❸ **The Squares within Squares,** Nancy Cabot, *Chicago Tribune,* Aug 1, 1936.

❹ **Cross Block,** *Farm and Home,* Feb 15, 1915.
"Eight pieces of the dark and 18 of the light goods, each two inches square, compose this block, and when a number of them are put together a very pretty effect of five-square and eight-square crosses is brought out. The order of the colors may be reversed. These blocks should be sewn together without strips of cloth between to produce the intended design." *Farm and Home,* Feb 15, 1915

❺ **Building Blocks,** Nancy Cabot, *Chicago Tribune,* Jan 15, 1938.

❻ **Tete-a-Tete,** Nancy Cabot, *Chicago Tribune,* Nov 13, 1935. Also known as:

Crossword Puzzle, *Farm Journal and Farmers Wife,* ca. 1957.

❼ **Nine Patch Variation,** *Q Book 109, Early American Quilts,* date unknown.

❽ **Irish Chain,** *The Patchwork Book,* 1932.

❾ **Forty Niner,** *Detroit Free Press,* Oct 26, 1934.

❶ 3 x 3 grid

❷ 4 x 4 grid

❸ 4 x 4 grid

❹ 5 x 5 grid

❺ 5 x 5 grid

❻ 8 x 8 grid

❼ 9 x 9 grid

❽ 9 x 9 grid

❾ 9 x 9 grid

Note: Since one-patch designs achieve their pattern as a result of the arrangement of multiple patches of identical shape but varied color, the grid drawings in this section are not unique to each design; many are used over and over again and are a guide to color placement not to patch shape.

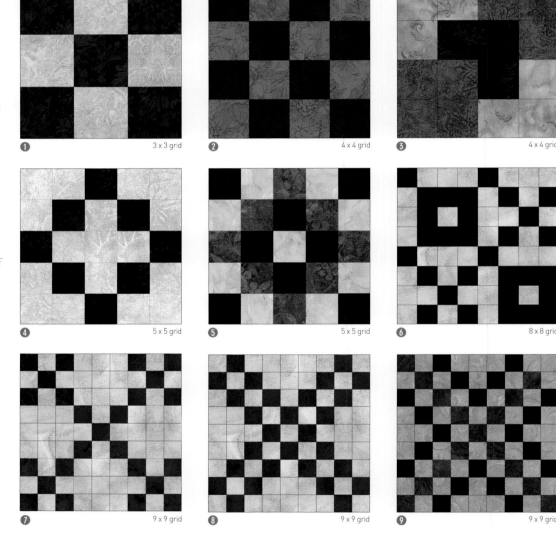

❶ ❷ ❸ ❹ ❺

❻ ❼ ❽ ❾

1. **Crossroads,** *Farm Journal and Farmers Wife,* ca. 1957.
2. **Golden Glow,** Hall, 1935.
3. **Double Irish Chain,** Laura Wheeler, *Cincinnati Enquirer,* Aug 6, 1933.
4. **Steps to the Garden,** Nancy Cabot, *Chicago Tribune,* Feb 20, 1935.
5. **Summer Garden,** Nancy Cabot, *Chicago Tribune,* Jan 20, 1935.
"'Summer Garden' was one of the first quilt patterns designed after the period of the crazy quilt died out. Squares and triangles were experimented with to create something a bit more unusual than anything previously made, and it remained for a young southern woman to create a 'pieced' block of outstanding simplicity and exquisite beauty. Of the original pieced blocks no two were alike, and they were pieced in both figured and plain materials and set together with bands of red." Nancy Cabot, *Chicago Tribune,* Jan 20, 1935
6. **Beautiful Mosaic,** *Farm Journal and Farmers Wife,* ca. 1941.
7. **Crossword Puzzle,** Hall, 1935.
8. **Triple Irish Chain,** Nancy Cabot, *Chicago Tribune,* Nov 26, 1935.
9. **The Irish Chain Quilt,** *Kansas City Star,* Dec 13, 1944.
10. **Homespun,** Nancy Cabot, *Chicago Tribune,* Jan 27, 1935.
11. **Mosaic Block,** *Old Fashioned Quilts,* ca. 1931.
12. **Washington Stamp Quilt,** *Kansas City Star,* Feb 23, 1944.
13. **Steps to the Altar,** *Mrs. Danner's Fifth Quilt Book,* 1970.

❶ **Postage Stamp Quilt,** *Kansas City Star,* Feb 18, 1942.

❷ **Postage Stamp,** Hall, 1935.

❸ **London Stairs,** *Kansas City Star,* Jan 20, 1934. Also known as:
- **Endless Stairs,** Nancy Cabot, *Chicago Tribune,* Mar 7, 1934.

❹ **Interlocked Squares,** Edna Marie Dunn, *Kansas City Star,* Sep 10, 1932. Also known as:
- **A 4 Part Strip Block,** *Kansas City Star,* Jan 28, 1948.
- **Fence Posts,** Holstein, 1973.
- **P Block,** *Kansas City Star,* Jan 28, 1948.
- **Roman Square,** Orlofsky, 1974.
- **Roman Stripe,** *Capper's Weekly,* ca. 1960.
- **Roman Stripe Zig Zag,** Gutcheon, *The Perfect Patchwork Primer,* 1973.
- **Spirit of St. Louis,** Nancy Cabot, *Chicago Tribune,* Apr 28, 1934.
- **Tricolor Block,** Nancy Cabot, *Chicago Tribune,* Sep 12, 1936.

❺ **Rail Fence,** Martens, 1970. Also known as:
- **Fence Rail,** *Q Book 108, Centennial Quilts,* date unknown.

❻ **Five Stripes,** *Ladies Art Company,* 1897.

❼ **Hit and Miss,** Finley, 1929.

❽ **Brickwork Quilt,** *Ladies Art Company,* 1897. Also known as:
- **Brick Wall,** Finley, 1929.
- **Brick Work,** Hall, 1935.
- **Streak of Lightning,** date unknown, per Holstein.

❾ **Depression Quilt,** *Kansas City Star,* May 27, 1942.

"Mrs. John L Waller, Farmington, Mo, gives us the Depression Quilt pattern. Her quilt of this design was made of tobacco sacks, which she ripped apart, washed and dyed. For a lining she used feed sacks. Mrs. Waller prefers this pattern done in a 2-tone color scheme." *Kansas City Star,,* May 27, 1942

❿ **Diagonal Pattern Patchwork,** *Weldon's Practical Patchwork,* ca. 1890.

⓫ **Fine Woven,** *Ladies Art Company,* 1897. Also known as:
- **Coarse Woven,** Hall, 1935.
- **Fine Woven Patchwork,** Hall, 1935.

⓬ **Chevron Patchwork,** *Weldon's Practical Patchwork,* ca. 1890.

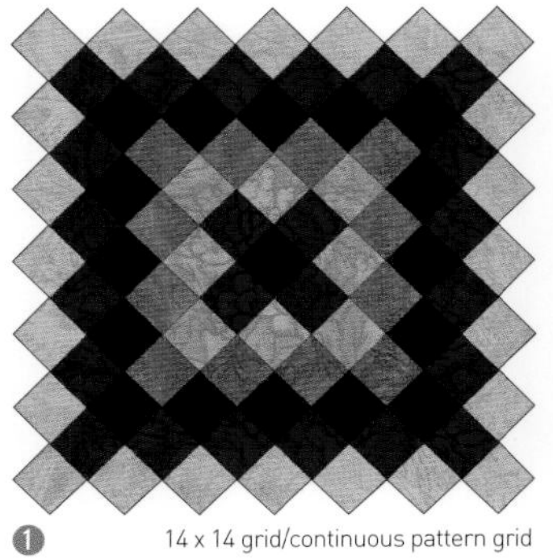

❶ 14 x 14 grid/continuous pattern grid

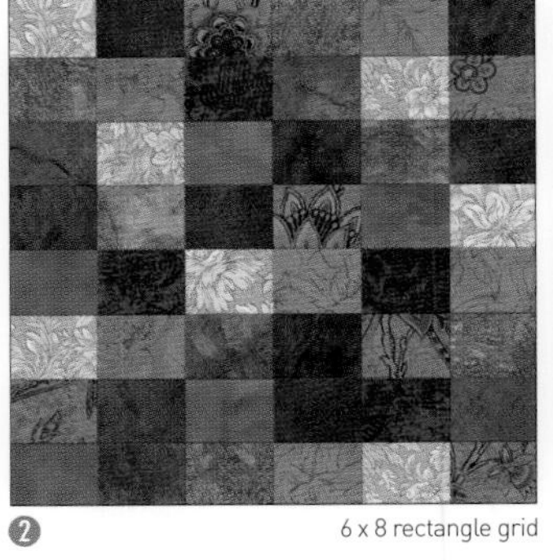

❷ 6 x 8 rectangle grid

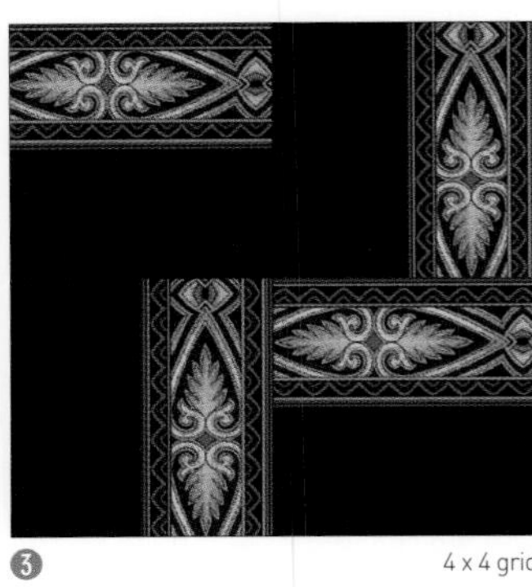

❸ 4 x 4 grid

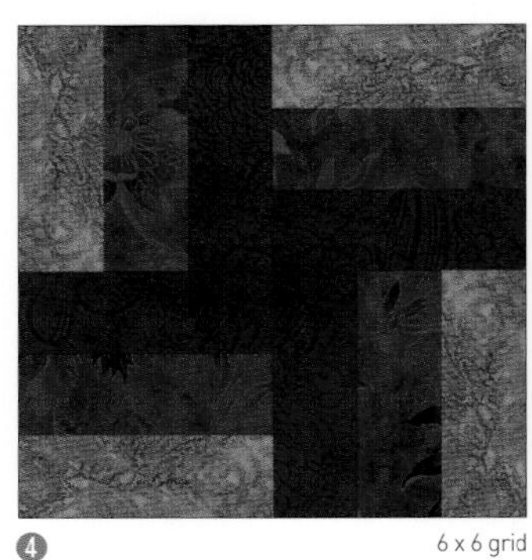

❹ 6 x 6 grid

❺ 8 x 8 grid

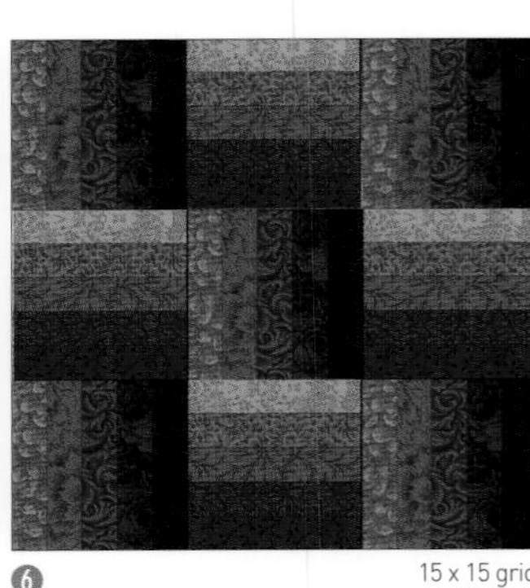

❻ 15 x 15 grid

❼ 6 x 6 grid

❽ 8 x 8 grid

❾ 12 x 12 grid

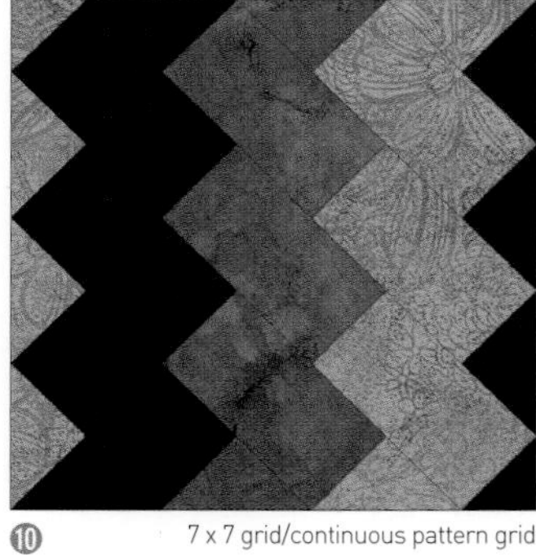

❿ 7 x 7 grid/continuous pattern grid

⓫ 12 x 12 grid/continuous pattern grid

⓬ 15 x 15 grid/continuous pattern grid

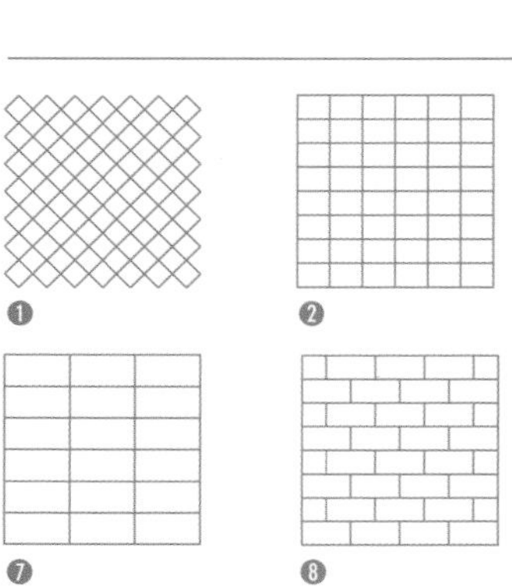
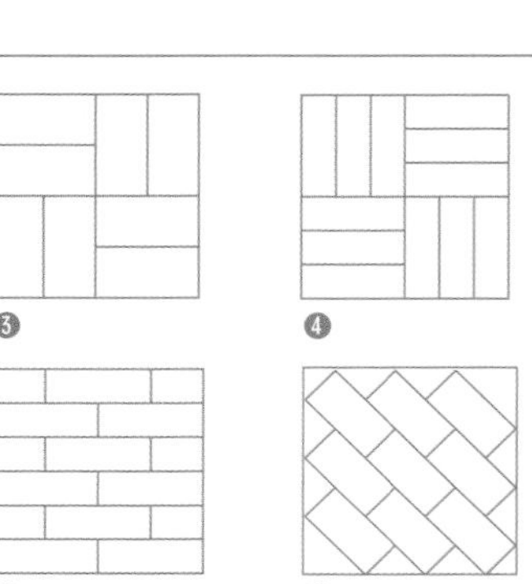

❶ ❷ ❸ ❹ ❺ ❻

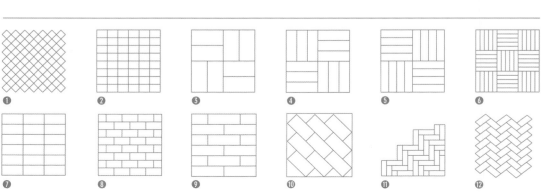

❼ ❽ ❾ ❿ ⓫ ⓬

❶ **Orange Pekoe,** Nancy Cabot, *Chicago Tribune,* Dec 28, 1935.

❷ **Picture Frames,** *Kansas City Star,* Feb 28, 1951.

❸ **The Broken Wheel,** *Dakota Farmer,* Jun 1, 1929. Also known as:

- **Corn Design,** *Dakota Farmer,* Jun 1, 1929.
- **Crow's Foot,** Hall, 1935.
- **Fan Mill,** Hall, 1935.
- **Fly,** Hall, 1935.
- **The Gay Pinwheel,** *Q Book 107, A B C Quilter,* date unknown.
- **Kathy's Ramble,** Hall, 1935.
- **Mill Wheel,** Finley, 1929.
- **Old Crow,** *The Patchwork Book,* 1932.
- **Sugar Bowl,** Hall, 1935.
- **Water Mill,** Finley, 1929.
- **Water Wheel,** Finley, 1929.
- **Windmill,** Finley, 1929.
- **Windmills,** Orlofsky, 1974.

❹ **Shadows,** ca. 1938, per Havig.

❺ **Broken Dishes,** Ruby McKim, McKim, 1931. Also known as:

- **The Double Square,** *Kansas City Star,* Feb 25, 1953.
- **Pretty Triangles,** date unknown per Brackman.
- **A Simple Quilt Block,** *Orange Judd Farmer,* date unknown, per Brackman.
- **Small Triangle Quilt,** *Kansas City Star,* Nov 7, 1945.
- **Triangle Combination,** date unknown, per Brackman.
- **Triangle Design,** *The Patchwork Book,* 1932.

❻ **A Victory Quilt,** *Kansas City Star,* Apr 8, 1942.

❼ **Mrs. William's Border,** Nancy Page, *Birmingham News,* May 18, 1943. Also known as:

- **The Fence Row Quilt,** *Kansas City Star,* Oct 6, 1943.

❽ **Ocean Waves,** *Ladies Art Company,* 1897.

❾ **Big Dipper,** *Ladies Art Company,* 1897. Also known as:

- **Bow Ties,** Nancy Cabot, *Chicago Tribune,* Jul 9, 1938.
- **Crazy Quilt,** *Q Book 102, Grandmother's Patchwork Quilts,* date unknown.
- **Electric Fan,** Clara Stone, *Practical Needlework,* ca. 1906.
- **Envelope Quilt Pattern,** *Kansas City Star,* Feb 10, 1943.
- **Hour Glass,** Eveline Foland, *Kansas City Star,* Feb 13, 1932.
- **One Patch,** Laura Wheeler, unidentified newspaper clipping, date unknown.
- **One Patch Quilt,** Alice Brooks, unidentified newspaper clipping, date unknown.
- **Pinwheel,** source unknown, date unknown.
- **Triangles,** Alice Brooks, unidentified newspaper clipping, date unknown.
- **The Whirling Blade,** *Kansas City Star,* Mar 8, 1944.
- **Yankee Puzzle,** Finley, 1929.

❿ **Design No. 3,** *Q Book 105, Covered Wagon,* date unknown.

⓫ **The Wild Goose Quilt,** *Kansas City Star,* Dec 28, 1938.

⓬ **Little Cedar Tree,** *Kansas City Star,* Feb 28, 1940. Also known as:

- **Seesaw,** Gutcheon, *The Perfect Patchwork Primer,* 1973.

❶ **Mosaic No. 17,** *Ladies Art Company,* 1897. Also known as:

- **Ann and Andy,** date unknown, per Brackman.
- **Design No. 1,** *Q Book 105, Covered Wagon,* date unknown.
- **Geese in Flight,** Orlofsky, 1974.
- **Mosaic No. 10,** Nancy Cabot, *Chicago Tribune,* Sep 28, 1934.
- **Triangle Charm,** Jinny Beyer, Jinny Beyer Studio design, 2006.

❷ **Mosaic No. 9,** *Ladies Art Company,* 1897. Also known as:

- **Double Windmill,** Nancy Cabot, *Chicago Tribune,* May 29, 1935.
- **Milly's Favorite,** Nancy Cabot, *Chicago Tribune,* Dec 6, 1933.
- **Mosaic No. 15,** ca. 1938, per Havig.
- **Pinwheel,** *Grandmother's Patchwork Quilt Designs, Book 20,* 1931.
- **Pinwheel and Square,** *Progressive Farmer #1816,* date unknown.
- **Pinwheels and Squares,** Nancy Cabot, *Chicago Tribune,* Jul 21, 1937.
- **Windmill,** Nancy Cabot, *Chicago Tribune,* Nov 19, 1934

❸ **Balkan Puzzle,** Nancy Cabot, *Chicago Tribune,* Mar 23, 1934. See 60-4 and 66-12.

❹ **Whirligig,** *Michigan Farmer,* 1926. Also known as:

- **Design No. 2,** *Q Book 105, Covered Wagon,* date unknown.
- **Devil's Puzzle,** Finley, 1929.
- **Fly Foot,** Finley, 1929.
- **Swastika,** Eveline Foland, *Kansas City Star,* Oct 5, 1929.
- **The Whirlwind,** *Farmer's Advocate,* Apr 27, 1933.

❺ **Old Tippecanoe,** *Ladies Art Company,* 1897. Also known as:

- **Bow Ties,** *Kansas City Star,* Jun 2, 1943.
- **The Broken Dish,** *Kansas City Star,* Jun 2, 1943.
- **Broken Dishes,** Ruby McKim, *Kansas City Star,* Sep 20, 1930.
- **An Envelope Motif,** *Kansas City Star,* Aug 19, 1942.
- **Flying Colors,** *Kansas City Star,* Nov 5, 1958.
- **The Four Patch Fox and Goose Quilt,** *Kansas City Star,* Dec 24, 1940.
- **The Old Windmill,** Hinson, 1973.
- **Port and Starboard,** Nancy Cabot, *Chicago Tribune,* Apr 5, 1937.
- **Tippecanoe and Tyler Too,** Finley, 1929.
- **Wheel of Time,** Beyer, Jinny, *The Quilter's Album…,* 1980.

❻ **Annie's Choice,** Clara Stone, *Practical Needlework,* ca. 1906. Also known as:

- **Anna's Choice,** *Kansas City Star,* Feb 26, 1941.
- **Arrow Point,** ca. 1938, per Havig.
- **Constellation,** *Q Book 109, Early American Quilts,* date unknown.
- **Margaret's Choice,** *Ladies Art Company,* 1922.
- **Pieced Star,** *Q Book 109, Early American Quilts,* ca. 1938.

❼ **Old Maid's Puzzle,** *Grandmother Clark's Patchwork Quilt Designs, From Books 20-21-23,* 1932. Also known as:

- **Reverse X,** *Grandmother's Patchwork Quilt Designs, Book 20,* 1931.

❽ **Depression,** *Kansas City Star,* Mar 20, 1937.

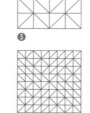

❶ 4 x 4 grid

❷ 4 x 4 grid

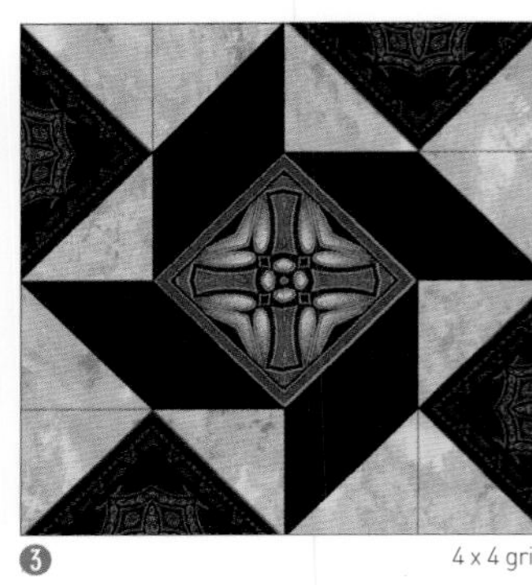

❸ 4 x 4 grid

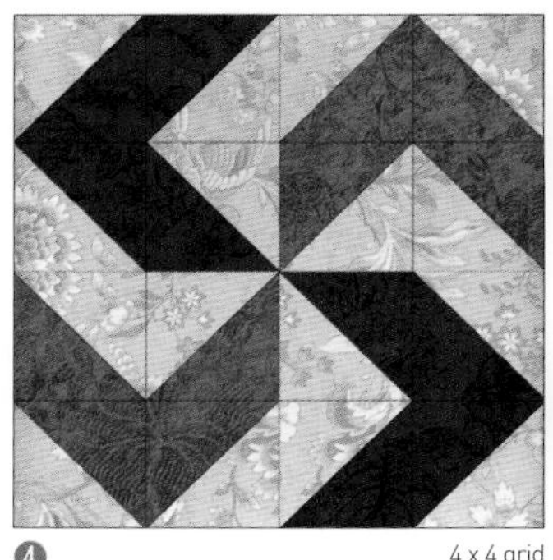

❹ 4 x 4 grid

❺ 4 x 4 grid

❻ 4 x 4 grid

❼ 4 x 4 grid

❽ 8 x 8 grid

❾ 8 x 8 grid

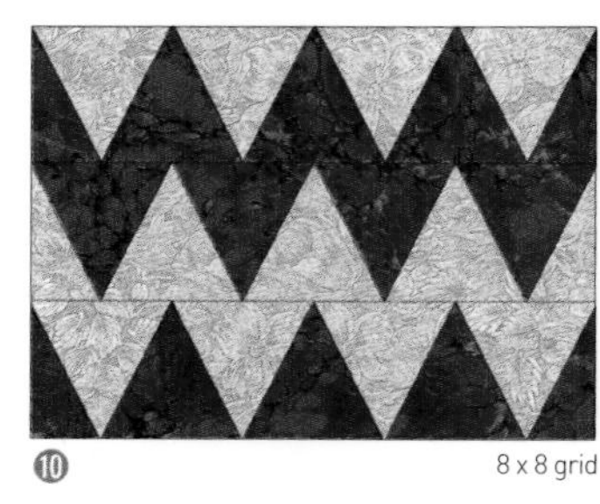

❿ 8 x 8 grid

⓫ 8 x 8 grid

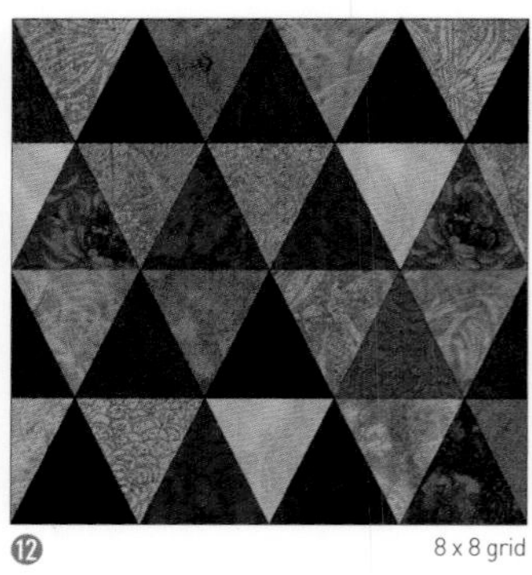

⓬ 8 x 8 grid

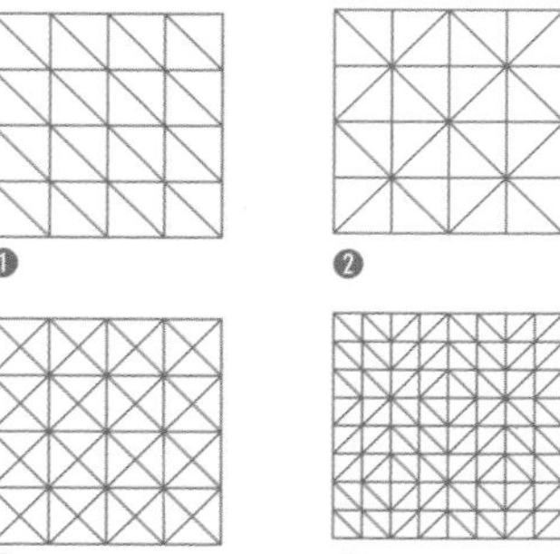

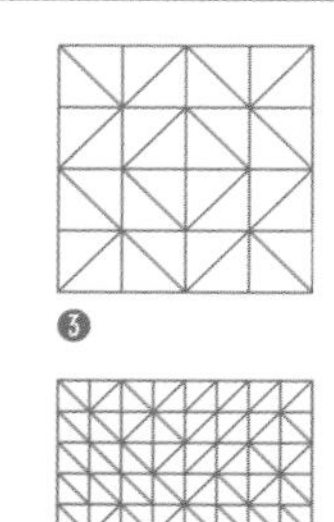

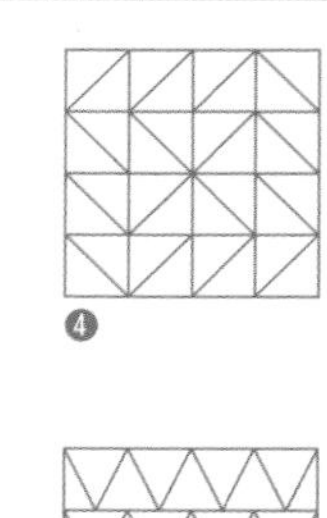

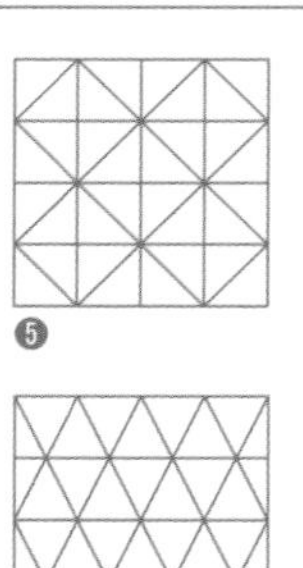

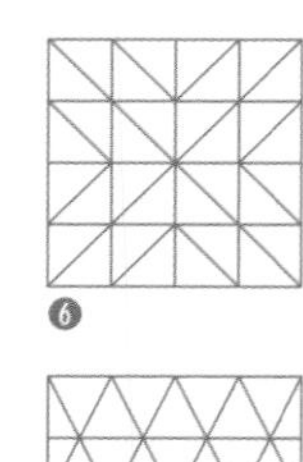

Quick Reference: Birds

"The high spots of our country's history have always been commemorated in quilt designs. 'The Blue Eagle' is an original 1933 contribution to the historical quilt album." Nancy Cabot, *Chicago Tribune*, Oct. 8, 1933

As part of his New Deal, the Roosevelt administration created the National Recovery Administration to administer the National Industrial Recovery Act, passed on June 16, 1933. The purpose was to jump start the economy. Through the NRA, codes were approved that dealt with unions, minimum wages, workweek hours and much more. As part of the push the Blue Eagle logo was adopted and businesses that followed the NRA codes were allowed to display posters with the eagle in their windows; "good Americans" would boycott businesses that failed to show the eagle. (*U.S. News and World Report*, Aug 10, 2003)

There was initially great excitement about the program, thus the interest in a quilt block commemorating the NRA. But the Blue Eagle did not prove to be a lasting "high spot" in our country's history. The NRA was controversial, and the Supreme Court later ruled that the code system was an unconstitutional abuse of federal power. (American Law Association, Schechter Poultry Corp. v. United States, 295 U.S. 495, 55 S. Ct. 837, 79 L. Ed. 1570, 1935). On September 5, 1935, the blue eagle was officially killed.

Other blocks depicting birds appeared in various newspapers and catalogs, but perhaps none so colorful as the *Blue Eagle*.

Chimney Swallows, *Birmingham News.* **See 358-12.**

Swallows in Flight, *Quilting.* **See 220-8.**

Swallow's Flight, *Prize Winning Designs.* **See 179-1.**

Blue Eagle, *Chicago Tribune.* **See 439-2.**

Swallow's Flight, *Chicago Tribune.* **See 123-8.**

Red Robin, *Indianapolis Star.* **See 341-9.**

Spring, *Detroit Free Press.* **See 317-11.**

9 **Merry Go Round,** *The Patchwork Book,* 1932. See 101-5 and 101-6.

10 **Streak O' Lightning,** Finley, 1929.
Also known as:
- **A Thousand Pyramids,** Nancy Cabot, *Chicago Tribune,* Oct 27, 1933.
- **Land of Pharaoh,** Nancy Cabot, *Chicago Tribune,* Aug 23, 1937.
- **Lightning,** Nancy Cabot, *Chicago Tribune,* Jan 18, 1937.
- **Rail Fence,** Finley, 1929.
- **Snake Fence,** Finley, 1929.
- **Streak of Lightning,** Hall, 1935.
- **The Lace Edge Quilt,** *Kansas City Star,* Mar 23, 1949.
- **Zig Zag,** Finley, 1929.

11 **Red Shields,** Nancy Cabot, *Chicago Tribune,* Jan 4, 1936.
"'Red Shields,' like Cardinal's Cap,' is one of the ancient designs which always are made up of red and white patches. There is only one pattern required." Nancy Cabot, *Chicago Tribune,* Jan 4, 1936

12 **Thousand Pyramids,** Finley, 1929.
Also known as:
- **The Mowing Machine,** Aunt Martha series: *Patchwork Simplicity,* ca. 1977.
- **Triangles,** Aunt Martha series: *Patchwork Simplicity,* ca. 1977.

❶ **Pyramids of Egypt,** Nancy Cabot, *Chicago Tribune,* Jun 24, 1935.

❷ **Cupid's Darts,** Nancy Cabot, *Chicago Tribune,* Oct 16, 1935.

❸ **Diamonds,** *Ladies Art Company,* 1897.

❹ **Diamond Net,** Nancy Cabot, *Chicago Tribune,* Nov 19, 1935.

❺ **Diamond Design,** *Ladies Art Company,* 1897. Also known as:
- **Springtime in the Ozarks,** *Kansas City Star,* Dec 18, 1940.

❻ **Fence Row,** ca. 1938, per Havig.

❼ **Godey Design,** *Godey's Lady's Book,* 1851. Also known as:
- **Baby Blocks,** Hall, 1935.
- **Block Pattern,** Orlofsky, 1973.
- **Block Puzzle,** *Grandmother Clark's Old Fashioned Quilt Designs, Book 21,* 1931.
- **Box Pattern,** date unknown, per Brackman.
- **Box Upon Box,** Nancy Page, *Birmingham News,* Aug 24, 1937.
- **Builder's Blocks,** *Kansas City Star,* Oct 22, 1947.
- **The Builder's Blocks,** *Kansas City Star,* Dec 16, 1953.
- **Cube Illusion,** Holstein, 1973.
- **Cube Work,** Orlofsky, 1973.
- **English T Box,** Orlofsky, 1973.
- **Hexagonal Star,** Hall, 1935.
- **Pandora's Box,** Holstein, 1973.
- **Rising Star,** Hall, 1935.
- **The Seven Sisters Quilt,** *Kansas City Star,* Apr 9, 1941.
- **Star and Box,** Nancy Cabot, *Chicago Tribune,* Nov 18, 1936.
- **The Star and Box Quilt,** *Kansas City Star,* Sep 20, 1939.
- **Steps to the Altar,** Orlofsky, 1973.
- **Texas Star,** *Q Book 110, Star Quilts,* date unknown.
- **Tumbling Blocks,** *Mrs. Danner Presents Quilt Book 7,* 1975.

❽ **Diamond Cube,** *Ladies Art Company,* 1897. Also known as:
- **Block Design,** *The Country Gentleman,* Jul 1930.
- **Diamond and Cube,** Hall, 1935.
- **Tea Box,** *Farm Journal Quilt Patterns,* 1935.

❾ **Variegated Diamonds,** *Ladies Art Company,* 1897. Also known as:
- **Baby's Block,** unidentified newspaper clipping, date unknown.
- **Baby's Blocks,** Ruby McKim, McKim, 1931.
- **Cubes and Stars,** *Grandmother's Patchwork Quilt Designs, Book 20,* 1931.
- **Tumbling Block,** Alice Brooks, unidentified newspaper clipping, date unknown.
- **Whirling Diamonds,** *Kansas City Star,* Nov 24, 1948.

❿ **Seven Stars,** *Ladies Art Company,* 1897. Also known as:
- **Building Blocks,** Nancy Cabot, *Chicago Tribune,* May 1, 1933.

⓫ **Dutch Tile,** Eveline Foland, *Kansas City Star,* Oct 31, 1931.

⓬ **The Dutch Tile Quilt,** Home Art Studios, *Cincinnati Enquirer,* Jan 24, 1933. Also known as:
- **Arabian Star,** Hall, 1935.
- **Dutch Tile,** Hall, 1935.
- **Gay Dutch Tile,** Kansas City Star, Oct 5, 1949.

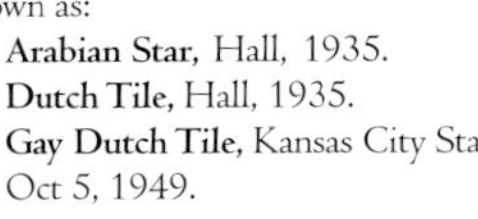

❶ 12 x 12 grid

❷ 8 x 8 grid

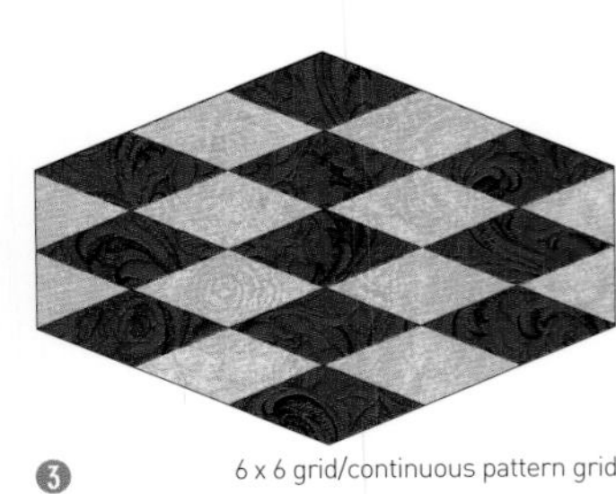

❸ 6 x 6 grid/continuous pattern grid

❹ 24 x 24 grid

❺ hexagon grid

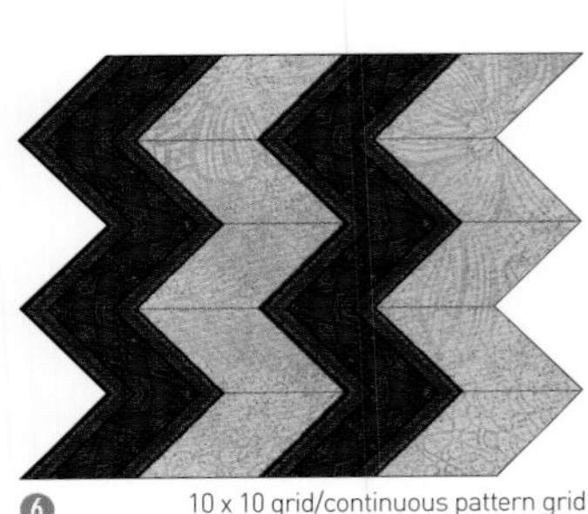

❻ 10 x 10 grid/continuous pattern grid

❼ hexagon grid

❽ hexagon grid

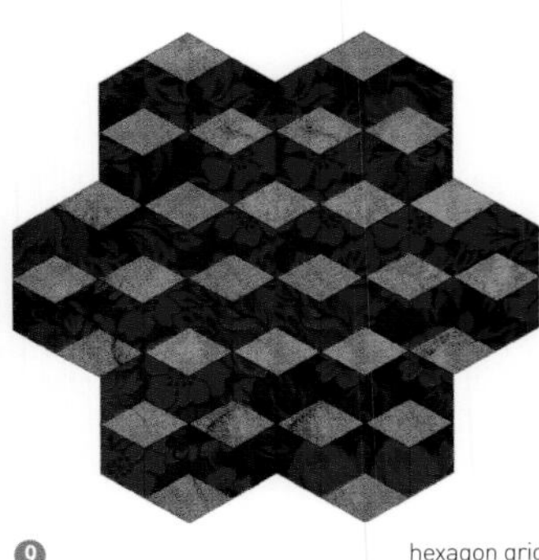

❾ hexagon grid

❿ hexagon grid

⓫ hexagon grid

⓬ hexagon grid

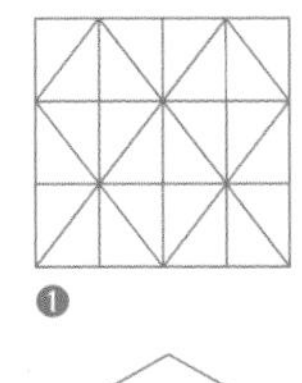

❶

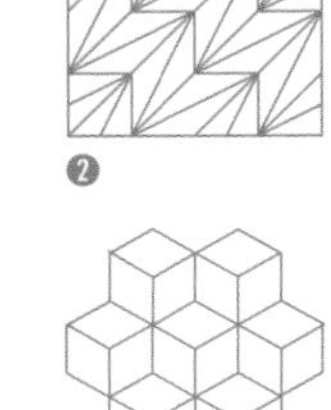

❷

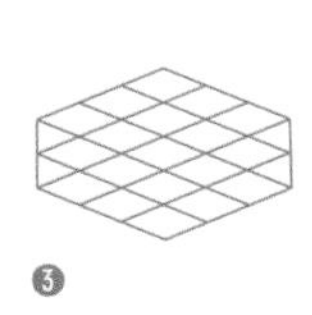

❸

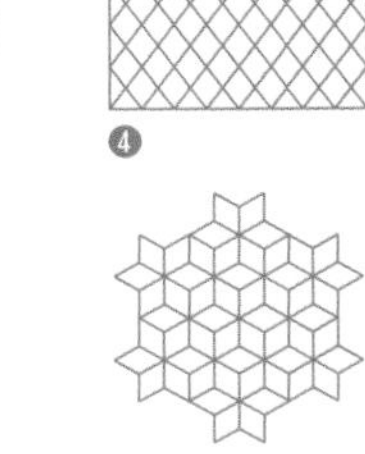

❹

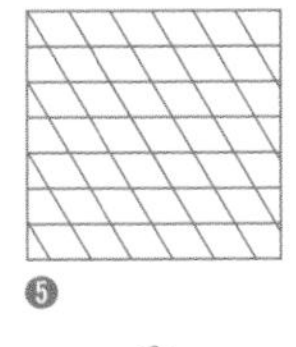

❺

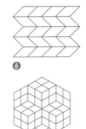

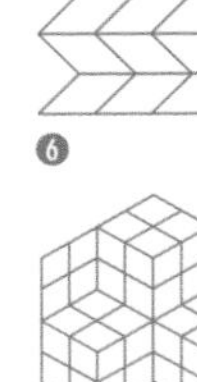

❻

❼

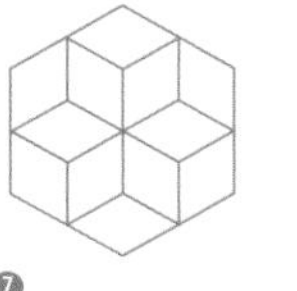

❽

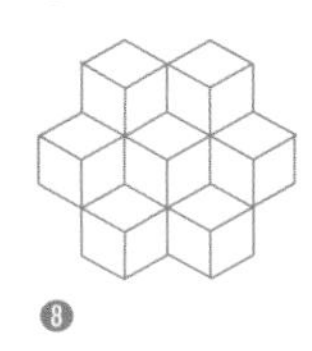

❾

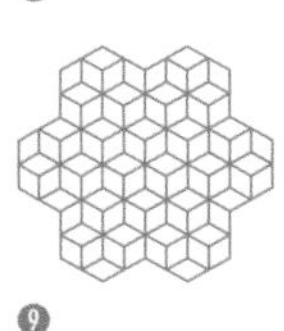

❿

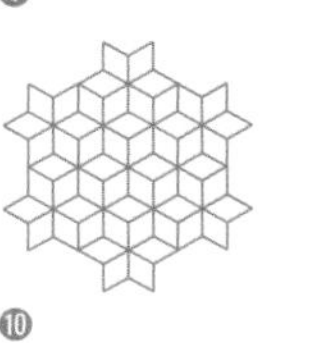

⓫

⓬

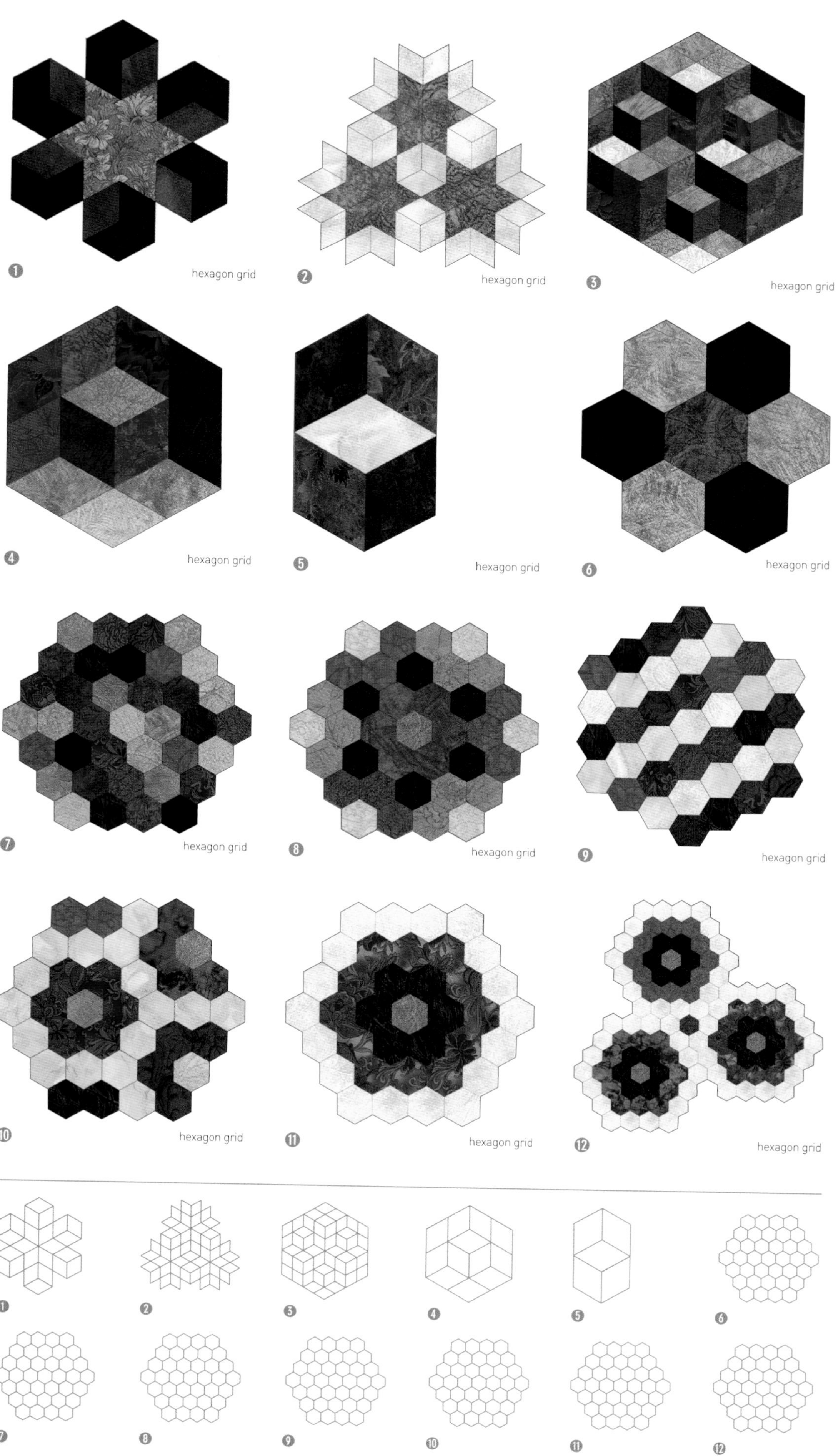

1 **Building Block Quilt Pattern,** Nancy Page, *Detroit Free Press,* Feb 15, 1934. Also known as:

- **Tumbling Blocks,** Nancy Page, *Birmingham News,* Jun 20, 1939.

2 **Tiny Star,** Hall, 1935.

3 **Enchantment,** Jinny Beyer, Hilton Head Seminar design, 1998.

4 **Block Party,** Jinny Beyer, Hilton Head Seminar design, 2003.

5 **Box Blocks,** *Ladies Art Company,* 1897.

6 **Endless Chain,** *Quilt Blocks from The Farmer's Wife,* 1932. Also known as:

- **Grandmother's Garden,** Alice Brooks, *Detroit Free Press,* Dec 23, 1934.
- **Honeycomb,** Laura Wheeler, *Indianapolis Star,* May 11, 1933.
- **Simplicity's Delight,** *Kansas City Star,* Mar 6, 1946.

7 **Hexagon Patchwork,** *Godey's Lady's Book,* Jan 1835. Also known as:

- **Honeycomb,** *Godey's Lady's Book,* Jan 1835.
- **Six Sided Patchwork,** *Godey's Lady's Book,* Jan 1835.

"'The Honeycomb', was made of hexagon patches sewed together without any attempt at color arrangement. But these six-sided patches were too suggestive of design not to invite experiment at the hands of the color-loving women who worked with them." Finley, 1929

8 **Colonial Bouquet,** *Grandma Dexter's New Appliqué and Patchwork Designs, Book 36b,* ca. 1932.

9 **Variegated Hexagons,** *Farm and Home,* ca. 1890

10 **Tumbler,** *Old Time New England,* April, 1927 Also known as:

- **Country Tile,** Alice Brooks, *Detroit Free Press,* date unknown.
- **The Garden Walk,** *Q Book 118, Grandmother's Flower Quilts,* date unknown.
- **Grandmother's Flower Garden,** *Virginia Snow Studio Art Needlework Creations,* 1932.
- **Mosaic,** Finley, 1929.
- **Old Fashioned Flower Garden,** *Ten Piecework Quilts for Southern Homes,* ca. 1936.
- **Old Fashioned Garden,** Laura Wheeler, *Indianapolis Star,* Apr 27, 1937.

11 **Garden Walk,** *Q Book 109, Early American Quilts,* date unknown.

12 **French Bouquet,** Eveline Foland, *Kansas City Star,* Mar 21, 1931. Also known as:

- **Grandma's Flower Garden,** *Quilt Blocks from Grandma Dexter,* ca. 1932.
- **Grandmother's Flower Garden,** Hall, 1935.

❶ **Flower Garden,** *Grandmother Clark's Old Fashioned Quilt Designs, Book 21,* 1931. Also known as:

- **French Bouquet,** Ruby McKim, McKim, 1931.
- **Grandma's Garden,** *Grandmother Clark's Old Fashioned Quilt Designs, Book 21,* 1931.
- **Grandmother's Flower Garden,** Ruby McKim, McKim, 1931.
- **Grandmother's Garden,** Nancy Page, *Nashville Banner,* Nov 14, 1933.
- **Grandmother's Rose Garden,** ca. 1938, per Havig.
- **Hexagons,** Laura Wheeler, *Nashville Banner,* date unknown.

❷ **The Rainbow Tile Quilt** Eveline Foland, *Kansas City Star,* Aug 30, 1930. Also known as:

- **The Diamond Field,** Eveline Foland, *Kansas City Star,* Apr 9, 1932.
- **Field of Diamonds,** date unknown, per Holstein.
- **Honeycomb,** *Quilt Blocks from The Farmer's Wife, Book 3,* 1932.

❸ **Twin Stars,** *The Patchwork Book,* 1932.

❹ **Mella Mosaic,** Hall, 1935.

❺ **Fascination,** Jinny Beyer, Hilton Head Seminar design, 1998.

❻ **Right Angles Patchwork,** Saward, 1882. Also known as:

- **Ecclesiastic,** Nancy Cabot, *Chicago Tribune,* Apr 19, 1935.
- **Ecclesiastical,** *Ladies Art Company,* 1897.
- **Inner City,** Jinny Beyer, Beyer, Jinny *Patchwork Patterns,* 1979.
- **Monk's Puzzle,** Nancy Cabot, *Chicago Tribune,* Sep 29, 1937.

❼ **Crazy Tile Quilt,** *Kansas City Star,* May 24, 1939.

❽ **Spellbound,** Jinny Beyer, Hilton Head Seminar design, 1998.

❾ **Colonial Garden,** *Grandmother Clark's Patchwork Quilts, Book No. 19,* 1932.

❿ **Rose Star One Patch,** Laura Wheeler, *Cincinnati Enquirer,* Sep 7, 1933. Also known as:

- **Rose Star,** Alice Brooks, Alice Brooks Designs, ca. 1950.

⓫ **Honeycomb Patchwork,** *Ladies Art Company,* 1897. Also known as:

- **Honeycomb,** Hall, 1935.

⓬ **Lucky Charm,** Jinny Beyer, Hilton Head Seminar design, 1998.

❶ hexagon grid

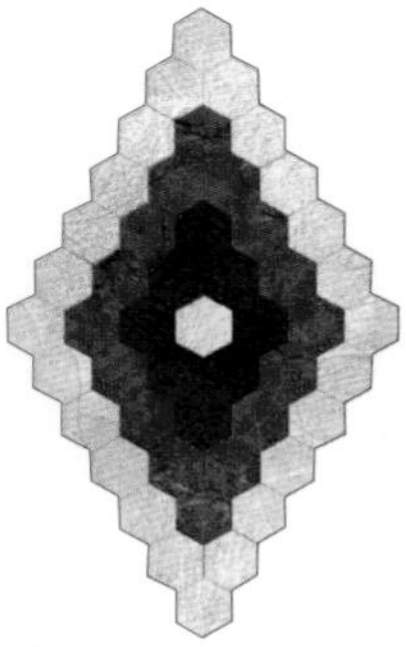

❷ hexagon grid

❸ hexagon grid

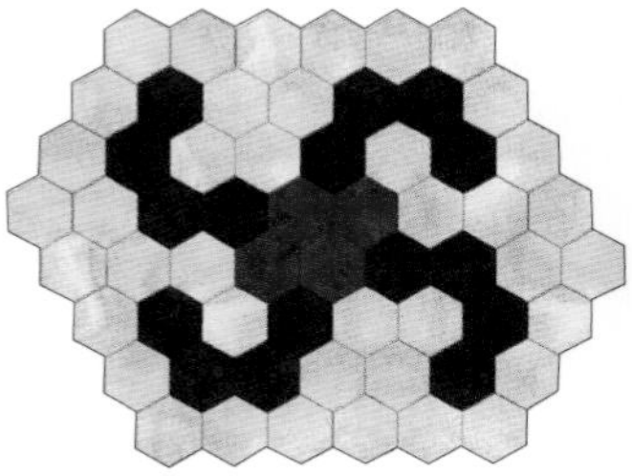

❹ hexagon grid

❺ hexagon grid

❻ hexagon grid

❼ hexagon grid

❽ hexagon grid

❾ hexagon grid

❿ hexagon grid

⓫ hexagon on 6 x 6 grid

⓬ hexagon on 6 x 6 grid

❶ ❷ ❸ ❹ ❺ ❻

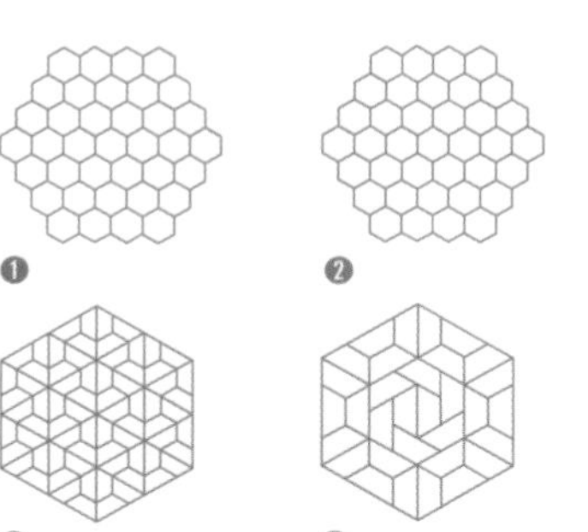

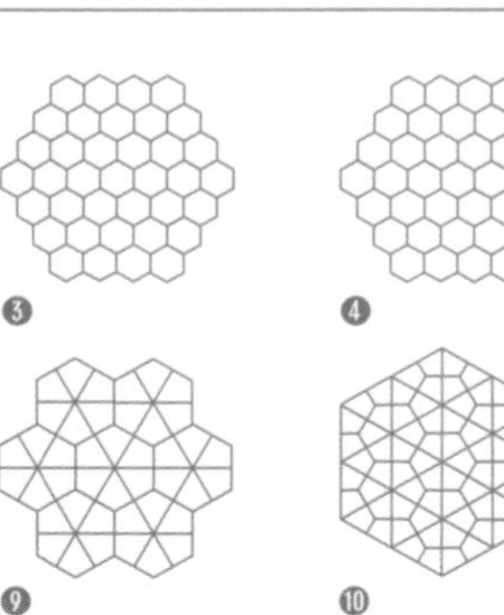

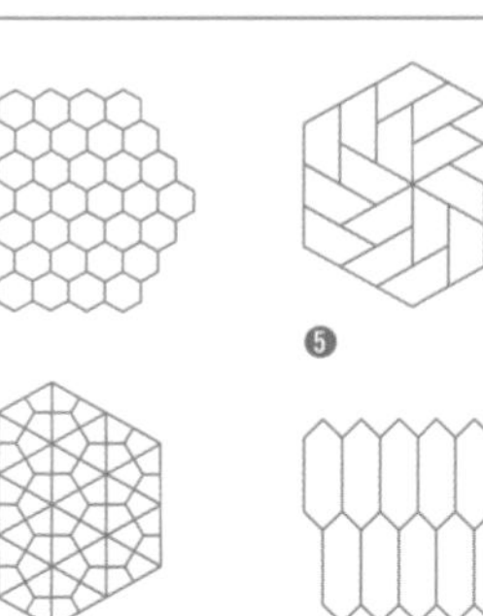

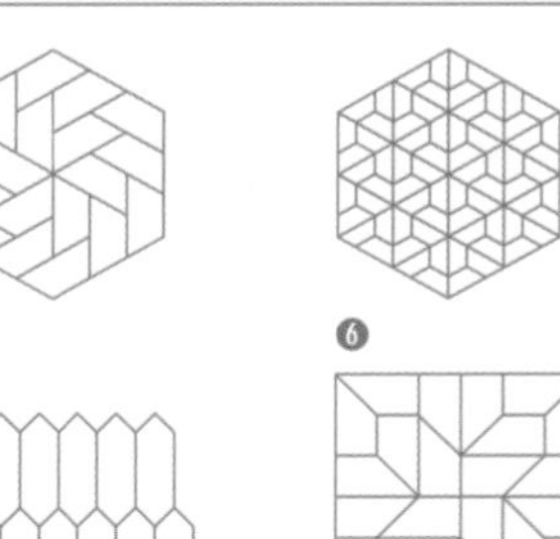

❼ ❽ ❾ ❿ ⓫ ⓬

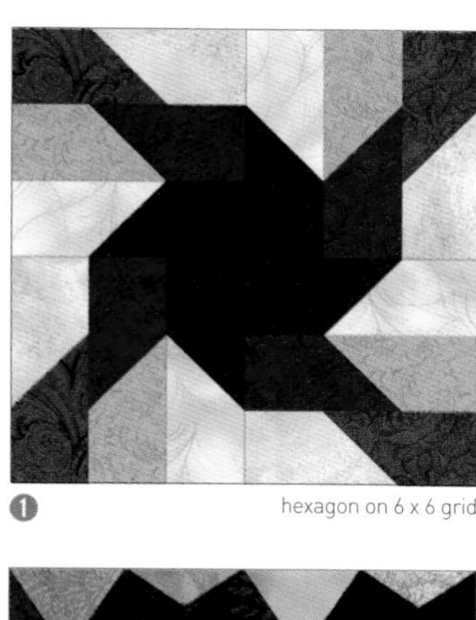

1 hexagon on 6 x 6 grid

2 one-patch design

3 one-patch design

4 one-patch design on 12 x 12 grid

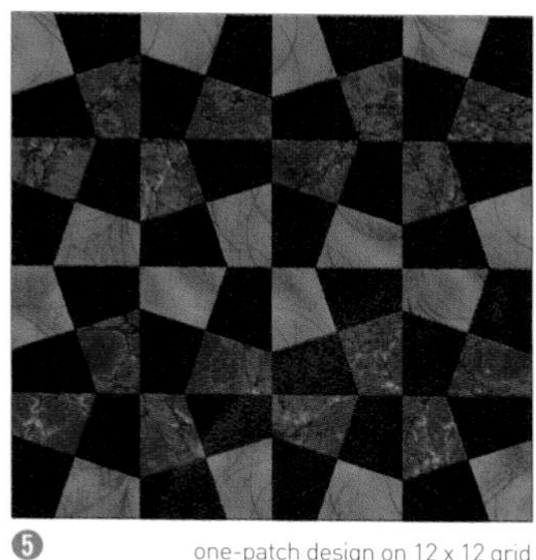

5 one-patch design on 12 x 12 grid

6 one-patch design on 6 x6 grid (curves)

7 one-patch design (curves)

8 one-patch design (curves)

9 one-patch design (curves)

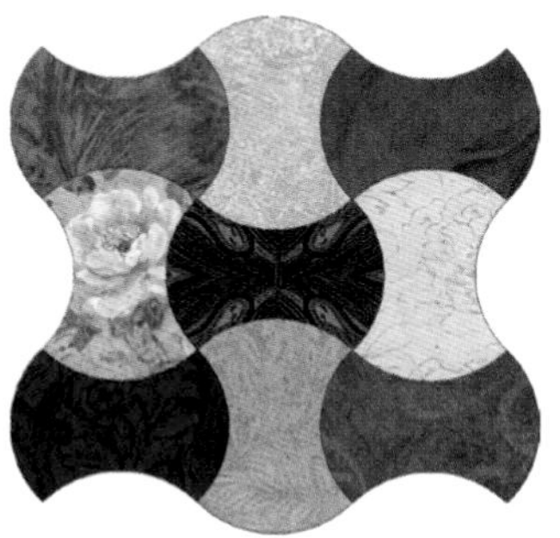

10 one-patch design on 3 x 3 grid (curves)

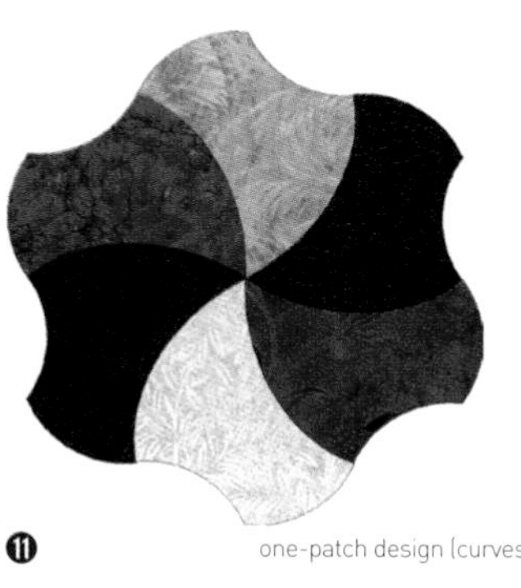

11 one-patch design (curves)

12 one-patch design on 8 x 8 grid (curves)

1 Amulet, Jinny Beyer, Hilton Head Seminar design, 1998.

2 The Picket Fence, *Kansas City Star,* Jan 6, 1954.

3 The Tumbler, *Ladies Art Company,* 1897. Also known as:

- **Flower Pot,** *Grandma Dexter Appliqué and Patchwork Designs, Book 36a,* ca. 1932.
- **Tumbler,** *Farm Journal Quilt Patterns,* ca. 1935.
- **Tumbler Block,** Nancy Cabot, *Chicago Tribune,* Feb 25, 1938.

4 Bat Wings, Nancy Cabot, *Chicago Tribune,* Jun 25, 1937.

5 Broken Rainbows, Nancy Cabot, *Chicago Tribune,* May 29, 1937.

6 Shell Chain, *Ladies Art Company,* 1897. Also known as:

- **Clam Shell,** Finley, 1929.
- **Clam Shells,** Eveline Foland, *Kansas City Star,* Oct 29, 1932.
- **The Clam Shell Quilt,** Home Art Studios, *Cincinnati Enquirer,* Mar 3, 1933.
- **The Shell,** *Q Book 130, Keepsake Quilts,* ca. 1990.
- **Shell Quilting,** Nancy Page, *Birmingham News,* Dec 9, 1941.

7 Sea Shells, *Grandmother's Patchwork Quilt Designs, Book 20,* 1931. Also known as:

- **Sea Shells on the Beach,** *Kansas City Star,* Jun 24, 1953.

8 Shell Chain, ca. 1938, per Havig.

9 Clamshell, *Quilts Heirlooms of Tomorrow,* ca. 1935.

10 The Friendship Quilt, Eveline Foland, *Kansas City Star,* Nov 15, 1930. Also known as:

- **Apple Core,** source unknown, date unknown.
- **Always Friends,** Jinny Beyer, Beyer, Jinny, *The Scrap Look,* 1985.
- **Badge of Friendship,** Jinny Beyer, Beyer, Jinny, *The Scrap Look,* 1985.
- **Charm Quilt,** *Kansas City Star,* Dec 30, 1933
- **Friendship Quilt,** Hall, 1935.
- **Mother's Oddity,** Jinny Beyer, Beyer, Jinny, *The Scrap Look,* 1985.
- **Jigsaw,** Jinny Beyer, Beyer, Jinny, *The Scrap Look,* 1985.
- **Spools,** Hinson, 1973.

11 Sea Charm, Jinny Beyer, Hilton Head Seminar design, 1998.

12 The Quilter's Fan, *Kansas City Star,* Aug 28, 1940.

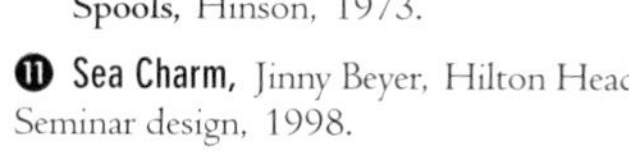

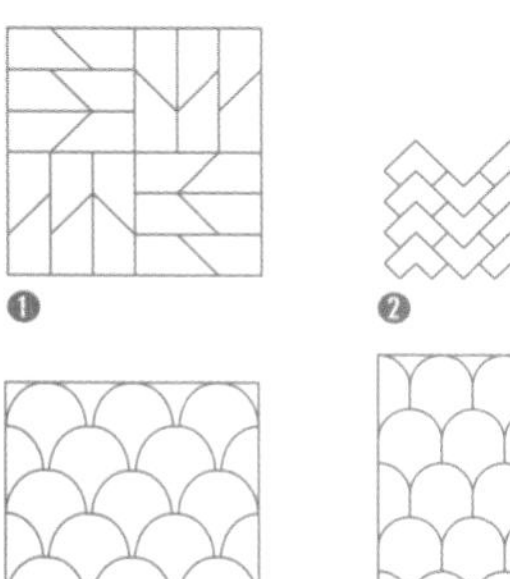

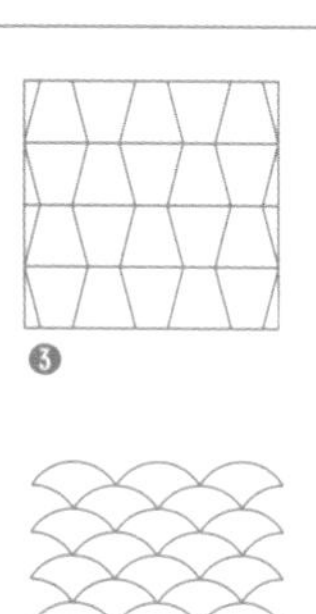

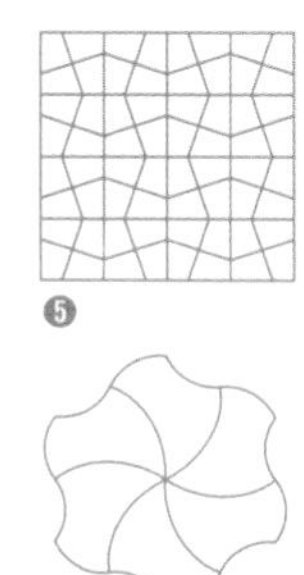

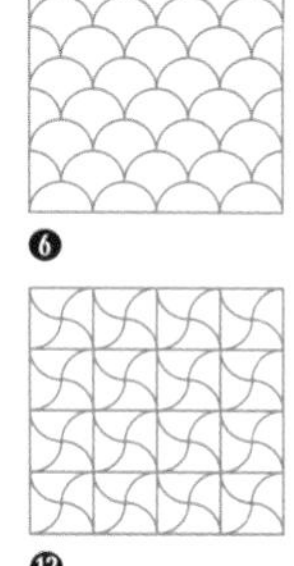

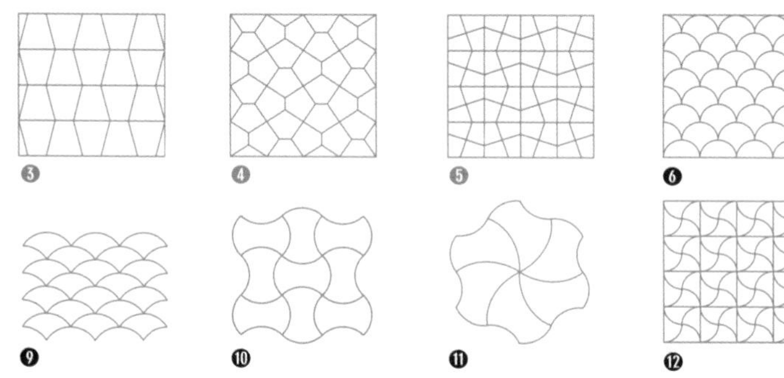

1 2 3 4 5 6

7 8 9 10 11 12

Autumn Splendor, Jinny Beyer, 2009

PART 6

Miscellaneous Blocks

"[This quilt] is an outburst of joy. . . . At the sight of it, every face brightens. How can . . . mere pieces of cloth sewed together have this power to lift the human spirit? No one can explain this; it is the mystery of art."

ROSE WILDER LANE, *THE WOMAN'S DAY BOOK OF AMERICAN NEEDLEWORK*, 1964

Additional Categories

Includes ● pentagon grid, ● 7-pointed star grid, ● non-symmetrical patterns, and ● non-symmetrical patterns (with curves)

1. **Evening Star,** *The Patchwork Book,* 1932.
2. **Five Pointed Star,** *Ladies Art Company,* 1897.
3. **Star in a Square,** *Kansas City Star,* Mar 21, 1951.
4. **Eastern Star,** Nancy Cabot, *Chicago Tribune,* Mar 15, 1935. Also known as:
   Five Pointed Star, Ickis, 1949.
5. **Star of the West,** Ickis, 1949.
6. **Union Star,** *Ladies Art Company,* 1897.
7. **Star of the West,** *Ladies Art Company,* 1897.
8. **The Twentieth Century Star,** Clara Stone, *Practical Needlework,* ca. 1906.
9. **Star of the West,** Hall, 1935. Also known as:
   Union Star, Hall, 1935.

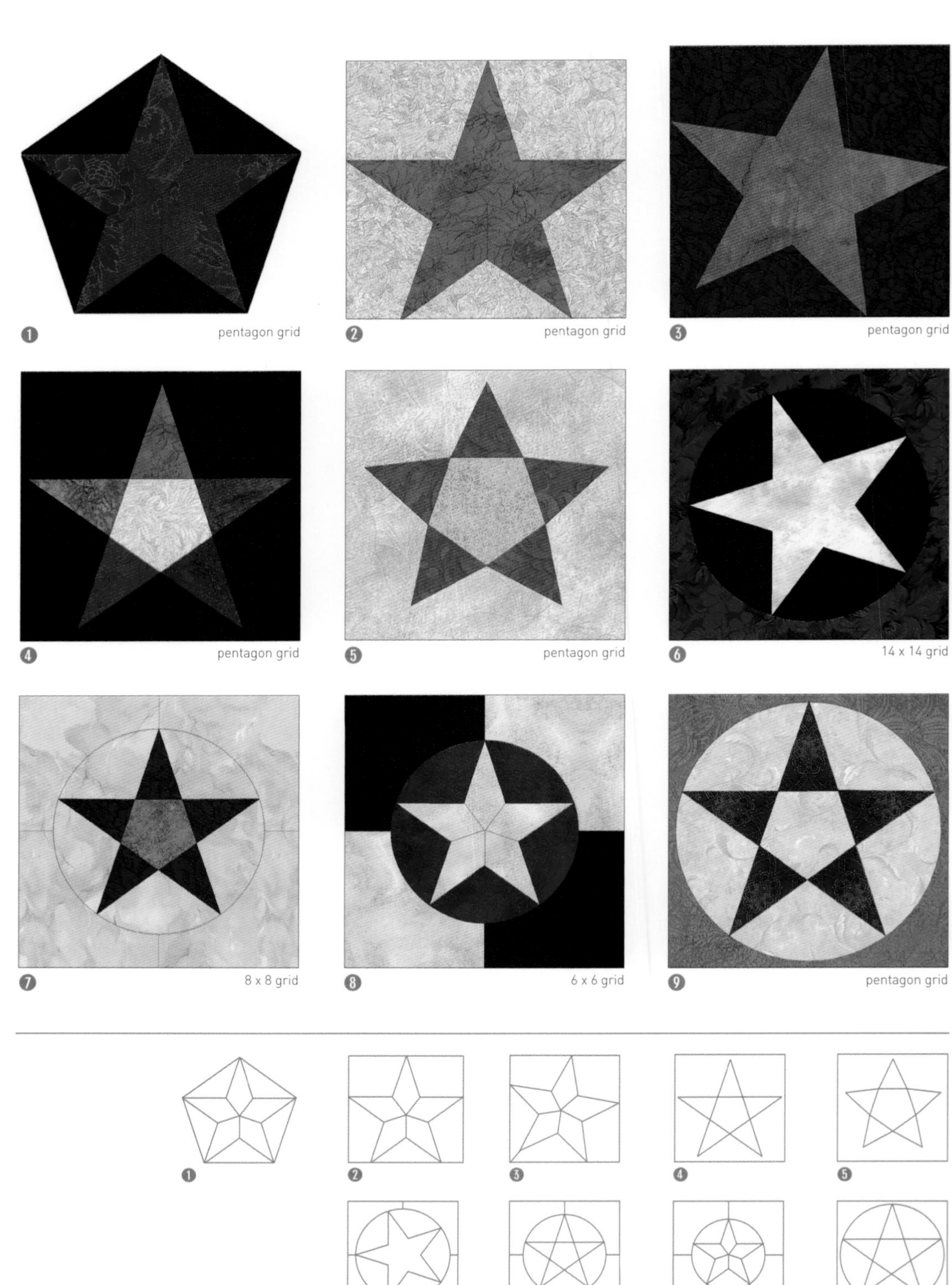

1 pentagon grid

2 pentagon grid

3 pentagon grid

4 pentagon grid

5 pentagon grid

6 pentagon grid

7 pentagon grid

8 pentagon grid

9 7-pointed star grid

10 7-pointed star grid

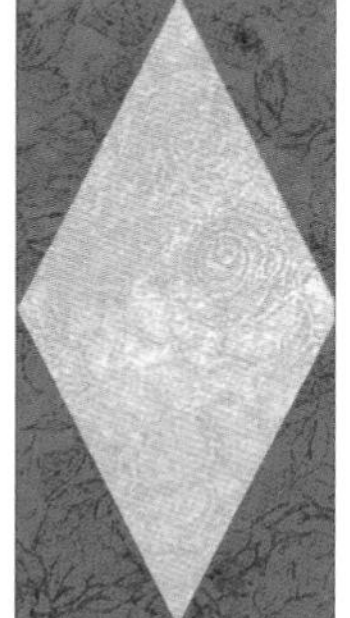
11 non-symmetrical design on 2 x 4 grid

12 non-symmetrical design on 3 x 4 grid

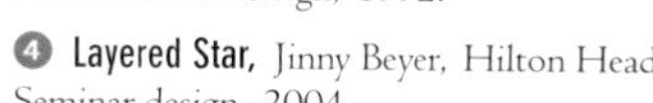

1. **Morning Star,** Jinny Beyer, Hilton Head Seminar design, 1992.
2. **Star upon Star,** Ickis, 1949.
3. **Exploration Point,** Jinny Beyer, Hilton Head Seminar design, 1992.
4. **Layered Star,** Jinny Beyer, Hilton Head Seminar design, 2004.
5. **Venetian Star,** Jinny Beyer, Hilton Head Seminar design, 2003.
6. **Starburst,** Jinny Beyer, Hilton Head Seminar design, 2003.
7. **Cob Web,** Jinny Beyer, Hilton Head Seminar design, 2004.
8. **Pine Cone,** Jinny Beyer, Jinny Beyer Studio design, 2004.
9. **Summer Rays,** Jinny Beyer, Hilton Head Seminar design, 2007.
10. **Autumn Splendor,** Jinny Beyer, Hilton Head Seminar design, 2007.
11. **A Friendship Block in Diamonds,** *Kansas City Star,* Sep 24, 1958.
12. **Salute to Loyalty,** *Kansas City Star,* Apr 7, 1943.

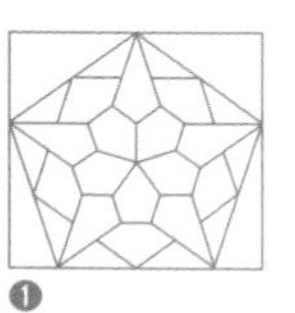
1

2

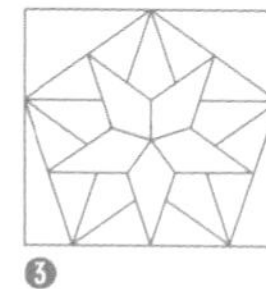
3

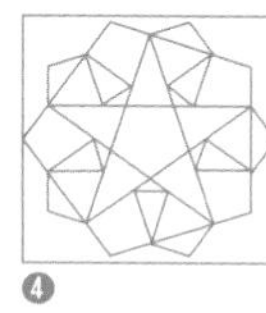
4

5

6

7

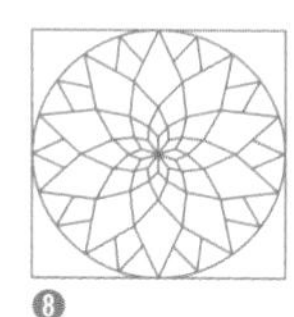
8

9

10

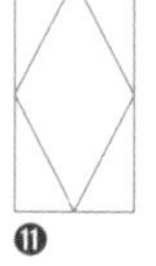
11

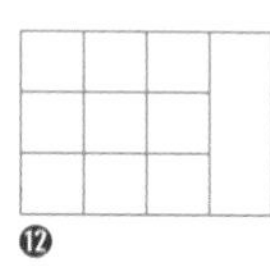
12

❶ **Hour Glass in a New Picture,** *Kansas City Star,* Aug 20, 1958.

❷ **Jerico (sic) Walls,** *Kansas City Star,* Dec 2, 1942.

❸ **Brickwork Block,** Nancy Cabot, *Chicago Tribune,* May 6, 1935.

❹ **Bat's Wings,** *Ladies Art Company,* 1897.

❺ **Bats' Wings,** Nancy Cabot, *Chicago Tribune,* May 8, 1934.
"Individual in shape, the 'Bats' Wings' block is one of the loveliest in existence. The completed rectangle is 8 by 10 inches, and the coverlet has pieced and plain blocks so alternated as to form a most unusual design." Nancy Cabot, *Chicago Tribune,* May 8, 1934

❻ **The Envelope Quilt,** *Kansas City Star,* Sep 20, 1944.

❼ **The White Cross,** *Kansas City Star,* Aug 14, 1946.

❽ **An Irish Chain Hint,** *Kansas City Star,* Aug 31, 1955.

❾ **A Butterfly in Angles,** *Kansas City Star,* Feb 2, 1944.

❿ **Star Fish,** Hall, ca. 1938. See 410-2.

⓫ **Dove in the Window,** ca. 1938, per Havig.

⓬ **Sylvia's Bow,** *Kansas City Star,* Dec 20, 1939.

❶ non-symmetrical design on 3 x 4 grid

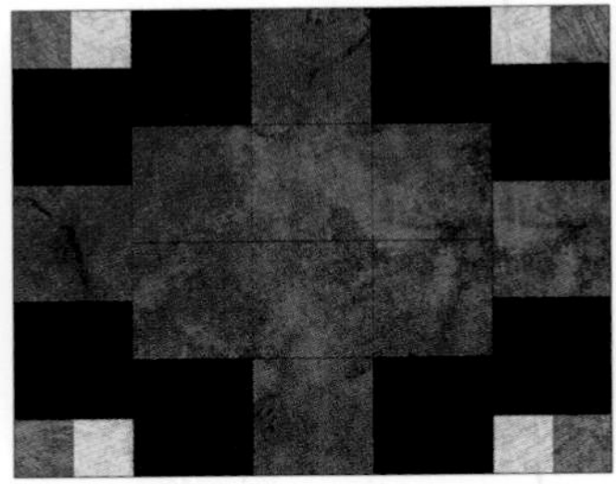

❷ non-symmetrical design on 16 x 20 grid

❸ non-symmetrical design on 13 x 14 grid

❹ non-symmetrical design on 8 x 10 grid

❺ non-symmetrical design on 8 x 10 grid

❻ non-symmetrical design on 15 x 22 grid

❼ non-symmetrical design on 27 x 38 grid

❽ non-symmetrical design on 7 x 13 grid

❾ non-symmetrical design on 6 x 8 grid

❿ non-symmetrical design on 15 x 20 grid

⓫ non-symmetrical design on 18 x 20 grid

⓬ non-symmetrical design on 13 x 10 grid

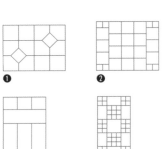

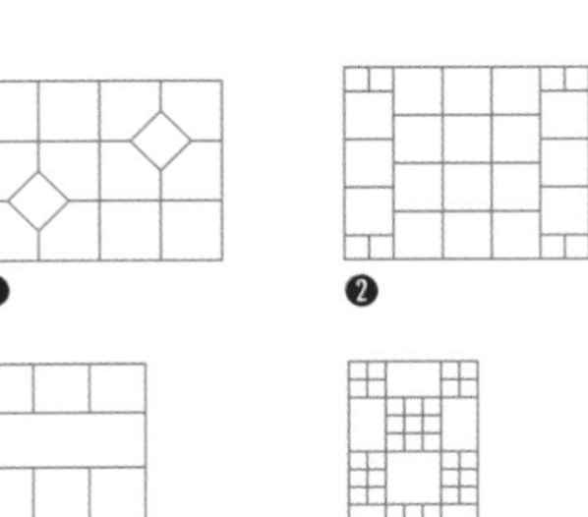

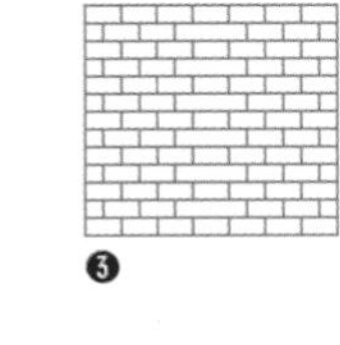

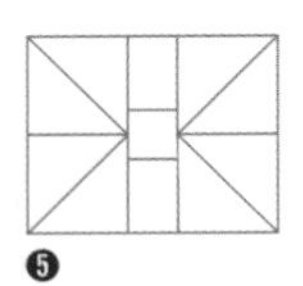

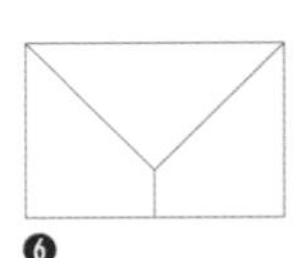

❶ ❷ ❸ ❹ ❺ ❻

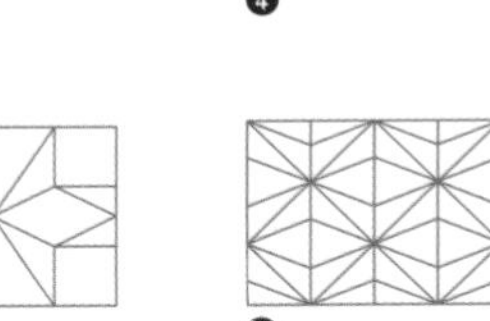

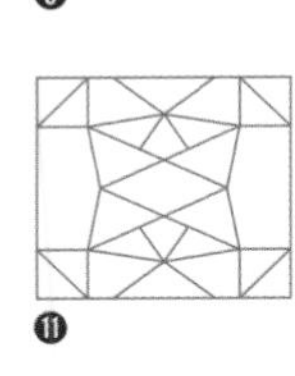

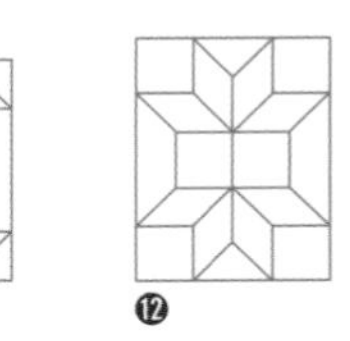

❼ ❽ ❾ ❿ ⓫ ⓬

1 non-symmetrical design on 20 x 28 grid

2 non-symmetrical design on 6 x 18 grid

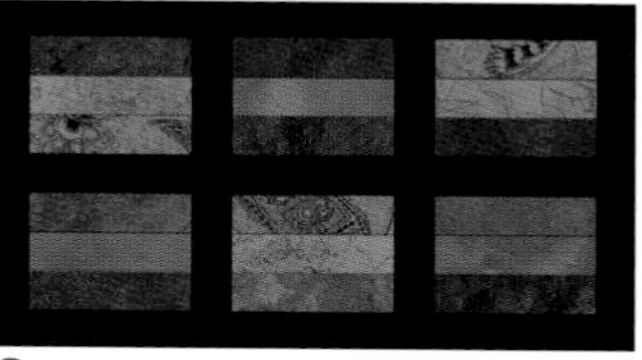

3 non-symmetrical design on 9 x 16 grid

4 non-symmetrical design on 16 x 18 grid

5 non-symmetrical design on 16 x 23 grid

6 non-symmetrical design on 24 x 28 grid

7 non-symmetrical design on 24 x 36 grid

8 non-symmetrical design on 26 x 32 grid

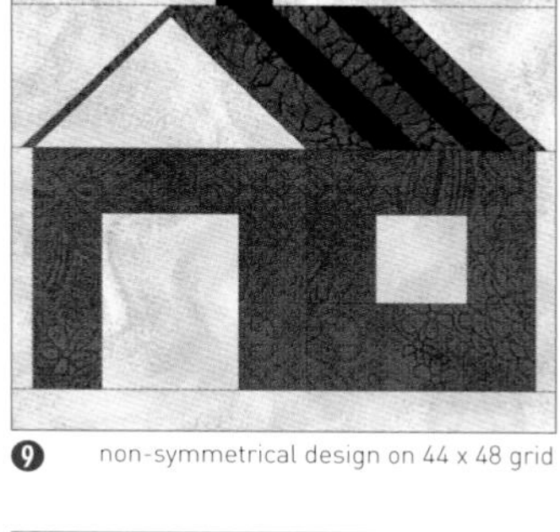

9 non-symmetrical design on 44 x 48 grid

10 non-symmetrical design on 59 x 64 grid

11 non-symmetrical design on 32 x 44 grid

12 non-symmetrical design on 18 x 27 grid

13 non-symmetrical design on 10 x 11 grid

1 **The Flowing Ribbon,** *Kansas City Star,* Apr 22, 1933.

2 **Blue Eagle,** Nancy Cabot, *Chicago Tribune,* Oct 8, 1933.
"The high spots of our country's history have always been commemorated in quilt designs. 'The Blue Eagle' is an original, 1933 contribution to the historical quilt album." Nancy Cabot, *Chicago Tribune,* Oct 8, 1933

3 **Roman Square,** Finley, 1929.

4 **The Goose Track,** *Kansas City Star,* Oct 25, 1944.

5 **Tree of Paradise,** *Farm Journal Quilt Patterns,* ca. 1935.

6 **Snowflake,** *The Patchwork Book,* 1932.

7 **Cranberry Patch,** Nancy Cabot, *Chicago Tribune,* Dec 24, 1935.
"Today is an especially good day to present this old quilt block, 'Cranberry Patch,' because it proves to be a gentle reminder of that commodity essential to the complete success of that big Christmas dinner in process of preparation." Nancy Cabot, *Chicago Tribune,* Dec 24, 1935

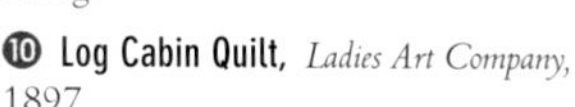

8 **Little Red Schoolhouse,** Aunt Martha series: *Bold and Beautiful Quilts,* ca. 1977.

9 **Early Colonial Cottage,** ca. 1938, per Havig.

10 **Log Cabin Quilt,** *Ladies Art Company,* 1897.

11 **Honeymoon Cottage,** Hall, 1935.

12 **Village Church,** ca. 1938, per Havig.

13 **Victory Quilt,** *Kansas City Star,* Apr 22, 1942.

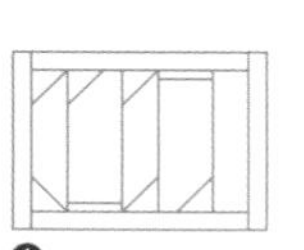

1

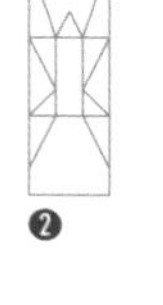

2

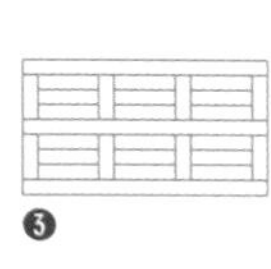

3

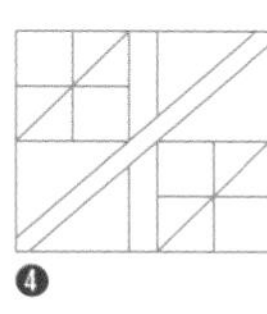

4

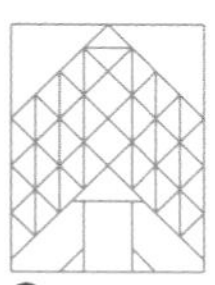

5

6

7

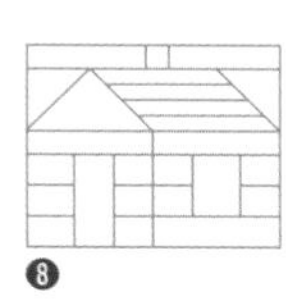

8

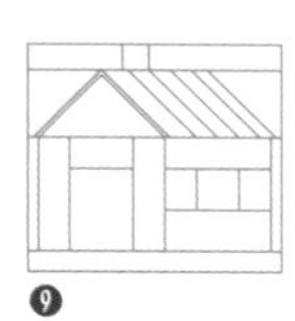

9

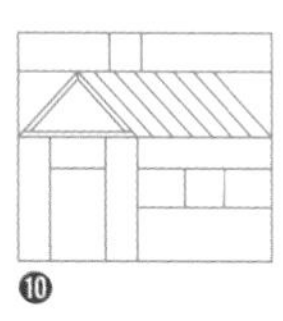

10

11

12

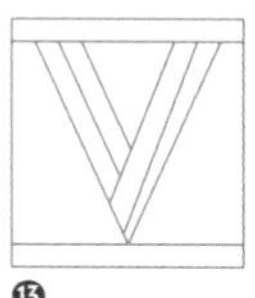

13

❶ **Soldier Boy,** *Kansas City Star,* Aug 2, 1944. Also known as:
The Soldier Boy, *Kansas City Star,* Jun 6, 1951
Soldier at the Window, *Kansas City Star,* Jul 10, 1957.

❷ **Oklahoma Bloomer,** *Ladies Art Company,* 1897.

❸ **The Dog Quilt,** *Kansas City Star,* May 2, 1936. Also known as:
A Scottie Quilt for Boys, *Kansas City Star,* Jun 28, 1950.

❹ **Giddap,** Eveline Foland, *Kansas City Star,* Jul 18, 1931. Also known as:
Democrat Donkey, Hall, 1935.

❺ **Elephant Ararat,** Eveline Foland, *Kansas City Star,* Jun 6, 1931. Also known as:
Ararat, Eveline Foland, *Kansas City Star,* Jun 6, 1931.

"Little did Ararat, slow old elephant that he is, ever think he would find himself gracing a quilt block when he came to live in the Swope Park zoo, there to become enthroned in the hearts of Kansas City children." *Kansas City Star,* Jun 6, 1931

❻ **Tea Leaf,** Hall, 1935.

❼ **Oriental Tulip,** Nancy Cabot, *Chicago Tribune,* Aug 20, 1933.

❽ **Tulip,** McKim, 1931. Also known as:
Modernistic Tulip, Hall, 1935.

❾ **Iris Quilt,** McKim, 1931. Also known as:
Modernistic Iris, Hall, 1935.

❿ **Modernistic California Poppy,** Hall, 1935.

⓫ **Japanese Lantern,** Hall, 1935. See 324-3 and 339-4.

⓬ **Rainbow,** Hall, 1935.

⓭ **Rainbow,** *Ladies Art Company,* 1897.

❶ non-symmetrical design on 6 x 15 grid (curves)

❷ non-symmetrical design on 18 x 20 grid (curves)

❸ non-symmetrical design on 10 x 13 grid (curves)

❹ non-symmetrical design on 13 x 15 grid (curves)

❺ non-symmetrical design on 11 x 14 grid (curves)

❻ non-symmetrical design on 16 x 20 grid (curves)

❼ non-symmetrical design on 30 x 44 grid (curves)

❽ non-symmetrical design on 6 x 10 grid (curves)

❾ non-symmetrical design on 32 x 40 grid (curves)

❿ non-symmetrical design on 24 x 32 grid (curves)

⓫ non-symmetrical design on 20 x 24 grid (curves)

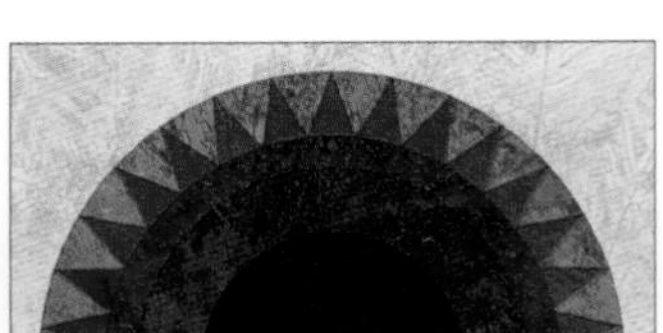
⓬ non-symmetrical design on 10 x 20 grid (curves)

⓭ non-symmetrical design on 16 x 30 grid (curves)

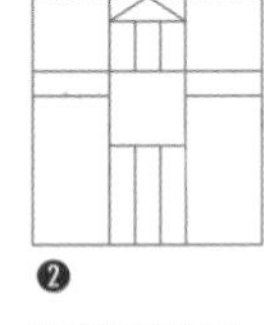
❶

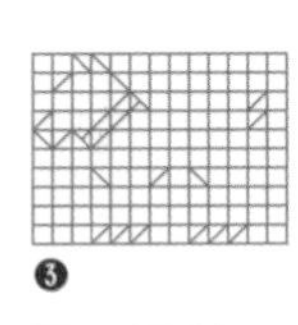
❷

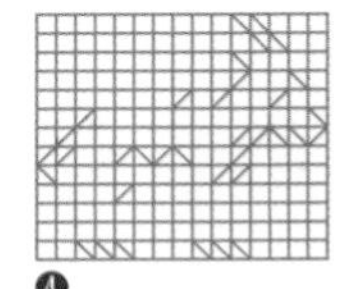
❸

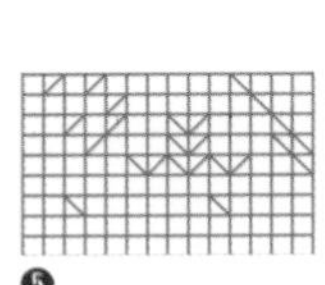
❹

❺

❻

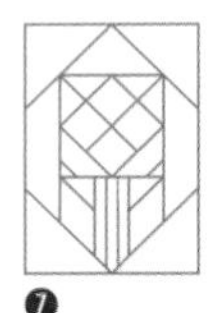
❼

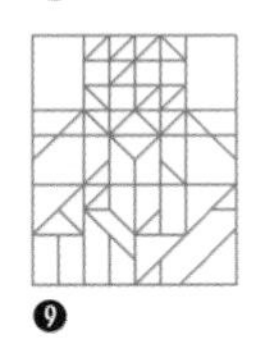
❽

❾

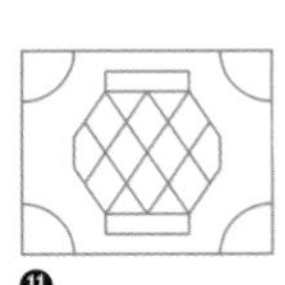
❿

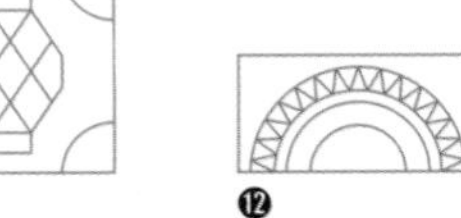
⓫

⓬

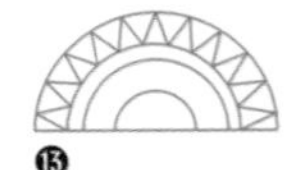
⓭

Bibliography

Block Sources

The primary bibliographic sources listed here are the earliest references I could find for publication of each block.

15 Quilts for Today's Living, Quilt Book 3, Graphic Enterprises, Inc., New York, 1968. One of several vintage booklets published by Graphic Enterprises, Inc. during the 1950s and '60s. According to notes by quilt researcher Cuesta Benberry, these pamphlets were published from 1968 to 1980 or later. Graphic Enterprises, Inc. also published the Laura Wheeler and Alice Brooks patterns (see page 8). See also Graphic Enterprises, Inc.

Alan, Jane, *Quilt Designs: A Rare Collection of Historical Interest,* John Dille Co., Chicago, 1933. A vintage pamphlet of quilt designs.

Alboum, Rose Lea, *American Legacy Quilt Index Series..* An ongoing series of quilt indexes compiled by quilt block researcher Alboum. Available are individual booklets of hand-drawn illustrations of patterns from most of the major newspaper, pattern, or catalog sources from the late 1800s to the 1970s.

Alice Brooks Collection of Needlecraft Masterpieces, Vintage pamphlet attributed to Alice Brooks, publisher unknown, ca. 1958. See also Graphic Enterprises, Inc.

Alice Brooks Designs, Graphic Enterprises, Inc, New York, date unknown. One of several vintage pattern booklets books published by Graphic Enterprises, Inc., during the 1960s and through to the 1980s. See also Graphic Enterprises, Inc.

American Heritage Quilt Book, Graphic Enterprises, Inc., New York, date unknown. One of several vintage books published by Graphic Enterprises, Inc., during the 1960s and through to the 1980s. See also Graphic Enterprises, Inc.

American Woman, The. Incomplete bibliographic information on the March 1902 issue of this publication came from photocopies of three unidentified clippings sent to me by quilt researcher Cuesta Benberry.

Americana Designs Quilts, Studio Publications, Inc., ca. 1954. Incomplete information on this publication came from an unsourced, undated quilt pamphlet.

Anne Cabot's Album, ca. 1952. This is possibly a later edition of *Anne Cabot's Fall and Winter Album* (see below). The front of the pamphlet reads: "Address all orders to: Grit, Williamsport, PA, All patterns 20c each."

Anne Cabot's Fall and Winter Album, ca. 1950. Incomplete information on this publication came from an unsourced, undated quilt pamphlet. The front of the pamphlet reads: "Address all orders to Mrs. Anne Cabot, Lancaster New Era, 106 Seventh Ave., New York 11, N.Y., Price of pattern 10c each, plus 1c postage for each pattern ordered."

Antique Quilts, McCall's Needlework & Crafts, New York, 1974.

Aunt Martha series. The name "Aunt Martha" appears on a series of vintage booklets published by Colonial Pattern Company, Inc., of Kansas, Missouri, between 1933 and 1977. This company is still in existence today (see also Colonial Patterns, Inc.). Several blocks are sourced to the booklets listed below. A more complete list is provided in the list of Secondary Sources on page 445.

Aunt Martha's Favorite Quilts, ca. 1953.

Aunt Martha's Workbasket, ca. 1933.

*Bold and Beautiful Quilts,*1977.

Easy Quilts, ca. 1958.

Quilt Designs: Old Favorites and New, ca. 1952.

Quilts, ca. 1963.

Quilts: Heirlooms of Tomorrow, 1977.

The Quilt Fair Comes to You, ca. 1933.

Patchwork Simplicity, 1977.

Bacon, Lenice Ingram, *American Patchwork Quilts,*William Morrow & Company, Inc, New York, New York, 1973.

Beyer, Alice, *Quilting,* South Park Commissioners, Chicago, Illinois, 1934.

Beyer Jinny, *Mystery Quilt Guide,* Breckling Press, Elmhurst (Chicago), Illinois, 1994.

Beyer, Jinny, *Patchwork Patterns,* EPM Publications, McLean, Virginia, 1979.

Beyer, Jinny, *Patchwork Portfolio,* EPM Publications, McLean, Virginia, 1989.

Beyer, Jinny, *The Quilter's Album of Blocks and Borders,* EPM Publications, McLean, Virginia.

Beyer, Jinny, *Quiltmaking by Hand,* Breckling Press, Elmhurst (Chicago), Illinois, 2004.

Beyer, Jinny, *The Scrap Look,* EPM Publications, McLean, Virginia, 1985.

Beyer, Jinny, *Soft-Edge Piecing,* C&T Publishing, Concord, California, 1995.

Birmingham News. Daily newspaper, Birmingham, Alabama.

Bismarck Tribune. Daily newspaper, Bismarck, North Dakota.

Blue Ribbon Patterns, Vol. 2, Tower Press, Cleveland, Ohio, 1970.

Brackman, Barbara, *The Encyclopedia of Pieced Quilt Patterns,* American Quilters Society, Peducah, Kentucky, 1993.

Capper's Weekly. Magazine published by Ogden Publications, Inc., Topeka, Kansas.

Chicago Tribune. Daily newspaper, Chicago, Illinois.

Chunn, Connie. See www.ladiesartcompany.com/index.htm. Chunn is a quilt researcher who has spent several years researching Ladies Art Company.

Cincinnati Enquirer. Daily newspaper, Cincinnati, Ohio.

Colonial Patterns, Inc. This is the current name of the company that is best known for its Aunt Martha's series of patterns, pamphlets, and quilt kits. According to the current owner Edward C. Price II, the original name was Colonial Company, founded by John E. Tillotson and his wife, Clara. In the late 1920s or early 1930s, the company began selling quilt patterns and kits and eventually attached the Aunt Martha byline to the patterns. Mrs. Tillotson created all the original Aunt Martha art. In October 1935 the Tillotsons launched *Workbasket* magazine which grew to be the largest circulation magazine in the needlework field. The Tillotsons later launched *Flower and Garden* and *Workbench.* All three magazines were published by their company, Modern Handcraft, Inc. The Colonial Company was sold in 1948 to Clifford and Alma Swenson, who changed the name to Aunt Martha's Studios, Inc. That name remained until April 1, 1974, when the company sold to Edward C. Price II, who changed to the current name, Colonial Patterns, Inc. Mr. Price still owns the company and continues to sell the Aunt Martha booklets and other embroidery and needlecraft patterns bearing the Aunt Martha name. (The information here was provided by quilt historian Wilene Smith, and supplemented by an interview with Edward C. Price II, the current owner of Colonial Patterns, Inc. Also helpful was the obituary of John E. Tillotson, founder of the company, in the *Kansas City Star* in late September 1999.)

Colonial Quilts, Home Art Studios, Des Moines, Iowa. Founded by Hubert Ver Mehren, Home Art Studios sold quilt patterns and catalogs, including this one and *Hope Winslow's Quilt Book.* Ver Mehren's designs advertising the patterns appeared in many periodicals in the early 1930s. See also page 7.

Columbus Evening Dispatch Daily newspaper, Columbus, Ohio.

Comfort. Vintage magazine published in the 1930s by Gannett Publishing Company, Augusta, Maine.

Country Gentleman, The, Curtis Publishing Company, Philadelphia, Pennsylvania. Vintage magazine established in 1890s.

Dakota Farmer. A newspaper founded in 1881 in Alexandria, South Dakota (now Hanson County, South Dakota). The paper moved in 1883 to Aberdeen, South Carolina. During the late 1920s it featured a quilt column to which readers would submit designs. In 1979 the publication was purchased by Webb Publishing, St. Paul, Minnesota.

Dayton News. Daily newspaper, Dayton, Ohio.

Des Moines Register. Daily newspaper, Des Moines, Iowa.

Detroit Free Press. Daily newspaper, Detroit, Michigan.

Detroit News. Daily newspaper, Detroit, Michigan.

Eight Star Quilt Designs for Piecework Quilts, ed. Sallie Hill, *Progressive Farmer,* Birmingham, Alabama, ca. 1935. See also *One Dozen Quilt Patterns.* and *Ten Piecework Quilts for Southern Homes.*

Evening Independent, Daily newspaper, Massillon, Ohio.

Farm & Fireside, The. A semi-monthly farming magazine published between 1878 and 1939 by Crowell-Collier Publishing Co., Springfield, Ohio.

Farm and Home. Semi-monthly newspaper from the 1890s, published by Phelps Publishing Company, Springfield, Massachusetts.

Farm Journal and Farmers Wife: Quilt Patterns Old and New. The patterns sourced to this vintage publication originated from two separate periodicals, one named *Farmer's Wife* and the other *Farm Journal. Farmers Wife* was published by Webb Publishing Co., St. Paul, Minnesota; *Farm Journal* had an address in Philadelphia, Pennsylvania. Some time between 1935 and 1941, the two publications merged to become *Farm Journal and Farmer's Wife.* Both magazines offered quilt patterns at one time or other. I have sourced several blocks to the following specific issues or named publications. According to Barbara Brackman, *Farm Journal* was established in March 1877 and later absorbed at least three other pattern sources (*Country Gentleman, The Farmers Wife* and *Household Journal*). In the twentieth century, the periodicals offered mail order patterns and booklets. Some of the patterns are reproduced in Rachel Martens, *Modern Patchwork.* Several publications I researched for this book are listed below.

The Farm Journal Quilt Patterns, The Farm Journal, Philadelphia, Pennsylvania, ca. 1935,

Farm Journal and Farmer's Wife: Quilt Patterns Old and New, Philadelphia, Pennsylvania, ca. 1941

Farm Journal and Farmer's Wife: Quilt Patterns Old and New (Silver Anniversary issue), Philadelphia, Pennsylvania, 1945.

Farm Journal and Farmer's Wife Quilt Patterns, Philadelphia, Pennsylvania, ca. 1957.

The Farmer's Wife Book of New Designs and Patterns, Book No. 3, The, (also titled *The Farmer's Wife New Book of Quilts—No. III With Complete Pattern Instructions*), Webb Publishing Co, St. Paul, Minnesota, 1934.

Quilt Blocks from the Farmer's Wife: Farmer's Wife New Book of Quilts, The Farmer's Wife, Webb Publishing Co, St. Paul, Minnesota, 1932.

Quilts: The Farmer's Wife Book of Quilts with Complete Patterns and Instructions for Making Them, The Farmer's Wife, Webb Publishing Co, St. Paul, Minnesota, 1931.

Farmer's Advocate, The,. I found this periodical referenced on an otherwise unidentified newspaper clipping, with no further publication information. I came across a periodical with the same name, published by Dawson and Bro, City of London, Canada West, between 1866 and 1965. However, I have no way of knowing if the clipping came from this periodical or another by the same name.

Finley, Ruth E., *Old Patchwork Quilts and the Women Who Made Them,* Charles T. Branford Co., Newton Center, Massachusetts, 1929. Reprinted by Howell Press, 1992.

*Frank Leslie's Modewelt,*1871. While I was unable to track down detailed publication information on this book, my research shows that Frank Leslie was a pseudonym for Henry Carter, a newspaper illustrator born in England in 1821. Carter came to New York in 1848 and began his own illustrated publication, *Illustrated Newspaper.* It was the first periodical to successfully bring pictures and news together in the same publication.

Fremont News Messenger. Daily newspaper, Fremont, Ohio.

Godey's Lady's Book, A popular magazine published by Louis A. Godey in Philadelphia, Pennsylvania, from 1830 to 1878.

Goodman, Liz, ed., *All About Patchwork: Golden Hands Special, #10,* Marshall Cavendish Publications, New York,1973.

Grandma Dexter publications: Virginia Snow Studios was a name associated with the Collingbourne Mills thread company of Elgin, Illinois. As early as 1913 the name Virginia Snow Studios began appearing on instruction booklets for embroidery, crocheting, and knitting, printed by the company to help promote its threads. In 1927, after Collingbourne purchased the Dexter Yarn Company of Rhode Island, the name "Grandma Dexter" was printed on the booklets, too. In the early 1930s a series of quilt pattern catalogs was printed and sold under the Grandma Dexter/Virginia Snow name. Among them are:

Grandma Dexter Quilt Patches and Blocks, 1932.

Quilt Blocks from Grandma Dexter, ca. 1932.

Grandma Dexter Applique and Patchwork Designs, Book 36a, ca. 1932.

Grandma Dexter New Applique and Patchwork Designs, Book 36b, ca 1932.

Grandmother Clark publications: W.L.M. Clark, Inc., of St. Louis, Missouri, published a series of booklets titled *Clark's Series of Art Needlework Books.* Book 21 lists 21 of these booklets, covering topics such as crochet, tatting, knitting, rag rugs, transfer designs for appliqué, cross-stitch, and embroidery. Some of the quilt booklets I referenced include:

Grandmother Clark's Authentic Early American Patchwork Quilts, Book No. 23, 1932.

Grandmother Clark's Patchwork Quilt Designs, From Books 20-21-23 and Quilting Patterns from Book 22, 1932.

*Grandmother Clark's Patchwork Quilts, Book No. 19,*1932.

Grandmother Clark's Old Fashioned Quilt Designs, Book No. 21, 1931.

Grandmother's Patchwork Quilt Designs, Book 20, 1931.

Graphic Enterprises, Inc. According to quilt researcher Cuesta Benberry, Graphic Enterprises Inc. was a mail-order pattern syndicate based in New York, also variously known as Needlecraft Service, Inc, and Old Chelsea Station, New York. It was best known for its quilt features dating from the 1930s which included distribution of patterns by Laura Wheeler and Alice Brooks (see page 9). Its services were advertised in newspapers nationwide and also in various magazines. The company published at first a semi-annual catalog from which various patterns could be ordered. Later on, the catalog was published annually. Always a general needlework resource, the company offered patterns for dressmaking, knitting, crochet, tatting, and embroidery, as well as quilting. Grit Patterns may also have been connection with this company. According to Cuesta Benberry, the pamphlets include two of my primary sources (listed here), as well as several others listed under Secondary Bibliographic Sources.

15 Quilts for Today's Living Quilt Book 3, 1968.

Museum Quilts, Book 2 #102, date unknown.

Grit Patterns. Vintage mail-order sewing pattern company. See also Graphic Enterprises, Inc.

Gutcheon, Beth, *The Perfect Patchwork Primer,* David McKay Co., Inc., New York, New York, 1973.

Gutcheon, Beth, and Gutcheon, Jeffrey, *The Quilt Design Workbook,* David McKay Co., New York, New York, 1976.

Hall, Carrie A. and Rose G. Kretsinger, *The Romance of the Patchwork Quilt in America,*The Caxton Printers, Caldwell, Ohio, 1935.

Happy Hours, publisher and date unknown. Vintage periodical referenced by Wilene Smith in *Uncoverings,* ed. Laurel Horton, American Quilt Study Group, Lincoln, Nebraska, 1990. See also Wilene Smith.

Havig, Bettina, *Carrie Hall Blocks: Over 800 Historical Patterns from the College of the Spencer Museum of Art, University of Kansas,* American Quilters Society, Peducah, Kentucky, 1999.

Hearth and Home, Vickory Hill Publishing Company, Augusta, Maine, date unknown. One of several magazines published by Vickery Hill Publishing Company in the 1890s. This magazine had a needlework column that sometimes featured quilt blocks. See also Wilene Smith.

Hilton Head Seminar designs. A series of patterns distributed at Jinny Beyer's annual Hilton Head Seminar, Hilton Head Island, South Carolina, from 1981 to 2009.

Hinson, Delores A., *A Quilter's Companion,* Arco Publishing, Georgetown, Connecticut, 1973.

Holstein, Jonathan, *The Pieced Quilt, An American Design Tradition,* New York Graphic Society, Greenwich, Connecticut, 1973.

Horton, Laurel, *Uncoverings, Volume 11,* American Quilt Study Group, Lincoln, Nebraska, 1990. See also Wilene Smith.

Ickis, Marguerite, *The Standard Book of Quilt Making and Collecting,* General Publishing Company, Toronto, Ontario, 1949. Reprinted by Dover Publications, Mineola, New York.

Illinois State Register. Newspaper established in Springfield, Illinois, in 1839.

Indianapolis Star. Daily newspaper, Indianapolis, Indiana.

James, Michael, *The Quiltmaker's Handbook,* Prentice-Hall Direct, New York, New York, 1978.

Jinny Beyer Studio designs. A series of quilt patterns produced by Jinny Beyer Studio, Great Falls, Virginia.

Kansas City Star Daily and weekly newspaper, Kansas, Missouri.

Kentucky Farmers Home Journal. Newspaper, Louisville, Kentucky.

Khin, Yvonne M., *The Collector's Dictionary of Quilt Names and Patterns,* Portland House, New York, New York, 1980.

Kiracofe, Rod, and Mary Elizabeth Johnson, *The American Quilt,* Clarkson Potter, New York, New York, 1993.

Ladies Art Company. A pattern company established in 1889 in St. Louis, Missouri, that offered quilt patterns for sale through their catalogs from 1897 until the 1930s. See page 7.

Ladies' Home Journal. A vintage periodical, originally named *Ladies' Journal and Practical Housekeeper,* established in 1883.

Ladies World Magazine. A vintage periodical, established in New York in 1886 by S. H. Moore & Co. It started as a mail order magazine, published on newsprint. In 1912 it was bought by McClure Publications, New York, and was published from then onwards in magazine format.

Lansing State Journal. Newspaper, Lansing, Michigan.

Laura Wheeler Catalog. See Graphic Enterprises, Inc.

Laura Wheeler Collection of Needlecraft Masterpieces. Vintage pamphlet attributed to Laura Wheeler, ca. 1958, publisher unknown. See also Graphic Enterprises, Inc.

Lima News. Newspaper, Lima, Ohio.

Louisville Farm and Fireside. A farm journal established in 1878 in Louisville, Kentucky.

Lowell Sun. Daily newspaper, Lowell, Massachusetts.

Manitoba Free Press. Newspaper, Winnipeg, Canada.

Martens, Rachel, *Modern Patchwork,* Countryside Press, Philadelphia, Pennsylvania, 1970. See also *Farm Journal and Farmer's Wife.*

McCall's Needlework & Crafts Antique Quilts, McCall Pattern Company, New York, New York, 1974.

McCalls Quilting, CKMedia, Golden, Colorado.

McKim, Ruby Short, *101 Patchwork Patterns,* McKim Studios, Independence, Missouri, 1931. Reprinted by Dover Publications, Meneola, New York.

Miall, Agnes, *Patchwork Old and New,* The Woman's Magazine Office, London, 1937.

Michigan Farmer. The name appears on an undated newspaper clipping I came across, but I was unable to track down bibliographic information.

Minneapolis Star. Newspaper, Minneapolis, Minnesota.

Modern Priscilla, The. A vintage home, garden, needlecraft magazine published from the late 1800s to 1930. The magazine was founded in Lynn, Massachusetts by The Priscilla Company, and moved to Boston in 1894.

Modesto Bee. Newspaper, Modesto, California.

Morning Herald. Daily newspaper, Uniontown, Pennsylvania.

Mountain Mist Blue Book of Quilts, The. A pattern collection that began in 1929 and was published intermittently in volume form by Stearns Technical Textiles Co., Cincinnati, Ohio.

Museum Quilts, Quilt Book 2, Graphic Enterprises, Inc., New York, undated. One of several vintage books published by Graphic Enterprises, Inc., during the 1950s and '60s. See also Graphic Enterprises, Inc.

Mrs. Danner publications: A series of booklets originally published by Scioto Imhoff Danner in El Dorado, Kansas, between 1930 and 1970. Some were reprinted by Helen M. Ericson, Emporia, Kansas, in the 1970s. The series includes:

Mrs. Danner Presents Helen's Book of Basic Quiltmaking, 1973.

Mrs. Danner's Third Quilt Book, 1954.

Mrs. Danner's Fourth Quilt Book, 1958.

Mrs. Danner's Fifth Quilt Book, 1970.

Mrs. Danner's Quilts Presents Book Six: Helesn's Book of Basic Quiltmaking, ed. Helen M. Ericson, 1973.

Mrs. Danner's Quilts Presents Book 7: Quality Quiltmaking, ed. Helen M. Ericson, 1975.

Mrs. Danner's Quilts, Books 1 & 2, combined and edited by Helen M. Ericson, 1971.

Nashville Banner. Daily newspaper in Nashville, Tennessee from 1876 to 1998.

National Weeklies, Inc. Vintage periodical publisher, based in Winona, Minnesota.

Needlecraft: The Home Arts Magazine. Monthly periodical published by Needlecraft Publishing Company, Augusta, Maine, and New York, New York.

Needlecraft Services, Inc. A mail-order fulfillment company established in New York in 1932 to service several newspapers. Columns offering patterns for sale asked readers to send orders to Needle Craft Service, Inc. in New York for fulfillment. As explained on page 8, some people referred to the company as Old Chelsea Station Needlecraft Services. See also Graphic Enterprises, Inc.

Nelson, Cyril I. and Carter Houck, *Quilt Engagement Calendar Treasury,* E. P. Dutton, New York, New York, 1982.

New Cyclopaedia of Domestic Economy, The. Henry Bill Publishing Company, Norwich, Connecticut, 1873.

New York Times. Daily newspaper, New York, New York.

Oakland Tribune,. Daily newspaper, Oakland, California.

Ohio Farmer. Farm magazine established in 1851 in Cleveland, Ohio.

Old Chelsea Station Needlecraft Service. See Needlecraft Services, Inc.

Old Fashioned Quilts. A pattern catalog published by *Rural New Yorker* magazine in New York, New York, 1931.

Old Time New England. Vol. XVII, No 4, April, 1927. An issue of *The Bulletin of The Society for the Preservation of New England Antiquities,* Boston, Massachusetts.

One Dozen Quilt Patterns, ed. Sallie Hill, *Progressive Farmer,* Birmingham, Alabama, 1946. See also *Eight Star Quilt Patterns* and *Eight Star Quilt Designs for Piecework Quilts.*

Orange Judd and Company. Publisher of *The Hearth and Home* magazine, based in Niagara Falls, New York during the 1880s.

Orlofsky, Patsy and Myron, *Quilts in America,* McGraw Hill, New York, 1974. Reprinted by Abbeville Press, New York, 1992.

Paris News. Newspaper, Paris, Texas.

Pasadena Post. Newspaper, Pasadena, California

Patchwork Book, The, Women's World Service Library, Manning Publishing Company, 1932. I could not trace the place of publication of this booklet. Inside, however, patterns are advertised for sale, available from *Woman's World,* Chicago, Illinois.

Pioneer Press. Daily newspaper, St. Paul, Minnesota.

Peto, Florence, *American Quilts and Coverlets,* Chanticleer Press, New York, New York, 1949.

Port Arthur News, Newspaper, Port Arthur, Texas.

Prairie Farmer, A periodical published in Chicago which sold mail-order patterns. See *Quilt Booklet No. 1.*

Prize Winning Designs, Sovereign Visitor, Colonial Pattern Company, Kansas, Missouri. See also Aunt Martha series.

Progressive Farmer. Farm magazine founded in Winston, North Carolina in 1886, now published monthly and based in Birmingham, Alabama. (According to Barbara Brackman, during the 1930s and '40s, the magazine sold mail-order patterns from The Spinning Wheel Company. The patterns were identical to Nancy Cabot blocks.)

Q Book series: According to quilt researcher Cuesta Benberry, the series was published by *Capper's Weekly,* a periodical established in Topeka, Kansas, in 1879. From 1935 onwards, the company offered various syndicated columns and a syndicated mail-order service through which readers could buy pattern booklets from a New York address. Some pattern collectors refer to these booklets as the Q Books, since each number is preceded by a Q. They began to appear in the 1940s. Several blocks are sourced to the booklets listed below. A more complete list is provided in *Secondary Bibliographic Sources* on page 445. (The gaps in the numbering occur because the company also produced other needlework books on knitting, crocheting and sewing.)

Q Book 102, Grandmother's Patchwork Quilts, ca. 1960.

Q Book 103, All-Year Quilts, ca. 1960.

Q Book 105, Covered Wagon, ca. 1960.

Q Book 107, The ABC Quilter, ca. 1960.

Q Book 108, Centennial Quilts, ca. 1960.

Q Book 109, Early American Quilts, ca. 1960.

Q Book 110, Star Quilts, ca. 1960.

*Q Book 112, One-Piece Quilts,*ca. 1960.

Q Book 116, Blue Ribbon Quilts, ca. 1970.

Q Book 118, Grandmother's Flower Quilts, ca. 1970.

Q Book 121, Bicentennial Quilts, ca. 1970.

Q Book 124, White House Quilts, ca. 1970.

Q Book 125, Rose Quilts, ca. 1970.

Q Book 126, All Time Quilt Favorites, ca. 1970.

Q Book 130, Keepsake Quilts, ca. 1990.

Quilt Blocks from The Farmer's Wife, Farm Journal and the Farmer's Wife, Philadelphia Pennsylvania, 1932. *See also Farm Journal and the Farmer's Wife.*

Quilt Book Collection 1, Graphic Enterprises, Inc., date unknown. A pamphlet of quilt patterns containing no bibliographic information. There is second publication, *American Heritage Quilt Book,* which is obviously from the same publisher, since the photograph on the cover is identical. In the interior, some of the patterns and artwork are also the same. According to quilt researcher Cuesta Benberry, the publisher was most likely Graphic Enterprises, Inc., New York, There is no date, but judging by the photograph on the cover and by the dates of similar publications, the pamphlet was probably published sometime in the 1980s. See also Graphic Enterprises, Inc.

Quilt Booklet No.1, ed. Lois Schenk, *Prairie Farmer,* Chicago, Illinois, 1931. *Prairie Farmer* was a periodical published in Chicago which also sold mail-order patterns.

Quilts Heirlooms of Tomorrow, Colonial Pattern Co., Kansas, Missouri, ca. 1977. See also Aunt Martha series.

Quilts, Coats & Clark, 1945. A pamphlet produced by needlework company Coats & Clark.

Quilts of Virginia, compiled by Virginia Consortium of Quilters, Shiffer Publishing, Atglen, Pennsylvania, 2006.

Quilter's Newsletter Magazine, CKMedia, Golden, Colorado.

Quilter's Quest designs: Several Northern Virginia/Maryland quilt shops hold a "shop hop" over the Veteran's Day weekend each year. Shops give away a pattern with the idea that quilters participating in the quest can make a quilt commemorating the event. I have designed several of these Quilter's Quest patterns, which are usually based upon a theme, such as trees, flowers, fans, baskets, etc.

RJR Patterns, Torrance, CA. An imprint of RJR Fabrics, producing patterns to accompany fabric lines by signature designers, including Jinny Beyer.

Rural New Yorker. A farm magazine established in 1850 by *The New Yorker,* New York.

Saward, Blanche C., Sophia Frances, and Anne Caulfield, The Dictionary of Needlework, Hamlyn, London, 1882.

Sioux City Journal. Daily newspaper, Sioux City, Iowa.

Smith, Wilene, "Quilt History in Old Periodicals: A New Interpretation," *Uncoverings,* ed. Laurel Horton, American Quilt Study Group, Lincoln, Nebraska, 1990. This article includes quotes from a vintage periodical named *Happy Hours* as well as references to other early publications, including *Hearth and Home.*

St. Louis Post Dispatch. Daily newspaper, St. Louis, Missouri.

Stockman's Journal. Vintage farm magazine. No further bibliographic information available.

Stone, Clara, Practical Needlework, C. W. Calkins & Company, Boston, Massachusetts, ca. 1906.

Syracuse Herald. Newspaper in Syracuse, New York.

Taylor, Barbara, *Barbara Taylor's Book on Quilting.* Taylor Bedding Manufacturing Co., Taylor, Texas, ca. 1970.

Taylor, Barbara. *The New Barbara Taylor Book on Quilting,* Taylor Bedding Manufacturing Co., Taylor, Texas, ca. 1970.

Ten Piecework Quilts for Southern Homes, ed. Sallie Hill, *Progressive Farmer,* Birmingham, Alabama, date unknown. Vintage pattern booklet. See also *Eight Star Quilt Designs for Piecework Quilts* and *One Dozen Quilt Patterns.*

Tulsa Tribune. Newspaper, Tulsa, Oklahoma.

US News & World Report. Bi-weekly national news magazine, Washington, DC.

Virginia Snow Studio Art Needlework Creations,. A name appearing on several of a series of pamphlets published by Collingbourne Mills, Elgin, Illinois, 1932. See also Grandma Dexter series.

Virginia Snow's Patchwork Designs. See above.

Waldvogel, Merikay, *Childhood Treasures: Quilts by and for Children,* Good Books, Intercourse, Pennsylvania, 2008.

Waldvogel, Merikay and Barbara Brackman, *Patchwork Souvenirs of the 1933 World's Fair,* Thomas Nelson, 1993.

Waldvogel, Merikay, "Also Known as Patty Shannon," *Quilter's Newsletter Magazine,* CKMedia, Golden, Colorado, pp. 38-41, October 2004.

Wallaces' Farmer,. Farm magazine established in 1898 in Iowa.

*Washington Post.*Daily newspaper, Washington, D.C.

Webster, Marie D., *Quilts: Their Story and How to Make Them,* Doubleday Page & Co., Garden City, New York, 1915.

Weldon's Practical Needlework, Weldon & Co, London, England. A series of books each consisting of twelve monthly newsletters published by Weldon & Co in the late 1800s. Reprinted by Interweave Press, Loveland, Colorado, 1999.

World Herald. Morning and evening editions of daily newspaper, Omaha, Nebraska.

Women's Household Needlecraft Service. A catalog mail-order company run by *Women's Household* magazine during the 1960s.

Workbasket. Vintage magazine launched in 1935 by Colonial Patterns, Inc, Kansas, Missouri. See also Colonial Patterns, Inc.

Secondary Bibliographic Sources

The following are sources referenced in Part 1 or in the text sidebars and quick reference sections. They also include several publications of special interest to quilters, designers, or quilt historians.

Aunt Martha series. The name "Aunt Martha" appears on each of a series of vintage booklets published by Colonial Pattern Company, Inc., of Kansas, Missouri, between 1933 and 1977. The booklets include:

- *Aunt Martha's Favorite Quilts,* ca. 1953.
- *Aunt Martha's Workbasket,* ca. 1933.
- *Bold and Beautiful Quilts,* 1977.
- *Easy Quilts,* ca. 1958.
- *Quilt Designs: Old Favorites and New,* ca. 1952.
- *Quilt Lover's Delights,* ca. 1960.
- *Quilts,* ca. 1963.
- *Quilts: Heirlooms of Tomorrow,* 1977
- *Star Designs,* ca. 1942.
- *The Quilt Fair Comes to You,* ca. 1933.
- *Patchwork Simplicity,* 1977.

Beyer, Jinny, *Designing Tessellations.* Contemporary Books, Chicago, Il, 1999. Reprinted by McGraw-Hill Company, New York. New York.

Brackman, Barbara, *Clues in the Calico,* Howell Press, Charlottesville, Virginia, October 1989.

Brackman, Barbara, "Who Was Nancy Cabot?," *Quilter's Newsletter Magazine,* CKMedia, Golden, Colorado, January/February 1991, pp. 22-24.

Brackman, Barbara, Jennie A. Chinn, Gayle R. Davis, Terry Thompson, Sara Reimer Farley, Nancy Hornback, *Kansas Quilts & Quilters,* University Press of Kansas, 1993.

Carleton L. Safford and Robert Bishop, *America's Quilts and Coverlets,* E.P. Dutton & Co., Inc., New York, 1972.

Colby, Averil, *Patchwork,* B.T. Batsford Ltd, London, 1958.

Cummings, Sue, *Album Quilts of Ohio's Miami Valley,* Ohio University Press, October 2008.

Fitzrandolph, Mavis, *Traditional Quilting,* B.T. Batsford Ltd, London, 1954.

Fox, Sandi, *Small Endearments,* Charles Scribner's Sons, New York, 1985.

Graphic Enterprises, Inc. A publisher of several vintage booklets from 1968 to 1980, based in New York. Graphic Enterprises, Inc. also published the Laura Wheeler and Alice Brooks patterns (see page 8). Grit Patterns may also have been connection with this company. According to quilt researcher Cuesta Benberry, the pamphlets include:

American Heritage Quilt Book, date unknown.

14 Quick Machine Quilts #134, date unknown.

15 Quilts for Today's Living Quilt Book 3, 1968.

Add A Block Quilts #131, 1979.

Decorate With Needlecraft, date unknown.

Envelope Patchwork Quilts #128, 1978.

Fashion Home Quilting, 1980.

Museum Quilts Book 2 #102, date unknown.

Nifty-Fifty Quilts #116, 1974.

Petal Quilts #125, 1977.

Pillow Show-Offs #121, 1977.

Quilt Book Collection 1, ca. 1975.

Quilt Originals #132, 1980.

Stuff 'N" Puff Quilts, #122, 1976.

Stitch 'N' Patch Quilts, #123, 1976.

Hechtlinger, Adelaide, *American Quilts, Quilting, and Patchwork,* Stackpole Books, Harrisburg, Pennsylvania.

Hope Winslow's Quilt Book, Home Art Studios, Des Moines, Iowa. Founded by Hubert Ver Mehren, Home Art Studios sold quilt patterns and catalogs, including this one and *Colonial Quilts.* Ver Mehren's designs advertising the patterns appeared in many periodicals in the early 1930s.

Kansas City Star Quilt Block Collection Volumes I – V, Central Oklahoma Quilters Guild, Inc., Oklahoma City, 1987.

Lemonie, E, *Géométrographie ou Art des Constructions Géométriques,* C. Naud, Paris, 1902.

Murdock, Catherine Gilbert, *Domesticating Drink, Women, Men, and Alcohol in America, 1870-1940,* Johns Hopkins University Press, Baltimore, Maryland, 2001.

Peterson's Magazine. Popular vintage magazine for women, published in Philadelphia from 1842 to 1898.

Q Book series: According to quilt researcher Cuesta Benberry, the series was published by *Capper's Weekly,* a periodical established in Topeka, Kansas, in 1879. From 1935 onwards, the company offered various syndicated columns and a syndicated mail-order service through which readers could buy pattern booklets from a New York address. Some pattern collectors refer to these booklets as the *Q Books,* since each number is preceded by a Q. They began to appear in the 1940s. They include the following. (The gaps in the numbering occur because the company also produced other needlework books on knitting, crocheting and sewing.)

Q Book101, Flower Quilts, ca. 1960.

Q Book102, Grandmother's Patchwork Quilts, ca. 1960.

Q Book 103, All-Year Quilts, ca. 1960.

Q Book 104, Crib, ca. 1960.

Q Book 105, Covered Wagon, ca. 1960.

Q Book 106, Bible Favorites, ca. 1960.

Q Book 107, The ABC Quilter, ca. 1960.

Q Book 108, Centennial Quilts, ca. 1960.

Q Book 109, Early American Quilts, ca. 1960.

Q Book 110, Star Quilts, ca. 1960.

Q Book 111, Round the World Quilt Book, ca. 1960.

*Q Book 112, One-Piece Quilts,*ca. 1960.

Q Book 116, Blue Ribbon Quilts, ca. 1970.

Q Book 117, Quilts on Parade, ca. 1970.

Q Book 118, Grandmother's Flower Quilts, ca. 1970.

Q Book 121, Bicentennial Quilts, ca. 1970.

Q Book 124, White House Quilts, ca. 1970.

Q Book 125, Rose Quilts, ca. 1970.

Q Book 126, All Time Quilt Favorites, ca. 1970.

Q Book 130, Keepsake Quilts, ca. 1990.

Q Book 134, Slumbertime Coverlets, ca. 1990.

Q Book 137, Plain and Fancy Flower Quilts, ca. 1990.

Q Book 139, Treasure Quilts-Mostly Pieced, ca. 1990.

Q Book 140, Quilts Plus, ca. 1990.

Q Book 141, Quilts of the Ozarks, ca. 1990.

Smith, Wilene, *Quilt Patterns, An Index to The Kansas City Star, The Weekly Kansas City Star, Weekly Star Farmer Patterns 1928-1961,* Mennonite Press, Inc. North Newton, Kansas, 1985.

www.illinoisquilthistory.com. A website by quilt historian Susan Wildemuth of Atkinson, Illinois, dedicated to research of quilts in Illinois. The site includes information on Loretta Leitner Rising (aka Nancy Cabot).

www.quiltershalloffame.net. The official website for the Quilters' Hall of Fame, a center for quilt research located in the historic home of Marie Webster in Marion, Indiana

www.wctu.org. Source of information on Carrie Nation and the Women's Christian Temperance Movement and Carrie Nation.

www.whitehouse.gov/history/firstladies/lh19.html. Source of information on Lucy Hayes, wife of President Rutherford B. Hayes. See also page 308.

Appendices

Appendix 1
Ladies Art Company Blocks

The 485 pieced blocks listed here appeared in issues of Ladies Art Company catalog. (See page 3 for an explanation of catalog numbers. The earliest date for the first printed catalog is 1897, even though some of the patterns with earlier numbers may have been offered for sale as early as 1895.) An asterisk next to the block name means that Ladies Art Company is not the earliest source I found for a particular block. To find the earlier sources, look up each of these blocks in the book. (For asterisked names, the Ladies Art Company source does not appear within the block listing, since the block is identically named in the earliest source.)

4 E Block, catalog #335, 1897, 206-11
A, catalog #421, 1906, 234-1
Air Castle, catalog #101, 1897, 143-2
Album, catalog #378, 1897, 205-2
Album Blocks, catalog #352, 1897, 175-2
Album Quilt, catalog #267, 1897, 263-2
All Kinds, catalog #377, 1897, 199-11
All Tangled Up, catalog #309, 1897, 123-5
American Log Patchwork, catalog #374, 1897, 250-10
Annapolis Patch, catalog #471, 1922, 113-2
Arabic Lattice, catalog #413, 1901, 210-4
Arkansas Traveler, catalog #205, 1897, 144-1
Art Square, catalog #324, 1897, 57-12
Aunt Eliza's Star, catalog #13, 1897, 124-9
Aunt Sukey's Patch, catalog #327, 1897, 407-11
Autumn Leaf, catalog #502, 1928, 333-2
B, catalog #422, 1906, 234-2
Baby Bunting, catalog #493, 1922, 384-9
Bachelor's Puzzle, catalog #34, 1897, 193-5
Barrister's Block, catalog #63, 1897, 105-12
Base Ball, catalog #179, 1897, 350-3
Basket Lattice, catalog #417, 1901, 408-7
Basket of Lilies, catalog #55, 1897, 367-11
Basket Quilt, catalog #316, 1897, 311-7
Bat's Wings, catalog #43, 1897, 438-4
Baton Rouge Block, catalog #474, 1922, 94-3
Bear's Foot, catalog #357, 1897, 223-9
Bear's Paw, catalog #162, 1897, 101-3
Beautiful Star, catalog #1, 1897, 297-1
Beggar Blocks, catalog #68, 1897, 242-1
Big Dipper, catalog #320, 1897, 427-9
Bird's Nest, catalog #256, 1897, 194-9
Blackford's Beauty, catalog #388, 1897, 87-8
Blazing Star, catalog #372, 1897, 277-8
Bleeding Heart, catalog #501, 1928, 360-2
Blindman's Fancy, catalog #201, 1897, 121-9
Block Patchwork, catalog #361, 1897, 416-1
Boston Puzzle, catalog #249, 1897, 350-9
Box Blocks, catalog #64, 1897, 431-5
Box Quilt Pattern, catalog #351, 1897, 224-12
Boxed T's, catalog #379, 1897, 166-8
Boy's Nonsense, catalog #153, 1897, 126-1
Braced Star, catalog #486, 1922, 139-5
Brick Pile, catalog #410, 1901, 406-3
Brickwork Quilt, catalog #293, 1897, 426-8
Brunswick Star, catalog #21, 1897, 415-10
Burnham Square, catalog #232, 1897, 176-8
C, catalog #423, 1906, 234-3
Cake Stand, catalog #59, 1897, 190-6
California Rose, catalog #184, 1928, 355-9
California Star Pattern, catalog #167, 1897, 266-3
* Capital T, catalog #84, 1897, 139-7
Carpenter's Square, catalog #395, 1897, 254-10
Cats and Mice, catalog #317, 1897, 132-6
Centennial, catalog #158, 1897, 78-5
Charm, catalog #96, 1897, 173-3
Cherry Basket, catalog #58, 1897, 322-11
Chicago Star, catalog #22, 1897, 156-4
Children's Delight, catalog #319, 1897, 192-3
Chimney Swallows, catalog #355, 1897, 326-6
Churn Dash, catalog #112, 1897, 84-12
Circle within Circle, catalog #42, 1897, 371-1
Cleveland Lilies, catalog #53, 1897, 367-1
Clown, catalog #524, 1928, 192-8
Cluster of Stars, catalog #393, 1928, 164-11
Coarse Woven Patchwork, catalog #242, 1897, 407-12
Cockelburr, catalog #505, 1928, 336-10
Cog Wheels, catalog #41, 1897, 380-6
Columbia Puzzle, catalog #31, 1897, 116-6
* Columbia, The, catalog #109, 1897, 400-3
Columbian Star, catalog #50, 1897, 156-6
Combination Star, catalog #19, 1897, 137-6
Compass, catalog #218, 1897, 419-2
Corn and Beans, catalog #100, 1897, 130-9
Country Farm, catalog #209, 1897, 406-8
Coxey's Camp, catalog #95, 1897, 85-2
Crazy Ann, catalog #165, 1897, 99-12
Crazy House, catalog #516, 1928, 188-5
Crib Quilt, catalog #415, 1901, 115-10
Cross and Crown, catalog #151, 1897, 194-3
Cross Roads to Texas, catalog #235, 1897, 165-12
Cross Within Cross, catalog #313, 1897, 112-5
Cross, The, catalog #407, 1901, 151-10
Crossed Canoes, catalog #89, 1897, 80-8
Crosses and Losses, catalog #251, 1897, 73-9
Crosses and Star, catalog #12, 1897, 193-8
Crow's Foot, catalog #118, 1897, 98-3
Cube Lattice, catalog #412, 1901, 406-7
Cube Work, catalog #228, 1897, 398-9
Cut Glass Dish, catalog #80, 1897, 150-2
D, catalog #424, 1906, 234-4
Devil's Claws, catalog #142, 1897, 97-6
Devil's Puzzle, catalog #24, 1897, 90-9
Diamond and Star, catalog #481, 1922, 413-11
Diamond Cube, catalog #91, 1897, 430-8
Diamond Design, catalog #312, 1897, 430-5
Diamond Star, catalog #244, 1897, 96-11
Diamonds, catalog #49, 1897, 430-3
Disk, The, catalog #138, 1897, 74-8
Domino, catalog #172, 1897, 153-10
Domino and Square, catalog #278, 1897, 203-10
Double Irish Chain, catalog #60, 1897, 209-5
Double Peony, catalog #178, 1897, 366-3
Double Squares, catalog #225, 1897, 217-10
Double Wedding Ring, catalog #512, 1928, 420-7
Double Wrench, catalog #148, 1897, 184-2
Double X, No. 1, catalog #78, 1897, 126-8
Double X, No. 2, catalog #76, 1897, 74-1
Double X No. 3, catalog #78, 1897, 73-12
Double X, No. 4, catalog #79, 1897, 130-5
Double Z, catalog #192, 1897, 75-12
* Double Z, catalog #360, 1897, 154-1
Dove in the Window, catalog #215, 1897, 224-2
Dover Quilt Block, catalog #470, 1922, 311-12
Drunkard's Patchwork, catalog #243, 1897, 354-8
Drunkard's Path, catalog #220, 1897, 352-7
Duck and Ducklings, catalog #245, 1897, 184-6
Dutch Mill, catalog #451, 1922, 82-10
Dutch Rose, catalog #185, 1897, 289-7
Dutch Windmill, catalog #520, 1928, 100-10
Dutchman's Puzzle, catalog #26, 1897, 68-10
E, catalog #425, 1906, 234-5
Ecclesiastical, catalog #295, 1897, 432-6
Economy, catalog #264, 1897, 58-4
Eight Hands Around, catalog #149, 1897, 79-3
Eight Point Design, catalog #323, 1897, 124-7
Eight Pointed Star, catalog #261, 1897, 276-1
Eight Pointed Stars, catalog #450, 1906, 160-6
Enigma, catalog #400, 1897, 283-9
Evening Star, catalog #5, 1897, 62-3
F, catalog #426, 1906, 234-6
* Fair Play, catalog #454, 1922, 371-9
Fan, catalog #143, 1928, 387-11
Fan Patchwork, catalog #296, 1897, 386-3
Fanny's Fan, catalog #143, 1897, 387-11
Fanny's Fan, catalog #143, 1897, 213-3
Fanny's Favorite, catalog #464, 1922, 84-5
Fantastic Patchwork, catalog #290, 1897, 407-3
Farmer's Daughter, catalog #419, 1901, 185-7
Feather Star, catalog #9, 1897, 272-6
Fine Woven, catalog #240, 1897, 426-11
Five Patch, catalog #82, 1897, 240-7
Five Pointed Star, catalog #18, 1897, 436-2
Five Stripes, catalog #139, 1897, 426-6
Flagstones, catalog #514, 1928, 153-4
Flower Basket, catalog #57, 1898, 74-10
Flutter Wheel, catalog #39, 1897, 128-6
Flying Bat, catalog #44, 1897, 278-2
Flying Dutchman, catalog #247, 1897, 146-2
Flying Squares, catalog #233, 1897, 188-2
Flying Swallow, catalog #503, 1928, 303-10
Fool's Puzzle, catalog #29, 1897, 353-3
Fool's Square, catalog #259, 1897, 186-1
Forbidden Fruit Tree, catalog #224, 1897, 307-11
Fortune's Wheel, catalog #521, 1928, 373-5
Four Little Baskets, catalog #305, 1897, 339-1
Four Points, catalog #106, 1897, 167-9
Four Points, catalog #306, 1897, 160-4
Four Stars Patchwork, catalog #311, 1897, 291-10
Four X Star, catalog #163, 1897, 185-12
Four Z Patch, catalog #375, 1897, 207-2
Fox and Geese, catalog #458, 1922, 337-5
G, catalog #427, 1906, 234-7
Garden of Eden, catalog #204, 1897, 183-2
Garfield's Monument, catalog #136, 1897, 218-10
Gentleman's Fancy, catalog #208, 1897, 140-6

Shoo Fly, catalog #276, 1897, 124-5
Shooting Star, catalog #16, 1897, 70-5
Simple Design, catalog #321, 1897, 204-4
Single Sunflower, catalog #367, 1897, 381-9
Sister's Choice, catalog #257, 1897, 185-10
Slashed Album, catalog #37, 1897, 101-9
Slashed Star, catalog #266, 1897, 378-10
Snail Trail, catalog #504, 1928, 93-11
Snow Ball, catalog #104, 1897, 350-5
Snowflake, A, catalog #277, 1897, 61-6
Solomon's Temple, catalog #193, 1897, 265-11
Some Pretty Patchwork, catalog #287, 1897, 107-2
Spider's Den, catalog #190, 1897, 177-2
Spider's Web, catalog #191, 1897, 292-10
Spools, catalog #398, 1897, 172-2
Springfield Patch, catalog #472, 1922, 103-4
Square and a Half, catalog #246, 1897, 186-8
Square and Star, catalog #263, 1897, 60-10
St. Louis Block, catalog #491, 1922, 276-8
St. Louis Star, catalog #275, 1897, 204-9
Star A, catalog #399, 1897, 176-4
Star and Chains, catalog #6, 1897, 289-3
Star and Cross, catalog #284, 1897, 166-10
Star Lane, catalog #403, 1901, 203-7
Star of Bethlehem, catalog #3, 1897, 399-8
Star of Hope, catalog #523, 1928, 189-9
Star of Many Points, catalog #2, 1897, 299-6
Star of North Carolina, catalog #473, 1922, 285-1
Star of the West, catalog #274, 1897, 436-7
Star Puzzle, catalog #10, 1897, 64-2
Starlight, catalog #528, 1928, 286-4
Stars and Cubes, catalog #15, 1897, 292-2
Stars and Squares, catalog #11, 1897, 79-2
Stars upon Stars, catalog #211, 1897, 278-5
Steps to the Altar, catalog #206, 1897, 152-1
Stone Mason's Puzzle, catalog #457, 1922, 223-3
Storm at Sea, catalog #135, 1897, 114-4
Strawberry, catalog #212, 1897, 356-7
Strip Squares, catalog #226, 1897, 258-3
Sugar Loaf, catalog #370, 1897, 192-6
Sunflower, catalog #448, 1906, 381-12
Sunflower, The, catalog #73, 1897, 356-2
Sunshine, catalog #121, 1897, 92-6
Susannah Patch, catalog #485, 1922, 62-2
Suspension Bridge, catalog #488, 1922, 384-4
Swastika Patch, catalog #455, 1922, 246-4
Sweet Gum Leaf, catalog #71, 1897, 173-13
Swing in the Center, catalog #252, 1897, 135-1
Swinging Corners, catalog #401, 1901, 358-9
T, catalog #440, 1906, 235-7
T Quartette, catalog #86, 1897, 151-5
'T' Quilt, catalog #369, 1897, 119-2
Tallahassee Quilt Block, catalog #469, 1922, 410-11
Tangled Garter, catalog #124, 1897, 242-5
Tangled Lines, catalog #484, 1922, 169-12
Tassel Plant, catalog #389, 1897, 171-4
Tea Leaf, catalog #69, 1897, 318-2
Texas Flower, catalog #304, 1897, 178-5
Texas Star, catalog #466, 1922, 399-11
Texas Tears, catalog #105, 1897, 166-6
Three Flowered Sunflower, catalog #74, 1897, 366-7
Tick Tack Toe, catalog #227, 1897, 258-2
Tile Patchwork, catalog #390, 1897, 412-2
Toad in a Puddle, catalog #150, 1897, 77-8
Tree of Paradise, catalog #260, 1897, 220-2
Trenton Quilt Block, catalog #476, 1922, 322-9
Triangle Puzzle, The, catalog #33, 1897, 192-10
Triangles and Stripes, catalog #229, 1897, 85-3
Triangular Triangle, catalog #103, 1897, 409-7
True Lover's Knot, catalog #263, 1897, 77-3
Tuip in Vase (sic), catalog #273, 1897, 368-3
Tulip Basket, catalog #518, 1928, 305-12
Tulip Lady Finger, catalog #394, 1897, 109-6
Tumbler, The, catalog #368, 1897, 433-3
Turkey Tracks, catalog #155, 1897, 244-11
Turnstile, catalog #519, 1928, 66-2
Twin Sisters, catalog #213, 1897, 66-1
Twinkling Star, catalog #301, 1897, 269-5
Twinkling Stars, catalog #406, 1901, 344-3
Twist and Turn, catalog #98, 1897,
* Twist Patchwork, The, catalog #294, 1897, 411-12
U, catalog #441, 1906, 235-8
Union, catalog #160, 1897, 136-7
Union Star, catalog #381, 1897, 436-6
V, catalog #442, 1906, 235-9
V Block, The, catalog #483, 1922, 114-5
Variegated Diamonds, catalog #288, 1897, 430-9
* Variegated Hexagons, catalog #292, 1897, 431-9
Venetian Design, catalog #115, 1897, 294-6
Vestibule, catalog #383, 1897, 173-10
Vice President's Quilt, catalog #298, 1897, 168-8
Village Church, catalog #123, 1897, 337-2
W , catalog #443, 1906, 235-10
W.C.T. Union, catalog #161, 1897, 249-11
Walk Around, catalog #527, 1928, 409-3
Washington Sidewalk, catalog #175, 1897, 91-9
Washington's Puzzle, catalog #32, 1897, 265-10
Wedding Ring, catalog #48, 1897, 184-11
Whale Block, catalog #490, 1922, 315-4
Wheel of Fortune, catalog #40, 1897, 294-11
White House Steps, catalog #221, 1897, 246-3
Widower's Choice, catalog #248, 1897, 209-9
Wild Goose Chase, catalog #94, 1897, 173-8
Winding Walk, catalog #409, 1901, 310-13
Winding Ways, catalog #463, 1922, 326-7
Windmill, catalog #127, 1897, 58-7
Wings, catalog #529, 1928, 325-4
Wonder of the World, catalog #46, 1897, 354-2
Work Box, catalog #358, 1897, 218-13
World's Fair Block, catalog #66, 1897, 106-10
World's Fair Puzzle, catalog #30, 1897, 108-5
World's Fair, The, catalog #134, 1897, 326-4
Wyoming Patch, catalog #494, 1922, 382-6
X, catalog #444, 1906, 235-11
Xquisite, The, catalog #281, 1897, 105-8
Y, catalog #445, 1906, 235-12
Yankee Puzzle, catalog #28, 1897, 68-5
Z, catalog #446, 1906, 235-13

Appendix 2

Laura Wheeler and Alice Brooks Blocks

Several pattern companies sold quilt block designs through advertisements in newspapers. Needlecrafts Services, Inc. of New York City, offered quilt patterns under various names, by far the most popular of which were Laura Wheeler and Alice Brooks (see page 8). Often, the same pattern was credited to Wheeler and Brooks, usually with a different pattern number and sometimes with a different block name. The pattern numbers are provided in these two indexes, so you can see which blocks were duplicated. Note that some blocks have multiple pattern numbers. I have found more than 325 blocks attributed to Laura Wheeler and more than 230 blocks attributed to Alice Brooks. The asterisk next to particular listings indicates blocks that were published elsewhere, either under the same or a different name, before they appeared in the periodical listed here. Note, too, that some blocks were published more than once in a particular periodical, but only the earliest dates are provided.

Laura Wheeler Blocks

Album Flower, #547, *Cincinnati Enquirer*, Sep 23, 1933, 300-7
America's Pride, #766, *Indianapolis Star*, Jul 1, 1934, 326-2
Ann's Scrap Quilt, #600, *Cincinnati Enquirer*, Nov 24, 1933, 162-1
Around the World, #1659, *Sioux City Journal*, Jan 10, 1938, 341-11
Aster, #578, *Kansas City Star*, Nov 13, 1933, 372-6
* Attic Window, #660, unidentified clipping, date unknown, 318-2
* Autumn Leaf, #406, *Illinois State Register*, Apr 22, 1933, 333-2
Autumn Leaf, #406, *Cincinnati Enquirer*, Dec 15, 1933, 335-7
Basket, #405, *Cincinnati Enquirer*, Dec 29, 1933, 190-6
Bear's Paw, #452, *Illinois State Register*, Jun 5, 1933, 223-9
Beginner's Choice, #2699, *Sioux City Journal*, Nov 9, 1940, 145-12
* Beginner's Joy, #987, unidentified clipping, date unknown, 57-11
Beginner's Luck, #567, *Columbus Evening Dispatch*, Mar 20, 1943, 337-7
Beginner's Pride, #743, unidentified clipping, date unknown, 78-11
Bell Flower, #642, *Cincinnati Enquirer*, Feb 18, 1934, 365-6
Betsy's Lattice, #512, *Cincinnati Enquirer*, Aug 20, 1933, 132-4
Bird of Paradise, #602, unidentified clipping, date unknown, 316-2
Blazing Star, #463, *Illinois State Register*, Jun 13, 1933, 114-11
Blazing Star, #2920, *Sioux City Journal*, Aug 2, 1941, 266-1
Bouquet, #735, unidentified clipping, date unknown, 223-2
Bowknot, #521, *Indianapolis Star*, Aug 21, 1933, 226-2
* Bride's Bouquet, #890, unidentified clipping, date unknown, 307-5
Bride's Prize, #1506, *Indianapolis Star*, Jun 10, 1937, 389-1
Bride's Quilt, #, *State Journal*, Apr 9, 1934, 388-10
Bright Star, #503, unidentified clipping, date unknown, 268-6
Brilliant Star, #538, unidentified clipping, date unknown, 290-10
Brunswick Star, #412, *Illinois State Register*, Apr 20, 1933, 286-1
Butterfly, #663, *Cincinnati Enquirer*, Nov 4, 1934, 181-3
Butterfly, #1408, *Minneapolis Star*, Feb 10, 1937, 317-10
Cactus Basket, #426, *Illinois State Register*, May 4, 1933, 306-8
Calla Lily, #972, *Cincinnati Enquirer*, May 7, 1935, 370-5
Carolina Favorite, #638, *Cincinnati Enquirer*, Feb 15, 1934, 336-3
Chained Star, #592, *Cincinnati Enquirer*, Jan 7, 1934, 330-9
Checkered Star, #624, *Cincinnati Enquirer*, Jan 16, 1934, 248-8

Star and Crown, #406, *Sioux City Journal*, Mar 31, 1938, 293-11
Star Flower, #844, *Cincinnati Enquirer*, Sep 2, 1934, 369-12
Star Flower Wreath, #625, *Cincinnati Enquirer*, Jan 28, 1934, 122-6
Star Flowers, #425, *Illinois State Register*, May 5, 1933, 345-12
Star of Spring, #1162, *Indianapolis Star*, Mar 12, 1936, 219-11
Star of the East, #387, *Sioux City Journal*, Apr 14, 1939, 211-8
Star of the East, #760, unidentified clipping, date unknown, 78-10
Star of the Night, #684, *Cincinnati Enquirer*, Apr 29, 1934, 274-7
Star of the West, #1222, *Indianapolis Star*, Jul 18, 1936, 256-3
Star Studded Beauty, #854, *Collection of Needlecraft Masterpieces* ca. 1958, 393-4
* Starlight, #496, unidentified clipping, date unknown, 286-4
* Starry Path, #514, unidentified clipping, date unknown, 144-4
Starry Pavement, #599, *Cincinnati Enquirer*, Jan 21, 1934, 324-6
Summer Fancy, #768, *Indianapolis Star*, Jul 8, 1934, 383-11
Sunbonnet Girl, #1274, *Indianapolis Star*, Jul 29, 1936, 338-11
Sunburst Quilt, #712, *Stockman's Journal*, date unknown, 298-3
Sunburst Star, #441, *Illinois State Register*, May 24, 1933, 278-6
Sunflower, #490, *Cincinnati Enquirer*, Jul 19, 1933, 175-9
Sunflower, #1088, *Cincinnati Enquirer*, Dec 7, 1935, 369-10
Sunset Star, #1547, *Indianapolis Star*, Aug 6, 1937, 323-11
Swing In The Center, #404, *Illinois State Register*, Apr 24, 1933, 134-10
T Block, #442, *Illinois State Register*, May 27, 1933, 134-11
Tangled Briars, #532, *Cincinnati Enquirer*, Sep 10, 1933, 150-11
Three Patch, #775, unidentified clipping, date unknown, 226-4
* Three Patch, #893, unidentified clipping, date unknown, 371-6
Three Patch, #1147, *Cincinnati Enquirer*, Dec 15, 1936, 394-3
* Three Patch Quilt, #534, unidentified clipping, date unknown, 73-2
Thrifty, #711, unidentified clipping, date unknown, 84-8
Tiger Lily, #651, *Cincinnati Enquirer*, Mar 4, 1934, 113-9
Tree of Life, #580, *Cincinnati Enquirer*, Nov 9, 1933, 274-11
Tulip, #508, *Cincinnati Enquirer*, Aug 12, 1933, 307-9
Tulip Garden, #920, *Cincinnati Enquirer*, Feb 9, 1935, 370-6
* Tumbling Blocks, #722, *Laura Wheeler Catalog*, date unknown, 431-1
Twist and Turn, #1217, *Cincinnati Enquirer*, May 23, 1936, 324-10
Two in One, #854, *Laura Wheeler Catalog*, 1959, 314-7
Vase of Flowers, #640, *Indianapolis Star*, Feb 20, 1934, 369-2
Wagonwheel, #2712, *Sioux City Journal*, Nov 29, 1940, 294-9
Washington Pavement, #257, *Indianapolis Star*, Aug 11, 1933, 302-11
Water Beauty, #792, *Cincinnati Enquirer*, Sep 14, 1934, 255-5
Water Lily, #696, *Cincinnati Enquirer*, May 8, 1934, 363-9
Water Wheel, #422, *Illinois State Register*, May 1, 1933, 305-2
Waving Plumes, #683, *Cincinnati Enquirer*, May 3, 1934, 311-4
Western Rose, #557, *Kansas City Star*, Nov 15, 1933, 359-3
Wheel of Fortune, #226, *Cincinnati Enquirer*, Aug 16, 1933, 377-10
Whirlaway, #223, *Columbus Evening Dispatch*, Aug 19, 1942, 317-12
Whirling Star, #530, *Cincinnati Enquirer*, Aug 31, 1933, 304-2
White House Steps, #531, *Paris News*, Aug 31, 1933, 220-11
* Wild Goose Chase, #443, *Illinois State Register*, May 22, 1933, 184-4
Wild Goose Chase, #443, *Illinois State Register*, May 22, 1933, 269-10
Wild Rose, #1296, *Pasadena Post*, Sep 17, 1936, 364-1
Windflower, #550, *Cincinnati Enquirer*, Sep 28, 1933, 311-2
Winged Square, #614, *Cincinnati Enquirer*, Jan 26, 1934, 175-11
* Wonder of the World, #656, unidentified clipping, date unknown, 353-2
* World without End, #483, *Sioux City Journal*, Jul 30, 1933, 226-12
World's Fair, #507, *Cincinnati Enquirer*, Aug 10, 1933, 121-10
Wreath, #479, *Sioux City Journal*, Jul 2, 1933, 303-10
Young Man's Fancy, #439, *Illinois State Register*, May 20, 1933, 201-5
Your Lucky Star, #985, unidentified clipping, date unknown, 284-9

Alice Brooks Blocks

American Rose Bud, *Detroit Free Press*, Jan 31, 1933, 223-11
Anchors Aweigh, #7418, *Washington Post*, Oct 29, 1942, 265-6
Aster, #5077B, *Detroit Free Press*, Feb 11, 1934, 367-9
Attic Window, #7196, unidentified clipping, date unknown, 318-2
Autumn Leaves, *Detroit Free Press*, Mar 30, 1934, 236-5
Baby's Block, #5502, unidentified clipping, date unknown, 430-9
Basket, #5066, *Detroit Free Press*, Jan 5, 1934, 190-12
Basket of Lilies, #5210, *Detroit Free Press*, Sep 26, 1934, 369-4
Bed of Tulips, #5132, *Detroit Free Press*, May 20, 1934, 361-12
* Beginner's Delight, #7176, unidentified clipping, date unknown, 68-1
Beginner's Delight, #7278, unidentified clipping, date unknown, 158-7
Beginner's Joy, #7359, unidentified clipping, date unknown, 206-8
* Beginner's Joy, #7388, unidentified clipping, date unknown, 206-8
Beginner's Quilt, #7188, unidentified clipping, date unknown, 184-2
* Beginner's Quilt, #7388, unidentified clipping, date unknown, 57-11
Beginner's Star, #7222, unidentified clipping, date unknown, 96-3
Border Block, #5077G, *Detroit Free Press*, Mar 18, 1934, 246-2
Bride's Quilt, #5844, *Detroit Free Press*, Apr 22, 1937, 388-11
* Brunswick Star, #5249, *Detroit Free Press*, Nov 11, 1934, 286-2
Butterfly, #5094, *Detroit Free Press*, Feb 19, 1934, 123-7
Butterfly, #5663, *Detroit Free Press*, Jul 25, 1936, 341-8
Cactus Basket, #x, *Detroit Free Press*, 29-Sep-34, 305-10
Calico Cat, #5707, *Detroit Free Press*, Oct 16, 1936, 332-3
Canterbury Bells, #5182, *Detroit Free Press*, Aug 26, 1934, 363-6
Chrysanthemum, #5194, *Detroit Free Press*, Aug 13, 1934, 261-4
Colonial Basket, #5072, *Detroit Free Press*, Jan 8, 1934, 369-6
Colonial Basket, #5832, *Detroit Free Press*, Apr 8, 1937, 325-3
Colonial Pavement, #5501, *Detroit Free Press*, Dec 24, 1935, 118-8
Colorful Scraps, #7230, unidentified clipping, date unknown, 78-2
Country Tile, #7464, *Detroit Free Press*, date unknown, 431-10
Dahlia, #5023, *Detroit Free Press*, Apr 8, 1934, 363-2
* Dahlia, #7367, unidentified clipping date unknown, 311-5
* Day or Night, #7151, unidentified clipping, date unknown, 58-2
Delectable Mountains, #7324, unidentified clipping, date unknown, 136-6
Dogwood, #5376, *Detroit Free Press*, Jun 13, 1935, 370-7
Double Pinwheel, #6851, *Bismarck Tribune* Dec 18, 1940, 145-1
Double Pinwheel, #7367, unidentified clipping, unknown, 311-5
Double Wedding Ring, #5101, *Detroit Free Press*, Mar 26, 1934, 419-10
Double Windmill, #5038, *Detroit Free Press*, Mar 25, 1934, 246-5
Dream Garden, #5119, *Detroit Free Press*, Aug 5, 1934, 361-6
Dresden Plate, #6702, *Detroit Free Press*, May 11, 1940, 375-9
* Dutch Windmill, #5195, *Detroit Free Press*, May 22, 1936, 389-6
Eastern Star, #5042, *Detroit Free Press*, Dec 15, 1933, 393-9
Endless Chain, #6564, *Detroit Free Press*, Jun 5, 1940, 401-1
Evening Flower, #5189, *Detroit Free Press*, Jul 18, 1934, 364-3
Evening Star, #6013, *Detroit Free Press*, May 4, 1940, 82-2
Fancy's Favorite, #6033, *Detroit Free Press*, Mar 22, 1938, 303-12
Five Patch, #7185, unidentified clipping, date unknown, 210-2
Five Patch, #7188, unidentified clipping, date unknown, 202-5
* Flower Basket, #5066, *Oregon State Journal*, Jan 5, 1934, 190-12
Flower Basket, #5848, *Detroit Free Press*, Dec 2, 1934, 307-7
* Flower Garden, #7193, unidentified clipping, date unknown, 432-1
Flower of Spring, #5296, *Detroit Free Press*, Feb 7, 1935, 363-8

Flower of the Morning, #5074, *Detroit Free Press*, Jan 19, 1934, 103-5
Flower of the Woods, #5367, *Detroit Free Press*, May 22, 1935, 365-7
Flowery Field, #5270, *Detroit Free Press*, Feb 16, 1935, 365-5
Flying Birds, #5131, *Detroit Free Press*, Apr 30, 1934, 324-3
Flying Geese, #7018, unidentified clipping, date unknown, 199-1
Flying Geese, #7242, unidentified clipping, date unknown, 206-9
Flying Geese, #7299, unidentified clipping, date unknown, 112-8
Fortune's Fancy, #5034, *Detroit Free Press*, Dec 14, 1933, 268-8
Four Patch, #7121, unidentified clipping, date unknown, 249-10
* Four Patch, #7194, unidentified clipping, date unknown, 96-4
Four Patch, #7235, unidentified clipping, date unknown, 300-1
Four Patch Beauty, #7305, unidentified clipping, date unknown, 102-4
Four Patch Star, #7357, unidentified clipping, date unknown, 78-12
Friendship Bouquet, #5060, *Detroit Free Press*, Mar 20, 1934, 225-9
Friendship Chain, #5096, *Detroit Free Press*, Feb 28, 1934, 328-4
Friendship Chain, #no pattern number, *Alice Brooks Collection of Needlecraft Masterpieces*, ca. 1958, 211-3
* Friendship Chain, #no pattern number, *Alice Brooks Collection of Needlecraft Masterpieces*, ca. 1958, 264-6
* Friendship Fan, #7022, unidentified clipping, date unknown, 385-12
Friendship Knot, #5058, *Detroit Free Press*, May 4, 1934, 336-2
Friendship Lily, #5076, *Detroit Free Press*, Jan 28, 1934, 123-1
Friendship Plate, #5002, *Detroit Free Press*, Nov 9, 1933, 375-10
Friendship Quilt, #7205, *Alice Brooks Designs*, date unknown, 128-1
* Friendship Ring, #7141, unidentified clipping, date unknown, 356-4
Friendship Rose, #5067, *Detroit Free Press*, Jan 29, 1934, 361-10
Garden Favorite, #5177, *Detroit Free Press*, Jul 9, 1934, 364-6
Garden of Friendship, #5787, *Detroit Free Press*, Feb 11, 1937, 369-3
Garden Treasure, #5452, *Detroit Free Press*, Oct 2, 1935, 370-4
* Gay Pinwheel, #7445, unidentified clipping, date unknown, 114-6
Grandmother's Fan, #5009, *Detroit Free Press*, Jan 10, 1934, 386-6
* Grandmother's Fan, #5887, *Detroit Free Press*, Jun 25, 1937, 386-7
Grandmother's Garden, #5259, *Detroit Free Press*, Dec 23, 1934, 425-6
* Grandmother's Garden, #5802, *Detroit Free Press*, Dec 23, 1934, 432-1
* Grandmother's Pride, #7278, unidentified clipping, date unknown, 256-10
Grandmother's Scrap Quilt, #5887, *Detroit Free Press*, Jun 25, 1937, 386-7
Grandmother's Two Patch, #5233, *Detroit Free Press*, Oct 19, 1934, 81-9
Gypsy Trail, #5246, *Detroit Free Press*, Nov 2, 1934, 388-4
Heirloom Quilt, #7189, *Modesto Bee*, Apr 4, 1942, 198-3
Heirloom Quilt, #7299, unidentified clipping, date unknown, 318-6
* Hexagons, #7062, *Detroit Free Press*, date unknown, 432-1
* Hidden Flower, #5401, unidentified clipping, date unknown, 339-2
* Imperial Fan, #7431, unidentified clipping, date unknown, 386-11
Jewel Quilt, #7284, unidentified clipping, date unknown, 160-10
Joseph's Coat, #5152, *Detroit Free Press*, Jun 20, 1934, 309-5
* Lady Slipper, #x, *Detroit Free Press*, May 26, 1933, 225-7
* Lafayette Orange Peel, #5152, *Detroit Free Press*, Jun 20, 1934, 309-5
Lily, #5070, *Detroit Free Press*, Jan 13, 1934, 361-11
Lily, #5077E, *Detroit Free Press*, Mar 4, 1934, 367-7
Lily Album, #5052, *Detroit Free Press*, Apr 22, 1934, 331-5
* Link of Friendship, #7402, unidentified clipping, date unknown, 316-7
* Log Cabin, #7287, unidentified clipping, date unknown, 254-6
Lone Star, #5110, *Detroit Free Press*, Apr 7, 1934, 111-12
Lotus Blossom, #5196, *Detroit Free Press*, Aug 10, 1934, 232-4
Lover's Knot, #5556, *Detroit Free Press*, Mar 21, 1936, 121-6
Lucky Clover, #5141, *Detroit Free Press*, May 9, 1934, 330-12
* Lucky Star, #7275, unidentified clipping, date unknown, 80-6
Lucky Star Quilt, #7089, unidentified clipping, date unknown, 304-1
Magnolia, #5115, *Detroit Free Press*, Apr 1, 1934, 257-8
* Magnolia, #7021, unidentified clipping, date unknown, 152-6
Maltese Cross, #5008, *Detroit Free Press*, Jan 1, 1934, 299-2
Mariner's Star, #6776, unidentified clipping, date unknown, 202-8
* Maryland Beauty, #x, *Detroit Free Press*, Apr 19, 1933, 189-10
* May Basket, #5557, unidentified clipping, date unknown, 74-12
* Merry Go Round, #5892, unidentified clipping, date unknown, 334-9
Milky Way, #5059, *Detroit Free Press*, Feb 17, 1934, 416-13
* Millwheel, #7029, unidentified clipping, date unknown, 371-11
* Modern Quilt, #7050, unidentified clipping, date unknown, 76-2
Moonflower, #5092, *Detroit Free Press*, Apr 16, 1934, 360-11
Morning Glory, #5211, *Detroit Free Press*, Aug 30, 1934, 370-2
Morning Star, #7447, unidentified clipping, date unknown, 305-1
Night and Day, #5810, *Detroit Free Press*, Mar 12, 1937, 160-1
Night and Day, #no pattern number, *Alice Brooks Collection of Needlecraft Masterpieces*, ca. 1958, 328-9
* Nine Patch, #5540, unidentified clipping, date unknown, 424-1
Nosegay, #5419, *Detroit Free Press*, Aug 22, 1935, 250-2
Nosegay, #7093, unidentified clipping, date unknown, 190-4
Old Fashioned Garden, #5175, *Detroit Free Press*, Jul 3, 1934, 364-7
* Old Fashioned Nosegay, #7010, unidentified clipping, date unknown, 307-5
One Patch Quilt, #7260, unidentified clipping, date unknown, 427-9
* One Patch Star, #7275, unidentified clipping, date unknown, 394-6
Orange Peel, #6907, unidentified clipping, date unknown, 309-3
Patchwork Quilt, #7080, *Wichita Eagle*, date unknown, 300-7
Patchwork Quilt, #7428, unidentified clipping, date unknown, 415-11
Patchwork Quilt, #7437, unidentified clipping, date unknown, 323-6
Peony, #5176, *Detroit Free Press*, Sep 23, 1934, 326-3
Peony, #5401, *Detroit Free Press*, Jul 20, 1935, 335-2
Philadelphia Pavement, #5109, *Detroit Free Press*, Mar 23, 1934, 112-8
Pine Tree, #5934, *Detroit Free Press*, Aug 18, 1937, 122-10
Pineapple, #5008, *Detroit Free Press*, Jan 1, 1934, 302-12
Pinwheel, #5345, *Detroit Free Press*, Jul 13, 1935, 158-11
Pinwheel, #7011, unidentified clipping, date unknown, 82-9
Pinwheel, #7056, *Washington Post*, Mar 16, 1947, 377-11
Pinwheel, #7101, *Washington Post*, Sep 22, 1943, 326-9
Poppy, #5077F, *Detroit Free Press*, Mar 11, 1934, 367-6
Potholder Patch, *Alice Brooks Designs*, date unknown, 93-5
Prairie Flower, #5335, *Detroit Free Press*, Apr 25, 1936, 364-9
Prairie Queen, #5003, *Detroit Free Press*, Apr 25, 1934, 135-3
Pride of the Bride, #5916, *Detroit Free Press*, Oct 6, 1937, 389-1
Pride of the Garden, #5067, *Detroit Free Press*, Mar 2, 1934, 344-7
Pride of the West, #5589, *Detroit Free Press*, May 15, 1936, 363-12
Prudence's Choice, #5005, unidentified clipping, date unknown, 206-4
Pudding and Pie, #6291, unidentified clipping, date unknown, 143-8
Quilter's Pride, #5465, *Detroit Free Press*, Nov 1, 1935, 339-3
Quilting Party, #7075, unidentified clipping, date unknown, 189-8
Ragged Robin, #5019, *Detroit Free Press*, Jan 23, 1934, 167-1
Rainbow, #5050, *Detroit Free Press*, Jan 5, 1934, 340-4
Rainbow Scrap Quilt, #7138, *Alice Brooks Designs*, date unknown, 387-8
Regal Lily, #5127, *Detroit Free Press*, Apr 18, 1934, 363-7
Rising Sun, #5346, *Detroit Free Press*, May 16, 1935, 336-12
Road to Oklahoma, #5033, *Detroit Free Press*, Dec 16, 1933, 106-3
Rose, #5684, *Detroit Free Press*, Sep 26, 1936, 364-11
Rose, #5077D, *Detroit Free Press*, Feb 25, 1934, 367-10
Rose in Summer, #5078, *Detroit Free Press*, Jan 25, 1934, 332-5
Rose Star, #7172, *Alice Brooks Designs*, ca. 1950, 432-10
* Rose Star One Patch, #7172, unidentified clipping, date unknown, 432-10

Round Robin Scrap Quilt, #5123, *Detroit Free Press*, Apr 10, 1934, 331-9
Scottie Quilt, #5673, *Detroit Free Press*, Aug 5, 1936, 335-4
* Scrap Happy, #7221, unidentified clipping, date unknown, 309-1
Shasta Daisy, #5100, *Detroit Free Press*, Mar 5, 1934, 196-3
* Ship o' Dreams, #x, *Detroit Free Press*, Sep 13, 1934, 76-6
* Ships at Sea, #7221, unidentified clipping, date unknown, 72-8
Shooting Star, #5030, *Detroit Free Press*, Feb 1, 1934, 118-12
Snowball, #5001, *Detroit Free Press*, Nov 7, 1933, 350-4
* Snowball, #7065, *Washington Post*, Jun 15, 1951, 350-1
Snowdrop, #5077A, *Detroit Free Press*, Feb 4, 1934, 367-5
* Southern Moon, #6651, unidentified clipping, date unknown, 310-9
Southern Pine, #5359, *Detroit Free Press*, Sep 14, 1935, 190-1
Southern Rose, #5045, *Detroit Free Press*, Dec 20, 1933, 330-11
Spider Web, #5057, *Detroit Free Press*, Apr 29, 1934, 259-5
Spring, #5580, *Detroit Free Press*, Apr 29, 1936, 317-11
* Squares and Diamonds, #7001, unidentified clipping, date unknown, 158-12
* Star and Crown, #7328, unidentified clipping, date unknown, 293-11
Star Flower, #5073, *Detroit Free Press*, Jan 4, 1934, 331-7
* Star of Friendship, #5051, *Detroit Free Press*, Dec 21, 1933, 70-1
* Star of the East, #6422, unidentified clipping, date unknown, 78-10
Star of the West, #5124, *Detroit Free Press*, Apr 2, 1934, 175-7
* Starfish Quilt, #x, *Detroit Free Press*, Oct 12, 1934, 75-8
Starry Chain, #5121, *Detroit Free Press*, May 6, 1934, 334-12
Starry Crown, #5106, *Detroit Free Press*, Sep 7, 1934, 294-5
Starry Field, #5044, *Detroit Free Press*, date unknown, 286-2
Starry Path, #5514, *Detroit Free Press*, Jan 23, 1936, 144-4
Starry Path, #7701, *Alice Brooks Designs*, ca. 1950, 180-2
Stars, #7121, unidentified clipping, date unknown, 287-3
Summer and Winter, #5867, *Detroit Free Press*, Jun 3, 1937, 312-10
* Sunburst Quilt, #7408, unidentified clipping, date unknown, 298-3
Sweet Sultan, #5138, *Dayton News*, Jul 1, 1934, 317-9
Three Patch, #5566, *Detroit Free Press*, Apr 2, 1936, 326-8
Three Patch, #5821, *Detroit Free Press*, May 20, 1937, 311-1
Three Patch, #7003, *Alice Brooks Designs* date unknown, 85-12
* Three Patch, #7144, unidentified clipping, date unknown, 226-4
Three Patch, #7198, *Detroit Free Press*, Jul 1, 1934, 371-6
* Three Patch Quilt, #7120, unidentified clipping, date unknown, 73-2
Three Patch Quilt, #7372, *Alice Brooks Designs*, date unknown, 138-10
Treasure Chest, #5099, *Detroit Free Press*, Mar 8, 1934, 263-8
Triangles, #5040, unidentified clipping, date unknown, 427-9
Tulip, #5077C, *Detroit Free Press*, Feb 18, 1934, 367-8
Tulip Garden, #5666, *Detroit Free Press*, Sep 7, 1936, 370-1
Tulip in Patchwork, #7412, *Alice Brooks Designs*, 1935, 370-6
Tulip Patch, #5327, *Detroit Free Press*, Mar 20, 1935, 363-10
Tumbling Block, #5502, unidentified clipping, 430-9
Tumbling Blocks, #7441, unidentified clipping, date unknown, 394-6
Turkey Tracks, #5004, *Detroit Free Press*, Nov 2, 1933, 358-11
Turnabout, #5992, *Detroit Free Press*, Dec 18, 1937, 193-4
Turnabout, #7071, *Washington Post*, Dec 28, 1949, 117-1
Turnabout, #7122, unidentified clipping, date unknown, 318-2
* Two in One, #7301, unidentified clipping, date unknown, 66-9
Two in One Design, #7098, unidentified clipping, date unknown, 79-1
Two Patch, #7523, unidentified clipping, date unknown, 84-8
Vase of Flowers, #5204, *Detroit Free Press*, Sep 12, 1934, 369-1
* Washington Pavement, #7026, unidentified clipping, date unknown, 302-11
* Waving Plumes, #6831, unidentified clipping, date unknown, 311-4
Wheel of Fortune, #5104, *Detroit Free Press*, Mar 16, 1934, 372-7
* Wheel of Fortune, #7192, unidentified clipping, date unknown, 377-10
Whirling Fans, #5118, *Detroit Free Press*, Apr 4, 1934, 388-2
Whirling Square, #5053, *Detroit Free Press*, Dec 19, 1933, 256-5
Whirling Star, #5523, *Detroit Free Press*, Feb 26, 1936, 336-11
Windmill, #5903, *Detroit Free Press*, Jul 21, 1937, 339-5
Windmill, #6777, unidentified clipping, date unknown, 118-3
Wonder of the World, #5183 and 7048, *Cincinatti Enquirer*, Jul 14, 1933, 353-2
* Your Lucky Star, #7454, unidentified clipping, date unknown, 284-9

Appendix 3

Nancy Cabot Blocks

There are more quilt blocks with the name of Nancy Cabot, in this book than any other designer or source. I have listed more than 1360 designs attributed to that name. Most of the blocks were first published in *Chicago Tribune*. The dates they first appeared in that newspaper are provided in this index. However, if you look up the block in the book, you will often find that *Chicago Tribune* was not always the earliest source. The first block in the list, for instance, An 'A' Star, was first published in *Ladies Art Company* under a different name, *Star A*. This is the design's primary source, while *Chicago Tribune* is a later, secondary source (see 176-4). In this index, the asterisk next to particular listings indicates blocks that were published elsewhere, either under the same or a different name, before they appeared in *Chicago Tribune* on the date given here. Note, too, that some blocks were published more than once in *Chicago Tribune*, but only the earliest dates are provided.

'A' Star, An, Feb 11, 1935, 176-4
Aerial Beacon, Apr 18, 1938, 298-11
African Daisy, Jun 4, 1935, 375-12
* Air Castle, Jul 30, 1934, 143-2
Alabama Beauty, Jun 6, 1933, 309-7
Alabama Rambler, Oct 3, 1936, 78-1
* Album, Jan 24, 1933, 146-10
Album Block, Jun 5, 1935, 175-1
Alcazar, Jun 1, 1938, 357-3
* Algonquin Charm, date unknown (per Alboum), 185-5
Alpine Cross, Sep 11, 1936, 269-11
Altar Steps, Sep 16, 1936, 152-1
Amazing Windmill, Sep 29, 1936, 292-9
Amethyst Chains, Apr 17, 1936, 242-11
Annapolis Block, Jun 10, 1937, 88-4
* Annapolis Patch, Jan 25, 1934, 113-2
Antique Tile Block, May 3, 1938, 154-3
Apache Trail, Jan 5, 1938, 177-11
Arab Tent, Nov 2, 1937, 346-5
* Arabic Lattice, Sep 24, 1934, 210-4
* Arkansas Traveler, Dec 11, 1936, 144-4
Around the Corner, Apr 8, 1936, 94-11
Arrant Red Birds, Jan 2, 1936, 123-10
Arrowheads, Mar 1, 1933, 114-8
Arrowheads, Sep 30, 1937, 238-2
* Art Square, Jul 9, 1934, 57-12
Aster, Jun 21, 1933, 376-8
Asters, Oct 29, 1935, 376-8
Attic Stairs, Nov 13, 1937, 412-11
Attic Window, Jan 2, 1935, 150-8
Attic Windows, Aug 31, 1936, 149-12
Aunt Dinah's Hunt, Jul 17, 1938, 359-2
* Aunt Eliza's Star, Aug 13, 1934, 124-9
Aunt Lottie's Star, Sep 4, 1936, 124-9
Aunt Patsy's Pet, Aug 25, 1936, 153-4
Aunt Polly's Puzzle, Feb 9, 1936, 352-4
Aurora Stars, Feb 26, 1936, 132-9
Autumn Leaf, date unknown (per Alboum), 314-6
Autumn Leaves, Feb 13, 1933, 333-2
Autumn Leaves, Jun 8, 1936, 181-5
Autumn Stars, Nov 19, 1937, 103-12
* Autumn Stars, Nov 20, 1937, 138-1
* Baby Bunting, Apr 7, 1935, 384-9
* Bachelor's Puzzle, Sep 28, 1933, 66-10
* Balkan Puzzle, Feb 15, 1933, 60-4
Balkan Puzzle, Mar 23, 1934, 428-3
* Balkan Puzzle, Jul 24, 1936, 66-12
Balsam Fir, Feb 17, 1938, 179-3
* Barbara Frietschie Star, Mar 18, 1933, 64-2
Barn Bats, Oct 19, 1935, 173-4
* Barrister's Block, Feb 6, 1933, 105-12
Basket of Tulips, Jun 3, 1934, 368-3
Bat's Block, The, Feb 9, 1937, 141-2
Bats' Wings, May 8, 1934, 438-5
Bat Wings, Jun 25, 1937, 433-4
Baton Rouge, Jan 27, 1934, 94-3
* Baton Rouge Block, Jan 27, 1934, 94-3
Baton Rouge Square, May 22, 1936, 183-11
Battle of Alamo, Mar 26, 1933, 150-1
* Beach and Boats, Aug 21, 1937, 413-8
Bear's Paw, Mar 23, 1933, 223-10
* Beautiful Star, Feb 8, 1933, 297-1
Beech Tree, Mar 25, 1935, 314-11
Beg and Borrow, Nov 25, 1937, 99-4
Beggar's Block, Jun 30, 1933, 242-1
Bird and Kites, Apr 10, 1937, 99-5
* Birds in the Air, Feb 18, 1933 150-5
* Bird's Nest, Dec 13, 1934, 194-9
Bishop Hill, Oct 7, 1935, 255-6

Bismark, Mar 29, 1938, 105-7
Black Beauty, Jul 14, 1933, 87-8
Blackford's Beauty, Apr 19, 1934, 88-1
Blacks and Whites, Nov 4, 1936, 105-3
Blazed Trail, Jul 23, 1937, 108-7
Blazing Star, Feb 25, 1933, 202-2
* Bleeding Heart Feb 12, 1934 360-2
Blind Man's Fancy, Oct 14, 1934, 121-9
* Blindman's Fancy, Oct 14, 1934, 121-9
Blockhouse, Dec 22, 1936, 247-7
Blue and White, Jan 19, 1934, 101-2
* Blue Bell Block, Feb 9, 1937, 141-2
Blue Boutonnieres, Jun 26, 1936, 149-8
Blue Chains, Mar 7, 1936, 147-1
Blue Eagle, Oct 8, 1933, 439-2
Blue Fields, Oct 27, 1936, 113-5
Blue Heather, Feb 10, 1936, 198-9
Blue Heaven, Jun 23, 1936, 202-7
Blue Meteors, Feb 8, 1936, 133-4
Bluebell Block, Nov 28, 1935, 195-11
Boston Commons, Feb 5, 1935, 224-11
Boston Corners, Feb 10, 1934, 409-3
Boston Streets, Mar 16, 1936, 413-3
Bow Knots, May 30, 1936, 409-12
Bow Ties, Jul 9, 1938, 427-9
Bowknot, May 19, 1933, 269-12
Bowl of Fruit, May 6, 1938, 151-12
Bows and Arrows, Mar 6, 1934, 350-3
Box Car Patch, Nov 10, 1934, 224-12
Boy's Nonsense, Jul 25, 1936, 113-4
Boy's Playmate, Feb 23, 1935, 126-1
Brick Pavement, Jun 9, 1938, 167-4
Brickwork Block, May 6, 1935, 438-3
Bride's Bouquet, Jan 11, 1945, 307-5
Bright Star, Aug 29, 1934, 146-8
Bright Stars, Apr 21, 1936, 97-6
Broad Arrow, Jul 21, 1936, 174-2
Broken Dishes, Jan 29, 1937, 203-1
Broken Irish Chain, Mar 9, 1938, 203-11
Broken Rainbows, May 29, 1937, 433-5
Broken Sash, Jan 30, 1935, 119-7
Broken Spider Web, Aug 3, 1935, 297-3
Broken Star, Jul 17, 1936, 78-8
Broken Windmills, Feb 5, 1936, 254-5
* Brown Goose, Mar 9, 1934, 76-1
* Brunswick Star, date unknown (per Alboum), 286-2
Buckeye Beauty, Dec 27, 1933, 114-9
* Buckeye Block, Feb 2, 1937, 340-5
Buckwheat, Mar 4, 1937, 154-8
Buffalo Ridge, date unknown (per *Quilter's Newsletter Magazine*), 85-9
Building Blocks, May 1, 1933, 416-1
Building Blocks, Oct 31, 1934, 424-5
Building Blocks, Jan 15, 1938, 430-10
Bull's Eye, Feb 17, 1933, 262-8
* Bull's Eye, The, Feb 17, 1933, 262-8
Burgoyne's Surrender, Nov 24, 1933, 180-7
Burr, Nov 27, 1935, 420-5
Bursting Star, Apr 30, 1937, 204-2
Butterfly, Sep 30, 1935, 156-8
Butterfly Block, Aug 12, 1937, 161-3
Butterfly Bush, Oct 8, 1934, 180-12
Byrd at the South Pole, Nov 14, 1934, 335-12
Cabin in the Woods, Mar 15, 1937, 174-3
Cactus Basket, Jan 23, 1933, 305-8
Cake Stand, Nov 18, 1933, 191-1
Calico Bouquets, Apr 27, 1937, 213-4
Calico Bush, Nov 27, 1933, 306-2
Calico Compass, Nov 17, 1937, 373-3
Calico Fan, Mar 8, 1936, 386-9
Calico Mosaic, Nov 5, 1935, 161-12
Calico Plant, Jun 3, 1938, 364-4
Calico Star, Dec 5, 1933, 162-9
California Rose, Jun 26, 1933, 355-8
* California Rose, Dec 27, 1936, 355-9
California Star, Mar 21, 1935, 266-3
* California Star Pattern, Mar 21, 1935, 266-3
Carnival, Mar 18, 1938, 211-7
* Caroline's Choice, Apr 13, 1936, 73-8
* Carpenter's Square, Feb 12, 1935, 254-10
* Carpenter's Wheel, Mar 4, 1934, 289-6
Cartwheel, Jan 25, 1935, 335-11
Castle Garden, Jan 12, 1937, 98-5
Castor and Pollux, Nov 30, 1935, 414-2
Cat and Mice, Jul 25, 1934, 132-6
Catalpa Flower, May 25, 1935, 296-10
Cathedral Window, Apr 13, 1933, 205-6
Cathedral Windows, Dec 12, 1934, 205-11
Celestial Problem, May 4, 1935, 249-11
Celestial Sphere, Jun 19, 1935, 344-3
Centennial, Oct 29, 1934, 78-5
Century of Progress, Oct 22, 1933, 111-3
Century of Progress, Jul 21, 1934, 399-4
Chained Dominos, Oct 10, 1933, 153-10
Chained Star, Nov 28, 1934, 289-4
Chariot Wheel, May 31, 1935, 268-3
* Charm, Jun 15, 1934, 173-3
Checkers, Nov 15, 1934, 222-4
* Cherry Basket, Mar 21, 1933, 322-11
* Chicago Star, Dec 24, 1934, 156-4
Chieftain, The, Oct 17, 1936, 110-10
Children of Israel, Dec 16, 1933, 264-12
* Children's Delight, May 14, 1934, 192-3
Chimney Swallow, Feb 16, 1933, 346-5
Chimney Sweep, Jul 3, 1935, 92-3
Chinese Coin, Apr 7, 1934, 184-5
Chinese Coin, Aug 19, 1936, 184-2
Chinese Gongs, Jan 7, 1937, 330-7
Chinese Holiday, Feb 13, 1936, 165-11
Chinese Waterwheel, Oct 5, 1936, 377-8
* Chosen Children, Dec 31, 1933, 264-12
Chuck a Luck Block, Mar 29, 1937, 166-3
Church Windows, May 31, 1938, 205-7
* Churn Dash, Feb 28, 1934, 67-5
* Churn Dash, Apr 20, 1937, 66-2
Circle within Circle, Jan 8, 1935, 371-5
City Streets, Dec 21, 1937, 241-12
* Clay's Choice, Apr 5, 1933, 70-5
* Clay's Compromise, Apr 9, 1933, 72-9
* Clay's Favorite, Dec 13, 1937, 70-5
Cleopatra's Puzzle, Jun 5, 1933, 351-8
Climbing Roses, Dec 5, 1935, 205-12
Clown Block, Jun 2, 1937, 192-7
Clowns, Nov 13, 1934, 183-9
Cluster of Stars, Oct 26, 1933, 330-4
Coarse Patchwork, Nov 30, 1934, 407-12
Cobblestones, Jun 30, 1937, 198-9
Cock's Comb, Aug 28, 1935, 93-8
Cocklebur, Aug 28, 1935, 331-11
* Cog Wheels, Mar 4, 1935, 380-6
Cogwheels, Aug 24, 1935, 380-5
* Colonial Garden, Dec 30, 1934, 432-9
Colonial Pineapple Block, Jun 2, 1933, 303-4
* Columbia Puzzle, Dec 3, 1934, 116-6
* Columbian Chain, May 27, 1935, 271-13
* Columbian Star, May 11, 1935, 156-6
* Combination Star, Mar 28, 1935, 137-6
Compass, Jun 27, 1933, 373-3
* Compass, The, Jun 27, 1933, 373-2
Conch Shells, Mar 29, 1936, 119-5
Cone Tree, Jun 12, 1937, 232-11
Confederate Rose, 1936, 203-2
Constellation, Jan 7, 1936, 83-11
Corn and Beans, Oct 16, 1934, 329-10
* Corn and Beans, Feb 9, 1935, 130-9
* Coronation, Feb 20, 1934, 346-6
Coronation Block, Mar 19, 1937, 195-1
Counterpane, Apr 4, 1934, 155-11
County Fair, Oct 2, 1937, 205-10
County Farm, Oct 7, 1934, 205-10
Court House Lawn, Mar 8, 1937, 91-6
Coxey's Army, Jun 19, 1934, 85-2
* Coxey's Camp, Nov 23, 1936, 85-2
Cranberry Patch, Dec 24, 1935, 439-7
Crazy Ann, Aug 2, 1934, 99-11
Crazy Loon, Apr 24, 1937, 108-12
Crazy Quilt Bouquet, Oct 24, 1933, 107-5
Crazy Quilt Star, Aug 3, 1933, 176-5
Crazy Star Quilt, Apr 15, 1935, 82-4
Creole Puzzle, Mar 24, 1938, 167-5
* Cross and Chains, Feb 10, 1938, 156-9
Cross and Crown, Dec 8, 1934, 227-5
* Cross and Crown, Oct 7, 1936, 194-3
Cross and Diamond, Mar 27, 1937, 85-11
Cross and Panel, Dec 23, 1936, 193-9
Cross and Square, Nov 23, 1937, 79-5
Cross of Geneva, Apr 26, 1938, 157-5
Cross of Tennessee, Jun 22, 1935, 254-2
Cross Roads, May 16, 1935, 383-7
* Cross Stitch, Aug 19, 1937, 61-6
* Crossed Canoes, Jun 10, 1933, 80-8
Crossed Chains, May 12, 1938, 170-8
Crossed Squares, Dec 24, 1936, 203-12
* Crosses and Losses, Oct 10, 1934, 73-9
* Crossword Puzzle, Nov 13, 1935, 424-6
Crowfoot, Dec 16, 1937, 98-3
Crown of Stars, Dec 10, 1935, 231-4
Crowned Cross, The, May 26, 1933, 157-3
* Crow's Foot, Dec 13, 1933, 98-3
* Cube Lattice, Mar 23, 1935, 406-7
Cubes and Tile, Dec 15, 1933, 292-3
Cubes and Tile, Sep 7, 1936, 406-7
Cubic Measure, Jan 23, 1936, 324-11
Cubist Rose, Oct 20, 1933, 110-12
Cumberland Gap, Dec 7, 1935, 410-1
Cupid's Darts, Oct 16, 1935, 430-2
Custer's Last Stand, Apr 30, 1933, 98-12
* Cut Glass Dish, Nov 26, 1934, 150-2
Daisy Swirl, Apr 25, 1933, 377-7
Dancing Cubes, May 8, 1937, 408-9
Dancing Pinwheels, Dec 19, 1935, 154-11
David and Goliath, Sep 6, 1936, 262-8
David and Goliath, Feb 17, 1933, 141-9
Decorated Basket, Nov 22, 1933, 311-8
Delaware Crosspatch, Sep 18, 1937, 189-4
Delectable Mountains, Nov 12, 1933, 216-10
Delft Mill, Apr 7, 1937, 100-9
Desert Rose, Apr 4, 1936, 159-11
Devil's Claw, Jun 18, 1934, 97-7
Devil's Claw, Oct 23, 1936, 228-9
Devil's Footprints, Jul 17, 1938, 359-2
Devil's Puzzle, Oct 19, 1934, 90-8
Diagonal Paths, Apr 18, 1936, 84-1
Diamond Chain, Oct 13, 1937, 121-4

* Magic Cross, Jan 27, 1937, 61-3
Magical Circle, Oct 25, 1933, 77-3
Magnolia Block, Jan 28, 1936, 172-12
Magnolia Bud, Feb 19, 1934, 116-7
* Magnolia Leaf, Apr 10, 1933, 178-3
Maiden's Delight, Oct 30, 1937, 228-1
Maltese Cross, Jun 11, 1938, 322-1
Maltese Cross Block, Dec 26, 1936, 266-2
Many Paths, Dec 18, 1933, 415-3
* Maple Leaf, Apr 10, 1933, 178-3
* Maple Leaf, Nov 30, 1936, 146-8
Marietta Blockhouse, Nov 14, 1935, 269-6
Mariner's Block, Mar 2, 1936, 379-3
Mariposa Lily, Feb 23, 1933, 367-4
Market Square, Mar 14, 1936, 111-11
Martha Washington Star, Jun 28, 1933, 78-9
Martha's Choice, Aug 19, 1934, 389-6
Martha's Choice, Dec 28, 1936, 389-5
Martha's Choice, Nov 11, 1937, 388-11
Mary's Block, Jul 28, 1937, 140-6
May Basket, Aug 21, 1936, 306-1
Mayflower, Jul 27, 1934, 131-10
Mayor's Garden, Jun 2, 1938, 133-8
Medieval Mosaic, Mar 30, 1936, 243-1
Medieval Walls, Mar 30, 1936, 243-1
Meeting House Square, Dec 31, 1935, 242-12
Melon Patch, Aug 2, 1933, 309-5
Melon Patch, Mar 29, 1934, 310-1
Memory Block, Jun 16, 1938, 95-5
* Memory Blocks, Jul 19, 1934, 204-12
Merrie England, Oct 4, 1935, 178-1
Merry Go Round, Oct 2, 1935, 292-9
* Merry Kite, Oct 18, 1933, 135-4
Mexican Siesta, Mar 18, 1936, 336-7
* Mexican Star, The, Jun 19, 1933, 199-9
Midnight Sky, Feb 1, 1938, 291-7
Midsummer Night, May 13, 1935, 294-8
Milady's Fan, Nov 7, 1934, 387-2
Milky Way, Jun 20, 1934, 102-12
Mill and Stars, Sep 26, 1936, 134-5
Mill Wheel, Mar 17, 1934, 143-6
Miller's Daughter, Sep 9, 1937, 185-6
* Millwheel, May 3, 1937, 67-11
Milly's Favorite, Dec 6, 1933, 428-2
*Milwaukee's Own, Apr 13, 1935, 359-6
Milwaukee's Pride, Dec 3, 1936, 359-6
Mississippi Oak Leaves, Apr 5, 1933, 359-7
* Missouri Daisy, Jun 4, 1933, 340-11
* Missouri Daisy, Jul 24, 1938, 343-4
Missouri Puzzle, Jan 21, 1935, 258-5
Missouri Star, Jul 24, 1933, 78-6
Missouri Trouble, Jun 26, 1935, 341-3
Mixed T Blocks, Mar 26, 1935, 151-2
Modern Corsage, Oct 10, 1936, 181-2
Modern Daisies, Sep 17, 1935, 362-9
Modern Daisy, Jul 27, 1937, 362-9
Modern Peony, Apr 20, 1935, 347-1
Modernistic Pansy, Sep 30, 1933, 178-10
Modernized Poppy, Nov 8, 1934, 362-3
Mohawk Trail, Aug 9, 1933, 351-10
* Mollie's Choice, Apr 25, 1934, 242-3
Monastery Windows, May 27, 1936, 111-2
Monday's Block, Jun 1, 1936, 210-6
Monk's Puzzle, Sep 29, 1937, 432-6
* Monkey Wrench, Feb 8, 1934, 93-11
Montana Maze, Jun 21, 1938, 224-9
* Moon and Stars, Feb 21, 1935, 317-6
Moon and Swastika, May 2, 1935, 318-8
Moon Block, Oct 12, 1937, 339-7
* Moon Flower, Aug 12, 1936, 361-2
Moorish Mosaic, Aug 26, 1936, 287-12
Morning Star, Feb 26, 1937, 398-7
Morning Star, Jun 17, 1937, 260-7
Morning Star, Jul 5, 1937, 278-2
* Mosaic No. 1, May 11, 1934, 75-6
Mosaic No. 2, May 19, 1934, 94-8
* Mosaic No. 3, Jan 17, 1934, 58-12
* Mosaic No. 4, Jun 22, 1934, 67-1
* Mosaic No. 5, Jun 29, 1934, 68-12
* Mosaic No. 6, Jul 23, 1934, 60-7
* Mosaic No. 7, Aug 8, 1934, 61-5
* Mosaic No. 8, Sep 1, 1934, 60-1
* Mosaic No. 9, Sep 11, 1934, 68-12
Mosaic No.10, Sep 28, 1934, 428-1
* Mosaic No. 11, Jun 17, 1937, 70-4
* Mosaic No. 12, Oct 4, 1934, 60-8
Mosaic Rose, May 19, 1938, 93-10
Mosaic Squares, Jun 2, 1936, 164-4
Mosaic Squares, Jul 1, 1936, 97-12
Moss Rose, Feb 27, 1936, 172-6
Mother's Choice, Mar 25, 1938, 164-6
* Mother's Fancy, Dec 10, 1934, 176-11
Mountain Homespun, Jun 7, 1935, 272-10
Mountain Pink, Jun 3, 1933, 373-1
Mrs. Cleveland's Choice, May 8, 1933, 175-12
Mrs. Morgan's Choice, Dec 25, 1934, 145-3
Mrs. Morgan's Choice, Nov 25, 1936, 145-5
My Favorite, Aug 8, 1933, 84-5
Mystic Maze, Mar 15, 1933, 292-9
Mystic Maze, Sep 29, 1936, 292-12
Mystic Star, Dec 18, 1937, 173-2
* Nameless Star, Oct 20, 1934, 62-3
Nauvoo Lattice, Apr 19, 1937, 411-7
Navajo, Aug 30, 1934, 109-9
Navajo, Sep 10, 1935, 123-4
Nebraska, Jul 22, 1933, 271-10
* Necktie, May 13, 1933, 61-11
* Necktie, Jul 23, 1936, 127-10
* Necktie Pattern, Jul 23, 1936, 127-10
Net of Stars, May 9, 1936, 414-8
* New Album, Oct 1, 1934, 57-7
New Barrister's Block, Jan 24, 1938, 106-1
New Double Irish Chain, Sep 15, 1936, 198-10
New Log Cabin, Jul 18, 1935, 233-9
New Moon, Apr 13, 1938, 311-10
* New Star, May 15, 1934, 216-3
New Star of North Carolina, Apr 2, 1938, 211-6
New Waterwheel, Apr 8, 1938, 241-6
* Next Door Neighbor, Jan 16, 1934, 68-3
Night and Day, Apr 2, 1934, 195-8
Night Heavens, Mar 27, 1936, 115-2
* Nine Patch, date unknown (per Alboum), 124-4
Nine Snowballs, Aug 20, 1935, 296-12
Nocturne, Jun 28, 1934, 328-1
Noon Day Lily, Feb 23, 1933, 367-4
Noonday, Feb 26, 1934, 382-7
Nora's Choice, Jan 1, 1938, 163-12
North Carolina Beauty, Jul 10, 1935, 265-3
North Carolina Lily, Feb 23, 1933, 367-4
North Carolina Star, Dec 21, 1933, 238-8
North Carolina Star, Feb 18, 1938, 285-2
Northern Lights, Jul 12, 1938, 226-11
Norway Pine, Aug 27, 1936, 208-5
Nosegay, Apr 12, 1933, 86-4
Nosegay, Mar 19, 1934, 255-1
Nosegay, Jul 22, 1936, 255-8
* Ocean Wave, Apr 6, 1933, 159-3
* Ocean Wave, Aug 22, 1936, 93-3
* Ocean Waves, Oct 30, 1934, 427-8
* Ocean Waves, Oct 14, 1936, 74-4
* Ocean Waves, May 13, 1937, 159-4
Octagon Block, Dec 14, 1937, 412-4
Octagonal Block, Aug 6, 1934, 411-1
Odd Fellow's Chain, Mar 8, 1935, 98-7
Odd Fellow's Cross, Feb 3, 1933, 200-10
Odd Patchwork, An, Dec 23, 1934, 248-10
* Odd Scraps Patchwork, Jun 16, 1934, 184-11
Odds and Ends, Mar 19, 1935, 105-4
* Ohio Star, date unknown (per Alboum), 124-7
Old Antique, Apr 28, 1933, 196-1
Old Fashioned Daisy, Jul 29, 1934, 196-4
Old Fashioned Pieced Block, Apr 17, 1935, 172-7
Old Favorite, Aug 5, 1937, 84-5
Old Glory, Jan 23, 1937, 394-6
* Old Gray Goose, Jan 27, 1933, 76-1
Old Italian Block, Jul 28, 1936, 132-2
Old Maid's Patience, Jun 24, 1933, 97-9
Old Maid's Ramble, Jul 31, 1934, 77-9
* Old Maid's Puzzle, Jun 15, 1933, 73-10
* Old Maid's Puzzle, Nov 22, 1934, 74-2
* Old Poinsettia Block, Dec 31, 1937, 70-4
Old Snowflake, Mar 12, 1937, 271-5
Old Staffordshire, Apr 21, 1937, 296-11
Old Time Block, Jan 30, 1938, 172-7
* Old Windmill, The, Jul 9, 1938, 428-5
One Dozen Napkins, May 22, 1937, 177-4
Open Windows, Jun 5, 1937, 101-10
Orange Peel, Mar 29, 1934, 310-1
Orange Peel, Jan 10, 1937, 359-1
Orange Pekoe, Dec 28, 1935, 427-1
* Oregon, Sep 9, 1937, 185-6
Oriental Puzzle, Jun 22, 1938, 163-10
Oriental Rose, Oct 13, 1933, 369-7
Oriental Splendor, Dec 18, 1933, 415-3
Oriental Star, Aug 10, 1933, 257-4
Oriental Star, Mar 26, 1936, 295-12
Oriental Tulip, Aug 20, 1933, 440-7
Original, The, Sep 17, 1933, 121-8
Ozark Mountains, Jan 9, 1936, 110-5
Pacific Railroad, Oct 9, 1936, 147-1
* Paddle Wheel, Apr 9, 1937, 145-4
Paducah Peony, Mar 24, 1937, 329-2
Painted Snowball, Jul 25, 1933, 357-6
Palm Leaf Block, Jun 27, 1937, 314-4
Panama Block, Aug 3, 1937, 199-9
Paneled Roses, Jun 11, 1937, 323-7
Parasol Block, Feb 5, 1937, 374-7
Path and Stiles, Apr 17, 1937, 241-11
Path of Fans, Aug 26, 1937, 351-10
Pathfinder, Jul 13, 1935, 189-3
* Patience Corners, Mar 1, 1934, 408-10
Pattern Lacking Name, Sep 9, 1935, 219-9
Peary's Expedition, May 12, 1933, 325-9
* Peek Hole, May 13, 1933, 61-11
Peeled Orange, Oct 11, 1933, 421-2
Penelope's Favorite, Sep 3, 1934, 315-7
Penn's Puzzle, Feb 11, 1938, 324-4
Pennsylvania Hex, Nov 1, 1935, 287-7
Peony and Forget Me Nots, Nov 19, 1936, 103-10
* Perpetual Motion, Aug 29, 1936, 144-6
* Perpetual Motion, Jan 16, 1937, 76-5
Philadelphia Block, Jan 19, 1938, 84-4
Philadelphia Pavement, Mar 7, 1933, 253-3
Philadelphia Pavement, Jan 19, 1938, 84-4

Pickle Dish, Nov 24, 1934, 325-6
Pieced Bouquet, Sep 21, 1933, 171-5
Pieced Butterfly, Jun 11, 1933, 173-1
Pieced Eight Point Star, Dec 11, 1933, 283-3
* Pieced Star, date unknown (per Alboum), 64-2
* Pilot Wheel, Jan 7, 1934, 325-8
Pin Cushion, Jul 15, 1934, 318-3
Pine Cones, Apr 19, 1938, 340-8
*Pine Tree, Jan 22, 1933, 255-2
* Pine Tree, Nov 4, 1934, 179-4
* Pine Tree, Nov 4, 1934, 179-5
* Pine Tree, May 10, 1937, 245-7
Pineapple Block, Apr 2, 1936, 271-2
Pineapple Squares, Jan 26, 1937, 273-8
Pink Magnolias, Jul 26, 1936, 228-5
Pinwheel, Feb 15, 1935, 99-11
Pinwheel and Vine, May 28, 1938, 207-4
* Pinwheel Quilt, Oct 18, 1933, 135-4
* Pinwheel Star, Apr 30, 1935, 286-8
Pinwheels, Jan 30, 1933, 206-6
Pinwheels and Squares, Jul 21, 1937, 428-2
Pioneer Block, Jan 20, 1938, 189-3
Plaited Block, Feb 12, 1937, 411-12
Point and Feather, Oct 13, 1936, 194-5
Port and Starboard, Apr 5, 1937, 428-5
Pot of Gold, Aug 10, 1937, 383-11
Potted Roses, Oct 31, 1936, 107-4
Potted Star Flower, Mar 31, 1935, 307-1
Potted Star Flower, Aug 18, 1936, 368-2
Practical Orchard, Jun 5, 1934, 124-4
* Prairie Queen, Feb 9, 1933, 128-7
* Prairie Queen, Mar 26, 1934, 130-7
Premium Star, Mar 5, 1935, 85-10
President's Block, Sep 19, 1937, 251-6
* Primrose Path, May 20, 1933, 105-7
Priscilla Alden, Mar 12, 1933, 377-5
* Priscilla, The, Aug 10, 1934, 226-12
* Priscilla's Dream, ca. 1938, *Detroit News* (per Brackman), 82-11
Prosperity, Jul 20, 1938, 276-5
* Prosperity Block, The, Jun 7, 1933, 244-1
Providence, Jul 3, 1933, 186-12
* Providence Quilt Block, Jan 3, 1938, 186-12
Pullman Puzzle, Nov 27, 1934, 312-2
Puritan Maiden, Jun 3, 1935, 328-5
Puss in Corner, Sep 3, 1935, 265-2
Puss in Corner, Dec 20, 1937, 240-2
* Puss in the Corner, Feb 16, 1937, 131-1
Puss in the Corner, Jul 27, 1938, 105-1
Pyramids, Jun 18, 1936, 172-10
Pyramids of Egypt, Jun 24, 1935, 430-1
Pyramids, The, Jan 11, 1936, 95-12
Quatrefoils, Jun 29, 1936, 141-4
Quatrefoils, Jun 14, 1937, 322-7
Quebec, May 21, 1938, 263-12
Queen Anne's Crown, Feb 3, 1937, 356-12
Queen Charlotte's Crown, Apr 17, 1933, 191-12
Queen's Crown, Jun 18, 1933, 263-5
Quilter's Delight, Apr 12, 1936, 353-10
Quilter's Delight, Dec 21, 1936, 193-10
Quilter's Delight, Jul 10, 1937, 268-3
* Rail Fence, May 15, 1935, 109-1
Rail Fences, Jan 3, 1936, 407-2
Railroad, Apr 11, 1934, 105-9
Railroad Block, Jul 10, 1936, 106-10
* Railroad Crossing, Feb 21, 1934, 206-2
Railroad Crossing, Jan 1, 1937, 166-12
Rainbow Block, Sep 7, 1934, 383-11
Rambler, The, Apr 11, 1933, 77-9
Rambler, The, Nov 16, 1938, 77-8
* Red and White Cross, May 26, 1936, 64-6
Red Buds, Dec 22, 1935, 332-7
Red Peony Buds, Jun 15, 1936, 110-2
Red Shields, Jan 4, 1936, 428-11
Reel, May 11, 1933, 354-12
* Reel, The, Dec 18, 1936, 355-2
Regal Cross, Sep 2, 1937, 322-5
* Ribbon Border, Jul 11, 1934, 413-8
Ribbon Square, May 8, 1935, 176-12
* Right and Left, Aug 21, 1934, 57-13
* Right Angles Patchwork, Sep 29, 1937, 432-6
Rising Sun, Mar 17, 1933, 374-3
Rising Sun, Jan 30, 1937, 294-12
Rising Sun, Aug 31, 1937, 378-10
Riviera, Mar 12, 1938, 122-1
Road Home, The, Sep 25, 1937, 354-7
* Road to California, May 15, 1941, 147-2
* Road to Oklahoma, Nov 6, 1933, 70-11
* Road to Oklahoma, Aug 16, 1937, 70-12
* Road to the White House, Jul 13, 1936, 146-11
Rob Peter to Pay Paul, Feb 4, 1933, 318-2
* Rob Peter to Pay Paul, Aug 5, 1936, 77-4
* Rob Peter to Pay Paul, Sep 22, 1937, 326-7
Rockingham Beauty, Dec 27, 1933, 114-9
Rockingham's Beauty, Sep 14, 1934, 114-9
Rocky Glen, May 27, 1933, 107-10
Rocky Mountain Puzzle, Jun 22, 1933, 105-2
Rocky Road to Dublin, Aug 15, 1933, 147-4
Rocky Road to Dublin, Jun 14, 1938, 242-10
* Rocky Road to Kansas, Mar 6, 1935, 65-2
* Rolling Pinwheel, date unknown (per Alboum), 145-10
Rolling Squares, Sep 19, 1936, 135-2
* Rolling Star, Mar 27, 1933, 286-2
* Rolling Stone, Mar 8, 1933, 114-4
* Rolling Stone, Oct 25, 1934, 131-11
Roman Courtyard, Apr 9, 1936, 164-9
Roman Cross, Nov 11, 1934, 91-9
Roman Pavement, Mar 4, 1938, 135-1
Roman Pavements, Nov 27, 1934, 312-3
Roman Roads, Jul 23, 1935, 213-1
Rope Block, Mar 9, 1937, 407-8
Rose Album, Jun 11, 1935, 355-9
Rose Garden, Jun 22, 1936, 265-12
Rose Point, Apr 21, 1938, 344-2
Rose Trellis, May 14, 1936, 206-5
Rosebud, Aug 27, 1934, 247-1
Royal Cross, Dec 15, 1934, 322-5
* Royal Japanese Vase, Jun 3, 1934, 368-3
* Royal Star Quilt, Jul 2, 1934, 168-4
Ruby Roads, May 8, 1936, 88-3
Ruins of Jericho, Nov 27, 1937, 85-6
Rustic Wheel, Jul 2, 1936, 244-7
Sacramento City, Jul 28, 1938, 328-2
* Sail Boat in Blue and White, A, Jan 4, 1937, 76-6
Sally's Favorite, Jun 1, 1934, 77-7
Santa Fe Trail, Feb 17, 1934, 251-3
Sapphire Net, May 12, 1937, 212-2
* Sarah's Favorite, Jun 1, 1934, 77-7
Saturn's Rings, May 28, 1937, 325-11
Savannah Beautiful Star, Jan 19, 1935, 402-3
Sawtooth, Jul 25, 1935, 270-12
Sawtooth Patch, May 17, 1934, 128-11
Schoenrock Cross, Jun 24, 1937, 224-6
Scotch Heather, Apr 24, 1936, 243-3
* Scotch Squares, Apr 6, 1935, 94-10
Scrap Bag Tree, Mar 14, 1933, 330-2
* Sea Shells, Jan 24, 1934, 433-7
Seasons, The, Mar 7, 1938, 243-5
Seminole Block, Dec 9, 1937, 195-3
Sentry's Pastime, Jun 12, 1936, 159-7
Seven Sisters, Mar 13, 1933, 394-12
Shaded Diamonds, Oct 27, 1937, 110-1
Ships at Sea, Mar 16, 1934, 107-8
Ships at Sea, Aug 9, 1936, 107-7
Ships in the Night, Oct 21, 1934, 270-10
* Shoo Fly, Jul 19, 1933, 124-5
* Shooting Star, Aug 12, 1933, 169-10
* Shooting Star, Aug 25, 1934, 70-7
Shooting Stars, Aug 12, 1933, 70-5
Shooting Stars, Feb 1, 1937, 169-10
* Silver and Gold, May 7, 1938, 276-4
* Simple Design, Jul 28, 1934, 204-4
* Simple Flower Basket, Jan 26, 1938, 75-1
Single Chain and Knot, Mar 25, 1937, 197-8
Single Irish Chain, Jul 13, 1933, 173-7
Single Lily, Aug 16, 1933, 365-9
* Single Sunflower, Mar 18, 1935, 381-9
* Single Wedding Ring, May 6, 1933, 184-11
* Sister's Choice, Jan 4, 1935, 185-12
* Six Pointed Star, Oct 26, 1934, 192-12
* Six Pointed Star, Jan 9, 1935, 399-9
* Sky Rocket, Dec 17, 1936, 157-11
Skyrocket, Apr 24, 1933, 157-11
Skyrocket, Dec 17, 1936, 157-12
* Slashed Album, Feb 4, 1935, 157-11
* Slashed Star, Dec 23, 1933, 378-10
Snail's Trail, Mar 11, 1934, 108-8
* Snow Block, Sep 29, 1934, 61-6
* Snow Crystal, Aug 3, 1936, 291-4
* Snow Crystal, Mar 20, 1934, 393-12
Snowball, Feb 2, 1933, 351-6
Snowball, May 18, 1933, 350-6
Snowballs, Jul 16, 1938, 77-4
Solar System, Jan 25, 1938, 402-12
Solomon Puzzle, Jan 7, 1934, 352-10
Solomon's Garden, May 31, 1936, 398-12
Solomon's Puzzle, May 24, 1933, 352-9
Solomon's Seal, Oct 25, 1937, 397-4
Solomon's Temple, Sep 23, 1934, 177-9
Southern Cross, Dec 4, 1935, 414-3
Spanish Squares, Dec 1, 1937, 207-12
Sparkling Dew, Feb 23, 1937, 401-5
Sparkling Jewel, Mar 11, 1937, 138-7
* Spider Web, Jan 29, 1934, 292-11
* Spider's Den, Sep 30, 1934, 177-2
Spinning Arrows, Feb 25, 1936, 146-5
Spinning Hour Glass, Nov 5, 1936, 103-8
Spinning Jenny, Oct 12, 1936, 103-2
Spinning Tops, Dec 7, 1937, 192-2
Spirals, Nov 21, 1936, 116-9
Spirit of 1849, Jan 29, 1936, 329-11
Spirit of St. Louis, Apr 28, 1934, 426-4
Spool and Bobbin, May 15, 1936, 106-9
Spool and Bobbin, Dec 9, 1936, 242-1
Spools and Bobbins, Dec 9, 1936, 242-1
Spool Block, Apr 1, 1938, 186-2
Spools and Bobbins, Dec 9, 1936, 242-1
Spring and Fall, Sep 23, 1937, 233-6
Spring Blossoms, Dec 28, 1936, 389-6
Square and Compass, Mar 4, 1933, 338-2
Square and Crosses, Sep 12, 1935, 337-3
* Square Cross, May 25, 1934, 173-10
Squares upon Squares, May 27, 1937, 411-5
Squares within Squares, The, Aug 1, 1936, 424-3

St. Elmo's Cross, Apr 30, 1938, 224-10
St. Elmo's Fire, Apr 14, 1936, 288-1
St. Louis Block, Oct 22, 1934, 276-6
* St. Louis Star, Jul 11, 1933, 204-9
Star and Arrow, Feb 20, 1937, 286-7
Star and Box, Nov 18, 1936, 430-7
* Star and Chains, Jun 16, 1937, 289-3
Star and Corona, Jun 24, 1938, 206-1
* Star and Crescent, Apr 14, 1933, 343-9
Star and Cross, Feb 7, 1933, 334-3
Star and Cross May 21, 1934 166-11
Star and Cross, Apr 27, 1936, 199-12
Star and Diamonds, Jul 24, 1937, 398-10
Star and Mill Block, Jul 3, 1936, 207-3
* Star and Pinwheels, Jul 3, 1937, 70-9
Star and Stripe, Feb 24, 1938, 87-8
Star and Wreath, May 24, 1938, 286-8
Star Cluster, Dec 21, 1934, 164-11
Star Flower, Oct 14, 1933, 361-3
Star Kites, Dec 25, 1937, 160-4
* Star Lane, Sep 18, 1934, 203-7
Star Net, Apr 2, 1937, 203-6
Star of '49, Apr 22, 1937, 231-5
* Star of Bethlehem, Dec 14, 1934, 399-8
Star of Erin, Apr 10, 1936, 142-6
Star of Magi, Feb 24, 1937, 289-5
Star of Many Points, Jul 4, 1933, 248-3
Star of Many Points, Sep 6, 1936, 141-9
* Star of North Carolina, Jan 23, 1934, 285-1
Star of St. Louis, Aug 9, 1937, 276-6
Star of St. Louis, Mar 2, 1938, 204-9
* Star of the East, May 7, 1938, 276-4
Star of the Orient, Jan 11, 1938, 257-5
Star of the Sea, Mar 22, 1933, 161-3
Star Puzzle, Sep 15, 1937, 283-8
Star Tulip, May 2, 1938, 324-7
Star within Star, Mar 13, 1937, 296-2
* Starlight, Mar 28, 1934, 286-4
* Starlight, Jul 12, 1935, 291-6
* Starry Crown, Apr 26, 1933, 338-8
* Starry Crown, Apr 19, 1936, 357-4
Starry Night, Dec 14, 1935, 413-13
Stars, Jan 5, 1935, 140-8
* Stars and Cubes, Sep 26, 1934, 292-2
* Stars and Planets, Jan 3, 1934, 402-11
Stars and Stirrups, May 6, 1937, 356-11
Stars and Stripes, Jul 4, 1936, 264-3
* Stars Patchwork, Sep 26, 1934, 292-2
Stars within Stars, Jul 4, 1934, 193-10
State Fair, Apr 14, 1938, 130-1
State House, Jun 22, 1937, 106-10
Steeplechase, Mar 6, 1934, 350-3
Steps to Glory, May 1, 1937, 108-3
Steps to the Altar, Apr 27, 1934, 152-1
Steps to the Garden, Feb 20, 1935, 425-4
Stone Mason's Puzzle, Apr 18, 1934, 223-4
Stonewall Jackson, Apr 23, 1933, 278-6
* Storm at Sea, Jun 14, 1934, 114-4
Storm Signal, Oct 16, 1937, 133-7
Straight Furrow, Mar 30, 1934, 111-6
* Strawberry, Dec 27, 1936, 355-9
* Strawberry Patch, May 24, 1935, 356-1
Strength in Union, Jan 8, 1938, 191-6
Stripes and Squares, Apr 24, 1935, 258-3
* Sugar Bowl, Jul 9, 1936, 74-11
* Sugar Bowl, May 6, 1941, 57-13
* Sugar Loaf, Dec 4, 1934, 192-6
Sultan's Block, Dec 3, 1937, 406-9
Summer Clouds, Apr 5, 1938, 90-2
Summer Garden, Jan 20, 1935, 425-5
Summer Sun, Mar 22, 1936, 278-11
Sun Dial, Mar 3, 1934, 274-4
* Sunbeam, Jul 31, 1933, 113-8
* Sunbeam, Aug 8, 1935, 300-3
Sunbeam Crossroad, Dec 25, 1935, 212-7
* Sunburst, Mar 5, 1933, 379-10
* Sunburst, Mar 20, 1933, 380-3
* Sunburst, Sep 18, 1935, 380-7
* Sunburst, Aug 31, 1937, 378-10
Sunburst and Mills, Feb 22, 1936, 304-11
Sunflower, Jul 9, 1933, 361-5
Sunrise, Dec 9, 1934, 384-8
Sunshine, Jul 14, 1934, 92-7
Sunshine, Dec 25, 1936, 92-8
Sunshine and Shadow, Dec 27, 1937, 317-5
* Susannah, May 17, 1933, 62-2
* Susannah Patch, Sep 18, 1936, 62-2
* Susannah's Patch, Sep 18, 1936, 62-2
* Suspension Bridge, Feb 6, 1935, 384-4
Swallow, May 16, 1933, 107-1
Swallow's Flight, Dec 28, 1933, 123-8
Swallows, Jul 18, 1936, 216-12
Swallows' Flight, Feb 21, 1938, 220-8
Swamp Angel, Jul 14, 1938, 124-8
* Swastika, Feb 27, 1933, 68-10
Sweet Gum Leaf, Aug 17, 1936, 97-5
Swing in the Center, May 15, 1933, 98-4
Swinging in the Center, Apr 30, 1934, 135-1
T Block, Jun 26, 1934, 139-7
* T Quartette, Jul 17, 1934, 151-4
* T Quilt, date unknown (per Alboum), 72-7
Talahhassee Block, Sep 4, 1937, 410-11
* Tallahassee Quilt Block, Nov 23, 1934, 410-11
Tangled Garter, Mar 3, 1934, 274-4
Tangled Lines, Apr 12, 1935, 169-12
Tangled Squares, Dec 17, 1935, 410-5
Tangled Trails, Jun 11, 1936, 314-10
* Tea Box, Apr 27, 1935, 430-8
Tea Leaf, Mar 19, 1933, 123-6
Tea Leaves, Mar 1, 1937, 153-7
Tea Party, Mar 19, 1933, 123-6
Tea Time, Jul 8, 1937, 266-5
Tennallytown Square, Jul 8, 1938, 91-9
* Tennessee Circles, Feb 14, 1933, 322-5
Tennessee Puzzle, Jun 22, 1935, 254-2
* Tennessee Star, Sep 8, 1933, 282-11
* Tete-a-Tete, Nov 13, 1935, 424-6
Tete a Tete Block, Apr 3, 1937, 161-7
Texas Cactus Basket, Feb 3, 1936, 120-3
* Texas Flower, Sep 15, 1934, 178-4
* Texas Ranger, Feb 1, 1935, 80-4
* Texas Star, Apr 23, 1934, 399-11
* Texas Tears, Jul 13, 1934, 166-6
Texas Tulip, Jun 8, 1933, 362-8
Thousand Islands, Apr 9, 1938, 248-2
Thousand Pyramids, A, Oct 27, 1933, 428-10
Three and Six, Sep 21, 1936, 126-8
* Thrift Block, Jun 16, 1934, 184-11
* Thrift Block, Sep 6, 1937, 58-5
Tic Tac Toe, Aug 18, 1934, 198-5
* Tile Puzzle Mar 1, 1935 153-6
Tinted Chains, Feb 19, 1938, 91-5
* Tippecanoe and Tyler Too, Jul 9, 1938, 428-5
Tirzah's Treasure, Mar 3, 1934, 274-4
Token of Affection, Jun 5, 1935, 175-1
Top Hat, Mar 1, 1936, 256-8
Topaz Trail, Nov 9, 1935, 407-1
Towers of Camelot, Jul 14, 1937, 143-2
* Tree Everlasting, Jan 16, 1937, 76-5
Tree of Life, Jan 22, 1933, 255-2
Tree of Life, Apr 27, 1938, 152-12
* Tree of Paradise, Sep 23, 1935, 218-1
* Tree of Paradise, Aug 11, 1936, 210-5
Trenton Patch, Jan 31, 1934, 322-9
Triangle Puzzles, Oct 5, 1933, 192-10
Triangle Trails, Aug 25, 1937, 192-11
Tricolor Block, Sep 12, 1936, 426-4
Tricolor Star, Jul 31, 1937, 175-1
Triple Irish Chain, Dec 3, 1933, 250-5
Triple Irish Chain, Nov 26, 1935, 425-8
Triple Sunflower, Mar 24, 1933, 366-1
Trout and Bass Block, Oct 1, 1937, 288-11
True Lover's Knot, Jun 1, 1933, 318-2
True Lover's Knot, Jan 22, 1937, 312-5
Tudor Rose, Nov 20, 1936, 196-7
Tuip in Vase (sic), Jun 3, 1934, 368-3
* Tulip in a Vase, Jun 3, 1934, 368-3
* Tulip in Vase, Jun 3, 1934, 368-3
* Tulips in a Vase, Jun 3, 1934, 368-3
Tulip Wheel, May 23, 1935, 332-6
Tumbler Block, Feb 25, 1938, 433-3
Turk's Cap Lily, Apr 16, 1936, 377-6
Turkey Giblets, Feb 8, 1938, 294-3
Turkey in the Straw, May 15, 1933, 98-4
Turkey Tracks, Aug 20, 1934, 266-4
Turkey Tracks, Jul 17, 1938, 359-2
Twelve Crosses, Aug 16, 1936, 115-12
* Twin Sisters, Sep 10, 1934, 66-1
Twinkling Star, Apr 22, 1935, 277-7
Twinkling Star, Aug 31, 1937, 378-10
Twinkling Star, Jun 28, 1938, 81-4
* Twinkling Star, date unknown (per Alboum), 138-12
* Twinkling Stars, Nov 3, 1936, 344-3
* Twist Patchwork, Apr 4, 1935, 411-12
Twisted Ribbons, Nov 4, 1937, 413-5
Two Crosses, Sep 28, 1936, 185-7
Unfolding Star, Apr 1, 1936, 305-6
Union Block, Dec 17, 1934, 137-3
Union Square, Jul 16, 1937, 133-6
Upstairs and Down, Oct 12, 1935, 106-4
V Block, The, Jan 15, 1935, 226-10
* Variable Star, Jan 28, 1933, 124-7
* Variable Star, Aug 27, 1933, 204-9
Variegated Diamonds, Mar 13, 1935, 406-5
Vice President's Block, Jul 8, 1934, 168-8
Victorian Maze, May 19, 1937, 411-6
Victorian Rose, May 5, 1936, 263-11
* Victoria's Crown, Jan 5, 1934, 357-1
* Village Square, Jul 13, 1937, 57-12
Vine Block, May 14, 1938, 252-3
Vines at the Window, Dec 4, 1937, 228-8
Vineyard, May 25, 1937, 210-3
Violet Blossoms, Jun 9, 1937, 360-3
Virginia's Choice, Nov 11, 1937, 388-11
Wagon Wheel, The, Sep 26, 1937, 372-1
Walls of Jericho, Oct 28, 1935, 227-3
Wampum Block, Apr 16, 1938, 153-11
Wandering Foot, Feb 5, 1933, 357-12
Wandering Paths, Jul 30, 1937, 416-1
* Washington Sidewalk, Jun 2, 1934, 91-9
* Washington's Puzzle, Oct 15, 1934, 56-2

Appendix 4

Nancy Page Blocks

Nancy Page (see page 6) was the pen name of prominent columnist Florence La Ganke, credited with blocks that appeared in several different newspapers. I have found more than 550 designs attributed to Nancy Page, most of which appeared first in the *Birmingham News.* The following index lists the blocks and the newspapers in which I found them. The asterisk next to particular listings indicates blocks that were published elsewhere, either under the same or a different name, before they appeared in the periodical listed here. Note, too, that some blocks were published more than once in a particular periodical, but only the earliest dates are provided.

* Cluster of Stars, *Birmingham News*, Aug 14., 1933 and Sep 17, 1933, 164-11
Cobblestones, *Birmingham News*, Sep 13, 1932, 411-1
* Combination Star, *Birmingham News*, Feb 22, 1938, 137-6
* Connecticut, *Birmingham News*, May 24, 1938, 60-8
Coronation, *Birmingham News*, May 29, 1934, 106-5
Cowboy's Star, *Birmingham News*, May 26, 1936, 80-7
* Coxey's Camp, *Birmingham News*, Apr 24, 1934, 85-2
* Crazy House, *Birmingham News*, Sep 6, 1932, 188-5
Crimson Rambler, *Birmingham News*, Apr 12, 1938, 94-1
Criss Cross, *Detroit Free Press*, Apr 6, 1937, 182-5
Crooked Path, *Birmingham News*, date unknown, 353-1
* Cross and Crown, *Birmingham News*, Dec 1, 1936, 194-4
Cross Bars, *Birmingham News*, Jun 11, 1935, 193-2
Cross within Cross, *Birmingham News*, Jul 7, 1942, 212-11
* Cross, The, *Birmingham News*, Aug 4, 1942, 151-10
* Crossed Canoes, *Birmingham News*, Apr 23, 1940, 138-12
Crosses and Losses, *Nashville Banner*, Nov 28, 1933, 206-6
* Crosses and Losses, per Alboum, Jun 6, 1939, 73-9
Crossroads, *Birmingham News*, May 9, 1939, 242-5
* Crossroads to Texas, *Birmingham News*, May 6, 1941, 165-12
Crossword Puzzle, *Birmingham News*, May 22, 1934, 258-4
Crow's Foot, *Birmingham News*, Jun 7, 1938, 136-5
Crown and Cross, *Birmingham News*, Aug 30, 1932, 194-4
Crown of Thorns, *Birmingham News*, Oct 31, 1939, 98-2
Crowned Cross, *Nashville Banner*, May 17, 1938, 166-7
Crowned Cross, *Birmingham News*, Dec 14, 1943, 166-7
* Cube Lattice, *Birmingham News*, Nov 2, 1943, 406-7
* Cut Glass Dish, *Birmingham News*, Dec 25, 1934, 150-2
Dallas Star, *Birmingham News*, Apr 20, 1943, 199-9
Danger Signal, *Birmingham News*, Aug 2, 1932, 159-1
Darting Birds, *Birmingham News*, Aug 23, 1932, 151-6
Darting Minnows, *Birmingham News*, Nov 3, 1942, 132-12
David and Goliath, *Birmingham News*, Apr 12, 1938, 194-6
Depression, *Birmingham News*, Sep 12, 1939, 199-2
Devil's Claw, *Detroit Free Press*, Jul 13, 1937, 97-6
Dewey, The, *Nashville Banner*, Dec 9, 1941, 167-11
Diamond Hexagon Quilt, unidentified clipping, Aug 25, 1942, 415-1
Diamond String, *Nashville Banner*, Oct 8, 1940, 397-5
Diamonds, *Nashville Banner*, Apr 3, 1934, 409-2
* Dolly Madison Star, *Nashville Banner*, Feb 28, 1939, 251-6
* Dolly's Favorite, *Nashville Banner*, Jul 19, 1938, 204-1
* Domino, *Birmingham News*, Oct 10, 1939, 153-10
* Domino and Square, *Birmingham News*, Oct 26, 1937, 203-10
* Double Four Patch, *Birmingham News*, Oct 13, 1942, 73-6
* Double Hour Glass, unidentified clipping, Jun 21, 1938, 245-4
* Double Irish Chain, *Birmingham News*, Sep 25, 1934, 209-5
* Double Irish Chain, *Birmingham News*, Mar 2, 1937, 223-3
* Double Nine Patch, unidentified clipping, Sep 17, 1935, 240-8
* Double Pyramid, *Birmingham News*, Mar 29, 1938, 170-6
Double S, *Birmingham News*, Jan 19, 1943, 101-5
Double Saw Tooth, *Birmingham News*, Jan 31, 1939, 191-8
* Double T, *Nashville Banner*, Nov 6, 1934, 139-7
* Double Triangle, *Birmingham News*, Sep 6, 1938, 77-11
Double Trouble, unidentified clipping, May 16, 1939, 128-8
* Dover Quilt Block, *Birmingham News*, Oct 27, 1933, 311-12
Dover Square, *Birmingham News*, Jun 26, 1934, 87-8
Doves in the Window, *Birmingham News*, Nov 13, 1934 and Aug 5, 1941, 224-2
* Dresden Plate, unidentified clipping, Apr 2, 1940, 375-1
Drunkard's Path, *Birmingham News*, Apr 23, 1935, 352-12
Dublin Road Quilt, *Nashville Banner*, May 28, 1940, 147-1
Duck Tracks, *Birmingham News*, Sep 8, 1936, 104-4
* Dutch Windmill, *Nashville Banner*, Mar 21, 1933, 389-6
* Dutchman's Puzzle, *Birmingham News*, Jul 2, 1940, 68-10
Easter Morning, *Birmingham News*, Mar 19, 1940, 84-8
* Eight Pointed Star, *Nashville Banner*, Nov 5, 1940, 276-1
Empty Spools, *Birmingham News*, date unknown, 244-2
* Endless Chain, unidentified clipping, Jun 2, 1942, 226-9
* English Ivy, *Birmingham News*, Aug 30, 1932, 178-7
English Wedding Ring, unidentified clipping, Jul 4, 1939, 184-11
Fanny's Fan, *Birmingham News*, Jun 25, 1935, 194-5
* Fanny's Favorite, per Alboum, May 12, 1936, 84-5
Field of Stars, *Birmingham News*, Nov 26, 1940, 243-2
* Fifty Four Forty or Fight, *Birmingham News*, Jun 10, 1941, 133-3
Fish Quilt, *Birmingham News*, Aug 5, 1941, 288-11
Fish Tails, *Nashville Banner*, Feb 5, 1935, 259-6
Fishnets, *Nashville Banner*, Aug 27, 1935, 411-12
* Five Patch, *Birmingham News*, Apr 11, 1939, 240-7
Flaming Star, unidentified clipping, Jun 1, 1943, 164-1
Flock of Birds, *Nashville Banner*, Aug 14, 1934, 165-10
* Flock of Geese, *Birmingham News*, May 31, 1938, 73-11
Flower Show, *Birmingham News*, May 31, 1938, 83-4
* Fly Foot, *Nashville Banner*, Apr 29, 1941, 68-10
* Flying Bats, *Birmingham News*, Feb 6, 1934, 101-9
Flying Birds, *Birmingham News*, Oct 18, 1937, 149-1
Flying Checkers, *Birmingham News*, Oct 1, 1935, 90-2
* Flying Clouds, *Nashville Banner*, Mar 23, 1937, 90-2
* Flying Dutchman, *Birmingham News*, Jan 7, 1936, 146-2
* Flying Squares, per Alboum, May 4, 1943, 188-2
Flying Triangles, *Birmingham News*, Mar 5, 1940, 137-11
* Flying X, *Birmingham News*, Jul 9, 1935, 127-3
Folded Stars, *Birmingham News*, Apr 27, 1943, 175-2
* Follow the Leader, *Birmingham News*, Jul 30, 1935, 188-6
* Fool's Puzzle, *Birmingham News*, Jun 12, 1934, 353-5
Forget Me Not, *Birmingham News*, Aug 25, 1933, 126-1
Formal Garden, *Birmingham News*, Oct 31, 1933, 205-9
Four Doves, *Nashville Banner*, May 14, 1934, 278-2
Four H Quilt, *Birmingham News*, Dec 28, 1937, 244-10
* Four Points, *Birmingham News*, May 16, 1933, 167-9
* Four Points, *Birmingham News*, Mar 6, 1934, 160-4
Four Stars, *Birmingham News*, Apr 3, 1934, 97-6
Four Stars, *Lowell Sun* Nov 7, 1933, 291-10
Four Winds, *Nashville Banner*, May 30, 1933, 344-1
* Four Winds, unidentified clipping, Apr 20, 1943, 146-7
* Fox and Geese, *Birmingham News*, Jan 2, 1941, 74-1
Framed Puzzle, *Birmingham News*, Jun 16, 1936, 99-8
Framed Squares, *Birmingham News*, Oct 27, 1936, 149-10
French 4's, *Nashville Banner*, Dec 19, 1933, 184-2
* French Bouquet, *Nashville Banner*, Dec 10, 1940, 432-1
Friendship Hexagon, unidentified clipping, Sep 20, 1938, 399-11
Frontier Fiesta, *Birmingham News*, Mar 7, 1939, 413-11
* Fruit Basket, *Birmingham News*, Date unknown, 190-10
Garden Paths, *Birmingham News*, Apr 16, 1935, 242-7
George B., *Birmingham News*, Apr 12, 1938, 414-10
* Georgetown Circle, *Birmingham News*, date unknown, 95-6
Glitter, *Birmingham News*, Apr 21, 1936, 97-6
Going to Chicago, *Detroit Free Press*, Aug 20, 1940, 106-10
* Golden Gates, *Birmingham News*, Feb 15, 1939, 248-9
Golden Wedding, *Detroit Free Press*, Jan 1, 1935, 202-4
Golden Wedding, *Nashville Banner*, date unknown, 226-12
Golden Wedding Quilt, *Nashville Banner*, Nov 4, 1941, 226-12
Goose Creek, *Birmingham News*, Jul 16, 1940, 247-5
* Grandmother's Flower Garden, *Nashville Banner*, Mar 27, 1934, 432-1
Grandmother's Garden, *Nashville Banner*, Jun 25, 1934, 432-1
Green River, *Birmingham News*, Jun 13, 1933, 127-9
Green Springs, *Birmingham News*, Feb 11, 1936, 240-8
Hamilton Gardens, *Birmingham News*, date unknown, 302-10
Happy Birthday, *Birmingham News*, Mar 3, 1942, 84-2
Happy New Year, *Birmingham News*, Sep 28, 1943, 204-4
* Hen and Chickens, unidentified clipping, Sep 26, 1939, 131-10
Henry of the West, per Alboum, Aug 12, 1941, 124-7
Hexagon Stars, *Birmingham News*, Dec 5, 1939, 399-11
Hexagons, *Nashville Banner*, Nov 3, 1936, 392-3
* Hickory Leaf, *Birmingham News*, Date unknown, 355-2
* Hill and Valley, unidentified clipping, Aug 2, 1938, 155-1
Hills of Vermont, *Birmingham News*, Apr 28, 1936, 191-9
Home Treasure, *Birmingham News*, Jun 14, 1932, 79-6
Homespun, *Birmingham News*, Dec 3, 1935, 242-1
* Honey Bee, *Birmingham News*, Dec 12, 1933, 324-1
Hopeful Star, *Birmingham News*, Dec 17, 1935, 168-5
* Hour Glass, *Nashville Banner*, Aug 8, 1933, 60-9
Hour Glass, unidentified clipping, Nov 21, 1939, 149-1
* Hovering Hawks, *Birmingham News*, Mar 19, 1940, 74-3
Hubbard's Cupboard, unidentified clipping, May 21, 1935, 128-8
Idaho, *Birmingham News*, Mar 27, 1934, 97-1
* Indian Hatchet, *Birmingham News*, Jun 15, 1937, 74-7
* Indian Trail, *Nashville Banner*, Nov 9, 1937, 101-2
Interwoven, *Birmingham News*, date unknown, 241-12
* Irish Puzzle, *Birmingham News*, Mar 26, 1940, 101-2
Jack and Six, per Alboum, Jan 5, 1943, 126-8
* Jack in the Pulpit, *Birmingham News*, date unknown, 167-10
* Jacob's Ladder, *Birmingham News*, Nov 5, 1935, 147-1
Jewel Boxes, *Birmingham News*, date unknown, 157-11
Joan's Doll Quilt, per Alboum, Aug 21, 1934 and Jan 6, 1942, 128-8
Johnny Round the Corner, *Birmingham News*, Sep 23, 1941, 185-1
* Joining Star, *Lowell Sun* May 21, 1934, 62-7
* Joseph's Coat, *Birmingham News*, Feb 25, 1941, 60-10
Jubilee, *Birmingham News*, Jan 15, 1935, 93-2
* July Fourth, *Birmingham News*, May 9, 1933, 68-2
* July Fourth, *Birmingham News*, Apr 13, 1943, 68-3
Jungle Paths, *Birmingham News*, Jun 25, 1940, 168-4
Kaleidoscope, *Birmingham News*, Nov 26, 1935, 103-1
* Kansas Troubles, *Birmingham News*, Apr 4, 1933, 100-12
Katie's Favorite, *Birmingham News*, May 7, 1935, 194-6
* Key West Beauty, *Birmingham News*, Mar 14, 1944, 82-7
King David's Crown, *Illinois State Register*,Nov 23, 1937, 204-8
King's Crown, *Birmingham News*, Sep 26, 1933, 136-6
King's Highway, *Birmingham News*, Aug 18, 1936, 155-12
Kite Tails, *Birmingham News*, Sep 11, 1934, 87-1
Ladies' Wreath, *Birmingham News*, May 5, 1942, 134-12
Lady of the Lake, *Nashville Banner*, Dec 5, 1933, 201-3
Lattice, *Nashville Banner*, Jan 4, 1934, 90-7
* Lawyer's Puzzle, *Birmingham News*, Oct 2, 1934, 105-12
* Leap Frog, *Birmingham News*, Nov 28, 1939, 209-12
Lemon Peels, *Birmingham News*, date unknown, 318-2
Lenox Plate, *Birmingham News*, Nov 23, 1943, 376-1
* Letter T, The, *Nashville Banner*, May 28, 1934, 151-3
* Lily of the Field, *Birmingham News*, Oct 28, 1941, 251-12
* Lily Pond, unidentified clipping, May 14, 1935, 223-8
Lily Quilt, *Birmingham News*, Nov 17, 1942, 97-5
* Lincoln's Platform, *Birmingham News*, Feb 23, 1943, 222-8
Linda's Favorite, *Birmingham News*, Jun 17, 1941, 84-5
Linked Petals, *Birmingham News*, Jan 7, 1941, 318-2
Linoleum, *Nashville Banner*, Mar 28, 1933, 132-10

Little Red Schoolhouse, *Birmingham News*, Mar 30, 1937, 265-9
* London Roads, per Brackman, Apr 30, 1940, 241-7
Lone Star, *Birmingham News*, Sep 5, 1933, 415-5
* Lost Ship Pattern, unidentified clipping, Aug 29, 1939, 150-4
* Love Ring, *Birmingham News*, Dec 28, 1937, 352-1
Lover's Knot, *Birmingham News*, Mar 10, 1942, 122-7
* Lover's Knot, unidentified clipping, Mar 28, 1939, 389-7
Lucasta's Block, *Birmingham News*, Feb 16, 1937, 100-12
* Lucky Pieces, *Birmingham News*, Sep 3, 1940, 70-8
Lucky Star, *Nashville Banner*, May 25, 1937, 344-1
Magic Box, *Birmingham News*, Jun 25, 1934, 85-3
Maine Woods, *Birmingham News*, Date unknown, 183-8
Maltese Cross, *Birmingham News*, Dec 26, 1933, 85-7
* Maple Leaf, *Birmingham News*, Sep 14, 1937, 178-3
Maple Leaf, *Birmingham News*, Mar 9, 1943, 180-6
* Marion's Choice, *Birmingham News*, Oct 23, 1934, 60-6
Mariposa Lily, *Birmingham News*, Dec 19, 1933, 367-2
* Martha's Choice, *Birmingham News*, Nov 14, 1933, 60-6
* Maud's Album Quilt, *Birmingham News*, May 10, 1938, 61-6
Mayflower Quilt, *Detroit Free Press*, date unknown, 226-7
* Melon Patch, *Birmingham News*, Aug 17, 1937, 309-5
Memory Blocks, *Birmingham News*, Jan 21, 1936, 204-11
* Merry go Round, *Birmingham News*, Mar 10, 1936, 101-5
* Meteor Quilt, unidentified clipping, May 5, 1936, 70-5
Milford Center, *Birmingham News*, Jun 28, 1938, 77-5
Military Cross Roads, *Birmingham News*, Dec 10, 1935, 91-10
* Milky Way, *Nashville Banner*, Mar 6, 1934, 206-6
Mill Wheel, *Birmingham News*, Dec 15, 1936, 184-11
Mineral Wells, *Birmingham News*, Jul 4, 1933, 92-12
Minnesota, *Birmingham News*, Sep 2, 1941, 199-2
* Missouri Puzzle, *Birmingham News*, Jan 1, 1934, 176-10
* Missouri Star, *Birmingham News*, Aug 16, 1932, 78-6
Mixed T, *Nashville Banner*, Dec 7, 1937, 151-3
Mona and Monette, unidentified clipping, Jun 20, 1939, 193-11
* Monkey Wrench, *Nashville Banner*, Mar 21, 1933, 206-6
* Monkey Wrench, *Nashville Banner*, Feb 1, 1938, 93-11
Monterey, *Birmingham News*, Aug 16, 1932, 103-4
Morning Patch, *Birmingham News*, Nov 2, 1937, 96-10
Morning Star, *Birmingham News*, Nov 14, 1933, 161-10
* Morning Star, *Nashville Banner*, Oct 22, 1940, 246-12
Mosaic, unidentified clipping, Nov 29, 1938, 139-10
* Mosaic No. 3, unidentified clipping, Oct 16, 1934, 58-12
* Mosaic No. 8, per Alboum, date unknown, 241-7
* Mother's Dream, *Birmingham News*, Nov 14, 1933, 247-10
* Mrs. Lacey's Choice, *Birmingham News*, May 1, 1934, 60-9
* Mrs. Morgan's Choice, *Birmingham News*, Mar 19, 1935, 145-4
Mrs. Thomas, *Birmingham News*, Jul 27, 1943, 204-10
Mrs. William's Border, *Birmingham News*, Nov 24, 1942, 427-7
Mrs. Young's Basket, *Birmingham News*, Jan 3, 1939, 190-8
* Navajo, *Birmingham News*, Date unknown, 109-8
* Necktie, *Nashville Banner*, Apr 2, 1935, 77-3
New Hampshire, *Birmingham News*, Date unknown, 94-5
New Jersey, *Birmingham News*, Apr 17, 1934, 216-9
New Mexico, *Birmingham News*, Oct 24, 1933, 157-1
* Next Door Neighbor, *Birmingham News*, Mar 24, 1942, 68-3
Noon and Night, unidentified clipping, Jan 20, 1942, 154-10
Noon Day Lilies, *Birmingham News*, Jul 21, 1942, 156-12
Noon Day Sun, *Birmingham News*, Aug 9, 1938, 186-6
North Carolina, *Birmingham News*, May 7, 1940, 141-12
North Carolina Lily, *Birmingham News*, Jun 13, 1939, 367-3
North Dakota, *Birmingham News*, Oct 7, 1941, 186-12
North Star, *Birmingham News*, Feb 9, 1943, 283-9
* North Wind, unidentified clipping, Apr 7, 1936, 126-10
Northern Lights, *Birmingham News*, Jul 27, 1937, 164-1
Nosegays, *Birmingham News*, Jan 30, 1934, 194-7
Ocean Wave, *Nashville Banner*, Jun 11, 1934, 140-5
Octagons, *Birmingham News*, Dec 28, 1937, 126-2
* Odds and Ends, *Birmingham News*, date unknown, 105-4
Off to San Francisco, *Birmingham News*, Apr 14, 1936, 147-1
Ohio Shade Tree, *Birmingham News*, Oct 6, 1936, 275-9
Ohio Star, *Birmingham News*, Nov 21, 1933, 83-6
Old Fashioned Frame, *Birmingham News*, Feb 8, 1939, 85-4
Old Fashioned Garden, *Birmingham News*, Jun 3, 1941, 251-3
* Old Gray Goose, *Birmingham News*, date unknown, 76-1
Open Box, *Nashville Banner*, Jul 16, 1935, 96-11
* Orange Peel, *Nashville Banner*, date unknown, 309-6
Oregon, *Birmingham News*, Sep 5, 1939, 185-6
Over and Under, *Detroit Free Press*, Feb 26, 1935, 241-12
Over and Under Quilt, *Detroit Free Press*, Jan 30, 1934, 242-1
Over the Sahara, *Birmingham News*, Apr 30, 1935, 101-11
Ozark Maple Leaf, *Birmingham News*, Aug 1, 1939, 150-10
Paisley Shawl, *Lowell Sun* Dec 3, 1940, 115-8
* Pale Stars, *Birmingham News*, date unknown, 70-3
Paper Flowers, *Birmingham News*, Sep 4, 1934, 97-1
* Paper Pinwheels, *Birmingham News*, May 21, 1934, 67-3
Path of Thorns, *Birmingham News*, Oct 15, 1935, 85-10
Peach Basket, *Birmingham News*, Sep 3, 1935, 191-3
Pennsylvania, *Birmingham News*, Jul 3, 1934, 128-1
Pershing, *Nashville Banner*, Jun 2, 1932, 137-5
Persian Squares, *Birmingham News*, Jul 3, 1934, 230-7
Peter's Neckties, *Birmingham News*, May 27, 1941, 155-3
Picnic Basket, *Birmingham News*, Nov 26, 1935, 191-3
* Pieced Star, *Birmingham News*, Feb 25, 1936, 70-8
Pine Burr, *Nashville Banner*, May 11, 1937, 264-5
* Pine Burr, *Birmingham News*, Oct 5, 1943, 196-9
Pine Cones, *Birmingham News*, Jan 18, 1938, 208-1
Pine Tree, *Birmingham News*, Jun 19, 1934, 217-12
Pine Tree, *Birmingham News*, Dec 11, 1934, 218-2
Pine Tree, *Birmingham News*, Aug 13, 1935, 171-1
Pineapple Quilt, *Birmingham News*, Jun 9, 1942, 271-1
Pinwheel Quilt, *Nashville Banner*, Jan 16, 1934, 135-4
Polk Ohio, *Birmingham News*, Jan 12, 1943, 276-2
Polka Dots, *Nashville Banner*, Jan 16, 1934, 350-9
Postage Stamp, *Lowell Sun* date unknown, 115-8
* Prairie Queen, per Alboum, Mar 14, 1939, 128-7
* Premium Star, *Birmingham News*, Dec 5, 1933, 193-12
* Primrose Path, *Birmingham News*, Aug 29, 1933, 105-7
* Propeller, per Alboum, Mar 24, 1936, 185-4
Puss in the Corner, *Birmingham News*, Jun 16, 1942, 142-2
Queen's Crown, unidentified clipping, Jun 5, 1934, 131-12
Queen's Crown, *Detroit Free Press*, Apr 13, 1943, 191-12
* Queen's Favorite, The, *Capper's Weekly* (per Brackman), Jun 21, 1930, 131-12
Quintettes, *Birmingham News*, Jun 30, 1936, 407-4
Quita's Favorite, *Birmingham News*, Jun 27, 1939, 95-10
Rachel's Garden, *Birmingham News*, May 28, 1935, 159-8
Railroad Crossing, *Birmingham News*, Aug 15, 1933, 77-10
Rain or Shine, unidentified clipping, Oct 29, 1940, 158-3
Rainbows, *Birmingham News*, Mar 2, 1943, 419-4
Red Cross, *Birmingham News*, Oct 9, 1934, 182-6
Red Cross, *Birmingham News*, date unknown, 91-1
Red White and Blue, *Birmingham News*, Feb 9, 1937 and Dec 20, 1938, 147-6
Resolutions, *Birmingham News*, Jun 15, 1943, 244-11
* Ribbon Border, unidentified clipping, Dec 30, 1941, 413-8
Ribbon Quilt, *Birmingham News*, Nov 3, 1942, 146-6
* Ribbon Star, per Alboum, May 8, 1934, 62-7
Ribbon Twist, *Birmingham News*, Mar 28, 1933, 411-12
* Rising Star, *Birmingham News*, Dec 20, 1938, 79-2
Rising Star, *Nashville Banner*, Apr 31, 1934, 277-7
Rising Sun, *Birmingham News*, May 13, 1941, 87-6
Road to California, *Birmingham News*, Jul 10, 1934, 263-7
Road to Tennessee, *Birmingham News*, date unknown, 411-2
Robbing Peter to Pay Paul, *Birmingham News*, May 21, 1940, 353-4
* Robert's Choice, *Birmingham News*, Aug 27, 1940, 62-8
* Rocky Glen, *Nashville Banner*, Feb 21, 1939, 107-11
Rolling Pinwheels, *Birmingham News*, date unknown., 145-7
Rolling Stars, *Nashville Banner*, Sep 24, 1940, 202-4
* Rolling Stone, *Birmingham News*, Feb 27, 1940, 286-2
* Rolling Stone, *Nashville Banner*, Nov 16, 1943, 131-11
* Roman Cross, *Nashville Banner*, Apr 25, 1933 and Apr 28, 1942, 91-10
Rosebuds, *Birmingham News*, Sep 21, 1937, 224-1
Round the Corner, *Birmingham News*, Dec 26, 1933, 185-1
Ruth's Favorite, *Birmingham News*, Dec 10, 1940, 231-7
Sailboat Quilt, *Birmingham News*, Mar 3, 1936, 110-8
* Sally's Favorite, *Birmingham News*, Aug 28, 1934, 77-7
San Diego, *Birmingham News*, Oct 30, 1934, 98-6
Sawtooth, *Birmingham News*, Oct 30, 1934, 128-11
* Scrap, *Nashville Banner*, Apr 10, 1934, 93-10
Scrapbag, *Birmingham News*, Apr 9, 1935, 115-8
Seven Great Lights, *Birmingham News*, Jan 5, 1937, 395-1
* Seven Stars, *Nashville Banner*, May 14, 1940, 395-1
* Shaded Stars, *Birmingham News*, Jun 24, 1941, 211-10
* Shell Quilting, *Birmingham News*, May 10, 1938, 433-6
Signal Bars, *Birmingham News*, Sep 22, 1933 and Jan 26, 1943, 194-11
* Signal Lights, *Birmingham News*, Jan 27, 1942, 80-5
Single Irish Chain, *Birmingham News*, Jan 28, 1935, 182-5
* Single Wedding Ring, *Nashville Banner*, date unknown, 184-11
Sister's Choice, *Birmingham News*, Oct 29, 1935, 185-12
* Sky Rockets, *Birmingham News*, date unknown, 66-8
* Skyrocket, *Nashville Banner*, Feb 13, 1934, 157-10
* Snail's Trail, *Birmingham News*, Jan 11, 1944, 93-11
* Spinner, The, *Birmingham News*, Oct 21, 1941, 66-3
* Spinning Stars, *Birmingham News*, Aug 30, 1932, 70-4
Spokane, *Birmingham News*, Aug 4, 1936, 165-6
Spring Garden, *Birmingham News*, Feb 13, 1940, 178-9
Spring Has Come, *Birmingham News*, Jun 12, 1934, 92-9
* Square and Star, *Lowell Sun*, Sep 10, 1940, 60-10
Square on Square, *Nashville Banner*, Aug 16, 1938, 93-10
Squares and Square, unidentified clipping, Aug 13, 1940, 182-9
Squares and Stripes, *Birmingham News*, Nov 11, 1941, 85-3
* Squares and Triangles, per Alboum, Feb 12, 1935, 131-12
* St. Louis Star, *Birmingham News*, Dec 26, 1940, 204-9
* Star, *Birmingham News*, Aug 15, 1933, 276-1
* Star and Chains, *Nashville Banner*, Jun 25, 1934, 289-3
Star and Cross, *Birmingham News*, Nov 3, 1936, 199-9
Star and Diamond, *Nashville Banner*, Oct 18, 1938, 104-12
* Star Lane, *Birmingham News*, Jun 6, 1933, 203-7
* Star of Beauty, *Birmingham News*, Aug 30, 1932, 68-3
Star of Hope, *Detroit Free Press*, Aug 20, 1935, 124-7
* Star of Many Points, *Lowell Sun*, date unknown, 299-6
* Star of the East, per Alboum, Apr 20, 1937, 276-1
* Star of the West, *Birmingham News*, Mar 1, 1938, 75-5
Star Rays, *Nashville Banner*, Jun 4, 1935, 397-5
* Stardust Quilt, *Birmingham News*, Apr 21, 1942, 70-5
Starflower, *Birmingham News*, Aug 22, 1939, 81-5

* Starlight, *Nashville Banner*, Mar 7, 1933, 157-10
* Starry Crown, *Birmingham News*, Jun 18, 1934, 338-8
Stars and Cubes, *Birmingham News*, Apr 2, 1935, 97-8
* Stars and Squares, *Nashville Banner*, Aug 19, 1941, 79-2
* Steeple Chase, *Birmingham News*, date unknown, 350-3
Stepping Stones, *Nashville Banner*, Aug 31, 1937, 87-1
Stepping Stones, unidentified clipping, Aug 11, 1942, 87-10
* Steps to the Altar, *Detroit Free Press*, Jun 21, 1932, 152-1
Steps to the Light House, *Nashville Banner*, Jun 16, 1934, 253-8
Steps to the White House, *Birmingham News*, Apr 31, 1934, 115-8
Straw Flowers, *Birmingham News*, Sep 17, 1940, 146-9
* Strip Squares, *Birmingham News*, Apr 6, 1943, 258-3
Subway Turnstile, *Birmingham News*, Dec 26, 1939, 112-11
Sugar Bowl, *Nashville Banner*, Jul 22, 1941, 318-2
Sugar Loaf, *Birmingham News*, Jul 11, 1939, 409-5
Summer Breezes, *Birmingham News*, May 18, 1943, 102-9
Summer Winds, unidentified clipping, Jul 2, 1935, 130-4
* Summer's Dream, *Nashville Banner*, Jun 4, 1940, 175-10
Sun and Shade, *Birmingham News*, Sep 1, 1942, 200-7
Sunburst, unidentified clipping, Feb 11, 1936, 415-5
Sunflower, *Birmingham News*, Mar 21, 1939, 164-7
Sunny Lanes, *Birmingham News*, Sep 20, 1932, 106-11
* Sunshine and Shadow, *Nashville Banner*, May 2, 1939, 155-2
Susannah Patch, *Birmingham News*, Oct 12, 1943, 78-4
Swallow, The, *Birmingham News*, Aug 15, 1939, 107-2
Swastika, unidentified clipping, Feb 29, 1944, 99-9
* Swing in the Center, *Birmingham News*, Mar 22, 1938, 134-12
Table for Four, *Birmingham News*, Mar 8, 1938, 86-3
Tall Pines, *Birmingham News*, Jun 4, 1940, 410-6
* Tassel Plant, *Birmingham News*, Jul 21, 1942, 171-4
Tea for Four, *Birmingham News*, May 20, 1941, 139-8
Tea Leaves, *Birmingham News*, Mar 15, 1938, 123-12
* Ten Inch Border, *Birmingham News*, Aug 26, 1941, 75-5
Tennessee, *Birmingham News*, Dec 22, 1936, 126-8
Texas, *Port Arthur News* date unknown, 133-3
Texas Cheers, *Birmingham News*, Sep 19, 1939, 199-6
Texas Treasure, *Birmingham News*, date unknown., 159-8
Tic Tac Toe, *Birmingham News*, Jul 27, 1937, 153-6
Tiny Pine, *Birmingham News*, Jul 28, 1936, 179-2
* Toad in a Puddle, *Birmingham News*, Feb 20, 1934, 77-8
Treasure Box, *Birmingham News*, May 15, 1934, 134-8
Tree of Heaven, *Birmingham News*, Oct 24, 1939, 225-11
Tree of Paradise, *Birmingham News*, Apr 4, 1939, 171-1
Trellis Quilt, *Birmingham News*, Apr 11, 1933, 409-1
* Triangle Puzzle, The, *Birmingham News*, Oct 22, 1935, 192-10
* Triangles, *Birmingham News*, Jul 15, 1941, 76-4
Triple Irish Chain (Large), *Birmingham News*, Mar 23, 1943, 250-6
Triple Irish Chain (Small), *Birmingham News*, Jul 29, 1941, 250-7
* Tulip Lady Finger, *Birmingham News*, Apr 11, 1933, 109-6
Tulip Time, *Birmingham News*, Jun 20, 1933, 190-2
Tumble Weed, *Birmingham News*, Nov 24, 1936, 99-7
Tumbling Blocks, *Birmingham News*, Jan 30, 1934, 431-1
Turnstile, *Birmingham News*, Jan 30, 1934, 199-11
Twenty Tees, *Birmingham News*, Mar 30, 1943, 159-10
* Twin Sisters Quilt, *Detroit Free Press*, May 13, 1941, 66-1
Twinkling Stars, *Birmingham News*, Mar 5, 1935, 289-6
Two Canoes, *Birmingham News*, Aug 6, 1934, 138-12
Under and Over, *Birmingham News*, May 30, 1939, 242-2
Urn, The, *Birmingham News*, Jul 18, 1939, 196-9
V for Victory, *Birmingham News*, Jul 12, 1938, 233-1
Variable Star, *Birmingham News*, Aug 6, 1935, 124-9
Vermont, *Birmingham News*, Feb 15, 1938, 77-11
Victorian Cut-outs, *Birmingham News*, Jun 9, 1936, 164-5
Victorian Frame, *Birmingham News*, Aug 22, 1933, 85-4
Victory Garden, *Birmingham News*, Jul 28, 1942, 142-7
Village Green, *Birmingham News*, Apr 14, 1942, 242-6
Walled Garden, *Birmingham News*, Jul 25, 1939, 244-2
Washington, *Birmingham News*, Jun 14, 1938, 91-9
Washington Pavement, *Birmingham News*, Mar 13, 1934, 302-10
Waste Not Want Not, *Birmingham News*, Aug 13, 1940, 134-4
Waving Grain, *Birmingham News*, Feb 6, 1940, 149-10
Wedding Bouquet, *Birmingham News*, Apr 20, 1943, 136-2
West Wind, *Birmingham News*, Dec 11, 1934, 127-5
Western Star, per Alboum, Jun 9, 1942, 124-7
Whirling Squares, *Birmingham News*, Mar 14, 1939, 91-7
* Whirlpools, *Birmingham News*, Feb 24, 1942, 60-4
* Wild Duck, *Birmingham News*, Jul 5, 1932, 72-3
Wild Geese, *Birmingham News*, Oct 13, 1936, 409-10
Wild Goose Chase, *Birmingham News*, Sep 27, 1932, 87-1
Willy Nilly, unidentified clipping, Feb 16, 1943, 102-10
* Windmill, *Birmingham News*, Aug 6, 1934, 58-6
* Winged Arrow, *Quilter's Newsletter Magazine*, Sep 21, 1943, 68-4
* Winged Arrows, *Birmingham News*, date unknown, 68-4
* Winged Square, unidentified clipping, Jul 12, 1932, 74-5
* World Without End, *Birmingham News*, Jul 26, 1938, 226-12
* Yankee Pride, unidentified clipping, May 25, 1943, 231-8
* Yankee Pride, per Alboum, date unknown., 292-2
* Yankee Puzzle, *Birmingham News*, Mar 31, 1936, 68-7
* Young Man's Fancy, *Birmingham News*, date unknown, 263-4
* Zig Zag Tile, *Nashville Banner*, Sep 5, 1937, 67-1

Appendix 5

Kansas City Star Blocks

Kansas City Star ran columns featuring quilt blocks from 1928 to 1961 (see pages 4 to 5). In this book, I have included more than 880 pieced blocks that were published with patterns at one time or other in *Kansas City Star*. This index lists the designs, along with the dates they first appeared in the newspaper. Those marked with an asterisk were first published elsewhere before they appeared on the date listed here in *Kansas City Star.*

4 H, Jan 24, 1940, 143-11
4 Part Strip Block, A, Jan 28, 1948, 426-4
4 Square Block with Diamonds, A, Jul 11, 1951, 194-10
4 H Club Quilt, Apr 30, 1932, 166-4
6 Point Flower Garden, Jul 22, 1959, 392-9
8 Point Snowflake, The, Apr 8, 1953 and Jun 10, 1953, 300-6
1941 Nine Patch, Sep 17, 1941, 246-8
Adaptation of The Indian Trail, Mar 10, 1943, 219-4
Air Plane, The, Jul 28, 1934, Jan 3, 1940, and Jun 3, 1942, 265-5
Air Port, The, Jul 11, 1936, 113-10
Air Ship Propeller, Jul 8, 1933, 372-8
Aircraft Quilt, The, Jul 13, 1929, 269-8
Airplane Motif, Apr 2, 1947, 288-11
Album, Sep 26, 1928, 146-10
Album, The, Oct 30, 1935, 91-10
Album, The, Jun 5, 1937, 157-11
All-Over Pattern of Octagons, An, Sep 23, 1942, 411-1
Amethyst, Feb 7, 1931, 82-4
Anna's Choice, Feb 26, 1941, 428-6
Anna's Pride, Aug 1, 1936, 336-5
Apple Leaf, The, Sep 14, 1935, 178-2
* Arabic Lattice, Jan 5, 1935 and Mar 27, 1935, 210-4
Ararat, Jun 6, 1931, 440-5
Arkansas, Dec 9, 1933, 340-7
Arkansas Centennial, Jan 9, 1937, 315-2
Arkansas Cross Roads, The, Mar 19, 1941, 70-12
Arkansas Meadow Rose, Oct 9, 1935 and Jul 10, 1946, 370-11
Arkansas Snow Flake, Feb 9, 1935, 117-5
Arkansas Star, Feb 9, 1935, 117-5
Arkansas Star, The, Jan 14, 1933, Mar 4, 1933, and Oct 6, 1948, 343-1
* Arkansas Traveler, Aug 22, 1945, 144-1
Army Star, The, May 26, 1943, 114-2
Around the Chimney, Jul 7, 1932, 101-9
Around the World, May 15, 1940, 337-11
Arrow Head, Jan 18, 1936 and Sep 22, 1937, 122-8
Arrow Head Star, Jul 11, 1931 and Oct 26, 1949, 299-6
Arrow Heads, Jan 21, 1942, 393-10
Arrow Star, The, Oct 20, 1934, 64-5
Arrowhead, The, Mar 26, 1941, 61-8
Aster Quilt, The, Feb 22, 1930, 375-5
Autograph Quilt, Feb 6, 1932, 229-9
Autograph Quilt, The, Mar 2, 1949, 229-9
* Baby Bunting, Feb 28, 1931, 384-9
Baby Fan Applique, Oct 3, 1945, 388-5
Bachelor's Puzzle, Aug 8, 1931, 206-7
Basket of Bright Flowers, A, Apr 24, 1946, 367-12
Basket of Diamonds, Aug 28, 1937, 110-9
Basket of Diamonds, Sep 5, 1936, 305-9
Basket of Flowers, Dec 14, 1935, 367-12
Basket of Lilies, Apr 4, 1931, 120-4
Basket Quilt in Triangles, A, Dec 16, 1942, 152-4
Basket Weave Friendship Block, The, Jul 1, 1953, 91-10
Basket Weave Friendship Quilt, The, Apr 9, 1958, 91-10
Basket, The, Apr 16, 1938 and May 15, 1946, 250-1
* Bear's Paw, Sep 15, 1937, 223-9
* Beautiful Star, Mar 16 1929, 297-1
Beggar Block, Mar 30, 1929, 242-1
Bell, Mar 15, 1961, 333-7
Bethlehem Star, Apr 30, 1938, 289-5
Betty's Delight, Jan 12, 1949, 86-1
Big Bear's Paw, The, Jun 15, 1960, 223-9
Bird's Nest, Jun 15, 1929, 194-12
* Blazing Star, Nov 18, 1953, 297-1
Blazing Star, The, Feb 15, 1930, 286-3
Block of Many Triangles, A, Oct 3, 1951, 109-3
Block of Many Triangles, A, Sep 17, 1952, 262-6
Blockade, The, Jun 4, 1938, 58-10
Blue Blades Flying, Jul 19, 1944, 263-10
Bluebell, Jan 24, 1940, 362-4
Bouquet in a Fan, Mar 18, 1933, 256-9
Boutonniere, Sep 26, 1931 and Mar 10, 1948, 393-7
Boutonniere, Sep 19, 1931, 415-9
Boutonniere, A, Mar 10, 1948, 415-9
Bow Tie in Pink and White, Feb 22, 1956, 77-3
Brave Sunflower, A, Dec 26, 1951, 381-8
Bridal Stairway Patchwork Block, Jul 1, 1933, 408-1
Bridle Path, The, Mar 9, 1935, 155-9
Bright Jewel, Sep 28, 1949, 183-7
Bright Morning Star, The, Sep 14, 1960, 277-7
Broken Branch, The, Nov 30, 1935, 218-3
* Broken Circle, Mar 23, 1929, 384-2
Broken Circle, Mar 24, 1934, 325-1
Broken Circle, The, Dec 17, 1952, 383-8

Broken Crown, The, May 6, 1933, 372-12
Broken Dish, The, Aug 21, 1937, 241-8
Broken Dish, The, Apr 30, 1952, 58-10
Broken Dish, The, Jun 2, 1943, 428-5
Broken Dishes, Sep 20, 1930, 428-5
Broken Path, The, Oct 25, 1939, 172-1
Broken Square, The, Apr 9, 1938, 312-5
Broken Stone, The, Jan 4, 1950, 318-1
Broken Stone, The, Sep 2, 1933, 383-5
Broken Sugar Bowl, The, Jul 22, 1942, 146-11
Broken Wheel, The, Sep 29, 1943, 84-11
Broken Window, Sep 8, 1937, 130-11
* Buckeye Beauty, Nov 15, 1939, 73-6
Builder's Block Quilt, The, Mar 31, 1943, 207-9
Builder's Blocks, Oct 22, 1947, 430-7
Builder's Blocks, The, Dec 16, 1953, 430-7
Butterfly, Apr 4, 1936, 220-4
Butterfly, Oct 17, 1931, 245-10
Butterfly in Angles, A, Feb 2, 1944, 438-9
Buzz Saw, The, Nov 5, 1941, 376-11
Cabin Windows, Apr 17, 1940, 168-10
Cactus Flower, Jul 4, 1931, 152-5
Calico Puzzle, The, Sep 13, 1930, 124-2
Caps for Witches and Dunces, Aug 15, 1956, 312-12
Car Wheel Quilt, The, Sep 4, 1940, 344-8
Carnival Time, Sep 9, 1959, 305-4
Carrie Nation Quilt, Dec 4, 1940, 170-5
Carrie Nation Quilt, The, Nov 12, 1947, 170-5
Casement Window, The, Mar 28, 1931, 91-5
Castle Wall, The, Oct 10, 1931, 295-1
Cat's Cradle, The, Sep 21, 1960, 126-8
Cat's Cradle, The, Feb 24, 1934, 149-1
Century Old Tulip Pattern, A, Sep 24, 1947, 314-5
Chain Quilt, Feb 25, 1942, 353-9
Charm Quilt, Dec 30, 1933, 433-10
* Cherry Basket, Oct 24, 1928, 322-11
Cheyenne, Sep 16, 1933, 57-9
Chinese Block Quilt, The, Jul 13, 1938, 130-3
Chinese Puzzle, Sep 19, 1936, 412-1
Chips and Whetstones, Sep 19, 1931 and Jun 22, 1949, 378-6
Chisholm Trail Quilt, May 31, 1939, 72-2
Christmas Star, Dec 19, 1931 and Dec 17, 1947, 288-5
Christmas Tree, Jun 2, 1934, 170-12
Christmas Tree, The, Dec 24, 1932 and Nov 8, 1950, 179-4
Churn Dash, Jan 04, 1930 and May 8, 1935, 184-2
Circle and Square, Nov 21, 1936, 355-3
Circle in a Frame, Oct 24, 1945, 325-7
Circle Saw, Jan 25, 1936, 289-6
Circle Saw, The, Jun 30, 1954, 374-3
Circle Upon Circle, Dec 2, 1933 and Feb 18, 1948, 418-1
Circular Saw, The, Jan 9, 1932, 340-3
Clam Shells, Oct 29, 1932, 433-6
* Clay's Choice, Jul 26, 1930 and Oct 9, 1937, 70-5
Cluster of Lillies (sic), Dec 22, 1934, 272-4
Coffee Cups, Jan 12, 1935, 341-5
Cog Block, Jul 27, 1955, 62-7
Cog Wheels, Nov 9, 1935, 83-12
Colorado Quilt, The, Jan 8, 1941, 64-2
Comfort Quilt, The, May 8, 1940, 174-9
Compass and Chain, The, Nov 23, 1935, 414-4
Compass Quilt, The, Aug 16, 1930 and Oct 8, 1947, 331-8
Contrary Husband Quilt, Nov 9, 1938, 224-12
Contrary Wife Quilt, Aug 27, 1941, 126-7
Corn and Beans, Jan 11, 1930, 130-10
Corner Posts, Dec 3, 1932, 185-7
Corner Star, The, Aug 9, 1939, 97-3
Cornerstone, The, Dec 23, 1942, 141-1
Cottage Tulips, Nov 7, 1931 and Aug 27, 1947, 358-2
Cotton Boll Quilt, The, Feb 12, 1941, 61-9
Coverlet in Jewel Tones, A, Jan 14, 1959, 231-1
* Cowboy's Star, Jun 4, 1932, 297-7
* Crazy Ann, Oct 15, 1932, 188-6
Crazy Ann, Oct 15, 1932, 188-6
Crazy Anne, Jun 15, 1949, 265-4
Crazy Tile Quilt, May 24, 1939 and Jan 21, 1948, 432-7
* Cross and Crown, Apr 26, 1930, 194-3
Cross and Crown, Aug 10, 1929 and Apr 26, 1930, 194-4
Cross Is Mother's Choice, Jan 8, 1958, 193-1
Cross Patch, The, Nov 16, 1955, 245-1
Cross Roads, Aug 1, 1931, 383-8
Crossed Canoes, May 18, 1929, 138-12
* Crosses and Losses, Jun 22, 1929, 73-9
Crow's Nest, Nov 25, 1933, 241-5
Crow's Nest, The, May 21, 1932, 112-4
Crown of Thorns, The, Nov 1, 1939 and Jan 5, 1949, 355-10
Crystal Star, Jun 16, 1934 and Mar 10, 1954, 64-1
Cup and Saucer, The, Feb 27, 1946, 341-5
Cupid's Arrow Point, Apr 6, 1929, 412-3
Cups and Saucers, May 23, 1936, 134-3
Cypress, Sep 9, 1933, 227-12
Cypress, The, Mar 9, 1960, 227-12
Danish Stars, Jun 10, 1942, 193-3
Depression, Mar 20, 1937, 428-8
Depression Quilt, May 27, 1942, 426-9
Design for Patriotism, A, Aug 20, 1952, 120-7
Design in Geometrics, A, Oct 24, 1956, 57-10
Dessert Plate, Jun 23, 1954, 374-10
Diamond Circle, The, Aug 14, 1935, 138-3
Diamond Cluster in a Frame, Mar 21, 1956, 285-12
Diamond Cross, The, May 22, 1937, 227-6
Diamond Field, The, Apr 9, 1932, 432-2
Diamonds and Arrow Points, Feb 21, 1945, 392-8
Diamonds in the Corners, Sep 5, 1956, 291-8
Diversion Quilt, The, Jul 11, 1945, 182-2
Dog Quilt, The, May 2, 1936, 440-3
* Dogwood Blossom, Feb 17, 1934, 384-10
Dogwood Blossom, A, Sep 17, 1958, 311-9
Dolly Madison Pattern, Apr 10, 1937, 392-9
Double Anchor, The, Nov 30, 1955, 171-12
Double Arrow, The, Jun 24, 1933, 156-3
Double Cross Quilt, The, Sep 7, 1938, 158-4
Double Irish Chain, Jan 13, 1934 and Apr 3, 1946, 233-3
Double Irish Chain, The, Jul 14, 1948 and Oct 21, 1953, 233-3
Double Irish Cross, Jun 7, 1930, 209-5
Double Nine Patch, Feb 16, 1929, 240-5
* Double Nine Patch, Jul 23, 1932, 240-8
* Double Pyramid, Aug 5, 1933, 170-6
Double Square, Jul 10, 1937, 300-5
Double Square, The, Feb 25, 1953, 427-5
Double Star Quilt, The, Jun 29, 1929, 289-6
Double T, Nov 28, 1928, 78-7
* Double T, Jul 19, 1939, 139-7
Double T Quilt, The, Dec 10, 1947, 139-7
Double T, The, Mar 27, 1937 and Jul 19, 1939, 139-7
Double V, The, Jul 24, 1940, 192-5
Dove at the Window, Nov 28, 1945, 172-5
Dove at the Window, Apr 11, 1936, 299-5
Dove at the Window, Jun 6, 1936, 278-2
Dove in the Window, Mar 9, 1929, 278-2
* Dove in the Window, Sep 17, 1932, 106-6
Dragon Fly, The, Oct 24, 1936 and Feb 17, 1954, 201-8
Dresden Plate, Aug 29, 1931, 375-5
Drunkard's Trail, The, Sep 16, 1942, 383-4
* Drunkard's Path, Mar 11, 1959, 352-6
Duck and Ducklings, May 4, 1929, 174-10
Ducklings, Jun 11, 1932, 184-4
Ducklings for Friendship, Oct 19, 1949, 184-4
Dutch Tile, Oct 31, 1931, 430-11
Dutch Tulip, May 23, 1931, 357-8
* Dutchman's Puzzle, Mar 29, 1930, 68-10
E Z Quilt, The, Aug 7, 1940, 236-3
Economy, Aug 12, 1933, 161-6
* Eight Pointed Star, Feb 23, 1929, 276-1
Eight Pointed Star, Feb 23, 1929, 286-2
Eight Pointed Star, Mar 17, 1934, 344-12
Eight Points in a Square, Sep 29, 1954, 344-11
Electric Fan, The, Feb 5, 1938, 345-5
End of the Road, Nov 9, 1955, 172-1
English Ivy, May 9, 1931, 178-7
Envelope Motif, An, Aug 19, 1942, 428-5
Envelope Quilt Pattern, Feb 10, 1943, 427-9
Envelope Quilt, The, Sep 20, 1944, 438-6
Evelyne's Whirling Dust Storm, May 5, 1943, 377-12
Evening Star, Nov 28, 1931, 283-5
Evening Star, The, May 18, 1960, 174-11
Evening Star, The, Mar 29, 1944, 351-6
Fair and Square, Mar 16, 1938, 195-9
Fan and Ring, Mar 27, 1940, 385-8
Fan of Many Colors, A, May 24, 1961, 386-3
Fan Quilt, Jan 26, 1935, 388-6
Fans and a Ring, Aug 11, 1948, 385-8
Farmer's Fields, Apr 5, 1939, 248-6
Farmer's Wife, Sep 3, 1932, 346-8
* Farmer's Daughter, Mar 16, 1935, 185-7
Feather Bone Block, A, Nov 15, 1950, 212-6
Feather Edge Star, Aug 11, 1934, 274-9
Fence Row Quilt, Apr 25, 1931 and May 21, 1941, 412-10
Fence Row Quilt, The, Oct 6, 1943, 427-7
Ferris Wheel, Jul 29, 1959, 376-3
Fish Block, Sep 21, 1929, 288-11
Fish Quilt, The, Jun 11, 1941, 288-11
Flag In, Flag Out, Nov 8, 1939, 232-2
Flash of Diamonds, Apr 6, 1949, 291-12
Floating Clouds, Nov 23, 1938, 416-9
Florida Star, Sep 24, 1932 and Jun 19, 1935, 396-3
Flower Basket, Jul 31, 1935, 305-9
Flower Garden Block, The, May 8, 1937, 392-9
Flower Garden, The, May 9, 1951, 392-9
Flower Pot, Aug 31, 1929, 305-8
* Flower Pot, Jan 17, 1931, 306-1
* Flower Pot, Apr 11, 1956, 305-12
Flower Pot, The, Jan 16, 1937, 190-11
Flower Ring, The, May 29, 1940, 419-5
Flowering Nine Patch, May 19, 1934, 113-3
Flowers in a Basket, Aug 20, 1941, 306-3
Flowing Ribbon, The, Apr 22, 1933, 439-1
* Flying Bats, Jul 2, 1932, 101-9
Flying Colors, Nov 5, 1958, 428-5
Flying Kite, Jul 7, 1937, 231-12
* Flying Swallows, Jul 29, 1933, 358-10
Flying X Quilt, The, Oct 26, 1938, 67-9
* Fool's Square, Jul 5, 1955, 185-9
Formal Flower Bed, The, Dec 1, 1943, 371-13
Formosa Tea Leaf, Nov 14, 1931, 277-12
Four Buds Quilt, The, Oct 1, 1941, 359-11
Four Corner Puzzle, A, Jul 21, 1943, 58-10

Appendix 6

Jinny Beyer Blocks

Here is an index of 495 blocks of my own design. The sources are provided, but you will need to look up the blocks to find the dates. From 1981 to 2009, I conducted an annual quilting seminar on Hilton Head Island. Each year, the participants received a group of pieced quilt blocks designed specifically for the seminar. On page 470, all 223 of the blocks are listed by year.

Hilton Head Seminar Blocks

1981
Compass Rose, 381-2
Lighthouse Tower, 295-6
Mariner's Wheel, 380-8
Palmetto, 167-6
Sea Pine, 110-11
Star Sapphire, 285-11
Atlantic Star, 201-11

1982
Atlantic Star, 201-11
Carolina Pinwheel, 162-2
Eastern Sunrise, 117-2
Mariner's Rose, 380-9
Rolling Compass, 380-12
Safe Harbour, 133-11
Sea Crystal, 298-1
Swallow Tails, 64-3

1983
Captain's Wheel, 298-4
Island Compass, 380-11
Kiran's Choice, 295-9
Lagoon Rose, 134-9
Reflecting Star, 86-5
Sea Crest, 201-9
Sea Pines Star, 285-10
Water Lily, 295-7

1984
Atlantic Jewel, 285-4
Carolina Compass, 381-1
Cave Crystal, 227-9
Crow's Nest, 201-12
Dragon Fly, 224-5
Sandpiper, 80-12
Sandy's Star, 237-5
Treasure Chest, 297-10

1985
Atlantic Aster, 380-10
Beach Rose, 284-4
Carolina Crossroads, 90-10
Clam Bake, 141-3
Crystal Flower, 179-11
Facets, 297-12
Ocean Star, 293-12
South of the Border, 227-10

1986
Beacon, 196-12
Breakwater, 224-7
Halley's Comet, 91-4
Pilot's Wheel, 194-1
Sand Castle, 96-9
Sand Dollar, 282-7
Sea Lily, 284-10
Surf Star, 115-1

1987
Cove Cross, 230-5
Crosswind, 90-11
Ellen's Dream, 205-3
Harbour Lights, 223-7
Mariner's Delight, 282-8
Reef Rose, 282-4
Riptide, 116-11
Sea Mark, 118-1

1988
Arrow Crossing, 196-11
Calibogue Sound, 90-6
Carolina Crown, 168-3
Feathered Square, 157-8
Inspiration Point, 80-10
Lead Glass, 81-1
Sheltered Cove, 160-2
Skipping Stones, 87-7

1989
Arrow Head, 204-7
Big Bang, 230-12
Moonstone, 142-5
Sand Dollar, 138-11
Sherwood Forest, 204-3
Variation IV, 299-1
Water Lily, 295-7
Whirlwind, 82-3

1990
Diamond Radiants, 1990, 381-3
Mariner's Beacon, 1990, 379-1
Mariner's Whirl, 1990, 382-12
Nautilus, 1990, 383-1
Seaflower, 1990, 381-10
Star Illusion, 1990, 381-4

1991
Bachelor Bouquet, 1991, 236-10
Chelsea, 1991, 83-8
Deco Tulip, 1991, 83-2
Facets, 1991, 160-3
Irish Star, 1991, 162-6
Nouveau Rose, 1991, 345-8
Signal Light, 1991, 159-5
Sunset Star, 1991, 287-2

1992
Espana, 1992, 393-8
Exploration Point, 1992, 437-3
Horizon, 1992, 287-5
Morning Star, 1992, 437-1
New World, 1992, 393-1
Poinsettia, 1992, 195-7
Robert Mourning's Centennial Star, 1992, 289-1
Santa Maria, 1992, 200-3

1993
Alhambra, 1993, 299-3
Jig Saw, 1993, 142-11
La Mancha, 1993, 87-3
Mediterranean Puzzle, 1993, 397-10
Moroccan Garden, 1993, 395-12
Roman Mosaic, 1993, 394-7
Seville, 1993, 283-10
Tsunami, 1993, 396-2

1994
Diamond Facet, 1994, 289-8
Emerald City, 1994, 158-8
Fox Fire, 1994, 158-9
Northern Lights, 1994, 213-12
Prism, 1994, 237-6
Star Sapphire, 1994, 84-10
Tiger Eye, 1994, 229-12
Topaz, 1994, 231-3

1995
Bellflower, 1995, 283-11
Centennial Star, 1995, 289-2
Charlotte's Webb, 1995, 195-10
Ferris Wheel, 1995, 87-4
Mystery Rose, 1995, 195-6
Prairie Points, 1995, 197-6
Stacked Crystals, 1995, 96-7
Turnabout, 1995, 286-9

1996
Clematis, 1996, 230-1
Forget Me Not, 1996, 398-4
Geode, 1996, 102-3
Prairie Points, 1996, 225-1
Spinning Wheel, 1996, 169-11
Sport, 1996, 398-3
Water Wheel, 1996, 397-11
Wind Blades, 1996, 103-3

1997
Arrowhead, 1997, 172-11
Desert Sun, 1997, 140-9
Discovery, 1997, 233-5
Lone Pine, 1997, 170-11
Origami, 1997, 398-1
Rocket Fire, 1997, 157-9
Spinning Sunflower, 1997, 398-2
Tetra, 1997, 99-13

1998
Amulet, 1998, 433-1
Enchantment, 1998, 431-3
Fascination, 1998, 432-5
Lucky Charm, 432-12
Moonstone, 1998, 195-4
Sea Charm, 1998, 433-11
Spellbound, 1998, 432-8
Talisman, 1998, 140-3

1999
Crystal Star, 1999, 396-4
Galaxy, 1999, 213-6
Garden Star, 1999, 285-9
New Horizon, 1999, 227-11
New Millennium, 1999, 285-8
Quasar, 1999, 81-11
Shooting Star, 1999, 285-7
Sunburst, 1999, 379-5

2000
Andromeda, 138-4
Aquarius, 244-9
Nova, 230-11
Orion, 211-4
Polaris, 81-7
Pulsar, 231-11
Quasar, 83-7
Vega, 138-8

2001
Cobblestone, 93-9
Distant Star, 246-11
Gyro, 211-9
Jack in the Pulpit, 189-2
Rolling Road, 230-10
Rubic's Cube, 227-8
Spider Web, 169-9
Woven Walk, 169-8

2002
Corsican Crystal, 290-2
Granada Star, 300-10
Lisbon Lattice, 169-3
Majorca Maze, 304-8
Palace Parquet, 142-9
Roman Road, 304-9
Terrazzo, 305-7
Tuscan Tile, 256-4

2003
Block Party, 431-4
Command Star, 395-7
Cubicle, 394-2
Global Star, 397-7
Hollow Cube, 394-1
North Star, 393-3
Starburst, 437-6
Venetian Star, 437-5

2004
Cactus Star, 271-6
Cob Web, 437-7
Facets, 271-4
Golden Compass, 379-4
Golden Puzzle, 217-7
Golden Tile, 100-8
Layered Star, 437-4
Nautilus, 354-6

2005
Beacon Star, 297-2
Cart Wheel, 284-1
Desert Star, 287-12
Gift Box, 281-11
Illusions, 297-6
Ribbon Star, 284-5
Silver Star, 290-6
Snow Flake, 288-4

2006
Aztec Steps, 121-1
Border Sea, The, 253-6
Bows and Arrows, 117-12
Cactus Flower, 302-8
Eternity, 400-7
Mission Stairs, 170-3
Triangle Maze, 400-8
Twister, 398-6

2007
Autumn Splendor, 437-10
Brewster's Choice, 396-9
Crystals, 290-4
Dahlia, 402-1
Shattered Star, 396-7
Spring Fancy, 401-9
Summer Rays, 437-9
Winter Fantasy, 396-8

2008
Alexandrite, 219-5
Carnelian, 163-3
Citrine, 396-6
Garnet, 396-12
Heliotrope, 397-2
Jasper, 219-1
Lapis, 395-6
Malachite, 395-9

2009
Coosawhatchie, 260-1
Emporia, 259-11
Exit 8, 260-12
Marion, 260-3
Rocky Mount, 260-13
Santee, 259-12
Selma, 260-2
Stony Creek, 169-6

Index